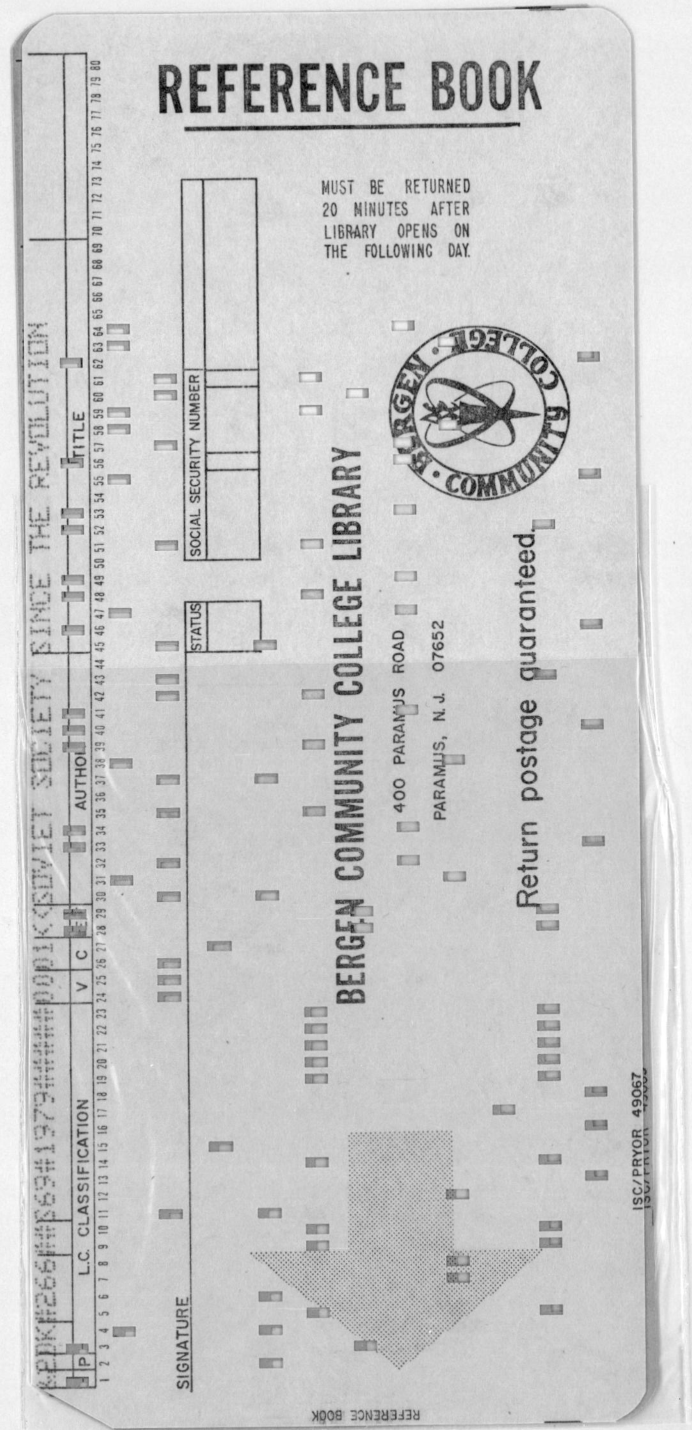
REFERENCE BOOK
MUST BE RETURNED 20 MINUTES AFTER LIBRARY OPENS ON THE FOLLOWING DAY.
BERGEN COMMUNITY COLLEGE LIBRARY
400 PARAMUS ROAD
PARAMUS, N.J. 07652
Return postage guaranteed.

# SOVIET SOCIETY SINCE THE REVOLUTION

## THE GREAT CONTEMPORARY ISSUES

### OTHER BOOKS IN THE SERIES

DRUGS
*Introduction by J. Anthony Lukas*
THE MASS MEDIA AND POLITICS
*Introduction by Walter Cronkite*
CHINA
O. Edmund Clubb, *Advisory Editor*
LABOR AND MANAGEMENT
Richard B. Morris, *Advisory Editor*
WOMEN: THEIR CHANGING ROLES
Elizabeth Janeway, *Advisory Editor*
BLACK AFRICA
Hollis Lynch, *Advisory Editor*
EDUCATION U.S.A.
James Cass, *Advisory Editor*
VALUES AMERICANS LIVE BY
Garry Wills, *Advisory Editor*
CRIME AND JUSTICE
Ramsey Clark, *Advisory Editor*
JAPAN
Edwin O. Reischauer, *Advisory Editor*
THE PRESIDENCY
George E. Reedy, *Advisory Editor*
FOOD AND POPULATION
George S. McGovern, *Advisory Editor*
THE U.S. AND WORLD ECONOMY
Leonard Silk, *Advisory Editor*
SCIENCE IN THE TWENTIETH CENTURY
Walter Sullivan, *Advisory Editor*
THE MIDDLE EAST
John C. Campbell, *Advisory Editor*
THE CITIES
Richard C. Wade, *Advisory Editor*
MEDICINE AND HEALTH CARE
Saul Jarcho, *Advisory Editor*
LOYALTY AND SECURITY IN A DEMOCRATIC STATE
Richard Rovere, *Advisory Editor*
RELIGION IN AMERICA
Gillian Lindt, *Advisory Editor*
POLITICAL PARTIES
William E. Leuchtenburg, *Advisory Editor*
ETHNIC GROUPS IN AMERICAN LIFE
James P. Shenton, *Advisory Editor*
THE ARTS
Richard McLanathan, *Advisory Editor*
ENERGY AND ENVIRONMENT
Stuart Bruchey, *Advisory Editor*
BIG BUSINESS
Leon Stein, *Advisory Editor*
THE FAMILY
David and Sheila Rothman, *Advisory Editors*
TERRORISM
Dr. Michael Wallace, *Advisory Editor*

THE GREAT CONTEMPORARY ISSUES

# SOVIET SOCIETY SINCE THE REVOLUTION

The New York Times
ARNO PRESS
NEW YORK/1979

HARRISON E. SALISBURY
Advisory Editor

GENE BROWN
Editor

**Library of Congress Cataloging in Publication Data**

Main entry under title:

Soviet Society since the revolution.

(The Great contemporary issues)
Articles from the New York Times.
Bibliography: p.
Includes index.
1. Russia—History—1917—Addresses, essays, lectures. I. Salisbury, Harrison Evans, 1908— II. Brown, Gene. III. New York Times. IV. Series: Great contemporary issues.
DK266.R83 1979 947.08 78-19596
ISBN 0-405-11526-1

Manufacutred in the United States of America

The editors express special thanks to The Associated Press, United Press International, and Reuters for permission to include in this series of books a number of dispatches originally distributed by those news services.

Book design by Stephanie Rhodes.

# Contents

# Publisher's Note About the Series

It would take even an accomplished speed-reader, moving at full throttle, some three and a half solid hours a day to work his way through all the news The New York Times prints. The sad irony, of course, is that even such indefatigable devotion to life's carnival would scarcely assure a decent understanding of what it was really all about. For even the most dutiful reader might easily overlook an occasional long-range trend of importance, or perhaps some of the fragile, elusive relationships between events that sometimes turn out to be more significant than the events themselves.

This is why "The Great Contemporary Issues" was created—to help make sense out of some of the major forces and counterforces at large in today's world. The philosophical conviction behind the series is a simple one: that the past not only can illuminate the present but must. ("Continuity with the past," declared Oliver Wendell Holmes, "is a necessity, not a duty.") Each book in the series, therefore has as its subject some central issue of our time that needs to be viewed in the context of its antecedents if it is to be fully understood. By showing, through a substantial selection of contemporary accounts from The New York Times, the evolution of a subject and its significance, each book in the series offers a perspective that is available in no other way. For while most books on contemporary affairs specialize, for excellent reasons, in predigested facts and neatly drawn conclusions, the books in this series allow the reader to draw his own conclusions on the basis of the facts as they appeared at virtually the moment of their occurrence. This is not to argue that there is no place for events recollected in tranquility; it is simply to say that when fresh, raw truths are allowed to speak for themselves, some quite distinct values often emerge.

For this reason, most of the articles in "The Great Contemporary Issues" are reprinted in their entirety, even in those cases where portions are not central to a given book's theme. Editing has been done only rarely, and in all such cases it is clearly indicated. (Such an excision occasionally occurs, for example, in the case of a Presidential State of the Union Message, where only brief portions are germane to a particular volume, and in the case of some names, where for legal reasons or reasons of taste it is preferable not to republish specific identifications.) Similarly, typographical errors, where they occur, have been allowed to stand as originally printed.

"The Great Contemporary Issues" inevitably encompasses a substantial amount of history. In order to explore their subjects fully, some of the books go back a century or more. Yet their fundamental theme is not the past but the present. In this series the past is of significance insofar as it suggests how we got where we are today. These books, therefore, do not always treat a subject in a purely chronological way. Rather, their material is arranged to point up trends and interrelationships that the editors believe are more illuminating than a chronological listing would be.

"The Great Contemporary Issues" series will ultimately constitute an encyclopedic library of today's major issues. Long before editorial work on the first volume had even begun, some fifty specific titles had already been either scheduled for definite publication or listed as candidates. Since then, events have prompted the inclusion of a number of additional titles, and the editors are, moreover, alert not only for new issues as they emerge but also for issues whose development may call for the publication of sequel volumes. We will, of course, also welcome readers' suggestions for future topics.

# Introduction

On the eve of World War I and the Revolution which lay directly ahead, Alexander Blok, one of Russia's great poets, saw in the new industrial pants being built across the Russian steppes, in the new coal mines that pocked the Ukranian landscape and in the chimneys of factories in Moscow, the first signs of "a new America."

So rapidly was Russia advancing into the industrial age that she had become the fastest developing nation in Europe; a country at the take-off point, ready to emulate the enormous expansion of England, Germany, France and the United States. This fact is well kept in mind when examining the 60 years of Soviet power which began November 7, 1917 and is continuing even now.

In trying to evaluate the social and economic progress achieved under the Communist regime it is sometimes supposed that 1917 was Year One in the transformation of Russia from the most backward power in Europe to the World's No. 2 power. Russia *was* backward by many standards in 1917, but she was moving forward with express-train speed and this momentum had even been accelerated by the enormous demands of World War I.

Russia had a population of about 139,700,000 in 1914, excluding Poland, the Baltic States and Finland which were separated from the Russian Empire at the time of the Bolshevik Revolution. The territory of the new Soviet comprised 8,125,000 square miles. There were 60 major nationalities in the Soviet Union and 28 per cent of the population was neither Russian nor Ukrainian. It was composed of a variety of ethnic peoples, Kazakhs, Uzbeks, Kirghis, Georgians, Armenians, Azerbaijani and others.

There were, at the time of the Bolshevik takeover, just short of 8,000,000 industrial, mining, railroad and village industry workers. The rest with the exception of civil servants, the military and a small professional group, were peasants, that is, farm laborers, only a small percentage of which owned their own farms. It is probable that Russia was almost 80% illiterate by contemporary standards. The country under the 300 years of Romanov rule was an absolute monarchy. In every respect—education, industry, science, health, agriculture—Russia lagged behind England, France and Germany.

In 1917 Russia was what we would today call an underdeveloped or emerging country, yet she was a powerful state with vast resources, a highly developed government, a large military establishment, a rapidly growing railroad system, an agriculture which though primitive, produced a large surplus for export, and an excellent but very small university system. A rudimentary parliament called the *Duma* had been instituted in 1905, but was sharply restricted by the Czar and had hardly begun to make a mark on the nation's political consciousness.

World War I hit Russia like a hurricane. The country mobilized nearly 16,000,000 men. The losses may have been five or six million lives, possibly more. Bodies piled up at the front lines like cordwood. Industry, railroads, food distribution, agriculture—the whole system broke down. By the time Vladimir Ilyich Lenin and his Communist Party took power in an almost bloodless coup d'etat on November 7, 1917, the Germans held most of Russia up the Petrograd approaches, all of Poland, most of Byelorussia and soon they advanced on through the Ukraine, took Kiev and penetrated to the north Caucasus.

It was a country in ruins. Revolution and civil war in which the British, French, Japanese and Americans intervened and fought against the Bolsheviks, took an added toll.

This was only the beginning of a succession of human tragedies which Russia was to suffer over the next half-century. Population specialists in 1978 were to estimate that had it not been for World War I, the losses of the Revolution, civil war, famine in the 1920s and 1930s, Stalin's purges of the mid-1930s, World War II and the new purges and famine thereafter, Russia today would have a population double its present size—approximately 500,000,000 instead of 250,000,000.

Lenin and his Communists clung to power during the Civil War by the most radical of expedients. They imposed what they called "war communism." Every industrial establishment, store, shop, bank and restaurant was taken over by the government. Military expeditions plundered the countryside "requisitioning" grain and food for the cities. Battles were fought with the peasants to seize their supplies. Millions of starving city residents abandoned the metropolises for the countryside.

Military operations were directed by Leon Trotsky, Lenin's number two man, who had joined him in 1917 after many years as a political opponent. Trotsky's rival in the military field was Josef Stalin, an obscure bureaucrat, a non-Russian, born in Georgia in the Caucasus and educated for the priesthood.

With the end of Civil War, Lenin instituted NEP, the "New Economic Policy," to try to get Russia on her feet. This was a partial return to capitalism. Foreign companies came back and often took over their former enterprises which had expropriated. Small-scale Russian entrepreneurs were encouraged. Peasants were paid again for their food and badly needed goods were sent to the villages.

By the time Lenin, worn from the strain of the Revolution and its aftermath, died in January 1924, after 18 months of paralysis, Russia was reviving. Some strides had been made at expanding the school system. The arts were flourishing—new plays, new theaters, new experimental writers—and life had become more easy though still far from normal.

Lenin had created the Communist party in his own image. He encouraged discussion within the ranks but once a decision was made everyone follow it with military discipline. He applied ruthless terrorism to those he regarded as enemies of the Revolution, executing Czar Nicholas II and his family, many of the nobility and the wealthy, important industrialists. But within his own party he was notably conciliatory remaining on good terms with his opponents. Even before he died, he became concerned that his death would split the Party. He warned particularly against Stalin whom he felt had concentrated too much power and would use it improperly. His fears were well founded.

When Lenin died, Stalin launched a savage campaign to become dictator. His chief opponent, Leon Trotsky, was immensely popular in the country, but had little support in the Party where he was regarded as a Johnny-Come-Lately. First Stalin formed a coalition with the other powerful Bolsheviks, particualrly Zinoviev, the Leningrad leader (Petrograd had been renamed after Lenin's death), and Kamenev, the Moscow chief.

Stalin and his allies drove Trotsky out of the Party into exile in remote Alma Ata, and then abroad to Turkey, Norway and finally to Mexico. He was killed there by one of Stalin's assassins in 1940. Stalin then moved against Zinoviev, Kamenev and ultmately all of the Old Bolsheviks, the men who had been closely associated with Lenin. By 1928 or 1929, Stalin had made himself master of Russia, but this was not immediately apparent either to the people in Russia or to those outside.

At about the same time Stalin launched two forced-draft movements: the so-called "collectivization of farming" and the first five-year plan for industry. The agricultural plan was designed to force all peasants into collective farms and bring an end to private farming in Russia. Many large agricultural estates had long since been turned into state farms run by the government. Now all the rest were to be organized. The thrust of Stalin's drive was against *kulaks,* the richer, more prosperous, more able farmers. Communist Party teams and Red Army units swept into the country side. They compelled the peasants to leave their farms and shipped them with their families to Siberia and Central Asia. Millions died and the disruption of agriculture was so acute that more millions died of famine the next year.

The collectives were instituted but agriculture had suffered such savage wounds that half a century later it was still a slow child in Soviet economy. The Soviet was compelled every year to import hundreds of millions of dollars worth of foodstuffs. Many economists felt she would never be able to establish a food industry productive enough to feed her population.

The achievements on the industrial front were more notable. The base for Russian industrial expansion had been laid before World War I, and many of the projects launched by Stalin had actually been on the drafting boards of engineers in the last years of the Czarist regime.

Stalin was enormously eager for the quickest possible results because he felt taht Europe was drifting toward war and he needed to expand basic industries like steel, machinery and armaments to meet the threat. By 1932 he had boosted steel production to nearly six million tons compared with a little more than four million before World War I. Coal production had been raised to 63,000,000 tons, more than double the pre-war figures, and oil to 21.3 million tons, compared with 9.3 in 1913. On the eve of World War II in 1938, he had raised steel production to 18,000,000 tons; coal to 133,000,000 tons; and oil to 32 million tons. The working force rose to 27 million and by 1938, 31.5 million persons were in schools and higher educational institutions.

Stalins's paranoid persecution complex had cost his country dearly. He had killed off most of the Old Bolshevik leadership after a staged series of trials. He had wiped out the total leadership of the Red Army on false charges of collaboration with the Nazis. He had executed thousands of ordinary Communist Party members and whole leadership groups of cities and provinces. Millions of persons had been sent to forced-labor camps. The police "industrialization" department had been placed in charge of great industries—gold and other mining operations in Siberia, the entire Soviet timber and lumber industry. Canals like the Volga-White Sea and the Moscow-Volga were built by prison labor. In some Red Army divisions the highest surviving officers were captains.

The stage was being set for one of Russia's most tragic and heroic epics. Stalin's fears over the rise of Hitler and the danger of Nazi Germany had proved correct and in 1939 Europe stood at the verge of war. First, Stalin opened negotiations with England and France for a united front against Germany. Then he switched and in August the two deadly enemies, Germany and Russia, made a pact which unleashed Hitler against Poland and World War II was on.

Stalin managed to stay on the sidelines until June 22, 1941 when he was astonished to find Hitler attacking the Soviet Union on a 1,200 mile front. He had hoped to double-cross Hitler but Hitler had double-crossed him. Despite all of Stalin's concerns, the Germans caught Russia unprepared. Nazi forces swept into the Soviet Union. Stalin had a nervous collapse and vanished for several weeks but his associates carried on. The Germans swept up to the gates of Leningrad and subjected it to a 900-day siege. They swallowed Byelorussia and the Ukraine, capturing Kiev and inflicting a million casualties on the Russians in a single blow. They plunged to the suburbs of Moscow but were turned back. They drove to Stalingrad and here in 1942-43 suffered a critical defeat. They had to pull back from the Caucasus. Gradually the Russians drove them back, inflicting terrible losses on the Nazis in the battle of Kursk-Orel in the summer of 1943, the greatest armored battle ever fought. By the spring of 1945 the Red Army had swept through the Balkans, Poland, the Baltic states and in May, Nazi Germany fell; Hitler a suicide in the Reichs chancellory bunker.

Once more the Soviet faced a colossal task. She had lost 20,000,000—and perhaps twice that number if all those who had died of disease, starvation, cold and Hitlers' death camps were counted—nearly 1,500,000 in Leningrad alone. All of European Russia lay in devastation, the cities smashed, the factories blasted to bits, the dams destroyed, the farms without tractors, horses or human power to plant the crops. Steel production in 1946 was hardly greater than it had been before the first five-year plan and even with food and aid from the United States and UNRRA Russians again starved in the countryside.

When Stalin had heard the news of Hitler's attack on the morning of June 22, 1941, he had exclaimed: "Now we have lost all that Lenin gave to us." The war had not been lost but no modern nation had suffered worse devastation.

In the task of rebuilding and rehabilitation, Stalin again utilized his secret police. Many millions of citizens were sent to Siberian labor camps, particularly almost all returning Soviet POW's. They were shipped straight from Hitler's concentration camps to Stalin's. Stalin decided he could trust no one who had been in the West, even in a prison camp. He lashed out at the intellectuals who had won a brief respite during World War II. Now they were savagely repressed and purged. All of Russia's physicists were put to work to match America's A-bomb, including some who were confined to police laboratories.

The A-bomb was produced in record time—October 1949—yet the general population was still kept on scant rations. Housing was built only in devastated towns and cities; overcrowding in Moscow steadily worsened. Stalin's own policies had provoked the Cold War. Now he drove his scientists and industries harder than ever in fear of war with the U.S.A.

A garrison mentality descended on the Soviet Union. No visitors came into Russia, no Russians went out. The Iron Curtain, as Winston Churchill christened it, descended. Russians hardly talked with each other, so fearful did they become of the police informers. The Siberian labor camps burgeoned. Lavrenti P. Beria, Chief of Police Services, became Stalin's right-hand man. The arts and literature were subjected to strictest controls. Great poets like Anna Akhmatova were suppressed. The satirist Mikhail Zoschenko was forbidden to write. The composer, Dmitri Shostakovich was censured. Operas like *The Great Friendship* were suppressed. Foreign Communist leaders vanished into concentration camps or were shot. Jews were persecuted and subjected to public abuse. Leaders of the Jewish Anti-Fascist Committee were secretly shot. The whole Leningrad Party leadership was shot.

In January 1953, Stalin prepared to launch a new and terrible purge, the one directed against most of his associates in the Politburo. He planned to arrest all the Jews in Russia and deport them to Siberia. The purge which he was planning would out-do all those he had conducted in the past. His plans rapidly matured but in the first days of March 1953 he suffered a stroke. On March 5, 1953 he died.

Stalin's death brought a new era to the Soviet Union, an era which in a sense is still in progress. Stalin's successors moved swiftly to reverse all of his cruelest terroristic policies. They released millions of prisoners from the concentration camps and closed the great bulk of the camps. Police Chief Beria and many of his most notorious associates were shot. Major efforts were made to improve Soviet living standards. More consumer goods appeared in the shops than had been seen for years. Food which had been in short supply, such as flour—which had normally been available in stores only once or twice a year—suddenly reappeared. The enormous expenditures for military arms were cut back.

The inevitable struggle for power got underway and Nikita Khruschchev emerged as the winner over Stalin's immediate successors, the triumvirate of Beria, Foreign Minister V.M. Molotov and Georgi Malenkov. Krushchev sought to revive Soviet agriculture. He revealed that

Russia's livestock census was no larger than it had been in the last Czarist year of 1916. He sponsored a vast program for plowing up steppe lands in Kazakhstan and western Siberia and sowing them with wheat—a risky gamble since the area got no more moisture than the Oklahoma dustbowl.

A great revival got underway in Soviet art and literature. Boris Pasternak published Doctor Zhivago abroad and won a Nobel Prize which caused great controversy within the Soviet. Brilliant new poets like Andrei Voznesensky, Yevgeny Yevtushenko and Bella Akhmadulina gave public informal readings in Pushkin Square attended by thosands. New painters and sculptors like Ernst Neizvestny, breaking with the sterile conventions of what was called "socialist realism" emerged. Suddenly, all of Russia seemed in ferment.

Khrushchev channeled large sums into new housing in Moscow, into making automobiles available for the first time on a major basis to private buyers, producing large quantities of radio and TV sets and embarking on-widespread cultural exchanges, particularly with the United States which for the first time brought leading American artists to the Soviet Union.

Khrushchev's extensive opening up of Soviet society was part of a major diplomatic effort which kept him travelling around the world and particularly to the United States where he was determined to inaugurate a new and more friendly relationship. He failed to achieve this goal after the shooting down of a U.S. U-2 reconnaisance plane over Russia caused the cancellation of a return visit by President Eisenhower in 1960.

Perhaps the high water mark of Khrushchev's liberalization was set by two events: his 1956 denunciation of Stalin, and revelation of Stalin's "secret crimes" against the Soviet people, and his permission for the publication in 1962 of the brief novella by Alexander Solzhenitsyn, *One Day in the Life of Ivan Denisovich.* This classic tale of a day in a Soviet concentration camp instantly produced world fame for Solzhcnitsyn who went on to win the Nobel Prize for literature with the publication (outside of the Soviet Union) of *The First Circle, The Cancer Ward* and finally his classic study of Stalin's camp system called *The Gulag Archipelago.*

But Khruschchev's personal diplomacy with Eisenhower, Nixon, Kennedy, Tito, Nehru and others did not suit his Politburo bureaucrats. Nor did they like his freewheeling politicking at home. The Soviet military establishment was incensed at his wholesale retirement of officers and his cuts in the standing army. In 1964 Khruschchev was deposed and replaced by a coalition headed by Leonid Brezhnev.

The Brezhnev era was characterized by a more bureaucratic approach. The liberal internal order sponsored by Khrushchev was carefully and selectively watered down. Experimentation in the arts was for the most part ended. Solzhenitsyn was expelled from the Soviet Union as were an increasing number of so-called dissidents, Soviet citizens, usually members of the intelligentsia and often Jewish, who protested Soviet policies, sometimes by street demonstrations, often through underground letters and newspapers.

At the same time every effort was made to continue to expand Soviet industrial and technological clout. In 1957 Russia had won the race into outer space with her first *sputnik.* She struggled to keep pace with the overwhelming technological assets of the U.S.A. When this became impossible the two countries signed a pact under which they, in effect, agreed to be partners in future space exploration.

The inadequacies of Soviet agriculture became more and more apparent and in order to maintain the relatively high consumption level to which Soviet society had become acc ustomed, Moscow began to rely more and more on extremely large-scale purchases in the United States. Soviet industry, which had scored spectacular increases in the first decade-and-a-half after World War II as new and rebuilt factories came on line, began to flag. In an effort to revive expansion ratios the Soviets more and more sought large-scale imports of foreign technology, particularly from the United States and Japan. Whole factories such as the enormous Kama River Fiat automobile plant were imported and put into production.

With the advent of the Nixon administration, the Soviet and the United States embarked on what was called detente, an effort to resolve major differences, particularly over arms, by negotiation. Moscow wished to link these talks to large-scale expansion of trade with the U.S.A. However, these efforts hit a snag due to the increasing internal friction in the Soviet over the Jewish question. Thousands of Jews sought to emigrate from Russia to Israel or the United States. For the first time since the 1920s some thousands were permitted to leave but then the policy began to come apart. Jews and other intellectuals demonstrated and protested against Soviet restrictions. Feelings abroad and in the United States supported the Jews and the other dissidents.

Apparently unable to cope with the domestic repercussions by ordinary means, the Soviet leaders fell back on elements to Stalin's policies; use of the secret police, arrests, harsh interrogations, and sentences to prison camps. And a new tactic was evolved—the sentencing of protestors to police psychiatric institutions.

Agitation over the Jewish question stimulated revival of nationalist tendencies. Ukrainians, members of the Baltic nationalities and Georgians began to stage manifestations against the authorities. Incidents of violent police repression and even street battles including shooting occurred. But alongside these repressive tendencies, the material conditions of life improved. More cars, even at costs of $112,000 after three and four year waits for delivery, appeared in the streets. The first super-highways were built and smog was noted in the Moscow atmosphere.

After sixty years the Soviet Union had created a stable but hardly dynamic society. Its standards of living had improved vastly but still had not reached the level of the advanced European countries. They were below those, for example, of Italy and not as high as those of East Germany, Czechoslovakia or Hungary.

The regime was still striving to cope with the natural and normal desires of Soviet citizens for more and easier contact with people beyond their borders, and with the problems of a free interchange of culture. New and significant Soviet writers, artists, composers and film directors were notable by the continued absence. Moscow was importing and printing a good deal of contemporary American literature with only minor censorship but was not producing Russian works which aroused much interest beyond her borders. Her mathematical and physical scientists numbered in the first ranks of the world but her biologist, biochemists and natural scientists were far behind. Social science was hardly extant and her higher education institutions accomodated only a fraction of that percent of the population enrolled in the United States.

In industry, pace and development were slow, design inferior, production badly hampered by bureaucracy. Soviet wage scales were still only a percentage of western pay scales. Agriculture seemed bogged down with no likely chance of ever attaining a production or efficiency level equal to the United States and other western countries. The revolutionary spark which Lenin had fanned into flame in 1917 had sputtered out and a slow rise of bourgeois acquisitive instincts seemed to be replacing it. A revolutionary society in 1979 the Soviet Union was not; a capitalist state she was far away from becoming.

Harrison Salisbury

CHAPTER 1

# Lenin, Trotsky and Stalin

Evil despot or father of Soviet modernization? Stalin was both. He presided over the industrializaton of a largely backward country. He also was responsible for a reign of terror that still casts its shadow over the U.S.S.R.
NEW YORK TIMES PICTURES

# REVOLUTIONISTS SEIZE PETROGRAD; KERENSKY FLEES

## MINISTERS UNDER ARREST

### Winter Palace Is Taken After Fierce Defense by Women Soldiers.

### FORT'S GUNS TURNED ON IT

### Cruiser and Armored Cars Also Brought Into Battle Waged by Searchlight.

### TROTZSKY HEADS REVOLT

### Giving Land to the Peasants and Calling of Constituent Assembly Promised.

**PETROGRAD, Nov. 8.**—With the aid of the capital's garrison complete control of Petrograd has been seized by the Maximalists, or Bolsheviki, headed by Nikolai Lenine, the Radical Socialist leader, and Leon Trotzsky, President of the Central Executive Committee of the Petrograd Council of Workmen's and Soldiers' Delegates. Their action has been indorsed by the All-Russia Congress of Workmen's Councils.

A proclamation has been issued declaring that the Revolutionary Government purposes to negotiate an "immediate democratic peace," to turn the land over to the peasantry, and to convoke the Constituent Assembly.

Premier Kerensky has fled. He is variously said to be headed for Moscow and the northern front of the army, and orders for his arrest have been issued. Last night he was reported to be at Luga, eighty-five miles southwest of Petrograd. Several members of his Cabinet have been taken into custody.

The Preliminary Parliament is declared dissolved.

Little serious fighting has attended the revolt so far. The Provisional Government troops holding the bridges over the Neva and various other points yesterday were quickly overpowered, save at the Winter Palace, the chief guardians of which were the Women's Battalion. Here last night a battle royal took place for four hours, during which the Bolsheviki brought up armored cars and the cruiser Aurora and turned the guns of the Fort of St. Peter and St. Paul upon the palace before its defenders would surrender.

Prior to the attack the Workmen's and Soldiers' leaders sent the Provisional Government an ultimatum demanding their surrender and allowing twenty minutes' grace. The Government replied indirectly, refusing to recognize the Military Committee.

Vice President Kameneff of the Workmen's and Soldiers' Delegates told The Associated Press today that the object of taking possession of the posts and telegraphs was to thwart any effort the Government might make to call troops to the capital. The Russkia Volia and the Bourse Gazette have been commandeered.

The city today presented a normal aspect. Even the noonday band accompanying the guard of relief under the previous administration continued its function. There were the customary lines in front of the provision stores and children played in the parks and gardens. There was even a notable lessening of the patrols, only a few armed soldiers and sailors moving about the streets

**How the Revolt Developed.**

The Maximalist movement toward seizing authority, rumors of which had been agitating the public mind ever since the formation of the last Coalition Cabinet, culminated Tuesday night, when, without disorder, Maximalist forces took possession of the Telegraph office and the Petrograd Telegraph Agency.

Orders issued by the Government for the opening of the spans of the bridges across the Neva later were overridden by the Military Committee of the Council of Workmen's and Soldiers' Delegates. Communication was restored after several hours of interruption. Nowhere did the Maximalists meet with serious opposition.

An effort by militiamen to disperse crowds gathered in the Nevaki and Letainy Prospekts during the evening provoked a fight in which one man is reported to have been killed. Minor disturbances, some of them accompanied by shooting, occurred in various quarters of the city. A number of persons are reported to have been killed or wounded.

Yesterday morning found patrols of soldiers, sailors, and civilians in the streets maintaining order. Further than a continuation of suppressed excitement, the streets of the city presented no unusual aspects. The shops and banks which had opened for business began closing up about noon.

Shortly after noon a Soviet force occupied the telephone exchange, where a small guard had been stationed for weeks. An effort by Government forces to retake the exchange led to a brief fusillade, by which it is believed a number of casualties was caused. The Maximalists remained in possession of the building.

Toward 5 o'clock in the afternoon the Military Revolutionary Committee issued its proclamation stating that Petrograd was in its hands. It read:

> To the Army Committees of the Active Army and to all Councils of Workmen's and Soldiers' Delegates and to the Garrison and Proletariat of Petrograd:
>
> We have deposed the Government of Kerensky, which rose against the revolution and the people. The change which resulted in the deposition of the Provisional Government was accomplished without bloodshed.
>
> The Petrograd Council of Workmen's and Soldiers' Delegates solemnly welcomes the accomplished change and proclaims the authority of the Military Revolutionary Committee until the creation of a Government by the Workmen's and Soldiers' Delegates.

Announcing this to the army at the front, the Revolutionary Committee calls upon the revolutionary soldiers to watch closely the conduct of the men in command. Officers who do not join the accomplished revolution immediately and openly must be arrested at once as enemies.

The Petrograd Council of Workmen's and Soldiers' Delegates considers this to be the program of the new authority:

First—The offer of an immediate democratic peace.

Second—The immediate handing over of large proprietarial lands to the peasants.

Third—The transmission of all authority to the Council of Workmen's and Soldiers' Delegates.

Fourth—The honest convocation of a Constitutional Assembly.

The national revolutionary army must not permit uncertain military detachments to leave the front for Petrograd. They should use persuasion, but where this fails they must oppose any such action on the part of these detachments by force without mercy.

The actual order must be read immediately to all military detachments in all arms. The suppression of this order from the rank and file by army organizations is equivalent to a great crime against the revolution and will be punished by all the strength of the revolutionary law.

Soldiers! For peace, for bread, for land, and for the power of the people! (Signed)

THE MILITARY REVOLUTIONARY COMMITTEE.

Delegates from the three Cossack regiments quartered here declared they would not obey the Provisional Government and would not march against the Workmen's and Soldiers' Delegates, but that they were prepared to maintain public order.

**Council Welcomes Lenine.**

The Petrograd Council of Workmen's and Soldiers' Delegates held a meeting at which M. Trotzky made his declaration that the Government no longer existed; that some of the Ministers had been arrested, and that the preliminary Parliament had been dissolved. He introduced Nikolai Lenine as "an old comrade whom we welcome back."

Lenine, who was received with prolonged cheers, said:

"Now we have a revolution. The peasants and workmen control the Government. This is only a preliminary step toward a similar revolution everywhere."

He outlined the three problems now before the Russian democracy. First, immediate conclusion of the war, for which purpose the new Government must propose an armistice to the belligerents; second, the handing over of the land to the peasant; third, settlement of the economic crisis.

At the close of the sitting a declaration was read from the representatives of the Democratic Minimalist Party of the Workmen's and Soldiers' Delegates, stating that the party disapproved of the coup d'état and withdrew from the Council of Workmen's and Soldiers' Delegates.

Later it was announced that the split in the Council had been healed and that a call had been sent out for a delegate from each 25,000 of the population to express the will of the Russian Army. Following is the text of this document:

> To All Army Corps and Divisional Committees:
>
> Today there is a reunion of the Workmen's and Soldiers' Delegates. The army committees are ordered to send delegates for expressing the will of the army. We suggest to you to send delegates immediately from your midst. To refuse to take part in deciding the destiny of the revolution is a sin which history will not pardon. Elect a delegate from each 25,000 and send them to the reunion.
>
> (Signed)
>
> THE PETROGRAD WORKMEN'S AND SOLDIERS' DELEGATES.

**Congress of Councils Approves.**

Subsequently the General Congress of Workmen's and Soldiers' Delegates of all Russia convened with 200 out of 560 delegates in attendance. The Chairman declared that the time was not propitious for political speeches, and the order of business of the congress approved was as follows:

First—Organization of power.

Second—Peace and war.

Third—A constituent Assembly.

The officers elected comprise fourteen Maximalists, including Nikolai Lenine and M. Zinovieff, an associate of Lenine, and Leon Trotzky. In addition seven revolutionary Socialists were appointed.

A delegation was named to initiate peace negotiations with the other revolutionary and democratic organizations "with a view to taking steps to stop bloodshed."

A resolution proposed by the Minimalists that an effort would be made to reach an agreement with the Provisional Government was voted down.

Of the 560 members of the Congress, 250 are Bolsheviki, 150 Socialist revolutionists, sixty Minimalists, fourteen of the Minimalist-Internationalist group, six of the Nationalist-Socialist group, three non-party Socialists, the others being independent.

The official news agency today made public the following statement:

"The Congress of the Councils of Workmen's and Soldiers' Delegates of all Russia, which opened last evening, issued this morning the three following proclamations:

> To All Provincial Councils of Workmen's and Soldiers' and Peasants' Delegates.
>
> All power lies in the Workmen's and Soldiers' Delegates. Government commissaries are relieved of their functions. Presidents of the Workmen's and Soldiers' Delegates are to communicate direct with the Revolutionary Government. All members of agricultural committees who have been arrested are to be set at liberty immediately and the commissioners who arrested them are in turn to be arrested.

"The second proclamation reads as follows:

> The death penalty re-established at the front by Premier Kerensky is abolished and complete freedom for political propaganda has been established at the front. All revolutionary soldiers and officers who have been arrested for complicity in so-called political crimes are to be set at liberty immediately.

"The third proclamation says:

> Former Ministers Konovaloff, Kishkin, Terestchenko, Malyanovitch, Nikitin, and others have been arrested by the revolutionary committee.

Mr. Kerensky has taken flight and all military bodies have been empowered to take all possible measures to arrest Kerensky and bring him back to Petrograd. All complicity with Kerensky will be dealt with as high treason.

**Capture of the Winter Palace.**

While the All-Russian Congress of Councils had been deliberating the Government forces, including the Women's Battalion, which had been guarding the Winter Palace had been driven inside in the course of a lively machine-gun and rifle battle, during which the cruiser Aurora, that had been moored in the Neva at the Nicolai Bridge, moved up within range, firing shrapnel, and armored cars swung into action. Then the guns of the Fortress of St. Peter and St. Paul, across the river, opened on the structure.

The palace stood out under the glare of the searchlights of the cruiser and offered a good target for the guns. The defenders held out for four hours, replying as best they could with machine guns and rifles, but at 2 o'clock this morning were compelled to surrender.

Meanwhile there had been spasmodic firing in other parts of the city, but the Workmen's and Soldiers' troops took every means to protect citizens, who were ordered to their quarters. The bridges and the Nevsky Prospect, which early in the afternoon were in the hands of the Government forces, were captured and held during the night by the Workmen's and Soldiers' troops.

November 9, 1917

# LENINE HEADS NEW CABINET

## Trotzky in the Foreign Office—Sailor on the War-Marine Board.

### MOVE TO CONFISCATE LAND

LONDON, Sunday, Nov. 11.—Premier Kerensky arrived at Luga, eighty-five miles southwest of Petrograd, last Wednesday and the garrison there attested its loyalty to his Provisional Government, according to a Petrograd dispatch yesterday to The Weekly Dispatch.

Yesterday morning he reached Gatchina, thirty miles southwest of Petrograd, where the same thing happened.

The newspaper's advices add that troops loyal to the Provisional Government are known to be near Petrograd, and a division of Cossacks is on the march from Finland. This news was given out at the Smolny Institute, headquarters of the Workmen's and Soldiers' Congress.

The garrison at Petrograd, which two days ago was solid for the extremists, is now said to be wavering in its allegiance.

The Weekly Dispatch's advices say that at the Town Hall it was rumored Friday night that most of the Moscow garrison had retransferred allegiance to the Provisional Government after fighting the Extremist supporters at the Kremlin, where they had taken refuge.

M. Skobeleff, Minister of Labor in Kerensky's Ministry, in addressing a meeting Friday night at the Town Hall, said that the Railway Workers' Union, which at first had worked under the instructions of Nikolai Lenine, now declared itself wholly on the side of the Committee of Public Safety and that it would not obey further orders of the Bolsheviki. This is the heaviest blow that the movement of the extremists has yet received.

In sixteen Ministries the Union of Government Servants has instructed its members to strike, thus paralyzing the whole Governmental machinery.

**The Bolsheviki Cabinet.**

PETROGRAD, Friday, Nov. 9.—The All-Russian Congress of Workmen's and Soldiers' Delegates is reported unofficially to have named a Cabinet composed of Bolsheviki and then adjourned. The Cabinet is headed by Nikolai Lenine as Premier and Leon Trotzky holds the post of Foreign Minister.

The Cabinet will serve until the Constituent Assembly approves it or selects a new one. In addition to Lenine and Trotzky the other members are reported to be as follows:

Minister of the Interior—M. RICKOFF.
Minister of Finance—M. SVORTZOFF.
Minister of Agriculture—M. MILIUTIN.
Minister of Labor—M. SHLIAPNIKOFF.
Committee on War and Marine—M. OVSIANNIKOFF, M. KRYLENKO, and M. BIBENKO.
Minister of Commerce—M. NOGIN.
Minister of Education—M. LUNACHARSKY.
Minister of Justice—M. OPPOKOV.
Minister of Supplies—M. THEODOROVITCH.
Minister of Posts and Telegraphs—M. AVILOFF.
Minister of Affairs of Nationalities, (a new post in charge of the affairs of the different nationalities within Russia)—M. DZHUGASHVILI.
Minister of Communications—M. RIAZANOFF.

The Cabinet members are all Bolsheviki and are supported by the Left and the Social Revolutionist Party, the other parties having withdrawn from the Workmen's and Soldiers' Congress. Bibenko is a Kronstadt sailor, while Shliapniko is a laborer.

In reply to a question from a peasant Deputy, who protested against the arrest of the former Ministers, Trotzky announced that the Socialist members of the Kerensky Cabinet would be released from the Fortress of St. Peter and St. Paul pending an investigation. He said that the other would be held.

The Congress took action to turn over to the Land Committees for distribution the landed estates and State and church lands. The lands of the Cossacks and the peasants will not be confiscated.

The entire staffs of the Foreign Office and the Ministries of Finance and Commerce have quit work.

The banks in Petrograd reopened today. The city is quiet.

November 11, 1917

### PEOPLE WANT A STRONG MAN.

**Kerensky Has Lost His Hold—All Sympathy for Government Gone.**

By HAROLD WILLIAMS.

Special Cable to THE NEW YORK TIMES.



PETROGRAD, Monday, Nov. 12.—Returning from a short visit to the northern Caucasus I traversed Russia from south to north. Rumors of the Bolsheviki rising had reached Kislovodsk before I left on Thursday—rumors wildly contradictory, exciting, and alarming. Throughout the ten Kuban territories order was undisturbed. At Rostoff on Friday I learned a few details of the rising of the garrison, while the workers were in a state of ferment and had passed Bolsheviki resolutions. But in the neighboring town of Novotcherkask, capital of the Don Territory, the Cossack Government under Kaledines had immediately declared for the Provisional Government, assumed full power in its own territories and established contact with the Cossack Governments of the neighboring territories.

Shortly before the rising the Cossacks of the Don Kuban Ter and Astrakhan territories, the Kalmyks of the Steppes, and the mountain tribes of Daghestan and the Black Sea coast had formed a league of autonomous units with a common federal government over the whole territory north of the Caucasus between the Caspian and the Black Sea. The existence of this league guarantees complete order in that territory, which includes the richest granary of Russia.

On Thursday the Kaledines Government declared martial law in the disturbed mining area of Donets Basin and an engineer whom I saw later in the train declared that the miners had resumed work.

The Cossack Congress which happened to be sitting in Kieff immediately took command of the situation there and arrested the Ukrainian Council and suppressed Bolsheviki. The last I heard in Rostoff was that the Cossacks were arresting the Bolsheviki at Novotcherkask.

From Rostoff onward there was a complete absence of definite news. Order prevailed at all the stations and fewer soldiers than usual besieged the train. The more intelligent soldiers with whom I talked were indignant with the Bolsheviki and although the Socialists declared for Korniloff, other and simpler men knew little of politics and cared less.

Nowhere throughout the journey did I hear a word of sympathy for Kerensky. Educated passengers were infuriated by his laxity in permitting the Bolsheviki agitation, and soldiers were indignant that he was unable to maintain authority and order. One railway man said that Kerensky, Lenine, and Trotzky ought all to be thrown into the Neva.

There was not a trace of enthusiasm for the Provisional Government, which was felt to have deserved its fate. But everywhere along the line was expressed a longing for real order, for real authority, for some one who could save Russia from her terrible fate.

At Kharkov Station on Saturday there was again a scarcity of news owing to a local newspaper strike.

A Bolsheviki committee had appointed its own commissary as Governor, but a passenger from Kharkov declared that there was no outward change and that the banks were open for business as usual.

At Kursk and Orel again I found complete order, but there were vague rumors and contradictory reports from Petrograd. Once we heard that the Cossacks had got the upper hand and again that the Bolsheviki were still in power.

At Tula we had news of trouble in Moscow. Approaching Moscow on a bright sunny afternoon we looked across the low-lying meadows and scanned the towers and cupolas of the city for traces of the smoke of battle. But the old capital stood out still resplendent, with no outward sign of any war.

On the outskirts the train stopped. We heard the sound of guns, and were told the officers' training school was being bombarded. Women told terrible stories of the fighting and bloodshed throughout Saturday and Sunday, and declared that whole lines had been mowed down by machine guns.

At the station there was not a single intelligent person, and all we could gather was vague rumors of continuous fighting, of houses destroyed by artillery and fire, of thousands of killed and wounded.

The streets near the station were lined with persons listening for the sound of firing, but we were told that further on the streets were empty.

As the train glided out of the station the sound of a volley came up from somewhere near the central post office. The only passenger who joined the train at Moscow was a soldier whose information was confused and fragmentary. He said that foreign soldiers were helping the Government troops.

At all stations further on we again heard contradictory reports, and I got no idea of the real situation until passengers from suburban stations joined the train this morning.

At the Petrograd station there were no visible signs of traffic. The streets looked bedraggled and grimy. There were shutters on most of the shops, and many were closed, but the trams were running as usual. Near my house I met a squad of red guard on patrol work. At the entrance to my flat two young men, residents of the house, were on guard. Residents of each house now take turns in policing the doors and gateways. We are all special constables now.

And then I plunged into the thick of Petrograd rumors and party wrangling and furious recriminations, and felt again the bitterness of the Russian tragedy as I had not felt it through all the long journey over the plain. Outside of Petrograd it is easier to believe in Russia: here the atmosphere of catastrophe is stifling.

### BOLSHEVIKI PRESS GERMANS.

**Say Prompt Action by Internationale Will Decide Civil War.**

Special Cable to THE NEW YORK TIMES.

LONDON, Nov. 17.—The Chronicle publishes two dispatches from Stockholm, dealing with the Russian situation, both being dated Friday. The first says:

"News has begun to arrive from Petrograd after a week's silence. Today's Stockholm Tidinge reports from an authentic source the actual situation in Petrograd is that the town is in the main controlled by the Bolsheviki, but that some quarters are in the hands of Kerensky forces. Kerensky's supporters are developing some degree of activity even in South Russia. It is said that the Bolsheviki troops are characterized by utter lack of discipline and are without officers to lead their operations.

"Travelers from Petrograd informed the Dagbiad that, in their opinion, Kerensky would succeed in mastering the situation. Popular sympathy has turned toward him, and there seems to be a common desire for a strong head at the helm and a restoration of the death penalty.

'Representatives here of the Bolsheviki have wired to the German minority leaders, Haase, Ledbour and Mehring: 'Your telegrams and the manifestations of the other brother parties have been sent in by courier, as telegraphic communications are cut. The whole struggle will not be concluded by victory or defeat. A lasting civil war is impending in Russia and its issue depends on swift and decisive effort by internationale.' "

The second dispatch reads: "The Italian Minister at Petrograd has arrived in Stockholm on leave from considerations of health. He left Petrograd Saturday and on Sunday evening was in telegraphic communication with Petrograd from Tornea. Interviewed by your correspondent, the Minister made the following statement:

"'The rapidity with which Maximalism has been able to spread in Russia may be explained by the fact that it makes an appeal to the ignorant masses in virtue of two ideas, which they easily understand and accept. These are: 1, distribution of land, and 2, immediate peace. Nevertheless, as these two ideas are as difficult to realize as they are easy to talk about, disappointment will come soon and the disorganization of the Maximalists will then be as rapid as its progress had been.

"'The Maximalists will have still another disappointment: They have promised a revolution in Germany. On this illusion they have based all their hopes regarding their "democratic peace." The fact is, however, that revolution in Germany is not only not in sight, but even unthinkable. German socialism is solidly behind the imperialistic Government and will be unmoved by the proclamations of Lenine.

"'The present crisis in Russia will end by clarifying and demonstrating these three huge errors of the Bolsheviki and by opening the eyes of the people.

"'On the other side the Central Powers are making a fundamental mistake if they think the real Russia has lost all consciousness of its mission and its power. Real Russia knows very well that it cannot defend its freedom and its future in any other way than by weapon in hand and by defending the common cause of the Allies.'

November 18, 1917

# Bolsheviki Catechism from Lenine's Pen

**By ABRAHAM YARMOLINSKY, Instructor in Russian at the College of the City of New York.**

**THE following attempt to formulate the platform of the socialistic faction which calls itself the Communistic Party, but which is commonly known as "Bolsheviki," is based on a pamphlet on the political parties in Russia, written by Nikolai Lenine, the Radicals' Premier of Russia. It is presented in the form of questions and answers. The wording closely follows that of Lenine.**

**Q.—What social class do we represent?**

**A.—We represent the class-conscious proletaries, hired laborers, and the poorer portion of the rural population.**

**Q.—What is our attitude toward socialism?**

**A.—We stand for socialism. The**

**Workmen's Councils must at once take the necessary practical steps for the realization of the socialistic program. They must immediately take over the control of the banks and capitalistic syndicates, with a view to nationalizing them; that is, making them the property of the whole people.**

**Q.—What form of State organization do we advocate?**

**A.—We advocate a republic of Councils of Workmen, Soldiers, Peasants, &c. All the power must belong to them.**

**Q.—Should we support the Provisional Government?**

**A.—No. Let the capitalists support it. Our aim is to make the councils the only authority and power in the country.**

**Q.—Is it necessary to convoke the Constituent Assembly?**

**A.—Yes, and as soon as possible. The guarantee of its success lies in the growth of the councils in number and power, and in the arming of the masses of workmen.**

**Q.—Does the State need a police force of the usual type and a standing army?**

**A.—Not at all. The people must be made synonymous with the army and militia. The capitalists must pay the workmen for their service in the militia.**

**Q.—Should the army officers be elected by the soldiers?**

**A.—Yes. Furthermore, every step of the officers and Generals must be verified by special deputies from the soldiers.**

**Q.—Should the soldiers oust their superiors without authority?**

**A.—Yes. This is useful and necessary in every respect. The soldiers only obey and respect the authorities they elect.**

**Q.—Are we against this war?**

**A.—Yes, we are. We are emphatically against this imperialistic war and the bourgeois Governments conducting it, our own Provisional Government included.**

**Q.—What is our attitude toward the predatory international treaties (about the dismemberment of Persia, China, Turkey, Austria, &c.) made by the Czar with England and France?**

**A.—We are against them. It is our task to make it plain to the masses that it is hopeless to expect anything in this respect from the capitalistic Governments, and that it is necessary to transfer the power to the proletariat and the poorer element among the peasants.**

**Q.—What is our attitude toward annexations?**

**A.—We are against them. All the promises of the capitalistic Governments to renounce annexations are false. There is but one means to expose the fraud, namely, to demand the emancipation of the people, oppressed by their own capitalists.**

**Q.—What is our attitude toward the Liberty Loan?**

**A.—We are against it, for the war remains imperialistic, waged by capitalists, allied to capitalists for the interest of capitalists.**

**Q.—Can the capitalistic Governments body forth the will of the nations to peace?**

**A.—No. Conscious workmen cherish no illusions on this score.**

**Q.—Should all monarchs be deposed?**

**A.—Yes.**

**Q.—Should the peasants immediately take possession of the private lands?**

**A.—Yes, the land must be seized immediately. Strict order should be established through the agency of the Councils of Peasants' Deputies. The production of bread and meat should be increased, for the soldiers must be better fed. The damaging of cattle, implements, &c., cannot be allowed. It is necessary to organize the poor peasants and the agricultural laborers.**

**Q.—Should the fraternization at the front be encouraged?**

**A.—Yes. This is both useful and necessary. It is absolutely necessary immediately to encourage attempts at fraternizing between the soldiers of the two belligerent sides.**

**Q.—What color is our flag?**

**A.—Red, for the red flag is the flag of the universal proletarian revolution.**

November 18, 1917

## CHAOS IN RUSSIA IS GETTING WORSE

### *Monopoly in Advertisements—How Attempt to Get Bank's 10,000,000 Rubles Failed.*

**By HAROLD WILLIAMS.**



Special Cable to The New York Times.

PETROGRAD, Nov. 21.—This combination of the sixteenth and twentieth centuries grows disconcerting. One has to develop new mental kinks to secure a grip on the situation. Russia is now made up of incoherent, complex, diverse political units, which are neither at war nor at peace with each other, which are connected by the old administrative and economic mechanism, but which recognize no central Government and have temporarily lost the secret of combination.

The habit of thinking in terms of Russia continues and is not easily eradicated, even by the whirlwind that has dissipated the central authority. Transcaucasia is governed by a local committee of moderate Socialists, and the Caucasian Army has just won a considerable victory over the Turks on the River Diala, on the borders of Mesopotamia, taking 1,600 prisoners. Kaledines's Government is master of the southeastern Cossack territories. In Kiev after a few days' fighting the staff escaped from the town, and the Ukrainian Rada took entire political and military charge of Ukraine, their War Minister promising to see to supplies for the southwestern front. In Helsingfors during a general strike the Socialists seized all Government institutions, and have established what they call the Red Government, and here in Petrograd we are living in wonderland.

That elusive and variable quantity, the Bolshevik Government, daily issues proclamation and decrees. Its latest effort is a decree establishing Government monopoly of advertisements; that is to say, advertisements are only to be published in the Soviet organs, and the penalty for disobedience is entire confiscation of the property and three years' imprisonment. Yet, in spite of all these stern prohibitions, the papers are creeping out one by one. All the Socialist papers are published daily. A Cossack paper has reappeared. The popular non-party sheets, Listok and Gazeta, are now immune, and it is only the big non-Socialist organs, the Rech, Bourse Gazette, and Novoe Vremya that are still under the ban; but the printers' union is threatening a general strike if the ban is not lifted.

The State Bank continues to be the scene of bloodless warfare. At 2 o'clock yesterday afternoon the Bolshevik Minister of Finance came to the bank with four soldiers and an order from Milrevcom for 100,000,000 rubles. One of the soldiers of the guard told him, "This is brigandage," to which the Minister replied, "That is a strong expression." Soon a detachment of soldiers, sailors, and Red Guard appeared with band playing and tried to enter the bank, but the Bolshevik Commander in Chief, Colonel Muravieff, was summoned and agreed that the guard be not removed.

Delegates from the regimental committees met in the bank, where two documents were read, one an order from Muravieff appointing Captain Mironoff commander of the detachment sent to open up the bank, and the other a proclamation from Milrevcom to the bank employes. The assistant director of the bank pointed out that this proclamation was unsigned, whereupon the Bolshevik Minister of Finance took a pen and signed it. Then a representative of the Peasants' Council read a resolution protesting against the criminal campaign of the Bolsheviki, and a representative of the Government department where paper money is manufactured declared that if an attempt were made to rob the bank all the workmen of the department would strike.

Eventually Muravieff went to the Smolny Institute, explained the circumstances, and returned with a resolution from the Bolshevik Government to the effect that in view of the fact that the demand for the money was not legally formulated the question would be left open and the demand would not be repeated until it could be made in legal form. The soldiers on guard declared that they would only admit to the bank persons legally authorized.

The minds of the Bolshevik followers are exercised by the question of the promised immediate peace. To calm them a long confused report on the peace situation was issued in the Pravda today by a new arrival, one Radek, representative of the Stockholm Bolsheviki and an intimate associate of Parvus. The report includes a proclamation from the German independent Socialists urging a mass demonstration in favor of immediate peace, and a leading article from the Leipziger Volkszeitung in a similar sense.

More important is the assertion, for the entire accuracy of which it is unwise to vouch, that the Scheidemann group sent a delegate to Stockholm to confer with the Russian Socialists there, and that as a result of the negotiations the delegate declared that the German majority Socialists wished the Russian workers to know that the majority party was prepared to support the demand for an armistice and peace negotiations on the lines laid down in the Bolsheviki decree. Scheidemann and Ebert were to begin a campaign on these lines last Sunday.

What all this means only experts in Stockholm diplomacy and in the psychology of Parvus and his associates can approximately determine.

November 23, 1917

# KALEDINES HEADS REVOLT AGAINST BOLSHEVIST RULE

## Supported in Great Movement by Conservatives, Lenine's 'Government' Announces.

## KORNILOFF HAS JOINED HIM

## Cossack Generals Supplied with 'Scores of Millions,' Petrograd Proclamation Says.

## RED ARMY ON THE MARCH

### Extremist Troops Ordered to Attack the Counter-Revolutionary Forces Anywhere on Sight.

LONDON, Dec. 9.—A proclamation to the Russian nation has been issued by the Russian Government announcing:

"Kaledines and Korniloff, assisted by the Imperialists and Constitutional Democrats, have raised a revolt and declared war in the Don region against the people and the revolution."

The proclamation adds that the Constitutional Democrats and bourgeoisie are supplying the revolting Generals with scores of milions.

"The Workmen's and Soldiers' Delegates have ordered the necessary movements of troops against the counter-revolution and issued decrees authorizing the local revolutionary garrisons to attack the enemies of the people without awaiting orders from the supreme authorities and forbidding any attempts at mediation."

**Kaledines Hope of Conservatives.**

General Kaledines. the Cossack chieftain who leads the new revolt against the Bolshevist Government, had originally at his immediate command an army of from 30,000 to 40,000 Don Cossacks. Aside from these professional warriors, however, General Kaledines has been systematically winning to himself in the last two months the support of those factions of the bourgeoisie and Constitutional Democrats who saw nothing but disaster for Russia if the Bolsheviki were permitted to take control of the Government. Accounts of Kaledines's activities, in Russian newspapers which have recently been received here, clearly indicate that the failure of the Korniloff revolt in September turned the eyes of the conservative elements to Kaledines as the last and only hope, and that these elements, by every means available, have endeavored to convince him that he could succeed where Korniloff had failed.

To this end he has been supplied, according to reports, not only with ample funds for the purchase of munitions and supplies, but an active propaganda has been undertaken right in the ranks of the army, especially since the Bolsheviki came into power, to win the peasantry over to his support. The peasants, being the future landholders of Russia, have been consistently appealed to by the emissaries of Kaledines on the ground that the Bolshevist rule eventually meant a complete dissolution of property interests, or, at the best, a communal system like the old Mir, which would leave the poorer peasants no better off after the revolution than they had been before the revolution.

As early as last August there was evidence that the peasants were inclined to swing into a strong allignment, with General Kaledines as their leader. The Knights of St. George, representing peasant landholders of some 80,000,000 acres, were organizing themselves into military leagues. All the peasant Cossacks, and Kirchiz and Caucasian tribes banded themselves together in defense of their homes and property against the Maximalists. From Lake Baikal to the Dniester, from the Don to the Persian border, it was evident that a great force was welding itself to oppose and crush the elements of disintegration.

Moscow was Kaledines's great stronghold. In the recent provincial elections the bourgeoise elements which wanted him to take control defeated the Bolsheviki at the polls. In Petrograd during the same elections the bourgeoisie and Constitutional Democrats ran very close to the Bolsheviki, showing even there the presence of a strong bloc upon which Kaledines could rely, and apparently did rely in the organization of the present revolt.

The preliminary steps in the revolt, though not officially recognized as such by the Bolsheviki, occurred in the middle of last month when General Kaledines with his Cossacks, according to reliable reports, seized the great Donetz coalfield, a position of great strategic advantage because it gave him control of the whole Russia system of railway communications, as well as the direct approach to the wheat and great food centers of Southern Russia, upon which the rest of Russia had to depend for its supplies. If these conditions have not changed it would be virtually in Kaledines's power to starve or freeze Petrograd out.

Even in November he announced that he would do that very thing. At Kharkov he stopped 200 wagons loaded with food for Petrograd, and announced his intention, it was reported, of stopping the whole transport of food to the capital, in order to subdue the Bolsheviki faction.

Kaledines, in his present position, is also favored by the fact that he has a direct line of communication with the British armies operating in Mesopotamia, so that if the Allies come to his support, he will be able to receive munitions and other supplies via the Persian Gulf and the Caucasus. In the most recent British reports of operations in Mesopotamia much emphasis has been laid on the active participation of Russian troops.

General Kaledines first came into prominence during the Korniloff revolt, when he backed Korniloff with his entire Cossack organization. After the Korniloff débâcle, the Kerensky Government demanded that the Cossack Council place Kaledines under arrest. The Cossacks refused to comply with the order and Kaledines remained in command. He continued to maintain an uncompromising position toward the Kerensky Government, and when the Bolsheviki took control he openly declared himself their enemy and retired to Southern Russia and the region of the Don, which was his stronghold. His headquarters are at Novo-Tcherkask.

General Korniloff, who, according to yesterday's dispatch, has come to the assistance of Kaledines in the new revolt, narrowly escaped death at the hands of Bolshevist soldiers on Dec. 4, when General Dukhonin, former Commander in Chief, was thrown from a train and beaten to death after the Bolshevist forces had captured the army headquarters at Mohilev. Before the Bolsheviki arrived, General Korniloff, anticipating their approach, fled from the headquarters, and, it appears, joined Kaledines in the south. It was General Korniloff's flight, in fact, that prompted the Bolshevist soldiers, according to reports, to wreak their vengeance upon Dukhonin.

December 10, 1917

# *Japanese Occupy Vladivostok Terminal; Foil Bolshevist Plan to Seize Supplies*

*Special to The New York Times.*

WASHINGTON, Dec. 11. — Authentic information reached Washington tonight that troops of the Japanese army have occupied the great railroad works at Vladivostok, the Pacific terminal of the Trans-Siberian Railway.

The importance of this action at this juncture cannot be overestimated. It means that the vast quantities of supplies assembled at Vladivostok for use by the Russian Provisional Government will not fall into the hands of the Bolsheviki, who have been casting eager eyes toward these for use in the civil war that has been precipitated throughout Russia by the action of the Bolshevist Government in seeking to negotiate a separate peace with the Central Powers.

The railroad works which the Japanese have occupied have been the place where all the imported railroad cars and locomotives shipped from the United States under the Russian credit purchases in this country have been assembled. There are also at Vladivostok great supplies of other kinds of stores, including ammunition. The possession of the railway yards and the railway equipment at the Vladivostok terminals will make it absolutely impossible for the Bolshevist Government to move these cars and stores without the consent of the Entente powers.

Aside from the necessity of preventing the supplies from being used against the Cossack and other elements that are endeavoring to overthrow the Bolsheviki, their protection is necessary to preclude the possibility of their falling into the hands of the Germans through the Petrograd extremists.

It would not be necessary for the Japanese to send troops by sea to Vladivostok. By reason of their control over the Dalny Peninsula and Korea, it would be possible for them to move troops from Chan Chun, in Manchuria, to Harbin, by rail, and thence eastward by rail to Vladivostok, and thus avoid the frozen condition of the port.

December 12, 1917

# *RUSSIAN OFFICERS ILLTREATED BY MEN*

## *Some Made to Change Places with Their Orderlies Under New Elective System.*

Special Cable to THE NEW YORK TIMES.

PETROGRAD, Sunday, Dec. 16.—Yesterday was a painful day for the officers of the Russian Army. The decree of Lenine came into force abolishing all military ranks, titles, and decorations. Henceforward officers will be elected by the men. The officers who are not re-elected to their duties become privates, with their pay correspondingly lowered. Privates prefer to elect officers from among themselves, and former officers are therefore almost always degraded. There were several cases yesterday of officers publicly assaulted by soldiers, who tore off their epaulettes and medals, using considerable violence and every insult contained in the luxuriant vocabulary of the Russian private.

On the front, or what remains of it, matters are even worse. With the active encouragement of German spies, the soldiers have introduced every possible means of degrading their officers. Colonels and their orderlies have been made to exchange functions. Officers of many years' service have been forced to clean out stables. An army whose soviets are unanimously opposed to the death penalty has no hesitation in its application to its own officers. The drastic reduction in pay is the last straw. Ranks have virtually ceased to count. An officer cannot desert, like a private. His country is still theoretically at war, and his fellow-soldiers would not hesitate to punish him and his family if he escaped. So officers now frequently wear civilian overcoats and invariably present a depressed appearance.

December 18, 1917

# BOLSHEVIST RULE MENACED BY FOES

**Social Revolutionists in Majority.**

Special Cable to THE NEW YORK TIMES.

PETROGRAD, Jan. 14.—At present 520 members of the Constituent Assembly have been elected. Of these 161 are Bolshevist and 267 are Socialist Revolutionaries. The other parties are small and mainly representative of the Maximalists. Forty-one Ukrainians form the largest group. All the important nationalities are represented down to Chuvashes and Bashkirs. There are only 15 Cadets, all told.

The Socialist Revolutionaries consequently have it in their control. It is uncertain how many of their left wing will vote with the Bolsheviki and how many of their right will not attend.

If the local Soviets can retain their hold on the Donetz Basin, important results will certainly follow. The Donetz region supplies the greater part of the coal used in Russia. Owing to the recent disturbances, the output has practically ceased, with disastrous consequences to transport of food and other necessaries.

Owing to lack of fuel, Petrograd's supply of electricity has almost given out. Current for lighting is available for only a few hours daily. The telephones work intermittently, and the tramways are held up by uncleared snow and lack of energy.

Moreover, daily reports are received of the closing down of factories owing to the shortage of fuel and of raw material, which does not arrive because of insufficient fuel for the railways.

The Bolshevist Government has passed a new decree making the State a publisher. In order to spread culture, the author's copyright expires fifteen years after death, when the State may, if it wishes, assume a monopoly of the publication of his works for a period of five years after his copyright becomes public property. The Government publisher is to proceed immediately to the publication of a series of Russian classics.

January 15, 1918

# *BOLSHEVIKI PREPARE DEMANDS ON ASSEMBLY*

## *Want Recognition of Soviet Authority and the Present Peace Program.*

By ARTHUR RANSOME.

Special Cable to THE NEW YORK TIMES.

PETROGRAD, Jan. 17.—The Central Executive Committee of the Soviet has published a declaration which will be read by a representative of the Government, who will open the Constituent Assembly. The declaration is in four parts.

The first part declares that Russia is a republic of Soviets. Both the Central and local Governments are to be in the hands of these organs. The basis of the Republic is a free alliance of free nations, a federation of national republics of Soviets.

The second part provides for the complete socialization of the country, including the nationalization of forests, mines, waters, banks, land, factories, railways, etc., industrial conscription, the arming of the whole working class and disarmament of the propertied classes.

The third part expresses the Constituent Assembly's approval of the Soviet policy, fraternization, publication of secret documents, and the ending of the war with a democratic peace on the principle of no annexations and no indemnities, and self-determination of peoples. It insists on a complete break with the barbarous bourgeois policy of keeping in subjection millions of working folk in Asia, in colonies generally, and in the small countries.

It approves the recognition of Finnish independence, the removal of troops from Persia, and the Armenians' right to self-definition, and expresses the belief that the Soviet Government will continue by the same road until it reaches "final victory" through an international labor revolt against the yoke of capital.

The fourth and most significant part includes recognition by the Assembly that it was elected on party lists prepared before the October revolution, and that it therefore is not justified in opposing itself to the Soviet Government. This indicates clearly the line of Bolshevist policy. In case the Assembly does not prove obedient, the Bolsheviki will probably look up Cromwell in English histories and learn what to do. From a rigid standpoint of theoretic democracy it is difficult to defend them. But the motives of the probable majority against them are neither idealistic nor patriotic. The Bolshevist motives also have nothing to do with patriotism, but they have ideals, and the present struggle is really an attempt to force these ideals on the apathetic multitude.

Anti-Bolshevist preparations for a deminstration continue, while the Bolsheviki urge that the people should stay at home and not lend themselves to be the tools of the so-called Socialist parties which have themselves become tools of the now desperate propertied and privileged classes.

Again throughout the town is that strange tension in the air which was noticeable before the previous rows. Yesterday at the Tauris Palace, where the Constituent Assembly is to meet, the Deputies were talking excitedly about machine guns and thinking that it was possible that the Assembly would not meet at all.

The Bolsheviki are quite confident of weathering the crisis.

January 19, 1918

# LENINE DISSOLVES RUSSIAN ASSEMBLY

## Sailor Guards Turn Members Out of Tauride Palace at 4 in the Morning.

PETROGRAD, Jan. 20, (Associated Press.)—The Constituent Assembly has been dissolved. The decree of dissolution was issued last night by the Council of National Commissioners and passed early this morning by the Central Executive Committee of the Workmen's and Soldiers' Deputies.

At 4 o'clock yesterday morning the Assembly was closed by sailor guards.

Following is the text of the decree of dissolution:

"When the Constituent Assembly voted against the declaration made by the President of the Central Executive Committee after an hour's deliberation the Bolsheviki left the hall and were followed by the Social Revolutionists of the Left on the Assembly showing its unwillingness to approve the manner in which the peace pourparlers were being conducted. At 4 o'clock this morning the Constituent Assembly was dissolved by sailors. Today a decree dissolving the Assembly will be published."

The first hint the newspaper men received that extreme measures were contemplated was at 6 o'clock yesterday morning, when they were informed that the Tauride Palace, where the Assembly began its sessions on Friday, would be closed to the members of the Assembly, to the newspaper men, and to every one else.

**Railway Men Hostile.**

Meanwhile the All-Russian Railway Men's Congress had passed by a vote of 273 to 61 a resolution supporting the Constituent Assembly and calling upon the People's Commissaries to agree with the majority with a view to the formation of a Government responsible to the Assembly.

Additional details of the opening of the Assembly on Friday are now available. Nikolai Lenine, the Bolshevist Premier, and other of the Government Commissioners attended. M. Sorokin, formerly Secretary to Kerensky, and other Social Revolutionary members who had been arrested were escorted under guard from their prison to the Tauride Palace to take part in the meeting. M. Tseretelli, former Minister of the Interior, although seriously ill, occupied a seat with the Social Revolutionary Left. Nearly half the Assemblers' Delegates stipulating that all authority was vested in that body, the Social Revolutionists proposed the cheer, "All power to the Constituent Assembly." This was enthusiastically given by the Social Revolutionists and hissed by the Bolsheviki.

January 21, 1918

# ECONOMIC CRISIS WORRYING LENINE

## Land-Owning Peasants as Well as Bourgeoisie to be Deprived of Their Estates.

## PAPER MONEY BIG PROBLEM

PETROGRAD, Feb. 6.—The distribution of land as the Spring planting season approaches and the increasing volume of paper money are furnishing grave problems for the Bolshevist authorities.

Unemployed workmen, who are leaving the cities for their native villages to get land, rapidly are spreading the economic struggle throughout Russia. The All-Russian Congress of Workmen's and Soldiers' Delegates adjourned without adopting the plans of M. Kalegayev, the Minister of Agriculture, for the apportionment of the land. Consequently, no definite legislation has been established for the method of division.

The land-owning peasants as well as the bourgeoisie are to be deprived of their estates. Premier Lenine today addressed a large gathering of agitators who are to depart soon for the provinces to lead the confiscation campaign. He urged them to make war on all village exploiters and rich peasants as they did on the wealthy landowners.

"We have taken the land to give it to the poor peasants," the Premier said. "Do not let the rich peasants or exploiters get the agricultural implements. Pit ten poor peasants against every rich one. The police are dead and buried and the masses must take affairs in their own hands.

"External war is finished or is being finished now. Internal war begins, but not a war with arms. This is an economic war. The masses must take back what has been stolen from them. The rich, who have hidden their wealth, think the masses will pull them through. Somehow, we must uncover the hidden wealth or, otherwise, the Bolshevist Government is banrupt.

"The republic needs 28,000,000,000 rubles annually. Its prospective income is only 8,000,000,000 rubles. The hidden wealth must be uncovered and placed at the disposal of the Government."

Increasing distrust of paper money is helping to make the economic and food conditions worse in Petrograd and elsewhere. There is no hard money, and the little paper money of the old régime is eagerly sought.

The circulating medium now chiefly is poorly printed bills, two inches square, and in denominations of 20 and 40 rubles. This money is referred to contemptuously as "Kerensky money," and is discounted in many places. The situation is rendered still more serious by the appearance of much counterfeit money.

Discussing the flood of paper money, the Izvestia estimates the present amount of Russian paper at 18,000,000,000 rubles as against 1,633,000,000 rubles before the war. The gold reserve before the war, which the newspaper says is now much less, was 1,604,000,000 rubles. The Izvestia estimates that the national debt of Russia is now about 80,000,000,000 rubles, of which 41,000,000,000 is war expenses contracted in thirty-seven and a half months.

The war increased the amount of paper money more than ten times, but the Izvestia points out that prices of manufactured articles have increased thirty to forty times. Izvestia declares that it would be impossible to liquidate the results of the war under a capitalistic régime, and says it is necessary to take immediate measures during the transition period to protect the public against the consequences of a flood of paper money.

It suggests the revaluation of the ruble, but says that such a course is impossible until the end of the war and until the gold reserve is increased. The Izvestia says that the leaders who frame a commercial treaty between Germany and Russia should keep in mind the "possibility and even the inevitable necessity of legal revaluation." It also suggests the revision of all tariff schedules and salary lists.

LONDON, Feb. 6.—A Reuter dispatch from Petrograd says that the Moscow branch of the State Bank has been closed indefinitely because of lack of funds.

February 8, 1918

# CHAOS IN RUSSIA AS GERMAN SEES IT

## Country's Industrial Production Has Sunk to 5 Per Cent. of Normal, He says.

AMSTERDAM, Feb. 24.—The state of chaos in Russia is described by an eyewitness in the Tageszeitung. Passengers on trains have been frozen to death owing to the lack of glass in the car windows. When the German and Austrian delegates left Petrograd they had not eaten bread for days. There are only two locomotives in Petrograd, one of which is capable of only ten miles an hour.

Repairs formerly costing 30,000 rubles now cost 500,000 rubles. The riveting of a boiler costs 70,000 rubles, which, says the correspondent, is not surprising, as the riveter gets forty rubles for a day's work of three or four hours. There are half a million unemployed in Petrograd, and the industrial production of the country has sunk to 5 per cent. of the normal.

In some of the districts most of the blast furnaces have been extinguished. Sugar production has been reduced from one hundred million poods, (a pood is about thirty-six and a half pounds,) to forty million poods, and next year will not reach ten million.

The Chief of the Finance Ministry is a college student. The Fifth Army Chief is a former actor. The Chief of Telegraphs is a clerk. The Government's reporter of the Financial Commission at Brest-Litovsk was a clerk, who, says the writer, "hadn't the faintest notion of the simplest exchange problems." The commander of the noted Pavloff Regiment is a woman.

A Dutch resident of Petrograd, in a long letter published in The Hague Nieuwe Courant, says that lynching occurs daily. After detailing seizures at the capital and many extravagances, he concludes: "Russia is so completely disorganized that it will be years before she recovers."

## MARTIAL LAW IN PETROGRAD.

### Bolsheviki Talk of "Passionate Desire" to Defend the Capital.

PETROGRAD, Feb. 23. — Petrograd was placed under martial law today. The following proclamation was issued by the General Staff of the Petrograd military district:

1. The City of Petrograd is declared to be under martial law.

2. All persons caught in the act of stealing, pillaging, attempting expropriation, or otherwise committing reprehensible deeds will be shot without pity by detachments of the revolutionary army.

3. Every individual, organization, or institution not having special permission must hand over to the Council of Workmen's and Soldiers' Delegates of the district all bombs, grenades, projectiles, and other explosives, which the Workmen's and Soldiers' Delegates will send to army depots. Every person who does not conform within forty-eight hours with this paragraph will be declared an outlaw.

4. All journals and other organs of the press are obliged strictly to verify all news given regarding the activities of the Government, as well as information coming from the theatre of war. The Extraordinary General Staff gives notice that refusal to submit in all respects to this order will involve suppression of the offending journal and the arrest of the editor and his collaborators.

5. Documents dealing with produce arriving or which has arrived or is retained in Petrograd or its environs must be presented to the Extraordinary General Staff. All produce will be paid for at rates fixed by the Food Controller. Any person who refuses to submit to this order or is convicted of concealing provisions will be shot as a speculator.

6. Counter-revolutionary agitators, German spies, and other persons who rise against the Government of revolutionary Russia will be shot.

7. All orders issued by the Extraordinary General Staff enter into force on the day of publication in the press organs of the Government.

8. All newspapers are compelled to publish the orders of the Extraordinary General Staff in heavy type on the first page.

In consequence of the declaration of a state of siege six of the most important Petrograd newspapers, which opposed the authority of the Workmen's and Soldiers' Delegates, have been suppressed. If attempts are made to reissue them the entire staffs will be arrested. The proprietors are ordered to pay full wages to the workmen during the period of suppression.

Formation of an army of volunteers to defend Petrograd has been begun, the Bolshevist Telegraph Agency announces.

"This crisis of irresolution in the spirit of the population is definitely at an end," the statement says. "The wave of panic has changed to a passionate desire to defend Socialist Petrograd by all means and to ward off attacks made against it. The appeal of the Council of Commissioners, beginning 'The Socialist Fatherland is in danger,' has caused an outburst of enthusiasm among the masses.

"Enrollment of large numbers of volunteers has begun. In a few days there will be under arms not less than 50,000 fighters, without counting soldiers who desire to fight. Special regiments are being formed, consisting of Socialist nationals from Esthonian, Lettish and Mussulman regiments in Petrograd. These Socialist regiments will be called regiments of defense of the Socialist Fatherland. Many women are expressing their desire to be armed and lend their aid to fighters marching against the Germans and supporters of General Kaledine.

"It is the same in the towns of Kiev, Moscow, and Pskov."

February 25, 1918

# PEACE SIGNED

BERLIN, March 3, (Via London.)—"By reason of the signing of the peace treaty with Russia," says the official communication from headquarters tonight, "military movements in Great Russia have ceased."

PETROGRAD, March 3.—The peace treaty with Germany has been signed.

The following message, addressed to Premier Lenine and Foreign Minister Trotzky, had been received yesterday at the Smolny Institute from the delegation at Brest-Litovsk:

As we anticipated, deliberations on a treaty of peace are absolutely useless, and could only make things worse in comparison with the ultimatum of Feb. 21. They might even assume the character of leading to the presentation of another ultimatum.

In view of this fact, and in consequence of the Germans' refusal to cease military action until peace is signed, we have resolved to sign the treaty without discussing its contents, and leave after we have attached our signatures. We, therefore, have requested a train, expecting to sign today and leave afterward.

The most serious feature of the new demands compared with those of Feb. 21 is the following:

To detach the regions of Karaband, Kars, and Batoum from Russian territory on the pretext of the right of peoples to self-determination.

March 4, 1918

# RUSSIANS MOVING CAPITAL TO MOSCOW

PETROGRAD, March 5.—Moscow is to be declared the new capital of Russia, and the Government purposes to publish a statement to this effect immediately. Petrograd will be proclaimed a free port.

Notwithstanding the signing of peace, the Government is determined to transfer all the State institutions to Moscow, Nizhni-Novgorod, and Kaza. The removal of the Ministries of Foreign Affairs, Communications, and Finance began today. The population of Petrograd is hastily quitting the city, but there are many transportation difficulties, and already the roads leading from Petrograd are crowded with all sorts of vehicles.

The Russian delegates returned from Brest-Litovsk today, and will report to the Executive of the Soviets as soon as possible. According to the latest reports here, hostilities have been suspended on all fronts, the Germans having halted on the northern front along the line comprising Narva, Pskov, Vitebsk, Mohilev, and Orsha.

The Bolshevist leaders are prepared to withdraw even as far as to the Ural Mountains rather than submit to the defeat of the revolution, said Leon Trotzky, Bolshevist Foreign Minister, in an interview today with The Associated Press. If the Bolsheviki could go back to the state of affairs which existed last October, just before they overthrew the Kerensky Government, he asserted, they would repeat the whole program which had been put through since that time.

March 7, 1918

## NEW POST FOR TROTZKY.

### Chosen to Head Petrograd Military Revolutionary Committee.

PETROGRAD, March 11.—In consequence of the departure of the Government Commissaries to Moscow, a special Petrograd Military Revolutionary Committee of seven members has been formed, with Leon Trotzky as President. Another committee of ten members, representing the Council of Commissaries, also will be formed, with Mr. Zinovieff, a Lenine adherent, as President.

The neutral legations have decided to remain in Petrograd.

The typhus epidemic in Petrograd is increasing. The anathema against the Bolsheviki pronounced by Dr. Tikhon, Patriarch of All-Russia and Metropolitan of Moscow, was read in all the churches Sunday.

The Germans advancing on Odessa are meeting with determined resistance along the Slobodka-Tznamenka line.

Reports received here say that Austria is isolating all prisoners of war who have returned in order to prevent propaganda.

March 13, 1918

## TROTZKY FOR A BIG ARMY.

### Says Only Trained Officers Can Successfully Oppose Germans.

MOSCOW, March 20 (Associated Press.)—Leon Trotzky delivered an address before the Moscow Soviet tonight and declared unequivocally for a new army of 300,000 to 750,000, commanded by trained officers and strictly disciplined. He said it was foolish to suppose that officers could be improvised and denounced guerrilla warfare as useless and undisciplined. He said the Bolshevist army was helpless against skilled troops.

"We need a strong army to defend ourselves in this critical world-position," he said. "From east and west enemies are upon us. According to news reports, Germany has proposed peace without annexations or contributions to the western powers, with Alsace to be returned to France and Belgium to be restored. This is unconfirmed, but probable. It means peace at Russia's expense. There is a struggle between two currents in England. One favors a compromise at Russia's expense, and the other reckons with a powerful development of the laboring masses, which warn against an alliance with Germany. We are surrounded by enemies on all sides. If it were proposed to France to return Alsace the French Bourse would sell Russia tomorrow."

M. Trotzky denied the charge that the Bolsheviki had wrecked the old army, but said that it was disorganized and enfeebled by three years of war, and when false war aims were made clear the complete collapse ensued.

A Russian woman doctor, who has returned to Moscow from Dvinsk, tells of conditions there after the Germans entered the city. Municipal officials and persons of all classes, tired of disorder and confusion, welcomed the Germans, gave flowers to the officers and paid them every courtesy.

The Germans were kind the first day, but the second day they commandeered all food supplies, reduced food allowances to Russians by one-half, and shipped supplies out of the city. The Mayor of Dvinsk offered the German Commander bread and salt, according to the Russian custom in greeting visitors, but feeling soon changed toward the invaders, who became harsh and enforced compulsory labor for twelve hours a day upon skilled workmen, the highest pay being three rubles ($1.50 at normal exchange) per day.

Russian officers were ordered by the Germans to restore their shoulder straps and then were made prisoners.

The daily food allowance now is a small piece of bread and a quarter of a pound of pork. Clerks receive from 40 to 60 rubles monthly, and physicians 30 rubles for the same time. The value of a ruble is now about 10 cents. Mohilev, Reval, Narva, and Kiev, as well as other occupied cities, report Germans commandeering and shipping out food supplies.

March 24, 1918

## *Japanese and British Land Troops at Vladivostok; Bolshevist Government Orders Siberians to Resist*

MOSCOW, April 6, (Associated Press.)—The British, as well as the Japanese, landed forces at Vladivostok yesterday. The local authorities had no warning of this action.

LONDON, April 6.—According to a semi-official dispatch from Moscow, the following official statement has been issued there:

"In reference to the landing of Japanese at Vladivostok, the Council of People's Commissaries is undertaking political steps, and at the same time orders all the Soviets in Siberia to offer armed resistance to an enemy incursion into Russian territory."

April 7, 1918

## RUSSIA'S OFFICIAL FLAG RED.

### Trotzky Appointed Joint Minister of War and Marine.

MOSCOW, April 9, (Associated Press.)—Russia's national flag henceforth will be red with the inscription "Rossiskay Sotzialyiticheskaya Federativnaya Sovietskaya Respublika" (Russian Socialistic Federative Soviet Republic). This was decided upon today in a resolution passed unanimously by the Central Executive Committee of the All-Russian Soviets.

Chairman Sverdloff, proposing the resolution, said it was imperative to decide the question of the flag immediately, as "the Russian flag will have to wave over the embassies in Berlin and Vienna, and we cannot have the old tricolor, so I think it most proper to adopt the red flag under which we fought and gained victory."

Leon Trotzky, former Foreign Minister, has been appointed Joint Minister of War and Marine. He has been acting as Minister of War since the Government was removed to Moscow.

April 11, 1918

## ASSERTS RUSSIA VIOLATES TREATY

### Berlin Protests Against Allies in Murmansk—Black Sea Fleet Reported Seized.

### TROTZKY PLANS BIG ARMY

MOSCOW, April 23, (Associated Press.)—Germany has protested to the Bolshevist Foreign Minister, M. Tchitcherin, against the landing of 6,000 allied troops at Murmansk, declaring that permission for such landing was a violation of the Brest-Litovsk treaty, which stipulated peace with Finland and non-interference in its internal life. It was denied in the protest that Germans had participated in the raid of the Finnish White Guards upon Kem, and the presence of Russian troops between Petrograd and Finland was objected to on the ground that they threatened to cross the frontier. Mediation of the Russo-Finnish conflict was promised if the Government prevented violations of the treaty.

The German advance in Russia continues uninterruptedly. The German forces have captured several cities and are nearing Kursk, capital of the Government of the same name, with a population of more than 50,000. This city is being evacuated. Leon Trotzky, in reply to a question, said that the advance would probably continue until peace with Ukraine has been effected.

There has been a report here that the entire Black Sea fleet has been captured by the Germans.

Leon Trotzky the Bolshevist Minister of War and Marine, speaking at a meeting of the Central Executives last night urged the issuance of a decree for compulsory military service.

"Fearing destruction, Russia must have an army," he said. "We do not know the hour when we will be openly challenged by the imperialistic enemy threatening us in the east."

The Central Executives adopted a resolution to this effect. The measure provides for the training of workmen, peasants, and unemployed from 18 to 40 years of age for eight consecutive weeks, for at least twelve hours weekly. Schoolboys from 16 to 18 will be trained in similar manner, while other children at school will be trained in accordance with the rules of the Department of Education.

Women may volunteer. The enlistment will be for a minimum of six months, and desertion will be punishable by imprisonment and loss of citizenship.

May 1, 1918

## *LITTLE PLANTING DONE IN RUSSIA*

### *Less Than Half of the Land Usually Tilled Will Be Cultivated This Year.*

SAMARA, Russia, May 2.—(Associated Press.)—Much of the fertile land of European Russia will go uncultivated this year. Less than half the land, which has in times past produced large quantities of grain and other crops, now remaining in control of the Soviet Government will be tilled, owing to the shortage of seed, horses, and implements, and the unsettled conditions brought about by the land division.

Peasants have hidden their seed and resisted the food committees. Many districts, consequently, have seed potatoes, wheat, barley, and oats, but the peasants are not willing to plant all the acreage possible, fearing the future disposition of the land and the control of the harvested crop. The hostility of the farmers toward city workers generally is shown by their unwillingness to surrender grain to the food committees and their hesitation to plant extensively lest their crops be requisitioned.

The wheat planting season ends this week in Central Russia, and in most of the districts less than half the grain land has been plowed. The exodus of city dwellers into the grain sections has been so large that breadstuffs are extremely scarce, even in grain centres like Samara, where bread sells for 2 rubles per pound. The price gradually rises approaching Moscow, and at some towns in the grain States children gather at the incoming trains and beg bread from the passengers.

Several provinces have issued their own money, but the peasants and merchants refuse to accept it, unless forced to do so by armed guards. Even the provincial cities are issuing their own money and are legalizing the circulation of officially indorsed checks on State banks, but the peasants do not willingly accept such mediums of exchange.

Samara Province has thousands of German colonists owning from sixty to eighty acres each, who have forcibly resisted the land committees and retain their property. These colonists are Russian citizens, and have been in Russia for several generations. The amount of land allotted to individual peasants varies in different sections, according to the density of the population, the nature of the land, and the size of the families. Two and a half to five acres is the average allotment in the grain-growing districts.

May 16, 1918

## RUSSIAN CITIES STARVING.

### Bread Ration in Petrograd Said to be Totally Exhausted.

**MOSCOW, May 11, (Associated Press.)—The food situation in Petrograd and other large cities of Russia instead of improving with the advent of Spring and river navigation is constantly growing worse.**

**The bread ration in Petrograd, which had been one-eighth of a pound weekly, now is totally exhausted. Other products are scarce.**

**In Moscow the food situation is somewhat better. The bread ration is a quarter of a pound and other food is obtainable at high prices. Sugar is scarce.**

**Conditions in the country generally do not promise an improvement in the food situation in the near future.**

May 20, 1918

## *ACCUSES RICH FARMERS OF STARVING RUSSIANS*

### *Lenine Organizes 'Food Expeditions' of the Poor to Seize Supplies.*

By ARTHUR RANSOME.


Special Cable to THE NEW YORK TIMES.

MOSCOW, June 5.—Yesterday, at a united meeting of the Executive Committee with representatives of other labor organizations, Premier Lenine outlined the Soviet policy against hunger. He pointed out that all the anti-Soviet parties were hoping that starvation would produce anarchy, which might or might not be profitable to them, and he proceeded to discuss means of dealing with the food supply, emphasizing the fact that raising prices and allowing the independent dragging of sacks of flour to market by individuals who traveled with their sacks and engaged in speculation would make the task of reorganization impossible, and at the same time strengthen the capitalistic system in the villages. This, he said, would afford new means of profiteering by rich peasants, and still further enslave the poor.

In the towns the factory workers, he said, better understood what they stood to gain by the revolution than did the country people. There must be a campaign of agitation in the country, a general organization of poor peasants for the final destruction of the autocracy of the rich peasants in the villages. It was the rich peasants, he said, not the poor, who were holding up food supplies.

He replied to the criticism of the behavior of some food-seeking expeditions by saying that the old principles of the capitalist régime still affected them. He called for unity of the workers and workers' expeditions from the non-agricultural districts, where starvation was threatened, for bread crusades against speculators and against the rich peasants, whose interests were naturally to uphold the system that had made them rich, and for established order in the place of the present disorder, and the holding up of stores that kept some districts fed and doomed others to death by hunger, and increased the power of the rich over the poor.

This, he said, would not only put an end to hunger, but also carry class-consciousness, which was necessary for the final triumph of the revolution, into the country as distinct from the town.

**MOSCOW, June 12, (Associated Press.)—The Central Executive Committee tonight voted to create committees of poor peasants for the purpose of taking a census of grain and other food necessities in villages, confiscating all in excess of that above requirements, and distributing food and agricultural machinery among the needy. The committees, which are to be permanent, will be formed by the local Soviets, and only the poor can become members. Their activities are to be directed exclusively against rich peasants, who are declared to be hiding grain, and against the bourgeois opposed to the Soviet Government.**

**To help these committees enforce the measure armed detachments of workmen have been formed in Petrograd and Moscow, 5,000 in each city, and more are to be formed and will be sent to various villages. Notwithstanding the severe criticism of the measure by the Opposition, particularly the Social Revolutionists, who pointed out that it would cause civil war among the peasants and announced that they would oppose its enforcement when passed because they regarded it as injurious, it was adopted by a large Bolshevist majority.**

June 16, 1918

## BOLSHEVIKI OUST RIVALS.

### No Other Party Now Represented in the Soviets.

**LONDON, June 18.—The Central Executive Committee of the Russian Soviets took a drastic step Friday in deciding to expel those of its members representing the Social Revolutionists, the Right, the Centre, and the Mensheviki, according to a Russian wireless message received here. All local Councils are to be asked to expel representatives of the same parties. Explaining the step, the message says:**

**" The authority of the Councils presiding through an extremely difficult period is being attacked simultaneously by international imperialism on all fronts and its coadjutors within the Russian Republic who are in conflict against the Government of the workmen and peasants. They employ the most contemptible means, including shameful calumny, conspiracy, and revolt."**

**It is declared also that it has been established clearly that representatives of the ousted parties, including the most responsible members, have been found guilty of organizing an armed revolt against the workmen and peasants, and in it acted in alliance with the counter-revolutionaries, " on the Don in conjunction with Generals Kaledines and Korniloff, in the Urals in conjunction with General Dutoff, in Siberia in conjunction with Semenoff, Horvath, and Koltchak, and in the last few days with the Czechoslovaks and their supporters, the black band."**

June 19, 1918

## BOLSHEVIKI CAN'T GET SIBERIAN GRAIN

By ARTHUR RANSOME.


Special Cable to THE NEW YORK TIMES.

MOSCOW, June 10.—The Czechoslovak revolt is increasingly serious because compromise has been made almost impossible by the anti-Soviet minorities in Western Siberia, who have seized authority wherever the Czechoslovaks are in the ascendency. In this way, from small beginnings, the Czechoslovak rising is turning into a movement on a considerable scale.

Even this would not matter so much if only the area of operations were anywhere else; but it not only cuts off the Soviet's line of retreat in case of a break with Germany, but also their food.

Cossack troops with German officers are reported to be advancing on Tsaritzen, while the Czechoslovaks dominate Samara, thus cutting off Russia from the lower Volga.

Strong Soviet forces have been sent to the scene, and the Soviet leaders profess confidence in their ability to suppress the movement. But the Czechoslovak troops are certainly the best disciplined in Russia, and from the point of view of European Russia, whose relations with Germany become more and more strained every day, the delay in reopening Siberian communications has a serious effect.

**Czechoslovaks Control Grain Routes.**

MOSCOW, June 14, (Associated Press.)—Czechoslovak control of sections of the Trans-Siberian Railway has completely cut all rail and wire communications between Siberia and Russia and has resulted in depriving European Russia of the Siberian grain supply.

The Czechoslovaks now control the southern section of the Trans-Siberian Railway from Samara, on the Volga River, to Tcheliabinsk and the Siberian main line on the east to Hovo Nikolaievsk, also the northern branch from

Tcheliabinsk to Yekaterinburg.

The conflict between the Czechoslovak forces and the Soviet Government began on May 26, when the Soviets attempted to enforce the order of Leon Trotzky, Minister of War, to disarm all the Chechoslovak forces on their way to Vladivostok for transportation overseas. Fighting occurred at Penza, Samara, Sigpane, Tcheliabinsk, Novo Nikolaievsk, Omsk, and several other points.

The Czechoslovak organizations originally numbered about 40,000 men. Of these, nearly 20,000 reached Vladivostok. The remainder, involved in an effort to resist disarmament, are chiefly centered about Tcheliabinsk.

Trotzky has ordered the mobilization in the Volga region of all men of the last five military classes to move against the Czechoslovak forces.

June 21.—The President of the commission appointed to combat counter-revolution has defined the procedure which of late has ordered numerous executions as "organized terror against enemies of the Soviet rule." Prisoners, says the commission, are shot only if the vote is unanimous. "We judge quickly; in most cases one day, or a few days at most, have elapsed between arrest and sentence," he adds.

Maxim Gorky's newspaper, Novaia Zhizn, protesting against these inquisitions, says that almost invariably the accused are hemmed in by a wall of evidence and forced to confess.

June 22, 1918

## SOVIETS TAKE INDUSTRIES.

### Nationalize All Big Enterprises—Fear Menshevist Terrorism.

LONDON, July 3.—All important industrial enterprises within the jurisdiction of the Soviet Government have been nationalized by a decree of the Government Council, according to a Russian official dispatch received here by wireless. Included in the decree are all coal, iron, copper, silver, lead, and salt mines, nearly all the gold mines, all metallurgic, textile, electrical, explosive and wood enterprises, and the tobacco, rubber, glass, pottery, leather, and steam mill trades.

Municipal undertakings, gas and water supply systems, canals and railways, whether in use or in the course of construction, will come under the provisions of the order.

The murder of M. Volodarsky, Bolshevist Commissioner for Press Affairs, in Petrograd on June 21, is very significant as a symptom of the growing discontent among the workmen and the opposition political parties, says the Petrograd correspondent of The Times under date of June 23. The Bolsheviki threaten vengeance, and party passions are running high among them.

The Bolsheviki regard the assassination of Volodarsky as the first terrorist act against their supremacy by the Mensheviki and Social Revolutionists. The correspondent says that they even endeavor to implicate Englishmen in the counter-revolutionary movement, with which they consider the murder is connected intimately.

Captain Stchasnig, former commander of the Russian Baltic Fleet, who was convicted of having opposed and agitated against the Bolshevist Government, has been put to death. The sentence of the court was carried out on June 22, according to a Moscow dispatch to the Exchange Telegraph Company. The Revolutionary Socialists of the Left, the advices state, who have supported the Bolsheviki, have entered a protest and recalled their representatives from the tribunal. Indignation is expressed by the independent press.

July 4, 1918

## STREET BATTLE IN MOSCOW

LONDON, July 8.—A formidable counter-revolution was attempted in Moscow on Saturday at the time of the assassination of Count von Mirbach, the German Ambassador, according to dispatches received here today. These dispatches indicate that the outbreak was suppressed with much bloodshed.

The Russian wireless circulated the following, signed by M. Araloff, the chief Moscow Commissioner:

"The Social Revolutionists, by fraudulent means, captured for a few hours a small part of Moscow and the Government telegraph office, whence they issued false reports of the suppression of the Soviet in Moscow. I beg to announce that the mutiny was caused by a group of cheeky fools, and was suppressed without difficulty by the Moscow garrison. The mutineers have been arrested, and order has been restored.

"The counter-revolutionary rising in Moscow has been suppressed, and the Social Revolutionaries are making a most ignominious fight. Orders have been issued to arrest and to disarm all members of the Social Revolutionary detachments and to shoot on the spot all who resist.

"Several hundred participants in the rising have been arrested, among them Vice Chairman Alexandrovitch, while special orders have been issued to secure all members of the Executive Committee of the Social Revolutionary Party.

"The Red Guards must continue watchful. The mobilization of our forces must continue, and all Social Revolutionaries must disarm to the last man."

### Fierce Fighting in Streets.

The Moscow outbreak was a "serious counter-revolution," according to a German semi-official Wolff Bureau telegram dated on Sunday from Moscow, and transmitted to London by the Exchange Telegraph Company's correspondent at Copenhagen. Fighting of great severity took place in the streets between the Bolshevist troops and Social Revolutionaries.

German newspapers are now pointing to General Savinkoff, who was War Minister in the Kerensky Cabinet, as the man behind the von Mirbach plot, which is being gradually developed by the Teuton press into a great anti-German movement backed by all those men whom Germany has found to be hindrances in her plans of aggression in Russia. A Moscow telegram circulated by the Wolff Bureau says:

"Savinkoff is considered to be responsible for the deed. He is, moreover, said to be closely connected with the Czechoslovak and Social Revolutionary movements. His whereabouts is unknown."

The German press is preparing the public for a radical move against Russia as punishment for the Mirbach affair. Exactly what this move will be is not as yet indicated, but Dutch and Scandinavian newspapers hint at a March on Moscow. Dispatches are printed showing that German forces are now about 300 miles west of that city and are being heavily reinforced.

German newspapers give many columns to developments in the Mirbach case, particularly long telegrams from Moscow praising the work that Count von Mirbach did there, and describing the alleged treacherous manner in which the assassins gained entrance to his office by posing as delegates of a commission for combating the social revolutionist movement. It is stated that they fired their revolvers, not only at Count von Mirbach, but also at German Councillor Kiezler and Lieutenant Müller, who were in the room. Immediately after the firing they jumped out of a window, hurling hand grenades back of them as they jumped. They leaped into a waiting automobile and escaped.

### Trying to Put Blame on Allies.

Nikolai Lenine, the Bolshevist Premier, is endeavoring to placate the Germans by appointing an "extraordinary commission of investigation" to probe the death of Count von Mirbach. The commission is headed by "Comrade Peters." A German official account of the assassination concludes:

"The result of a preliminary inquiry permits the assumption that agents in the service of the Entente are implicated in the affair."

As soon as Emperor William heard of the assassination of Count von Mirbach, according to an Exchange Telegraph dispatch from Amsterdam, he ordered Foreign Secretary von Kühlmann to break off negotiations with the Russian delegates in Berlin. A strong guard has been placed before the house of the Bolshevist Ambassador in Berlin, as it is feared that the populace of the capital will inaugurate anti-Russian demonstrations.

The assassination of Count von Mirbach is seen as an event of great importance, which may have far-reaching results, by the newspapers here. The Daily Mail and The Daily Express agree that the assassination may have momentous consequences, and compare it to the murder of Archduke Francis Ferdinand at Sarajevo four years ago. The Express adds:

"German influence (in Russia) can only be established on a solid basis by the maintenance of a great army of occupation. Russia may once more play a part in the war."

July 9, 1918

## REDS EVICTING BOURGEOISIE.

### Terrorism and Hunger Increase—Hostility to Germany.

AMSTERDAM, July 11.—Telegraphing from Moscow, the correspondent of the Frankfurter Zeitung says:

"The bourgeoisie are experiencing a veritable reign of terror. They are being turned out of their houses, which are being used for the billeting of troops. Furniture and valuables are being removed to cellars and to other hiding places.

"Rich people, in order to avoid attracting attention, go about dressed in the poorest clothes and live in daily fear of being evicted from their homes by armed workmen and soldiers.

"The cost of living is extremely high. The cost of food is the highest. Flour rose in a few days from 200 to 380 rubles. No bread is obtainable. Grain supplies from the Ukraine, Northern Caucasus, and Siberia to Northern and Central Russia have completely ceased.

"No one could assert that the relations between the German authorities and the Soviet Government are normal or friendly."

July 12, 1918

# EX-CZAR OF RUSSIA KILLED BY ORDER OF URAL SOVIET

## Nicholas Shot on July 16 When It Was Feared That Czechoslovaks Might Seize Him.

## WIFE AND HEIR IN SECURITY

## Bolshevist Government Approves Act, Alleging Plot for a Counter-Revolution.

LONDON, July 20.—Nicholas Romanoff, ex-Czar of Russia, was shot July 16, according to a Russian announcement by wireless today.

The former Empress and Alexis Romanoff, the young heir, have been sent to a place of security.

The message announces that a counter-revolutionary conspiracy was discovered, with the object of wresting the ex-Emperor from the authority of the Soviet Council. In view of this fact and the approach of Czechoslovak bands, the President of the Ural Regional Council decided to execute the former ruler, and the decision was carried out on July 16.

The central executive body of the Bolshevist Government announces that it has important documents concerning the former Emperor's affairs, including his own diaries and letters from the monk Rasputin, who was killed shortly before the revolution. These will be published in the near future, the message declares.

The text of the Russian wireless message reads:

"At the first session of the Central Executive Committee, elected by the fifth Congress of the Councils, a message was made public that had been received by direct wire from the Ural Regional Council concerning the shooting of the ex-Czar Nicholas Romanoff.

"Recently Yekaterinburg, the capital of the Red Urals, was seriously threatened by the approach of Czechoslovak bands and a counter-revolutionary conspiracy was discovered which had as its object the wresting of the ex-Czar from the hands of the council's authority. In view of this fact, the President of the Ural Regional Council decided to shoot the ex-Czar, and the decision was carried out on July 16.

"The wife and the son of Nicholas Romanoff have been sent to a place of security.

"Documents concerning the conspiracy which was discovered have been forwarded to Moscow by a special messenger. It had been recently decided to bring the ex-Czar before a tribunal to be tried for his crimes against the people, and only later occurrences led to delay in adopting this course.

"The Presidency of the Central Executive Committee, having discussed the circumstances which compelled the Ural Regional Council to take its decision to shoot Nicholas Romanoff, decided as follows:

"'The Russian Central Executive Committee, in the person of its President, accepts the decision of the Ural Regional Council as being regular.'

"The Central Executive Committee has now at its disposal extremely important documents concerning the affairs of Nicholas Romanoff—his diaries, which he kept almost up to his last days, the diaries of his wife and his children, and his correspondence, among which are the letters of Gregory Rasputin to the Romanoff family. These materials will be examined and published in the near future."

July 21, 1918

# AMERICAN TROOPS LANDED AT ARCHANGEL

## RUSSIANS WELCOME US

## Archangel Regards Presence of Our Troops as Allied Guarantee,

## JAPAN TO LEAD IN SIBERIA

KANDALASKA, Aug. 4, (Associated Press.)—American troops participated in the landing of the allied forces at Archangel last week.

The first detachment of the international forces included members of the Russian Officers' League.

The participation of the Americans in the landing has been greeted enthusiastically in Northern Russia. The people consider that the United States is absolutely without selfish interests as regards Russia, and look upon the Americans as a guarantee of the friendliness of the Allies toward the country.

The population of Archangel received the troops with cheering. The men debarked and advanced toward Archangel, where already an anti-Bolshevist revolution had taken place. The leaders in this movement invited the protection of the allied troops.

The final resistance of the Bolsheviki occurred Saturday. They were definitely defeated at the station of Ysakagorka, on the left bank of the Dvina.

In their flight from Archangel the Bolshevist forces carried away 40,000,000 rubles in money and much other treasure, but left many supplies behind them. The bridges and railway lines were not damaged.

The new Provisional Government at Archangel, which has assumed power throughout "the region of the north," is receiving the volunteer support of the village soviets in the country adjoining Archangel.

The Government includes the following nine persons, all of whom are members of the Constituent Assembly: Tchoikawski of Viatka Government, Nomoff of Archangel, Masloff of Vologda, Gorkorsky of Novgorod, Kartacheff of Kazan, Stansenko of Samara, Sikhatcheff, who was the constituent representative from the Northern Russian front; Zoubof, former Assistant Mayor of Vologda, and Starzof, former President of the Archangel Duma.

**Siberian Expedition Plans.**

WASHINGTON, Aug. 5.—Plans for the organization and dispatch of the American military contingent to Russia to co-operate with the forces of the allied nations in support of the Czechoslovaks at Vladivostok are being worked out by the army General Staff.

At the War Department today it was said that by next Wednesday General March, Chief of Staff, would be able to give out a statement of as much of the plans as safely may be disclosed at that stage.

Meanwhile there is no objection to the statement that if the military laws that govern joint action by international military forces are to be observed in the case of this Siberian operation, and as there is good reason to believe that they will, the senior officer of the international force will be in supreme command. It is assumed that as Japan by reason of her proximity to the scene of action will supply the largest single body of troops in the undertaking, she will naturally assign to their command an officer of higher rank than those in command of the smaller American and Entente forces. In the opinion of officials here this officer will be General Baron Uyehara, Chief of Staff of the Japanese Army.

The fact is recalled that the only notable violation of this international rule of courtesy was on the occasion of the joint expedition against the Boxers in China more than a decade ago. Then, the Kaiser, though his contingent was less than some of the others, rushed a Field Marshal all the way from Europe to China in order, through his superior rank, to be able to claim Germany's right to command the expedition. No such small statesmanship is expected to be displayed on this occasion.

The Red Cross has been forehanded in arranging for the participation of that organization in the Siberian enterprise, and already has arranged for the shipment to the Far East of quantities of supplies likely to be needed. This is to be done in addition to the usual hospital service which falls to the Red Cross.

Admiral Knight, commanding the American naval forces on the Asiatic station, already is at Vladivostok on his flagship, and is in communication twice each day with the Navy Department here. It was said that he would of course co-operate fully with the military authorities in the execution of their program, using for this purpose the vessels of his fleet.

**Vladivostok Will Not Resist.**

There will be no armed resistance to the landing of the international soldiers at Vladivostok, as the port practically is dominated by the Japanese and British naval and military forces already there, though so far these have not interfered with the functions of the local authorities.

Assurance that no trouble is to be expected on this account has been received by the Russian Embassy here in the shape of returns from the result of the municipal elections. These showed that the Bourgeoisie and Moderate Socialists polled 69 per cent. of the votes, while the Bolsheviki received only 31 per cent.

The Czechoslovak forces in Siberia will remain there and co-operate fully with the allied forces being sent to their assistance, according to orders issued today by Professor T. G. Masaryk, President of the Czechoslovak National Council and Commander in Chief of the Czechoslovak armies.

Through the commander of the forces in the region of Vladivostok, General Diterichs, the Czechoslovaks are reminded that they are in the territory of a friendly nation, and that they are to oppose in the first place the Austrians and Germans, but also any Russian faction allying itself with their enemies or the enemies of the Allies. They are requested by the orders, however, to continue their policy of neutrality in Russian internal administrative affairs.

August 6, 1918

## GERMANS MASS FOR MARCH TO PETROGRAD

### Lenine, Made Member of Autocratic Triumvirate, Urges Extermination of Foes.

LONDON, Aug. 13.—The Germans intend to occupy Petrograd, a dispatch to the Copenhagen Poletiken from Helsingfors declares, the Exchange Telegraph correspondent in the Danish capital reports. Troops for this purpose are already being brought toward the objective, it is added.

AMSTERDAM, Aug. 13.—Because of the counter-revolutionary movement in Russia the "Second Soviet Congress" has placed the execution of power in the hands of a triumvirate composed of Premier Nikolai Lenine, Leon Trotzky, Minister of War, and M. Zinovieff, an associate of Lenine, according to Moscow advices to the Rhenish Westphalian Zeitung. Unlimited power has been given to them to take all measures necessary to gain victory in the fight of the Soviet Republic against its enemies.

A new manifesto advocating the pitiless annihilation of all counter-revolutionaries has been issued by Premier Lenine, according to the same paper. Peasants retaining grain beyond their personal needs will be arraigned before revolutionary courts as enemies of the people. Capital punishment will be inflicted on illicit traders.

The advices add that leaders of the Kerensky party, who had been kept under strict Soviet observation, have suddenly disappeared. It is believed in Moscow that they have fled abroad.

The German newspapers show much perturbation over the situation in Russia as it affects Germany.

"Inexorable fate is driving Germany toward a fresh state of war with Russia unless a remedy shall be found at the last moment," says the Vossische Zeitung of Berlin.

The newspaper describes the German Embassy's flight from Moscow to Pskov as "a retreat from Russia," and continues:

"The Russian nation, torn asunder by a thousand conflicts and weakened by revolution and civil war, has yet found the energy and enough unanimity to tear up the Brest-Litovsk peace treaty. This much is clear. The peace made at Brest-Litovsk no longer exists."

August 14, 1918

## FIRST REGIMENT OF AMERICANS IN VLADIVOSTOK

*Special to The New York Times.*

WASHINGTON, Aug. 15.—Coincident with the Tokio announcement that General Otani had on Monday left for Vladivostok to direct the operations of the Japanese Expeditionary Force in Siberia, formal announcement was authorized by Secretary Baker late this evening that the first American contingent of troops "is now arriving at Vladivostok."

This contingent is the 27th Regular Infantry Regiment of the United States Army. It is commanded by Colonel Henry D. Styer, a West Point graduate, who was at the Army War College in 1914 and is a seasoned infantry commander. The 27th, like the 31st Regiment of Infantry, which is also en route to Vladivostok, was sent from the Philippines, where both units have been serving since 1916. The arrival of the 31st has not yet been announced.

Neither of these regiments is at full war strength. They are on a peace footing. The 27th and 31st Regiments will be supplemented by other troops to be sent from the United States. Secretary Baker and General March, the Chief of Staff, have requested that the size of the Expeditionary Force be not mentioned at this time, but it can be stated with official sanction that the size of the expedition will not be in excess of 10,000 Americans.

Japan, it is understood, will send to Vladivostok an expeditionary force identical in size with that which the United States is forming.

August 16, 1918

## LENINE WOUNDED TWICE BY ASSASSIN

### Attempt on Red Premier's Life at Moscow—Commissary Uritzky Murdered at Petrograd.

LONDON, Aug. 31.—Criminal attempts have been made on the life of Nikolai Lenine, the Bolshevist Premier, at Moscow, according to a Russian wireless message received here today from the Russian capital under date of Aug. 30.

Lenine was wounded in two places, but did not lose consciousness.

An attempt on the life of a British General has been made at Murman, according to a dispatch to the Exchange Telegraph from Copenhagen, quoting a Moscow telegram.

AMSTERDAM, Aug. 31.—Moses Uritzky, People's Commissary for Home Affairs at Petrograd, has been assassinated. The assassins, according to Russian advices received through Berlin, were arrested.

Several attempts have been made against the life of Lenine since he became Bolshevist Premier in November, 1917. Lenine's real name is Vladimir Ilitch Ulianoff. He was born of a noble family at Simbirsk, on the River Volga, about 1870.

On Jan 16 last an attempt was made to assassinate Lenine at Petrograd while he was going to the Smolny Institute in an automobile. Several shots were fired, but Lenine was not injured. On the night of Jan. 31 a young man in a student's uniform entered the Bolshevist headquarters at the Smolny Institute and fired a shot from a revolver at Lenine. The bullet did not take effect.

Lenine and Leon Trotzky, the Bolshevist Minister of War, were reported by the semi-official Wolff Bureau of Berlin early in August to have fled from Moscow to Kronstadt, the naval base near Petrograd, but no confirmation of this report has been forthcoming.

September 1, 1918

## SOVIET GOVERNMENT TRIES REIGN OF TERROR

### Decrees Summary Execution for All Persons in Moscow Found with a Weapon.

LONDON, Sept. 3.—The attempted assassination of Nikolai Lenine, the Bolshevist Premier, has been followed by drastic measures on the part of the authorities in Moscow, according to the Helsingfors correspondent of the Hamburg Fremdenblatt, who reports that, in addition to the removal of thousands of persons from Moscow to Petrograd, the following proclamation has been issued by M. Peters, Chief of the Extraordinary Commission in the Russian capital:

"The criminal adventures of our enemies force us to reply with measures of terror. Every person found with a weapon in his hand will be immediately executed. Every person who agitates against the Soviet Government will be arrested and taken into a concentration camp and all his private property seized."

The Russian newspaper Pravda says that numerous officers and members of the Social Revolutionary Party have been arrested at Moscow in connection with the attempt to assassinate Lenine.

In connection with the assassination at Petrograd on Aug. 31 of Moses Uritzky, the People's Commissary for Home Affairs, the Pravda says that numerous houses were searched. They included the building of the British Embassy, where an exchange of shots took place. Two persons were killed, one of them being a Britisher whose identity has not yet been established.

September 4, 1918

## THOUSANDS KILLED BY REDS IN RUSSIA

### In Petrograd Alone 812 Persons Have Been Put to Death in a Week.

### HUNDREDSHELD IN HOSTAGE

STOCKHOLM, Sept. 17.—Wholesale executions are increasing in Petrograd, according to private telegrams received here by the way of Helsingfors. During the past week 812 persons were executed, and more than 400 others are on the prescribed list. Most of them have already been made hostages.

All persons of rank of Councilors of State have been imprisoned regardless of their political views.

WASHINGTON, Sept. 17.—Information reaching the State Department today from a neutral country threw new light on the situation in Central Russia, where a reign of terror conducted by the Bolsheviki has made the position of the populace tragic in the extreme and is endangering citizens of the Entente Powers who have been unable to leave the country.

Declaring that the outside world cannot have a true conception of the actual conditions, the dispatches say that since May, the Bolshevist Extraordinary Commission Against the Counter-Revolution has conducted a campaign of wholesale murder. Thousands have been shot without even a form of a trial and many of them probably were innocent of the political views for which they were executed.

The assassination of Moses Uritsky, head of the Commission Against the Counter-Revolution, and the attempt on the life of Premier Lenine were direct results of this condition of tyranny, say the advices. Besides the 500 persons who were shot in connection with the death of Uritsky, a large number of other persons are held for execution in the event that further attempts are made on the lives of the Bolshevist leaders.

A general search is being made of the homes in Moscow of the well-to-do and of former officers in an effort to obtain any shred of evidence upon which to make arrests. The prisons are filled to overflowing and executions continue daily. In many cases, it is said, sentences are passed upon the slight grounds that the accused might be dangerous to Bolshevist power.

In addition, irresponsible and avengeful gangs are venting on innocent persons their desperation over the daily declining power of the Bolsheviki, while the Socialists, who are opposing the Soviet Government, have adopted the same methods that they once used against the tyranny of the Imperial Government.

All newspapers in Moscow, except the Bolshevist organs, have been suppressed since July 1, and in these are to be published the names of persons executed or held prisoners in connection with the killing of Uritsky.

September 18, 1918

# KOLCHAK IS MADE DICTATOR AT OMSK

## Power Vested in Admiral by Three Members of Siberian Directorate of Five.

## THE TWO OTHERS ARRESTED

VLADIVOSTOK, Nov. 19, (Associated Press.)—Though a coup on the part of the Council of Ministers of the new All-Russian Government at Omsk, Admiral Alexander Kolchak has become virtual dictator and commander of the All-Russian army and fleet. Two Ministers, M. Avksentieff and M. Zenzenoff, who opposed Admiral Kolchak's dictatorship, have been arrested. A portion of the directorate of the erstwhile Ufa Government, which formed the administrative body of the new Government, and to which the Ministry was responsible, supports Admiral Kolchak.

Telegrams received here from Omsk state that the move was "due to extraordinary circumstances and danger menacing the State." The Council of Ministers has assumed authority and transferred it to Admiral Kolchak. The latter has accepted the responsibility, and, it is announced, has entered upon his duties as "Supreme Governor." General Horvath, General Ivanoff, Minister of War of the Omsk Government, and General Renoff, former Commander of the All-Russian forces, announce that they recognize the new authority.

The coup occurred on Nov. 18.

**Vologodsky Still Premier.**

M. Vologodsky, head of the Western Siberian Government, who is a member of both the Directorate and the Council of Ministers, retains his post as Premier. General Boldereff is absent from Omsk, and his attitude is unknown. He is expected at Ufa shortly, and negotiations are proceeding to bring him into line. French Commissioner Renault is at Omsk, and British Commissioner Elliott will leave immediately for that city.

While there have been rumors that such a development might occur at Omsk, credence was not given to them, and the news came as a distinct surprise to allied commanders and representatives at Vladivostok. The local Zemstvo, Provisional Council, and other minor organizations, held a conference early this morning. It is indicated that there is at present a disposition not to recognize the Kolchak Government. The change was accepted by the people and troops without disorder.

The activities of the radical wing represented in the All-Russian Government forced the militarist and conservative elements to adopt countermeasures, according to Lieut. Gen. Horvath, prominent among the leaders in the anti-Bolshevist movement in Siberia, who gave his view of the coup when seen on his train at his headquarters. These measures, he said, included the arrest of many members of the Left of the Social Revolutionists, among them four Ministers and Assistant Ministers.

"The Government, in the face of this accomplished fact," General Horvath explained, "found it advisable to declare the Directorate abolished and to transfer temporarily the superior authority to a supreme Governor, whose power is limited by the Council of Ministers. In other words, there is mutual responsibility."

The success of the coup, in the opinion of General Horvath, rests with the United States. France and England, he believed, would not withhold recognition of the new order, since the personnel of the Ministry and the policy of the Government remained unchanged. He cited the example of the events of the French Revolution, in which the Directory was supplanted by a single head. He expressed the opinion that the majority of the Russians would welcome the present substitution, as it left the situation more easily comprehended than that under the previous form of government.

To M. Tchernoff, Minister of Agriculture in the Kerensky Cabinet, most of the propaganda leading to the coup is attributed. He had been retained in a minor capacity in the present Cabinet where he was enabled to carry on this work.

Admiral Kolchak, whose dictatorship over the Omsk Government is announced, was commander of the Russian Black Sea fleet before the revolution. He was compelled in June, 1917, to surrender command of that fleet to the revolutionists. He did this after throwing overboard his sword, which the Japanese had left him when the Russians evacuated Port Arthur in the Russo-Japanese War. Later in 1917 he visited this country at the head of a naval commission from the Kerensky Government and discussed possible co-operation between the Russian and allied fleets.

After the Bolsheviki gained the ascendancy in Russia he went to Siberia, where in May of this year he was elected Director of the Chinese Eastern Railway and co-operated with General Orloff in an effort to free the eastern portion of that railway from the Bolsheviki. In this connection he came into contact and clashed with General Semenoff, anti-Bolshevist leader in Siberia, now in command of the anti-Bolshevist army in the Baikal region. General Semenoff, however, was recently reported as recognizing the authority of the Omsk Government.

Admiral Kolchak, in a press dispatch during last July, was quoted as declaring belief in the necessity for an allied expedition into Russia to suppress Bolshevist outlawry and render possible representative elections, so as to secure proper self-government to the country.

M. Avksentieff, one of the men arrested, was a member of the Directorate of Five in the new Russian Government formed by the Pan Russian conference at Ufa, over which he presided.

November 22, 1918

# REPORT ALLIES MARCHING ON KIEV

## Skoropadski Said to Have Surrendered and Denikine to be in Control of Ukraine.

## NEW GOVERNMENT FORMED

BASLE, Nov. 22.—Entente troops are marching on Kiev, according to advices to newspapers in Switzerland. General Skoropadski, Ukrainian dictator, has surrendered and General Denikine, leader of anti-Bolshevist forces, has been named as his successor, with the consent of the Entente nations, it is said.

COPENHAGEN, Nov. 22.—An all-Russian Government, composed of the General Staff of the volunteer army, has been formed at Ekaterinodar, (capital of the territory of the Kuban,) with the object of re-establishing Russia on a federated principle, according to advices from Kiev. Former Foreign Minister Sazonoff is Foreign Minister of the new Government.

WASHINGTON, Nov. 22.—The report from Copenhagen that a new Government has been organized at Ekaterinodar, is accepted by officials here as indicating that this important centre in Southern Russia has been chosen as the seat of the new Government of the Cossacks under General Denikine.

While the new Government is styled all Russian, the belief here is that for the present, at least, it is clearly local, extending its authority only over the Ukraine and the territory controlled by the Don Cossacks. It is regarded as certain, however, that the new régime will endeavor to form a union with the Government at Omsk, under which Siberia and Northern Russia is governed.

Cable dispatches received at the Russian Embassy today from Siberia throw a new light on the changes that took place recently in the All-Russian Government of Omak and brought to the front Admiral Kolchak as dictator with the approval of the Government.

A group of three military officers, on the night of Nov. 18, according to these dispatches, arrested without authority two members of the directory, AVKsentieff and Zenzinoff and two prominent citizens of Omak, Argunoff and Rogovsky. The coup, the object of which is not entirely clear, was attempted without any participation or knowledge of the Government. It was promptly and emphatically disapproved by the Government.

In order to prevent further irresponsible activities and to maintain the principle of firm governmental power, the Council of Ministers urged energetic measures and issued a special decree authorizing Admiral Kolchak to take over the supreme power of the State. By his order the offenders were turned over at once for trial.

The chief aim of the authorities, it is reported, is to eradicate the possibility of further illegal actions or Bolshevist eruptions and the complete banishment of politics from the army.

November 23, 1918

# *ANTI-RED FACTIONS IN RUSSIA UNITING*

## *Three Cossack Chieftains Rally to Siberian Government and Semenoff Submits.*

OMSK, Siberia, Jan. 19, (Associated Press.)—The Omsk Government, headed by Admiral Kolchak, is rapidly increasing its authority both east and west of Omsk. During the last week the Omsk Government was advised of the adherence to the authority of General Denikine, the leader of the Omsk forces west of the Urals, of General Krasnoff, the Hetman of the Don Cossacks, and General Filimonoff, Hetman of the Kuban Cossacks.

Admiral Kanine, it is announced, has been appointed commander of the Russian Black Sea Fleet. He is subordinate to General Denikine, who now holds sway over Odessa, the Crimea, and Sebastopol.

It is announced in Government circles that the controversy with General Semenoff, the anti-Bolshevist leader in the region of Chita, is in a fair way to a settlement. Semenoff, it is said, has accepted the appointment of a commission to try charges against him and has signified his readiness to join General Dutoff in fighting the Bolsheviki. The commisson to try General Semenoff will meet in a week or so at Chita. It is understood that General Semenoff has informed Admiral Kolchak that he was the victim of a misunderstanding. The charges against Semenoff include that of interferring with the telegraph and railway lines, the seizing of money in banks, and the intimidation of railway employes. Allied officers in Omsk continue their good offices in the interest of a settlement.

M. Savinkoff and Vladimir Bourtzeff, well-known revolutionist now in Paris, have telegraphed offers of their support to Admiral Kolchak. The adherence of Savinkoff is regarded as adding important strength to the Omsk Government. Admiral Kolchak has telegraphed his thinks to Savinkoff, declaring:

"I consider your acceptance a sign of a distinct movement which is uniting all forces to save Russia in this critical hour."

It probably would be premature and over optimistic to declare that the Omsk Government has inaugurated a settled régime and that insurrections and civil conflicts in non-Bolshevist Russia are at an end. The country is too vast, and unknown political currents have not yet found complete expression.

In Omsk Russia is compared to an agitated river which will continue to be troubled until it finds a normal and peaceful level, but Russians seeking the highest interests of the country as well as foreigners who are studying the situation on the ground appear to be united in considering the Kolchak Government as a sincere and vigorous movement to rehabilitate the nation.

There is a unanimous feeling that a powerful personality like Admiral Kolchak is necessary to carry the Government over the present crisis. If he succeeds in holding and strengthening his position in the next six months, these observers believe he will have formed the nucleus of an orderly and permanent régime, whatever political form it may eventually assume.

The observers do not believe that Kolchak is conspiring to restore the monarchy, as some of his opponents charge. They look upon the Kolchak Government as the only group offering hope of a solution.

The correspondent visited the churches in Omsk during the services Saturday night and found them all crowded. The Cathedral was overflowing. Most of the worshipers were men, and all were standing quietly in prayer.

Just as along the four thousand miles of the Trans-Siberian Railway, so at Omsk the masses of the Russian people apparently crave only peace and order, opportunity to obtain the necessities of life and a fair measure of comfort and happiness. They say they are surfeited with suffering, war and sorrow. It is hard to reconcile the gentle, sympathetic, and hospitable Russians encountered everywhere in this region with the tales of ferocity coming across the Urals.

At this critical hour of reconstruction the people are turning trustingly to America and the Allies for help. Their leaders emphasize that help, to be effective, must be immediate.

January 25, 1919

## RED ARMY MADE STRONG BY COERCED OFFICERS

### *Families of Expert Commanders Are Held as Hostages for Their Conduct.*

COPENHAGEN, Feb. 4.—In their advance from Dvinsk the Bolsheviki have captured Vilkomir, forty-five miles north-northwest of Vilna, the capital of Lithuania, according to a report from Vilna.

LONDON, Feb. 4.—Bolshevist forces are now masters of almost the whole Eastern Ukraine, including the important centres of Kharkov, Poltava, Ekaterinoslav, and the Konetz mining region, according to a Helsingfors dispatch to The Mail. It is reported that a Soviet Government has been established at Kharkov, the President being M. Rakovsky, one of the signatories to the Brest-Litovsk treaty with Germany.

ARCHANGEL, Feb. 3, (Associated Press.)—Advices to the Allied Intelligence Department reveal some of the methods by which the Bolsheviki have been able to organize their army in such a way as to make possible the carrying on of a strong campaign in Northern Russia.

The principle of these methods, according to information received from the interior, lies in compelling the Generals and staff officers in the old Russian Army to serve the Bolsheviki by holding their families as hostages for the officers' conduct. Cases have occurred of officers' families being placed under close arrest, the women being treated as badly as the men.

The position of former Russian officers in the ranks of the Soviet Army is extremely difficult. They occupy posts as commanding officers and are trusted in all technical matters, but in regard to everything else are under constant suspicion and are controlled by Bolshevist Commissioners, who are permanently attached to the army and even control the carrying out of operations. Leon Trotsky, the Bolshevist Minister of War and Marine, has issued an order that families of officers who desert to the Allies are to be held responsible and will be prosecuted in some cases.

Military experts who have been forced to serve the Bolsheviki include some of the best men in field tactics, engineering, and ordnance to be found in Central Russia.

General mobilization of soldiers in all districts is being vigorously carried out, and all attempts to avoid service are being severely dealt with. The training of the Bolshevist Army is being assisted by special schools of instruction at Petrograd and Moscow for all non-commissioned officers and men belonging to the Bolshevist party. Generally, the army is growing stronger, and, although the new troops are far from being reliable, they, nevertheless, owing to the severe methods which have been adopted, form the main strength of Bolshevist power.

It is stated that this apparent increase in military strength has been taken by many to indicate that Bolshevist ideas are gaining favor with the population, but this is by no means true. The majority of the people are anti-Bolshevist, but are afraid to express their opinions. The entire strength of the Bolsheviki, it is averred, rests on their institution of Red terror.

February 5, 1919

## EXODUS OF WORKERS FROM RED CAPITALS

### *Life Intolerable in Moscow and Petrograd, They Go to Country to Become Peasants.*



Special Cable to THE NEW YORK TIMES.

GENEVA, May 13.—The revolt of the working classes in Russia against the tyranny of the Bolshevist dictators threatens soon to lead to a general economic catastrophe and to the definite collapse of Soviet rule.

Reliable reports received here state that during the last three months hundreds of thousands of industrial workers have deserted Moscow and Petrograd and returned to the country to become peasants. Their existence had become intolerable in the cities where they were subjected to continual official supervision and interference, and reduced to downright slavery. It is estimated that in Moscow alone 70 per cent. of the workmen fled, leaving hundreds of factories idle.

The fugitives in many cases carried off valuable raw materials and manufactured goods in order to exchange them in the villages for land and live stock with which to set up as farmers.

Drastic measures have been adopted by the Soviet to put an end to this flight en masse of the industrial proletariat. The workers who remained are closely watched. Innumerable Government spies and agents pervade the workshops and report all symptoms of unrest and discontent, whereupon the chief agitators are at once arrested.

In some State factories which manufacture ammunition and arms for the Red Army the workers are forced to take meals and sleep in specially constructed barracks adjoining the workshops. May receive visits from their wives and children, but are not allowed to leave the precincts, which are surrounded by barbed wire fences and guarded day and night by Chinese mercenaries, who have orders to shoot any workmen trying to escape.

A special commissary has been put in charge of each factory by the Soviet. These commissaries are invested with dictatorial powers over the workmen and are in truth little better than the overseers who used to drive the African negro to work in the days of slavery.

May 15, 1919

## BOLSHEVIKI IN GRIP OF KOLCHAK PINCERS

### Review of Military Situation as Denikin's Forces Sweep Up from South Russia.

### VOLGA RETREAT STRATEGIC

The Russian Information Bureau here gave out yesterday a review of the military situation on the various anti-Bolshevist fronts in Russia based on cabled information received from the headquarters of Admiral Kolchak and General Denikin. It reads:

"Since the beginning of March military operations have been carried on along all the anti-Bolshevist fronts. In spite of the extremely difficult conditions of liaison and communication between the different groups, the armies have been acting in accord.

"Last Winter the Bolsheviki announced their intention to free the fertile South of Russia. They began the Spring campaign by dealing a blow at General Denikin's army. Being greatly outnumbered, Denikin was obliged, after a series of battles, to cede a large territory to the Bolsheviki, and to condense his front within a limited area on the lower reaches of the Don River and the Kuban territory. The position of his army was a difficult one. At this very moment the Siberian Army began its advance.

"The Bolsheviki stopped their operations against Southern Russia, concentrated their principal forces in the mid-Volga region in May, and advanced on the Eastern and Southeastern fronts. There is no doubt that at the beginning their principal object was to cut in between Kolchak's left (Southern) flank and Denikin's right (Eastern) flank, in order to prevent the junction of these armies. This advance had two results: The general retirement of the Siberian Army, which avoided decisive actions with an enemy clearly superior in force, and the advance of Denikin, who skillfully took advantage of the principal Bolshevist forces having been transferred to another front.

"At the present time the Siberian Army, resisting the strong pressure of the Bolsheviki, has retired to the line of the middle Kama, the Belaya, and the upper Ufa rivers. Denikin's army, after winning a series of brilliant victories, taking over 30,000 prisoners, guns, etc., has greatly extended its field of action. The capture of Tsaritsin is its latest striking success. The 10th Bolshevist Army is beaten, having lost three-quarters of its men. The 14th, 23d, and 16th Divisions have likewise been almost annihilated. An advance of from 150 to 200 miles has been made.

"While this was going on in the South and East, a new front was formed in the Northwest by General Yudenich. The Russian Northern Corps, supported by the Esthonians, who are aided by the Allies, has occupied the approaches to Petrograd. Thus Denikin's and Yudenich's armies are like a pair of pincers held by Admiral Kolchak, the head of the All-Russian Government at Omsk, and the Commander in Chief of the Russian armies."

July 16, 1919

## KOLCHAK BEATEN, MAY BE DEPOSED

### Supreme Ruler's Situation Is Serious, and Troops Are Deserting Him.

*Special to The New York Times.*

WASHINGTON, Nov. 25.—Fear as to the future of the Kolchak Government in Siberia is entertained in official and diplomatic circles in Washington as a result of the forced evacuation of Omsk and the deep retreat which the forces of the All-Russian Government have been compelled to make.

The best canvass of the situation that can be made here indicates that the situation of Kolchak from a military point of view is worse than at any time since he assumed the supreme command. It is now considered a possibility, with the collapse of his army, that Kolchak will shortly occupy the rôle only of nominal dictatorship. His downfall is expected to be decided by the attitude of the municipalities, Zemstvos, co-operative associations, and semi-Eastern Chieftains in Eastern Siberia. One of these Chieftains is the Buriat Hetman Semenoff, who in the past has given nothing more than nominal allegiance to the Kolchak Government and has been in control of territory between Irkutsk and the frontier of Manchuria.

**Kolchak's Rear Guard Stampeded.**

TAIGA, Siberia, Nov. 18 (Associated Press).—Eight thousand wives and children of officers making an eleventh-hour flight from Omsk are reported to have been captured by the Bolsheviki ten miles east of Omsk. The retreat of the rearmost units of the Siberian army from the all-Russian capital became a stampede, the troops throwing away their guns and commandeering locomotives, trains and carts in which to escape.

Fifteen trains carrying officers and their families, besides scores of other trains filled with refugees, ammunition and merchandise, which were blocked by wreckage and lack of motor power, fell into the hands of the Bolsheviki, who followed up the Cossacks by a cavalry pursuit.

One year after assuming the supreme rulership, Admiral Kolchak today is on his way eastward, facing the necessity of re-establishing his seat of Government on the shore of Lake Baikal and reconstructing his army, which has been badly shattered.

**Northwest Army Dwindled Away.**

REVAL, Esthonia, Nov. 24.—The Russian Northwest Army, which attempted recently to capture Petrograd under General Yudenitch, has virtually gone out of existence, according to General Soots, Chief of the General Staff of the Esthonian Army. He made this statement on the basis of a report brought in by Colonel Rink of the General Staff, who returned from the Narva front on Sunday.

According to Colonel Rink's report, the army was in a bad condition during the retreat following the attempt on Petrograd. General Yudenitch and his staff lost all connection with the army, which was left to its fate, unable to resist the Bolshevist attack. The Yudenitch troops retired in disorder and sought protection on Esthonian territory. Part of the Russian troops, with 10,000 refugees, have settled south of Narva. Some of the soldiers have already been disarmed, and the remainder will be deprived of their weapons in the near future.

"Four Russian divisions which retreated from Yamburg to Narva are now organized under General Tonnison," said General Soots. "They willingly obey the orders of the Esthonian chief and are now protecting the positions below Narva. General Yudenitch and his staff are now unemployed. The present critical condition of the Russian troops was caused by the incompetence of the Russian Chief Command.

"The troops had to mix flour with snow, owing to the scarcity of bread. Many refugee children died of hunger and cold, but we made conditions better for the survivors."

November 26, 1919

**Reds Claim War Is Won.**

LONDON, Jan. 13.—A wireless dispatch received from Moscow, reviewing the successes of the Red armies, says:

"The enemy's technical forces were destroyed when the Reds captured the Donetz Basin and captured enormous quantities of materials. The Red cavalry created in answer to General Mamontoff's raid, achieved exploits under Budenny and Dumenko which will be a proud record in military history.

"The Turkestan front may be regarded definitely as liquidated. Orenburg and the Ural regions being completely cleared of the enemy.

"The Polish-Lett attacks in the Dvinsk region are merely local.

"The liberated regions are precisely those which will permit of the restoration of industry and transport and promote the well-being of the country by peaceful work.

"A Soviet army will soon arrive in proximity to the Japanese but will not undertake any aggressive action calculated to provoke a collision with the Japanese. But the menace of the Japanese and of the vassals of the Entente in the West still compel the Soviet authority to devote a great part of its forces to military purposes.

"We are already forty versts beyond Krasnoyarsk. Our victory over Admiral Kolchak was mainly due to support given us by the Siberian peasants."

January 14, 1920

# DENIKIN RESIGNS; HIS CHIEF AID SLAIN

## Wrangel to Take Command of the Anti-Bolshevist Forces in Crimea.

CONSTANTINOPLE, April 5 (Associated Press).—General Wrangel, commander of the volunteer army of Russia, has been appointed by the anti-Bolshevist leaders to relieve General Denikin as commander of the anti-Bolshevist forces in the south of Russia.

Denikin's former Chief of Staff, General Romanovsky, who had resigned, was murdered tonight in the Russian Embassy here shortly after his arrival in Constantinople. There is no clue to the murderers. General Mokrov has succeeded him. General Ichilling has resigned as commander of the Crimean troops.

General Wrangel is of Norwegian blood and is such a forceful character that the Russians fighting against the Reds are said to believe he can reorganize the shattered volunteer and Cossack forces better than the Generals who participated at Odessa and Novorossisk, where the volunteers showed no desire to fight.

Volunteer troops are to occupy Simferopol and Sebastopol. General Alexieff's division is to occupy Kertch. Don and Kuban Cossacks are at Eupatoria, on the western coast of the Crimea.

The Bolsheviki are not yet making any headway in the Crimea. In the Caucasus they are advancing rapidly toward Azerbaijan and Georgia. From Petrovsk on the Caspian Sea they have reached Derbent on the Baku Railroad. They also are moving speedily along the railroad from Armavir to Tuapie, the next important port on the Black Sea south of Novorossisk. The Don and Kuban Cossacks fighting in that section are being forced into Taupie, from which place it is probable that the women and children will be evacuated to Theodosia. The Bolsheviki are only about thirty miles from Tuapie.

April 7, 1920

# POLES ATTACKING TO FREE UKRAINE

## Petlura Issues Declaration of Independence and Urges People to Aid Troops.

## PILSUDSKI LEADS FORCE

WARSAW, April 28 (Associated Press).—General Pilsudski, as Commander in Chief, is leading the Polish army in its drive toward the Dnieper River, which began on last Monday. By the capture of Owrucz, Jitomir and other railroad centres the Poles now control the two main lines leading to Kiev.

Jitomir was taken after a brief but fierce fight. The Poles announce that the Bolshevist 58th Infantry and 17th Cavalry Divisions were destroyed in the combats in this region.

The Bolsheviki then began a general retreat, offering resistance at only a few scattered points. Many prisoners and much material were taken, the material including sixteen locomotives and 2,000 railway cars.

The Kosciusko Squadron, composed of American aviators, is taking part in the advance into the Ukraine, notwithstanding the unfavorable weather.

Along the 300-kilometre front (187 miles) the advance is continuing. The Poles have been held up at a few points by the resistance of small forces of the Bolsheviki having machine guns. The Reds have adopted the machine gun method of the Germans for their rear-guard actions in order to permit withdrawals without endangering larger forces. The Poles are using armored trains and armored motor cars, which are particularly effective against the machine gunners, many of whom have been captured or killed.

A War Office communication issued today says the Bolsheviki began concentrating six weeks ago for a drive in the south, and that the Reds evidently were determined to attain a decisive military victory.

"In view of this fact," says the communication, "the Poles planned a counteraction under Pilsudski's leadership. The first day they reached Owrucz, Kremmo and Godnow. Then, taking advantage of the confused Bolshevist retreat, they proceeded further in the direction of their objectives. By the general advance the Poles now virtually control all the railroads extending southward from Mozir to the region of Winnica."

In connection with the drive to free the Ukraine of the Reds and Poland's recognition of Ukrainia's independence, as announced in General Pilsudski's proclamation, General Petlura, the Ukrainian leader, has issued a declaration of the independence of the Ukrainians.

The declaration gives assurance of the gratefulness of the loyal Ukrainians for Poland's assistance in the campaign against the "Red Imperialists," and appeals to the people to give the troops every consideration.

The declaration says that for three years the Ukrainians endeavored to gain their independence, fighting alone and forgotten by the world's nations. By hard fighting against the invaders, it adds, the Ukraine is prepared to prove to the world that the Ukrainians are ready for independence and prepared to direct State affairs. It also announces that a call for a National Assembly will be issued shortly.

April 30, 1920

# ANTI-RED FORCES ADVANCE IN CRIMEA

## Wrangel Captures Towns, 5,000 Prisoners, 27 Guns and 5 Armored Trains.

## POLES EVACUATE KIEV

LONDON, Sunday, June 13. — The Polish Army, The Sunday Observer says it understands, evacuated Kiev on Friday, owing to the continued menacing advance of the Bolshevist Army, which threatened to cut off the Polish line of retreat. The source of this information is not given by the newspaper.

LONDON, June 12.—Capture of Melitopol, in the Crimea, by General Wrangel, who succeeeded to the command of the Denikin forces in Southern Russia, is reported in a Reuter message from Constantinople. Five thousand prisoners, 27 guns and 5 armored trains were taken.

An Associated Press dispatch from the Turkish capital says:

"The first considerable offensive by the forces of General Wrangel, anti-Bolshevist leader on the Crimean front, is reported to have been successful.

"On June 4 large detachments of Wangel's troops left Theodosia by sea and landed June 6 at Berdiask and Marioupol, ports on the Sea of Azov. The forces of General Wrangel were not attacked while passing through the Strait of Kertch. They landed with slight opposition and captured both ports easily.

"The movement was designed to coordinate the anti-Bolshevist forces in the Don and Kuban country and strengthen the defense of the Crimea by cutting off the Bolshevist retreat and communications. General Wrangel's landing party included adequate forces of artillery, cavalry and infantry."

The Polish lines both north and south of Kiev on the west bank of the Dnieper are being driven in by the Bolsheviki, who are cutting the Polish railway communications with the city, according to Friday's official statement from Moscow. The statement says:

"Outside of Kiev, on the right bank of the Dnieper, we are driving back the Poles from the north and the south. A number of villages along the Korosten-Kiev Railway, together with Fastova, are in our hands.

"West of Bisna (on the Dvina, seventy miles southeast of Dvinsk) our troops occupied a series of points fourteen miles from the town. North of the railway (the Dvinsk-Vitebsk line), fighting is continuing with varying success. Fighting also continues in the direction of Dokchitcha (Upper Beresina). Along the River Beresina enemy attempts to advance have been checked.

"In the Crimean sector fighting is continuing north of the isthmuses of Sivatch and Perekop."

June 13, 1920

**UPS AND DOWNS IN POLAND.**

The Polish counter-offensive has had sudden and startling success, but it is well not to be too optimistic. Warsaw is safe for the time being, but this year's campaign has proved that the Russians are numerous enough to beat the Poles in the long run, and that most of them are willing to fight for any Russian Government against Poland. Dispatches from Warsaw represent the Polish successes as highly important, but a few days ago the Russians were winning victories just as overwhelming. The suspicion has been expressed by military men that in this particular war whichever army gets the worst of the first hour or so quits fighting for the day. But there is a more plausible explanation of the reverse of fortune.

The Russians have been driven back from the neighborhood of Warsaw, and also along the German frontier; but they are advancing in Galicia. The Galician front stood firm while everything was in collapse further north because the best Polish troops were there. General WEYGAND insisted that Warsaw could be saved by bringing these troops up to the defense of the capital, and he seems to have been right. The menace to Warsaw has been thrust off, and with it falls a good deal of the widespread fear of a Bolshevist tidal wave that would sweep clear to the Rhine. That danger was never so great as excited persons believed during the advance on Warsaw, and a good many fears must be calmed by this proof that the Bolshevist army is not invincible.

August 20, 1920

## *Reds Sign Armistice With Poles; Also Make Peace With the Finns*

Copyright, 1920, by The New York Times Company.

Special Cable to THE NEW YORK TIMES.

LONDON, Oct. 6.—The Government today received a telegram from Riga stating that the heads of the Polish and Russian delegations there had agreed to the signing of an armistice and of the fundamental preliminaries of peace.

The terms agreed to, it is understood, are the terms offered by the Poles. The success of the negotiations has owed much to the influence of Prince Sapieha. It is probable that the armistice line will run through Boronovitchi, Pinsk and Rovno. East of that line the Poles, it is understood, will acquiesce in whatever government the Russians may set up in White Russia and the Ukraine and will not insist on any special form of government.

The chief provisions of the agreement include a demand that the Bolsheviki shall desist from propaganda in Poland and restore Polish national treasures. Russia, of course, is to recognize fully the independence and sovereignty of Poland.

The question of East Galicia, it is expected, will be settled between the Allies and Poland. The Russians abandoned their demand with regard to East Galicia.

WARSAW, Oct. 6 (Associated Press).—Dispatches from Riga say that hostilities between the Poles and Russian Soviet forces will cease Friday under an armistice signed by the Polish and Soviet peace delegates yesterday.

RIGA, Oct. 6.—It was said this morning at the headquarters of the Polish delegation that M. Joffe, head of the Russian mission, had accepted virtually as a whole the Polish peace draft based on the eleven points framed by the Riga delegation and made public at the beginning of the Riga conference.

There are understood to be fifteen points in the new draft. The details of two of these points have not been worked out, although the points have been accepted in principle. The working out will probably be completed today.

The Poles have defined a boundary based on ethnographic lines which has been accepted but not yet written into the draft by the secretariat.

The boundary will cut off Lithuania entirely from Russia, granting Poland a corridor between, it was authoritatively stated at the headquarters of the Polish peace delegation here.

The line as virtually agreed upon begins to the east of Dvinsk, runs south through Baranovitchi, Luniniets and Sarny and practically along the German line of 1915 to the Rumanian boundary.

HELSINGFORS, Finland, Oct. 6.—The Russo-Finnish peace treaty has been accepted by both the Russians and the Finns at the Dorpat conference. It will be signed as soon as it has been printed.

October 7, 1920

## *SAYS WEYGAND GOES TO HELP WRANGEL*

COPENHAGEN, Oct. 6.—The French General Weygand has left for South Russia to take supreme command of the anti-Bolshevist troops of General Wrangel, the National Tidende says today.

Recent dispatches from Paris asserted that the French Government was considering the sending of General Weygand to South Russia to advise General Wrangel, whose Government has already been recognized by France. It is to General Weygand's strategy that the successful counterstroke of the Poles which relieved Warsaw and drove the Soviet troops from Polish territory is credited.

October 7, 1920

**Makno's Desertion Doomed Army.**

Copyright, 1920, by The New York Times Company.

Special Cable to THE NEW YORK TIMES.

LONDON, Monday, Nov. 15.—Some days ago it was announced that Trotzky in person was directing the Red army's advance against General Wrangel, which is only explainable on the hypothesis that final success was hoped for.

One of the most serious blows suffered by Wrangel at the height of his successes against the Bolsheviki was the defection some weeks ago of General Makno, the Ukranian peasant leader, whose forces were operating in conjunction with Wrangel's army in the region to northeast of Crimea. He went over to the Reds and took command of a section of the front against the volunteer army.

The Daily Chronicle's military correspondent, discussing the collapse of Wrangel's army, says:

"Wrangel's idea was that the volunteer army should as far as possible seek to fight on a narrow front, utilizing large rivers and other natural obstacles to protect its flanks against the numerically superior Bolsheviki.

"When he succeeded Denikin in command of his army, or rather of such relics as survived Denikin's collapse, he set to work upon these theories, always handicapped, however, by very inadequate numbers and resources. He planned to use the Crimea as a base, as a sort of Torres Vedras with sea communications open behind him to the French and the narrow isthmuses of the peninsula heavily fortified against attack.

"During the Summer, while the Bolshevist armies were busy with the Poles, he sallied forth on to the mainland and gained considerable successes, which, however, he was careful to exploit with great prudence, always bearing in mind the probability of another retreat to the Crimea.

"After the Bolsheviki signed peace with Poland this need soon arose. Very large Bolshevist forces were concentrated against him, but he seemed without any crushing loss to have made good his retreat and to stand firm on the isthmuses. By an unexpected ruse the Bolshevist cavalry succeeded in outflanking him. Favored by hard frost, they crossed the shallows of the so-called Putrid Sea and took the isthmus defenses in the rear. The result seems to have been rapid and irremediable collapse.

"It should be added that Wrangel differed from his predecessor not only on strategy but on politics. Denikin's political administration during his advance last year developed on frankly reactionary lines and hopelessly antagonized the peasants. Wrangel, on the other hand, enlisting the services of such men as Krivochin, the famous ex-Minister of Agriculture, and Struve, the Constitutional Democrat leader worked out a land program which was genuinely popular with the peasants. This, however, was much disliked by many of the reactionary officers in his force and their discontent may have contributed to the final breakdown."

The Chronicle in an editorial says that if three years of government by Lenin and his associates prove anything it is that they are not to be ousted by arms—neither by foreigners, nor by White Russians.

"Fighting has only strengthened them," it says, "and peace may have the opposite effect. Whether or not that be so, peace ought to come. We hope that French statesmen may now be led around to what has throughout the present year been the conviction of British statesmenship on this subject. If so, we may see not only considerable simplification and strengthening of relations between the two allied pillars of Western Europe, but a vital advance toward an economic resettlement of the continent as a whole.

"Nor is the true interest of Russia different. If Bolshevism is a disease, as we suppose, it is by nursing and tonics, not by fresh surgical operations, that the Russian body politic is likeliest to be enabled to shake it off."

November 15, 1920

# SOVIET LABOR DRAFT TAKES BOTH SEXES

## All Males 16 to 50 and Females 15 to 40 Required by New Order to Register.

## TROTZKY FOR LABOR ARMY

### Workmen Must Be Treated Like Soldiers, Says His Report, Made Public by State Department.

PETROGRAD, May 21.—The Soviet Government is taking steps to insure the full utilization of industrial power and the elimination of parasitic elements by ordering the registration of all males between the ages of 16 and 50 years, and of females between the ages of 15 and 40.

Each person registering is to furnish a book containing full particulars regarding the nature and the place of their employment, together with data giving a description of themselves, to establish their identity. No other identification cards are to be valid in the future.

A similar system of identification cards is to be established in Moscow and other Russian cities.

*Special to The New York Times.*

WASHINGTON, May 23.—The State Department has made public a report on the militarization of labor in Soviet Russia, made by Leon Trotzky, the Bolshevist Minister of War, at the ninth congress of the Russian Communist Party. The report was published in the Izvestia, the official Soviet organ in Moscow, on March 21.

The report, in dealing with the necessity for the mobilization of Russian labor on a military basis, confirms reports received here recently of the progress of disintegration within Soviet Russia and consequent decrease of Soviet authority through the failure of the system to work. Trotzky, in the report, refers to what he characterizes as the "conditions of starvation and disorganization existing today" in justification of extreme measures considered in well-informed circles here a vain efort to prevent ultimate collapse.

The opinion was expressed in a high quarter here today that Trotzky's report of the manner in which the Bolshevist authorities shuffle the working classes about as they see fit, with scant regard for their rights and liberties as individuals, should have a salutary effect upon the elements of American labor who are inclined to look with sympathy upon the Bolshevist Russian political order.

Trotzky's report says:

"At the present time the militarization of labor is all the more needed in that we have now come to the mobilization of peasants as the means of solving the problems requiring mass action. We are mobilizing the peasants and forming them into labor detachments which very closely resemble military detachments.

"Some of our comrades say, however, that even though in the case of the working power of mobilized peasantry it is necessary to apply militarization, a military apparatus need not be created when the question involved skilled labor and industry because there we have professional unions performing the function of organizing labor. This opinion, however, is erroneous. At present it is true that professional unions distribute labor power to the social economic organizations, but what means and methods do they possess for insuring that the workmen who are sent to a given factory actually reports at that factory for work?

"We have in the most important branches of our industry more than a million workmen on the lists, but not more than eight hundred thousand of them are actually working, and where are the remainder? They have gone to the villages or to other divisions of industry or into speculation. Among soldiers this is called desertion, and, in one form or another, the measures used to compel soldiers to do their duty should be applied in the field of labor.

"Under a unified system of economy the masses of workmen should be moved about, ordered and sent from place to place in exactly the same manner as soldiers. This is the foundation of the militarization of labor, and without this we are unable to speak seriously of any organization of industry on a new basis in the conditions of starvation and disorganization existing today.

"In the period of transition in the organization of labor compulsion plays a very important part. The statement that free labor, namely, freely employed labor, produces more than labor under compulsion is correct only when applied to feudalistic and bourgeois orders of society."

May 24, 1920

# SOVIET INDUSTRIES SHOW HUGE DEFICIT

## Nationalization Results in Loss of 23,756,700,000 Rubles for Current Year.

LONDON, May 31.—The official organ of the Russian Bolshevist Government reports an estimated deficit for 1920 on the operations of nationalized industries of 23,756,700,000 rubles, according to a Berlin dispatch to the Exchange Telegraph Company.

The total includes 5,650,000,000 rubles spent on official salaries and on organization of the industries, 14,393,000,000 rubles lost owing to production cost exceeding sale prices and 1,210,000,000 rubles spent on political measures which were found necessary to keep the workmen quiet.

The political measures, the dispatch says, consisted chiefly in stationing soldiers and gendarmes in the most turbulent factories.

June 1, 1920

# INDUSTRIAL CHAOS IN SOVIET RUSSIA

## Conditions Described by a Traveler Who Left Moscow in May.

## NOTHING THERE TO SELL

### People Live by Bartering Last Possessions for Food—Workmen Forced to Steal.

The most authentic news about industrial and trade conditions in Soviet Russia received in many months is contained in the following letter (translated from the German), written by a merchant in Moscow in the latter part of May and brought out of the country by hand, so that it escaped the Bolshevist censor. The letter, the original of which reached the Moscow merchant's brother, who is now in the United States, about a week ago, after dealing with personal matters, says:

"The journey from Reval to Moscow can now be made in a direct train; the railway line has been restored and the great bridge near Jamburg has been repaired. Jamburg is a great centre of exchange. The Esthonians supply potatoes and the Soviet Government gives small quantities of timber and flax in exchange.

"The foreigner who deals for the first time with the Soviet authorities receives a somewhat ludicrous impression. The representatives of the Soviet Government do not appear to be in a position to carry on a serious conversation and pass everything with a certain amount of frivolity. That is true to such an extent that it is, for instance, quite immaterial whether, in discussing a business transaction, 100 or ten millions are mentioned as a consideration. It is even doubtful whether any business even after being validly entered into ever materializes, for the subordinate officials will use boycott and sabotage.

"The greatest obstacle, however, in transacting commercial business is the lack of business knowledge possessed by the Soviet representatives. By order of the Soviet Government negotiations have to be conducted concerning business transactions, but there is no one there who understands anything about the particular business, for all those who knew have either escaped or have been assassinated, or do not wish to work for the Soviet Government, as they are unwilling to support régime that has ruined Russia. It is obvious that in these circumstances any working with the Soviet Government is rendered extremely difficult.

"The demand for goods in Russia is so enormous that huge quantities of any article, whatever its nature, could be sent there, for they would all find a market. But owing to a complete lack of means of payment and of exchange commercial business is out of the question.

"At every occasion of negotiations the Bolsheviks attempt to impress the foreigner by offering such compensation as crops in Turkestan, the Ural, South Russia, &c. Naturally, no serious man can entertain such proposals, for those same regions of Turkestan, the Ural and South Russia, which are now under the domination of the Bolsheviks, may pass tomorrow into other hands, to say nothing of the fact that those famous stocks of grain simply cannot be transported.

"The stocks offered by Krassin and other Bolshevist emissaries, are not produce, but goods that have been confiscated from private owners, that is to say, taken by force, and which cannot be utilized for lack of fuel and of competent technical personnel and even skilled labor.

"Naturally, even if these goods could be transported, the stock would soon run out without any sensible diminution of Russia's enormous requirements.

"Any materials that could be used as a means of payment are lacking. The stocks of platinum and gold, for instance, that have been taken away from private owners, are so insignificant that they would not suffice to pay for one-tenth part of the rolling stock that would be necessary to make even a modest beginning in rehabilitating transportation. What still remains of articles of value in private possession, such as imperial paper money, gold, silver, jewelry, &c., is buried by their owners, because nobody believes that the Soviet Government will last. Enormous capital is thus entirely withdrawn from circulation and will remain dead until trade, private property and other inducements for production are again called into being.

"The many promises of the Bolsheviki to supply goods are only intended for the diplomatists of other nations who do not know Russia, and are therefore taken in. How can Russia export timber, when even in the houses occupied by Soviet officials, all waterworks, pipes, as well as central heating pipes—where they existed—have burst in the Winter frost for lack of wood to burn, while it is useless to put any portable stoves in rooms, since no fuel is available even for central heating? In Moscow and Petrograd thousands of wooden houses have been demolished and blocks of streets destroyed because the wood of which they were built was the only kind of fuel that could be procured.

"The Bolsheviki speak of supplies of naphtha, while 75 per cent. of the Russian population must do without any artificial light, must go to bed at dusk, and the others only possess tiny oil lamps, something in the nature of glimmering night lights, which are yet considered a great luxury. They speak of exporting fats, while the whole population looks like negroes in the Winter for want of soap that cannot be manufactured because there are no fats, while faces and hands get black owing to the smoky oil stoves where such are available.

"It might be possible for Russia to export flax, and the reason for this is that the textile industry came to a standstill owing to lack of fuel, and thus the raw materials could not be utilized, not because there is any surplus of such raw material.

"Moreover, when contemplating exchange of goods, due attention must be paid to the question of transport. The state of affairs on the railways, not withstanding all the achievements of the Bolsheviki who have been masters now for over two and a half years, is such that for the ordinary mortal it is quite impossible today to book a ticket anywhere. Traveling is only possible for persons sent on a mission by the Soviet Government. Even in the local traffic of the Moscow suburbs, there are such regulations during the Winter that only employes of the Soviets, or members of the Communist Party, can travel. All others have to go on foot, even if it is hundreds of miles.

"This opportunity may be taken for remarking that not everybody is allowed to join the Commercial Party, but the great majority of the whole population feels it a shame or an insult to be called 'Communist' or 'Comrade.' The very word 'Comrade' has become an insult.

"At first the Bolsheviki suppressed every sort of private trade, and even the smallest shops were 'nationalized,' so as to prevent any speculation, but lately they have had to allow small shops to be conducted under the name of 'Kustarny shop'—that is to say, 'home industry shop.' The Bolsheviki shut not only one eye, but both eyes, if these so-called 'home industry shops' also offer for sale articles of luxury of French or German origin, or any other goods of whatever kind. The magnanimity of the Bolsheviki goes so far as to allow even in their own Soviet institutions, where formerly speculation was punished by death, goods to be bought in the so-called 'home industry shops' at free commerce prices—that is to say, at the highest profiteering prices. They had to admit that the monopoly of State trade was impossible, as nothing could be bought at the officially fixed maximum prices, and so the Bolsheviki authorities had to yield.

"In addition to these shops there are in Moscow and Petrograd, almost in every large square, so-called Sukharevkas, a motley collection of market booths where, at enormous profiteering prices, everything can be obtained that was formerly obtainable in shops, from furniture to the costliest diamonds and pearls, and also articles of food. The Sukharevka in Moscow itself, which formely occupied the space of about two-thirds of a mile, now occupies a length of nearly three and a half miles in the street. It begins in the Karetny-Sadovaya and continues right up to the Red Gate, and we may notice as really original the so-called Bourgeois Avenue, where the bourgeoisie bring their last belongings for sale. This avenue trades exclusively in personal articles of luxury, pearls, diamonds, watches, linen, silk dresses, stockings, shoes, dancing pumps, &c. The owners sell successively their last possessions simply in order to be saved from death by starvation. It is characteristic of the kind of purchaser that they will pay for a gramophone 60,000 rubles, while for a piano only 30,000 rubles would be paid, because a gramophone can be played by any proletarian.

"The Soviet Government could not help seeing that industry cannot be kept alive on the principles maintained hitherto, and has therefore at its last Congress withdrawn the management of those concerns from the Communist Councils and has placed it in the hands of individual experts, as in former times. It hopes thereby to revive industry. It is particularly interesting to know that after the decision had already been promulgated, the heads of the Soviet Government have not yet come to a uniform view as to what extent these individual managers might endanger the Soviet policy or the domination of the Bolsheviki, but the opinion was expressed that no choice is possible, for it is a case of force majeure.

"The great majority of the population, after all businesses had been nationalised, had become employes of the Soviet authorities. Every workman and employe is supposed to be mobilized, and is not allowed to give up his work or situation. His salary may vary between 2,400 and 4,200 rubles per month. That amount, in the present circumstances in Russia, is, of course, ludicrous, and everybody is compelled to depend on the so-called State rations which he receives free of charge at his place of employment.

"The ration consists of millet soup without meat and millet porridge, alternating only with beetroot and beans and about half a pound of black bread per day. In many places it is the practice to distribute at the end of the month to every person employed one pound of flour, strictly checked, and occasionally some meat or butter. If these rations were not provided no one could have been found to enter the service of the Bolsheviki. For even when receiving a monthly salary averaging 3,000 rubles, the most abstemious man is unable to feed himself.

"As an instance, it may be said that for 1,000 German marks (old paper money with red stamp) 80,000 to 90,000 rubles are paid in Moscow. That rate of exchange corresponds very closely to the prices of victuals in Russia as compared with those in Germany. Thus, for instance, black bread with an admixture of straw and certain other grains cost 350 rubles per Russian pound (409 grams); our gray bread costs 800 rubles; butter, 3,000 rubles; pork, 2,300 rubles; beef, 1,200 to 1,500 rubles, and so on.

"Today everybody, even the workman who at first was so devoted to the Bolsheviki, is an enemy of that Government, for he is compelled every day to sell something of his remaining slender possessions in order to keep himelf alive. We need only compare the exchange to form an opinion of the earnings of a Russian workman. Three thousand rubles corresponds to a monthly wage of 30 marks. Consequently everybody is compelled to steal, and again the Soviet Government shuts one eye, for finally men must do something to find food, and if a piece of bread or a potato is "embezzled," well, the authorities cannot help it.

"In these circumstances it is useless to talk of any productive work, whether by the Soviet institutions or by factories. Everybody is compelled to neglect his work, for he must, in order not to starve, do something in addition to his regular employment.

"Officially the eight-hour working day still exists, and therefore, so-called supplementary work has been introduced, and on Saturdays and Sundays workmen are seen by hundreds in the streets, where they are compelled by armed soldiers to do such work as scavenging or removing débris of destroyed houses, disincumber railway lines, &c., without any pay. This forced labor is called euphemistically "Communist Sabbath." It can be easily imagined how enthusiastic the workmen are over the fate that the Bolsheviki have provided for them.

"The much-vaunted 'liberty' consists in the fact that at meetings where, for instance, 5,000 railway workers were present, including at the utmost some 300 Communists, only Communists were allowed to speak. Resolutions are not voted upon, but immediately after the last Communist has concluded his speech they are announced as having been passed unanimously under pressure of the omnipotent and omnipresent Chrezvychaika (Extraordinary Commission).

"Trotsky's energy has nevertheless achieved the result that many railroad cars have been repaired and certain trains leave and arrive on time. This had led to the hope in many places that the crisis was over, but it is necessary to take into consideration that the railway transport has been reduced to a minimum fraction of what would be necessary to maintain passenger and freight traffic. Moreover, the railways constituted only a small portion of the diversified economic life of Russia and the success achieved at isolated points, with great energy and still greater severity, is not proof that other difficulties have been overcome.

"Above all, the attitude of all those who do not belong to the Soviet Government or the Communist Party, or the Military Staff, that is to say, the attitude of 90 per cent. of the inhabitants, is inimical to the Bolsheviki, although at the commencement of the Bolshevist reign, the majority of the work people were favorably disposed toward them. It is, however, impossible to expect any improvement of conditions under the system of the Soviet Government, and so long as the Soviets adhere to their principles neither order nor productive work nor any well-being is possible in Russia."

July 24, 1920

## RUSSIA FACES FAMINE.

### Drought Causes Failure of the Grain and Hay Crops.



Special Cable to THE NEW YORK TIMES.

COPENHAGEN, Sept. 17.—A special dispatch to the Berlingske Tidende from Kovno says that, according to the Bolshevist organ Isvestia, a crisis is impending in the food situation in Russia, an unusual drought having upset all calculations.

Especially have the grain-producing districts round the Volga River suffered and in many places the harvest is so bad that there will be insufficient seed for the coming year. Also the hay crops failed, which, combined with the failure of the grain harvest, threatens livestock with starvation.

September 18, 1920

# REPORT RED ARMY CLAMORS FOR PEACE AS WORKERS REBEL

### Twelve Soldier Delegates Sent to Moscow with Demands Summarily Shot.

LONDON, Oct. 2.—Reports of serious disturbances in industrial establishments in Soviet Russia and of a peace movement in the army on the Western Russian front are contained in a Reuter dispatch from Helsingfors, dated Friday, based on advices received there from Narva, near the Russo-Esthonian border.

Two commissaries were killed in the factory outbreaks, it is declared. Nearly all the factories in Petrograd are affected, the workmen striking with the object of overthrowing the Soviet Government, according to the reports.

Large meetings are being held among the troops of the western Soviet army, demanding peace, it is asserted. Twelve delegates from the army who were sent to Moscow to urge the making of peace, however, were summarily shot, it is declared.

"Consternation reigns in the Moscow Government," the Narva reports add.

COPENHAGEN, Oct. 2.—Reports that a strike movement is rapidly spreading in Russia, resulting in serious disturbances in various parts of the country, have been received by the National Tidende from its Helsingfors correspondent. He declares travelers from Russia confirm the recent reports that street conflicts had occurred in Petrograd, in which several of the Soviet commissioners were killed by a mob. (The previous reports had it that six of the commissioners were drowned in the Neva.)

Persistent rumors that Leon Trotzky, the War Minister, had been wounded, and that General Budenny, the noted cavalry leader, was being court-martialed, also were in circulation, the travelers reported.

At a mass meeting, which was largely attended by Petrograd people, a resolution is declared to have been unanimously passed in favor of immediate peace with the rest of the world.

October 3, 1920

# PEASANTS INDICT RULE OF SOVIET

## Communities Throughout Red Russia Adopt Resolutions Setting Forth Their Wrongs.

## WORSE THAN UNDER CZARS

*Special to The New York Times.*

WASHINGTON, Oct. 18.—Peasants in Soviet Russia are engaged in a powerful and widespread anti-Bolshevist movement, according to official advices received here. In many communities they have adopted resolutions indicting the Soviets under twelve counts. After declaring that scarcely any of the evils which they endured under the Czar have been righted, they demand a national election in secret ballot to create a Constituent Assembly.

It is reported that these resolutions have been adopted at numerous meetings and are being circulated for action throughout Soviet Russia. The resolutions assert among other things that there is no free press in Russia and that there is no place now, because only an official government press exists, wherein to oppose official wrongs and abuse. The resolutions further contend that there is no equitable distribution of land, and that lands without redemption were promised but the price of redemption has been collected in taxes and confiscations.

Chaos exists everywhere, the resolutions declare, and incompetent officials have been sent into communities by the soviet authorities who abuse their powers and have no control over themselves. The city is living at the expense of the country, and the peasants have no say as to who shall represent them or what laws shall be passed dealing with their welfare.

"Small wonder, under these circumstances, if everybody is talking about a new soviet serfdom, and there are even such as regret the passing of the old Czarist bureaucratic rule," say the resolutions.

**Text of the Demands.**

The complete text follow:

"We, working peasants, citizens of the village (name), in village council assembled (date, and number of persons present,) have adopted the following resolution.

"To declare to the Council of People's Commissaries and to the Central Executive Committee of the Soviets which are ruling in Russia, that we had expected a happy and free life after the fall of the old Czarist and bureaucratic Government; nevertheless, we see that after a brief respite all the burdens and all the oppression of the old order are being restored in a new form. We have, therefore, resolved to state all our woes, grievances and complaints, point by point, as follows:

"1. We were promised by the present Government land without redemption payments. Since that time, however, the price of redemption has been collected from us over and over in the shape of all kinds of levies, requisitions, regular and extra taxes, payments, confiscations, duties and services, and still the land is not ours. The Soviet officials may always, whenever their fancy strikes them, cut it off, and they do, in point of fact, cut it off for various communes and Soviet farms in which we fail to observe anything but mismanagement and loafing, wasteful to the people as well as to the Government.

"2. The present Government has failed from the very beginning to carry out all over Russia a proper and equitable distribution of land among those who are in need of it, thereby starting among us land feuds, inequality, envy and estrangement. Meanwhile, the authorities, taking advantage of this state of affairs, are forever interfering with our land settlement, making various reallotments, curtailments and grants without any definite and equal law, acting entirely arbitrarily. Therefore none of us feels secure of the morrow, and without that no proper farming is possible.

"3. Among the local authorities appointed over us we hardly ever find people who know and understand our agricultural life, but instead we find mostly bungling, inefficient, incompetent persons, real good-for-nothings, who are meddling in everything, causing confusion, abusing their powers, rendering no account to us, and having no control over themselves. Nobody respects them and no one could ever regard them as real authorities.

"4. Therefore we never get any needed help from the authorities in the matter of seeds, provisions, textiles, oil and salt, and in renewing our worn-out implements. Roads, schools and hospitals we find totally neglected. In a word, the existing authorities are useless to us, and we see nothing but endless demands for further exertions and services.

"5. For the fruits of our weary toil taken from us at fixed prices they not only fail to supply us at equally fixed prices with goods from the city, but we are even prevented from acquiring them at free market prices. Worse than in the times of the feudal barons, all of Russia has been criss-crossed with toll-barriers by the so-called food control detachments of which we shall say nothing except that they are everywhere called robber detachments.

"6. We are so much overburdened with all manner of payments in kind that we call them by their old name of landlord serfdom. We, toilers of the soil, do not refuse to work our share for the needs of the State. But we only observe throughout the country disorder and chaos, and the cessation of all normal production; the cities are filling up with people who live at the expense of the State, either entirely without work or else merely loafing on empty jobs, while all of them have to be sustained again by the farmer.

"7. Still we see the all-sustaining farming communities have absolutely no share in the administration of State affairs. New ordinances, laws and decrees are being passed all the time, but no one ever asks us whether they are convenient to us, and how we fare under them. They always descend upon us like snow from the sky, and none of our elected representatives are previously notified about them, nor are they asked for their approval.

"8. Although officially there are supposed to exist among us our own freely elected soviets, they exist merely on paper; we are forever being coerced and told whom we may and whom we may not elect, and we are being threatened and intimidated; besides, there are now to be found no willing candidates for public office, since our representatives are anyway prevented from above from doing anything. They are now accepting public offices as it used to be before, under the autocracy, unwillingly, reluctantly, often taking turns, as if they had to render some hard and onerous state duty.

"9. Another great evil we find in the fact that no free press has been left in Russia, and that only the official Government press exists, so that there is no place left where any abuse or wrong might be revealed and brought to light. Every free man has his mouth shut now closer than ever before, and who ever dares open his mouth against any injustices is seized immediately, carted off and put away, no one knows where. As of old, our country is getting to be without a law and arbitrariness is taking the place of justice.

"10. Worst of all are we, common folk, suffering from those gentry wearing leather jackets who call themselves agents of the extraordinary commissions. These fellows are acting toward us as if they were in a conquered country, and nobody can feel safe before them; no law exists for them, while their own will is law to everybody.

**Exhausted by Civil War.**

"11. Small wonder, under these circumstances, if everybody is talking about a new Soviet serfdom, and there are even such as regret the passing of the old Czarist and bureaucratic rule. But we, who are not in favor of a return to the former slavery, we do not blame these people for it. The fault rests with those who, holding the reins of power, have tolerated so many oppressions and wrongs against the common folk of the villages that life has become unbearable to them. Thus it is but necessary for some bold General like Denikin, Kolchak or Yudenitch to take the field when there are at once found so many who are disaffected with the present Government that civil war begins and brother goes against brother and son against father. We declare that we are utterly exhausted by this civil war, which has drenched all Russia with the blood of our sons and the tears of parents and which is taking from the farms the best labor power and is ruining the whole country.

"12. In conclusion, we declare that we had expected after the fall of the old régime a new life and justice among men; we expected ourselves to be regenerated, to lay aside malice and selfishness and to begin to live like brethers, in truth, conscience and love. We had expected the new Government to guide us along that path, bringing light to us from above and showing us an example of justice and love of truth. But we had to convince ourselves with pain in our hearts that from above they are bringing us only lawlessness, greed, disregard for human life, brutality and coarseness. And, instead of sacred joy over the triumph of liberty and truth, we behold all about us in all hearts a growing exasperation, brutality and bitterness.

"Such are, in twelve points, our complaints, grievances and discontents."

In demanding a Constituent Assembly the resolutions urge that the Soviets order throughout Russia on one day a general popular election, "to see who approves of the acts of the Council of People's Commissaries, who is satisfied with its officials and the system they have set up, who desire that they remain in power and, on the other hand, who is not satisfied with them and wants them to abdicate and turn over the power to those chosen by the people."

"To our mind," the resolutions continue, "it seems that all should have the right to vote. Of the working people there is an immense mass in Russia, while of the bourgeoisie and 'koulaki' (wealthy farmers) there is but a handful. If, however, it should be decided to disfranchise them, we fear that the very opposite result may be obtained; the real bourgeois and 'koulaki' who have managed to join the soviet forces will be voting, but under the pretext of disfranchising the 'koulaki' they themselves will disfranchise the most genuine, honest, working farmers.

"Furthermore, the balloting must be secret, so that there may be no room for any intimidation, and that everybody may cast his ballot as his conscience bids him to without fear of punishment. We have witnessed enough elections and votings that have been nothing but pure frauds and lies which disgrace the liberty we have won.

"We also have decided to appeal to our brothers of toil, the city workers, requesting them to lend their support to our just complaints and demands."

October 19, 1920

## PEASANTS TORTURE REDS.

### Soviet Troops Retaliate by Destroying Rebellious Villages.



Special Cable to THE NEW YORK TIMES.

COPENHAGEN, Nov. 4.—According to a Riga dispatch bread transports from Siberia and Volga districts being impossible owing to traffic difficulties the Government made requisitions in Middle Russia, where the harvest, however, was exceedingly bad.

In consequence of the requisitions peasant rebellions have broken out in fifteen Governments. The Isvetia narrates an especially cruel insurrection in the Government of Tcherigoff where peasants saw off arms and legs of Communists, killing them under terrible tortures.

In return the Soviet Government shells the villages, destroying them completely. Moscow is feverishly excited. The social revolutionaries have issued a call to the people to crush Soviet rule.

November 5, 1920

## BIG CITIES PARALYZED BY FAMINE, LENIN SAYS

LONDON, Nov. 5.—Nikolai Lenin, the Russian Bolshevist Premier, frankly admits the seriousness of the food situation in Russia. A Central News dispatch from Copenhagen quotes him as writing in the Russian newspaper Proletaskaja Pravda as follows:

"Soviet Russia never before has experienced such a food crisis. Moscow and other cities are paralyzed by famine and the army is becoming famished. It is necessary for us to use all means in our power to enforce delivery of foodstuffs by the peasantry."

Writing in the same paper, Leon Trotzky, the Bolshevist Minister of War and Marine, says:

"We want to see rebellions in other countries, so as to render an attack upon our country impossible. The Red Army is in dire need of food and clothing. If these needs are not supplied immediately, all our efforts will be futile."

November 6, 1920

# COMMUNIST CHIEF HITS BUREAUCRACY

## Suggest Manual Labor to Keep Bolshevist Leaders in Touch with Masses.

Power and iron discipline have sadly changed the enthusiastic spirit that prevailed in the ranks of the Russian Communist Party in the days of its early triumphs, according to an article entitled "The Average Communist," printed in the Moscow Pravda, the official organ of the Communist Party, and reprinted in the Berlin Freiheit of Oct. 10. The author of the article, M. Preobrashensky, secretary of the Central Committee of the Russian Communist Party, says:

"The unity and comradely ties that existed in the ranks of the party in 1917 and 1918 are no longer to be found. It is true that the party discipline has grown, but it rests more upon external force. The party life is dying away right among the broad masses of the comrades. Formerly the average Communist knew that he, too, co-operated in the molding of the party's will; now all he has to do is to execute the decisions of the party committee.

"Indeed, the reason for such centralization is to be found in the life-and-death struggle that the Soviet republic has to carry on, but nevertheless in this connection the necessary and permissible measure has been exceeded. The work of the party is saturated with bureaucracy and this evil cannot be remedied overnight, as it is to be attributed to the lack of men qualified to handle the enormous amount of party work. The average Communist is also spiritually far removed from the leading party members. This is due to the fact that the leading party members display slight interest in the education of the masses of the party, and also to the difference between the living conditions of the two groups, which, although at first regarded as of little consequence, is contributing a great deal to this development and in the course of time also produce a difference in the points of view.

"What does the most toward estranging the masses from the party is the fact that the party is being invaded by ambitious and avaricious elemenes which are far removed spirtually from it. Because of the lack of qualified persons, we have to make the best of such individuals, but if we now have to choose between them and the workers, we prefer the workers. But even in the case of what fortunately is thus far a small number of old-time Communists the proletarian spirit is disappearing. When a person in his daily work and his private life no longer mixes with the workers, but only with the bourgeoisie and the bourgeois intellectuals, a person cannot deny, if he wishes to remain a Marxist, that this is bound to have its effect in the long run. The leading party members must be made to do common manual labor for from a month to a month and a half each year, or, in case of bodily weakness, at least be sent to the provinces. The conditions described above have caused large numbers of workers who announced their readiness to join the party during the great recruiting week to remain away from the general party registration in the end."

November 7, 1920

## Trotzky Bids for Capital As Distress in Russia Grows


Special Cable to THE NEW YORK TIMES.

COPENHAGEN, Dec. 16.—The Politiken's Riga correspondent says Trotzky everywhere lately has been spreading propaganda for peace and work for economics rebuilding. He declares the Soviet Government has resolved at any cost to get work and peace, the country being poorer and distress more terrible than ever before. The Soviet Government therefore is willing to give concessions to foreign capitalists.

The provisional concession in Kamchatka to Americans is without danger, he says, as Japan would see that Americans did not bring arms there. The duration of the concession is also without danger, as the world revolution would doubtless break out before the expiration of the concession.

December 17, 1920

## SOVIET TO JAIL STRIKERS.

### Long Sentences and Loss of Food Cards Decreed as Punishment.


Special Cable to THE NEW YORK TIMES.

COPENHAGEN, Jan. 14.—A dispatch from Helsingfors says the Soviet Government has issued a new decree prohibiting strikes in Russia. Offenders are to be sentenced to imprisonment from one to five years and their families lose their food cards.

January 15, 1921

# RUSSIA COLLAPSING UNDER SOVIET RULE

## Transportation Breaking Down on Top of Crop Failure and Coal Famine.

## NO MORE MONEY CURRENCY

*Special to the New York Times.*

WASHINGTON, Jan. 20.—Authentic information just received by the United States Government regarding conditions in Soviet Russia show that there has been a further collapse of the already broken down system of transport which, on top of the crop failure and the coal famine, have developed a most deplorable internal situation as a result of the communistic experiment.

All things in Russia are combining to make it the hardest Winter the Russian people have been compelled to face in more than a century.

Practically all of the mines in the Don region have been shut down because of water in the pits resulting from lack of sufficient fuel with which to operate machinery for pumping out the water. The coal shortage has cut down the number of trains in operation, forced the closing of some of the factories in operation, and even limited the amount of available electric current. Formerly two trains a day had been in operation between Moscow and Petrograd. Now this has been reduced to only two trains a week with an occasional extra train operated under special orders only of the commissariat.

Only five cables for the transmission of electric power are now in use in Petrograd. These five cables furnish current for use only by five services, these being the offices of the Extraordinary Commission, the Smolny Institute, the flour mills, the bakeries, the street railways and the radio station. The street cars are operated only four hours daily in Petrograd, between the morning hours of 7 and 11 o'clock. The report says the street railways face a complete suspension of operation unless fuel is obtained immediately.

Factories that failed to obtain sufficient coal last Summer, the report says, have been obliged to shut down. Repair work on ships has also been abandoned because of lack of fuel, and Odessa and other ports are clogged with vessels for that reason.

The week of Jan. 10-17 was set apart as "fuel week," during which, under orders from Moscow, an attempt was made to take a census of all fuel stocks in Russia. This term has been extended for another week. The reports indicate that all over Russia there is a breakdown of transportation, worse than before, and these on top of poor crops and the fuel shortage have made the situation very difficult.

Beginning with Jan. 1 all currency was abolished as a medium of exchange in Russia and the only such medium now in work takes the form of "work cards" which pass as currency. The existing economic breakdown is the severest Russia has ever experienced, and is regarded as revealing the utter incapacity of the Bolshevist régime to care for the economic necessities of the nation, as well as the failure of the Soviet economic system as an experiment.

January 21, 1921

# KRONSTADT REBELS TRAIN THEIR GUNS ON PETROGRAD

## Warship Threatens Soviet Forces in the City—Neighboring Port of Oranienbaum Shelled.

LONDON, March 6.—Confirmation of reports that Russian revolutionists have taken possession of Kronstadt, the fortress and seaport at the head of the Gulf of Finland near Petrograd, is given in the most recent advices received in Copenhagen by way of Helsingfors, says the Copenhagen correspondent of the Exchange Telegraph today. The revolutionaries have made Kronstadt the centre of their organization, the correspondent asserts.

"The rebels have trained the guns of the warship Petropavlovsk on Petrograd," the correspondent continues, "and have sent the ice-breaker Jermak to Oranienbaum (on the Gulf of Finland opposite Kronstadt.) The Soviet authorities have suspended the Petrograd-Oranienbaum rail service.

"The revolting sailors sent delegates to Petrograd, but it is not certain whether to negotiate with the Soviet officials or to confer with fellow revolutionists.

"Moscow reports say the Bolsheviki overpowered the rebels there with the most sanguinary terrorism."

Soldiers and sailors from Kronstadt, says a dispatch to The London Times from Riga, attacked Oranienbaum Friday across the ice, but were repulsed by the batteries there. Four ships fired on Oranienbaum.

The sailors have sent a message to Petrograd demanding the expulsion of General Avoroff, the dictator in Petrograd, and the execution of M. Zinovieff, the Governor of Petrograd.

HELSINGFORS, Finland, March 6.—Advices from Reval, Esthonia, say that Leon Trotzky, the Bolshevist Minister of War, has assumed the direction of the operations which are being carried on against the insurgents.

March 7, 1921

# BOLSHEVIKI CRUSH MOSCOW UPRISING

## Official British Reports Show Workers Still Threatening—Kronstadt Rebels Hold Out.

## PEASANTS GREATER MENACE

LONDON, March 10 (Associated Press).—After ten days of coonflicting reports regarding events in Russia, information received in British official circles today are believed to give something of a true picture of conditions there.

It is stated that the anti-Bolshevist risings in Moscow which were more in the nature of trade unionist strikes than military operations, have been liquidated, and that the communists are continuing their rule. The belief is expressed, however, that settlement of the trouble was by force, rather than by an amelioration of the economic difficulties, and that strikes may be expected to occur at any time with increasing seriousness.

The situation in Petrograd remains obscure, official circles limiting definite statements to the fact that Kronstadt and several fortresses on the south shore of the Gulf of Finland are holding out against the Bolsheviki.

The first information concerning the exact nature of the Kronstadt revolt is reported to have been received in Finland in a newspaper published by the Kronstadt revolutionists.

In this paper it is stated that no attempts are being made to re-establish anything approaching the Czarist régime or even to overthrow the Soviet system, but that the revolt is against what is termed the military dictatorship of Lenin and Trotzky, by which the people have been robbed of the benefits of the Russian revolution.

This newspaper disclaims the leadership of General Kozlovski and names M. Petrichenko as the leading member of the revolutionists.

It declares that the association by the Bolsheviki of the names of Czarists and such reformers as Alexander Kerensky with the revolutionists is a dodge on the part of the Bolshevist propagandists to obscure the real nature of the Kronstadt revolt and make it appear to be the work of foreigners and Czarists rather than of the Russians themselves.

The presence of Kerensky in London, which became known today, after he had been reported to be in Kronstadt leading the revolutionists, is considered in some quarters here an indication of the truthfulness of the statement of the newspaper.

The greatest importance is being attached here to Wednesday's official Bolshevist wireless dispatch admitting that communication between Moscow and Siberia had been cut off for a fortnight and indicating that the smouldering opposition of the peasants was becoming active. The belief was expressed here today that peasant uprisings would be more dangerous to the Bolshevist régime than active military opposition from an isolated fortress such as Kronstadt, where, if immediate success did not attend the mutineers, the result would be starvation and ultimate surrender, while no such success could be hoped for in a Bolshevist campaign against the rural populations.

**Revolts Are Spreading.**

Trustworthy news received from the interior of Russia, says a dispatch to The London Times from Reval, shows that anti-Soviet revolts are spreading throughout the country. The food situation is described as catastrophic, no food trains having reached the country from Siberia since Feb. 11. The situation is made more serious through the congestion of the transport system. On the main railway from Perm to Vologda 300 trains are being held up.

March 11, 1921

# KRONSTADT YIELDS TO SOVIET FORCES

## Red Army of 60,000, Favored by Fog, Overcomes the 16,000 Defenders.

## REBELS DESTROY WARSHIPS

## Gen. Koslovsky, with Revolutionary Committee and 800 Soldiers, Reaches Finland.

HELSINGFORS, March 17 (Associated Press).—Kronstadt has surrendered to the Soviet forces. This announcement is made by the Revolutionary Committee of Kronstadt, which has arrived in Finland, accompanied by 800 soldiers.

Before retreating from Kronstadt the revolutionists blew up the warships Petropavlovsk and Sebastopol.

General Koslovsy, leader of the revolutionists, has also arrived in Finland.

STOCKHOLM, March 17.—Kronstadt was taken by the Soviet forces at 2 o'clock this afternoon, according to a Bolshevist news agency.

The report of the arrival of the Kronstadt Revolutionary Committee and 800 soldiers at Terioki, on the Finnish frontier, is confirmed.

Since the revolt began there has been no such heavy cannonade as Kronstadt launched today against Krasnoya Gorka, according to advices received here. Throughout Wednesday night and Thursday fires burned furiously for miles around. They broke out in the centre of Kronstadt, flared up at Krasnoya Gorka and swept to many other points.

For the assault Trotzky had concentrated the whole of the new Seventh Army, consisting of Red cadets from all the Russian cities and other troops, totaling 60,000.

Favored by fog, the attacking forces advanced, led by a white-clad detachment in open formation and followed by heavy columns.

Kronstadt fired its ten-inch guns, and when the attacking forces were near enough opened with a machine gun fire, causing severe losses.

Nevertheless the survivors managed to force an entrance through the Petersburgski Gate into the town, where the local communists joined them. But after two hours of fighting they were ejected, and at 7 o'clock nearly all the attacking forces had been killed or wounded.

Meanwhile Kronstadt's obsolete batteries Nos. 4, 5 and 6 on the small islands near the Karelian coast were blown up and the defenders were obliged to retreat. The obsolete forts of Todleben, Obrutcheff and Schantz held out longer.

The Kronstadt garrison consisted of between 15,000 and 16,000 men, of whom 10,000 were sailors. They were exhausted through lack of sleep for several days.

Soon after the fall of the fortress groups of fugitives from the abandoned forts were seeking safety across the ice toward Finland.

March 18, 1921

# TELLS HOW LENIN IS LOSING CONTROL

## Petrichenko, Kronstadt Leader, Says Fighting Men Now Know His Tyranny.

## LEAVES FATAL TO LOYALTY

## When Men Visit Their Homes They Learn the Facts Previously Hidden by the Censorship.

TERIJOKI, Finland, March 30 (Associated Press). — Throughout Russia soldiers and sailors for the first time in years are receiving leaves of absence or are being temporarily demobilized and are learning from the people the facts of the tyranny of the communists. The Kronstadt and Petrograd revolts were due to this cause, and similar movements are now spreading to every troop and sailor centre, when the men return to them from leaves of absence. Thus demobilization is daily growing more dangerous for the Bolsheviki.

These and other inside facts, constituting the latest developments in Russia, were given The Associated Press today by Stephan Maximovitch Petrichenko, a plain petty officer from the Russian battleship Sebastopol, who led the Kronstadt revolutionists and who was interviewed today in the Terijoki refugee camp.

It was Petrichenko, and not General Kozlovsky, the commander at Kronstadt, who was the central figure in the latest attempt by the Russian workingmen to overthrow Communist tyranny. Kozlovsky was only a technical man in the affair.

"For years," said Petrichenko, "the happenings at home while we were at the front or at sea were concealed by the Bolshevist censhorship. When we returned home our parents asked why we fought for the oppressors. That set us thinking."

Petrichenko described dramatic meetings on the quarterdecks of the battleships Sebastopol and Petropavlovsk. The meetings on both vessels simultaneously drew up resolutions demanding freedom of speech and of the press, freedom of individual workers from the tyranny of the communists, and calling for a constituent assembly. The resolutions spread to other ships, to the Kronstadt garrison and to the workers in Petrograd, and the revolt resulted.

"We are defeated," said Petrichenko, "but the movement will proceed, because it comes from the people themselves."

March 31, 1921

## CAN'T MAKE SOCIALISM REAL AMONG PEASANTS

Special Cable to THE NEW YORK TIMES.

LONDON, March 22.—A Stockholm dispatch to The Morning Post says:

"According to Moscow agency messages the Tenth Communists' Congress concluded its sittings on the day of Kronstadt's surrender. The final sitting witnessed heated struggles with regard to domestic questions, but finally Lenin emerged victorious.

"It was decided to abolish grain confiscation and to introduce a tax, payable in grain, and to allow free commerce. The old dispute regarding trade unions was decided in Lenin's favor by 569 votes to 50 for Trotzky. A decision of the preceding Congress to abolish co-operative organizations was canceled.

"In concluding his speech, Lenin said:

"'Those who believe that in this Russia of peasants Socialism can be realized, simply believe in a Utopia.'"

March 22, 1921

## SOVIET RESTORES COINAGE SYSTEM

### Establishment of Silver Currency Is Forced on the Bolsheviki by the Peasantry.

### BANKS AND INTEREST NEXT

RIGA, May 2.—Coinage of silver has been authorized by the Russian Soviet Government, it is said in Moscow newspapers received here, the Bolshevist Government having completely reversed its position after having held out for a long time for a complete abolition of money.

This was due, it is said, to the desire of the Government to satisfy the peasants, whose ascendency in Russian affairs is becoming increasingly evident daily. The peasants were for a long time distrustful of paper money, which was turned out so rapidly that an armful of ruble notes was needed for the purchase of a simple article such as a pair of shoes.

Moreover, the Moscow newspaper Economic Life has been permitted to print a lengthy article advocating the resoration of the savings banks in Russia and even the payment of interest in connection with the proposed new coinage of silver.

"It is considered," says the newspaper, "that the establishment of a wide network of savings banks, separately or jointly with the co-operative societies, would be a most useful measure. In order to draw money into such banks, there should be some privileges, or even the payment of interest.

"From the economic viewpoint there could be no objection, because it is clear the republic would gain more if it paid interest, which would save money, being more profitable than constantly issuing new billions of exchange tokens."

Economic Life asserts that the establishment of the banks would have a great psychological effect on the peasants by preventing them from hoarding silver money. It concludes with the statement that such a change would be unavoidable as soon as financial relations are founded "on the sound basis of exchange of goods."

Finally the Moscow Izvestia, a copy of which has been received here, says a new decree issued by Nikolai Lenin, the Russian Soviet Premier, giving the trades unions, instead of the Government, the right to fix the pay of workmen.

Following the restoration of free trade to co-operative societies, the establishment of a system of taxation in kind and other recent concessions, the decision to restore the coinage of silver marks, according to recent arrivals from Moscow, Premier Lenin's final admission of the impossibility of the original Communistic theories at this time.

May 3, 1921

## LENIN DIDN'T SCRAP WORLD REVOLUTION

### Text of Famous Speech Shows He Reported Its "Great Step Forward."

### CONCESSIONS TO PEASANTS

#### Those Recommended Apparently Only Exceptions to His General Policy of Communism.

The text of the speech delivered by Nikolai Lenin, the Russian Premier, before the Tenth Congress of the Communist Party, as printed in the official Bolshevist newspaper Pravda of March 10, was made public yesterday by A. J. Sack, Director of the Russian Information Bureau in the United States, representing in this country the Russian democratic anti-Bolshevist forces. This is the speech which led to reports that Lenin had repudiated a world revolution and communism for Russia.

Referring to the question of world revolution, Lenin said:

"Aid is coming to us from the Western European countries. It is not coming as fast as we should like it, but it is coming, nevertheless, and gathering strength. Of course, the world revolution has made a great step forward, in comparison with last year. Of course, the Communist International, which last year existed merely in the form of proclamations, is now existing as an independent party in every country. In Germany, France and Italy the Communist International has become not only the centre of the labor movement but the focus of attention for the whole political life of those countries. This is our conquest, and no one can deprive us of it. The world revolution is growing stronger, while the economic crisis in Europe is getting worse at the same time.

"But, at any rate, were we to draw from this the conclusion that help would come to us from there within a brief period in the shape of a solid proletarian revolution, we would be simply lunatics. We have during these three years learned to understand that the staking of the game on the world revolution does not imply any figuring on a definite date, and that the pace of its development, growing more and more rapid, may bring us the revolution in the Spring, or may not. We must, therefore, know how to adapt our activity to the mutual class relations existing within our own and other countries, that we may be able for a long time to retain the dictatorship of the proletariat, and, at least gradually, to cure all the ills besetting us. Only such a view of the problem will be correct and sober."

The most urgent problem now in Russia, according to Lenin, is the relations between the working class and the peasantry. "These relations," he said, "are not what we had believed them to be. These relations represent a peril many times greater than all the perils threatened by the Denikin, Kolchak and Yudenitch campaigns put together.

"The peasants are not satisfied. They do not care for the economic forms we offered them. We must not conceal anything, but admit that a form of relationship which the peasantry does not care for will never exist. The peasantry has become far more middle-class than before. The village has been leveled down. The middle-class peasant now predominates. We must, therefore, see what this peasant wants. He demands: (1) A certain freedom in his economic turnover; (2) opportunity to market his products in exchange for goods."

In conclusion, Lenin recommended concessions amounting to granting to the peasant the right to dispose freely of that surplus of his products which would be left him after giving to the Bolshevist Government what would be levied on him as taxation in kind. Besides "freedom in local trade for small farmers," nothing is mentioned in Lenin's speech about any other concessions or changes in the fundamentals of the existing Bolshevist economic policy.

Commenting upon Lenin's speech, Mr. Sack said it was clear that the main Russian industries and Russia's transport system would continue to operate on communistic principles.

May 4, 1921

# LENIN TO ENCOURAGE SMALL CAPITALISTS

## But Government Will Retain Control of Transportation and Big Industries.

## UNIONS WILL FIX WAGES

RIGA, June 1 (Associated Press).—The congress of the Communist Party closed its sessions at Moscow on Monday with a declaration of approval of the program expounded by Nikolai Lenin and his lieutenant, Miliutin, Minister of Agriculture in the Soviet régime, who is now the ruling spirit so far as economic questions are concerned. The policy thus approved was outlined by Lenin and Miliutin during the discussion and was accepted in silence by Zinovieff, Soviet Governor of Petrograd, who has heretofore been regarded as head of the irreconcilable element.

The policy as outlined by Lenin and Miliutin consists mainly in the following points:

First, collection from the peasants of a fixed amount of grain by a system of tax in kind, estimated by Miliutin to amount to about one-third of the crop. The remaining two-thirds of the crop is to remain at the disposal of the peasant for trading through the newly restored co-operatives, whose power is to be extended. The former system of requisitions, which made the peasants the ardent and sometimes the fighting foes of communism, permitted the peasant to keep only a small quantity of grain for his personal consumption, while the State forcibly took the rest.

Second, retention in the hands of the State of the largest industries and means of transportation, particularly the leather, salt and textile industries. These latter are turning out the manufactured goods now most needed by the peasants. They are to be speeded up in order to satisfy the peasants' needs, and the workmen are to be encouraged by a bonus system and other inducements which will increase production. Supervision is to be under the trade unions, which will fix the rates of pay instead of the Government, as heretofore. These large industries and transportation facilities, as well as natural resources, such as mines, &c., are regarded as strong influences in maintaining the present régime.

Third, encouragement of small and medium-sized co-operatives and private industries. Factories will be leased to these smaller industries, and even financial assistance will be given. The trade unions will fix the wages, the Government retaining the right of factory inspection. Personal initiative of workers will be suitably rewarded and will supplant equal pay. Government officials in charge of factories who prove lax in their management will be strictly prosecuted. The chief purpose throughout will be to increase production.

Besides the foregoing, there will be general relaxation of prosecution and of hindrances to free trade.

In the course of his speech on Monday Lenin said that the development of capitalism, through the small industries and agriculture, was not to be feared, for the reason that the proletariat always held firmly in its hands all the large sources of industry. It must be remembered, he went on, that the peasants' economy could not be stabilized without certain freedom of barter and without those capitalistic relations connected with barter. He therefore urged the collection of taxes in kind, in order to leave the peasant freedom to barter the remainder of his crops.

June 2, 1921

## SOVIET'S FAMINE DECREE.

### It Grants Wide Powers to Non-Partisan Committee Formed for Relief.

Soviet Russia, the Bolshevist organ left behind here by Ludwig C. A. K. Martens, gave out the following yesterday as having been received by cable from Moscow under date of July 24:

"A decree of the All-Russian Central Executive Committee has granted wide powers to the recently organized Non-Partisan Public Famine Relief Committee, which comprises sixty-three representatives of all classes and political parties in Russia. The committee will conduct its activity under the Red Cross emblem, and will enjoy full legal rights and self-government. The committee is authorized to acquire independently Russian and foreign foodstuffs, medicines, &c., for the starving population in the famine regions, and is empowered to open branches in Russia and in foreign countries and to send commissioners abroad.

"The veteran Russian writer, Vladimir Korlenko, has been appointed Honorary Chairman, and Maxim Gorky is being sent abroad as High Commissioner. The committee has elected a non-partisan Executive Committee comprising the following: Chairman, Kamenev, President of the Moscow Soviet; Rykov, former Chairman of the Supreme Council of National Economy; Kishkin, prominent leader of the Cadet Party; Prokopovich, Moderate Socialist; Korobov and Tcherkassev, well-known non-Communists.

July 27, 1921

# TOTAL CROP FAILURE REPORTED IN RUSSIA

## Data Compiled by the Soviet Officials Show an "Unprecedented" Shortage of Grain.

## NEXT YEAR PROBABLY WORSE

Data on food conditions throughout Soviet Russia, as compiled by Soviet officials who are seeking to stay the famine that grips the land, reached this city yesterday, disclosing that "the whole of food-producing Russia is stricken with a total failure of crops."

Communications to the Volja Rossii, organ of the right wing social revolutionists in Prague, by the Soviet leaders themselves, indicate that next year Russia's plight will be even worse, for there is an unprecedented shortage of grain seed. Only in the provinces near Petrograd and other large cities were the crops of any avail, but, as officials reluctantly admitted, the food-producing acreage of these provinces is small.

The conditions portrayed by Soviet officials—Lenin, President Kalinin of the All-Russian Central Executive Committee, and M. Ossinsky, temporary Commissar of Agriculture—were those prevailing two weeks ago.

The information disclosed by the Prague social revolutionists was gathered by members who attended the third session of the All-Russian Central Executive Committee, which began its meetings in Petrograd on May 30. At that time, the Prague radicals reported, the Bolsheviki had made no mention of the possibilities of a famine along the Volga or in Southeastern Russia. But when Kalinin made his report to the committee he found it expedient to speak of the famine. He discussed the "activities of the Help Commission for the starving peasants," and added:

"Although the commission tried hard to alleviate the pangs of hunger, it could accomplish little because of the extent to which starvation had gone. This is especially true in five provinces, and there has lately been added another, Cherepovesk, where conditions are frightful. The others are Kaluga, Tula, Riazan, Orlov and Zarizin.

### Peasants Were Skeptical.

"In the beginning even the commission was viewed skeptically by the peasants, and they used to say that the organization of feeding stations 'smelt commune.'"

The Prague newspaper, quoting the Soviet publication, Isviestia of Moscow, on the proceedings of the All-Russian Central Executive Committee, attributed to President Kalinin this statement:

"It must be mentioned that at present such cities as Moscow, Petrograd and other large labor centres are passing through the greatest famine, no less than the one through which all the rest of Russia was passing during the severest period of starvation."

Continuing, the organ of the Prague social revolutionists reported:

"When Kalinin had concluded his report, Mr. Ossinsky, the Acting Commisar of Agriculture, made a formal report in which he drew a horrible picture of the common failure of crops, basing his statements on the amounts of grain seed that had been gathered for sowing in the fields.

"'In a whole series of provinces, especially along the Volga,' he reported, 'in the Provinces of Samara, Simbirsk and Saratov there was an insufficiency of grain seed. In Samara there were gathered 2,000,000 poods (a pood being equivalent to 36 pounds) of seed, which is only one-quarter of the amount necessary for the sustenance of the inhabitants. This figure is very significant and shows that there is almost a dearth of grain seed in this province.

August 10, 1921

# Our Aid to Russia: A Forgotten Chapter

**In 1921-22, millions of Russians were saved from starvation by swift American action.**

By GEORGE F. KENNAN

THE exchange that took place recently between Soviet First Deputy Premier Kozlov and Secretary of State Herter over the question of who paid for the American relief action during the Russian famine of 1921-22 suggests that few people now recall the detailed circumstances of this episode into which so much American interest and effort were poured at the time. Since this is one of those points at which the Soviet historical image is beginning to diverge rapidly from that of historians in this country, it might be worth while today to review the facts of this episode.

During World War I, up to 1917, the area under cultivation in Russia declined by about 25 per cent. For this, the Bolsheviki were in no way responsible. But after their assumption of power, this decline continued unchecked until 1921, so that by that year the area sown to crops can scarcely have been much more than half of the prewar figure. There is solid evidence to show that while the civil war played a part in this further decline of agricultural production after the revolution, the major cause of it lay in the reckless and ill-advised policies of the Soviet Government itself, and particularly in its failure to provide adequate incentives for the individual peasant.

In 1921 Russia was struck by a first-

GEORGE F. KENNAN, a former Ambassador to Russia, is the author of a history entitled "Soviet-American Relations, 1917-1920."

class drought in certain of the main grain-growing regions, notably the Trans-Volga district and the southern Ukraine. In the prevailing conditions, the effects of this drought were serious in the extreme. The total crop in the year 1921 fell short by some seven million tons of the minimum amount required for feeding the country. Had there been normal reserves and distribution facilities, famine might still have been prevented. But, in addition to the lack of reserves, Russia was at that time in a general state of economic ruin.

AGAINST this background, the effects of the drought were appalling. By midsummer an estimated fifteen million persons were threatened with sheer, stark starvation; and there was absolutely no prospect that this disaster could be appreciably mitigated by action undertaken within Russia itself.

At some time in the late spring or early summer of 1921, the Soviet Government became at least partially aware of the dimensions of the catastrophe and also of its own inability to remedy it. How seriously the Soviet leaders viewed the situation we do not know. This was a bad time for them. They had just been severely rocked by the Kronstadt mutiny. They had already been sufficiently sobered by the general economic breakdown to inaugurate the New Economic Policy in March. The famine now came as a new blow.

Walter Duranty, the well-known correspondent of The New York Times, wrote that the Soviet leaders were aware "that the whole machinery of state * * * was liable to be wrecked on the rocks of the food shortage." Others took a less serious view of the political dangers which the famine presented for the regime. However that may be, the extremity in which the leaders found themselves must really have been great.

THE appeal for help was not made in the name of the Soviet Government. It was made by Maxim Gorki, the writer, who, while close to the Communists, was known and respected as a literary figure far beyond Russia's borders. Gorki issued his appeal on July 11, 1921. Hinting that he himself did not believe in humanitarian impulses, he pointed out that the Russian famine nevertheless presented "a splendid opportunity" for those who did so believe to apply their convictions. He invoked the images of Tolstoy, Dostoevski, Mendeleev, Pavlov, Mussorgski and Glinka as bonds likely to appeal to cultured European and American people. He ended with the bald injunction: "Give bread and medicine." Two or three weeks later, Lenin, in his own name, issued a similar appeal to the international proletariat for aid to the Russian comrades.

Gorki's appeal aroused the immediate interest of Herbert Hoover and those who had previously been associated with him in the work of famine relief. Mr. Hoover, though by now Secretary of Commerce in the new Republican Administration, was still head of the American Relief Administration, usually known as the A. R. A. The A. R. A., following completion of its famous wartime program in Belgium, had administered post-hostilities relief, mostly for children, in some twenty-three countries.

THE idea of work in Russia by the A. R. A. had come up at the time of the Paris Peace Conference, but had been vitiated by the fact that the offer to Russia was coupled with conditions which were wholly unacceptable to the Soviet Government. The matter had come up in the following year, 1920, during the Russian-Polish war, when the advance of the Red Army into Poland had interrupted the work of the A. R. A. feeding stations in that country. The retreat of the Red Army from Poland had been followed by talks between A. R. A. officials and the Soviet authorities in Moscow about possible A. R. A. work in Russia. But these had broken down because the Soviet Government insisted on complete control of actual supplies brought in, and refused to guarantee the protection of any A. R. A. personnel in Russia unless the United States Government would enter into official relations with the Soviet Government.

Following the breakdown of these talks, Communist-controlled organizations had kept up a drumfire of criticism of Hoover for failure to send food to Russia on Soviet terms. Now, with the evidences of the Russian famine, and the news of Gorki's appeal, it seemed to Hoover that there might be a real chance of agreement.

The State Department, on being consulted, made only one condition. This was that the Soviet Government release a number of Americans, whom it was holding in its prisons as hostages in order to bring pressure to bear toward the resumption of official relations. These were men who had fallen foul of the Soviet authorities in one way or another between 1919 and 1921.

ON July 22, 1921, Hoover replied to Gorki's appeal, explaining that the prisoners would first have to be released before any American aid could be extended, and then listing the technical conditions on which the A. R. A. would consider extending aid. These were, in fact, exactly the same conditions on which the A. R. A. had been distributing food in a number of other countries. This offer was promptly accepted by Maxim Litvinov as a basis for negotiations; and a batch of six American prisoners was released across the Estonian border the next day as a starter. About 100 were finally released.

Two days later at Riga there began negotiations which ended with the signing, on Aug. 20, of a curious sort of treaty between the A. R. A. and the Soviet Government. This agreement defined the conditions under which the A. R. A. might act within Russia to bring aid to famine sufferers, particularly children.

The A. R. A. operation in Russia lasted roughly a year and a half. About one-fifth of the total dollar costs, running to some sixty-two million dollars, were covered by the Soviet Government itself which released some twelve million dollars from its gold reserve for this purpose. Of the remainder, about one-half was put up by the American Government. The rest came from private donations in the United States. In addition, the Soviet Government expended an estimated fourteen million dollars on behalf of the program in local currency.

THE American staff of the A. R. A. in Russia numbered something less than two hundred Americans. Within a few weeks after inauguration of the program, i.e., by February, 1922, as a result largely of exertions by these Americans that were little short of heroic, some 1,200,000 Russian children were being fed. By August, the figure had grown to a peak of 4,173,000 children, plus over six million adult sufferers whose condition was too urgent to be ignored—a total of over ten million people.

There were at one time 18,000 feeding stations in operation. In all, some 788,000 tons of food were imported and distributed by the A. R. A. alone. Medical relief was brought to many millions to control the raging typhus which accompanied the famine. The program lasted, so far as the adults were concerned, until the relatively favorable harvest of 1922 had been gathered. Long before the A. R. A. program was finished, the Soviet Government had resumed export of its own grain.

The A. R. A. was not alone in this work. Valuable independent contributions were made by other American and European organizations, including the Quakers, but these were on a far smaller scale. The Soviet Government, too, stimulated—one senses—by the A. R. A.'s example and competition, greatly increased and improved its own efforts to meet the situation.

It has been soberly and authoritatively estimated that, as a result of the A. R. A.'s efforts alone, approximately

**MEMENTO**—A scroll presented in 1923 to Herbert Hoover, A. R. A. chairman, says Russians will never "forget the aid rendered to them."

eleven million lives were saved, of which at least a third were those of children and young people.

The Soviet Government plainly wished to see the A. R. A. succeed in bringing famine relief to certain of the stricken districts (for some reason, the southern Ukraine does not seem to have been included in this benevolent intention) and in many basic respects it supported the A. R. A.'s operations. But the memories of the recent civil war were still fresh, and the Soviet leaders made it a principle, then as later, to put the preservation of Soviet power ahead of every other consideration. Their view of world capitalism, furthermore, left no room for the possibility that Americans might be sincere in the humanitarian sentiments on which they based their readiness to extend this aid, and made it necessary to search for ulterior motives on the American side.

FOR these reasons, the dominant consideration underlying Soviet treatment of the A. R. A. and its doings—a consideration overshadowing any interest in its success as a famine-relief agency—appears to have been an absurdly overdrawn concern lest the operation should become a focal point for opposition to the Soviet regime. To this end, efforts were put in hand (a) to intimidate the A. R. A.'s local employes to a point where they would, while nominally serving A. R. A., take their orders actually from Communist commissars sent out for the purpose and (b) by this and other means to bring distribution of the food under direct Soviet control. The A. R. A. had no choice but to resist these efforts, and it was generally successful in doing so.

By the same token, official liaison with the A. R. A. was entrusted to the organization whose main function was to see that it did not become the seat of conspiracy: the secret police. The A. R. A. was obliged, throughout the major period of its existence, to deal with the organs of the central government through the agency of a senior official of the dreaded "Cheka" (special secret police). He was A. V. Eiduk, a man known during the civil war for his merciless severity to the enemies, or supposed enemies, of the revolution. From the A. R. A.'s standpoint Eiduk had the advantage that, whenever he could be persuaded to issue an order on A. R. A.'s behalf, he had the means to make it respected. But he was suspicious and hostile, and obviously took more seriously the duties of surveillance and penetration of the A. R. A. operation than he did the task of assisting the Americans with their work.

THE head of the mission, Col. William Haskell, was repeatedly obliged, in his dealings with Eiduk, to come to the verge of closing up the entire program (at one time he even had to stop all shipments from the United States for a considerable period) in order to protect the integrity of the operation.

The treatment of the A. R. A. in Soviet public statements was varied and contradictory. Lenin, for his part, seems to have kept scrupulously aloof from the American relief undertaking and to have avoided committing himself in its favor or disfavor. Other Soviet leaders did not hesitate, even while the program was in progress, to impugn the A. R. A.'s motives and to encourage hostility to it and suspicion of it among the population.

At the farewell dinner for the senior A. R. A. staff in 1923, Leonid Kamanev, one of the senior Soviet figures of the time, spoke warmly of the A. R. A.'s work, and presented Colonel Haskell with a Resolution of the Soviet of People's Commissars professing most profound gratitude and declaring that the Soviet people would never forget the help given by the American people. Yet historians note that at about this same time Kamenev's wife (Trotsky's sister) was saying in speeches that foreign relief was just a subterfuge for the penetration of Russia and for getting rid of undesirable food surpluses.

RECENT Soviet historical works do indeed mention the famine, but they ignore Gorki's appeal; they portray the A. R. A. as having taken the initiative in proposing American assistance; they show the Soviet Government as having graciously accepted the proposal while rejecting the A. R. A.'s efforts to encroach on Soviet sovereignty. They slide quickly over the question of what the A. R. A. really did in the way of famine relief (one recent book says cryptically that the A. R. A. "gave a certain help to the starving") and they go on to tell at length of what the Soviet Government itself did, and of the assistance given by the foreign proletariat. The latter assistance, measured against the A. R. A.'s, was in a ratio of about one to fifty.

The best that may be said in retrospect is that, despite all the friction and difficulty, both sides got, basically, what they most wanted. The A. R. A. did not become a source of conspiracy; the Soviet Government was not overthrown. Several million children, who would otherwise have died, were kept alive.

July 19, 1959

# LENIN CONFESSES ECONOMIC DEFEAT

## Tells Communist "Missionary" Meeting: "We Are Now Making a Strategic Retreat."

## RETURNING TO CAPITALISM

## "Not the Re-establishment of Private Ownership, but of Personal Communistic Interests."

By WALTER DURANTY.



Special Cable to THE NEW YORK TIMES.

MOSCOW, Oct. 19.—"The real meaning of the new economic policy is that we have met a great defeat in our plans and that we are now making a strategic retreat," said Nikolai Lenin in one of the frankest admissions of the failure of his policies ever made by a leader of a great nation.

He was speaking last night about the economic change to the delegates from the instruction centres which have recently been established for workers and peasants all over Russia. The delegates represented the active or missionary element of the Communist Party, which has undertaken the task of making communist doctrine in a sense the official religion of the new Russian State.

"Before Lenin spoke," says the official newspaper, the Isvestia, "there had been a somewhat acrid discussion regarding the new policy, which many communists cannot fail to regard as an abjuration of their dearest ideals. But, as usual, Lenin's logic vanquished opposition. His statement is clearly intended to close the discussion definitely."

"Our defeat in the economic field, whose problems resemble those of strategy, though even graver and more difficult," said the Soviet chief, "is more serious than any we suffered from the armies of Denikin or Kolchak. We thought the peasants would give us sufficient food to insure the support of the industrial workers, and that we should be able to distribute it. We were wrong, and so we have begun to retreat. Before we are utterly smashed let us retrace our steps and begin to build on a new foundation.

"It is doubtless inevitable that some of the comrades will not be pleased with the situation, and even get panicky about it. Yet it happened that all of our military successes were preceded by similar retreats and that the same state of panic was then noticeable in certain quarters. Afterward we began a slow, systematic and cautious advance, finally crowned by victory. We must follow the same plan in the economic field, where the prime cause of our defeat lay in the fact that our economic policy up above wasn't adequately connected with the lower spheres and thus failed to bring about that revival of productive forces which was considered the principal and urgent part of our plan. The supplying of manufactured goods to the country and its direct relation with the problem of reconstruction in the cities were chiefly responsible for the economic and political crisis of the Spring of 1921."

Lenin thus admits that his change of economic front is due to recognition of the fact that communism is at present inadequate to supply the peasants on the one hand with manufactured goods and the urban workers on the other with food. The latter are in much the worse position of the two, for the farmer can wear home-made boots or resharpen his broken knife, but the workman cannot live without food. There are thousands of workers' homes in Moscow today where no meat is eaten from one month's end to another's, where even bread is too dear, and tea and potatoes are almost the sole diet. Men say that they would be glad to work if there were regular work for them to do, but owing to lack of machinery and raw materials—to say nothing of the deficiency of technical staffs—there is not enough employment for them to earn a proper living wage.

The problem is further complicated by the fall in the purchasing value of the ruble, due to the steady issue of new paper money, which has caused incessant disputes and even strikes over a wage that a month before seemed at least acceptable.

But while my observation tends to show that for some time, at least, Russia has little to hope for from foreign concessionnaires in the way of stimulating industry, owing to the fact that details of their dealings with the State and their employes are still to be worked out in practice, the fact remains that the intense demand from the thousands of newly opened stores of all categories is bound to resurrest native industry, which the State is doing its utmost to aid with credits and promises, and as far as possible with raw materials, technicians, machines, &c.

### "Re-establishing Capitalism."

MOSCOW, Oct. 19 (Associated Press). Nikolai Lenin, in a speech delivered here today on Russia's new economic policy, declared:

"We must face the fact that we are re-establishing capitalism, and also the question of whether the peasantry will follow the capitalists or the communists. If the capitalists organize quicker and better they will send us communists to the devil.

"Our problem," continued the Soviet Premier, "is to make the future capitalism subject to the State and serve it. We are now surrounded by forces stronger than ourselves, and in order to gain victory we must use the last of our forces and convince the peasantry, and also the workers, of the necessity of our aims and of their advantages to the common good.

"The present return to capitalism is not the re-establishing of private ownership, but of personal communistic interests. In order to reorganize our economic life we must interest every specialist; and in this we have failed so far by direct attack. Now we must make a turning movement. If we again fail every one of us will go to the devil and be hanged, and will deserve it.

"I say to you: 'Go into business. Work with the capitalist by your side, both Russian and foreign, who will get 100 per cent. out of you. Let him get rich. But learn from him, and only then will the true communistic republic be created. It is hard, difficult, wrenching toil, but all of us must do it, as there is no other way out.'

"The time for drawing political pictures of great aims is now past. We must put theories into practice. We must do much cultural work and also digest our political experience in order that our political coup d'état may be saved."

October 22, 1921

## 1,000-Ruble Note Smallest Legal Tender in Moscow Now

MOSCOW, Feb. 3. — Five-hundred-ruble notes are no longer legal tender in Moscow. A recent decree of the Moscow Soviet announces that hereafter street railways and other Government institutions will accept nothing less than thousand-ruble notes.

A thousand-ruble note is worth half an American cent at the present legal rate of exchange.

At the old par of Russian exchange a thousand-ruble note would be worth $515.

February 4, 1922

## ARMY SOVIETS' POWER CUT

According to new regulations in effect since Jan. 1, reported in a Moscow dispatch to the German press, the functions of the Soldiers' Councils of the Red Army are materially restricted, and any attempts on their part to interfere with matters outside their sphere will be regarded as mutiny. The officers' authority is fully restored, it being explained that this is possible because the present officers of the Russian Army are practically all trained proletarians and not former servants of the Czar, as was the case for a long time after the Bolshevist revolution.

February 5, 1922

## BOLSHEVIKI DROP TERRORIST SYSTEM

### Decree Grants the Right of Trial and Reforms the Secret Police.

By WALTER DURANTY.



Special Cable to THE NEW YORK TIMES.

MOSCOW, Feb. 8.—The Russian right of habeas corpus goes into effect today with the publication of a decree of the Supreme Council proclaiming that no one is to be held in prison more than two months without trial. From the American viewpoint this may seem but a limited version of the famous act guaranteeing the individual liberties of the Anglo-Saxon race for hundreds of years, but in Russia, newly emerged medieval feudalism, it is epochmaking progress.

From today the Cheka (all-Russian extraordinary commission) ceases to be the direct instrument of uncontrolled authority the human race has known since the Spanish inquisition and becomes a special State detective force not greatly different from the American Department of Justice or the French Sûreté Generale. The decree enjoins the Cheka henceforth to be a new department in the Ministry of the Interior called the Political State Department—just as France has the Sûreté Generale under the Ministry of the Interior. Special Cheka tribunals that during the last four years have been able to arrest, condemn and shoot, all in a few hours without saying why or wherefore to the rest of the country, are now abolished. In special cases of counter-revolution, banditism, espionage, for protection of railroads and waterways defense of Russian frontiers against smuggling and passage of persons without proper authorization, for execution of orders of the Supreme Council and exceptional military offenses, the body may continue the Cheka system of search, arrest, &c., without warrant—though a warrant must be procured within forty-eight hours—but always the runs decree: "The arrested persons must be informed the reasons for the arrest within two weeks; the arrested persons must be within two months either released or brought to trial in the ordinary courts. If there is reason why the said trial is to be delayed, the new Political State Department must get a special permit to that effect from the Supreme Council."

February 11, 1922

## RUSSIAN WEALTH CUT HALF.

### Farmers Have Only 13 Per Cent. of Pre-War Implements.

MOSCOW, Feb. 10.—Russia has only 13 per cent. of the agricultural implements her farmers owned in prewar times, according to a recent report of M. Kameneff, head of the famine relief work.

The towns and cities have only one-fifth of their prewar wealth, while the wealth of the country is only one-half what it was before the war opened.

February 11, 1922

## EXPORTS AND IMPORTS FREED.

### Soviet Decrees Foreign Firms May Operate in Russia.

MOSCOW, March 17 (Associated Press).—A decree announcing the opening of free import and export trade with Soviet Russia was published today by the Izvestia.

Under the provisions of the decree co-operatives and private persons receive the right independently to purchase abroad and import goods into Soviet Russia, and foreign firms are permitted to carry on import and export business in Soviet Russia on their own account.

March 18, 1922

## Lenin Plans to Remove Communists From Thousands of Managerial Posts

MOSCOW, March 19 — (Associated Press).—Contentions that Russia has reached the limit of her retreat toward capitalism, but that nevertheless it is needful to remove thousands of Communists from important posts and to substitute efficient managers, will be made by Nikolai Lenin, the Bolshevist Premier, and other Soviet leaders before the All-Russian Communist Congress which is due to open here tomorrow.

Difficulties in reconciling these apparently divergent principles are expected to bring forth an interesting debate; but the leaders are confident that opposition which may be expected particularly from the Radical Left group, will be unimportant.

A year ago, following the Kronstadt revolt, the Communist Congress approved the initiation of Lenin's new policy. After a year, though a majority of the Russian public finds freedom for individual efforts a relief from the previous rigid state of control, there still are a number of Communists who have become increasingly discontented over the resurrection of the bourgeoisie.

Lenin himself in a recent speech said the change had gone too far, and that the coming congress would be asked to set rigid limits for capitalistic development.

March 20, 1922

## COMMUNIST CONGRESS BACKS LENIN'S POLICY

### Approves His Statement That the Retreat Toward Capitalism Is Finished.

MOSCOW, March 30 (Associated Press).—After hearing the grievances of malcontents concerning the recent changes toward capitalism, the Communist Party Congress again resolved today to follow the lead of Premier Lenin and approved his statement that "the retreat is finished."

A suggestion by M. Ossinski was also approved, to the effect that the power of the Council of Commissars should be confined to executive duties, and that the Commissars should not encroach upon the legislative powers which the Soviet Constitution gave to the Executive Committee of the All-Russian Soviet.

Lenin, appearing for the second time in the final debate over his previous speech, deprecated attempts at opposition within the party, even though there was disappointment over the turn economic terms had taken.

"With power in our hands, it is unnecessary for us to fear anything," he said. "To conclude that we are returning to capitalism is laughable. If we do not make political mistakes, then I say it is ninety-nine to one we will surmount this crisis, and the whole party, as well as most of the non-party workers and peasants, will be with us."

M. Larin, former head of the Economic Council, as one of the chief critics of the new policy, wanted to know if the people would fight for the restaurant-keepers and speculators, who had been restored to prosperity, if Soviet Russia were attacked.

April 1, 1922

# SOVIET 'SURRENDER' ON PROPERTY RIGHTS

**Decree on Which Russia's Future Dealings With Capital Depend Is Adopted.**

**STRING TO CONCESSIONS**

MOSCOW, May 22 (Associated Press).—A fundamental decree recognizing property rights within certain limits, and upon which Russia's future dealings with American and other foreign and local capital depend, unanimously passed the Executive Committee today.

While wide latitude is given capitalistic and industrial effort, the decree nevertheless provides that everything must be limited to the Soviet laws and gives the Soviet the right to void any agreement which "obviously is directed to harm the State."

A special clause was added to the law on motion of the Communistic faction at the last moment which makes it non-retroactive. It specifically denies rights under the law to previous owners whose property was expropriated on the grounds of revolutionary law up to the time of the issue of the decree and does not give them the right to demand return of the property.

Foreigners under the decree have the same rights as Russian citizens, if they previously have secured permission from the proper authorities to operate in Russia. The right of the protection of the Russian court is given to persons abroad suing on contracts and other matters in Russia, only in the event that Russian citizens similarly have access to the courts of the nationals who sue in Russia.

Soviet officials today told the Associated Press they considered this decree largely meets the condition of Secretary of State Hughes for American trade in Russia. They further declared that the law expressed the maximum of surrender to capitalism Russia is ready to make, and that its limits define the limits of retreat which Nikolai Lenin in a recent speech mentioned as having ended.

Regarding the ownership rights in buildings not nationalized up to date, M. Kursky, Commissar for Justice, told The Associated Press that virtually all large structures in Russia had been nationalized, thus leaving few of them affected by the new law.

The committee also unanimously passed the Government's new land policy, reiterating the principle of State ownership of all lands, but providing life tenure for peasants working it. The measure provides that none may buy or sell land, but that it may remain indefinitely in the possession of those cultivating it.

In addition to the above the new land law provides persons may be deprived of land if they leave it voluntarily and fail to cultivate it for three consecutive years; if they try to sell or pawn their holdings; they they emigrate, or if the plots are wanted for State purposes.

Peasants temporarily unable to cultivate the land themselves may lease it for a maximum of the two sowing seasons. Communes working the land themselves are permitted in certain cases to hire labor.

May 23, 1922

## SEES FAMINE ROUTED.

**Soviet Organ Says Rye Crops Indicate "Startling" Yield.**

MOSCOW, July 9 (Associated Press).—Combining comment on the Russian harvest outlook with editorial opinion on The Hague conference, the Pravda declares that "a sound harvest provides the basis for the Russian delegation at The Hague speaking clearly, decisively and with a firm tongue."

"We cannot say our economic condition is light, our way is strewn with roses," adds the paper, "but we can say we can continue to wait. The worst now is behind us. Our economic State is not falling, but, though slowly, is improving.

"The famine is ending, and reports from the Southern Provinces show that the rye harvest already has begun to indicate startling yields in the areas sown. Though too early to say there will be a big harvest, one thing is certain—that this year will be a grain year and that the famine is ending and will not be repeated.

"Throughout the famine areas nature appears to be trying to make up for what it did to Russia last year. First reports from the Saratov district show yields of ninety poods of rye per dessatine, in some localities 150 poods. In Rostov the yield is also ninety poods. In normal years sixty-five poods per dissatine was considered a medium average."

(A pood is about thirty-six pounds. A dessatine measures about 2.70 acres.)

July 10, 1922

## MOSCOW TO BAN RELIGION.

**It Must Not Be Taught to Children In Schools of Any Kind.**

*Special to The New York Times.*

WASHINGTON, Aug. 14.—Punishment of forced labor up to one year for those giving religious instruction to children or minors in educational institutions, either national or private, will be administered by the Russian Soviet Government, according to a Moscow dispatch received today, which stated that such a provision had been inserted in the Soviet's new criminal code.

This is declared to be another step forward in the campaign being waged by the Bolsheviki for the stamping out of the Church in Russia. The next step contemplated is said to be the issuance of orders prohibiting the baptism of children, the theory of the Soviet authorities being that, while it is admittedly impossible completely to eradicate religion from the Russian character in this generation, by forbidding it to be taught to children the next generation can be made non-religious, or at any rate anti-Christian.

The destructive activities of the Bolsheviki, the Moscow dispatch states, are to some degree camouflaged by the setting up of a "Free Church" to be led by Bishop Antoninus, who by many is held largely responsible for the overthrow of the Patriarch Tikhon. It is Bishop Antoninus who is stage managing the convocation of the new Sobor—the conclave of the Orthodox Church.

August 15, 1922

## *Banishment Penalty Restored In Russia by Soviet Decree*

MOSCOW, Aug. 19.—Exile, one of the chief punishments resorted to under the Czarist régime, which banished many of the present Soviet leaders, appears to have been adopted again in Russia, as banishment abroad or within Russia of political offenders without trial is decreed in an order by the Central Executive Committee, just published in Izvestia. The term of banishment by the decree is limited to three years.

A special commission, under the presidency of the Commissar of Interior, is charged with the banishment, and the State political police will take charge of the exiles on their arrival at the place to which they are sent.

August 20, 1922

## THE "NEPMAN."

We have all got to get acquainted with a new word coming out of Russia. Let us introduce the "Nepman." He is the little trader, the small shopman, now springing up in the Russian cities since individual enterprise in commerce has ceased to be the horrible crime which the Bolsheviki at first thought it. This new figure is a result of what is called the New Economic Policy. For short it is known as the N. E. P. Hence the "Nepman."

Some searching questions about him and his activities were recently put to Lenin in Moscow by the friendly interviewer, Mr. Arthur Ransome, who wrote out the answers of the Dictator and sent them to The Manchester Guardian. The inquiries related partly to the economic aspects of the Nepman and partly to the political. Did not Lenin fear that this bustling and prosperous class of traders might become a political force hostile to the Soviet Government? No more than the shopkeepers in a London street, was Lenin's reply. Another question was whether the prosperity of the small traders was not a refutation of Communist doctrines. In answering, Lenin made a careful distinction between business on a small scale, in which personal initiative might be admitted, and the "heavy industry," where State control must be rigorously continued. Finally Mr. Ransome wanted to know if there was any truth in the rumors flying about Moscow that the Government was going to restore the "card system" this Winter, and make a wholesale requisition on the shops of the Nepmen. Lenin indignantly denied that he was dreaming of anything of the sort. He declared the reports to be malicious inventions, and asserted that measures of that kind were not to be thought of in "contemporary Russia." Apparently, therefore, the Nepman has come to stay.

December 6, 1922

# SOVIET CONGRESS SITS IN MOSCOW

**All-Russian Gathering, 90 Per Cent. Communist, Reviews 1922 Developments.**

By WALTER DURANTY.
Copyright, 1922, by The New York Times Company.
Special Cable to THE NEW YORK TIMES.

MOSCOW, Dec. 22.—The tenth All-Russian Soviet Congress will open at the Grand Opera House tomorrow. There will be more delegates than last year—more than 3,000, instead of 2,600. The great majority, of course, are Communists—fully 90 per cent.—who are holding a preliminary meeting tonight.

The rigid discipline of the Communist Party insures the acceptance of the Government program and removes from Congress the function of a free Parliament in the Western sense. But Russia is not a Western country, anyway, and the opportunity for individuals or groups to voice heterodox opinions, even though their vote be orthodox, has no small importance.

It is certain, for instance, that there will be speeches by peasant delegates, who form the majority of the Congress, to emphasize the peasants' demand for more and cheaper manufactured goods than the present system of State-controlled production is able to supply. They will point out, too, that it is impossible to expect the peasants to be the mainstay and sole real source of revenue of the Soviet Government unless their demands are satisfied, and that the excessively high standard of prices and taxation have resulted in driving them back to lower production, whereas it is the Government's purpose to increase their production to the utmost. Such statements are incontrovertible.

I am informed that the Government in reply will give them a frank exposition of the national situation which can be assumed to be pretty much along the following lines:

The Communist Party is more firmly in the saddle than ever, and the red flag now waves over a unified country, from the Arctic to Odessa, from Petrograd to Vladivostok.

The army is loyal and effectively reorganized, and, most important of all, from the Government point of view, there has grown up a generation inspired with national patriotism whose adherence to the new régeme may be conveyed in the statement that for its members the red flag has become the flag of Russia, as the tri-color of the French Revolution became the flag of France.

**Agriculture Recovering.**

Agriculture has recovered to a considerable degree, the production being within 35 or 40 per cent. of the pre-war figures, and, unless the weather is unfavorable, is likely to get within 25 per cent. of these figures next year.

That is on the credit side of the Russian balance. But there are debit items also.

The system of State-controlled industry is not yet a success to put it mildly. According to figures given at the recent Congress of Trade and Industrial Departments, the industrial assets of the country have decreased by nearly 40 per cent. in the last year. The number of factories working has also decreased, though to a smaller degree, and there is a considerable amount of unemployment in Moscow, Petrograd, and other cities.

What is worse, the project, described in a recent cable to THE NEW YORK TIMES for the amalgamation of the Foreign Trade Monopoly, the Bureau of Internal Trade Administration and the Supreme Council of National Economy into one organization, on the lines of a Western Department of Commerce, has been quashed by the influence of the Foreign Trade Monopoly Bureau. Official reports about the monopoly's system were as critical as any foreign business man could desire. The monopoly still stands.

The year's work of the State Bank has resulted in a large decrease of the bank's liquid assets and the fall of the paper ruble has continued—the rate today is around 50,000,000 to the dollar, as against 500,000 at this time last year—although real progress has been made in the way of repudiation of this base paper and the substitution of something not far removed from the gold standard.

It is unquestionable that the material condition of the great majority of the Russian people has shown a marked improvement in the past year, and banditry in the outlying areas and robbery in the urban centres have undergone a corresponding decrease. The aftermath of the famine still remains, but American and other foreign and native relief agencies appear to be in a position to prevent any deaths from starvation. The sanitary conditions are much better, for which credit is chiefly due to the Medical Department of the American Relief Administration, which successfully carried out a huge and magnificent program.

**General Feeling of Hope.**

Above all, there is a great and general feeling of hope throughout the country. Even the most determined adversaries of the Government are united in admitting that Russia has turned the corner and is on the upward road.

December 24, 1922

# RIGID COMMUNISM GAINING IN RUSSIA

**Manifest Reaction Against the Concessions Made to "Capitalism."**

By WALTER DURANTY.
Copyright, 1923, by The New York Times Company.
By Wireless to THE NEW YORK TIMES.

MOSCOW, Jan. 4.—The new year finds a distinct tendency in Russia toward reaction—that is, toward the maintenance of Socialist principles by the Soviet Government and away from further concessions to the "capitalistic" or Western system of political thought, economics and government.

Four recent very obvious indications of this tendency are: 1. The constitution of the relatively loose Federation of Soviet republics, which converts the former relatively loose Federation of Soviet Russia—including the former Far Eastern Republic—the Ukraine, White Russia and the Caucasian group of Soviet republics into one highly centralized body.

2. The retention of the foreign trade monopoly, despite widespread and in many cases justified criticism, both from foreign business men and the Right and Left Communists.

3. The permission given the Komsomol, as the young Communist organization is termed, to carry out an anti-religious demonstration here on Saturday, the old Russian Christmas Eve.

4. The decision, communicated to me by one of the highest authorities of the Foreign Office that the Soviet Government purposes to take no initial step toward starting or strengthening political or commercial relations with the Western powers, although, of course, the official in question added that this decision must not be taken to mean that Russia would refuse to consider suggestions in this direction that might be made from outside.

**American Parallel for New Constitution.**

To discuss these four points in detail would require too much space. The new Constitution alone is so complicated and so far-reaching in its possible effects as to demand a separate dispatch. It is enough for the present to say that in addition to concentrating power over the whole territory of the union in the hands of a central group whose devotion to Communist principles is better assured than that of the autonomous local groups, the new Constitution offers an interesting, and to all appearances a technically perfect, parallel of the American "compartment" system of factory construction, permitting that extensions or new "compartments" be added with minimum expense, owing to the previously standardized construction, and almost no increase in the central staff and overhead.

In other words, if Poland or Latvia, Finland or Turkestan should desire at any time to join the Union of Soviet Republics, they could do it, so to speak, automatically, without political complications, with a minimum increase of Federal administrative machinery and with great and financially profitable decrease of their own administrative burdens.

Points 2 and 3 are self-explanatory so far as indications of a reactionary tendency are concerned, although it is understood that Saturday's fixture is for a demonstration only, and that no aggression or violence toward the clergy or religious buildings will be permitted.

Point 4 is significant in view of recent rumors about the Russian desire to repair the error of refusing the American suggestion last Summer that a commission of investigation be received in Russia. The Soviet Government does not admit that it made an error or that it refused the suggestion. It is also whispered that the experience of the Russian delegation at Lausanne, to say nothing of the recent disarmament conference here, has led the Government to believe that any initial step it might take would be doomed to failure at present.

It may be suggested that all this is just bluff to hide the desperate economic situation and dispel in the minds of the Western powers conviction on which England, at any rate, is believed here to act, that Russia will soon be on her knees begging for help at any price. That the economic situation is bad no one here will deny. Indeed, the official organ of the Council of Labor and Defense, Economic Life, has printed statistics about Russia's commerce and industry more damning than the worst reports of any economic spy—if the Russians still believe that there are any such concealed in the hard-worked ranks of the American Relief Administration—could have transmitted to Mr. Hoover's Department of Commerce. But statistics do not tell the whole truth, and there are two additional factors which explain and prove the reality of the reactionary tendency now apparent there.

The first is the experience in business methods acquired by the ruling Communist class during the past eighteen months. The second is the assurance in the mind of that ruling class that it can depend upon the support of the peasant. Both factors are fated to crystallize into the sentiment, at present general in high Communist circles, that the Soviet Government can stand on its own feet and stick to its principles without further concessions.

Naturally I don't mean that State control of business and industry is now on the point of becoming a success—far from it. But few will deny that the Russian Communist Party has energy and brains—and fanatical courage and self-confidence. Just as its leaders made a success of the army despite terrific handicaps, so they feel they are bound to make a success of industry. I saw the Red Army in the early part of 1920. It was a pretty sight. I have seen the Red Army lately, and it is good enough. So, why not industry? With faith, youth, brains and energy you can work miracles—even in Russia.

**Peasants the Decisive Factor.**

But that is relatively insignificant compared with the question of the peasants. If the peasants of Russia support the Soviet régime it can afford to disregard the rest of the world. Rightly or wrongly—such investigation as I have been able to make incline me to believe rightly—the Communist leaders now are convinced that the peasants do and will support them. That would mean that, even if industry for some years proved so inefficient that prices remained high, or that the bulk of the real revenue of the Soviet Government must still be drawn from the peasants, or that the number of the industrial proletariat continued to dwindle as the number of factories in operation was reduced, there would be no real danger for the Soviet Government.

Finally, it is worth remembering that this Government is composed almost entirely of enthusiasm—men who throughout their lives have endured hardships for the sake of the principles they hold. The position last year and the year before was that rather than risk the loss of all those principles, the leaders were willing to sacrifice part of them, at least temporarily. In 1923 it looks as if they thought the possibility of total loss practically negligible. Therefore, why sacrifice further.

January 6, 1923

# RUSSIAN OPPOSITION KEEPS TCHEKA BUSY

**Strikes, unemployment and more or less open political opposition continue to harass the Bolshevist Government of Russia and furnish the re-organized "Tcheka" (political police) with plenty of work, according to reports trickling over the border and printed in German and Swiss Socialist newspapers.** Some of these papers remark that while Premier Lenin and his advisers have compromised with capitalism to the extent of giving a wide range to private industry they are still maintaining a strict censorship over the press and are emulating the Japanese Government in trying to keep the Russian masses from being contaminated by "dangerous thoughts."

December was an extraordinary hard month for the Russian workers, says a report from Moscow found in the Berner Tagwacht of Jan. 12. Strikes became more numerous and the big metal works of Sormovo were closed down. The Soviet authorities were especially worried at the unrest among the postal and telegraph employes and arrested large numbers of them, some 400 being held in jail in Moscow alone. In Petrograd many striking metal workers were arrested and deported to Orenburg in the Urals.

On Dec. 18 the political police made wholesale arrests in Moscow of the leaders of the unemployed, who had planned to hold a big demonstration during the fourth congress of the Communist International and present demands to the delegates of the Communists of the world including the right to work and to exercise freedom of speech, press and assembly. The Tcheka had got wind of the plan in time to prevent its execution, so the visitors from abroad were not annoyed. The subsequent arrests seemed to be for the purpose of making an example of the leaders and stifling any further demonstrations. According to reports received by the Berlin Vorwärtz, there were 100,000 persons out of work in the principal Ukrainian cities in October, while the newly erected unemployment insurance machinery was functioning but feebly and the 50,000 rations per day being supplied by the Government were far from sufficient. In Moscow 45,000 persons were unemployed on Nov. 1, against 34,000 on Oct. 1.

From Yekaterinoslaf comes a report of a victory over the Soviet authorities won by the local section of the Metal Workers' Union. It appears that seventeen of the section's members had been exiled to Vyatka and Tobolsk for having led a movement which resulted in the expulsion last June of the Communist "cell" from the Nizhni-Dneprovsky shops. Their comrades insistently demanded their return and the authorities gave way and sent them back to Yekaterinoslaf, where they were made the objects of a great ovation.

Persecution of the Social Democrats and Social Revolutionaries continues, according to reports telling of the ousting of these non-Communists from the service of the State and of frequent arrests. In Kharkof thirty-five Social Democrats were arrested at one stroke, twenty-six of whom were banished to distant towns, while nine were turned over to the courts to be tried on charges of possessing forbidden literature and living under assumed names.

In a letter recently addressed to Leon Trotzky, Russian Minister of Defense, in reply to a plea for a united labor front made by the Communist International, Emile Vandervelde, the Belgian Socialist leader, reproaches the Bolshevist chief for keeping Social Revolutionaries in jail under inhuman conditions. He reminds Trotzky that some of the prisoners fought valiantly against Czarism and that they helped Trotzky to return from exile during the Kerensky régime.

February 4, 1923

## Lenin Suffers a Stroke, Condition Is Serious; Announcement Causes a Sensation in Moscow

By WALTER DURANTY.
Copyright, 1923, by The New York Times Company.
Special Cable to THE NEW YORK TIMES.

MOSCOW, March 12.—A single sheet of a special edition of the Pravda carrying a Government communiqué stating that Lenin had had a relapse and a doctors' bulletin in big type two columns wide appeared on the streets a few minutes before 6 o'clock this evening and caused an immediate sensation.

People gathered in knots to discuss the news, which certainly came as a shock to the general public and caused obvious emotion. The gay holiday air of the streets on a fine March evening suddenly vanished.

Still more startling was the effect of the announcement by Rykof to a plenary session of the Moscow Soviet.

Although today (Monday), was a holiday—the sixth anniversary of the downfall of the Czar—upon which no newspapers were to be published, the Government deemed it necessary to issue a special edition of the Pravda. The official communiqué follows:

"On Oct. 3 the President of Council of Commissars, Vladimir Ilyitch (Lenin) returned to his duties. After two months' work he again began to show weakness and signs of fatigue. The doctors recommended a lengthy rest and ordered absolute abstention from work, even newspapers being forbidden. They only allowed him to consider such general questions as reorganization of the State apparatus and peasant workers inspection or educational reforms. Vladimir Ilyitch strictly followed the régime set by his physicians—Minkowski Foerster, Kramer and Kozevnikoff—and his health improved until it was hoped he would be allowed to return to work in the very near future.

"In the last few days, however, a serious set-back occurred. The Government consequently judges it necessary to publish medical bulletins."

Today's doctors' bulletin is of ominous brevity. It runs:

"Lenin's health has markedly worsened. Symptoms of blood vessel rupture again appeared, causing certain interference with the power of movement of the right arm and leg. The general condition is satisfactory. Heart is good, temperature 27.1 Centigrade (98.7 Fah.); pulse, 96."

M. Rykoff, one of the Deputy Presidents of the Council of Commissars, also announced that Lenin was worse during a meeting which was being held to celebrate the anniversary of the overthrow of the Czar, and also the twenty-fifth anniversary of the organization of the Communist Party.

In the big theatre where the celebration was held one could have heard a pin drop, so intense was the interest of the gathering when Rykoff said Lenin was in a serious condition, but not fatally ill. He added that daily bulletins would be issued regarding the condition of the patient.

Rykoff's announcement was the first official statement, although there ha been many rumors of the serious illness of the Premier. It cast gloom over the gathering.

March 14, 1923

## RUSSIA'S NEW CIVIL CODE

THE Civil Code of the Russian Socialistic Federated Soviet Republics went into effect the first of the year. A translation by Acting Commercial Attaché H. B. Smith of the decree putting the code into effect in a report to the Bureau of Foreign and Domestic Commerce from Warsaw, is as follows:

"(a) All controversies in private legal relations, which have arisen before Nov. 7, 1917, may not be brought up before the judicial or other official institutions of the republic.

"(b) Controversies in private legal relations which may have arisen from date of Nov. 7, 1917, up to the date of the bringing into force of the new Civil Code, must be regulated according to the laws in force at the date of the beginning of the controversy.

"(d) If these legal relations allowed by the laws in force at the date of the controversy are not sufficiently clearly decided by the laws then in force, such cases may be brought up again.

"(e) Interpretation enlarging the attributes of the Civil Code of the R. S. F. S. R. may only be admitted in such cases when such interpretation is demanded for the defense of the interests of the workmen and peasant state and of the working classes.

"(f) The interpretation of the code on the basis of the laws of the pre-revolutionary courts is prohibited.

"(g) The general three years' prescription of civil lawsuits concerns also the legal cases which may have arisen before the introduction of the new code.

"(h) The rights of foreign citizens belonging to States with which the R. S. F. S. R. have entered into certain conventions are regulated on the strength of these conventions. Unless the rights of foreign citizens are foreseen in the treaties between the Soviet Government and the States in question, viz., rights of free passage on the territory of the R. S. F. S. R., the choice of an occupation, the founding and purchase of commercial and industrial enterprises, the acquisition of the building rights, the right to own land—these rights may be given to foreigners only by the decision of the responsible authorities of the Soviet Government.

"Remark 1. Foreign limited companies, associations, &c., acquire the right of legal parties only on the basis of special permits of the Government.

"Remark 2. Foreign legal parties who have not the permits to operate on the territory of the R. S. F. S. R. possess the right of legal defense in cases originated outside the frontiers of the R. S. F. S. R. but only on the basis of reciprocity."

March 18, 1923

## NEW BODY TO RUN SOVIET INDUSTRY

### State Control Commission Plans to Do So Independently of Foreign Capital.

### 50 NAMED, ALL COMMUNISTS

MOSCOW, April 27 (Associated Press).—The work of putting into effect the decisions of the Communist Congress—in substance, that Russia endeavor to rehabilitate herself without the slightest surrender of proletarian dictatorship, and enforce more vigorous communistic control of industrial and economic life—was begun today.

Though Leon Trotzky's thesis on the subject of reconstruction of heavy industries was approved, it is not yet certain whether Trotzky himself will take over this work. It may be left to the present State machinery, which, however, the correspondent was informed today, will be closely inspected by the new State Control Commission.

At its first meeting today the commission elected Valerian Kubichoff Chairman and proposed that he be appointed to the all-important post of Commissar of State Control. Kubichoff, a former cadet in the Czar's Army, is 35 years old. He was exiled to Siberia in his youth for revolutionary activities. He has taken a prominent part in the Communst Party and won Bokhara and Turkestan to the Soviet Federation. He is noted for his stern efficiency.

Fifty ardent Communists were elected members of the commission, which will have the right to investigate all departments of the Government in an endeavor to bring about what is described as Lenin's idealism. These Commissioners were relieved of all other duties.

As defined in a resolution printed today, the duties of the State Control Commission include merciless punishment of Soviet employes for every case of snobbishness, no matter how small, or disregarding questions of workers and peasants; investigating bribery or bureaucracy and selecting the personnel for important posts.

This plan Premier Lenin dictated from his sick bed months ago in an effort, as he put it, "to save the Soviet State from on the one hand losing communism entirely and on the other hand from further ruination by inefficient management of affairs."

The resolution embodying M. Stalin's plan for welding Russia's 60,000,000 non-Russian inhabitants into a United States of Russia without racial jealousies was printed today. M. Stalin is Commissary for National Minorities and one of the most prominent men of the Soviet Government.

In addition to proposing a sort of Senate in which all the small republics, and even the national minorities within these republics, would be equally represented, the plan makes concessions to the national feelings of the Georgians and other peoples in the Southern Soviet Republics. It is proposed that State business, the work of the schools and all the departments of these republics be conducted in their own language, and that the State officials be chosen by their own people. It is expected that considerable liberty will be allowed these Governments in working out their own economic policies and constituting their national military units.

The scheme for taxing the peasants has not yet been worked out definitely, but generally it provides for three-fifths payment in cash and the balance in produce, with the likelihood of the tax amounting to about 20 per cent. Educational work among the peasants will be broadened.

Trotzky's industrial plan proposes the complete shutting down of non-profitable factories, with concentration of work on the productive ones, and the substitution of responsible individual managers for the workmen's committees.

April 28, 1923

## RUSSIA ORGANIZES TWO FEDERAL BODIES

### Upper House, of 57 Members, Has the Only Real Authority —Other Is Advisory.

By WALTER DURANTY.
Copyright, 1923, by The New York Times Company.
By Wireless to THE NEW YORK TIMES.

MOSCOW, April 28.—Reorganization of the Communist Party administrative apparatus, voted by the party congress just ended, may have far-reaching effects not only on the party itself but on the whole governmental system of Russia.

The controlling authority of the Communist Party, already existent in fact, is being more formally organized, and this affirmation for Communist authority and co-ordination thereto constitute what is practically a Federal Constitution.

Hitherto Soviet Russia has been governed by a sort of dual control for which there is no parallel in foreign systems of government. Henceforth there are to be two Communist Party Central Committees, one executive, of forty members and seventeen associate members or "candidates," as they are termed here; the other a control board of fifty members and ten associates. Roughly they may be said to correspond to a Senate and a lower house, with the difference that the real power and initiative will be vested exclusively in the former, and the latter's functions will be purely critical and controlive.

The latter includes none of the best known Bolshevist leaders, but will have a far greater percentage of provincial members than the former.

In practice, all power is concentrated in the hands of the political bureau which actually governs Russia with dictatorial authority. The only limitation on its power is the annual party congress, which is required to set the seal of its approval on projected policies and also on the personalities of its leaders, whom it elects to the Central Executive Committee by the only numbered secret ballot in all Russia today.

The new Federal Constitution involves the reorganization of the former fifty provinces of Russia into twenty-one departments with a new system of centralized control similar to that of France.

At present the political bureau consists of Lenin, Trotzky, Statlin, Kyenef, Zinovief and Rykoy. Lenin may not die, but he certainly will be unable to work for many months—if ever. Djerjinski, Burkharin, Radek, Tsurupa, Rakowski and perhaps one or two others will form a sort of informal group of associate members, upon whom the bureau may call any time it deems fit.

It is understood that there will be more specialization in the political bureau than before. That is, the Central Committee will be divided into sections, economical, political, national, military, &c., whose Chairmen will be representatives of that particular department in the bureau. For instance, Stalin will specialize on inner national questions; Trotzky on military and probably, with the collaboration of Rykov, on economic and industrial; Zinovieff on matters pertaining to the workers in Russia and the Communist international abroad; Kamenef, with perhaps the assistance of Djerjinski, on political and internal security affairs. Thus each would present a report on the subject under his charge and it would serve as a basis for subsequent discussion.

The question remains who will be the dominant force in the bureaus, or Lenin's successor. In the latter form the question annoys the Russian Communists exceedingly, because they say it implies a sort of dictatorial authority non-existent in theory, but actually wielded by Lenin through the "fortuitous circumstance" of his ability to analyze the situation and forecast the wisest policy.

April 29, 1923

## RUSSIAN RUBLE GIVES WAY TO A NEW MEDIUM

There is considerable interest in international circles in the "chervonetz," the new Russian standard of value, and intense efforts are being made by the State Bank of Russia to popularize this new standard. The President of the Russian State Bank declared that although the chervonetz is secured by gold and stable foreign currencies to practically the whole amount of the issue, none the less gold cannot be obtained for it, but only Soviet rubles at a rate fixed daily by the "official" Bourse.

For some months the State Bank was able so to manipulate dealings on various currencies as to maintain the chervonetz at approximately what they considered should be its value (in Soviet rubles) in relation to the pound, namely, 111 per cent. At the end of March the chervonetz stood as high as 117 per cent. of the pound, but toward the end of April it went below 100 per cent., and only thanks to great efforts on the part of the bank was it maintained at slightly over 100 per cent. for a short time. About May 8, however, the bank quite lost control and pounds were dealt in on the "black" bourse during the next two weeks at a figure of which the official chervonetz quotation was at one time below 70 per cent. At the time when the interview was given the chervonetz was quoted at about 90 per cent. of the pound, that is, 20 per cent. below the figure regarded by the State Bank as its true value.

The chervonetz thus cannot yet be considered a currency of stable value expressed in pounds sterling or dollars. It is, however, more easily exchanged into Soviet rubles than sterling or dollars, as a large proportion of shops and institutions will accept it instead of Soviet rubles at the rate of the day.

July 15, 1923

## SOVIET STILL BARS FREEDOM OF SPEECH

### Press and Public Meetings Are Under Strict Control, and No Opposition Is Allowed.

### ALL DISPATCHES CENSORED

### Foreign Correspondents Work Under Difficulties Like Those Encountered During the War.


Special Cable to The New York Times

LONDON, Sept. 12—Freedom of speech as the term is understood in America does not exist in Russia. Newspapers all are State-controlled and nothing may appear that does not meet the approval of the censorship. The same applies to all public speaking—indeed, even private meetings are strictly controlled.

Putting it in a nutshell, no opposition to the Government, either written or spoken, is allowed. In this respect anyway the Communists admit their "Dictatorship of the Proletariat" is a despotism, but they defend it on practical grounds.

"There are potential enemies in our midst," said Trotsky a year ago in reply to remonstrances from foreign correspondents about the harsh treatment of certain professors. "At present our position is secure enough to ignore them, but should the European situation become critical these internal enemies might be dangerous. It therefore is wiser and more merciful to expel them from Russia now than to imprison or perhaps shoot them later."

Special pleading this, it may be objected, but it exactly represents the Bolshevist viewpoint. Many Communists advance another argument.

"Freedom of speech and the press in America and England," they say "are the slow outcome of a centuries' long fight for personal liberty. How can you expect Russia, just emerged from blackest tyranny, to share the attitude of Anglo-Saxons who struck the first blow against royal tyrants a thousand years ago at Runnymede? Our revolution is so recent we still may be considered in a virtual condition of war, and Western nations admit the necessity of press control when the safety of the State is at stake."

The third argument put forward is that a majority of the Russian people are in such a backward position as to fall an easy prey to any cunning speaker or writer, and must therefore be protected against such in their own interest—the same reasoning, as shown in a previous dispatch, which was used to justify the Communist dictatorship.

One high Russian official put it more bluntly:

"The real truth of the matter is that the press and speech restrictions like terrorism proceed in the first instance from fear. When a régime is sure of its position and knows it is supported by a majority of the people it does not care what the minority says. When it is new or grows anxious and uncertain it tends to limit opposition or even criticism. Only time and the continued stability of the Soviet régime will bring us gradually into line with Western standards."

**Censorship of News Dispatches.**

The question of press censorship as applied to foreign correspondents falls in a somewhat different plane. Generally speaking nothing they write meets the eyes of the Russian public—although foreign newspapers may now be received through the open mail despite the fact that officious custom men still sometimes confiscate them at the frontier. Nevertheless, censorship exists. Litvinoff told THE NEW YORK TIMES correspondent before entering Russia two years ago there would be no censorship of foreign news except as regards military matters, which he said were taboo without special permission of the War Department. For nearly a year the Foreign Office maintained in principle at least that, although they supervised foreign news messages, there was no actual censorship. Gradually, however, a censorship did become a definite and concrete thing, with the usual characteristic faults.

In five years' experience of French censorship in civil and military affairs THE TIMES correspondent found these results followed:

Overnervousness—Censors as relatively subordinate officials would suppress anything they were doubtful about rather than assume the responsibility or keep referring the matter to superiors.

Overzeal—Censors would grow to want everything submitted to them to be favorable to the French cause and tend to suppress criticism, however honest or harmless.

Overtenderness for Superiors—As minor officials the censors would suppress anything that might give offense to greater powers above them. Which leads up to the worst fault of the censorship as experienced in France and Russia—the inevitable tendency on the part of the censor to feel he somehow is responsible for the news passed by him, that his stamp in somehow gave it a sort of official standing. This, of course, is entirely false, as the whole reason for a censorship is the suppression of information that may injure the State and that alone. But the censor's personal equation becomes too strong.

One of the Moscow censors remarked naively to THE TIMES correspondent after suppressing a dispatch: "I wouldn't mind so much if it was written from London or Paris. But the people you are attacking are friends of ours and I don't like that kind of thing to go out with a Moscow date line"—that is, with the stamp of Moscow official approval.

On the whole, however, experience with the Russian censorship is favorable enough. The censors would not only say what was suppressed before the dispatch was sent—which the French declined to do save in exceptional cases for the first three years of the war—but would listen to argument and often permit modification of the offending passage so as to maintain all or part of the news value.

**News of Famous Trial Suppressed.**

In a trying position they are courteous and tactful and, generally speaking, there is little to complain of. Until the Butchkavitch affair. Then the element of fear came into play and the work of the foreign correspondents became virtually impossible. In a subsequent dispatch to THE NEW YORK TIMES a brief outline of this unhappy business was given. Enough to say now that a combination of circumstances had produced a state of ferment in Soviet Government circles not far removed from panic. This was especially true of the Foreign Office, which handles the censorship, and where the consequences abroad of action the Government contemplated taking, and did in fact take, perhaps were more fully realized than in the other departments.

Any accurate presentation of the facts involved an explanation of the existing ferment and the conflict of forces. For some reason the authorities declined to permit this in the slightest degree. In plain English, the fear complex dominated their usual prudence. It was not long before they realized the error, and Litvinof, on behalf of the Foreign Office, gave representative American correspondents a solemn promise that henceforth nothing should be suppressed in a news message save facts whose accuracy the writer was unable to substantiate. The promise has been kept, but the damage was done.

Favorable news from Moscow rests under suspicion, whereas unfounded reports about events in Russia broadcast by anti-Bolshevist Emigrés from Riga, Helsingfors, Reval, &c., find ready acceptance. The excuse the Soviet officials offer, that they have been so much injured in the past by malicious lies or perversions of truth, is human but won't mend matters, and the position will remain unsatisfactory until they realize that conditions in Russia now being so much better than the majority of people abroad believe, the entire absence of restrictions on foreign news would do them infinitely more good than harm.

September 13, 1923

## CHEKA TERROR RULE PUT 50,000 TO DEATH

### Bolshevist Forces Struck in the Night to Plant Fear in the Hearts of the People.

### MYSTERY ADDED TO HORROR

### No One Knew Who Might Be Its Agents and a Careless Word Might Bring Terrible Fate.

By WALTER DURANTY.


Special Cable to THE NEW YORK TIMES.

LONDON, Sept. 13.—The "Cheka," or Extraordinary Commission for the Suppression of Counter-Revolution, to give it its full official title, ceased to exist as such in the early part of last year when it was brought under the control of the Ministry of the Interior on the same lines as the American Department of Justice or the British Scotland Yard. A new title, "Gay-Payoo," or State Political Administration, is now in common use, but few non-Communist Russians can speak the word "Cheka" without a shudder.

Created soon after the Bolshevik revolution, the "Cheka" was developed by Dzerzhinsky—the mild-eyed enthusiast of ruthless and fanatic energy—with the same executive efficiency as he has shown in the past two years in reorganizing the railroads. In his hands it became not a political police force alone, but the veritable sword of the Soviet Government. Its picked battalions rushed to every danger point, first in the cities and later on to the front against the White generals. Its armed agents were in every large town and on every railroad. It conducted court-martials in the army through "flying tribunals," where they came unheralded to crush mutinies before the plotters knew they were suspected. Finally it carried as a great political organization its own prisons, its own tribunals and its own firing squads.

To this day there are people in Moscow who make a detour rather than walk the pavement in front of 2 Lubianka, the headquarters where the prisoners of the "Cheka" were first examined, so deep was the terror it evoked.

**Created Terror Deliberately.**

There is no doubt that Bolshevist leaders deliberately created this feeling in the minds of the superstitious Russians. The "Cheka" operated by night, arrested persons and vanished and their fate remained a mystery. Its very name was taboo, and strange, horrible stories were told of the manner of its executions. No man knew who might be one of its agents, nor into what a careless word might involve him and his family.

Valuable as the effect thus produced may have been to the Soviet Government in difficult days in 1919 when its fate seemed hanging by a hair, the subsequent reaction in Russia, and more especially abroad, did it infinite harm. The bogy it had created became the symbol of its murderous rule and fantastic stories were told of millions of "Cheka" victims, hideous blood baths and executions en masse.

In point of fact, it is doubtful whether the total number of "Cheka" executions throughout the whole period up to 1922 surpasses 50,000. I once asked a group of bitterly anti-Bolshevist Englishmen, most of whom were in Russia when the revolution occurred, in which all lost dear friends or property, what they estimated the total "Cheka" executions at. No one put the figure higher than 100,000 for the whole country. The majority placed it much lower; one quoting as an analogy the French Revolution, whose victims the great historian Michelet estimates at 4,000—put it as low as 20,000.

Though lives were cheap in Russia and the "Cheka" leaders pitiless in defending the revolution when in danger, they would have defeated their own object by the wholesale slaughter of workers and peasants on the scale reported abroad. Nor are such men as Dzerzhinsky or Latsis, now head of the State Salt Trust, or Unschlitt, the present chief of the Gay-Payoo, the bestial butchers they have been depicted. In a remarkable monograph on terrorism Latsis declared that the object of "terror" is to create the maximum effect at the minimum cost. "Thus it is better," he said, "to execute ten, twenty or even one hundred persons immediately at a critical moment than by hesitation, either merciful or anxious, to allow a rebellion to break out, which would cost thousands of lives before it was suppressed."

On these grounds Latsis is said to have given an opinion against the death sentences on the Catholic priests last Summer. "They should have been killed when arrested or not at all," as my informant repeated his words. But this I was unable to confirm.

The Bolsheviki make little attempt to defend the "Cheka" on moral grounds.

"It was a matter of practical necessity," they said. "The safety of the revolution was at stake. Robespierre fell because he had no such organization to defend him." But, they add, "Remember the actual revolution did not cost many lives—a few score in Petrograd and not many hundreds in Moscow. This is apart, of course, from the murder of land owners by the peasantry or officers by the soldiers.

They further add that the "Red terror did not begin until the Summer of 1918, when anti-Bolshevist agitation culminated in the attempted assassination of Lenin on Aug. 30, 1918."

That there is considerable truth in this statement has been admitted by foreign officials in Moscow and Petrograd up to that period. It was in 1919, 1920 and 1921 that the terror became most dreadful, for then the suppression of "speculation," which meant any form of buying or selling, and the concealment of money or valuables—both penal offenses under the strict Communist régime — were added to the "Cheka's" activities.

According to creditable evidence, life in the Russian cities must then have been a perfect hell of "smelling out witchcraft" with none knowing when the "witch doctors" might descend upon them.

**Denunciation Added to Horror.**

A terrible factor aided the "Chekists" and increased the horror of that time, namely denunciation. Thousands of letters, often anonymous, or whispered informations poured in to the "Cheka's" offices, denouncing this man or that woman as a "speculator" or a concealer of valuables. Hunger or overstrained nerves sent whole families to prison. Few if any such cases swelled the list of actual executions—the offense was venial and universal—but thousands packed in jails died of disease and starvation.

Where the vengeance of the "Cheka" claimed hundreds of victims, private spite took a toll of thousands and tens of thousands. Just imagine what it meant in practice. If a wife was tired of her husband, or a husband of his wife, if a servant had a grudge against a former master or an employe against a former boss it meant a few words to the "Cheka" and then—silence. Of course the "Cheka" bears the responsibility before history, but the blame rests not entirely on the "Cheka."

Today things are quite different. I venture to say that no one who behaves himself has any more to fear from the "Gay-Payee" than the average American citizen from the Department of Justice. Much has been written about spies surrounding foreigners in Russia—foreign correspondents in particular. It is all rubbish. I lived in Moscow several months with an American capitalist and a former intelligence officer of the British Army. None of us was plotting a counter-revolution and none of us was bothered by the "Cheka" at any time on any pretext.

September 14, 1923

# NEW SUPREME CHEKA FOR SOVIET RUSSIA

***Decree Establishes the Communist Inquisition in All of the Allied Republics.***


Special Cable to THE NEW YORK TIMES.

RIGA, Nov. 23.—By a special decree the Soviet Government has created a new Supreme Cheka which is called the O. G. P. U. [Unified State Political Department]. The decree proclaims the O. G. P. U. as the supreme institution for combatting political and economic counter-revolution, espionage and brigandage throughout the territories of all the Soviet republics. This body has the full control and management of all similar institutions and of the military forces of such institutions now working independently in the separate republics.

The O. G. P. U. is to have its own special military forces under the immediate command of the President of the O. G. P. U. One of its principal functions is to guard the frontiers of the Union of Soviet Republics. All agents and employes of the O. G. P. U. are subject to the same discipline and enjoy the same privileges as persons on active military service.

The name of the President of the O. G. P. U. has not been announced.

November 24, 1923

# REPORTS RUSSIA GAINING.

**Congressional Party Observes Signs of Economic Recovery.**

LONDON, Oct. 8.—The Congressional party consisting of Senator Ladd of North Dakota, Senator King of Utah, Representative Frear of Wisconsin, A. A. Johnson and Frank Connes, which spent two months in Russia, is sailing for home tomorrow on the Leviathan.

All the members of the party were greatly impressed by Russia's progress toward economic recovery, according to Senator King, who said the "waves of Russian life are bearing with telling effect against the walls of the abnormal conditions that have existed under the Soviet régime."

October 9,1923

# MOSCOW PROHIBITS ALL PRIVATE SCHOOLS

***Religious Instruction Is Banned—Atheistic Christmas Reported a Success.***


Special Cable to THE NEW YORK TIMES.

RIGA, Jan. 2.—Prohibition against the teaching of children in private institutions, that is to say, of giving religious instruction, which long has been in existence, has been extended by a new decree in Russia which absolutely forbids teaching of any sort except in the Communist schools.

All private schools are thus abolished. Persons, teachers or parents who violate this regulation are liable to severe penalties, especially if they have given instruction to groups of more than three children.

Soviet official circles explain this measure as intended to combat "pernicious non-Communist influences," but the real reason is to be found in the fact that private schools in Moscow and all the provincial towns are very numerous, the parents clubbing together to engage teachers to instruct their children with a resultant emptying of the Communist schools.

At the same time the Government publishes new statutes for the Soviet schools, one of which prohibits punishment of any kind whatsoever.

The Government reports that the anti-religious Christmas campaign was a great success, though less demonstrative than former campaigns. About 70,000 Moscow children and adults attended the Komsomoltsi's (League of Communist Youth) athletic entertainment.

January 3, 1924

# SOVIET OUSTS 100,000 FROM UNIVERSITIES

***Excludes Bourgeois Students in Plan to Proletarianize All Russian Education.***

MOSCOW, May 17 (Associated Press) —In line with its policy of purifying the Communist Party and strengthening its hold on all departments of Russian public life, the Soviet Government today issue a degcree which virtually eliminates students of the bourgeois class from the high schools and universities and proletarianizes all education.

This measure is made necessary, Soviet officials say, by the overcrowded condition of all the universities and by the need for giving the youth of the peasant and proletarian classes the educational facilities which were denied them under the Czarist régime.

"In coming years," the decree says, "the Soviet Republic will not be in a position to utilize the special knowledge of the bulk of students who are now completing their education."

Nearly 100,000 students of non-proletarian origin will be affected in Russia proper, while a much greater number will be involved in the other republics of the Soviet Federation when the present decree is extended to them.

As this year only those students designated by the Communist Party and the trade union organizations will be eligible to enter the universities, the younger generation of students who are now completing secondary school courses will be deprived of the opportunity of getting higher education.

The new decree is corollary to the campaign undertaken by the Communist Party after the death of Nickolai Lenin, which resulted in the expulsion of those who, it believed, had lost touch with party affairs and showed inclinations toward the New Economic Policy, and in the admission of nearly 300,000 new members drawn from the factories and other proletarian walks of life.

May 18, 1924

# CATHEDRAL TO BE MUSEUM.

**Decreased Attendance May Close Many Churches in Russia.**

LENINGRAD, July 3 (Associated Press).—Church attendance in Bolshevist Russia has decreased to such an extent that many churches are on the point of closing their doors. The religious authorities say that contributions from the congregations are so meagre that they scarcely are able to maintain the churches and pay the slender salaries of the clergymen.

St. Isaac's Cathedral, the most magnificent in all Russia, is a striking example of the changed order since the separation of the Church and State. Finding the collection baskets almost empty each Sunday, the governing body of the cathedral has decided to convert the superb edifice, erected at a cost exceeding $11,000,000, into a museum and offer it as a great relic of the past to the "Old Petrograd Society," a non-religious organization.

The plan, as outlined by the governing body, is to have the society convert the cathedral into a public museum and charge a sufficient fee to support the institution.

Americans who have visited Leningrad when it was known as St. Petersburg or Petrograd, will remember this famous cathedral. Memory may recall to them its superb columns of red granite, its enormous golden dome, the colossal doors of solid bronze, pillars of lapis lazuli and malachite, rich sculptures in striking bronze relief, magnificent paintings, exquisite mosaics, priceless ikons and huge ecclesiastical vessels of gold and silver. Forty years were required to build this great structure.

July 4, 1924

# RED MAJORITY WINS IN ECONOMIC REVOLT

## Insurgents, Scoring State Inefficiency in Industry, Lose and Face Punishment.

## BLOW IS AIMED AT TROTSKY

### Stalin Accuses Him of Six Offenses —Propaganda in His Red Army Curbed.

By WALTER DURANTY.

Copyright, 1924, by The New York Times Company.
Special Cable to THE NEW YORK TIMES.

MOSCOW, Jan. 19.—The Communist party conference ended last night with an overwhelming victory for the machine against the opposition as expected. The policies of the Central Executive Committee were approved in a unanimous resolution and the amendments offered by its critics were rejected by all save two or three last ditch supporters.

The insurgents were branded as "factionaries," and the small bourgeois as heretics, while Stalin, chief of the machine leaders, gratified himself and his hearers by reciting "six errors" he attributed to Trotsky as though they were the seven deadly sins.

Bukharin, whose method of reporting the whole discussion as managing editor of the Pravda seemed to impartial observers anything but impartial, was honored with praise for the manner in which the machine organ upheld the machine interests, and altogether "it was a famous victory."

But there are one or two points worth nothing, nevertheless. First, it is a truism that any one who "bucks" a political machine, especially such a well-oiled machine as the Russian Communist Party, is doomed to failure from the outset unless he can stir up the party masses sufficiently to produce a change in the composition of the upper strata of the party hierarchy or scare the latter into submission.

This the insurgents failed to do, because the masses were aghast before the spectre of a factionary split in the party ranks called up by the machine leaders, with perhaps greater political acumen than justification. From that moment it was obvious that the party conference would be a machine affair.

But the very success of the machine in crushing so-called factionism may be a source of subsequent danger. Relieved by the exorcism spectre, it is inevitable that a widespread demand for freedom from machine "instructions" in the election of local party group leaders will be renewed with greater force than ever.

Secondly, the machine failure to solve the economic problems, which was the real cause and foundation of the insurgent attack, won't necessarily be remedied by the fact—which some insurgent speakers carefully pointed out —that it was incorporated in the program number of their suggestions.

Thirdly, as another insurgent remarked, it is not a question of hair-splitting over the reasons for the economic crisis—whether it is due to overproduction above the demands of the market, or under production, resulting in prices that the market cannot swallow—that really matters, but "how to correct the basis of the evil, namely, that private enterprise at present in Russia, despite the taxes and other handicaps, is managing to make a profit while State enterprise records a loss.

This point really is the most important of all, because it goes right to the heart of the social experiment now being carried on in Russia.

Stripped of all political claptrap, the rivalries of persons, Russian verbosity and Marxist phraseology, it comes to this:

Is not private enterprise more successful than inefficient State management? The Russian Communist machine accuses its critics of small Bourgeois heresy for daring to ask this, but the latter reply:

"Please note that we emphasize the word inefficient. We are just as good Marxists as you, and accept no less fully the Marxian dogma that State monopoly and control must prevail over, and supersede the wasteful and competitive—that is, mutually injurious—private enterprise. But on one absolutely essential condition, that State management be no less efficient than private enterprise, which yours is not."

Here is the crux of the whole problem —can State management be elevated to the required pitch of efficiency? The rest of the world says no, at least not yet; the Russians say it can because, even supposing State management less efficient than private, its monopoly advantages should more than compensate the difference.

It is unnecessary to cite the statistics that have been used in terrific volume in the present controversy in order to show that Russia, under the management of the existing machine, has not reached that minimum pitch of efficiency. Whether Trotsky and his supporters could reach it, or whether the machine, under the spur of their criticisms, will reach it are open questions.

But one thing is certain, if the machine does not succeed in reaching it, or reasonably near it, before long the peasant masses, and workers too, for that matter, will make their voice loud and clear.

This won't mean the downfall of the Communist Party control of Russia. The Bolsheviki are too united against the outer danger, too well organized, too popular as compared with an alternative régime, with its inevitable return to bloodshed and general disturbance, for that.

But it will mean either that Trotsky and his friends will get a chance to make good or that the existing leaders will retain control at a sacrifice of a pretty large and unpalatable gulp of their Marxist principles.

---

MOSCOW, Jan. 19 (Associated Press). —The facts in the dispute within the Communist Party became clearer today with the publication of a resolution adopted by the party conference paving the way for the stringent punishment of discipline breakers, and with the publication also of a speech by M. Stalin, which in effect lays the blame for the entire affair upon the shoulders of Trotsky.

The resolution aims at Trotsky's pet institution, the Red Army, in which it is declared special attention should be paid to putting the work of propaganda on a "healthier footing." Many units in the Red Army prior to the present party conference adopted resolutions favoring the platform of the faction opposing the party leaders.

For any attempt to conduct factional work in the army, the offenders must be seriously punished, says the resolution.

January 20, 1924

# LENIN DIES

## SOVIET CONGRESS IN TEARS

### Mass Hysteria Only Averted by a Leader's Brusque Intervention.

By WALTER DURANTY.

Copyright, 1924, by The New York Times Company.
By Wireless to THE NEW YORK TIMES.

MOSCOW, Jan. 22.—Nikolai Lenin died last night at 6:50 o'clock. The immediate cause of death was paralysis of the respiratory centres due to a cerebral hemorrhage.

For some time optimistic reports had been current as the effects of a previous lesion gradually cleared up, but Lenin's nearest frends, realizing the progress of the relentless malady, tried vainly to hope against hope.

At 11:20 o'clock this morning President Kalinin briefly opened the session of the All-Russian Soviet Congress and requested every one to stand. He had not slept all night and tears were streaming down his haggard face. A sudden wave of emotion—not a sound, but a strange stir—passed over the audience, none of whom knew what had happened. The music started to play the Soviet funeral march, but was instantly hushed as Kalinin murmured brokenly:

"I bring you terrible news about our dear comrade, Vladimir Ilyitch." [Nikolai Lenin was his pen name.]

High up in the gallery a woman uttered a low, wailing cry that was followed by a burst of sobs.

**Kalinin Breaks the News.**

"Yesterday," faltered Kalinin, "yesterday, he suffered a further stroke of paralysis and——" There was a long pause as if the speaker were unable to nerve himself to pronounce the fatal word; then, with an effort which shook his whole body, it came—"died."

The emotional Slav temperament reacted immediately. From all over the huge opera house came sobs and wailing, not loud nor shrill, but pitifully mournful, spreading and increasing. Kalinin could not speak. He tried vainly to motion for silence with his hands and for one appalling moment a dreadful outbreak of mass hysteria seemed certain. A tenth of a second later it could not have been averted, but Yunakidze, Secretary of the Russian Federal Union, thrust forward his powerful frame and with hand and voice demanded calm. Then Kalinin, stumbling, read out the official bulletin.

" 'Jan. 21 the condition of Vladimir Ilyitch suddenly underwent sharp aggravation. At 5:30 P. M. his breathing was interrupted and he lost consciousness. At 6:50 Vladimir Ilyitch died from paralysis of the respiratory centres.

" 'Dated 3:25 A. M., Jan. 22.

" 'Signed:

" 'Drs. OHUNK [Lenin's personal physician and chief of the Moscow Health Department, who gave Lenin first treatment when wounded Aug. 30, 1918.]

" 'SEMISKO [a close personal friend of Lenin, and Minister of the Health Department],

" 'FOERSTER,

" 'GTYE,

" 'OSIGOF,

" 'YEWISTRATOF.

"We propose," continued Kalinin, "that the twenty-first day of January henceforth be set aside as a day of national mourning." By a tragic coincidence today—Jan. 9, old style, is a similar Bolshevist holiday in memory of Father Gapon's petitioners, massacred by the Czar's troops in the courtyard of the Winter Palace on "Bloody Sunday," 1905.

"Do you agree?" questioned Kalinin.

A confused sound, half sob, half sigh, was the only assent.

**Whole Congress Gives Way to Grief.**

Kalinin tried to tell the funeral arrangements, but broke down completely.

Kamenief and Zinovief, equally unnerved, and other members of the Presiding Committee had laid their heads on the table and cried like children. Even the daredevil Cossack leader Budyenny was weeping unrestrainedly, while the delegates in the body of the theatre stood motionless, sobbing, with tears coursing down their cheeks.

January 23, 1924

# LENIN LIVED TO SEE HIS THEORIES FAIL

Implicit belief in his own principles and absolute good faith in carrying them out have been the sources of power—in the opinion of intelligent, even of unfriendly critics—which enabled Lenin for over six years to retain his hold on Russia while that country sank from lower to lower depths.

While Russia declined into economic ruin, while millions starved to death within short distances of rich lands which were formerly the greatest wheat producing regions of Europe; while civilization disappeared and some districts fell even into cannibalism; while the country with the greatest agricultural resources in the world had to be fed from abroad; while preventable disease made havoc such as has been unknown for centuries—all this time Lenin easily held his power in Russia, and even kept international followers, who pleaded with their own countries to follow the example of Russia.

Lenin remained an idol with much of the population even while it was being cut to pieces by disease and hunger. According to one acute critic, the Russian masses had the same feeling toward Lenin which they had formerly had toward the "Little Father." They used to revere the Czar and to find excuses for him while hating his functionaries. In the same way the ordinary Russian found no fault with Lenin and laid the ruin of the country to those around him and to circumstances that he could not control.

While the peasant and workingmen had a superstitious reverence for Lenin those who were nearer to him had a loyalty founded on their knowledge of his absolute disinterestedness and the intensity of his convictions. They felt that he worked hard, lived ascetically, scorned riches and was inspired by a fierce enthusiasm unmixed with baser motives. Trotsky might be accused of making himself wealthy, and many of those about Lenin might be accused of lining their own nests in one way or another. But Lenin was never suspected. It was evident that he was true to himself, that he did not care for ease, glory or flattery, and that he cared for nothing except to make his doctrines work.

The fact that his doctrines did not work had been several times reported to be a contributing cause to his fatal illness. No amount of fanaticism could blind him to the fact that they had not worked out right. He had readjusted those doctrines and temporarily suspended some of his axioms, in the hope of reviving industry and keeping the people fed during the interim caused by some inexplicable delay in the arrival of Utopia. These compromises had not saved the situation. His final illness was caused, in part, according to some accounts from Russia, by the fact that he finally saw things as they were and realized that he had failed.

For every one legally assassinated in the French Revolution, he had caused the judicial murder of hundreds—all, of course, for the good of Russia. This was frankly admitted and defended as an essential step in clearing the stage for the communistic millennium. The age of blood was to be a preliminary to the age of gold. It took a long time to convince Lenin—if he was ever convinced—of his error.

His greatest disappointment was the failure of the international movement, the inability of Communists in other countries to overthrow their Governments and put the world under the rule of Soviets in the early stages of the revolution. For a long time he counted on this with certainty and bent all his energies in this direction.

But temporizing with "capitalistic" Governments has been allowable, under Lenin's system of conduct, from the beginning. The memoirs of Ludendorff and others have thrown light on this point, showing that Lenin was deliberately placed in Russia by the German General Staff in 1917 in order to put Russia out of the war.

He was in Geneva when the Czar's Government broke down. His transportation across Germany was arranged by the German high command as a strategic manoeuvre. Lenin was perfectly willing to accept this help from a capitalist Government. He knew the hopes which Germany founded on him. He had no idea at all of fulfilling them, as his later speeches and writings show. He believed that the Russian revolution which he foresaw would be followed by uprisings of the proletariat all over the world, the German revolution being one of the first. But the event proved that the Germans had calculated the chances correctly. Lenin did put Russia out of the war. He did not succeed in his hope of a proletarian triumph in Germany. The German revolution came later from military and economic causes, not as a result of Soviet infection.

At two periods in his career Lenin has been the most important man in Russia. The earlier time was during the attempted revolution of 1905. He left his mark on Russia heavily in 1905, because the insurrection which he then led checked the steps which had been taken to put Russia on a constitutional basis. Lenin was a perfect specimen of the doctrinaire in 1905, as in 1917. His devotion to dogma would not permit him to look with favor on half measures. At a later period he was ready to barter and trade in practical measures, but he would hear of no compromise where a political dogma was involved.

**Always for Rule of the Minority.**

Already in 1905 Lenin and the Social Democratic Party, which he founded, had worked out the theory of government by a small revolutionary minority, commanding the majority and working in their interest. The movement was not to be a democratic movement, but a movement where the masses would be led for their own interest, as that interest was conceived by the small intellectual minority. The masses were not to vote or express their will in any way, but to be pawns in the game played for their interest. The attitude of this minority toward the proletariat was: "They don't know what they want. We know what they want, and we will get it for them."

The first Soviet was formed in Petrograd in 1905 after the granting of the Constitution. It was to the activity of this Soviet and the influence of Lenin that Russia owed the gradual curtailment of the Constitution granted by the Czar in 1905. The actual uprising by the followers of Lenin was quickly suppressed, but it gave reactionaries the argument that any concessions offered to the Russian people would cause revolt, and that the safety of the Government lay in the practice of despotism according to the old rules.

Lenin was 54 years old. He belonged to the class known as the small nobility. He was brought up in the Orthodox faith. He was educated to be a professor. His father was a State Councillor. The family name was Ulianoff. "Lenin" is a pen name.

When he was 17 years old, Lenin's brother Alexander was executed for complicity in a terrorist plot against the life of Alexander III. In the same year Lenin finished his course in the Simbirsk Gymnasium and entered the Kazan University. He was banished from Kazan a few months later for taking part in a students' riot.

His offense was overlooked, however, and in 1891 he was a student in the University of St. Petersburg, where he studied law and economics. He also studied in Germany.

**Exiled to Siberia in 1895.**

In 1895, arrested in St. Petersburg as a dangerous Socialist, he was exiled to Siberia for three years. In 1900 he went abroad. His writings, especially developing the Marxian theory, made him known throughout the world and gave him a leading position as an international Socialist. His work, "The Development of Capitalism," became a standard Socialist textbook. This was one of a long series of books from his pen. From year to year he gained note at the international Socialist conferences. Living much of the time in Switzerland, he was the head of the group of exiled and condemned revolutionists of Russia and other countries. He spent much of his time in Galicia, a vantage point from which he maintained close contact with the revolutionary movement in Russia. Of Lenin's life in Switzerland, M. J. Olgin wrote:

"A smoky back room in a little café in Geneva; a few score of picturesque-looking Russian revolutionary exiles, men and women, seated around uncovered tables over glasses of beer or tea; at the head of the table a man in his forties, talking in a slow yet impassioned manner; and now and then an exclamation of disapproval, an outburst of indignation among a part of the audience, which would be instantly parried by a flashing remark of the speaker, a striking home with unusual trenchancy and venom—this is how I see now in my imagination the leader of the Bolsheviki, the great Inquisitor of the Russian social democracy, Nicolai Lenin.

"There is nothing remarkable in the appearance of this man—a typical Russian with rather irregular features; a stern but not unkindly expression; something crude in manner and dress, recalling the artisan rather than the intellectual and the thinker. You would ordinarily pass by a man of this kind without noticing him at all. Yet, had you happened to look into his eyes or to hear his public speech, you would not be likely to forget him.

"His eyes are small, but glow with compressed fire; they are clever, shrewd and alert; they seem to be constantly on guard, and they pierce you behind half-closed lids."

**Back in Russia After the Czar's Fall.**

With the overthrow of the Czar the Russian revolutionaries returned to Russia. Kerensky fell in November, and Lenin and Trotsky set up the "dictatorship of the proletariat," maintaining themselves in power by the slaughter of tens of thousands as counter-revolutionaries. In the matter of maintaining their power, Lenin and Trotsky showed themselves to be thoroughly practical men, shrinking from nothing to destroy opposition. At the same time, according to most of their critics, they sought to apply Socialist principles without change to the rest of Russia. The conflict between theory and the selfishness and other defects of human nature has continued in that country ever since, until recently, when, in order to resurrect Russia after her economic suicide, Lenin offered concessions of many kinds to capital.

The beginnings of Bolshevist power were marked by threats of the destruction of all government, by appeals to the proletariat all over the world to rise in the manner prescribed in the International Socialist books, by the promise to wipe out capital and to destroy money. Lenin showered the nations of the world with appeals to their workingmen to follow the example of Russia.

At home Lenin met and defeated plots and counter-revolutions until his enemies gave up in despair. The source of his power has remained somewhat mysterious, in spite of attempts to explain it on the ground that the slaughter and exhaustion in Russia had left all factions so weak that none could make any effort to throw off Bolshevist tyranny.

Maxim Gorky described the work of Lenin as an experiment in a laboratory, with the exception of the fact that it was performed on a living thing, and that, if the experiment did not have the expected success, the outcome would be death.

**Disasters of Bolshevist Rule.**

An almost complete stoppage of production, chaos in the transportation system, famine in the big cities, then in the country districts, all accompanied the Bolshevist régime almost from the beginning—effects largely due, according to outside observers, to the belief that work was no longer a necessity, but that all could live off those richer than themselves. Lenin and the other Bolshevist leaders from the beginning laid the blame for the condition of things in Russia to the Czarist régime, and the steady deterioration has been attributed to the action of the counter-revolutionaries and of the nations which declined to recognize Russia.

Spasmodic efforts to bring back production by introducing martial law with the nationalization of industries, compelling workers to do a hard day's work at peril of their lives, were announced from time to time, but proved not to be enduring or of wide application.

Lenin's literary output, explaining and recommending the Russian system to the rest of the world, went on unabated, in spite of the Russian collapse. The real condition of starvation and ruin in Russia was denied, and the reports of it attributed to the malice of the capitalist press up to the very time when the Russian Government was compelled to appeal to the outside world, America in particular, in order to have food sent to some of the greatest food-producing districts, where the Bolshevist rule brought about famine in the midst of what used to be the granary of Europe.

Lenin as he was in the third year of his absolute dictatorship was described by H. G. Wells as follows in an article printed in THE NEW YORK TIMES:

"I had come expecting to struggle with a doctrinaire Marxist. I found nothing of the sort. I had been told that Lenin lectured people; he certainly did nothing of the sort on this occasion. Much has been made of his laugh in the descriptions—a laugh which is said to be pleasing at first and afterward to become cynical. The laugh was not in evidence. His forehead reminded me of some one else—I could not remember who it was—until the other evening I saw Arthur Balfour sitting and talking under a shaded light. It is exactly the same domed, one-sided cranium.

"Lenin has a pleasant, quick-changing brownish face, with a lively smile and a habit (due, perhaps, to some defect in focusing) of screwing up one of his eyes as he pauses in his talk. He is not very much like the photographs you see of him, because he is one of those persons whose change of expression is more important than their features.

"He is like a 'techy' housewife who wants you to recognize that everything is in perfect order in the middle of an eviction. He is like one of those now-forgotten suffragettes who used to promise us an earthly paradise as soon as we escaped from the tyranny of 'man-made' laws."

Lenin told Wells that Russia was to be rehabilitated by turning her water-power into electricity.

"For Lenin," Wells continued, "who, like a good orthodox Marxist, denounces all Utopians, has succumbed at last to a Utopia, the Utopia of the electricians. He is throwing all his weight into a scheme for the development of great power stations in Russia to serve whole provinces with light, with transport and industrial power. Two experimental districts, he said, had already been electrified.

"Can you imagine a more courageous project in a vast, flat land of forests and illiterate peasants, with no water power, with no technical skill available, and with trade and industry at their last gasp? Projects for such an electrification are in process of development in Holland, and they have been discussed in England, and in those densely populated and industrially highly developed centres one can imagine them as successful, economical and altogether beneficial. But their application to Russia is an altogether greater strain upon the constructive imagination."

**His "Strategic Retreat" in 1921.**

In addressing the Russian Assembly of Political Education in 1921, Lenin, for the first time, made a partial admission of defeat and error in the Bolshevist governmental policy, although throwing the blame for the economic collapse mainly on the civil wars.

"In part," he said, "under the influence of military problems which were showered upon us and of the seemingly desperate condition in which the republic found itself under the influence of these circumstances, we made the mistake of deciding to pass immediately to communistic production and distribution.

"We decided that the peasants, according to the system of requisition of surplus, would give us the needed quantity of bread, and we should distribute it to the factories and workshops and arrive at communistic production and distribution. I cannot say that we drew up thus definitely and clearly any such plan, but we acted in that spirit.

"This, I am sorry to say, is a fact. I say I am sorry because an experience which did not take long has convinced us of the mistakenness of the proceeding, which was in contradiction to what we had previously written in regard to the transition from capitalism to socialism and has convinced us that without passing through a phase of socialistic supervision and control you cannot rise even to the first degree of communism.

"In theoretical literature, from 1918 on, when the problems of taking over authority came up and were revealed by the Bolsheviki before the whole people our literature emphasized precisely the need of a long and complicated transition through socialistic supervision from a capitalistic society to even an approach to a communistic society.

"This, in a way, was forgotten by us when we had to take the necessary steps toward construction in the midst of the fever of civil war. Our new economic policy is in substance a consequence of the fact that, in this respect, we met with a bad defeat and have undertaken a strategic retreat. Before they have thrashed us definitely, let us retreat and construct everything over again, but more solidly.

"There can be no doubt of the fact that we suffered an economic defeat on the economic front, and the defeat was severe; and we are raising quite consciously the question of a new economic policy. Naturally it is inevitable that a part of our comrades should fall into a very disturbed, almost panic-stricken, state of mind. These people will begin to relapse into a feeling of panic on account of the retreat. That is unavoidable."

The main features of the new policy as outlined later by Lenin included "the partial restoration of freedom of trade in agricultural products, abandonment of the practice of unrestricted requisition of labor and the substitution of a fixed labor tax, abandonment of uniform wages for employes of the same grade in enterprises operated by the State and the substitution of compensation according to the service rendered; leasing to private individuals of certain industrial establishments hitherto controlled by the State."

Attempts of the Soviet Government to interest American capitalists and manufacturers in Russia had failed, both because of lack of support from the American Government and because an exploring party of American manufacturers came to the conclusion that Russia had nothing with which to pay them except promises. When hope to tempt this country to resume trade was at an end, the Soviet Government made its plea for provisions, which resulted in the sending of the American Relief Administration to Russia and the feeding of millions in that way.

In the effort to start business and manufacture and reopen foreign trade, many compromises were struck with foreign capitalists, and Lenin's later policy has been described as a retreat from all his textbook principles.

During the latter part of his active life Lenin was the leader of this movement in Russia to resume trade relations with foreign Governments. The granting of concessions to foreign capital within the last two years has been largely due to his influence. It is a dramatic coincidence that his death was announced on the same day that a Labor Government committed to a recognition of and trade with Soviet Russia, assumed power in Great Britain, with which Lenin had been most anxious to trade.

The initiation of the "Nep," or the new economic policy, and the encouragement of foreign trade with capitalist as well as socialist countries were the last great things done by Lenin. He insisted that these steps were not a return to capitalism. In a speech at the Communist Party Congress on March 30, 1922, he declared that the "Nep" had been only a retreat, and that "the retreat is now finished."

When he made this speech Lenin was already on the verge of breaking down. He had collapsed early in the month after addressing a meeting of metal workers, and had been taken to his country place. Despite previous announcements that he would head the Russian delegation at the Genoa Economic Conference, he was unable to attend when the rest of the delegation left late in March.

From this time until his death Lenin, although he remained the titular head of the Russian Government, was obliged to give over the active leadership of affairs, except for brief intervals in which he was able to return to Moscow, only to be driven back to the country again by the recurrence of his illness.

Lenin's physicians admitted in June, 1922, that the Premier had suffered an apoplectic stroke late in the previous month. It was also announced at this time that Lenin had undergone an operation for the removal of a bullet with which he had been shot by Fanny Kaplan in 1918.

**Resumed Work Till Relapse Came.**

In the Fall of 1922 Lenin again returned to his desk in Moscow. He appeared in good health and seemed to make a point of seeing strangers to convince them that reports that he was at the end of his rope were unfounded. This return to activity, however, lasted only a few months. Early last January it was announced that Lenin had had a relapse, and was again at death's door.

An ominous silence reigned for two months, when it was officially announced that Lenin had suffered another stroke, and that he had difficulty in speaking as well as in moving his right arm and leg.

Since then it has been only a question of time. Last April Lenin's physicians announced that they had detected a catarrhal affection of his left lung in addition to his other ailments. In May plans were considered for his removal to the Crimea for the sake of the warm climate, but they were not carried out. Acting President Kamenief, addressing the Communist Party of Moscow, announced last June that Lenin was improving.

There has been very little about Lenin in the news from Russia in the last few months until very recently, when there have been hints of discussion among the Communists as to who his successor would be.

## RYKOFF IS ELECTED TO SUCCEED LENIN

**Announcement Made of His Appointment as Chairman of Federal Commissars.**


By Wireless to The New York Times

MOSCOW, Feb. 2.—Alexis Ivahovitch Rykoff has been appointed President of the Council of Commissars in Lenin's place, with the Ukrainian Chubar and Georgian Orkalasvili assistants.

Rykoff, former head of the Supreme Council of National Economy, an old revolutionary and a friend of Lenin, is of pure Russian extraction, an engineer by profession, and a man of great perseverance and industry, but no outstanding capacity.

Less widely known or popular than Lenin, Trotsky, Kemenief and Kalinin, he has shown during a year or more, as one of Lenin's three substitutes, administrative qualities of a high order. Last Summer already Rykoff was gradually assuming the position of "chairman" in the discussions of the Political Bureau which is the real Government of Russia. Quietly and imperceptibly it came about. He would say, "Comrades, we are wasting time. Let's get down to brass tacks and decide one way or the other."

Physically he is tall, slim, dark, with a pale face and short dark goatee. Like most Bolsheviks, he is a fluent speaker but his oratory is marred by a slight stammer. Last Summer when he opened the Moscow Agricultural Exhibition he stumbled sadly over "Association of Soviet Socialist Republics," which it was unhappily necessary to mention several times. Kemenief will be named head of the Council for Labor and Defense.

Most interesting of all is the forthcoming appointment of Dzerzhinsky as head of the Supreme Council of National Economy in Rykoff's place. Dzerzhinsky is not only the creator and chief of the dreaded Cheka but the extraordinarily successful reorganizer of the Russian railroad system.

February 3, 1924

# THE HEIRS OF LENIN

***The Ruling Triumvirate of Kamenev, Zinoviev and Stalin, and Who's Who Among the Other Soviet Leaders***

*The world is watching Russia, more intently than ever, for she is about to choose the successors of Lenin. What follows is an intimate picture of the outstanding personalities today in the Soviet Republic. It is written by a man who is still in Russia, and whose name, for obvious reasons, cannot be given. For twenty years he has known the men whom he describes, and he has been in a position to observe first hand the course of events in Russia.*

What does the administrative machinery of Soviet Russia look like behind the scenes? And what are the relative positions of the leading personalities and factions, within the Bolshevist political "general staff"? These questions may be answered without difficulty.

Every oligarchy is supposed to be made up of a number of concentric circles the last of which represents the exact centre, the very core of the regime. Thus, while Lenin had been that core until his physical failure, his place had been occupied for some time by a triumvirate of successors, acting, so to speak, as his political heirs. This triumvirate, which is still the core, consists of Kamenev, Zinoviev and Stalin. With the death of Sverdlof they became Lenin's closest political lieutenants. In the name of Lenin's mere shadow, these three men practically ruled the Communist Party and, through that, all of Russia. Access to the stricken chief had been virtually monopolized by these three men, and they were regarded as his closest and most trusted aids. They acted as the conveyers and interpreters of his wishes, counsels and instructions; and some evil tongues insist that they were even worse than careless conveyers, very often. Of course, they were absolutely free to interpret their chief as they saw fit.

However that may be, the fact remains that they were accepted by the party as the genuine spokesmen of Lenin.

But what of the future? As long as Lenin lived and the state of his health permitted him to appear in public on the most important and solemn occasions, that sufficed for all practical purposes. For it is almost inconceivable how unchallenged was the sway this man exercised over the Bolshevist ranks! They looked up to him as to some idol, and even his closest collaborators, with but few exceptions, appeared as mere nothings, when compared with the authority he wielded.

The last time that Lenin had one of those "bright spells" and was able to return for a short period to the affairs of state, he surprised everybody by his cheerful, vigorous manner, joking and laughing a great deal. At an extraordinary meeting, attended by members of the Council of People's Commissaries, the General Committee of the Communist Party, the Supreme Council of National Economy, numerous representatives of various other departments and organizations, and all kinds of individual experts—a meeting called to settle a great many disputed matters, including the famous Urquhart concessions case—there was an interesting chance to observe the process by which important decisions of the Soviet Government are arrived at.

The first thing to attract attention was the fact that the speakers did not seem to be addressing the audience at all, but Lenin personally. He, in turn, acted as if this were the natural thing to do. Some of the speakers he would encourage with remarks such as "That's right," "Correct," "Quite right," etc., deciding, in a tone that seemed plainly to brook no contradiction, what part of the speaker's topic was to be considered as definitely settled and what was to be discussed further. Other speakers, again, he would curb, and challenge their statements unceremoniously, in the same peremptory fashion.

His conduct of the meeting was of a strict, military style; often he would announce a simple, arbitrary rule like this: "The speaker has two minutes, his opponent two minutes, discussion is superfluous; we shall now vote." The speaker and his opponent, expecting anything but this, would struggle for two minutes in vain attempts to say something important in the defense of their propositions, and then Lenin would hand down his Presidential opinion, proposing its unanimous adoption by all who had the right to vote on the matter.

In this way it happened that Lenin literally "pushed through" at the same meeting the plea for the private syndicate of the timber industry, permitting foreign capital to share against the strenuous opposition of some very prominent Communists, in its organization. On the other hand, he vetoed, just as arbitrarily, the Urquhart concession, which had already been considered as good as granted. This was done very simply, in the following words:

"Well, let us, then, wait for better offers. This Urquhart scheme is already a step forward, and others will follow. We are not in such great need of it just now, and we are strong enough to afford the luxury of waiting a little longer. We now take up our next question."

I had occasion after that to talk to some prominent Englishmen who were fully informed of the impression that had been created in their own country by the failure of the Urquhart plan. "Great Britain," one of them told me, "is not interested in the Urquhart-deal, anyway. And, besides, Urquhart does not play in his own country the important part with which people in Russia so often credit him. In this case he acted upon his own initiative and at his own risk. I must say, however, that this unexpected decision, coming as it did after your authorized representative, Krassin, had given his consent—quite within the bounds of his plenipotentiary powers—to this so long and so carefully prepared compromise plan, will make us lose all further interest in trying to restore mutual intercourse.

"We expect the State, just as much as any individual citizen, to be as good as its word, and it must not break it if it hopes to have any dealings with outsiders. As matters stand now, a person really never can tell with whom he is dealing here and what surprises there may be in store for him. After this, no serious business man will care to have anything to do with you. And as for Krassin, his prestige among us has been hopelessly destroyed now."

Still more characteristic is probably the fact that Krassin himself, notwithstanding this heavy blow dealt by Lenin to his prestige, declared shortly after the Twelfth Communist Congress, last April, while speaking to a large gathering of friends, that he was staking all his hope only upon a possible recovery--

*(Continued)*

of Lenin's health. "Only Vladimir Ilitch," said Krassin, "has the courage to follow the path which, under existing conditions, would be the only one to lead us out of this blind alley in which we find ourselves. His greatest asset is the fact that he is, in truth, a master opportunist. Just think: Who else would have dared at that particular moment (i. e., in the Spring of 1921—Translator's note) to propose the new economic policy? No other man that I can think of! And if any one but himself should have dared take a step like this, why, he would have been nagged to death as a spineless compromiser, perhaps even a dangerous renegade and traitor. Even if a whole faction composed of our most prominent members should have attempted to lead the party along this road, they would have gained nothing except splitting the ranks of our organization. But Lenin was followed without question; he was opposed by no one. Ah, if he could only get well again, everything would be altogether different!"

If we see even Krassin himself afflicted with that peculiar mental twist which made old grandmother Nanilla (a character in Nekrassov's "Forgotten Village") place all her confidence in the lord of the manor, saying, "Just wait till the master gets back, he will settle our dispute!"—what may be expected of the Bolshevist rank and file? All of their recent past has been one continuous chain of adventures, desperate situations and risky undertakings of one kind or another. On more than one occasion they found themselves standing upon the verge of the yawning abyss, looking down into its depths with a shudder, while the abyss, in turn, was searching their own souls: and more than once they had already resigned themselves to an inevitable end.

Thus far, however, something or other has always been sure to turn up at the last moment to save them from utter perdition. Mostly, this was due to the unforeseen mistakes of their enemies. Lenin's happy trait—not to abandon hope till the very last, or, in any event, to keep it alive among his followers—often seemed under these circumstances, in the eyes of his loyal supporters, as nothing short of prophetic inspiration.

"We can follow Ilitch blindfolded; he can foresee all things! How many times have our insurgents opposed him, only to see him come out victorious in the end, and compelled themselves to admit that they had 'made a mistake!' We have been in situations that it seemed as if nothing more hopeless could be possible, yet he never failed to pull us through safely, and he will surely do it again."

This manner of reasoning I have had occasion to observe among the Bolshevist rank and file, not once and not twice, but all the time.

It will now be easily seen what it meant to be governing "in the name of Lenin's mere shadow." In order to do this, it was, of course, indispensable that the reliability of the men who acted as the executors of the political testament of that "living corpse" should not be subject to the slightest doubt. At the Twelfth Communist Congress, however, they came dangerously near being discredited. An article of Lenin's, directed against one of the triumvirs, Stalin, was making the rounds among the delegates. This article attacked Stalin in such vitriolic terms that it seemed as if Lenin were bent on killing him politically. There was a great deal of excitement, and finally a signed statement was obtained from Lenin "rehabilitating" his sinning lieutenant and asking that he be treated with absolute confidence.

In this way the incident was closed. But it proves that the triumvirate cannot hope to feel quite as secure as the leader whom it represents. Even with Lenin alive it was bound to reckon with such influential party "bosses" as Trotsky, Dzerzhinsky and Bukharin, who may now not that he is dead prove strong enough to undermine the authority of the triumvirate.

However, let us consider the triumvirate itself.

Zinoviev was once nicknamed "gramophone for Lenin's records." For a long time he enjoyed neither love nor authority among the Bolsheviki, and it required all the persistence of Lenin himself to overcome this general antagonism to Zinoviev and drag him through to the Central Committee. The moral aspects of Zinoviev's personality are far from causing enthusiastic admiration. * * * People who have watched him in "action" think him a good deal of a coward. On one occasion only did he dare come out openly against Lenin: that was during the November revolution. The scale had suddenly tipped against the Reds as Kerensky was reported to be marching on Petrograd at the head of a loyal army, and other unpleasant events had occurred just then. And thus it was that Zinoviev, like a drowning person catching at a straw, decided to grasp at the idea of a compromise with the hated moderate Socialist parties.

However, no sooner was the danger safely past than he became, without the slightest compunction, their bitterest enemy and persecutor, far surpassing in ferocity not only Volodarski, but even Uritsky. For his momentary insubordination he was now making liberal amends by redoubled zeal in the inauguration of Lenin's policies.

This is the real explanation why Zinoviev, and not Trotsky or Radek, both of whom are far more capable, but also more independent characters, was pushed through by the chief to fill the position of President of the Communist International. Gradually Zinoviev's prestige increased; he grew to be more self-confident; and his oratorical skill, too, seems to have improved a little. Of the members of the triumvirate, he is undoubtedly the most "convenient" to his comrades. Having been presented with Petrograd as a kind of princely "appanage," and busy with his work in the International, he always manages to go hand-in-hand with his colleagues and adjusts himself to their policies without friction.

Kamenev is the most tractable and diplomatic member of the triumvirate. The lessons in opportunism which Lenin has been teaching have appealed very strongly to his nature. His opponents think him double faced, and they call him a "sweet-spoken Jesuit." Undoubtedly he lacks strength of character. It is likely that he is in fact less double faced than submissive and fickle. He would like to please all, and he is lavish with promises which he is unable, and sometimes none too willing, to carry out. And what if he "keeps the word of promise to the ear, but breaks it to the hope"? What can he do against his more stiff-necked comrades? All he can do in such circumstances is to wash his hands in innocence like Pilate.

He is always ready to follow the line of least resistance. This sometimes puts him into a rather awkward situation. During the World War, when he was surprised by the Czarist police at a secret pacifist gathering of Bolsheviki, he wriggled and turned during his trial in such a way as to lose a great deal of the respect he had enjoyed, not only within the party, but even among outsiders. He was reproached for having shown too little political courage and then lacking personal dignity.

In the trying period between March and November, 1917, he did not show any greater strength of character. But when the political horizon finally cleared for the Bolsheviki he became invaluable to them in more than one sense—he knew better than any one else how to "grease the creaking axles"; he understood the art of getting along with everybody; he knew how to be amiable and charming. Indeed, he knows just how to stroke the fur of stubborn comrades, finally coaxing them, as one does mettlesome horses, into place between the shafts. He is very useful in maintaining contact with the outside world, to which he is always glad to present Bolshevism in its "most reasonable" and attractive aspects.

People who have known Kamenev previously cannot help observing that he has greatly added to his political stature and that he has become a past master in the political game. In short, he represents a perfect example of the astute politician, somewhat feminine by nature, with a hint of treachery and much inclined to play in the game of politics the part of a "lady pleasant with everybody," as Gogol would have said.

Stalin, or to give him his real name, Dzhugashvili, is less widely known than his comrades, but is undoubtedly their superior as far as strength of character is concerned. His is the most vivid personality in the triumvirate. Although less endowed with purely superficial accomplishments than his colleagues, he has advanced through persistence, firmness of purpose and mental alertness. He possesses to the superlative degree the gift for pulling, behind the scenes, all the wires that have been carefully and skilfully connected with the living puppets cast for one part or another. Whenever the need arises for quietly preparing the ground within the party for a certain purpose, to create the desirable atmosphere; to help or to harm some particular individual; to undermine a reputation or enhance a person's prestige; to inaugurate and carry through within the ranks of the party a regular campaign against some particular tendency or faction—in all such undertakings Stalin is an expert hand.

He shows traits that are generally associated with a typical Oriental politician being crafty, tenacious, determined, and knowing how to bring people around to his views either quite imperceptibly or by undisguised aggressiveness. Selfish and quite conscious of his own importance this scheming politician can on occasion be very temperamental and bold, not disinclined to a certain adventurousness. His was almost the greatest part of all in plotting the November revolution. An indefatigable worker of the type to be seen in general staffs, he does not loom so large in the public eye; but at his desk he certainly amounts to a great deal more than the more showy and picturesque "talkers," Kamenev and Zinoviev.

Such is our "centre of centres," our fundamental, governing triumvirate. Of the other prominent persons in the party it is with Trotsky, Dzerzhinsky and Bukharin, partly also with Radek, on the one hand, and—especially in recent months—with Krassin, on the other, that the triumvirate has had to reckon—and presumably must still reckon if it survives.

Trotsky's place is in the second parallel circle, as represented by the Political Bureau of the Communist Party, without whose sanction nothing is done. There exists between him and the triumvirate something like an alliance. As long as Lenin was still able to work Trotsky was a brilliant second to him. Twice he attempted to play an independent part, to defend his own position, but was forced on both occasions to retreat and surrender. Ever since he has acted so much more carefully that he did not even try to take advantage of Lenin's virtual retirement to step into his place.

None the less it must be said that, up to a certain point, Trotsky follows his own lights. He feels strongly the importance of his position, which made him the next powerful leader alongside the living Lenin, and he never misses an opportunity to impress others with a proper sense of "respectful distance." The rank and file of the party accepts this without complaint. But higher up, among the "staff officers" of the party, Trotsky is not liked, only feared. He is harsh, domineering, prone to be peremptory, unkind and vindictive by nature. Those who knew him years ago can observe how much he has changed as a public speaker. Previously, he would be at his very best in shooting off temperamental, dazzling oratorical fireworks; today, on the contrary, he has elaborated a style that appears to be in keeping with his exalted rank, deliberate and weighty in tone solemnly slow, ponderous and hard.

His popularity is still as great as it used to be among the military experts, especially those inherited from the Czarist army. These persons cannot find enough praise for the firmness with which he has weeded out in the Red Army the public meeting habit of the first Bolshevist period, sternly suppressing every attempt at restoring an electoral system of choosing officers, as well as at discussing orders from superiors, instead of executing them without hesitation, as was the case before. He is, furthermore, praised for the ruthlessness with which he has restored the old iron discipline in the army. And, finally, he is given credit for having put an end to all manner of "Socialist Utopias" about popular armament, national militia, and other such ideas, and for simply going back to the usual type of regular army, kept in barracks by conscription, with the only difference that, instead of serving an autocratic Emperor, the army now serves the autocratic Soviet of People's Commissaries.

Trotsky knows very well how to take proper advantage of this sentiment in military circles. It may be that his lack of victories in foreign wars (also, perhaps, his Jewish descent, which is still held against him in many circles) hinders him from assuming a stronger and autocratic position in the State. To be sure, a mere Corsican was able to become a Napoleon, but this was possible only because that Corsican had known how to win the crown of martial glory and how to lean upon a victorious army covered with fame and rich in victories. Trotsky is perfectly well aware that he cannot boast of such success, and he is therefore wise enough to curb his vaulting ambitions.

Dzerzhinsky is another leader of vast influence and power. This man represents virtually a Communistic Torquemada, a saintly executioner, an immaculately pure shedder of blood. There is absolutely nothing Russian about him, for he is a Pole not only by birth, but in his whole psychology. Speaking for myself, I should say that I consider him abnormal, though the abnormality is not the kind for which it would be easy to send a person to the insane asylum. His appears to be that form of insanity which makes it so easy to send people, without the slightest moral scruples, to prison, to hard labor, to torture, to the executioner, or to slow death in some remote concentration camp where all the horrors of Schluesselburg Fortress, Cayenne, and all the Devil's Islands of the world pale into insignificance by comparison.

It is really a fact that he is absolutely unselfish and honest. He forced himself and all the members of his household to live with truly Spartan rigor solely on the official Government rations ("payok") at a time when it was scarcely possible to subsist, and nobody, in fact, did subsist, on thhese rations; this, when all the members of the Administration, even the frugal Lenin himself, had to make extensive use of private shipments of foodstuffs and all kinds of testimonial gifts presented to them by various regular army and Cheka regiments, &c.

There is no doubt that he harbors no personal enmity against any particular victim of his ruthlessness, and he is really a very pleasant person in private life, studiously correct in manners, and often even chivalrous, like so many Poles, and this by no means in the merely pretentious, outward sense of the word. Yet he is implacable like a soulless machine, like fate and destiny itself! He showed his organizing talent not only in that first product of his genius, the Cheka, but also in extirpating graft on the railroads, where corruption had spread into every part of this arterial system of the country.

One can see that Dzerzhinsky has suffered much in his life, that the iron has entered his heart, snapping something within his soul, and that the loss of this little screw—whatever it may have been—has turned him into a sinister monster, as if in diabolical mockery of the by-name of "Golden Heart" glibly bestowed upon him by that idle talker, Lunacharski.

Of Bukharin it must be said that he is a demagogue of clearest water, a turbulent, reckless and ruthless character, but a hard worker and far from being a fool. He is very democratic in his personal life, having few demands and no attachment for material things. Once he tried to start a row against Lenin himself, but "steep roads have tamed the fiery horse," as they say in Russia. He has now subsided a great deal and allowed himself to be backed into the shafts. At the Twelfth Communist Party Congress one could see clearly that his ostensible "left" criticism of the party centre was in fact calculated very cunningly to advance the interests of this very faction.

Whenever it is attacked by the "rights," that is, the moderate, businesslike Communists known as "Krassinites," for its stubbornly uncompromising attitude toward the urgent demands of practical life, and the lessons of practical experience, we can see Bukharin jump into the fray as if some one had pulled him by a string, and he forthwith assails the "centre" with charges of the very opposite nature. Thus the centre finds itself compelled to neutralize one faction with the other. As for Bukharin's irresistible "turbulence," a special safety valve has been provided for that: he has been put in charge of the affairs of the Communist Youths' League, with its rabid anti-religious campaign, after the fashion of the French Revolutionist atheists. And here he finds himself in his native element. The following incident, trifling in itself, serves as a characteristic illustration:

When Vandervelde, Liebknecht and Rosenfeld arrived at Moscow (during the famous trial of the Social Revolutionists last year—Translator's note) Bukharin in person, leading a riotous mob of Communists to demonstrate their hostility to the arrivals, practiced his skill as a shrill whistler by using two fingers in his mouth, like some street rowdy. * * * It must be admitted, however, that he does not lack some ability as a theoretician of Communism. No better man could really be found to watch over the purity of the Communist doctrine, at the head of the daily paper of the central committee of the party, the Pravda.

The one who is most remote from the concrete problems of every-day life is Radek. On more than one occasion I heard him say that his mind was working too much on "Western" lines to suit it to Russian conditions. His chief interest lies in problems of industrial, proletarian Socialism. But in a peasant country like Russia all these problems are too intimately linked with rural problems, and here he is no specialist, here he feels not at all at home. He, therefore, gladly permits his Russian comrades to attend to these questions. His particular sphere of activity lies in the domain of foreign relations, especially as represented by the Communist Internationale, in so far as it deals with the West.

All these people, however, are only "side horses," after all. As for the real "shaft horses," and pretty mettlesome at that, Trotsky and Dzerzhinsky alone may be classed as such. Besides, the former has in his control the Red Army, and the latter, the Cheka. These two represent the most formidable forces that will have to be reckoned with in case of any trouble. They are therefore to be taken into consideration above all.

Altogether different is the situation of that other great Bolshevik, Krassin. Thus far, there has seemed to be no solid influence behind him. And yet he kept on advancing all the time, simply because he has been able to make himself the spokesman of an imponderable, yet most powerful force—the logic of life itself. To the Bolsheviki this logic appears in the formula of a consistently carried out "down-grade movement with our hands on the brakes." The successors of Lenin, as well as all those who were most closely linked with him in authority, are gliding down this grade against their will, struggling against it with might and main forever hopeful of being able to halt the movement somewhere along the road and entrenching themselves in some strong position from which not a step further should have to be conceded, in order to make such a position serve, after that famous "breathing space," as the starting point of a fresh offensive.

Krassin, on the other hand, considers all such talk as a mere survival of Communistic conservatism, and he insists upon a consistently followed, uninterrupted course towards private economic enterprise, attracting foreign investments, and favoring peaceable co-operation with the capitalistic neighbors of Soviet Russia. And he stands, accordingly, for the ruthless suppression of everything in the Soviet methods that may hinder such a development.

Now, as a matter of fact, Krassin's views are coming to be accepted more and more, but not without tremendous struggles, impediments, delays and side-trackings and postponements at every stage, often nullifying the effect of the measures finally permitted to be taken. Krassin represents the common, irrefutable logic of the evolution going on in the ranks of the Soviet Administration, which resembles in this respect the Termidor of the French Revolution.

Naturally the dogmatical conscience of Simon Pure Communism is at odds with that logic. Theoretically, as far as mere words are concerned, they have been getting the best of Krassin, leaving him in the minority, yet the very Bolsheviki who have been voting against him can be heard now and then ruminating sadly: "Still, Krassin is the only one who has any carefully planned and well thought out program!" As a matter of fact, Krassin is favored by all the "economically thinking" Bolsheviki; but to make public admission of that, or even to admit it to themselves—is something to which only a few can bring themselves.

Krassin has too much of a reputation as a heretic. He did not sympathize with the November revolution. He only joined the party afterward, as a practical man of affairs anxious to go on with his work and seeing that the only way to do so would be to accept that revolution and make the best of it.

Nevertheless, there is being formed around the nucleus of Krassin's ideas a certain group which, although not yet quite clearly defined and formulated, places great hopes in Krassin. This group avoids all open expression of opinion, being mortally afraid lest it be mistaken for another one of those "conspiracies," for the powers that be are only too suspicious and watchful.

Such are our leading personalities. And such are their mutual relationships. We have seen that they have their individual shadings, their personal disagreements. But we must once for all remember this: All these differences of opinions and policies are only "family affairs," and they do not in the least prevent the "family" from facing the outside world as a compact block. Nay, more; in the matter of granting political liberty to the people, there is absolutely no difference between the extremly "left" Bukharin, "right" Krassin, and middle-course Kamenev. They are all exactly alike in that they take no stock in democracy. The only question on which they differ is that of how best to carry out their program, essentially bureaucratic as far as methods are concerned. None of these men deserves the slightest confidence on the part of those who hope for a political emancipation in Russia. In this respect one of them is not better than another. Only worse.

Outside of Russia, as far as we are able here to judge, some hopes are occasionally expressed for a split in the Bolshevist Party, or for the victory of some faction or tendency that may open vast possibilities of peaceful evolution away from the dictatorship toward democracy. All such hopes are absolutely baseless. Within the party there exists no force capable of fundamentally changing it. It is under the sway of a conservative, stabilized spirit. And this spirit is still further upheld by the instinct of self-preservation, which makes these people hold on tightly to one another and tells them plainly that regeneration is impossible without a split, and a split means death. There will be no split. There can be only a chopping off. Everything that is independent, everything that will dare to start any serious opposition, will be suppressed at its very inception and cut off without mercy.

The rank and file of the party will remain intellectually browbeaten and accustomed to being reduced to a "common denominator" by those higher up. You will perhaps say that such a party can have no future. I shall not dispute that. But it can rest satisfied with the present, as long as it succeeds, by taking good advantage of all circumstances in prolonging the present indefinitely.

February 3, 1924

# COMMUNISTS RENEW FIGHT WITH TROTSKY

**By WALTER DURANTY.**


By Wireless to THE NEW YORK TIMES.

MOSCOW, May 28.—Last Winter's controversy between Trotsky and the other Communist Party leaders was renewed at yesterday's session of the Congress, although in much milder terms than six months ago.

In a speech on Saturday Zinovieff had invited those members of the party who had been disapproved by the special party conference summoned early in the Spring to discuss the controversy to come forward at the present Congress and admit their errors frankly. Trotsky, evidently regarding this as a challenge, yesterday attempted to explain his position and the criticism he though fit to make. Last Winter he offered a somewhat caustic distinction between the duty of all members of the party to follow the party decisions without questioning and the duty of the individual member to point out what they honestly believed to be errors in the party policy. On the latter basis they made criticisms, but not as adversaries charged with a spirit of disloyalty or "factionism."

Though greeted with applause at the beginning and end of his speech, Trotsky failed to carry his audience with him. Succeeding speakers assailed his defense. Uglanof, an influential party worker in Leningrad and Nijni Novgorod, replied it was not a question of the duty of individual members of the party, but of the real attitude of Trotsky himself, who was not a simple member of the party, not a soldier in the ranks, but one of its greatest leaders, its General. Others followed the same line and made it clear how MOMENTOUS to Soviet Russia is the question whether Trotsky will drop his independent policy, even though he thinks it better than the policy adopted by the party, and co-operate in carrying out the latter's policy to the best of his ability, because that, it was declared, is what Communist Party discipline means.

In concluding speeches today Stalin and Zinovieff reiterated their opinion that Trotsky was wrong in trying to defend his independent line and appealed to him and the rest of the former opposition henceforth to work hand in hand with the party. A resolution to this effect was carried unanimously.

It is now evident that behind the whole controversy lay one of the present subjects of dissension between the Russian Bolsheviki and the Mensheviki. The former always insisted that criticism of any proposed policy should be changed to enthusiastic support in the event that policy was adopted by the party. The Mensheviki claimed a greater degree of latitude for individual judgment, thus leading to divisions and "factions" which reduced them to impotence in comparison with the iron bound unity of the Bolsheviki when the time for action came. Trotsky was never a Menshevik, though not a member of the Bolshevist party until 1917, but he occupied a sort of independent position of his own between the two. Now he is playing true to his individualist type in trying to defend by dialectic, his standpoint of last Winter, which aimed at reconciling rigid party discipline with the right of criticism. But his older Bolshevist colleagues of the Lenin school won't admit this distinction. Hence the accusations of "Menshevist heresy" they have launched against him.

May 29, 1924

# PRIVATE TRADERS QUIT ENTERPRISES IN RUSSIA

## Soviet Campaign for State and Cooperative Business Drives Out Small Capitalists.

MOSCOW, June 17.—Reports from many provincial centres say hundreds of private traders and wholesale and retail business houses are suspending operations owing to the Government's determination to support only State and cooperative enterprises.

At Vitebsk some forty firms have closed and at Vladimir twenty-five traders have ceased business. Fifteen per cent. of the entire number of independent commercial firms at Yaroslav are liquidating, while at Irkutsk private trading has ceased altogether. Similar reports have been received from Tiflis and other Caucasian centres.

The refusal of the State and cooperative concerns to sell merchandise to private wholesale dealers leaves the independent business men no alternative except to close their doors. In Moscow and other large cities State and coöperative stores are rapidly supplanting concerns supported by private capital.

June 18, 1924

# SAYS SOVIET INDUSTRY HAS HAD GREAT GAINS

## Dzerjinsky Reports That Subsidy This Year Can Be Cut Two-Thirds.

Copyright, 1924, by The New York Times Company.
Special Cable to THE NEW YORK TIMES.

MOSCOW, June 19.—An optimistic report of Russian industry has been given to the Council of Commissars by Dzerjinski, President of the Supreme Council of National Economy. He declared that whereas last year industry received a State subsidy of 133,000,000 gold rubles, the present year it required only 64,000,000. Furthermore, in the current year the State should get back from industry 40,000,000 profit—including 21,000,000 from the textile trust—reducing the total subsidy to 24,000,000 against last year's 133,000,000.

This marked alleviation of the national budget Dzerjinski attributed to an improvement in banking and credit facilities, which this year had begun to assume in Russia position of assistance to industry similar to that played by private finance in Western countries. Thus, instead of 250,000,000, which represented the total bank credits to industry at the beginning of the current fiscal year, the figure six months later, on April 1, was 350,000,000. If the harvest doesn't fall materially below expectations, Dzerjinski concluded, the only branch of State industry that will need a subsidy next year will be the metallurgical, although the State will still have to assist the building and electrification program.

The harvest prospects, though less hopeful than six weeks ago, appear better than at the beginning of June. There have been heavy rains in Southern Ukraine, which quite removed the fear of a crop failure in that important sector and reports from Siberia are excellent.

South of the Volga is much below average, and in the Province of Tsaritsin the crop is virtually ruined by fifty days of drought. But on the whole the harvest will not be far below expectation, perhaps 3,200,000,000 poods instead of 3,500,000,000.

June 20, 1924

# SPEEDING UP LABOR UNDER SOVIET RULE

## Coal Mines and Steel Works Report Greater Productivity in Recent Months.

By WALTER DURANTY.

Copyright, 1924, by The New York Times Company.
Special Cable to THE NEW YORK TIMES.

MOSCOW, Aug. 24.—The Bolsheviki appear to have taken a step toward overcoming what are perhaps the most serious obstacles in the path of the Socialist State, low productivity of labor, lack of initiative and the bureaucracy which generally characterize State-run enterprises.

Since early Spring this year, Dzerjinski, former Chief of the Cheka, who is one of the strongest personalities in the new Russia, has been wrestling with this problem, as President of the Supreme Economic Council. Labor unions here, as elsewhere, resent attempts to speed up the productivity of their members. But here they are so influential as to have resisted them successfully until Dzerjinski was appointed.

It is announced today that the Don coal mines since the beginning of August have increased their weekly output by more than 30 per cent., although in same period the number of workers has increased only 4 per cent. In the operating year of 1922-3 the Don mines produced 305,000,000 poods of coal [a pood is thirty-six pounds]. In 1923-4 the output was 485,000,000 poods. For the coming year it will be 600,000,000, the official statement says. The number of "white collar" employes in the mines is now within a fraction of the pre-war figure.

What the reduction of the productivity of labor means and what Dzerjinski has to contend with may be gathered from the experience of a large steel plant in the same region. The per capita production is almost exactly half that of 1913. Although it must be remembered that the day was then twelve hours long and is now eight. In this factory wages, including compulsory insurance, &c., amount to 81 per cent. of the pre-war figure. Here, too, however, an improvement in individual productivity is noticeable—from 10 to 13 per cent.—for the past two months.

Almost all branches of industry estimate an increased production for the coming year of from 10 to 35 per cent.

There are better reports, too, about the harvest, which Premier Rykov, in a speech delivered yesterday, put at the total figure (for grain) of 2,640,000,000 poods, which, with the 150,000,000 pood surplus from last year, will amply meet the needs of the population in the bad harvest region and leave a margin for export.

August 25, 1924

# BOLSHEVIKI ACCUSE TROTSKY OF HERESY

## Stalin Charges War Minister With Trying to Appropriate the Mantle of Lenin.

## URGES WAR AGAINST HIM

MOSCOW, Nov. 27 (Associated Press).—The full text of the reports of Leo Kameneff and M. Stalin attacking War Minister Trotsky have just been published. These reports heretofore have been confined to the inner circle of the Communist Party.

Trotsky's career, prior to the 1917 revolution and during and after the Bolshevik coup d'état, is carefully surveyed in forty columns of printed matter. Both Kameneff and Stalin, the Soviet leaders, strive to show that Trotsky always has acted as a Menshevik and now has departed from pure Bolshevism and party idealism.

Kameneff explains that the Central Committee of the party was compelled to inaugurate a campaign against Trotsky because his recent book, "Lessons of the 1917 Revolution," was being published under the ostensible protection of the Communist Party and, coming from a member of the party's political bureau, which directs the work of the Communist International, the book creates a danger for the party.

It cannot, therefore, Kameneff says, be allowed to pass unchallenged. If no exception is taken to the book, he added, it might be accepted as a manual for young Communists and members of the Communist International.

### Stalin Charges "Heresy."

While Kameneff confined his general criticism of Trotsky to his own self-defense, Stalin, who is a member of the Executive Committee of the Communist Party, dwells unsparingly upon the War Minister's "heresy" and his alleged abandonment of orthodox Bolshevik principles. He accuses Trotsky of attempting to take Lenin's mantle for himself. He also urges members of the party to wage a relentless war against the military leader, as "otherwise Trotsky's ideas may become the concentration point for all non-proletarian elements who strive to disintegrate the proletarian dictatorship."

Although Trotsky's friends believe that the present movement is intended to render him politically innocuous, Stalin says he does not favor reprisals or harsh treatment of party opponents. He declares there is no danger in the present controversy of splitting the party, adding "We have only to struggle against Trotsky and eliminate his Menshevik ideas."

### Few Support Trotsky.

The whole campaign has been introduced, it is said, to avoid renewed dissension within the Communist ranks. Unlike last year's controversy, however, when Trotsky found support in many quarters, especially among the young Communists and military cadets, the War Minister this time is almost deserted. There are few even of his avowedly outspoken supporters who dare take up his defense in view of the all-powerful elements in the Communist Party which are arrayed against him.

Numerous resolutions are coming in daily from the provincial branches of the Communist Party pledging the fullest support to the Central Committee's attitude toward Trotsky. Following his tactics of last year, the War Minister maintains a discreet silence. He has not yet uttered a single word, either in speeches or in the press, and there are indications that he does not even attend to the ordinary routine of business in his office. The executive work of the War Council is now directed by M. Frunze, Trotsky's assistant.

Political observers seem to think that Trotsky's adversaries have scored a complete victory over the war chief, but they believe that the party leaders will not attempt to dethrone him altogether, for such a measure would undoubtedly produce a profound reaction among the rank and file of the army, who regard their leader very highly. Also deep resentment could be looked for among certain sections of the population which consider the War Minister the most able member of the present Government.

November 28, 1924

## CANCEL RED ELECTIONS WHEN UNSATISFACTORY

### Moscow Authorities Order 'Strictly Controlled' Polling Throughout All Russia



By Wireless to The New York Times

RIGA, Jan. 2—M. Kalinin, President of the Union of Soviet Republics, has signed a decree instructing the central executives of all the numerous republics of the union to cancel all elections and, under strict control, elect new Soviets in all places where recent elections had unsatisfactory results and where the electors who are not "class conscious" had elected candidates of whom the Communist authorities cannot approve.

This decree follows measures taken last November to avoid "mistakes" in the rural elections, the "unsatisfactory" results of which necessitated the postponement of the Soviet Congress from January to April.

From the point of view of the Government the elections have proved particularly difficult to direct, and elections have been going on for several months. The official announcement now explains that the authorities must quash not only the original elections but also subsequent new elections where results are insufficiently auspicious. The statement says:

"It is clear we must correct our blunders here. Let us speak plainly. We must hold new elections everywhere where elections turned out badly and where they gave undesirable results, regarded strictly from the standpoint of consolidating the Soviet authority."

By the side of these announcements the Soviet newspapers publish complaints that local Communists use pressure to compel the peasants to elect officially approved candidates, and curiously admonish the agents to use every possible means to guide the electors in their choice and combat every effort to abuse the "rights of free elections which the peasants enjoy."

January 3, 1925

## TROTSKY DROPPED FROM WAR COUNCIL

### He Is Warned That Defiance of Party Will Cost Him Other Places in Soviet System.

### REFUSES TO ADMIT ERRORS

MOSCOW, Jan. 18 (Associated Press).—Leon Trotsky will not be permitted to remain on the Soviet War Council, and he is warned that a continuance of disobedience will culminate in his being expelled from the Political Bureau and the Soviet Executive Committee.

These facts became known today in a semi-official communication issued here.

The communication says that at a plenary meeting of the Executive Committee and Control Commission of the Communist Party, held on Friday, it was decided, almost unanimously, first, to invite Trotsky to submit effectively to party discipline; second, that his retention on the War Council must be regarded as impossible, and, third, that the question of the further employment of Trotsky on the Executive Committee be postponed until the next party congress, with a warning that his continued disobedience would entail his removal from the Political Bureau and the Executive Committee.

According to the communication, Trotsky wrote to the committee regretting his inability, owing to his illness, to attend its session, and declaring that he had kept silence in order to spare the Communist Party. He vigorously denied he favored revising Leninism or that he belittled the rôle of Lenin.

Trotsky added that he, himself, regarded "Trotskyism" as ended politically, and said he had not foreseen that his book on the revolution would be made use of on the political platform. Regarding the accusations against him of lack of discipline, Trotsky wrote:

"I reply emphatically that I am ready for any task, in any post or outside any post and under any control imposed by my party. It is useless to emphasize, that after recent discussions, our cause necessitates that I should be relieved of my post of President of the Revolutionary War Council."

The resolution adopted by the commission declares that Trotsky's anti-Leninist views regarding the peasants constituted a special danger to the Communist Party, as his attitude had undermined the confidence of the peasants in the Soviet policy. Further, the resolution observes that Trotsky's letter fails to admit his errors and maintains his anti-Bolshevist attitude, thus making his submission a pure formality.

January 19, 1925

## BOLSHEVIKI ADOPT OLD WAGE SYSTEM

### Return to Piecework and Remove All Limits on Production and Workers' Earnings.



By Wireless to THE NEW YORK TIMES.

RIGA, Jan. 30.—During the last fortnight the Bolsheviki have decided to introduce unobtrusively several measures to invigorate the economic life of Soviet Russia, some of which are in striking contradiction to the doctrines they hitherto have professed.

The most noteworthy is perhaps the supreme trade unionist authority's scheme to raise the productivity of labor by enforcing the application of the piecework system as much as possible in all industries. The scheme explicitly removes all maximum production limits and consequent wage limits, and definitely expresses the hope the workers will increase both their output and earnings to an indefinite extent. Piecework payment, which in the realy years of the revolution the Bolsheviki condemned, gradually has crept in since they began a campaign a year ago to spur the workers to greater production as the only means of bringing prices down and saving Soviet industry from total ruin.

The Currency Department of the Soviet Government has decided to abolish the existing prohibition and henceforth allow private persons and enterprises to conclude agreements not only in Tchervontsi but also in foreign currencies.

The Central Committee of the Communist Party recently held a special meeting to consider ways and means of overcoming the widespread evil of non-payment of workers' wages, which they considered one of the chief obstacles to the increase of the industrial output because it fostered discontent among the workers and conflicts. The trust directorates' figures produced at the meeting show some progress has been made during the last few months in dealing with this problem.

On Jan. 1 Soviet industries, apart from chemical concerns, still owed their workers £312,000, whereas in October the arrears of wages amounted to £1,419,700 and in July £1,307,600. The greatest debtors to the workers were the metal industry and the Don coal mines.

The Soviet press announces the arrival at Leningrad from Birkenhead and London of the first cargoes of flour purchased abroad, amounting to 6,300 tons.

January 31, 1925

## STALIN PROMISES LAND TO PEASANTS



By Wireless to THE NEW YORK TIMES.

BERLIN, April 14.—According to reports from Moscow, Stalin, chief of the Communist Party, is promising the peasants great land reforms which may ultimately return land to private ownership. This step is regarded as a natural result of the economic reforms promising restoration to private ownership of factories, mines and houses and re-establishment of the freedom of trade.

Stalin's important announcement was made at a Moscow meeting of provincial representatives of the peasants. Among the complaints was the statement that the peasants would not plant crops or improve the land unless possession of the land for a long term of years was guaranteed. Stalin authorized the representatives to carry the message to their provinces that land would be granted to peasants for a period of at least twenty years and perhaps forty. He also stated there was a possibility of the land being returned to private ownership without restriction.

Representatives of the peasants asked Stalin how his promises could be fulfilled when such action was contrary to the Soviet Constitution. Stalin answered: "We wrote the Constitution. We can change it also."

Stalin also promised the peasants in addition the franchise and representation with privileges in the Government. The peasants now elect one representative for every 40,000 inhabitants, while the cities are allowed a representative for every 25,000. Peasants at present are not eligible to hold office except in the provincial committees. The peasants now demand equal representation and eligibility to the country's highest executive committees.

Stalin instructed the representatives to inform the peasants these election reforms would be granted and that the peasants would be admitted to the eligible list for the country's highest offices.

These promised reforms, which are expected on account of the recent concessions granted to private capital, are considered the greatest step the Soviet Government has made toward the abolition of Marxist dreams since the Government was formed in 1917.

Great importance is attached to the promises as coming from Stalin, who is the Communist Party chief and successor to the power formerly held by Lenin.

April 15, 1925

## Soviet Decree Lets Peasants Hire Hands; Drops 8-Hour Limit, Permits Child Labor

By Wireless to THE NEW YORK TIMES.

MOSCOW, April 22.—In pursuance of its policy of attracting the peasantry to the Soviet régime, the Government passed today a decision permitting farmers to employ hired labor on their allotments. This is probably the greatest concession to the peasantry since the decree for the socialization of the land in 1917, which, simultaneously with the abolition of private land ownership, annulled the application of hired labor in agriculture.

According to the Soviet land laws, the whole land is considered State property and is distributed to the peasantry in proportion to their families and capacity for working it by their own means. The leasing of additional plots is also prohibited. Only the Soviet Communes possessing large areas were permitted to employ hired labor. The peasant farmers had the limited right to engage outsiders only temporarily in emergency cases, especially during the harvest season.

Inasmuch as the redistribution of the land after the revolution left some groups of peasants deficient in their holdings and at the same time forbade the hiring of labor, unemployment continued to increase in the villages. This added to the general dissatisfaction of the peasants, who were unable to manage without permanent employment of hired labor, and at the same time had a disastrous effect upon the agricultural situation throughout the country.

The new ruling published today is regarded as a measure which will remove the conditions which have hindered the development of national agriculture in Soviet Russia and will regulate the relations between the middle class of peasantry and the so-called groups of poor peasants.

The decree permits farmers to hire labor all the year round. It makes provision for increasing the working day beyond eight hours, as decreed by the Soviet labor code, and allows the employment of children over twelve for light work. The number of agricultural workers is not limited, but contracts cannot exceed the period of twelve months and must be registered with village authorities.

Sickness insurance must be provided by employers and wages cannot be lower than the State minimum fixed by the Labor Commissariat for the respective districts.

Certain Orthodox Communists do not deny that this new measure is a radical departure from the fundamental positions proclaimed by the Communists immediately after gaining power. The modification of policy, however, is considered as absolutely necessary in the interest of national economy as well as for the attainment of unity with the peasantry.

April 23, 1925

## SOVIET NOW RETURNS FACTORIES TO OWNERS

### Berlin Hears Moscow Is 'Leasing' Plants Without Termination Date, 3 Years Tax Free.


By Wireless to THE NEW YORK TIMES.

BERLIN, May 2.—The Soviet Government has decided to return all factories, plants and institutions to former owners, thus moving further toward abolishing the communistic idea of common property, according to information from Moscow. M. Dzerzhinsky, Chief Commissar of Public Economy, made this important announcement, it is reported, stating that 80 per cent. of the members of the Soviet Congress now in session favored returning the property and abandoning the idea of State ownership. The reason given is that the Government has been unable to operate the plants at a profit.

The Soviet Constitution permits no private ownership, the property is being turned over to original owners on a lease bearing no termination date. On account of the rundown condition of the plants, the Government announces the owners will not be taxed for three years in order to allow them to make necessary repairs.

After the announcement of property return, the Government gave over leases of more than 2,000 apartment houses in Moscow alone to the original owners or heirs, allowing them to rent the apartments without permission of the Government's housing committee. These properties also are declared free from taxes for a three-year period in order to give the owners a chance to make repairs.

Labor unions believe permissions granted to employers to hire men without Government restriction on wages will cause a demand for workers and will increase the present low pay, making the lot of laborers better.

May 3, 1925

## Trotsky Elected Member of Soviet Cabinet; Gets Most Applause in Party Congress

Special Cable to THE NEW YORK TIMES.

MOSCOW, May 13.—Leon Trotsky made today his first public appearance since he returned from the Caucasus and after a period of nearly eight months by attending the opening meeting of the annual Federal Congress of the Soviets at the Grand Opera House, together with all the other leaders of the Government and the Communist Party.

He was elected a member of the Presidium, which numbered seventy-five.

When his name was announced after those of Stalin, Kalinin, Kemenief, Rykoff and Zinovief, and Trotsky stepped out briskly from behind the platform, the whole house broke into tremendous applause, which was more prolonged than that received by any other leader.

Trotsky took his seat at a table next to Tomsky, leader of the trade union who, with another member, separated him from Zinovief who is regarded as Trotsky's uncompromising adversary.

Trotsky remained on the platform during the session, which lasted more than three hours. He remained silent, not engaging in the proceedings. He looked rather concentrated, probably feeling that the attention of the house, including the members of the Diplomatic Corps who were present, centred upon his predominant figure.

It is very doubtful whether he will address the convention on any subject in the agenda. He certainly is not listed to report on any question but might possibly be elected to work on committees to which will be entrusted the framing of resolutions on Government proposals.

The state of Soviet industry and finance also will be discussed and a new Central Executive Committee of the Soviet Federation, possessing the functions of a parliament, will be erected at the closing of the convention.

According to current rumors, Trotsky will have the post of Minister of Foreign Trade, while other Ministers might change posts.

May 14, 1925

## CURRENT SUPPLIED TO RUSSIAN VILLAGES

### Communist Party Organ Reports Big Industrial Gain Through New Lighting and Power.

### PEASANTS STILL DUBIOUS

### They Believe Lights Are Fairy Lamps or Demons to Be Exorcised When Users Are Shocked.

By WALTER DURANTY.
Special Cable to THE NEW YORK TIMES.

MOSCOW, Aug. 22.—Despite setbacks and a shortage of money, the Soviet authorities are now going ahead quite fast with "electrification" of the rural districts of Russia, which was one of Lenin's ambitions. What he really wanted was the introduction to Russian villages of labor-saving machinery and he chose electric light and power as a striking symbol of the wonders of the new machine world. Under the caption, "Rural Electrification" the Communist Party organ, Pravda, runs, three or four times weekly, accounts of the establishment of small electric plants, averaging fifty horsepower, in villages mostly in the central districts. The stories vary little—incredulity and even fear of the peasants at the outset, then enthusiasm and a rush to install the new light in every cottage. The peasants are so ignorant that in many cases they thought "electrification" was the name of a fairy or djinn whom the Bolsheviki had enslaved by magic arts.

Invariably the construction engineers have to convince the elders by putting an electric bulb in a truss of hay, that the new light is not incendiary nor dangerous. Cases have occurred where an unwise peasant got a shock and gathered his comrades to riot and destroy the power station. In other places they summoned the priest to exorcise the demon with prayer and holy water.

Today the Pravda describes the installation of plants in villages of the Province of Pensa Bahenki, the Province of Moscow and the Peskovutka Province of Tambov. It is interesting to note the evidence of "Lenin Cult" that in the two latter provinces the electric light is spoken of as "Ilyich light," Ilyich being Lenin's middle name. All three villages average around two to three thousand population and before the war did a fairly good business in home industry products—shoes, embroideries, wood carving, toy making and carpentry. This business died during the revolution, but now, with electric light, Baenki has a home-workers cooperative of 500 members, making an average of $40 a head monthly—higher wages than skilled artisans obtain in the cities.

In Peskovatka the cost of thrashing grain is said to have been reduced 50 per cent. In Lad instead of as formerly one-third of the adult male population going each Winter to seek ill-paid work in the cities it is claimed that every one now spends the long Winter, "bright as daylight," in cottages producing a monthly output of evening homecraft worth $12,000.

August 23, 1925

# BOURGEOIS RUSSIANS TO HAVE NEW RIGHTS

## Communist Party Favors Removal of Restrictions on Specialists and Managers.

## AIMS TO AID INDUSTRY

### Closer Cooperation of "White Collar" Men and Proletarians Is Expected to Result.

By WALTER DURANTY.

Special Cable to THE NEW YORK TIMES.

MOSCOW, Aug. 23—Another step forward on the road of Russia's return to normal conditions of economic life was made by the resolution of the Central Executive Committee of the Communist Party published today regarding better treatment of "specialists," that is, technicians and "white collar" men in Soviet business and industrial administrations.

Isvestia, which is the organ of the Communist Party, describes the resolution editorially as "of exceptional importance." It sets the definite seal of Communist Party approval on the change that has been going on here for the last four years from so-called militant communism to the present condition of State socialism—controlled, it is true, by the dominant Communist Party.

The system in industry now has come to be that while the State owns a majority of large enterprises the actual management is given over to a board of "specialists," controlled by a small number of trusted Communists, who, by the way, have now learned to cooperate without much friction. Hitherto one of the main difficulties in this system has been the distinction made between manual workers and white-collar clerical staffs, technicians and managers. The former were considered proletarians, the latter bourgeois. The resolution published today—not of the Soviet Government but of the Central Executive Committee of the Communist Party, which is above and behind the Government—aims at wiping out this distinction and putting specialists on a special footing equal to manual workers. It is the abolition of the stigma of "bourgeoisism" for the specialists.

"To improve conditions of life and work for specialists," the resolution reads, "the Central Executive Committee considers necessary the following measures: (1) Admission of children of specialists to all branches of the educational system"—two years ago children of the bourgeoisie were ejected from the universities, &c. (2) Admission of specialist representatives as assistant judges in law cases concerning specialists and their work. (3) Improvement of housing conditions for specialists, that is, lower rent, &c., and for granting to them of tax exemptions. The committee thinks it extremely important to arrange a satisfactory general tariff for specialists instead of individual or collective agreements and to give them facilities of all kinds which will contribute to the accomplishment of their work."

The resolution then insists on the necessity of close cooperation between the old pre-revolution specialists who are now working for the Soviet Administrations and the younger post-revolution men, and demands that both groups receive free access to foreign technical knowledge, publications, &c.

All this is tantamount to recognition of specialists as valuable to the proletarians. It may well appear as the final capitulation of so-called communism in the face of economic realities which have brought about such changes in the last four years. On the other hand it may equally be said it marks the free and willing acceptance of the Communist régime by bourgeois economic elements.

During the last week THE NEW YORK TIMES correspondent talked with a number of specialists, especially those connected with textile enterprises. In positions of trust there are such persons as Morosoff, a member of an immensely rich family that formerly controlled the pre-war textile trust of Russia; Kotusoff, who is managing director of one of the biggest textile factories, &c. They appear well enough satisfied and claim that rivalry between the different groups in the same trust or for results between different trusts can be an outlet for individual initiative and will require all the work and interest the individual can demand.

August 25, 1925

# 'BONUS' BY SOVIET SPEEDS WORKERS

## *Profits Are Indirectly Turned Back to State Employes Through Labor Guilds.*

By WALTER DURANTY.

Copyright, 1925, by The New York Times Company.
Special Cable to THE NEW YORK TIMES.

MOSCOW, Sept. 10.—The Academy of Science celebration is one more proof that Soviet Russia is undergoing a second grand transformation since the revolution. The first began in 1921, when civil war and pure communism were replaced by "the new economic policy" and peace. The "new economic policy" produced a wild scramble in private trading and speculation, which was more or less forcibly suppressed in the Winter of 1923-24 in favor of State enterprise. All this period was complicated by an internal controversy of the Communist Party, between followers of Trotsky and the Old Guard, which for a time hindered normal development.

The beginning of the present year saw an end of the controversy, leaving Communist Party leaders free to continue the new economic policy, as they now declare, "along lines originally laid down by Lenin." Viewed from the non-Communist standpoint, however, the new policy in itself was a concession to the peasants in particular and economic law in general—that is to say, acknowledgment that pure communism, for the time being at least, had been discovered impracticable. It is therefore logical to suppose that in continuation of the new economic policy there will be further concessions.

This is precisely what is occurring today. Russian economics are being transformed from the communist theory and socialist hypothesis to practical, workaday business, whose universal label of "State Socialism" means that what is known in America as "big interests" is here represented by Government officials instead of private individuals.

Of course Communists say that this distinction makes an enormous difference. Also it must be remembered that the Communists absolutely control politics in Russia. But a brief resume of concessions they have made in the past few months will show how surely the economic life of the country—and it is an article of the Marxist faith that economics dominate politics—is tending to run along the same lines as the rest of the world. Thus the peasants did not own land, according to the Communist theory, but merely worked it. Now they can lease and rent, which, in practice, establishes legal tenure. In theory they could not hire additional labor. Now they can hire and fire. Technicians and white collar employes were regarded as a hostile element. Now the Communist Party itself announces they are to be treated as brothers instead of pariahs.

The same thing has just happened with the Academy of Science in Leningrad, and Leningrad offers yet another and more interesting example of the change. The whole city that was practically dead eighteen months ago, is now throbbing with activity. Where one shop was open, there are now ten streets where the houses are being furiously repaired, the population has increased fully 50 per cent., formerly comatose factories are working and new buildings, especially or the outskirts, are rising apace. Why? Chiefly because there has been found a workable compromise between capital—as represented here by the State—and labor.

Now when the State wants to build or repair, or to increase the output of a factory, it applies to "artels"—small or large groups, or guilds, of workers. The artel, as a legal person, accepts a contract for building or for a job in a factory. It pays its members a regular labor federation tariff, just as the American contractor would do. But if they work hard and quickly, there remains quite a fat profit, which goes to the coffer of the artel to be divided among its members.

An American visitor, ex-Governor James P. Goodrich of Indiana, was surprised to see Russian bricklayers laying 2,000 bricks per man per day. He saw, too, street paving being done at a speed America. no longer knows and the Butiloff steel works driving faster than Pittsburgh. This may not sound like Bolshevist Russia, but it explains why things here have now really begun to go ahead.

September 11, 1925

# LENIN CULT GROWS THROUGHOUT RUSSIA

## His 'Corner' Becomes Shrine in Schools, Factories, Clubs and Even Railroad Stations.

## CONSTANT THRONG AT TOMB

By WALTER DURANTY.

By Wireless to THE NEW YORK TIMES.

MOSCOW, Sept. 2.—The Lenin cult has made big strides in the past year.

In every Government administration, every school and factory, in all the clubs of peasants, soldiers and workers and even in the railroad stations and restaurants there is a "Lenin Corner," with big photographs of the dead leader draped with fir branches, flowers and red and black ribbon and with a selection of his works and other communistic literature. In theory it is a place for quiet study of the basic principles of communism's creed; in practice it is almost a shrine.

Indeed one "Lenin Corner" in Tiflis was found to have a tiny subdued electric light glowing before Lenin's picture—a sheer modernized replica of the sacred lamp which orthodox Russians keep ever burning before the holy ikon. This electric light was immediately ordered extinguished, but the spirit that prompted it remains.

### Pilgrims Coming All Day Long.

Not the least characteristic manifestation of this spirit is the daily attendance of the public at Lenin's mausoleum in Red Square. From early morning there is an irregular progress of special delegations—workers' and peasants' groups from the country, visiting foreigners, &c.—but the evening, between 8 and 9 o'clock, is reserved for the people of Moscow.

It was a curious sight yesterday. The rain was falling heavily and the high electric arc lamps reflected a thousand puddles amid the cobblestones of the great square, throwing into stark relief the reddish white wall of the Kremlin like a cliff, with the whole square and the pyramid of the mausoleum at its foot. On the outskirts of the square the high spires of the churches and monasteries and the Kremlin towers were faintly outlined against the sky. Atop the highest central tower fluttered a red flag illuminated by the light from below like a flame against the blackness of the sky.

### Girl Says Tomb Visits "Help Her."

At 7:45 the already long line of waiting people, a thousand or more in number, began winding across the square from the low iron railing round the mausoleum. On the other side of the square, along the front of an ancient style but modern building, which is the chief Government department store in Moscow, there is a similar long line waiting patiently for permits.

There is no pushing or noise and very little conversation. Most of the crowd are young—17 to 25 years old. They advance slowly and are admitted to the permit bureau in groups of a dozen.

In front of me was a typical Communist girl in a black leather jacket, with a red handkerchief round her head. She had visited the mausoleum, she said, six times in the last three months. She found it difficult to explain just why—partly in tribute to the dead leader—but more than that. She said it helped her somehow—life isn't always easy—and—and—it helped her.

The average simple-minded believer in any faith would speak much the same of a pilgrimage to a saint or a temple.

The permit bureau was conducted by uniformed soldiers of the Political Detective Administration. They gave passes without delay on the production of identity papers, but foreigners were also required to sign their names in a book. Mostly the visitors, in groups of four to six, were from factory, club or school.

By 8:30 I had joined the line at the mausoleum, now shorter as the soldiers hurried us through fifty or more a minute. The guard at the gate took the rain-soaked pass swiftly and automatically, repeating in a low voice, "Admit six—admit ten—admit two."

### Body Remains Unchanged.

Under a sort of flat table supported by columns at the top of the mausoleum four lights glowed in yellow, and other yellow lights showed up the deep black letters, "Lenin," carved above the low entrance.

There was no sound as the public descended the shallow staircase, red-carpeted and red-walled, save the slow shuffle of feet and the purr of the electric fan in the central chamber below. At the foot of the staircase four chemical fire extinguishers on the wall struck an incongruous note.

We turned to the right into the little square cellar where Lenin lies in khaki tunic with the Order of the Red Flag on his left breast on a simple couch beneath a glass pyramid and mounted on a low gallery running around three sides. Sentries with fixed bayonets stood motionless at the head and foot.

The walls of red and black were unrelieved save by the purple and gold splash of a single large flag and the little brown stain of a wooden thermometer. The electric fan purred louder and the soft light filtered yellow and brown through the marble bowls.

Lenin's body has remained quite unchanged since my last visit over a year ago. It seemed very small and lonely among all the faces staring so intently as the people sidled round.

No one spoke as we filed upstairs again and out, but there was a queer collective sigh, as if all of us had been holding our breath.

The throng streamed across the square to the gate where stands the most famous religious emblem in Russia, the minute shrine to the Iberian Virgin, ablaze with lights, silver and gilt ikons, and colored stones. A little group bowed before the figure and pressed on devoutly to the narrow door.

September 3, 1925

# COMMITTEE FINDS SOVIETS INACTIVE

## Russian Communist Investigators Confirm Charges Made by Critics.

## ARE DECORATIVE BODIES

### Executives Run Administration, and Councils Merely Approve Their Acts.

Critics of the Bolshevist Government of Russia have frequently raised the charge, especially during the last few years, that the much-lauded Soviet system does not function, either in local or national matters. It is asserted that the masses of the people, and even many Communists, have become so disgusted at the farce of electing members of councils that do nothing but O. K. the acts of their executive bodies that very few bother to vote in the periodical elections of the various local State and national soviets.

That there was a certain justification for this criticism was recognized at the last conference of the Russian Communist Party and a committee was named to investigate conditions bearing upon the workings of the Soviets and the failure of the workers and peasants to participate in the elections and to recommend ways and means of reviving the people's original enthusiasm. This committee has been at work for some time and has published the first instalment of its report in the Krassnaya Nove of Moscow.

According to this report, as summarized by the Berner Tagwacht of Aug. 22, the Soviets were great, stormy, popular assemblages during the early years of the revolution. But about the end of 1920 "the Soviets were practically shoved aside by their own executive bodies, made up of a ring of a few persons." The report explains this change by saying that "political circumstances demanded the greatest possible concentration of power, the nearest approach to an autocracy." After the close of the civil war these extraordinary conditions disappeared, but even today "the Soviets actually no longer exist as organs of the proletarian democracy."

**Councils Seldom in Session.**

The ruling power in Russia lies in the hands of the Presidium of the Soviet, the committee reports, adding: "The Soviets are only seldom called into session and then generally for purposes of information or decoration." The Moscow Soviet, for instance, was convened only ten times in 1924. Seven sessions were merely ceremonial affairs, having nothing to do with administration, so only three were devoted to work. In Yekaterinoslaf, eight sessions out of twelve were purely ceremonial, in Kursk, five out of seven, &c. On an average the Soviets meet once in two months in a session lasting only two or three hours. The investigating committee says that "the reports of the head of the administration to the Soviets are of a formal and useless nature."

In only a single case did the committee find a Soviet expressing dissatisfaction with the activities of its Presidium. But the committee is of the opinion that this apparent harmony does not at all agree with the facts. It declares that "in general the reports are not discussed at all. Under the most favorable circumstances the meeting asks questions. The resolutions that are presented are unanimously approved."

In all Russia only four of the presidiums, which really have done away with the Soviets, have presented reports of their work to the plenary meetings of the Soviets. The committee considers itself obligated to emphasize the fact that, with the degrading of the Soviets to purely decorative bodies, their law-making powers have also been reduced to practically nil, because "in no law are the rights of the Soviets mentioned. On the contrary, everything that saw the light of day from 1922 to 1924 was left to the executive committees and the presidiums for their action."

The effect of all this upon the voters is revealed in the falling off in their participation in elections. In 1922 the percentage of the electorate that voted was 36; in 1923 it was 32 and in 1924 it was only from 24 to 30. The report adds that "under these conditions the attendance at meetings of the Soviets is very low and is getting more so from meeting to meeting."

**Right of Recall Unexercised.**

The right to recall members of the Soviets is also said to exist merely on paper. The committee remarks: "Unfortunately, we do not know of a single case where the voters have exercised their right and recalled a member of the Soviets for not having done his duty. And still there are some such members."

In order to put life into the Soviets it was resolved three years ago that every member of a Soviet must be a delegate to some subdivision or section of the Soviet. But the committee found that this innovation had not strengthened the influence of the Soviets. The sections cannot function as bodies keeping check on administrative activities because the "cells" of the Communist Party are in the way. They cannot bring any enthusiasm into the work as they are hidebound themselves and are foreign to the masses. The committee notes that "There are numerous complaints that the sections are lifeless and constitute nothing but useless links in the administration."

The committee has not finished its work, so its suggestion for the tempering of the Russian bureaucracy with a little democracy are yet to be made public.

September 6, 1925

# RUSSIAN YOUTH MOVEMENT SHOWS GROWING STRENGTH

When The New York Times correspondent in Russia returned recently to Moscow after a year's absence, one of the things that attracted his attention was the remarkable increase in the membership of the "Comsomol," or Communist Union of Youth. With the 1,500,000 boys and girls making up this organization rests the future of communism in Russia, according to the views of many of their older comrades. The nature of this body was described by Fritz Scholthöfer in a recent issue of the Frankfurter Zeitung. He said:

"One can hardly make comparisons with similar organizations of Western Europe. The spiritual content of the movement is Marxism. This is dogmatically laid down and nobody questions it. There is no sign of that intensive striving after new ideals, regardless of clarity of unity, with which our German youth is filled. In Russia it is a matter of bringing young folks of both sexes into the organizations and training them to defend the Communist conception of the world and the Communist idea of the State. But this doesn't hinder the movement from being led with all the fire of youthful enthusiasm.

"The 'Comsomols,' in their public appearances, remind me of what I saw of the Fascista 'giovinezza' in Italy. Everything is organized along military lines. School children are taken into the ranks early, boys and girls together. With gold-trimmed red flags and drums the detachments march through the streets. They have their own songs, all of which exalt the proletarian struggle.

**Replica of Communist Party.**

"There was recently held a big national conference of the 'Comsomol' societies. One of the speakers opposed shaping the youth organizations and their activities too much after the model of the Communist Party. The warning, however, came too late. For, in every way the 'Comsomol' is a replica of the party. It carries the latter's political activities into the ranks of the children and youth, not merely in the form of agitation and education, but also practically. It is conscious and active political propaganda among the young people. For two months now the society has had its own daily newspaper. There is life in every line, and there is the inspiration needed when now and then a local society grows sleepy.

"Children are enrolled when they reach school age and are kept in the societies until they are 23 years old. The first division is called the 'Octoberists'; the second (embracing members from 9 to 14) the 'Pioneers'; the third consists of the real 'Comsomols.' Upon becoming 23, they may remain attached to the society as passive members. The worthy ones—those, that is, who have made good through active work and political reliability—then join the Communist Party.

"Youthful workers and peasants are admitted to the 'Comsomol' without hesitation, but children from other classes must bring good recommendations and undergo a period of probation. The composition of the 'Pioneer' societies at present is 45 per cent. workers' children, 31 per cent. peasants' children and 24 per cent. children from other classes. If a person asks whether the non-partisans could not attain considerable influence or even control of the society, the answer is that Communist leadership is absolutely assured.

"The 'Comsomol' remains in close touch with the local and central management of the Communist Party all over the country. Thus there is a concentrated, methodical activity, corresponding in every place and at all times with the permanent aims and the sometimes changing tactics of the party itself. This is true of the clubs, of the lecture courses and especially of the 'cells,' which carry on the strongest and most effective propaganda.

**Spreading the Doctrine.**

"The 'cells' are found in factories, schools, unions and the army. Theirs is the task of 'taking active part in the whole life of the establishments, the villages and the schools.' They spread the doctrine and recruit members. I learn from persons who have watched the work of these 'cells' that they are not functioning in vain and that they are winning a dominating influence over their fellow young people, which accounts for the rapid growth of the organization.

"In country districts the 'Comsomols' have produced astonishing changes. I have heard that in a number of villages in Central Russia, mainly near industrial centres, the local groups function as independent economic units. They are composed of the children of rich and poor peasants and of farm laborers, who leave their parents' homes and cultivate together the land assigned to them. They receive credit from the cooperatives, and the result of the harvest is used to buy agricultural machinery which increases the land's productivity.

"The rich peasant has to hire a farmhand in place of the son who is working in the 'Comsomol.' The fathers stick to the old style of farming, while the boys become exponents of technical progress and of nationalized agriculture. The training of 'tractorists' (young fellows who know how to handle farm machinery) is part of the official program of the Union of Youth."

September 13, 1925

# RUSSIAN COMMUNISTS ARE 'PURGING' PARTY

## Leaders Expel All Members Who Are Found Guilty of Any 'Bourgeois Taint.'



By Wireless to The New York Times.

LONDON, Sept. 22.—Just as doctors at Ellis Island ask would-be immigrants, "Are you ill?" lynx-eyed watchers over the purity of the Russian Communist Party ask members who have fallen under suspicion, "Are you bourgeois?" If the answer does not serve to calm their suspicions, the watchers promptly "fire" the suspect from the party or otherwise punish him.

According to advices reaching here from Riga, Russian Communist Party authorities recently examined 100,000 persons haled before it on suspicion of not being simon pure Communists and found 20,000 wanting. Of the latter no fewer than 8,500 were expelled from the party, having been pronounced guilty of "bourgeois taint, breach of discipline, mentality alien to communism, lack of real sympathy with the party ideals, political illiteracy, un-Communist behavior, maintaining relations with non-Communists, &c." The remaining delinquents received milder punishments, such as "party censure."

One hundred thousand more are now being examined for signs of the "bourgeois disease" and similar things horrible in Communist eyes.

It is stated that these "purging" tactics now are a regular thing in the Communist Party's internal policy, having been found necessary in order to maintain discipline and obedience to the supreme leaders.

September 23, 1925

# SOVIET CHIEFS ROW OVER THE PEASANTS

## Communists Clash at Red Congress Over Suppressing Rich Farmers.

## ZINOVIEFF HEADS MINORITY

### Shakes His Fist at Group Led by Stalin and Bukharin in First Serious Split.


Special Cable to THE NEW YORK TIMES.

MOSCOW, Dec. 21.—The new Communist dispute raised by the Leningrad faction at the All-Russian Communist Congress meeting in the Kremlin culminated yesterday in a controversial minority report read by G. S. Zinovieff and sustained by forty-three delegates, an event unprecedented since the October Revolution.

The general trend of M. Zinovieff's speech was to point out the danger from the Kulaks, or "Fists," the wealthy peasant group, and to demand a more complete measure of Socialism as distinguished from State capitalism. The climax was reached when M. Zinovieff, shaking his fist, cried:

"We proclaim a sacred war against all daring to identify the N. E. P. (New Economic Policy) with Socialism."

The discussion turned out to be more serious than had been anticipated. The cause of the controversy was the growing doubt whether the building of a Socialist State was feasible in a country surrounded by a hostile capitalistic world.

The peasant still remains the Communist Party's unsolved riddle, with one party group prone to underestimate the danger from the Kulaks while another faction headed by M. Zinovieff demands their forceful suppression. The majority of the Central Executive Committee, headed by Joseph Stalin, advocates aid for the poor peasant and consolidation for middle class farmers against the Kulaks.

**Bukharin Denounces Use of Force.**

Vigorously replying to M. Zinovieff and speaking for the majority of the Central Executive Committee of the Communist Party, N. J. Bukharin said:

"To destroy whatever methods are still left from Military Communism must be our fundamental policy. The party must not be dragged back. We must fight the Fists with other methods."

Stressing the unprecedented nature of the minority report M. Bukharin said:

"Our party is facing an acute crisis. The very fact that there is a minority report is an event of vast political importance. We have had conflicts in recent years, but never has the Opposition demanded the right to submit a minority report. This shows that the party faces a serious situation."

M. Stalin, who continues to dominate the Congress, speaking yesterday, said:

"There are two factions in the Communist Party. One is inclined to ignore the Fist danger, denying the presence of the class struggle. The other faction overestimates the danger, contending that the overwhelming factor in the situation is the recovery of capitalism in the village, bringing a sharp class cleavage between the Fists and the poor, while the middle class peasant fades rapidly.

"The latter faction tends to kindle a new class struggle in the village, leading to committees of poor peasants and civil war. Such defection, if unchecked, may destroy the party.

**Stalin Warns of "Democracy."**

M. Stalin next attacked those who were working for a democracy, saying:

"Some of our non-communist intelligentsia hold that the Communists should reform and consolidate with the Bourgeoisie. We must then approach the threshold of a Democratic Republic, overstep it and with the aid of some Caesar become an ordinary Bourgeoisie Republic. But the make-up of our Party and its builder are a guarantee against such an eventuality."

Explaining the Communist Party's sanction of the sale of vodka, M. Stalin said: "Some people think you can build Socialism with kid gloves. This is a mistake.

"If we have no loans and cannot accept the enslavement of concessions, we must seek means elsewhere. Here we must choose between slavery and vodka."

Touching on the party's make-up, M. Stalin gave the following interesting figures:

Out of 54,000,000 adult peasant population, ranging in age from 18 to 60, only 202,000 are Communists. In July, 1925, the total of Russian workmen, including farmhands and small trades, was 6,500,000. Of these 2,094,000 were workmen employed in key industries, of whom 534,000, or 25 per cent., were Communists.

December 22, 1925

# RED MAJORITY WINS IN MOSCOW DISPUTE

## Communist Congress Rejects Minority Amendments to Platform, 559 to 65.

## DISSIDENTS ARE CENSURED

### Strengthening of Armed Forces and Measures for Russian Industrial Independence Are Called For.


Special Cable to THE NEW YORK TIMES.

MOSCOW, Dec. 25.—At 1 o'clock this morning the political and economic dispute, which for the past several days has divided the All-Russian Congress of the Communist Party, came to a head in a vote of 559 for the platform adopted by the Central Executive Committee and 65 against it.

The test came in a ballot resulting in the rejection of the amendments to the platform offered by Leon B. Kameneff in behalf of the Leningrad Opposition.

The platform as adopted censures the minority faction for overestimating the danger from the Kulaks (the wealthy peasants) and for underestimating the importance of cooperation with he middle class peasants. It instructs the Central Executive Committee to take all steps to strengthen the Red Army and the sea and air fleet. It also instructs the committee to follow a reconstruction policy with a view to industrializing Russia to the extent where the country would manufacture heavy machinery and equipment, thereby assuring independence from capitalist countries.

**Asks "Peaceful Foreign Policy."**

The platform calls for discounting political stabilization in Europe; warns of the growing American rôle in international affairs, amounting to "financial and economic world domination"; takes note of the "pacific manoeuvring for another world war" by the Locarno Conference and the League of Nations; points to the contradictions between victor and vanquished States and the imperialist colonial policy "awakening semi-colonial peoples" in China, India, Syria and Morocco, and urges support of the struggle for the unity of all labor unions.

The Congress further directs the Central Executive Committee to consolidate by all means the Soviet Republic as the base of a future world revolution with the Western proletariat and the oppressed colonial peoples, simultaneously instructing the Soviet Government to pursue a peaceful foreign policy.

**Cleavage in Leadership.**

When the party battle was over, the array of the opposing forces appeared to be of greater significance in the division of leadership rather than in the relative numerical strength.

Joseph Stalin, N. I. Bukharin, Alexis I. Rykoff and Michael Kalenin, leading the triumphant majority, faced among their opponents Mme. Nadejda Constantinova Krupskaya, the widow of Nikolai Lenin; Leon B. Kameneff, G. S. Zinovieff and G. Y. Sokolnikoff, the Finance Minister whom M. Stalin charged yesterday with attempts to "Dawesize" Soviet Russia, meaning that if M. Sokolnikopf's theories were adopted they would subject Russia to a process similar to the operation of the Dawes plan in Germany.

Paradoxical as it may seem, M. Kameneff and M. Zinovieff, who a year ago fought Leon Trotsky when the latter championed the cause of party democracy and the right of the minority to self-assertion, have presently found themselves proclaiming the slogan of "live and let live," demanding for their faction its own newspaper for threshing out party disputes, and advocating kindred measures which, according to their opponents, they vigorously opposed when advanced by M. Trotsky.

**Session Full of Fireworks.**

The charges frequently made in the foreign press that all Soviet assemblies are mere rubber stamp affairs certainly could not be applied to this convention, which in point of verbal fire and ungloved attacks, accusations and interruptions, has yielded nothing to any American political gathering.

Though there was little indulgence in sentiment, it also played a part. M. Zinovieff, M. Kameneff and Mme. Krupskaya, who spent the greater part of their lives with Lenin in exile and heretofore have been considered his best disciples, while admitting M. Stalin's ability, resented iron party discipline. Thus M. Kameneff and Mme. Krupskaya charged that the Pravda recently refused to publish their articles.

With M. Trotsky and other former leaders now temporarily in the background, M. Stalin's strength has been vastly enhanced. Yesterday after M. Stalin's concluding speech the delegates rose and sang the "Internationale."

December 26, 1925

# RED RULERS BOW TO PEASANT POWER

## Moscow Decree Ordering Cut in Prices Forced From Leaders by Rural Population.

## ELECTIONS SHOW STRENGTH

By WALTER DURANTY.


By Wireless to THE NEW YORK TIMES.

MOSCOW, July 7.—A row of facts like sign posts pointing the way to Russia's future evolution is revealed today in a leading editorial in Pravda on the elections for town and village Soviets now being held throughout the country. Pravda strips off the veils of optimism and delusion and reveals the naked truth.

"There is thrown in our faces the great growth of political interest and activity in the villages as compared with that among the urban populations, particularly the urban proletariat," says Pravda, which continues:

"The correct (that is, Communist) policy in our country can be ensured only by reinforcement in a proletarian direction.

"The results of the electoral campaign to an evident degree contradict the line of policy adopted at the last Communist Party congress.

"In the towns the result of the elections demonstrates the political interests and activity of the small bourgeois elements.

"In the villages the elections show that the poor and middle-class peasants are much less politically active than are the prosperous sections.

**Appeal Made to Communists.**

"There is a growth of small bourgeois 'Nepmen,' and the prosperous peasants are striving to penetrate every pore of our administrative apparatus and are displaying sometimes amazing dexterity."

The rest of the article is devoted to an appeal to the members of the Communist party to redouble their energies to meet the danger.

It is more interesting to consider what the facts cited mean at this juncture. The first deduction is that the invincible Russian revolution, like the French Revolution, has cleared the road for the hitherto virtually enslaved mass of the country and the urban population.

Once free, this mass disregards theories, whether they be those of Robespierre or Rousseau, Marx or Lenin, and drives solidly toward the ordinary human pursuit of happiness which, in the modern world, means first and foremost the accumulation of surplus money.

**Russia is 90 Per Cent. Peasant.**

With regard to the Russia of today, however, the accumulation of money is hampered by a number of socialistic restrictions, which at the same time hinder the peasant's pursuit of happiness by making him pay an exorbitant price for the various things he needs to be happy.

The would-be accumulator in the towns does not yet matter much politically. Although, as Pravda admits, his activity is growing, his individualism can still be swamped by the larger collectivist vote.

But in the villages it is a different story. The peasants form almost 90 per cent. of the Russian population, and, although more of them are poor than prosperous, the poor want much the same thing as the prosperous, namely, high grain prices and cheap manufactured goods.

In other words, the prosperous peasants elected village or county Soviets, which genuinely represent all their electors, whether rich or poor, and therefore cannot be ignored by the Communist rulers of Russia.

**Six Years of Compromise.**

**It is the artificial collectivism of Marx confronting the practical collectivism of the peasant population. This confrontation of opposites has been more or less openly existent since 1920 brought peace to Russia.**

**The history of those six years is one of compromise and concession to peasant pressure. Today the pressure seems greater than ever, and the Communist rulers reply by issuing a decree that the prices of goods needed by the peasants must fall 10 per cent. within three weeks. Like Canute, they order the tide of supply and demand to cease to ebb and flow.**

**But suppose the tide flows on. There is a temporary remedy possible in the shape of diversion of part of German credits for the purchase of machines to buying manufactured goods. But the whole purpose of the Russian acceptance of German credits was to buy machines and increase home production. The only possible solution seems to be further concessions and further compromises.**

July 8, 1926

# FINDS LABOR LOSING GRIP ON THE SOVIET

## Social Democratic Organ Says Petty Officials Are Gaining Communist Party Power.

## BUREAUCRACY IS STRONGER

### Industrial Workers, Peasants and Farmhands, It Is Said, Are Being Relegated to Second Place.

During the nearly nine years that have elapsed since the Bolsheviki overthrew the Kerensky Government and seized the reins of power in Russia, the Communist Party has been transformed from a small body of industrial workers, led by a handful of intellectuals, into a mass party made up largely of State employes and in which the percentage of actual manual workers is rapidly falling. Such is the conclusion arrived at by a writer in the Berlin Bulletin of the Russian Social Democratic Party, following a study of a report in the Moscow Pravda, the official Communist Party organ, of the composition of the party's membership.

The Pravda's figures, which are confirmatory of occasional items in the Russian press during the last couple of years indicating that the original proletarian party was fast becoming a bureaucracy, show that last year the Communist Party registered a big gain in recruits from among petty officials, while the recruiting of members from the ranks of the industrial workers suffered a sharp falling off. The report refers to the "excessive growth of the party organizations through the influx of officials."

In the Urals the number of officials in the party was increased by 55 per cent. last year, while that of the workers increased only 22 per cent. In the Novgorod district the percentage of workers in the party fell from 45.1 to 43.6 during the last five months of the year, while that of petty officials made a corresponding gain. In Krasnoyarsk 49 per cent. of the new members were officials.

Even in industrial regions, such as in the Baku oil country and the Donyets coal district, the Communist Party organizations among the manual workers in the big establishments have barely managed to hold their own, while the organizations of petty officials and clerks have grown rapidly.

In treating the statistics on the Communist Party membership among the peasants, who embrace about 85 per cent. of the 140,000,000 persons living under the Soviet régime, it is noted by the Social Democratic writer that many of the "peasant" members of the party are petty village officials who formerly were farmers, but now are parts of the State machinery. In the party organizations in the country part of the Leningrad district the percentage of peasant members fell from 52 to 45 in the latter half of 1925, while the percentage of officials rose from 17 to 23.

**Farmhands Fail to Join Party.**

Attempts to enlist the actual wage-working farmhands have not met with much success, judging from figures giving their percentage of the total Communist membership as only 2.8 in the Leningrad Government and 4.5 in Poltava.

The present situation is summed up by the Social Democratic writer as follows:

"The great party machine is above the State and is financed by huge sums from the State Treasury. Under these circumstances the advantages connected with membership in this party are enormous. Within the colossal official machine tendencies may be observed that do not so much signify political reconciliation with communism as they do the need of a calm way of living, permanent income and regular work.

"In this way the Communist Party has developed into a party of officials, the roots of which are still to be found in the party of the workers, but in which the influence of the proletarian elements is steadily declining.

"And here one must remember that there is a material difference between Russian and Western European State officials. In every democratic, even in every parliamentary, country the officials are under control of the press, of the parties, of public opinion.

"In Russia of today, on the contrary, the Communist body of officials is self-governing. It controls everything, but itself is under no sort of control by any one. For the 'dictatorship of the proletariat,' which is in reality nothing but a dictatorship of the Communist Party, has as the result of nine years' development degenerated into a dictatorship of the party bureaucracy that stands above all classes and all laws.

"Still a few years more of such development and the influence of the working class will equal zero. The State apparatus snaps the ties that bind it to the class from which it sprang and gradually develops into a new dictatorship which from its nature will signify a bourgeois dictatorship. This can only be hindered by the rise of a mass movement for the democratization of the country. The beginnings of such a movement are already plainly apparent among the peasants as well as among the workers."

August 1, 1926

## *Zinovieff Ousted*

MOSCOW, Russia, July 24 (AP).—Gregory Zinovieff, who gained much international notoriety for his direction of Communist activities in foreign fields, has come to a fall in his own country.

The Red crusader has been expelled from the Political Bureau of the Central Executive Committee of the Communist Party, perhaps the most important political organization of the whole Soviet State.

M. Rudzutak, the Soviet Commissar for Transport, has been chosen in Zinovieff's place.

Zinovieff is accused, as Chairman of the Communist International, of sending out secret proclamations and other documents in code to members of various branches of the Communist party. It is charged this was done with a view to undermining the present Central Executive Committee of the Communist Party, of which M. Stalin is the dominant member.

July 25, 1926

# STALIN, RED 'BOSS,' OUTWITS HIS FOES

By WALTER DURANTY.


Special Cable to THE NEW YORK TIMES.

MOSCOW, July 30.—They play clever politics, these Communists. Boss Croker or Charles Murphy would turn over in their graves if they could see how Joseph Stalin and the Communist Party Administration are dealing with Leon Trotsky and the lesser members of the opposition. The Administration controls the press and has a firm grip on the party machine. So its tactics are sharp and savage.

The first machine attack was directed against Zinovief M. Lashevich and the other opposition extremists who seemed to be deliberately trying to split the party. They were easily beaten. Thereupon the Administration press proceeded to lump all the rest of the Opposition together and to claim that the resolution from Communist units all over the country disapproving the extremists implied the condemnation of the Opposition as a whole.

The Opposition group centered around M. Trotsky, M. Preobrajenski, M. Radek and M. Piatakof had little sympathy with M. Zinovieff, who had been one of their bitterest adversaries two years ago. But now they are suffering for his failure by being involved in the condemnation of him. This is an admirable object lesson in the present-day political strategy of Moscow.

**Stalin Leaves Foes Out in Cold.**

The fact is, M. Stalin, the Administration "boss," has more political sense than the rest of the Communist Party put together. He is a remarkable personality, this son of a Georgian cobbler who veils his cold-blooded astuteness behind an apparent brusque simplicity.

"I am a plain, rugged fellow," he told the Communist Party Congress last Winter. "You must forgive my lack of tact or delicacy."

But he has most of his opponents bluffed to a standstill. M. Trotsky is far abler and more popular, M. Piatakof and M. Preobrajensky have far more brains and M. Radek has a far greater knowledge of European affairs, but they sit out in the cold. They are reduced today to speculating on their misfortune.

"If there is an economic crisis this Fall," they say, "through disproportion of the prices of foodstuffs and manufactured goods—if the peasants are dissatisfied and the workers are grumbling—then our chance will come."

**Opposition Planks Taken U-.**

Meanwhile the Administration is unobtrusively stealing their thunder. M. Trotsky in his chief argument in the recent party controversy was for the "rationalization of industry." Today the Pravda, the Administration organ, puts forward industrial rationalization as one of the chief planks of the Administration's platform. [Rationalization just means more efficient methods which are obviously desirable.]

Another section of the Opposition advocated slackening the activity of the Communist International. The Administration calls this heresy, but gives the Communist International President, M. Zinovief, a resounding smack on the nose which cannot fail to add to the confusion of the Communist Parties outside of Russia.

Yet another group of the Opposition demands reconciliation with foreign capitalists in order to solve the Russian problems by the help of foreign money. The Administration calls this "Menshevism"—which is one of the ugliest expressions a Russian Bolshevik can apply to a fellow Bolshevik.

July 31, 1926

## *Red Leaders Drive Kameneff From Cabinet; Suspend Piatakof From Economic Council*

MOSCOW, Aug. 14 (AP).—Ianasthasius Mikoian has been appointed Commisar of Trade to succeed Leon B. Kameneff.

M. Mikoian is a member of the Central Executive Committee of the Union of Soviet Socialist Republics.

He is the youngest member of the Soviet Cabinet, being only 31 years old.



MOSCOW, Aug. 14.—M. Piatakof, one of the close friends of Trotsky and a leading member of the Communist Party Opposition, today was relieved for two months of his duties as Vice President of the Supreme Council for National Economy.

This prolonged "holiday" is not surprising in view of his attitude during the recent party discussion toward his then chief, Dzerjinski, who was recently succeeded by another of Stalin's supporters, Quibeshef.

The appointment of M. Mikoian to succeed M. Kameneff and the suspension of M. Piatakof make it clear that the Administration does not intend to compromise with the Opposition, as was expected in some quarters here.

Indeed, another but more extreme Oppositionist, Ossovski, today was expelled from the party altogether for a "heretical" pamphlet advancing the thesis that the present state of affairs justifies the existence of a legitimate opposition, that is, a real two-party system, in the Soviet Union.

M. Kameneff was made Commissar of Trade, a Cabinet position, early in the present year. He belongs to the "die hard" group of extremists, who oppose State capitalism, the policy to which the dominant chiefs of Communist Russia now tend.

At the Congress of the Communist Party late last year an open break occurred among the "Big Seven," Stalin, Kameneff, Zinovieff, Bukharin, Rykoff, Trotsky and Tomsky.

They accused each other of hypocrisy, intrigue and distortion of the doctrines of Lenin.

The Opposition, headed by Zinovieff, charged that the leaders, headed by Stalin, were taking the party back to the "slough of capitalism."

During the Congress Kameneff was denounced as a heretic and expelled from the Political Bureau.

Stalin emerged from the conference supreme.

As a penalty for his defections, Kameneff was relieved of the highly important posts of Chairman of the Council of Labor and Defense and Vice Premier and made head of the Trade Department, a position of far less political weight than his former post.

August 15, 1926

## RUSSIAN PEASANTS STILL HOLD GRAIN

### Editorial in Isvestia Discloses That August Purchases Are Only Half of Program.

### 1925 STAND IS REPEATED

By WALTER DURANTY.



MOSCOW, Aug. 21. — "Peasant pressure," which many observers of Russian affairs believe will be the decisive factor in the long run in shaping the country's destiny, is now being applied in no uncertain form. The leading editorial in Isvestia today makes public news of alarming portent to Soviet plans, only superficially concealed by the moderate tone in which it is presented.

The editorial reveals that the State grain purchasing program for the first ten days of August has been fulfilled to only 16 per cent. of the monthly plan instead of 33 per cent.; that is less than half. In the same period last year the program was fulfilled to 23 per cent., 7,000,000 bushels then being purchased against 4,500,000 this year. This may not sound particularly ominus, but when it is realized that the peasants' unwillingness to part with grain last year threw the whole national financial business and industrial scheme out of gear and produced a prolonged economic crisis, the fact that this year begins 50 per cent. worse is writing on the wall that needs no prophet to decipher.

Peasants last year refused to sell grain in expected quantities because they could not buy what they considered an adequate quantity of manufactured goods with the proceeds. Grain prices, generally speaking, are a little higher than pre-war. Goods, as Dzerjinski stated, are three to four times higher. The peasant prefers to keep his grain for his family, cattle, poultry, &c., and make shift with such goods as he can provide for himself—there is a growing tendency to revive village industries of spinning, weaving, shoe and tool making, &c.—or do without.

Last year the authorities explained the peasants' reluctance to sell by the fact that there had been a series of poor harvests and the peasants felt it necessary to accumulate stocks. This year the harvest is as good or better than last year, and if grain is not forthcoming another explanation cannot be avoided. Last year we were told there was mismanagement and unnecessary competition between different State purchasing bodies, and much was said of the pernicious influence of private dealers. This year there are complaints, but the grain is not forthcoming.

Perhaps it is early to cry, "wolf"—though Isvestia cries it clearly enough for those that have ears to hear—and it must be remembered that the above mentioned stocks accumulated last year give the peasants plenty of time to wait and see how the market will develop.

**Reserves Make Peasants Independent.**

It is also true that today's cabled reports from the provinces indicate an increasing flow of grain to the purchasing centres, but it is no less true that possession of reserve stocks gives the peasants economic independence in addition to the personal freedom which they took for hemselves even before the Bolshevist revolution, and which the Bolsheviki confirmed and reiterated.

If the present tendency to withhold grain continues it is hard to calculate the consequences. That they may menace the Soviet régime as such is quite absurd. But that they involve further modifications of Soviet methods is far less unlikely. Ninety per cent. of the total population holding on to the basic sources of national wealth is a force not easily to be ignored.

August 22, 1926

## LENIN 'TESTAMENT' AT LAST REVEALED

### Letter, Hidden After Leader's Death, Warned Against Stalin and Extolled Trotsky.

### MAX EASTMAN HAS TEXT

### He Also Exposes Secret Rule of Seven Members in Dominant Soviet Group.

By MAX EASTMAN.
Author of "Since Lenin Died."



The most important thing happening in the world today is the struggle between two groups of Bolsheviki for control of the Russian Communist party, and thus of the entire territory of the former Russian Empire. The group now holding the power is dominated by Stalin, and comprises in its General Staff Bukharin, Rykoff, Kalinin and Tomsky. The late Djerzinsky was, after Stalin, the most forceful man in it. The belief of this group is that the victory of the revolution and its future development can be defended only by holding the power firmly in their own hands, employing every conceivable device to prevent a régime of free discussion in the rank and file of the party and a real democratic election of the officials who shall control it.

The dominating personality in the opposition group is Trotsky, whose authority among Communists has increased during these two years of disciplined silence and hard work. He now has with him in a solid oppositional bloc not only Radek, Rakovsky, Sokolnikoff, Piatakoff, Preobrazhensky, Krestinsky and Krupskaya, the wife of Lenin, but also his most bitter opponents of two years ago, Zinovieff and Kameneff. This group believe that the revolution can be preserved and made to move forward only if the power is taken away from that small class of bureaucrats and professional party officials systematically appointed and controlled by Stalin from above and restored to the rank and file members of the party. (There is no question with either group of a democracy which shall extend beyond the limits of the Communist Party, which has about a million members.)

The attitude of the ruling group toward the opposition may be inferred from the words uttered by Djerzinsky shortly before his death last August:

"Keep your powder dry for the Autumn."

**Story of Suppressed Letter.**

The attitude of the opposition is firm and determined. They declare their absolute devotion to the unity of the party but no less absolutely demand that the bureaucratic dictatorship, established by Stalin in his all-powerful position as General Secretary, shall be broken and a régime of sincere and real party-democracy forthwith established. Such a régime would doubtless transfer a predominant influence from the Stalin to the Trotsky group, if only because of the persuasiveness and popularity of Trotsky. The personality of each of these leaders is thus in a peculiar manner bound up in the programs he represents. Stalin survives by the perfection of his bureaucratic machine. Trotsky's influence would probably become paramount if a régime of party democracy were established.

Three years ago, lying on his deathbed and deprived of the power of speech, Lenin wrote a letter predicting this struggle between Trotsky and Stalin, analyzing the characters of the two men and indicating the action which the party ought to take to avoid a split. The almost uncanny political sagacity of Lenin was never more clearly revealed than in that brief letter, which has been called his "Testament," to the party. It sounds today like the speech of a prophet.

The letter was locked up in the safe and declared non-existent by Stalin and his associates in power, because it contained a vigorous criticism of Stalin himself and a demand that he be removed from his commanding position as General Secretary of the party. I gave correct citations from the letter a year ago last Spring in my book "Since Lenin Died," but I was compelled to give them on my own authority. My citations were denounced and denied all over the world by the official Communist press, obeying orders from the ruling group in Russia. The Politburo itself issued from Moscow a document declaring in the same breath that the letter did not exist and that I had quoted it incorrectly! I am now able to quote the "Testament of Lenin" in full. The translation is my own and this is the first time this document has been published in any language:

**LENIN'S "LAST TESTAMENT."**

By the stability of the Central Committee, of which I spoke before, I mean measures to prevent a split, so far as such measures can be taken. For, of course, the White Guard in Russkaya Mysl (I think it was S. E. Oldenburg) was right when, in the first place, in his play against Soviet Russia he banked on the hope of a split in our party, and when, in the second place, he banked for that split on serious disagreements in our party.

Our party rests upon two classes, and for that reason its instability is possible, and if there cannot exist an agreement between those classes its fall is inevitable. In such an event it would be useless to take any measures, or in general to discuss the stability of our Central Committee. In such an event no measures would prove capable of preventing a split. But I trust that is too remote a future, and too improbable an event, to talk about.

I have in mind stability as a guarantee against a split in the near future, and I intend to examine here a series of considerations of a purely personal character.

I think that the fundamental factor in the matter of stability—from this point of view—is such members of the Central Committee as Stalin and Trotsky. The relation between them constitutes, in my opinion, a big half of the danger of that split, which might be avoided, and the avoidance of which might be promoted, in my opinion, by raising the number of members of the Central Committee to fifty or one hundred.

Comrade Stalin, having become General Secretary, has concentrated an enormous power in his hands; and I am not sure that he always knows how to use that power with sufficient caution. On the other hand Comrade Trotsky, as was proved by his struggle against the Central Committee in connection with the question of the People's Commissariat of Ways of Communication, is distinguished not only by his exceptional abilities—personally he is, to be sure, the most able man in the present Central Committee; but also by his too far-reaching self-confidence and a disposition to be too much attracted by the purely administrative side of affairs.

These two qualities of the two most able leaders of the present Central Committee might, quite innocently, lead to a split; if our party does not take measures to prevent it, a split might arise unexpectedly.

I will not further characterize the other members of the Central Committee as to their personal qualities. I will only remind you that the October episode of Zinovieff and Kameneff was not, of course, accidental, but that it ought as little to be used against them personally as the non-Bolshevism of Trotsky. [The fact is that Trotsky stood outside the Bolsevik party until the Summer of 1917.—M. E.]

**Estimate of Younger Leaders.**

Of the younger members of the Central Committee I want to say a few words about Bukharin and Piatakoff. They are, in my opinion, the most able forces (among the youngest), and in regard to them it is necessary to bear in mind the following: Bukharin is not only the most valuable and biggest theoretician of the party, but also may legitimately be considered the favorite of the whole party; but his theoretical views can only with the very greatest doubt be regarded as fully Marxist, for there is something scholastic in him (he never has learned, and I think never has fully understood, the dialectic).

And then Piatakoff—a man undoubtedly distinguished in will and ability, but too much given over to administration and the administrative side of things to be relied on in a serious political question.

Of course, both these remarks are made by me merely with a view to the present time, in the assumption that these two able and loyal workers may not find an occasion to supplement their knowledge and correct their one-sidedness.

25/XII/22.

**A Significant Postscript.**

*Postscript*: Stalin is too rough, and this fault, entirely supportable in relations among us Communists, becomes insupportable in the office of General Secretary. Therefore, I propose to the comrades to find a way to remove Stalin from that position and appoint to it another man who in all regards differs from Stalin in one superiority—namely, more patient, more loyal, more polite and more attentive to comrades, less capriciousness, &c., This circumstance may seem an insignificant trifle, but I think that from the point of view of preventing a split and from the point of view of the relation between Stalin and Trotsky which I discussed above, it is not a trifle, or it is such a trifle as may acquire a decisive significance. LENIN.

Jan. 4th, 1923.

October 18, 1926

# TROTSKY ADMITS DEFEAT, BOWS TO STALIN GROUP AS THE REAL RED CHIEFS

## HIS ASSOCIATES JOIN HIM

### All Opposition Leaders Agree to Obey Rules of the Party.

### CONFESS ERROR PUBLICLY

By WALTER DURANTY.

Copyright, 1926, by The New York Times Company. By Wireless to THE NEW YORK TIMES.

MOSCOW, Oct. 17.—The terms of the settlement arrived at between the Communist Party Central Committee, led by Joseph Stalin, and the opposition, led by Leon Trotsky, reveal complete defeat for Trotsky and his associates. Instead of being a compromise which rumor reported was the outcome of Trotsky's two weeks' fight against the Central Committee in violation of its laws, there has been unconditional capitulation by the insurgents.

Two weeks ago the Trotsky-Zinovieff group of minor leaders made their first public attack against the Central Committee in a meeting which was denounced as illegal and in a manner which the Central Committee called "a shameless violation of party discipline." Today the six leaders of the opposition—Trotsky, Zinovieff, Kameneff, Pyatikoff, Sokolnikoff and Yevdokimoff—publicly repudiated their actions in the press.

They admit their conduct was calculated to split the party, confess they violated discipline and promise to dissolve their fractional organization and submit without reserve to the decisions of the Central Committee.

**Details of the Capitulations.**

The six leaders preface their declaration with the statement that they continue to hold their own views, but then proceed to surrender all the machinery they had carefully constructed for the purpose of making these views effective. Promising to confine their opposition opinion "within the limits of the party constitution and the decisions of the Central Committee," they give up their claim to the right to defend their standpoint after the majority has voted them down and insure their silence at the fifteenth session of the party conference on Oct. 25, when the Central Committee has decreed there shall be no discussion of the points nearest the opposition's hearts.

"We disagreed with the majority of the Central Committee of the Congress on a number of principal problems," the six declare. "These views we still retain. But we categorically repudiate the theory and practice of the freedom of forming groups and fractions. At the same time we consider it our duty to openly recognize before the party that in the fight for our views we and our followers on a number of occasions after the Fourteenth Congress permitted ourselves to take steps which are in violation of party discipline and which tend to split the party.

"Considering these steps unconditionally wrong, we declare that we definitely give up fractional methods of defense of our views because of the danger of such methods for the unity of the party.

"We call for the same act from all comrades who hold our views. We call for the immediate dissolution of all the fractional groups formed around the views of the opposition."

The six leaders disavow fellowship with the opposition groups in the foreign Communist parties, specifically throwing overboard a number of foreign Communist leaders who had depended upon them for support.

**Call Two-Party Theory Wrong.**

"We consider deeply wrong the theory of two parties, the gospel about the liquidation of Communist International and Red Trade Union International, all attempts to create union with the Social Democratic parties and any widening of the concession policy beyond the limits set by Lenin.

"We consider unconditionally binding upon ourselves the resolutions of the Fourteenth Congress and Central Committee, and will unconditionally subordinate ourselves to them and work actively for their realization."

The six conclude with the expression of the firm hope "that their associates recently expelled from the party for sharing their opinions and following their example may be readmitted to membership in consideration of the sincere submission of their leaders."

In a resolution printed simultaneously with the declaration of the opposition the Central Committee states that from 53,208 Communists voting in party meetings during the campaign of opposition only 171 openly sided with Trotsky.

Today's declaration by Trotsky and his associates indicates that they realized that they were leaders without active followers and could fight no longer. Whatever concessions may have been made privately to the opposition leaders, for the rank and file of the party they appear to have rescued very little from the wreck. It is not, however, impossible that the penitent oppositionists may now be allowed to retain some party posts and even participate in the Government.

October 18, 1926

## *Communist Party Expels Trotsky and 81 Associates*

MOSCOW, Nov. 12 (AP).—The Central Communist Committee tonight expelled Leon Trotsky, Gregory Zinovieff, Leo Kameeff, Karl Radek, M. Smilga and M. Preobrashensky from the Communist Party.

It was the original intention of the Central Committee to lay the question of expulsion before the Communist Congress [which convenes Dec. 15], but the Oppositionists precipitated matters by organizing counter demonstrations, as well as illegal meetings, and taking possession of the meeting halls by force.

The Central Committee also expelled today seventy-six adherents of the rank and file of the Opposition. They were charged with ing a series of underground op- organizing a series of underground opposition meetings addressed by M. Trotsky, M. Kameneff and Christian Rakovsky, the former Soviet Ambassador to France.

November 13, 1927

## Trotsky Banished as Menace to Soviet Unity, Says High Russian Official Arriving at Berlin

By The Associated Press.

KOVNO, Lithuania, Jan. 30.—Late advices from semi-official sources in Moscow said that the Communist party had decided that because of Leon Trotsky's continued meddling with internal party affairs, it would be necessary to remove him from Soviety territory in order to preserve national unity.

It was understood that his family would be allowed to accompany him on the condition that he would never attempt to return to Moscow.

BERLIN, Jan. 30 (Jewish Telegraphic Agency).—Leon Trotsky has been banished from Russia, according to a leading Soviet official who has arrived in Berlin from Moscow.

He said the decision to exile Trotsky was taken by the Politbureau, the most important branch of the Soviet government. Of the ten members five voted for Trotsky's banishment, one abstained from voting and four voted against it.

Those who voted against Trotsky's exile, he said, were Kalinin, Rykof, Bucharin and Tomsky. The resolution was proposed by Joseph Stalin, Trotsky's principal foe.

After the decision was reached, according to this official, the Angora Government was approached for an arrangement to admit Trotsky to Constantinople. Mustapha Kemal Pasha, however, had informed Stalin, he said, that the admission of Trotsky to Constantinople would involve many delicate problems. He would, however, agree to admit the exile to Angora provided Trotsky were kept strictly within the grounds of the Soviet Embassy and when visiting the city be accompanied by guards.

The Soviet official further said that rumors prevalent in Moscow indicated that Trotsky had been seen in Tiflis on his way to Batum, whence he would be transported to Constantinople.

January 31, 1929

## Secrecy Surrounds Red Rulers in Kremlin; Publicity Stops at the Walls of the Fortress

MOSCOW (AP).—What goes on in the Kremlin has become a closed book of mystery to most of Russia and all the rest of the world.

All except a few men in the little group of communists who hold the nation in their grip live within its walls. The fortress of Moscow has become the fortress of communism, and only a few persons can enter the gates.

Of what sort are the men who live with their families in the Kremlin, in the old palace of the Czar and the houses that once sheltered his courtiers and his guards?

What do these men do with their evenings? How do they amuse themselves? What are their habits at work and at play? What are their tastes, their caprices, hobbies, failings? The world would like to know, perhaps, but it can't find out.

The light of publicity that beats upon thrones, on presidents, on oil kings and actors in the Western world is very, very dim in Russia. Its rays do not penetrate the guarded Kremlin at all, for the men who live there control the press and have the power to silence a wagging tongue.

Of one high official it is gossiped that he likes liquor inordinately; of another that he goes several times a week with his cronies to one of the aristocratic country homes near Moscow, now a recreation centre for the higher-ups, and there enjoys drinking bouts that are not particularly proletarian, and that is about all.

Of Stalin, the real ruler of the country—although his post is in the Communist party and not in the government at all—hardly anything personal is heard or said. He remains out of sight.

Stalin's office is in a building of steel-gray color, and his home inside the Kremlin walls. He has a wife and two children. Several commissars also have their wives and children with them in the Kremlin. They come and go, as do high military officers and others of importance, in American and British cars.

They are never dressed as other men one sees elsewhere in such expensive cars; but almost always in unpressed clothes, soft collar, usually colored, and a cap. Hats are bourgeois, they say in Red Russia.

Some of the little children who live within the Kremlin have French and German governesses, teaching them foreign tongues, just as the children of the aristocrats used to have.

How do their fathers provide such things when no Communist is allowed to have a salary of more than 225 rubles ($112.50) a month?

Well, that is just another one of the Kremlin's many mysteries.

July 21, 1929

## Bucharin Ousted From Communist Party Post; Rykoff and Tomsky Warned Against Dissent

By The Associated Press.

MOSCOW, Nov. 17.—Nikolai Bucharin today was expelled from the powerful political bureau of the Central Committee of the Communist party as the leader of the Right Wing opposition in the party.

For more than ten years M. Bucharin has been one of the most prominent leaders of the Communist party. He was for many years editor of Pravda, the official organ of the party, until removed early this year. He had also been a member of the executive committee of the party and a member of the Presidium Council of Supreme Economy.

At the same time today Alexis Rykoff and Michael Tomsky, also members of the political bureau, who hold besides important posts in the Soviet Government, were warned that if they continued to oppose the present policy of the party similar measures would be immediately taken against them.

N. A. Uglanov, Commissar of Labor, and several others broke with the Right Wing after admitting their "mistakes" before a plenary session of the Central Committee of the Communist party. In forecasting today's events, the official government organ Izvestiya nearly two weeks ago said that the results of the first year of the five-year industrialization plan had proved that members of the Right Wing were more in the wrong.

M. Bucharin, considered the greatest authority on Communist theory, was once an intimate friend of Joseph Stalin, strong man of the party, but is now stripped of almost all power. The Central Committee has been in session here since Nov. 10 and took the drastic step of expelling him from the political bureau because he "persisted in his mistakes."

Much surprise was caused by the stern warning to M. Rykoff, who is President of the Soviet Cabinet and chairman of the Council of Defense and Labor. The action against M. Tomsky, now department head in the Council of National Economy, who was once before punished for political heresy and then pardoned, created no surprise.

The committee decided to call the next All-Union Party Congress in 1930.

November 18, 1929

# STALIN DISMISSES RYKOFF

### MOLOTOFF NAMED TO POST

### People's Commissars' New Head Is Known as Firm Supporter of Stalin's Theories.

### UNITY OF RULE NOW EVIDENT

Special Cable to THE NEW YORK TIMES.

MOSCOW, Dec. 19.—Alexei Rykoff, whose prestige had almost vanished since his alleged connection with the recent espionage trial in Moscow, has been relieved of his office as president of the people's Council of Commissars, which corresponds to the office of Premier, and also of his post as president of the Council of Labor and Defense. Viacheslav Molotoff, one of Joseph Stalin's right-hand men, has succeeded him.

It is officially announced that M. Rykoff was relieved of office at his own request. Interest in the future of the man who during the last few months was regarded here as the chief opponent of M. Stalin, took a lively turn when M. Rykoff some weeks back announced he was going to the Caucasus for a "rest cure" but never reached his destination. He was said to have been taken off a train not far from Moscow early in November at M. Stalin's orders and brought back to the seat of government, where some said he was under preventative arrest awaiting trial for activities against the International. Around this time his name was associated with that of Sokonikoff, the Soviet Ambassador in London, as being concerned in a Right Wing plot against M. Stalin, who now seems to govern the country as head of the Communist party.

As against the Premiership, the head of the Communist party outside of the government seems to be the more powerful office. It is from this party and not from a government office that M. Rykoff's successor comes. M. Rykoff is the last of Lenin's colleagues in the Soviet Government that came to power in 1917 and was chosen to succeed Lenin as Premier.

Ever since his student days at Kazan this politician of peasant stock has spent periods in prison and exile and it looks now as if he had spent his revolutionary force.

December 20, 1930

# RYKOFF AGAIN WINS HIGH RUSSIAN POST

Bucharin and Tomsky Also Are Returned to Favor by Vote of All-Union Congress.

SOVIET HARMONY REGAINED

MOSCOW, March 17 (AP).—The restoration of Alexei Rykoff, recently deposed as Premier, and several others who were removed from their posts was one of the surprising developments of the Sixth All-Union Soviet Congress, which adjourned tonight.

Rykoff does not come back as Premier, but he was elected to the important Central Executive Committee, along with Nickolai Bucharin and Michael Tomsky. Not long ago both Bucharin and Tomsky appeared to be in as great disfavor as Rykoff himself.

Harmony appears to have been reestablished between the Rights and the Lefts and there was much handshaking as the Congress broke up so the delegates could go back home for the Spring planting.

The three outstanding Rights who have been reinstated are the forerunners of others who will be returned to grace, observers are saying, and the action of the Congress is interpreted as an indication that Joseph Stalin is still the strong man of Russia.

March 18, 1931

# STALINISM SHELVES WORLD REVOLT IDEA; TO WIN RUSSIA FIRST

Success of Socialism at Home Held Best of Propaganda for Conversion of Others.

VIEW IS DEEMED ORTHODOX

Huge Extent of Country Cited as Giving Possibility for Full Development of Marxism.

CAPITALISM HELD DOOMED

So Stalinists Feel They Are Not Violating Ideals in Diverting Efforts to One Nation.

By WALTER DURANTY.

Special Cable to THE NEW YORK TIMES.

PARIS, June 17.—The essential feature of "Stalinism," which sharply defines its advance and difference from Leninism and is the key to the comprehension of the whole five-year plan, is that it frankly aims at the successful establishment of socialism in one country without waiting for world revolution.

The importance of this dogma, which played a predominant rôle in the bitter controversy with Leon Trotsky and later with the "Rights" [Right-wing Russian Communists], cannot be exaggerated. It is the Stalinist "slogan" par excellence, and it brands as heretics or "defeatists" all Communists who refuse to accept it in Russia or outside.

**Marx Once Attacked View.**

Curiously enough, Karl Marx himself, in one of his earlier letters, described this theory as a fallacy and an illusion. Lenin, too, in his early belief that the World War would end in a stalemate from which a proletarian revolution would be the only issue, was reluctant to admit that a single Socialist State could flourish in a capitalist—therefore hostile—world. Trotsky after characteristic indecisiveness (he once told a Communist Youth meeting in Moscow that world revolution was "far, far beyond the mountains") tried to use Marx and Lenin to convict Stalin of heterodoxy.

Stalin had a clearer perception of Russia's possibilities and the reserves of untapped energy in her people, hardly less "virgin" than her soil. He saw, too, that the Soviet Union was not "one country" in the sense in which Marx wrote but a vast self-sufficing continent far more admirably fitted by its natural configuration and resources and by the character and ways of its population for a Communist experiment than what Marx prognosticated in a compact industrial State like England.

It can fairly be argued, no doubt, that Stalin may have been pushed further by the controversy with the Trotskyists and the Rights and by the enthusiasm of his younger followers than orthodox Marxism would approve. Indeed, such noted revolutionaries as Emma Goldman and Angelica Balabanoff, with whom the writer recently talked, unite with Trotsky in accusing Stalin of "perverting" or even "betraying" the revolution.

But development along Stalinist lines became inevitable from the day the United States broke the war deadlock and brought about a post-war "capitalist stabilization," which, though they called it temporary, the Bolsheviki even now do not believe to be fatally shattered by the current world depression. For that matter, too, Lenin's new economic policy was a flagrant retreat from orthodox Marxism, and if Stalin has had the will and strength to correct that change of the compass and bring the Soviet ship back to the Marxist course he may surely be pardoned for a doctrinal adjustment required and justified by circumstances.

It does follow, however, that the theory of "Soviet Socialist sufficiency," as it may be called, involves a certain decrease of interest in world revolution—not deliberately, perhaps, but by force of circumstances. The Stalinist socialization of Russia demands three things, imperatively—every ounce of effort, every cent of money, and peace. It does not leave the Kremlin time, cash or energy for "Red propaganda" abroad, which, incidentally, is a likely cause of war, and, being a force of social destruction, must fatally conflict with the five-year plan, which is a force of social construction.

The writer ventures to say that at the present moment the Communist International's activities are confined to the Communist parties of other countries and to a small group of zealots in Moscow, whose influence and importance are much more theoretical than real. Of course, Stalinism refuses to admit this openly, and takes refuge behind two theses—first, that world revolution is inevitable anyway as a result of capitalist economic rivalries (this is pure Marxist dogma which even zealots must accept); second, that the success of socialism in Russia is the best possible propaganda for the rest of the world.

But facts are facts, whether one admits them or not, and it is quite on the cards that the real source of the quarrel of Trotsky and foreign Marxist theoreticians with Stalinism is their realization that Stalinism, while retaining world revolution as an ultimate goal, has abandoned it as an immediate practical issue little less completely than the early Christian Church abandoned the millennium or second advent when Constantine made it the official faith of the Roman Empire.

June 18, 1931

# HOW RUSSIA CHARTS HER ECONOMIC COURSE

## Sixteen Men Sit in Moscow and Plan Fifteen Years Ahead for The Future Welfare of a Nation of 146,000,000 People

***IN Soviet Russia the industry, trade and farming of the nation is planned for and charted by a small committee in Moscow. Stuart Chase, economist and certified public accountant, has recently returned from an extended first-hand study of the famous Gosplan, its aims, its methods and its achievements. The following article gives a summary of his views of this dramatic experiment.***

**By STUART CHASE.**

SIXTEEN men in Moscow today are attempting one of the most audacious economic experiments in history. As the presidium of the State Planning Commission, responsible to the Council of People's Commissars and popularly known as the Gosplan, they are laying down the industrial future of 146,000,000 people and of one-sixth of the land area of the world for a period of fifteen years. They are making a careful and immensely detailed plan for a year in advance, a careful but less detailed plan for the next five years, and are blocking out the general economic development for the next fifteen years. Not only industry, but agriculture, transportation, superpower, exports, imports and the Government budget, all come within their purview.

Here in America we can sometimes coordinate production to demand, or "balance the load," as the engineers say, in a single factory; less frequently we can balance it in a single strong industrial monopoly, like the American Telephone and Telegraph Company, but in Russia they are trying to balance it for the whole economic structure, particularly as a protection against crises and speculative booms. The Gosplan is our War Industries Board of 1918 carried several dizzy leaps into the future. It is an experiment so immense, so novel and so courageous that no student of economics can afford to neglect it. Whether it transcends the limits of human administrative capacity and fails, or whether it meets this challenge and succeeds, it has much to teach us. It is something new in the world.

**Wholesale Control the Aim.**

Suppose you were asked tomorrow to take a train to Washington, to sit at a desk in a Government bureau, to take pencil and paper and tell the railroads, the power companies, the steel mills, the coal mines, the oil fields, the Secretary of the Treasury, the banks, the wholesale houses, the farmers, the ship lines and the automobile factories how to order their capital investments and their raw materials, how to plan their production and distribution—for the next five years. One suspects that even Henry Ford would quail before the order. For lesser mortals a journey to the moon would seem about as feasible. Yet here are men who have accepted the challenge in a larger though less industrially complicated country.

The Gosplan would be impossible without a high degree of economic socialization through which its mandates can be put into practical operation. Russia is far from a Communist, or even a pure Socialist, State, but it does carry on with a larger amount of socialization than any other modern community, except possibly Denmark. According to Government statistics not over 10 per cent. of the agricultural output of Russia which finds an outside market is socialized; that is to say, it is not in the hands of Government farms or producers' cooperative societies. Ninety per cent. is the work of the individual peasant, who is in effect a private trader. To get his wheat and milk and pork upon the open market, however, the peasant must sell a large fraction of his produce to Government-controlled wholesale houses at prices that are largely fixed in advance. Nor can he export any of his produce except through the Government export monopoly. So, while the bulk of agricultural production is not socialized, its distribution is.

Of industrial production it is estimated that 83 per cent. is publicly controlled. If we exclude the output of local handicrafts the percentage will be higher. The private factory owner and foreign concessionaire probably do not manufacture more than 5 per cent. of the present factory output. It is said that more than 90 per cent. is in the hands of the Government trusts. There are several hundreds of these trusts; they are semi-independent, legal entities responsible for their own obligations, making their own agreements with the labor unions and committed to the earning of profits. But instead of going to stockholders the profits go into the Government budget.

Trust managers are appointed by the Supreme Economic Council of the Government, while prices of trust products are frequently controlled, and the disposition of fixed capital is always controlled—three vital factors which with other regulations tie the whole trust structure closely to the State. You can call it State socialism or State capitalism, as you prefer, but it is certainly industrial socialization on an enormous scale.

**The Government Trusts.**

Wholesale trade is largely in the hands of the "syndicates," which are the selling houses of all the trusts in one field—the textile syndicate and the sugar syndicate are instances. The Soviet authorities figure that approximately 70 per cent. of all retail trade in industrial goods, excluding local barter and trading in the villages, is in the hands of Government stores, trust stores or cooperative stores. The private shopkeeper has less than a third of the trade now, and is losing, relative to the cooperatives, every year. Thus distribution, both wholesale and retail, is largely socialized.

Finally, the Government—either central or local—operates directly the railroads, steamship lines, telegraph and telephone services, and all public utilites, including large scale electric power developments. It also controls prices, money, banking and credit and has a monopoly of export and import trade.

On the whole, the system is a curious mixture of socialization with State socialism, State capitalism, cooperation, controlled concessions—all in the kettle; but this brief sketch makes it clear that save for the peasant producers—whose markets are tied up in the system—socialization is the rule in Russia. The Gosplan accordingly has plenty of channels through which it can work.

The goal to be achieved by the central plan is simple and straightforward: A maximum production of necessities and plain comforts for the producing population of Russia at a minimum of human effort, while at the same time scrupulously safeguarding the health, safety, education, opportunity for leisure and working conditions of those that labor. In other words, however great the benefits of low cost production, it must not be obtained at the expense of the fundamental health and welfare of the workers.

In achieving this maximum production with a minimum of waste, it is proposed to locate industries near their sources of raw material, which already is being done; to eliminate competitive crosshauling, advertising, salesmanship; to encourage by grants of new capital to those industries (like iron and steel) which have hitherto been underdeveloped; to discourage any duplication or excess capacity of industrial equipment by withholding capital; to build no more shoe factories than are sufficient to provide shoes for the people of Russia, no more textile mills, no more sugar factories; to encourage electrification as the basic source of power; to exploit oil fields and coal fields as a unit without the interference of property lines (the Baku oil field is already operated on this basis). In brief, to try and do the job right from the engineering point of view. Whether it is right from the psychological point of view, only time can tell.

**The Shortage of Capital.**

War communism, which was in effect from 1918 to 1921, was largely a planless chaos. The new economic policy inaugurated by Lenin in the latter year set up a host of boards and commissions to deal more pragmatically with harsh realities. Interests began to clash, particularly as the economic structure started to revive and capital was available for the expansion of industry. This capital was severely limited. Would it go to electrification, to the railroads, to agricultural experiment stations, to canals, to the iron and steel industry, to the drilling of new oil wells? The Russians are passionate pleaders and one can imagine the officers of the budget sitting amid a flow of rhetoric and sweating large drops. Twenty billions called for, and only one to give. Nor is America the only country where town boosters are eloquent. From the Yellow Sea to the Baltic the "grandest little burg on earth" pleaded for its power station or fleet of tractors or new housing project.

It was a case either of flip a coin for it or deliberately and intelligently plan. Only so could be created a first line of defense against the piteous wails of every industry and every geographical section.

The early work of the Gosplan was concerned with laying a statistical basis for its future tables and diagrams and with organizing subsidiary groups throughout the country. Every one admits that the first statistics of the young republic were sketchy and unreliable. They gave only the crudest notion of what was actually happening. Obviously this situation had to be corrected if curves for the future, which were based on past performance, were to be worth more than so much waste paper. For the fiscal year 1926 (and thus prepared in 1925) a rough national plan was worked out, but I was told that the basic statistics were too poor to make it of much value. A year later (1926) the authorities believed that the statistical situation—that is, the reliability of crop reports, factory production figures, trade turnover figures, &c.—had so far improved that it would be possible to lay down an integrated plan for 1927. Then they began to set up workable standards for the various branches of industry to meet. Finally, in the Spring of this year, a five-year plan was published in a book of 300 pages, and on this five-year plan industry is now operating.

### Genesis of the Gosplan.

The gentlemen who run Russian economics do not labor on the flip-a-coin basis. They proceeded to get together a group of able economists, engineers and statisticians and ordered them—as President Wilson ordered the War Industries Board—to outline a program: a plan for next year, a plan for the next five years, a plan for the next fifteen years. And so, in 1922, the Gosplan came into being. It was paper work, inevitably abundant with theory and speculation, but at the same time it was an answer to a tangible, immediate crisis.

The national Gosplan at Moscow now has a large building to itself not far from the Kremlin. The atmosphere reminded me strongly of the old Food Administration barracks in which I worked at Washington—the temporary partitions, the hurrying messengers, the calculating machines, the telephones, the cleared desks, the unending panorama of charts and maps. It is an atmosphere tense with effort, in which 500 men and women take their work with the utmost seriousness. They feel, and one feels with them, that they are challenged by a problem that lies at the borderline of the capacity of the human intellect.

There are at present over 500 persons on the central staff in Moscow, headed by a governing board of sixteen, who are appointed by the Council of People's Commissars. In addition there are a number of consulting experts on a part-time arrangement. The staff is divided into a Reconstruction Division, a Production Division and an Economic Division. A monthly statistical review is published, much of the data for which are kept up to date by information wired from the outlying local districts.

To coordinate its activities local planning boards (little Gosplans) have been set up all over the country. Each constituent republic has such a board, each major district, each smaller provincial area. Every agricultural centre, every factory, prepares reports that ultimately come into the Gosplan calculations. No major step in industry, agriculture, transportation, superpower or finance can be taken without the visa of the Gosplan. It is the clearing house for the whole industrial structure. Yet, legally, it is only an advisory body—one arm of the Council of Labor and Defense. It can promulgate no legislation, issue no "cease and desist" orders. Its power comes from the fact that the supreme administrative body of the republic, the Council of People's Commissars, will not normally act on economic matters until it has obtained the approval of the Gosplan. Its real power, as opposed to its legal authority, is accordingly very great. It charts the course upon which the ship of state is steered.

### Powers of the Gosplan.

It would be a mistake to suppose, however, that the Gosplan is the sole agent for economic coordination and forward planning; it is rather the court of last resort. The Supreme Economic Council, which directs the trusts and operates industry, has a whole series of planning boards connected with its administrative branches. These boards work out operating schedules for the future, propose the allocation of new capital, industry by industry, and make detailed proposals of what they think should be done. When such proposals are finally thrashed out, then they go to the Gosplan for acceptance or revision. The Gosplan has itself been following industry closely; it has on the table, furthermore, the current proposals for agricultural development, the proposals for new railway lines, for power sites, for exports; finally, it has its own one-year and five-year programs as a bench mark. As a resultant of all these forces it is the only body in the State which can intelligently accept or revise the proposals of the planning boards of the Supreme Economic Council, or of the railroads, or of any other operating group. It alone can fit the jigsaw puzzle together.

The objectives of the Gosplan appear to have been two: To bring Russian economic output up to the pre-war basis of productivity and to make Russia economically self supporting so far as is reasonably possible. These two objectives, furthermore, are not in complete harmony, because self sufficiency means a greater relative expenditure on capital goods than on goods for immediate consumption, and thus delays the attainment of the pre-war output capacity.

Despite this handicap, the Gosplan officials report that the pre-war level for all industry combined has been reached and passed, with specific industries still below and others far above the 1913 standard. Therefore these officials feel the first objective of the Gosplan, broadly speaking, has been attained, though much remains to be done in pulling up the lagging minority.

### The Problem of Machinery.

The second objective is far more complicated and difficult. Russia has more than enough foodstuffs with which to feed herself. But industrially she has always drawn heavily on other countries in exchange for her food surplus. Somewhere within her far-flung borders there is nearly every sort of raw material, or the means to mine it or grow it; but the specific development for all sorts of essential manufactured goods has hitherto been lacking. Cotton can be grown in Russia, but the bulk of the material for her textile mills has always come from America, and still does.

> ## *HOW COMMUNIST IS RUSSIA?*
>
> *According to Soviet Government records the following proportion of the economic activities of the nation are publicly operated:*
>
> ***All the railroads, steamship lines, telegraph and telephone services, electric light and power plants; all of the export and import trade, and all of the banks are controlled directly by the central or local Governments.***
>
> ***Of industrial production 83 per cent. is controlled by Government trusts or syndicates.***
>
> ***Of retail trade in industrial goods 70 per cent. is in the hands of Government, trust or cooperative stores.***
>
> ***Of the agricultural output 10 per cent. is in the hands of Government farms or producers' cooperatives.***

Meanwhile, the mill machinery has crossed the border from England or Germany, or elsewhere. To grow cotton and make textile machinery in sufficient quantities to meet national requirements is a large and complicated problem. Behind it march in dismal phalanx the problems of rubber, chemicals, tractors, motor cars, coal cutting machinery, locomotives, trolley cars, steamships, mill machinery of all kinds, instruments of precision, and what not. For many commodities, the cost of economic self-sufficiency, particularly at the present time, is vastly higher than the import cost—if the goods could be readily obtained on the world market. For some commodities it is positively prohibitive.

It thus devolves upon the Gosplan to lay down the general policy and to determine how far economic self-sufficiency shall go. There may be a concrete and comprehensive determinant, but I could not find it. Broadly speaking, we know it goes all the way in respect to iron and steel and electrification. There is no phase of either industry that is not planned to bear the trade-mark, "Made in Russia." Rubber, cotton and cork plantations are being experimented with. There is talk of large silk farms, of a huge automobile plant, of tractor factories. But it would take a year to find, and a book to tell the exact status of the plans and the tangible achievement of the policy of economic self-sufficiency. Meanwhile an increase in foreign trade is planned for the next few years rather than the reverse.

The five-year program of the Gosplan covers the period Oct. 1, 1926, to Oct. 1, 1931. During that period it calls for a 78 per cent. increase in the physical volume of industrial production, against a 30 per cent. increase in agricultural production. With industry growing faster than agriculture, it is hoped to close the famous "scissors," and to give the peasant an adequate flow of textiles and hardware in return for his wheat and his beef, as well as to bring industrial prices into reasonable alignment with agricultural prices. One year of the five is nearly completed, and figures are available, based on performance to date, to tell whether the program as outlined is actually being carried out.

### Forecasts and Results.

Industrial production was budgeted to increase by about 15 per cent. as an average for the five years. Actually, according to Gosplan data, it has increased 13.7 per cent. The aggregate of agricultural production, which is not locally consumed but finds a market, was budgeted to increase by 6 per cent.; on the average its increase is put at 8.7 per cent. The shooting is thus not bullseye work, but, if these figures are correct, it is close enough to make the five-year plan look as if it had a fighting chance, particularly as heavier relative revenues are planned in the later years.

On Sept. 9, 1927, the Gosplan released its conclusions for the fiscal year 1927, and its proposals for the year 1928. Perhaps there is no better way to show the scope of its work than briefly to summarize that report.

It starts with a list of five major difficulties. Russian statisticians have a genius for being gloomy. The Gosplan finds that relative to needs the industrial structure is growing all too slowly and it sees no turning point in this relative backwardness for years to come. The second black mark is the fact that population is growing faster than it can adequately be cared for, with a very serious unemployment situation as a result. The third is the lack of alignment between agricultural and industrial production—the "scissors" are still open. The fourth is the difficulty in knowing where to draw the line between industry producing capital goods and industry producing goods for immediate consumption. The fifth is the difficulty in finding the technical ability to carry out the immense projects in new capital construction, for which a part of the funds is available. Money is ready but not the full engineering staff.

Then the report proceeds to more cheerful matters. The mass of agricultural and industrial products that entered trade in 1927, it states, amounted to $9,606,000,000. It estimates that in 1928 the total should reach $10,874,000,000, an increase of 13.2 per cent. Prices are to be cut in 1928, however, which will bring the gross volume down to $10,323,000,000, or a money increase of 6.4 per cent. (The physical volume, it is estimated, will remain at 13 per cent, and thus roughly approximate what the authorities believe will be a second successful year on the original five-year program: a 15 per cent. increase in industrial goods and a 6 per cent. increase in agricultural goods.) The productivity of labor is scheduled to increase 12 per cent. in 1928, and manufacturing costs to decline 6 per cent. on the average. Transportation is to increase 12 per cent.

In 1928 consumption goods will not be increased as fast as the ratios of the previous years. A relatively greater effort will go into capital goods. Officials admit that this will cause some dissatisfaction, but they point out that there is now at least enough to go around on a modest standard of living, and capital goods (new machinery and tools) are urgently needed. In respect to consumption goods, they think that the first six months of 1928 will be harder sledding for consumers than the second six months.

**The Capital Invested.**

The total capital investment in 1928, it is estimated, will be $2,678,000,000 an increase of 13.8 per cent, in money total over 1927. Of this total, Government industries are allowed $630,000,000, transportation $385,000,000, electrification projects $144,000,000. About 1,000,000 men, it is figured, will be engaged in construction work. Construction costs are scheduled to come down at least 8 per cent. during the year. The total credit facilities of the nation, it is planned, will expand 23.2 per cent, in 1928 to a total increase of $605,125,000, with a relatively greater share for long term credits available.

Of all hired manual labor at the present time, Gosplan records show, 80.6 men out of 100 work for the Government or the cooperatives, leaving only 19.4 men working for private industry. According to the report these ratios should rise during 1918, forcing private industry to even lower percentages. In respect to distribution, the present share controlled by the Government and cooperatives is said to be 72.6 per cent. It is due to rise to 84.5 per cent in 1928.

**Charting the Future.**

And finally, the Gosplan executives believe that the coming year will proceed "on a non-crisis course on the basis of economic equilibrium."

A more audacious document it would be difficult to imagine. These sixteen men salt down the whole economic life of 146,000,000 people for a year in advance as calmly as a Gloucester man salts down his fish. Furthermore, what I have seen of the actual working of the economic structure in Russia leads me to suppose that, failing acts of God, the actual performance for the year 1928 will not be so very far from the prophecies and commandments so calmly made.

For the last century men have been arguing as to the relative merits of a collectivist versus an individualist economic system. Millions of words have been printed, millions of cubic feet of hot air have been discharged into the atmosphere, and nobody really knows anything about it. Russia is beginning—just beginning—to provide an enormous experimental station in which the interminable and fruitless argument can perhaps some day be settled on the basis of cold facts.

December 11, 1927

# SOVIET HOME POLICY TURNS TO THE LEFT

## Victory Over Rich Peasants in Grain Collection Fight Brings Positive Radical Trend.

## DRASTIC PROGRAM DRAFTED

### Peasant Tax, Hitting the Wealthy 'Kulaks,' Will Be Increased 35 Per Cent. and Industry Advanced 23.

By WALTER DURANTY.

By Wireless to THE NEW YORK TIMES.

MOSCOW, March 8.—The Soviet's internal policy has taken a definite trend to the "Left," a trend that is not a mere matter of appearances and one that is likely to continue for several months at least.

This course is made abundantly clear by the following four facts:

1. The Communist Party is positively committed to a strong campaign against the Kulaks, or richer peasants, throughout the country.

2. There is a new and vigorous campaign in the town and country alike against private traders, or so-called "speculators."

3. The important Peasants' and Workers' Inspection Commissariat has issued recommendation in the strongest terms that the peasant tax be increased 35 per cent., pressing, of course, most heavily upon the Kulaks.

4. It was recently decided to increase industrial production 23 per cent., in terms of the pre-war ruble, as compared with last year, whereas the initial program of the State Planning Committee last Fall called for an increase of only 14 per cent.

**Similar To Opposition's Program.**

This naturally means a greater expenditure upon industry with a corresponding benefit to urban industrial workers, which is strangely reminiscent of the program of the late lamented Opposition.

Indeed it might almost seem as though the Opposition had guessed the opinion of the dominant proletariat and its elite, Communist Party, more accurately than their adversaries, despite the fact that the latter won an easy victory as a result of the Opposition's fatal error in adopting factional methods which threatened seriously to disrupt the whole party.

Though this is partly true, it is not the whole truth, nor even the most important part of the truth. It must be admitted that this swing to the "Left" was decided upon only recently, after considerable hesitation on the part of the important members of the Soviet Administration. What really brought it about was the striking change in the past two months in the grain collection situation.

At the end of the year the grain situation, which is the foundation of the Soviet's national economy, was little short of catastrophic. Something like a panic ensued in certain quarters and there was talk of sending M. Solonikoff abroad to secure a rapid supply of manufactured goods "on the best terms possible," a phrase with obvious implications.

**Stalin Wins Fight With Kulaks.**

Then Joseph Stalin put his foot down and refused to capitulate before the Kulaks without a fight. Every instrument of Soviet power was mobilized throughout the country and the grain was collected by fair means, or, as the Pravda admitted, by means less fair.

And the grain came in. On March 1 the collection total was only 4 per cent. below the figure for the same period last year. The Kulaks had tried to sabotage the collections and had failed. So why fear them any longer. That is the real basis of today's internal policy, especially if it is understood that the Kulaks in Bolshevist eyes stand for the whole system of private capitalism wihch Bolshevism is pledged to overthrow.

This success gave fresh vigor to that still existant pure Communist sentiment which M. Stalin, astute politician though he be, genuinely represents against the weaker vessels who feel it inevitable that the Soviet Union, with its 85,000,000 peasants, is gradually developing into a petitbourgeoise State with a system of mild paternalistic Socialism, now exemplified on a tiny scale by Latvia.

Everything now depends upon the extent to which the Kulaks really have been beaten, and, what is more, upon the extent which the Soviet Administration's estimate of the Kulaks as a small section of the peasantry unpopular with their fellows is really correct.

The Pravda admits that the Kulaks were trying to sabotage the grain campaign, but hopes that they will be again defeated by the increased area sown by the poor and little peasants or will themselves surrender.

The answer will be known in June orJuly, but if, for any reason whatsoever, the harvest is poor, the present difficulties of the Soviet Government will be increased enormously.

March 9, 1928

# STALIN DENOUNCES 'TECHNICIANS' PLOT'

## Calls It a New Form of Foreign Intervention in Speech on Internal Policy.

## URGES CONTACT WITH MASS

### Rejects Capitalistic Remedies for Economic Crisis—Would "Re-energize" Communists.

By WALTER DURANTY.

Wireless to THE NEW YORK TIMES.

MOSCOW, April 18.—A speech by M. Stalin is always something of an event, because the General Secretary of the Communist Party is markedly less talkative than the majority of his colleagues in the Kremlin. The speech by M. Stalin which is published today is especially interesting because it was delivered at the recent mixed plenary session of the Central Committee and the Central Control Committee of the Communist Party. It is the voice of the Kremlin speaking through its influential mouthpiece.

M. Stalin discussed three topics—self-criticism, grain collections and the Shakhta affair or the "technicians' plot." His statement reveals much that was hitherto obscure in respect to the Kremlin's internal policy.

A few days ago another prominent spokesman of the Kremlin, M. Bukharin, made the assertion that the counter-revolutionary activities of the technicians, discovered in the Shakhta coal region, exists perhaps also in the chemical and munitions industries. Others have declared that they are present in the metallurgic industry besides.

M. Stalin sweepingly describes the Shakhta affair as "new foreign intervention." Military intervention of the period of 1918-20 failed, so the hostility of foreign capitalists, he says, took the fresh form of "economic intervention" through bourgeois technicians.

It is not fortuitous that the Shakhta molehill is presented as an intervention mountain. It is not fortuitous that elsewhere in the speech the grain collecting crisis in the last three months of 1927 was presented as an attempt by "Kulak speculators" to disrupt national economy and starve the urban proletariat and the Red Army.

**Warns Against Stifling Criticism.**

It is not fortuitous that M. Stalin warns against leaders who lose contact with the masses, who ignore or stifle criticism, who fail to foresee difficulties; or that he emphasizes the Kremlin's recent decision that all important Bolshevist executives must spend at least one month every year in local work in the provinces.

All this means that the Kremlin has finally emerged from the fog of ideological discussion with the opposition that has obscured its vision for the past two year, and is now facing the facts. It now seems that while the Communists argued, things were happening. Not the former owners of concessions or foreign foes alone have been active, but every element hostile to the Kremlin's power.

The forces of religion have grown stronger and bolder as pressure against them relaxed. The newspapers today carry full stories of Easter drunkenness, accidents, disorder and a sharp increase in absentees from work.

And M. Bukharin himself is scheduled to speak tonight at a special meeting of the society for the struggle against alcoholism.

The richer peasant opposition probably is due more to economic than political reasons, but it is among this section of the rural population that religious influence is the greatest, as M. Stalin remarks. And the fact that it is these who are economically unsatisfied is precisely the most dangerous feature of the situation.

April 19, 1928

# NEW SOVIET TAXES HIT RICH PEASANTS

## Moscow Congress Adopts Plan Increasing Revenues and Relieving Poor Farmer.

By WALTER DURANTY.

Wireless to THE NEW YORK TIMES.

MOSCOW, April 20.—The new peasant tax was last night approved "basically" by the joint Central Executive Committee and Council of Nationalists, which consttiute the Congress of the Soviet Union, but a commission of fifty-nine members was appointed to introduce certain corrections before the measure takes effect. Thus mildly the Soviet press announces the conclusion of one of the hottest and most prolonged debates in recent years.

According to a spokesman for the Kremlin, the new tax law, which it is estimated will bring in 25 per cent. more revenue than last year, or 400,000,000 rubles, compared with 320,000,000, would free 35 per cent. of the peasantry, the poorest, from any payment whatever and would reduce the proportion paid by 53 per cent. more, the middle peasants, from half of the whole revenue to 38 per cent. The remaining 12 per cent. the richer peasants or Kulaks, who last year paid the other half, will now pay 62 per cent.

If Mr. Garvin, Arthur Ransome or other pundits abroad still imagine that the Kremlin's internal policy is toward the Right, or toward the Left only in semblance, these figures may undeceive them.

The project, which will go into effect with only minor modifications during the fiscal year from Oct. 1, 1928, to Sept. 30, 1929, in regard to 85 per cent. of the total population of the Soviet Union, has raised class discrimination, against the Kulaks, to the highest point since the introduction of the Nep, or new economic policy.

April 21, 1928

# 178,000 FIRMS QUIT BUSINESS IN RUSSIA

## Private Traders With Capital of $500,000,000 Forced Out in the Past 18 Months.

## AIM IS TO END ALL BY 1930

By WALTER DURANTY.

Wireless to THE NEW YORK TIMES.

MOSCOW, April 29.—In the fiscal year ending Sept. 30, 1927, 108,000 private firms were put out of business, according to the Workers' Gazette. Later figures show that 70,000 more, or 28 per cent. of the private firms, were closed down during the first half of the present fiscal year, between Oct. 1 and April 1.

Moreover, the State Planning Commission hopes that the private firms will be entirely eliminated by Jan. 1, 1930. That is the present status of the unrealized "swing to the Right" so confidently predicted by foreign optimists as a result of the downfall of the Trotsky Opposition.

Estimates vary as to the total of private capital thus forced out of activity. It is probably not less than 1,000,000,000 rubles [$500,000,000].

A recent decree of the Soviet Government offering favorable terms to private house builders evidently aims to push private money in that direction. But private capital has been short enough to become shy.

According to your correspondent's information, the private capitalists are now investing money in State loans which pay from 10 to 15 per cent. and are tax free. This robs the State of the benefit of private initiative and obliges the State to pay large annual interest to the private capitalists.

There are other adverse portents. The April grain collections have fallen down deplorably, not only below a third of this year's program but far below last year. It appears as if the peasants, who have been successfully sat upon during the past three months, were beginning to kick against the pricks.

The Spring grain-sowing campaign, according to the Pravda and other official newspapers, is not going too well. The sovereign Communist Party has bitten off this year an exceeding large mouthful. It is sometimes easier to bite than to chew.

April 30, 1928

# *PEASANTS IN RUSSIA ARE TO BE SOCIALIZED*

## *Finding Them Immune to Communism, Soviet Government Will Try Another Method.*

Recent numbers of Pravda, the official organ of the Russian Communist Party, have expounded a new project for Russian unification by which it is hoped the peasants, who compose 80 per cent. of the population of the USSR, may be brought under the control of the Soviet Government, if not of the Communist Party. As is well known, the peasants have all along rejected Communism, except in so far as it pertained to a redistribution of land, while the "kulak," or wealthy peasant, has even more power and wealth today than he had in Czarist days.

According to Pravda, the kulak must be destroyed, while the poorer peasants are to be socialized, and in the following manner: The destruction of the kulak will be effected by the compulsory confiscation of his stocks of production, and heavy fines for not using the soil to its best advantages. It will be made impossible for him to hire labor or to sell his surplus produce to the middleman. The cooperative societies will take the place of the middle man and any cash profits from the transaction must be used by the kulak to purchase bonds in the peasant loan, which will be devoted to the benefit of the poorer peasant.

Meanwhile, this poorer peasant, who even in Czarist days regarded the kulak with respect, hoping to become one himself some day, will receive greater facilities in the way of being exempt from land taxes for certain periods and supplied with modern agricultural machinery purchased by the State out of the funds of the peasant loan. Closer contact between the cooperatives and the State will be established, and selling will only be possible through the medium of these organizations.

Although the revolution, for the time, destroyed the power of the kulak, particularly in the great grain districts of Russia, his superior education and defiance of Communism caused him to win in the race with the Government to capture the adhesion of the poorer peasant and to emerge from the five years of chaos still defying the Soviet and more powerful than ever.

Soviet officials have persistently closed their eyes to this situation and accepted the killing of tax collectors as a matter of course. In certain respects the kulak has even been encouraged, as were the private merchants or "nepmans" after the new private trading laws of 1922. In certain cases he has even been allowed to abuse his privileges. There being no possibility or even object in Soviet Russia of investing profit in real property, the kulak, like the nepman, either hoarded his wealth or spent it in living and dressing better than his neighbor. Subtle Communist agents were then instructed to agitate against these kulaki as capitalists living as bourgeoisie on the blood and toil of their poorer neighbors. But as these poorer neighbors had been bound to the richer by centuries of land traditions the agents were not successful.

May 27, 1928

# PEASANT OFFENSIVE ON MOSCOW GROWS

## Assassinations of Bolshevist Agents in Villages Are Double Last Year's, Pravda Says.

By WALTER DURANTY.

Wireless to THE NEW YORK TIMES.

MOSCOW, Nov. 11.—"Class warfare" in Russian villages is rapidly becoming more than a Marxist formula. The Moscow press is full of stories of the "kulak," or wealthy peasant counter-offensive, or the "fiery activity of anti-Soviet elements" expressed not only in widespread arson but in bloody affrays and in assassinations of social workers or Bolshevist correspondents.

Since the November holidays Izvestia has reported six such killings and five cases of persons seriously wounded. Pravda recently stated that fifty social workers were killed and many wounded in the two months from Aug. 15 to Oct. 15. Today it adds that the number of such killings this year is double that of the preceding year.

The Soviet newspapers present this somewhat warning phenomenon as a "kulak revenge against new taxation and successful measures to socialize villages." In other words, as a stabbing in the back by a cowardly and defeated foe.

My knowledge of Russian character forces me to question this viewpoint. Oriental fatalism makes for passivity in defeat, and it is my personal conviction that the present symptoms have a distinctly aggressive character and represent a mass movement—confined, it is true, to a certain section of peasant society—demanding serious consideration.

It is no secret that some economic experts have feared that the process of socialization of the villages was being pushed too rapidly among peasants already disgruntled by the "extraordinary measures" undertaken earlier in the year to complete grain collections. On the other hand, it is wrong to exaggerate the danger or to attempt to regard it as a precursor of revolt against Soviet power. But is certainly looks like one of those "warnings" to which in the past the Kremlin's ear has shown itself to be far from deaf.

Whether my opinion is right or wrong, there is for the Kremlin one reassuring factor in the situation: the October grain collections reached the record figure of 1,750,000 tons, surpassing even the bumper collections of October, 1926.

November 12, 1928

# RUSSIA WILL PUSH RURAL COMMUNISM

## Congress Votes Five-Year Program of Socialization Despite Peasant Discontent.

## BIG CROP INCREASE ONE AIM

### Move Held of Great Importance Because It Is an Effort to End Capitalism Everywhere in Russia.

By WALTER DURANTY.

Wireless to THE NEW YORK TIMES.

MOSCOW, Dec. 16.—The session of the Soviet Congress that terminated last night still further emphasized the Kremlin's intentions of carrying our rural socialization as rapidly as possible. Despite widespread peasant discontent due to the "extraordinary measures" used in the State grain collections in the Spring and Summer, despite the fact that this year's grain collections so far are only a trifle above last year's level for the same period (which was so low as to lead it to the said extraordinary measures after the new year) and despite the competition of private traders who offer the peasants from 70 to 150 per cent more for their grain than the "fixed prices" paid by the State's collecting organizations, it is clear that Congress has decided to follow to the letter the agrarian policy outlined by the November plenary session of the Communist Party Central Committee.

The Congress unanimously adopted a resolution to introduce a five years' agrarian plan, corresponding to the five years' plan for industrialization, whereby it is proposed to increase the crop total 30 to 35 per cent between 1929 and 1934.

This very parallel is a very significant feature because the basic purpose of the industrialization program is to complete the socialization of the urban centres. It is hoped that in five years the agrarian program will do the same for the country.

**Would End Incongruity.**

This has enormous importance for the future because it indicates that the Kremlin is now fully aware of the incongruity of two opposing systems of economy—capitalism and socialism—side by side in the same country. The point is that the methods contemplated by the five-year agricultural plan is essentially socialist in character, namely, an enormous extension of State farms, State-aided "collectivities" (groups of small peasant units for cooperative working), communal farms and State-aided "metayage," here called "contractation."

In other words there is now being carried on in the rural areas the same sort of drive against private capitalism as occurred in urban centres in 1924-25 when it was realized that the "nepmen" were getting dangerously strong.

At that time the Kremlin was content to let the "individual peasant producer," that is, the small private capitalist or rural nepman, prosper unmolested. The Kremlin has now decided that he, too, is a source of potential danger unless checked.

Had Lenin lived, the delicate balance between socialism and capitalism inside Russia, which was the true essence of Lenin's own creation, the Nep, might have been maintained, but his successor has been compelled by circumstances to choose between one or the other. Naturally enough they have chosen socialism.

The question remains whether they can make it work. The analysis of the Soviet budget figures recently cabled to THE NEW YORK TIMES shows that State industry and transport is being run at a loss, although it must be admitted that expenditure on these counts includes a large amount of capital investment under the five years' industrialization plan which may be a producer in the future. Is there ground for believing that the State will be more successful with agriculture?

**Arguments on Both Sides.**

On the one hand there are all manner of arguments about the individualist character of the Russian peasant. The communal and collective farms, it is held, penalize, and so discourage, industrious farmers for the benefit of their lazier or less efficient brethren. It is argued that "contractation" does not produce results and is simply a disguised form of subsidy to the poorest villagers, and that State farms become a part of a national "pork barrel" giving fat jobs to bureaucrats but making little profit.

On the other hand, there are many reasons for believing that the optimism expressed by Soviet agricultural experts in speeches to the Congress regarding the possibility of a 35 per cent increase in harvest within five years is justified. About seven-tenths of all farm land worked in the Soviet Union still adheres to the ancient "three-field" system, in which one-third is unused every year. It is calculated that the adoption of Western crop rotation methods would alone increase the harvest by 25 per cent, and that, after all, is merely a matter of education.

Again, the practice of using cleansed and sorted seed and fertilizers has hardly scratched the surface of the Russian farmer's mind. This is also a matter of education. Finally, more than 33 per cent of Russian farms, it was stated at the Congress, are without any form of animal or mechanical traction and lack the most elementary implements. This the State proposes to remedy by supplying tractors and equipment to the farms grouped in cooperative units.

December 17, 1928

# HUGE INDUSTRIES PLANNED BY SOVIET

## 5-Year Construction Program Is Outlined at Moscow Communist Conference.

## SUPER-STATE IS ITS AIM

### Krijanovsky's Ambitious Scheme Stills for the Moment the Opposition's Criticism.

MOSCOW, April 25 (AP).—A vast project entailing a huge five-year industrialization program was announced in detail before the All-Russian Communist Conference sitting in the Kremlin today.

The announcement of the program, which seeks to remake primitively agrarian Russia into an industrial super-State, stilled for the moment the discordant note in the Kremlin opposition fight which had developed in the conference between the dominant Stalin group and the leaders of the so-called Right Wing.

M. Krijanovsky, president of the Soviet Union Planning Commission, voiced Soviet Russia's readiness to fulfil the dream of Lenin of a Russia turned into an industrial giant.

"We must build the Ural-Siberian super-road, linking Kuznetsky coal with Ural metallurgy and be able to throw Siberian grain into the central regions," he said. "We shall dig the Volga-Don channel and link Donetz coal to the central industries. The cheap water route will stimulate the speed of industrialization of the central areas.

"The great Balakhinsky power plant will get into full swing supplying cheap electricity. Leningrad and the central and south industrial region will remain our base. Herein we have 67 per cent of our fundamental industrial funds. The Don Basin production must double, meaning that we must do in five years what has been done in the forty preceding years.

"In Central Russia we will build a gigantic automobile plant. We shall invest a billion dollars in Lenigrad industries. Our five-year plan provides for stimulating the industries of the Eastern and frontier region as well as the allied national republics."

M. Krijanovsky then concluded with an appeal for unity, declaring that the big plan could be fulfilled only in the circumstances of party unity.

April 26, 1929

# SOVIET INDUSTRY GETS AMERICAN AID

## Contracts Involving Millions With Industry Here Are Disclosed.

## FORD COOPERATION LAUDED

Details of Soviet contracts with more than fifteen American concerns, involving millions of dollars, were made public yesterday in a joint statement issued by Valery I. Meshlauk, vice chairman of the Supreme Economic Council of the Soviet Union, and Saul G. Bron, chairman of the board of the Amtorg Trading Corporation, 261 Fifth Avenue.

Among the outstanding of these contracts is the one with the Ford Motor Company, signed at Dearborn, Mich., last Friday, at which time it was announced that this agreement calls for the purchase of $30,000,000 worth of Ford cars and parts by the Russian interests within the next four years. The other contracts call for designing of plants, technical assistance and exchange of patents.

The statement issued yesterday at the offices of the Amtorg Trading Corporation which was one of the parties to Ford Motor Company contract, said that "it is significant that American engineering skill is being utilized on many of the principal Soviet industrial projects now under way."

The Ford contract, which is for a term of nine years, provides for technical cooperation between the Ford Motor Company and the Soviet Automobile Trust for five years after the completion of a factory at Nizhni-Novgorod, which is expected to be put in operation within four years, and which will produce annually 100,000 Ford cars and trucks. This plant will produce more trucks than passenger cars.

The statement pointed out that the Soviet Union possesses only 20,000 cars "and is probably the least advanced in this respect of any of the large European countries." The statement added that "an indication that the problem is receiving adequate attention is the fact that this year $150,000,000 has been appropriated for road construction" by Soviet Federal and local authorities.

Other contracts have been made with the following:

Hugh L. Cooper Company, New York, consulting engineers on a $100,000,000 hydro-electric power plant in the Ukraine, claimed to be the largest in the world.

International General Electric Company, for exchange of patents and technical assistance.

Radio Corporation of America, for exchange of patents and other technical information.

du Pont de Nemours Company, for technical assistance in building ammonia fertilizer factories.

Freyn Engineering Company, New York, consulting engineers in the designing of steel mills to cost more than $1,000,000,000.

Stuart, James & Cooke, New York, consulting engineers, for building new coal mines, rebuilding old mines and installing up-to-date equipment.

Nitrogen Engineering Company, New York, for technical assistance in constructing a nitrogen fertilizer factory.

Longacre Engineering and Construction Company, New York, for technical assistance and supervision on the erection of apartment houses in Moscow.

McCormick Company, New York, for the designing of a large baking plant in Moscow.

Albert Kahn, Inc., Detroit, for designing the Stalingrad tractor factory to produce 40,000 tractors a year.

Arthur P. Davis, Oakland, Cal., chief consulting engineer on irrigation projects in Soviet Central Asia.

The statement issued yesterday said in part:

"We wish to state that in all of our conversations and negotiations with Mr. Ford he afforded us the maximum of cooperation and evinced a great interest in our industrial development, particularly in the application of automotive power to large-scale farming.

"The construction of the new automobile plant is a part of the general Soviet program for the inauguration of many new industries in the country. A tractor factory with a capacity of 40,000 machines per year was started last year at Stalingrad, and construction of another tractor factory with a similar capacity is to be commenced shortly. The tractor plants at Leningrad and Kharkov are being re-equipped for larger capacities. Several large power plants are under construction, as well as many factories for the production of fertilizers, paper, electrical equipment and other products."

June 4, 1929

# WAGE CUTS ROUSE PROTEST IN RUSSIA

## Union Officials Voice Indignation Felt by 10,000,000 Organized Workers.

## LABOR DISPUTES INCREASE

### In the Meantime a Marked Rise in the Cost of Living Is Noted in the Cities.

Competition among factories for the purpose of speeding up production is all right and the recent introduction of drastic discipline into the big Russian industrial plants may be excused by the Soviet workers in the interest of the Communist Fatherland, but when it comes to cutting wages, even in an indirect way, the officials of the trade unions find themselves obliged to inform the Soviet authorities that there is a limit to the patience and patriotism of the some 10,000,000 members of organized labor in the Soviet Union.

Such is the conclusion arrived at after an examination of recent comment in the Russian trade union press on the fact that the Supreme Economic Council, headed by V. Kuibyshef, has found itself obliged to raise the standards of individual output and to reduce piecework rates in order to increase production according to its plans without exceeding the total sum allotted by the budget for the payment of wages.

According to an article in Trud, the central organ of the Russian trade unions, summarized by the Geneva Bureau of the International Labor Organization of the League of Nations, there exists a difference of opinion between the executive officials managing industry and the trade unions on the question of methods of application of the revised wage scales and standards of production. While the unions admit the necessity of an increase of individual output on the basis of the stabilized wages, and State industry is seeking economies by the reduction of wages while maintaining the present level of output, certain trusts have decided to carry out an automatic reduction of wages, without prejudice to further reduction by a rise in the standards of output.

**Moscow Workers Hard Hit.**

This system, against which the unions have protested, consists in determining the total sum of savings to be made in the sphere of wages for a given group of undertakings. The next step is the distribution of the sums to be saved according to individual undertakings. The workers of the clothing trust of Moscow, for instance, find themselves threatened by this policy with a reduction of wages of from 30 to 35 per cent. In the chocolate factories and pastry cooks' establishments of Moscow the reduction would amount to 29 "tchervonets rubles" a month per worker, or more than 30 per cent of present wages.

The economic and political danger to which such tactics on the part of the industrial bodies would give rise is pointed out by the trade unions, and attention is drawn to the growing number of labor disputes provoked by it. It is declared that a stubborn resistance must be opposed to all efforts to revise the totals of output and the piecework scales by means of an automatic reduction of wages. It is added that certain unions have unfortunately already signed supplementary collective agreements giving such powers to the management of industry.

The trade union press admits the necessity in many cases of raising the standards of output, and even of reducing piece-work rates, but only after a thorough study of the position of each undertaking, and only when improvements in the process of manufacture, such as mechanization and rationalization, justifying such measures, have been brought about. Hardly anything, it is said, has as yet been done in the sphere of rationalization, and the study of the standards of individual output is still in an undeveloped condition.

In these conditions the General Council of Trade Unions categorically opposes any precipitate change in the standards of wage scales, and especially opposes the growing tendency of the managers of State industry to seek economies by reducing wages.

**Cost of Living Rising.**

That the lot of the industrial workers has not been improved of late would seem to be indicated by the fact that the Soviet press has been drawing attention for some time to the steady rise in the cost of living. It is pointed out that the index numbers of the cost of living, calculated on the basis of the minimum monthly budget of a worker, increased by 6.3 per cent during the first half of the financial year 1928-1929. (The Soviet financial year begins on Oct. 1.) The increase was 6.5 per cent in Moscow and 7.4 per cent in Leningrad.

The highest increase, amounting to from 9 to 10 per cent is shown in agricultural produce, while the prices of industrial products have risen by 2 per cent.

The General Council of Trade Unions has examined the question and arrives at the conclusion that these figures do not give an exact indication of the position, since the consumers' cooperative societies are only increasing to a relatively slight extent the prices of the products of which the worker's minimum monthly budget is composed while making much greater increases in other goods. According to Trud the minimum monthly budget of a worker includes a very limited selection of goods.

Moreover the Moscow worker has long ago replaced most of these goods by objects of better quality. For instance, the budget includes kitchen utensils of cast iron, while the worker prefers aluminum. It includes the commonest quality of soap and high boots, while the worker prefers shoes and a better quality of soap. Again, the budget only makes provision for coarse woolen stuffs, while the worker generally buys ready-made clothes.

August 18, 1929

# RED WORKERS TOLD TO OBEY SHOP HEADS

## Soviet Order Gives Managers Supreme Control, Regardless of Employes' Party Rank.

## FACTORY POLITICS ENDED

### Unions and Other Groups Lose Former Power to Influence Employment and Dismissals.

Wireless to THE NEW YORK TIMES.

MOSCOW, Sept. 7.—An order that is likely to astonish many American radicals was published today by the Bolshevist party's Central Committee. It provides that Soviet factory managers must be obeyed by all workers, whatever rank these may happen to hold in the local Bolshevist party or in their trade union section. It is decreed that a real single command must henceforth exist in all factories; and that trade unions, shop stewards' committees, &c., are curtly told to cease attempting to usurp managerial functions.

In each factory the Bolshevist leaders must explain to the workers that measures taken by the management to restore discipline, increase output and rationalize production are all for their good.

This probably refers to the present policy of compulsory overtime and "voluntary" Sunday work.

**Wide Powers Granted.**

The managers are to have full powers personally to appoint and dismiss all members of the administrative and technical staff. Still more astonishing is the equal right granted to them to dismiss ordinary workers or put them on any job or transfer them to any shop. And although the managers are advised to consult the local party units and trade union sections on this point, the latter are reminded that they have absolutely no veto power whatsoever, but only the right to send up a report to the higher powers.

Similarly the shop managers are to have wider discretion in choosing their own assistants and foremen. The factory managers must receive contracts guaranteeing a long term of office, and can only be dismissed by the high industrial authority which appointed them. In addition to their regular holiday, the Supreme Council of National Industry must arrange to give them six to eight weeks special leave yearly to improve their technical knowledge.

This measure shows how far the Stalin Administration is both ready and forced to go in its fight against drunkenness, absence from work without permission, insubordination, hooliganism, manager-baiting and other practices which seriously affected the output of the factories last year. But it also marks a further stage in the final centralization of all things here, which seems to be the immutable rule of Russian life.

**Tomsky Ousted From Power.**

In order to take this step, it was first necessary to remove Tomsky, who at bottom is more of a syndicalist than a Communist, and his chief lieutenant, from trade union headquarters, for their policy, although honest, had encouraged the short-sighted attitude of the local workers toward the general output plans.

It is a curious fact that while the Bolsheviki have been denouncing American labor leaders for sacrificing the real, permanent, corporative class interests of the workers to "capitalistic rationalization of industry," an exactly parallel process has been taking place here.

In America, England and elsewhere industry is being rationalized by trusts under private capital or on a national basis. Here in Russia we have a similar rationalization in State trusts under a system of State capitalism. True, the factory managers here are members of the Bolshevist party, but the organic laws at work are the same. Under the new order Soviet trade unions have practically become company unions, according to the American model.

September 8, 1929

# SHORTAGE OF FOOD DISTURBS MOSCOW

### Soviet Transportation and Distribution System Is Blamed as Inefficient.

### CURRENCY IS NOW INFLATED

By WALTER DURANTY.

Wireless to THE NEW YORK TIMES.

MOSCOW, Oct. 10.—As Soviet industrial production reaches record figures, as "Dnieperstroy" beats the world record for monthly tons of cement, as the coal, oil and timber outputs surpass the previous highest, and the five-year plan estimates grow ever more ambitious there has grown also a food shortage in Moscow, and one commodity after another is added to the rationing list.

The most recent is milk, which can only be sold on "children's cards," while cream and cheese have practically disappeared, and butter is lamentably scarce. At present almost every edible of popular consumption is rationed, with the exception of salt. Fruit, vegetables, and even potatoes, are lacking at most of the cooperatives, despite the fact that Moscow and the northwestern provinces generally had the best potato crop in years.

The authorities defend the ration system on the ground that "it prevents speculation" and "insures food for the workers at reasonable prices;" but when the workers' wives must stand four in line to get food against their coupons, and often find the commodity they want is not obtainable, it seems that "there's something rotten in the State of Denmark."

**Conclusions From a Survey.**

It is a pretty serious matter, this food shortage at the beginning of what is called here the "decisive year of the five-year plan," but a comprehensive analysis of the food situation made during the past week from newspaper reports, stores, interviews in competent quarters and other sources produces rather curious conclusions, the first of which is that the shortage is much less real and much less serious than it appears. That is to say, there is plenty of food in the country, and no danger of starvation anywhere and, no less important, the public seems aware of this and is neither panicky nor more than mildly annoyed by the present conditions.

Three other conclusions are, from the Soviet point of view, less optimistic. First, there is a weakness at times approaching a breakdown in the Soviet system of food transportation and distribution. Second, the currency inflation, which undoubtedly exists, is affecting the food markets adversely. Third, and worst, the peasants are selling less of their products, and in some cases reducing output deliberately.

The first conclusion finds ample confirmation in the newspapers. Whereas ninety-two carloads of potatoes are needed daily for Moscow, the city is only receiving an average of fifty-nine, while literally hundreds of carloads are delayed at various junctions. This transport weakness is affecting the whole commercial and industrial life of the country, and there seems no one capable of organizing transport to satisfy a great new increase demanded by the successful harvest and rapidly growing program of industrialization.

**Cooperative Distribution Blamed.**

Meanwhile cooperative distribution has come under fire from many quarters. A recent legal process which put the blame for meat shortage on a small group of minor officials of the cooperatives was quashed by the High Court in Moscow, which ordered that the central cooperative organization be held responsible in a new trial. So far as one can judge, it is neither graft nor red tape that is to blame, but the apathy of men who have become petty functionaries uninspired by individual initiative or hope of personal profit.

Currency inflation, as experience in Germany and Austria has shown, produces a "flight from the market" of goods whose prices are controlled. Whither they fly may remain a mystery, but their disappearance is certain. At this moment Russia has a total currency circulation of 2,500,000,000 rubles, compared with a little more than 1,500,000,000 a year ago. That the five-year plan required this increase is true, and it doubtless is equally true that the country can "absorb the black" in the near future, but for the time being it is inflation and the Soviet ruble has decreased in purchasing power.

Thirdly, the disparity of prices between foods and manufactured goods has led the peasants to keep much of their produce for themselves and their stock instead of selling it. In consequence they live better than ever before—which politically is important—but the urban centres go short. Then, too, the present system of rural taxation puts a much heavier burden on the peasant who has two cows than on the peasant who has one, so he slaughters the second cow and sells the meat.

This would seem to be the gravest danger to the success of the five-year plan. The State and collective farms at best amount to only 16 per cent of the agricultural total while the rest of the peasantry tends to reduce production to the limit of its own needs in order to escape taxation.

October 13, 1929

# RED PRISON FUGITIVES TELL OF SUFFERINGS

### Thirteen Refugees Near Exhaustion Reach Finland—Report 100 Killed in Jail.

Wireless to THE NEW YORK TIMES.

HELSINGFORS, Finland, Nov. 3.—Thirteen Russian refugees, including one woman, entered Finnish territory in Lapland today after an exhausting and adventurous march for a fortnight through forests and marshes in Russian Carelia.

The refugees say they served many years in the notorious Solovetsk prison colony, where they were sentenced by the Bolsheviki, and were recently employed in building houses near the Murmansk Railway.

Early in October, they said, they were shifted nearer to Finland and there conceived the plan to escape. They wounded their keepers, and after taking a little food started westward.

When discovered by Finnish frontier guards the refugees were almost collapsing from starvation and fatigue. They described conditions in the Solovetsk prison as terrible, saying that the authorities resorted to torture for the slightest offense, and that the death rate among the prisoners is excessive owing to filthy conditions, poor food and cold. Women, they said, are particularly persecuted.

In their report to Finnish authorities the refugees declared that one day last Winter a massacre of more than 100 prisoners belonging to some religious brotherhood was perpetrated. All were sentenced to death and ordered to prepare their own graves, and, then, the refugees said, their hands and feet were cut off and the bleeding prisoners were put into their graves to freeze to death.

November 4, 1929

# SOVIETS RUTHLESS IN WAR ON KULAKS

### Stalin Explains "Liquidation" of Rich Peasants Means Complete Dispossession.

### "NEPMEN" ALSO INCLUDED

#### Huge Head of Lenin Is Unveiled in Moscow on Sixth Anniversary of His Death.

By WALTER DURANTY.

Wireless to THE NEW YORK TIMES.

MOSCOW, Jan. 23.—Last Wednesday was one of the five annual holidays provided under the new Soviet calendar and "nonstop week" system. It was in commemoration of the death of Lenin in 1924 and of the massacre of workers in the courtyard of the Winter palace in St. Petersburg (now Leningrad) in 1905.

In place of the memorial services that would be held on such occasions in other countries, Communist and workers' organizations throughout Russia held meetings in "the Lenin corner" which exists in every club and factory and there undertook some voluntary work for the public benefit. Thus in Moscow tens of thousands of young Communists spent the day collecting old iron, bottles and the like in fulfillment of a pledge made by the Moscow Communist youth organization to provide enough such material before the Spring sowing to buy 500 tractors.

In front of the grand opera house, there was a brief ceremony of the unveiling of a colossal head of Lenin, above which in huge red letters is written, "Lenin lives in the hearts of all the workers of the world."

The head, which is about twelve feet high and rests on a twenty-foot black-draped scaffolding, is made of gray canvas. The features, with their narrow, half-closed eyes, suggest a death mask and the impression is heightened by the color. The raised right eyebrow gives a slightly cynical expression.

It is like a new sphinx brooding over the inscrutable future, and the crowd stared up awe-stricken. Grotesque as the idea of this bodyless head may sound, its effect is portentous and grim.

The anniversary was also notable for an editorial signed by M. Stalin which appeared in the Red Army newspaper Red Star, in which the Communist leader carefully explained the meaning of the phrase, "liquidation of the kulak [rich peasant] as a class," which is the keynote of the Kremlin's revised economic policy. M. Stalin said:

"It is necessary to smash in open combat the opposition of this class and to deprive it of the productive sources of its existence and development—the free use of land, the means of production, the right to hire labor, &c. The present policy in the country is not a prolongation of this policy, but a violent change from the old policy of limiting capitalist elements in the villages to a new policy of liquidating the kulak as a class.

A recent editorial in THE NEW YORK TIMES discussing M. Stalin's agrarian policy charitably assumed that the process of liquidating the kulaks would mean their reduction to the average present status by deprivation of their land and other provileges, after which they could enter the collective movement as poor or middle peasants. Nothing could be further from the truth. It is proposed to stamp them out root and branch, so that the place where they were may know them no more. Not only are they refused admission to the collectives, but they are being expelled if they manage to join.

**Exile or Death Offered.**

The press here Wednesday carried a resolution adopted by 450 delegates from the collectives of one of the counties of Moscow Province. The delegates resolved to "devote all efforts to this achievement by the end of Spring—that not one kulak, priest, nepman or trader be left in our country."

To define further the brutal truth, take the conclusion to an article in the Red Star in which that writer says:

"What will become of the kulak after his liquidation as a class? To us it is all one—let him fall under the first passing automobile or spend the rest of his life in exile—anything, provided he disappears from our midst."

The fact is that the revised policy puts the kulaks, private traders and servants of the religious cults up against a wall. In the urban centres the nepman, or small capitalist, is deprived of his apartment, his property, including his furniture, and is even forbidden to live in any large city. It is done legally on a taxation basis, but it amounts to expropriation, differing only in form from the nationalization of apartments and other property, which occurred in the early days of the revolution.

The same things happen to the kulaks in the villages. It is a wholesale and ruthless carrying out of what the word "liquidation" means in Russian. Lenin's widow, Mme. Krupskaya, alone has raised her voice in protest, not against liquidation as such, which she declares she approves, but on behalf of the children of the "doomed classes."

"To expel the children of the class enemies from the crowded schools in order to give places to the children of workers and peasants," writes Mme. Krupskaya, "is correct enough, but it is time to consider the social problem involved. Do we wish to create millions of new homeless waifs as a shame and a burden to the country?"

**Say Dispossessed May Work.**

In answer to your correspondent's inquiries, the authorities said the "dispossessed classes" could gradually regain their standing by work in the lumber camps or on construction projects where the labor demand exceeds the supply. In any other country the problem would seem terrific, but actually in Russia things do not move with the implacable rapidity of the Kremlin decrees. The liquidation process probably will be gradual and its aftermath less difficult than it would be elsewhere. During the early years of communism the same process occurred on a greater scale working worse hardships.

From the general standpoint the revised economic policy seems far from unpopular. In the cities the overcrowding is so great that the news that hundreds or thousands of apartments will be vacated by the expulsion of nepman tenants is good news to all. Similarly, the poor peasants are delighted to hear that the best land in the village, with a mill or dairy attached, is to become the property of the new collective.

Nor does the anti-religious movement seem to meet opposition. On the contrary, the workers of one factory in Moscow celebrated Lenin's anniversary by tearing down the famous monastery of Saint Simon in order that it may be replaced by a communal house with a clubroom, theatre, restaurants, nurseries, sports centres and a park.

January 26, 1930

# SOVIET SANCTIONS EXILING OF KULAKS

## Poor Peasants Encouraged to "Hunt" the Richer Ones in Ruthless Class War.

## 'HOOLIGANISM' IS ATTACKED

### Labor Code Is Amended to Check Damage to Factories by Making Workers Responsible.

Wireless to THE NEW YORK TIMES.

MOSCOW, Feb. 2.—The class war in the villages becomes more ruthless daily. A decree promulgated today by the Council of People's Commissars empowers local executives to evict and exile the kulaks (rich peasants), thus sanctioning measures already in widespread practice.

In all regions where the Soviet intends to develop full collectivization all leasing of lands and hiring of labor are forbidden. The kulaks' entire possessions—house, stock and implements—will be handed free over to the nearest collective farm after the State has taken the share which the tax collector holds is due. These gifts to the collectives are to be regarded as contributions made by the "village poor," who thus are stimulated to hunt the kulaks.

The term "kulak" is used elastically here according to the exigencies of the mass agitation campaigns. The last clear definition which your correspondent has seen was in the fiscal law of 1928, when kulak meant any peasant family living on one farm and producing on the tax collector's own assessment not less than 500 rubles (about $250) worth of foodstuffs annually, all told, after twenty rubles (about $10) per head had been deducted for food.

The average value of a kulak family's "means of production," including live stock, has been estimated at about 1,400 rubles ($700). So the press justifies the new decree by declaring that liquidation of the kulak farms must proceed concurrently with the creation of collectives and that the kulaks must be liquidated as a class because if they are allowed to remain in the villages they will become an element of discontent.

Pravda justifies the order of War Minister Voroshilof to send 100,000 specially trained soldier, to the villages this year to manage the collectives by asserting that they will still be soldiers, remobilized at any moment, and that therefore the national safety will not be endangered.

The efforts of the Bolsheviki to hammer discipline into the Russian workers and thus check carelessness and rowdyism, which are the twin enemies of production, are shown by a stiff amendment to the labor code announced today. Any worker or clerk who is found guilty of damaging plant or office equipment through carelessness or disobedience to rules must make good the damage up to one-third of his total wage or salary.

This clause will not modify the wage contracts already existing in many factories, under which the workers are held responsible for such unwillful damage up to their entire wages. Moreover, the workers are held pecuniarily responsible for all acts of rowdyism or disorder outside of factory hours for the total cost of the damage done, not merely up to the totality of their wages.

February 3, 1930

# RED CHIEF EXPLAINS NEW KULAK POLICY

## Stalin Says Soviet Did Not Have Strength Three Years Ago for Attack.

## TROTSKYISM IS CRITICIZED

### Communist Secretary Says Exiled Former Leader Wanted to Start Campaign Too Soon.

Although Leon Trotsky, one-time head of the Red Army, is living in exile from his Soviet Fatherland, and Gregory Zinovief, erstwhile chief of the Communist International, has made his peace with the "powers that be" in Russia and is holding a minor Government post in comparative obscurity, Joseph Stalin, triumphant Secretary of the Communist party of the Soviet Union, still considers it necessary to remind his old political enemies that their "Left Wing" policy was all wrong in 1927, from the Communist view, while at present his own extreme plans for "liquidating" the more comfortable peasants and the remaining private traders are quite feasible.

In a speech recently delivered by Secretary Stalin before a conference of students of Marxian economics as applied to the problem of agriculture, on Dec. 27, briefly summarized in a Moscow wireless dispatch to THE NEW YORK TIMES, he took pains to emphasize the "mistakes" of the former Opposition. While defending the Kremlin's new policy of wiping out the "kulak" (the more prosperous farmer) as rapidly as possible, M. Stalin also pointed out that up till new economic conditions had forced the Communist Government to temporize and merely try to "restrict the exploiting tendencies of the kulak," instead of waging vigorous war upon the richer peasants as a class. Then, as quoted in official Soviet publications, M. Stalin continued:

"Was this policy correct? Yes, it was indubitably correct. Could we perchance, five or three years ago, have undertaken such an attack upon the kulak as we are carrying on today? Could we at that time have reckoned on such an attack being successful? No, we could not. That would have been the most dangerous adventurism. That would have been an exceedingly dangerous playing at attack. We would certainly have come to grief and thereby strengthened the position of the kulaks. Why? Because we had not yet at our disposal those points of support in the villages in the shape of a broad network of Soviet estates and collective farms upon which we could rely in the decisive attack on the kulaks. Because at that time it was not possible for us to substitute for the capitalist production of the kulak the Socialist production in the shape of the collective farms and Soviet estates.

**Party Not Ready in 1927.**

"In 1927 the Zinovief-Trotsky Opposition wanted at all costs to force upon the party the policy of an immediate attack on the kulaks. The party did not enter upon this adventure, as it knew that serious persons do not play at attack. The attack on the kulaks is a very serious matter. One must no diffuse it with declamation against the kulaks, which the Zinovief-Trotsky opposition energetically endeavored to force upon the party.

"To attack the kulaks means to smash the kulaks, to liquidate them as a class. * * * To attack the kulaks means to make proper preparations and then to deliver the blow, such a blow that they are not able to recover. That is what we Bolshevists call a real attack. Could we have undertaken such an attack five or three years ago with any prospect of success? No, we could not.

"In the year 1927 the kulak produced over 600,000,000 poods [a pood equals about 36 pounds] of grain, 150,000,000 of which he got rid of by exchange outside the village. That is a fairly serious force with which one must reckon. And how much did our Soviet estate and collective farms produce at that time? About 80,000,000 poods, of which they threw 35,000,000 upon the market. Judge for yourselves whether at that time we were in a position to replace the production and the commodity grain of the kulaks by the production and commodity grain of our Soviet estates and collective farms. It is clear that we could not have done so. * * *

"And how does the matter stand at present? We now have an adequate material basis for a blow against the kulak, to break his resistance, to annihilate him as a class and to replace his production by the production of the Soviet estates and collective farms. You are aware that the grain produced on the collective farms and Soviet estates amounted in 1929 to no less than 400,000,000 poods. You also know that in 1929 the collective farms and Soviet estates delivered more than 130,000,000 poods of commodity grain. In 1930 the total production of the collective farms and the Soviet estates will amount to no less than 900,000,000 poods and they will supply not less than 400,000,000 poods of commodity grain.

"As is to be seen, today there exists the material basis for replacing the big peasant production by that of the collective farms and Soviet estates. That is why our attack on the kulak has now met with undeniable success. * * *

"It is for this reason that we recently have gone over from the policy of restricting the exploiting tendencies of the kulak to the policy of liquidating the kulak."

February 23, 1930

# STALIN URGES SOVIET TO SLOW UP DRIVES

## Communist Party Chief Holds Gains Are Endangered by Extreme Peasant Policy.

## CHIDES CHURCH WRECKERS

## He Suggests Little Is to Be Won by Their Work—Says Small Traders Will Stay.

By WALTER DURANTY.
Wireless to THE NEW YORK TIMES.

MOSCOW, March 2.—Joseph Stalin, general secretary of the Communist party, put the brake on Communist enthusiasm in a remarkable article published in all newspapers here to-day. Its statesmanship appears to put Stalin on a level with Lenin himself, and it is unquestionably the most important pronouncement made in Russia for several years.

Under the title "Dizziness From Successes," Stalin begins by saying that more than 50 per cent of the peasant holdings now have been collectivized and more than 3,500,000 tons, or more than 90 per cent of the program, of cleaned seed already have been distributed to the collectives for Spring sowing. Such a result appeared quite impossible three weeks ago, and it is perhaps the greatest tour de force in the whole history of the Bolshevist party, as Stalin and his readers well know.

**Sees Dangerous Overconfidence.**

"Our success," Stalin continues, "already is producing a dangerous spirit of glorification and overconfidence. Communists are beginning to feel and say, 'We can work miracles—nothing is too hard for us.' Optimism is good, but to let it turn our heads is bad. Some of our comrades have already had their heads turned and have begun to make errors, which are not only not practical and non-Leninist, but they are actually playing into the hands of our enemies. This tendency must be checked immediately."

Stalin goes on to point out the two principal dangers of an overconfident attitude as, first, the idea that collectives can be successfully established in regions as yet economically unsuitable, such as Turkestan or the extreme northern part of Russia, and, secondly, that collectivization must be pushed immediately to the extreme of communism and even pigs, poultry and dwellings shared in the collective. It is a dangerous mistake and it is playing the enemy's game, says Stalin, to try to collectivize "by military force" unsuitable regions.

It is equally wrong, he says, to attempt suddenly to change the artel system—the artel is the typical peasant collective under which land, horses, cows, plows and the like are united for the common benefit; but homes, sheep, goats, pigs and poultry remain individual property—into a 100 per cent commune in which everything is shared with every one. Stalin slashes at those "comrades who seem to believe that a Communist Utopia can be established in the villages by bureaucratic ordinances," and he warns them that the untimely attempts at supersocialization must be stopped at once.

The basic success of the collective movement, he says, lies in the fact that it is largely voluntary on the part of the peasants. To force them further, he holds, would be a fatal and autocratic error and would imply a rupture between the Communist party and the masses it controls, whereas in reality its strength and its whole reason for existence are based upon a close connection with and work for the masses.

"Some of our comrades," says Stalin sarcastically, "think they can start a collective by pulling down church bells [that is, demolishing the churches] and then they call themselves r-r-revolutionaries [with three r's]."

Taken as a whole, Stalin's pronouncement means, if not back pedaling, at least soft pedaling. A fortnight ago he indicated that the measures against "nepmen," or private traders, in urban centres were being pushed too far and that at least small private traders still had a rôle to play in the national economy. Now he says the same for the villages—that the peasants may retain their pigs or poultry or even milch cows. Indirectly, he soft pedals the anti-religious campaign also.

To believe that this is due to the foreign outcry is entirely to misunderstand both Stalin and the Soviet State. Nevertheless his article makes it clear that the Kremlin has its ear pretty close to the Russian ground and will not risk its gains by trying to overplay its hand.

March 3, 1930

# RED PRESS ADMITS RURAL RESISTANCE

## Izvestia Says Obstinacy Is Wide and "Subkulaks" as Well as Kulaks Are Recalcitrant.

## FINDS GAINS EXAGGERATED

## Paper Says Farm Socialization Figure of 57 Per Cent Is Too High—Red Organizer Slain by Mob.

By WALTER DURANTY.
Wireless to THE NEW YORK TIMES.

MOSCOW, March 24.—Fresh light is thrown on the situation in the villages and the motives behind the recent decisions of the Communist party and the government by the leading editorials today in Izvestiya and Pravda, both of which are devoted to the peasant question.

Izvestiya, the official organ of the government, stresses the importance of stimulating Spring sowing in the "individual sector" by providing good seed, by developing the contract system under which a farmer or group of farmers gets an advance in seed, implements or goods in return for a promise to pay back a certain proportion of his or their crops, and by spreading the news that all increases over last year's sowing by individuals will be exempt from taxation.

**Admits Wide Opposition.**

Izvestiya makes three significant admissions—first, that the official collectivization figure of 57 per cent for all Russian farms, as of March 10, may be somewhat exaggerated; second, that "kulak [richer peasant] opposition" is actively trying to reduce the area sown by individuals; third, it is not only "kulakism" but "subkulakism" that is the enemy.

Pravda, official organ of the Communist party, elucidates the latter point by the frank statement that "excesses of overzealous Communists has tended to give to the kulak allies in the ranks of the peasantry as a whole.

"We are still far from attaining the isolation of the kulak from the peasant masses," Pravda says. "Our errors have hindered that isolation and much work still remains to be done."

"We must struggle resolutely," the editorial continues, "with the tendencies directed against participation by the middle peasants in the collectives. But the kulak is not only trying to spoil the collective movement—he is trying to spoil the sowing campaign altogether. To members of collectives, he says, 'Once you have joined the collective, make the government supply everything.' He advises individuals to cut sowing to a minimum.

"In this game the kulak is aided by Communist hotheads on the one hand, who describe our policy of correcting their errors as cowardice or a 'step backward,' and by 'Right opposition' Communists on the other, who advocate capitulation before the kulak, and say they warned us beforehand of what would happen."

One can read between the lines in the Pravda editorial that for the present, at any rate, the recent "soft-pedaling" measures certainly do not mean a definite change in policy, but both Pravda and Izvestiya make it clear that some anxiety exists and that peasant opposition is stronger and more widespread than either newspaper would have admitted six weeks ago.

If further proof is needed, take an obituary notice appearing in today's Literary Weekly, which runs:

"Krasnodar [a town in Northern Caucasus, on the Kuban River]. March 20.—This morning at the station of Petrovsk a savage mob incited by Kulaks killed the Red proletarian writer, F. A. Makayef, active Communist and social worker. Death found Makayef at his post of duty.

"He was engaged in explaining to peasants the decision of the county authorities regarding collectives."

March 25, 1930

# REDS USE SCHOOLS TO AID 5-YEAR PLAN

## Education in Russia Is Being Made a Propaganda Machine, Columbia Professor Reports.

## TEXTBOOKS ARE ALTERED

## All Problems and Illustrations Deal With Soviet Economic Theories, Dr. Counts Asserts.

Education in Soviet Russia has discarded most of traditional formulae and substituted the problems of the five-year plan for economic rehabilitation as the principal course of study, according to Dr. George S. Counts, associate director of the International Institute of Teachers College, Columbia University. Dr. Counts recently returned from a seven-month tour of inspection through Russia.

Courses and textbooks, he said, are being revised, and every agency for disseminating information and propaganda is taking part in the general movement of educating the Russian masses in the doctrines of communism.

Speaking of the "systematic efforts that have been made to popularize the plan through the various arms of the education system," Dr. Counts said:

"In the primary school, secondary school, technical school and university, provision is made everywhere for the study of the five-year plan. For an individual to pass through any one of these institutions without becoming familiar with the major provisions of the plan is practically impossible.

"For the lower schools courses and textbooks are being revised to include material dealing with the plan, and for the higher schools special lectures on the plan are being organized. To an even greater extent the school for adults, and particularly the Soviet party schools and Communist universities, are assuming responsibility for the propagation of the plan.

"When peasants learn to read they read about the five-year plan, and when they study arithmetic they wrestle with the figures of the plan. The non-scholastic agencies are also brought into service. The press is literary pouring forth books, brochures, articles and placards about the plan. There are huge volumes of a technical nature designed to furnish guidance to the specialists; then there are small pamphlets dealing in popular fashion with every phase of the plan.

"The newspapers and journals are filled with news items, articles and editorials about the program of construction. Artistically executed placards dealing with the plan are distributed to schools, clubhouses, reading rooms, libraries and wherever people congregate. Also the moving picture, the radio and the museum are doing their bit. Moreover, special lecturers are being trained and sent into the more backward areas to propagate the plan."

The educational system, apart from its preoccupation with the plan, is of tremendous scope and breadth, Dr. Counts said, and differs radically from the Western systems of education.

"In the existing schools old courses are being shortened and new courses are being added. Also new agencies of training are being organized in great numbers and special courses of many types are being arranged by correspondence. And in those fields where the need is particularly urgent, maintenance stipends for students have been increased in number and amount."

March 9, 1930

# SOVIET SLOWS REDS IN THE FACTORIES

## Latest Decree Puts Ability Above Politics in Selection of Industrial Leaders.

## WORKER INTERFERENCE CUT

By WALTER DURANTY.
Wireless to THE NEW YORK TIMES.

MOSCOW, April 12.—The series of "soft-pedaling" decrees or manifestos issued recently by Communist leaders, Soviet Government departments and the Central Committee of the Communist party was supplemented by the Central Committee today in an order relating to factory management, particularly in the metallurgic industry.

The first of the series of measures ordering a slowing down in the campaign for 100 per cent communism was Joseph Stalin's "warning" of March 2. Then came decrees for the relief of persons unduly deprived of their civic rights, for the equalization of meat rations in the provinces between manual and other **workers; one giving permission to physicians to resume private practice, which had been forbidden, and other relaxations from the militant Communist program introduced in the beginning of the year.**

**The question every one is asking is whether these measures mean a change of policy and whether history is repeating itself from 1921, when Lenin in March made a statement implying regressions from militant communism and a series of other relaxation measures followed, culminating in the new economic policy of Aug. 9, 1921, which definitely ended that period of militant communism.**

**Your correspondent's opinion is that the parallel should not be pushed too far. What is occurring now is not a change of policy, but, as Stalin himself has said, "a correction of errors." The tremendous strain upon the nation, caused by "pyatiletka" (the five-year plan), both in agriculture and in industry, had reached a state of tension which was becoming intolerable and the Kremlin found it necessary to loosen up somewhat. The collectivization program was slowed down in agriculture and today's decree implies a similar admission of the dangers of overzealous communism to industry.**

The decree occupies nearly three columns and is couched in somewhat obscure language, but reading carefully one can detect three important points.

First, factory managers and department heads henceforth will be selected for executive ability rather than for their political standing.

Second, factory executives henceforth will be freed to a considerable extent from interference by workers' committee and other more or less political investigations which waste their time.

Third, no one shall be nominated **for "special work" without the approval of the factory manager or department chief concerned. This last order refers to all sorts of "stunts" organized by Communist groups in the factories, such as sending off "shock brigades" to the "collective farm front" or the "lumber front," which, however admirable in intention, grievously disorganize factory routine.**

**All three measures are really designed to strengthen the authority of the factory bosses, which seems to show that even Soviet Russia is not blind to the importance of individual initiative and competence. Here, perhaps, one gets the key to the reason for some of these new measures.**

**Without a definite political change "pyatiletka" has forced the Kremlin, for the time being at least, to pay more attention to economic results than to politics.**

April 13, 1930

# REDS SEIZE ON PLOT TO JUSTIFY REGIME

## Alleged Sabotage of Engineers in Wide Conspiracy Held to Account for Shortcomings.

## MASSES' SUPPORT RALLIED

### Accused Russians Are Said to Be the Victims of Emotions Played on by Emigres.

By WALTER DURANTY.
Wireless to THE NEW YORK TIMES.

MOSCOW, Nov. 12.—The unusual publicity given the alleged plot among engineers to overthrow the Soviet Government is far from accidental, though it is a novelty to publish a whole document of indictment here ten days before a trial. **An editorial in today's Economic Life makes clear two of the reasons and there are others. The editorial says:**

**"If, despite the damaging activities revealed by the plot, our industrial achievements are already so great, how vast would have been our success had no damaging occurred?"**

And a few lines further:

"In many respects the damaging ideology coincides with ideology of Right and Left 'opportunists' inside the Communist party."

When any country, not only one with a proletarian dictatorship, experiences hard times, it has a natural desire to visit the blame on some one. In the Soviet Union, where there is no "closed season" for bourgeois scapegoats and where life is excessively difficult, the tension enormous and the achievements, however wonderful, cannot in the nature of things bring about much general improvement in living stands for a year or so to come, this natural desire is intensified.

**Emigré Origin Is Suggested.**

It was served in the timeliest manner by the incurable romanticism of the former ruling and bourgeois class. That Russian émigrés in Paris have "learned nothing and forgotten nothing" is explicable, but that the men who chose to stay here and work for the Soviet and who have gone to and from Europe freely should stake their lives on such fantastic dreams is hard for an Anglo-Saxon to understand.

Without attempting to suggest that the indictment against them is untrue or unfounded, your correspondent does believe they are in a great degree the victims of circumstances and of their own temperament. They meet old friends abroad who ask about "things in Russia." "Pretty hard," they reply, quite honestly, and as the conversation continues with lavish drinks in the Russian manner they soon find themselves listening to wild talk about what will happen when "they" smash and how so and so, a member of a foreign cabinet or of a general staff, has promised such and such support. And before the evening terminates the whole crowd is pledged to some desperate endeavor.

It sounds ridiculous, but it is true of Russians, as Dostoievsky shows, and of the whole strange story of Russian conspirative effort before and after the Bolshevist revolution—with the exception for the most part of the Bolsheviki themselves because they have been drawn not from the intellectuals who plotted in vain and of whom Dostoievsky wrote but from the peasant or semi-peasant proletariat or from oppressed races whose lives were too hard for fantasy.

And Bolshevist discipline is so stern withal that the weaker and looser vessels are soon cracked under the strain.

Economic Life's second allusion stresses the coincidence between the publication of the indictment and the renewed attack on intra-party opposition. Today the Moscow Communist party issues a manifesto calling for severe disciplinary measures, even exclusion from the party, against MM. Sertzof and Lominadze and other "Oppositionists," who only recently were holding high positions, and adds:

"Their factional activities make the conduct of Rykof, Bukharin, Tomsky, &c., insufferable."

When such important Communists are involved it does not hinder the Kremlin's repudiation of them and their policies to make public the fact that the said policies and much of their "ideology" were based on the "expert" advice and suggestions provided by self-confessed traitors to the Soviet régime.

**Reds Glad to Show Menace.**

The Soviet Union is not the only country where political opponents risk being tarred publicly by any dirty brush that offers. Nor is it repugnant to the Soviet rulers to have open testimony, however second-hand and unwarranted by proof, of capitalist hostility, notably on the part of France, and of fresh schemes for military intervention.

The alleged confessions of Leonid Ramsin, Victor Laritcheff and M. Kalmanikos justify in the eyes of the Soviet masses all the emphasis that has been placed on the alleged risk of a new attack upon the "Socialist fatherland" to rub home the lesson that that emphasis was meant to inculcate—that the Communist party and the proletariat must rally solidly round the Kremlin.

How far the alleged confessions will "stand up" during the trial is another story, and foreign diplomats here are rather skeptical. But from the internal political viewpoint four important ends have already been achieved, no matter how the trial goes.

**First, the alleged plot is held to show why there have been shortcomings in the five-year plan; second, that the intra-party opposition has been wrong and misled, if not worse; third, that the recent sweeping changes in high administrative posts had a sound basis; fourth that the Soviet's enemies still are active and vigilant.**

November 13, 1930

# SOVIET WILL IMPORT 13,000 TECHNICIANS

## Native Schools Fail to Produce Experts to Meet Demands of 5-Year Plan for 1931.

By The Associated Press.

MOSCOW, Jan. 25.—The Soviet Government will continue to look to foreign specialists for the necessary technical skill in carrying out the five-year industrialization plan.

Government officials estimated today that 13,000 additional foreign engineers, technicians and skilled workers would be needed in 1931 if the scheduled construction was to be accomplished.

At present there are more than 4,000 foreign specialists employed under individual contracts with the Soviet Union, in addition to the 2,000 or more employes of 124 large foreign companies having technical-aid contracts with the government.

Efforts to develop native talent by intensive training methods have met largely with failure. Technical schools generally cut their courses from three years to six months, with students working day and night in order to qualify in the various technical professions. But a majority of the students were found unable to stand the strain and the large classes were reduced greatly before completion of the courses.

The 13,000 additional men needed in 1931 include 3,000 engineers, 3,000 foremen and 7,000 skilled workers. Europe is expected to supply about 2,600 of the engineers and the same number of foremen and about 5,000 skilled workers. The others are expected to be obtained in America.

The unemployment situation in the rest of the world puts the Soviet Union in a favorable position to employ foreign help, as applicants for the most part are willing to work for less than in more prosperous times.

Practically all foreigners are under contract whereby they receive part of their salaries in the currencies of their countries and part in rubles. The government has been trying to do everything possible to make the foreign employes satisfied. Shops have been opened in the various industrial centres for foreigners where only they can buy food and other commodities at lower prices than in the open market.

How many of these foreigners become converted to the theories of Marx and Lenin is not known, but few Americans embrace the doctrines. The Germans, however, who are in the majority among foreign employes, are said to be more or less sympathetic.

In the elections which now are in

progress throughout the country, the foreigners are being urged to vote and even propose their own candidates for the Soviets, a procedure permissible under the Constitution.

**Orders New Drive on Kulak.**

Joseph V. Stalin, head of the central committee of the Communist party, and Viacheslaf Molotoff, chairman of the Council of People's Commissars of the Soviet Union, have appealed to all Communist and government economic organizations to speed up the collective farm program this Spring.

Their note declares that the aim is the further collectivization "of the poor middle class peasants and to realize the liquidation of the kulaks as a class." This is interpreted as a further move in the long strife against the kulaks, who are prosperous and independent peasants, thus standing in the way of the Communist collective ideal. All economic bodies are urged to pay greater attention to the Spring grain-sowing program this year.

The movement for production of more cotton in the union also is being pushed. Government experts predict that about 233,000 bales will be taken from the 3,000,000 acres under cotton cultivation at present.

January 26, 1931

# STALIN SETS DECADE FOR 100 YEARS' WORK

## Russians Must Acquire Technical Knowledge or Perish in Hostile World, He Says.

## CITES HISTORY AS WARNING

## Calls for Further Sacrifices by Masses to Bring Soviet Abreast of Other Nations.

By WALTER DURANTY.
Wireless to THE NEW YORK TIMES.

MOSCOW, Feb. 5.—In a speech made recently before the first conference of the All-Union Communist industrial executives, but published only today, Joseph Stalin, virtual dictator of Russia, demanded intensification in the Socialist drive to teach Russians what other nations know in the way of technical knowledge.

"Russia is from fifty to a hundred years behind the rest of the world in knowledge," he asserted. "It is our job as Bolsheviki to make up arrears in these ten years, because laggards always suffer. That is what happened in Old Russia—she was always backward and paid for it dearly. Mongols beat her, Turks beat her—and Swedish feudalism and Poles. Anglo-French capitalists beat her—and Japanese barons.

**Gives "Law of Capitalism."**

"They beat her because of backwardness – military backwardness, cultural backwardness, governmental, industrial and agricultural backwardness. They beat her because it was profitable and they could get away with it. That is the law of capitalism—to beat the backward and the weak. 'You're right if strong; if weak you're wrong'—that is the wolf law of capitalism. And that is why we must make up arrears. As Lenin said, 'We must die or catch up and surpass them.' We must do that or they will smash us."

In the old days, Stalin said, the Russian masses had no country, no fatherland. Today they have the greatest country in the world—a fatherland of the working masses everywhere and where all workers are at home, he said. But that position carries obligations.

"We, who first conquered the capitalist masters, who first set up workers' power, first began to build socialism—we have a duty to our fellows abroad," Stalin continued. "The job we are doing, if it succeeds, will overturn the whole world and free the whole working class. For that we must learn and learn and learn and master the technique of industrial management and overcome our backwardness.

"This is our duty not to the U. S. S. R. [Union of Socialist Soviet Republics] alone, but to the workers of the whole world, who now regard us as their vanguard, their 'shock brigade' in the battle against capitalism, their fatherland. Can we justify their hopes? We can and will—that is our duty."

The conference of the industrial executives discussed the prospects of accomplishing the current year's industrial program, which calls for a 45 per cent increase in production, and what is needed to accomplish it. In Lenin's manner Stalin hammered home his points in the simplest language by repetition, until it seemed to Lenin's hearers like a teacher instructing a class. Stalin would be the first to admit he lacks Lenin's exceptional gifts, but it is clear he has studied Lenin to good purpose.

He is a comporatively young man—in his fifty-second year—and his friends say he steeps himself constantly in Lenin's speeches and writings and tries to follow Lenin's example always and to act and believe as Lenin would have acted. Even his opponents admit he is succeeding.

**Follows Lenin Closely.**

A former "oppositionist" told your correspondent ruefully not long ago that Leon Trotsky and the rest of them made the fatal mistake of underestimating Stalin. The man has grown tremendously in recent years. He has followed Lenin so faithfully and studied him so well that he has acquired much of Lenin's force and "qualities."

In his speech published today, Stalin begins with the bold assertion that accomplishment of this year's program means that the "pyatilatka" (the five-year plan) will be carried out in three years in its main fundamentals. What, he asked, was needed to do this? Two conditions—first, physical, or as the Bolsheviki call them, "objective" possibilities, such as natural resources, centralized authority supported by adequate man power, and a coordinated plan. The second is the will, intelligence and knowledge to utilize said possibilities.

In language so plain that a child could follow his argument, Stalin held that the objective possibilities did exist and that the program of their utilization as devised and directed by the Communist Party was good enough to have raised an outcry and caused dismay in the whole capitalist world.

"What about the second condition—that is, have we got the proper management for our industry?" Stalin continued. "We have the will, but have we got the competence? Unhappily, things are not wholly satisfactory in this respect, and as Bolsheviki we must say so openly and straight."

Stalin said that all too often Communist executives thought the signing of papers was the beginning and end of factory management. Making use of popular phrases in Lenin's manner he drove home to his hearers the lesson that successful factory management meant the mastery of technique—this phrase he repeated a dozen times at least—and that one of the chief reasons why the damaging activities of "class enemy" engineers had gone so far was the passive attitude toward technical knowledge on the part of Communist executives.

"You must learn it," he told them. "You must master technique; you as Bolsheviki, as the leaders of Russia, must really lead. And to lead you must have knowledge."

February 6, 1931

## *Soviet Now Makes It a Crime For a Worker to Be Careless*

By The Associated Press.

MOSCOW, May 22.—Because of recent numerous breakages of machinery in factories and collective farms, the Supreme Court has issued instructions to officials of district courts throughout the Soviet Union that henceforth "carelessness" will be considered a crime and all offenders must be tried under criminal statutes.

Conviction would carry with it imprisonment or exile.

When tried by factory courts these offenders usually were acquitted on a plea of "accident." Under the new court rulings it will be unnecessary to prove the intention of workers who damaged machines or set fire, but only that he was careless.

May 23, 1931

# STALIN GIVES RUSSIA 'NEW ECONOMIC PLAN' WITH UNEQUAL WAGE

## Tells Planners of Nation's Work That More Individuality Is Needed in Industry.

## BOURGEOIS WELCOMED BACK

## Ban Is Removed From Expert Class Recently Accused of Sabotage of Projects.

## 5-DAY WEEK IS CHANGED

### It Can Be Turned Into a 6-Day Week With a Full Holiday if Factories So Desire.

Special Cable to THE NEW YORK TIMES.

MOSCOW, July 5.—What is already called "Stalin's New Economic Policy" completely occupies the front pages of the most important newspapers, such as Pravda and Izvestia, today. It virtually sanctions inequality of wages, establishes individual responsibility of directors of industry and workers, and readmits engineers of the old régime into industry.

The point which has attracted most attention here, however, is a practical order to abandon the five-day week in factories—with continuous operation of the plants—wherever this system has been found unsatisfactory, and the substitution of a six-day week—five days' work and one free day, which every one will share.

This programme is set forth in a speech which Joseph Stalin made before a meeting of the industrial directors—the men who are planning the conduct of the industry of the country. It was delivered on June 23. No reason is given why it is published so late or for the fact that it appears on the same day as the opening of the plenary session of the central committee of the Communist party.

It has attracted great attention among the workers and the Russian people generally and also among foreigners here, because M. Stalin speaks rarely and when he does speak his words carry a weight that almost amounts to orders.

His virtual sanction of piece work methods and the system of unequal wages is regarded as signii. ant. Literal interpretation of the Ma: ist dogma means that under communism every one should work according to his ability and receive according to his needs. Since everybody's needs are practically the same and only ability varies, this would mean that every one should receive almost equal wages or the equivalent of wages.

M. Stalin, however, defends his view that wages should not be equal, but should be paid according to a difficulty of the work and the skill of the worker, by saying that this period of the socialization of industry and agriculture is not communism—and is a stage in which emergency measures are necessary.

Another outstanding and new point of M. Stalin's declaration is that every ruling class must develop its own intelligentsia and that the proletariat—that is on the understanding that the proletariat is the ruling class here—must bring forth its own intelligentsia. By this M. Stalin means an industrial intelligentsia of engineers and specialists which in the past has been made up largely of foreign experts or experts left over from the old régime.

The higher technical schools for a long time have been open mostly to sons of the proletariat but M. Stalin now says that, in addition, workers on the job who prove themselves worthy must be promoted to positions where they can use their ability to the utmost.

He also recommends clemency to the engineers of the old régime and says they are now joining the workers' mass movement. This attitude comes as a surprise after the many trials of such experts for sabotage and damaging industry and the imprisonment of antagonistic individuals. It shows that M. Stalin is sure of his position.

He says in substance that the sharpest fangs of these enemy elements have been drawn. In the past this warring contingent depended on the dissatisfaction of the peasant masses with the administration of agriculture over the grain situation. Now he considers that the grain question is settled and the majority of the peasant population satisfied by the establishment of more than 75 per cent of collectivization in the chief grain growing areas. Therefore he considers that the danger of intervention on the part of these elements is over.

### Likened to American Business.

Establishment of individual responsibility for workers and directors and other measures outlined calls forth this comment from foreign observers here: "Why, those are just like American big-business methods."

So far as the six-day week is concerned, it is remarked that if this plan is generally introduced it will mean a great crowding of street cars, parks, movies and theatres in general on the free day.

Some observers here see in M. Stalin's plans a project for consolidating and increasing the tempo of Soviet industry and agriculture as a counter move on the part of the Kremlin to a supposed new anti-Soviet combination, an effort to prepare for expected onslaughts either economic or actual by recruiting and disciplining their own strength.

The Pravda editorial today sees the Hoover plan and the discussions with France regarding it as a struggle between these two countries for hegemony in an anti-Soviet attack. Pravda says further that the reparations negotiations and conferences among the big nations have as an end the forming of a united offensive front against the Soviet Union.

### Six Points in Stalin Program.

MOSCOW, July 5 (AP).—A general overhauling of conditions applying to labor and industry, representing significant changes and in some cases wide differences from previous practices of socialistic development, was proposed by Joseph Stalin in his latest public pronouncement.

He called for a reversal of the policy of the "iron fist" toward members of the "old bourgeois industrial intelligentsia" and adoption of an attitude welcoming them into the service of the State.

He outlined a future program, embracing the following six points:

Readjustment of wages to make the scale commensurate with the type of labor performed; the halt of workers from shifting from one place to another to improve their living conditions.

Remedy of the growing labor shortage by attracting more peasants to industries as agriculture progresses toward mechanization.

Improvement of the organization of labor in industry in order to distribute the proper strength among factories and to end "irresponsible" methods.

To have the working class develop its own "intelligentsia" of such skilled workers as engineers and technicians.

To change the policy toward specialists of the old order to attract more of them to industry.

To increase the interior sources of industry and develop the piece-work system.

### For Individualism in Industry.

He also proposed the reversal to individualistic from collective business administration, saying that "new conditions demand new methods of work and leadership."

Reorganization of the present system of wages is necessary, he added, if the shifting of labor is to be prevented.

"In many of our factories the wage system is such as to leave no difference between the skilled and unskilled worker and between hard and easy labor," he said. "This leads to unskilled workers showing no interest in raising their qualifications, and skilled workers move from factory to factory in search of a place where their qualifications will be more valued.

"To give this shifting a free hand would undermine our industry, wreck our plan of production and stop improvement in the quality of manufactured goods. We must destroy such equal wages. It is unbearable to see the locomotive driver receiving the same wages as a bookkeeper."

July 6, 1931

# COMMUNISM BUILDS ITS CITY OF UTOPIA

## Russia's Ideas of a Model Community Will Be Tested in a Vast Project For Thousands of Families

*The author of the article that follows is a member of a Cleveland firm of engineers and builders which is engaged in constructing the remarkable new Russian city which he describes. When completed the city will include an automobile plant capable of turning out 150,000 Ford cars and trucks annually, a steel plant and accommodations for 48,000 men and women workers and their dependents. Mr. Austin believes the success or failure of the new community, the first of its kind ever created, will be a factor of decisive importance in the future of Soviet Russia.*

*By ALLAN S. AUSTIN*

ON the north bank of the Oka River, a little more than six miles above its junction with the Volga at the historic market town of Nizhni Novgorod, is rising a new city for 60,000 inhabitants in which American engineers are translating into brick and concrete the social theories of the Soviet Government. Here, in a land of forests, through which four centuries ago the traders were floating their rich cargoes of furs, the old Russia, the new Russia and modern America have flowed together like the rivers themselves.

The new city, carved out of what a year or two ago was almost wilderness, will be Communist Russia's conception of what a community ought to be. If it succeeds it will affect the future mode of life of the 150,000,000 people now inhabiting the Soviet Republics. On that score as well as because of the sheer magnitude of the enterprise it is second to no physical undertaking now under way in Russia. Here we see concretely expressed the theories of communism with regard to family life, education, recreation and labor. The city is a Communist utopia, built so from the ground up.

Because of the significance attached by the Soviets to their first brand-new socialistic city neither money nor thought has been spared. Leading professors of economics and sociology were invited to contribute their ideas. Six of the foremost architectural societies and institutions in Russia submitted plans in a competition which was finally won by the High Technical School.

The problem was one to stir the enthusiasm of any architect or engineer. The city was planned as a complete industrial unit. An automobile plant to be built near by was to employ 18,000 workers, one-third of whom would be women. Six thousand additional women would be employed in the kitchen factory, bread factory, clubhouse and similar institutions. An allowance of 25 per cent was made for dependents, minors and other non-producers, making a total of 30,000 people. A steel plant not yet started was to employ an equal number of workers, bringing the total population, when everything was completed, to 60,000.

The High Technical Commission laid down the fundamental requirements of size, area per person and the number and kind of functions to be provided for in the city. It then turned to American architects and engineers to "rationalize" the project, to use the pariance of the moment in Russia. Of this process of "rationalization" nothing has been more striking than the improvements made to the water, plumbing, heating and lighting systems.

The chief problem which confronted the designers was the proper density of population. Overcrowding is still one of the major concerns in the older and larger cities of Russia. Quite probably most of the Soviet officials interested in the development were only too familiar with the stuffy rooms, dark hallways and inadequate sanitation arrangements of the older communities. They desired for the new city abundant sunshine, fresh air and ample modern conveniences. Throughout the planning there was a conscious effort to raise the standard of living for the working people to a new level.

For social and practical reasons it was decided to divide the housing facilities into units for 1,000 persons each. Elevators were ruled out, both because of the extra expense and because of the frankly acknowledged fact that the Russian people are still distrustful of such contrivances. The housing units therefore took the form of five houses each, each house four stories high, connected with the other buildings of the unit by enclosed passages and accommodating 200 persons. In addition each "community unit" includes a clubhouse, a nursery building and a kindergarten building.

About ten acres of ground is allotted to each unit. Of this a little less than two acres is building area, the remaining eight acres being permanently reserved for lawns, walks, playgrounds and park space. One can picture the benefits to any large American city which this breathing space would give. No longer would there be the rush to the country on Sunday, or children growing up in ignorance of flowers and tadpoles and grasshoppers. The Soviet's attention to youth is practical and significant.

• • •

THE life in any one community unit of the new city will be very much like that in any other. Let us look at one of these units in detail. The clubhouse is its most significant feature and is really the nerve centre of the group. In this building, 300 feet long and two stories high, provision is made for all social, educational, recreational and gastronomic needs of the adult population. Directly off the lobby into which one enters is a large dining hall which will accommodate one-third of the population of the unit at one time. There is also an open-air dining balcony for use during the Summer months. The club kitchens are on the order of serving pantries, since most of the food for the entire city is prepared in the central kitchen factory and sent out in a cooked or semi-prepared condition. As there are no regular kitchen facilities in the community houses, the club's kitchens supply every one, including those who for one reason or another do not use the club dining room.

Next in importance to the dining room is the auditorium, which serves also for a gymnasium and motion-picture theatre. Adjoining it on the first floor are locker and shower rooms for men and women, and above these are the projection and film-storage rooms. In the hands of the Soviets the movie is a most important branch of education, instructing even those who cannot read. Even the posters, signs and graphs are so well adapted to the still widespread illiteracy that we foreigners, illiterate in Russian, can grasp their meaning as well as though they were printed in English.

Steel Against the Sky—Building an Auto Assembling Plant at Nizhni Novgorod.

*Photo From Press Cliche.*

The club buildings also contain a library, reading room, chess room, game room, telephone and telegraph room, notion shop, a political science study room, a laboratory for inventive experiments and a room for the study of military science. They seem to justify, from the Soviet point of view, the title of "headquarters of civilization" which a young "comsomol" bestowed upon a club building of similar type in a near-by town.

The club is not a school in the ordinary sense, but facilities for the stimulation and molding of adult minds are so conveniently provided that communism can hardly help taking root. The science laboratory is particularly noteworthy. There is a well-developed policy in the Soviet Government to encourage individual initiative along scientific and engineering lines, so that Russia will not have to depend upon foreign specialists.

• • •

SO many functions are concentrated in the clubhouse that the only remaining use for the five community houses in the unit is as dormitories. These buildings are about 40 feet wide, 200 feet long and four stories high, and are constructed with brick sidewalls and concrete frame. The windows are double, as is necessary in the severe Winters of this latitude, but are larger than the ordinary Russian window. The walls are insulated against the cold with a composition of wood chips and shavings, cemented by an impregnating compound which makes the whole virtually fireproof, and floors and walls are soundproofed, so that the occupants may live with as little interference from one another as possible.

The first three floors are arranged alike, with single and double rooms alternating. Nine square meters (96.87 square feet) was fixed by the High Technical Schools Commission as the allowance for each person, and the sleeping rooms are all too small to permit of any other use than that for which they are designed. This limited amount of privacy is all that is permitted to the worker under the new scheme of living. Each room has a wardrobe and wash-basin, and each floor has a central lobby or lounging room and hot-plates for a limited amount of light cooking.

The fourth floor of each building is composed of larger rooms, the size of a double and single room combined. These are intended to be occupied by "Communes"—groups of three or four young men or women who work, study and live together. Nobody worries about any moral questions that may arise from housing groups of both sexes on the same floor. So far as I know, there is no chaperonage of any kind, nor any restrictions covering the assignment of rooms. Beyond this fact we can only conjecture. We do find a good many young people who have been married twice or even three times before they are 30. On the subject of morals in general there is just as much dissension and divergence of opinion here among the Russians as there is over prohibition at home. There are those who believe in the freedom the present laws allow and those who do not.

• • •

THE nursery and kindergarten buildings are an integral part of each complete unit. The nursery is designed for children from 3 months to 3 or 4 years of age, of whom it is estimated that there will be about eighty-five in each unit. The building is planned to be an actual, full-time home for these children, with eating and sleeping quarters, and a staff of child specialists and nurses in charge. The degree of separation between children and parents will be largely a matter of choice on the part of the parent. Many fathers and mothers, I believe will be quite satisfied to have the government take over in large measure the care of their children. This would apply especially to the younger couples when both parents are working in the plant. Another inducement is that the nursery can often provide better or more suitable foods than the individual families are able to procure. For example, hospitals and nurseries share the limited supply of fine white flour and always receive preference in case of a shortage of milk. By many such indirect ways are the objects of the Soviets attained.

The kindergarten is planned for children between 4 and 7 years of age. Here emphasis is laid on project work, as it is in our own progressive schools; a woodworking shop is one of the principal features. Children are taken to visit factories where the Communist system may be seen at work, or to inspect some great construction project. I have seen dozens of groups of youngsters with their teachers visiting the site of the new town and being told of the important differences such enterprises will make in their own lives. The slogan, "the Five-Year Plan in four years," is everywhere.

* * *

THE new city will not be limited to the units I have described. The new scheme of life is frankly admitted by the Soviets to be experimental. While its practicability is being demonstrated, workers who so desire will be allowed to live in apartment houses, identical in size and capacity with the community houses, but divided into apartments of three rooms with kitchen and bath. Each room is large, containing about twenty square meters. But unlike American practice, each family has one room rather than one apartment, and each kitchen has to serve for three families. This is not an innovation but is the plan generally followed in the cities at the present time.

In these apartment groups the clubhouses and school buildings are left unbuilt. The Soviet sociologists are not interested in putting more of their government's money into clubs, nurseries and kindergartens than is necessary to prove the correctness of their ideas. The city at first will be two-thirds apartment construction and one-third community units. But as soon as the practicability of the community unit plan has been demonstrated the apartment houses can be transformed into units by adding partitions and erecting the club and school buildings.

Now let us take a look at the city as a whole. It covers an area of about 3.66 square miles, has an extreme length of three miles and contains about twenty-five miles of roadways. It is so oriented that each building has an east and west exposure, getting direct sunlight into every room. A large central square forms the hub of the city. Here is the Palace of Culture, which supplements the functions of the clubs and is the administrative headquarters for all cultural development throughout the community. Adjoining this building is the governmental and political headquarters and on other sides of the square are situated a department store and a hotel. The fire department occupies a prominent corner, as is fitting for an organization whose members are on a par, roughly speaking, with Governors of American States. The brightness of their brass helmets establishes their position in no uncertain way.

From the central square a double boulevard about a mile and a half long runs to the Oka River, where there will be a yacht basin and docking facilities for the river boats. The boulevard runs through a park, which comprises about one-third of the entire area of the city and which has sites for a university and future public buildings. At one side of the city and convenient to the industrial plant are various service buildings, including the kitchen factory, the bread factory, the slaughter house, the laundry and bath house, and food-storage buildings. Well isolated from the city proper and in attractive wooded surroundings is a polyclinic hospital. A large athletic field has one stadium big enough for football and track events, a smaller stadium for tennis matches, and locker and bath houses.

* * *

THE hours of work and leisure in the Russian Utopia will probably be much the same as those of working people in the United States. The eight-hour day is in effect rather generally, with a seven-hour day being introduced in some places. Some figures I recently saw indicate that out of about 16,000,000 organized workers in the Soviet Union all except a little more than 1,000,000 were working eight hours a day. This is the length of the work day in the city under construction. One hour is generally taken for lunch. Lunch rooms in the industrial plant, supplied from the central kitchen factory now being erected near the city, will serve the noon meal, making it unnecessary for the workers to carry a lunch or return home for it.

Recreation after working hours will probably consist largely of sports, for there is a great popular interest in games, gymnastic drills and all sorts of out-of-door activity. The entire field of sports is enthusiastically encouraged by the Soviets and is characteristically fostered by the formation of outing and sporting clubs, to some of which are assigned instructors. I was surprised to observe the complete stocks which sporting goods stores carry in contrast with the meager variety of wares in the average store. And it is interesting to note that most all sport terms are English words. Tennis and volley-ball are popular. The proximity of the river makes swimming and boating, in Summer, very convenient, and with but few exceptions the condition which Will Rogers summed up as "not a bathing suit in Russia" still prevails. There is an organization called Dynamo which fosters all kinds of sports, organizes teams and competitions and occasionally sponsors a tour of foreign athletes through Russia. Recently we witnessed an exhibition of boxing by a group of Swedish boys, followed by an exhibition of "physico-culture" put on by the Dynamo group.

The Russians, workers and peasants alike, seem to have a passion for singing beautiful minor harmonies which are wholly unlike our music. This singing, with accordion accompaniment, is to my mind one of the most attractive features of Russian life. Every night, now that it is warm weather, we hear groups of men wandering about singing. There used to be a great rivalry between the villagers over their singing, and each village would have its characteristic song. Since much of our labor comes from these villages, we still hear the old refrains.

* * *

IF family life among the workers now engaged on the model city is an indication of what may be expected later on, I should say that it would be, from our point of view, quite normal among the older engineers and mechanics. There is, however, a large group of young people of both sexes apprentices or "comsomols," who have left their parents' homes and are embarking on careers of their own under the guidance of the Soviets. Their presence in large numbers is probably the most noticeable feature of the social life, and they are most typical of what might be called the New Russian. Stepping into one of their rooms, one finds the walls covered with revolutionary posters and pictures of Soviet leaders, and on the tables are pamphlets of the same order. As I said before, there does not seem to be any system of chaperonage, and the young people's morals are their own concern.

As a footnote to my mention of family life, I should add that in spite of the publicity usually given to the subject of birth control by journalists writing of Russia, there is not the slightest evidence of race suicide. There are babies in abundance and the nurseries and kindergartens should have plenty of customers.

So, to sum up, sports, amusements, home life, education, work, all phases of existence in fact, are here molded to fit the socialistic concept. This doctrine will soon be practiced here on a scale never before attempted, with people educated to it for a decade and under conditions as favorable as can be prepared.

Sitting here in the midst of construction activities, one is apt to become absorbed by the problems of providing housing and complete facilities for 50,000 persons in a year and a half, of the shortage of skilled labor due to the unprecedented amount of construction now under way in the U. S. S. R., of the corresponding shortage of materials, and dozens of other distractions quite familiar to any one working in Russia. Perhaps the carpenters never worked on any but log houses in their own village before; perhaps the plasterers were laborers at the dock three weeks ago, before they went to school a few nights; perhaps an electric saw is new to every one. Well, so is a socialistic city new to them all, and if they are to obtain the unusual benefits and vastly improved living conditions which have often been promised them, they must resort to unusual methods and make unusual sacrifices to achieve these extraordinary ends.

Is the game worth the candle? Will the experiment succeed? No prudent person is answering these questions at the present time. But the socialistic city at Nizhni Novgorod is giving to the Soviet Government a proving ground for its theories. Here they will fail or triumph. They have not had this chance before.

August 9, 1931

# SOVIET IN NEW BID FOR FOREIGN MONEY

## Stores Selling Goods for "Valuta" Only Will Start a Mail-Order Business.

## AMERICANS WILL BE AIDED

### Those Working in Russia Will Be Able to Get Goods Formerly Unobtainable There.

By WALTER DURANTY.

Wireless to THE NEW YORK TIMES.

MOSCOW, Aug. 20.—About a year ago there opened in the centre of Moscow a fine new store called Torgsin (a combination word meaning trade with foreigners) to sell antiques and other valuable articles for foreign money, checks and drafts.

It contained also, for the convenience of foreign specialists, a clothing and dry goods department, toys, carved peasant work and at first a tiny section for the sale of foreign wines from pre-war Russian supplies, candy and canned goods.

The prices on the whole were moderate, and the provision department grew by leaps and bounds. It now handles bread, cheese, fruit, tobacco, groceries and a wide variety of products from new Soviet canneries.

Whereas Russians originally were not encouraged to buy at the new Torgsins, no restrictions were made, provided payment was in foreign money. Today the Industrial Gazette publishes an interview with the President of the Torgsin division, M. Sklar, who states that thirty stores are now open from Vladivostok and Archangel to Baku and Tiflis, where, in addition to direct sales for foreign money "to all citizens without exception," a mail-order business will be conducted on a nation-wide scale through foreign banks or foreign money orders.

Thus Americans with relatives in Russia can insure the delivery of food packets by sending orders to the nearest Torgsin store. M. Sklar added that while Torgsin hitherto has handled only Russian products "of export quality"—which means more here than outsiders may realize—henceforth it will carry some imported goods, which strikes a welcome chord in American hearts, for Americans in Russia are homesick for cigarettes, coffee, breakfast food, sauces and pickles, which are not obtainable here.

The fall in world market prices owing to the glut of food products has played havoc with Soviet export plans at a time when three years of hard work has made it highly desirable to improve the living standard of the population, and the Torgsin "home-export" plan will do double service in providing foreign valuta and keeping much-needed food at home.

A possible objection that a privilege will thus be given to that section of the population with friends or relatives abroad—that is, on the whole to others than the working class—is less serious here than might be imagined.

The workers on the whole are fairly well provided through factory and other "closed distribution centres," and any addition to the general food supply would have a favorable effect everywhere. What is more, the local Torgsins have already begun the practice of selling goods for rubles, provided the purchaser has a certificate from a bank or a State finance bureau showing he has received them in return for articles or old coinage of gold or silver.

It is probable, too, that there is quite a large amount of hoarded foreign money in Russia, which thus could be put into circulation for government uses. It is quite possible to expect that business running into tens of millions of dollars will be done by the Torgsin stores in the coming twelve months, provided the mail order deliveries are handled efficiently. This would make a vital difference in a rather critical situation.

August 20, 1931

# MOSCOW LIFTS BAN ON SMALL TRADERS

## Decree Allows Peasants to Sell Part of Grain in the Open Market at Own Prices.

Wireless to THE NEW YORK TIMES.

MOSCOW, May 7.—A stimulus to agriculture, more bread for individuals and a spur to petty trade generally are foreseen as a result of a decree just signed jointly by Joseph Stalin, Communist party chief, and Premier Molotoff.

The decree first reduces the total government grain collections this year by about 20 per cent, thus leaving more grain in the hands of the growers, and second, it gives freedom and encouragement to collective farm members and individual peasants to sell their grain in the open market at their own prices, not the government fixed prices.

Issued by the Council of Commissars and the Central Executive Committee of the party, it was displayed on the front pages of all the newspapers today, and as one of the grain trust officials remarked, "naturally, it will make the peasants happy," for they will have more grain for their own use and will be able to indulge in one of their favorite pastimes by bartering it at bazaars.

It is thought here that the sale of this grain will encourage the individual to manufacture such needed articles as cloth and tinware. The fact that a large amount of consumers' goods was made by petty artisans before the revolution and during the period of the NEP [New Economic Policy] often has been neglected in attempts to explain the present goods shortage 'n the ..ace of the increased factory production.

**To Trade Manufrctures for Grain.**

Bootmakers and others will now trade their wares for grain. Just now it is next to impossible to get shoes unless they are made by independent cobblers, and even the peasants' bark sandals are scarce. In connection with this new poli~y of free trade it is interesting to note the agricultural tax will exempt profit derived from goods sold in the markets.

May 8, 1932

# RUSSIAN FARMERS WARY OF MARKETS

## Fearing Confiscation, They Do Little to Add to Amount of Foodstuffs Available.

## SPECULATORS ARE SEIZED

### Gang Is Captured After It Gets Funds for Its Operations by Fraud on Building Trusts.

By ROBIN KINKEAD.

Wireless to THE NEW YORK TIMES.

MOSCOW, June 17.—The decree allowing collective farm members and individual peasants to trade freely at the bazaars has been in effect more than a month, but the general supply of foodstuffs and other goods has not increased appreciably.

More people are buying and selling at the markets, but thus far the peasants have not completed the year's harvest nor had time to grow potatoes or other vegetables. The meat supply also has failed to gain much ground because the peasants are short of cattle, pigs and poultry as a result of the wide slaughtering in 1930, when they thought all live stock would be seized. Now they are commencing to sell to the markets what meat they have instead of selling it secretly or eating it themselves, as in the past. The markets are growing slowly, and it is safe to say this new form of trading will not throw any considerable weight on the food balance for at least six months.

Not only is it hard to get food to sell at the bazaars just now, but it is difficult to get the machinery of trade functioning. The peasants are suspicious by nature because of the treatment they received in the old days, so instead of rushing to the markets, they are circling warily around the tempting bait to make sure there is no trap.

**Distrust Is Emphasized.**

One old peasant said to your correspondent:

"I trust the government all right. I am sure they are sincere in allowing us to trade, but some of my friends are not convinced. They say they might be allowed to trade for a time and when they have made some money and raised some stock for the market a new decree would be passed and the results of their efforts seized."

But the government and the Communist party are making the biggest efforts to start the ball rolling and encourage the peasants to come in. That the matter is considered important is seen by looking into the newspapers. Day after day two subjects always take up considerable space—the drive for a new loan and the effort to get the peasants into the markets.

Some of the articles exhort the Communist party members, village Soviets and collective farm leaders to explain the situation to the coy peasants and convince them that the government is really sincere. Others expose the mistakes made by officials and others in trying to start markets or reprimand villages which have not made proper provisions for trading.

**More Bazaars Demanded.**

For instance, in Izvestia today there is an article saying there are not enough bazaars in the Moscow region, and insisting that more must be opened. There is another article attacking officials of the Tamboff district for mistakes made in the bazaars. Militiamen there arrested a group of peasants for killing cows and marketing the meat and confiscated their goods. These militiamen evidently had not heard of the new decree and were acting in accordance with former rules.

Elsewhere, instead of letting the peasants make their own prices, the village Soviets set prices too low, thus discouraging any trading. In another instance, tax collectors extracted a 25-ruble tax instead of a levy of 1 ruble from the traders.

It was revealed yesterday that there were many speculaters hanging about the markets to buy things as cheaply as possible and then resell them at higher prices elsewhere. Moscow detectives caught one gang which had forged documents indicating that the members were carpenters and stone masons. With these false papers these men made contracts with various building trusts for work in Siberia and elsewhere where skilled labor is in great demand. With the money advanced to them they speculated in produce.

This conduct is condemned as "unsocial" and unlawful.

June 19, 1932

# PRIVATE FOOD TRADE ABOLISHED IN RUSSIA

## Soviet Ends System of Peasant Sales—Meat Collections to Be as Rigid as Taxes.

## SHORTAGE CAUSES MOVE

By WALTER DURANTY.

By Wireless to THE NEW YORK TIMES.

MOSCOW, Sept. 24.—The Kremlin has decided upon a strong forward policy regarding the Soviet food difficulties. Two decrees published today mark the abandonment of the "Rightward swing" inaugurated by the measure adopted early in the Summer.

The new step is a reversion to a reinforced system of State food collections as opposed to allowing peasant producers to conduct private trade. As Lenin found in the months preceding the formal introduction of the new economic policy in the Summer of 1921, private trade without private traders is an anomaly.

**Stalin Revokes Private Trade.**

The circumstances then were such that he was forced to take a "backward" step, from a Bolshevist point of view. Faced with the same anomaly, Joseph Stalin moves forward and revokes private trade—for that is what today's measures come to, though they do not say so expressly.

One decree, issued by the Council of Labor and Defense, of which Stalin is a member, abolishes the decree issued earlier in the Summer which released peasants in a fifty-kilometer radius of the principal cities from State food collections, except grain, with the idea that they would sell their own produce in the markets instead.

To make its meaning clear the new decree is reinforced by an order from the Moscow Provincial Soviet, which declares that Summer relaxation has been abolished because it was "used for speculation in foodstuffs." In other words, private trade inevitably brought private traders, or middlemen, to say nothing of slick peasants withholding their supplies until prices soared.

For weeks it looked as if a new NEP might be on the way despite the denials of Kremlin spokesmen. Today's decisions show the opposite.

**Decree on Meat Collections.**

The second decree, signed by Stalin and Premier Molotoff, at first sight appears to be simply what the preamble states—"a means of regulating and facilitating State meat collections in the reduced quantities fixed in the decree of May 10," which raised the proportion of meat to be collected from State cattle ranches but lowered the proportion from collective and individual farms.

But additional clauses of the new decree say that the collections will "have the force of tax obligations" and that non-delivery will be punished by a fine to make the "collections" virtually "requisitions."

If the system of general food collections in the suburban areas, as reinstituted by the Council of Labor and Defense, carries a similar proviso, as may well be the case, the result will be something equivalent on a modified scale to the food tax policy of the militant Communist period, which failed through the weakness in distribution and the shortage of consumers' goods, both consequent on the civil war. The chances of a similar policy are now incomparably better, but it is a bold move.

September 25, 1932

# SOVIET DEDICATES DNIEPROSTROY DAM

## Thousands Wave Red Flags as Kalinin Names Huge Power Plant After Lenin.

## TOWN BRILLIANTLY LIGHTED

## Electric Letters 10 Feet High Across the Dam Flash Words of Victory to Spectators.

## SIX AMERICANS HONORED

DNIEPROSTROY, U. S. S. R., Oct. 10 (AP).—Bands blared the "Internationale," red flags waved and thousands of spectators cheered today as the Soviet Government dedicated the largest hydroelectric plant in the world to the cause of socialism.

The occasion was the formal opening of the gigantic Dnieprostroy dam, which eventually will supply an area of 70,000 square miles and a population of 16,000,000 with electric power. One of the features of the ceremony was the formal announcement by Mikhail Kalinin, President of the Soviet Central Executive Committee, that the Order of the Red Banner of Labor had been awarded to Colonel Hugh L. Cooper, constructor, and five other Americans who participated in the building and equipping of the great enterprise.

**Americans Honored.**

The Americans honored, besides Colonel Cooper, are Frank Eieer, a member of Colonel Cooper's New York staff; Fred Winters and George E. Binders of the Newport News Shipbuilding and Drydock Company, and Charles Thompson and William Murphy of the General Electric Company. The same award went to Alexander Winter, also an American, who was the government's chief engineer in the building of the dam. He has been named Vice Commissar for Heavy Industry, despite the fact that he is not a member of the Communist party.

The ceremony was held in the shadow of the dam in a natural amphitheatre adjacent to the power house containing the world's largest generators and turbines, manufactured by the General Electric Company. The rest of the work was done by the Newport News Company.

The participants in the ceremony were workers and officials actually employed in the construction, several battalions of soldiers and detachments of sailors, and a group of officials both of the U. S. S. R. and the Ukrainian Government.

The plant has been only partly completed. Two of the five generators already in place hummed an accompaniment to official declarations that Dnieprostroy marked the greatest step toward realization of Lenin's dream of an electrified Russia. Four other generators remain to be installed. The full capacity of the power plant probably will not be realized until next year, when floodgates on the dam will be constructed to raise the level of the river and provide more pressure.

Formally dedicating the project with the name "Lenin's Plant," M. Kalinin contrasted the depression and the closed factories in other parts of the world with the gathering speed of Socialist construction in the Soviet Union. He quoted Joseph Stalin, head of the Communist party, thus:

"There is no fortress which the Bolsheviki cannot conquer."

**Praise American Aid.**

Other speakers included G. K. Orzhonikidze, Commissar for Heavy Industry, Mr. Winter and President Chubar of the Council of People's Commissars of the Ukrainian Republic. Each of them paid tribute to the American technical assistance that had been received.

On a speaker's stand decorated with red banners bearing the hammer and sickle insignia was Colonel Cooper, who made a brief speech through an interpreter in which he said the plant "stands as a challenge to all those of your country and elsewhere who previously doubted the wisdom of your government." In an earlier statement to newspaper men Colonel Cooper advocated recognition of the Soviet Union by the United States.

"Lack of understanding between the two countries is the greatest plague in the world today," he said. "I hope this work of mine will help to abolish misunderstanding and to bring about American recognition, which is one of the greatest international problems now facing the two countries."

M. Stalin was unable to attend personally, but he telegraphed his congratulations. He joined with Premier Molotoff in a recommendation that a monument to Lenin be placed on the top of the dam.

Tonight the whole town, now housing 125,000 persons—it used to be a village of 400 in a barren steppe—was brilliantly lighted with power from the plant. The dam itself flashed, in letters ten feet high, the words' "Soviet power plus electrification and bolshevism."

October 11, 1932

# *SOVIET UNION PERMITS PRIVATE GRAIN SALES*

## *Peasants in Moscow Province and Tartar Republic Get Right to Sell Surplus.*

MOSCOW, Dec. 2 (AP).—The Council of People's Commissars and the Central Committee of the Communist party issued an important decree today permitting all collective and individual peasants in Moscow Province and the Tartar Republic to sell their surplus grain in private markets immediately.

Although these regions contribute relatively small proportions of the nation's total grain, the order was significant in that they are the only ones which have supplied all the government's grain "collections"—that is, the part of the crop the State requires peasants to deliver at fixed prices.

Under regulations announced last May, which authorized peasants to sell their surplus in the open market, it was stipulated that no grain could be marketed until Jan. 15, 1933, which is the date set by the government for the completion of nation-wide collections.

Collections, on the whole, have been notoriously backward in 1932. There have been unofficial predictions that some concessions to the peasantry would be necessary to speed them up.

In some quarters it was predicted that today's decree was the beginning of the alteration of Soviet Russia's agricultural policy respecting collections.

December 3, 1932

# EVENTS IN SOVIET DIFFICULT TO WEIGH

## Conflicting Outlook of Western Nations, Censorship and the Crucial Period Are Obstacles.

## NEW FOOD DECREE ISSUED

## Factories Will Take Over on Jan. 1 Stores Operated by Cooperatives —Aim Is to Spur Efficiency.

By WALTER DURANTY.

By Wireless to THE NEW YORK TIMES.

PARIS, Dec. 5.—The task of the foreign correspondent in the Union of Socialist Soviet Republics has never been easy because he must try to report a vast, bewildering country, full of contradictions and in a perpetual state of flux, to readers whose social system, conditions of life and actual habit of thought are immeasurably different.

But recently, since the food shortage and its effects have grown manifest, the serious reporter's position has become delicate and difficult, not only on account of the censorship but for more profound reasons.

On the whole the Soviet censorship is fair and reasonable. According to Foreign Commisar Litvinoff, its purpose is to prevent the cabling of information that is false, malicious or persistently hostile in tone, while mailed articles are subject to no restrictions save that the writer later will be called to account if they are held to infringe any of the points barred by cable censorship.

**Put Burden on Reporter.**

The censors always inform the correspondent if they wish to delete a passage on the grounds that it is incorrect, or, more frequently, that its truth cannot be immediately established, which places the onus of proof on the reporter and frequently leads to vexatious delay if one gets a "beat" on a news item not yet confirmed by publication in the official press.

But the censors will usually allow modification in such form as not to spoil the sense and sequence of the rest of the despatch. On the other hand, they are only human and share the viewpoint that the writer has observed in censors everywhere, whether civil or military. That is to say, they tend to this view:

"This may be true and, I daresay, it is, but its publication may get me into trouble. Therefore, I prefer to delete it."

In other words, personal responsibility is shifted from the correspondent, who is a more or less free agent and doubtless is quite willing to take chances, to the censor, who is a government official most reluctant to risk his official head.

This is particularly the case in Moscow in a period of difficulty and tension like the present, when a lapse might cause consequences to a Communist official, whereas the worst a foreign reporter is likely to incur is a warning that he will be forced to leave the country if the incident is repeated. But that is only a minor difficulty.

There is another, much more serious—namely, to determine the extent and character of events as they occur and to gauge their effects with accuracy. For instance, take the present food shortage. The first thing one finds on investigation is that a phenomenon apparently most disquieting—an exodus of about a million peasants from the Ukraine, driven by fear of hunger—began a full year ago and practically ended by the first of May.

It was due to the fact, now freely admitted, that Ukrainian reserves of food and seed grain were overdepleted to meet the needs of the Far Eastern army, but the exodus at first was so gradual the authorities themselves could hardly distinguish it from the seasonal movement that has always been a feature of Russian village life. It was only when the Spring sowing began that the shortages were realized and the seed provided.

Even then the local authorities, anxious to make a good showing, reported that the acreage sown was about equivalent to that of the previous year, although they must have known a large part of the area was sown much too light. When the harvest came in July and August it appeared, first, that the yield per acre was only half what was expected and secondly, that there was a considerable shortage of labor.

Simultaneously, the vanguard of Winter fugitives began to reach Moscow begging for help from the State and individuals alike. This time lag between cause and effect presents an incredible difficulty for the foreign observer. Similarly, it may soon be generally known that "incidents," involving in some cases violence, occurred in the North Caucasus six weeks ago.

The newspaper Pravda referred cryptically to the backsliding of some Communist Youth members who championed the kulak cause.

The Economic Life made scant mention of the party "purging" in the same region, and the army newspaper, Red Star, referred briefly to cases of "successful sabotage."

But before these disjointed indications appeared, the authorities had taken steps to redress the grievances and the "situation was liquidated." It is perfectly absurd for a reporter now to postulate the consequences of a state of affairs that has already ceased to exist. The best one can do is to refuse to be influenced by isolated information, however authentic, and to try to strike a balance on general conditions.

Even if this can be done successfully there arises a final bugbear. Are the food shortage and its effects lasting or temporary? How far do they affect the national efficiency and the socialization program? With the following additional delicate point, which no conscientious American reporter in Europe can neglect nowadays, when statesmen everywhere are playing the diplomatic poker game with their cards mighty close to their chest:

To what extent is one justified in suggesting that this or that card in one player's hand is weak when one cannot be absolutely sure about it? Compared with that problem in reportorial ethics, the thought of unpleasant personal consequences of an error becomes insignificant.

**Factories to Take Over Stores.**

Wireless to THE NEW YORK TIMES.

MOSCOW, Dec. 5.—All newspapers here today feature a decree issued jointly by the central committee of the Communist party and the Council of People's Commissars and signed by Joseph Stalin and Premier Molotoff. The decree provides that factories and similar institutions shall supply from the "closed" stores only workers (and their families) who are employed there. It will go into effect Jan. 1.

Moreover, food cards will be issued monthly by the factories. In case a worker quits his job he must hand in his card when he leaves the factory.

The decree also appoints a commission to consider means of supplying those who do not work in factories or institutions and, therefore, do not have special stores. Formerly the closed stores were under the control of the cooperative societies and supplied workers belonging to the cooperatives.

The decree has two main purposes—to improve the means of supplying workers with food in a period when that task is becoming difficult, and to increase labor discipline. It is felt that stores selling only to members of one factory or institution can plan and supply food and goods more efficiently, eliminating queues and waste.

Secondly, by putting the control of food supplies in the hands of factories, the managements will have a powerful weapon to insure labor discipline. If workers are absent without reason or loaf on the job they can be squeezed in a tender spot. It is believed also that this move will tend to halt drifting from one job to another, now one of the main labor problems confronting the Soviet Union, because the food supply will be cut off the minute a worker quits.

The newspaper Izvestia says in an editorial accompanying the decree that formerly workers could take jobs in one factory and receive a ration of potatoes, then change their jobs to get another ration to sell in the open markets, thus causing much speculation in food.

Cafeterias are being installed in many factories to improve the efficiency of the mass-feeding system. A group of fourteen American specialists is directing this work.

December 6, 1932

# SOVIET TO 'ANCHOR' LABOR BY PASSPORT

## Orders All Citizens Over 16 to Get Documents, With Secret Police Directing Operation.

## SEEKS RETURN TO FARMS

## Hopes to Rid Industrial and Urban Centres of "Useless Mouths" and Class Enemies.

## DECREE CLIMAX OF DRIVE

By WALTER DURANTY.

By Wireless to THE NEW YORK TIMES.

MOSCOW, Dec. 28.—In an effort to "anchor" industrial labor and force former farm workers back into rural life, the Soviet Government today issued a decree that goes further than anything it has yet attempted.

The decree orders every citizen over 16 years old to get a passport and instructs the militia, under the authority and direction of the O. G. P. U., the secret police, to examine and verify said passport with the expressly stated purpose of removing "useless mouths" and surreptitious class enemies from the urban and industrial centres.

The decree completes and, above all, puts teeth in previous measures in the same direction. From the Western standpoint it is a shocking infringement of individual rights and freedom, but the Soviet does not think in Western terms and the decree is regarded simply as a vigorous step toward the improvement of discipline and the living conditions of the genuine or permanent workers which the laboring masses not only desire themselves but believe the Bolsheviki are trying to produce.

**Lack of Training Weak Point.**

The Russian Worker's weak point, lack of training and economic or industrial discipline, has become particularly apparent under the pressure of recent difficulties. Throughout the country, in towns and villages alike, labor has become fluid, trickling here and there like water in search of the level where the difficulties are least, that is, where food, housing and goods are most plentiful and easiest acquired.

To reduce labor fluidity is the Bolsheviki's chief problem today, and they are attempting to solve it by a double method:

First, by the increase and better distribution of the supply of food and goods, especially for the towns and factories. Factory and other "socialized" restaurants now feed 14,000,000 persons daily, including 2,000,000 children in the schools, and factory and other "closed distributing stores" supply goods for fully four-fifths of the population of the urban and industrial centres and the construction camps.

Second, now in progress and exemplified by today's decree, a nationwide drive to keep industrial labor stationary and force back to the farms people attracted by reports of better conditions in town or construction camp, who have left rural life in such numbers as to produce an actual shortage of agricultural labor.

Among these is a considerable proportion of almost professional work shirkers and such "class enemies" as kulaks—the term now covers any peasant opposed to rural socialization — and "speculators," petty private traders, who have managed to get a foothold in factories and other enterprises.

**More for Real Workers.**

Their removal would leave more food, goods and housing for distribution among the regular workers, which explains why recent decrees to this purpose have caused not resentment but satisfaction among the permanent working masses.

The Soviet has immense natural resources and the biggest single supply of white man-power in the world. But the resources are useless unless they are developed and their development is hampered by distance and climate.

They are also imperfectly known, but doubtless far greater than is generally estimated. Thus critics of the Magnitogorsk metallurgic project in Central Siberia argued from earlier Soviet reports, first, that there was no coal within several hundred miles, and second, that the total ore deposits proved and probable amounted to only 93,000,000 tons, whereas latest investigation shows ore of 300,000,000 tons and a new field of excellent coking coal less than 100 miles away.

But the utilization of these resources depends on man-power, which therefore takes precedence in the analysis of Soviet prospects.

Russian labor is docile and enduring and demands less than white labor anywhere. One might almost say that the Russians accept worse conditions of food and housing than Negro labor in American towns and factories.

This, no doubt, is partly because of previous low standards, but still more because of the fact that the Bolsheviki have convinced leading laborers—not labor leaders, but the youngest, strongest and most educated section of the laboring masses—that the Socialist edifice is being built for them in their interest and that present sacrifices and hardships are worth while for the sake of future benefits.

People talk about minority rule, about the army and the Gaypayou terror, but the greater proportion of factory workers and a large and important section of the peasants are thoroughly "sold" on the Communist program. They may grumble, as soldiers and civilians in France and Germany grumbled during the war, but they remain loyal and steadfast.

December 29, 1932

# SOVIET HOLDS GOAL ACHIEVED BY PLAN

## Figures Show Program Was Not Met, but Leaders Find Industrial Base Is Laid.

## GAINS BRING SUFFERING



MOSCOW, Dec. 30.—Soviet Russia's Five-Year Plan for economic construction, shortened to four years and three months, ends with the old year in undoubted industrial, agricultural and social achievements for the world's first Socialist State, but fulfillment only in part of the definite objectives it laid down.

From the viewpoint of Soviet leaders the plan has been successfully carried out in the attainment of its broad general aim of establishing a base for industrialization of the country. The nation now has a foundation of heavy industry, they assert, on which can be built future means of production without relying on foreign imports.

Until complete figures are published it will be impossible to strike a balance of the actual successes and failures under the plan. A fair index for industry, however, can be found in the record of the greater part of this year, showing less than 20 per cent increase over 1931 in all industrial production, whereas a 34.7 per cent increase actually was required to fulfill the general plan.

**Gains Fail to Meet Plan.**

Almost without exception, the yearly control figures were not met. On the other hand, every year has shown substantial production gains over the previous year. These increases, rather than the actual relation of accomplishments to the plan, furnish the yardstick by which officials measure progress.

As the Five-Year Plan ends the Russian masses are faced with a severe food shortage, which is the worst since the plan began and responsibility for which can be traced directly to the subordination of light industry, producing consumption goods, to what the State felt was the larger necessity of creating its own heavy industry first.

The extent of the spread between these two branches of economy is shown in the fact that 87 per cent of all capital investments in industry during the Five-Year Plan was allotted to heavy industry. While not minimizing the seriousness of the present food situation, leaders justify their position by asserting that heavy sacrifices were necessary on the part of the population during the first five-year period to give the nation the necessary means for future development.

The growing extent of the human strain may have played no small part in the decision of the leaders in 1930 to end the Five-Year Plan nine months short of the original five-year period so that a quicker start could be made in the improvement of living standards—one of the primary aims of the second Five-Year Plan beginning with the new year.

Of the basic key industries—coal,

pig-iron, steel, electrification and transport—all are considerably behind the plan, and among other heavy industrial branches only oil, and possibly machine building, can claim fulfillment. In the case of oil, the Five-Year Plan production was accomplished in half that period and is still running ahead of a program revised upward.

Light industry, despite its relatively insignificant rôle in the Five-Year Plan and notwithstanding that several of its branches more than fulfilled the program, failed to accomplish the plan as a whole by 7.7 per cent, although it showed a total production gain of 64 per cent for the four-year period.

The food industry continues badly in arrears, barely showing a gain over the 1931 production and making the worst showing this year of any branch of economy.

In terms of world production, Soviet Russia during the Five-Year Plan, according to official figures, jumped from sixth to third place in coal, although the daily output now is averaging only about 18,000 tons. The year's program called for 90,000,000 tons.

In pig-iron the nation jumped from sixth to second place, although the present daily average output of 17,000 tons is considerably behind the 9,000,000 tons planned for the whole year. In oil the country rose from third to second place, with 22,300,000 tons in 1932, compared with 21,700,000 planned; in machine building, from fourth to second place, with the 1932 output totaling 5,700,000,000 rubles, compared with 6,800,000,000 planned; in electric energy, from eighth to third place, with 13,500,000,000 kilowatt hours, compared with 17,000,000,000 planned.

The most phenomenal success under the plan is found in agricultural collectivization, which now amounts to 80 per cent of the entire cultivated area, compared with 17 per cent anticipated originally for the end of the Five-Year Plan.

The country now has 211,000 collective farms and 5,820 State farms, compared with 33,000 and 3,000, respectively, at the beginning of the plan. It has 147,800 tractors, against 26,740 in 1928, and the cultivated area has increased from 113,000,000 hectares (279,110,000 acres) to 136,000,000 hectares (335,920,000 acres), while individual farms have been reduced from 24,000,000 to 9,000,000.

**Ruble at Low Point.**

Against these successes, however, must be balanced the growing sluggishness on the part of the peasants due to the government's inability to supply sufficient manufactured goods. This condition also is responsible for the sharp decline in the purchasing power of the ruble, which now is at the lowest point since it was stabilized in 1924.

During the last five years more than 100 cities, formerly non-existent, with populations ranging up to 40,000, have been reared to support the newly created industries which have spread across the Urals into Siberia. Equally important in the minds of officials is the coincident metamorphosis of the Russian masses into a nation of workers, when before they were ignorant of the first elements of manual labor.

"For the first time, the Russian masses have been taught to use their hands in modern industrial pursuits," said one Soviet authority. "That probably is one of the most outstanding achievements of the Five-Year Plan."

On the credit side of the ledger must also be listed the complete abolition of unemployment, the eradication of illiteracy among more than 50 per cent of the illiterate part of the population, and, in international affairs, wide successes in the conclusion of non-aggression pacts with neighboring countries in pursuance of the Soviet policy of peace.

Meanwhile, however, the Soviet State is faced with a mounting unfavorable foreign-trade balance, which has forced it to curtail drastically its purchases abroad and to dispense with all except the absolute minimum of technical assistance from foreign engineers requiring gold payments.

December 31, 1932

# MOSCOW DOUBLES THE PRICE OF BREAD

By The Associated Press.

**MOSCOW, Aug. 20.—Foreign correspondents here were warned individually today by the press section of the Foreign Office not to attempt to travel in the provinces or elsewhere in the Soviet Union without first submitting an itinerary and outlining the purpose of the trip and obtaining formal permission. Although it was said officially that this was not a new rule, it seldom has been applied to restrict the movements of foreign newspaper men.**

**Despite published claims of a bumper crop this year, the Foreign Office without explanation refused permission to William H. Chamberlain, Christian Science Monitor correspondent, to visit and observe the harvest in the principal agricultural regions of the North Caucasus and the Ukraine. Mr. Chamberlain, one of the best known American correspondents, who has lived here eleven years, had often traveled in those regions. There was a food shortage there the past Winter.**

**Several months ago two other American correspondents were forbidden to make a trip to the Ukraine.**

**The price of bread suddenly and without public announcement was increased 100 per cent today in all government cooperative stores. Black bread was raised from 6 to 12 kopecks for 400 grams (nearly one pound) and white bread from 16 to 32 kopecks.**

August 21, 1933

# SOVIET FOOD DOLES GIVEN IN CAUCASUS

## Peasants Who Are "Diligent" Receive Aid—All Others Are Threatened.

## SOWING PLANS LAGGING

MOSCOW, March 10 (AP).—The Soviet Government now is feeding some of the peasantry in the North Caucasus region, where the agrarian situation is acute because of failure of last year's crops due to reluctance of the farmers to produce.

The action, following a recent government decree granting seed loans for Spring planting in the North Caucasus and the Ukraine, was revealed only casually in a provincial newspaper reaching here today from Rostov-on-Don.

The North Caucasus regional Communist party committee, the newspaper revealed, had threatened a stoppage 'of food assistance" as one of the measures taken against collective farms and villages failing in proper preparations for planting.

"Food where needed will be allowed only to those showing diligent work," the edict added.

This was the first open acknowledgment that the State had been compelled to go to the assistance of farmers in this respect, although there have been indications for some time that a large section of the peasantry in the chief grain-producing areas were in sore straits. How long the feeding had been in progress and the number of persons affected was not revealed.

It was pointed out that, in a number of districts and villages as well as collective farms, tractor stations were poorly prepared for Spring planting. The party committee gave the backward collectives ten days to improve their work. Otherwise they will face dissolution, distribution of their lands and property to worthier workers and exile of the entire offending populations.

One whole village and three collective farms were placed on the dreaded "black board" as a warning, accompanied by the withdrawal of the government's food doles and loans for seed and fodder.

At the same time it was announced that four district party secretaries and one tractor station director had been expelled for improper organization of the sowing campaign.

BERLIN, March 10 (AP).—The newspaper Boersen Zeitung today quoted the Oslo (Norway) journal Aftenposten, which carried a dispatch from Archangel, Russia, saying that a large lumber depot there had been afire for fourteen days and that thirty persons accused of being counter-revolutionaries had been shot.

March 11, 1933

# FAMINE IN RUSSIA HELD EQUAL OF 1921

## Witnesses Describe Starvation Among People in Ukraine and Other Regions.

By FREDERICK T. BIRCHALL.

Wireless to THE NEW YORK TIMES.

BERLIN, Aug. 24.—The food scarcity in Russia is beginning to attract general attenion in Germany. The papers are printing news about the terrible conditions known to exist in Russian agricultural sections, where food should be plentiful, but is not, even yet, owing to last year's collections by the government of all available grain.

The German collection of funds to relieve distress among Russo-German inhabitants of the Ukraine and other sections is being intensified, although at this time the new Russian grain crop should become available. There is some apprehension here that the new crop may be insufficient.

As no publication takes place in Germany without a motive, this one may be due to the fact that the prospects for the coming Winter in Germany are none too roseate. It may be desired to show the people how much worse they could be under communism that under Hitlerism.

It is a fact that conditions under the two outstanding dictatorships in Europe are pretty doleful, and here they may become worse.

**Travelers Tell of Sights.**

Yesterday, on the invitation of the German Evangelical Press Association, several travelers just back from Russia told German newspaper men some of the things they had seen there. Their talk was widely published today, and the revelations of what they had seen in the last few weeks indicate that the recent estimate of 4,000,000 deaths due indirectly to malnutrition in agricultural Russia in recent months may be rather an understatement than an exaggeration.

The speakers were two Russo-German fugitives and an American, Walter Becherer, of the First Wisconsin National Bank in Milwaukee. As witnesses of indescribable misery, they were united in the assertion that the present Russian famine, euphemistically called a food shortage, has equaled if it has not exceeded the catastrophe of twelve years ago, with consequences which cannot wholly be wiped out even by the good harvest in Southern Russia this year.

All had traveled in the flat country and beyond Odessa, and they reported that the further they went into the interior the greater was the misery. They spoke of starved children with emaciated limbs and swollen abdomens who were seen along the railroad track, not occasionally, but as a common spectacle; of field mice being in demand for food and of thousands unable to work from undernourishment and being, therefore, deprived of rations on the ground of laziness.

One of the Russo-Germans told of two German villages in Southern Russia in which half the population had died of starvation. They had letters and photographs of villages, women and children to support their stories. Dr. Ehrt, leader of the Evangelical Press Association, announced that the Reich committee for "brothers in need" had already helped 12,000 German families and that the region was still collecting funds.

To the writer today Mr. Becherer, who was in Russia as a tourist under regular auspices, said it was almost impossible to exaggerate the seriousness of present conditions in the Ukraine, but that it was most difficult to give details owing to obstacles placed in his way. In Odessa he complained to his guides that they always took him from his hotel through the same streets. They replied that tourists were not permitted to go into side streets. The reason, Mr. Becherer said, was obvious.

He visited the children's hospital outside the city and was appalled by the spectacle of the undernourished children he saw there. There were many stories of cannibalism in the region which he believed to be authentic, he said. In fact, while he was there a mother was on trial for killing and eating her four children. The disappearance of three children was admitted, but the evidence concerned the killing of the fourth, and the woman's only defense was that this child would have died in a day or two anyway.

Mr. Becherer confirmed the Russo-German fugitives' stories on the wiping out of two German Ukrainian villages with populations averaging about 1,000. In one village, he said, there had been nearly 400 deaths from malnutrition and in the other not quite so many. The survivors were transported to labor camps in the Urals.

He emphasized, however, that statistics were not available and that detailed observation was difficult. In the cities spies were at every corner. Red Army detachments were omnipresent, and even in the country airplanes were constantly flying over the fields. He was told that the planes were on guard against "enemies," but he deduced from the fact that assemblies of every kind were forbidden that the planes were there to prevent the people from meeting, even out in the open in the fields.

**Holds Worst Is Over.**

Whiting William of Cleveland, known in the United States as a compiler of surveys of industrial and labor conditions, also returned from Russia today. He declined to discuss what he had seen, explaining that he intended to write his observations for American consumption. But his conversations generally confirmed what had been told by other travelers. He did indicate that in his opinion, owing to the very good harvest, the worst was over.

Travelers generally stress the statement that nobody will ever know how many people have died of starvation in Russia this year because the victims, after collapsing in their homes or in the open, are certified to have died of heart disease or exposure or other ailments.

It has been known here for some time that travel in Russia has been greatly restricted. Even foreign correspondents are forbidden to leave Moscow without special permission. A NEW YORK TIMES correspondent in another capital who recently wished to spend a holiday in Russia applied for the usual tourist's visa but was informed it could not be granted as there was a general prohibition against journalists traveling as tourists.

An American correspondent stationed in Moscow who asked for a visa to return there via Odessa was told it would be granted to him there but on condition that he pledge himself not to leave the train en route.

August 25, 1933

# BIG SOVIET CROP FOLLOWS FAMINE

## Grain Packs Storehouses After Hunger Decimated Peasants in the Ukraine.

## KREMLIN WINS ITS BATTLE

## Nearly a Third of the Populace of Kharkov Was Mobilized for Work in Fields.

By WALTER DURANTY.
Special Cable to THE NEW YORK TIMES.

KHARKOV, U. S. S. R., Sept. 15.—Here, too, in the Ukraine the Kremlin has won the battle with the peasants. The harvest is so good that grain elevators, depots and delivery points are overcrowded to bursting.

At stations along the railroad one sees grain piled up in sacks or lying in heaps under quickly constructed roofs shored up with planks—scarcely protected from theft or bad weather. But the cost has been heavy and the effort tremendous.

During three days in July—from the 19th to the 21st—200,000 of Kharkov's population of 750,000 were "mobilized" for harvest work. It sounds incredible, but the information is confirmed in foreign sources here. From Young Pioneers, Communist children 12 or 13 years old, to old Communist party members, the city population went out to help and stimulate in the collection of the harvest, as three months earlier they had cooperated in the Spring sowing.

**Peasantry Was Decimated.**

It was a triumph, one might say, of organized effort and Soviet mass enthusiasm. Quite true, and that is what won the battle. But at the same time one asks the question, Why was such an effort necessary? Here one gets the other side of the medal.

It was necessary because hard conditions had decimated the peasantry. Some had fled. There were Ukrainian peasants begging in the streets of Moscow last Winter, and other Ukrainians were seeking work or food, but principally food, from Rostov-on-Don to White Russia and from the Lower Volga to Samara.

Already last year there was mass emigration from the Ukraine, and those who have read Pearl Buck's "The Good Earth" will know what that means—peasants will not leave the land unless conditions are deadly hard.

The blunt fact is that early last year, under the pressure of the war danger in the Far East, the authorities took too much grain from the Ukraine. Meanwhile, a large number of peasants thought they could change the Communist party's collectivization policy by refusing to cooperate. Those two circumstances together—the flight of some peasants and the passive resistance of others—produced a very poor harvest last year, and even part of that was never reaped.

The situation in the Winter was undoubtedly bad. Just as the writer considered that his death-rate figures for the North Caucasus were exaggerated, so he is inclined to believe that the estimate he made for the Ukraine was too low. [That estimate was three times the normal death rate.]

As he said in an earlier dispatch, this has been a struggle comparable in effect and intensity with the battle of Verdun. And victories cost lives. On the one side was the firm determination of the Kremlin to socialize agriculture at any cost; on the other, peasant hatred of new ways, peasant conservatism and peasant inertia, and at the beginning of this year a mass flight of peasants from a grave lack of food and seed and animal traction. The animals died or were eaten.

It was a tragic situation, but the Kremlin met it. The Kremlin pumped in new forces—500,000 tons of grain for seed and food, tens and hundreds of thousands of volunteer workers, and tractors by the thousands. The grain was sown right up to the program, and with favorable weather it grew and ripened.

The news spread that the harvest would be good, and back from Samara and Moscow, from White Russia and Rostov-on-Don came Ukrainian refugees desperately eager to work on any terms. Hunger had broken their passive resistance—there in one phrase is the grim story of the Ukrainian Verdun.

So now there is a bounteous crop, and the Ukraine is assured of food for the coming year. Through the tractor stations and the political sections the Kremlin has absolute control, and there is plenty for food and seed for the Autumn sowing, which is already in full swing.

Above all the peasants have learned a lesson—a lesson written in letters of stone on the obelisk fronting the Moscow Soviet—"Those who do not work do not eat."

September 16, 1933

# SOVIET REDS DROP MANY FROM PARTY

## Expulsions Are Expected to Total 750,000 in 'Cleansing' Now Being Concluded.

By WALTER DURANTY.
Special Cable to THE NEW YORK TIMES.

MOSCOW, Sept. 28.—The great "cleansing" of the Communist party that has been in progress for three months is now drawing to a close, and it is possible to give a general picture of the methods and results.

If Moscow may be taken as a fair cross-section of the whole country, as doubtless it may, the expulsions ran about 18 per cent—that is, upward of 750,000. Most of them, however, were probationary—that is, the expelled members have the opportunity of rejoining the party by better conduct in the coming six months or year.

Two new features have marked this cleansing. First, non-party persons have been encouraged to attend the examinations. Previously such persons merely received permission to attend. Second, in addition to the previous tests of individual faith and works, much stress has been laid this year on the results achieved by the factory, office or collective farm to which the party member belonged.

Thus a "comrade" might have an irreproachable personal record but find himself subjected to sharp criticism for his backward organization. The purpose of this is to make the cleansing not merely an individual test but a means of education and propaganda amid the non-party public and a means of improving work and aiding economic progress.

The cleansing method is simple. Three examiners are appointed by the "centre." They have no connection with the local party branch. Any one present at the examination may ask any question about the private life, habits, morals, work and play as well as party conduct of the members being examined. The examiners decide whether the questions should be answered or not, but the examiners give extraordinary latitude, and the meetings sometimes are hilarious.

For instance, when the Odessa Torgsin—where there had been flagrant speculation in foreign money—had its cleansing in a large hall there was queue at the doors, like a theatre on a first night, and the movies and other places of amusement did a poor business. It is said that 60 per cent of those Torgsin comrades were expelled and the whole organization was put up to public shame.

The possibilities of a situation where any one from an office boy upward can take free cracks at the bosses are obvious.

Among the lower ranks the majority of the expulsions were due to insufficient knowledge of Marxist doctrines. Drunkenness and improper absence from work also took a heavy toll. Higher up it was rather a question of works and the results achieved, with great stress laid on "conduct unbecoming a Communist" both on the job and in private life.

**Reprimanded for Arrogance.**

One highly efficient young official received a severe reprimand and was nearly placed on probation for "habitually assuming an arrogant manner" toward messengers and girls who brought glasses of tea—which is no less a feature of Russian offices than English offices.

His excuse, that he was working so hard that he had no time to smile and say "Thank you," brought this stern reply from the examiner:

"Comrade, that savors of the capitalistic mentality. Here you have no class superiority over your subordinates and cannot treat them as inferiors because you have a more important job."

Sometimes, though rarely, there is an attempt to "frame" an unpopular comrade, but as all the members expelled have the right of appeal, such schemes, if temporarily successful, generally get readjusted with unpleasant consequences to the framers.

From a certain angle the cleansing may seem a rather schoolboyish performance, and it is true there is much that is juvenile in the New Russia. On the other hand, the value of the cleansing in keeping the party members up to the mark, in educating them and outsiders in Communist principles and duties, and in consolidating the party ranks in iron discipline cannot be overestimated.

October 1, 1933

# SOVIET THREATENS INDUSTRIAL HEADS

### Decrees Prison for Those Who Permit Further Output of Inferior Goods.

### INEFFICIENCY STILL RIFE

### Products for 'Defense of the Country' Are Among Those Held Poor.

Special Cable to THE NEW YORK TIMES.

MOSCOW, Dec. 9.—A decree issued today and signed by President Mikhail Kalinin, Premier Molotoff and A. S. Yenukidze, secretary of the Soviet Central Executive Committee, places responsibility for the poor quality of goods and inefficiency in factories on managers and other executives.

This is another Kremlin measure to tighten up industry, which must pay for the increases in the production of raw materials and agricultural products. When the collective farms produce their quotas, as a large number did this year, they are in a position to demand quality in commodity goods.

Hence "managers of trusts, directors of factories and members of administrative and technical personnel who are guilty of producing poor or incomplete products," the decree says, "shall be held criminally responsible and be liable to legal repression [that is, imprisonement] for a period of not less than five years."

The second part of the decree states that the prosecuting authorities of the Soviet Union shall be charged with the steadfast enforcement of the decree. It is not uncommon that an automobile or tractor arrives at its destination minus carburetor, sparkplugs and even wheels.

If enforced, the decree should be effective in eliminating not only inefficiency but bureaucracy by placing the responsibility directly on the shoulders of managers. Incompetent executives who hitherto have been able to evade responsibility must now produce usable goods or find other jobs.

By The Associated Press.

MOSCOW, Dec. 9.—Aroused by the continued failure of Soviet industry to improve the quality of its products, particularly in those branches producing the means for "the defense of the country," the Soviet Central Executive Committee decreed today criminal prosecution for officials and employes found guilty of turning out inferior materials.

The order declared "bad and incomplete machines, accessories and materials produced by our factories are causing considerable loss to the government."

"Especially intolerant and criminal," it continues, "is the issue of bad articles by industries charged with producing goods dedicated to the defense of the country."

December 10, 1933

# SOVIET'S NEW PLAN TO AID CONSUMERS

### Half of Huge Increases Called For in Second 5-Year Program to Be in Goods.

### 240% OUTPUT GAIN IS AIM

### Auto and Tractor Production to Be Trebled—6,831 Miles of Railways to Be Built.

By WALTER DURANTY.
Special Cable to THE NEW YORK TIMES.

MOSCOW, Dec. 30.—The Soviet Government published today the basic figures and an outline of the second Five-Year Plan as it is to be presented for the consideration of the Communist party congress the end of the month by Premier Molotoff and V. V. Quibysheff, president of the State Planning Commission.

This prodigious program contemplates an increase in annual industrial production in the period from the end of 1932 to the end of 1937 of 2.4 times, or, in price terms, from 43,000,000,000 rubles to 103,000,000,000. Of this more than half, or 54,300,000,000 rubles' worth, will be goods of popular consumption.

Other staggering facts emerge from the mass of statistics. The annual production of coal, oil, pig iron, machines and the production of means of production are to be more than doubled. Steel, copper and chemical production and the output of automobiles, tractors, combines and other agricultural machinery, freight cars and locomotives are to be trebled or more.

**Farm Output to Be Doubled.**

Electric power is to increase by 180 per cent. Agricultural production is to be doubled—from 13,000,000,000 to 26,000,000,000 rubles in price terms of 1927. The grain crop is to be raised to 110,000,000 metric tons, chiefly by improving quality rather than increasing the sown area, with similar increases in other products.

Machine-tractors stations are to be increased from 2,400 in 1932 to 6,000 in 1937, with a tractor "park" of 8,250,000 horsepower, as compared with 2,250,000 in 1932.

There is to be an advance in the mechanization of agriculture, in the supply of fertilizer and sorted seed and in improved methods of cultivation. The amount of freight carried by the railroads is expected to rise from 169,000,000,000 kilometer tons in 1932 to 302,000,000,000 in 1937. River transport is scheduled to increase from 26,000,000,000 tons to 64,000,000,000, sea transport from 18,000,000,000 to 51,000,000,000 and auto transport from 1,000,000,000 to 16,000,000,000 kilometer tons.

In the five-year period there will be new railroad construction of 11,000 kilometers [6,831 miles], including the Donetz-Moscow coal line and the strategically important line from Central Siberia along the north of Lake Baikal to the Okhotsk Sea, which road is already about half built.

**Educational Rise Planned.**

It is expected that the number of workers and employes engaged in industry will increase 30 per cent, with a corresponding improvement in training and technical qualifications, and the number of students at all schools—primary to universities—is to grow from 24,200,000 to 36,000,000. Real wages are planned to double in the five years as a result of increases in food supplies and consumers' goods two to threefold and a 30 to 40 per cent drop in prices.

The turnover of goods is to increase two to three times and the national income is to mount from 45,500,000,000 rubles to 108,000,000,000. It is most interesting to note that about half the whole capital investment in heavy industry, including mines and railroads, during the five years is to be placed east of the Urals, which region will be the future industrial heart of the Soviet Union and virtually impregnable to enemy attack. It also is significant that of fifteen great textile plants to be constructed by 1937, ten will be located in Central Asia, near the sources of the cotton supply.

The program declares the second plan will go far to solving the ancient rivalry between town and country by assimilating social and labor conditions of the peasants to those of factory hands and by strengthening the link between urban and rural workers. It admits, however, that the Soviet ideal of a classless society will hardly be attained so soon and that vigilance is still needed against "kulaks" [individualist farmers] and other "class enemies."

December 31, 1933

# STALIN DISCLOSES LIVESTOCK LOSSES

## Number of Horses, Cattle, Pigs, Sheep and Goats Cut About 50% by Collectivization.

## FARM OFFICIALS SCORED

By WALTER DURANTY.

Special Cable to THE NEW YORK TIMES.

MOSCOW, Jan. 28.—Joseph Stalin's speech before the All-Union Communist Congress occupies no fewer than thirty-eight columns in the Soviet press today. The Bolshevist leader, who spoke before the congress Friday night but whose speech was not made public until yesterday, viewed the country's progress with legitimate pride, but he did not fail to mention with strong emphasis and biting irony, arousing shouts of laughter and applause, Soviet weaknesses and shortcomings.

He attacked particularly bureaucracy, transportation failures, shortcomings in goods exchange and distribution, talkative if honest nincompoops in responsible positions and the tendency of executives to "grow dizzy from success" or alternately to rest on their laurels and imagine all difficulties overcome.

**Reveals Livestock Losses.**

He slashed into the mistakes of agricultural authorities and for the first time revealed the full measure of the livestock "casualties" in the collectivization campaign. The number of horses dropped from 34,000,000 in 1929 to 16,500,000 last year, cattle from 68,100,000 to 38,600,000, sheep and goats from 147,200,000 to 50,600,000 and pigs from 20,900,000 to 12,200,000.

Apart from these tragic figures there is nothing specifically new in the speech, although M. Stalin made an interesting analysis and explanation of the reasons, meaning and purpose of the Communist party reforms and governmental reforms which the congress is expected to approve. He also stressed the fact that this congress, unlike its predecessors, met without the existence of intraparty opposition.

M. Stalin made a fresh departure in Marxist theory by the statement that there was no "greater" danger between Left and Right deviations, which were equally anti-Marxist and anti-Leninist, and that the so-called greater danger existed only when any form of deviation, either to the Right or the Left, was neglected and allowed to gain undue strength. Then, indeed, he said, the deviation became a danger.

Similarly, he maintained that there was no essential distinction between local nationalism, such as occurred in the Ukraine and White Russia, and broader national chauvinism—both were anti-Leninist and anti-internationalist phenomena.

M. Stalin concluded with the assertion that fascism had not conquered Marxism, as had sometimes been declared abroad. Marxism, he asserted, had been in existence for eighty years and its enemies had often said they had conquered it, but it still remained in the hearts of the workers. The proof of its vitality, he said, was in the Union of Soviet Socialist Republics, which occupied a sixth of the earth's land area and was the leader and "udarnik" [shock worker] of Marxist workers throughout the world.

**Livestock Slaughtered by Peasants.**

The livestock losses which have occurred in Soviet Russia since 1929 are the result of wholesale slaughtering by peasants to prevent authorities from forcing them to pool their animals in collective farms. Whether such slaughtering is still going on is not made clear in the foregoing dispatch.

However, the Soviet authorities assert the problem of collectivization has been solved and imply that no such large-scale resistance is now taking place. When the collectivization campaign was put into full swing in the Winter of 1929-30 the peasants fiercely resisted it by slaughtering their livestock, and M. Stalin had to call a halt upon zealous Communists who were forcing peasants and all their chattels into the collective groups.

At that time he issued his decree entitled "Dizziness From Success," in which he rebuked Communists for spreading terror among the peasants and bringing the country to the verge of a meat famine. He set forth that the peasants must be persuaded rather than forced to enter the collectives and that they need not collectivize all their livestock.

Since then collectivization has proceeded apace, until now more than 80 per cent of the peasants are included. The State has hoped to overcome the livestock shortage through large State farms as well as renewed confidence on the part of the peasants.

January 29, 1934

# STALIN SAYS FEARS MADE SOVIET RISE

## Explains to Red Army Cadets That Industrialization Was Vital as Defense.

By HAROLD DENNY.

Wireless to THE NEW YORK TIMES.

MOSCOW, May 6.—Joseph Stalin, Soviet dictator, has at last explained why the Bolshevist régime has driven the Russian people into industrialization and collectivized agriculture regardless of privation and hardship and despite protests within the country against the punishing pace. It is because the fear of war has hung over Soviet Russia ever since its birth. The country has been mechanized and socialized regardless of cost to prepare it to resist attack.

M. Stalin revealed this in an address Saturday to the graduating Red Army cadets in the great Kremlin Palace. The most significant sentence in this address, which was made public today, probably was the following:

"We had either to solve the task [industrialization of a backward, disrupted country] and establish socialism in our country in the briefest possible time or our country—technically unadvanced and of low culture—would lose its independence and become the plaything of imperialist powers."

**Reviews Terrific Struggle.**

He reviewed the terrific struggle to bring the Soviet Union to the present level and to create a strong Red Army with a strong industry behind it. Between the lines, and sometimes in the lines, he was pleading Bolshevist justification for the sacrifices exacted from the people and for the severity with which those who have objected to so fast a tempo have been treated.

The struggle for industrialization and mechanization has required hardship and rigid economy, he stressed.

"We had to economize on food, schools and textiles to accumulate the means necessary for the establishment of industry," he went on. "There was no other way to wipe out our technical poverty.

"There were comrades who were frightened and called to the party to retreat. They said, 'Why do we need your industrialization, collectivization, machinery, metallurgy, tractors, combines and automobiles? It would be better to give us more textiles, to buy more raw materials for manufacturing articles for general consumption and to give the people more of the little things that make life beautiful. It is a dangerous dream to attempt to create industry—and more so modern industry—with our backwardness.'

"True, we could have used the 3,000,000,000 rubles of foreign exchange which we raised by the most rigid economy and which was expended by our industry to import raw materials and permit greater production of articles of general consumption. But that would have not given us metallurgy, the machine-building industry, tractors, automobiles, airplanes and tanks. We would have been disarmed to our external enemies. We would have undermined the bases of socialism here. We would have found ourselves at the mercy of the foreign and internal bourgeoisie."

May 7, 1935

# *Many Soviet Workers Gain Overnight Fame As Exponents of Stakhanoffite 'Speed-Up'*

By The Associated Press.

MOSCOW, Jan. 18.—Sudden fame has come to half a hundred Soviet workers, taken from factories, farms and mines to be pacemakers for the Stakhanoffite speed-up movement.

Names that a few months ago were known only within the narrow limits of workshops or villages today are symbols of a nation-wide "over-the-top" push for all lines of laboring activity.

Outstanding among the new famous are:

Alexei Stakhanoff, miner, who started the movement by hewing out 102 tons of coal with a pneumatic drill in one workday of six hours.

Peter Krivonos, locomotive engineer, who increased the average speed of freight trains to that of passenger trains on the Donetz Railway.

Alexander Busygin, smithy of the Gorky automobile plant, who forged 1,115 crankshafts in a single shift.

Boris Smetanin of the Leningrad shoe factory, who put lasts on 1,820 pairs of shoes in one day.

Evdokia and Maria Vinogradova, textile mill employes, who tend 144 looms.

Maria Demchenko, who obtained a yield of more than 20,000 pounds of sugar beets an acre on a Soviet collective farm.

Mamlakat Nahangova, 11-year-old girl, who doubled adult averages by picking more than 220 pounds of cotton in one day.

The Stakhanoffite movement, forging with official backing through a wave of opposition, will, the government has promised, "revolutionize" Soviet industry, greatly increase production and improve the Russian workman's standard of living. It is described as "rationalization" of labor and full utilization of technical equipment.

"Stakhanoff's followers," said an official explanation, "correctly distribute labor, use to the full their working time and operate their machines to maximum efficiency."

Further light may be cast on the underlying reason for the opposition by a subsequent statement that Stakhanoff's "secret" consisted of an ability to make his pneumatic drill "work all the 360 minutes of the six-hour working shift."

Enemies of the Stakhanoffites have sought in various ways, even to the point of committing murder, it is said, to stop the movement. The government has quickly retaliated, ordering the offenders severely punished.

Those who have followed Stakhanoff into fame are men and women generally recognized as having more than ordinary capacity for work. Joseph Stalin, the Communist leader, calmed fears to some extent by publicly promising that all workmen would not be required to duplicate the performance of the Stakhanoffites.

January 19, 1936

# SOVIET PAY SCALES CUT TO AID OUTPUT

**Production Norms Per Worker in Heavy Industry Held to Be Far Too Low**

**TOTAL WAGES WILL RISE**

**But New Quotas Are Likely to Cause Dismissal of Many Employes**

By HAROLD DENNY

Special Cable to THE NEW YORK TIMES.

MOSCOW, April 3.—The Commissariat of Heavy Industry announced today it would reduce pay scales and increase production "norms"—namely, the individual worker's standard daily output, above which higher pay per piece is given—in order to fulfill the government's demand for higher labor productivity and lower production costs.

As a result of this the Commissariat expects to discharge many workers from over-manned plants, freeing them for enterprises that are under-manned.

The government's radical upward revision of production schedules in most industries for this final year of the second "Pyatiletka" [Five-Year Plan], ordered earlier in the week to overcome the slump, called for a 19 per cent increase in labor productivity and a 3 per cent reduction in costs.

**Global Wage Rise Provided**

It also provided for a total wage increase of 8 per cent in heavy industry. Just how the increased total wages are to be reconciled with lower pay rates is not made clear in the new order, but presumably industrial leaders believe that attainment of new norms by increasing the number of workers who are yearly mastering the processes of modern industry will make this possible.

The Heavy Industry Commissariat's order is predicated on the conviction that the norms in a vast number of processes were ridiculously low. The introduction of Stakhanoffism late in 1935 showed that skilled, conscientious workers were capable of far higher production than the norms then existing, and when it got well under way the norms were increased.

Now, according to the heavy industry leaders, the present norms in many instances are far below the workers' capacities. They assert surveys now being made disclose whole industries in which the norms are outlandishly overfulfilled—accordingly necessitating higher wage expenditures for output over the norms.

Industrial leaders also point out that the Soviet Union has spent billions of rubles both for raising the skill of workers and for carrying on technical reconstruction, thus laying the basis for greater productivity. These measures, they report, are constantly diminishing the amount labor needed for production.

**Executives Criticized**

In the struggle to overcome the handicaps of past inefficiency and sabotage and to fulfill the second Pyatile'ka, the entire industrial personnel, from Commissars down, are now under heavy pressure. Meetings are being held everywhere, at which active workers are criticizing executives and even Commissars for shortcomings. Rebukes from headquarters follow, if such criticism is not severe enough.

The uproar over sabotage that followed January's treason trial is having one bad effect. Industrial executives are reporting that many engineers are afraid to undertake anything in the least risky for fear they may be called wreckers if a project fails. To safeguard themselves against unjust accusations, engineers are piling up mountains of paper in recording every step they make.

The anxiety of these engineers is reminiscent of the situation following the wreckers' trials in the early days of Soviet industrialization, when initiative for a long time was smothered by this same fear.

April 4, 1937

# SOVIET STANDARDS FOR WORKERS RISE

**Living Conditions Improve as 'Real Wages' Gain With Decrease in Costs**

**FREE SCHOOLING HELPS**

**Medical Treatment and Cultural Advantages Bring Up Level of Russian Life**

By WALTER DURANTY

Special Cable to THE NEW YORK TIMES.

MOSCOW, March 24.—The improvement in living standards and increase in "real wages" in Soviet Russia are growing more evident daily as the second Five-Year Plan augments the quantity of food and consumers' goods.

In 1928, when the first Five-Year Plan was initiated, the number of workers and employes in the Soviet Union was approximately 12,000,000. Today it is 26,000,000. In 1928 the workers received 8,000,000,000 rubles annually in wages; now 71,000,000,000.

In 1926 there were an estimated 1,500,000 unemployed; now there are none. More important still are the facilities given young and unskilled workers to improve themselves and their position.

**Free Night Schooling Aids**

Free night classes and all manner of technical education—not to mention the complete absence of the difficulties in joining labor unions that still maintain the gulf between skilled and unskilled labor in many Western countries—have produced remarkable results here.

Investigation of a group of 7,000 young workers in nine leading industrial centers showed that their average wage increased threefold between January, 1931, and December, 1935, as a consequence of improved qualifications through special instruction. It goes without saying that free medical treatment, sports and holiday advantages have vastly improved in the past five years—as well as housing—although Soviet "self-criticism" maintains that all four still leave much to be desired.

There has been a significant improvement also in the food and clothing of Soviet workers, and a steady reduction of prices. Thus the average individual consumption of Moscow workers has increased, in a comparison of 1936 with 1909 as follows:

Meats and fats, doubled; fish, five times greater; butter, 35 per cent more; sugar, three and a half times more; bread, one and a half times, and potatoes 64 per cent. The consumption of clothing has increased an average of 40 per cent in the past two years, which is estimated to be nearly three times more than the pre-war figure.

**Cultural Help in Easy Reach**

Last but not least, there are social insurance and what are called here "cultural conditions," which include everything from indoor swimming pools, skating rinks, football stadiums to opera houses, theatres and movies at rates within the reach of the poorest workers.

According to the latest statistics the average monthly wage of a Soviet worker is around 230 rubles. He still gets less for it in consumers' goods than the American earning the nominal equivalent of $46, but the reduction in prices and cultural and medical facilities and low room rent nearly balance the account.

March 25, 1937

# LOW SOVIET WAGES LINKED TO UNREST

***The writer of the following uncensored article is a reporter, columnist and drama critic of The Cleveland Plain Dealer, who has made several visits to Russia and has now returned there after two years to observe the changes that have taken place.***

**By WILLIAM F. McDERMOTT**

**Copyright, 1937, by the North American Newspaper Alliance, Inc.**

**MOSCOW.—There are those who suspect that low wages and high prices may have something to do with the great blood-bath and purge that now washes every part of Russia. Faced with discontent and inertia on the part of large bodies of workers, the Soviet regime has had to fix the blame on leaders and conspirators, for a proletarian State cannot admit that it is having trouble with the masses for whom it was theoretically created and to whom it owes its existence.**

**On the basis of what you can see and guess here, I believe the situation is not to be so simply explained. A good deal more is involved than an effort to shift culpability for certain admitted failures.**

**But, if there is not some dissatisfaction among the mass of the Russian citizens over their condition of life, they are different from the masses everywhere else in the world. Despite the undeniable increase in the variety and amount of goods available, and notwithstanding monumental achievements in engineering and building, the scale of living in Russia for the multitude remains shockingly low. Prices are still fantastically high; wages are pitifully low.**

**Gives Official Figures**

**I will give you only official and verified figures, or such as I have collected at first-hand from my own observation. The national economic plan for the U.S.S.R., printed by Gosplan in 1937, states that the average yearly wage for all Russians in 1936, including white-collar workers, artists and so on, was 2,770 rubles. This excludes farm laborers, who are much more poorly paid.**

**Let us take the higher figure. A wage of 2,770 rubles a year means 231 rubles a month. At the official rate of exchange a ruble is worth a little less than 20 cents, so 231 rubles would be about $46.**

**But a ruble is worth very much less than 20 cents in purchasing power. It is reasonable to estimate that its buying value in Russia is about 5 or 6 cents, as measured in world prices. What the average Russian workman gets in real money is between $12 and $14 a month.**

**A few price quotations will make the situation clear. A pound of coffee in Moscow today costs 24 rubles, or nearly $5. Sugar to sweeten the coffee comes cheaper at 40 cents a pound. A cut of beef costs about $1.30 a pound. Pork chops are just above $1 a pound. Butter is $2 a pound.**

**Eggs at the moment are ten for $1, cheese $2.50 a pound and milk 32 cents a quart. Russians with a taste for such luxuries as chocolate candy can indulge themselves at an outlay of $4.50 a pound.**

When it comes to a suit of clothes, you get into real money. What is described as the "best" suit of ready-made woolen clothes is priced at 1,065 rubles, or $213. An "ordinary" suit comes to $110. A passable woolen overcoat comes to $280, and no fur or gold braid either. The cheapest overcoats for these Arctic Winters are about $100.

Woolen underwear is unavailable at the moment, but the last recorded price is $28 a suit, a circumstance that may have had something to do with the disappearance of woolen underwear from the market. It is harder to do without shoes, though some Russians you see on the streets manage to get along with a kind of burlap wrapping. Men's shoes are priced from $35 to $48.

Women must be hard put to it to maintain a chic air, and the miracle is that a few of them almost manage to achieve it. Light wool for dresses costs $25 a yard. Crêpe de chine is cheaper at $13 a yard. Rayon stockings are $8. Kid gloves have been drastically reduced and are now available at $5 a pair.

These prices are translated into dollars at the current rate of exchange. When you translate wages into dollars at the same rate of exchange, you can see how far the average worker's $46 a month will go.

Leaving the dollar out of it entirely and comparing ruble prices with ruble wages, it is mathematically demonstrable that an average Russian must work three days to earn the money for a pound of coffee. He must labor more than four months for a good suit of clothes and more than two months for an ordinary suit of clothes, and both suits are pretty sleazy by the standards of the American workman.

### Pair of Shoes Is 3 Weeks' Work

A pair of shoes will cost him from three weeks to a month of toil, and an overcoat will keep his nose to the grindstone for as long as six months.

The critical point is that these prices have recently been advancing after a period of decline. For the most part, they are substantially lower than they were two years ago, but they are generally higher than they were last year.

Obviously, the great majority of Russians are not able to buy these expensive suits and shoes and they do not drink coffee or milk or eat much butter. They wear what they have to wear and they live on black bread, which is relatively cheap, and on cabbage and a little tea, without sugar—if they can afford tea, for it is far from cheap.

The special shops from which workers could buy at less than the market rate have disappeared as an important factor in Russian economy. The prices quoted above are the prices charged at stores where the general population does its shopping.

In a department store my attention was attracted by a line of perhaps 200 men waiting at one of the counters. I worked over into the mob to see what they were after. It seemed that the store had received a new shipment of fancy double-breasted suits, and they were waiting to buy these sartorial triumphs at $160 a copy.

### Take Suits Without Fitting

Nobody was trying a suit on. They were just guessing at the size and taking them as fast as they could be handed out. Somebody has the money for these exorbitantly priced articles. Where do they get it?

Well, everybody in a Russian family works, wives and others, as well as children as soon as they are old enough. The family income is larger than suggested by the average wage of individual workers.

Moreover, there is a relatively small, but numerically large, proportion of skilled workers, artisans and specialists who receive many times the average wage, and have more money than they know what to do with in Russia. These folks absorb the goods that are out of reach of the rank and file.

This inequity may conceivably be one of the causes of the current Russian restlessness. When everybody is getting approximately the same wages only the minority of specially skilled or specially industrious people are dissatisfied. When great differences in income reappear after such a period of leveling off, it is the masses that are likely to be uneasy and resentful.

I do not know that this is the case in Russia. But it is reasonable to believe that extremely high prices and very low wages for the great majority of the population are not conducive to enthusiasm for any system or regime, particularly at a time when the disparity between income and living costs is growing.

### Differences in Wages Great

An ordinary unskilled laborer will get as little as 150 rubles a month, which is a usual wage. A writer or an actor may earn 10,000 or 15,000 rubles a month, or more. An especially skilled and quick mechanic will be paid several thousand rubles a month. Shock-brigade workers in the mass industries will get ten or twenty times as much as slower and less efficient laborers.

Such differences in wages create economic classes as inevitably as differences in the possession of property. There is no private ownership of the means of production in Russia. No individual owns a factory, a railway, a mine or any part of one. Nobody owns a store, a warehouse, a hotel or anything else necessary to the distribution of goods or the rendering of services.

But if I am paid twenty times, or fifty times as much in wages as you are, I can buy things that you cannot afford and I can live an altogether different kind of life in relation to material wants. Russia today is divided into a great many diverse economic classes. There are people who can afford things and there are people who cannot.

### Profit Motive for Farmer

In addition to the private and personal incentive to produce stirred up in the farmer by the piece-work system, he also has a profit interest in the success of the collective farm as a whole. After the State takes its share of the crop, after the 3 per cent taxes are paid, after the nurseries, club rooms and tractor services are paid for, the remainder of the harvest is divided among all the farmers according to the amount of work they have individually done.

Some of the crop may be sold on the open market and the money divided, or the farmer may take his pay in grain, hay, potatoes or some other produce that he or his privately owned cow and chickens can eat.

It was interesting to see that the constitution for model collective farms stated that one of the reasons for the organization of a collective was to make all the farmers "well to do." That seemed a curious word to be employed by a regime that theoretically disdains private riches and has so often been severely contemptuous of the well to do created by other forms of society.

However, the theorists will not have to worry very soon about the problem created by the well-to-do collective farmer. No general figures are available as to the wages and rewards of the communal plowmen, but you can get some idea of what they are by some figures printed in Pravda on June 30 in relation to the wages on a collective farm near Moscow.

### Farmer's Yearly Earnings

In 1935 the workers on this farm earned three pounds of grain a day and 29 kopecks in money. Twenty-nine kopecks is less than 7 cents at the official rate of exchange, but it will not buy more than about 2 cents' worth of goods.

Last year the workers on the same farm earned one-third of a pound of grain a day and 2 cents a day in cash value. If a farmer worked every day in the year, snow rain or shine, his total income in practical cash would be $7.30 for twelve months, and his present payment in grain would be about enough to keep a chicken alive.

This farm was cited as a horrible example, intended to illustrate the results of mismanagement, but the existence of such wage scales is suggestive of the general standards of pay on the collective farm.

Conditions may be better than they were. They are still appalling.

You have all the concomitants of an ordinary economic system. You will see ragged boys and men looking longingly into bakery shop windows for cheap cakes and rolls they cannot buy, and, on the same street, you will visit a restaurant crowded with Russians tossing out fistfuls of greasy bills in payment for champagne.

This growing disparity in the economic status of the population probably explains the new respect for clothes, the new emphasis on decoration and finery. It may also help to account for a great many other things that are happening in Russia.

I wondered how the piece-work system could be applied to the collective farms. Ninety-nine per cent of all the Russian farm land is now collectivized. In America, the custom is to pay farmhands by the month, regardless of the work performed. Not in Russia.

On the collective farms, all the farmers are paid on a piece-work basis. A certain norm is set for an honest Soviet day's work, depending on the character of the soil, the equipment and other individual circumstances. A man or woman must milk so many cows, plow or plant so many acres in a normal day's work.

If the laborer does two days' work in one day, he is paid for two days' work, and, conversely, if he does only half a day's work in a full day on the job, he is paid only for the half day. He may work every day for a full month on the farm and get paid for only fifteen days' production.

Not only that, but deduction of 10 per cent will be made from the wages of farm laborers whose work is considered to be below standard. Premiums of 10, 15 and 20 per cent are paid to workers, to managers and to whole brigades when the sowing, or the reaping, is completed in unusually quick time. You can see that there must be plenty of hopping on a Soviet farm.

The intangible moral changes that have come over Russia in the years I have been traveling here are marked and significant. I do not mean merely the restrictions on divorces, or the new attitude toward the family or the admitted evidence of a revival of religion, or the changed emphasis on the value of maternity.

The amended divorce laws involve only a penalty of $10 for the first divorce, $25 for the second and so on, with the additional injunction that you must notify your spouse that you are contemplating a divorce. Formerly divorce was free and casual. It is still cheap, quick and popular.

The new laws forbidding abortions are not so much an acknowledgment of the sacredness of maternity as they are a boast that Russia is now able to feed her increasing population and has need of material for building socialism and creating armies.

I mean something less ponderable. You feel these impalpable spiritual changes very strongly. I think they come mostly from a sense of further order and increased discipline. Their whole effect is to make life seem more normal as we, in democratic countries, conceive of normality.

That is another paradox in the Russian situation. As life is violently disturbed at the top with executions and arrests, it becomes outwardly more orderly at the bottom. People go about their business and their play as they do everywhere else in the world.

The girls and boys hold hands and go to dances in the evening. There are now dozens of dance restaurants in Moscow, and even the movie theatres provide floors for the fox-trotters.

The Soviet woman bedecks herself with cosmetics and has her fingers manicured and highly rouged at a beauty parlor. There is a waiting line at every beauty parlor and barber shop, and many of the barbers are women.

The other evening I saw a comrade, dressed in shirt-sleeves and a pair of pants sadly soiled with the grime of his hard labor, seated fastidiously at a table in a beauty parlor while the manicurist attended to his nails and about a dozen women customers waited their turn. This is something new here, something that did not exist and could not happen a few years ago.

The arrangement of society is solidifying into distinct classes and the distinction here, as elsewhere, is based on money.

The general level of dress is makeshift and shabby, but within the limits of this poverty of material there is an enormous range of difference, a difference, I should say, much greater than you would find between the chic promenades and the slums of New York.

Discipline, ideas of service, are unrecognizably improved. Moscow's streets are spotlessly clean; the shop windows are spruced up; the lines of people waiting to buy commodities are smaller and wholly orderly.

The longest line I have seen ran, single file, for almost a block. But the line was waiting not for food for the stomach but for mental nourishment, or at least such mental nourishment as is provided by a Moscow newspaper.

The waiters in the hotels used to have a half-dead appearance and they went about their labors in a gentle daze. They come running now, or running as fast as their ancient legs will carry them, and they pant with an eagerness to serve.

You can see that the incentive of reward or the fear of a figurative lash has completely changed their attitude and set a new value on life. That change, you sense, is going on all over Russia, for you see evidence of it everywhere you look.

August 29, 1937

# THIRD 5-YEAR PLAN EVOLVED BY SOVIET

Program Designed to Overtake and Surpass U. S. Is in Hands of Industrial Leaders

TO GO INTO EFFECT JAN. 1

Prime Goal to Be to Increase Productivity of Labor—High Standard Set for Drive

By The Associated Press.

MOSCOW, June 6.—The Soviet Union's third Five-Year Plan, designed this time "to overtake and surpass America," today was taking form in the hands of the nation's industrial leaders.

It probably will go into effect next Jan. 1, immediately on completion of the second Five-Year Plan.

Although the plans which must be submitted to the Kremlin by July 1 are incomplete, figures published indicate the government hopes to accomplish more in the third period than the combined achievements of the first and second Five-Year Plans.

The second plan already has been pronounced a success by Soviet officials and the nation's industrial architects are looking forward to the seventh and eighth Five-Year Plans that will not be finished until 1960 and 1965.

The planners assume a population increase of 125,000,000 within the next twenty-five years to raise the present 175,000,000 to 300,000,000. The Russian birth rate has nearly doubled since the 1936 decree encouraging large families.

The prime goal of the next period will be increase of Russian labor's productivity, still admittedly inefficient when compared with American labor standards.

"The American's labor efficiency is two or three times higher than ours" is a frequent declaration of industrial officials who have been sent in a constant stream to the United States to learn about American production.

The Russians already are a little disdainful about the rest of Europe, asserting that in key industries they lead all other European nations.

"Europe can teach us little more; America can teach us much," Anasthasius I. Mikoyan, Commissar of the Food Industry, declared when he returned from the United States recently. Many others have echoed his statement.

Some observers believe this means the Soviet Union will concentrate its buying in the United States during the next five years, turning from Great Britain and Germany. Already there is a trend in that direction, the Russians showing their feeling that only the United States is big and experienced enough to appreciate Russia's gigantic industrial problems.

The Soviet Union hopes to lead the world in gold, coal and steel production, civil aviation and agricultural production before 1942. Leadership in tractor and threshing combine production already is claimed and airplane production is believed to be ahead of any other country.

Although a big increase in automobile production is planned, it is believed the Russians will trail the United States in this field for many years, although now they are second only to Great Britain in Europe.

The complex State Planning Commission coordinates the national program. Thousands of engineers under orders from the Kremlin work out both broad principles and essential details years in advance.

Soviet economists expect consumers' goods—commodities which fill the ordinary needs of the average man—to become more plentiful, better and cheaper in the next five years. The Russians have encountered difficulty in this branch of industry, which was somewhat neglected while capital-goods industries were pushed.

June 7, 1937

# MECHANIZING GAINS IN SOVIET FARMING

32,000 Harvesting Combines Working Two Years Ago Have Risen to 121,000

TRACTORS ALSO INCREASE

Average Acreage Covered Has Mounted Rapidly — Defects Being Steadily Overcome

Wireless to THE NEW YORK TIMES.

MOSCOW, Sept. 19.—Recent years have witnessed a very rapid increase in the mechanization of Soviet agriculture. Take as a single example that whereas there were 32,000 harvesting combines working two years ago, they had risen by Aug. 1 of this year to 121,000, which are scheduled to reap more than 42 per cent of the current grain crop.

There has been a similar increase in tractors, which now total 350,000 machines in active use, although many are obsolescent.

Like every branch of Soviet industry, mechanized agriculture is characterized by extraordinary ups and downs. One harvester group will reach the unusual average per machine of 3,000 acres during the harvest month, whereas another only twenty miles away cannot surpass 500 acres.

Nevertheless, there is steady progress because the nation-wide average, which was under 200 acres per machine per month in 1932, now approximates 900 acres.

Mechanized agriculture suffers from four defects: Inadequate organization, which carries with it two other defects, a shortage of parts, oil and gasoline at the points where they are needed and faulty repair facilities, and a lack of trained personnel.

All four are being steadily overcome as Russia grows more machine-minded to a degree that can be appreciated only by a family that allowed a young son to buy a rickety auto with the fear that he would break his neck, only to find in a few months that the youngster was not only driving the car expertly but had patched it up in good running order.

In this direction much is being done by industrial Stakhanoffists and mechanical students, who are making a habit of spending their vacations at tractor stations, where they earn good money fixing machines. Today there are upward of 4,000 of such stations, compared with 1,500 in 1933, when Joseph Stalin devised them as an expedient to save the collective farm situation.

It was one of the shrewdest measures ever adopted in the U.S.S.R., because it simultaneously brought order out of the collective chaos and put the all-vital traction into the hands of the State, as animal traction at that time had been reduced to negligible proportions by Kulak opposition—they killed the animals—and famine conditions.

Since 1933 the total number of tractors has increased sixfold and the big caterpillar tractors eightfold in the country, which is now 99 per cent "socialized" agriculturally, with 92 per cent of the peasantry enrolled in collective farms.

September 20, 1937

# SOVIET SHORTAGES CAUSING MURMURS

Long Queues Still a Feature of Russian Life—Textile Output Below Plan

MORE TRIALS THREATENED

Wireless to THE NEW YORK TIMES.

MOSCOW, Oct. 10.—Official data on textile production, just published, help to explain why the average Soviet citizen is so inadequately dressed, although much better than three or four years ago. The figures also explain why long lines of would-be purchasers, standing patiently for hours, are still a conspicuous feature of Moscow life.

According to a statement by I. E. Lubimoff, Commissar of Internal Trade of the Russian Socialist Federated Soviet Republic, the largest unit in the Soviet Union, the textile industry is short 200,000,000 meters of cloth for the first half of this year, and the mills are still falling far behind their schedules.

He adds that a large proportion of the textiles produced is of bad quality, containing streaks, rips and tears, or it fades or ravels after brief use. One State trade organization in a large district of Moscow had to scrap as unusable 3,100 meters of 6,900 meters of cotton cloth received from one textile factory during August.

**Trials Are Indicated**

Such instances are not exceptional, Mr. Lubimoff said, and he indicated legal action would be taken against textile executives responsible for putting out unusable goods.

His findings accord with an exposé published last week in the organ of the Commissariat of Light Industry, in which it was asserted the textile program was behind 364,000 meters of standard quality cloth for the first four months of this year.

It was charged in that exposé also that the government's plan for a higher quality and greater variety of textiles had been ignored. It was said confusion in distribution had added needlessly to the shortage and that shortages in textiles and other most important necessaries among consumer goods were becoming chronic despite steady driving by the government to put goods into the hands of the people.

Shoes and stockings along with dress goods and ready-made clothing of most sorts are now extremely difficult to buy even in Moscow. Soviet apologists partly explain the shortages on the grounds that there is now a much greater demand owing to a higher cultural level of the masses of the people. Rising wages, which have given the people more money to spend, are also cited. There is undoubtedly much validity in that view.

It is also asserted that, now that the harvest is coming in, goods are being diverted to villages. But in attacks by executives on the situation responsibility is being put squarely up to the textile industry.

**Department Store Unstocked**

A visit to Mostorg, the leading government department store in the center of Moscow, gives a visual demonstration of the shortage against which the people are murmuring and the authorities are thundering. No textiles except some embroidery and linen are to be found there after early morning hours.

There are yards and yards of vacant counters and sleeves. Good-natured clerks stand or sit idle or chat with loitering shoppers. The shoe department has only a few stray pairs. There was a supply of women's felt boots, however, which a line of customers was snapping up against the fast-approaching cold weather.

Counters in the women's stocking department were bare. Hangers stood completely denuded in the women's ready-made clothing departments. There was an assortment of men's ready-made clothing, however, with the customers, many obviously from villages, standing five deep in front of the counter.

So great is the demand for all these staples that would-be purchasers go from one section of town to another when word spreads by grapevine that dress goods, shoes or stockings will be received by some particular store.

Passing through Moscow streets late at night one constantly encounters lines forming in front of shoe and textile stores, even as early as midnight, the customers hoping to buy something when the stores open.

Meanwhile there appear to be good supplies of less-urgently required goods. For instance, in Mostorg there are large stocks of men's neckties—hardly Fifth Avenue style, it is true, but nevertheless neckties—toys, dolls, costume jewelry of metal or semi-precious stones, and many sorts of notions and knick-knacks.

A brisk business was being done today in big, gaudy, tasseled, rayon lampshades, which Muscovites love to suspend over their dining tables.

October 11, 1938

# SOVIET CUTS DOWN WORKER BENEFITS

## Sharply Reduces Maternity Absence With Pay and Curbs Vacations and Sick Leave

## FIXES PENALTY FOR TARDY

## Campaign Against Religion Resumed With Approach of Russian Christmas

By HAROLD DENNY
Wireless to THE NEW YORK TIMES.

MOSCOW, Dec. 28.—The highest Soviet authorities adopted measures today to tighten up labor discipline by reducing the amount of time lost through unjustifiable absences and unearned vacations and by discouraging a tendency of Soviet workers to leave one job for another elsewhere, where they have heard that better housing or better supplies are available.

These new measures, embodied in a resolution effective Jan. 1, include many of the recent demands for labor reforms which had been obviously dictated by high authority and which had been voiced by workers at meetings in various parts of the Soviet Union.

The object of these demands is to increase labor productivity, which is obstinately low here, and thereby decrease manufacturing costs, which, together with other factors, make the ordinary Soviet citizens the worst supplied in consumption goods at the most exorbitant prices paid by ordinary citizens in any important country in the world.

**Signed by Three Leaders**

The resolution embodying this new labor code was promulgated by the Council of People's Commissars, the Central Committee of the Communist party, and the Central Trade Union Council and was signed by Premier Vyacheslaff Molotoff for the Commissars, by Joseph Stalin for the party and by U. M. Shvernik for the trade unions.

One of the most interesting features of the new labor laws, in view of the great amount of publicity that has been given to the extremely liberal Soviet laws now in force, concerns expectant mothers. According to many recent accusations in the official press, many women have been using these laws for a kind of racket.

It has been alleged that many women who have been merely housewives for husbands in upper income brackets have taken jobs when they learned they were to be mothers, solely to get the four months' maternity leave with full pay given to women in manual work or the six weeks' leave for office workers. Then, after collecting this, they would quit and go home. The abuse of the current maternity regulations naturally has put heavy financial burdens on the industries that have had to pay their wages.

The new regulations cut the maternity leave virtually in two. From the beginning of next year a woman will not be able to qualify for maternity leave unless she has worked for one concern for seven months. Then her paid leave will be reduced to thirty-five days before the birth of her child and twenty days afterward.

**The New Labor Provisions**

In general, the labor regulations provide:

First, if a worker is late three times in one month or four times in two consecutive months he will be discharged.

Second, vacations will be given only after a worker has been employed for eleven consecutive months in the same institution.

Third, social insurance for temporary disability will consist of 50 to 100 per cent of the workers' wage, depending on the length of his employment, his membership in a trade union and similar considerations.

The obvious hope of Soviet authorities is that these new regulations will increase production. Figures on truancy and reduced output have recently been published here to prove that high labor turnover and unnecessary absences have a direct relation to the slumps in production.

**Anti-Religious Drive Pressed**

The approach of the Russian Christmas, which for the remaining devout will be celebrated Jan. 7, with elaborate Orthodox rites in the churches on the preceding evening, is being made an occasion for intensified anti-religious agitation.

This time complaints against the activites of religious sects are being tied up with the campaign to reduce the number of absentees from work. There have been a number of articles in the Soviet press recently asserting that religious festivals are accompanied by an increase in the number of people failing to report for duty in factories or on collective farms, but today Gudok, the organ of railway transport, carries a lengthy attack on religious persons as deliberate disruptors of traffic, and it enumerates several allegedly treasonable plots inspired by the religious.

"Understanding the tremendous importance to the national economy of the uninterrupted activity of transport, priests and other are directing their energies to disrupting railroad work," says the Gudok article. "An ecclesiastical holiday—Christmas—is now approaching. There is no doubt the clergy are preparing for many-sided activity.

"Already this year they have attempted to disrupt transport. Nowhere and in no way must even the slightest interruption of the movement of railway facilities be permitted. There must not be one case of truancy or one case of tardiness.

"All social organizations must promote active anti-religious agitation. A high quality of atheistic propaganda is needed to counteract the cunning and subtle intrigues of the clergy. Our railroad press, motion pictures, clubs, red corners, radio stations, etc., must all develop anti-religious work, which is weak in many places."

December 29, 1938

# SOVIET FARMS GET NEW QUOTA ORDER

## State Demands Are Based on Acreage to Force Backward to Produce More

## HERDS WILL BE INCREASED

By G. E. R. GEDYE
Special Cable to THE NEW YORK TIMES.

MOSCOW, April 7—A decree that revolutionizes the whole system of collective farming was issued by the Council of Peoples Commissars today. It abolishes obligatory deliveries to the State of crops on the basis of sowings and substitutes fixed quantities according to acreage.

The decree also imposes the obligation on all collective farms to breed quotas of horses suitable for military purposes.

A Pravda editorial points out that the decree is a fundamental change in the policy of collecting and purchasing agricultural products. It will presumably operate as a speeding up process, forcing backward farms to rise gradually to the yield of advanced farms.

The decree's preamble declares the existing system is obsolete. Basing the obligatory quantities of meat, milk and wool to be surrendered on the herds owned by each farm set a premium on the possession of small herds or even none while good farms that increased their herds had to surrender constantly raised quotas.

The new system, based on acreage, the preamble declares will be a powerful stimulant to livestock breeding. The new principle also is applied to hides and eggs. The old system, it is stated, was responsible for the absence of poultry on most collective farms. Similarly the system requiring military horses only from farms having them militated against increasing herds.

The result of fixing obligatory deliveries according to sowings, the preamble continues, was that collective farms reduced areas sown and were not stimulated to bring fresh areas under cultivation. The existing system was said to have provided too many collecting organizations for meat, vegetables and other supplies.

The decree retains the old system for cotton, tobacco, fruits and berries.

The quotas for grain and rice will total 3,700,000,000 pounds. Increased deliveries are demanded from several republics and Khabarovsk and Leningrad Provinces because the existing quotas are too small.

Beginning this year there will be obligatory deliveries of hay. Beginning next year compulsory deliveries of milk, ewes and cheese will be based on the areas of collective farms.

Breeding of horses suitable for the army will be compulsory next year.

The acreage principle will be applied to meat deliveries. Meat produced in excess of the State quota will be available for local consumption. Farmers furnishing hides will be allowed to purchase leather goods.

April 8, 1940

# *Text of New Soviet Constitution Designed to Set Up More Democratic Rule*

*Following is the draft of the Constitution of the Union of Soviet Socialist Republics, submitted by the Constitution Commission of the Central Executive Committee of the U.S.S.R. and approved by the Presidium of the Central Executive Committee of the U.S.S.R. to be presented for consideration by the All-Union Congress of Soviets, as received from Moscow:*

## CHAPTER I

### Social Organization

Article 1: The Union of Soviet Socialist Republics is a socialist state of workers and peasants.

Article 2: The political foundation of the U.S.S.R. is formed by the soviets of toilers' deputies which have grown and become strong as a result of the overthrow of the power of the landlords and capitalists and the conquests of the dictatorship of the proletariat.

Article 3: All power in the U.S.S.R. belongs to the toilers of the town and village in the form of soviets of toilers' deputies.

Article 4: The economic foundation of the U.S.S.R. consists in the Socialist ownership of the implements and means of production, firmly established as a result of the liquidation of the capitalist system of economy, the abolition of private ownership of the instruments and means of production, and the abolition of exploitation of man by man.

Article 5: Socialist ownership in the U.S.S.R. has either the form of State ownership (public property) or the form of cooperative and collective farm ownership (property of individual collective farms, property of cooperative associations).

Article 6: The land, its deposits, waters, forests, mills, factories, mines, railway, water and air transport, banks, means of communication, large agricultural enterprises organized by the State (State farms, machine and tractor stations, and so on), as well as the essential part of housing in the cities and industrial centers, is State property, that is, public property.

Article 7: Public enterprises in collective farms and cooperative organizations, with their livestock and implements, products produced by the collective farms and cooperative organizations, as well as their public buildings, constitute the public, socialist property of the collective farms and cooperative organizations.

Each collective farm household has for its own use a plot of land attached to the household and, as individual property, subsidiary establishments on the land attached to the household, a house, productive livestock and poultry, and minor agricultural implements—in accordance with the statutes of the agricultural artel.

#### Land Held Forever

Article 8: The land occupied by collective farms is secured to them for use without time limit, that is, in perpetuity.

Article 9: Alongside the socialist system of economy, which is the dominant form of economy in the U.S.S.R. the law allows small private economy of individual peasants and handicraftsmen based on individual labor and excluding the exploitation of the labor of others.

Article 10: The personal ownership by citizens of their income from work and savings, home and auxiliary household economy, of objects of domestic and household economy as well as objects of personal use and comfort are protected by law.

Article 11: The economic life of the U.S.S.R. is determined and directed by the national economic State plan for the purposes of increasing public wealth, of a steady rise in the material and cultural level of the toilers, of strengthening the independence of the U.S.S.R. and its defense capacity.

Article 12: Work in the U.S.S.R. is the obligation of each citizen capable of working, according to the principle: "He who does not work shall not eat." In the U.S.S.R. the principle of socialism is being realized: "From each according to his ability, to each according to his work."

## CHAPTER II

### State Organization

Article 13: The Union of Soviet Socialist Republics is a federal State, formed on the basis of the voluntary association of the Soviet Socialist Republics with equal rights:

Russian Soviet Federated Socialist Republic,

Ukrainian Soviet Socialist Republic,

White Russian Soviet Socialist Republic,

Azerbaijan Soviet Socialist Republic.

Georgian Soviet Socialist Republic,

Armenian Soviet Socialist Republic,

Turkmenian Soviet Socialist Republic,

Uzbek Soviet Socialist Republic,

Tajik Soviet Socialist Republic.

Kazakh Soviet Socialist Republic,

Kirghiz Soviet Socialist Republic.

Article 14: The jurisdiction of the Union of Soviet Socialist Republics, as represented by its supreme organs of power and organs of State administration, extends to:

(a) representation of the Union in international relations, conclusion and ratification of treaties with other States;

(b) questions of war and peace;

(c) admission of new republics into the U. S. S. R.;

(d) control of the observance of the Constitution of the U. S. S. R. and insuring conformity of the constitutions of the Union republics with the Constitution of the U. S. S. R.;

(e) approval of alterations of boundaries between Union republics;

(f) organization of the defense of the U. S. S. R. and the direction of all the armed forces of the U. S. S. R.;

(g) foreign trade on the basis of the State monopoly;

(h) protection of State security;

(i) establishment of the national economic plans of the U. S. S. R.;

(j) approval of the unified State budget of the U. S. S. R. as well as the taxes and revenues entering into the U. S. S. R., Union-republic and local budgets;

#### Trading Enterprises Controlled

(k) administration of banks, industrial and agricultural establishments as well as trading enterprises of all-Union importance;

(l) administration of transport and means of communication;

(m) direction of the monetary and credit system;

(n) organization of the State insurance of property;

(o) contracting and granting loans;

(p) establishment of the fundamental principles for the use of land as well as the exploitation of deposits, forests and waters;

(q) establishment of the fundamental principles in the field of education and protection of public health;

(r) organization of a unified system of national economic accounting;

(s) establishment of basic labor laws;

(t) legislation on judicature and legal procedure, criminal and civil codes;

(u) laws on citizenship of the Union, laws on the rights of foreigners;

(v) passing all-Union amnesty acts.

Article 15: The sovereignty of the Union republics is restricted only within the limits set forth in Article 14 of the Constitution of the U. S. S. R. Outside of these limits, each Union republic exercises independently its State power. The U. S. S. R. protects the sovereign rights of the Union republics.

Article 16: Every Union republic has its own constitution, which takes into account the specific features of the republic and is drawn up in full conformity with the Constitution of the U. S. S. R.

#### Republics Free to Secede

Article 17: Each Union republic retains its right freely to secede from the U. S. S. R.

Article 18: The territory of the Union republics may not be changed without their consent.

Article 19: The laws of the U. S. S. R. have the same force in the territories of all Union republics.

Article 20: In the event of a law of a Union republic differing from an all-Union law, the all-Union law is operative.

Article 21: A single Union citizenship is established for all citizens of the U. S. S. R. Every citizen of a Union republic is a citizen of the U. S. S. R.

Article 22: The Russian Soviet Federated Socialist Republic consists of the following Territories: Azov-Black Sea, Far East, West Siberia, Krasnoyarsk, North Caucasus. Provinces: Voronezh, East Siberia, Gorky, Western, Ivanovo, Kalinin, Kirov, Kuibyshev, Kursk, Leningrad, Moscow, Omsk, Orenburg, Saratov, Sverdlovsk, Northern, Stalingrad, Cheryabinsk, Yaroslavl. Autonomous Soviet Socialist Republics: Tatar, Bashkir, Daghestan, Buryat-Mongolia, Kabardino-Balkaria, Kalmuck, Karelia, Komi, Crimea, Marii, Mordva, Volga German, North Osetia, Udmurt, Chechen-Ingush, Chuvash, Yagut. Autonomous Provinces: Adygei, Jewish, Karachayev, Oirot, Khakass, Cherkess.

Article 23: The Ukrainian Soviet Socialist Republic consists of the following provinces: Vinnitsa, Dniepropetrovsk, Donets, Kiev, Odessa, Kharkov, Chernigov and the Moldavian Autonomous Soviet Socialist Republic.

Article 24: The Azerbaijan Soviet Socialist Republic includes the Nakhichevan Autonomous Soviet Socialist Republic and the Nagorno-Karabakh Autonomous Province.

Article 25: The Georgian Soviet Socialist Republic includes the Abkhazian A. S. S. R., Ajarian A. S. S. R., South Osetian Autonomous Province.

Article 26: The Uzbek Soviet Socialist Republic includes the Kara-Kalpak A. S. S. R.

Article 27: The Tajik Soviet Socialist Republic includes the Gorno-Badakhshan Autonomous Province.

Article 28: The Kazakh Soviet Socialist Republic consists of the following provinces: Aktyubinsk, Alma-Ata, East Kazakhstan, West Kazakhstan, Karaganda, South Kazakhstan.

Article 29: The Armenian S. S. R., White Russian S. S. R., Turkmenian S. S. R. and Kirghiz S. S. R. do not include any autonomous republics or territories and provinces.

## CHAPTER III

### The Supreme Organs of U.S.S.R.

Article 30: The supreme organ of State power of the U.S.S.R. is the Supreme Council of the USSR.

Article 31: The Supreme Council of the U.S.S.R. exercises all rights vested in the Union of Soviet Socialist Republics according to Article 14 of the Constitution, in so far as they do not enter, by virtue of the Constitution, into the competence of those organs of the U.S.S.R. subordinate to the Supreme Council of the U.S.S.R.: the Presidium of the Supreme Council of the U.S.S.R., the Council of People's Commissars of the U.S.S.R., and the People's Commissariats of the U.S.S.R.

Article 32: The legislative power of the U.S.S.R. is exercised exclusively by the Supreme Council of the U.S.S.R.

Article 33: The Supreme Council of the U.S.S.R. consists of two chambers: the Council of the Union and the Council of Nationalities.

Article 34: The Council of the

Union is elected by the citizens of the U.S.S.R. on the basis of one deputy per 300,000 of population.

Article 35: The Council of Nationalities consists of deputies appointed by the Supreme Councils of the Union and autonomous republics and soviets of toilers' deputies in the autonomous provinces: on the basis of ten deputies from each Union republic, five deputies from each autonomous republic and two deputies from each autonomous province.

Article 36: The Supreme Council of the U.S.S.R. is elected for a period of four years.

Article 37: Both chambers of the Supreme Council of the U.S.S.R., the Council of the Union and Council of Nationalities, have equal rights.

Article 38: Legislative initiative belongs in equal degree to the Council of the Union and the Council of Nationalities.

Article 39: A law is considered approved if adopted by both chambers of the Supreme Council of the U.S.S.R. by simple majority vote in each.

Article 40: Laws adopted by the Supreme Council of the U.S.S.R. are published over the signatures of the Chairman and Secretary of the Presidium of the Supreme Council of the U.S.S.R.

Article 41: Sessions of the Council of the Union and the Council of Nationalities begin and terminate concurrently.

Article 42: The Council of the Union elects the chairman of the Council of the Union and two vice chairmen.

Article 43: The Council of Nationalities elects the chairman of the Council of Nationalities and two vice chairmen.

**Presiding Officials Named**

Article 44: The chairmen of the Council of the Union and of the Council of Nationalities direct the sessions of the corresponding chambers and regulate their inner arrangements.

Article 45: Joint sessions of both chambers of the Supreme Council of the U.S.S.R. are directed in turn by the chairman of the Council of the Union and the chairman of the Council of Nationalities.

Article 46: Sessions of the Supreme Council of the U.S.S.R. are convened by the Presidium of the Supreme Council of the U.S.S.R. twice a year.

Extraordinary sessions are convened by the Presidium of the Supreme Council of the U.S.S.R. at its discretion or on the demand of one of the Union republics.

Article 47: In case of disagreement between the Council of the Union and the Council of Nationalities the question is referred for settlement to a conciliation commission established on the basis of equal representation. If the conciliation commission does not come to an agreement upon a decision, or if its decision does not satisfy one of the chambers, the question is considered for a second time in the chambers. In the event of the two chambers not agreeing upon a decision, the Presidium of the Supreme Council of the U.S.S.R. dissolves the Supreme Council of the U.S.S.R. and fixes new elections.

Article 48: The Supreme Council of the U.S.S.R. elects, at a joint session of both chambers, the Presidium of the Supreme Council of the U.S.S.R., composed of the Chairman of the Presidium of the Supreme Council of the U.S.S.R., four Vice Chairmen, the Secretary of the Presidium and thirty-one members of the Presidium.

The Presidium of the Supreme Council of the U.S.S.R. is accountable to the Supreme Council of the U.S.S.R. in all its activities.

**Powers of Presidium**

Article 49: The Presidium of the Supreme Council of the U.S.S.R.

a) Convenes sessions of the Supreme Council of the U.S.S.R.;

b) Interprets laws in operation by issuing appropriate instructions;

c) Dissolves the Supreme Council of the U.S.S.R. on the basis of Article 47 of the Constitution of the U.S.S.R. and fixes new elections;

d) Conducts a referendum on its own initiative or the demand of one of the Union republics;

e) Rescinds decisions and orders of the Council of People's Commissars of the U.S.S.R. and the Councils of People's Commissars of the republics in the event that they are not in accordance with the law;

f) Between sessions of the Supreme Council of the U.S.S.R. relieves of their duties and appoints the various People's Commissars of the U.S.S.R. at the instance of the Chairman of the Council of People's Commissars of the U.S.S.R. to be later submitted for confirmation by the Supreme Council of the U.S.S.R.;

g) Awards decorations of the U.S.S.R.;

h) Exercises the right of pardon;

i) Appoints and replaces the supreme command of the armed forces of the U.S.S.R.;

j) Between sessions of the Supreme Council of the U.S.S.R. declares a state of war in the event of an armed attack on the U.S.S.R.;

k) Declares general or partial mobilization;

l) Ratifies international treaties;

m) Appoints and recalls plenipotentiary representatives of the U.S.S.R. to foreign States;

n) Accepts the credentials of diplomatic representatives of foreign States.

Article 50: The Council of the Union and the Council of Nationalities elect Credential Commissions which verify the authorization of the deputies of each chamber.

On representation from the Credential Commission the chambers decide either to recognize the authorization or annul the elections of the individual deputies.

**Inquiries and Audits**

Article 51: The Supreme Council of the U.S.S.R. appoints, when it deems necessary, investigating and auditing commissions on any question.

All institutions and officials are obliged to comply with the demands of these commissions and to supply them with the necessary materials and documents.

Article 52: A deputy of the Supreme Council of the U.S.S.R. cannot be prosecuted or arrested without the consent of the Supreme Council of the U.S.S.R. and, in the period when the Supreme Council of the U.S.S.R. is not in session, without the agreement of the Presidium of the Supreme Council of the U.S.S.R.

Article 53: After the authority of the Supreme Council of the U.S.S.R. has expired or after the Supreme Council has been dissolved before the expiration of its term, the Presidium of the Supreme Council of the U.S.S.R. preserves its authority until the formation by the newly elected Supreme Council of the U.S.S.R. of a new Presidium of the Supreme Council of the U.S.S.R.

Article 54: When the authority of the Supreme Council of the U.S.S.R. expires or in the event of its dissolution before the expiration of its term, the Presidium of the Supreme Council of the U.S.S.R. fixes new elections within a period of not more than two months from the date of the expiration of its authority or the dissolution of the Supreme Council of the U.S.S.R.

Article 55: The newly-elected Supreme Council of the U.S.S.R. is convened by the former Presidium of the Supreme Council of the U.S.S.R. not later than a month after the elections.

Article 56: The Supreme Council of the U.S.S.R. at a joint session of both chambers forms the Government of the U.S.S.R.—the Council of People's Commissars of the U.S.S.R.

## CHAPTER IV

## Supreme Organs of The Union Republics

Article 57: The supreme organ of State power of a Union republic is the Supreme Council of the Union republic.

Article 58: The Supreme Council of the Union republic is elected by citizens of the republic for a period of four years.

The ratio of representation is determined by the constitutions of the Union republics.

Article 59: The Supreme Council of the Union republic is the sole legislative organ of the republic.

Article 60: The Supreme Council of the Union republic:

a) adopts the Constitution of the republic and amends it in accordance with Article 16 of the Constitution of the U.S.S.R.;

b) ratifies the constitutions of the autonomous republics belonging to it and defines the boundaries of their territories;

c) approves the national economic plan and budget of the republic;

d) exercises the right of amnesty and pardon to citizens sentenced by judicial organs of the Union republic.

Article 61: The Supreme Council of the Union republic elects a Presidium of the Supreme Council of the Union republic composed of: the chairman of the Presidium of the Supreme Council of the Union republic, his deputies, and members of the Presidium of the Supreme Council of the Union republic.

The powers of the Presidium of the Supreme Council of a Union republic are determined by the constitution of the Union republic.

Article 62: The Supreme Council of the Union republic elects the chairman and his deputies to conduct its meetings.

Article 63: The Supreme Council of the Union republic organizes the government of the Union republic—the Council of People's Commissars of the Union republic.

## CHAPTER V

## Organs of Administration Of U.S.S.R.

Article 64: The supreme executive and administrative organ of State power in the Union of Soviet Socialist Republics is the Council of People's Commissars of the U.S.S.R.

Article 65: The Council of People's Commissars of the U.S.S.R. is responsible to the Supreme Council of the U.S.S.R. and accountable to it.

Article 66: The Council of People's Commissars of the U.S.S.R. issues decisions and orders on the basis of and in fulfillment of laws in effect and controls their execution.

Article 67: Decisions and orders of the Council of People's Commissars of the U.S.S.R. have obligatory force and must be carried out throughout the entire territory of the U.S.S.R.

Article 68: The Council of People's Commissars of the U.S.S.R.

a) unites and directs the work of the all-Union and Union-republic People's Commissariats of the U.S.S.R. and of other economic and cultural institutions under its jurisdiction;

b) takes measures to realize the national economic plan and State budget and to strengthen the credit-monetary system;

c) takes measures to ensure public order, to defend the interests of the State, and to safeguard the rights of citizens;

d) exercises general direction in the realm of relations with foreign States;

e) determines the annual contingent of citizens subject to be called for active military service and directs the general upbuilding of the armed forces of the country.

**Council's Veto Rights**

Article 69: The Council of People's Commissars of the U.S.S.R. has the right in respect to those branches of administration and economy which fall within the jurisdiction of the U.S.S.R. to suspend decisions and orders of the Councils of People's Commissars of the Union republics and to annul orders and instructions of the People's Commissars of the U.S.S.R.

Article 70: The Council of People's Commissars of the U.S.S.R. is formed by the Supreme Council of the U.S.S.R. and is composed as follows:

The Chairman of the Council of People's Commissars of the U.S.S.R.;

The Vice Chairmen of the Council of People's Commissars of U.S.S.R.;

The Chairman of the State Planning Commission of the U.S.S.R.;

The Chairman of the Soviet Control Commission;

The People's Commissars of the U.S.S.R.;

The Chairman of the Committee for Purchasing Agricultural Products;

The Chairman of the Art Committee;

The Chairman of the Committee for Higher Education.

Article 71: The Government of the U.S.S.R. or the People's Commissar of the U.S.S.R. to whom any question of a deputy of the Supreme Council is addressed is obliged to give an oral or written reply in the respective chamber within a period of not more than three days.

Article 72: People's Commissars of the U.S.S.R. direct the branches of State administration which come within the jurisdiction of the U.S.S.R.

Article 73: The People's Commissars of the U.S.S.R. issue within the limits of jurisdiction of the respective People's Commissariats orders and instructions on the basis of and in fulfillment of laws in effect, as well as of decisions and orders of the Council of People's Commissars of the U.S.S.R. and verify their fulfillment.

**Status of Commissariats**

Article 74: The People's Commissariats of the U.S.S.R. are either All-Union or Union-republic.

Article 75: The All-Union People's Commissariats direct the branch of a State administration entrusted to them in the entire territory of the U.S.S.R. either directly or through organs assigned by them.

Article 76: Union-republic People's Commissariats direct the branch of a State administration entrusted to them through identically named People's Commissariats of the Union republics.

Article 77: The following People's Commissariats comprise the All-Union People's Commissariats:

Defense;
Foreign Affairs;
Foreign Trade;
Railways;
Communications;
Water Transport;
Heavy Industry.

Article 78: The following People's Commissariats comprise the Union-republic People's Commissariats:

Food Industry;
Light Industry;
Timber Industry;
Agriculture;
State Grain and Livestock Farms;
Finance;
Home Trade;
Home Affairs;
Justice;
Health.

## CHAPTER VI

## Organs of Administration Of Union Republics

**Article 79: The supreme executive and administrative organ of State power of a Union republic is the Council of People's Commissars of the Union republic.**

**Article 80: The Council of People's Commissars of a Union republic is responsible to the Supreme Council of the Union republic and is accountable to it.**

**Article 81: The Council of People's Commissars of a Union republic issues decisions and orders on he basis of and in fulfillment of the laws in effect in the U.S.S.R. and the Union republic, and of decisions and orders of the Council of People's Commissars of the U.S.S.R., and verifies their execution.**

**Article 82: The Council of People's Commissars of a Union republic has the right to suspend decisions and orders of the Councils of People's Commissars of autonomous republics and to rescind decisions and orders of executive committees of Soviets of toilers' deputies of territories, provinces and autonomous provinces.**

**Composition of Council**

**Article 83: The Council of People's Commissars of a Union republic is formed by the Supreme Council of the Union republic and is composed of:**

**The chairman of the Council of People's Commissars of the Union republic;**
**The vice chairmen;**
**The Chairman of the State Planning Commission;**
**People's Commissars:**
**Of the Food Industry;**
**Of Light Industry;**
**Of the Timber Industry;**
**Of Agriculture;**
**Of State Grain and Livestock Farms;**
**Of Finance;**
**Of Home Trade;**
**Of Home Affairs;**
**Of Justice;**
**Of Health;**
**Of Education;**
**Of Local Industry;**
**Of Communal Economy;**
**Of Social Welfare;**

**A representative of the Committee for Purchasing Agricultural Products;**

**Chief of the Art Administration;**

**Representatives of the All-Union People's Commissariats.**

Article 84: The People's Commissars of a Union republic administer branches of the State administration which come within the jurisdiction of the Union republic.

Article 85: The People's Commissars of a Union republic issue within the limits of jurisdiction of respective People's Commissariats, orders and instructions on the basis of and in fulfillment of the laws of the U.S.S.R. and the Union republic, decisions and orders of the Council of People's Commissars of the U.S.S.R. and the Union republic, and of orders and instructions of the Union-republic People's Commissariats of the U.S.S.R.

**Article 86: The People's Commissariats of a Union republic are either Union republic or republic.**

Article 87: Union republic People's Commissariats administer the branch of a State administration entrusted to them, being subordinate both to the Council of People's Commissars of the Union republic and corresponding Union republic People's Commissariat of the U.S.S.R.

**Article 88: Republic People's Commissariats administer the branch of a State administration entrusted to them, being subordinate directly to the Council of People's Commissars of the Union republic.**

## CHAPTER VII

## Supreme Organs of Power of Autonomous Republics

Article 89: The supreme organ of State power of an autonomous republic is the Supreme Council of the A.S.S.R.

Article 90: The Supreme Council of an autonomous republic is elected by the citizens of the republic for a period of four years in the ratio of representation established by the constitution of the autonomous republic.

Article 91: The Supreme Council of an autonomous republic is the sole legislative organ of the A.S.S.R.

Article 92: Each autonomous republic has its own constitution which takes into account the specific features of the autonomous republic and is drawn up in full conformity with the constitution of the Union republic.

Article 93: The Supreme Council of an autonomous republic elects the Presidium of the Supreme Council of the autonomous republic and forms a Council of People's Commissars of the autonomous republic, in accordance with its constitution.

## CHAPTER VIII

## Local Organs of Power

Article 94: The organs of State power in territories, provinces, autonomous provinces, regions, districts, cities and villages (stanitsas, khutors, kishlaks, auls) are soviets of toilers' deputies.

Article 95: The soviets of toilers' deputies of territories, provinces, autonomous provinces, regions, districts, cities and villages (stanitsas, khutors, kishlaks, auls) are elected by the toilers of the respective territory, province, autonomous province, region, district, city or village for a period of two years.

**Article 96: The ratio of representation in the soviets of toilers' deputies are determined by the constitutions of the Union republics.**

Article 97: The soviets of toilers' deputies direct the activities of the organs of administration subordinated to them, ensure the maintenance of State order, observation of the laws and the protection of the rights of citizens, carry out local economic and cultural construction and draw up the local budget.

Article 98: The soviets of toilers' deputies adopt decisions and issue orders within the limits of the powers vested in them by the laws of the U.S.S.R. and the Union republic.

**Article 99: The executive and administrative organs of the soviets of toilers' deputies of the territories, provinces, autonomous provinces, regions, districts and cities are the executive committees elected by them, composed of the chairman, the vice-chairmen and members.**

**Article 100: The executive and administrative organ of village soviets of toilers' deputies in small localities, in accordance with the constitutions of the Union republics, are the chairman, vice-chairmen and members elected by them.**

**Article 101: The executive organs of the soviets of toilers' deputies are directly accountable both to the soviets of toilers' deputies which elected them and to the executive organ of the higher soviet of toilers' deputies.**

## CHAPTER IX

## Court and Prosecution

**Article 102: Justice in the U.S.S.R. is administered by the Supreme Court of the U.S.S.R., the supreme courts of the Union republics, territory and province courts, courts of the autonomous republics and autonomous provinces, special courts of the U.S.S.R. which are created by decision of the Supreme Council of the U.S.S.R., and People's Courts.**

**Article 103: In all courts, cases are tried with the participation of the people's associate judges, with the exception of cases specially provided for by law.**

**Article 104: The Supreme Court of the U.S.S.R. is the highest judicial organ. It is charged with supervision of the activity of all judicial organs of the U.S.S.R. and Union republics.**

**Article 105: The Supreme Court of the U.S.S.R. and special courts of the U.S.S.R. are elected by the Supreme Council of the U.S.S.R. for a period of five years.**

**Article 106: The supreme courts of Union republics are elected by the Supreme Councils of the Union republics for a period of five years.**

**Article 107: The supreme courts of autonomous republics are elected by the Supreme Council of the autonomous republics for a period of five years.**

**Article 108: Territory and province courts, and courts of the autonomous provinces are elected by territory or province soviets of toilers' deputies or by soviets of toilers' deputies of the autonomous provinces for a period of five years.**

**Election of Courts**

**Article 109: People's courts are elected by secret ballot for a period of three years by citizens of the district, on the basis of universal, direct and equal suffrage.**

**Article 110: Court proceedings are conducted in the language of the Union or autonomous republic or autonomous province, persons not knowing this language being ensured the possibility of fully acquainting themselves with the material of the case through an interpreter as well as having the right to address the court in their native language.**

**Article 111: In all courts of the U.S.S.R. cases are heard openly, except when otherwise provided for by law, and the accused person is ensured the right of defense.**

Article 112: Judges are independent and subject only to the law.

Article 113: Highest supervision of the exact observance of the laws by all People's Commissariats and institutions under them, as well as by individual persons holding official posts, and also by citizens of the U.S.S.R., is vested in the Prosecutor of the U.S.S.R.

Article 114: The Prosecutor of the U.S.S.R. is appointed by the Supreme Council of the U.S.S.R. for a period of seven years.

Article 115: Prosecutors of republics, territories and provinces, as well as prosecutors of autonomous republics and autonomous provinces, are appointed by the Prosecutor of the U.S.S.R. for a period of five years.

Article 116: District prosecutors are appointed for a period of five years by the prosecutors of the Union republics with the approval of the Prosecutor of the U.S.S.R.

Article 117: The organs of prosecution perform their functions independently of any local organs whatsoever, being responsible to the Prosecutor of the U.S.S.R. alone.

## CHAPTER X

## Citizens' Basic Rights And Obligations

Article 118: Citizens of the U.S.S.R. have the right to work—the right to receive guaranteed work with payment for their work in accordance with its quantity and quality.

The right to work is ensured by the socialist organization of national economy, the steady growth of the productive forces of Soviet society, the absence of economic crises, and the abolition of unemployment.

Article 119: Citizens of the U.S.S.R. have the right to rest.

The right to rest is ensured by the reduction of the working day to seven hours for the overwhelming majority of the workers, establishment of annual vacations with pay for workers and employes and provision of a wide network of sanatoriums, rest homes and clubs for the accommodation of the toilers.

Article 120: Citizens of the U.S.S.R. have the right to material security in old age as well as in the event of sickness and loss of capacity to work.

This right is ensured by the wide development of social insurance of workers and employes at the expense of the State, free medical aid, and the provision of a wide network of health resorts for the use of the toilers.

Article 121: Citizens of the U.S.S.R. have the right to education.

This right is ensured by universal compulsory elementary education, free of charge, including higher education, by the system of State stipends for the overwhelming majority of students in higher schools, instruction in schools in the native language, and organization of free industrial, technical and agronomic education for the toilers at the factories, State farms, machine and tractor stations and collective farms.

**Equal Rights for Women**

Article 122: Women in the U.S.S.R. are accorded equal rights with men in all fields of economic, State, cultural, social and political life.

The possibility of realizing these rights of women is ensured by affording women equally with men the right to work, payment for work, rest, social insurance and education, State protection of the interests of mother and child, granting pregnancy leave with pay, and the provision of a wide network of maternity homes, nurseries and kindergartens.

**Article 123: The equality of the rights of citizens of the U.S.S.R. irrespective of their nationality or race, in all fields of economic, State, cultural, social and political life, is an irrevocable law.**

**Any direct or indirect restriction of these rights, or conversely the establishment of direct or indirect privileges for citizens on account of the race or nationality to which they belong, as well as any propagation of racial or national exceptionalism or hatred and contempt, is punishable by law.**

Article 124: To ensure to citizens freedom of conscience the church in the U.S.S.R. is separated from the State and the school from the church. Freedom to perform religious rites and freedom of anti-religious propaganda is recognized for all citizens.

Article 125: In accordance with the interests of the toilers, for the purpose of strengthening the socialist system, the citizens of the U.S.S.R. are guaranteed:

a) freedom of speech;

b) freedom of the press;

c) freedom of assembly and meetings;

d) freedom of street processions and demonstrations.

These rights of the citizens are ensured by placing at the disposal of the toilers and their organizations printing presses, supplies of paper, public buildings, streets, means of communication and other material conditions necessary for their realization.

Article 126: In accordance with the interests of the toilers and for the purpose of developing the organizational self-expression and political activity of the masses of the people, citizens of the U.S.S.R. are ensured the right of combining in public organizations: trade unions, cooperative associations, youth organizations, sport and defense organizations, cultural, technical and scientific societies, and for the most active and conscientious citizens from the ranks of the working class and other strata of the toilers, of uniting in the Communist Party of the U.S.S.R., which is the vanguard of the toilers in their struggle for strengthening and developing the Socialist system and which represents the leading nucleus of all organizations of the toilers, both public and State.

Article 127: The citizens of the U.S.S.R. are ensured the inviolability of the person. No one may be subjected to arrest except upon the decision of a court or with the sanction of the prosecutor.

Article 128: The inviolability of the homes of citizens and the secrecy of correspondence are protected by law.

Article 129: The U.S.S.R. grants the right of asylum to foreign citizens persecuted for defending the interests of the toilers or for their scientific activity or for their struggle for national liberation.

Article 130: Every citizen of the U.S.S.R. is obliged to observe the Constitution of the Union of Soviet Socialist Republics, to carry out the laws, observe labor discipline, honestly fulfill his social duties, and respect the rules of the socialist community.

Article 131: Every citizen of the U.S.S.R. is obliged to safeguard and consolidate public, socialist property as the sacred inviolable foundation of the Soviet system, as the source of wealth and might of the fatherland, as the source of the prosperous cultural life of all the toilers. Persons attempting to violate public socialist property are enemies of the people.

Article 132: Universal military service is the law. Military service in the Workers and Peasants Red Army represents the honorable duty of the citizens of the U.S.S.R.

Article 133: The defense of the fatherland is the sacred duty of every citizen of the U.S.S.R. Treason to the fatherland: violation of oath, desertion to the enemy, impairing the military might of the State, or espionage for a foreign State, is punishable with the full severity of the law as the most heinous crime.

### CHAPTER XI

## Electoral System

Article 134: Deputies to all soviets of toilers' deputies, the Supreme Council of the U.S.S.R., Supreme Councils of the Union republics, territorial and province soviets of toilers' deputies, Supreme Councils of autonomous republics, soviets of toilers' deputies of autonomous provinces, regional district, city and village soviets of toilers' deputies (stanitsas, villages, khutors, kishlaks, auls), are elected by the electors on the basis of universal, equal and direct suffrage by secret ballot.

Article 135: Elections of the deputies are universal: all citizens of the U.S.S.R. who in the year of the elections reach the age of 18 have the right to participate in elections of deputies and to be elected, with the exception of the mentally deficient and persons deprived of electoral rights by the courts.

Article 136: Elections of deputies are equal: every citizen has the right to elect and be elected irrespective of his race or nationality, his religion, educational qualifications, residential qualifications, his social origin, property status and past activity.

Article 137: Women have the right to elect and be elected on equal terms with men.

Article 138: Citizens serving in the ranks of the Red Army have the right to elect and be elected on equal terms with all other citizens.

Article 139: Elections of deputies are direct: elections to all soviets of toilers' deputies from the village and city soviets of toilers' deputies up to the Supreme Council of the U.S.S.R. are effected by the citizens voting directly.

Article 140: Voting at elections of deputies is secret.

Article 141: Candidates are put forward for election according to electoral districts.

The right to put forward candidates is granted to social organizations and societies of the toilers: Communist Party organizations, trade unions, cooperatives, youth organizations and cultural societies.

Article 142: Every deputy is obliged to render account to the electors of his work and the work of the soviet of toilers' deputies, and he may at any time be recalled in the manner established by law upon decision of a majority of the electors.

### CHAPTER XII

## Emblem, Flag, Capital

Article 143: The state emblem of the Union of Soviet Socialist Republics consists of a hammer and sickle against a globe depicted in rays of the sun and surrounded by ears of grain with the inscription "Workers of the World, Unite!" in the languages of the Union republics. Above the emblem is a five-pointed star.

Article 144: The state flag of the Union of Soviet Socialist Republics is red cloth with the hammer and sickle depicted in gold in the upper corner near the staff and above them a five-pointed red star bordered in gold. The relation of the width to the length is 1:2.

Article 145: The capital of the Union of Soviet Socialist Republics is the city of Moscow.

### CHAPTER XIII

## Procedure for Amending The Constitution

Article 146: Amendment of the Constitution of the U.S.S.R. is effected only by the decision of the Supreme Council of the U.S.S.R. when adopted by a majority of not less than two-thirds of the votes in each of its chambers.

June 26, 1936

# PARTY DEMOCRACY ORDERED IN RUSSIA

By The Associated Press.

MOSCOW, March 5.—A reform of the Communist party to introduce democracy and secret, direct voting for lower officials of the party was announced tonight at the conclusion of a secret session of the central committee of the party, which had been in session in the Kremlin for ten days.

The same body announced the expulsion of Alexei I. Rykoff and Nikolai Bukharin from the party. Their trial on charges of treason is expected soon.

The new Constitution is responsible for the voting reform. It guarantees direct and secret voting for all except those specifically disfranchised. The announcement immediately preceded elections to be called shortly to name members of the Supreme Council, which will be the Soviet Parliament.

**Reform Rules Adopted**

A communiqué declared the Communist party would continue leadership of national affairs, but said the undemocratic régime in lower ranks must be eliminated. Seven reform rules were announced, but these will not affect the power of the party at the top.

The party central committee, of which Joseph Stalin is secretary general, will continue to be appointed by delegates to the party congress, who, however, hereafter must be chosen by secret vote.

The announcement said all lower party officials henceforth must be elected by secret vote, not appointed as heretofore. Elections must be held yearly, except for provincial party elections, which must be held every eighteen months.

Members of the party receive full right to criticism and the privilege of removing any candidate from the list of party officials if they disapprove of him. The communiqué stated:

"The introduction of the new Constitution of the U.S.S.R. means a change in the political life of the country. It introduces democracy and the elective system. It means the control of the Soviet masses over Soviet organs.

"Political activity of the masses consequently is expected to increase. The dictatorship of the proletariat becomes more elastic. The party must lead this change in order to guarantee its domination in the coming elections for the Supreme Council."

March 6, 1937

# STALIN CALLS HALT ON FULSOME PRAISE

By HAROLD DENNY

Special Cable to THE NEW YORK TIMES.

MOSCOW, March 28.—Joseph Stalin is fed up with the personal adulation that has been heaped upon him in increasing measure in recent years and he has decided to have it modulated, if not completely ended. This is according to many indications here.

It is given as one reason, but only one, for the campaign launched publicly and vigorously today by the Communist party to "omit flowers" in speeches, editorials and the like dealing with the Communist party and government officials, from the highest to the lowest.

It was confirmed inferentially also in a speech by Stalin before the Central Committee of the party on March 3, which was made public for the first time tonight, and by means of an electrical transcription broadcast in Stalin's own voice throughout the Soviet Union.

**Warns on Complacency**

Stalin's speech counseled against complacency and overconfidence regarding the progress of industry and agriculture and warned the people to increase their vigilance against wreckers inspired by Trotskyists and other enemies of the Soviet Union abroad, reminding the people once more that Soviet Russia is a single Socialist country in a world of capitalism, some of whose governments wish the downfall of the Soviet Union and have filled this country with spies and saboteurs.

He described carelessness, complacency, self-satisfaction, excessive self-assurance, conceit and braggadocio as companion vices that fertilized the ground in which such enemies flourished.

But though Stalin in his speech as made public touched lightly on the insidious effects of flattery and overconfidence the newspaper Pravda, organ of the Communist party, in an editorial that is almost equally an expression of Stalin's will, swung hard on the same subject.

"Florid sentences, sugary reports and immoderate applause dull the edge of Bolshevist vigilance and lead people to substitute drum-beating for daily work," said Pravda. "Servility follows the trail blazed by conceit and carelessness."

According to insiders, Stalin means this is to apply to himself as much as to any lesser leader. Fulsome flattery of the leaders has been until now one of the most striking superficial phenomena of the present régime. Speeches and editorials on almost any subject, from Arctic exploration to Marxian dialectics, almost invariably have included panegyrics to Stalin strikingly at variance with his demeanor, which, as the writer has observed many times, is invariably modest, self-effacing and, on great occasions, such as his presentation of the new Constitution to the Congress of Soviets, actually diffident.

Many Russians say Stalin personally disliked but realized the Russian people must have an ikon and permitted himself to be so utilized. Now apparently Stalin believes the necessity for that is past.

March 29, 1937

# Soviet Elections Will Give One-Man Slates to Voters

## Vast Majority of Districts Nominate Solitary Candidates for Dec. 12 Polls—People Puzzled—Economic Council Set Up

By HAROLD DENNY

Wireless to THE NEW YORK TIMES.

MOSCOW, Nov. 24.—President Mikhail Kalinin in a speech in Leningrad yesterday—which was prominently published here today —gave the Soviet explanation of a surprising fact, just now become conclusively evident. That fact is that in only a negligible handful of the Soviet Union's 1,143 districts will there be more than one candidate for the Supreme Council [Parliament] in the widely heralded secret election on Dec. 12 under the new Constitution.

The Supreme Council will be a bicameral parliamentary and executive body, composed of the Council of the Union and the Council of Nationalities, which, according to the letter of the new Constitution, will hold supreme power.

The almost complete absence of even a show of contests has surprised foreign observers, who had expected two or more dependable candidates to be put up in each district. It has caused wonderment also in Soviet minds.

President Kalinin dealt with such doubts in his speech before the workers of the Red Putiloff plant in Leningrad, which was a storm center of revolt in 1917 and in which he worked as a youth. The workers there have nominated him as a candidate for the Council of Nationalities. The President's speech was a brief for the superiority of "Soviet democracy" over the procedure in capitalist countries.

Mr. Kalinin remarked that some Soviet citizens were asking:

"What is the use of my going to vote? There is only one candidate, and he will be elected anyway."

The President continued:

"It is a grave mistake to think this. In capitalist countries it also happens that there is only one candidate. It mostly happens in out-of-the-way places where there are fifty electors of local gentry and one lord whom they 'elect'.

"But if in our country in a number of places candidates withdraw their names for the benefit of some candidate, it is a result of their social kinship and common political purpose. Tens and hundreds of thousands of electors after considerable discussion have agreed on one candidate. It is a sign of socialism—a sign of the impossibility of differences among the working masses, such as there are in bourgeois society."

This statement was greeted with loud applause.

### Would Show the World

"I will tell you frankly," Mr. Kalinin went on, "that if an overwhelming majority of our electors go to the polls many Fascist gang leaders will stop and think, 'Look—not only is their army strong, but even greater power stands behind the army.' We will show the whole world how great is the unity of the working masses and the Communist party.

"In bourgeois countries election campaigns take much less time than ours is taking. When the ruling classes of capitalist countries carry out an election campaign their only purpose is to get a majority and gain seats in Parliament. The bourgeois parties do not care what trickery they use. Their only purpose is to overwhelm the working people and win the elections.

"The question may arise—we are sure the working masses of the Soviet Union will retain their power, then why should we need such a long election campaign? The election campaign must serve as a great school of education for the masses and for the leaders who will emerge from these masses. Socialism demands the utmost organization of the working masses."

In another section of his speech Mr. Kalinin said the tasks of the Soviet proletariat were enormous and would be difficult so long as the Soviet Union remained encircled by capitalist States.

Moscow newspapers for some days now have been publishing lists of candidates from various parts of the Soviet Union. These candidates will be the first to be voted on by the secret ballot as provided for in the new "Stalin Constitution," instead of by a show of hands in open meetings as heretofore at Soviet elections.

### Nominations in the Open

The candidates for the forthcoming elections, however, are chosen by a show of hands at open meetings of trade unions and other authorized nominating bodies. Hundreds of these meetings have nominated incumbent Soviet leaders beginning with Joseph Stalin—who was nominated by 1,564 such meetings—and including Premier Vyacheslaff Molotoff, L. M. Kaganovitch, Commissar of Heavy Industry; Klementy E. Voroshiloff, Commissar of Defense; Nikolai Yezhoff, Commissar of Internal Affairs; Andrey Andreyeff, member of the Communist Political Bureau; Maxim Litvinoff, Soviet Foreign Commissar, and every other important figure.

November 25, 1937

# STALIN WINS POLL BY A VOTE OF 100%

## No Opposition Is Shown in Count of One Precinct in Area Where Leader Ran

## COUNT HELD UNEQUALED

By HAROLD DENNY

Wireless to THE NEW YORK TIMES.

MOSCOW, Dec. 13.—Fully 95 per cent of the Soviet Union's voters cast ballots in the election of the Supreme Soviet yesterday, it was announced today by the Central Election Commission on the basis of preliminary estimates. Late tonight the commissioners, still tabulating the ballots, said they would have no additional information before tomorrow.

As the Stalin ticket was the only one in the field, it is evident that nearly every able-bodied man and woman over 18 years old responded to the most powerful campaign to "get out the vote" ever conducted. It is unthinkable that very many scratched their one-man tickets.

The returns were being hurried to the election commissions today throughout the Soviet Union by every form of conveyance, including 200 airplanes and 100,000 automobiles and trucks.

### Write Praise of Stalin

It was disclosed today that most of the voters in the "Stalin district" of Moscow, which the leader had chosen as his own constituency among the hundreds originally nominating him, wrote on the envelopes in which the ballots were sealed such phrases as "Hurrah for Comrade Stalin!" "Long live Comrade Stalin!" and "Best wishes to you, Comrade Stalin."

The whole election procedure is being carried out to the last with the same meticulosity as if a real election contest were being waged.

Pravda today carried the following description of the ceremony of counting the ballots in the Seventy-fifth Precinct of the Stalin district, where every elector voted and voted for Stalin, who, of course, was unopposed for the Soviet of the Union:

"Midnight has struck. The twelfth of December, the day of the first general, equal and direct elections to the Supreme Soviet, has ended. The result of the voting is about to be announced.

"The commission remains alone in its room. It is quiet, and the lamps are shining solemnly. Amid the general attentive and intense expectation the chairman performs all the necessary formalities before counting of the ballots—checking up by list how many voters there were and how many have voted—and the result is 100 per cent. 100 per cent! What election in what country for what candidate has given a 100 per cent response?

"The main business starts now. Excitedly the chairman inspects the seals on the boxes. Then the members of the commission inspect them. The seals are intact and are cut off. The boxes are opened.

"It is quiet. They sit attentively and seriously, these election inspectors and executives.

"Now it is time to open the envelopes. Three members of the commission take scissors. The chairman rises. The tellers have their copybooks ready. The first envelope is slit. All eyes are directed to it. The chairman takes out two slips—white [for a candidate for the Soviet of the Union] and blue [for a candidate for the Soviet of Nationalities]—and reads loudly and distinctly, 'Comrade Stalin.'

**Everybody Up Applauding**

"Instantly the solemnity is broken. Everybody in the room jumps up and applauds joyously and stormily for the first ballot of the first general secret election under the Stalinist Constitution—a ballot with the name of the Constitution's creator."

The account goes on to tell of the ovation that greeted the announcement of each Soviet of the Union ballot—every one for Stalin.

The official press today called the election a victory of the "bloc of party and non-party Bolsheviki," which was stressed heavily in the latter days of the drive to get out the vote. This emphasis that many candidates loyal to the regime were not members of the Communist party was in harmony with Stalin's announcement about two years ago that there were good Bolsheviki outside the party as well as within it.

December 14, 1937

## 700,000 SCRATCHED THE SOVIET BALLOT

### Proportion Higher Than Was Expected—98 Per Cent Voted 'Stalin Ticket'

Wireless to THE NEW YORK TIMES.

MOSCOW, Dec. 17.—There was an opposition vote, after all, in the Soviet general elections last Sunday, although it was probably smaller in proportion to the total number of votes cast than in any other large national election ever held.

Fuller election statistics made public today show a total of 1,334,124 votes were "scratched"—that is, the name of the candidate was crossed out. Except for very few districts there was only one candidate in each, so crossing off the name was the only way a voter could protest except by staying away from the polls in the face of a strenuous drive. More than 2,000,000 votes were also invalidated in some manner.

The total of votes scratched, however, was probably almost twice the number of citizens who went to the trouble to protest in this manner against the "Stalinist ticket." Each voter voted for two candidates for the Supreme Soviet—one for the Council of the Union and one for the Council of Nationalities—so it is likely that most of the persons scratching one candidate scratched both. This would reduce the number of voters scratching to, say, 700,000.

Even this number was larger than most foreign observers here had expected. The Soviet press, however, hailed this as further proof of the Soviet masses' loyalty to the present regime. Izvestia calculated that of the voters 98.6 per cent voted for the Stalinist candidates for the Council of the Union and 97.8 per cent voted for the Stalinist candidates for the Council of Nationalities.

December 18, 1937

# A REIGN OF TERROR

## RUSSIAN REDS WAR ON PARTY 'HERETICS'

### Stalin Heads Drive Against All Who Fail to See Marxism in the Official Light.

### SOME LEADERS UNDER FIRE

### "Masked Trotskyism" and "Luxemburgism" Are Chief Offenses Against "Party Line."

Wireless to THE NEW YORK TIMES.

MOSCOW, Dec. 18.—A new crusade against factions is now under way within the highest ranks of the Communist party after a period of calm and apparent harmony. The campaign, accompanied by verbal bombshells and broadsides, is resulting in expulsions from the party, and Joseph Stalin is Commander-in-Chief of the offensive.

The moot point is the correct interpretation of the history of the Communist party before the revolution and just after it. The trouble started with the publication last March of an article in the magazine, Protection of the Revolution, by Anatole Slutsky, discussing Lenin's position in relation to the German Social Democrats.

**Stalin Scores "Liberalism."**

But nothing came of it until November, when Stalin published an article in the magazine, Bolshevik, charging that a spirit of "rotten liberalism" was tainting the minds of certain Bolsheviki and, more particularly, that Slutsky was heretical in intimating that there was anything wrong with Lenin's Bolshevist behavior.

Stalin said further that such an article was evidence of the existence of Trotskyist tendencies within the party, masked under the cloak of seemingly orthodox views. This sort of thing Stalin termed "masked Trotskyism" and the holders of the refractory views "Trotsyist contrabandists."

Now, with the regional Communist party conferences under way and the national conference in the offing, Communist leaders are following Stalin's signal by denouncing "Trotskyist contrabandists" in speeches and in the press. In a recent address before the Institute of Red Professors, Lazar Kaganovitch, one of Stalin's right-hand men and a member of the Communist Political Bureau, severely criticized any deviations from that intangible thing called the party line.

He said the class struggle was still going on in the corners of the country and, therefore, that merciless crushing of any heretical elements in the party was necessary in order to maintain a united front against the "class enemy." He also delivered a tirade against Emelyan Yaroslavsky and Karl Radek for incorrect interpretations of Communist history.

M. Radek was formerly an ally of Leon Trotsky, but has since recanted publicly many times, admitting an erroneous understanding of Lenin's principles and expressing his desire to conform to the party line. But it is interesting to note that M. Yaroslavsky, who is head of the Godless Society and one of M. Trotsky's bitterest enemies, is now himself under fire for masked Trotskyism.

M. Kaganovitch also attacked "Luxemburgism," an interesting new disease attributed to those who attempt to justify their stand by citing the career of Rosa Luxemburg, spectacular German revolutionist. M. Radek has asserted that she acted as a bridge to bring over the masses to communism.

M. Kaganovitch counters that they need no bridge and that it is precisely because Fraulein Luxemburg was so near to the Communists that her errors must be exposed mercilessly. This illustrates one of the reasons for the seemingly unimportant wrangles and hair-splittings among the Communists.

**Absolute Harmony Demanded.**

They hold that only by a full understanding and correct interpretation of Communist history can the foundation for future progress be laid and mistakes avoided both in developing Russia and in furthering world revolution. Another reason for jumping on dissenters is to eliminate warring factions which hold up progress by quarreling and giving "class enemies straws to seize upon."

Expulsion from the party and from the Institute of Marxist History has been the penalty of Comrade Slutsky and of many lesser lights for their "rotten liberalism." That punishment means something in a country where to be a Communist is one of the highest honors. So far criticism has been the sole punishment of others—for instance, Eugene Preobrezhensky, an eminent Marxist theoretician and co-author with Nicolai Bukharin of "The A B C of Communism."

Foreigners, whose ears are untrained in the music of Marxian dialectic and Bolshevist doctrine, cannot hope to hear the subtle shadings which cause such intraparty strife. The most interesting thing to them is the importance attached to these differences and the punishment meted out to those whose tone is slightly off the official key.

December 20, 1931

# COMMUNISTS EXPEL 24 SOVIET LEADERS FOR PARTY 'TREASON'

Zinovieff and Kameneff Said to Have Known of a Plot to Re-establish Capitalism.

By WALTER DURANTY.
By Wireless to THE NEW YORK TIMES.

MOSCOW, Oct. 11.—Gregory Zinovieff, long a holder of high Soviet offices; Leo Kameneff, brother-in-law of Leon Trotsky, and eighteen less known Communists were expelled by the Communist party today as "traitors to the party and the working class for trying to form by underground ways a counter-revolutionary organization to re-establish capitalism in the U. S. S. R."

Four others, of whom the best known is Nicolay Uglanoff, who formerly held a high position in the Moscow party organization, were expelled for tacit participation and aid to the "conspiracy," as the newspaper Pravda terms it.

**Had Pledged Loyalty to Party.**

M. Kameneff and M. Zinovieff are not accused of active participation in the plot, but it is charged that they received counter-revolutionary documents and were in touch with the movement despite their promise three years ago, on their readmission to the party, to give unswerving loyalty. They had been expelled as followers of Leon Trotsky.

Pravda says the plotters who violated their pledge deserve no mercy. The expelled Communists belong to the Right and Left sections of the intraparty opposition, which corresponds significantly to the attempt M. Trotsky is now making abroad—especially, Pravda states, in Poland—to unite all former Communist opposition groups under his own banner.

As in the case of previous opposition movements, the conspirators tried to capitalize the immediate difficulties of the Soviet, and declared the farm and collective system proved a failure. They demanded a return to kulak methods of individual farming and "a transfer to capitalists as concessions of enterprises created by the heroic labor and enthusiasm of the working class." This would have gone further than the New Economic Policy (Nep).

**Dangers in "Defeatism."**

Leaders of the party held that these "defeatists" were wrong and merited punishment, especially because the agrarian revolution of the past three years has been carried out with so much difficulty and involved so much loss that any weakness of nerve or attempt to impair party unity is nothing less than treachery.

"Either you are building socialism or not," it was said, "and why wail over broken eggs when you try to make an omelette?"

October 12, 1932

# FORMER FOES SEEK PEACE WITH STALIN

Bucharin, Rykov and Tomski Confess Error in Regard to Industrialization Need.

PRAISE SPIRIT OF CHIEF

But Only Bucharin Appears to Have Convinced Party of His Complete Sincerity.

By WALTER DURANTY.
Wireless to THE NEW YORK TIMES.

MOSCOW, Jan. 20.—A strange and peculiar Bolshevist ceremony occurred at a recent meeting of the Central Committee of the Communist party in the shape of formal "peccavi" speeches by three leaders of the former Right Opposition, Nicolai Bucharin, Alex Relykov and M. Tomski, which subsequently were pupblished in the Pravda.

As a result, M. Bucharin was adjudged to have atoned for his earlier errors, but MM. Rykov and Tomski are still held to be wanting and have received sharp warning to watch their steps most carefully in the future. Superficially, all three speeches were much the same: They confessed grievous misjudgment of the agrarian situation five or six years ago and failure to realize the need for intensified industrialization and voiced full present adherence to the party policy, giving almost fulsome praise to its guiding spirit, Joseph Stalin. Last, but not least, all three agreed to the present Kremlin thesis that the fight for rural socialization had produced something like a "state of war"—that is, class war—wherein any opposition was equivalent to high treason.

M. Bucharin specifically stated that some oppositionists had attacked the "barracks régime" of the Kremlin, but said he considered the Kremlin's forcefulness justified by the acute character of the class struggle.

**Replies Unsatisfactory.**

Read more carefully, however, it appeared that M. Bucharin had honestly convinced himself of the Kremlin's rightness and his own error, whereas the "true meat of doctrine," as old Scots theologians used to say, was lacking in his colleagues.

M. Bucharin's exposition of how he reached the conviction that M. Stalin and his supporters had "become" leaders by a sort of natural logical development of circumstances was worthy of the Athanasian Creed. M. Rykov, on the other hand, made a clever forensic defense which seemed to lack sincerity and once or twice seemed to verge on sarcasm.

M. Tomski's speech sounded genuine, and in places rose to touching eloquence, but he, too, failed to convey the impression that he really was sure the party majority had been correct throughout. His rebuke to those who said he had been backward in confessing error was:

"Do you think it a light matter for a veteran Bolshevist revolutionary like me to admit I was false to the ideals of the revolution—that such things are said easily, with smiling lips?"

This was as striking as his bold explanation of why he had attacked M. Stalin, "not from doubt of his personal character of devotion to the Communist cause, but because I believed it my duty to point out his errors of policy."

**New Opposition Assailed.**

Although all three disavowed connection or sympathy with the new opposition, which they heartily condemned, it is interesting to note that they and, for that matter, the Kremlin spokesman also seem to take for granted that these periodic outbursts of intra-party opposition are, in a sense, an expression of resistance to anti-Socialist forces in the country which somehow influence the weaker vessels, even among the elect of the Central Committee. Here, again, there is a curious parallel with theology, as if the spirit of anti-socialism had become personified like Saint Paul's devil and was always seeking to corrupt those whose faith was not wholly pure.

What seems the simpler explanation is that intra-party opposition is a more or less natural reflection of partial popular discontent reminiscent of the days when the children of Israel "murmured" against Moses in the wilderness and longed for Egypt's lost fleshpots.

The Russians can see the promised land of socialism near before them, but up to the present moment its quest has brought much hardship, while the "milk and honey" are still to come.

January 22, 1933

# SOVIET ABOLISHES ITS SECRET POLICE

Judicial Powers of the Ogpu Are Given to Regular and Military Tribunals.

NEW BODY REPLACES IT

By HAROLD DENNY.
Special Cable to THE NEW YORK TIMES.

MOSCOW, July 10.—The Ogpu, the State secret police organization, was abolished tonight by a series of decrees from the Kremlin. In its place a new department of the government, the People's Commissariat of Internal Affairs, was created. Genrikh G. Yagoda, acting chief of the Ogpu, was named Commissar of Internal Affairs.

The chief change brought about by this reorganization is the transferring of the judicial functions of the Ogpu, which summarily tried suspects whom it arrested, to the regular courts and to the military tribunals.

Under the decrees, Commissariats of Internal Affairs are created in all component republics of the Soviet Union.

The new organizations are charged with making secure the revolutionary order and preserving the security of the State; protecting public property; registering all civil data, including births, deaths, marriages and divorces, and guarding the country's borders. They will also have charge of correctional labor camps, of fire protection and of handling exiles.

The collegium of the Ogpu—the division that tried the persons brought before it by the secret agents—is abolished by the decrees. The Commissariat of Internal Affairs and the local organizations under its authority are to carry on the investigating activities of the Ogpu. However, the new organizations must turn their evidence over to regularly formed courts "in accordance with the established law."

Matters involving the security of the State are to be referred to the Supreme Court of the U. S. S. R. Crimes such as espionage and the betrayal of the fatherland are to be tried before a military collegium of the Supreme Court or before military tribunals.

One significant section of the decrees provides for the organization in the Commissariat of Internal Affairs of a special body having the right to exile or imprison persons in labor camps for a maximum term of five years or to deport them from the U. S. S. R. by administrative order.

Additional courts will be formed in the ordinary judicial system to deal with cases heretofore tried by the Ogpu courts. A special Court of Appeals will be created having the right to reverse decisions of all other courts, including the Supreme Court of the U. S. S. R.

The decisions of this court in turn can be appealed to the Central Executive Committee of the U. S. S. R., thus giving final power into the hands of the highest officials of the Soviet State.

By tonight's decrees the new commissariat becomes, next to the Commissariat of Defense, the most powerful body in the Soviet Union.

July 11, 1934

# *Kiroff, High Soviet Leader, Slain; Assassin in Leningrad Is Arrested*

***One of Ten Members of Communist Political Bureau, the Real Ruling Power of Russia, Mourned by Country—Death Laid to 'Enemies of Working Class.'***

**By HAROLD DENNY.**

**Special Cable to THE NEW YORK TIMES.**

MOSCOW, Dec. 1.—The first assassination of an important political figure in the Soviet Union since 1918 occurred at 4:30 P. M. today. The victim was Sergei Mironovich Kiroff, a member of the Political Bureau of the Communist party, the group of ten which is the real ruling power of the Soviet Union. M. Kiroff was one of Joseph Stalin's principal aides.

He was shot and killed in the quarters of the Leningrad committee of the Communist party, the former Smolny Institute, which was the headquarters of the Bolshevist revolution when Nicolai Lenin lived there and directed the overthrow of the Kerensky Government.

Few details of the crime have been given out. It was merely said that the assassination had been "instigated by enemies of the working class." The murderer has been arrested and his identity is being sought.

M. Kiroff was 46 years old. He had been a member of the Bolshevist party since 1904. He was a revolutionary leader in Tomsk, Siberia, and conducted an underground printing shop for circulating revolutionary literature.

He was arrested in 1905 at the time of the famous December revolt, which was suppressed with great bloodshed. He served five years in prison and afterward worked in Irkutsk and Vladikavkaz. He took a leading part in the Bolshevist revolution and served in the Red Army from 1918 to 1920 during the civil war.

After the civil war he served as secretary of the Communist party in Transcaucasia. Since 1926 he had been secretary of the Leningrad regional party committee and secretary of the Northwestern bureau of the central committee. He was a member of the presidium of the central executive committee of the government.

December 2, 1934

# SOVIET ARRESTS 71 IN WAR ON 'TERROR'; BARS MERCY PLEAS

**Speedy Trial Ordered for All With Appeal From Death Sentences Suspended.**

**By HAROLD DENNY.**

**Special Cable to THE NEW YORK TIMES.**

MOSCOW, Tuesday, Dec. 4.—Spurred by the assassination of Sergei M. Kiroff, the Soviet Government has struck its heaviest blow in years at those whom it regards as plotters of terroristic acts against Soviet officials.

With dramatic suddenness it was announced early this morning that seventy-one persons had been arrested and haled to trial before the military collegium of the Supreme Court of the Union of Soviet Socialist Republics. Thirty-two of these were seized in the Moscow region and thirty-nine in the Leningrad region. They are stigmatized as "White Guards" and accused of plotting terroristic activities.

Stern action was also taken against Leningrad officials of the Commissariat of Internal Affairs for alleged negligence making possible the assassination of M. Kiroff. F. D. Medved, Chief of Internal Affairs in Leningrad, was summarily removed. He was replaced temporarily by J. Agranov. M. Medved's assistant, F. T. Fomin, and six other responsible officials also were removed. All will be brought to trial.

The government announced other drastic measures to nip in the bud any further attempts on the lives of officials.

By the terms of a decree adopted by the central government immediately after the Kremlin received the news of M. Kiroff's death, terrorists and plotters are to be tried swiftly and to be executed immediately without opportunity for appeal.

This decree, to which the government gave the fullest publicity yesterday, modifies the existing judicial procedure in all cases of terrorism. Its principal provisions, as stated in the official communiqué, are as follows:

"Investigation of terroristic acts, whether planned or actually carried out, shall be conducted speedily.

"Execution shall not be postponed when clemency is asked by criminals of this classification, because the presidium of the Central Executive Committee of the U. S. S R. deems it impossible to consider such appeals.

"Departments of the Commissariat of Internal Affairs concerned shall carry out the execution of criminals in this category without delay."

December 4, 1934

# ZINOVIEFF AND 18 GET PRISON TERMS

**Ex-Leader of the Communist International Sentenced to Ten Years, Kameneff Five.**

**By HAROLD DENNY.**

**Special Cable to THE NEW YORK TIMES.**

MOSCOW, Jan. 17.—Gregory Zinovieff, a former president of the Communist International, was sentenced in Leningrad today to ten years' imprisonment as the organizer of a counter-revolutionary effort against the present Soviet Government. Lev Kameneff, a former Vice Premier of the Soviet Union, was sentenced to five years' imprisonment as a less active counter-revolutionary.

The other seventeen members of the so-called Moscow Centre who went on trial were also sentenced to prison terms varying from five to ten years.

Seventy-eight others, whose cases were considered by a special council of the Commissariat for Internal Affairs [which replaced the Ogpu, Soviet secret police], have been exiled—forty-nine to concentration camps and twenty-nine to administrative exile, that is, to exile in specified towns where they will have limited freedom. Thirteen women are among the seventy-eight.

**Others in the Group.**

Their number also includes G. I. Safaroff, A. P. Zalutsky and I. V. Vardin, who were arrested at the same time as M. Zinovieff and M. Kameneff. M. Safaroff gave damaging testimony against the Moscow Centre, which evidence was used in the Leningrad trial just concluded.

Most of the ninety-seven persons convicted today were members of the Communist party up to the time of their arrest, and all were listed as members of the Trotsky-Zinovieff opposition.

Thus today, although it added no names to the list of 117 persons executed since the assassination of Sergei Kiroff on Dec. 1, completed the final and catastrophic downfall of M. Zinovieff, M. Kameneff, G. E. Yevdokimoff and others who were once intimate friends of Nikolai Lenin and who were revolutionists in the days of the Czar and Alexander Kerensky.

It brought to a bloodless climax the greatest purge within the Communist party since 1927, when Leon Trotsky was driven out of the party and into exile after he had matched strength with Joseph Stalin.

About 1,500 persons who had thrown in their lot with M. Trotsky, including M. Zinovieff, M. Kameneff and others among those sentenced today, were expelled from the party then for accepting M. Trotsky's thesis that a Socialist revolution must be world-wide and could not be made successfully in a single country. Nearly all of those persons, including M. Zinovieff and M. Kameneff, subsequently recanted and were readmitted to the fold. About 2,500 others avoided expulsion by formally repudiating the Trotsky-Zinovieff opposition.

The decision of the court in Leningrad upheld the accusation in the indictment that the nineteen defendants composed a counter-revolutionary group headed by M. Zinovieff in Moscow and, furthermore, asserted the belief that the Moscow group guided the Leningrad Centre, fourteen of whose alleged members, including Leonid Nikolaieff, the assassin of M. Kiroff, were executed as terrorists on Dec. 29.

**Evidence of Dead Men Cited.**

The decision cited testimony by some of those who have been executed that the Moscow Centre had tried repeatedly to organize a bloc to oppose actively the present régime. However, it absolved M. Zinovieff and his companions of actual responsibility for the assassination of M. Kiroff in the following words:

"The court investigation has not established facts justifying the conviction of members of the Moscow Centre as the instigators of the murder of Kiroff. The investigation has fully proved, however, that members of the counter-revolutionary Centre knew of the terroristic attitude and encouraged it."

Those besides M. Zinovieff sentenced to ten years in prison are A. M. Gertik, A. S. Kuklin and M. Sakhoff. Those sentenced for eight years are M. Yevdokimoff, who confessed fully in the court and testified against his companions; J. V. Sharoff, M. Y. Bakayeff, I. S. Gorsheni and N. A. Tsarkoff. Six-year terms were imposed on G. F. Feodoroff, A. V. Hertsberg, S. M. Hessen, I. I. Tarasoff, A. V. Perimoff, A. I. Anisheff and L. J. Faivilovich. Five-year terms were given to A. F. Bashkiroff and B. L. Bravo. The property of all of them was confiscated.

Today's decision was the first by a military tribunal since the round-up began, following the assassination of M. Kiroff, that brought no death penalties.

January 18, 1935

# STALIN DISSOLVES REDS' 'OLD GUARD'

## No Explanation Is Given for Disbanding of Society of Old Bolsheviki.

## GROUP ONCE HELD IN AWE

By HAROLD DENNY.
Special Cable to THE NEW YORK TIMES.

MOSCOW, May 26.—A unique and picturesque organization, the Society of Old Bolsheviki, many members of which had been in jail or exile under the Czar, was dissolved today by a decision of the Central Committee of the Communist party, of which Joseph Stalin is the leader.

No reason was given for the dissolution, but the text of the party decision says the society in a plenary session decided it should be dissolved. Membership in the society had been restricted to persons who had been members of the Communist party continuously since before the 1917 revolution.

Thus it constituted a sort of Bolshevist "Old Guard" devoted to basic communistic principles, since it had sacrificed and fought for them before bolshevism triumphed here. The membership included M. Stalin, President Mikhail Kalinin, Foreign Commissar Maxim Litvinoff and other famous veterans, but as it numbered about 600, the majority of its members was not prominent in Soviet affairs.

**Organized Thirteen Years Ago.**

The society, organized in 1922 with 200 members, rapidly grew in strength and influence. It conducted benevolent activities for needy members, and among its objects was "to establish opinion on current problems from the viewpoint of long revolutionary experience and to impress young workers and students with the traditions of old revolutionaries."

Old-fashioned as many of them no doubt became in the industrialized society for which their revolution had laid the basis, they occupied conspicuous posts of honor in the Soviet State.

Originally they had their headquarters in the Kremlin, but later they were housed in their own building in Moscow. They had their own publishing house, theatre, museum and libraries, and there were branches in many large cities throughout the Soviet Union. A committee including Andre Andreyeff, former Commissar for Transportation, and Emil Yaroslavsky, head of the League of Militant Atheists, was appointed to dispose of the society's property.

**Check-Up on Reds Ordered.**

Another interesting action of the Communist party today was to order a careful check-up of members before the forthcoming issuance of new membership identification cards to replace the old ones. According to Pravda, chief Communist party organ, a shocking carelessness in keeping membership records has been found in many places, with the result that hundreds of disloyal and questionable elements have crept in.

"It must be remembered that the Soviet Union is encircled by capitalism," says Pravda. "Spies, terrorists and deceivers, sent by the secret service of certain countries, try to use their poisoned weapons. There are still hidden counter-revolutionary Trotskyists, White Guards and Zinovieffists. It must be remembered that they attempt to enter the party ranks to strike at the proletarian cause. The party must be put in order."

May 27, 1935

# SOVIET INDICTS 16 AS A TERROR BAND GUIDED BY TROTSKY

## Zinovieff, Kameneff and Four Others Already in Prison Are Among the Accused.

By The Associated Press.

MOSCOW, Aug. 14.—The Soviet Government charged tonight that its former War Commissar and revolutionary zealot, Leon Trotsky, sought to foster a rebellion from his Norway exile. The government jailed ten of his asserted colleagues and indicted, besides these, six persons already in prison.

Direct responsibility for the assassination of Sergei Mironovitch Kiroff, colleague of Joseph Stalin, was attributed to Mr. Trotsky, Leon Kameneff and Gregory Zinovieff. Mr. Kiroff was slain in 1934.

The three, most powerful enemies of Stalin in his fight for power after the death of Nikolai Lenin, were charged with planning a campaign of terror and attacks upon leaders of the Soviet régime.

**Trotsky Declared Leader**

The government asserted that under "the direct direction of Trotsky and the leadership of the so-called united centers, the Trotsky-Zinovieff gang, prepared a number of terroristic actions against Communist leaders."

"Trotsky sent five agents from abroad into the Union of Soviet Socialist Republics," the government charges.

The communiqué did not name the leaders against whom the new plot allegedly was directed.

Both Mr. Kameneff and Mr. Zinovieff now are serving ten-year prison sentences for counter-revolutionary activities coincident with the assassination of Mr. Kiroff. Bitter opponents of Stalin in party councils, Mr. Zinovieff and Mr. Kameneff joined with him to direct the nation after the death of Lenin in 1924.

August 15, 1936

# BOLSHEVIK LINKED IN PLOT ENDS LIFE

## Tomsky, Head of the State Publishing House, Named by Prisoners at Trial.

## DEATH FOR 16 DEMANDED

## The Prosecutor Exhausts His Vocabulary Reviling Accused, Who Break in Ordeal.

By HAROLD DENNY
Special Cable to THE NEW YORK TIMES.

MOSCOW, Aug. 22.—Mikhail Tomsky, whose alleged connection with the Trotskyist bloc was under investigation by Soviet authorities, committed suicide today at his country house at Bolshevo, near Moscow, it was announced here tonight.

The announcement was made at the close of the night session in the trial of Gregory Zinovieff, Leon Kameneff and fourteen others accused of plotting to kill Joseph Stalin and other Soviet leaders. No further word was heard in regard to Nikolai Bukharin, Karl Radek, Alexei Rykoff and the two other "Old Bolsheviki" under investigation because their names as well as Mr. Tomsky's were mentioned by some of the prisoners on trial.

**Prosecutor Cows Prisoners**

Andrei Vishinsky, the prosecutor, completed this afternoon the State's case against the sixteen with a demand for the death penalty. He was so vehement the prisoners slumped back in their chairs and some buried their heads in their hands and wept for the first time since the trial began.

"The mad dogs must be shot—all sixteen of them," cried the prosecutor.

Then all evening these men in the expectation of death made their last statements in as dramatic courtroom scenes as can well be imagined. They were permitted to speak as fully as they wished. Even here there is free speech in the shadow of the executioner.

"I never interfere with last words," blandly said Chief Judge V. V. Ulrich, who has probably sentenced more persons to death than any other living judge, when one defendant asked how long he could talk. Only once did he interrupt a defendant, and he was reciting party history.

So these men, some of them fainting at times, others choked by sobs or stopping to wipe tears from their eyes, but upheld by the Russian talent for the theatrical, delivered their own funeral orations before a hushed audience of their enemies.

Before this long and moving scene each defendant in turn had declined Judge Ulrich's invitation to speak in his own defense. There had been not a single defense witness and no prosecution witness except the defendants themselves and two other confessed conspirators. By their own wish the defendants were not represented by counsel.

"The accusation against me is correct and just," said Zinovieff in a faint, high-pitched voice. "I have no intention of defending myself. I will only make a last statement."

**None Pleads Extenuation**

Kameneff and others replied similarly.

Their statements revealed a psychology incomprehensible to most Western minds. Although their sentences have not yet been passed, none tried to lighten his confessed guilt or plead extenuation. Only two, T. Bakaieff and R. Pickel, revealed the faintest hope that their lives would be spared.

Of the six who spoke tonight, all the rest declared they must bare their souls of everything in their last hours. Moved both by emotion and a sense of drama they confessed their sins sobbingly, like camp-meeting converts, and applied to themselves more scathing epithets than Mr. Vishinsky had used. The prosecutor sat silent while the defendants further clinched the cases against them, if that was possible.

Often the mutual hatred of this ill-assorted group, who had united only in hatred of the Stalin régime, flared up in bitter new accusations against each other.

"If we Trotskyists and Zinovievists had succeeded in winning power at noon, at five minutes past 12 we would have been fighting among ourselves for offices in the new administration," said S. Mrachkovsky, once a corps commander in Trotsky's Red Guard. "In these last hours of my life I am happy there is a Stalin and that he will continue to lead our country along the path of progress."

T. Reingold turned upon his fellow prisoners like a fury, denouncing Zinovieff and Kameneff as cowardly, lying hypocrites. He amplified his accusation that Trotsky had planned to defeat the Soviet Union war as a step to restoring himself to power.

"In 1931," said Reingold, "Zinovieff told me:

" 'We must admit Trotsky is right. We are for a defeat that will remove the present leadership even though it may cost us some land in the Far East. Stalin costs us more. We have plenty of land.' "

Bakaieff, who according to the alleged plot was to have been made head of the Ogpu and to have destroyed the actual assassins, strongly hinted Zinovieff murdered his private secretary, who is supposed to have committed suicide rather than carry out instructions to kill Stalin.

Almost hysterically Bakaieff cried that Zinovieff had ordered him, Bakaieff, to kill Stalin, with the words, "Let Stalin have Bakaieff's bullet."

"Now I realize that this was a sadistic phrase," sobbed Bakaieff. "I had been Stalin's pupil and worked hand in hand with him under his guidance. And so Zinovieff wanted me, Stalin's pupil, to be also his killer."

Today the levity that has been such a strange phenomenon in this assassination trial—levity in which even the prisoners joined—was completely gone. In its place in the prisoners' box there was brooding and despair.

August 23, 1936

# RUSSIA EXECUTES 16 IN ANTI-SOVIET PLOT

MOSCOW, Tuesday, Aug. 25 (AP).—Sixteen men convicted of a plot to overthrow Joseph Stalin and the Soviet Government have been executed, it was officially announced today.

A terse statement said the Central Executive Committee of the Soviet Union had declined an appeal for mercy and that all sixteen, convicted and sentenced early yesterday, had been shot.

The defendants—including Leon Kameneff and Gregory Zinovieff, once high in Bolshevist councils—had been sentenced to suffer "the highest measure of social defense—death before a firing squad."

All had confessed their participation in the plot, and many had even admitted they "deserved" death, in a series of self-accusations that even surpassed the prosecutor's charges.

No mention was made of where or how the executions were performed, nor why the action was so sudden. A previous announcement had said the men would have seventy-two hours of grace.

August 25, 1936

# SOVIET TERRORISM SEEN BY TROTSKY

## Exile Attacks the Constitution Plan Because All Opposition Is Crushed by Moscow.

## HARSH MEASURES LISTED

## Many Foreign Communists Are Among 300,000 Victims of Last Nine Months.

By LEON TROTSKY



HOENEFOSS, Norway, Aug. 15 (By Mail).—Wide publicity has been given by the press of America and the world to the preparations being made for a new Constitution in the Soviet Union.

The Soviet leaders have stated that this Constitution is going to be "the most democratic of all constitutions in the world," and that from now on elections are going to be carried out by universal, equal, direct and secret ballot.

A few press interviewers have asked whether, in view of the existence of only one party, the elections could truly be regarded as free. It is necessary to ask another question:

In what manner is the only party in existence preparing the constitutional reform?

The answer is: by unheard-of and uninterrupted acts of repression, not against the enemies of the Soviet Union but mainly against those elements which, while remaining absolutely loyal to the régime, find themselves in opposition to the top which it is impossible to depose or even to control.

### Repression Aids Bureaucrats

It is perfectly safe to state that nine-tenths of all the acts of political repression are serving not the defense of the Soviet State but the defense of the autocratic government and the privileges of the bureaucratic section within the State. Thus, the only political party in existence becomes the exclusive tool of the governing group.

Until recently, the "isolator"—the prison—has been regarded, next to the death sentence, as the severest form of punishment. The inhabitants of the political "isolators," since 1928, are in the main former members of the governing party who, without having in any way broken discipline, have taken a critical stand in relation to the governing group or Stalin personally.

However, the latest developments show that the "isolators," owing to their limited capacity and the high cost of their maintenance, are being rapidly replaced by concentration camps, where prisoners are forced to live under inhuman physical and moral conditions.

The concentration camps are now spread over the whole periphery of the country and are an imitation of the camps in Hitler Germany. Prisoners regard the transfer from an "isolator" to the concentration camp as a condemnation to slow death.

In consequence, during recent months in the Soviet Union, there have been numerous hunger strikes of political prisoners who thereby back their demand to stay in prison. The hunger strike, generally recognized as a last act of desperation, has now become the most common method used by political prisoners.

Taking as a basis for calculation the news published in the official Soviet press, during the last nine months far more than 300,000, possibly up to half a million, members have been expelled from the Communist party, and this form of "party cleaning" is being constantly developed further.

### No Work for Oppositionists

In the majority of cases, the expelled are arrested, one section being sent to concentration camps, the other into exile. Stalin's organ, the Pravda, of March 15, publishes instructions to local authorities, prohibiting them to give employment to political oppositionists.

In a country where the State is the only employer this decree means starvation to the victims. Hundreds of remote miserable hamlets in Siberia and Central Asia are inhabited by tens of thousands of former members of the Bolshevist party who are leading the life of Hindu pariahs. A single word of protest, the mere demand for work, will send them into concentration camps, into the worst form of katorga (hard labor).

Those who succeed in surviving their periods of imprisonment or exile receive a "wolf's passport," an identity paper that actually outlaws its bearer. No one will house him and he is condemned to the life of a homeless vagabond.

The object of all these measures is to break the spirit of these people, to force them into line with the official views, at least to make them pretend by an open declaration that they endorse the policy of the ruling power. By this method the bureaucracy hopes to be able, before the introduction of the "universal, secret ballot," to smother every spark of critical thought in the country and thereby to make sure that those types of plebiscites can be put into operation which are sufficiently well known to us in the history of present-day Germany.

The exiles are deprived of the privilege of corresponding with each other or with relatives. Families who remain in contact with the exiled relatives are in turn persecuted. Even mutual aid of the exiles is regarded as a crime.

### Many Foreign Reds Jailed

I have to add that in the Solovietsky "isolator" and possibly also in others a large number of oppositionist foreign Communists are kept in prison, Hungarians, Bulgarians, Rumanians, Poles and in general those nationalities whose governments are harldy expected to raise a protest.

Foreign oppositionists are simply condemned by the G. P. U. [secret police] as "spies." By this method the Moscow leadership of the Communist International is able to rid itself of all those members who have become disgruntled and critical.

I need not emphasize that I am fully aware of the gravity of my statements, and that I take the unqualified political and moral responsibility for them.

I suggest that an unbiased international commission, composed of trustworthy persons who have the confidence of the public and in particular of the workers' organizations, could find the means of investigating on the spot all these facts in order to bring into this matter absolute clarity.

In all countries are societies of Friends of the Soviet Union. If they are in fact composed of true friends of the Soviet people, and not of the ruling bureaucratic clique, it is their duty to raise with us a loud demand for such a commission.

August 30, 1936

# SOVIET TRIES RADEK AND 16 ON SATURDAY AS TROTSKY'S AIDES

## Former Moscow Commentator and Other Prominent Men Are Accused of Treason

## BUKHARIN LOSES HIS POST

By WALTER DURANTY

Special Cable to THE NEW YORK TIMES.

MOSCOW, Jan. 19.—Another great public treason trial will begin here Saturday, when Karl Radek, former Soviet commentator, and sixteen others will face the military collegium of the Supreme Court.

Simultaneously with the announcement today of the start of this trial it became known that Nikolai Bukharin, well-known Bolshevik, had just been removed from the editorship of Izvestia, Soviet Government organ. Since last Friday the name of Mr. Bukharin had not appeared in Izvestia as the "responsible editor" but had been replaced by the words, "Editorial Council."

Among those who will go on trial with Mr. Radek are Gregory Piatakoff, former Assistant Commissar for Heavy Industry; Gregory Sokolnikoff, former Ambassador to Great Britain, and L. Serebryakoff, former Assistant Commissar for Communications.

**Trotsky Again Is Linked**

In a communiqué announcing the trial Andrey Vishinsky, Attorney General, states:

"Investigation has established the existence of a 'parallel center' organized on Trotsky's instructions in 1933 in connection with the Trotskyist-Zinovieff center. Investigation has established that the parallel center on the direct instructions of Trotsky organized subversive terroristic groups in a number of enterprises especially important to national defense to carry out subversive and sabotage action and prepare terroristic acts against the leader of the Communist party and the Soviet Government."

The communiqué adds that the "parallel center" further engaged in espionage on behalf of foreign powers to ruin the Soviet military force, hasten armed aggression against the Soviet Union and dismember it and replace it by capitalism and bourgeois power.

Although only four of those accused are named as members of the parallel center, the others are declared to have participated in espionage, terrorist sabotage and conspiracy. Four of them—N. I. Muraloff, Y. N. Drobnis, A. A. Shestoff and S. M. Stroiloff— were mentioned in the sabotage trial of a German engineer at Novosibirsk, Siberia, and it is expected the charge of sabotage will play a prominent part in the trial, especially in regard to the chemical industry, of which Mr. Piatakoff was formerly chief.

The fact that the trial will be public and that the words "on the instructions of Trotsky" appear thrice in today's communiqué may be taken to indicate that Soviet authorities are convinced the recent unsatisfactory phenomena in important branches of industry, despite the general progress, have had an artificial origin of the gravest and most widespread character, closely connected with foreign enemies.

January 20, 1937

# SOVIET DOOMS 13; RADEK AND OTHERS GET 10-YEAR TERMS

## Sokolnikoff, Former Envoy to Britain, Among Four to Escape With Their Lives

## CONDEMNED ASSERT GUILT

By WALTER DURANTY

Special Cable to THE NEW YORK TIMES.

MOSCOW, Saturday, Jan. 30.—Thirteen of the seventeen defendants in the "Trotskyist" treason trial here were sentenced to death at 3:30 A. M. today. The four others, including Karl Radek and Gregory Sokolnikoff, received prison terms up to ten years.

Judge Vassily V. Ulrich, president of the military collegium of the Supreme Court, began the reading of the verdict at 3 A. M. with all in the courtroom standing. The reading lasted for thirty minutes. Then the Judge pronounced the sentences.

Radek and Sokolnikoff, although among the leaders of the conspiracy, were sentenced to ten years in prison, as was V. V. Arnold. M. S. Stroiloff, who had pleaded that he had engaged in espionage only under blackmail methods of Germans and did not know of a general plot, was sentenced to eight years. Radek and Sokolnikoff escaped the death penalty because, although admitting all the charges, they had not organized acts of terrorism or engaged in sabotage.

The thirteen men sentenced to death have seventy-two hours in which to appeal to the Soviet Central Committee for clemency.

Curiously enough, the best phrases in the "last words" of the "Trotskyist" prisoners yesterday were uttered by A. A. Shestoff, former coal mine manager, who had admitted he was the blackest scoundrel of the whole lot. In a bold, ringing voice Shestoff concluded his statement thus:

"I ask no consideration or mercy. No proletarian court can spare my life. I want only one thing—when I stand at the place of punishment. I want to wash away with my blood the dark stain of treason against my country."

The four principal accused, save perhaps Sokolnikoff, former Ambassador to Great Britain, likewise made no appeal for clemency. The court room was more crowded than ever before when Gregory Piatakoff, former Assistant Commissar for Heavy Industry, rose to speak with the same firmness and clarity as he had previously shown. Piatakoff devoted his last words to a refutation of Prosecutor Andrey Vishinsky's statement that he was still a Trotskyist.

He said his confession, although it had come very late—here he paused for nearly a minute—"too late for any good to result to me"—proved he had genuinely broken with Trotskyism. He affirmed that no pressure had been brought on him to confess, and he added with defiantly upraised head:

"No pressure in the world could make a man like me confess—nothing save sincere repentance. Therefore, I have a right to claim that I have broken with my evil past. Trotsky will doubtless deny everything and continue his action against the U.S.S.R., but I reject it.

"I stand before you crushed and covered with filth, deprived by my own crime of everything. I have lost my party, friends, family and myself, but"—here he turned direct to the prosecutor—"you have no right to deprive the court of knowing that I found at the end the courage to break completely with the past."

Radek's final speech produced a strange and not wholly pleasant impression. He dragged in somewhat unnecessarily the names of Nikolai Bukharin, former Izvestia editor, and General Vitovta K. Putna—both under arrest—as Leon Trotsky's conspirators and seemed to be trying to suggest in an ambiguous fashion that other centers of Trotskyist activity of which the authorities were ignorant still existed here.

**Misgivings Among Observers**

Then he went on with such a verbatim adoption of the whole thesis of the prosecution about Trotskyist activities in general as to provoke the thought that the trial might not, after all, be so genuine as it seemed. Several of the most experienced observers of Soviet affairs among the diplomats and reporters were led to question whether Radek's last words were not a final circuitous counter-attack, instead of an apology. Especially when he concluded:

"Trotsky has become the center of all the counter-revolutionary forces. There are people in this country who, from liberalism or any other form of dissatisfaction with the régime, may tomorrow become oppositionists and regard Trotsky as their leader. What is more, the Trotskyists in France, Spain and elsewhere are still dangerous, and Trotskyism still remains an instrument that may fire up war."

Sokolnikoff objected to two of Mr. Vishinsky's assertions—that the accused had perhaps not yet told the full truth and that they were a gang of bandits without a political basis. Radek had also attempted to refute the latter assertion. Sokolnikoff said he had made a declaration in 1926 that contained the basic idea of restoration of capitalism, and although the fourteenth Communist party congress had rejected it he had reverted to the same views in 1932.

**Mentions the Late Tomsky**

This, he said, had been the determining factor in his junction with the Trotskyists, although he was personally inclined to the "Right," and had been closely associated in 1935 with Mikhail Tomsky, who committed suicide last August while under investigation.

Sokolnikoff said the conspirators did have a political program but that the "logic of struggle" had led them fatally step by step to an alliance with outside anti-Soviet elements and finally to spying and treason on behalf of Fascist enemies without whose support their movement could not have existed.

"In their hands," Sokolnikoff concluded, "we became helpless tools. Nevertheless I feel I have broken now with Trotskyism because I gave honest evidence and told all."

L. Serebryakoff, former Assistant Commissar for Communications, said briefly that for twenty years he had been loyal and for three years a traitor because he had made a political error, which he had admitted in full.

M. S. Boguslavsky, former member of the presidium of the Moscow Soviet, followed—a strange little hunchback man of 60, who caused some unfeeling laughter among the audience by saying he would prefer to die a natural death and devote his remaining years to honest work that would atone for his sins.

He took up Sokolnikoff's phrase, the "logic of struggle," and asserted it had led Mr. Trotsky to fool the conspirators as they had fooled the authorities here. This, Boguslavsky said, gave him the right to say he was not a real criminal—again derisive laughter—and to beg the court's mercy.

**Recalls His Years in Czarist Prisons**

J. N. Drobnis, former secretary of the Moscow Soviet, also appealed for clemency on the grounds that he was an old party member who had spent six years in Czarist prisons and had thrice been sentenced to death.

N. I. Muraloff spoke his last words with soldierly courage and brevity, thus:

"I blame no one save myself for my part in this conspiracy. I have been a member of the [Communist] party since 1903, and for more than twenty years I was a loyal soldier of the Bolshevist party. For more than ten years I was a loyal soldier of Trotsky. That is my nature—I cannot help it—and I have no excuse to offer, nor do I care to ask for your mercy."

B. O. Norkin, former head of the munitions trust, begged for his life on a plea "to fight the agents of fascism, Trotskyism and the German Gestapo [secret police]." He spoke in a tone of emotion that aroused a murmur of contemptuous disapproval among the audience.

Stroiloff repeated his earlier assertion that he had been forced into espionage work by blackmail methods of his German connections abroad, that he had taken no part in terrorism and sabotage and knew little of the real motives of the conspiracy. He asked for his life on the ground of valuable services and inventions that had brought him the highest honors in the past.

The other defendants all asked clemency but said little of special interest, with the exception of Arnold, whose plea was at least original. He said:

"I was born illegitimately and remain illegitimate and have acted like an illegitimate. I admit it. But it is not my fault but the fault of Czarist society, which,. unlike the Bolsheviki, who do not recognize illegitimacy, never gave an illegitimate a chance of becoming decent citizen."

None of the accused beat his breast in self-condemnation or indulged in the fulsome praise of Joseph Stalin that disgusted observers at the previous trial. All spoke with dignity, restraint and courage and gave a genuine impression of telling the truth.

Nevertheless, it is a pity from the Soviet viewpoint that no documentary evidence was produced in open court, as a letter and a photostat copy of a letter from a Japanese envoy and, it is said, other important material held back for the secret session last Wednesday night. Moreover, Mr. Vishinsky in his speech Thursday made too many references to the secret session that had no convincing effect.

Taken all in all, however, the trial did "stand up" and should go far to justify Sokolnikoff's statement that Mr. Trotsky is now revealed before the workers of the Union of Soviet Socialist Republics and the rest of the world as an ally of fascism and a preparer of war and, therefore, definitely finished as a force of international importance.

January 30, 1937

# COUNCILS TO CURB SOVIET GENERALS

## New Military Groups Formed to Minimize Chances of Army Opposition

## LEAD DRIVE AGAINST SPIES

## Direct Recruiting and Training and Are in Supreme Charge of Defense Program

By The Associated Press.

MOSCOW, May 17.—Russia enlisted her great Red army of 1,300,000 men today in a fight against followers of Leon Trotsky and against "espionage and sabotage."

A Kremlin decree established supreme military councils to dominate the army in both its new task and its normal defense functions and to provide a check against army commanders.

The hitherto dominant army commanders will be members of the new councils, but their orders must be countersigned by at least one other member of the council who will have close contact with the Communist party.

Thus, no single officer is in supreme command of troops, an action designed to minimize chances of any opposition developing within the army.

**Result of Sabotage Trials**

Designation of the councils was seen as a direct outgrowth of the disclosures of sabotage and espionage set forth in the series of trials of confessed Trotskyist conspirators—who named the exiled revolutionary leader as chief conspirator, despite his repeated disavowal of all charges of seeking to foster overthrow of the present Communist régime.

Reorganization of the Red war machine was foreshadowed last week by the demotion of Marshal Mikhail Tuckachevsky, First Vice Commissar of War, whose name was mentioned in the January conspiracy trial.

The new councils will have supreme command in recruiting and training of all forces for national defense, and in control over civilian communications and labor which is connected with defense work—subject to the Commissar of War.

They are responsible solely for political education and the morale of troops, and are ordered to direct "the merciless struggle against the enemies of the people—spies, wreckers and diversionists."

They will have command of civilian gas and air defense, will recruit and train territorial and volunteer troops, direct sanitary operations, medical training, distribution of supplies and defense of military and private property.

The government announced also that millions of copies of a new spy manual would be distributed to aid every one in recognizing espionage acts by Soviet enemies.

The decree said "the War Council is the highest representative of the military power, and all troops and military establishments are subordinate to the councils."

**Similar to Early System**

The war council system is similar to the system used during the early years of the Russian revolution when a Red army was being welded under old Czarist officers. Then war councils were named to check on the activities of the army commanders.

Before the military decrees came the announcement that four more alleged sympathizers with Trotsky had been arrested.

The central committee of the Communist party charged the four —officials of the All-Union Council of Trade Unions—with bureaucratic mismanagement, embezzlement of State funds and sabotage of plans for protection of workers.

An official announcement said the trade unions would be reorganized, with an attempt to increase workers' interest in them.

In addition, a leading Soviet playwright, Vladimir Kirshon, and three of his associates were ordered tried on charges of criminal responsibility for wasting funds of the Copyright Union of Soviet Writers.

The accusations were linked with the recent removal of Henry G. Yagoda, once head of the Secret Police, from his post as Commissar of Communications.

Yagoda, who is under arrest, is charged with embezzlement of State funds. The government accused Kirshon of maintaining his divorced wife and children on rations provided by Yagoda.

It also is alleged that Kirshon took royalties from plays by dead or unprotected authors and paid them to associates, who in some cases used the money for elaborate parties.

May 18, 1937

# RED ARMY MARSHAL, ACCUSED, ENDS LIFE

## *Gamarnik Was Vice Commissar of Defense—11 More Russians Executed as Trotskyists*

MOSCOW, Tuesday, June 1 (AP).—Marshal I. B. Gamarnik, 43, Vice Commissar of Defense and one of the leading officials of the Communist party, committed suicide yesterday, the party central committee announced today.

The terse announcement said Marshal Gamarnik was involved with anti-Soviet elements in a plot against the government, but did not give details of the accusations against him. The Vice Commissar, who was head of the political department of the Red army, joined the Communist party in 1916 and played an important revolutionary rôle as War Commissar on the southern front. Subsequently he helped organize the Communist party in Odessa and Kharkov. He was appointed to the central committee in 1930.

The execution of eleven more persons accused of railway sabotage under the direction of a "Japanese intelligence organization" at Khabarovsk, Siberia, was disclosed yesterday, bringing to sixty-six the total executed during May in the Far East.

Those executed, all former railway officials, were convicted at a session of the military collegium of the Supreme Court on charges that they were "participants in a Trotskyist spy and terroristic organization which acted under the control and on the orders of a Japanese intelligence organization in the Far East."

June 1, 1937

# 8 SOVIET GENERALS DOOMED AS SPIES AIDING ALIEN FOES

## Military Court Sentences High Officers Speedily, Without Presence of Counsel

## TRIAL IS HELD IN SECRET

## All of Accused Are Said to Have Confessed Giving Data to a Foreign Power

By HAROLD DENNY

Special Cable to THE NEW YORK TIMES.

MOSCOW, Saturday, June 12.—Marshal Mikhail N. Tukhachevsky and seven other generals who had been high in the councils of the Red Army were sentenced to death by shooting yesterday at a closed trial on charges of treason.

The sentences must be carried out immediately under the law of Dec. 1, 1934, decreed after the assassination of Sergei Kiroff, Leningrad Communist leader. Under the same law no appeal is permitted, and neither a prosecuting attorney nor defense counsel was present at the trial.

A communiqué issued early this morning made no mention whether the sentences had yet actually been executed. Besides ordering death, the special session of the military collegium of the Supreme Court of the Soviet Union stripped the accused of all military titles, including Tukhachevsky's lofty one of Marshal of the Soviet Union.

Judge Vassily V. Ulrich, famous as the man who has sentenced

Times Wide World Photo.
M. N. Tukhachevsky

scores to death on charges of treason, espionage and wrecking, presided over the military court, composed of high-ranking generals.

**Reports All Pleaded Guilty**

The communiqué said that after the reading of the indictment all the defendants—who had previously confessed—pleaded guilty. The communiqué added that the court established that all eight had been in the employ of the "intelligence service of a foreign State carrying on an unfriendly policy toward the Union of Soviet Socialist Republics," that they had "systematically supplied military circles of that State with espionage information, committed sabotage for the purpose of undermining the power of the Red Army, prepared for the defeat of the Red Army in the event of a military attack on the U.S.S.R., and pursued the aim of dismembering the Soviet Union and restoring a government of landowners and capitalists in the U.S.S.R."

Nothing more of the proceedings was made public.

The eight officers sentenced to death were:

Marshal Tukhachevsky, former Vice Commissar of Defense, who had been slated to command the western front in the event of war.

General A. I. Kork, former commandant of the Frunze Military Academy.

General I. E. Yakir, former commander of the Leningrad military district.

General I. P. Uborevitch, former commander in White Russia.

General Robert P. Eideman, former head of Osoaviakhim, organization for training military reserves in various defense measures.

General B. M. Feldman, former chief of the personnel section of the general staff.

General K. V. Putna, former military attaché in London, Berlin and Tokyo.

General V. M. Primakoff of the Kharkov military district.

**Editorials Cry, "No Mercy"**

The official press in scathing editorials yesterday cried, "Down with traitors! No mercy to spies and betrayers!" and declared danger of a counter-revolutionary attack on the Soviet Union by imperialist powers was steadily growing. The vehemence of the press comment was at least equal to that shown during the Moscow treason trials of last July and January, which resulted in the shooting of twenty-one of the forty-three defendants.

There was complete quiet in Moscow, however. Except for long queues at newspaper kiosks, there was no evidence that the people were taking any great interest. The crowds on the streets went about their business as casually as ever. Popular reaction, if there was any, was one of calloused indifference.

The newspaper Pravda said yesterday:

"The Soviet people will try the band of spies in full harmony with Article 133 of the great Stalinist Constitution, according to which 'treason to the fatherland'—violation of the oath, desertion to the enemy, impairing of the military might of the State or espionage—is punishable with the full severity of the law as the gravest crime."

Calling the roll of the eight defendants, Pravda, which is the organ of the Communist party, referred to them as "the thrice-despised and hated names of the participants in this now crushed kernel of Fascist spies."

"Great and holy is the hatred of the toilers of our fatherland toward enemies of the people—spies, traitors, wreckers, all who wish to besmirch the prospering Soviet land with the foul boot of German and Japanese fascism," Pravda continued. "Scouts of the capitalist world do not receive and never will receive any mercy in our country.

"The reptile of Fascist espionage has many heads, but we will cut off every head, paralyze and sever every tentacle and extract the snake's venom. The vigilance of the Soviet secret service, the vigilance of the organs of the Commissariat of Internal Affairs, headed by Comrade Yezhoff, whose words harmonize with his actions, have interrupted the base activity of eight Fascist spies.

"This destruction of a military espionage group brilliantly shows the crisis and decline of the bourgeois secret service and proves that every new attempt to send spies and diversionists into the U.S.S.R. will be stopped in time. The Soviet secret service is becoming stronger. Let all spies, diversionists and murderers tremble. The Soviet secret service will show what it is capable of."

**Germany Is Suggested**

The foreign State to which the defendants were accused of giving State military secrets was not specifically named, but the Red Army's organ, Krasnaya Zvezda, pointedly asserted that preparations for aggression by Germany had greatly increased since the accession of the Nazi régime.

That paper declared the Red Army was still unconquerable and that "under the leadership of the party of Lenin and Stalin and under the command of its beloved People's Commissar, Marshal of the Soviet Union, Comrade Voroshiloff, the Red Army will go on to new victories."

Pravda derided German interpretations that the arrests and trials of leading Red Army figures revealed weakness in Soviet power. Instead, their detection, said Pravda, demonstrated the strength of the Soviet Union and the weakness of capitalist intelligence services.

June 12, 1937

# *Soviet Purge Cuts Young Communist Ranks; Eight High Officials Removed as Enemies*

By HAROLD DENNY

Wireless to THE NEW YORK TIMES.

MOSCOW, July 23.—The Soviet purge has taken a new turn into the field of youth training, it was disclosed today in an unexpected announcement that eight important officials of the Young Communist (Komsomol) organization had been removed for corrupting Soviet young people toward Troskyism and other heresies in order to use the youths for "criminal purposes."

While these criminal purposes were not specified, Mr. Dedikoff, head of the Department of Agitation and Propaganda of the Moscow City Communist party committee, said in a report on the dismissals that special attention was being paid to the work of Komsomol organizations in connection with the forthcoming secret elections under the new Constitution and to the struggle "against enemies of the people—Japanese, German, Trotskyists and Bukharinist spies and wreckers."

It is among the youth—reared under the Bolshevist régime and presumably indoctrined with Stalinism—that loyalty to the present régime apparently is soundest. Any attempt to sow the seeds of heresy among them naturally would be considered very seriously by the authorities.

The removed officials are Messrs. Feinberg, Ilyinsky and Lukyatoff, secretaries of the central committee; V. M. Bubekin, until recently editor of the Komsomolskaya Pravda, chief organ of the league; Andreieff and Vlinkoff, secretaries of the central committee of the Ukrainian Komsomol.

These men were publicly denounced today as "enemies of the people," which implies that they were arrested and accused of conducting hostile activities. Mr. Schorkin, secretary of the Moscow city committee, and Mr. Sidoroff, secretary of the Moscow district committee, also were removed for "displaying impermissible political carelessness."

Under the heading "To Uproot Completely Agents of Enemies in the Komsomol," the Komsomolskaya Pravda today declared:

"Recently exposed spying and wrecking gangs of Trotskyists, Bukharinists and other hirelings of Fascism had their agents not only in party, economic and State organisms but in the Komsomol organ as well. The enemies tried to get hold of the youth because the youth are less hardened in the class struggle, less experienced politically and less sturdy.

"By various treacherous provocative manoeuvres the enemies tried to corrupt the Komsomol in order to use the youth for their criminal purposes."

Fascist agents, Komsomolskaya Pravda went on, got in leading positions, especially in the Moscow Sverdlovsk and Azov-Black Sea regions, and tried to undermine Communist education of youth.

Mr. Klinkoff and Mr. Andreieff were accused also of attempting to corrupt the Young Pioneer organization, the Communist society for children.

July 24, 1937

# RUSSIANS ARE TOLD INFORMING IS DUTY

## People Are Exhorted to Watch Neighbors and 'Tell on' Them if Suspicious

## IMMUNITY IS SUGGESTED

By HAROLD DENNY
Wireless to THE NEW YORK TIMES.

MOSCOW, July 30.—The whole population of the Soviet Union was called on today to act as informers against suspicious neighbors in order to strengthen Bolshevist vigilance against spies and saboteurs and help the government "smoke out all Fascist agents and destroy them as mad dogs."

Citizens were reminded in a special article in Pravda, Communist party organ, that the new Soviet Constitution made defense of the fatherland a sacred duty and warned that failure to report any suspicious occurrence to the NKVD [the secret police] was a crime against the Soviet State and the Soviet people and traitorous to the fatherland. Scruples against betraying friends must be abandoned as philistinism.

That declaration in Pravda, which is the authoritative mouthpiece of the Kremlin, begins with a condemnation of "chatterers and over-curious people" who wittingly or unwittingly serve foreign intelligence services.

"It is the duty of the Soviet citizen to view his surroundings critically and to know well the people with whom he works or is friendly," Pravda continues. "The honest Soviet citizen must not only beware of spies; he must actively aid in the revelation of the undermining activity of agents of foreign intelligence services.

"No matter in what field the Soviet citizen works he must always be vigilant and always watch carefully for enemies and intrigues. The first duty of the Soviet citizen who has found the tracks of a spy or saboteur is immediately to warn the organs of State security.

"Some one in a neighboring apartment may have peculiar visitors and carry on anti-Soviet conversations with them. That should be reported to the organs of State security. Yet some people who are sunk in the mire of philistinism think differently. They do not like to 'tell on' a neighbor.

"If an acquaintance has committed a petty deception in his work they hush it up in order not to 'give up' a friend. This false conception of giving up and telling on must be done away once and for all.

"On the other hand, it must be remembered that only an honest admission of guilt to the organs of public safety will help the man who finds himself caught in a spies' net. While punishing the hardened criminal with all the severity of the law, the Soviet State will yet always help the man who became snared in a cobweb woven by public enemies."

July 31, 1937

# UKRAINE PREMIER SUICIDE

## Liubchenko Declared Involved in Anti-Soviet Activities

MOSCOW, Sept. 2 (AP).—The newspaper Pravda, official organ of the Communist party, announced today that Panas Petrovich Liubchenko, Premier of the Ukrainian Republic and an old-time Bolshevik, had committed suicide because he was involved in anti-Soviet activities.

Mikhail Bondarenko, an unknown in politics, was appointed Premier to succeed Mr. Liubchenko. Mr. Bondarenko is the son of a worker and was brought up in the Soviet ranks.

The execution of ten "Trotskyists" by a firing squad was reported from Leningrad following their conviction by a court martial. They were accused of injuring workers by their wrecking activities in a Leningrad factory.

September 3, 1937

# Soviet 'Cleansing' Sweeps Through All Strata of Life

## *Starting With Generals and High Leaders, Stalin's Purge Is Now Hitting Cooks and Nurses—People Getting Inured to Arrests*

By HAROLD DENNY
Wireless to THE NEW YORK TIMES.

PARIS, Sept. 12.—Dramatic and bewildering is the twelvemonth in the history of the Soviet Union that has just drawn to a close. It has been a year of considerable positive accomplishment, despite recessions in many key industries and disorganization of much of the Soviet economic and political machinery. But most of all it has been a bloody year, the bloodiest since the early years of the Bolshevist revolution.

It has been a year of startling contrasts. Early on the morning of Aug. 24, 1936, sixteen men, including the world-famous old Bolshevist leaders Gregory Zinovieff and Leo Kameneff, were convicted of plotting to assassinate the present Soviet leaders, from Joseph Stalin down, to seize power and betray the country to capitalism. They were led stumbling out forthwith to be shot.

On Dec. 5, 1936, the last Congress of Soviets tumultuously adopted Stalin's new Constitution, advertised by Soviet spokesmen as the most liberal and most democratic in the history of mankind.

Then, in March of this year, Stalin in a speech before the central committee of the Communist party demanded genuine democracy within the party, and at the same time in a little noted part of his speech he called for cleansing the country of all disloyal elements, which, though not realized then, was the signal for the wave of executions, imprisonments, dismissals and degradations that are continuing unabated to this day. The twelvemonth just concluded also brings the Soviet regime close to its twentieth birthday, for on Nov. 7 the country will elaborately celebrate the seizure of power by a little group of determined men, high among whose councils were leaders who now are dead at the hands of their one-time comrades or in jail awaiting whatever inglorious fate.

Thus now is an appropriate time to review the situation and weigh the possible reasons for this drastic and continuing purge. These possible reasons are beginning to emerge from obscurity. They are still regrettably vague and incapable of concrete proof in a land where the simplest affair is often veiled in semi-Oriental mystery, where in treason cases all but the "show trials" are held behind closed doors and their evidence not revealed, and where foreigners are now objects of suspicion, cut off to a large degree from personal contacts and compelled to live their lives in Moscow beyond an invisible pale.

Yet we have the Soviet press, which in recent months has been filled with amazingly frank information; we have eyes to see with and ears to hear with, and so, though much information is denied us, much filters through, and we do get the feel of things.

### The Hunt Goes On

The dead of this past twelve months—those names actually announced in the limited number of provincial newspapers reaching our Moscow desks—number many hundreds and the toll is increasing almost daily. The hunt for "spies, wreckers and diversionists" is now dredging into the humbler strata of the population.

Whereas a year ago the Soviet authorities were shooting the bearers of names famous in bolshevism and less than three months ago the greatest generals the Red Army had developed were executed, now the Government has got down to shooting cooks as terrorists because they put rotten meat in officials' stew, and women attendants in a nursery for poisoning children's foods for counter-revolutionary purposes.

In between the one-time leaders of a world revolution and the restaurant help lie those hundreds of big and little men shot for varying crimes, ranging from wrecking trains at the behest of foreign spies to abusing the peasantry and disrupting agriculture in order to discredit the Soviet regime and lay the basis for a return to capitalism.

Untold thousands more have been arrested in every part of the Soviet Union, one deduces from reading between the lines of the Soviet press, for arrests are rarely announced in so many words. Innumerable others have been dismissed from their jobs under circumstances that will militate against their getting desirable jobs again. And those expelled from the Communist party in recent months are legion.

### Fields Hit By the Purge

The Soviet purge is affecting almost every conceivable field of life.

Those that have already felt it include:

1. Old Bolsheviki, men who helped to make the revolution but fell out with Stalin on doctrinal issues or came to be regarded as politically untrustworthy, so that they were either accused of counter-revolution or shelved.

2. The Red Army, eight of whose greatest generals, headed by Marshal Mikhail N. Tukhachevsky, were executed last June on the amazing charges of selling military secrets to Germany.

3. The People's Commissariat of Internal Affairs (NKVD), which has taken the place and functions of the old Ogpu. Its higher ranks, from Henry G. Yagoda, the commissar, down, have been combed, and since the downfall of the sinister figure of Yagoda last Fall hundreds of its higher officials are reliably reported to have followed him to prison—a feature of the purge that apparently is popular with Moscow's general public.

4. The Commissariat of Foreign Affairs, a number of whose highest officials, including Nikolai Krestinsky and Leo M. Karakhan, assistant commissars, and three members of the Press Bureau, which includes the censorship, disappeared under circumstances suggesting their arrest.

5. The governing organs and Communist party leadership of constituent republics, notably White Russia, Georgia and the Ukraine, where there have been mass arrests and dismissals, together with suicides and executions.

6. The Communist party, from members close to the seats of power in Moscow to local officials in remote provinces.

7. The Young Communist League—charged with the vitally important task of educating Soviet youth in loyalty to the Stalin regime—many of whose leaders have been removed, some under the ominous accusation of being "enemies of the people."

**Reserve Corps Is Winnowed**

8. Osoaviakhim, organization containing millions of members devoted to training army reserves, whose former chief, General Robert P. Eideman, was one of the generals executed with Marshal Tukhachevsky.

9. Local agricultural administrations, from regional officials to chairmen of collective farms and agronomists, a number of whom have been shot recently for alleged anti-State activities.

10. Industries of all sorts, resulting in a general shifting of commissariats as well as numerous dismissals.

11. Railway transport, which alone has provided hundreds of firing squads with victims, especially in the Far East.

12. The State Planning Commission, which is the brain of this vast State-controlled economic organism.

13. Foreigners. There has been a general, though by no means complete, "liquidation" of foreigners in Russia. It started with citizens and former citizens of potentially hostile countries, such as Germany, Japan and Poland, and has spread to citizens of other countries with which the Soviet Union has no quarrel.

Most foreigners who had retained their foreign citizenship were simply asked to leave the country. Many foreign radicals, however, who had entered Russia and taken Soviet citizenship were arrested. The most notable of these was Bela Kun, one-time leader of the short-lived Soviet regime in Hungary. More than a hundred Hungarians he induced to take refuge in Russia are reliably reported to be under arrest.

**Communist International Hit**

Even the Communist International staff is reported to have been heavily raided and many of its German members put in jail. And now a young Englishman has been arrested in Leningrad on charges of espionage.

There has been a general clearing out of American and other foreign engineers. Some American engineers of high ability are still employed, however, in airplane manufacturing, radio installation and ice cream-making, in which the Soviet Union still desires foreign technical aid. These report they are receiving every courtesy.

Even this long list is incomplete. Inroads have been made into the fields of education, journalism, literature and drama, though apparently not on a mass scale. The editor of the Komsomolskaya [Young Communist] Pravda was among those denounced as "enemies." Another Soviet writer who has disappeared is accused of spreading Nazi propaganda, because in articles and books on Germany, on which he was an authority, he quoted from Adolf Hitler too fully.

The political director of the famous Moscow Art Theatre was brusquely removed, as were the director of the Mali Theatre and Natalie Sachs, internationally known director of the Children's Theatre. Even the Park of Culture and Rest has not been spared, a woman director and lesser executives having been removed, if not arrested.

**No General Breakdown Near**

So extensive a purge in so many fields would seem to indicate a general breakdown. But the significant thing is that it has not occurred and there is no reason now to believe it will occur. True, many industries are seriously lagging, but, ridden as they are with fantastic inefficiency, most of them are functioning fairly well by previous standards in the Soviet Union, and there is no reason to believe the country will not struggle through.

In any judgment of Russia one must bear in mind that the country itself is enormously large and enormously rich, with every essential raw material and adequate food supplies. It must be remembered also that the Russian people have enormous powers of resistance. They can "take it," else they would never have survived the frightful years through which they have passed.

One would think, too, that the waves of arrests, in which so many are losing relatives or friends, would stir up dangerous resentment. Worry is apparent in Moscow, but, strangely enough, the tension when I left Moscow a few days ago seemed less than it was immediately following the Tukhachevsky execution.

The people have become used to it. Their sensibilities have been dulled, and, I think, there is a certain fatalism in their attitude. Arrests are commonplace in Russia. The Russians have always been subject to political persecution, and being arrested is certainly no disgrace. The Russians appear to accept it with amazing equanimity.

Recently a simple artisan was arrested as he went with a card of introduction from one foreigner to another to do a job of manual work. He was turned over to the Secret Police, who, believing him an important spy, threw him in a cell with some intellectuals, similarly suspected. After two days and nights he was turned loose.

An American would have been hopping mad at such treatment, but not this Russky [Russian]. He was very cheery at the fact that he had got out at all and flattered at being enabled to associate with cultured company for the first time in his life.

September 13, 1937

# SOVIET ENDS PURGE IN RANKS OF PARTY

## Orders the Reinstatement of Thousands of Communists Wrongfully Expelled

## PURGERS NOW UNDER FIRE

By HAROLD DENNY

Wireless to THE NEW YORK TIMES.

MOSCOW, Jan. 18.—The High Command of the Soviet dictatorship suddenly called off the purge within the Communist party today. It issued a series of peremptory orders to the entire party organization throughout the country to reinstate thousands who had been expelled from the party and to restore their jobs to all who had been dismissed as a result of their expulsion.

These measures were adopted at a plenary session of the central committee of the party today and were transmitted to the country late tonight in a special radio broadcast. Joseph Stalin, of course, attended the session and took a dominant part in it.

Today's orders to the country, with their frank revelation of wholesale injustices operating to the detriment of the Soviet Union itself, as well as individual victims, appears to form a perfect parallel with Stalin's "Dizziness From Success" address in 1930.

In that address Stalin slowed down collectivization of the peasantry, confiscation of food products and liquidation of Kulaks (wealthier peasants) when the excesses with which those policies had been applied brought the countryside to passive revolt and laid the basis for the famine of 1932-33.

The report of the Communist party committee's session, officially broadcast tonight, frankly admitted that thousands and tens of thousands had been expelled from the Communist party en masse without consideration for individual cases and asserted, furthermore, that this ruthlessness had created discontent, playing into the hands of Trotskyists, who then enlisted unjustly expelled people into their own ranks.

The broadcast cited several instances of mechanical mass expulsions and set such things down to careerists in party posts who were willing to sacrifice dozens of their comrades to demonstrate what good Communists they were, making a show of "vigilance" to distract attention from their own shortcomings.

**Orders Action on Appeals**

The broadcast forbade further mass expulsions, ordered reinstatement in their jobs for all arbitrarily expelled, prohibited dismissals from jobs as a corollary to expulsions and ordered action on all appeals from expulsions within three months.

At the same time it became known tonight that the Supreme Court of the Soviet Union had held a plenary session at which unwarranted dismissals from posts were denounced as the work of public enemies. The Supreme Court ordered lower courts to prosecute administrators guilty of illegally discharging employes and to oblige organizations to pay illegally discharged persons for the time lost.

Authenticated cases of unjust dismissals from jobs or expulsions from the Communist party in the course of the Soviet purge are coming to light in great volume, with the consequent probability that some of the purgers will themselves be purged. These abuses have been perpetrated upon the government's incessant urging of the whole populace to "vigilance against Trotskyist-Bukharinist wreckers" and other malefactors. On the authority of the Soviet Union's premier official organ, Pravda, this vigilance has been perverted, as foreign observers here have long been convinced, by persons anxious to curry favor, to pay off private scores or to insure themselves.

The situation prompted Pravda to put Mikhail Koltzoff, one of this country's most brilliant journalists, to work on it. A month ago he published a feuilleton condemning silly exaggerations of "vigilance." This emboldened many citizens to send in details and examples of malice and stupidity.

Mr. Koltzoff draws the conclusion that much of this persecution is done by persons who themselves are enemies of the people and are trying to make a smoke-screen to cover their own crimes, and he adds significantly:

"The NKVD [Commissariat of Internal Affairs, or secret police department] will unfailingly get all those who, instead of giving honest assistance to the Soviet secret service try to create confusion and surround themselves with fog by slandering perfectly innocent people and depriving them of work."

Here are a few typical instances gathered by Pravda:

In the city of Ufa, in Eastern Russia proper, a student with a good work record and the son of a miner, was expelled from a pedagogical university because he once visited the apartment of a teacher later accused of being a bourgeois nationalist. Then the expellers demanded that the student's wife either divorce her husband or lose her party ticket. At first the couple considered getting a divorce. Then they became determined to fight. The wife was allowed to remain in the party, but with a severe reprimand; the husband has not yet been reinstated in school.

A young technician at a Sverdlovsk factory was fired because some one "exposed" the fact that he had somewhere at some time bought phonograph records from a man later accused as a wrecker. Other factory managers refuse to hire him lest they should get into trouble. Authoritative proofs that the technician has never had any traffic with wreckers have made no difference.

In the Novosibirsk region a man who had struggled with wreckers in a bread factory was expelled from the party for alleged concealment of his social origin and kinship with a wrecker. He denied the allegations and ascribed them to revenge motives. Meanwhile, his wife has also been expelled from the party and dismissed from her job; his sister in Saratoff has been expelled and dismissed likewise, and the expelling officials have even written to Leningrad University demanding that his son be expelled from school.

**Accused Criticized Officials**

The director of Perm University, who by many accounts is a highly efficient executive who has built up the institution, is accused of wrecking, double-dealing, shielding enemies of the people and undermining university work because, it is alleged, he criticized drinking and street-fighting of leaders of district Communist party committee.

Persons who cause unjust expulsions and dismissals belong in three categories, according to Mr. Koltzoff's analysis.

In the first are malicious letter writers, who use office time and office typewriters and interrupt office work to write slanders on coworkers or others, sending carbon copies of the letters to NKVD agencies or prosecutors. Such poison pen letters, says Mr. Koltzoff, are made up of rumors, suspicions or downright inventions. Some of these letter writers are themselves now being investigated, and Mr. Koltzoff states that many of them turn out to have very shady records.

The second category is composed of careerists who, having neither ability nor a desire to work, try to establish themselves as exemplars of vigilance by digging up all kinds of gossip, no matter how old.

The third type is the self-insuring bureaucrat who thinks it safer to expel or dismiss an honest man than stand up for him and consequently acts on every irresponsible or malicious accusation.

Today brought news of seven executions. One is of a drunken and reckless chauffeur who was shot after a long lethal career. Another is of a Siberian miner shot for wrecking. Five persons were executed in Tadjikastan, where they had been accused of wrecking agriculture since 1934.

All five had been officials of the Tadjikastan Agricultural Commissariat and all had been accused of participating in a Trotskyist counter-revolutionary plot. The leader, named Droznoff, the former head of the planning department, was alleged to have participated in Trotskyist demonstrations in Moscow and to have ridden with Leon Trotsky, Gregory Zinovieff and Leo Kameneff as evidence of his long connection with Trotsky.

January 19, 1938

# *21 Soviet Ex-Leaders Face Trial; Charges Include Murder of Gorky*

## *Rykoff and Bukharin Head List to Be Arraigned Wednesday—3 Doctors Accused in Deaths of Writer and 2 Officials*

By WALTER DURANTY

Special Cable to THE NEW YORK TIMES.

MOSCOW, Feb. 27.—The greatest and most startling of the Soviet treason trials will begin publicly in Moscow on Wednesday. The list of the twenty-one accused includes names that once stood highest in the Soviet land, but in addition to charges of espionage, sabotage, etc., there is a grim new accusation—of murder by doctors of such former eminence as L. G. Levin, former chief of the Kremlin Hospital.

It is charged that Dr. Levin, Dr. I. N. Kazakoff, noted endocrinologist and head of a large clinic, and Professor D. D. Pletneff, famous heart specialist, "organized and accomplished the nefarious murders of Menzhinsky [Vyacheslaff Menzhinsky, former head of the Secret Police], Kuibesheff [chief of Russia's first Five-Year Plan] and Maxim Gorky."

Mr. Gorky's personal secretary, P. P. Kruchkoff, figures among the list of the accused.

The list of the accused is headed by Alexei I. Rykoff, former Premier of the Soviet Union, Nikolai I. Bukharin, former editor of the government newspaper Izvestia, and Henry G. Yagoda, former head of the Ogpu and former Commissar of Communications.

Others facing trial are:

Nikolai Krestinsky, former first assistant to Foreign Commissar Maxim Litvinoff.

K. G. Rakovsky, former Soviet Ambassador to France and a long-time Bolshevik active in Russia's diplomatic affairs.

A. P. Rosengoltz, once Commissar of Foreign Trade.

Vladimir I. Ivanoff, former Chief of the Timber Industry.

Gregory T. Grinko, former Finance Commissar.

Akmal Ikramoff, former leader of the Uzber Soviet Republic, in Central Asia.

Faysulla Khodjaieff, former President of Uzbek, who was removed from office in June, 1937.

Mikhail A. Chernoff, former Commissar of Agriculture.

I. A. Zelensky, ex-head of Consumers Cooperatives.

S. A. Bessonoff, V. F. Sharangovich, P. T. Zubareff, P. P. Bulanoff and V. A. Maximoff.

The indictments are terrific and comprehensive. They state that a "conspirative group called the 'Right-Trotskyist bloc,' organized, on the instructions of foreign intelligence services of countries hostile to the U. S. S. R., for espionage, sabotage and terrorism, to rupture the Soviet military power for provocation of military attacks of the said countries against the U.S.S.R., for the ruin of the U. S. S. R., for the dismemberment of the U. S. S. R. and for the severance from it of the Ukraine and the republics of Armenia, Azerbaijan, Georgia and the Far Eastern maritime provinces for the benefit of the above-mentioned foreign countries and finally for the overthrow of the Socialist regime of the U. S. S. R. and the reestablishment of capitalism and the power of the bourgeoisie."

FORMER SOVIET LEADERS TO BE TRIED

Associated Press

Nikolai I. Bukharin

Times Wide World

Alexei I. Rykoff

**Depended on Armed Force**

The accused, it is stated, relied "exclusively upon the armed force of foreign aggressors to accomplish their aims." It is further stated that many of the accused have long been agents of foreign intelligence services of hostile powers and that their chief, Trotsky, "as now established, was connected as a spy with one foreign intelligence service as far back as 1921, and with another since 1926."

It is added that "some of the accused were provocators and agents of the Czarist secret police; it has been established that a majority of the leaders of the 'Right-Trotsky Bloc' carried on their hyphenated activities under the direct orders of Trotsky, Bukharin and Rykoff, according to plans broadly conceived and worked out by the general staffs of certain foreign governments."

"It is also established," the indictment adds, "that in addition to the murders of Kuibesheff, Menzhinsky and Gorky, with the aid of the doctors, the murder of Kiroff was accomplished by the decision of the Right-Trotskyist Bloc."

Then comes the most shocking accusation of all:

"In 1918, shortly after the Bolshevist revolution in the period of the negotiations of the Brest-Litovsk peace, Bukharin and his group of so-called Left Communists and Trotsky and his group, together with the Left 'Social Revolutionaries,' organized a plot against Lenin as head of the Soviet Government. Bukharin, Trotsky and other conspirators, as is evident from the materials of the present investigation, aimed at breaking the Brest-Litovsk peace treaty, upsetting the Soviet Government, arresting and killing Lenin, Stalin and Sverdloff and forming a new government from the Bukharinites, Trotskyites and Left Social Revolutionaries."

February 28, 1938

# *Bukharin Says He Led Coup Plot, Aiming to Set Up Fascist Regime*

## *Denies Part in Kiroff Murder—Yagoda Gives Lie, Charging Bloc Prepared Slaying*

By HAROLD DENNY

Wireless to THE NEW YORK TIMES.

MOSCOW, March 5.—Nikolai I. Bukharin, former member of the Communist Political Bureau, who after the assassination of Sergei Kiroff in 1934 demanded in a bloodthirsty editorial in Izvestia the destruction of all concerned in that crime, was called for the first time tonight as a direct witness in the treason trial of twenty-one men.

He assumed full responsibilty for all the crimes committed by the Rightist-Trotskyist bloc, even those in which he personally did not participate, because he was the head of that bloc.

[Mr. Bukharin, in explaining in the Moscow court his aims as a member of the Oppositionist bloc in Russia, said the kind of regime he sought was "fascism," according to an Associated Press dispatch from Moscow.]

He denied having been concerned in the plot to kill Mr. Kiroff who was the Leningrad Communist leader, and the plot in 1918 to kill Lenin, Joseph Stalin and Jacob M. Sverdloff, but Henry G. Yagoda, testifying for the first time at any length and admitting association with the Rightist conspirators, implicated Mr. Bukharin in the Kiroff murder.

Mr. Yagoda said flatly that Mr. Bukharin and Alexis I. Rykoff, former Premier, who also had denied participating in terrorist activities, had finally approved a plan to kill Mr. Kiroff, although they had both originally condemned it as too dangerous, as had Mr. Yagoda also.

Mr. Yagoda, incidentally, who was then Commissar of Internal Affairs, which includes the political police, accompanied Stalin, who obviously did not suspect him, on a hurried journey to Leningrad on the night of the assassination, Dec. 1, 1934, to investigate the affair.

Mr. Bukharin, though he admitted most of the charges against him, was a spirited witness. He replied to Andrey Y. Vishinsky's rapid-fire questions with equally rapid-fire answers, arguing points of fact and even insisting on telling something of his ideology as an Oppositionist and describing the steps whereby he—once revered as the great proletarian philosopher—now found himself in the prisoners' dock.

He did not beat his breast in self-denunciation as so many defendants have done in treason trials here. But he shot back the answer, "Yes, counter-revolutionary," to Mr. Vishinsky's query whether that was not his status and added more detail to the mosaic of treason, sabotage and conspiracy that the prosecution has built up.

### Would Restore Capitalism

The purpose of the Rightist group of which Mr. Bukharin confessed having been the leader was the restoration of capitalism in Russia, Mr. Bukharin asserted. Questioned by Mr. Vishinsky, he went on to say that his organization had intended to accomplish this by forcible overthrow of the Soviet Government, to be brought about by taking advantage of the government's difficulties, by means of a war in which the Soviet Union would be defeated and even by sacrifices of territory.

"In other words," Mr. Bukharin went on, "by dismemberment of the U. S. S. R., with the ceding of the Ukraine, the maritime provinces, White Russia, etc."

"To whom?" Mr. Vishinsky asked sharply, gesturing at Mr. Bukharin with his hand.

"To capitalist countries who are interested in those territories because of their geographical position—to Germany, Japan and, in a lesser degree, to England," Mr. Bukharin responded quietly, yet almost defiantly. "Wrecking was to be used extensively. This was mostly prompted by the Trotskyist section of the bloc.

"I did not do much personally about wrecking and sabotage, but I am naturally responsible for all because it was part of the work of the organization of which I was the leader. Personally I was occupied with general supervision and with the ideological side."

At another point Mr. Bukharin remarked that he did not know of many crimes because he was the leader, not the switchboard operator, of that organization.

### Takes Up Kiroff Murder

Mr. Vishinsky stated accusingly that the "assassination of Kiroff was carried out under instructions of the Rightest-Trotskyist bloc."

"I know nothing about it," said Mr. Bukharin.

Mr. Vishinsky called up Mr. Rykoff, sitting near Mr. Bukharin in the front row, and made the same assertion to him.

"I took part in the organization of terrorist groups, but I did not have any connection with the assassination of Kiroff. That was committed without the knowledge of the Rightists."

Mr. Rykoff then sat down and Mr. Yagoda was called up in his third-row place, for it is a custom in Soviet trials often to have as many as four defendants standing at once, contradicting or confirming each other's testimony.

Mr. Yagoda rose and stood stoop-shouldered, a wreck of a man—he who so recently was a commanding if sinister figure in a smart uniform standing at the base of Lenin's tomb, presumably immediately to mobilize the uniformed NKVD men [troops of the Commissariat of Internal Affairs] instantly if any attack were made on the lives of the Soviet leaders. He stood and implicated Mr. Bukharin and Mr. Rykoff in the Kiroff assassination, by saying:

"Bukharin and Rykoff lied. I, Bukharin, Rykoff and Yenukidze [Avel S. Yenukidze, one-time secretary of the Central Executive Committee of the government and recently executed as a traitor] were involved in that assassination."

Mr. Yagoda spoke in a low and spiritless voice.

"Yenukidze," he continued, "proposed the assassination of Kiroff. I objected, feeling it was too dangerous."

Mr. Yagoda admitted that, knowing of the plot to kill Kiroff, he had issued instructions through one of his aides that the assassination not be prevented.

### Tells of Two Plots on Lenin

Mr. Bukharin was sternly questioned on whether he had had any part in the alleged conspiracy to assassinate Lenin in 1918. Mr. Bukharin admitted he had heard of two plots at that time (when he was an intimate of Lenin) and that he had warned Lenin about the first plot but not about the second. He said it would have been easy to assassinate Lenin because he knew Lenin never carried a pistol.

Mr. Bukharin began sparring with Mr. Vishinsky from the moment he was called up to give evidence.

"I have two pleas to demand before starting to give evidence," the defendant said. "The first is that I be allowed to tell a connected story, the second that I be allowed to tell something of the ideological side of the conspiracy."

Mr. Vishinsky sharply argued that the prosecutor had a right to ask any questions he liked under the criminal code. Presiding Judge Vassily V. Ulrich confirmed this, but told Mr. Bukharin he certainly could tell a connected story. Mr. Bukharin then asked:

"May I say a few words about the restoration of capitalism?"

This was greeted with an outbreak of laughter from the audience.

"That has certainly been your chief occupation," said Mr. Vishinsky.

### Speaks of Public Interest

"I don't wish to speak about the ideological part of this conspiracy in order to lessen my responsibility," said Mr. Bukharin. "I thought this trial had a public interest, and I wanted to present the platform of the restoration of capitalism as we visualized it. I especially have wished to do so since so little has been said about it here.

"Watching this trial, the public opinion of our country and of the world may ask how people of my type have become criminals and violent counter-revolutionaries. They may ask what our purpose was in perpetrating these foul crimes.

"A popular answer to this is that we tried for power, but that is wrong. There never has been a sheer fight for power among political parties.

"I would like to halt at this, although I realize the term 'ideological position' is ill-applicable to us here in the dock. But I wanted to speak about the objective side of the case.

"Our original differences from the party developed into outright counter-revolution. Overnight we found ourselves on the other side of the barricades, on the side of kulaks [richer peasants], private traders, etc. Our original over-estimation of the individual peasant became an idealization of him.

"In 1917 we, myself included, would not have thought of pitying White Guards, but in 1929 and 1930 we felt actual pity for the kulak, on the ground, as it seemed to us, of humaneness. The kulak became a tactical point in our program.

"Psychologically, we who were once the preachers of industrialized socialism looked first with irony and then with rage and fury on the growth of Socialist factories, which we thought were crushing the peasants."

At this point Judge Ulrich tried to check Mr. Bukharin's ideological exposition with an ominous remark: "You will have your last word, in which you may say all that you like. Now tell us about your anti-Soviet activities."

Mr. Vishinsky then interposed:

"Tell us how this platform of yours found expression in practical counter-revolutionary work."

Mr. Bukharin responded:

"I wish at least to outline the main points of our program—freedom for the Kulak, freedom for individual traders, foreign concessions, slower industrialization, freedom of parties; a coalition, which is the logical conclusion of any alliance."

Mr. Bukharin went on to tell how in 1928 when the attack on kulaks was started he had formed an opposition. He said Mr. Yagoda had provided specially selected material for his use in compiling his speeches. Mr. Yagoda was not in Mr. Bukharin's actual group, Mr. Bukharin said, but was connected with it and because of his position as head of the political police, it developed in other testimony, he had to maintain only the most discreet connection with the Rightist-Troskyist bloc. Then Mr. Bukharin told of the formation of the bloc and of meetings with Lev Kameneff and Gregory Piatakoff, since executed.

"I drew up the 'platform of 1928' and discussed it with Zinovieff and other Trotskyists," Mr. Bukharin testified, adding:

"In 1930 and 1931 the next phase developed. The class struggle in the country was intense. The proletariat was making an onslaught on the villages. The kulaks were being liquidated and were resisting.

### Changed to Double-Dealing

"We changed our tactics and reverted to double-dealing. We gave instructions to our people who were being sent to the provinces to recruit adherents."

Mr. Bukharin went on to say that after about the Fall of 1932 they adopted tactics for the forcible overthrow of the Soviet Government.

Mr. Vishinsky, who had listened with nervous politeness to this long ideological recitation, broke in to say:

"I must again remark that I am interested in your actual crimes."

Mr. Bukharin, his whimsical wit still active in this tragic session, replied:

"There were so many. One must needs select them."

Mr. Bukharin then spoke briefly of the illegal conferences of counter-revolutionary representatives and of counter-revolutionary work and of his participation with others, also once great, in preparations for a coup d'etat against the Stalin regime.

Mr. Bukharin was stiffly questioned by Mr. Vishinsky in an endeavor to elicit whether he had had espionage contacts with foreign powers. He was questioned about his connection with the political police of Austria, where he had spent some time before the revolution. His response was that his only connection with the Austrian police was that they had arrested him as a revolutionary.

He then was asked whether he had had connections with the United States Secret Service in the few months he had spent in America, to which he responded, "No." Following that, he was asked how he had been "recruited by the Japanese" during his stay in Japan on his way from the United States. He responded that he had never been recruited.

The court adjourned late tonight until Monday.

March 6, 1938

## 18 RUSSIANS EXECUTED

### Moscow Announces Sentences of Court Have Been Carried Out

MOSCOW, March 15 (AP).—The execution of eighteen confessed conspirators against Soviet Russia was officially announced tonight. A terse communiqué announced the death sentences, imposed at the end of Moscow's greatest treason trial, March 13, had been carried out, without disclosing the exact time or place.

High on the list of those executed were Nikolai Bukharin, chronicler of the Red revolution, and Alexis I. Rykoff, once Premier of Russia.

The Presidium of the Supreme Soviet, Russia's highest nominal authority, last night denied clemency appeals of seventeen of those doomed to the firing squad.

March 16, 1938

## RUSSIA BUILDS UP BY FORCED LABOR

### Army of Political Prisoners and Exiles Toil on Vast Public Works

### NKVD THEIR TASKMASTER

### More Than 2,000,000 Persons Constructing Dams, Canals and Power Projects

MOSCOW (AP).—Victims of Dictator Joseph Stalin's "purges" who escape execution do not escape punishment. Stalin makes them work.

Hundreds of thousands of political prisoners and exiles are building power dams, railroads, highways, coal mines and oil fields under police bosses.

The vast scope of work in labor camps—foreigners estimate that 2,000,000 or more persons are engaged on projects under the control of the NKVD, the former OGPU, or political police—has been revealed by the newspaper Rabochaya Moskva. It praised the police as "excellent managers and brilliant organizers of socialist industry."

**Jobs Already Completed**

The Baltic-White Sea and Moscow-Volga Canals and a new railroad line of great military importance in the Far East are among the jobs completed with convict labor, and still greater tasks are contemplated during the third Five-Year Plan which began this year.

Two huge power dams, at Rybinsk and Uglich, on the Volga and Sheksna Rivers, are supposed to be built by 1940. Another big project, with a hydro-electric station to provide power for industrial enterprises in the Ural Mountains, is being formed in the watershed of the Kama, Pechora and Vychegda Rivers.

One group of Chekists (so called from the political police's former name of Cheka), headed by S. Y. Zhuk, who built the Moscow-Volga Canal, has been entrusted with the building at Kuibyshev, on the Samara Bend of the Volga, of what the Soviets say will be the largest hydro-electric station in the world.

Canals will be dug for the irrigation of hundreds of thousands of acres of Steppes east of the Volga for the production of millions of bushels of wheat.

**Work in Arctic Tundra**

In the Arctic tundra, where temperatures go to 58 degrees below zero, prisoners are digging coal for the Soviet enterprises in the Far North, drilling for oil, laying railroads and building a nickel plant. It took five years of intensive work to sink one mine.

Prisoners are laying the first two motor highways in Soviet Russia, from Moscow to Minsk, capital of White Russia, and to Kiev, capital of the Ukraine.

The Georgian military highway, 130 years old, is being reconstructed by them. And another highway, 819 kilometers (495 miles) long, is being laid across Kirghizia, from Frunze to Osh, through mountains covered with eternal snows down to valleys where cotton grows, almost at the Chinese frontier.

Not all the workers on these far-flung industrial projects are prisoners. Many are persons exiled from their homes by the Russian method of giving them passports requiring them to live in a certain region. Upon arriving there they must work to live. The only available jobs are the construction projects.

March 27, 1938

## STALIN SAYS PURGE DIDN'T HURT SOVIET

### Stresses Benefit in Removal of 'Murderers, Wreckers' and 'Other Monsters'

By HAROLD DENNY
Wireless to THE NEW YORK TIMES.

MOSCOW, March 11.—The Soviet Union is stronger because of the purgings of recent years and the Communist party has now reached a state of stabilization where methods of mass purging are not needed, according to Joseph Stalin, secretary general of the Communist party, in an address before the party congress last night. The end of his long report was released for publication today.

"The chief internal task of the Soviet State now lies in peaceful, economic-organizational and cultural-organizational work," he said. "Concerning our army, punitive organs and the political police, they will address their spearpoint now, not at the interior of the country, but without, at external enemies."

But in this address—his first public reference to the treason trials of Marshal Mikhail Tukhachevsky, Vice Commissar Gregory Piatakoff and Nikolai I. Bukharin—he made it clear that there would be no relaxing of vigilance against foreign spies and Soviet citizens whom they may enlist as tools, for such will be a source of danger to the Soviet regime as long as it is encircled by capitalist States.

Mr. Stalin's report on behalf of the party's central committee, containing a hopeful statistical analysis of the country's economic development in comparison with capitalist countries, was delivered, as are all his speeches, quietly and with an entire absence of bombast or hysteria.

**Receives Ovation at End**

He was interrupted at times with stormy applause and received a tumultuous ovation at the end when he said:

"We must admit the bourgeoisie and its agents in the working class succeeded to a certain extent in contaminating the spirit of the working class by the poison of doubt and mistrust. If the successes of the working class in our country, if its struggle and victory serve to raise the spirit of the working class in capitalist countries and strengthen its faith in its own power, its faith in its own victory, then our party can say that it does not work in vain."

As he concluded and turned away to his seat on the dais the 2,000 delegates and alternates leaped to their feet shouting, "Hurrah! Long live the great Stalin!" "Hurrah for our beloved Stalin!"

In commenting on the treason trials Mr. Stalin said:

"Certain writers in the foreign press babble that the cleansing of Soviet organizations of spies, murderers and wreckers such as Trotsky, Zinovieff, Kameneff, Yakir, Tukhachevsky, Rosengoltz, Bukharin and other monsters allegedly 'shook the Soviet structure and introduced disintegration.' Such vile chatter deserves only ridicule.

"How could the cleansing of Soviet organizations of harmful, disintegrating elements shake or disintegrate the Soviet structure? The Trotskyist-Bukharinist gang of spies, murderers and wreckers, groveling before foreign States, permeated with a slavish desire to bow down before every foreign petty official and prepared to offer him their services as spies—a band of people failing to understand that the least Soviet citizen, free from capitalist chains, stands a head higher than any highly placed official of a foreign country, dragging the yoke of capitalist slavery—who heeds the pitiful band of bribed slaves, what value can they have for the people and whom can they 'disintegrate'?"

**Stresses Vote After Purges**

Mr. Stalin cited as proof that the purge had not shaken the country the fact that after the shooting of Red army generals Soviet citizens had given a 98 per cent vote in the Soviet elections to the Stalinist bloc—the only ticket running—and after the shooting of Bukharin and his associates had cast a 99 per cent vote in the election to the Soviets of the constituent republics, held under similar conditions.

"Listening to these foreign babblers one might conclude that if one were to let spies, murderers and wreckers go free then the Soviet organizations would be much stabler and firmer," Mr. Stalin continued amid laughter. "Are not these gentlemen giving themselves away too early by thus brazenly defending spies, murderers and wreckers?

"Would it not be truer to say the cleansing of the Soviet organizations must lead and really did lead to a further strengthening of these organizations. Of what, for example, do the events at Lake Khasan [fighting with the Japanese on the Siberian frontier last Summer] speak if not that the cleansing of the Soviet organizations was the truest method of strengthening them?"

Mr. Stalin apparently made a distinction between the party purge of 1933-36 and the purge on treason charges that followed. Too many members were admitted between the Sixteenth and Seventeenth Congresses when the party membership totaled 1,800,000. The party purge was renewed and intensified after the assassination of Sergei Kiroff and now the All-Union Communist party has 1,600,000, a net loss of 270,000 since the last Congress in 1934.

"As a result of all these measures," Mr. Stalin went on, "the party cleansed its ranks of chance passive careerists and directly inimical elements, leaving the firmest, most devoted people. It cannot be said the purge was conducted without serious mistakes. Unfortunately there were more mistakes than we could have foreseen. Undoubtedly we have no more need for the method of mass purging."

He said the reduction in the party membership had been on the whole a good thing since the party now, though smaller in number, was higher in quality.

Mr. Stalin explained at some length the new Communist "line," that even though the exploiting classes have been suppressed here the State cannot wither away as Karl Marx had expected. He said it would be absurd to think that Marx could have foreseen nearly a century ago the present international situation and the capitalist encirclement of this lone Marxist State. Therefore, he said, the State apparatus must be maintained, including the army, navy and political police, to protect the State from foreign enemies.

Reviewing the Soviet's internal situation, he said the most important accomplishment of the period since the last Congress in the field of development of national economy was the reconstruction of industry and agriculture on the basis of modern technique. The Soviet Union is foremost in this field, he said.

Next, in the field of social-political development the chief results, he said, were the liquidation of the remnants of the exploiting classes, consolidation of the people, morally and politically, and full democratization of the country's political life by the creation of the new Constitution.

"None dares question the fact that our Constitution is the most democratic in the world," said the Soviet leader.

Though boasting of large production gains for Soviet economy, Mr. Stalin derided former members of the staff of the State Planning Commission who were removed two years ago for, among other things, setting unachievable goals. The planning of 60,000,000 tons of pig iron yearly at the end of the second five-year plan he termed "a fantasy if not worse." He also ridiculed these planners for planning a population increase of 3,000,000 to 4,000,000 annually.

He called on the party to lead the country in overtaking capitalist countries, industrially and economically, in the next ten or fifteen years.

"From the point of view of the cultural development of the people in the period [the past five years] under report it was truly a period of cultural revolution," he said. "The putting into practice of universal compulsory primary school education, a rise in the number of schools and students of all grades, a rise in the number of specialists graduated from higher institutions, the creation and strengthening of a new Soviet intelligentsia—such is a general picture of the cultural upsurge of the people."

Considerable speculation was occasioned today by the lack of mention of Nikolai Ivanovitch Yezhoff who prepared the last three treason trials and conducted the purge of 1937-38, though at last reports he was secretary of the central committee, chairman of the control commission and Commissar of Water Transport, he was the only one of the Politburo group not decorated in honor of the party congress. He was not chosen as a member of the presidium of thirty-five for the congress, though this honor was paid Lorenti Beria, who succeeded him last December as Commissar for Internal Affairs.

March 12, 1939

# STALIN IS PLACING NEW MEN IN POWER

## Getting Rid of Bureaucrats Is Thought to Have Been One of His Purge Objectives

## LENIN FAILED IN ATTEMPT

By WALTER DURANTY
Wireless to THE NEW YORK TIMES.

MOSCOW, April 30.—That red tape, bureaucracy and politics curse every government will be no news to Americans. But it is particularly true in a socialist State that owns and directly manages finance, industry, trade, agriculture, railroads, shipping, mining and all other branches of national life.

Ask Wall Street how it would like that as an "injection" of politics into business.

In 1921 Lenin launched a big drive against bureaucrats, that is, men holding executive jobs by virtue of political qualifications rather than of practical experience and technical capacity. The drive flared along for three months, when lo, it was found that the number of "bureaucrats," according to Lenin's definition, had increased by 11.8 per cent.

In 1926 Joseph Stalin stated:

"In order to carry out the objectives of the Communist party in industrialization, it is especially necessary to create 'cadres' [executive personnel] of new men, cadres of new builders in industry."

Mr. Stalin's greatest quality is his unflinching adherence to purpose. Once at Easter in 1905 the Tsarist police gave the First Company of the Salyansk Regiment a treat by making some political prisoners, including Mr. Stalin, run the gantlet between two lines of soldiers armed with sticks and brass-buckled belts. Mr. Stalin walked the line, his head erect, holding a book in his hand.

Yet it took him thirteen years and a drastic remedy (to put it mildly), known abroad as the purge, to get his new executive personnel —which, by the way, it is now becoming evident was not the least of the purge's objectives.

Last January one of the shrewdest foreign observers here expressed the opinion that the struggle henceforth was not against the Opposition, which the purge had eliminated, but between technicians and bureaucrat-politicians. The new central committee of the Communist party and the Council of Commissars answer that criticism.

From two-thirds to three-quarters of both bodies, which represent the tops in the party and the government, respectively, are men with thorough technical training, many of whom have been directors of factories and trusts. The same lines are being followed down to the local party leaders and managers of collective farms and factories. In short Mr. Stalin has replaced the old bureaucrats by his young "new cadres."

May 1, 1939

# TROTSKY, WOUNDED BY 'FRIEND' IN HOME, IS BELIEVED DYING

By The United Press.

MEXICO CITY, Aug. 20—Leon Trotsky was struck many times in the head with an axe today by a man who called at his suburban home "so frequently he seemed to be one of the family," and physicians at the Green Cross Emergency Hospital said the exiled Communist leader might not live through the night.

Mr. Trotsky was operated upon and immediately placed in an oxygen tent. The surgeons said it was too early to determine the results of the operation. They said the most serious wound was one that pierced the skull and entered the brain, causing a hemorrhage. The operating surgeon added that the chances are "90 to 10 that he cannot live."

The 60-year-old former Soviet War Commissar's assailant was tentatively identified as Frank Jackson, was later found to be Jacques Monard van den Dreschd, 36 years old, said to have been born in Persia.

Guards at Mr. Trotsky's home who rushed into the study and overpowered van den Dreschd when they heard the famous exile scream, said the assailant probably was a member of the OGPU (Russian Secret police).

August 21, 1940

# TROTSKY'S CAREER A REBELLIOUS ONE

### Wandered in Exile From Youth, Became Right-Hand Man of Lenin, Headed Red Army

### RIFT WITH STALIN ENSUED

### He Resumed Exile in Turkey, Norway, Then Mexico—Once Lived in New York

**DIES OF WOUNDS INFLICTED BY ASSASSIN**

**Leon Trotsky as he appeared at a press interview early this month**

Associated Press

Leon Trotsky, whose real name was Leba Bronstein, was born of Jewish parents in 1879 in a small town in Kherson, Russia, near the Black Sea. His father was a chemist. He received his education in the local schools, but did not attend the university. He was expelled from school at the age of 15 for desecrating a sacred ikon, an image of the Orthodox Russian Church, thus giving an early indication of his radical temperament, which led him throughout his life to attack religion as well as the other factors in the existing order of things.

While still in his teens Trotsky became a revolutionist, and began to write articles, make speeches and help in the organization of revolutionary movements. He became a disciple of Karl Marx, and gradually formulated the communistic ideas which he and Lenin later were to put into practice in Russia. At the age of 22 he was banished to Siberia for four years for participating in a workmen's revolutionary movement in Odessa, but he escaped from Verkholensk, where he was exiled, after three years and lived in France and Germany.

Trotsky returned to Russia at the time of the uprising of 1905, which was the forerunner of the 1917 revolution, and became president of the Council of Workmen in what was then St. Petersburg. He was again arrested when the 1905 rebellion was put down and was exiled to Siberia for life this time. But he escaped after six months on a false passport made out in the name of Trotsky, said to have been the name of a guard. This was the way in which Trotsky got the name which has become known throughout the world ever since.

**First Fame As Writer**

Trotsky lived in France, Switzerland, Austria and Germany during his second exile, and supported himself by writing for radical publications He wrote a pamphlet called "There and Back," describing his imprisonment and his escape from Siberia, which brought him considerable prominence in Russia.

When the war started, Trotsky was editing a newspaper in Berlin, where he had found many friends among the radicals and had had help in writing a history of the first Russian revolution. The espousal of the German national cause by the German Socialists led Trotsky into violent controversies, in which he denounced them freely for their lack of international-mindedness, and he was finally exiled from Germany as a "dangerous anarchist." Going to Vienna, he found refuge with Dr. Victor Adler, whose son Fritz, in 1916, assassinated Count Stuergkh.

Next he went to Zurich, Switzerland, and then on to Paris. There were frequent reports in later days, when he became prominent, that he had acted as a German agent, and that the Germans had financed him, as well as Lenin and other Bolshevist leaders, in a plot to get Russia out of the war. Nothing has ever come out to stamp Trotsky definitely and conclusively as a German agent, however, and the United States Secret Service in a very thorough investigation of his life in this country found no proof of the charge.

In Paris Trotsky began the publication of a radical sheet called Our World, but it was suppressed, and Trotsky was expelled from France. He was escorted to the Spanish frontier, but was arrested and lodged in jail. On his release he sailed for New York with his wife and two sons, Leo and Sergius. Trotsky's wife had become a member of the Russian revolutionary group in Switzerland in 1901, when a student in Geneva, and was said to have smuggled pamphlets and messages from the exiles in Switzerland into Russia, and to have helped radical leaders enter Russia secretly. She met Trotsky in Paris in 1903 and aided him in the spread of revolutionary propaganda, which once caused her arrest and imprisonment in Russia.

Trotsky and his family arrived here on the steamship Monserrat from Barcelona, Spain, on Jan. 14, 1917, and they went to live in a three-room apartment on Vyse Avenue, the Bronx. He found work as an editorial writer on the Russian radical daily Novy Mir, published in St. Mark's Place, at $20 a week, and also wrote editorials for the German socialistic publication, the Volkszeitung, and other similar journals He received $10 to $15 for each editorial written for papers other than the Novy Mir, and also earned about $300 by delivering about thirty lectures during the two months and a half he was in New York. His editorials and lectures were chiefly devoted to espousals of peace and socialistic theories. While he was here he predicted that the war would result in revolution among the working classes in the warring countries.

After he left America a story was told that he had worked in the Bronx as waiter in a cheap restaurant. No proof has ever been submitted to substantiate the tale.

**Stopped by British, but Released.**

Following the overthrow of the Czar, Trotsky and his family left New York to return to Russia. He sailed on the Kristianiafjord on March 27, 1917, with his wife and children, but was detained by the British authorities when the ship stopped at Halifax. The Russian Government requested his release, particularly in a message from Kerensky, head of the Provisional Government, later overthrown by Lenin and Trotsky. Accordingly, Trotsky continued his voyage to Russia in April, 1917, after having been held in a military internment camp in Nova Scotia.

On his arrival in Petrograd Trotsky joined Lenin and the other Maximalists, or Bolsheviki, in the Left Wing of the Russian Socialists. They first supported the Kerensky government, but gradually broke away on the issue of peace. Lenin and Trotsky insisted on immediate peace, while Kerensky held out for remaining in the war at the side of the Allies.

In July, as a result of the Bolshevist uprising in St. Petersburg, as it was still called, Kerensky ordered the arrest of Trotsky and the Communist leaders. Lenin fled to Finland, but Trotsky was imprisoned. In September, the judge before whom he was tried held that he had taken no part in the uprising and he was released.

The November revolution, in which the Kerensky government was overthrown, brought Lenin and Trotsky to the top. One of their first measures was the negotiation of the Brest-Litovsk treaty with the Central powers ending Russian participation in the World War. Trotsky bitterly opposed accepting the Germans' terms and yielded only under pressure by Lenin.

In the new government Trotsky became Lenin's right-hand man, taking the post of Minister of Foreign Affairs and then Minister of War. It was in the latter capacity that his monumental achievement of reorganizing and directing the Red Army took place. In all the bitterness of later internal conflict not even Trotsky's enemies tried to take from him the credit that was his due for welding the disordered remnants of the Czarist Army, reduced in numbers, poorly equipped, broken in morale, into an efficient fighting force.

The numerical strength of the army he organized was about 1,500,000. In four years of almost constant fighting on various fronts it defeated the forces under Yudenitch, Kolchak, Denikin, the "White Army" of Wrangel in the the Crimean, and the Polish Army. Trotsky was often at one or another of the fronts, riding in a special armored railway train. In forming the Red Army he had resorted to compulsory military service, and ruthlessly restored the old iron discipline of the Czarist Army, thus putting an end to all manner of "Socialist Utopias" about popular armament and national militia. It was the same old army system except that instead of serving the Emperor it served the Soviet.

Once the army was functioning smoothly Trotsky was able to turn his efforts to other fields. In 1919 he started to reorganize the railroad system, but his severe tactics alienated the employes and Lenin ultimately removed him in summary fashion. It was the first of many rumored quarrels with Lenin. Trotsky was reputed by his enemies in the Communist camp to have been jealous of Lenin's power and discontented with the fact that he did not have an equal share in controlling Russian destinies. The same charge was made by the Trotskyists against Stalin. When Lenin became incapacitated by illness in 1923 and it was obvious that he had not very long to live, Trotsky was expected to step into Lenin's shoes. His failure to do so ultimately caused his political ruin.

While Lenin was still alive, but unable to carry on his work, the All-Russian Congress named a triumvirate to take his place. It consisted of Kameneff, Zinovieff and Stalin, the General Secretary of the Communist party, who was later to prove Trotsky's conqueror in the struggle for power.

Lenin died in January, 1924, and the inevitable fight for control of the Communist party began almost immediately after. It soon became evident that the triumvirate was too strong for Trotsky. A year later he was removed as chairman of the Revolutionary War Council, which meant his automatic dismissal as Minister of War and the beginning of the end of his political career.

The crux of his opposition, then and afterward, was on the question of "right" and "left." Trotsky always stood for communism in the strict sense of the word, without compromise. Russia should have nothing to do with capitalistic systems of government or economics, he believed; the "world revolution" should be fostered; the well-to-do peasants should not be favored at the expense of the poorer. He urged an aggressive policy toward Great Britain, the helping of China to become "Red," and no conciliating of America. The fact that his policies were adopted later demonstrated that he was opposed as a personal factor, not as a Communist.

**Trotsky Lacked Audacity.**

With so much right on his side, from the Communist point of view, it was later held by many critics that Trotsky could not have been a skillful politician, otherwise he would have gained the ascendency in the party which Stalin won. According to Kerensky, Trotsky lacked audacity.

He was in an even better position to assume leadership than was generally known at the time, because, as it developed in the Fall of 1928, when Trotsky's book, "The True Situation in Russia," was published, the Communist party was warned against Stalin by Lenin in his last political will and testament, in which Lenin had urged Stalin's removal as General Secretary. With remarkable prescience, Lenin predicted the feud between Trotsky and Stalin, which, he said, was the "chief danger" to the Communist party. Of Trotsky he wrote:

"Comrade Trotsky is not only remarkably clever—he certainly is the cleverest man in the Central Committee—but he knows his own value and possesses a complete understanding of the admistrative side of State economics. The difference between these two most important leaders in the Central Committee may bring about an involuntary cleavage, which will take place quite suddenly, if the party does not take any steps to prevent it."

Despite his strategic position, however, Trotsky was outmanoeuvred by the clever tactics of Stalin, who during the years of Lenin's illness had managed to obtain control of the party machinery.

In January, 1925, Trotsky went to the Caucasus, ostensibly for his health but really as an exile. Within four months he had submitted with good grace and by the end of the year had regained much of his old power and seemingly healed the breach with Stalin, who had come definitely to the fore.

Trotsky undertook a new field of work as chief of the Scientific and Technical Branch of the Supreme Economic Council and head of the Russian Concessions Committee. His endeavors were now in the direction of industrial expansion and the mechanization and electrification of industries. In December, 1925, he was re-elected to the Central Executive Committee.

On the surface internal dissension had ceased, but it was only a truce before the resumption of hostilities. Stalin all along had been consolidating his power. The triumvirate no longer existed. Kameneff had been discarded and Zinovieff had joined forces with Trotsky in an opposition that gradually gathered force. It had early become evident that either Stalin or Trotsky must go. The former became outspoken in his attacks on Trotsky.

"He is a heretic," he said. "Trotsky never was a Bolshevik. We must stamp out Trotskyism."

Trotsky's efforts were utterly futile. On Oct. 17, 1926, with Zinovieff and others of the Opposition, he capitulated unconditionally and publicly repudiated his actions.

Trotsky's capitulation, however, did him no good. A week later he was ousted from the Political Bureau. The next month he was removed from the Supreme Economic Council. Once more he came out openly in opposition to Stalin, and, as always, he got the worst of it. Most of his honors and high offices had been taken from him. In June, 1927, the Central Control Committee recommended the expulsion of Trotsky and Zinovieff from the Central Committee, but Trotsky escaped with a reprimand. Within a month, however, the mills of Stalin began grinding again and did not stop until Trotsky, deprived of every office and honor was simply a "man in the street." He was expelled from the Communist International Executive Committee after the discovery of an "underground" printing office for producing Opposition documents. In October he was ousted from the Central Committee of the Communist party.

**Watched "His" Army Pass By.**

When the tenth anniversary of the establishment of the Soviet was celebrated, in November, 1927, and a great parade of the Red Army was held in Moscow, Trotsky, who had organized the army and was once its beloved idol, stood in the street with other spectators, almost unnoticed, and watched it march by. A few days later he was removed from his last office as head of the Concessions Committee, and was expelled from the Communist party.

In January, 1928, strict censorship was imposed on all news emanating from Russia, but gradually, through London and Berlin, news leaked out that Trotsky and others of the Opposition had been exiled to Siberia. When the news was confirmed, Trotsky was an exile at Alma Ata, in the city of Vierny, on the Chinese-Turkestan frontier in the remotest depths of the wild and uncivilized Russian Central Asiatic domain, 400 miles from the nearest railway station.

His sojourn at Alma Ata lasted about one year. Although the Opposition press outside of Russia printed many stories of his hardships, failing health and ill-treatment, Trotsky does not seem to have spent a partcularly unhappy year. His wife and two sons accompanied him; he had servants, an adequate income and a certain amount of freedom. Except for an attack of malaria, his health, always delicate, steadily improved. Most of his time was spent in writing his memoirs, several books, and, as it transpired later, pamphlets against the ruling faction, which were surreptitiously circulated both in and outside of Russia.

If the news emanating from Russia in January, 1929, is to be trusted, Trotsky was, in fact, preparing for a return to power by means of a revolution. At any rate, on Jan. 23 it was suddenly announced that 150 followers of Trotsky had been arrested and after summary trial sent into "rigorous isolation" in a number of prisons as "enemies of the proletarian dictatorship" for plotting a civil war against the State. It was charged that they were secretly carrying out Trotsky's orders by circulating handbills and other propaganda, particularly among the Communist youths and the army.

Once again Stalin had proved too quick and strong for Trotsky. With one powerful blow he had put an end to the secret adherents of Trotsky, who had remained inside the Bolshevist party, and launched a new offensive against all Trotskyists, which was to end in the expulsion of Trotsky from Russia.

In the days succeeding the wholesale arrests, rumors came thick and fast from Riga, Berlin, London and Constantinople that Trotsky was en route to Turkey, whence he had been banished. Official Moscow kept silent, but on Feb. 1 THE NEW YORK TIMES correspondent definitely annbunced that the decision to send Trotsky out of the country had been taken.

Thus Trotsky, who in 1917 was being hailed as the "Napoleon of the Revolution," ended, like Robespierre, a victim of the very forces he had done so much to create.

**Passed His Exile in Turkey.**

On Feb. 6, 1929, Trotsky arrived at Constantinople with his family. He at once asked permission to be admitted to Germany, pleading ill health and suggesting sanatoriums such as Wiesbaden or Baden-Baden. The request was rejected after a bitter fight in the Reichstag and Trotsky continued his appeals to other countries, invariably meeting defeat. In turn Austria, France, Spain, Italy, Czechslovakia, Norway and Holland refused to allow the creator of the Red Army to live within their respective frontiers.

When he appealed to England, the country noted for its hospitality to political exiles, he suffered the same rebuff. British labor gave him "the cold shoulder," and on July 11, 1929, after much debating with members of the Extreme Left in the House of Commons, Trotsky's request was definitely refused.

At Prinkipo, one of the suburbs of Constantinople, Trotsky busied himself with writing his memoirs and pamphlets by the hundred. Shortly after his arrival in Turkey he wrote a series of articles bitterly denouncing Stalin, saying that the present strong man of Russia was "without creative force and headed for reaction." He also described Stalin as "a mediocre politician pursuing a zigzag policy, ignorant of world affairs."

In 1931 it was reported that Trotsky was suffering from tuberculosis and bronchitis and that he was dying. His health was bad and he again pleaded for asylum in Germany. An appeal to Maxim Gorky to extend him hospitality at Capri was denied by the author of "Chelkash."

It was during his stay at Prinkipo that he wrote his voluminous "History of the Russian Revolution," a work that bitterly attacked Stalin and sought to prove that there were two great men of New Russia—Lenin and Trotsky.

**Daughter Committed Suicide.**

His daughter, Zinaide Wolkow, committed suicide in a Berlin rooming house in 1933. Trotsky blamed it on Stalin, because the dictator had refused to admit her to citizenship in the Soviet land.

Traveling correspondents and magazine writers interviewed the exile at Prinkipo from time to time, and never failed to get material about Trotsky's views on world affairs in general and Russian affairs in particular.

In July, 1933, he arrived at Marseilles, via Naples, and received sanctuary through the French Government, then headed by Camille Chautemps. His whereabouts were mysterious until he was found living in a villa at Fontainebleau in the Barbizon district, near Paris. Less than a year later he was ordered to be expelled because he had "not observed the duties of neutrality." Every revolt that occurred was laid to his machinations, but it is doubtful whether he had anything to do with them. He was hounded by creditors and then sought domicile in Great Britain and later the Irish Free State. This was denied him.

In France he wrote a life of Lenin, a eulogy to the father of the Russian revolution. In June, 1935, Trotsky, accompanied by his family, arrived in Oslo and found a haven of refuge in Norway.

In August, 1936, however, after a period of comparative quiet, Trotsky was again in the midst of turmoil, the greatest since his exile from Russia. This emanated from the trial of sixteen Bolsheviks in Moscow, the so-called Zinovieff-Kameneff trial, which resulted in the execution of the accused, including a number of outstanding leaders of the October revolution, after their conviction for "treason." They were accused of conspiring with Trotsky to assassinate Stalin and other Soviet leaders and restore capitalism in Russia. Trotsky was in reality the chief defendant, for although tried in absentia he was pictured as the villain of the alleged conspiracy.

The verdicts of guilty were founded wholly upon confessions of the accused, which Trotsky denounced as false, characterizing the trial as a frame-up. He demanded an impartial investigation of the charges and threatened to sue a Communist paper in Norway for libel because it repeated these accusations as proven. The Norwegian Government, however, forbade him to bring the suit.

After the Zinovieff-Kameneff trial Trotsky's situation in Norway took a distinct turn for the worse. The Soviet Government demanded his expulsion, and although at first Norway declined to accede to the demand on the ground that it interfered with the principle of political asylum, it finally declined to renew his residence permit. Eventually the Mexican Government, under President Cárdenas, permitted him to come to live in Mexico on condition that he would not interfere in Mexican affairs. For this relief Trotsky was indebted to Diego Rivera, the Mexican mural painter, an admirer of the fallen Bolshevik leader, and a friend of President Cárdenas. Trotsky arrived in Mexico on a Norwegian tanker in January, 1937.

**Another Treason Trial**

He had no sooner taken up residence in a villa outside Mexico City than his peace was again disturbed by another treason trial in Moscow, this time of seventeen Bolsheviks, accused of counter-revolutionary activities, sabotage, assassination plans and betraying Russia in deals with Germany and Japan. Most prominent among the new group of defendants were Karl Radek, Piatakoff, Sokolnikoff and Serebriakoff, all former leading figures in the Soviet hierarchy. They, too, confessed, involving Trotsky as their leader. This trial was likewise denounced by Trotsky as a frame-up. For weeks he supplied the American and world press with statements and articles refuting the charges, accusing Stalin of deliberately concocting the trials in order to complete the political ruin of his opponents. Trotsky charged that Stalin was liquidating the Communist party and the revolution, accusing him of establishing a Red fascism in Russia.

On Jan. 9, 1937, Trotsky was to address a meeting in New York by long-distance telephone from Mexico, in which he was to discuss the Moscow trials. He was unable to speak in person because of a breakdown in the technical arrangements. His address was read to the audience from an advance copy. He again challenged the veracity of the Moscow accusations, demanding an impartial investigation and offering to surrender to the Soviet Government if proven guilty in such an investigation.

Trotsky's reputed heading of his own counter-revolutionary movement received wide publicity. As a result of statements made in the confessions of defendants at the Moscow trials, Trotsky denied that he had ever received $1,000,000 from Soviet officials who wished to promote his work. He denied also another allegation that he had conspired with the defendants then on trial.

In May, 1940, Trotsky narrowly escaped death when machine-gun bullets swept through the bedroom of his home on the outskirts of Mexico City. Later, Robert Sheldon Harte of New York, who had been his guard, was found dead in a Mexican farmhouse, to which he apparently had been taken after being kidnapped at the time of the assault on Trotsky. Mexican police were unable to find the machine-gunners, and Trotsky accused Stalin of instigating the assassination plot.

During the Mexican Presidential election two months later, supporters of the Mexican Government accused Trotsky, according to dispatches from Mexico City, of taking part in a Fascist plot with supporters of General Juan Andreu Almazan, oppositionist candidate.

To the last moment of his life Trotsky remained a stormy petrel, clinging to his extreme Communist ideas, particularly his theory of permanent revolution. Few men have ever provoked such hatred in some and such devotion in others as Trotsky. Whatever history's verdict upon him may be, it will not fail to record that he helped fill some of its most colorful pages.

August 22, 1940

# Text of the Berlin-Moscow Treaty

By The Associated Press.

*MOSCOW, Thursday, Aug. 24.—The text of the German-Russian non-aggression pact announced here today follows:*

The German Reich Government and the Union of Soviet Socialist Republics, moved by a desire to strengthen the state of peace between Germany and the U.S.S.R. and in the spirit of the provisions of the neutrality treaty of April, 1926, between Germany and the U.S.S.R., decided the following:

### Article I

The two contracting parties obligate themselves to refrain from every act of force, every aggressive action and every attack against one another, including any single action or that taken in conjunction with other powers.

### Article II

In case one of the parties of this treaty should become the object of warlike acts by a third power, the other party will in no way support this third power.

### Article III

The governments of the two contracting parties in the future will constantly remain in consultation with one another in order to inform each other regarding questions of common interest.

### Article IV

Neither of the high contracting parties will associate itself with any other grouping of powers which directly or indirectly is aimed at the other party.

### Article V

In the event of a conflict between the contracting parties concerning any question, the two parties will adjust this difference or conflict exclusively by friendly exchange of opinions or, if necessary, by an arbitration commission.

### Article VI

The present treaty will extend for a period of ten years with the condition that if neither of the contracting parties announces its abrogation within one year of expiration of this period, it will continue in force automatically for another period of five years.

### Article VII

The present treaty shall be ratified within the shortest possible time. The exchange of ratification documents shall take place in Berlin. The treaty becomes effective immediately upon signature.

Drawn up in two languages, German and Russian.
MOSCOW, 23d *of August*, 1939.

*For the German Government:*
RIBBENTROP.

*In the name of the Government of the U.S.S.R.:*
MOLOTOFF.

August 24, 1939

# STALIN BECOMES SOVIET PREMIER

## MOLOTOFF SHIFTED

### Remains as the Foreign Commissar, Becomes Vice Premier

### NO NEW POLICY INDICATED

### Washington and London Wary of Interpreting Change—Blow to Red Party Held Sure

By The United Press.

MOSCOW, May 6—Joseph Stalin tonight became Premier of the Soviet Union after the resignation of Vyacheslaff M. Molotoff, who had served both as Premier and Foreign Commissar.

By assuming the Premiership, or chairmanship of the Council of People's Commissars, the 62-year-old Mr. Stalin achieved the same vast leadership and power held by V. I. Lenin before the latter's death in 1924.

Mr. Stalin, son of a Tiflis cobbler and a revolutionary since he was 17 years old, now is leader of both the government and the Communist party. Mr. Molotoff, who retains his post as Foreign Commissar, has long been urging the Supreme Soviet to accept his resignation as Premier because of the pressure of duties in handling the affairs of both that office and directing Russia's foreign policy, it was stated officially.

**Molotoff Is Vice Premier**

The Supreme Soviet has accepted the resignation of the 51-year-old Mr. Molotoff as Premier—a position he held for ten years as the titular head of Russia—and "appointed" Mr. Stalin to the office, it was said. Mr. Molotoff becomes Vice Premier in addition to retaining the portfolio of Foreign Affairs.

The official announcement, blared over all Russian radio stations late tonight, said that Mr. Molotoff had been "overburdened" in his dual role and had "repeatedly asked" to be relieved of the Premiership.

The President of Russia is Mikhail I. Kalinin, President of the Presidium of the Supreme Soviet of the U.S.S.R., created under the Soviet Constitution of 1936, but the office carries little authority.

The official Tass agency announcement of Mr. Stalin's replacement of Mr. Molotoff said the shift was carried out by means of three decrees. It read:

"The Presidium of the Supreme Soviet of the U.S.S.R. has issued the following three decrees:

"Decree 1—In view of Molotoff's repeated statements to the effect that it is difficult for him to fulfill the duties of Chairman of the Council of People's Commissars of the U.S.S.R. simultaneously with the duties of People's Commissar of Foreign Affairs, to comply with Molotoff's request to relieve him of the duties of Chairman of the Council of People's Commissars of the U.S.S.R.

"Decree 2—To appoint Joseph Visarionovitch Stalin Chairman of the Council of People's Commissars of the Soviet Union.

"Decree 3—To appoint People's

RUSSIA'S NEW PREMIER AND HIS ASSISTANT

Joseph Stalin

V. M. Molotoff
Times Wide World

Commissar of Foreign Affairs Vyacheslaff Mikhailovitch Molotoff as Vice Chairman of the Council of People's Commissars of the U. S. S. R."

**No Change in Policy Indicated**

It was indicated that, although Mr. Stalin's formal authority was now as broad as it could be, there would be little change in Russian policies inasmuch as Mr. Molotoff in handling both internal and foreign affairs had worked in close co-operation with Mr. Stalin and under his supervision.

In this connection it is recalled that in many recent developments of Russian foreign policy, such as the recent signing in the Kremlin of the new pact with Japan, Mr. Stalin appeared as the key figure in the ceremonies and has sat in on frequent international conferences here.

Tonight's announcement came as a distinct surprise, as do most Russian official decisions.

However, the announcement stressed that Mr. Molotoff would remain in direct supervision of Russia's foreign policy at a grave moment when all Russian leaders are warning of the threatened spread of the "second imperialist war" and its menaces to Russia's own frontiers.

Only last night Mr. Stalin, in a speech at graduation exercises for sixteen Red Army military academies and nine military departments of civil higher educational establishments, had told of Russia's swelling defense preparations and determination to be prepared for "any surprises." He added that the Red Army had now been rebuilt on the basis of experience in the latest types of warfare and had been considerably rearmed.

Mr. Stalin has been secretary of the Central Committee of the Communist party since 1922, a member of the Presidium of the Supreme Soviet of the U. S. S. R. and a member of the Executive Committee of the Communist International.

The Presidium on which he sits is composed of a President—Mr. Kalinin—and eleven Vice Presidents, one for each constituent republic of the Soviet Union, and twenty-four members. The body serves, in effect, as an administrative group under the Supreme Soviet made up of 569 members from all parts of Russia's realm.

Mr. Molotoff, Premier since 1931 and re-elected by the Supreme Soviet in January of 1938, became Foreign Commissar on May 4, 1939, just four months before the outbreak of the war, when he suddenly was chosen to replace Maxim M. Litvinoff.

In August of 1939 Mr. Molotoff played a chief role in the conclusion of the Russian-German pact. Later he handled the diplomatic angles of the conflict with Finland, visited Berlin for consultations several months ago and more recently signed Russia's name to the new friendship pact with Japan.

Mr. Molotoff formerly was secretary of the Central Committee of the Communist party.

Mr. Stalin's assumption of the position of Premier marks another step in his expansion of power, which began after Lenin's death in 1924, followed by the late Leon Trotsky's banishment to Siberia and subsequent expulsion from Russia.

### MOLOTOFF LED APPEASING

**Took Over Post From Litvinoff to Push Deal With Germany**

Vyacheslaff Mikhailovitch Molotoff, who succeeded the comparatively pro-British Maxim Litvinoff as Commissar for Foreign Affairs of the U. S. S. R. on May 4, 1939, and took charge of steering the new Soviet policy of "appeasement" toward Nazi Germany—which succeeded Mr. Litvinoff's policy of collective security—has been since 1935 an advocate of "dealing" with the Fascist powers to keep Russia out of war.

It was he who gave the world the first explanation of the new Russian policy toward Germany in his speech before the Supreme Soviet when the treaty of neutrality with Germany was ratified on Aug. 31, 1939, enabling Adolf Hitler to launch his attack on Poland the following day. It was he who announced over the radio on Sept. 17 that the Red Army had crossed the Polish frontier and was proceeding to occupy the White Russian and Ukrainian territories which Poland had held since 1918. It was he whose public addresses built up the Soviet's justification of its new foreign policy by representing Poland as the aggressor and Britain and France as waging war for imperialistic reasons and therefore no more deserving of sympathy than Germany.

Before he succeeded Mr. Litvinoff Mr. Molotoff was little known to the outside world. It was only later that realization became general that his appointment meant a complete reversal of Mr. Litvinoff's anti-Fascist policy. Then it was brought out that back in 1935 Mr. Molotoff had made the following statement:

"We have never had any other desire than good relations with Germany. We profoundly desire to develop relations with every State, not excluding those with a fascist regime."

In 1939 he asserted that "a strong Germany is an indispensable condition for durable peace in Europe," and that "only the enemies of Germany and the U. S. S. R. can strive to create and foment enmity between the people of these countries."

May 7, 1941

# HITLER BEGINS WAR ON RUSSIA

## BAD FAITH CHARGED

By C. BROOKS PETERS

By Telephone to THE NEW YORK TIMES.

BERLIN, Sunday, June 22—As dawn broke over Europe today the legions of National Socialist Germany began their long-rumored invasion of Communist Soviet Russia. The non-aggression and amity pact between the two countries, signed in August, 1939, forgotten, the German attack began along a tremendous front, extending from the Arctic regions to the Black Sea. Marching with the forces of Germany are also the troops of Finland and Rumania.

Adolf Hitler, in a proclamation to the German people read over a national hook-up by Propaganda Minister Dr. Joseph Goebbels at 5:30 this morning, termed the military action begun this morning the largest in the history of the world. It was necessary, he added, because in spite of his unceasing efforts to preserve peace in this area it had definitely been proved that Russia was in a coalition with England to ruin Germany by prolonging the war.

**Saw Stalemate in West**

Herr Hitler, in his proclamation as reported here, made one vitally interesting statement, namely, that the supreme German military command did not feel itself able to force a decisive victory in the West—apparently on the British Isles—when large Russian troop concentrations were on the Reich's borders in the East.

The Russian troop concentrations in the East began in August, 1940, Herr Hitler asserted. "Thus, there occurred the effect intended by the Soviet-British cooperation," he added, "namely, the binding of such powerful German forces in the East that a radical conclusion of the war in the West, particularly as regards aircraft, could no longer be vouched for by the German High Command.

[The German radio announced early today that documentary proof would shortly be given of a secret British-Russian alliance, made behind Germany's back.]

**Designed "to Save Reich"**

The German action, Herr Hitler explained to his fellow-National Socialists, is designed to save the Reich and with it all Europe from the machinations of the Jewish-Anglo-Saxon warmongers.

The German Foreign Minister, Joachim von Ribbentrop, followed Dr. Goebbels on the air with a declaration of the Reich Government read before the foreign correspondents in the Foreign Office. Herr von Ribbentrop said he received V. G. Dekanosoff, the Russian Ambassador, this morning and informed him that in spite of the Russian-German non-aggression pact of Aug. 23, 1939, and an amity pact of Sept. 28, 1939, Russia had betrayed the trust that the Reich had placed in her.

"Contrary to all engagements which they had undertaken and in absolute contradition to their solemn declarations, the Soviet Union had turned against Germany," the Reich note asserted. "They have first not only continued, but even since the outbreak of war intensified their subversive activities against Germany in Europe. They have second, in a continually increasing measure, developed their foreign policy in a tendency hostile to Germany, and they have third massed their entire forces on the German frontier ready for action."

The Soviet Government, it was charged, had violated its treaties and broken its agreements with Germany. This was characterized as evidence that Moscow's "hatred of National Socialism was stronger than its political wisdom." Recalling the enmity between bolshevism and nazism, it was asserted that Bolshevist Moscow was "about to stab National Socialist Germany in the back" while the latter was "engaged in a struggle for existence."

"Germany has no intention of remaining inactive in the face of this grave threat to her Eastern frontier," it was proclaimed. "The Fuehrer has therefore ordered the German forces to oppose this menace with all the might at their disposal. In the coming struggle the German people are fully aware that they are called upon not only to defend their native land but to save the entire civilized world from the deadly dangers of bolshevism and clear the way for true social progress in Europe."

Continuing his allegations, Herr von Ribbentrop declared that the German High Command had repeatedly directed the attention of the German Foreign Office to the steadily increasing menace of the Russian Army to Germany. These communications from the High Command will be published in detail, it was declared.

All doubts of the aggressive intention of the Russian concentration were dispelled, it was declared, by the news that the Russian general mobilization was complete and that 160 divisions were concentrated facing Germany.

This apprehension was heightened, it was stated, by news from England concerning the negotiations of Sir Stafford Cripps with a view to establishing closer collaboration between Britain and the Soviet Union and the appeal of Lord Beaverbrook to support Russia in her forthcoming conflict.

June 22, 1941

**WHERE GERMAN ARMIES MARCH ON RUSSIA**

Shown on the map is the western frontier of the Soviet Union, a battle line of more than 2,000 miles. Berlin indicated an attack from Norway to Rumania.

# STALIN, ON RADIO, RALLIES THE SOVIET

## PREMIER CONFIDENT

### Warns of 'Grave Danger,' but Holds No Army Has Been Invincible

### CONCEDES SOVIET LOSSES

### Reports Best German Units Crushed—Urges Destruction of Endangered Property

By The Associated Press.

MOSCOW, Thursday, July 3—Premier Joseph Stalin warned his people in a broadcast today that Nazi troops were inside White Russia and the Ukraine, but promised that "Hitler's army will be beaten like those of Napoleon and Kaiser Wilhelm."

He said German troops had occupied Lithuania, the greater part of Latvia and the western parts of White Russia and the Ukraine.

Mr. Stalin, who rarely speaks on the radio, said that "the enemy continues to push ahead, sending fresh forces to the front * * * despite the heroic resistance of the Red Army and despite the fact that the enemy's best divisions and best units of his air force have already been crushed and found their grave on the field of battle."

"Fascist aviation has enlarged its field of action, bombarding Murmansk, Orsha, Mogilev, Smolensk, Kiev, Odessa and Sevastopol," the Premier added. "A grave danger hangs over our country."

**Invincible Armies Decried**

But, he added, "history shows that invincible armies do not exist and never have existed."

"The army of Napoleon was considered invincible," the Premier declared, "but he was defeated finally by Russian, English and German troops. The German army of Wilhelm II also was considered invincible during the first imperialist war. Nevertheless it submitted several times to defeats inflicted by Russian and Anglo-French troops and finally was crushed by Anglo-French troops."

Mr. Stalin answered the question of why Russia ever signed her now shattered non-aggression pact with Germany by saying:

"No peaceful nation could refuse a peace accord with a neighboring power even if such monsters and cannibals as Hitler and Ribbentrop [German Foreign Minister Joachim von Ribbentrop] were found at its head."

**"Aggressor" to World**

Mr. Stalin said Germany, in breaking the pact by invading Russia, had gained temporary military advantage, but now was marked "in the eyes of the entire world as a bloody aggressor."

"Our cause is just," the Premier added. "The enemy must be crushed. We must win. Because of the war forced upon us, our country has entered into a battle to the death with the most ferocious and perfidious enemy. * * * Our troops are fighting heroically against an enemy armed to the teeth. * * * Thousands of Soviet tanks and airplanes are in action."

Mr. Stalin declared that a German victory meant restoration of great landed estates such as existed under the Czar, "slaves of German princes and barons," and said that therefore "it is necessary that Soviet citizens understand" what is at stake.

**Material Increase Asked**

He called for a ruthless campaign against defeatists, saboteurs and spies, and appealed for revitalized munitions and factory output and better transport organization.

The Premier mentioned the historic speech of Prime Minister Winston Churchill of Britain in which he promised all possible aid to the Soviet, and also the favorable attitude of the United States in the fight against Reichsfuehrer Hitler.

These statements, Mr. Stalin said, "create grateful sentiments in the hearts of the peoples of the Soviet Union."

Then, swinging into a recital of what Russians could actively do to aid in the war besides working in their shops and fields, he suggested these courses:

1. Destruction of every bit of equipment and foodstuffs likely to fall into German hands.
2. Retreat into the eastward vastnesses of Russia with all available supplies and transports at the approach of German troops.
3. Organization of local militias to fight with the regular army. He said Leningrad and Moscow workers already had so organized.
4. Organization of Russia's own system of underground saboteurs, spies and wreckers in German-occupied zones.

"All Soviet citizens must defend each inch of soil and fight until the last drop of blood for our villages," the Premier added.

July 3, 1941

# ALL VOLGA 'GERMANS' EXILED TO SIBERIA

## SHIFT IS DECREED

### Soviet Takes Sweeping Step to Forestall a Fifth Column

### NAZI FOMENTATION FEARED

### Action Impelled by Failure of District to Report Any Dissident Activity

By CYRUS L. SULZBERGER

Wireless to THE NEW YORK TIMES.

MOSCOW, Monday, Sept. 8—In a sweeping move designed to obviate permanently any dangers of a fifth-column movement in the Volga German Republic, which has housed hundreds of thousands of Germans since the latter part of the eighteenth century, when Catherine the Great invited in settlers from South Germany, the Soviet Supreme Council has signed a decree ordering the resettlement of that population in Siberia.

This predominantly farming folk will be moved eastward as soon as possible. A decree signed by President Mikhail I. Kalinin on Aug. 28 indicates its obvious purpose by stating:

"According to reliable information received by the military authorities, thousands and tens of thousands of diversionists and spies among the German population of the Volga are prepared to cause explosions in these regions at a signal from Germany."

**Easternmost German Colony**

The Volga settlement is the easternmost colony of Germans. The accent of the Volga settlers, however, is markedly different from that of the inhabitants of the present Reich

When this war started there was considerable speculation as to how extensively the Nazis were seeking secretly to organize dissent among this racial element. President Kalinin's decree now indicates that the government is taking no chances.

Russia watched with interest the uprisings of German settlers in the Yugoslav Banat during the Nazi invasion last April. Although the German Army's drive toward the Volga is a tremendous distance from its possible eventual objectives, it is clear that steps toward preventing present or future trouble are already being taken.

The decree, whose existence was made public today, is based on the theory that possible German efforts to muddy the waters in the Volga Republic might necessitate a Soviet action against the entire population in that region and that therefore to avoid such a predicament it is more advisable to resettle that population on Siberian land. This area is not only far from any danger of such interference but needs development.

It is stated that no Germans from the Volga have reported the existence of the purportedly large numbers of dissidents who have been uncovered.

"If diversionist acts took place," the decree said, "under orders from Germany by German dissidents or spies in the Volga German Republic or in neighboring regions, and bloodshed resulted, the Soviet Government would be forced under martial law to adopt reprisal measures against the entire Volga German population.

"In order to avoid such an undesirable occurrence and to forestall serious bloodshed, the Presidium of the Supreme Council of the U. S. S. R. has found it necessary to resettle the entire German population of the Volga regions to other districts under the condition that the resettled peoples be allotted land and given State aid to settle in the new regions. The resettled Germans will be given land in the Novosibirsk and Omsk districts, the Altai region of the Kazakhstan Republic and neighboring localities rich in land.

"In connection with this, the National Defense Council is instructed to resettle as soon as possible all Volga Germans who will be given land estates in new regions."

Nothing has been said about whether the regions evacuated by these Germans will be settled by new inhabitants, but because of the great industrial and agricultural importance of the Volga settlement it is most likely that this will take place. Hundreds of thousands of persons have been removed successfully from White Russia and the Western Ukraine and it is not impossible that some of them will be deposited in the Volga strip.

September 8, 1941

# HARD RUSSIAN CAMPAIGN BRINGS MANY SURPRISES

### Both Reds and Germans Have Acted In Ways That Were Not Expected

By HANSON W. BALDWIN

Special to THE NEW YORK TIMES.

LAKE CHARLES, La., Sept. 20—The first snows of Winter have covered the tundra and the forests of the Soviet north, but for the Allies the Winter's prospects are not cheerful.

Three months of the greatest campaign in military history have ended; Russia has been seriously hurt, and though the Germans may still be some way from decisive victory, time may well be not on the Allied, but on the Nazi side.

Winter is almost at hand in much of the vast land of the Soviets, yet its delaying influence upon German tactics during certain months and in certain theatres of the 2,000-mile front cannot be expected to prove a dominant factor. With much of Russian industry and raw material centers in German hands and more of it threatened, with the losses of the Red Army probably far greater than those of the German, Soviet strength is ebbing far more rapidly than the Nazi strength.

**Need for Support**

A "blood transfusion" of American and British aid, sent chiefly by the Iranian gateway, may delay the Nazi conquests and cost the Germans dearly. But unless prodigies of production, transportation and supply are performed with great speed in the United States and Great Britain and in Russia and over the land, ocean and air routes connecting the three countries, the Germans will almost certainly accomplish eventually their primary aim—destruction of most of Russia's western armies and conquest of the industrial heart of Russia west of the Volga.

**What is the present situation and what are the prospects?**

It would be impossible to assay those prospects without first referring to the tactical and technical surprises the Russian campaign already has provided. The Russians unquestionably have given the Germans the stiffest opposition Adolf Hitler's troops have

THE GERMAN - RUSSIAN FRONT AFTER THREE MONTHS OF WAR
1ST MONTH (JUNE 22-JULY 22)
2ND MONTH (JULY 22-AUG. 22)
3RD MONTH (AUG. 22-SEP. 21)
Last week's main drives
Railways
Miles 100 200 300
FINLAND
Lake Ladoga
Viborg
HELSINKI
KRONSTADT
LENINGRAD
Hangoe
G. OF FINLAND
TALLINN
Novgorod
DAGOE
Estonia
OESEL
Staraya Russa
Kalinin
Yaroslavl
GORKI
Pskov
BALTIC SEA
RIGA
Latvia
Rzhev
MOSCOW
Dvinsk
Ryazan
SOVIET
Vyazma
Memel
Lithuania
Vitebsk
Tula
Ryazsk
KAUNAS
Smolensk
Orsha
VILNA
UNION
EAST PRUSSIA
Mogilev
Bryansk
Orel
MINSK
Don
Bobruisk
Gomel
Kursk
Voronezh
Bialystok
Pripet Marshes
Pinsk
Pripet
Konotop
WARSAW
Bug
Brest-Litovsk
POLAND
Kowel
KHARKOV
KIEV
Zhitomir
UKRAINE
DONETS INDUSTRIAL BASIN
Berdichev
Kremenchug
Dniepropetrovsk
Vinnitsa
CRACOW
LWOW
Stalin
Slovakia
Taganrog
Krivoy Rog
Mariupol
BESSARABIA
Nikolaev
Melitopol
Kherson
SEA OF AZOV
ODESSA
Perekop
CRIMEA
AREA SHOWN IN INSET MAP
Galati
Sebastopol
Danube
Constanta
BLACK SEA
NIKOLAEV
KHERSON
Melitopol
Berdyansk
NOGAIS STEPPE
Chalbasi
Kirilovka
SEA OF AZOV
RYE, MAIZE, WHEAT
CRIMEA
IRON MINES
Theodosia
SIMFEROPOL
SEVASTOPOL (NAVAL BASE)
5,060 FEET
Roads
Railways
9-21-41

## A LONDONER CONTEMPLATES THE APPROACHING RUSSIAN WINTER

Illingworth in The London Daily Mail

"Cold comfort."

yet encountered, and in so far as the world is concerned, the length of time the German victories have already required has been a surprise. There is little doubt that the Russians were underestimated.

The surprises they have provided—surprises that may continue to be factors in the future progress of the war are several:

(1) The Russians evidently had far larger reserves of material—particularly planes and tanks—than had been believed.

(2) The qualities of Red Army command and staff work seem to have been better than anticipated.

(3) There have been no evidences of effective fifth - column movements or, as yet, of political dissidence.

(4) The army has shown what is apparently a greater capacity for manoeuvre than it was believed it possessed.

(5) Anti-aircraft and anti-tank defenses — both formerly described as Soviet weaknesses—have been shown to be fairly strong.

On the other hand, the Germans—the basis of whose military system, contrary to many misconceptions in this country, is flexibility and initiative—have also provided some surprises:

(1) They apparently have shown a considerable desire to economize and husband their military forces; victories have been achieved, where possible, by manoeuvre rather than frontal assault. In some instances where frontal assault was necessary, the Rumanians and the Finns have been assigned to some of the more costly sectors, as at Odessa and on the Karelian Isthmus. Air forces have been conserved as much as possible, and this, plus poor air fields and supply difficulties, may explain in some measure the relatively light German raids against Moscow.

(2) German Army communiqués which in previous campaigns had acquired a reputation for military exactitude, became at times in July, and occasionally since, political hyperbole. The Germans in Russia have not only been conducting a military offensive, but, as Herr Hitler has emphasized, they have been trying to stir up a "world crusade."

(3) The Germans as yet have made relatively little attempt to dispute with air power the Russian Black Sea superiority, probably because of the immense need for air power upon the land fronts.

These are some of the surprises of the Russian campaign—a campaign the details of which are, as yet, little known to the outside world. They are merely indicative of the surprises that are certain to come—surprises that make any precise forecast obviously impossible. Enough tangible results are evident, however, after a campaign of three months to permit an estimate.

**First, economically, industrially and for the military support of her armies, navies and air forces, Russia is chiefly dependent upon the area west of the Volga—specifically upon the Ukraine, Moscow, Leningrad and Kola Peninsula areas up in the far north. About half the Ukraine is in German hands, the rest imperiled.**

**The Ukraine industries were dependent on a triumvirate of power—the iron ore of Krivoy Rog, the electrical power furnished by the Dnieper dams and the coal of the Don Basin. Krivoy Rog is in German hands; the largest of the Dnieper dams has been blown up, the others are in German hands; only the coal remains.**

### Sources of Ore

**There are many other sources of iron ore in Russia, but most of them have not been developed in proportion to Krivoy Rog, and the re-routing of iron ore transportation and the construction of new steel mills offer tremendous problems. One such region—the Kerch area in Crimea—is already apparently partially cut off by the new German drive.**

Leningrad, which produces about 14 per cent by value of Soviet industrial output, is encircled; that output is lost to Russia. The Kola Peninsula production is isolated; many Russian western industrial cities are in German hands; only the Moscow area, nexus of the aircraft industry, and the partially developed mining and industrial areas west of the Volga are free for the moment from threat; the heart of Russian industry is already in German hands or is directly imperiled.

Secondly, Russian military losses have been huge, probably as much, in comparison to the German losses as one and one-half or three to one. And those losses are likely to increase; great sections of the Russian Army are apparently now cut off in Leningrad and Odessa, at the bottom of the Kiev pocket, and perhaps in the Smolensk area.

The situation of the Russians is, therefore, as a London spokesman pointed out last week, extremely grave. Yet Winter is approaching, and German communication lines are stretched thin; Russian guerrilla warfare continues in the German rear, while the stout Russian peasants in the uniforms of the Red Army still oppose the German advance.

The outlook, therefore, remains unchanged; the odds of military victory are still strongly upon Germany, although it is a victory that may well not reap its final fruits—capture of Moscow, an extension of German control to most of the area west of the Volga—until next year.

### The Ultimate Victory

But military victory does not necessarily mean ultimate victory. Guerrilla warfare, even opposition by armies of smaller size than at present, might be continued indefinitely, perhaps, if Russian troops could be supplied from outside Russia and from the industries west of the Volga. And economic consolidation of their military gains in Russia may be a problem too big for the Germans.

Everything in the future of the Russian campaign—which is to say, in one sense, the future of the world—depends, therefore, as it has depended for these last three months, on what Joseph Stalin and the Russian masses may choose to do. If they resist to the death, the German victories may eventually reap bitter fruits; if they surrender, Germany has won the Continent of Europe.

September 21, 1941

# MOSCOW PARLEY PLEDGES HUGE AID

## Talks Ended Speedily as U. S. and Britain Agree to Supply Almost All Soviet Asks

By The Associated Press.

MOSCOW, Thursday, Oct. 2—The United States and Great Britain agreed to fill virtually every Soviet need for war supplies in exchange for "large quantities" of Russian raw materials at the concluding session last night of the three-power conference.

The conference closed two days ahead of schedule after only three days of sessions — probably the shortest international council of such dimensions ever held. A communiqué issued by the British and United States delegations and one by the Russians announced its results.

For the United States and Great Britain, W. Averell Harriman and Lord Beaverbrook, heads of their delegations, promised "to place at the disposal of the Soviet Government practically every requirement for which the Soviet military and civil authorities have asked."

In return, said the communiqué issued by Mr. Harriman and Lord Beaverbrook, "the Soviet Government has supplied Great Britain and the United States with large quantities of raw materials urgently required in those countries."

Arrangements were said to have been made to "increase the volume of traffic in all directions."

The Soviet communiqué stressed the "atmosphere of perfect mutual understanding, confidence and good-will," and said that the delegates had been "inspired by the eminence of the cause of delivering other nations from the Nazi threat of enslavement."

In a speech to the closing session Foreign Commissar Vyacheslaff M. Molotoff said that the conference had shown that "deliveries of arms and most important materials for the defense of the U. S. S. R., which were commenced previously, must and will become extensive and regular."

Mr. Molotoff added that "these deliveries of airplanes, tanks and other armaments and equipment and raw materials will be increased and will acquire growing importance in the future."

October 2, 1941

# *Moscow Relieved and Gay After Beating Off Nazi Tide*

By C. L. SULZBERGER

Wireless to The New York Times.

**MOSCOW, Dec. 14—This is the story of Moscow and its people, who for ten bitter weeks gallantly withstood the greatest massed military assault in all history. Seven hundred and fifty thousand men, bearing with them a monstrous array of tanks, aircraft and** all the many death-dealing instruments conceived by the ingenious Nazi mind, thundered close to the city limits and beat savagely upon the gates. They did not pass.

Today, after weeks of bitter cold and lowering snowstorms, the sun rose propitiously, shining on the placid white streets while the inordinately gay Muscovites, relieved of strain, bustled about doing their Sunday shopping and jesting at the latest posters ridiculing the retreating Germans.

The Ballet presented a gala performance. Women waited outside shops with loaded market bags. Soldiers back on leave ambled along with their wives, girls or mothers. Uniformed peasant lads from the provinces got their first awed glimpse of the Kremlin's crenelated walls and the snow-laden, bulbous turrets of magnificent St. Basil's Church.

Along the broad avenues cavalrymen riding in pairs patrolled their beats, for the city still is under martial law. At each corner stood infantrymen—usually non-commissioned officers—still on the alert with bayoneted rifles. Readiness remains the watchword. Overhead was the constant drone of fighter patrols in the bright, clear sky, and occasional flights of bombers roared back from their assignments in the west.

### Bomb Damage Not Great

Squads of women workers cleared snowdrifts from the sidewalks. Repair platoons were taking care of the amazingly slight bomb damage in that rapid fashion that has kept Moscow spic and span, despite the German Air Force's most persistent efforts.

The writer walked past the university, which was hit directly by a giant bomb some weeks ago. Reconstruction was proceeding. The Bolshoi Theatre, although it was struck twice, shows few scars. A magnificent anti-aircraft barrage protected the center of the capital, and only the outskirts suffered more than minimal damage. I have not seen a single area that even remotely compares with the wreckage shown in photographs of London.

All morning long I strolled about the streets, regarding the cheerful crowds. There were fewer children playing with sleds and skis than in normal times. There were more women. There were more soldiers. There were infantrymen in fleece-lined leather coats with yellow fur calpacs; women auxiliary workers with skirted uniforms with gray squirrel caps; provincial levies wearing quilted jackets, mittens, boots and spiked woolen forage caps emblazoned with the Red Star; Cossack officers in gay dress costumes, with blue capes, spurred knee-boots and high astrakhan hats, strutting about with handsome girls on their arms.

As I walked along the sidewalk, a talkative and grinning young man with one extra drink under his belt grabbed my arm.

"You are happy," I said. "Why?"

"It is Moscow," he said. "Here we are in Moscow."

A woman I know, who had just come back to the capital, said:

"I am glad to have seen this day. You foreigners cannot understand. Of course, my family is not here. Most of my friends are gone. But this is Moscow. If you foreigners could only understand what that means."

### Beaten Germans Retire

Many miles to the west, beaten German troops are retreating slowly, harried by the Russian cavalry and pounded by the great shells of heavy artillery, which Joseph Stalin once called the god of war. Passing constantly through the streets of Moscow are Red Army trucks, staff cars and motorcycles on their way to the front, where the Russians are moving in hard on the enemy's heels.

Just two months ago the Germans pierced the Soviet lines near Mozhaisk and stormed down the main highway toward the city gates. Later they came closer. They bombed the city, dropping new explosives contained in concrete shells calculated to kill as many civilians as possible while saving metal for dwindling reserves.

The Germans pounded close to the capital's water supplies. They brought up the largest tank army ever assembled, in an effort to batter down the stanch Red Army lines. They failed. Now, with reserves of gasoline depleted, they are leaving dozens of tanks behind as they withdraw slowly westward. Also left behind are soldiers frozen at their posts.

December 15, 1941

# *Soviet's Social Outlook Altered In Fixing Public Interest on War*

## *Zeal for Combat, Tolerance of Religion and Glorification of Individual Stand Out—Popular Cultural Interests Are Kept*

Wireless to The New York Times.

KUIBYSHEV, Russia, April 24—Without underestimating the privations that the Soviet people have accepted in their war effort, it may be said that it is in their finer habits of mind rather than of body that those not serving in the army have been most profoundly affected.

Today the Soviet citizen reads, sees around him in the form of popular poster art, watches in the cinema and the theatre and hears by radio little that does not have some connection with the war or with the Russian tradition that the people are being called upon to defend. This does not mean a complete interruption of general cultural interests, however. The ballet, the opera and concerts are crowded, while this year's publishing list includes 50,000 copies of Chaucer's "Canterbury Tales," 100,000 of Mark Twain and 50,000 of Stendhal's "La Chartreuse de Parme," as well as many classical reprints not even remotely connected with war.

But, except for a constant interest in the classics—you still find the hotel doorboy reading "Hamlet" and the street bookstalls sell not detective stories but cheap editions of "War and Peace" and Lermontoff's poems—little is being published that gives the reading public any escape from the events overshadowing their lives.

Take, for example, Krokodil, a

weekly with nearly 250,000 circulation. It is rare to find on any of its eight pages a drawing or joke not connected with the war. The current issue is made up entirely of material that is funny, usually cruelly so, at the expense of the Germans. Unlike Punch and The New Yorker, it has no jokes against its own readers.

All forms of popular art link the present war with Russian historic tradition, from the odes of the ancient Kazakstan bard, Dzhambul—the Russian Homer, as he is sometimes called—to the latest production of Moscow's Stanislavsky's Theatre, where scenes from Suvoroff's last campaign against Napoleon are presented operatically.

The heroic defense of Sevastopol in the Crimean War is recalled in 100,000 copies of Tolstoy's "Sevastopol Tales," and the Battle of Borodino in 250,000 copies of relevant chapters from "War and Peace," sold at a few cents a copy in paperback editions, while partisan warfare in the past, the people's wars under Pojarsky, and the victories of Alexander Nevsky, Suvoroff and Kutuzoff are revived in countless pamphlets and film exhibitions.

This is the first time in the Soviet Union's history that war has become a popular subject, though tales of adventure and daring always have been widely read. Indeed, many of the achievements of Soviet workers, explorers, scientists and airmen have been presented in heroic style. It is significant that Jack London and Kipling have long been highly popular authors in Russia.

The great task of directing public attention exclusively to war meant certain modifications in the official attitude toward certain subjects, the most striking being religion and personal heroism. Antireligious voices have been completely silenced and the flood of literature once devoted to this subject has ceased. It is realized that religious faith—not necessarily with any powerful church influence—is part and parcel of the national Russian make-up, as also of other nationalities fighting beside the Russians in the Red Army.

As a Russian writer put it to this correspondent: "I always hated bortsch. But when I go to the front and get it for dinner, I now eat it willingly because I feel it is a Russian national dish. Many of us feel the same way about religion now."

**Church Earns Tolerance**

The church has earned this tolerance. Particularly in the occupied regions, priests and believers have stoutly resisted German attempts to use them politically in an anti-Soviet sense. A story is told of a high personage who while decorating partisans stepped before a shaggy-headed and bearded hero and said kindly, "But you know you ought to have your hair cut." The reply was, "But I am not allowed to; I am a priest."

There was a time when the glorification of personal deeds of bravery were frowned on officially. It is said that the writer of a children's book about a little boy who killed a crocodile met disapproval because he overstressed individual action. That time is past.

Today every Soviet newspaper is packed with tales of individuals' exploits—the soldier who kills single-handed a record number of Germans, the pilot who sacrifices his life by crash-landing his plane on a concentration of German tanks at a gasoline dump. The example of these men and women is help up before the nation and the army.

It would be wrong to think that these modifications are sudden or temporary. They have been going on gradually for several years in preparation for national defense and the mobilization of the country's full force. But the war has hastened the process and made them more apparent.

April 25, 1942

# RUSSIANS SEE STALINGRAD AS KEY TO THE WAR

## To Make Sure of Holding the City They Call Urgently for a Second Front

By RALPH PARKER

Wireless to THE NEW YORK TIMES.

MOSCOW, Sept. 12—The Soviet press does not hide the great importance that the government attaches to retention of control of the Volga. It is now more than two months since the Soviet people were told that the giving up of further territory would reduce the country's fighting capacity and threaten centers and communications vital to Russia's continued existence. They were told: "The motherland is in mortal danger. The Germans must not reach the Volga." Since then the Don and Kuban granaries have been lost, the Maikop oil field has been lost, the enemy has strengthened his grip on the Black Sea coast, fascist mountaineers are planting the swastika on the Caucasian heights and Stalingrad is imperiled.

**Food Losses**

So far Russia's most serious losses have been in food. On the Don steppe the Germans are reported forcing the peasants to transport the harvest to central depots where the grain is sent westward. Fruit and dairy produce is being requisitioned wholesale by the Wehrmacht. That is so much loss to Russia, so much gain to Germany. But Stalingrad's loss would outweigh all previous losses in this campaign, for Stalingrad is the Volga; Stalingrad, in the words of Red Star, the Army newspaper, is Grozny, Baku and Transcaucasia. To lose Stalingrad is to lose for the Red Army fighting above and below it the bulk of the wealth that lies beyond it.

With the Germans firmly established on the Volga the war both for Russia and her allies would take on a new aspect. At no time during the present war has it been truer that the Red Army men—those gray-eyed, broad-faced, frowning, sweating, swearing Russians—are fighting and dying to save the future prosperity of America and the future existence of England.

The loss of Stalingrad would remove from the Red Army the only large city in a very wide area. There is no other city within 200 miles where an army powerful enough to organize a counter-offensive could winter and it seems doubtful, after the tremendous strain of many weeks of unabated battle, absorbing so many reserves, that a determined counter-offensive on the Volga front could be organized before Winter. Once in firm possession of Stalingrad the Wehrmacht could count on a period of recuperation for a large part of its weary forces and set about the consolidation of its grip on the lower reaches of the Volga, the Kuban and North Caucasia.

It is true that the Wehrmacht's failure before Voronezh and the vigorous local pressure that the Red Army has maintained along the Don at various points between Voronezh and Kletskaya suggests that there is a menace to von Bock's Volga salient from the north and should the German Marshal falter at Stalingrad, we may see this menace increase and the roof of the salient come crashing down on the twenty-five German divisions within the salient. But should Stalingrad fall, von Bock might well decide to aim at outflanking those Russian armies below and beyond Voronezh by striking northward up to the neck of the egg cup formed by the Don and Volga.

**Junction and Shield**

There are two aspects of the Volga's strategic importance—the Volga as a line of communication and the Volga as a shield. German possession of the Volga around and south of Stalingrad would not, of course, deny the Russians its use as far as the intermediate stages. The river has enormous importance in the middle and upper reaches which the loss of the lower reaches would not affect.

The whole elaborate riverine economy of the vast valley would continue during the remaining two months of navigation—important months for wheat and timber moving to the cities. But 7,000,000 tons of oil which (to use the peacetime estimate) were towed upstream annually past Stalingrad would have to seek other more limited overland routes from Emba and Zhilaya Kosa and Krasnovodsk on the Caspian—routes quite incapable of carrying more than a small fraction of the river-borne quantity.

The gravity of the loss of the main communications in connection with Russia's future strategy is relative to the size of reserves of grain and oil, and the possibilities of alternative sources of supply. The crucial question is whether the Red Army would be able to launch a crushing offensive against the Wehrmacht next year in coordination with the Allies if Stalingrad fell and the Germans established themselves on the Volga. If not, then the Allies' chances of defeating Germany next year are slight and the cost of the ultimate victory will be high—a cost not in Russian but in British and American lives.

However burning Russian hatred for Germany, however resolutely the nation stood behind the government, however sullenly the peoples of the occupied Soviet land endured the German yoke, the Allies would draw no real aid in their ultimate reckoning with Hitler if Russia were too enfeebled in manpower, too deficient in arms and too ill-placed strategically to force the enemy to keep at least half his forces in the East.

It does not need a large force to garrison the occupied territory. People who have been wandering about in the inferno behind the German lines and found their way to Moscow state that except in towns and at communication knots the Germans are thinly dispersed in the depth of the occupied region. Theorists who maintain that even if Russia is beaten to a standstill she would still absorb huge German forces in the East are drawing dangerous analogies from the last war. Nazi organizations already have shown near Leningrad how ruthlessly and effectively they are prepared to deal with rebellious villages.

### Germans Facing West

**If then the Nazis could establish themselves on a tenable line and, satisfied that the Red Army was too enfeebled to launch a counter-offensive on a massive scale, withdrew the bulk of their forces from Russia, the Allies would have to face in the West a formidable foe consisting of several millions, including the fighting elite of the veterans. And not only in the West. With its left flank secured, the Wehrmacht could confidently deliver blows at the Middle East from the Black Sea region. The outlook would be black.**

**Stalingrad may well be decisive and turn the hypothesis into cold, blunt fact, for with Stalingrad in** German hands, large-scale fighting on the Volga front would probably diminish and any scaling down of the war's intensity is a German gain and an Allied loss. With Stalingrad firmly held, the process of attrition which the Wehrmacht can barely stand would be prolonged, the enemy would be forced back across the Don steppe to the cities where lie the nearest quarters where the Army could maintain itself over the Winter.

If von Bock is able to bring the Don campaign to an end within the next two or three weeks his forces would be in fair shape again for campaigning next Spring, while the Red Army would be cut off from the supplies of the South. In such an event Allied chances of rapid success in the West would be far from bright.

### Desire for Second Front

It is the realization that the whole issue of the war may depend on the result of the present operations that gives so keen an edge to the general desire here for the immediate opening of a second front in Europe. Mr. Churchill's phrase about the Russian front, "This is Sept. 8," puzzled the people here, for at that date last year Moscow still stood before its worst ordeal. Optimists interpret it to mean that four months remain of the year in which all Russia looks to Britain and America to fulfill the expectation of their intervention in Europe. There are others whose reaction is: "Yes, Sept. 8, and Molotoff was in the West in May. Where are your armies?"

There is a general foreboding that when the Allies feel strong enough to strike it will be too late to save themselves. Maybe it is too late to save Russia from days even darker than today, but nevertheless there is the utmost determination to continue wearing down the enemy in the great battle in progress at Stalingrad, where Red Star believes Germany's hopes already have been frustrated and a period of siege warfare opened.

In the belief that the enemy can be beaten if he is worn down, even though Russia herself may be worn down, nothing is being spared at Stalingrad, for Russia knows that when the final victory crowns the Allies' efforts, Russia will share it, just as when the Soviet frontiers are re-established the contribution of occupied regions will not be forgotten in Moscow. For the Russian people are confident that the peoples of all Allied lands recognize the imperishable service Russia has done for the United Nations, and Russia trusts peoples' conscience as she trusts their instinct.

September 13, 1942

# ALL OF RUSSIA'S LOSS IS NOT HITLER'S GAIN

## Germany Must Fight On Against a Foe Who Still Has Vast Resources

By CHARLES HURD

**WASHINGTON, Sept. 19—The German sweep through the Caucasus has reached Stalingrad and choked off the river traffic of the Volga,** but it would be a mistake to think that all of the military and economic lifeblood thus drained from Russia is flowing into the veins of Hitler's war machine.

Russia has lost a great deal in resources but Hitler has hardly gained a tithe of that loss. Viewed from the standpoint of the coming fourth year of the war on the Western Front, he now seems to have achieved little more than a stalemate.

No informed observer minimizes the size of the blow dealt to the United Nations in the pushing back of the southern Soviet armies, but the actuality is much less critical than was the anticipation in the broad view of the world picture. Russia has been badly beaten in the campaign season now closing, but Russia is not conquered.

What, therefore, is the net result? What have the Russians lost and what have the Germans gained? And, most important, what is left to the Russians?

### Scorched Earth

The Germans have gained rich territory, but it must be assumed that this area has been scorched and destroyed with the same dogged stubbornness with which Soviet citizens have joined their soldiers in fighting every mile of the German advance. Grain fields, factories and railway rolling stock have been the victims of the Russian torches, to say nothing of the normal mass destruction of warfare.

The German Army, while depriving Russia of vast oil resources by blocking transit on the Volga, actually holds only the Maikop fields, which are among the smallest of the producing regions. These fields probably can be put into operation in about six months, but in the meantime they yield nothing, except the debatable margin of probable future supplies that may make the Germans feel more secure in drawing on their current reserves.

The German Armies, at terrible cost to themselves, have inflicted heavy casualties on the Russians, but there has been no German claim or other evidence that any main Russian Army has been destroyed.

This means that the Germans have been forced for a second year to trade their primary objective for a secondary one. They set out to destroy the Soviet Armies and instead have won only territory. The Soviet Armies, possibly hurt badly in the loss of equipment, still remain intact, and with sufficient strength to launch irritating counter-attacks along the line to the northward.

### Unrelenting Struggle

No one can estimate the strength of the Russian Army as of today, but the German communiqués themselves testify to the manner in which the Russians are fighting. This fighting in itself prevents the establishment of a static line, which Hitler would hope to hold with a fraction of current forces employed against the Russians in order to prepare for the coming struggle in Western Europe.

Thus it is apparent that Hitler has won from Stalin very little beyond potential supplies for the future and the prospect of another Winter in Russia.

And what is left of Russian resources? The industrial position of Russia today might be compared with the industrial position of the United States if we had lost the industry, mines and oil fields of Pennsylvania and New England, but still hold the resources of the Middle West. This constricted Russia may expect to supplement its supplies with whatever trickles in through the northern ports of Murmansk and Archangel and the southern route from Basra, on the Persian Gulf, north across Iran and by transport through the Caspian Sea.

The Russian battle lines now extend southward from Leningrad to a point west of Moscow and southeastward then to a line running east and west between the Don and Volga Rivers. A strong force holds the eastern end of the Caucasus.

Henceforth the supply of these armies must come largely from the industrial region east of Moscow, which extends to the Urals. The distance provides considerable protection from German bombers but makes a headache of transport, in which Russia is weak.

### Moscow Industry

The Russian forces still hold the wealthy industrial district around Moscow, but for a year industries in this locality have been moved to the eastward, mainly to Gorki, formerly the seat of the Russian automobile industry. It may be assumed, however, that Moscow is still the heart of the industrial community that supplies munitions, machinery, arms and transport to the Soviet forces.

In this region also are produced textiles, chemicals, metal ware and electrical equipment. This region appears to be secure until next year. Along the Volga River are spaced great oil refineries, together with hydroelectric plants and shipyards.

### Manufacturing Power

Great as has been the loss of industry to the Soviet, Russia still has an immense reserve of manufacturing power; the supply of raw materials has become its principal worry with the loss of the iron mines near Kerch and the stopping of oil shipments from Baku via the Volga.

For oil, the Russians must fall back on the relatively undeveloped fields near Kazan and Sterlitamak and other pools in the western reaches of the Urals. These fields promise very great production, but development of them has been slow. The main iron reserves now left to the Russians lie far to the north of Leningrad and in the Urals, except for one field south of

## *SOVIET RESOURCES: THOSE CONQUERED AND VITAL ONES REMAINING*

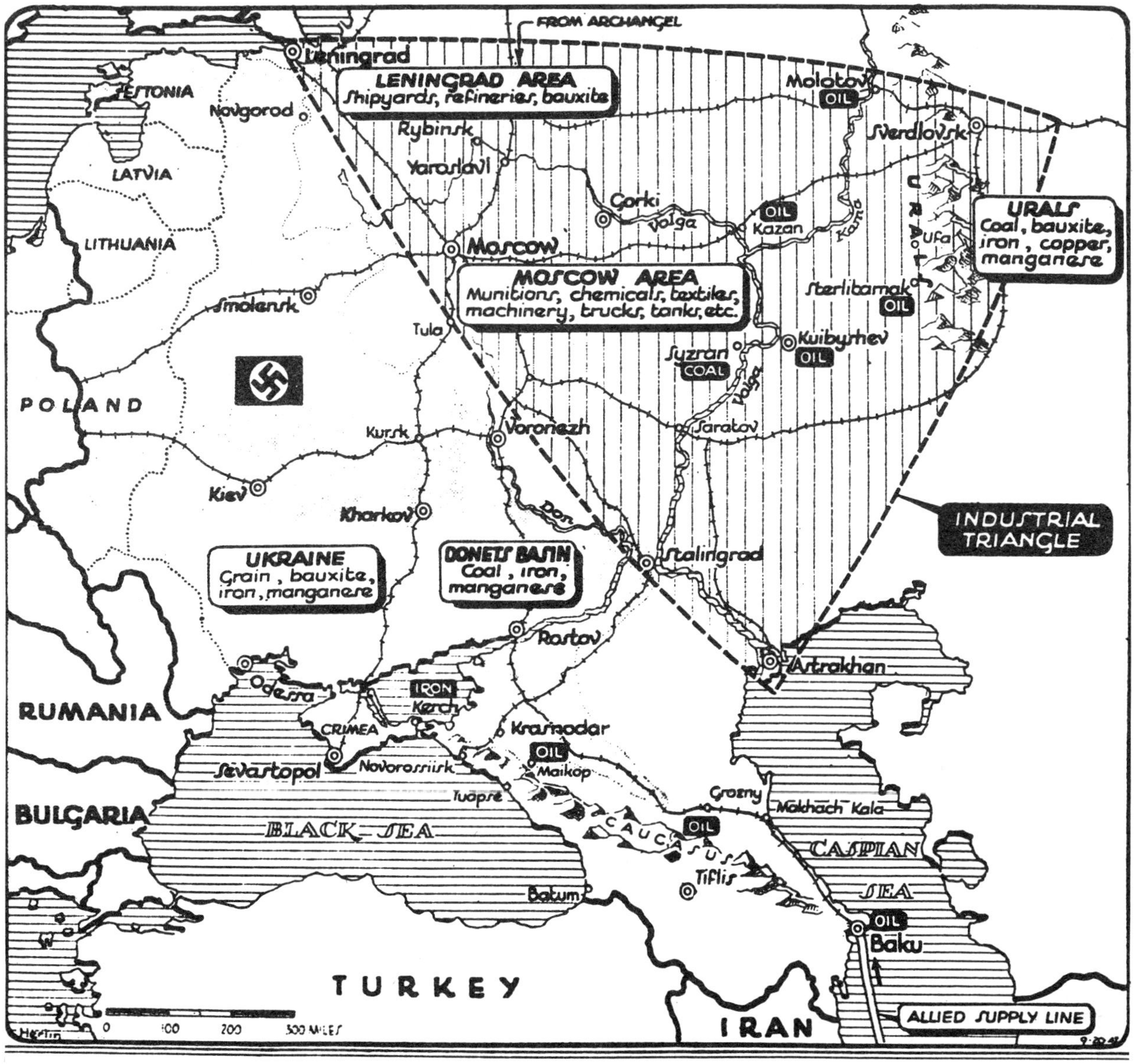

Moscow. Coal must be shipped from the fields of Syzran, on the banks of the Volga, to supply the industries in the neighborhood of Moscow, although this field is easily convenient for the Ural industries.

The effective industrial region of Russia today consists of a triangle considerably less than the area of the United States, but with a population that probably is greater. In this region, incidentally, are relatively few farms, so the question of food to maintain this working and fighting population is grave, unless there are large reserves carried out of the occupied region and placed in storage.

**Productive Area**

The ordinary maps of Russia give a false impression of the productive area of that country. As of today, this area begins with Leningrad in the northwestern corner, where the Soviet forces stand with their backs against precious shipyards, oil refineries and aluminum mines. It extends eastward along the Trans-Siberian Railway to the city of Sverdlovsk, railway junction and heart of the oil, coal, aluminum and iron mines of the Urals. The eastern side of the triangle runs southward to the Caspian Sea and the western side extends northwestward from the mouth of the Volga through Moscow to Leningrad.

The fact that the river traffic of the Volga no longer flows unimpeded from the Caspian northward does not mean that the commerce of this river is paralyzed. The river still is the great interior artery of commerce, with 50,000,000 workers living and working in its valley.

Starting at a point a little north of Stalingrad this traffic goes unimpeded northward along the western edge of the Ural development, and then the broad sluggish waters turn northeastward to flow through Gorki, Yaroslavl and Rybinsk. An eastern arm of the river, named the Kama, flows northeastward along the southern boundary of the Kazan oil field and through another great potential oil deposit near Molotov.

Thus the river is still a vital transport factor, particularly in a country where railway lines are scanty. The value of the Russia served by the Volga and the Kama as a productive arsenal depends largely on the organizing genius used to extend its resources since June of last year.

September 20, 1942

# RED ARMY REDUCES COMMISSARS' RANK

### Associate Political Command Abolished, but Leaders Will Become Junior Officers

### STALIN UNIFIES AUTHORITY

By RALPH PARKER

Wireless to THE NEW YORK TIMES.

MOSCOW, Oct. 10—The lodging of full powers of command in the hands of Red Army officers by bringing the political commissars under their control was decreed today. The measure will unify command, removing ambiguities and causes of delay. At the same time it will increase the prestige of the commanders and deepen the influence of the political staffs, which in the future will have military rank and be fully trained fighting men.

The step was not unexpected. It has grown out of the circumstances of the war, which demand speedy decisions and in which fighting men wish to be addressed in language they understand and by men who share their dangers. The greater part of the present commissars will immediately, or after a short training course, take posts of command. Others. who lack flexibility and are unwilling to learn the practical lessons of war, will cease to play a role in the political education of the Red Army.

[The political commissars' power was suspended after the war with Finland in 1940, but was restored after Germany attacked Russia.]

The decree, far from meaning an end of Red Army political education, should strengthen it, and may be a considered further step in the full mobilization of Russian strength in offensive spirit.

**Order Signed by Stalin**

The decree was published by the Presidium of the Supreme Soviet and put into effective operation by an order signed by Premier Joseph Stalin in his capacity as People's Commissar of Defense. The decree vests full authority of command in the Red Army's officers, abolishing the institution of military commissars, though at the same time creating a class of political workers under the control of the military commanders.

Those political commissars who have already acquired complete military experience in operations will be transferred immediately to appropriate military posts. The lowest grade of political worker will become a subaltern, the battalion commissar a major, the regimental commissar a colonel and so on. Those who have not acquired full military education will learn it in short courses at the front.

Mr. Stalin's order removes all authority from commissars, naming them as aides to their commanders. Military posts are to report on the military qualifications of the higher-ranking commissars. The Soviets are ordered to advance experienced political workers in the lower ranks to positions of military authority at the greatest possible speed and to organize courses for the creation of cadres of company, battalion and regimental commanders.

In a preamble to the decree, the Supreme Soviet points out that the establishment of political commissars in the Red Army dates from the civil war, when there was a certain distrust of commanders, among whom some were skeptical or hostile toward the Soviet power. The political commissars played a decisive role in strengthening the Red Army's political education and military discipline.

**New Leadership to Fore**

The civil war was followed by a period in which new officers' cadres were formed and the present war brought much new talent to the surface. The Red Army's commanders now have proved in battle their devotion and political and military maturity. The decree emphasizes that the commissars have gained military experience and that some already hold positions of military command.

The commissars thus have become superfluous, the decree continues. Indeed, they might have become an obstacle in the way of improved leadership and have placed the commanders in embarrassing positions.

Abolition of the autonomous powers of the Red Army's political staff is regarded here as evidence of the keen sense of realism of Russia's military and political leaders. It marks an even closer identification of the people with the regime, and it has become possible only through the growth of political knowledge in the army and the emergence in battle of a keen young reliable corps of officers, who constantly have been fed from the ranks.

It is to free these responsible commanders from any hindrances in carrying out their duties and to add to their ranks that the present decree is issued. It will immediately add to the Red Army's fighting forces thousands of men with high leadership qualifications, many them close friends of the commanders and beloved by the men.

**Trend to Unity Long Seen**

At the same time the decree removes certain handicaps and corrects certain abuses. Today it is far less necessary than in the civil war to divide military and morale leadership in the army.

"The regimental commissar is the political and morale leader of the regiment, the first to defend material and spiritual interests," Mr. Stalin wrote in 1919. "The regimental commander is the head of the regiment; the commissar must be the father and soul of the regiment."

But since then Mr. Stalin has taken a keen personal interest in training educated commanders able to take full responsibility. His concern has been that they should be men of strong will, devated to the cause of socialism, able to lead troops fully equipped with modern means of warfare and train them properly. An increase of officer cadres also has been a paromount concern of Mr. Stalin.

"If our army possesses genuinely steeled cadres in sufficient numbers it will be invincible" he said in an address to graduates of Red Army acedemies seven years ago.

The reforms in the Red Army were foreshadowed by a Red Star editorial on Wednesday, which strongly criticized political commissars who neglect military knowledge. The army newspaper urged that all political workers strengthen their knowledge of military matters and be able to take command if neccessary. Their value was not measured by the number of their meetings and reports, but by their discipline and success in battle, it asserted. The commissar should know how to handle arms, fight and dig before he could urge men to shoot straight, fight toughly or dig in well, the editorial continued, for the main power of agitation is in personal example.

Red Star declared some political commissars had no military knowledge and did not want any, relying on their civil war reputations of political capabilities.

Another indication of the way things were running was the extraordinary publicity given to a play, "The Front," Alexander Korneichuk's remarkable exposé of fault and error in the Red Army. It is a morality play; that is, its characters are composite, not based on any individuals, but personifying certain tendencies, good and bad, in the Red Army.

A careful analysis of "The Front" was published in every Soviet newspaper a fortnight ago, and it caused widespread discussion. Ivan Gorloff personifies in the play all the harmful tendencies referred to in the Red Star editorial.

"The trouble with Gorloff," the critique said, "is that he did not want to study, missed opportunities to travel abroad and learned nothing, though he was brave, had a good record and fought very well in the civil war. An enemy is not beaten by radio communications, but by heroism and valor."

The Red Army command considered that the commissars put too much emphasis on their men's spirit at the expense of realism. At the same time the role of the commissars during the long retreats of the Summers of 1941 and 1942 was most valuable. Without their example and encouragement, the picture today would have been very different. But today the situation is different.

"Political work in attack has to be different than in defense," Red Star asserts. "The people are strong because they know the direction is not in the hands of men like Ivan Gorloff. Their liquidation will lead to the Red Army's strengthening."

October 11, 1942

# 9-DAY FIGHT RAGES FOR RUSSIAN HOUSE

## Stalingrad Apartment Building Becomes Red Army Citadel in Swaying Battle

## TANK CHARGE FRUSTRATED

MOSCOW, Oct. 14 (U.P.)—Its windows are shattered, the doors blown off and corners wrecked by bombs. Russian women and children who once lived peacefully in its room are dead—slaughtered by the Germans. But today Russian machine guns, anti-tank guns and rifles point through the bricked-up windows of this four-story apartment building in the outskirts of Stalingrad known as 217 Bar A.

The story of the nine-day battle that raged in and around the building is the story of the defense of Stalingrad. It was told today by the newspaper Pravda's special correspondent, Boris Polyevoy, as it was related to him by the apartment's commander, Lieutenant Tzvetkoff.

Once the house had modern flats and wide stairways. Now, again in Russian hands, it is wrecked, surrounded by a network of trenches. The Germans occupy a building diagonally across the way.

The Germans captured the street in mid-September after artillery and aerial attacks, and then occupied 217 Bar A.

**Germans Driven Out**

They dug a maze of trenches in its inner courtyard and put a strong artillery emplacement behind a pile of kindling wood. Russian Guards counter-attacked, reoccupied the street and entered the house, which they took by fighting their way through the corridors. Then they dug in to await a German counter-attack, which came the next morning.

Artillery shelled the approaches of the building. Ten waves of divebombers rained down explosives. Then twenty heavy tanks, carrying German tommy-gunners, moved forward.

Russian anti-tank riflemen opened fire and five tanks went up in flames. The others kept coming. The riflemen, having exhausted their ammunition, rushed into 217 Bar A and began hurling grenades from the windows. Three more tanks went up in flames. The others kept moving.

Machine guns in the windows of the lower floors poured a hail of lead into the tommy-gunners, but they, too, soon ran short of ammunition. The tanks kept coming.

One tall, unnamed soldier, clutching a tank mine at his breast, shouted "I won't let you pass, you skunks!" and threw himself under the leading tank. Three tanks were left. They broke through the barricade and approached 217 Bar A.

The defenders threw benzine bottles, but the German tommy-gunners burst into the building's entrance. Fighting raged on the stairway. The Germans outnumbered the Russians three to one.

They tried to ascend the stairway, but one Russian tommy-gunner, lying on the landing, held them off.

Running short of ammunition, the Russians on the stairs hurled grenades until a group of Germans who had gone up the fire escape to the second floor attacked them from the rear. The defenders retreated to the third floor.

**Grenades and Epithets Fly**

A Soviet tommy-gunner named Tchepournine, who had been wounded in the shoulder and hip, was carried along. He was put on the kitchen floor of one flat to guard the fire escape from another rear attack. The others built another barricade on the third landing.

The Germans tossed up grenades, but the Russians caught them and hurled them back, shouting, "Here's one for Stalingrad—here's one for the Ukraine." Unable to make any headway, the Germans descended to the lower apartments.

The next morning at dawn the Germans renewed the assault. They opened it with a ten-minute mine-thrower attack on the stairway and through the windows. The exploding mines filled the stairway with brown smoke and plaster dust. But when the Germans tried to crash through they were mowed down by accurate rifle shots.

Their cartridges almost gone, the Russian riflemen were getting ready for a hand-to-hand struggle when they heard shouts from across the rooftops. They came from other Russian troops who had crawled across the roofs of near-by houses to relieve their beleaguered comrades.

They leaped into the house through trap-doors in the roof and began showering the Germans with grenades. The enemy began fleeing from the house. The battle cost the Germans fifty-two men and two officers.

And 217 Bar A still stands.

October 15, 1942

# *NAZIS' GRIP ON STALINGRAD BROKEN; 15,000 SLAIN AS SOVIET PUSH GAINS*

## 12,000 MORE TAKEN

### Russians Smash Ahead, Capture Many Places in Multiple Drive

### HELP REACHES VOLGA CITY

### Column Arrives From North—Three Divisions With Generals Among Forces Encircled

By The Associated Press.

MOSCOW, Wednesday, Nov. 25—The three-month-old Nazi grip on Stalingrad was weakening today after a swiftly advancing Red Army had killed 15,000 more Germans yesterday and captured 12,000, including three divisional generals, in a great Winter offensive rolling so fast that some Nazi units were cut down from behind in panicky retreat.

Russian official announcements raised the toll of Nazis to 77,000 dead or captured, not counting huge numbers of wounded who apparently are freezing to death on the frozen steppes, as did other German units last Winter in the rout from Moscow.

The Red Army's effort to encircle the entire Nazi army stalemated before Stalingrad, estimated at 300,000, clearly was gaining in power. Two communiqués told of vast stocks of war equipment falling to the Soviet tide, of at least one enemy airdrome being seized so swiftly that scores of German planes were unable to take to the air.

**Stalingrad Defenders Gain**

Inside Stalingrad the Russians in frontal assaults also were gaining against Nazi detachments whose rear communications had been slashed by Russian flanking armies sweeping across the Don River far to the west.

[The German High Command admitted the gravity of the situation by acknowledging the penetration of Nazi defenses southwest of Stalingrad. But it said "countermeasures" were under way and reported "savage battles" in the Don bend region. The London Express quoted a Stockholm report that the Germans had "begun to pull out of Stalingrad."]

The midnight Soviet communiqué said 900 Germans were killed and dozens of enemy blockhouses occupied in a slow but steady advance inside Stalingrad, while in the Caucasus Red Army units cut down additional hundreds of Nazis in successful stands in the Nalchik and Tuapse sectors.

This bulletin added some details to the striking Russian successes above and below Stalingrad and inside the Don River bend, as announced in a special communiqué. One Red Army unit captured a Nazi airdrome so swiftly, it said, that forty-two enemy planes did not have time to take to the air. Twenty-five of these planes were destroyed and the seventeen others were captured intact.

In some sectors there was evident Axis demoralization, because hundreds of fleeing Germans were being struck down from behind as the Red Army rolled onward.

This was the third special communiqué in three days and it told this story of increasing Red Army successes:

One Red Army gained twenty-five miles northwest of Stalingrad, another drove an additional twelve miles ahead to the southwest on a line paralleling the Stalingrad-Novorossiisk railroad in an apparent attempt to drive straight across the Northern Caucasus to the Black Sea and shatter communication lines of the German Mid-Caucasian army.

In the Don River elbow, directly west of Stalingrad, the Red Army already had cut direct Nazi army's communications with its faltering forces inside Stalingrad. It was inside the strategic Don loop that the three Nazi generals were seized. Twelve more Russian villages were taken in this huge pincer movement.

The Russians announced that in one day they had captured 1,164 guns of various caliber; 431 tanks, many in full working order; eighty-eight planes, many of them intact; 3,940 trucks, more than 5,000 horses, 3,000,000 shells, 18,000,000 cartridges and large numbers of infantry arms and other equipment and provisions, which "still are being counted."

In the twenty-five-mile advance northwest of Stalingrad a significant subsidiary action was mentioned by the Russians. One Red Army column driving straight down the western banks of the Volga captured the villages of Tomilin, Akatovka and Latashanka to link up directly with Red Army troops who for three months have held the northern factory district of Stalingrad.

This presaged an early rout of Nazi forces still entrenched in the ruins of that industrial city, in the opinion of observers. The greater arms of the offensive undoubtedly also will force an imminent decision on Nazi chieftains who have been told by Adolf Hitler to take Stalingrad at all costs. The Russians also had reached the town of Surovikino, seventy-five miles west of Stalingrad.

The central army, after slicing from the Volga to Kalach on the easternmost point of the Don bend, crossed that river, apparently to make a junction with other Red Army units crossing in the Kletskaya region, seventy-five miles northwest of Stalingrad.

With Nazi railroad arteries cut both above and below Stalingrad, these central armies now were severing road links that ran straight eastward in the Don elbow and crossed that river by Nazi pontoons at a point only twenty-five miles short of Stalingrad.

A six-mile advance in the Don loop area found the Russians occupying the villages of Zimovsky, Trekh Ostrovyanskaya and Sirot-Trekh Ostrovyanskaya and Sirotinskaya.

The southern Red Army fanning out along the Stalingrad-Novorossiisk railway reached Sadovoe in a twelve-mile advance from Aksai. This village is more than fifty miles below beseiged Stalingrad. The villages of Umantsevo and Peregruzny also were taken in this advance.

The momentum of the Russian offensive and its direction suggested that the ultimate intent might be to drive clear across the top of the Caucasus peninsula to Rostov to trap Germans below the Don. At Chernyshevsk, the Russians were within 240 miles of Rostov.

November 25, 1942

# SOVIET FARMS AID ARMY NEAR FRONT

## State Center Resumes Work of Backing Fighting Men as Soon as Nazis Leave

## CATTLE DRIVEN TO REAR

## Girls Saved Prized Herd From Invaders by Long Trek While Battle Raged

By RALPH PARKER

Wireless to THE NEW YORK TIMES.

BEHIND THE RUSSIAN LINES, on the Central Front, Dec. 8—This morning we left a small market town thirty miles behind the central front and drove westward. The town was astir when we crossed the broad marketplace, with its depressing piles of shattered masonry and its many pathetic traces of private patching and mending after three months of German occupation. Woodsmoke curled lazily from chimneys and its sharp, clean scent reached us as we trudged through the fresh snow to the garage. We passed a "brotherly grave" where several hundred Red Army men and murdered civilians were buried and a freshly painted memorial, with its balance sheet and its careful calculation of German damage.

Last night Ivan Skatchkoff, the town's Communist party secretary, told us in terse phrases what the occupation had meant—loss of manpower and transport, robbery and humiliation of the local population—"people had forgotten how to smile when we came back," he said—obliteration of thousands of little lopsided timber houses, famine, disease and cold. Now we were on the way to what had been the most prosperous state farm in the region, the winner of the Moscow district competition for dairy farms.

The road, lined with windbreaks, ran straight as an arrow westward. Every now and then, nailed to telegraph posts, were notice boards with patriotic slogans. The woods were sadly thinned by last year's shellfire. At the foot of a monument of Napoleonic War days a burned-out German tank was rusting.

### Not Improved by Nazis

A Russian farm in Winter never is an attractive place and one in which the Germans have spent three months is very much less so. The buildings were widely scattered in the shallow fold into which the forest protruded, and shabby and unpainted, with many broken windows. But when we reached the nerve center of the farm, the manager's office, we found it comfortable enough.

It was a big room with whitewashed log walls, on which portraits of Lenin and Maxim Gorky and a huge red velvet banner hung beside charts of production statistics. From the windows tall, easy mannered, loose-limbed Ivan Nyechyeff, which means "the unexpected man," could see the cattle sheds, clover fields and stables and a little central patch, around which, oddly like the stations of the cross, were fancy notice boards with newspapers, cautionary messages, announcements, exhortations and all those manifold printed words that at every turn impinge on the Soviet man, even out in the fields.

As we sat in this office, within hearing of the business of the general office, where half a dozen girls were attending to the administration, the manager sketched the recent history of the Alexandrovo State Farm [the Sovkhoz is a State enterprise, the farmers being employes, not collective owners as in the Kolkhoz].

The bulk of the farm had been evacuated in the week before the Germans entered the region. Only fifteen cows were left of the original 650. Sixty per cent of the houses were destroyed and nearly half of the cattle sheds, while from the remaining houses the Germans on retreating stole all the household utensils.

What was remarkable about the farm—and this is typical of the whole front's hinterland—is that, despite the devastation and evacuation, it is now helping to support the Red Army. Nyechyeff arrived about three days after the last green-uniformed German had left and immediately set about converting the farm to fodder production and little else. Being better provided with repair facilities, the farm also became a center for putting damaged tractors in order for the neighboring collective farms and lending out of its surplus.

Meanwhile, he told us, the farm's life was gradually recovering. They had found one case of typhus and there was much unnatural swelling from hunger and frostbite after the German occupation. Health now was normal.

### Woman Doctors Animals

While we were talking, a broad-faced woman with her head neatly bound with a scarf brought in bowls of hot milk and small, crisp pancakes. With her was Olga Shcherbakova, 28-year-old veterinary doctor of the farm. It is a responsible job and she earns good money—550 roubles monthly—in addition to an apartment, food, fuel and electric light.

It was hard enough before the Germans came, especially hard on the women, for most of the men had gone to the rear. Olga Shcherbakova expected a baby. Her husband was at the front. Then when she normally would have started taking things easily, war—in the form of three-day tank battles over the fields, of weeks of incessant cannonade and of dive-bombing the barns and cattle sheds—swept over the adjacent region.

On Oct. 8 the manager called a meeting of the entire farm and announced that he had received instructions from the regional executive committee for the immediate evacuation of all cattle according to a prearranged plan.

Olga Scherbakova knew what was expected of her. Her job was to see that all those 650 cattle reached their destination 150 miles beyond Moscow in good health. But she was not to leave with them. Even if the Germans overran the farm, there was work for her in connection with the partisans forming in the forests and work, too, in sabotaging German plans and rallying any waverers.

Early on an October morning, when normally the farm women would be out mushrooming, all but fifteen of the cattle or the Alexandrovo State Farm began the trek eastward with fifty women and three tractors. For a day Olga Shcherbakova accompanied them and supervised the milking and roadside feeding. Then she trod back to Alexandrovo to wait for the Germans.

The trek lasted twelve days, taking a zigzag course to avoid the main roads reserved for the Army. Sick cattle were left with farms where they had passed the night. Children were crowded on the tractors. On the first two days the long column of cattle was dive-bombed and had to disperse in the forest. But they passed through the defenses of Moscow, then manned for the most critical period of the battle for the capital, and twelve days after leaving Alexandrovo reached their destination with the loss of ten head of cattle.

Olga Shcherbakova's baby was still-born. When she told us that it was the only time her voice faltered as she unfolded the whole tale of courage, painstaking organization and devastation.

Red Army men were rebuilding the foundations of the stables and in the repair shop Alexei Alexeivitch was putting a tractor together.

"Thank them in America for these socks," he shouted, pulling up a trouser leg to show us.

"And tell them," the manager said as we took our leave, "that we are doing our bit for the Red Army, even if we are merely a skeleton farm."

December 9, 1942

# RUSSIANS BREAK LENINGRAD SIEGE

## SOVIET GAINS GROW

By The Associated Press.

MOSCOW, Jan. 18—The historic siege that Leningrad, Russia's second largest city, has undergone for seventeen months was broken today by a Red Army offensive south of Lake Ladoga that shattered the German ring around the city, it was announced officially tonight.

The ancient fortress city of Schluesselburg, on Lake Ladoga east of Leningrad, where the Germans closed their ring in August, 1941, was recaptured by Russian forces under Marshals Gregory Zhukoff and Klementi Voroshiloff, the communiqué said.

This news was greeted with rejoicing throughout the country as other Russian troops operating in Southern Russia steadily smashed ahead toward Kharkov, in the Ukraine; Rostov, at the mouth of the Don River, and the Maikop oil fields in the Caucasus.

Moscow residents hearing the announcement shouted with joy and hugged each other. Workers in Russian arms factories, toiling day and night to supply the armies engaged in seven great offensives on the snow-swept plains and swamps, heard the news over loudspeakers and kept on working.

The Russians battered their way through almost nine miles of tremendous German fortifications and crossed the Neva River to end Leningrad's blockade. In a week of

## RUSSIANS SMASH SEVENTEEN-MONTH BLOCKADE

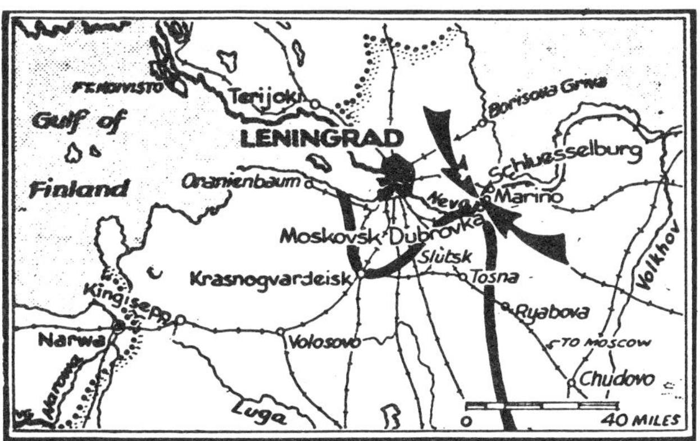


Jan. 19, 1943

**A junction of Soviet troops from immediately around Leningrad and others from the Volkhov front to the east cleared a railway running east and ended the siege of the former capital. The troops from the west crossed the Neva River and the combined forces occupied Schluesselburg, Marino, Moskovsk Dubrovka and other points. A map of the entire Russian front is on Page 3.**

bitter fighting, the Russians announced, the Germans left 13,000 dead on the battlefield and four German divisions and remnants of other detachments were routed. More than 1,260 prisoners were taken.

**Zhukoff Promoted for His Work**

Marshal Zhukoff, the hero who led the Red Army that rolled back the Germans from the gates of Moscow last Winter, has received his present rank for his work at Leningrad. Marshal Voroshiloff commanded Leningrad's hard-fighting garrison during the first months of the city's siege, when the Germans threw hundreds of thousands of men against the strategic city, but failed to crack it.

Leningrad is a vital lever in the defense of Northwestern Russia because of its proximity to the Gulf of Finland and the Baltic States. Ever since its envelopment the Germans had repeatedly maintained that it was doomed.

Further striking Russian victories were announced from the Voronezh, Stalingrad, middle Don and Caucasian fronts.

The Fourth Italian Army Corps was reported to have been smashed as the Russians fought their way into Kamensk, eighty-five miles above Rostov. The Red Army spilled across the Donets River in this area, and Likhaya, about fifteen miles south of Kamensk on the important railway to Rostov, apparently was its next goal.

**Red Army Crosses Manych River**

In the Caucasus the Russians crossed the Manych River to capture Divnoe, the railhead for a line running westward to the Rostov-Baku railway. Farther south the Russians captured Cherkessk, on the way west from Pyatigorsk toward the Maikop oil fields.

At all these points the latest successes meant not only the occupation of vitally important points but also the breaking of the main German defense lines, opening the way for further advances.

In some sectors the Axis troops were reported to be in hasty flight. German troops re-formed at every possible point where the terrain offered some defense advantages, only to be sent fleeing again by the massed weight of Soviet tanks, tommy-gunners and cavalry, front reports said.

Hit repeatedly on all sides, the German Army seemed unable to cope with the staggering succession of offensives.

**The Leningrad blow was the seventh major Russian move this Winter, one that meant the relief of the city from suffering unsurpassed by any in this war, even at Odessa, Sevastopol and Stalingrad. Less than half the original population of the city lived through last Winter under siege, supplied only across the frozen Lake Ladoga. Last month they still were being shelled by German siege guns. Now the isolation has ended.**

**The news of the relief of Leningrad was given in a special communiqué broadcast at 11 o'clock tonight and relayed over the public loud-speaker systems in streets and squares in every city and town.**

**The Germans still clung around Leningrad on its west and south sides, but their line had been pierced on the east side and their grip was being shaken loose.**

**Millions of Persons Relieved**

LONDON, Jan. 18 (AP)—The seventeen-month-old German siege of Leningrad, Russia's second largest city, was broken today.

Breaking the blockade of Leningrad brings relief to millions of persons and also releases the Nazi grip on the flow of Soviet armaments and other industrial facilities in the big city on the Gulf of Finland. Observers also foresee a new turn in the entire war, because Leningrad is a springboard for reconquest of the Baltic States.

This great news, announced in a Moscow broadcast heard here by the Soviet monitor, was a further damaging blow to German morale, because Leningrad had been in a powerful Nazi vise since Aug. 21, 1941.

"After seven days' fighting the troops of the Volkhov and Leningrad fronts united on Jan. 18 and so broke the blockade of Leningrad," said the communiqué.

Schluesselburg, big Nazi fortress on the south shore of Lake Ladoga, about twenty-five miles east of Leningrad, was among a dozen places stormed and captured by Russia's Winter-hardened troops.

The Russians hit the fortress from two directions, fighting their way through about eight miles of mine fields, barbed wire, steel and concrete pillboxes. One Red Army column fought eastward from Leningrad along the west bank of the Neva River, the other struck west along Lake Ladoga after crossing the Volkhov River.

Schluesselburg had been under sporadic Red Army attacks since the fall of 1941. By capturing it the Russians regained a railway running from Leningrad through Schluesselburg to connect with a line to Moscow, and another to Murmansk in the far north. Murmansk is the chief Arctic port for American and British supplies to Russia.

In their long unsuccessful effort to take Leningrad the Germans have lost scores of thousands of men, the Russians said. Adolf Hitler ordered the city taken by storm in August, 1941, and the Germans hurled 300,000 men against it. The Nazi waves broke under resistance directed by Marshal Voroshiloff, but the siege has continued ever since.

The Russians have managed to fly supplies into the city and also opened communications across Lake Ladoga, small boat convoys in the Summer and railway tracks laid across the ice in Winter.

"It is necessary to bear in mind," the Russian communiqué said of the breaking of the siege, "that during many months of blockade of Leningrad the Germans converted their positions on the approaches to the town into a mighty fortified area with a network system of solidly constructed concrete and other erections with large numbers of anti-tank and anti-infantry obstacles."

In this week of savage fighting in piercing cold the Russians said their "God of War," their artillery, demolished 470 enemy fortified centers and dugouts, twenty-five strongly defended observation posts, and silenced 172 artillery and mortar batteries. Among the booty captured were 222 guns, 178 mortars, 512 machine guns, 5,020 rifles, twenty-six tanks, 17,300 grenades, seventy-two radio transmitting stations, 1,050 horses, 880 carts, forty various supply dumps, 36,000 mines, 150 trucks, 22,000 shells and 2,200,000 cartridges.

The break-through was carried out by Leningrad forces commanded by Col. Gen. Leonid Govoroff, who was elevated to his present rank a few days ago, and by Volkhov front troops commanded by General Kirkill A. Meretskoff.

The troops of Lieut. Gen. Romanovsky and Major Gen. Dukanoff distinguished themselves in the fighting that lifted the siege, the communiqué said.

General N. N. Voronoff also was promoted to marshal, the Moscow announcement said. An artillery specialist, he has played a leading part in Russia's huge southwestern drive, which still is rolling forward.

January 19, 1943

## ALL OF STALINGRAD RUINED BY BATTLES

**By HENRY SHAPIRO**
**United Press Correspondent**

STALINGRAD, Feb. 8—This city, once a vast industrial center whose name will always be a symbol of the triumph of men over metal, is a heap of ruins and rubble. Everywhere there is devastation.

Correspondents arrived in Stalingrad two days after Field Marshal General Friedrich von Paulus had laid down his arms in one of the most humiliating defeats a German army ever suffered. Overnight, it seemed, Stalingrad had turned from an active war front into a hinterland, 300 miles away from the Russian-German front, which is moving swiftly westward.

Indicating the great triumph in this sector, sixteen German generals were seen as prisoners in a village on the steppes in the Stalingrad area.

Soviet troops who survived the terrific battle at Stalingrad crawled from under ground and walked erect again just before we arrived. They said they stepped over the frozen bodies of Germans, hopped across deep craters, and avoided mountains of debris in their search for mines in every ditch, dugout and cellar that had been held by the Germans.

There are no streets, no avenues, no parks in Stalingrad. Millions of shell-pocked bricks and mountains of metal fragments are all that remain of such buildings as the Dzherzhinsky tractor plant.

**No Bricks Left Usable**

In the last fifteen months I have seen ruins of cities such as Serafimovitch and hundreds of villages on other fronts. In those places there are at least individual bricks that still are usable. That is not true of Stalingrad today.

Adolf Hitler boasted that when the Russians recaptured towns and villages they would find not towns and villages but ruins and debris. That is one promise he kept. The destruction of Stalingrad probably exceeds anything since Ghengis Khan swept down from the Mongolian Desert and laid waste to the great cities of Central Asia.

A typical scene in Stalingrad is the former central Heroes of the Revolution Square. Here was the Univermag department store, the cellar of which was Marshall von Paulus's last headquarters.

The magnificent square once was fringed with five-story buildings. These had been razed and the trees had been chopped down for fuel. The square and the adjoining streets are criss-crossed with trenches and tunnels connecting what is left of houses.

February 9, 1943

# KHARKOV 60% RUINED BY NAZI OCCUPANTS

## Russians Find Only Shell of City With but 300,000 People

KHARKOV, Russia, Feb. 27 (U.P.) —Kharkov, third city of the Soviet Union and the first of its size from which the Germans have been driven, today is an empty shell. It is a city of destroyed buildings, twisted steel girders and pocked streets, marks of sixteen months of German occupation and a final burst of vandalism as the Red Army closed in a little more than ten days ago.

Kharkov authorities estimated that between 300,000 and 350,000 of the city's original 900,000 to 1,000,000 inhabitants were left. They estimated that 60 per cent of its buildings had been destroyed or heavily damaged.

That is the picture of a once great "skyscraper city" of factories, thirty-five colleges, a university, twenty research institutes and 137 secondary schools.

Soviet officials said squads of Nazi firebugs raced through the city setting thousands of its buildings on fire as the Russian troops closed in. Dynamite charges left the main railroad station a mass of ruins. On Feb. 17—the day after the Russians reoccupied the city—twenty-eight German planes returned to dive-bomb the heart of it, smashing the best buildings still standing, according to the official accounts.

February 28, 1943

# KHARKOV TEACHERS SLAIN BY GERMANS

## Educational Institutions Were Razed to Reduce Ukrainian Center to Illiteracy

## CHILDREN TRAINED AS SPIES

## Nazis Began Mass Executions by Hangings From Balconies on a Two-Mile Route

KHARKOV, Russia, Feb. 28 (U.P.) —German forces, occupying Kharkov in a sixteen-month reign of terror, systematically destroyed the city's educational and cultural institutions in an effort to reduce the Ukranian population to illiteracy.

They burned and blasted the principal buildings of the University of Kharkov, closed twenty research institutes and shut the city's 107 secondary schools that had been attended by more than 100,000 students.

Dmitri Andrevitch Korneyenko, Professor of Organic Chemistry at the University of Kharkov and head of the city's Department of Education, said only the first five grades of Russian elementary schools were permitted to function and these only for two and a half of the sixteen months the Germans held Kharkov.

Professor Korneyenko said the Germans began by stripping the well-equipped laboratories, sending the most valuable equipment to Germany. He said platinum and silver instruments and quantities of equipment were looted from the laboratories and shipped to the Reich.

Then the reign of terror began. Twenty thousand volumes from Kharkov's scientific laboratories were burned. Newspaper files were destroyed. The principal university buildings, including the scientific buildings, law school and the University Club were burned and blasted. Time bombs were exploded in the biology, physics, mathematics, chemistry, geology and geography buildings.

**Professors Shot or Hanged**

Eminent professors were ferreted out of hiding by the Gestapo and shot or hanged because of their Jewish origin or their refusal to collaborate with the occupation authorities.

Professor Korneyenko named fifteen educational leaders and scientists who were among the hundreds of teachers and professors who were executed or died of starvation.

Thousands of professors were reduced to living by odd jobs. Others sold matches and soap. Most were reduced to selling their furniture and personal belongings on the open market to procure food.

[Professor Korneyenko lived by making matches that his 62-year-old mother sold in the streets, according to Reuter. "At first I hardly ever left my flat," he said. "With my knowledge as a chemist I made matches. Later, when some one denounced me and things got too hot, I had to change my abode almost every night."]

The Germans opened three schools for children between 10 and 15, in which the students were trained for use as spies in Russian territory.

Kharkov's medical services and hospitals suffered during the occupation. Dr. Alexander Butrin, a Ukrainian, said the Germans provided skeleton services but as a result of semi-starvation rations and the lack of medicine and hospital facilities the city's birth rate declined disastrously.

At first the local population was excluded from the hospitals but later the Germans reserved 200 beds for Kharkov residents and opened two maternity hospitals. The patients were required to pay for services and provide their own food.

**Ration for Hospital Patients**

The Germans finally relaxed to the extent of feeding hospital patients about 3.5 fluid ounces of soup and wheat husks daily and later added 3.5 avoirdupois ounces of horse meat daily.

Nine day nurseries and three orphanages were opened for children whose parents had been "sent to Germany." The Germans repaid such parents with small favors and discriminated systematically against the rest of the population.

The Nazi hangmen reveled in public executions. They would summon the populace under the balcony of the former Communist headquarters and proclaim the "crimes" of the victims. Then the victims would be pitched over the balcony rail at the end of a rope.

Two days after they took Kharkov the Germans staged their first mass hanging. Men and women were thrown from every balcony along a two-mile route. Their bodies dangled for days.

One of Kharkov's most frightful spectacles is the sight of Russian prisoners freed from German camps during the Soviet advance. Their heads are cadaverous. Their arms and legs are as thin as sticks and many walk with crutches.

March 1, 1943

## *Rank of Marshal Is Given to Stalin*

By The United Press.

LONDON, March 6—Premier Joseph Stalin has received the military title of Marshal of the Soviet Union from the Presidium of the Supreme Soviet, the Russian Parliament, the Moscow radio announced tonight.

In his capacity as Soviet Defense Commissar, Mr. Stalin has been Commander in Chief of the Red Army, a rank that he has used only recently in such documents as orders of the day.

Mr. Stalin's new rank of Marshal is regarded in military quarters here as emphasizing his active participation in the shaping of the strategy in the great Soviet drives against the Germans. Unlike Adolf Hitler, he prefers the seclusion of the Kremlin to the press-agented front headquarters affected by his adversary.

March 7, 1943

## SOVIET PARTISANS UPSET AXIS PLANS

### More Than 100,000 Fighting Behind Enemy Lines, Blocking All Steps for Collaboration

By C. L. SULZBERGER

Wireless to The New York Times.

MOSCOW, June 6 — The Red Army possesses more than 100,000 Partisan fighters who serve as an extremely valuable although highly secret patriotic mass, definitely collaborating with the High Command in the liberation of the country.

The exact number of Partisan fighters cannot be revealed and may never be known. Their ranks include active fighters as young as 11 years and as old as 80.

Their feats have not gone unrecognized by the general staff, even if many of them, for security reasons, are still unheralded in the public press. Special decorations have been given to Partisan heroes, many posthumously, and many more than the public realizes have been secretly bestowed to protect their clandestine movements.

The Partisan force, which emanates from conditions in this country and from traditions dating back to the times of Peter the Great, received a great impetus in Napoleonic wars. It was modernized in the civil wars fought while the Bolshevist regime was establishing itself.

The valuable work of these forces may be summed up as follows:

1. The Partisans serve as a scouting screen for the Red Army along the entire front.
2. They are a constant harassing force along the enemy's line of communications.
3. They hamper enemy offensive and defensive plans in effective cooperation with the Soviet High Command.
4. They cause a constant drain on enemy manpower, which is forced to distribute itself along lines of communication that would otherwise appear safe and is forced to organize punitive expeditions.
5. They are now an inspiring patriotic force, keeping the population keyed up, eliminating any Quislings and blocking any large-scale Axis efforts for collaboration.

Since the German invasion of the Soviet Union began almost two years ago there has been an improvement in the efficiency of the Partisans comparable to the improvement of the regular Red Army itself. The principal improvements have been in organization and in the efficiency of liaison contacts. Contact has been arranged through the distribution of radios, the use of army planes and other methods of delivering reports and instructions.

There appear to be no obstacles to Partisans when they seek to establish connections. During the recent All-Slav meeting here, Yugoslav and Czechoslovak Partisans, aided by Ukrainian and Russian guerrillas, were able to travel through hundreds of miles of enemy-held territory. One woman, who had escaped from a Munich concentration camp, arrived after a journey that was aided by Czech and Russian Partisans.

Some of the most effective Partisan activity is reported to be around Smolensk, Kiev, Pinsk, Gomel, Bryansk and Vitebsk and in Latvia, all either within or relatively near the edge of the great forest belt. But Partisans are not limited to such regions and some very valuable assistance has been given in the Kuban, where on plains that affording almost no cover there are loyal fighters.

There is a difference between Partisan and guerrilla warfare. The Partisan bands arose from the spontaneous resistance of the population of occupied areas, generally commencing to make itself felt five or six weeks after the occupation, and only later organized and coordinated with the full Red Army war effort.

The Partisan movement does not consist of guerrillas or Commandos attached as regular units to branches of the Red Army, but consists of volunteer patriots whose struggle usually began before there was any contact with the High Command. Raids by parties of Baltic or Black Sea sailors or sallies by special parties of scouts between Murmansk and Petsamo are of a different category.

June 7, 1943

## RED ARMY'S PLEA BACKED BY SERGIUS

### 'Real Help' From West Russia's Need, Says Acting Patriarch After Seeing Stalin

### CHURCH ACCORD PRINTED

### Soviet Press Gives Emphasis to Step for Re-establishing the Orthodox Holy Synod

MOSCOW, Sept. 5 (U.P.)—Acting Patriarch Sergius of the Russian Orthodox Church today called for "some real" military help from the Allies in a statement following the conference with Joseph Stalin in which the Premier gave his approval to the complete restoration of the church in the Soviet Union.

The 76-year-old Metropolitan of Moscow, who came to Moscow in a specia ltrain, ending his two years' semi-exile at Kazan in the Tartar Republic, said:

"I am not a military expert, but it seems to me that the time for the complete annihilation of Hitler has arrived. If the Red Army alone was able to force back the Germans, it is not difficult to predict how speedily the war will terminate when our troops receive some real help from the Allies.

"I refuse to believe that the mothers of English and American soldiers want this to drag on. Let us not prattle about patience. We Russians are the world's most patient people. But the cup of our patience is overflowing."

**Stalin Declared Sympathetic**

Premier Stalin and Foreign Commissar Vyacheslaff M. Molotoff received Acting Patriarch Sergius, Metropolitan Alexei of Leningrad and Nikolai, Primate of the Ukrainian Church, in the Kremlin yesterday. An official statement later said that Premier Stalin viewed sympathetically their proposal to elect a permanent Patriarch of all Russia and to re-establish a Holy Synod of Bishops, supreme executive council of the Russian Orthodox Church.

The announcement that the Soviet Government would place no obstacle in the way of the church reorganization had front-page prominence in all Russian newspapers today and the step was regarded as the most important development in relations between the Soviet State and the Church since the Holy Synod was disbanded in the early days of communism.

The three Metropolitans will soon call a national council of Bishops to elect the Patriarch—an action previously opposed by the government.

Sergius, who saw Premier Stalin three days after he came from Kazan, where he had been conducting efforts to restore the church to its ancient rights and privileges and had spurred the church's contribution to the Russian war effort, said that the church had contributed more than 8,000,000 rubles for a tank column.

Additionally, he said, priests and laity had donated personal savings amounting to tens of millions of rubles for aircraft squadrons, the relief of wounded anu orphans and for the restoration of liberated areas.

September 6, 1943

# Nazis Systematically Ruined Kiev As Red Army Watched Helplessly

MOSCOW, Nov. 7 (U.P.)—Battle-toughened Soviet veterans stood on the heights before Kiev Friday night with tears of blind fury in their eyes as they watched the destruction of the "mother of Russian cities" by ruthless German troops.

Awaiting the signal for the final assault, they watched helplessly while a sea of flames engulfed large areas of Kiev and great columns of fire shot into the sky as German demolition squads set off one explosion after another.

The signal for the attack came just before dawn yesterday. Aroused to unusual fighting pitch by the sight of the burning city, the Russians attacked with determination to save as much of the ancient cathedral town as possible.

These soldiers had seen the same sight scores of times in their 300-mile advance westward, but Kiev holds a special place in the hearts of all Russians. The country's history is inextricably linked with the history of Kiev. All Russian peasants—and 90 per cent of the Red Army are peasants—hold Kiev as the country's ancient religious capital.

Launching the final attack, Russians, Ukrainians, Georgians and representatives of many distant Soviet republics smashed forward with unprecedented bitterness.

The first tank units broke into Kiev shortly before 6 A. M., raced across the flaming city to the Vasilkov road and began a relentless pursuit of the fleeing Germans. The Nazis dashed down the road, hammered by Soviet bombers and Stormoviks and pursued by Red Army tanks.

"History has not known such a swift operation" as the penetration of Kiev, the Red Army newspaper Red Star said today. Soviet tanks crushed concentrations of German guns in the forests around Pusha-Voditza, northwest of Kiev, and cut through Nazi infantry positions.

Tanks poured into the city, racing down streets illuminated by the rays of the rising sun and the glare from sheets of flame pouring from buildings. Entire sections of Kiev are submerged under a mass of flames and smoke. The most important parts of the city were in ruins. Hollow shells of great buildings were monuments to Kiev's former grandeur.

Civilians and soldiers fighting the flames were handicapped by a lack of water, the Germans having destroyed the water system. Walls collapsed about the fire fighters and long tongues of flame shot out into the street.

The Germans destroyed Kiev's university, its electric plant, its public buildings and schools.

Everywhere the Russians found signs reading: "For Germans only; Ukrainians forbidden." Civilians reported that the German administrators had brought their families to Kiev and occupied the best apartments in the better sections of the town. The city's handsome government administrative buildings were a mass of debris.

November 8, 1943

# DONBAS INDUSTRIES RUINED, SOVIET SAYS

## Commission States Factories and Mines Were Wrecked by Retreating Nazis

## MACHINES TAKEN TO REICH

## 78 Officials, High and Low, Are Responsible, Moscow Finds—Many Murders Alleged

By RALPH PARKER

By Cable to The New York Times.

MOSCOW, Nov. 13—The State Commission for the Investigation of Atrocities and Damage inflicted on the Soviet Union's people and property by Germany today published a detailed report on the findings in Stalino Province of the Donets Basin.

According to the report, the German High Command issued orders for the complete destruction of the Donbas after the removal of whatever machinery, raw materials and labor power it was possible to carry away. In cold, precise phrases, the report reveals how the enemy was only too successful in carrying out his plans.

Stalino Province was described as the most important coal and metallurgical center of the Soviet Union. From 152 mines operated before the war, 140,000 tons of high grade coal were produced daily. Electrical power stations on the Donets River and at Zaparozhye, which were linked, had a capacity of three billion kilowatts. Eight and one half million tons of coke were produced each year. Twenty-two blast furnaces gave five million tons of iron a year. Forty-three Marten furnaces produced four million tons of steel. Rolling mills turned out three million tons of steel. The region had important building material, glass, fertilizer and machine tool enterprises as well as fifteen institutes and technical schools.

Stalino Province was the scene of great industrial expansion under the first Five-Year Plan, when foreign engineers helped the Russians build their plants and where, for the first time in Russia's history, heavy machinery of certain important types was produced within her frontiers.

### Specific Order Disclosed

According to the commission's findings, an order was circulated at the beginning of September by the economic department of the German group of armies in south Russia, then in charge of one Herr Nagel. The order was numbered 1-313-43 of the Ekonomische Abteilung and was reported to contain instructions to a number of German enterprises interested in the Donbas industries. The German firms included such concerns as Vostok, Kolin and Otto. They were told to take what they could and to destroy the rest.

Acting on these instructions, the commission's report states, the Germans destroyed 140 mines, leaving only twelve small mines with a total daily output of 500 tons intact. They blocked 154 pit tunnels and put out of working order many shafts, lifts, ventilators, conveyors, drills and pumps.

In all, the commission found, the Germans had inflicted damage roughly estimated at two thousand million rubles. The names of those held responsible for the demolitions are listed.

[Seventy-eight Nazi "criminals who must pay the penalty for their monstrous crimes committed against the Soviet people" were named by the Moscow radio yesterday, the Office of War Information reported. Among them were the commandants of many towns in Stalino Province, their deputies, police officials, factory heads, financial, military and technical advisers, and jurists and engineers. The list ended with the names "Corporals Johann Goltz and Hermann Zerrholz."]

Among the cities and towns cited as having suffered the most are Stalino, Kramatorsk, Gorlovka, Makeyevka, Yenakievo, Konstantinovka and Mariupol.

The Stalino metal works, where more than 12,000 workers formerly were employed, was described as wrecked, as were also 113 schools. Half a million books were said to have been burned at the institute there.

The report also stated that 125,000 Donbas inhabitants had been taken into Germany and many thousands had been found slaughtered in mine shafts, quarries and mass graves.

### "Scorched Earth" Was Strategic

German damage to the Donbas area differs radically from that inflicted by the Red Army and workers on their evacuation, it was pointed out recently in an authoritative article in the Moscow press. Confident that they would return, the Russians' interpretation of the scorched earth policy was to put factories out of commission by strategic wrecking. This was aimed at preventing the enemy from putting the industry back into commission without considerable delay. It did not consist of capital damage such as the Donbas suffered at German hands, for their policy, the commission's report makes clear, was intended to strike a blow at the Soviet Union that it was probably hoped would be felt for many years.

November 14, 1943

# SOVIET REBUILDING AHEAD OF PROGRAM

By W. H. LAWRENCE

By Wireless to The New York Times.

MOSCOW, Feb. 5—The Soviet Government reported today the progress it is making in rehabilitating devastated farms, factories and homes in the territories that have been liberated by the Red Army from German occupation.

The work is going forward despite the terrific demands of the war on men and materials, and the official report said it was ahead of plan. Efforts are being made first to restore the rich agricultural areas that were overrun by German troops, thus increasing the total food supply available for the Soviet peoples as well as reducing the amount of foodstuffs that must presently be shipped from other areas into the newly liberated districts.

The statistics presented in the official report to the Council of Peoples' Commissars, which covers two pages of today's Moscow newspapers, are indeed impressive, but there is no means of comparison with other accomplishments and other countries because the present rehabilitation effort is the largest the world has seen in the midst of war.

There is no indication what percentage of the total necessary rehabilitation work has been accomplished nor how long it will take to make these regions completely self-sustaining. In areas such as Stalingrad it will literally be necessary to rebuild completely from the ground up.

### The Regions Covered

The report records the progress in carrying out the Government's decisions of Aug. 23, 1941, and covers the regions around Kalinin, Smolensk, Orel, Kursk, Voronezh, Stalingrad, Rostov, Voroshilovgrad, Kharkov, Sumy, Stavropol and Krasnodar.

Among the more impressive statistics are the reconstruction of 326,461 structures housing 1,813,614 persons, many of whom had been forced to live in dugouts because their former homes had been destroyed in battle or sacked by the Germans.

Twenty-five building material factories and eleven lumber mills, which have a cutting capacity sufficient to produce lumber for the construction of standard houses containing 800 apartments monthly, have been built.

It is on the agricultural front that the greatest progress is being made because it has had priority. A total of 1,723,201 head of cattle and horses and 516,853 chickens, ducks and geese have been sent to collective farms in the liberated areas.

This includes the return of 630,830 head of cattle and horses that had been evacuated eastward in the van of the advancing Germans and whose return was a major task in view of the inevitable wartime transport shortage. That task included the organization of fifteen large crossings along the Ural, Volga, Terek and Oka Rivers. The animals returned included 209,453 large-horned cattle, 366,765 sheep and goats and 54,621 horses.

It was stated that a foundation for the complete re-establishment of cattle breeding in the liberated areas had been established and this included the reconstruction of breeding shelters, which had virtually all been demolished by the Germans. For this task alone the Government forests sent 1,610,000 cubic meters of timber.

A total of 96,324 tons of seed for the fall sowing has been made available and efforts are being made to provide sufficient machinery for the crops' cultivation and harvest. Thus far, 5,972 tractors have been returned from the east and workmen have reconstructed 575 machine tractor stations and 969 machine tractor repair shops. In addition, nine large repair stations have been built.

It is stated that tractor equipment valued at 18,620,200 rubles has arrived in the liberated areas and another 2,513,100 rubles' worth is en route.

The report said that a total of 3,587 specialists and leaders of agricultural work had been sent to the liberated territories, of whom 389 are administrators, 1,169 agronomists, 364 veterinarians and 499 mechanical engineers.

Railroads always are war targets and the destruction of transport facilities in the liberated regions has been very great. There are no figures given in today's report on the number of railway miles that have been restored to use, but it is stated that 122 stations have been reconstructed and 1,399 road-building barracks have been erected for the workers who are rebuilding the railroads.

February 6, 1944

# SOVIET UNION PAYS HOMAGE TO WOMEN

## Their Vital Role in Red Army, in Factories and on Farms Earns Nation's Plaudits

By Wireless to The New York Times.

MOSCOW, March 8—The Soviet Union is paying tribute today to its women who are fighting alongside the Red Army and playing a major role in the manufacture of munitions and material with which the army fights.

To any foreigner, it is obvious that the settled Soviet policy is to grant absolute equality of opportunity to women in Government and in industrial, cultural and social life, with an attendant equality of responsibility. And it is equally apparent that the policy has paid big dividends in the present war. As a result, women here are playing a greater part for victory than they are in any other country at war.

Much of the work behind the winning of the war has been theirs, and much credit will go to them—a fact that was evident in today's celebration of International Women's Day.

Women are among the leaders in every type of activity in the Soviet Union at war. According to the best available statistics, they undoubtedly constitute the majority of the Soviet Union's working force. In many branches of industry women had reached 45 per cent of the industrial force by October, 1941, four months after the invasion began.

Women fly fighter planes, keeping the aircraft in the air as many as seventeen hours a day on occasion. They serve as snipers and guerrillas, ruthlessly killing off German soldiers, deeds for which many have won the highest Government decorations. Behind the front, they run railroad trains, tend switches, mine coal, manufacture war material and work in the fields.

### Women Do Farm Work

Unlike the United States, where hundreds of thousands of able-bodied men have been deferred for work on farms, it is stated officially here that "the main burden of agricultural work has been laid on the shoulders of women." In addition, of course, they have continued and expanded women's work in the scientific field, such as in medicine, and have carried on the women's normal work, such as the organization of nurseries, group feeding and other activities upon which the war has placed a greater burden.

Women are doing the softest and toughest jobs with equal dispatch. On a recent trip to the Leningrad front, foreign correspondents talked in the Kiroff munitions plant with girls who had worked throughout the long months of the German siege, when artillery shells were constantly falling on the plant, which was only two and a half miles from advanced German positions. The girls used to go to work in the morning and find some of their comrades dead from hunger.

In the fields a few miles from Leningrad, as the correspondents toured the captured German fortifications, one saw girls trudging alongside boys, feeling their way through the snow and hunting for enemy mines that had been planted in large numbers.

### Snow Cleared Swiftly

One of the things that most impresses a foreigner in Moscow is the speed with which the city's streets are cleared of snow. Most foreigners have commented that the work is done faster than in New York City. And this primarily is the work of women. In coldest weather groups of five to seven can be seen chipping at the ice with sharp, pointed instruments and then taking shovels to load the snow and ice on trucks.

They drive buses and street cars, subject usually to the traffic direction of women police.

A current article by Klavdia Nikolayeva, active woman party leader, in a Moscow party magazine gives some idea of the contribution that women are making. Pointing out that women have taken over the majority of farm jobs since the war began, she offered these statistics of production increases: Grain, 100 per cent; potatoes, 76 per cent and vegetables, 86 per cent. Miss Nilkolayeva gives some idea of the increased number of women taking on the hardest farm jobs with these figures, based on the Krasnodar District, where in 1940 women had constituted 8.7 per cent of the tractor drivers, 40 per cent of the combine operators and 6.1 per cent of the transport drivers. In 1943 the percentage of tractor drivers had increased to 49.9 per cent, combine operators to 40 per cent and transport drivers to 40 per cent.

March 9, 1944

# SEVASTOPOL YOUTH WIPED OUT BY FOE

## Survivors Report Young Men Were Loaded on Barges and Drowned in Harbor

By W. H. LAWRENCE
By Cable to The New York Times.

MOSCOW, May 11—Soviet war correspondents reported today the story of the survivors of battered Sevastopol, who described the final German atrocity—loading the surviving young men of the city on barges, which were towed to the middle of the harbor and then sunk only a few days before the Red Army stormed the fortress.

This was described as a terrible tragedy dictated by the "helpless hate" of the remaining German and Rumanian troops, who knew their number was up because the powerful Red Army was quickly approaching and ready to break through the fortifications that ringed the city's mountainous approaches. No estimate was given of the number of young men thus exterminated.

From stories and maps printed in the Soviet press it is evident that once beautiful Sevastopol has been almost completely destroyed—perhaps replacing Stalingrad as Russia's most devastated city. This was a result of both the 250-day siege in 1941 and 1942, when the Germans dropped as many as 125,000 bombs in a single month and poured in countless artillery shells, and the latest siege, in which the Germans blew up as many of the remaining installations as they had time for.

### City Like Rocky Desert

The only important building mentioned as not blown up is the electrical plant on the south side of the city, which residents said the Germans did not have time to destroy.

Correspondent Eugenia Kriger wrote in Izvetsia that the center of Sevastopol was like "a rocky desert." He said "Frunze Street has become a graveyard" and that "on Lenin Street, where the Germans were, nothing is left alive." He reported that no large buildings or houses were left standing intact.

Writers for all the papers reported that thousands of dead German and Rumanian soldiers "lie everywhere, in gardens, in streets, on porches—revenge for the horrors of Sevastopol." The narrow streets were said to be littered with dead Germans and cars, guns and tanks destroyed by swiftly moving Red Army tanks and mobile guns. All the city's famous statues and memorials were reported destroyed.

Major Victor Koroteieff, writing in the army newspaper Red Star, described the joy of the residents on the arrival of the Red Army. Women brought them bouquets of red Crimean roses and other flowers.

May 12, 1944

# Soviet Edicts Tighten Divorce Law, Encourage Big Families by Grants

## Dissolutions Require Court Procedure, With Judge Urged to Seek Reconciliation—Special Medals Honor Mothers

By Wireless to THE NEW YORK TIMES.

MOSCOW, July 9—The Soviet Government issued a stringent decree yesterday making important changes in divorce procedure. In future, a divorce will be obtainable only after a decision of the courts. The old method of divorce by declaration and registration at the marriage bureaus has been superseded.

Prospective applicants for a divorce henceforth will be obliged to state their reasons and satisfy the courts those reasons are serious and valid. Courts are enjoined to reconcile the disputants wherever possible. The divorce fees, which formerly were fixed at a maximum of 500 rubles, have been raised to 2,000.

To protect health, certain changes in the law affecting abortion also were announced. The changes facilitate the obtaining of abortions for valid reasons connected with health and will operate to curtail illegal abortions.

Coincidentally, the Government has introduced new scales of family allowances, which will provide down payments and monthly grants to all mothers of families of four children and more. Family allowances previously were granted only after the birth of a seventh child.

The new scheme, which applies to unmarried mothers as well—an unmarried mother receives aid for the education and rearing of children from the first child—has been accompanied by measures increasing the holidays prospective mothers can claim and also provide for post-natal vacations.

Prospective mothers or five or more children will now qualify for medals. For rearing families of five and six, a Motherhood Medal is awarded; mothers of seven, eight or nine children will receive the Order of Glory, while mothers of ten or more children will in future be known as "Mother Heroines."

Simultaneously with the decree of the new measures, taxes previously imposed on bachelors have been extended to cover partners in childless marriages, who will pay 6 per cent of their income. Parents of one child will pay 1 per cent; parents of two children, one-half of 1 per cent.

There are many exemptions, including men serving in the Army and their wives.

### Divorce Now Hard to Obtain

MOSCOW, July 9 (AP)—The Supreme Soviet's new divorce decree, which went into effect yesterday, requires both parties to file a petition in court and appear personally before a Peoples' Court, which hears all the evidence, then seeks to determine it if cannot effect a reconciliation. If this is believed impossible, the petition can be carried to a higher court. Witnesses must be heard in both courts.

Should the higher court decide to grant a divorce, then the paper will be returned with signatures to the registration office, where it may cost the petitioner anywhere from 500 to 2,000 rubles.

The new divorce ruling is probably the most sweeping change made by the Russians toward establishing stronger family ties and is in keeping with the current emphasis on religion, children and motherhood.

It is taken as further evidence that the Russians are vitally interested in building up family life and the home.

From now on, to obtain a divorce in the Soviet Union, persons must have a good reason, and must prove it.

No longer will such explanations as "I can't get along with my wife" or "My husband gets on my nerves" do.

How long such a procedure will take was not indicated, but it would appear that considerable time would be needed.

The Government also enacted new exemptions for pregnant women. Their leave from work was extended from the present sixty-three days to seventy-seven—thirty-five before birth and forty-two afterward. Pregnant women will receive a double food ration after six months of pregnancy. New facilities in kindergartens and nurseries will be provided for nursing mothers.

July 10, 1944

# RUSSIAN MIGRATION NOT PLANNED AHEAD

## Removal of Men and Machines to Siberia and Urals Was Unforeseen by Red Army

## INDUSTRIES TO STAY THERE

## Many Refugees Already Have Returned to Seared Homes —Some Plants Will Stay

By W. H. LAWRENCE
By Wireless to THE NEW YORK TIMES.

TASHKENT, Uzbekistan, U.S.S.R., July 9 (Delayed)—For the first time foreign correspondents have been able to see and hear the details of the world's greatest industrial migration—the swift movement of men and machines from German-occupied or threatened industrial sections of the Soviet Union to the refuge of the Urals, Siberia and central Asia.

This is a story now two and one-half years old, but one that has never been told before and one that has lost none of its flavor through age. It is an accomplishment that entailed moving millions of men, women and children, hundreds of industrial plants and tens of thousands of machines within the space of a few weeks or a few months over rail systems already clogged with troops and supplies. It caused the creation of new cities or a tremendous overcrowding of old ones.

All details of what those operations involved cannot yet be told, but information gathered by this correspondent on the trip to Magnitogorsk, Sverdlovsk, Omsk, Novosibirsk, Alma Ata, Tashkent and Samarkand left no doubt that this tremendous movement of productive resources was one of the main reasons why the Red Army could fall back as far as the Volga and then turn on the Germans and defeat them decisively.

### Evacuation Not Anticipated

So far as this correspondent could learn there was no master evacuation plan for Russian industry in advance of the war. The speed, efficiency and thoroughness with which the original move was made had led many to think that even before the war the Soviet Government had marked machines in the Kharkov tractor plant, for example, for removal to a specific factory in a chosen remote town in case of emergency.

But, according to officials with whom we talked, the whole project was improvised and carried out under conditions of the greatest emergency and necessity for speed. According to Rodion M. Glukhoff, vice chairman of the Council of People's Commissars of the Uzbek Republic, his area usually had word that it would receive a specific factory only two weeks in advance of the arrival of the first trainloads of machines and of workers.

In that brief period, he said, factory space had to be provided for machines, and housing and food had to be arranged for the workers. Transportation arrangements had to be made to obtain raw materials for fabrication and to ship finished goods to the front.

Some performances were truly remarkable. A factory making complicated Douglas two-engined transports [DC-3's], and employing thousands of workers, moved all its machines and half its workers to central Asia, turning out its first plane thirty-five days after the arrival of the last equipment.

We saw the plant in operation during our tour. The final assembly line was in the former hangars on the airport, and despite the dispersed character of its new production facilities, the factory's output record was respectable.

In Siberia we saw a well-organized optical plant scattered through a series of buildings that formerly had been a technical institute. We were told it had been moved west in November, 1941, and had begun production twenty-two days after the arrival of machinery in Siberia. The factory turns out the most complicated gun sights and range finders and other optical equipment superior in quality to the captured German material we inspected in the same factory.

Because motion pictures play a large part in Soviet informational effort, officials in the stress of war even created a new Hollywood—they moved studios, artists, directors, composers, technicians and equipment from Leningrad and Moscow to far-off Alma-Ata, where twenty-five full-length pictures were produced during the war.

On the set of "Ivan the Terrible" we talked with the English-speaking Soviet director, Sergei Eisenstein, who said that two parts of this three-part story of Czar Ivan's life had been finished and when presented would give a new and more favorable impression of one of the Czars who materially expanded the territory of Russia.

But the big job, and the one that will receive important mention when the history of this war is written, was the removal of men and machines from overrun areas so that they could take up again the job of fashioning the implements of war for repelling the German invaders. It is not possible yet to tell that story for reasons of military security. Accurate over-all statistics concerning the number of factories and of people moved must wait, but these population figures for individual towns and areas will serve to illustrate the magnitude of the task:

| City. | Pre-War Population. | Today's Population. |
|---|---|---|
| Magnitogorsk | 160,000 | 240,000 |
| Sverdlovsk | 500,000 | 750,000 |
| Omsk | 320,000 | 514,000 |
| Novosibirsk | 450,000 | 700,000 |
| Alma-Ata | 180,000 | 400,000 |
| Tashkent | 700,000 | 850,000 |
| Samarkand | 140,000 | 160,000 |

Mr. Glukhoff told us that the Uzbek Republic, which formerly had a population of about 6,200,000, had received more than 2,000,000 refugees, or an influx of about one-third of its pre-war population.

Such tremendous population increases, even when spread out over a three-year period, would create major problems and worries for city administrators of any country, but the men who run Soviet cities had the problem of caring for the increases in the course of a few weeks or a few months.

Such a large-scale movement of peoples seeking refuge from the advancing German Army created problems of food, housing, fuel and water, to mention only a few. The problem of caring for them, important as it was, still remained secondary to the major task of keeping the Red Army in the field supplied and fed. For that reason, local and regional government units of the areas affected had to solve most problems with their own resources.

The major problems of resettlement have been solved. In fact, many, many thousands of those refugees—perhaps a large majority of them—already have left their temporary homes in the east and have gone to rebuild their war-seared dwellings in the liberated areas of the west.

In Uzbekistan we were told that more than 90 per cent of those who had been sent there had already left for their homes. Whether this condition is true throughout the Urals, Siberia and Central Asia we were not able to learn But the evacuated factories and the workers who toil in them, for the most part, will remain where they are now, thereby permanently building up the districts that gave them refuge.

In Tashkent we were told by Mr. Glukhoff that Leningrad was putting up an argument for the return of some factories and some workers that Tashkent wished to retain, but that the final decision on the relocation of these enterprises would be made by the Central Government in Moscow.

In assaying the worth of the evacuation job in its entirety, it is necessary to look not only at the arms and food thus produced for the Red Army, but to remember that the men and machines thus moved were denied to the German invaders. And it is important, also, to note that so far as is known there were no large-scale famines or epidemics of disease such as might be expected to accompany such a huge migration.

July 15, 1944

## RUSSIA REBUILDING INDUSTRIES FIRST

JERUSALEM, March 4 (U.P.)—A British Parliamentary mission to Russia reported today that priority for reconstruction there was being given to industrial enterprises, public buildings, schools and housing in that order.

Consequently, in Stalingrad, tractor plants are up to pre-war conditions but the people are still living in holes in the ground, the mission reported.

"We were permitted to see everything we wanted," John Parker, a member of the mission, said. "We visited Moscow and Leningrad, where part of the mission went to the Don Basin to see war industry, and Stalingrad and Baku.

"We were impressed particularly by industrial development in the Urals and central Asia. The housing problem in Russia will be enormous and even very old towns are overcrowded."

The mission, which spent six weeks in Russia, described the trip as successful and said that "we hope there will be an exchange of visits."

March 5, 1945

# MOSCOW JOY MAD AS BERLIN IS WON

### Stalin Announcement Starts Unprecedented Celebration in Honor of Victory

By CYRUS L. SULZBERGER

By Wireless to THE NEW YORK TIMES.

MOSCOW, Thursday, May 3—News of the fall of Berlin was received here with wild acclaim although it had been expected hourly for several days.

It was Marshal Stalin's order of the day officially announcing the capture of the Nazi capital which really set things off.

It is poetic justice that among the Soviet officers specially singled out in Marshal Stalin's order for participating in the conquest of Berlin was his son, Col. Vassily Stalin, who took part as a Red Air Force pilot in the aerial destruction of the city.

While the news electrified the already jubilant capital of the Soviet Union, which was concluding the two-day May Day holiday, it is noteworthy that no more than the usual salute given for the conquest of an enemy or the liberation of a friendly capital was ordered in the case of Berlin—324 guns firing twenty-four salvos each.

But never has this largest Soviet salute been received with more acclaim. Shouting Muscovites, usually quite restrained even with the best of news, hurled their hats high in the air in the streets and plazas near Red Square while powerful blue searchlights focused proudly on the Kremlin's towers.

**Berlin a Smoking Shell**

The Berlin that fell to the relentless Russian assaults was a flaming, smoke-covered shell of the city that the Fuehrer dreamed would be the world's center. More than two years of concentrated Allied bombing, which dug great chasms a hundred yards in diameter in the broad avenues, and sixteen days of Russian shelling—the battle started from the bridgehead west of Kuestrin on April 17—as well as twelve ghastly days of street fighting, have laid Berlin waste.

This was a desperate battle while it lasted and not the least of its features was the terrible dark underground warfare in the Berlin subways and sewers, where the Nazis time and again sought to break through to the Russians' rear and where special squadrons of Soviet sappers, wearing black rubber coats, crawled through after them with grenades, machine guns, tommy guns, small field pieces and even searchlights, determined that none should escape.

The center of the city, where the battle had been going on for the last few days around fortified strongpoints in and beneath the Tiergarten and large public buildings like the Reich's Chancellery and ministries, is a smoking shambles, with the Russians turning into smaller ruins the wreckage resulting from the Allied air attacks.

However, it has been reported that the outskirts are in relatively good condition and that Soviet officers already have set about establishing order there, opening emergency hospitals, bakeries and food stores.

So far there is no news as to who was captured in Berlin among the high Nazi party members and military leaders. It may take days to round up all the hunted war criminals believed to be hiding out in the shambles that was their capital. For days, it is reported, they have been donning civilian clothes and disguises and arming themselves with hidden weapons in desperate eleventh-hour preparations for escape.

But the Red Army, and especially the security troops, are looking for them. Russian justice is going to be meted out in revenge for Stalingrad, Kiev, Sevastopol, Leningrad and Smolensk and men from all those battered cities are in Berlin to see to that.

This is the absolute end, the Goetterdaemmerung of Nazidom. It is obvious that the formal announcement that the European war is over can be anticipated at almost any hour.

May 3, 1945

# 25,000,000 Homeless in Russia Only Fraction of German Damage

## 17,000,000 Head of Cattle and 20,000,000 Swine Carried Off by Invaders—Transport Strain Adds to Problems

By Air Mail to The New York Times

MOSCOW, Oct. 25—There is no doubt that hardship confronts the Russians this winter. More than 1,700 towns and 70,000 villages were destroyed or severely damaged, more than 6,000,000 buildings were destroyed and 25,000,000 persons were made homeless; this is a fraction of the damage inflicted by the Germans on Soviet soil.

The 25,000,000 homeless will be suffering the most. The problem facing the Soviet Government is one of housing, clothing and feeding the vast population. Seventeen million head of cattle and 20,000,000 swine—not to count horses, poultry, etc.—were killed or driven to Germany. It will take years for Russia to recover.

Transport that coped with the heavy traffic will again be strained this winter. Tens of thousands of miles of railroad tracks destroyed by the Germans are under repair and reconstruction.

This winter will nevertheless be easier than the war winters. Market prices, continually tumbling, are about one-quarter of last year's costs for staples. The lower prices are partly due to increased sown areas and good harvest prospects and partly to a Government policy of reducing prices on unrationed food and goods. Three reductions in prices have brought unrationed prime necessities and luxuries to an average of 40 per cent of last year's prices.

Optimism in the country is reflected by the many rumors that rationing will be abolished in the near future. A recent decision of the Central Council of Trade Unions calls for an increase in the network of open dining rooms, which means that it will be easier to get a meal when you want one. Restaurant prices have also fallen but are still beyond the reach of the average worker. A common sight in Moscow is trucks speeding up the roads and stopping in side streets to unload potatoes grown in individual gardens, which are highly popular all over the country as a standby for the whole year.

Markets are always crowded with collective farmers selling their produce and with customers. Prices are still high but far less than last year; money is coming into its own again.

The return of soldiers to farms and factories is resulting in greater production and facilitating the country's return to a peacetime footing. There is no question of unemployment; on the contrary, there is an acute labor shortage in all trades and professions, skilled and unskilled. Advertisements in all papers and huge posters everywhere attest this. The Government is planning to train up to 1,000,000 skilled young workers a year in trade schools.

### Building Goes On All Year

All over the country building is going on the year round. In most of the liberated towns the people are speeding building and repairs. Industrial employes may receive long-term credits of 10,000 rubles for building an individual house. American prefabricated houses are popular.

All this points to alleviation of the acute housing problem, which will last a long time.

The clothing shortage may be slightly alleviated by the construction of textile mills and repair of machinery all over the country. The trend is to smarter and better clothes and footwear.

Fuel presents another grave problem this winter. In some parts of Russia it is colder than at the North Pole.

The Germans did great damage to Soviet oil and coal fields, causing the loss of millions of barrels of oil and millions of tons of coal. Moscow, which is in the center of the Soviet Union, gives a picture typical of what is going on all over Russia.

Double windows are being sealed, central heating systems, where they exist, are being repaired, roofs mended and coal is being stored. It is common to see in Moscow, as elsewhere, people trundling pushcarts loaded with wood—logs of pine or birch or fir—for their Dutch stoves. This year's ration in Moscow is more than last year's. It is about three and a half cubic maters of wood for each twenty square meters of floor space in houses without central heating for the winter season, which lasts officially from Nov. 15 to March 15.

November 13, 1945

# Soviet's Scars of War Vanishing In Rebuilding at a Feverish Pace

By BROOKS ATKINSON

By Wireless to The New York Times.

MOSCOW, Jan. 30 (Delayed)—Look from the windows of the train during the thirty-hour journey from Moscow to Kiev. In a way, the scene may be symbolic of what is happening all over the world, where the pressure for resuming normal life is tremendous. Look out the window and you can see not only what has happened but what is happening now.

What happened during the violent days of war lies sprawling and forgotten in the snow—blasted railroad cars upended, rusty tank traps, tangles of barbed wire, lonely chimneys towering above ruins and fortified strong points that once were vibrant with life but now are deserted by men who have more constructive things to do.

What is happening now is associated with life. It shows how quickly the human urge for living possesses a ravaged land. All along the way there are innumerable new log houses—peeled, clean-looking logs. White smoke is hovering above the chimneys, looking almost gay. They are sturdy, neatly built houses that will last for years. Gradually they are becoming a part of the dark evergreen forest that surrounds them.

Since the railroad is the lifeline of the region, everything is concentrated around it. It attracts people like a magnet. The people are living in abandoned freight cars or in temporary huts hastily knocked together from the carcasses of destroyed railroad buildings. At every station, there are mobs of people bundled against cold in padded coats, winter helmets and felt boots. An impromptu cafeteria is open for business when the train pulls in. Peasant women stand beside the rails to sell bread, hot meat, boiled eggs, roast fowl and hot mlik. Boys sell cigarettes at emergency prices. Since the Kiev express carries no restaurant car, passengers descend on the food market with cups, tin plates, bottles and cans.

With one eye on the train, which may start again without notice, and the other on the food supply, they hastily buy enough to keep body and soul together.

The train is stuffed with passengers, for the railroads cannot keep pace with the demands for transportation. Everyone is carrying bags and bundles and everyone is excited. At least half the passengers are Red Army officers and men, who are already used to travel in mass migrations. Some of them, just discharged from the hospital, are going home or to rest camps in the South. Some of them are hobbling on crutches; some have lost an arm or a leg.

Although the cars are so full that it seems like a miracle that anyone can travel for long hours in cramped quarters, the war cripples take the traveling conditions for granted and are only too glad to be moving. A few hardy souls, unable to burrow into the cars, stand on the exposed steps or on couplings between the cars in weather amout 4 or 5 degrees below zero, Fahrenheit.

White frost encases the coat collars and mufflers where they have been breathing. When the train stops, they run up and down the platform, stamping their feet and swinging their arms.

Every railroad yard is filled with freight cars; every siding contains a freight train waiting to let the express through. People are riding the freight cars, too. The open freight cars contain a sample of all the things that this busy nation needs for reconstruction—coal, logs, planks, pipes, limestone, scrap metal, machinery, used motor cars, new trucks. Besides, there are items of German machinery including a large transformer and parts of a steel rolling mill.

By the end of January, Russia is frozen hard and swept with snow. The cold is the most important single fact in every aspect of life. But the overburdened railroad hums with the lumbering vitality of this nation, which is rapidly absorbing the ugly things that happened into the brighter pattern of the things that are happening now.

February 1, 1946

# 5-YEAR PLAN

## PREMIER HAILS GAIN

### Seeks Production Rise to 'Guarantee Against Any Eventuality'

### He Promises to End Rationing Soon, After Stressing Ability to Stand Recent Blows

By The Associated Press.

LONDON, Feb. 9—Premier Joseph Stalin announced tonight a new Five-Year Plan for the Soviet Union with huge production boosts "to guarantee our country against any eventuality," and asserted that the present capitalistic world economy sets the stage for war.

He predicted, too, that Soviet scientists could "not only catch up with but also surpass those abroad."

Premier Stalin set goals for steel, pig iron, coal and oil production close to the output of the United States which he said might require three new Five-Year Plans, if not more.

In a pre-election speech, broadcast by the Moscow radio, the Premier promised that "soon rationing will end," and that the Russian worker's standard of living would be raised.

**Blames Capitalism for War**

Declaring that the war was "the inevitable result of the development of the world economic and political forces on the basis of monopoly capitalism," he asserted:

"Perhaps the catastrophe of war could have been avoided if the possibility of periodic redistribution of raw materials and markets between the countries existed in accordance with their economic needs, in the way of coordinated and peaceful decisions.

"But this is impossible under the present capitalistic development of world economy. Thus, as a result of the first crisis in the development of the capitalistic world economy, the first World War arose. The second World War arose as a result of the second crisis."

Premier Stalin, making his first speech since Sept. 2, spoke on the eve of elections for the Supreme Soviet in the district where he is a candidate for re-election.

He called for an industrial output of 50,000,000 tons of pig iron a year, 60,000,000 tons of steel, 500,000,000 tons of coal, and 60,000,000 tons of oil. When these goals are reached, "only then can we consider our country guaranteed against any eventuality," he said.

[The Statesman's Yearbook of 1945 said Russia's estimated production in 1941 was 18,000,000 tons of pig iron, 22,000,000 tons of steel, 191,000,000 tons of coal, and 38,000,000 tons of oil. The American Iron and Steel Institute gives United States production of pig iron in 1944 as 61,007,000 tons and steel as 89,641,000 tons. The United States Bureau of Mines reported United States production of coal and coke in 1944 as 683,700,000 tons.]

February 10, 1946

# Russia Purges Plant Officials In Nation-Wide Fraud Inquiry

By DREW MIDDLETON
By Wireless to The New York Times.

MOSCOW, June 26—Widespread dismissals and fining of factory directors, engineers and accountants as a result of the discovery of evidence that industrial-production figures had been faked, bonuses had been distributed illegally and factory funds had been misappropriated was announced by the Ministry of State Control in all newspapers this morning.

The Ministry also charged that officials had been converting state property to their own use and shipping goods that were unfinished or below standard to customers. According to the announcement, purges have not taken place in any one industry or group of industries or in any one industrial region but have been distributed in such widely separated areas as Leningrad, Moscow, Stalinsk and Tomsk in Siberia. Nor is there any evidence of any connection between one group and another in the statement made today.

Industrial officials have been removed from their jobs and fined and in many cases they will be tried in court, the announcement stated. The removals have taken place in such important enterprises as the Russian Diesel plant in Leningrad; the Tula Coal Company in Tula, near Moscow, and at the Dniepropetrovsk metallurgical equipment and engineering plant in the Don Basin, according to the statement.

**Series of Investigations Made**

The Ministry announced that it had conducted a "series of audits of the financial and economic activities of certain enterprises and institutions" and that the auditors had discovered the "illegal acceptance of a bonus [on the basis of altered production figures], the improper use of bonus funds and the embezzlement of financial and material property of value by various responsible persons." The Ministry's report was divided into three sections, each of which dealt with a single category of offenses. The first is the falsification of production figures and the illegal distribution of bonuses. The second is the mismanagement of industrial plants and the poor quality of production including the falsification of figures, while the third category described various cases of embezzlement.

According to the charges, N. V. Solodukhin, director of the Russian Diesel plant, and its production manager, M. G. Solovyov, "during the whole of 1945 and the first quarter of 1946 arbitrarily increased wholesale fixed prices for Diesel spare parts" and "thereby artificially increased the indices of fulfillment of their plant's production." The charge added that they included "in their reports of production of spare parts those that had been produced before the war and had already been counted."

Thus Solodukhin was able to give "illegally large bonuses to various workers of the plant for overfulfilling the planned production quota." Moreover, Solodukhin "illegally spent state funds for his personal needs." Solodukhin has been removed from his job and is to pay a fine of 6,000 rubles, while Solovyov has been severely reprimanded and will pay a fine of 4,000 rubles.

**Mine Affairs Detailed**

The affairs of Mine No. 19 of the Stchekinougol Trust of the Tulaougol coal combination give a good example of what the Ministry rooted out in its investigations. At this mine Kamchatkov, its production head, and Petrashov, former chief engineer, "faked coal output figures and made false reports to the trust headquarters on the amount of coal mined. Thus, in February, 1945, the mine fulfilled its production quota by 98.3 per cent but the reports fixed the figure at 102.4 per cent."

These officials also tampered with the production figures for March and April, raising each in order, the Ministry said, "to get bonuses." The statement added that this was done "with the knowledge of Tronin and Solodky, respectively trust manager and chief engineer of the Stchekin coal trust." Kamchatkov and S. G. Lyakhov, head bookkeeper, have been removed from their positions and are to be tried, the statement added, while Tronin and Solodky were severely reprimanded and must pay fines of 7500 rubles each.

The conspiracy at the Dniepropetrovsk metallurgical equipment and engineering plant included Zhernovoi, the plant director; Chernyshenko, the chief engineer, and Olkhovik, the head bookkeeper. At this plant also the index of total production was raised and tubings produced before the war were included in the current inventory. Zhernovoi was dismissed and will be tried, while the others are to be fined. Here again production figures were falsified to permit the distribution of bonuses.

**Similar Pattern Shown**

The same pattern is evident in the report on the Katek automobile plant, where G. V. Bourakov, the director, falsely reported that the plant's planned production quota had been exceeded by 3 to 5 per cent in October and November of 1945 and January and March of this year. The Ministry also charged Bourakov and F. F. Aunapy, his chief engineer, with "not organizing proper control of technological discipline and specifications for the production of automotive electrical equipment" and

**with the "shipment of poor-quality products to customers." B. I. Bok, the head bookkeeper, falsified the books so that the production figure for 1945 was 20 to 25 per cent in excess of the actual production.**

**Four officials of Building Trust No. 14 of the Ministry of Aviation also submitted fraudulent reports on the progress of construction last November and December. Two officials were discharged; the others were reprimanded and fined.**

**The Ministry of State Control discovered forgery and embezzlement in the food processing industry. B. A. Goubichev, representing the Stalinsk collecting station of the Novosibirsk branch of the chief of the supply administration of the Meat and Dairy Produce Ministry, has been dismissed and will be tried for forging his signature to a fictitious list of workers entitled to food products and for falsifying accounts.**

**A. K. Solovyov, representing the Tomsk branch of the same department of the same Ministry, and his bookkeeper, N. A. Lazoskaya, together embezzled 40,000 rubles in 1945. Other embezzlers were discovered in the business manager's office of the Ministry for Agricultural Machinery. All officials accused of embezzlement have been removed from their posts and will be tried.**

June 27, 1946

# RUSSIA'S ECONOMY: A SURVEY OF ITS STRENGTH AND WEAKNESS

## While the Five-Year Plan Is Not Working Out as Expected The Soviet Has a Way of Driving Its Program Through

**By a Correspondent of The Economist, London**

It is perplexing to watch the strange changes in the general public's opinions on Russia's economic as well as military strength.

In the later phases of the war and for some time after it the popular imagination seemed hypnotized by the picture of the "Eastern giant" striding across the Continent with some inexplicable and irresistible force.

The fashion has since changed. In recent months Russia's weakness has been impressing itself upon the public mind and providing the topic for guesswork and comment. Attention has been centered on Russia's economic difficulties, now quite often seen through magnifying glasses.

Which of these pictures is the correct one? Each is partly true and partly misleading. An old Russian poet once epitomized the riddle in an apostrophe to Mother Russia: "Thou art so powerful and thou art so helpless; thou art so poor and thou art so plentiful, Mother Russia." The saying is not yet out of date—even after the Five-Year Plans and the hoisting of the Russian flag on the Reichstag. Any realistic appraisal of Russia must still balance its strength against its weakness.

The news that has come from Moscow in recent weeks has all tended to emphasize, even sensationally overemphasize, the elements of weakness. For several months a spate of grim statements and grave warnings about the economic situation has been coming from official Soviet sources.

Soon afterward came the announcement about the calamitous drought, "the worst since half a century." Simultaneously the Gosplan published the results achieved in industry in the first year of the new plan; it became known that in many branches of industry the planned "targets" had not been reached. Last month's budget session in the Supreme Soviet was filled with the most "alarming" statements and speeches the Russians had heard since the late Twenties.

At the same time the Central Committee of the party met, and Mr. Stalin apparently made several important speeches at its closed sessions—the speeches have not been reported in the press and only Mr. Andreyef referred to them in public. On March 1 the campaign culminated in a statement issued by the Cabinet itself. At the Supreme Soviet most Ministers responsible for economic departments were severely criticized by deputies—a most unusual thing in Russia—and, still more unusually, by their own colleagues in the Government.

There can be no doubt that the Soviet Union is in the throes of an economic crisis. The salient facts have been set out in the Government's statement of March 1. The reconversion of Soviet industry to peace has "in the main" been completed; but the process has not been carried out efficiently. "The gross output of the entire civilian production was 20 per cent higher in 1946 than in 1945."

This has a reassuring ring, but it really means that the first year of the new plan has ended in failure. Since plant and labor diverted to civilian production must have increased by much more than 20 per cent, the increase in gross output by only 20 per cent indicates a steep decline in productivity.

The situation is worst in the former occupied areas. There industrial output increased by 28 per cent, but it "did not even reach half the pre-war production." This is a euphemism—output is probably well below the 50 per cent. In the victorious Soviet Union the devastation and unsettlement of the war are being overcome at a pace not much quicker—so far—than the rate of economic rehabilitation in western Germany.

### Lack of Coal

As elsewhere, so in Russia; lack of coal is stated to be the chief problem. "The development of the coal industry, which is experiencing the greatest difficulties as a result of the war, is lagging behind and delaying the progress of the entire national economy." The criticism seems to be addressed to the central planning authorities rather than to the coal industry.

The fact is that the 1946 plan for coal output has been fulfilled. The Asiatic coal mines have fallen short of their target by 3 per cent, but the European ones, which must now produce about half of Russia's coal, have produced 5 per cent more than was planned.

The implication of the statement about the coal crisis is, therefore, that the planners in Moscow have not been bold enough. Even so, it must be doubted whether lack of coal has been the decisive reason for the slow rehabilitation of Ukrainian and south Russian industries.

It is more probable that stagnation in the former occupied lands is caused by a crisis in the morale of the working population, a crisis due to disastrous housing conditions, to shortages of food and consumers' goods, and also to general post-war frustration. "The housing plan for 1946 was not fulfilled; the housing space made available amounted to 6,000,000 square meters. Housing difficulties are delaying the creation of permanent cadres of workers and the raising of the productivity of labor."

Incidentally, the five-year target for housing is very modest. Even if the planned building by private persons (12 million square meters) is added to it, the average housing space which the twenty-odd million Soviet citizens made homeless by the war can hope to get by 1950 will at best be not more than 4 square yards per person; and this does not allow for any increase in population. The bottleneck is in the supply of cement, bricks and timber.

In some respects, then, the crisis appears to be milder than the wording of the official statements suggest; in others it is certainly even graver. But it should be remembered that the old Ukrainian and southern Russian centers of industry are no longer as important for the Soviet economy as they used to be: and the situation in the new centers in the east is incomparably better than in the formerly occupied provinces.

### Agricultural Status

The agricultural situation presents a similar difference between the west, stricken by war and drought, and the east, where life has not been so unsettled. Thus "in western Siberia and Khazakhstan the grain harvest increased by one and a half times compared with 1945." But the over-all situation is grim. Restoration of the pre-war grain output is not expected under three years; the figures of the last harvest have not been disclosed. The peasants have failed to deliver their quotas of grain to the Government.

By what means then does the Soviet Government intend to overcome the present crisis? The means recently adopted are not new—they have been used and tested in previous Five-Year Plans; but they have now been carried a few long steps further.

The current Five-Year Plan is based on a system of priorities in which the renewal and the expansion of industry's capital equipment is ruthlessly promoted to be the first and foremost objective of national economy. Even though in 1946 the plan was not fulfilled in many branches, the progress made in re-equiping industry was by far more rapid and energetic than the over-all increase in the output of consumers' goods.

The disappointingly slow increase in the gross output of civilian goods—20 per cent—is contrasted with a 50 per cent increase in machine building. In the long run the principle is certainly sound, and it is sure to pay handsome economic and political dividends.

### Producing Machines

Soviet planners prefer to have as many machines as possible produced now, even at a lower rate of efficiency, than to rely on the hypothetical higher efficiency that could be expected in the future from a better-fed, better-clad and better-housed working class. What one might call the anti-consumer outlook of Soviet planners has evidently been enhanced by the experiences of the war.

The shortage of manpower is being overcome by what looks like a real tour de force. The number of workers in industry was increased by three million people last year: for the current year the plan provides for total employment amounting to 31.6 million people. This is 1.2 million more than the total employment in 1940, Russia's

## THE CHANGING ECONOMIC MAP OF RUSSIA

Russia is facing many problems in reconverting her industry from a war-economy. The biggest difficulties have arisen in the areas (shown on the top map) invaded and devastated by Germany and her allies during the war. The million Russian troops on occupation duty in Europe constitute another important factor in the Soviet economy.

last year of peace.

Where does this new labor come from? In the main, from the armed forces; but even the most drastic demobilization would hardly have allowed Russia to keep her employment at a level so much higher than that of before the war, since Russia's manpower has been reduced by millions of casualties. Apparently most of the female and juvenile labor drafted into industry during the war will be staying on.

In addition, a drastic regrouping of the available labor resources is taking place which aims at transferring great masses of people from less to more productive jobs. Thus the establishment of the economic civil service has now been cut by 730,000 posts—the personnel thus released is to be employed in actual production.

### Farm Workers

A similar redistribution of workers, especially of the skilled ones, is taking place in agriculture. On Mr. Stalin's initiative, the salaries of agriculturists employed on administrative jobs will from now on be 25 per cent less than those of "agronomers" working in the field.

The whole set of measures designed to deflate economic bureaucracy is very characteristic. For many years the regime has had a vested interest in inflating the administrative cadres, since politically they have been its most reliable prop. But now that vested political interest has very obviously clashed with the demands of national efficiency, the regime has had to sacrifice a section of that social group whose privileged position it has hitherto carefully sheltered.

However, the most important emergency measures have been taken in wages policy. Payment by results, rewards for skill and efficiency, progressive piece rates have been the guiding principles ever since the inception of Stakhanovism in 1935. The policy is now being pushed to new extremes in both its positive and negative aspects. Output above the standard norms is to be even better rewarded than hitherto; the standard norms are to be raised; and often output below the standard norms is to be penalized through decreasing scales of payment.

But the most sweeping and thoroughgoing change—one that affects two-thirds of the Soviet population—is being made in the structure of agricultural wages. Until now the system of payment in the collective farms was a combination of time and piece rates.

The time rate was the pay for the so-called working day. The working day and its pay was equal for all; and all collective farmers were obliged to do an equal number of "working days" during the year. From now on the uniform payment per working day is abolished, and all agricultural wages are to be calculated on the basis of efficiency—that is, in relation to harvests.

April 13, 1947

# Soviet Statistics on Growth Found 'Biased' by Experts

By WILL LISSNER

The Soviet Union's economic potential as a great world power has been exaggerated by "biased" official Soviet statistics into a "badly distorted" version of economic growth, according to analyses by a group of leading statisticians made public yesterday by Prof. Seymour E. Harris of Harvard University.

The analyses are contained in reports by the economists and statisticians that will be published next month by the Department of Economics at Harvard University in its technical publication, The Review of Economic Statistics.

Obtaining their data by treating and analyzing the official Russian statistics by advanced techniques, they picture the Soviet Union as a poverty-stricken nation with an industrial output that is not large on American standards although "a very large part was devoted before the war to armaments and investments."

They portray the U.S.S.R. as a country with "a distressingly low level of welfare." This is indicated by an average consumption, measured in 1940 dollars, of $111 a year, against $600 in the United States (where, unlike war-devastated Russia, average consumption now has risen to 1,300 such dollars). Also, Russia's total output of goods and services on the outbreak of the war was roughly one-third that of the United States.

At the same time the statistics show Russia has made striking and important advances in certain fields, such as electric power, oil, coal and pig iron production, although not as much as has been claimed. Also, its military power appears greater than its economic position might indicate.

One of the statisticians reported that before the Nazi invasion devastated part of the Soviet economy, a loss which the Russians have sought mightily to make up, one-third of the total output of goods and services was devoted to the development and expansion of industry and to armament production.

The reports also indicate the output of all Soviet industry in 1945 declined to a greater extent than 8.3 per cent below the 1940 output, the drop announced by the Soviet Government, but this was partly because armament production required a greater expenditure of labor and other resources per unit.

### Five Leading Economists

The project that developed this picture of Russia was initiated by Professor Harris. Taking part in it were five of the world's leading students of Russian economy. They are Alexander Gerschenkron, Russian expert and economist of the Federal Reserve Board, Washington; Colin Clark, Australian Government financial adviser and an outstanding authority on comparative national income statistics; Paul A. Baran, an economist on the staff of the Federal Reserve Bank of New York; Prof. Abram Bergson of Columbia University, and Aaron Yugow of New York, a specialist on Russian industry. Drs. Baran and Bergson were Russian experts of the Office of Strategic Services during the war.

Having undertaken the studies as individuals, the statisticians take personal responsibility for the opinions expressed. Their views have no official sanction and are not necessarily those of the Government agencies and institutions with which they are connected, Dr. Harris explained.

The study is not presented as an exact one, Dr. Harris said, for important information is withheld by the Soviet Government as a matter of defense policy, and the material available does not yield precise results. It was offered, it was explained, as a scientifically valid approximation of the Russian economic position and a more realistic portrayal than has been available hitherto.

The statisticians believe their analyses explode not only the "glowing reports" coming from Russia about extraordinary gains in output and income, but many misconceptions about Russian industrial growth given currency in official reports by other Governments and in private studies.

As an example of the disposition of economists to accept Russian statistics "rather uncritically," Dr. Harris cited the League of Nations report on industrialization last year. This was an "excellent" study, he pointed out. Yet the League's experts estimated Russian industrial output in 1936-38 at 18.5 per cent of world output, and that of the United States at 32.2 per cent of the world figure. The findings of Mr. Clark, Dr. Gerschenkron and Dr. Baran indicate this estimate for Russia is wide of the mark. Dr. Baran puts the Russian output at one-third that of the United States, not at more than one-half.

As another example, Dr. Harris cited the famous Bombay Report for India, published by a group of Indian business men in 1944, which credited a report that the national income of the U.S.S.R. had increased "fivefold" in the twelve years after the beginning of the first five-year plan. Mr. Clark estimated the total Russian national income in 1934 and 1928 were at about the level of 1913, and by 1938 had risen 50 per cent.

The Harvard economist cited other recent examples—reports that Russian industrial output rose 650 per cent from 1928 to 1940, that Russian national income per capita rose 352 per cent in the same period, that labor productivity rose in each of the years from 1933 to 1937 at the rate of 8, 13, 21 and 9 per cent, respectively, whereas the consistent rate in the United States is 3 per cent a year.

The statisticians explained these estimates, which they held to be erroneous, by a number of technical analyses. A chief difficulty, they asserted, is that these estimates are based primarily on the U.S.S.R. index of industrial output expressed in 1926-27 prices. This index, Dr. Gerschenkron and Dr. Baran reported, has "a substantial upward bias," resulting from the practice of adding new products at current higher prices even though all products are presumably measured in the low 1926-27 prices.

Professor Bergson dealt with the shortcomings of wage and labor statistics. He reported that on the basis of a comparison of the Central Planning Board's figures for wages and workers with the correct total computed from other official statistics, the Russian manner of collecting statistical data is "suspect." Its concepts are not clearly defined and in some instances the data are "very misleading," he said.

### "Biased" Picture Presented

Noting from Mr. Yugow's report that Russian statisticians are aware of some of the shortcomings of their statistics and that they have made sincere efforts to improve them, Professor Harris said:

"It is not contended that the Soviet Government manipulates its statistical series, but the refusal to publish price indices, considered together with the so-called use of 1926-27 prices for the purpose of measuring output, suggests an intention to present a biased statistical picture."

Mr. Clark dealt in his study with general problems of the interpretation of Russian statistics, particularly with those relating to measures of the growth of national income and of productivity. Dr. Baran dealt with Russian income. In measuring the rise in Russian income, both statisticians applied unusual techniques.

Instead of depending exclusively on the Russian series, each constructed his own index of Russian output based on scattered Russian statistical data. Mr. Clark measured the Russian output by following the method of Prof. Michael Polanyi of the University of Manchester, England, in terms of "international units," an index number based on prices prevailing in other countries, one international unit being defined as the quantity of goods and services exchangeable for one dollar over the average of the years 1925-34. Dr. Baran measured the output in terms of the 1940 dollar.

### Gross Product Computed

Mr. Clark's result, that Russian national income had risen only 50 per cent by 1938, cannot be checked against Dr. Baran's work because the latter found that efforts to supply the shortcomings of Russian income statistics or make them comparable with United States income statistics yielded unsatisfactory or impracticable results.

Instead, Dr. Baran computed the gross national product of the U.S.S.R. from official reports and used the estimates of leading Soviet statisticians specializing in national income problems to achieve a basis for valuing gross output in United States dollars.

With this procedure he computed that the value of Russian gross national product in 1940 was 432,290,000,000 "current rubles" or $32,250,000,000 in 1940 dollars. Checking on the result, he found the "purchasing power parity" is 13.40 rubles per United States dollar and pointed out "that the 'courtesy rate' accorded by Soviet authorities to foreign diplomatic and consular agencies operating in the U.S.S.R. is 12 rubles per United States dollar," whereas the official rate is 5 rubles per United States dollar.

Dr. Baran presented this estimate of $32,250,000,000 as the Russian gross national product in 1940 so that its magnitude can be visualized. He does not claim that it is precise enough to warrant comparison with the corresponding United States figure, which is $100,000,000,000. He pointed out, however, that the smallness of the difference between his own underlying estimates and those of the Soviet State Planning Commission "would suggest that the estimates presented above cannot be very far off the mark."

He calculated further that out of a gross product of about $32,250,000,000, about $10,000,000,000 were spent in 1940 on investment and military preparedness, which left about $22,000,000,000 of goods and services for the civilian population.

Mr. Clark used the available statistics to investigate Russian productivity. He found, he reported, that real product per man-hour by 1928 apparently had just about been restored to the 1913 level.

"It is also clear that after 1928, during the First Five-Year Plan, real product per man-hour fell heavily, and reached its minimum in the period 1932-34," he said. "If we measure real product per man-hour actually worked, productivity in 1932-34 was only about two-thirds of that of 1913 or 1928."

Measuring the product per head of the population available for work, he concluded, "we still find productivity per man-hour falling 15 to 20 per cent between 1928 and 1932-34, recovering the 1928 level only in 1936, but rising 25 per cent above it by 1939."

Dr. Gerschenkron concluded it is probable that an accurate index of industrial output in Russia would have reached a level just before the war "somewhere between that of the official Soviet index and that of the physical indices of output of basic industrial raw materials." The latter are much lower.

### Inconsistency on Wages

Professor Bergson reported that he found "an obvious inconsistency" in the goals for employment and wages in the Fourth Five-Year Plan, published in 1946. The plan sets as the 1950 goal 33,500,000 wage-earners and salaried workers, with 6,000 rubles average annual earnings, which is a wage bill of 201,000,000,000 rubles, not 252,300,000,000, as the plan states.

The inconsistency arises, he asserted, because the reports of the Soviet Central Statistical Administration on labor statistics are interpreted abroad and used for planning within Russia as if they were comprehensive. Actually, scattered Russian reports, he said, cite omissions and deficiencies in these data.

In several of the Russian institutes that have been set up in recent years at American universities, similar studies of Russian statistics are going forward. Syracuse University recently published a survey of the Russian economic system by Prof. Harry Schwarz, and Ohio State University issued one on Russian foreign trade by Dr. Mikhail V. Condoide.

Dr. Harris expressed the hope that the studies of his colleagues reveal "the need of devoting greater resources in this country for the study of Russian statistics."

October 20, 1947

# SOVIET DEVALUES THE RUBLE AND ENDS RATIONING OF FOOD IN FIGHT AGAINST INFLATION

## CUTS RANGE TO 90%

## Cash Conversion Rate Is 1 for 10 in a Move to Curb Speculators

By The Associated Press.

MOSCOW, Dec. 14—The Soviet Union announced tonight it would begin the issuance of new currency on Tuesday and simultaneously would abandon all food rationing in a program to combat inflation.

The announcement was made to the nation by the Moscow radio in a decree of the Council of Ministers and the Communist party. It was signed by Premier Stalin and Col. Gen. Andrei A. Zhdanov, secretary of the Communist party Central Committee and a member of the Politburo.

[The action was the first admission that post-war inflation had affected the controlled Russian economy. It followed by ten days the statement in Washington by Acting Secretary of State Robert A. Lovett that something "in the nature of panic buying" had hit Russia over rumors of devaluation of the ruble.]

The decree for currency reform provides that rubles brought to banks for conversion will be exchanged at the rate of ten old rubles for one new one. Bank deposits and bonds will be converted at rates ranging from one for one to one for three old rubles. The exchange must take place in the week Dec. 16-22.

**Throngs Gather to Listen**

Rationing was ordered abolished on all "food and industrial goods," and consumer goods were brought under unified price control. The price of bread under the new program will be 12 per cent lower than the ration price and beer 10 per cent lower, the announcement said, but vodka and wine will be unchanged.

The object of the new program is to combat inflation and speculation which had increased the market prices of some commodities to ten or fifteen times their pre-war levels, the announcement added.

The abolition of rationing was received with expressions of joy by the citizens of Moscow. Yuri Levitan, the announcer who broadcast all the nation's important war communiqués, read the decree affecting every one of the Soviet Union's 200,000,000 inhabitants.

In Moscow, hundreds gathered at loudspeakers in public places to listen. When the import of the news dawned upon them, they pounded each other on the back, shook hands and met in groups to discuss the developments.

In addition to the 12 per cent reduction for bread and flour, a 10 per cent cut will take place for cereals and macaroni from the present ration price. Meat, fish, fats, sugar, confectionery goods, salt, potatoes and vegetables will remain at the present level.

**Effect of the Reform**

Tea, milk and certain other items were increased over their present "too low" ration price, but reduced well below the prices charged in the unrationed "commercial" stores. [The dispatch gave no specific prices for any item.]

Wages and salaries were untouched by the currency reform. All institutions were ordered to pay their employes wages and salaries for the first half of December between Dec. 16 and 20, thus assuring that everyone would have enough currency to make an adjustment from the old system to the new.

The currency reform affects those with bonds, savings accounts and cash. Those who present cash for exchange will receive one new ruble for ten old ones, regardless of the size of the sum they exchange.

Bank deposits up to 3,000 rubles will be exchanged on a one-for-one basis; accounts up to 10,000 rubles will be exchanged at a rate of one-to-one for the first 3,000 rubles and the remainder on a basis of two new rubles for three old; deposits of more than 10,000 rubles will be exchanged at the foregoing rates for the first 10,000 rubles and the remainder on a basis of one new ruble for two old.

The holders of ordinary state bonds will receive new bonds with a face value of one ruble for each three rubles of face value of the old bonds. Holders of the 1938 issue of state bonds, which were fully redeemable at any time, will receive one new ruble for each five of face value.

Thus, savings bank depositors with moderate deposits will fare the best under the reform and those who kept their cash in their pockets are the chief losers.

The Moscow radio announcement was the first official mention of inflation and speculation in the Soviet Union. Although a hint that rationing would be abolished was made Dec. 9 by Deputy Premier Georgi M. Malenkov, also a secretary of the Communist Central Committee.

Under the decree, the Soviet Union will become the first of the larger European countries to take off rationing completely all foodstuffs and consumer goods.

The Russian nation was told by the Government that any monetary losses suffered by individuals under the currency reform were "the last sacrifices" that would be demanded of them as a result of World War II.

The decree said currency reform was necessary to allow the end of rationing and to put the Russian economy on a sound basis. It said too much money was circulating throughout the Soviet Union as compared with goods to be bought, adding that the excess money was coming from two sources—immense military expenditures, which required putting large sums into circulation, and also from "counterfeit money in rubles" left by the German Army when it was occupying part of Russia.

December 15, 1947

# RUBLE CONVERSION HARD ON PEASANTS

By WILL LISSNER

The Russian peasant bore the brunt of the confiscation of savings that attended the recent conversion of the Soviet Union's currency, according to data that became available yesterday.

Information on the distribution of savings in cash, in bank deposits and in bondholdings, taken from official and other authoritative Soviet sources, was made available by Prof. Harry Schwartz of the Board of Russian Studies, Syracuse University. During the war Dr. Schwartz was an expert on Russia with the Office of Strategic Services. He has been carrying on research in recent developments in Soviet prices.

One source of information on the distribution of Soviet savings is the work of A. K. Suchkov, "Revenues of the State Budget of the USSR," published in Russian in Moscow in 1945 by the publishing house of the Ministry of Finance. It is a textbook for financial officers.

Mr. Suchkov reported that in 1944 about 80 per cent of the savings deposits in savings institutions were those of workers and salaried employes, Dr. Schwartz said. Mr. Suchkov made a point of noting that the savings deposits do not reflect the savings of collective farmers, implying that the latter, following the universal tradition of peasants, kept their surplus income in cash hoards. Government bonds, he added, were similarly distributed largely among the urban population.

In the conversion, holders of cash receive one new ruble for each ten old ones. Holders of savings deposits and state bonds fared much better.

Bank depositors receive one new ruble for one old one on the first 3,000 rubles on deposit, two new ones for three old ones on the next 7,000 rubles on deposit and one new one for two old ones on any balance above 10,000 rubles.

Holders of ordinary state bonds receive one new ruble for three old ones in the face value of the bond. Holders of 1938 state bonds receive one new ruble for five old ones of value.

Up to the beginning of the war the total of all bonds floated was 50,000,000,000 rubles. During the war 90,000,000,000 rubles of state bonds were floated. Meanwhile, deposits in savings institutions increased from 7,000,000,000 rubles in 1940 to 12,000,000,000 in 1947.

Among the classes that benefit from the more favorable treatment given bank depositors and bondholders than holders of cash are several that occupy strategic positions in the Soviet economy. First there are the millionaire Stakhonovites, the pace setters in the factories under the incentive wage system that is nearly universal in Soviet factories. Then there are factory managers and state administrators, who are rewarded with large bonuses when they attain or exceed goals. Then there are the intellectuals, who receive cash premiums as royalties and bonuses.

The extraordinary range of incomes in the USSR is reflected in the distribution of deposits, according to Dr. Schwartz's data. Z. M. Batyrev and V. K. Sitnin, in "The Financial and Credit System of the USSR," published in the Soviet Union in 1945, gave the following statistics:

Accounts of less than 100 rubles which comprised 57 per cent of all accounts, were 5 per cent of all savings on Jan. 1, 1938. Accounts from 100 to 1,000 rubles were 23 per cent of all accounts and 28 per cent of all savings. Accounts of more than 1,000 rubles were 10 per cent of all accounts but comprised 67 per cent of the total sum of savings.

At the beginning of the war the average of individual deposits in rural banks is believed to have been 134 rubles. Mr. Suchkov reported that at that time the average of all savings accounts was 417 rubles, which indicates the great disparity in the deposit holdings of rural and urban citizens in the USSR.

December 22, 1947

# Stalin Decrees Sweeping Price Cuts In Food, Clothing, Consumer Goods

By The Associated Press.

**MOSCOW, Feb. 28—Premier Stalin tonight proclaimed price cuts in forty-five classifications of food, clothing and other consumers' goods.**

**The decree said the changes would raise the ruble's purchasing power and strengthen Soviet money in relation to foreign currencies.**

**The price cuts, effective tomorrow in all retail stores, knock 10 per cent off the price of bread, fish, butter and canned goods, 20 per cent off the price of cheese and 12 to 20 per cent off many clothing items. Vodka will be reduced 28 per cent and timepieces 30 per cent.**

**Restaurants, tea houses and other catering establishments were ordered to make corresponding reductions in their prices.**

**Muscovites rejoiced as the decree—signed by Premier Stalin and Georgi M. Malenkov, secretary of the Communist party's Central** Committee—was broadcast by radio. The price reductions are a new step toward reattaining the Soviet Union's pre-war standard of living.

The first stage of post-war price reductions was announced in December, 1947, when money was revalued and many Soviet citizens had to exchange 10 old rubles for one new one. At that time derationing also was announced. Some further price reductions were made last April, but the changes decreed today are the most sweeping since December, 1947.

The announcement said:

"In connection with the further uplift of the national economy of the U.S.S.R., the growth in production of consumer goods and the new achievements in the field of reducing costs, it became possible in the latter part of 1948 to effect a new reduction of prices of consumer goods.

"The Council of Ministers of the U.S.S.R. and the Central Committee of the Communist party of the Soviet Union [Bolsheviks] have resolved to effect this new reduction of prices, which partly was started already in 1948, and to consummate it on March 1, 1949. This shall be the second stage in reducing the price of consumer goods.

---

The new Soviet price reductions in food and consumer goods reflect increased Soviet production of these items. The Central Statistical Administration of the Soviet Union announced announced late in January, last, that the grain harvest virtually equaled that of 1940, and was substantially above the previous year. Compared with 1947, the output last year of some of the price-cut commodities rose in the following percentages: Butter, 37, wool cloth, 28, and stockings 44. Alcohol production rose 50 per cent, explaining the very sharp reduction in the price of vodka and liqueurs.

Not all the basic cost-of-living items were reduced in price, however, since the list seems to omit leather shoes and clothing made of cotton textiles, though prices were cut on the less important wool and silk garments and on shoes made of textiles and mixed materials. Sugar also was unmentioned.

Despite the latest reductions Soviet prices are still far above pre-war levels. Bread sold for one ruble a kilogram in Moscow in 1940, but will be 2.7 rubles now. Butter was 23 rubles a kilogram before the war; the new price is about 57 rubles. Despite the new reductions in prices the most important foods continue to be almost triple pre-war prices, though wages have not even doubled, indicating that real wages in terms of food still are below the pre-war level.

March 1, 1949

# PROPERTY RIGHTS IN SOVIET DEFINED

## Press Says Citizens Can Have House, Furniture, Savings and Personal Objects

By HARRISON E. SALISBURY

Special to THE NEW YORK TIMES.

MOSCOW, June 25—The two leading newspapers of the Soviet Union—Pravda, organ of the Communist party, and Izvestia, organ of the Government—published today extensive articles emphasizing the right of Soviet citizens to own personal property and outlining the whole concept of personal ownership in the Soviet Union.

Both articles were answering questions of readers who wanted to know the difference between bourgeois ownership of private property and ownership of personal property under the Socialist system.

The articles stated that under socialism all means of production were owned by the state but at the same time the Soviet Constitution "protects the personal property of citizens and the rights of inheritance."

The articles said Soviet citizens have the right to their income and savings obtained from work, to own a house and domestic appurtenances, to own objects of domestic use and to own objects of personal use and convenience.

In the case of collective farmers, Pravda noted that a farmer had not only a household and personal garden plot but the rights to whatever is grown on his personal plot as well as personally owned cattle and poultry, structures for housing animals and small agricultural equipment.

Rather than discouraging ownership of personal property, Pravda said the Socialist system encouraged it by increasing the income and savings of citizens and presenting the possibility of buying greater quantities of valuable objects of consumption, service and convenience.

"Personal property of toilers is continuously growing in the post-war period," Pravda reported. "This was greatly helped by monetary reform and the abolition of the card system in 1947 and by the systematic reduction of prices for goods of mass consumption."

Pravda reported that after price reductions last March the sale of radio sets more than doubled, the sale of phonographs and bicycles increased five times, that of motorcycles three times and of watches four times. The demand for furniture, automobiles and musical instruments also jumped.

Furthermore, under last autumn's decree of the Supreme Soviet Presidium authorizing private building and ownership of houses, there has been a big increase in individual house construction.

Izvestia contrasted all this with private property in bourgeois society, which it described as "the right of unrestrained exploitation of the working class by bankers and manufacturers—the right of the rich, who live by clipping coupons, usury and speculation, to a parasitic way of life."

June 26, 1949

# SUPPLY WOES CUT SOVIET PRODUCTION

## Needed Materials Often Arrive Late, Forcing Factories to End or Curtail Output

By HARRY SCHWARTZ

The industrial supply system of the Soviet Union is apparently operating poorly, causing serious hindranee to production.

Leningradskaya Pravda recently printed an article by a factory director in Leningrad complaining of the harm done to production by supply difficulties. Needed materials often arrive late, forcing factories to cease or partly curtail output. Raw materials and semi-fabricated goods frequently do not meet specifications so that they cannot be used at all or must be further processed by the recipient.

In Leningrad alone, the article reports, hundreds of government offices employ thousands of persons who are supposed to facilitate necessary transactions between different enterprises. But these work so poorly and are of so little help that many factories have to spend large sums foraging for themselves so that their work can continue.

The situation is so bad, the director writes, that to meet its needs for electric lamps, motors, transformers, optical equipment and forgings, his factory has had to institute production of these items itself. At the same time, he says, Leningrad has large factories producing all these items, factories that are by no means always working at capacity.

At the root of the situation, he declares, is the overly bureaucratic organization of the Soviet industrial supply system. Factories adjacent to each other are not allowed to make arrangements directly to supply each other's needs if they belong to different ministries. These and other restrictions on enterprise managers' iniative tie them hand and foot, he complains, and must be removed if matters are to be improved.

A similar situation exists in the local consumer goods industry in Moscow, the newspaper Moskovskaya Pravda reports.

The supply system for these enterprises is working so badly that it is estimated that they will fail to receive about 600,000,000 rubles worth of raw materials that they require, about one-third their total needs. Because of the lack of materials, these enterprises will not be able to achieve this year's output plans for such goods as furniture, phonographs, children's bicycles, aluminum utensils and knitted goods.

To get around supply difficulties, some factories in Moscow do not produce articles for which they are best fitted, but only such goods for which they are able to obtain materials.

June 11, 1950

# SOVIET DATA SHOW SLAVE LABOR ROLE

## Force Administered by Secret Police Found Major Basis of Russian Economy

By HARRY SCHWARTZ

Special to The New York Times.

WASHINGTON, Dec. 16—Conclusive proof that the slave labor system administered by the Soviet Union's secret police is a major foundation of the country' economy has been made public by the United States Government. The proof is provided by a secret Soviet document that gives a comprehensive picture of the volume and geographical distribution of the work done by the economic organizations of the Soviet internal security organization.

The document is the "State Plan for the Development of the National Economy of the U. S. S. R. in 1941." It carries an official Soviet security classification "Not to be publicized" and is labeled, "Supplement to decision No. 127 of the Council of People's Commissars of the U. S. S. R. and of the Central Committee of the All-Union Communist Party (Bolshevik), January 17, 1941."

### N. K. V. D. Plans Detailed

A 750-page statistical compilation, the plan covers all phases of panned Soviet production for 1941 in great detail, including the production and construction activities of the N. K. V. D., the old title of the M. V. D.

The United States and British governments have been in possession of this plan throughout the post-war period but until recently have kept it hidden behind security restrictions. Knowledge of the facts it contains has been one of the reasons both countries have pressed the subject of slave labor in the Soviet Union before the United Nations.

The draft of the 1941 Soviet economic plan, which has never been made public in the U. S. S. R. was captured by German forces in the Soviet Union during World War II. It was obtained by Western intelligence officers when Germany surrendered and has since been painstakingly checked for authenticity and accuracy by American and British specialists on the Soviet economy.

### Largest Single Agency

The picture of the secret police economic activities that emerges from this plan indicates that this organization is the largest single construction division in the U. S. S. R. and also engages in large-scale production of a number of major commodities, including timber, coal, chromium ore and furniture. The plan also indicates that the M. V. D. productive activities are carried on throughout the Soviet Union, but mainly in the northern regions of both European and Asiatic Russia.

Regarding construction, the 1941 plan provided that the secret police be responsible for work valued at 6,810,000,000 rubles out of a total of new construction by all Soviet economic agencies valued at 37,-650,000 rubles.

The N. K. V. D. construction target was divided among three organizations. The chief administration for labor camps, Gulag, was responsible for 2,675,000,000 rubles worth of building. The chief administration for roads was assigned 550,000,000 rubles and the chief administration for railroad construction 1,350,000,000 rubles.

### 2% of All Soviet Output

Gross industrial production by the secret police in 1941 was projected at 1,969,000,000 rubles in terms of 1926-27 prices, almost 2 per cent of all industrial production. In the case of individual commodities on which the slave labor force was to have been employed, however, the percentage of its output was much greater.

The most important area of secret police production was lumber-cutting and wood manufacture. For 1941 the N. K. V. D. was scheduled to produce 34,730,000 cubic meters of timber out of a total planned production of 290,640,000 cubic meters.

In 1941 the N. K. V. D. was scheduled to turn out 10,500,000 railroad ties, more than 20 per cent of the Soviet total.

### Oil Production Scheduled

The forced labor coal production goal for 1941 was 5,325,000 metric tons, about 5 per cent of the national total. Of this, 3,625,000 tons was to come from the Khabarovsk territory in the Far East, 250,000 tons from the Krasnoyarsk territory in Eastern Siberia, 100,000 tons from Buryat Mongolia, 1,000,-000 tons from Chita Province, 50,-000 tons from Kazakhstan, and 300,000 tons from the Komi Republic in the far north.

Petroleum production by the N.K.V.D. in 1941 was planned at 250,000 metric tons, all of it to come from camps in the neighborhood of Ukhta and the Izhma River in the Pechora area of the far north.

December 17, 1950

# SOVIET CURB SEEN ON FARM-CITY PLAN

## Moscow Believed to Abandon Attempt to Concentrate Peasant Population

By HARRY SCHWARTZ

Special to The New York Times.

WASHINGTON, April 11—The Soviet Government has apparently decided to abandon for the time being its earlier plans to jam its peasant population into large "agrogorods" (farm cities) or to endanger the jealously held private garden plots on collective farms, information available here indicates.

At the recently concluded fifteenth congress of the Communist party of Armenia, G. A. Arutinov, its secretary, denounced "certain comrades" who "tended to disorient" the party's objectives by advocating that peasant households be amalgamated into large agrogorods. Instead, he urged that peasants be allowed to live near the fields they till, thereby implying that the enlarged collective farms formed during the past year might consist of several villages each rather than of one large agrogorod.

Mr. Arutinov also criticized Communists advocating that farmers be resettled in multi-family dwellings rather than their traditional one-family huts. He warned them against any action tending to deprive farmers of their private garden plots, saying that the collective farm population had not yet reached a sufficiently advanced political level.

### Position Unlike Khrushchev's

By these statements Mr. Arutinov took a position directly contradictory to many of the recommendations urged by Nikita Khrushchev, Politburo member, in Pravda early last month. There had been an earlier indication that Mr. Khrushchev did not have full Politburo backing for his recommendations. Pravda published a correction the day following the appearance of his article and said that it had appeared for "discussion" purposes only.

Observers here attributed this apparent change of policy to Politburo concern over peasant resistance to the measures proposed by Mr. Khrushchev. The Politburo member himself had hinted at such resistance in a speech late last year when he urged intensive efforts to educate farmers under the influence of "anti-collective farm elements."

There has been no evidence as yet, however, to suggest that the rapid amalgamation of Soviet collective farms that took place last year has evoked any substantial violent resistance. But this reform, which reduced the number of such farms by more than half, was largely juridical while the retreat that is now apparently taking place deals with matters that would have vitally affected the daily life and routine of Soviet farmers.

### Only Passive Resistance

The resistance that has been met thus far has been largely of a passive character. Farmers have stalled and delayed in choosing the sites of new agrogorods, in uniting the smaller fields of former independent farms, and in making other physical changes required to effectuate fully the measures urged by the Communist party for more than a year. Thus much of the farm enlargement program to date has been largely a nominal phenomenon and only partly realized in practice.

Those in touch with the situation here do not believe that the reform in collective farm organization and operation to date has sufficiently disturbed the countryside to act as a deterrent upon the Kremlin's foreign policy. The retreat initiated actively by Mr. Arutinov seems designed to forestall any such mass unrest among the farm population that would weaken the Soviet regime as it was weakened by resistance to mass collectivization in the early Nineteen Thirties.

A major consequence of the reform, however, has been to strengthen Communist party control over the countryside. When 252,000 separate collective farms existed over a year ago, most farms had few or no Communist party members and those with active party units were a small minority. As a result of amalgamation, however, party units have been formed on a much larger percentage of collective farms than ever before in Soviet history and these are being increasingly used as control mechanisms today.

April 12, 1951

# Soviet Reports 4th Five-Year Plan Exceeded Iron and Steel Targets

By The Associated Press.

LONDON, April 16—The Soviet Union declared tonight it had successfully completed its latest five-year plan for industrial expansion and boosted production by 73 per cent over 1940. The Moscow radio broadcast the Soviet announcement.

In the war-important steel industry the Russians listed three categories in which they said they had exceeded production estimates. Total iron and steel production had gone up by 45 per cent instead of the target figure of 35 per cent. Pig iron production was reported up 29 per cent, smelting of steel 49 per cent and production of rolled metal 59 per cent.

While it did not claim success in every field of production, the announcement said "the most important tasks of the plan have been considerably exceeded."

The Soviet Union said the target for boosting industrial production over the pre-war figures during the 1946-50 period had been 48 per cent. The broadcast also said the plan had been completed in four years and three months, rather than the five years it had been expected to take.

The broadcast confirmed reports that much of Soviet industry had been concentrated in the eastern part of the Soviet Union. It said pig iron production in the Urals had been boosted 160 per cent over 1940 and gave various percentages for increased iron and steel production in Siberia.

"Production of iron and steel has been organized in Transcaucasia and Central Asia," it added.

In the war-ravaged south, the announcement said, the metal industry had been completely rebuilt and "is giving more metal than before the war."

In spite of the production boosts, however, "the production of ferrous metals and especially certain kinds of rolled metal is lagging behind the increased demands of the national economy," the Moscow radio said.

The announcement said the Soviet Union had mastered improved techniques in iron and steel production and introduced labor-saving and automatic production devices. It said great production efficiency had been gained from both blast and open hearth furnaces.

No figures were given for non-ferrous metals and the announcement, perhaps significantly, did not say their production targets had been reached. It merely said production of copper, aluminum, nickel, lead, zinc and "other non-ferrous and rare metals has greatly exceeded the prewar level."

The broadcast said coal production had beaten the five-year target slightly, going up by 57 per cent over the pre-war figure, with the war-torn Donbas region in the south providing more coal than it had in 1940 and leading the Soviet mines in production.

The broadcast said that oil production last year had been 22 per cent above the pre-war figure and above the goal set. It added that "completely reconstructed and re-equipped is the oil industry of Maikop, which was destroyed during the war, and the Grozny oil areas and the oil industry of the Western Ukraine."

It asserted that new prospecting, drilling and production techniques had located new oil and gas reserves, boosted output of high-octane gasoline and aviation oils and improved their quality.

The broadcast said Soviet oil production in the east had been greatly increased, with the eastern regions providing 44 per cent of the output in 1950, compared with 12 per cent in 1940.

"The construction of enterprises for the production of synthetic liquid fuel was developed," the broadcast said.

Electric power production in 1950 was reported 87 per cent above the 1940 figure, beating the goal set, and reconstruction of hydroelectric plants destroyed during the war was completed. In addition, it said new hydroelectric plants had been built.

## Consumer Goods Low

The Soviet announcement on fulfillment of the fourth Five-Year Plan apparently confirms earlier indications that the U. S. S. R. equaled or exceeded in 1950 many of the goals set for heavy industry, but did much less well in the production of consumer goods.

Gross industrial output in the U. S. S. R. last year aggregated about 240,000,000,000 rubles in terms of 1926/27 prices, the percentages indicate. This compares with the 138,500,000,000 rubles produced in 1940 and the original 1950 goal of 205,000,000,000 rubles. United States analysts have long pointed out that the 1926/27 ruble measure tends to exaggerate the growth of Soviet output.

Steel production last year was about 27,400,000 metric tons as against 18,300,000 tons in 1940 and the original 1950 objective of 25,400,000 tons. Pig iron production was apparently at or slightly below the 1950 goal of 19,500,000 tons, or 4,500,000 tons more than in 1940. The disproportionate rise of steel output was made possible by increased use of scrap metals to augment pig iron.

The output of Soviet petroleum last year was about 37,500,000 metric tons against 31,000,000 tons in 1940. Oil production in the Volga River area and east to the Pacific Ocean, however, grew far more rapidly, totaling about 16,100,000 tons in 1950 as compared with 3,700,000 tons in 1940. Output in the Baku and other western regions, on the other hand, was only about 21,400,000 tons last year against 27,300,000 tons a decade earlier, indicating Baku output had failed to recover from wartime losses and regain the pre-war production level.

Production of petroleum at the Maikop and Grozny oil fields in the Caucasus was about 5,000,000 metric tons in 1940. This had been reduced to little more than 1,000,000 tons by 1945, but in 1950 the pre-war level was apparently regained.

Electric power generated in the U. S. S. R. last year aggregated about 90,000,000,000 kilowatt-hours, almost 10 per cent more than the 82,000,000,000 kilowatt-hours originally called for by the five-year plan.

April 17, 1951

# STALIN ENUNCIATES A NEW PARTY LINE IN ECONOMIC FIELD

## Revises or Rejects Theories Provided by Marx, Engels, Lenin and Himself

By HARRY SCHWARTZ

Revising or rejecting concepts and propositions enunciated earlier by Marx, Engels, Lenin and himself as he saw fit, Premier Stalin has produced what is virtually a new economic theory for Communists all over the world, one intended to displace the old masters and their works as the guide for future development of Stalinist-ruled states.

In Moscow yesterday Western diplomats concluded, after study of the Stalin statement, that the Soviet leader did not see any immediate prospect of war between the United States and the Soviet Union. Nor did the diplomats see any immediate likelihood of more cordial relations and diminished tension between East and West.

It was pointed out that nowhere in his statement did Mr. Stalin mention the possibility of war between the two most powerful nations of the world, an omission that was not considered accidental.

Mr. Stalin's 25,000-word statement in the magazine Bolshevik published in Moscow on Thursday represents his bid for primacy among great Socialist thinkers of the past, his version of an up-to-date "Das Kapital," without, however, the great abundance of evidence and elaborate logical reasoning assembled by Karl Marx in that foundation of modern Socialist economic theory.

The nineteenth Congress of the Communist party of the Soviet Union, centering current activities of the Moscow regime, will open in the Kremlin tomorrow.

Premier Stalin explicitly rejects Marx's analysis of labor under capitalism as inappropriate to conditions under communism or socialism. He asserts that Marx analyzed labor working under capitalist conditions to show how workers were exploited and how surplus value was extorted from them so they might have "a spiritual weapon for overthrowing capitalism." This analysis, Premier Stalin holds, cannot be retained under socialism, where, Mr. Stalin says, the working class holds power and owns the means of production.

On the same ground he rejects Marx's distinction between labor producing material goods and labor engaged in occupations such as military service, health protection, education and the like. Only under capitalism, the Soviet Premier implies, did Marx see the former kind of labor as higher and different from the latter kind. Under socialism, he says, citing one Marxian **work to support his view, that all types of labor satisfying the working class' needs are equally indispensable.**

**Premier Stalin argues that Engels' proposition that "once society takes the means of production, commodity production [that is, production of goods for purchase or sale on the market] will be abolished" cannot be applied in the Soviet Union. He argues in this way against "certain comrades" who saw the Communist party as having made a mistake in retaining production for market sale after it had nationalized the means of production in the Soviet Union.**

**Premier Stalin argues that Engels' formula is ambiguous and did not specify whether he had in mind the nationalization of all the means of production or only some of them. But, Mr. Stalin maintains, it is clear from other of Engels' writings that he had in mind complete nationalization of all the means of production and that this could be done only in Britain, which had and has the highest development of capitalism and concentration of production, both in industry and agriculture.**

**In the analysis of the current state of capitalism, Premier Stalin now rejects as outmoded a proposition of Lenin and one of his own. He asserts that Lenin's 1916 statement that capitalism "as a whole grows much faster than before" and his own pre-war assertion that capitalist markets had attained relative stability are theses that have lost their force because of new conditions.**

**The Soviet leader criticizes as imperfectly worded his previous assertions that for the attainment of communism the differences between industry and agriculture, and between mental and physical labor, must be wiped out. He did not mean that every difference must be wiped out, he now says, but only the elimination of essential differences, leaving some "non-essential differences" that are inherent in the nature of these activities.**

**By these and other revisions of past theory, plus restatement and elaboration of parts of Communist doctrine he considers still valid, Mr. Stalin's latest work provides the essentials of a comprehensive analysis of the economics of Stalinist states and also of what he regards as the essential features of current and future capitalist development.**

**The wide scope of the questions with which he deals and the vigor of his expression make clear that this latest pronouncement must be considered the final Communist authority on all economic questions, although he leaves for others the task of filling in the details and providing detailed factual material to substantiate his theories.**

**The chief propositions enunciated by Premier Stalin follow in the order of his presentation:**

**¶Economic laws reflect objective processes that take place independently of the will of people. Human beings can discover these laws and modify their action "but they cannot change or abolish these laws."**

**¶The Soviet Government was able to achieve economic success because it relied "on the economic law of the obligatory conformity of the relations of production with the character of the productive forces," that is, that the way in which human society is organized for production must conform to the nature of the actual productive process.**

**¶Even though a country may have a backward peasant agricultural economy, the working class must seize power when it is able to, nationalize means of production in industry, and strive gradually to unite the peasants into large collective farms. Here Stalin claims to be paraphrasing Lenin.**

**¶The purchase and sale of commodities in markets cannot disappear in the Soviet Union now because the collective farms are not state-owned and will surrender their produce only for other goods or the money to buy other goods. The market place can be done away with only when there is a "universal production sector with the right to distribute all consumer requirements of the country."**

¶The problem of how the universal production sector will be formed requires further consideration, but it is unlikely it will be by a simple state expropriation of the collective farms.

**¶A law of value operates in the Soviet economy, governing particularly the production and sale of consumer goods. But the law of value will disappear in the higher stage of communism when the production of goods will be measured directly by "the actual number of hours spent" on their production. By the law of value here, Mr. Stalin apparently means the process by which prices are set on goods so as to reflect, in total, the costs of production, as well as much of the cost of Government programs, such as armament, education, etc.**

**¶The Soviet Government, however, is the master of the law of value in the Soviet economy because it is able to continue and expand the production of unprofitable heavy industrial goods while curbing the output of relatively profitable consumer goods.**

**¶The law motivating the development of modern capitalism is the law that the capitalist always seeks "to secure the maximum capitalist profit through exploitation, ruination and impoverishment of the majority of the population of a given country; through enslavement and systematic robbing of other nations, especially of the backward ones; and in the end, through wars and militarization of national economy in order to secure the highest profits."**

**¶"The fundamental economic law of socialism is the law of planned proportional development of the national economy" in order to secure "the maximum satisfaction of the constantly growing material and cultural needs of the whole community" through the use of ever better technology.**

**¶In order to prepare the actual transition from socialism to communism it is necessary to organize productive forces rationally and secure the constant growth of production and to turn the collective farms into communal property "in a manner profitable to the collective farms." It is also necessary to obtain such a cultural development of society that all its members can receive adequate education to choose their own professions and not to be chained to one field for all their lives as the result of specialization. Housing conditions must be improved; real wages must be at least doubled; and prices of consumer goods must be systematically reduced.**

October 4, 1952

## FARM CENTRALIZING GAINS

### Soviet Amalgamation Policy Cuts Collective Centers 60%

The number of collective farms in the Soviet Union has been reduced 60 per cent since 1949, Georgi M. Malenkov revealed in his address to the nineteenth Congress of the Communist party in Moscow on Sunday.

From a peak of about 254,000 at the beginning of 1950, the number of collective farms has been reduced to about 97,000, he said, through the program of amalgamating small and medium-size farms into larger units.

Mr. Malenkov's report revealed that the amalgamation program had continued beyond early 1951. A year and a half ago, Minister of Agriculture Ivan A. Benediktov reported that the number of collective farms had been reduced to 123,000. Mr. Malenkov's latest statement indicates a still further reduction of 26,000 since early 1951.

As a result of this agricultural revolution, the typical collective farm in the Soviet Union now is a gigantic enterprise having an average of about 10,000 acres, of which about 3,000 are sown to crops. It seems clear, however, that the old pattern of scattered village settlement remains largely unchanged, so that the typical enlarged collective farm consists of several villages coordinated in one center. Last month Nikita S. Khruschev, Politburo member in charge of agricultural affairs, confessed that his earlier advocacy of the creation of large agricultural communities, called agrogorods, had been an error.

October 8, 1952

# THE PARADOXES OF A COMMUNIST WORLD

## Bolshevism Applied to Society and Morals in Russia Brings Startling Contradictions

*By ANNE O'HARE McCORMICK*

ANYTHING can happen in Russia. It is the mother country of the incredible. There are three-tent colonies in the arctic circle with their own Soviets: there are large settlements in the Siberian forests which, until their discovery this Summer, had never heard of Lenin; there are peoples like the Shapsougi, a little lost tribe in the Caucasus Mountains, 3,000 strong, that has been a going republic for 112 years in spite of and unknown to any Czar. Fifty thousand persons pass casually back and forth every year across the Polish frontier in defiance of the efforts of the strongest guard in Europe to keep them in and out. Strange sects perform illegal and secret rites and ancient superstitions flourish under the blind eyes of atheist and orthodox alike.

Back of the Russia that one sees is always a withdrawn and shrouded Russia that one never sees. Nobody knows how many hidden fastnesses are still untroubled even by rumors of world war or revolution. The regions the traveler explores are forever dwarfed by the regions neither he nor any one else has ever explored; his observations of communism are shadowed by the knowledge that there exist whole communities as isolated from communism as if they inhabited another planet.

That is what halts and qualifies the answers to all questions about Russia—especially when the questions go behind the economic and political and probe into the social and moral consequences of the Red Revolution. To the outside world, of course, no effects of applied socialism are so interesting and important as its effects on the home and the family, but those are just the effects impossible to determine without putting down at the beginning a very large X to express the unknown quantity in every speculation.

With that reservation, the observer pursues to unexpected conclusions his transient survey of Bolshevism in the uncertain field of domestic relations. He learns, for instance, that the Soviet Government has already passed the second of what is likely to be a long series of experimental marriage laws. It has farmed out to private families as many as possible of the abandoned infants it originally planned to have mothered and fathered by the State. It begins strongly to emphasize the advantages of "home training" and "family responsibility." It has recognized the family as the legal unit for holding and inheriting farm lands. In most of the new housing schemes "private kitchens" are exhibited as the chief improvement of the future over the present overcrowded and too-communal housekeeping.

He hears from a young bourgeois the strongest approval and from a young Communist the bitterest denunciation of the present code of marriage and divorce. The bourgeois declares that marriage is the one relation in life in which the Russian today is absolutely free. The Communist, a girl under 20, already divorced, vows that she and all her friends have resolved never again to marry one of their own generation. "Marriage to them," she says, "means no more and involves less thought and responsibility than going to the movies. It is degrading."

Add to these reversals and contradictions the constant preaching of austere standards of life and morals on the part of the older and more fervent Communists, and you perceive either that Communist precept is stricter than its laws, or that those laws in practice have shocked and embarrassed their authors. In the Ukraine I met a Communist who confessed that he had had his first child baptized secretly in violation of all Communist principles because she was a girl; reverting to the stock paternal pattern, he wished her to be brought up "in the old-fashioned way." For a similar reason the head of a village Soviet in the Moscow gubernia insists on maintaining a church where there never was a church before. "We must do something for the women and children," he said, "to counteract the new laws!"

FOR the large majority of the country folk the old tradition of the irrevocable marriage and the inescapable family resists all the relaxing legislation of the new régime. Church weddings and church christenings seem to be as frequent and as festive as they ever were. The moral standards of Russian villages were never high; now they are said to be lower, particularly among the young, but as the same complaint rises from the elders in every country under the sun, that world-wide decline, if it exists, can hardly be blamed on the Bolsheviki. They have enough to answer for in that the Russian rising generation, constantly instructed in the noble revolutionary duty of breaking down the past and destroying tradition, is rather more enthusiastic and thorough in attacking the family and smashing the Ten Commandments than their more romantic compeers in other lands.

The result is such that it forces communism into the anomaly of advocating the practice of a puritanism that it denies in principle. The country is noisy with educational campaigns waged by the Government to modify the effects of its own laws. Thus, although unregistered marriages and abortions are legalized, there is as strong a propaganda against them as if they were unlawful, as there is against vodka, the most profitable of all the State monopolies. In the economic order, the new Russia searches for rewards for invention and incentives to production that are not material; sometimes it finds such incentives. In the moral order the search is for sanctions and inhibitions that are not spiritual; it is significant that they seem to be found only among those Communists to whom communism is a religion.

The debate on the 1927 marriage and divorce law actually extended to some of those vague outposts that look on China or the polar region. It lasted for two years and was marked by the first appearance in Russian history of peasant women in a national congress. These women came from remote villages to say that while they knew nothing about speaking in public they knew there was something wrong with a law that reduced a marriage of many years and much shared labor to the status of a day's infatuation. The law was passed against their protests.

On its face it seems to allow even easier marrying and unmarrying than the other experimental law which it supersedes. The old law recognized as legal only registered marriages; it was intended primarily to abolish church marriages. The new law recognizes both registered and unregistered unions; a church marriage thus falls into the category of unregistered contracts and can be proved "actual" in case of dispute or divorce. No child born in Soviet Russia is ever illegitimate, but the new law, by legalizing every relationship, attempts to fix responsibility for the support and care of children born under any circumstances.

Thus its effect, in addition to relieving the State of the guardianship of an increasing family of abandoned babies, is more stringent than that of the old law. One may marry and divorce as breathlessly as he pleases under Soviet law, but so long as the obligation to support the children of every union is strictly enforced it cannot be done too promiscuously or uncalculatingly in a proletarian State where birth control propaganda has made little headway and the birth rate steadily increases. Most marriages are registered. A divorce, if both parties desire it, involves merely a second entry at the bureau of registration.

In case only one party seeks separation, the case goes to the People's Court. As the appeal is always granted on the ground that no marriage can exist without mutual consent, the procedure is simply for adjudication of disputed property rights and the care of children. Property owned by either husband or wife before marriage remains personal, property acquired during marriage is divided, and if the wife has a better job than the husband or he is unemployed or incapacitated, she pays the alimony.

A GREAT point is made of the perfect sex equality of communism. Women in Russia do enjoy the same freedom as men. A single standard of judgment is applied to both, and no one can fail to be struck by the frank matter-of-factness and healthy absence of emphasis on sex. "Suggestiveness" is never the note of Russian life or entertainment. The kind of drama censored in New York might have a chance in Moscow if it were good enough, but the Soviet capital would be shocked and bored by the uncensored shows that draw the biggest crowds on Broadway

Yet if any one imagines that the new marriage code establishes equality between men and women, he should talk with the older women, some of whom are rather tragic in their desire for security instead of freedom. Those who are peasants, broken by hard labor in the fields and the bearing of many children, complain that their husbands take strong wives for the harvest season. All are bitter that the law allows them to be so easily discarded for the young. Discussion of marriage has reached villages that care nothing for the eight-hour day or the dictatorship of the proletariat; it has made articulate what sounds like an entire population of outraged wives and rebellious husbands.

At that, however, I doubt that the divorce rate in Russia is higher than it is in the United States. The latest figures I was able to get for the R. S. F. S. R. are for 1925, when there was one divorce for every seven marriages. In the Ukraine for 1926 the proportion was only one to fifty, and in other parts of the union the number of divorces is still less. The automatic divorce of the Soviets is simpler, easier and cheaper than ours; we go to more trouble and expense to maintain the world's divorce record.

Women work on the same terms as men. They form fully half of the processions you see trudging back from the fields to the villages at night. About 45 per cent. of industrial workers are women. The mother who works in a factory gets two months' leave with pay both

A Rural Court in Russia Presided Over by Women. A Peasant Woman Is Laying a Complaint of Ill-Treatment Against Her Husband.

*Photograph Copyrighted by P. and A.*

before and after her child is born. When she returns to work she deposits the baby every morning in the day nursery most factories maintain for the young children of working mothers. Nursery care for children, whether in these factory crèches, kindergartens or pre-school institutions of one kind or another, is largely a State function and is more scientific and efficient care than could be given in the home.

The new family and the new home of the communistic ideal is based on the cooperation of men and women in industrial or agricultural labor for the workers' State, with the care of children and all household drudgery relegated to public agencies. "No nation can be free," said Lenin, "when half of the population is enslaved in the kitchen." Communism is against the kitchen; it is always bracketed with the altar as a stupefying and stultifying tradition.

WHAT Soviet Russia really aspires to, in fact, is a communal housekeeping startlingly similar to that of a city like New York. The ideal of domesticity that fires the imagination of the builders of a communistic world is the kitchenless, laundryless, nurseryless, vacuum-cleaned and cooperatively-owned home that is multiplying so rapidly on the fabulous shores of Manhattan Island. The American system is profitable enough to release nearly half the inhabitants of these capitalistic cells from any occupation other than that of being wives. In Moscow the wives have to work. They have to work because of the low wages of their husbands, and also because the collective State is an aggregation of economic units, male or female, and cooking for one man or caring for one's own children is not considered either an economic or a satisfying employment.

At the same time, as has been noted, the newest houses built by the collective State have private kitchens, and the public babies are being nursed by private mothers. Lenin's "large socialist households" replacing the "petty households" and "bourgeois cosiness" of the past are not fairly represented by the kind of communal living now experienced by the city proletariat, but it is understandable that ten years of such collectivism has restored an almost bridal glamour to the private cooking stove.

The only time I ever heard a Russian woman official become lyrical and romantic was over a new and unshared kitchen. They are not romantic, the women developed and developing in the equality of communism. They are not even romantic about realism, like the more poetic and sentimental sex. They represent a new type of woman, at once more independent and regimented than the old. No doubt the difference is partly a matter of clothes; their dress is almost as uniform as men's. You realize over and over again in Russia how distinguishing and extinguishing are fashions. Women dressed alike, dressed without regard to styles, are more like one another and more like men than any but the feminist would believe. I have often tried to guess which were men in a group of bloused Russians seated behind a table.

The Daughters of Revolution are a strong and formidable breed. They move across the Russian panorama like the Fates rather than the Graces, with the effect of a natural force. The switch-tenders, square and weatherbeaten, smoking cigarettes at their posts on the car tracks; the ghoul-like guards in museums, so much more vigilantly and aggressively passive than men; the overpoweringly informative guides; the indifferent and static clerks in the State shops; the solid delegate to a Soviet Congress, so much like an American clubwoman; the girl Comsomols, solemn, muscular, self-assured; the old village matchmaker, toothless from chewing life raw; the tall teacher who made Rasputin die again on the scene of his murder; the factory workers pouring into the Moscow stations on Sunday nights with sacks of food bought in the country loaded on their backs.

THEY are curiously neutral and curiously invincible as they move. The female of the proletarian species looks incapable of fear, of foolishness, or of charm. She will be a power, one feels, in the government of the future. Though she takes her place in all the village, factory, district and All-Russian Soviets, in the proportion of about 10 per cent., she has a surprisingly small place in the Government.

The Communists have produced no woman Commissar of the People. With the exception of Krupskaya, Lenin's widow, in charge of the Bureau of Political Education; Kameneva, wife of Kamenev and sister of Trotsky, Director of the Society of Cultural Relations, and Kollantai, twice Ambassador, no woman has held anything like a first-class post in the United States of Soviet Republics. Mme. Rosanova, formerly in the Soviet Embassy in London, energetically directs the foreign department of the Trades Union headquarters. Mme. Goldfarb acted this Summer as foreign press censor. Mme. Gorky heads a bureau in aid of political prisoners. Many libraries, small museums, public monuments and State institutions are in charge of women, but the number of women rulers in the proletarian dictatorship is conspicuously small in proportion to the number of women workers.

This is the more striking because communism is definitely out to smash woman's ancient "sphere." The home in the old Anglo-Saxon sense of castle and sanctuary, if it can exist anywhere in the modern world, certainly has no place in a strictly economic system. In Russia one decides that the Bolsheviki are right in attacking the home as a bourgeois institution. It is. The home demands a certain amount of space, a certain margin of leisure, a certain minimum of care and useless comfort. There will be better housing in the Russia of tomorrow, but the home is already as extinct as the Czar.

COMMUNISM is also out to shatter family solidarity. A revolution has intervened between two generations in Russia. That revolution was not a revolt of intolerant and war-embittered youth, like the Fascist uprising in Italy. All the leaders of the Bolsheviki were middle-aged men, expert and practiced revolutionists. They did not have to improvise a philosophy or invent a new theory of government. They had their law and prophets ready. They had to fit an empire into a formula. Compared to Mussolini, they had the great handicap of the sonneteer as against the verse libertine.

There are still no young men at the helm, either of the party or the Government. Yet they have engineered the most ruthless and the most successful of all the battles of youth against age. Bolshevism was never a youth movement; the generation it now inflames has been carefully kindled. The young Communists have learned the communist catechism and served their novitiate. They represent the first generation brought up by the State. They were taken young in order that they might be pure of any prejudice for the past. They belong to their parents and their families less than any youth in the world. The old idea of the family falls before them. Whether they will found a new one of their own remains to be seen. There are faint stirrings of reaction among the young, a timid swing away from realism toward romanticism. It would be almost too human if these youth or their children should develop a family complex and become defenders of the sanctity of the home.

There are about 2,500,000 Comsomols. They are the recruits for the governing party of the future, though not all of them either remain Comsomols or become Communists. They already take an active part in political life, particularly in the villages, the real battlefield between old and young. And side by side with them grows up a smaller but even more conspicuous flying column of youth, the so-called "bez prizorny," or homeless children. Nobody seems to know how many they are. Their number is put at between 300,000 and 500,000 in all parts of the Union. I was told by the earnest official in charge of reclamation work among them in Moscow that their number now, whatever it is, is 50 per cent. less than it was in the worst years, whatever that was.

They are explained as the orphans left homeless and destitute by the World War, the revolution and the famine. They look like ragged flocks of animated scarecrows flapping along the main streets of cities and the main routes of travel. They have Summer and Winter routes, like birds; they haunt every railway station: they beg and steal and curse and scavenger from Leningrad to Sebastopol. Sometimes they have the faces of evil old men and sometimes of tough and swaggering children challenging the world. In Moscow they sleep in doorways, in asphalt mixers, under heaps of rubbish, in the gutters. About 10 per cent. of them are girls.

When one asks why the authorities, so good at rounding up political suspects, do not gather in these wretched little vagrants, many of whom are diseased, are drug addicts, are ill and crippled, the answer is that only the criminals are arrested; the others must go voluntarily to the institutions provided for them. The work of reclamation began as early as 1917 and has been pursued steadily ever since, but no statistics have been kept as to results and no satisfactory explanation is made as to why there are still so many at large. I was informed that 27,000 are at present cared for in the Moscow district alone and that 4,000 left institutions last year and are now at work or in high schools. Thirty per cent. are Comsomols.

A Woman Worker of Leningrad.

No one can doubt the anxiety of the Government to liquidate this problem. Provision for the physical care of children under the Soviets is only limited by their resources; one sees evidences everywhere of a passion for child welfare. Russians are fundamentally kind, and they are kindest to children. We visited one of the shelters for the homeless children, a shabby but pleasant old country house on the banks of a river many miles from Moscow. Boys and girls ranging in age from 5 to 16 romped freely through the house and grounds, healthy, happy, remarkably at home.

SOME of them served us tea and slices of bread and butter and conducted us through their "laboratory schoolrooms. In one of which the United States was featured in a chart of "the history of imperialism." The institution was self-governing and no punishment was permitted. A committee of children sat with the teachers to decide on school politics. The Director declared that under this system he had no trouble with his 280 waifs, all fished from the streets of Moscow—a statement that makes it all the more mystifying that so many thousands choose and are allowed to starve and freeze rather than enjoy the benefits of this self-governing paradise.

We asked a group of "Octobers," the youngest children, what they imagined America was like. "Tall buildings, lots of automobiles and trains, people prettier and talking differently than Russians," snapped a 5-year-old. A yellow-haired girl of 12 interviewed us. She wanted to know if the workers were well treated and lived well in the United States. She politely doubted our answers, and hoped we would report what a good time Russian workers had.

It is plain that the reclaimed homeless children are good little propagandists. Why cannot an all-powerful Government devise some means to prevent the unreclaimed from being such bad propaganda? Into Greece, five years ago, were suddenly flung more than 100,000 orphans, naked, hungry and half dead from exposure. These 100,000 amounted to one-fortieth of the population of one of the poorest and most disorganized countries in the world, also in a chaos of civil war and revolution. In proportion to the population, a million homeless children constitutes for Russia only one-fourth of the number thrown into Greece from Asia Minor. It is true that Greece had help; the American Near East Relief took care of about one-fourth of the refugee orphans. But the help given to Greece by America was as nothing to the help given to Russia during the famine. There is not a homeless child in Greece today, and never has been since a month after the deluge. There are no homeless children wandering around in any other war-devastated country. What is the matter with Soviet Russia?

That is the inevitable question posed by these hordes of lost children. Why cannot a system that claims to be resolving so much bigger problems, that appears so zealous in every form of public welfare, do something about this one? Until it does the scarecrows of another young Russia deride the march of the Young Communists and set one wondering what other dark things lie behind this bright parade in that incredible country where anything can happen and perhaps everything does.

December 4, 1927

## SOVIET PUPILS TO LOSE THEIR FORMER LIBERTY

### New Decree Calling for Individual Instruction Also Will Change Curriculum.

Wireless to THE NEW YORK TIMES.

MOSCOW, Aug. 29.—The Soviet school year begins Sept. 1, but the days of revolutionary freedom will be gone for Soviet pupils. A decree of the central committee of the Communist party restores examinations and school discipline, with the penalty of expulsion for recalcitrant pupils, and stresses the teacher's authority and the need for personal attention for the pupils.

The curriculum also will revert somewhat to reading, writing, grammar, arithmetic, geography and the rudiments of physics, especially electricity, but the practical study in the fields and workshops, introduced after the revolution, will continue to hold an important place.

A total of 95 per cent of Soviet children, between the ages of 8 and 12, now attend compulsory school of four years' duration, which next year will be extended to seven years. The pupils total 23,750,000, as compared with 7,250,000 before the war. Henceforth all pupils in the secondary schools must learn a foreign language. English is the most popular and German is second.

August 30, 1932

## *Gains Are Found in Soviet Liquor Control; Temperance Is Taught and Excess Punished*

Wireless to THE NEW YORK TIMES.

HELSINGFORS, Finland, March 19.—The Russians are making determined efforts to solve the alcohol problem, says Everett Colby of New Jersey, who on the initiative of John D. Rockefeller Jr. has studied the liquor conditions in Russia for some time and is now returning home with an elaborate report.

Mr. Colby told interviewers that the Soviet Government, although it was anxious to increase the State revenue from liquor sales, carried out a vigorous campaign against every abuse.

Its propaganda includes the instruction even of small children and is continued in the schools, where the temperance courses are considered as important as the other lessons.

Special efforts are made to encourage workers to restrict their alcohol consumption, and everywhere posters are displayed warning against excessive drink.

The Russians have a special method of dealing with first-offense drunkards. Instead of putting them in cells, they give them warm baths, clean clothes and beds. Afterward they are sent home or to work in rural districts.

Habitual drunkards, however, are treated more severely. Leonard Harrison of New York, who was commissioned to study the effects of the abolition of prohibition in Finland, is arriving soon to collect material.

March 20, 1933

## CRIME DOESN'T PAY IN SOVIET CAPITAL

### Its Scarcity Is Due in Great Part to Fact That Those With Money Are Widely Suspected.

### OTHER DETERRENTS SEEN

### One in Five of the Inhabitants of Moscow Is Pledged to Inform the Authorities.

By WALTER DURANTY.

Special Cable to THE NEW YORK TIMES.

MOSCOW, Sept. 8.—There is no organized crime in Moscow nor commercialized vice—no racketeering nor kidnapping, no speakeasies, gambling hells nor brothels.

Full-blossomed "pinks" and other admirers of the Soviet régime may say that this admirable state of affairs is part and proof of the superiority of the Soviet system, but there are cruder if more truthful explanations.

First and foremost, there is no "percentage" in crime. Money does not mean much any more in the Soviet Union. And any one with large funds becomes the object of universal suspicion. That is the first deterrent.

Second, at least one in five of Moscow's inhabitants from the graybeards to the "little pitchers with long ears," owes allegiance to the Communist party or its junior branches. What this means can scarcely be measured in words.

The veteran American reporter William Shepherd wrote recently that the less prosperous city blocks in Chicago were the most fertile breeding ground for gangsters because every red-blooded boy regarded a gangster as a hero.

**None of That in Moscow.**

There is none of that in Moscow. The discipline of the Communist party and its junior branches demands not only complete support for the party policies, but that members immediately give information to the proper quarter about anything they think or suspect is likely to conflict with said policies.

In other words, one in five of Moscow's inhabitants is pledged to inform the authorities about anything he or she imagines to be an infringement of the law. There is no hero worship of lawbreakers in Soviet Moscow.

Third, there is literally no room for commercialized vice in Moscow. The city is so overcrowded that neither a speakeasy, a gambling hell nor a brothel can exist more than a few minutes without some one's knowing why and what it is all about. And if five persons know one of them informs the authorities in accordance with the party duties aforementioned.

That is the second deterrent. The third deterrent is the hand of the law, exercised through the police and the dreaded O. G. P. U., which work together on cases of organized crime and commercialized vice because such are regarded as anti-social offenses, although in theory the police authorities are concerned with ordinary crimes and misdemeanors—while the O. G. P. U. concerns itself with crimes against the State. But "anti-social" crimes are crimes against the State, which brings in the O. G. P. U.

**Has Unlimited Powers.**

The O. G. P. U. has unlimited powers, including those of summary arrest, trial and execution. Criminals cannot use slick lawyers or political pull to avoid punishment. Without delay or publicity they are tried, acquitted or condemned, and, in the latter case, shot or sentenced to terms of imprisonment.

For the latter Moscow has introduced something new. According to Soviet ideas, criminals fall into two classes—anti-social or counter-revolutionary, who are punished by death, and the others, who are "victims of economic environment."

In other words, the Soviet, with the rare exception of a sadistic or degenerate criminal, regards all lawbreakers as victims unless they have been proved to be anti-social elements—that is, counter-revolutionaries.

For the "victims," what is needed is not punishment but reform and a chance to live the decent life of a law-abiding citizen, of which they were deprived by their earlier environment. Accordingly, the Soviet prisons are not places of punishment but reform schools in the truest sense of the phrase.

There is a prison colony near Moscow where every one lives in perfect freedom without bars, cells, warders or restrictions save that they must spend the night on the premises. They have their own homes, workshops, factories, farms and kitchen, can marry and divorce and can go to Moscow as they please. They must work, but they receive union wages. All "prison discipline" is in their hands, under the supervision of no more than four O. G. P. U. officials.

They can escape at will, but they do not escape, and five years of practice in this and similar "reform schools" tend to justify the Soviet's contention that the average criminal would live an honest life if he had a proper chance.

September 10, 1933

## SOVIET PEASANTS NOW USING FORKS

### A Revolution Effected Since 1917 in Sales of the Complete Table Combination.

### 'STORE CULTURE' PUSHED

### Clerks Are Told They Must Be More Courteous to Customers

By The Associated Press.

MOSCOW, March 6.—One of the effects of the Bolshevist revolution was cited today by the newspaper Pravda, which reported that before the revolution only twenty-five forks were sold for every 100 knives, but now every one who buys a knife also wants a fork.

These figures were given in connection with statistics issued today showing the demand for urban products to be greatly increasing in the country areas. Increases were shown in orders for iron beds, phonographs, razors, tooth brushes and—table forks.

The newspaper Izvestia announced that Soviet shop employes must concentrate further in developing "store culture," the courteous treatment of customers. In many stores there are signs reading:

"Clerk, be polite to the customer. Customer, be polite to the clerk."

March 7, 1935

# LIFE IS CHANGING IN RUSSIA

## Gradations in Status, Based on Merit, Are Permitted in Soviet Classless Society

By WALTER DURANTY.

Special Cable to THE NEW YORK TIMES.

MOSCOW, Dec. 20. – One of the most interesting things about the Union of Soviet Socialist Republics is that it is dynamic and fluid. The Moscow of today is always a different city from the Moscow of three months ago.

Not only does the visual aspect of Moscow change with new buildings, new streets and squares and new stream-lined street cars—the finest in Europe, as long as subway cars, blue instead of maroon and running two together instead of three, with doors that open and shut automatically – but there are also changes of a less material character.

As superficial foreign observers put it, "Moscow is going bourgeois." That is to say, there are evident certain phenomena of comfort, or even luxury, which seem inconsistent with the Spartan régime of the proletarian revolution.

**Army Ranks Differentiated.**

Henceforth, for instance, army officers will be no longer addressed as "comrade commander," which term was applied universally to all ranks, from lieutenant to general, but by the specific designations of their rank, from lieutenant up to marshal, this last a revived title, now borne by five Soviet military leaders.

Then, too, there is the resurgence of the idea of patriotism, as exemplified by the word "rodina," meaning homeland or birthplace, instead of the phrase "Socialist Fatherland," always used before.

And there are private autos and comfortable apartments and high wage scales for men and women whose services to the State are greater than the average. There are manikin parades and silk stockings, lipsticks and cosmetics and jazz bands. There are scores of such bands in Moscow today, and every factory or regiment, almost every village or collective farm, has its own jazz orchestra. To jazz music thousands and tens of thousands of Moscovites dance every night on skating rinks throughout the city.

To take a different case, one night this week the American tenor Sergey Radamski, who has been a popular singer in Moscow for six or seven years, with his wife, Mary, gave a concert at the Moscow Conservatory of Music, singing Handel's "The Messiah" and Handel arias, sacred music. They sang in English and German, it is true, but fully half the capacity audience understood one or the other. Until quite recently Mr. Radamski had to submit every word of what he sang in any language to preliminary censorship and no sacred music was allowed. Now that does not matter, provided the music is good.

**City Not "Going Bourgeois."**

Must it be judged from this that Moscow is reverting to religion as well as to "bourgeois habits?" Nothing could be further from the truth. If one looks beneath the surface, it is not difficult to find out what is really happening in Moscow.

It all depends upon two comparatively simple factors. The first is that the present system in the U. S. S. R. is not Communist and does not pretend to be Communist, but Socialist. In other words, that principle enunciated by Joseph Stalin in 1931 of greater reward for greater service still holds good in place of the pure Communist principle of absolute equality. The latter may come later, but, in the present intermediate or Socialist state, inequalities are admitted and the better man or woman works, the more he or she receives in return.

Secondly, it is a fact that consumers' goods—the means and articles of comfort or luxury, from new apartments and furniture to bicycles, autos, clothes and cosmetics —are now being produced in considerable and constantly growing quantities. In the old days, when such things were the privilege of the rich alone, they were naturally taboo to the proletariat and to own them stamped the owner as a hated bourgeois. But now they are within the reach of the best workers throughout the country, and why should not the latter enjoy the fruits they have striven so hard to cultivate?

It may be argued that this very differentiation of wages, and by consequence of rewards for service, must lead to new class differentiations in what claims to be a classless society. It looks like that to outsiders. It seems as if there were growing up a new military class of officers, a new class of bureaucrats and directors of State enterprises, a new class of high-paid upper workers, all of whom together will form or are forming a new bourgeoisie.

**Bolshevist Explanation.**

The Bolsheviki deny this hotly. They say the present distinctions are not those of class but of rank, which is a very different thing. Rank, say the Bolsheviki, must exist in any society; there must be the leaders and the led, those who direct and order and those who follow and obey. But class, according to the Bolshevist idea, is a hereditary perpetuation of rank, for which they claim there is no place in the Soviet state.

A field marshal or the head of a great trust has a privileged position, but it is the reward of merit, and he cannot transmit it automatically to his children. He perhaps can give his children a better start than his lesser fellow-citizens, since after all "kissing goes by favor" the whole world over, but he is no more able to insure his children's position than a general in the United States Army can make his son also a general the day after the boy leaves West Point.

Time alone will show whether the Bolsheviki can succeed in preventing rank from transmuting itself into class, as has hitherto proved the case in all societies, however new or revolutionary. In their favor they have a strong trump card which is new in human history: the abolition of private property and the power of money. They have a second card, too: unlimited opportunity to all of education and advancement.

December 22, 1935

# NEW RUSSIA GRADUATES HER FIRST GENERATION

*By WALTER DURANTY*

MOSCOW.

EIGHTEEN and a half years have passed since the Soviet Revolution; and in the U.S.S.R. boys and girls "come of age," that is to say, have voting rights as citizens, on their eighteenth birthday. This means much in terms of human values. It means that there has grown up a new generation of Russian youth, which has nothing in its consciousness save the revolution.

One must add to the 18-year-olds the ones who were small children when the revolution occurred, from the age, say, of 1 to 12. That makes thirty years, which is accepted as the time-period of a generation. Children and young men and women under the age of 30 form half the population of any country, or more than that. In the present Soviet Union their numerical proportion is greater, because in Russia the life term has been shorter than in the West. What, then, are the thoughts and aspirations, the attitude toward life, of these young Russians who, as I said, have no political consciousness of Czarism and the "old days," but only of Soviet rule?

Before attempting to answer these questions it is necessary to remember that almost all these youngsters belong to families who never knew what it was to have property or possessions except in the narrowest sense. Before the revolution nearly everything was owned by less than 10 per cent of the population, while the remaining 90 per cent had little save the clothes they wore, and were fortunate if they received one square meal a day.

The poverty of the Russian masses was incredible and was indeed one of the chief reasons for the revolution, just as it was in France in 1789. These young Russians, therefore, "start from scratch," as one might say, and find nothing surprising or unnatural in State socialism and the abolition of the profit motive.

• • •

THE vast majority of Russian youth, therefore, face life from three definite—and, it would be considered in America, somewhat unusual—angles. First, they approve of the revolution because, having had nothing to lose, they have lost nothing; second, they are convinced that, instead of their country belonging to Them—meaning the landlords and capitalists—it now belongs to Us—meaning the people; third, they feel that before them lies unlimited opportunity, expressed in terms of free and equal education.

It is perhaps the greatest single achievement of the Bolsheviki that they have offered their people education, because that is the key which most truly unlocks the gate of life. To the men, women and children of the U.S.S.R. light has been brought, although perhaps, from an American standpoint, a light of no great brightness. Yet a beginning has been made, which is the essential thing, since young Russia starts from so low a position that even small advances seem gigantic by comparison.

I remember some years ago in Moscow talking to a boy of 19 who was studying in the university. He lived with three others of the same age in a small stuffy room in conditions which I regarded not only as most uncomfortable but little conducive to study. I said as much and he looked at me in amazement.

"What," he cried, "you don't see that we have steam heat and electric light and they feed us in the college dining room and give us books and clothing and thirty rubles a month for pocket money?" (At that time thirty rubles had the purchasing power of about eighty cents in this country.)

"You don't understand," he continued passionately, "of course you don't understand, how can you understand? But let me tell you that the first twelve years of my life were spent in a wooden shack no bigger than this room. It was built against the cottage of a richer peasant so that we could get warmth from his stove because we were too poor to have a stove of our own. There I lived with my father and mother and a grandfather who was paralyzed, and four brothers and sisters. The floor was neither brick nor wood, just plain earth.

"None of us went to school, of course, until the revolution. We were worse than slaves, we were animals. Then the revolution came and took us in its arms to teach and help us and make us learn. Do you realize," he concluded, "that there are millions of boys and girls in Russia today about whom that is true? Don't you know that we would fight for the revolution and die for it any time because it has given us this"—he waved his hand across the stuffy little bedroom of the Moscow University—"instead of that?"—the pigsty in a village.

* * *

THE revolution has given them that, and something more, much more. It has given them hope, which, second to health, is the prime condition for human happiness. Hope and opportunity for a better life.

In the United States today one hears frequently from young people that opportunity is denied them. They go to high school or college, in many cases at the cost to themselves and their parents of sacrifice and effort; they dig their teeth in the "hard granite of education," as Trotsky once called it, and they learn. They learn in order to improve themselves, to enjoy a full and better life, to have, in short, a greater chance for happiness, and to live usefully for their country and themselves, only to find, when they graduate from school or college and receive their diplomas all new and shining, that there is nothing for them to do.

In New York City alone there are thousands of young architects, engineers, doctors and lawyers who have qualified for professions that demand no small amount of skill and training, but who cannot get a job at any price. "Shovel snow or drive a truck," is what life tells them nowadays. "Don't you know that the skilled professions are hopelessly overcrowded already?"

How far this is due to economic conditions is more a matter for discussion than many young Americans would believe. From what I have been able to gather during the three months recently spent in the United States, the general impression among the younger generation appears to be that the world or society or the economic system—call it what you will—"owes them a living" and is failing to pay its debt. Do the facts justify this view?

It is immediately obvious that in a country hit by a colossal depression which causes millions of employed men and women to lose their jobs, which freezes credit in all directions and causes stagnation in such industries as building, metallurgy and mining, no one can expect that raw untested youth will find it easy to obtain employment. Furthermore it must be remembered that the great increase in national wealth which occurred in the decade following the war gave great and novel impetus to the natural human desire for progress and self-improvement.

Millions of boys and girls and millions of parents suddenly saw the chance of making a new generation better than its elders by education. Simultaneously there was a parallel increase in the volume of State aid for education in high schools and colleges. The combined effect of this was to persuade the "young generation" that it would have advantages and opportunities which its elders had not enjoyed. It worked to get them, and then suddenly on the very threshold of life, as one might say—I mean life as adult citizens—it found nullity and frustration and is outraged and bewildered in consequence.

Is it not possible, however, that there is also a psychological factor involved at this point; may it not be true that just because the youth of the country has prepared itself for "something better," it is now asking too much? In other words, could not some of the young unemployed people who have recently graduated find jobs if they were willing to take them? I do not necessarily mean shoveling snow in season, but other jobs, small ones that do not seem to rank with what one has wanted, and therefore are rejected.

This is an unpopular theory and may sound harsh, but is it entirely unwarranted? The day of the pioneer, the day of new frontiers, of sheer and rugged individualism, has passed. In consequence, the present generation no longer possesses the freedom of choice that was open to its parents. Twenty-five or thirty years ago it seemed that in almost any field for which a boy or girl wished to prepare, and did so conscientiously, there was unlimited opportunity. Perhaps the answer is that in those days there was less education, less competence, in short, less competition. Whatever the answer may be, the fact remains.

* * *

IN the Soviet Union conditions are immensely different. First and foremost, it is only just beginning the exploitation of its natural resources. That whole huge territory—greater in area than the United States, Canada and Mexico combined—has thus far barely been scratched. Each day brings discovery of new potential wealth—animal, vegetable and mineral.

The presence in the United States of the Russian pilot, Levanevsky, whom they call in Russia the "Arctic Ace," directed attention to the air exploration along the northern coast of Siberia which is adding untold wealth to the fishing and fur industries of the U.S.S.R. New forests, too, are being charted and cruised and fishing developed in lakes and rivers that were almost unknown to man.

The exploration of mineral wealth is even more startling. Vast deposits of coal, iron and copper, of oil, gold and silver and other metals, have been found in the past four or five years and are now in process of development. In industry the U.S.S.R. is in process of great expansion. The natural resources are so great and the country has been so backward industrially that one might almost say that any régime would provide unlimited employment for many decades to come, and that the Bolsheviki have simply accentuated the speed of development by centralized control and an organized system of planning.

* * *

SOVIET agriculture deserves a special paragraph to itself. Agricultural conditions were so low and backward that the field for improvement was enormous. Soviet economic experts have estimated that the modernization of Russian villages in terms of housing, lighting, water supply and sanitation is a task great enough to occupy the whole energies of the nation for many years. Small chance of unemployment here, despite the effects of mechanization and improved methods in reducing the demand for man-power in the fields themselves, especially when one considers that there is a steady flow of younger men and women from the country to the cities, towns and new industrial settlements in order to meet the ever-growing requirements of industrial labor.

Finally, there are the professions. Teachers, engineers, doctors, architects, writers, artists, actors are needed literally by millions to meet the cultural (in the widest sense of the word) needs of the new Soviet population. Here is, in short, the exact opposite of what is occurring in the United States. The demand is infinitely greater than the supply.

Of course it may fairly be argued, and the Bolsheviki themselves would not deny it, that the present unsatisfactory conditions for American youth are not necessarily permanent, that

*Sovfoto.*

A young Russian machinist.

they are the result of a temporary situation produced by one of the periodic economic crises, which are, according to Marxist doctrine, a more or less natural and inevitable feature of the capitalist system and do indeed imply its ultimate demise, but which are far from immediately fatal. In other words, the United States will shortly emerge from the depression, as it has emerged from depressions in the past, is indeed perhaps already emerging, and the situation of the younger generation, which now seems so hopeless will again become bright and cheerful.

Even Stalin has admitted that he does not believe that the present crisis will be the last, which indicates clearly his willingness to believe in the possibility of an upward swing. Nevertheless, even if one accepts this theory, there remains an element of uncertainty and the ever-present fear lest another depression—say fifteen or twenty years hence—may rob the youth of today of the fruits of its labors, just as it has robbed their elders in the past six years.

In the U.S.S.R., on the other hand, it is asserted that no such danger can possibly exist, that not only is employment insured for all who care to work but that it is permanent employment, that workers in any branch of life are taken care of in case of disability, and that adequate provision is made for them in old age, when they can work no longer. Their hours of labor, too, are strictly limited, and there can be no attempt by employers to lower their wages or reduce their living standards. Save for personal misconduct they have nothing to fear about losing their work or its fruits.

* * *

AT first sight, then, it appears that the position of Russian youth is far more satisfactory than that of its brothers and sisters in America. There are, however, other factors to be considered. First of all, there is the danger of war, to which young Russia is exposed but from which the United States is comparatively immune.

A foreign invasion can wreck lives and destroy the fruits of effort even more swiftly and cruelly than a capitalist depression. To meet this potential menace the need for military training and the necessity for national defense is being dinned continually into the ears of Russian boys and girls. Even children are being trained in the use of arms, and the older ones of both sexes drill and march in military formation and spend no small part of their time in preparation for war.

It is also possible that the insistence upon military or semi-military training is not only inspired by fear of war but by the wish to teach discipline to the Russian youth. A further important means toward this end is the development of games and athletic sports, which is being pushed vigorously and rapidly throughout the Union.

Each year in Moscow there is a great parade, in Red Square, of the athletic associations, in which a quarter of a million youngsters of both sexes march in orderly formation according to categories, each group carrying the "tools of their trade"—oars, footballs, boxing gloves, tennis racquets and so forth. The bright and variegated colors of blouses, jerseys and shorts produce an effect of picturesque animation, which is heightened by the eager faces of the paraders. It is an impressive sight.

* * *

THIS very parade, however, emphasizes a phase of Young Russia's life — regimentation. As I have said, the emphasis is placed on joint effort, on working together rather than on individual exploits. True to the Marxist theory, it is mass effort and mass success which come first, rather than the personal element. Regimentation extends not merely to games but to everyday life.

A boy or girl is comparatively free in choice of a profession or means of livelihood, provided, that is, that the necessary qualifications are present, that the chosen courses can be mastered and examinations passed. Once this is accomplished individual freedom of action is greatly restricted. The young engineer or doctor or agronome is given a post which may not in the least correspond with his or her wishes, but which virtually cannot be refused. Of course, it is often possible to arrange things; personal pull still counts in the Soviet Union.

What I mean is that if a young graduate physician is appointed to Tashkent but wishes to go to Sverdlovsk for family or other reasons, he is not forbidden to find, if he can, some colleague who has been appointed to Sverdlovsk but would like to go to Tashkent. Such a system is doubtless far less repugnant to Russians than it would be to American ideas of individual freedom, but it often causes grumbling and distress. In the case of the members of the Young Communist League, the matter is different because by joining the Communist party they put themselves as wholly at its disposition and agree to submit as fully to its orders as does a soldier in the army or a sailor in the navy.

# SOVIET MORALS LESS REVOLUTIONARY

By HAROLD DENNY

Wireless to THE NEW YORK TIMES.

MOSCOW, Nov. 26.—Official disapproval of moral laxity now being voiced here is another reminder of the fact that bit by bit Soviet morals are swinging around to the old-fashioned standards of bourgeois society. Soviet morals have a long way to go yet before they will cease to shock many conventionally minded people of other countries. But they have already come a long way since the early days of the revolution. Then many young people—and older ones too—engaged in a riot of amatory adventures in the belief that adherence to old convictions was somehow counter-revolutionary.

The issue of morals was debated by the early Bolshevist leaders and the bulk of the best thought—including Lenin's—was that promiscuity was not good Communist doctrine. But the soberer concepts then promulgated left a great deal of latitude and still do.

The Bolshevist concept of relations between the sexes in capitalist countries is one of prostitution and exploitation. It represents women as yielding to men, either in marriage or outside, because they are economically dependent on men.

## Communist Equality

The Communist aim was to build a state wherein women would be the economic equal of men and in which no woman need give herself to any man except from love.

The Bolsheviks have achieved their aim of economic equality of the sexes to a considerable degree. Every able-bodied Soviet woman can get a job, be it as street sweeper, subway digger or member of the government, although the proportion of women to men in the higher walks of life probably is considerably smaller here than in America.

The Soviet woman's relative economic independence has brought her sexual freedom also, enhanced by the Soviet marriage code and generally free and easy point of view. No stigma attaches to the relationship of a man and a woman outside wedlock. No stigma of illegitimacy attaches to a child born of such a union and the father must assist in its maintenance.

## Marriage and Non-Marriage

The institution of de facto marriage has been retained, notwithstanding persistent efforts of Soviet authorities in recent years to stabilize the family along merely conventional lines. The mere fact that a couple live openly together and assume the relationship of man and wife legally makes them so. If they wish to be normal about it—and often the woman thinks it offers her more protection—they register the marriage at the "Zags" (the Soviet Vital Statistics Bureau). But the marriage is prefectly legal without that.

It was the aspiration of the Soviet regime to do away completely with prostitution. It has made great progress in this direction. Moscow has far fewer prostitutes than most world capitals. But it still has some.

November 27, 1938

# *Births Up 35% in Russia; Bonus System Is Credited*

By The Associated Press.

MOSCOW, Nov. 21—Russia's birth rate, which before the war was one of the highest in the world, has increased more than one-third as a result of the 1944 decree giving cash awards to mothers of three children and more, it was announced today.

The Commissariat of Public Health withheld actual figures, but announced that during the first nine months of this year the Russian birth rate jumped 35.3 per cent over the same period last year.

The last recorded figures list Russia's 1935-39 birth rate as 44.1 for each 1,000 population, compared with 17.1 for the United States during the same period. Russia's last census, in 1939, disclosed a total population of 183,736,286.

Assistant Commissar M. D. Kovrigina attributed the increase to the decree awarding payments ranging from 400 rubles to the mother of three children to 5,000 rubles and 300 rubles monthly for each child in excess of ten.

November 22, 1945

# LIFE TERMED DRAB FOR SOVIET WORKER

### Factory Job and Bus Travel Keep Him Away From Home About 12 Hours Each Day

### HELD WEARY OF POLITICS

### Feeding and Clothing Family Is Main Concern—Believes What Press, Radio Tell Him

By DREW MIDDLETON

Ivan Ivanovich gets up before the light comes to the street in the Arbat quarter of Moscow where he lives. Gita, his wife, is still sleeping. She works part time at a factory, does the housework and spends hours standing in line to buy the household's food. These days she is always tired. So Ivan dresses in silence.

His two sons sleep together. There is space for a fourth bed in the room but now in winter it is cold and Vassily and Georgi would rather sleep in one bed. The bit of Pravda pasted over a gap in one of the windows does not keep the cold air out. Ivan has asked the house committee for repairs but nothing has happened.

In the kitchen, which he and his family share with four other families, Ivan finds Andrei, who works in the same factory. They have a glass of tea each, munch some black bread and divide a tiny segment of cheese. Through the thin walls they hear Serge and Simeon, who live with their families in the other two rooms, getting up.

When Ivan and Andrei reach the street the first light has touched the gray, unhealthy surface of the snow. In the center of the city plows and relays of old women have cleared the snow from the streets. Here, five minutes' walk from the Kremlin, it lies unbroken save for the footprints of the inhabitants of the quarter. Unless some official drives his car down the street, it will remain that way until spring, when it will melt and the cellars will flood.

Ivan is lucky. When he left the army he kept his boots. They are still fairly waterproof. Into them he has tucked his heavy black workman's trousers. They are patched at a couple of places but this is not extraordinary. Under his army overcoat Ivan wears an old quilted jacket and under that his threadbare, once warm, underwear. Soap is hard to come by and the underwear remains a dull gray despite Gita's exertions over the washtub.

## Much Shoving To Get on Bus

At the corner they wait for the trolley-bus. There are not enough buses in Moscow these days and the line is long. If they look across the square they can see the gold-topped towers of the Kremlin churches. But no one bothers to look. The most important thing is to get aboard the bus.

This Ivan does with a good deal of shoving and repeated cries of "Look out, citizen, you are pushing." When he finally finds a place he is next to the garrulous man who works in the bookkeeper's office at the factory, who is a Communist and who is always talking politics.

Ivan listens politely. But it is not a novelty to be told that the Americans are establishing new air bases in the Arctic or that the just demands of Comrade Molotov have been refused at the Council of Foreign Ministers. Ivan has read that himself or heard it over the radio. He seems to listen but he thinks of Vassily's cough and Gita's tired face.

The journey takes some time. This trolley-bus, like most in Moscow, suffers from the occupational complaint of not being able to keep its conducting arm on the wire. Twice it has come off with a flash and shower of sparks. No one in the trolley-bus remarks on it. It happens every day.

One day at the factory is pretty much like the rest. Ivan is in charge of a section charged with assembling the dials for radios. Recently there has been a shortage of tools but today things seem to be going fairly well. The section is made up of boys and girls from the labor reserves, willing enough but untrained. It is not work, Ivan thinks, for big youngsters from the farms.

## Extra Food as a Bonus

Last month Ivan's section overfulfilled its "norm" under the factory's part of the Five-Year Plan.

So this month he and the section get extra dishes at the factory restaurant. Today, in addition to cabbage soup, macaroni and tea, Ivan gets a small piece of meat. He pays for the meal at factory prices. It costs him about 90 cents.

Today is one of the "days." Ivan forgets, although the newspapers have reminded him, whether it is Army Day or Tank Day or Artillery Day or Navy Day. However, he goes along with some of the other section leaders to hear a speaker sent by the Central Committee of the Moscow Soviet expound the glories of the Soviet system and the danger to it of the imperialist aggressors in the United States.

When work is done Ivan starts home through the darkness. He works an eight-hour day but transportation is so bad that in all he is away from home nearly twelve hours. They are building some apartment houses for workers near his factory, but although he peers out at them from the window of his shop each day they do not seem to change much.

On the bus going home Ivan reads the Moscow newspaper, his favorite. It does not have as much international news or ideological articles as Pravda and Izvestia, which are morning papers, but it has more local news.

Not all Russians live Ivan's life. But the majority do. For the planned society has evolved the standard society and that standard is low. Ivan, compared to some, is relatively well off. He makes about $85 a month and Gita about $40.

There is an upper class that Ivan sometimes calls the "novi barri," the new nobles.

Composed of party officials, senior army and navy officers, the chieftains of the security police, factory managers and technicians, scientists, writers, artists and theatrical folk, it lives well.

Take M., a member of the novi barri, a Government official. As one of the prerequisites of office he has the use of a three-room apartment in a relatively new building. His position entitles him to trade at a well-stocked shop reserved only for officials of his grade and the apartment is furnished moderately well by Western standards. In addition, M., who spent some time in the West, acquired a table, two chairs, a very good sideboard and some dishes which, if they do not match in pattern, are better than those purchasable in Moscow.

But Ivan is the man the editorial writers of Pravda have in mind when they declare that "further sacrifices" will be required from "the patriotic Soviet people" during the next few years. M. is the man who will benefit from those sacrifices.

M. had managed to amass a considerable number of rubles. The devaluation of the currency probably has raised hob with his plans for the future. Even so, he was probably not as hard hit as a doctor friend. The doctor, who practiced privately at home after finishing his daily work at the clinic, made as much as 25,000 rubles a week in some weeks.

Neither M. nor the doctor allowed their Communist devotion to the Marxian ideal to prevent them from keeping an eye on the main chance.

One of the odd things about Ivan is that although he lives in an environment that is severely political he is not actively affected. For him the urgent objectives are the repair of that broken windowpane, the hope that there will be some more food in the stores and electric hot plates in stock.

Ivan accepts without surprise and without question most of what he is told over the radio and in the newspapers. Today he believes that the Soviet Union defeated Germany, liberated all of Europe and then turned east and struck the decisive blow in the war against Japan. Just the other night he saw a movie that showed the Japanese commanders signing the peace terms with the Russians aboard a battleship. The movie did not tell him that the battleship was an American one or that the Soviet officers were merely some of the representatives of the Allied powers aboard the U. S. S. Missouri. And if you told Ivan this, he would not believe you.

He is told that the system under which he lives is the most productive, freest and most civilized that the wit of man has yet devised. Since he is literally a prisoner within his country, he has no standards by which to judge this information.

Ivan has no tradition or background of people's rights and people's progress. If he thinks of his lot in comparison with that of others at all, it is to compare it with the life of his father and his grandfather. They, he has been told, worked under a harsh and restrictive system and were sweated by the bourgeoisie and the aristocrats. He grumbles about shortages but he is sure that his life is better than theirs.

Perhaps an old man may whisper in the factory canteen that under the Czars a man could at least protest. Even if he went to prison for protesting, his family might see him and his friends might help him.

Ivan doesn't want to listen to the old man. For, like every other Russian, he knows that "they" are always listening; that the old man himself may be one of "their" men. The best thing to do is forget.

**Role Accepted Humbly**

In that way things are a little better since the war. Occasionally Ivan and Gita go to the Bolshoi, the Great Theatre, to hear the opera or see the ballet. Since they are humble folk, their seats are never very good. However, Ivan is the last man to protest against such inequalities.

After all, there had always been persons who were sitting in the best seats, eating the best food, wearing the best clothes in Russia. They are the rulers and although Ivan grumbles, he believes beneath the grumbling that it is just.

Like many other Russians, Ivan and Gita have a sneaking and, by Communist standards, wholly unpatriotic fondness for moving pictures made in the West. Some time ago when the old British picture "Lady Hamilton" was being shown at a neighborhood theatre across town, they went over to see it. It offered escape.

These days escape is hard to find in Soviet films. They preach eternally and although Ivan will work hard under the Five-Year Plan he wants something more than a film about the glories when he relaxes.

Both Ivan and Gita are anxious that their sons shall have a better life than they. Nowadays the boys, if their grades are high enough, can go on from school to become engineers or doctors or lawyers. If their grades are not high enough they can be drafted into the labor reserves. Both parents want to avoid that.

Lately, however, Ivan has begun to wonder whether success for his boys will not in the end take them away from him.

A friend of his, a co-worker at the factory, has a daughter, a brilliant girl who received high marks in chemistry at the university and then went to a special school to study food processing. Unfortunately, she is not going to be allowed to stay in Moscow.

Huge new bakeries are being built in the east and she has been directed to one of them. It is a good job but Ivan wonders whether her parents will ever see her again.

Ivan's life is a drab one. But in the long run the worst thing about it is not its drabness, not the shortages, the crowding, the hunger, the lack of security inherent in a political system subject to periodic fits of industrial change, but the fact that Ivan and Gita and all the other millions of Ivans and Gitas have no means of changing it.

February 4, 1948

# REDS' TYRANT BIAS LAID TO BABYHOOD

**Russians Want Strong Regime Because They're Swaddled in Infancy, Study Indicates**

The age-old custom of swaddling infants in Russia may help to condition the Russians to demand strict state control over the individual, Dr. Margaret Mead, anthropologist, concludes.

A summary of Dr. Mead's analysis of the Russian character was published in the September number of Natural History monthly magazine of the American Museum of Natural History.

Before the Bolshevik revolution, Dr. Mead reported, the Russian baby was swaddled "day and night, only being undone to be fed, bathed or changed," for the first yea rof life. The baby was carried about by an old woman or child nurse, "experiencing but never touching" the external world. The battle of the Communist regime against swaddling failed, Dr. Mead wrote, "so that the bulk of Soviet children are still swaddled, though probably not as tightly or for as long a period."

Taking that and other factors in child training in the Soviet Union today into account, the anthropologist wrote:

"We may expect that the young Soviet citizen will have some of the traditional fear of his own ungoverned impulses and the corresponding belief in the importance of a strong state authority, reinforced by modern Bolshevik training in the value and importance of control.

"We may expect that there will be a strong potential revolt against authority and a corresponding demand for authority, so that young Soviet citizens will dream of throwing off the Soviet yoke, but only in order to establish some other absolute form."

Dr. Harry L. Shapiro, curator of anthropology at the museum, explained that Dr. Mead headed a group of a dozen social scientists who studied the Soviet character "at long range" for three years.

The group read masses of official documents, Soviet publications and commentaries by non-Soviet observers. Refugees were interviewed and Russian literature and movies were examined.

"This was not the ideal way to study the Soviet character, of course," Dr. Shapiro commented, "but it was better than nothing. To my knowledge, it is the first time such methods have been applied to so large a segment of society. We think it was quite a tour de force for Dr. Mead to have got as much data as she did."

Dr. Mead's full report will be published later. The first year's work will be detailed in a book, "Soviet Attitudes Toward Authority," to be published soon by McGraw-Hill. The study was indirectly financed by the Federal Government and partly sponsored by the museum, where Dr. Mead is associate curator of ethnology.

September 23, 1951

# Classes of 'Classless' Russia

**The old Communist principle has been converted to the rule 'to each according to his position in the social pyramid.'**

By HARRY SCHWARTZ

THE Bolshevik Revolution of 1917 was largely a revolt against the concept of a class society. Yet thirty-five years later, the Soviet Union is as markedly stratified as the Imperial Russia it replaced. Soviet theoreticians, far from denying this, make a point of the fact that the U. S. S. R. is not a classless utopia. Official theory now holds that the Russian people have not yet reached that stage of development required for ideal, classless communism; that they

Marshal (Zhukov)—pay, 1,000,000 rubles.

must still be paid or punished to produce. Hence the line now is: "From each according to his abilities, to each according to his work."

To this is added the comfortable rationalization that inequalities of power, income and comfort do not give rise to classes that are hostile toward each other, since there is no exploitation of man by man in the Soviet Union. There may be classes, but they are in harmony, all of them working tirelessly to achieve the final goal of classless equality.

THE realities of Soviet life are considerably different from the pleasant orthodox view. Briefly, the class structure of the U. S. S. R. is this: (1) At the very apex of the social pyramid are a few hundred families, members of the Politburo and their closest associates in the ruling clique of the Communist party, the Government, the military and the secret police; (2) immediately below is a much larger group whose members are numbered in the hundreds of thousands of families—perhaps a million at most—and who consist of the top rulers' most important servitors; they are the secondary echelons of party and Government bureaucracy, higher officers of the armed forces, many members of the secret police, the chief managers of the economy, leading writers, artists and musicians, scientists and intellectuals generally, and a few highly publicized Stakhanovite workers and farmers; (3) a much less affluent middle class consisting of intermediate officials of the party, Government and military, engineers and technicians, collective farm officials and the more fortunate workers and farmers; (4) the basic mass of workers and peasants, and (5) the millions of slave laborers.

Exactly what proportion of the Soviet population may be found in each of these groups it is impossible to say because of the Communist habit of withholding data, but some estimates can be made. There may be at most 5,000,000 persons, including family members, in the two top groups, or about $2\frac{1}{2}$ per cent of the population. The middle class may account for another 10,000,000 or 15,000,000. Thus the Soviet upper classes comprise less than 10 per cent of the population.

Just how much better off the Soviet upper classes are than communism's hoi polloi is reflected in every aspect of the life of these fortunate people. In the two top classes, in particular, real incomes are far greater than the Soviet average because the members receive high incomes and a great many perquisites of office not available to the average Communist working staff. They have at their disposal such state-provided facilities as automobiles, luxurious vacation resorts and similar white graft. Moreover, their high money incomes are not taxed away at the same rate as they would be in the United States: for most categories of Soviet citizens the income tax rate never exceeds 13 per cent.

IN terms of actual money, the difference may be estimated in this way: the average Soviet worker's income is about 8,000 rubles a year. At the level of the Pólitburo, the standard is about 1,000,000 rubles; in the group immediately below, it is in the hundreds of thousands of rubles; in the middle class, at about 20,000.

Ballerina (Ulanova)—pay, 100,000 rubles.

The differing levels of well-being are reflected also in the food, clothing, housing and other living components available. Meat, eggs, dairy products and fresh fruit, for example, are rare luxuries for the standard Soviet citizen. In the two upper classes they are daily staples. The wardrobe of the ordinary Soviet worker or peasant is limited, contains few changes and is of indif-

Farm manager—pay, 20,000 rubles.

ferent quality. Not so for the two upper classes: there, clothing is abundant; fur coats are not uncommon; at the very top those who wish have access to Parisian fashions or at least copies. Automobiles, washing machines and electrical appliances are frequently seen in the homes of upper-class Soviet citizens, while the great mass of people not only cannot afford them but may never have seen some of these articles.

In the field of housing, the social commodity most conspicuous by its lack in the Soviet Union, there are sharp contrasts between the upper classes and the rest of the population. Top-ranking Soviet officials luxuriate in spacious apartments, country villas and shooting boxes. Members of the middle class may be rich enough or lucky enough or both to find a separate apartment or a small house. But the bulk of city workers crowd into one or two rooms, depending on the size of a family, and must share a kitchen, bath and other facilities with other families.

Medical service for high officials, army officers, members of the secret police and others of the élite is much better than it is for the humble worker and peasant. Special clinics and hospitals are at hand for the upper classes, as are the finest physicians. At the very top, foreign medical specialists are made available if necessary.

HARRY SCHWARTZ of The Times staff regularly analyzes many Soviet publications.

Social life and recreational opportunities are more abundant, intensified and varied for the upper classes. They can afford to give lavish parties and dinners—and their homes contain the space for such gatherings. Special vacation resorts are set aside for them, while the ordinary worker's chance of getting to a Crimean spa is contingent upon his beating his work quota or upon his pull with trade union or other authorities.

What are the consequences of this class structure for the Soviet Union today and for its future?

It must be recognized that this class system is a source of strength for the ruling Politburo oligarchy. By sharing the country's consumption surplus with millions of privileged bureaucrats, party officials, military officers, secret police members and the like, Stalin and his colleagues have created a mass base for their power. Many of these people, therefore, must identify their own material interest with that of the oligarchy and have an incentive to perpetuate the present rule. For many in the lower classes, the ambition to rise must be a similar incentive to work harder, to win favor and to show devotion and loyalty.

However, the class system is also a major source of weakness. The great majority of the population is in the lower classes, in the groups which are ill-fed, ill-clothed and ill-housed. These people would not be human if they were not envious of those above them and resentful of their superior material status. Anger at the sharp inequities in Soviet society must be felt in tens of millions of hearts, bottled up but a source of never-ending tension and aggravation.

**Factory worker— pay, 8,000 rubles.**

THE Soviet Government undoubtedly realizes that this tension exists. It seeks to counteract it by propaganda directing its peoples' attention to the glorious Communist future when all will have what they need and none shall want. But after more than three decades of nonrealization, this propaganda must have lost much of its effectiveness.

What of the future? If present trends continue, the Soviet class system will tend to become evermore stratified and evermore nearly a caste rather than a class system. Each privileged group uses its influence to make certain that its children will occupy at least as good a place in society as the parents.

Stalin himself has set the example by making his son, Vassily, a lieutenant general at the age of 30; this example has not been lost upon the rest of the population. The result is that nepotism and favoritism are rife throughout the Soviet structure.

In sum, the bright idealism of the 1917 revolution has long since vanished in the U. S. S. R. under the impress of forces which have re-created a class pattern similar to that which the Bolsheviks destroyed. But where other modern class societies have developed institutions and laws lessening old inequalities, Soviet society has progressed in the other direction. Though the overt expression of the class struggle has been repressed in the U. S. S. R., the desire for such struggle exists and grows among its people. Under these conditions there must be fertile ground for the message from the free world that better methods of societal organization exist and can be won by those willing to fight for them.

March 2, 1952

# SEX NOT RESPECTED BY WORK IN RUSSIA

## British Writer Relates How Women Clean Streets as Well as Ply the Professions

*The following dispatch was written by Cyril Ray, a British correspondent, who spent eighteen months in Moscow.*

North American Newspaper Alliance
From Kemsley News Service

LONDON, May 3—"But what was Moscow like?" people ask me, and I never know where to begin.

I had left Moscow, as I had first seen it, in the hard, white hands of the Russian winter, and London, basking in its April sunshine, was all the gayer and brighter by contrast.

I came home by train by way of Helsinki, across 1,000 miles of endless snow—snow that stretched for many thousands of miles more, from Archangel to the Caucasus and from the Baltic to Vladivostok, but Moscow's streets had been clear, as they almost always are. Superbly efficient in some things, infuriatingly incompetent in others, the Russians have licked the problem of snow clearance in the big cities.

Motor-drawn snow plows and snow shovelers swing into action at the first snowfall. Fleets of trucks go off in convoy to dump the heaped snow into the Moskva River, or the fields outside the town.

**Women Chop Away Ice**

Metropolitan mountaineers clear the overhang from roofs and window ledges, and—most characteristic of all—in every important street and roadway of Moscow sturdy women, young and old, in head shawls, quilted coats, high felt boots and aprons (I never understood the aprons) chop with metal hoes at the icy underlay left by the snow shovelers, and sweep it into the gutters.

In the summer these same women will be sweeping the dusty streets and tidying the parks and gardens.

Once you have strolled the streets of Moscow, you realize that the equality of the sexes in Russia—for good or for bad—is a very real thing.

There are women bus drivers and taxi drivers; women lay bricks along with men; there are more women doctors than men doctors; and painting and plastering seem to be exclusively female occupations.

Women get the rate for the job, but they do the job for the rate—and nobody who has seen a load of heavy furniture being unloaded by women ever will doubt that in Russia a woman is held to be capable of the heaviest work—as, in fairness, she is held to be suitable for the most honorable and highly paid professions.

"Ah," I hear someone say, "so some jobs in the Soviet Union are more honorable and highly paid than others! What about the classless Communist society?"

**Only Moving Toward Communism**

The Russian answer to that is that the Soviet Union is not yet a Communist state, but is only progressing toward communism, and that meanwhile wide differences of pay are a necessary stimulus. But the large sums of money you would earn if you were a successful (and an orthodox Marxist) author, a ballerina, an electrical engineer, or a highly efficient coal miner cannot be invested in private enterprise, to give you control of or a profit from other people's labor, and cannot affect the accent or clothes or manners or title of your children. (They can now make it a little, but not much, easier to give them a university education.)

There are wide differences in income in Russia, and a Soviet Army general is more respected than a private because of his greater responsibility, but there are no inherited class distinctions—yet, at any rate.

Though a general may be able to afford to dine at Moscow's smart Ararat restaurant every night, and a factory worker once a month, you can dine there yourself any night and see both generals and mill hands eating the same food and getting the same service.

May 4, 1952

## REDS RUN TO CUBIST ART,

**Marinsky Palace, Petrograd, Daubed for May Day Celebration.**

Special Cable to THE NEW YORK TIMES.

LONDON, May 22.—The Petrograd correspondent of The Daily Express, describing the Bolshevist May Day celebrations, says a grotesque feature was the daubing of the Marinsky Palace—the House of Lords of the Romanoff days—the Winter Palace, and the Government offices in peculiar colors of a cubist scheme devised by Signor Marinetti.

A more ambitious note was struck by the allegorical presentation of the progress of the proletariat, after the style of a Bayeux tapestry. This embraced a weird picture of the Kaiser as a skeleton of death crowned with a German helmet and with an Iron Cross pinned to his ribs, and a scythe grasped in his bony fingers shown in the act of cutting down the red flowers of revolutionary Russia.

May 23, 1918

## RUSSIA.

**Communists Dissatisfied With Futurists.**

HITHERTO the Soviet Government patronized officially the art of the Russian futurists, whose avowed leader, the poet, Maiakovsky, published his poems in The Isvestia. All the placards used in the official manifestations and processions were painted also by futurists and cubists and the Government Publishing Company (Gessisdat) has published many a volume of "one word in a line" poems.

But at the present time the attitude of the Soviet Government toward the futurists seems to have changed. The Commissary of Education, Lunacharsky, made a statement to the effect that "we have had enough of that foolishness." The well-known Communist Sosnovsky published a long article in the Pravda ruthlessly criticising Maiakovsky and his friends. He asserts that the futurists, who three years ago were true supporters of the Communist Government, are now changing front. For instance, Maiakovsky dared to say that words like "red flag," "freedom," "revolutionary peoples," &c., became tedious banalities because the readers have had enough of them. This Mr. Sosnovsky describes as a "dangerous political tendency."

July 8, 1923

## *Soviet Now Bans Phonograph Jazz Records; Calls Our Dances "Bourgeois Music"*

MOSCOW, Jan. 8 (AP).—"Bourgeois music, unfit for proletarian society," is the description of the Soviet authorities for American jazz.

Recently the fox-trot, shimmy and other American dances were banned in Russia, and now the authorities have forbidden entry into the country of phonograph records from the United States containing fox-trots, Charlestons and similar pieces.

These dances likewise cannot be broadcast from Russian radio stations. When European stations are heard broadcasting jazz, or what passes for jazz, the local radio plants immediately do their worst to drown them out by setting up the weird, raucous discords of a "cat concert."

An interesting story of how an American correspondent who came to Moscow this week fooled one frontier guard shows that the meaning of the word "Charleston" is not generally known. When the American arrived at the frontier, the customs inspector discovered he had a dozen records in his baggage. Examining the labels on the fox-trots, the customs inspector said regretfully, "These are prohibited in the Soviet Union." Realizing argument would be futile, the correspondent replied dejectedly, "Very well."

Then the inspector took up the package of "Charleston" disks and, after pondering over the word "Charleston" for several minutes, asked the American, "What does Charleston mean?"

"Oh, that's a new form of American light operatic music," was the response.

"Classical music?" queried the guileless inspector.

"Yes," rejoined the correspondent.

"Well, you may take them; we have no objection to real classical music like this." As a further concession the inspector said, "No duty payable."

The triumphant journalist now is believed to have the only Charleston records in all Russia. His room in Moscow is the rendezvous for Americans who are oblivious to the existing ban on American dances. Nightly they fling their legs to the lively strains.

January 9, 1927

## MOSCOW IN THROES OF LITERARY 'WAR'

**Pilniak's Book on Struggle of Classes Brings Down Storm of Virulent Comment.**

**"WHITE PRESS" REJOICES**

**Unexpurgated Berlin Edition Rouses Ire of Foreign Office Against Famous Author.**

By WALTER DURANTY.

Wireless to THE NEW YORK TIMES.

MOSCOW, Sept. 5.—As the Far Eastern war clouds have grown less lowering, Moscow has started a little war of its own—a literary war in which accusations fly like bullets and ink is spilled like blood.

The "casus belli" or "corpus delicti"—these Latin terms are so confusing — is Citizen Boris Pilniak, president of the Soviet Society of Authors, hitherto one of the most popular post-revolutionary writers, whose "Naked Year" has been widely translated and cited as a typical and excellent product of the new Russian literature. Pilniak recently completed a new novel called "Red Wood," which he offered, according to his custom, simultaneously to a Soviet publishing house in Moscow and to the Russian publishers "Petropolis" in Berlin.

The theme of the book is "class warfare" in Soviet villages—an apposite and highly topical subject at present, but the Soviet publishers thought that Pilniak treated it with more sympathy to the kulaks—the rich peasants—than the facts warranted, and suggested certain cuts and changes, which delayed publication.

Meanwhile the book appeared in Berlin, to be saluted with howls of joy by the White Russian press abroad, although in justice to Pilniak it must be stated that he tried vainly to prevent the Berlin publication when he discovered that the book was unacceptable here.

**Storm Bursts on Pilniak.**

Whereupon the storm burst on Pilniak's head, led by Boris Volin, one of the principal officials of the Foreign Office Press Department, whose talents as polemist have ere this on occasion been used against the flock of foreign reporters he is supposed to shepherd. Volin represents the best type of new Russian culture, thoroughly familiar with three or four foreign languages and literatures, a devoted Communist and wielding a wicked pen. But he is a fair fighter, and once when the foreign correspondents thought he had made an unkind generalization in their regard from an individual case, he saw to it that the Izvestiya published their reply.

Anyway, he tore poor Pilniak wide open, and others followed his example. In vain Pilniak replied that half a dozen other well known Soviet writers had contracts with Petropolis, that he had tried to prevent publication, that an author had a right to present both sides of the picture and that he was as good a Sovietist as any one, and yielded to none in his faith in the Socialist success in Russia. That helped him not a whit. They called him traitor, backslider and, almost, counter-revolutionary.

Loudest of all was the poet Mayakovski, a big, beefy, noisy citizen, who signalized himself a few years ago on his return from America by issuing a hyperbolic denunciation of the United States and all its capitalist works. Mayakovski doubtless feels he would make a better president of the Soviet Authors' Society than Pilniak, whose action he calls "equivalent at the present moment to treachery on the war front." Which, Euclid said, is absurd.

**Symptomatic of Class Struggle.**

On the other hand, this whole storm in a teacup is a symptom of the bitter intensity of the class struggle in Russia today. Putting private envy or jealousy aside, Mayakovski voices the general Communist sentiment when he declares that any one who even unwittingly furnishes arms to hostile forces must himself be considered an enemy. Unhappy Pilniak faces the probability not only of removal from his presidency in the Authors' Society, but literary boycott as well.

September 8, 1929

# SOVIET DECREES END OF ABSTRACT SCIENCE

## Conference Is Now Being Held to Harness All Research to Socialist Ends.

## BUKHARIN LEADS ATTACK

By WALTER DURANTY.

Wireless to THE NEW YORK TIMES.

MOSCOW, April 8.—Not content with existing troubles—great enough in all conscience, though perhaps sometimes exaggerated—the Kremlin has now taken upon itself a new battle, namely, to harness science for Socialist service.

There is now being held in Moscow what is purposely entitled "A Conference for Planned Organization of Scientific Investigational Work." It is interesting to note that the principal speech was made by Nikolai Bukharin, co-member with Alexei Rykoff, who also was recently restored to grace, and Mikhail Tomsky of the Right Opposition "troika" [trio].

M. Bukharin proved worthy of the Kremlin's renewed trust. He declared:

"So-called pure science, that is science devoid of contact with practical life, is a figment. [Would Einstein agree to this?] The whole fabric of scientific investigational work in capitalist countries is a weapon in the hands of capitalist magnates and governments and their industrial and military organizations.

"We Bolsheviki, on the other hand, have demanded a gigantic increase of scientific effort in the whole system of Socialist construction in the Soviet Union. The problems before us require a decisive and categorical break with bourgeois traditions of old academism and their conversion to the task of solving immediate, practical difficulties."

M. Bukharin continued that Russian scientists must now choose whether to throw in their lot wholeheartedly with the Socialist system or "hide their hostility behind a screen of pure science and its abstraction from the national life."

In the discussion which followed, it appears from newspaper reports, the assembled scientists, whether of the old régime or Communists, were reluctant to accept M. Bukharin's challenge. The newspaper Economic Life states that the speakers without exception avoided the basic thesis which M. Bukharin had outlined and preferred to confine their remarks to matters of detail. It would thus seem that science is not much readier than Pegasus to be tied to the Soviet chariot.

Indeed, Economic Life rubs home this impression by a sarcastic article in an adjoining column about a department of the Leningrad Academy of Science "wasting a whole year" in abstruse investigation of the characteristics of an oakshoot grown in a dark cellar, and whether it is easiest to pull a round, a triangular or a square nail from a piece of wood.

However suitable the soil of Russia may be to Bolshevist doctrines, it is also congenial to the vaguer and more abstract manifestations of science and art. It will be interesting to see what success the Soviet Government will have in bending either or both to the utilitarian aims of Socialist construction.

April 9, 1931

# SOVIET ARTS WORKS FERVID BUT CRUDE

## 2,500 Paintings Exhibited in Moscow Reflect Course of the Country.

## PRESS LAUDS THE DISPLAY

### Russian Newspapers Hold It Shows 'Escape From Arid Formalism of Capitalist' Pictures.

By WALTER DURANTY.

Special Cable to THE NEW YORK TIMES.

MOSCOW, June 30.—"Fifteen years of Soviet Art" is the pretentious title of an exhibition of about 2,500 paintings, which was opened in the Historical Museum at Moscow this week. It is the first real big exhibition of painting in Russia since the revolution. Of the 339 artists represented only seventy-seven had pre-revolution training.

This exhibition and the articles about it in Moscow newspapers provide an admirable contrast between the fundamental truth that is art and the Soviet verbiage on the subject. There are columns of drivel about "the new creation," about "the artist in touch with the reality of life," about "the health and sun of the Bolshevist revolutionary effort," and about "the escape from the arid formalism of capitalist artistic production."

**Much of Work "Bourgeois."**

And what do you see to justify these pompous and self-congratulatory phrases? Acres of fourth-rate daubs—and bourgeois in the sense of the word in which real artists use it, that is, dull and stereotyped.

The writer has seen more "revolutionary" art in one room of the Paris "independents" or even in the Beaux Arts salon itself than in all the sixteen rooms of the Moscow exhibition, although here and there are pictures by the older artists that reach the Western European average and some work of younger men that really does stand out.

To begin with, the Russians for some reason are illustrators rather than painters. One need only see their "masters" in the Tretyakoff Gallery to know that. Is there one Russian, dead or alive, whose name would be included in a list of the world's 100 best painters? There are some good engravers, but the best talent develops along the lines of poster illustrations and cartoons, in which Soviet artists are finding the real expression of life and of revolution in a way that almost justifies the eulogies of the Pravda and the Izvestia.

Those eager scribes, however, do not seem to realize that the "subject of the painting does not matter one rap." To read them one would think they began with the idea that a picture of Lenin or Stalin or of a new factory or collective farm or of the Red Army winning a battle or of Communist Youth "physiculture" girls playing volley ball must ipso facto be a good picture.

And to prove it there stands at the foot of the staircase leading to the exhibition one of the most ghastly statues of Lenin in white plaster with a Red flag background that the writer has ever seen. That is saying a lot, for there is little more conventional, banal and frankly bad collection of statuary than his admiring fellow-countrymen have perpetrated to "honor" Lenin.

**Many Show Promise.**

These are harsh words, but they are justified, and this criticism of the "fifteen years of Soviet art" also is justified. Yet a professional art critic would find in this exhibition many pictures that show promise and that are not mere imitations of this or that foreign fad.

There is Dennika with an arresting statuesque quality of bodies in moments of physical tension—like Myron's Discobolus — expressed quietly and without violent colors and with a sober purity of line. And there is a curious picture by Yakovlef—hitherto best known as a restorer and copier of old masters—of an operation in a modern hospital, with ugly realism but honest force and composition.

Williams, also a pre-revolution painter, presents a yellow and brown study of a girl acrobat in a manner reminiscent of Whistler, which shows up the puerility of the surrounding canvases. And the novel color and perspective effects of the lumber-camp pictures by Svetkoff are there.

In short, the exhibition—far more than Soviet writers realize—is a true and just reflection of the nation's life today. Here are youth, ardor and courage; small but golden reserves of talent, great, if unskilled, effort, and amazing eagerness, but withal much ignorance, crudity and lack of technique.

July 2, 1933

# PROPAGANDA AND MUSIC

## Tchemodanoff's History of Music Betrays Logic Led Astray Through Dogma

By OLIN DOWNES.

No doubt it would be impossible and ridiculous to expect sound sense and balanced reasoning of a revolution. In such a moment an impulse more violent and explosive than sound reasoning is required, and at the necessary moment nature supplies it. For the moment such an immaterial and impractical thing as art is extinguished. It cannot defy the raging tempest, but must bend before it or disappear, to manifest a new growth when the cataclysm is over.

The music and literature about music which emanate today from Russia are in the great majority of instances the offspring not of musical inspiration, or logical thinking, or esthetic development; they are the superficial, ephemeral and distorted products of revolution. This powerful and fruitful revolution is accompanied by a certain naïveté. Ideas long entertained by the average intelligence are disseminated as if the disseminator had discovered a matter of the greatest novelty.

A résumé and certain quotations from "A History of Music in Connection With the History of Social Development," by S. M. Tchemodanoff, professor of the First Moscow State University, is before us. The terminology of this volume, as revealed in the excerpts submitted, is interesting and in itself indicative of the dominating trend of Russian "ideology," whether in politics or music.

Rightly or wrongly, the Russian State categorically refuses to separate musical expression from any other form of social manifestation in a modern State. Art and society are parts of a whole and subject to one set of definitions. No one could teach music or lecture about it in Russia or write a book on such a subject contesting these ideas and have the volume published. Of course, there is the practical solution. To what extent Professor Tchemodanoff is a Marxist musician or to what extent he has adapted a history of music to the demands of his environment cannot be determined here. Many of his statements follow modern opinions about music history and would not be strongly contested by any reasonable-minded student of the musical art—namely, that without doubt the development of an art and the evolution of its forms and styles are profoundly influenced by parallel social and cultural developments in a community.

We did not have to wait for Professor Tchemodanoff to acquaint us with this fairly patent fact, although it may be admitted that music critics and historians as a class were slow to recognize its fundamental place in any reasoned criticism. But to what an extent the correspondences between music and other arts and ideas can be literally demonstrated is a question yet to be decided. Beethoven had revolutionary emotion in much of his music. So did Verdi. But Beethoven did not imitate a cannon shot when he penned the first four notes of the Fifth symphony, and it is very doubtful whether he had the taking of the Bastile in mind when he composed the finale of that powerful work.

Mr. Tchemodanoff meets this asseveration. "An artist," he says, "as well as a philosopher, does not suspect that his creative ideas are influenced by the social conditions of this or that class. Moreover, he would deny this connection if some one were to point it out to him. He would insist that he was absolutely free in his creation and that he works only in the name of art and his own great ideas. Nevertheless, there is not a single artist, no matter how formally free he may be, who could escape the influence of the ideological atmosphere which surrounds him."

The measure of logic in such paragraphs as this is obscured by other statements typical of the determination of the present Russian régime to twist all facts and ideas to its service. Thus: "The bourgeoisie, true enough, from top to bottom (during the old order) was in accordance with Beethoven's rebellious tendencies, but in the epoch of decisive class struggles it could not think of music, since all its attention was centred upon social questions. As to the petty bourgeoisie, with whom Beethoven was most in accord, it could not give any serious material help to artists. Because of non-recognition, or lack of interest in his work (and both, as we have seen, are determined by the social conditions of the epoch, Beethoven remained forever poor. Also, his unrequited love, which was doomed because of social prejudices and Beethoven's poverty, was, as it is easily seen, directly or indirectly determined by the social conditions of that period during which Beethoven was creating his rebellious sounds."

It is well known that the upper classes in Beethoven's period, and not the lower ones, were quick to understand his genius and to honor the man, even when his unreasonable and arrogant behavior toward them would have instantly alienated any but those who by reason of culture and sensitiveness to the presence of genius were so generous in addition to being well-bred that they more than tolerated Beethoven's gaucheries. As for Beethoven's poverty, his circumstances were far better than those of the great majority of composers of his period.

It remains true that "not one composer was so closely related to the fate of the Revolution as was Beethoven." And that "he remains eloquent on the tribune of the twentieth century." Is his music "still capable of inspiring masses toward revolutionary action"? Did the crowd who stormed the Kremlin do so to the tune of the Ninth symphony? Or was it the Hammerklavier sonata? We thought these works had another significance. We thought Beethoven's battles were fought on other fields, and we do not believe that the author of the last quartets remotely conceived of Marxist propaganda.

It would pay composers and critics in Russia to do a little clearer thinking than they seem to permit themselves in this field. If a comparison is made between the music produced in Russia before the revolution and since the year 1917, the result is merely a humiliating spectacle for the Russian composers of the present day—humiliating because of the crassness, inexpertness and musical emptiness of nearly everything which has come from them. The Russian revolution needs a real musical prophet.

The lesson of this should be clear, which is that music must spring from the composer's consciousness with the same power and rectitude that a plant shows when it pushes up through the soil. There can be no forcing of expression in music, and any self-conscious attempt in this direction is completely powerless when confronted with the secrets of the human soul.

The heroic and altruistic motives back of the Russian revolution were acutely needed. They will profoundly modify, if they do not materially change, the Western world's conception of government and economics. But it must be acknowledged that with this holy and blazing fanaticism there is mingled, particularly when art is discussed, an incredible lot of nonsense, and that the Communist as a type is lamentably lacking in the conception of beauty and the sense of humor.

July 23, 1933

# Design for A Russian Setting

By LEE SIMONSON.

WHENEVER we speculate on life after a social revolution—and some form of social revolution seems to us more imminent today than it did five years ago—we are inclined to worry about the fate of the artist in the new state. We are certain he will lose his freedom, which with us at present consists largely of the privilege of doing hack work or starving. We are sure propaganda will destroy art, though our critics are constantly reminding us how little art, even without propaganda, we have produced. We are certain that a State determined to give work and food to every citizen will neglect the opportunities for culture that 10,000,000 or so of our unemployed no longer have, and which if they did have would consist of a weekly seat at the movies.

The Soviet theatre provides an effective answer to our doubts. For, under State capitalism, it does precisely what private capitalism pretends to do for the theatre and invariably fails to accomplish. Whatever the economic crisis the Soviet theatres have the wherewithal to stage superb productions. Classics, for which we cannot found endowed theatres, are revived regularly. Where a production is staged it is completely restaged. A fresh imagination directs the play: there are no second-hand ideas in evidence, no second-hand scenery and no second-hand costumes from the wardrobe room. Two opera houses, performing regularly in both Moscow and Leningrad, keep every opera of importance, whether native or foreign, in the repertory for a full season, which is more than our millionaires have succeeded in doing even after passing the hat. There are ballets—both classic and modern—circuses, vaudeville, comic operas, music halls and playhouses for children as well. In the theatres there is not one school of acting, or one theory of production, but a dozen—all accepted, and all successful so that one can often see the same play in turn done according to realistic, constructivist or expressionist principles, by different companies in different theatres, each renowned for its particular artistic method.

The competitive scramble of private capitalism has all but emptied our theatres. In Leningrad and Moscow they are full every night. They are free to do Shakespeare or Schiller, Eugene O'Neill or Sophie Treadwell, Russian classics such as Chekhov, Tolstoy and Ostrovsky, or plays by authors discovered the day before yesterday. And singers, composers, directors, actors and playwrights, designers and dancers by the hundred are kept continuously employed, receive higher wages and earn better livings than many of the commissars. This continued vitality and prosperity have been characteristic of the Soviet theatre before the Five-Year Plan, since the Five-Year Plan, in fact, without interruption for the last ten years.

I saw the Soviet theatre at first hand for the first time in 1926, in May at the end of a theatrical season, when most of the theatres in Moscow had already closed. The country was just beginning to get on its feet; the wreckage of the first of the White invasions had been just about cleared up; from my train window going south from Kiev to Odessa I saw an iron bridge still sprawling on its side, where it had been blown during the repulse of Petlura. But the theatre had a vitality that it rarely achieved anywhere under private capitalism in its heyday. The amazing variety of productions offered by the theatres was such that I was as distracted as the proverbial centipede before I could decide every night which one to go to see. And I ended by going to two plays a night, preferring to see half a production rather than miss it entirely. Ten days of this was more than enough to make obvious the fact that the iron hand of political dogma had not destroyed variety or individuality of artistic expression; in fact, it had encouraged it. There was far more subservience to formula, imposed from below if not from above, in the theatres of Paris, London and New York that I had just left. Even in the repertory of any single playhouse in Moscow there was more variety of method, more unabashed experiment and a greater range of subject-matter in the course of a week than repertory theatres in the rest of Europe or this country ordinarily achieved in the course of years.

* * *

You could have seen, in 1926, Eugene O'Neill's "The Hairy Ape" at Tairov's Karmerny Theatre; Wilde's "Salomé" and Lecoq's operetta "Giroflé-Girofla," with the chorus swinging from standing bars and trapezes as a substitute for dance routine. At Meyerhold's constructivist theatre "Roar China" was blazing its denunciation of foreign imperialism, and was followed by a revival of a Russian classic, Ostrovsky's "The Forest." At Stanislavsky's Moscow Art Theatre another Ostrovsky classic, Maeterlinck's "The Blue Bird," and the story of an unsuccessful revolt of liberal-minded nobles under Alexander I. At the Theatre of the Revolution the story of an incident of the revolution of 1917 acted with violent realism. At the opera houses a stupendous production of "Lohengrin," Tchaikovsky's "Pique Dame," with its background of prerevolutionary luxury, and ballets—traditional classic dancing in "Esmeralda" that filled an entire evening and modern choreography in "Potiphar's Wife." Every performance was played before a packed house and an enthusiastic audience. The vaudeville-circus was so popular I couldn't get a seat, largely on account of a visiting troupe of American Negroes singing and dancing jazz. The commissars who had imported them were said to be disappointed because they neither looked nor behaved like representatives of a subject people.

I have just seen the Soviet theatre at the beginning of a theatrical season (in mid-September) before most of the playhouses were open. Despite successive agricultural crises and the spartan régime that the effort of putting through the Five-Year Plan has imposed on the population, the theatre showed the same amazing vitality and variety. Every theatre was packed with an enthusiastic audience. After 2 o'clock in the afternoon it was difficult to get a seat. I was again hard put to it deciding which of half a dozen productions I would see on any one night, and again was finally forced to go to two a night as I had seven years ago. In Leningrad there was a nightly choice of opera or opera-comique. I could have seen "Pique Dame" still in the repertory. I went instead to a thoroughly modernized "Carmen," an entirely new production of "Boris Godunoff" sung to Mussorgsky's original score, and a revival of "William Tell" so dramatically staged that I forgot how old fashioned the music was.

* * *

But everything was not spectacle. At the Alexandrinsky Theatre I saw "Fear," a merciless but sympathetic study of the plight of a professor of the old régime and his failure, despite his best intentions, to adapt himself to the new order. It was acted with all the subtlety and all the force of traditional realistic methods of acting. I could have seen the same play at the Moscow Art Theatre a week later, but saw instead "The Days of the Turbins," an equally sympathetic study of the dilemma of two Czarist officers during the White invasion of the Ukraine, and "Bread," a picture of the revolt of the die-hard peasants against the Soviet grain collectors, which was as exciting as any melodrama. I missed a dramatization of Dostoivsky's "Crime and Punishment" in order to see a satiric version of "All's Well That Ends Well" elsewhere, and left a revival of Schiller's "Kabale und Liebe" with startlingly decorative sets and resplendent uniforms, acted with melodramatic fervor, to see two acts of Tolstoy's satiric "The Fruits of Enlightenment."

In order to see Stanislavsky's new opera troupe perform "Eugéne Onégin"—a troupe that has been trained to act as well as to sing—I had to miss a performance of the same opera at the big opera house on the same night. I saw one act of Tairov's opening bill, a play dealing with the corruption of a foreign engineer in the Caucasus, and then boarded a sleeper—incidentally as comfortable a sleeping car as I had anywhere else in Europe—which took me to Warsaw. But I saw the models for Tairov's recent productions of "Desire Under the Elms" and "All God's Chillun." Its first-act setting gives a better suggestion of a street under an "L" than any we have ever done here. The photographs of Sophie Treadwell's "Machinal," staged last season, show a background of towering skyscrapers more expressive of architecture than any production this country has ever projected.

* * *

All this was a mere foretaste of the coming season, which will include a production by Tairov to be called "Egyptian Nights." The first part is to be a condensation of Shaw's "Caesar and Cleopatra," the second part Shakespeare's "Antony and Cleopatra" performed in one evening! Meyerhold's new theatre was being rebuilt; the Theatre of the Revolution was being completely renovated and had not yet reopened. There were any number of important companies either on tour or not yet playing, including those given to musical satires and revues in both Leningrad and Moscow. But it was quite as obvious in 1933 as in 1926 that in no country where individualism is still a sacred shibboleth was there as much variety of method, as much liberty to experiment, as much freedom of expression, as much individuality in every form of expression adopted as in the first collectivist State. That conclusion becomes even more obvious after walking through any theatre museum—for every theatre and opera house has its own museum—where models of all its important settings are preserved in chronological order. In 1933 as in 1926 the Soviet theatre is still the most original, the most varied, the most daring and the most imaginative in the modern world.

* * *

It is not my purpose to analyze this in terms of stage-settings. These will be seen at the International Exhibition of Theatre Art that opens at the Museum of Modern Art on Jan. 8, where they will tell their story more vividly than I can here. What I am attempting to describe is the vitality of the Soviet theatre as an institution, its freedom from formula, its ability to avoid falling into grooves, its sense of alternatives, the range of its comment on life whether past or present. For a nation that has destroyed its past more completely than any other nation in the world today, the Soviet theatre manages to preserve the image of the past more faithfully than countries that worship it.

When, as in "Eugéne Onégin" or "Pique Dame," the swank of the old régime has to be revived, it is revived to the hilt of the last sword. The ballroom scene in "Onégin" is brilliant with uniforms and gold lace that would satisfy the ghost of any former governor general. The Byzantine splendor of Boris's court gleams and glows. The soldiers and courtiers of "Kabale und Liebe" were resplendent in patent-leather boots, gold epaulets, sashes and glittering stars and moved with a precision that could evoke a thrill in a Prussian officer eager to revive the military glories of Frederick the Great. It struck me that the audience enjoyed this spectacle quite as much as the singing or the acting and reveled in the opportunity to see in the theatre the glitter and glamour of an aristocratic era that it would never see again. These tyrants and sycophants of past eras of oppression are never caricatured or belittled. They are played "straight"; they have all the pomp, the dignity and presence they once had when they were rulers of the earth. When they are caricatured like the gentry in Tolstoy's "Fruits of Enlightenment" it is almost precisely to the degree that Tolstoy's text caricatures them as pretentious fatheads and stuffed shirts. The Soviet theatres provide a more convincing and historically accurate projection of former aristocracy than one could find anywhere else.

What they provide, however, is something more than an excuse for a costume parade or a resplendent stage picture. Soviet audiences transfer to every story of former oppression of an underdog, collective and individual, their emotions of having sustained a successful revolution. That is the excuse for reviving so banal an opera as "William Tell." The more authentically projected the tyrant and his bullying men-at-arms, the more authentic becomes their vicarious release: they have ratified, with their applause, the overthrow of a veritable oppressor, not a man of straw. Precisely because Czar Boris is invested with all his traditional pomp, does the moment become dramatic when they can indict him in the person of the mad monk who faces the Czar in front of the Kremlin and accuses him of murder. The enemy can be re-indicted and reconquered every night. The audience is able to point an accusing finger with impunity and gets an additional kick out of this scene because it was never allowed to be performed under the Czarist régime. When the hero of "Kabale und Liebe" defies his father and rushes off shouting something to the effect that he will tell the world what tyrants are, the house broke out into cheers and wild applause.

* * *

Whatever the precise control of official censorship may be—and there is no doubt that lately the censorship has been considerably relaxed—the Soviet theatre, in dealing with the actualities of its own revolution, seems singularly tolerant. In "Fear" the cards are not stacked against the professor, although he is an intellectual of the old régime: he is not presented as a hopeless relic. His struggle to adapt himself to the new state is genuine enough to make real drama. The force of the play's conclusion is rather that he is, in spite of his best efforts, hopelessly conditioned and that there is no alternative finally to putting him out of the way. Having read the play in translation and being exhausted that evening by too much theatre-going, I left before the last act. The cloak room attendant, an elderly man, protested vehemently. "You must go now?" [my guide translated for me]. "You're missing the best part—where they prove the professor is wrong." The play was more exciting even to a class-conscious proletarian because the opposition had had its say.

* * *

But even more surprising is the tolerance and detachment of "The Days of the Turbins," the story of two brothers, Czarist officers at the end of the great war during the struggle for Kiev. German regiments and their German staffs desert them. They are left with a company of cadets in the military school while Petlura's White Army approaches unopposed. The cadets, in a pathetic outburst of boyish fanaticism, welcome a Thermopolae. They assemble singing the Czarist hymns, prepared to die gloriously. The brothers force them at pistol point to rip off their uniforms and save themselves by flight. One brother is killed during the bombardment. The other escapes and remains in hiding in civilian clothes in his sister's apartment. Petlura and his White Army men mean nothing to him. The Czar has abdicated. There is no one to whom he can give allegiance, no cause which he can any longer acknowledge or for which he can risk his life. The last act is largely genre comedy as he and his friends dress a Christmas tree and celebrate the happy termination of the sister's love affair. But just before the final curtain the strains of the Internationale are heard in the street and word comes that the Soviet troops are entering Kiev. There is a long pause, as the last of the Turbins realizes his complete isolation and then remarks with listless melancholy: "For some this is a beginning, for others an epilogue."

The brothers are portrayed as courageous, intrepid and thoroughly likable human beings. In fact, the villains of the piece are the German staff who scuttle ignominiously rather than make a last stand, who betray the Czarist regiments they are commanding, and a brother-in-law who scuttles with them in order to save his skin. What gets over in both these plays is a respect for any individual courageous enough to risk his life even for the wrong cause. In 1926 I had seen the wreck of the railway bridge still sprawling across the embankment where it had been blown during the days of the Turbins. Seven years later the Soviet theatre can project with a certain degree of compassion the wreck of lost loyalties.

December 10, 1933

# REALISM IS URGED IN SOVIET WRITING

**Less Propaganda and Fuller Portrayals Forecast by Authors' Congress.**

**SATIRE ALSO EMPHASIZED**

**Moscow Press Gives Greatest Prominence to Proceedings of the Convention.**

By WALTER DURANTY.

Special Cable to THE NEW YORK TIMES.

MOSCOW, Aug. 24.—The Soviet press is treating the first All-Union Congress of Writers, now in session in Moscow, as an event of outstanding national importance, which, perhaps, it is.

Thus Pravda, which is the official mouthpiece of the all-powerful Communist party and which is probably read by 20,000,000 Russians daily, devoted six full pages yesterday to a report of the discussions of the congress.

If one could imagine three-quarters of a daily edition of THE NEW YORK TIMES taken up exclusively by news of an American writers' congress it would be possible to get an idea of the importance which the Soviet rulers attach to the process of forming the Soviet national mind along new lines.

**Wide Range Covered.**

Joseph Stalin has said, "the writer is the engineer of the spirit," and his phrase, which expresses the dominant Soviet theory of the need for technical knowledge, has become a slogan for the writers' congress. The congress includes all forms of literary activity, from books, the press, the theatre, movies and the radio to poems and songs of the minor nationalities in the Soviet Union.

Underlying or inspiring this congress are three essential factors. The first is that the population, which previously was 80 per cent illiterate, has now become 80 per cent literate and is incredibly eager to get reading material.

The second factor is that this change from illiteracy to literacy has taken place in a Socialist State, which deliberately aims at controlling and creating public opinion through its writers of all categories. Add to that the fact that 70 per cent of Soviet writers today are themselves Communists—that is to say, in sympathy with the sentiment that the authorities are trying to create.

Thirdly, the Soviet system appears to be providing a solution for the problem that has proved a stumbling block for the British Empire from Ireland to India despite British genius for compromise—namely, adjustment of the relations between "subject," or minor, nationalities and the central rulers.

The real secret of Soviet adjustment lies in the Communist party, which makes no distinctions of race or color. One might almost say that the new Russian conscience would esteem a Communist Hottentot, provided he were a real Communist, higher than Dr. Nicholas Murray Butler.

**Minority Races Encouraged.**

From this premise the Kremlin proceeds to give the utmost encouragement to the writers of the minor nationalities, provided always that they are, if not Communists, at least not in conflict with the Communist party line. The Communist party line thus becomes the axis of adjustment between the minor nationalities and the Soviet State.

So, putting these three factors together, one may take for granted, first, that the Kremlin knows what it wants the writers to write; second, that the writers themselves want to write it, and third, that the red thread of the Communist party in Soviet life provides the unified spirit according to which writing should be written.

But that does not solve the problem that is the fundamental one of the present congress—namely, What is the best way to do it? One thing seems clear enough and the congress appears to have realized it—that overmuch propaganda is not the best way.

There is a lot of loose talk in the congress about the marvelous opportunity that Soviet writers now have for realism and writing the basic facts about humanity as compared with the fake and falsehood of writing in bourgeois countries. As if Rabelais or Swift or Shakespeare or Goethe had never existed.

**More Satire Urged.**

Nevertheless, despite this loose talk there are some real ideas, after all, and talk, however loose, may help to clarify ideas. Soviet writing, one gathers, is beginning to contemplate a jump from partisanship propaganda and partial realism to the realism of painting the whole picture as it is, rather than part of the picture or the picture as the writer wants it to appear.

It is not a mere accident, for instance, that this congress is presided over by Maxim Gorki, who was always a rebel against the old social order and depicted the life of the "underdog" with stark fidelity. Nor is it an accident that the most popular Soviet "columnist," Mikhail Koltzoff, made a plea for satire in Soviet writing and repeated the old truism that ridicule may be a mighty weapon in the cause of truth and progress.

According to the Marxist philosophy, the occasion produces the man, but so far it must be admitted there are no signs of the genius who can symbolize and synthesize the new Russia.

August 26, 1934

# SOVIET CINEMA NEWS

## Career of Sergei Eisenstein, Who Is Now Preparing His Film, "Moscow"

Moscow.

If you ring the bell four times, Sergei Eisenstein, whose name is synonymous with Soviet cinema, will himself come to the door to let you in. He will invite you into a typical Moscow flat in which live several families, where he occupies one fair-sized room. The walls of his room are lined with books; on a large, flat-topped desk there is a perpetual disorder of stacks of current literary journals and books sent to him from friends he has made throughout the world. In the corner stands his bed. A few bric-à-bac which he brought home with him from Mexico hang on the walls. This is his home and his workshop.

Thirteen years ago, when the period of civil war was over and Eisenstein was demobilized from the Red Army, he came to live in this room in Moscow. At that time he was 22. He had broken with his life as a student of engineering and architecture. In the period of post-war revolutionary reconstruction he drew upon his talent as a painter and entered the "Proletcult" (organization for proletarian culture), where he made stage settings. Later he assumed the leadership of the organization and remained with it for three years; his next step was in the direction of the cinema. Eisenstein has a sentimental attachment for his room in Moscow, where he thought out his first cinema problems; the large desk near the window has charted the progress of his artistic career.

In the Soviet Union, Eisenstein's creative growth is not measured as the abstract artistic development of an individual. Here Eisenstein is judged only in relation to, and against, the social background of the Russian revolution. Eisenstein has himself expressed his position in the Soviet cinema by this statement:

"In the Soviet Union no artist, if he wishes to grow creatively, can cut himself off from the task of building socialism. To do so would be tantamount to cutting one's self off from life. The period we are living in represents the epoch of the struggle for a classless society; the artist who does not take part in that struggle blocks his own creativeness, for he has thereby cut himself off from all contact with reality."

Paradoxical as it may seem (to those who hold the opinion that Soviet films are only propagandistic and therefore not art), scenarists and directors are regarded as artists here. And Eisenstein is considered as outstanding among them. It has even been said that in the field of cinema art he holds a place comparable to that which is held in literature by Russia's great revolutionary poet, Mayakovsky. Eisenstein is thought of as the classicist of social cinema art—defined as art which fulfills a great social need, in contradistinction to films which are made for an individual type of film patron. Eisenstein's "Potemkin," "Ten Days That Shook the World" and "October," pictures which give the content and movement of the social revolution, are examples of social monumental films.

When Eisenstein returned to Russia in 1931 from his unsuccessful and now well-publicized trip to Hollywood and Mexico he credited that experience to education and settled down to new tasks. He wanted to produce a comedy. He planned to step out of his rôle as a creator of epics and try his hand at a new medium. The Russian press began to speak of an Eisenstein comedy which had the strange title "M. M. M." No one seemed to know what the theme was about and the director was unwilling to explain. "M. M. M." was never made and to this day Eisenstein will not lift the mysterious veil surrounding the comedy. However, in conversation he has said that making "M. M. M." would have been a luxury for him. The need of the times was another historical film and the comedy had to be abandoned.

"Moscow."

Eisenstein is now working on a new film. At no time in his career has he attempted so colossal a canvas as his forthcoming picture, "Moscow." He is gathering material and in the Fall of 1934 will probably be ready to begin production. Two articles written by the Soviet director, in which he makes known his preliminary concept of the film, have already appeared in the press, one in Lituraturni Gazetta (Literary Gazette), the other in Sovietskaya Iskustva (Soviet Art). Superficially Eisenstein's next picture can be described as a history of Moscow. But his own written statement is more revealing.

"Moscow as a theme," he wrote, "is most singular. Moscow is the centre of the Socialist future of the world. Moscow as a city is a living example of the road leading to a new social order."

In his cinematographic history of Moscow Eisenstein wishes to give form to the theory of the class struggle. Beginning with Moscow in the period of serfdom he will trace its history through the biography of four generations whose lives reveal the interaction of what the director regards as the opposing forces of society—the exploiters and the exploited. Out of this struggle emerges the victorious proletariat. Eisenstein's newest film will undoubtedly overflow all accepted cinematographic boundaries. A study of what he has already written about "Moscow" indicates that he is groping his way toward new cinema horizons.

In the realm of cinema science

Eisenstein is Russia's foremost theoretician. Through his years of film experience and his study of art he has painstakingly gathered a mass of notes out of which he has created, as he terms it, "the granite of cinema science." He plans to expound his theories in three volumes, the first of which will be ready for publication in January, to be printed in English and Russian.

**Eisenstein's Lectures.**

Eisenstein's scholarly tomes are not altogether the result of quiet meditation in an ivory tower. In his very busy existence he also finds time to be on the faculty of GIK (State Institute of Cinematography) and particularly during this past year he has spent a great deal of his time lecturing at the institute. Many of the conclusions which he arrives at in his book are a synthesis of discussions with his students and other members of the faculty, among whom are Pudovkin, Dovshenko and Romm. His association with the institute is characteristic of his own point of view and the point of view of the Soviet cinema industry as a whole. Eisenstein believes that personal successes are not sufficient, and that to guard the method of one's individual work jealously is not consistent with Soviet ideology. There are no secrets of the trade and all artistic and technical knowledge is pooled and passed on to the young students.

There are 600 students at GIK, as it is called here. They come from factories and offices from every corner of the Soviet Union and range in ages from 18 to 30. Among them are represented thirty-six Russian national minorities — Uzbeks, Georgians, Bashkirs, Tartars; and even a sprinkling of foreigners from abroad. Seventy-five per cent of the students live on government stipends and for the most part occupy student dormitories where they lead a Spartan existence.

The training courses are for directors, camera men, scenarists, actors and administrators. For directors the course is four years, for others it is three. The curriculum for all students includes among their special interests courses in political economy, the history of the Communist party and Leninism. Budding directors study psychology, sociology of art, music, literature, painting, scenario writing, theory of directing, work with actors and physical training. Komsomols (members of the Young Communist League) are given preference when there is a vacancy at the institute and they always constitute the major part of the student body.

BELLA KASHIN.

December 17, 1933

# 'FAIRY TALE' FILMS BERATED IN SOVIET

## Version of 'Ivan the Terrible' Banned as 'Anti-Historical' —5-Year Plan Stressed

## MOVIES CALLED A 'WEAPON'

### Episodes of Recent War, Job of Reconstruction Fixed as Subjects for 1946-47

By Wireless to THE NEW YORK TIMES.

MOSCOW, July 7—The second part of Sergei Eisenstein's three-part film, "Ivan the Terrible," on the life and times of the medieval Czar will not be released for distribution anywhere, Culture and Life, a weekly newspaper issued by the propaganda and agitation board of the Central Committee of the Communist party, has announced in its current issue.

Although there has been no official comment beyond this as yet, it is understood that work will not be started on the third and final part.

The ban was applied as the result of what the newspaper calls the "anti-historical and anti-artistic viewpoint of the film's second part, and its failure to portray "contemporary realism."

Mr. Eisenstein himself is still convalescing from a heart attack in a hospital near Moscow.

Oddly, heart attacks seem to haunt those interested in the life of Ivan the Terrible. Alexei Tolstoy suffered a heart attack just after he had finished the second volume of his trilogy written around Ivan's life, and Nicolai Khmelov, the actor portraying Ivan in the play written by Tolstoy, had a heart attack on the set one day. Mr. Eisenstein's attack came just after he had finished cutting Part Two of the film.

According to the newspaper, "Ivan the Terrible," is "cold and passionless historism."

**"Fairy Tale" Themes Assailed**

"Contrary to historic truth, Ivan the Terrible has not been shown as a progressive statesman, but as a maniac and like a scoundrel who behaves in a crazy manner, surrounded by many young cutthroats he has assembled. It is clear that this film is anti-historical and anti-artistic and could not be released for distribution," the paper says.

A long denunciation of the current trend of film producers to make pictures around the lives of historical and literary persons, and "fairy tale themes" was included in the newspaper article. These, it was felt, impede the portrayal of Soviet life of today and lack realism.

The Soviet film industry was warned: "The cinema is a sharp ideological party weapon, and departure from contemporary life would mean the loss of its principal valuable qualities."

What the board wants to see are pictures about "simple Soviet people, who are the real creators of history."

The newspaper revealed that the Council of Ministers and the party's Central Committee had approved the production of films this year and next in which valor in war and loyalty to the Soviet Union would be the main themes.

At present, it said, producers are interested in pictures that fail to make audiences think and are concerned with "insignificant topics." Comedies are classed as "primitive and bad."

**New Themes Are Functional**

Here are the themes that will be developed by Soviet producers in 1946 and 1947: The history of the Soviet State and Socialist development; the Great Patriotic War, that is, World War II; the development of the post-war economy and the rehabilitation of occupied areas; the work of Soviet intellectuals and scientists; the lives of the people in Latvia, Estonia and Lithuania; the smashing of the German armies at Stalingrad, Leningrad and in the Crimea; engineers who increase the technical efficiency of the Soviet Union; collective farmers and their lives under German occupation; the work of Partisan fighters on the restoration of collective farms; mother heroines, that is, women who have reared ten children; oil and metal workers; Georgian fruit farms and Uzbek collective farms.

The films will all be connected with the Five Year Plan, which affects every ramification of Soviet life today. But every film must be "ideological and a highly artistic production," the newspaper warns.

The program, as outlined in Culture and Life, will serve as an important propaganda aid in the completion of the Five Year Plan, toward which all Soviet efforts now are aimed.

Since the plan was announced, Moscow newspapers have featured at least four columns each day on it, exhorting the workers for greater and greater production and emphasizing how important it is for the Soviet Union to overhaul the United States lead in heavy industrial production.

July 8, 1946

# RUSSIAN MAGAZINE ORDERED TO CLOSE

## Second Severely Criticized for Publishing 'Decadent' and 'Bourgeois' Literature

By DREW MIDDLETON
Special to THE NEW YORK TIMES.

MOSCOW, Aug. 21—The literary magazine Leningrad has been suspended and Zvezda, another literary magazine also published in Leningrad, has been severely criticized by the Central Committee of the All-Union Communist party as a result of their publication of stories and poems described as "ideologically harmful * * * anti-Soviet attacks * * * ideologically alien."

This action was announced on the front page of Pravda this morning in a two-column article in bold face type. The article was reprinted from yesterday's edition of Culture and Life, publication of the Propaganda and Agitation Committee of the Central Committee.

The Central Committee also confirmed the appointment of A. M. Yegolin as chief editor of Zvezda. He will also continue as vice chief of the propaganda department of the central committee.

The committee's action is of great importance to the future development of Russian literature along the "principles of Leninism." In today's Pravda article these were reaffirmed. "Our journals, be they scientific or artistic, cannot be nonpolitical and stand aside from politics," it said.

**Two Writers Barred**

Mikhail Zostchenko, a writer, and Anna Akhmatova, a poet, were severely criticized in an article and the new editor was instructed to bar their writings in future in obedience to the Central Committee's injunction to "correct the line of this journal." Zvezda has recently "published many ideal-less and ideologically harmful articles," Pravda reported, and made a "gross error" in publishing the work of Mr. Zostchenko, "whose works are alien to Soviet literature."

According to the article, Mr. Zostchenko made a specialty of writing "empty, vulgar stories * * * of advocating rotten stupidity, vulgarity and political indifference calculated to disorientate our youth and to poison their minds. He paints the Soviet order and people in a distorted form, libelously describing the Soviet people as primitive, uncultured, foolish people with provincial tastes and morals. Zostchenko's viciously hooligan description of our actual life is accompanied by anti-Soviet attacks."

This is the most severe criticism leveled at a Russian writer in many years and may well presage the start of a drive for "efficiency" in literature as well as in industry and agriculture with a general demand that Russian writers rededicate themselves to the principles of Leninism and Stalinism and do their utmost in their writings to speed the success of the present five-year plan.

**Poetry Called Decadent**

Zvezda also popularized the work of Miss Akhamatova, whose works are a "typical representative of empty ideal-less poetry, alien to our people." Her poetry is "saturated" with a spirit of pessimism and decadence, reflecting the tastes of out-of-date salon poetry, which has frozen on the basis of a bourgeois-aristocratic esthetic and decadence—"art for art's sake."

Miss Akhmatova's poetry, it is charged, is harmful to Russian youth and "cannot be tolerated in Soviet literature." The frequent use of the writings of Mr. Zostchenko and Miss Akhmatova introduced "elements of ideological dispersion and disorganization" among Leningrad writers, the article continued, and articles and stories "cultivating a spirit of worship of modern bourgeois culture alien to the Soviet people" began to appear.

Such articles lowered the magazines' "ideological level" and permitted the penetration of "articles alien to the ideological sense." Pravda said that the Central Committee had pointed out that Leningrad was "particularly badly edited," for, like Zvezda, it permitted the publication of stories "imbued with the spirit of worshipping everything foreign."

August 22, 1946

# Science—and Ideology—in Soviet Russia

**Russian scientists are servants of the state and in their work must follow Marxian laws.**

By WALDEMAR KAEMPFFERT

WHERE does Russian science stand today? That question has particular importance because of a second question: Can Russia produce the atomic bomb? These questions are not raised in Paris or at the meetings of the United Nations, but they are surely in the minds of Byrnes, Attlee, Bevin, Evatt and others who are attempting to shape mankind's destiny.

Russia's achievements in science have been great. The Russians maintain that this success must be attributed to the acceptance of Marxist principles. There is no evidence to bear them out. The record of capitalistic science is equally brilliant. Soviet science has been a success not because it is shot through and through with Marxism, but in spite of it. Its results must be attributed entirely to organization, planning and centralized direction of a type that would be abhorrent in a democracy that still believes in free enterprise both in business and in research.

The results achieved by Soviet science are such that it seems certain Russia can develop an atomic bomb in not too long a time. The physicists who developed the bomb and who testified at Washington before several Congressional committees were almost unanimous in declaring that in a few years — the estimates varied from three to ten—any nation with the requisite knowledge and the technical resources could match our own achievement. Only a few scientists deny that Russia has the knowledge and technical resources, and even this group, which is not composed of physicists, gives Russia twenty years in which to make atomic bombs.

This matter of the bomb is of importance, for the reason that the release of energy from matter calls for scientific attainments of the highest order. The quality of Russian science can therefore be appraised by reviewing what has been done in atomic physics. Recently Dr. Gerald Oster of Princeton published such a review. His survey leaves no doubt that since 1932, the year when the neutron was discovered, Russian physicists have been hard at work on the atom.

ONE of Russia's best men, Dr. Ivanenko, "was the first to propose on well-founded theoretical grounds the present picture of the nucleus as composed of protons and neutrons"—a picture indispensable in duplicating our success. The theory of nuclear fission with which the names of Niels Bohr and J. A. Wheeler are associated was presented independently by the Russian, J. Fraenkel, in 1939, and that theory was applied in producing the material with which we load atomic bombs. The Russians do not know today as much as we, the British or the Canadians know about atomic bombs, but foremost scientists in this country say that Mr. Molotov's was no empty boast.

HOW is the quality of Soviet science not only in physics but in other fields to be appraised? Partly by the testimony of eminent scientists who have visited Russian laboratories and talked with the directors, partly by what the Russians have published. The visitors have recorded their impressions in the British scientific weekly Nature, to which every scientist turns for the first announcements of new discoveries in any field of science; and the Russians have published their accomplishments—not propaganda but sober, detailed accounts of techniques and results—in the same medium and in their own journals.

It is not difficult for an expert to evaluate what has thus been revealed. As soon as a scientist states in Nature or in any other reputable scientific periodical that he has discovered a new property of the cosmic rays or that he has developed a serum which will cure a disease, his experiments are repeated and a confirmation or denial appears. Whether claims are made by Russians, Englishmen, Frenchmen or Americans, they are subjected to merciless scrutiny. Russian science has met that scrutiny.

DR. V. K. ZWORYKIN, research director of the Radio Corporation's Laboratories and the man who put television on its feet, testifies to the high state of Russian electronics not only in radio but in metallurgical heating and industry. Dr. Charles E. Kellogg, the United States Department of Agriculture's Chief of the Division of Soil Survey, has nothing but praise for what Soviet Russia has done in soil science. Dr. W. A. Wooster finds that in crystallography Soviet physicists are the peers if not the superiors of their counterparts in Great Britain and the United States. Julian Huxley has an equally high opinion of Soviet biology. Dr. E. Rock Carling, a member of a British Surgical Mission to Russia, is convinced that Russian military medicine and surgery is in every way equal to that of the West and in some respects superior. Dr. E. M. Crowther of the Rothamsted Experiment Station speaks of "the high standard of work maintained in agrochemistry and of the revolutionary theories evolved by Russians engaged in what they call 'the chemization of socialist agriculture.'"

A spokesman for Russian science — Prof. Peter Kapitsa, physicist.

ALL this does not mean that Russian science is perfect. In some fields it lags; in others it leads the world. The progress made in twenty-five years was reviewed in all fields of Russian science as recently as last year in Nature. Drawing on the knowledge of the world and importing much apparatus it needed, Soviet Russia started virtually from scratch and in that short period made a record that has never been matched by any country.

In 1915 Czarist Russia had only 150 research centers, and these did virtually nothing to improve the country socially. Today there are over 2,250 scientific institutions in Soviet Russia, and the number of research scientists and engineers is well over 40,000.

State science is pursued in Soviet Russia on an unprecedented scale. At the outset (1927) Lenin and his associates decided that the individualistic method of research was too haphazard. Moreover, it led to the exploitation of physics and chemistry, in which profits lie, to the neglect of biology. Research was therefore to be conducted on all fronts. It was to be left not to individualists like Franklin or Faraday who followed their own bent or to inventors like Bell or Edison, but to laboratories, all organized and directed to carry out a plan.

The strategy and tactics of this huge organization are laid down by two important bodies. One is the Academy of Sciences, the other the State Planning Commission. Both are integral parts of the Government. The two are separate in function but one in purpose. The Academy rules in science, makes national surveys of resources and reports what can probably be done to reach the goal set by a given five-year plan; the commission formulates and carries out the plan. From one end of the country to the other there is social and economic purpose in science and direction from on high.

UNDER such a system can science be free? The Russians insist that their scientists are as free as any in the world. By "freedom" evidently the privilege of an investigator to solve an assigned problem in his own way is meant. Nothing is said of the ideological compulsion to which every scientist and every factory worker is subjected. Professor Peter Kapitsa, one of Soviet Russia's most distinguished physicists, states that "the Academy is called upon to direct all our science ideologically from top to bottom," and that "each of its separate institutes must pursue the same policy."

What does Kapitsa mean? He means the compulsory acceptance of Marxism, the belief in "class science." All this is based on dialectical materialism, the philosophy of strife formulated by Marx and Engels. The strife is between opposites, such as capital and labor. One opposite is called the "thesis," the other the "antithesis," and out of the struggle of the two comes the synthesis, which is something new in quality.

WHAT has this to do with scientific research? Nothing. It is not of the slightest help in dealing with atoms or plastics. Yet this Marxist doctrine of dialectical materialism must be accepted by every scientist; the alternative is disgrace, even imprisonment.

Politics and science are therefore inseparable in Soviet Russia. A scientist may be free to work out his problem in his own way, but he is not free to think as he pleases on political matters either inside or outside of the laboratory. A departure from the Marxist norm means the end of a career, unless there is an abject recantation and a promise of good behavior in the future. Dismissed for what is regarded as "counter-revolutionary" thinking he is helpless. For in Soviet Russia all research is government research, and all laboratories are closed to suspected "counter-revolutionists."

The Communist party is the severest critic of research policies. It has its organ, Pravda, in which dissatisfaction with Soviet science is usually first voiced, and other organs in which the work of research laboratories is praised or condemned. In every institute it has a cell to elucidate the meaning of the party, of the Government's prevailing policy, of Stalin's latest pronouncement. It lectures on Marx, on philosophy, on literature, on history and the correct Marxian interpretation of science. It is as much responsible for the success or the failure to achieve expected scientific results as the director of an institute.

According to J. G. Crowther, an English Communist who has visited Russia many times, all this lecturing "deepens the workers' understanding of the value of science and its role in social affairs," and he adds with a straight face: "It reveals, too, often unconsciously, the tendencies of the participator's doubts [in discussions that follow lectures]. Saboteurs may be discovered through the suggestiveness of their philosophical doctrines."

EVEN in Soviet Russia, with its one-party system, politics changes its thinking. Hence every laboratory worker keeps his ear to the ground, and hence the eminent physicist or biologist in high favor today may be indicted and on trial tomorrow. All this is puzzling to Americans who know nothing of Republican or Democratic science and who are reconciled to avowed Communists in professorial chairs. Steinmetz was a Socialist whose views did not prevent the General Electric Company from making the most of his rare scientific gifts, but a "bourgeois" Steinmetz in Soviet Russia is simply unthinkable.

The history of Soviet science speaks for itself in this political respect. Between 1917 and 1922, a period when it was necessary to make the most of the few trained Czarist scientists who were pliable enough to declare their allegiance to Marx, there was considerable liberality. After the New Economic Policy (1922-1927) was formulated the party asserted itself. The Academy was overhauled and suspected dissenters were dismissed or imprisoned. To prove their faith the zealots wrote articles on "Marxism and Surgery," "The Dialectics of Graded Steel," the "Dialectics of the Internal Combustion Engine," the dialectics of anything.

WHEN, in 1927, Trotsky lost his struggle with Stalin and was expelled from the party there were wholesale dismissals and imprisonments of scientists. From 1929 on, the year of Trotsky's exile, the persecution of "enemies of the people" increased in scope and intensity. Shostakovich was denounced for "decadent bourgeois formalism and naturalism" and his music disbarred and only before the war was he restored to favor. "Enemies" were discovered in the Pulkova Astronomical Observatory and "eliminated"; the director of the Soil Institute, Polynov, was disgraced because he was held to be a member of a counter-revolutionary organization; some distinguished physicists, Luzin among them, were accused of "wrecking mathematics and the physical sciences."

TOWARD the end of the Trotsky purge the Astronomical Division of the Academy of Sciences passed some impassioned resolutions, which were signed by the president and eighteen members and which declared that "modern bourgeois cosmogony is in a state of deep ideological confusion resulting from its refusal to accept the only true dialectic-materialistic concept, namely, the infinity of the universe with respect to space as well as time," and a belief in relativity was branded as counter-revolutionary.

Agol, an able biologist who had worked in America for a time, was arrested for "direct connection with the Trotskyite murderers." Nikolai Bukharin, Soviet Russia's leading theorist and one of Lenin's favorites, was expelled from the Academy for having "seized the leading posts in the Academy and with the acquiescence of the former directorate influenced its whole life and directed the efforts of that scientific center."

Nikolai K. Koltzov was denounced as "a fascist traitor" by the Academy of Agricultural Sciences because of his belief in eugenics, which to the party is merely a bourgeois invention to perpetuate class snobbery and ancestor worship. Psychologists must eschew the introspective approach (the study of mind as such) and confine themselves to behaviorism. Intelligence tests for children were abolished by decree of the party (1936) after Prof. G. P. Blonsky in a characteristic retraction declared: "I knew all along that bourgeois pedology does not accept the Marxist basis, but I continued using tests and measurements which are a means of bolstering up the exploiting class."

THE case of genetics, the science of heredity, is the one of which we have heard most. Biologists generally accept the theories of the Abbé Gregor Mendel as they were developed by Nobel Prize Winner Thomas Hunt Morgan and his school. The gene is to life what the atom is to inanimate matter. It accounts for stature, for hair and eye color, for any physical characteristic of a plant or animal. Exercise can modify man's stature, dyes can change the color of his hair, but none of these changes can be transmitted to succeeding generations. Cut off the tails of mice for scores of generations and their descendants will still be born with tails.

THE leading Russian figure in genetics was the late N. I. Vavilov, whose work is highly regarded the world over. His opponent was T. E. Lysenko, a plant cultivator of the Burbank type, who dismissed heredity as a "bourgeois fraud" and asserted that he had improved strains of grains, vegetables and fruits merely by controlling such environmental factors as temperature, moisture and nutrition, and that his new varieties bred true—a revival of the doctrine of Lamarck long repudiated in the best biological circles.

The controversy between Vavilov and Lysenko was staged by the party organ

Under the Marxist Banner, and it was followed much as a Presidential election is followed here. At its height the Government decided not to hold the International Genetics Congress scheduled for 1937. The reason given was inadequate preparation. In 1939 Vavilov was forbidden to attend the International Congress of Genetics held at Edinburgh, even though he had accepted the presidency months before. Vavilov vanished. His name did not appear in the footnotes of papers published in botanical periodicals. It was as if he had never lived. He died in 1943 or 1945 under circumstances that the Soviet Government has not seen fit to reveal.

Since the all-powerful party varies its policy from time to time, foreign observers are puzzled by its seeming inconsistencies. In periods of political calm there is more tolerance than in periods of tension. So it happens that despite the Vavilov-Lysenko controversy, which started while the hunt for Trotskyites was still in full cry, genetics is taught in the University of Moscow, and there are as many geneticists in the U.S.S.R. as there are in this country.

SIMILARLY, there are able relativists, despite the Academy's attack on Einstein's theories. In the last few years the political sea has been fairly serene, which helps to explain why Prof. Peter Kapitsa ventured in 1943 to voice some dissatisfaction with the Soviet fusion of theory and practice and to stress some of the shortcomings of the practical men with whom he had to deal in factories when he tried to develop a turbo-compressor needed to supply oxygen for the generation of gas in sealed coal mines.

English converts to communism are not wholly satisfied with this conception of freedom, if freedom it can be called. One of the most ardent of these, the distinguished crystallographer, Prof. J. D. Bernal, decries blind obedience to higher authority because it is likely to end in the Fuehrerprinzip, which is about what has happened in Soviet Russia. There is, moreover, an immense difference between the discipline that a scientist in a democracy imposes on himself and discipline imposed from the outside.

And yet there is the impressive Soviet record of success in science. How is it to be explained? Dialectical materialism is certainly not the answer, since it is of no help in devising or performing an experiment, nor a necessity in planning research. Nor is the abolition of capitalism and free enterprise. We are forced to the conclusion that the organization and the direct application of science are the secret of Soviet success.

We shall have to watch Russian science. It has a plan of research; we have none. It spends a larger proportion of the national income on science than we do. In metallurgy, crystallography, in soil science, in geochemistry, it has already surpassed us. In twenty-five years who knows but that it may outstrip ours? A race is already in progress—a race between Russian collectivistic and American individualistic research.

HOW far can we go in organizing research without sacrificing the principles of democracy and individual initiative? Can we preserve the tradition of freedom in science and still plan, organize and direct research under Government guidance? The atomic bomb, radar, the proximity fuse, TVA, the work of a hundred Government scientific bureaus, the control of epidemics—all came out of planning and concerted effort. Can teamwork give us "fundamental" discoveries without sacrificing scientific freedom?

Despite the industrial evidence that it can, those who oppose teamwork in "pure" science argue that it hampers the isolated genius. The same argument was advanced when the industrial laboratories were established. It was maintained that the highly individualistic inventor must work alone. But industry has proved otherwise. If cancer were to be attacked by the industrial method—and cancer research involves a fundamental study of normal and abnormal growth—something of importance would surely result from the cooperation of physicists, pathologists, biochemists, geneticists and mathematicians. Because planning and teamwork have never been tried here in "fundamental" research of this type, it is illogical to insist that they will not work.

OUR hope lies in a National Science Foundation with broader powers than those specified in the Kilgore Bill recently rejected by Congress. If such a foundation is to serve its purpose, its first task should be the mapping out of all science to reveal gaps in our knowledge that ought to be filled. The map would be kept constantly in mind when a grant of money or a contract for research is made. It would of necessity be flexible and all-embracing so that a good project submitted by some university professor but not so mapped could easily be fitted into the proper niche.

Ideas may originate either in the foundation or in outside laboratories. If a distinguished biologist or chemist declines an invitation to fill a gap in our knowledge, there will be regrets but no compulsion. If he accepts, he will be as free as ever to think and to experiment as he pleases.

Under such a system there is no reason why university professors may not investigate as they do now, why industrial laboratories should not follow their own ways, why philanthropic foundations should not grant money for research. American scientists will have to revise their thinking if such a system is ever introduced.

September 15, 1946

## ZHDANOV DENOUNCED 'BOURGEOIS' WRITERS

Special to THE NEW YORK TIMES.

LONDON, Sept. 21—The Moscow radio gave today for the first time the full text of the now famous lecture by Col. Gen. Andrei A. Zhdanov, chairman of the Soviet of the Union and secretary of the Central Committee of the Communist party, condemning the literary magazines Zvezda and Leningrad for "non-political" writings. The party, among other things, was told that Soviet writers must shun bourgeois culture, with its addiction to gangsters, girls and adultery.

When Pravda last month published the decree condemning the two magazines and their leading writers, it was realized abroad that the move represented an effort to clamp down the lid on literature in the Soviet Union.

The text of General Zhdanov's report issued today shows that it was one of the most important pronouncements on culture to come out of the Soviet Union in years. It took an hour to read over the radio.

"If feudalism and, later on, the bourgeoisie in the periods of their flourishings could create art and literature asserting the new systems and praising the flourishing of these systems," said General Zhdanov in a key passage, "then surely our new socialist system embodying all the best in the history of human civilization and culture is capable of creating the most advanced literature, which will leave far behind the best creations of olden times."

His primary accusation was that the literary group in Leningrad had strayed into "non-political channels, deprived of ideology and principles" and had lost the "sense of responsibility to their people, state and party."

Literature is a duty, said General Zhdanov, and it is up to writers to rebuff the "hideous slanders and attacks against our Soviet culture" and also to expose and attack bourgeois culture.

September 22, 1946.

## Soviet Denounces Its 'Big 3' In Music, Orders a New Line

By The United Press.

MOSCOW, Feb. 11—The Central Committee of the Communist party today accused Russia's three leading composers and the Soviet music world in general of creating and encouraging anti-democratic works.

In a decree behind which lay the latent threat of sterner measures, the committee laid down a four-part program that all concerned—composers, music critics, the Moscow Conservatory and the Arts Committee of the Government—must follow.

Dmitri Shostakovich, Aram Khatchaturian and Sergei Prokofieff, the "big three" whose works are played throughout the world, were attacked, along with four lesser composers — Vissarion Y. Shebalin, Gabriel Popov, Nikolai Miaskovsky and Vano Muradeli.

It was understood that the committee's action was the result of the new opera, "Great Friendship," by Muradeli. This work had its first — and only — rendition at a closed performance in the Bolshoi Theatre here on Nov. 7, the anniversary of the Bolshevik Revolution, with Premier Stalin and other Government leaders present. It was the only work specifically mentioned by the Central Committee.

The opera, composed by a man from the Premier's own native town of Gori, Georgia, was called historically and ideologically incorrect, with "inexpressive, poor, unharmonious, muddled" music.

M. P. Khrapchenko, who was dismissed last week as chairman of the Arts Committee, also was criticized by name.

The Central Committee's program for the Soviet music world—in operatic, symphonic, choral and dance compositions—is:

(1) "The development in Soviet music of realistic direction, the foundation of which is recognition of the huge, progressive role of the classic heritage and especially of the traditions of the Russian musical school."

(2) "The utilization of this heritage and its further development."

(3) "The combination in music of a high content of artistic perfection and musical form."

(4) The recognition of the "truthfulness and reality of music, of its deep organic connection with the people and their music and songs; and of high professional art with simultaneous simplicity and accessibility of musical works."

The Central Committee said that those criticized had ignored warnings and instructions it issued in September, 1946, for the elimination of "bourgeois" influences and the creation of real Soviet art.

The committee said the works of the three leading composers "smell strongly of the spirit of the modern bourgeois music of Europe and America, which reflect the marasmus (progressive emaciation or wasting away) of bourgeois culture, the complete denial of musical art" and of going up a musical blind alley.

Dmitri Shostakovich
The New York Times

The Moscow Conservatory was accused of following "this formalistic trend" and of turning out young composers "in blind imitation" of the big composers.

**Below the Classic Level**

"Lately there has not been created a single Soviet opera that stands on the level of Russian opera classics," the committee said. Operatic and symphonic music were especially condemned. Ballet music, for which Prokofieff is especially famous, was not mentioned specifically.

The critics were accused of failing to "smash harmful views and theories," of becoming "loudspeakers for separate composers and of slavishly praising everything their favorites wrote.

The blame for all this was laid at the door of Mr. Khrapchenko's Arts Committee and the Union of Soviet Composers, of which Khatchaturian is chairman. The Central Committee ordered "organizational changes" in these and other party and State organs dealing with music.

The Propaganda and Agitation Division of the Communist Central Committee was entrusted with the job of "correcting the situation, liquidating shortcomings and providing for the development of Soviet music in a realistic direction."

Composers in all fields must produce "a high quality" of "ideological works," the committee said.

The Soviet music world was censured for "formalistic distortions and anti-democratic tendencies alien to the Soviet people and their artistic tastes, denial of the main principles of classic music, propaganda of atonality, dissonance and disharmony which are alleged to be the expression of 'progress' and 'novelty' in the development of musical forms; renunciation of such most important foundations of musical creation as melody, a passion for muddled neuropathic combinations which transform music into a cacophonic and chaotic heaping of sounds * * *; renunciation of polyphonic music and singing which are based on the simultaneous combination and development of a number of independent melodic lines, and a passion for one-tone unisonal music and singing—often without words—which violates the many-voiced structure common to our people, and which leads to the pauperization and downfall of music."

The Central Committee recalled that the Communist newspaper Pravda issued the first warning against "formalistic distortion" in 1936 when Shostakovich's "Lady Macbeth of Mtzensk" was so severely criticised that the composer retired for nearly five years.

"Treating upon the best traditions of Russian and Western classical music," the committee said, "rejecting these traditions as allegedly 'outdated, old-fashioned and conservative,' treating haughtily composers who try conscientiously to master and develop methods of classical music as supporters of 'primitive traditionalism and epigonism (degeneracy),' many Soviet composers in a race for falsely understood novelty have torn away from the demands of the artistic taste of the Soviet people, have closed themselves in narrow circles of specialists and musical gourmets, have lowered the high public role of music and narrowed its significance, limiting it by the satisfaction of distorted tastes of esthetic individualists."

**"Rotten Theory" Charged**

The Composers Union praises unworthy works, the committee said, while composers who "desire to continue and develop the classical heritage are called secondary and are unnoticed and slighted.

"Composers who boast of their 'novelty and arch-revolutionarism' in the sphere of music speak out as supporters of a most backward and musty conservatism," the committee said, "displaying a haughty intolerance to the least manifestations of criticism."

To protect themselves, it was added, composers have circulated the "rotten theory" that people who do not understand their music "are not grown up and their music will win public acclaim in 100 years."

Muradeli, the committee said, has neglected "the best traditions and experience of classic opera in general and Russian classic opera in particular, in a race for false 'originality.'" Examination of his work by the Central Committee, it was said, showed that it was symptomatic of "the unsatisfactory state of modern Soviet music."

February 12, 1948

## *Prokofieff, Khachaturian Accept Moscow Rebuke*

By Reuters.

MOSCOW, Feb. 15—The composer Sergei Prokofieff today told Tass, the news agency:

"However hard it is for me to realize that I was among those who expressed a formalistic trend, I am convinced that the Soviet people and the musical public will help me to overcome this trend in my work, and that my future creations will be worthy of my people and my great country.

Condemnation by the central committee of the Soviet Communist party of formalistic trends in Soviet music "truthfully expresses the thoughts and sentiments which have for many years agitated the Soviet people" the composer Aram Khachaturian declared.

"At the same time the Soviet people sharply condemn and reject the degrading musical art of modern Western Europe and America, reflecting the decadence of bourgeois culture."

February 16, 1948

## *Shostakovich Welcomes Party 'Fatherly Concern'*

MOSCOW, Feb. 21 (AP)—Dmitri Shostakovich has accepted the recent criticism leveled at leading Russian composers by the Central Committee of the Communist party and announced that he will correct his mistakes.

Shostakovich was quoted by the magazine Culture and Life as having told a gathering of Soviet composers that he interpreted the party criticism as "fatherly concern for us—the Soviet artists."

The Central Committee on Feb. 11 accused seven composers of writing music that "follows the formalist trend—a trend against the people."

Serge Prokieff, also censured by the Central Committee, Wednesday thanked the party for helping him.

February 22, 1948

## SOVIET ACADEMICIAN CONFESSES HE ERRED

Special to THE NEW YORK TIMES.

MOSCOW, Oct. 30—Academician Georgi F. Alexandrov, whose book, "A History of Western European Philosophy," was assailed in 1947 by Soviet critics, said in a lecture here that the mistakes in his work were "precisely those concessions to bourgeois philosophy which followed the route of bourgeois objectivism."

Mr. Alexandrov said these mistakes must be corrected by "carrying out the directions which have been given by Lenin and Stalin."

In the first of a series of lectures on dialectical and historical materialism under the auspices of the All-Union Society for Dissemination of Scientific and Political Knowledge, Mr. Alexandrov said the present era marked "the collapse of capitalism." He declared that such a thing as an objective "non-party" philosophy did not exist. The entire policy of bourgeois philosophy, he charged, is the defense of the class interests of the bourgeoisie. The same condemnation applied, Mr. Alexandrov said, to the "alleged objectivity" of bourgeois science.

There are two philosophies, he declared, one serving the bourgeoisie and the other the proletariat. Mr. Alexandrov said it was especially important to stress the class nature of philosophy at this time, when what he called international reaction was trying to delay an advance toward communism. Any concessions to bourgeois philosophy, he asserted, would be a betrayal of the interests of the proletariat.

October 31, 1949

## RUSSIA TO PURGE LEXICON

### Use of Foreign Words in Science Is Called Intolerable

MOSCOW, March 16 (UP)—The Academy of Sciences of the Soviet Union is going to "cleanse" Russian science and technology of unnecessary foreign words, it was announced today. The academy met yesterday, the announcement said, and heard Academician A. M. Terpigorev say:

"A scientific terminology cluttered with foreign words is intolerable. In most cases these foreign words can be substituted by Russian words."

Other speakers said a terminology of physics, chemistry, geology and biology closely connected with Socialist production must be created.

March 17, 1950

## SOVIET EXPUNGING WEST'S PSYCHIATRY

### Drive to Liquidate Concepts of Freud and U. S. Behaviorism Is Launched by Savants

Special to THE NEW YORK TIMES.

MOSCOW, Oct. 15—A sharp, new and by all indications decisive drive has been opened to expunge from Soviet psychology, psychiatry and neurology the final remnants of support for such Western concepts as Freudian psychology and American behaviorism and psychosomatics.

The drive was launched in the past week at a joint session of the Soviet Academy of Medicine and the All-Union Society for Neuropathology and Psychiatry.

The chief targets of the critical attack include veteran psychiatrist V. A. Gilyarovsky, head of the All-Union Institute of Psychiatry and one of the oldest and known workers in the specialty; Prof. Mikhail Gurevich, a member of the Academy of Medical Sciences and a known worker in the field of brain pathology; A. S. Shmaryan; Prof. M. I. Sereiskii, author of standard texts of psychiatry and psychotherapy; G. E. Sukhareva, specialist in child psychiatry, and I. G. Ravkin, experimenter on the role of shock and pharmacological treatment of major psychic diseases, including schizophrenia.

The chief accusation brought against all these scientists at the current sessions was that while they were all criticized nearly a year and a half ago at the time of the memorial meetings commemorating the centenary of I. P. Pavlov, whose principles have been established as the basis of all Soviet psychiatry, they had not yet esponded with appropriate changes in their work and teaching.

The tone of the discussion, led by Academician A. G. Ivanov Smolensky, one of Pavlov's leading followers, has been extremely sharp.

The session was particularly dissatisfied with Professor Gilyarovsky's explanation that his mistakes were founded upon ignorance of Pavlov's discoveries and an overestimate of the importance of the reflex theories of Russian scientist Bekhterov and the American behaviorist school of psychology. The session found Professor Gilyarovsky's errors particularly serious because of his important influence upon teaching and research, exerted through the Institute of Psychiatry.

Nor was the session satisfied with the explanations of Professor Gurevich and Mr. Shmaryan, who were said "not to display an honest endeavor to break with the notorious 'brain pathology' but stubbornly did not want to acknowledge the complete rottenness of the theory," which was described as being ideologically similar to bourgeois psychology. The explanations of these men "by no means" satisfied the session.

The absence in these scientists of "even the consciousness of their responsibility for the severe damage which they dealt Soviet scientific and practical psychiatry and the cause of training psychiatric personnel naturally arouses the justified indignation of the medical profession," the session held.

#### Repression Versus Reflexes

According to the theory of Freudian psychology, abnormality of the mind stems from emotional shocks, primarily sexual in nature, suffered during past experience and then repressed.

Sigmund Freud, the Austrian psychiatrist responsible for this theory, said also that dreams were the partial remembrance of these emotional shocks in veiled, symbolic form and that, therefore, their analysis was important in the treatment of psychological abnormality.

Psychosomatics, which was also criticized by the Soviet scientists, refers to the relationship between the mind and the body and especially relates to a system of medicine that emphasizes the role the mind plays in causing physical illness.

The man upon whom the Soviet scientists now base their psychiatric theory, Ivan Petrovich Pavlov, was a physiologist, who, working with dogs, studied the action of the brain. From his experiments a theory evolved that all actions were reflexes based upon a history of association with certain stimuli.

This theory concentrates on the objective approach to the study of an individual rather than to the subjective approach, as in Freudian psychiatry, in which that which is within the individual is studied.

October 16, 1951

# POST-WAR POLITICS

## COMMUNISTS SHOW 60% RISE IN RUSSIA

By C. L. SULZBERGER

By Wireless to THE NEW YORK TIMES.

PARIS, June 3—One of the important internal changes that has taken place within the Soviet Union during the war is the growth in membership of the Communist party—despite its immense casualty figures—and the change in the character of its membership.

Although exact information on the secrets of the party organization and its role are difficult to obtain, it is evident that its development occupied the attention of Soviet leaders consistently during the conflict.

In 1940, before the German attack on the U.S.S.R., the party totalled 3,000,000 members and 400,000 "candidates," a membership that had remained fairly constant during previous recent years. It now is believed the party has considerably more than 5,000,000 members and probably 1,000,000 "candidates," or probationary members, which represents a considerable increase even over last year and reflects the expanding tendency.

Actually, the rate of increase has been much greater than this almost 60 per cent membership rise indicates. During the war, the death rate among party members was unusually high. A large proportion of party members are in the Red Army and it was their custom to volunteer for particularly dangerous assignments.

#### Figures Indicate Trend

The trend of replacement can be indicated by certain figures made available to this correspondent. In May, 1941, the month before the German attack, 16,617 new members were accepted by the party. This rose to 70,000 in January, 1942, and by August, 1943, 201,135 "candidates" and 110,038 full members were accepted in a single month.

This accelerated recruiting resulted from a deliberate policy. By the time the German-Russian war had lasted one year, secret organizational pamphlets were instructing the party to continually replenish its membership roster by admitting "the best people."

During the war it was obvious that patriotism, initiative and courage both at the front and in the rear work were eagerly sought after by the party. "Primary organizations" and party "groups" who select "candidates" in factories and geographical districts and in Army units all over the country, either approving their full membership or depriving them of candidates' cards after a year's trial, were enjoined after a few months of war that the recruiting was unsatisfactory and were urged to enlist new members, especially Stakhanovites, women and former Comsomols [members of Communist youth organizations].

The membership drive was especially accelerated in the Army and Navy. By February, 1943, the period of probation for candidates had been reduced from a year to three months for especially distinguished soldiers and sailors, and the voting procedure for their approval simplified.

The number of primary party organizations handling Communist affairs, recruiting and policy was almost quadrupled during the war. Since June, 1943, there has been one in every battalion and in recent months as many new candidates have been admitted from each battalion [625 men] as before the war from a division [10,075 men].

Clearly, there have been immense casualties among party members, perhaps especially among those of long standing. By autumn, 1943, 58 per cent of a battalion's "partorges" [secretaries of the primary organization] were Communists of less than one year's standing. Usually a Partorg is the unit member of longest standing.

Furthermore, there has been a close parallel between war decoration and party membership. It is believed more than 80 per cent of the party members in the Red Army have received decorations.

A special drive began two years ago to enroll decorated men, and indeed so much pressure was placed on a man who received a valor medal, according to French Normandie Squadron fliers, that it was difficult to refuse to become a member. The same pressure, it is believed, was exerted on officers whose competence caused their rapid promotion.

June 4, 1945

# MOSCOW REFORMS GOVERNMENT RANKS

## Stalin Now Heads Ministers, Not Commissars, in Change Voted by Supreme Soviet

MOSCOW, March 15 (AP)—The Supreme Soviet voted tonight to drop the title of "Commissar" and substitute the word "Minister" for the highest-ranking officials of the Soviet Government and to change the name of the Council of Peoples' Commissars to Council of Ministers.

Generalissimo Stalin, who is chairman of the Council of Peoples' Commissars, thus becomes chairman of the Council of Ministers. As chairman he is Premier and head of the Government.

The action of changing from the word "Commissar," used for more than a quarter-century by the Soviets, was taken by a rising vote of both houses of the Supreme Soviet in a joint session, which revised the Constitution of the Soviet Union to that effect.

March 16, 1946

# *Konev Now Heads Soviet Land Forces*

By Reuters

MOSCOW, Nov. 18—Marshal Ivan Konev has been appointed Commander in Chief of all Russian ground forces. He succeeds Marshal Georgi K. Zhukov.

The change was disclosed in a report of graduation exercises at the Frunze Military Academy, the Soviet Union's leading military school. An order was read to the graduating class from the "Commander in Chief, land troops, armed forces, U. S. S. R., Marshal of the Soviet Union Konev."

Reports that Marshal Zhukov had been appointed to command the Odessa military district, indicating he had fallen from favor, were circulated last July. In September, however, a dispatch to THE NEW YORK TIMES from Istanbul, Turkey, said that, while many believed he had been relegated to a second-class post by the Odessa appointment, he had actually been named to Russia's most important military region, in the opinion of Turkish observers.

November 19, 1946

# STALIN QUITS HELM OF ARMED FORCES

LONDON, March 3 (AP)—Prime Minister Stalin, after six years as commander of the vast Russian military organization, resigned his post as Minister of the Armed Forces today because of the "excessive pressure of his main work" and handed the job to Gen. Nikolai Alexandrovich Bulganin, the Moscow radio said tonight.

The change in the top military command came as the Soviet Union gradually was de-emphasizing military activities and demobilizing millions of soldiers to enter industry and speed up the country's current Five-Year Plan. Prime Minister Stalin stepped out of the military office only a week before the four-power Foreign Ministers' Conference was scheduled to open in Moscow.

The brief radio announcement, recorded here by the Soviet monitor, gave "pressure" of other work as Generalissimo Stalin's only reason for relinquishing one of his many State posts.

However, the tremendous task of guiding Russian military forces through the war with Germany undoubtedly tired the 67-year-old Prime Minister Stalin, who often has been reported ill since the end of the war.

March 4, 1947

# PENALTY OF DEATH BANNED BY RUSSIA

Special to THE NEW YORK TIMES.

LONDON, May 26—The Soviet Union has abolished the death penalty in peacetime in view of the "exceptional" devotion to the state displayed by the people during the war and because peace can now be regarded as certain for a long time, the Moscow radio announced tonight.

A decree of the Supreme Soviet said that crimes hitherto punished by death would henceforth be dealt with by confinement in "corrective labor camps" for twenty-five years. Death sentences not yet carried out are to be commuted to such confinement.

The text of the decree as broadcast in Russian and translated in London by the Soviet Monitor, an affiliate of the Soviet Tass news agency, follows:

"The historic victory of the Soviet people over the enemy has not only demonstrated the increased might of the Soviet state, but first and foremost the exceptional devotion of the entire population of the Soviet Union toward the Soviet motherland and Soviet Government.

**Peace Is Held Secured**

"Simultaneously, the international situation during the period after Germany's and Japan's capitulation shows that the cause of peace can be considered as secured for a long time, despite the attempts being made by aggressive elements to provoke war.

"Taking into consideration these circumstances, and meeting the wishes of the trade unions of workers and employes and other authoritative organizations expressing the opinion of the broad masses of the people, the Presidium of the Supreme Soviet of the

U.S.S.R. believed that application of death sentences is no longer necessary under peacetime conditions.

"The Presidium of the Supreme Soviet of the U. S. S. R. decrees:

"(1) Abolition of the death penalty in peacetime established for **crimes under the laws in force in the U. S. S. R.**

**"(2) For crimes punishable by the death sentence under the laws in force, application in peacetime of confinement in corrective labor camps for twenty-five years.**

**"(3) For death sentences not yet carried out to publication of the present decree, replacement of the death sentence on the decision of a supreme court by the punishments provided under Article 2 of the present decree."**

**Shvernik Signs Decree**

**The decree was signed by N. M. Shvernik, President of the Presidium of the Supreme Soviet, and A. F. Gorkin, Secretary of the Presidium.**

**The death penalty in the Soviet Union has been applied almost exclusively for offenses adjudged "crimes against the state." For the premeditated murder of a private individual, for example, the 1926 criminal code provided only one to ten years' loss of liberty.**

**The 1926 code characterized death by shooting as an "exceptional measure for protecting the state" against crimes threatening the "fundamentals of the Soviet authority and of the Soviet order." Theft of state property was put into this category.**

**The classes of offenses for which the death penalty might be applied were broadened legally under a decree of April 7, 1935, which provided that persons above the age of 12 could be put to death for crimes such as "thefts, assaults, injuries, mutilations, murder or attempt at murder." In practice, however, the death penalty continued to be reserved for offenses against the state.**

May 27, 1947

## *Use of the Death Penalty Revived in Soviet Union*

By The Associated Press.

LONDON, Friday, Jan. 13—Tass said today that the Soviet Union had revived the death penalty for use against traitors, spies and saboteurs. The death penalty had been abolished in 1947.

The Moscow dispatch of the Soviet news agency was distributed in London by the Soviet monitor. The death penalty was revived, the dispatch said, by the Presidium of the Supreme Soviet, which issued a decree dated yesterday.

There was some speculation in London that the decree might foreshadow a new series of prosecutions on the order of the 1937 treason trials.

January 13, 1950

# Beria, Russia's Mystery of Mysteries

### His dreaded power extends over the U.S.S.R. and its satellites, yet he is almost unknown.

By EDWARD CRANKSHAW

LONDON.

**IN a land where security, for centuries an obsession, has now become a mania, it is not surprising that the man who controls the whole apparatus of state security should himself be a mystery of mysteries. And, indeed, less is known about the life and character of Lavrenti Pavlovich Beria than about any of his colleagues under Stalin. Compared with Beria, Stalin himself is an open book, Molotov a babbler.**

**Yet this man, about whom so little is known, has swiftly risen from provincial obscurity until he now stands as one of the three pillars of Stalin's regime, towering above his seniors, and forming with Molotov and Malenkov the post-war *troika*, or triumvirate, which rules Russia in Stalin's name. He is 51, nineteen years younger than** Stalin, nine years younger than Molotov, three years older than Malenkov. In the Politburo itself Andreyev, Bulganin, Kaganovitch, Khrushchev, Mikoyan and Shvernik are all senior to Beria and have all been surpassed by him.

**TWELVE years ago he was not even a name to most Russians, though Stalin knew all about him. Then, suddenly, he found himself famous, or notorious, throughout the length and breadth of the U.S.S.R. That was in 1938, when Stalin called him up to Moscow from the mountains of Georgia to put an end to the great purges and take over the N. K. V. D. from the maniacal Yehzov. As far as the ordinary citizen was concerned, that made him,** after Stalin himself, the most powerful individual in the land, master of the midnight arrest, lord of the Siberian concentration camps and mines. But as far as the Politburo was concerned, he was still technically its servant. There had been men in that job before. They had come and they had gone, powerful and to be feared by even the highest after Stalin because they knew so much, but, in the last resort, removable. Yagoda and Yehzov had been removed.

But Beria was something other than these. He was more than the chief policeman. A fellow-countryman and

**EDWARD CRANKSHAW,** English journalist and author of "Russia and the Russians," served with a British military mission in Moscow for eighteen months during World War II.

confidant of Stalin's, he was also, in his way, a politician. He had even written a book to demonstrate the all-important part played by his chief in the early days of bolshevism, thus laying the first official foundations for the latter-day legend of Stalin as Lenin's right-hand man and natural successor. And for fifteen years, first as head of the Georgian G. P. U., then as Secretary of the Georgian Communist party, he had ruled, virtually as Stalin's regent, that most turbulent of all the Soviet republics. Now he was in Moscow, on Stalin's personal command, to take over the stabilization of a shattered and demoralized Russia, damaged sorely by the purges, and to restore some confidence in a land where no man could trust his neighbor.

It soon became clear that Lavrenti Beria was to be not merely the instrument of the policy-makers but one of their number. In 1939 he was promoted to the inner Committee of Defense, which ran the war. In 1946 he was a full member of the Politburo, and plainly closer to Stalin than most of his colleagues. At the same time he was put in charge of the development of atomic energy.

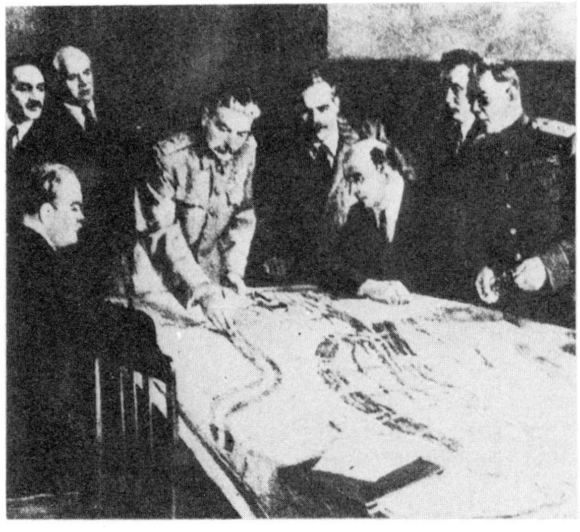

STALIN'S FRIEND—Significantly, Beria is seated at his mentor's left in a painting by D. Nalbandyan, "For the Happiness of the People."

When this happened, all the old People's Commissariats were converted overnight into ministries, and the old People's Commissariat for Internal Affairs, the N. K. V. D., was split into three ministries under three of Beria's loyal subordinates—the M. V. D., with responsibility for internal order and forced labor, under Kruglov; the M. G. B., with responsibility for espionage and counter-espionage, under Merkulov (later replaced by Abakumov); the M. G. K., with inspection rights over the whole apparatus of government, under Mekhlis, the only Jew still holding high position in the Soviet Union apart from Stalin's brother-in-law, Kaganovitch.

All these three new ministries—Internal Affairs, State Security and State Control—report to Beria. Today, still Russia's chief policeman, he runs, through the Cominform, the new Soviet empire and plays a decisive part in Soviet foreign policy.

This career, briefly sketched, is interesting not only in itself, but because it reflects with remarkable exactitude the development of the Soviet system during the past twelve years—since the day when Stalin called off the great purge, having destroyed every vestige of potential opposition, and set himself up as the absolute and undisputed dictator of the Russian people and the Communist world. The rise of Beria has been the history of Stalinism in its final phase.

His beginnings are obscure and do not matter in the least. The official story is that his father was a poor peasant eking out a wretched existence on the Black Sea coast. If this is true, it says a good deal more for czarism than the Bolsheviks usually care to say. For it is certain that young Beria received a first-class education, finishing at 20 with a first-class degree in architectural engineering from the Baku Polytechnic.

He is also supposed to have joined the Bolsheviks, a minority party detested by the older revolutionary parties, at the age of 18 in the year of the revolution, and to have worked underground while studying for his diploma—underground because in those days Baku was still an anti-Bolshevik stronghold, and remained so for three years after Lenin's revolution. But from the moment when Baku was won for the Soviets, there is no doubt about Beria's career. And in 1921 he volunteered for service in the Cheka—the successor to the Czarist Ochrana and the predecessor of the G. P. U.

It was not then a fashionable thing for ardent young Bolsheviks to join the Cheka. As a rule the more intelligent Communists were used to stiffen the Cheka, staffed by career policemen, for special tasks. Why the young architectural engineer sought out this odd vocation it is impossible to say. Since he was plainly consumed with ambition, it may well have been a cool and calculated move by one who saw the safest and surest way to the top through the backstairs influence of the one organization in Soviet Russia not subject to the arbitrary despotism of the Security Police—namely, the Security Police itself.

More than this was almost certainly his desire to serve the revolution most effectively; and to judge by his character as revealed in later life, it is probable that young Beria saw that rigid police discipline and an unsleeping watch over the potential enemy within the gates was going to cut more ice than any amount of demagogic oratory—especially in one who was neither a natural demagogue nor an orator. At any rate, he chose; and he stuck to his choice.

Shortish, bald today, thick-necked, the face pallid in the Kremlin manner, the nose a little like a duck's bill, but sharp, the mouth tight and thin, the manner gentle and coldly, abstractedly benign—the whole effect of that pedantic aloofness which makes people think of scholars when they should really think of fanatics of the most dangerous kind—it is only now that the outside world is beginning to see this familiar figure of a career policeman to be much more than that, to be a genius of some not easily apprehended kind. For the genius is certainly there.

It is equally certain that Beria is a man with a fixed idea—the guarding of the Soviet Union from all harm, from within and from without. The way he has set about this task is the story of the last twelve years of Stalinism. The irony of it is that in his first year as a national figure he was regarded by many as a liberator, come to scourge the tyrants and bring benevolence and mildness to the bleak rule of the Kremlin.

That idea resulted from three things. First, it was largely on his advice, it is popularly believed, that Stalin put a sudden end to the great purges which were turning the country into a shambles and bringing the work of the Government to a standstill; second, one of Beria's first actions was to purge the more notorious of the purgers and to amnesty thousands who had been exiled maliciously; third, at the Party Congress in 1939, when he was elected a candidate-member of the Politburo, he spoke out against the hysteria which attributed all the things wrong with the Soviet Union as being due to wrecking and sabotage, and strongly criticized the then current practice of attributing all muddle and inefficiency to conspiratorial activity against the state.

It was a curious legend, this story of Beria's mildness. People had only to reflect on his past career, first as the G. P. U. boss, then as the party boss of the Caucasus, to realize that he could not be mild. For throughout this varied, turbulent area—all important because it stood between Moscow and the oil of Baku—he had to carry out the harsh policies involved in the collectivization, the creation of irrigation works, the driving of mountain peasants into factories and disciplining them, the stepping up of the oilfields of Grozny and Baku, the introduction of new commercial crops in the teeth of bitter resistance from peoples wedded to immemorial practices of subsistence farming, the taming of wild mountain races and the breaking of Moslem influence in the Moslem strongholds.

The resistance flared up again and again. It was Beria who directed for the Moscow Government the civil war against the full-scale Georgian rebellion in 1924. It was he who suppressed the revolt of the Kuban Cossacks. And the tens of thousands of embittered and bewildered smallholders, labeled kulaks, who were herded off in box cars, away from the mountains to the endless plains of Siberia, were all set in motion by Lavrenti Beria—and on the orders of the men whom he was later to supersede.

For we have to remember that although Yehzov liquidated Yagoda, and although Beria himself in due time liquidated Yehzov, first Yagoda, then Yehzov, as heads of the whole apparatus of state, had been his master. In other words, he, Beria, benefited first from the holocaust of the purges and then, stepping forward, took the applause for stopping them.

THE machine he took over was already monstrous and colossal. Since then, although there has been no open opposition to Stalin of the kind Yagoda had to cope with, it has grown. In spite of the amnesties with which Beria, to calm the country, and for no other reason at all, celebrated his installation, there is nothing at all to suggest that he has ever tried to reduce the size and range of that machine. On the contrary, under his supreme direction it has spread and ramified until it now covers half of Europe as well as the U.S.S.R., has headquarters in every Asiatic capital, and controls the Communist parties of every country in the world.

At home he took over the immense complex of forced labor camps and prisons developed so amazingly under Yagoda, who, trying to find work for millions of deportees in the great struggle for collectivization, ended up by developing a vested interest in slave labor which had to be sustained by a ceaseless flow of new human material. The great construction works and the secret factories started for the purpose of employing prisoners had to be kept going when the original prisoners had died or served their turn. That meant a constant demand for prisoners.

Thus, what started as a temporary expedient became part of the economy of the state, so important that if all those prisoners now engaged in forced labor were tomorrow to be released it would throw the whole production plan completely out of gear. And it was under Beria that this system reached its present appalling and irredeemable elaboration.

WE shall hear a great deal of Beria as time goes on. There is little doubt that if Stalin died now, he, with Malenkov, would inherit all power, though Molotov would be the greatest name. Nobody knows for certain whether Beria and Malenkov, whose careers have run neck and neck, are allies or rivals. Beria has the power of the Security Police; Malenkov, the power of the party. Knowing what we do know of Stalin, it seems probable that he chose these two men to balance each other. What is quite certain is that together they could obliterate any attempt at organized opposition, but, at loggerheads, they could bring the whole country down in ruin.

**Beria's troops—Their job is to keep order in the capital.**

WE shall hear of Beria as a statesman. He has already begun to appear as a statesman in the Soviet manner. He was chosen on Stalin's birthday to write the Pravda article on the advance of world communism. As the man now in charge of the Cominform and of the Kremlin's fifth column everywhere, this was highly suitable. In the course of that article he said:

> Stalin has laid down a program of action for Communists. They must, he says: (1) exploit all differences and contradictions in the bourgeois camp; (2) take concrete action to unite the working classes of the economically advanced countries with the national liberation movements of the colonies and dependent nations; (3) complete the struggle for the unity of the trade union movement; (4) take active measures to bring together the proletariat and the small peasants; (5) support Soviet rule and disrupt the interventionist machinations of the imperialists against the Soviet Union, bearing in mind that the Soviet Union is the base of the revolutionary movement in all countries.

That is the new language of Russia's chief policeman. It is important because it is the most up-to-date statement of the Stalinist attitude toward the prosecution of the revolution. And when earlier I said that the last decade of Beria's career mirrors with exactitude the development of Stalinism, it was precisely because the whole trend of Soviet development since Stalin's apotheosis during the great trials of the middle Thirties has been to substitute policemen for ideologies, police repression for Bolshevik dynamism.

In country after country, as well as much earlier in the Soviet Union itself, devoted and ardent Communists have been used to prepare the way for the rule of unmitigated power in the traditional Russian manner and then have been destroyed by their creators, their purpose served. And the arch-destroyer has been Beria. Rajk of Hungary, Kostov of Bulgaria, Gomulka of Poland have been his victims.

Today, at 51, he is virtually the dictator of the satellites, a new kind of unofficial foreign minister working through his nominees, the ignoble corps of Communist Ministers of the Interior; working also in countries outside his control through agents—secret agents in embassies, missions, government offices and factories, more or less unconcealed agents in trade unions—working also through official diplomacy and in the conference rooms, playing off one power against another, working through threat and propaganda, through bullying notes and unctuous demonstrations [illegible]r world peace; working, above all, through the official Communist parties, and then, the purpose achieved, breaking their hearts and destroying them in all but name.

IT has been an extraordinary career, achieved without a single gesture, almost without a single public announcement of any kind. It has simply happened, very much as the breaking of millions of lives by his agents simply happened, with no public gestures and pronouncements and marked at the most by a stifled cry of terror in the darkness of the Russian night.

Some were misled by his years of obscurity. But it is clear now that Stalin had marked him as his own long before he called him to Moscow in 1938. The most remarkable thing about his background seemed to be its narrow specialization.

In that world of chaos and bold and blundering experiment which was the U.S.S.R. during the first twenty years of Bolshevik rule, the men who shone, the men who rose, were the able and adaptable toughs of genius, who never from one day to the next knew what they would be doing—organizing a production drive in industry, supervising the final stages of the collectivization, pushing through the Moscow underground, building a new steel center in the middle of the empty steppes, carrying out a party purge, crushing a rebellion in the Ukraine, and so on.

BERIA alone among the senior party leaders of today kept to one place and one job. But that made him in fact the uncrowned king of one of the most difficult and quite the most complex area inside the U.S.S.R. In that job he had to cope with every aspect of the economy of the U.S.S.R., so that when the time came for his appearance on the national stage he was ready, his only serious rival being Malenkov. We cannot predict the future of either of these two. The future of each depends on the other. Neither of them—and this is an alarming thought—has any experience of men and affairs outside the Soviet Union.

Meanwhile, one thing we say with certainty. And that is that Lavrenti Beria, the self-appointed guardian of the revolution from all dangers, internal and external, has, by the deepest irony, done more than any single man to destroy the revolution—by substituting the dead hand of police rule for the dynamism of an active if perverted faith wherever his shadow has fallen. And perhaps, after all, it is possible to find a phrase for his undoubted genius which, I said, was not easily to be apprehended; it is the genius of stupidity.

THE fixed idea, the idea of guardianship, has, behind that thin smile, the pale eyes and the balefully flashing pince-nez, become through routine identified with the idea of destruction. To guard you must be ready to destroy the enemy. Therefore to destroy the enemy is to guard. But who is the enemy? Obviously it is impossible always to say. So you destroy everyone who might possibly prove to be the enemy.

It is a simple formula. And it is only a very small step from seeing yourself as the guardian of the revolution, sweeping aside ruthlessly but regretfully and with no ill-feeling everyone and everything that may seem to stand in the way of the progress of the revolution, feeding where you will and can. And in no time, then, you yourself are the revolution, or Great Russia, or whatever label you care to use, which has no existence outside you.

Compared with this sort of megalomania, the sadism of a Yagoda, the degenerateness of a Yehzov, is no more than a nasty adolescent viciousness.

April 2, 1950

# Russian Jokes: Not Passed by the Censor

**The fifteen 'best,' satirizing the regime, are presented by an expert on Slavic affairs.**

Compiled by BERTRAM D. WOLFE

*Jokes about the Kremlin rule are legion. In the early years of the Soviet regime, before full totalitarian dictatorship had been reached, such jokes circulated among the Soviet people themselves. After it had become perilous to joke about the U. S. S. R. in that country, such anecdotes continued and still continue to be told outside the Communist sphere. Bertram D. Wolfe has made a hobby of collecting such jokes. Here are the fifteen he considers "best."*

### OF HOMES AND HOMAGE

THE teacher distributed pictures of Stalin to all her pupils and next day asked each to report what he or she had done.

"I hung the picture on the wall facing the door, so that every one who comes in can see," said one.

"I hung it in the corner of the room, where the ikon used to be, and lit a candle under it," said another.

But little Peter remained silent. "You, Peter," said the teacher gently. "Where did you hang the image of our leader?"

"Nowhere," stammered Peter.

"Nowhere! Why not?"

"Please, teacher, the other four families have the walls; we live in the center of the room."

### FALSE ALARM

THE hour of the midnight police visits. The Soviet apartment house was fast asleep. The janitor began rapping heavily on every apartment door. "Don't be frightened, Comrades," he shouted loudly as he knocked. "It's only a fire."

### FUTURE PERFECTED

CITIZEN PAVEL PAVLOVICH asked for information at the Kaunas railway station in Soviet Latvia. "What time is the train for Moscow leaving?"

"Oh, about 20 per cent earlier than it used to," said the attendant.

"What does that mean?" asked Pavel.

"Seventeen per cent earlier than by schedule."

"And what is the time by the schedule?" Pavel persisted.

"Well," said the attendant, "the Moscow train always tries to leave 10 per cent earlier than the express to Leningrad."

"And what time," asked Pavel, "does the express leave?"

"Exactly twenty-four hours earlier than is listed on the time table."

In desperation, Pavel demanded to see the time table himself. "I'm sorry," said the attendant, "but I can only let you have the one which we will use in

three years' time. You see," he said, "those who made up the time tables undertook to work 300 per cent ahead of their norms!"

### COWED—

ROOSEVELT, Churchill and Stalin were motoring on a country road near Yalta, when a cow blocked the path. Roosevelt got off and, using his gentleman-farmer skill, tried to persuade the cow to move on, but the cow would not budge. Next Churchill tried crisp, sharp commands, but the cow remained immovable. Finally Stalin whispered a few words in the cow's ear. The cow rushed off in a cloud of dust.

"Wonderful!" said Roosevelt. "Tell me, Generalissimo, what was the magic formula?"

"Simple," said Stalin. "I told the cow that I would put her on a collective farm."

### —AND COWRAFFES

AN agronomist, explaining the wonders of Soviet science, pointed out a rare specimen. "And this," he

said, "is the latest triumph of Michurinite biology. Our director, Lysenko, has succeeded in breeding a cow and a giraffe to produce a new species called the cowraffe."

"And what is the value of a cowraffe?" asked one of the audience.

"It is a herbivorous animal so constructed that it can graze in Bulgaria while it is being milked in Moscow."

### R.S.V.P.

TWO citizens were passing the famous Secret Police headquarters at Lubyanka prison. Involuntarily, one of them found his head drawn in that direction and read the sign: "Entrance strictly forbidden!" He thought it over reflectively. "And do you think," he said to his friend, "that if it read: 'The honor of your presence is requested,' I would go in?"

### IN OLD EDENGRAD

BEAMING happily, Molotov walked into Stalin's study one day and declared, "There's no doubt about it. Adam and Eve were both Russians. Now we can claim the invention of mankind along with the invention of radio, television, the airplane and everything else. Isn't that wonderful?"

Always cautious, Stalin inquired, "Are you sure of that? You know the Voice of America likes nothing more than to tear down our invention claims. We'll have to really back that one up."

"Nothing to it," was Molotov's confident answer, "just think about it for a moment. Adam and Eve had no clothing to cover their nakedness. They had no roof over their head. They lived on apples. Yet they thought they lived in Paradise. What else could they be but Russians?"

### TO EACH ACCORDING . . .

THE *Kolkhoz* was meeting one Nov. 6 for the annual holiday award of prizes. The chairman read: "Milkmaid Anastasia Ivanovna, for her exemplary care of the cows entrusted to her charge, receives as a prize a hen and a rooster." General applause. The orchestra breaks into a flourish.

"Stable-boy Vasili Petrov, for rearing a prize-winning horse, gets a new suit." Again applause, whistling, shouting.

"Shock-brigade harvester Ivan Rostov, for harvesting 190 per cent of his quota, for working Sundays and holidays, for displaying high political consciousness, for setting new speed records for all the other peasants to imitate, receives the grand prize of the complete works of Stalin!"

Dead silence, then a voice from the rear of the hall: "Serves him right!"

### INCREDULOUS

AN astonished border guard held up a horde of rabbits that were seeking to crash the Soviet border into Poland. He asked for documents. "We are going," said the rabbit leader, "on a G. P. U. order."

"What order?"

"The G. P. U. has just ordered the arrest of every camel found in the Soviet Union."

"But you are not camels!"

"Yes, but just try to tell that to the G. P. U."

DIALECTICS

ACADEMICIAN LYSENKO was performing an experiment on the auditory nerve of the flea. He put the flea on his right hand and bade it jump to his left. It jumped, then jumped back again in response to a second command. Carefully he removed the flea's hind legs.

"Jump right!" he commanded. "Jump left!" But the flea did not budge.

"This proves scientifically," he said, "that a flea loses its sense of hearing when its legs are removed."

Drawings by Gordon Hake.

COMRADE

MIDNIGHT. Two Soviet citizens are going on a diagonal across the vast and deserted Red Square. Midway one of them heaves a great sigh. "Sh-h!" cries the other, putting a finger athwart his lips.

"Why, what's the matter? In the first place I didn't say anything. In the second place, there's nobody here but me and you."

"Don't you know," retorts his companion, "that whenever two Russians get together, one of them is bound to be a member of the N. K. V. D.?"

PRODUCTION!

DURING the first Five-Year Plan an American pilgrim was ushered into the director's office of a model factory. He stared wide-eyed at the production chart hanging on the wall. "Oh, yes," said the director. "During the first year we produced only 5,000; the second year, 50,000; the third, 500,000. This year we'll probably make a million."

"Is that so? May I ask what you are producing?" asked the visitor.

The director reached out to the belt conveyor and pulled off a little brass tag for the visitor to inspect. It read: "The elevator isn't running."

CLASSLESS REUNION

THREE Soviet citizens who had somehow survived the purges were comparing notes in a forced labor camp.

"I am here," said the first, "since 1929, for calling Karl Radek a counter-revolutionary."

"And I," said the second, "since 1937, for saying that Radek was not a counter-revolutionary."

"And I," s·· the third, "am Karl Radek."

LINE OF SUCCESSION

THE old woman sighed "thank God!" as she finally managed to squeeze into a Moscow subway car.

"You shouldn't say that, citizen," a Red Army soldier rebuked her. "You should say, 'Thank you, Stalin, for the Moscow subway.'"

They rode in silence for a while, then the old woman asked, "But what if Stalin dies?"

"Oh, then," said the soldier, "you can say 'thank God.'"

INFLATION PERIL

"IT'S wonderful," a Lithuanian confided to a Russian friend, "it's a source of great pride to be a citizen of the New Lithuania, the largest country in the world."

"How do you make that out?"

"Why, our Western frontiers are on the Baltic Sea; our capital is in Moscow and the majority of our population is in Siberia."

July 22, 1951

# SOVIET CALLS PARTY CONGRESS OCT. 5; WILL ABOLISH POLITBURO IN SHAKE-UP

## New Presidium to Take Place of Old Bureau in Statute Revision

### PROGRESS REPORTS SET

By HARRISON E. SALISBURY

Special to THE NEW YORK TIMES.

MOSCOW, Aug. 20—Acting in his capacity of Secretary of the Central Committee of the All-Union Communist party, Premier Stalin announced today a call for a general party congress Oct. 5, at which Georgi M. Malenkov, Deputy Premier, will deliver the chief report. Mr. Stalin also may speak.

It is difficult to overestimate the importance of the October congress which will be the first to be held since the end of World War II. The last such meeting was held in 1939.

One of the proposals to come before the congress in a general revision of the party statutes is to eliminate both the Politburo and the lesser-known but equally key structure—the Organization Bureau of the party, or, as it is called, the Orgburo.

**New Groups to Get Duties**

The functions performed in the past by these mechanisms will be turned over in large part to a new creation—the Presidium of the Central Committee of the party, which will exercise authority in intervals between meetings of the full committee. Some organizational functions of the Orgburo will be vested in the party secretariat, which is the third of the important party inner mechanisms and which will continue under the new statutes.

[Another vital issue to come before the party congress will be a new five-year plan calling for a 70 per cent increase in the production of such products as iron, steel, coal, oil, electricity, shipping, chemicals and timber, news services reported. The new plan will cover the period from Jan. 1, 1951, to Dec. 31, 1955. It is customary in the Soviet Union to announce a five-year plan sometime after the plan period has actually begun.]

The Politburo of the Central Committee of the Communist party has existed since Oct. 23, 1917, a few days before the Bolshevik revolution seized power for the Communist party.

Since 1931 the party has been officially known as the All-Union Communist party (Bolsheviks). The new title is the Communist party of the Soviet Union. The word Bolshevik had popularly been applied to the Russian Communist party since the famous split within the Russian Social Democratic party in which Lenin's adherents held a majority.

There are other chances of even deeper significance to close students of the doctrine of Marxist-Leninist-Stalinist thought. In the past the party statutes gave the following definition of the party: "The all-union Communist party [Bolsheviks] is the vanguard of the working class or the U. S. S. R. the highest form of its class organization."

The new statute broadens this definition to read: "The Communist party of the Soviet Union is the voluntary militant alliance of like-minded Communists organized from people of the working class, working peasants and the working intelligentsia."

Thus the party under the new statutes is specifically defined to include not only the "working class" but working peasants and the intelligentsia as well.

While in practice the party has long included large numbers of working peasants and the intelligentsia, this is the first recognition in the statutes of their coequal status. To anyone versed in the long history of a party thought and debate on this question of composition, the change obviously is important and doubtless reflects the party's belief that the radical transformation of the class structure to one unified working base has been completed.

Significant, too, is the proposed change in the definition of a party member. The present definition reads that a "member of the party is considered one who recognizes the program of the party, who works in one of its organizations, who subjects himself to the decrees of the party and who pays membership dues"—a definition virtually identical with that proposed by Lenin at the famous London Party Congress of 1903, which played a major role in producing the split between the Bolsheviks and the Mensheviks.

The new definition reads: "A member of the Communist party can be any working citizen of the Soviet Union who does not exploit other persons' labor, who recognizes the program and statutes of the party, who actively assists their realization, who works in one of the organs of the party and fulfills all the decisions of the party."

Thus two new concepts are introduced — membership is limited to Soviet citizens and to Soviet citizens who do not exploit the labor of others.

August 21, 1952

Associated Press

STALIN AND PROTEGE: The Soviet dictator and Georgi M. Malenkov as they reviewed a May Day parade in 1949 in Moscow.

# 25-Man Presidium Headed By Stalin Replaces Politburo

By HARRISON E. SALISBURY

Special to THE NEW YORK TIMES.

MOSCOW, Friday, Oct. 17—A group of thirty-six prominent party and Government leaders was elected yesterday by the new Communist party Central Committee as members and candidates of the new Central Committee Presidium, which replaces the former twelve-man Politburo.

At the same time, the Central Committee named a new ten-man Secretariat to replace the former five-man Secretariat.

Premier Stalin was named chairman of the Presidium and first member of the Secretariat.

The new Presidium is made up of twenty-five full members and eleven candidates and includes ten former Politburo members as full members and one—Alexei N. Kosygin—as an alternate. Andrei A. Andreyev, a member of the former Politburo, was not named to the new Presidium.

The new Presidium provides a much broader representation of the leading Government organs than the former Politburo. It includes a substantial group of important regional party leaders as well as six important members of the Council of Ministers, including the Foreign Affairs Minister, Andrei Y. Vishinsky, as an alternate.

Another feature of the presidium was the fact that the new members were chosen largely from city and regional party organs. The Presidium included four Union Republic leaders, Otto V. Kuusinen of Karelo-Finland, who for many years has been closely associated with the ideological field; L. G. Melnikov, Secretary of the Ukraine; N. S. Patolichev, Secretary for Byelorussia and L. I. Brezhnev, Moldavian party secretary, who is now assuming duties in the central apparatus of the Secretariat.

The new Presidium included the following members:

Premier Stalin, V. M. Andrianov of the Leningrad party organization, A. B. Aristov of Chelyabinsk, Mr. Beria, Marshal Bulganin, Marshal Voroshilov, S. D. Ignatiev of the Moscow organization, Mr. Kaganovich, Demyan S. Korotchenko of Kiev, Vassili V. Kuznetsov, trade union leader; Otto V. Kuusinen, Karelo-Finnish leader.

Also Mr. Malenkov, Vyacheslav A. Malyshev, vice chairman of the Council of Ministers; L. G. Melnikov, Ukrainian party secretary; Mr. Mikoyan, Nicola A. Mikhailov, Communist Youth secretary; Mr. Molotov, Mikhail G. Pervukhin, Vice Chairman of the Council of Ministers; Gen. Panteleimon K. Ponamarenko, Maxim Z. Saburov, Chairman of State Plans; Mikhail A. Suslov, Mr. Khrushchev, D. I. Chesnokov, leading party philosopher, Mr. Shvernik and M. F. Shkiryatov.

Those elected candidate members of the Presidium were:

L. I. Brezhnev, Moldavian party secretary; Foreign Minister Andrei Y. Vishinsky, Finance Minister Arseny V. Zveryev, N. G. Ignatov, Krasnodar secretary; I. G. Kabanov, Mr. Kosygin, N. S. Patolichev, Byelorussian party secretary; N. U. Pegov, A. N. Puzanov, Ivan F. Tevosyan, vice chairman of the Council of Ministers, and Pavel F. Yudin, party ideologist.

The new Central Committee Secretariat is composed of:

Premier Stalin and Messrs. Aristov, Brezhnev, Ignatov, Malenkov, Mikhailov, Pegov, Ponamarenko, Suslov and Khrushchev.

### Infusion of Young Leaders

As chairman of the party Control Committee, the Central Committee elected Mr. Shkiryatov who had been chairman of the former Party Control Commission.

The outstanding feature of the elections is wholesale infusion of capable and energetic young regional party leaders and veteran administrators in the apparatus that will guide the work of the Communist party between sessions of the party congress.

It was also notable that in selecting the chiefs of the party apparatus the Central Committee drew exclusively from civilian ranks. The new members are almost entirely regional party leaders, the chief cabinet ministers and party specialists in ideology. The list includes no new military figures.

Among figures newly come to prominence, one of the outstanding is Mr. Aristov, named both to the Presidium and to the Secretariat. He has been the leader of the extremely important Chelyabinsk industrial region in the Urals and as such has been intrusted with some of the heaviest production responsibilities to fall on any regional party chief. Mr. Pegov, Br. Brezhnev and Mr. Ignatov are in much the same category.

Another feature immediately apparent is the very important role that is now assigned to those four vice chairmen of the Council of Ministers who had not been members of the old Politburo. They are M. Z. Saburov, head of the State Planning Commission; V. A. Malyshev, vice chairman of the Council of Ministers and a specialist in machine production, and M. G. Pervukhin, another vice chairman and specialist in chemical industries—all named full members of the Presidium. I. F. Tevosyan, another vice chairman and specialist in metallurgy, was named a candidate member of the Presidium.

October 17, 1952

# MOSCOW ARRESTS 9, LAYS MURDER PLOT TO JEWISH DOCTORS

## Asserts Zhdanov Fell Victim to Conspiracy by a Group Under U. S. Orders

## BRITAIN ALSO IS ACCUSED

## Broadcast Says Key Leaders of the Army and Navy Were the Intended Victims

By The Associated Press.

MOSCOW, Tuesday, Jan. 13—The Soviet press announced today the arrest of nine "terrorist Jewish doctors" on charges they plotted to kill top Soviet leaders on instructions from Zionist organizations, and the United States and British intelligence services.

The press accounts and a broadcast by the Moscow radio said the doctors had confessed they killed Andrei A. Zhdanov, a top member of the Politburo, who died in 1948, and Alexander S. Scherbakov, head of the chief political administration of the Soviet Army, who died in 1945.

Others marked by the plotters for death, the accounts said, were Marshal Alexander M. Vasilevsky, War Minister; Marshal Ivan S. Konev, commander of Soviet ground forces, and his chief of staff, Gen. S. M. Shtemenko; Marshal Leonid A. Govorov, who commanded the Soviet forces in Finland during World War II, and Admiral G. I. Levchenko, Deputy Navy Minister.

The radio broadcast said the doctors were "connected with the international Jewish bourgeois-nationalist organization 'Joint' set up by the American intelligence service."

[In New York, spokesmen for the American Joint Distribution Committee, which has sent millions of dollars to assist Jews in Europe, including those behind the Iron Curtain, said their organization was known in Europe as "Joint." They said that if the Moscow attack was directed at their committee, it was too ridiculous for comment. The spokesmen noted that the Kremlin had attacked their organization twice in the past.]

### Harmful Treatment Charged

Quoting a dispatch from the official Soviet news agency Tass, the broadcast said the doctors had admitted trying to kill off the top Soviet leaders by harmful treatment and bad diagnosis.

Regarding Mr. Zhdanov's death, the broadcast said:

"The criminals confessed they made an incorrect diagnosis of his disease and, concealing the miocardinal infraction from which he suffered, prescribed a regime which was contra-indicated for this serious illness and thereby killed Comrade A. A. Zhdanov."

The broadcast added that in the case of Mr. Scherbakov, the doctors "incorrectly applied strong medicines for his treatment, introduced an experimental regime and thus caused his death." At the time of the army official's death, it was said to have been caused by paralysis of the heart.

The radio said among those arrested were Profs. M. S. Vovsi, V. N. Vinogradov, M. B. Kogan, B. B. Kogan, P. I. Egorov, A. I. Feldman, Y. G. Etinger, A. M. Grinshtein and G. I. Mayorov. All were identified as "therapeutic doctors" except Professor Grinshtein, who was described as a neuropathologist.

The broadcast declared:

"Investigation has established that members of this terrorist group, by taking advantage of their positions as doctors and by violating the trust of ill people with premeditation, criminally undermined their health and deliberately made incorrect diagnoses and then, by incorrect healing methods, destroyed them."

### Fits Anti-Semitic Pattern

The reported arrest of Jewish doctors in the Soviet Union appears to tie in with the growing pattern of anti-Semitism in the Soviet Union and its satellites.

In the treason trial last December of prominent Czech Communists, eleven of the fourteen tried were Jews, including Rudolf Slansky, former Secretary General of the Czechoslovak Communist party.

In M. Slansky's confession he said that after Czechoslovakia's liberation he had placed in important posts "capitalist Jewish emigrants who returned to Czechoslovakia as imperialist agents" and allowed them to cultivate relations with Israeli organization that were "nothing other than camouflaged American spy networks."

In a recent speech, Czech President Klement Gottwald told his people that "all Zionist organizations have become espionage groups since the state of Israel was established."

Some time ago, the American Jewish Committee charged that tens of thousands of Soviet Jews were in slave labor camps because the Kremlin's suspicion that their loyalty could not be trusted.

### Reduced to Worst Status

In a report based on evidence gleaned from Soviet publications and from refugee journalists and other sources, the committee declared that as a group the Jewish population in Russia had been reduced to its worst status in many years.

Soviet suspicion of Jewish loyalty, according to the report, is based on fear that the Jews have a "Western" orientation incompatible with the Soviet chauvinism now being fostered by official propaganda. It also was said that Soviet authorities feared that Zionist sentiment was strong among Soviet Jews, who have been prohibited, with rare exceptions, from migrating to Israel.

The report also referred to a number of anti-Semitic outbreaks that had been reported from small Ukrainian towns, along with accounts of assaults on individual Jews in Moscow and Odessa.

January 13, 1953

# *Here Are 35 Red Ways To Catch a 'Heretic'*

By The Associated Press.

BERLIN, Jan. 24—The purge-ridden Communists have now figured out thirty-five different ways to denounce someone.

Goaded by Moscow's desire for violent purge, the Communist word-coiners are filling their controlled press with brand new words designed to catch anyone, however innocent, and indict him for "thought crime."

The United States High Commission in Berlin, scanning the Eastern press for clues to the reasons behind the purge, compiled today a survey that listed the kind of "isms" that mean heresy to the Kremlin:

Trotskyism, Zionism, cosmopolitanism, objectivism, particularism, burocratism, unionism, diversionism, schematism, imperialism, Titoism, pacificism, conciliationism, individualism, factionalism, practicism, neutralism, relativism, critical realism, militarism, chauvinism, Social Democratism, opportunism, careerism, equalitarianism, theoreticism, formalism, naturalism, collaborationism, opposition to internal party democracy, bourgeois attitude, kulak attitude, lack of vigilance, lack of class consciousness and uncritical attitude.

January 25, 1953

# STALIN DIES AFTER 29-YEAR RULE

## PREMIER ILL 4 DAYS

By HARRISON E. SALISBURY

Special to THE NEW YORK TIMES.

MOSCOW, Friday, March 6—Premier Joseph Stalin died at 9:50 P. M. yesterday [1:50 P. M. Thursday, Eastern standard time] in the Kremlin at the age of 73, it was announced officially this morning. He had been in power twenty-nine years.

The announcement was made in the name of the Central Committee of the Communist party, the Council of Ministers and the Presidium of the Supreme Soviet.

Calling on the Soviet people to rally firmly around the party and the Government, the announcement asked them to display unity and the highest political vigilance "in the struggle against internal and external foes." [No announcement was made of a successor to Premier Stalin.]

The Soviet leader's death from general circulatory and respiratory deficiency occurred just short of four days after he had been stricken with a brain hemorrhage in his Kremlin apartment.

Accompanying the death announcement was a final medical certificate issued by a group of ten physicians, headed by Health Minister A. F. Tretyakov, who cared for Mr. Stalin in his last illness under the direct and closest supervision of the Central Committee and the Council of Ministers.

**Pulse Rate Was High**

The medical certificate revealed that in the last hours Mr. Stalin's condition grew worse rapidly, with repeated heavy and sharp circulatory and heart collapses. His breathing grew superficial and sharply irregular. His pulse rate rose to 140 to 150 a minute and at 9:50 P. M., "because of a growing circulatory and respiratory insufficiency, J. V. Stalin died."

[The news of Mr. Stalin's death was withheld by Soviet officials for more than six hours.]

Pravda appeared this morning with broad black borders around its front page, which was devoted entirely to Mr. Stalin. The layout ir [illegible]led a large photograph of the F[illegible]ier, the announcement by the Gc[illegible]rnment, the medical bulletins and the announcement of the formation of a funeral comm[illegible]ion headed by Nikita S. Khruschchev, secretary of the Central Committee of the party.

**PREMIER JOSEPH STALIN**

*A portrait released by Sovfoto, Soviet picture agency*

Other members of the commission are Lazar M. Kaganovich, Premier Stalin's brother-in-law; Nikolai M. Shvernik, President of the Soviet Union; Alexander M. Vasilevsky, War Minister; N. U. Pegov, an alternate member of the Presidium; P. A. Artemyev, commander of the Moscow military district, and M. A. Yasnov, chairman of the city of Moscow.

Pravda's announcement said Mr. Stalin's body would lie in state in the Hall of Columns.

His death brought to an end the career of one of the great figures of modern times—a man whose name stands second to none as the organizer and builder of the great state structure the world knows as the Soviet Union.

[The United Press said members of Mr. Stalin's family and his closest associates in the Presidium and Central Committee were at his bedside.]

The Soviet leader began his life in the simple mountain village of Gori deep in poverty-stricken Georgia. He rose to head the greatest Russian state that has ever existed. For nearly thirty years, Mr. Stalin was at the helm of the country. No other statesman of modern times has led his nation for a longer period.

This morning's official announcement declared that the Government and party would strengthen "the defense, capacity and might of the Soviet state" in every manner, and in "every way" strengthen the Soviet Army, Navy and organs of intelligence "with a view to constantly raising our preparedness for a decisive rebuff to any aggressor."

The declaration comprised an important statement of policy, both external and internal. With regard to foreign relations, it declared that the party and Government stood by an inflexible policy of securing and strengthening peace, of struggle against the preparation and unleashing of a new war, and for a policy of "international collaboration and development of businesslike connections with all countries."

**Friendship for China Cited**

The second foreign policy point was the declaration of firm support for "proletarian internationalism," for the development of brotherly friendship with [Communist] China, with the workers of all countries of the "people's democracy" and with the workers of capitalist and colonial countries fighting "for peace, democracy and socialism."

The announcement of Mr. Stalin's death was made to the Soviet people by radio early this morning. The announcement was early enough so that persons going to work had heard the news before leaving their homes.

This correspondent circled the Kremlin several times during the evening and early morning. The great red flag flew as usual over the Supreme Soviet Presidium building behind Lenin's Tomb.

Lights blazed late as they always do in many Kremlin office buildings. Sentry guards paced their posts at the Great Kremlin Gate.

The city was quiet and sleeping, and in Red Square all was serene. The guards stood their duty at Lenin's Tomb, but otherwise the great central square was deserted, as it always is in the hours just before daylight.

The last medical bulletin before the announcement of Mr. Stalin's death was issued shortly before 9 o'clock last night, reporting his condition as of 4 P. M. yesterday. It said his condition had grown worse despite every method of therapy employed by Soviet physicians.

The bulletin revealed that, at 8 o'clock yesterday morning, there occurred a sharp heart circulatory collapse, which was corrected by "extraordinary curative measures."

A second "heavy collapse" occurred at 11:30 A. M., which "was eliminated with difficulty."

Pravda, organ of the Central Committee of the Communist party, and Izvestia, organ of the Soviet Government, called on the Soviet people yesterday to rally around the party and the Government in "these difficult days" and to display what Izvestia characterized as "heightened revolutionary vigilance." Pravda also demanded from all Soviet citizens "stanchness of spirit and vigilance."

Pravda's editorial appeal to the populace was read repeatedly over the radio. It was also read and discussed in factories, shops and offices throughout the country. Pravda had clearly sounded the theme of the day—vigilance and unity.

March 6, 1953

# Stalin Rose From Czarist Oppression to Transform Russia Into Mighty Socialist State

## DICTATOR RUTHLESS IN MOVING TO GOALS

### He Furthered Socialization and Industrialization of World's First Marxist Nation

### LED WORLD WAR II EFFORT

### Hard, Mysterious, Aloof, Rude, He Outlasted the Dreamers and Solidified Power

Joseph Stalin became the most important figure in the political direction of one-third of the people of the world. He was one of a group of hard revolutionaries that established the first important Marxist state and, as its dictator, he carried forward its socialization and industrialization with vigor and ruthlessness.

During the second World War, Stalin personally led his country's vast armed forces to victory. When Germany was defeated, he pushed his country's frontiers to their greatest extent and fostered the creation of a buffer belt of Marxist-oriented satellite states from Korea across Eurasia to the Baltic Sea. Probably no other man ever exercised so much influence over so wide a region.

In the late Nineteen Forties, when an alarmed world, predominantly non-Communist, saw no end to the rapid advance of the Soviet Union and her satellites, there was a hasty and frightened grouping of forces to form a battle line against the Marxist advance. Stalin stood on the Elbe in Europe and on the Yalu in Asia. Opposed to him stood the United States, keystone in the arch of non-Marxist states.

Stalin took and kept the power in his country through a mixture of character, guile and good luck. He outlasted his country's intellectuals, if indeed, he did not contrive to have them shot, and he wore down the theoreticians and dreamers. He could exercise great charm when he wanted to. President Harry Truman once said in an unguarded moment:

"I like old Joe. Joe is a decent fellow, but he is a prisoner of the Politburo."

But the Stalin that the world knew best was hard, mysterious, aloof and rude. He had a large element of the Oriental in him; he was once called "Ghengis Khan with a telephone" and he spent much of his life nurturing the conspiracies that brought him to power and kept him there.

#### Opinion of Leon Trotsky

Leon Trotsky, Stalin's brilliant and defeated adversary, regarded him as an intellectual nonentity who personified "the spirit of mediocrity" that impregnated the Soviet bureaucracy. Lenin, who valued Stalin highly as a party stalwart, characterized him as "crude" and "rough" and as a "cook who will prepare only peppery dishes."

But those who survived the purges hailed Stalin as a supreme genius.

Although he remained an enigma to the outside world to the very end of his days, Stalin's role as Russia's leader in the war brought him the admiration and high praise of Allied leaders, including President Roosevelt and Winston Churchill. And, indeed, only a man of iron will and determination like Stalin's could have held together his shattered country during that period of the war when German armies had overrun huge portions of Russian territory and swept to the gates of Moscow, Leningrad and the Caucasus. Like Churchill in England, Stalin never faltered, not even at moments when everything seemed lost.

When most of the Government machinery and the diplomatic corps were moved to Kuibyshev in December, 1941, in expectation of the imminent capture of Moscow, Stalin remained in the Kremlin to direct the operations that finally hurled the Nazi hordes from the frontyard of the capital. His battle orders and exhortations to the Russian armies and people to persevere in the fight contributed immensely to final victory. Repeatedly, Churchill referred to him in Parliament as Russia's "great warrior."

#### War Role Paramount

With the turn of the tide against the Germans, Stalin proclaimed himself marshal of the Soviet Union and later generalissimo. Surrounded by a galaxy of brilliant generals, whose names will go down in history as among the greatest of Russia's military leaders, Stalin was portrayed in the Soviet and foreign press as the supreme commander responsible for over-all strategy. To what extent this was true will have to be determined by the future historian, but that his role in the conduct of the war was paramount is undeniable.

The energy and will power he displayed both before and during the war confirmed the justification for his name, for Stalin in Russian means "man of steel," a nom de guerre he adopted early in his revolutionary career. Long before he dreamed of becoming the supreme autocrat of Russia he had displayed the steel in his character as a political prisoner under the Czarist regime. A fellow prisoner of that period gave an illustration of Stalin's grit. This was in 1909, in the prison at Baku. In punishment of rioting by the prisoners, the authorities ordered that they be marched in single file between two lines of soldiers who proceeded to shower blows upon them with rifle butts. With head high, a book under his arm, Stalin walked the gantlet without a whimper, his face and head bleeding, his eyes flashing defiance. It was the kind of grit he demanded from others, the kind that helped save Russia from Nazi conquest and domination. His experience under the Czarist regime and his Asiatic character taught him how to treat political opponents.

In his relations with the Allied powers during the war and in his diplomacy before and after the war Stalin won the reputation of a grim realist.

Joseph Vissarionovich Djugashvili, later to become famous under his revolutionary name of Joseph Stalin, was born in the Georgian village of Gori Dec. 21, 1879.

His father was an impoverished and drunken shoemaker who made him sullen and resentful by regular beatings. His mother, Ekaterina, a peasant's daughter, was a woman of singular sweetness, patience and strength of character who exercised great influence on her son. She called him Soso (Little Joe) and lived to see him dictator of the world's largest empire.

#### Attended a Seminary

When he was 6 or 7, young Stalin contracted smallpox, which left him pock-marked for life. Through the efforts of his mother, who worked as a part-time laundress, Stalin entered a church school at 9. He was remembered there as a bright, self-assertive boy who loved argument and who flew into a fury with those who did not agree with him. He remained in this school from 1888 to 1893.

By heroic exertions, Stalin's mother obtained for him a scholarship in the Theological Seminary at Tiflis, where he studied from October, 1894, to May, 1899. The seminary was a gloomy institution—a cross between a barracks and a monastery—where the students attended endless lectures on theology and spent their few spare moments plotting to obtain forbidden books from the outside.

Stalin was among the worst offenders. An entry against him in the seminary's book of discipline has been preserved:

"At 11 A. M. I took away from Joseph Djugashvili Letourneau's 'Literary Evolution of the Nations.' * * * Djugashvili was discovered reading the said book on the chapel stairs. This is the thirteenth time this student has been discovered reading books borrowed from the Cheap Library. * * *"

The official reason for Stalin's expulsion was that for "unknown reasons" he failed to attend examinations. He declared he was expelled for "propagating Marxism."

To support himself he obtained a temporary job as night attendant in the Tiflis Observatory, but he was more concerned with his observations at meetings of Tiflis railway workers during the day than of the stars at night. His revolutionary apprenticeship was served as an organizer of the Tiflis transportation workers. He helped stage street demonstrations and distribute revolutionary leaflets.

In April, 1899, he received his first baptism of fire at a demonstration he helped organize in the heart of the city. The demonstration was drowned in blood by Cossacks, and he went into hiding for a year to escape the police. At this time he assumed the nickname of "Koba," after a hero in Georgian mythology.

On Nov. 11, 1901, he was elected a member of the Tiflis Committee of the Russian Social Democratic Labor party, in his native Georgia. A few weeks later he was deputized to go to Batum, a thriving industrial and commercial center, to direct revolutionary activity. In March of that year he led a strike of oil workers in that city.

In April, 1902, he was arrested and lodged in the Batum prison, from which he was transferred to Kutais. While in prison he learned of the meeting in London, in 1903, of the second congress of the Russian Social Democratic party, at which the party split into Bolsheviks and Mensheviks—extremists and moderates — an event that subsequently determined the entire course of the Russian Revolution. Stalin allied himself with Nikolai Lenin, leader of the Bolsheviks. Trotsky was against Lenin, although in 1917, after the revolution, he joined Lenin and became his principal lieutenant in the October Revolution and in the establishment of the Soviet regime.

On July 9, 1903, while in prison in Kutais, Stalin was sentenced to three years of exile to Siberia, and in November of that year he was transferred to the bleak, remote village of Novaya Uda. There he received his first letter from Lenin in response to one posing certain questions concerning Bolshevist policy and tactics. The letter confirmed him in his adherence to Lenin, whom he glorified as "Mountain Eagle." Determined to escape, Stalin made his way safely to Irkutsk at the end of the year. From there he proceeded to Baku, in the Caucasus, where he experienced his second baptism of fire as leader of a strike of oil workers. It was part of a wave of strikes that swept Russia with her defeat by Japan, a wave that was the harbinger of the Revolution of 1905.

Shortly after the outbreak of the general strike, which was the key element in the revolution of 1905, Stalin met Lenin for the

# From the Pictorial Record of Three Generations of the Family of Joseph Stalin

Associated Press

**Stalin as a student at Tiflis Theological Seminary in 1894.**

Associated Press

**A photo of him taken by the Czar's secret police in 1915.**

Sovfoto

**When he returned from Siberia to Petrograd (now Leningrad) in 1917. He had been exiled for his revolutionary activities.**

Associated Press

**Nadya Alliluyeva Stalin, his second wife, died Nov. 8, 1932.**

**Lieut. Jacob Stalin, son, a prisoner of Nazis, after he was captured in 1941 in World War II.**

Sovfoto

**Lieut. Gen. Vassily J. Stalin, son, commander of the air forces in the Moscow district.**

first time at a party conference in Tammerfors, Finland.

From the Tammerfors conference Stalin returned to his activity in the Caucasus, where on June 26, 1907, on Erivan Square in Tiflis, he directed the celebrated "expropriation" which netted the Bolshevik party 340,000 rubles. There had been other such "expropriations," but this was the biggest and most dramatic. Formally, Lenin and his associates had frowned upon these acts, but they, nevertheless, accepted the proceeds to help finance the party's work. In the Erivan Square affair a band of revolutionists directed by "Koba" fell upon a convoy of two carriages carrying Government funds fron. the railway station to the state bank, and after bombing the Cossack guard escaped with the money, which was sent to Lenin.

Following the "expropriation," Stalin was arrested and lodged in Bailov fortress, in Baku, where the incident of his running the gantlet of rifle butts took place. Soon thereafter he was exiled for the second time to Solvychegodsk, in Siberia, from which he escaped on June 24, 1909. He returned to Baku to resume his revolutionary activity, but remained at liberty only eight months, when he was again arrested and sent back to Solvychegodsk. From that place he conducted a secret correspondence with Lenin and his staff at Bolshevik headquarters in Cracow.

Eager to attend a party conference in Prague, Stalin again escaped and made his way to St. Petersburg, where he was arrested and exiled to Vologda. Once more he escaped and reached St. Petersburg on the day of the notorious massacre of workers in the Lena goldfields in Siberia. In St. Petersburg he helped found Pravda, the official organ of the Bolshevik party, but on the day of its first issue he was arrested and exiled to Narym, in the Urals. On Sept. 1 1912, he escaped and returned to St. Petersburg to resume the editorship of Pravda. This time he was betrayed by the agent provocateur Malinovsky, who had him

Sovfoto

**With his daughter, Svetlana, at the opera in Moscow in 1937. Between them are Vyacheslav M. Molotov and Nikolai M. Shvernik. Molotov is Deputy Premier and Shvernikis President of U.S.S.R.**

The New York Times

**Mme. Ekaterina Djugashvili, his mother, hoped that he would be a priest. Her name for him was "Soso," meaning Little Joe.**

**arrested together with Jacob Sverdlov, the future first President of the Soviet Union, at a concert given for the benefit of Pravda, Stalin and Sverdlov were exiled to Turuchansk, in Siberia, from which they were taken to the outlying settlement of Kureika, 800** miles north of the Trans-Siberian Railway. After twenty years of revolutionary activity and repeated imprisonments and exilings, Stalin found himself at a dead end. Letters arrived from Lenin, but they seemed very remote and futile. Then came the news of the first World War in 1914, the war that Lenin predicted would bring the downfall of the Russian autocracy and world revolution.

Stalin was transferred to Atchinsk, on the Trans-Siberian Railway, and it was there he first received word of the revolution of March 12, 1917. Almost the very first act of the Provisional Revolutionary Government, in which Alexander Kerensky was at first Minister of Justice and later Premier, was to order the release of all political prisoners. Among the many thousands who profited by this decree signed by Kerensky was Joseph Stalin. He made his way speedily to Petrograd.

On his arrival in Petrograd in March, 1917, Stalin went directly to the office of Pravda, where he was met by V. M. Molotov and Leo Kamenev. Lenin and most of his staff were in Zurich, Switzerland. It was not until April 16, 1917, that Lenin arrived in Petrograd after his famous journey through Germany in a sealed car provided by the German General Staff. The journey led across Germany to Stockholm and through Finland. A month later Trotsky arrived from America.

Upon his arrival in Petrograd in May, 1917, from the United States, where he had lived for several months, Trotsky lost no time in associating himself with Lenin in his demand for the overthrow of the Provisional Government, conclusion of an immediate peace, a sweeping Socialist program and advocacy of world revolution. From the very beginning of this development Trotsky completely overshadowed Stalin and all others among Lenin's lieutenants. He became Lenin's "big stick."

**In the first Council of Commissars, formed upon the formation of the Soviet Government, Stalin was given the modest, obscure post of Commissar of Nationalities. Nevertheless, that post in the hands of Stalin became symbolic and significant, for it was under** Stalin as supreme dictator that the Soviet Union, conceived as a multiple state of nationalities, achieved its greatest expansion, territorially and politically.

In the October Revolution Stalin took a relatively modest part. Although his admirers picture him as taking the initiative with Lenin in planning and executing that historic unpeaval against the opposition of Trotsky and others in Lenin's immediate entourage, the minutes of the Central Committee of the party for Oct. 23, two days before the coup d'état, show clearly that Lenin and Trotsky took the lead in demanding approval of the uprising, while others were either opposed or hesitant. Stalin supported Lenin. On that occasion, the minutes attest, Lenin, angry and defiant over the refusal of his collaborators to approve the plans for the uprising, rose and, pointing to Trotsky, shouted, "Very well, then, he and I will go to the Kronstadt sailors," meaning that he would summon the sailors of the Baltic Fleet to rise in rebellion against the Kerensky regime. The Baltic Fleet played a leading role in the uprising. Later these same sailors, who had been glorified by Trotsky as "the pride and beauty of the Russian Revolution," were shot down en masse by Trotsky in their revolt against the Soviet regime in March, 1921.

During the civil war after the Bolshevik revolution Stalin and Trotsky were at loggerheads. This was particularly true during the fighting on the Tsaritsin and Perm fronts. Repeatedly Trotsky called him to order and on various occasions Lenin had to intervene to make peace between them. The enmity and hatred between Trotsky and Stalin dated from that period.

Already during Lenin's illness, which lasted about two years, Stalin began preparing for his future leadership of the party and of the Government. This he ultimately achieved by utilizing his new position as general secretary of the party in building a party machine loyal to him.

**Member of Triumvirate**

After Lenin's death, authority was vested by the party in the hands of a triumvirate, consisting of Stalin, Zinoviev and Kamenev. There were three principal factions in the party, the left, represented by Zinoviev; the right, headed by Rykov and Bukharin, and the center, of which Stalin was regarded as the spokesman. Trotsky, who was ill a good part of the time, so much so that he had been unable to attend Lenin's funeral, had plans of his own. He felt that ultimately, as Lenin's chief collaborator, he would inherit Lenin's mantle.

In the bitter factional polemics that ensued, Stalin played the left against the right and vice versa, and eventually defeated both, as well as Trotsky.

In 1936, during the period of purges, Stalin proclaimed a new Constitution for Russia, with promises of universal secret suffrage, freedom of the press, speech and assembly. It was interpreted to maintain the dictatorship and to stabilize the revolution.

Not since the days of Peter the Great, who sought to westernize Russia by force, had the country witnessed so violent a transformation. In fact, nothing in the history of revolutions could compare with the gigantic social and economic upheaval brought about under Stalin. Profound as was the

In 1929 Stalin began predicting a second world war and avowed that his purpose was to keep Russia clear of the conflict. Despite this policy, with the advent of Hitler to power he joined in collective security measures. He abruptly abandoned his advocacy of collective security in 1939, when he about-faced and signed a mutual nonaggression pact with Nazi Germany.

It led to World War II, into which Russia later was drawn by Hitler's attack on her. This onslaught forged a Soviet alliance with the West, an alliance that ultimately enlarged the Soviet sphere.

**70th Birthday Celebrated**

Stalin's fiftieth and sixtieth birthdays were celebrated, but the press prepared the Soviet public on his sixty-ninth anniversary for the grim reality that years had left their impress even on "the teacher and inspirer of the world proletariat." Pictures were published showing that Stalin's hair had whitened. Then on his seventieth birthday in 1949 his anniversary was celebrated in grand fashion.

It was the first occasion in which Stalin had permitted public participation in his private life, and hence little was known about his personal affairs. He married twice. His first wife was Ekaterina Svanidze, who died after a long illness in 1907. They had a son, Jacob whose fate has been unknown since he became a German prisoner during World War II.

In 1919 the Premier married Nadya Alliluyeva, the 17-year-old daughter of his old revolutionary crony, Sergei Alliluyev. She died in 1932 under mysterious circumstances. They had a daughter and a son. The latter, Vassily, is now a lieutenant-general in the Soviet Air Force. All that became known of the daughter was her name, Svetlana, and her intellectual interests.

March 6, 1953

# Russians Revered Man Who Ruled As 'Our Father' and Godlike Genius

## Communist Propaganda Built Up Stalin Cult of Omniscience—Religion, History and Science Turned to Party End

To an extent never before seen in modern history, Joseph Stalin was revered as a living god in the last decades of his life. In the Soviet Union and Eastern Europe the Communist party substituted the deified Stalin for the notion of a supernatural god which, together with all other aspects of formal religions, it rejected as "superstition."

The Stalin cult was propagated by every instrument of Communist propaganda. He was extolled as omniscient and omnipotent, the possessor of every virtue, and as the greatest genius that ever lived, as "our father," "our leader," "our teacher," "the sun of our lives." He was pictured as infallible.

Everything of which the Soviet Union could boast was credited to him. To him alone went credit for all Soviet economic progress, for triumph in World War II, for the achievements of Soviet science. Writers, scientists, sports champions, and other outstanding figures credited their achievements to "the inspiration of Comrade Stalin."

To replace the religious ikons of Czarist Russia, pictures and statues of Stalin were used everywhere in the Soviet Union.

Typical of the adulation given Stalin is this poem printed in 1946:

"I might have compared him to a white mountain—but the mountain has a top.
"I might have compared him to the depths of the ocean—but the ocean has a bottom.
"I might have compared him to the shining moon—but the moon glows at midnight, not at noon.
"I might have compared him to the sun's brilliance—but the sun glows at noon, not at midnight."

The highest mountain of the Soviet Union was named Mount Stalin. Among Soviet cities are Stalingrad, Stalino, Stalinsk, Stalinabad, Stalinogorsk. The Stalin automobile plant in Moscow made the best Soviet car, while of other Stalin factories, Stalin mines and Stalin farms there were thousands. The Stalin Prizes given each year were Soviet equivalents of the Nobel Prizes.

Stalin's every word was official doctrine and a citation from Stalin the highest authority on every subject. In 1950 when Stalin issued a pronouncement on philology, that pronouncement immediately swept away the last shred of authority from the doctrines of the late Prof. N. Y. Marr, the man whose writings had until then dominated Soviet philology.

Much of Soviet scholarship in the social sciences and the humanities consisted mainly of commentaries upon the writings of Stalin.

Stalin's biography and the early history of the Soviet Union were rewritten.

On Stalin's seventieth birthday, Dec. 21, 1949, the members of the Politburo delivered addresses paying homage to Stalin's genius in every field, attributing to his initiative every advance made by the Soviet Union.

In Soviet schools he was portrayed to the children as a second father, watching over them constantly, ready to praise or chastise as they deserved.

When Stalin partly weakened Soviet Government prohibitions on religious observance, instruction and the training of priests, he began a period in which Soviet priests, mullahs, rabbis and other clergymen called upon God to bless Stalin, identifying his will with the will of God and his policies with the policies that the faithful of all religions were bound to support.

March 6, 1953

## CHAPTER 2

# Khrushchev's Russia

Nikita Khruschchev addresses a large gathering at Moscow's Lenin Stadium in 1959. He is dwarfed by the giant portrait of Lenin in the background.
UNITED PRESS INTERNATIONAL

# MALENKOV IS NAMED NEW SOVIET PREMIER; WIDE CHANGES DISCLOSED TO AVOID 'PANIC'

## FOUR TO HELP RULE

### Beria, Molotov, Bulganin and Kaganovich Are Deputy Premiers

### TEN-MAN PRESIDIUM

### Molotov Is Again Foreign Minister—Vishinsky Demoted to U. N.

By HARRISON E. SALISBURY
Special to THE NEW YORK TIMES.

MOSCOW, March 6 — Georgi Maximilianovich Malenkov was named head of the Soviet Government tonight in place of the late Joseph Stalin in a series of changes in the highest Soviet leadership.

Mr. Malenkov has assumed the post of Chairman of the Council of Ministers, which was held by Stalin.

At the same time he was named as first in the list of the Presidium of the Central Committee of the Communist party, which is composed of ten members and four alternates.

Sovfoto

**NEW SOVIET LEADER: Georgi M. Malenkov, 51, who succeeded Joseph V. Stalin yesterday as Premier of Soviet Union.**

Standing beside him in the chief and most responsible posts of Government and party in this reorganized structure are four veteran Soviet leaders and co-workers of Stalin—Lavrenti P. Beria, Vyacheslav M. Molotov, Nikolai A. Bulganin and Lazar M. Kaganovich. Those four become the First Deputy Chairmen of the Council of Ministers and with Mr. Malenkov constitute its Presidium.

The announcement over the Moscow radio at 11:30 o'clock tonight was made in the name of the Central Committee of the Communist party, the Council of Ministers and the Presidium of the Supreme Soviet.

The changes in the directing bodies of the Government were made, it was announced, with the purpose of maintaining uninterrupted and correct leadership and avoiding "any kind of disarray and panic."

The announcement said the changes would secure the nation from any kind of interruption in directing the activity of state and party organs and "unconditionally secure" the successful carrying into effect of party and Government policies both internally and abroad.

The chief impression given by the Government both in tonight's announcement and in the proclamation of Stalin's death was one of firmness and the highest political vigilance, a sense of the rallying together of party and Government forces to withstand any threats from within or from without.

The Government was acting with the g[illegible]test resolution and with mark[illegible] vigor. Mr. Malenkov lost no tin[illegible] in demonstrating his will and determination to prove a worthy custodian of the policies of monolithic unity and steel resolution that marked the leadership of Stalin.

Without any question, the most important feature of the announcement was the placing of Mr. Malenkov at the helm of the Soviet State. He long has been one of Stalin's closest associates and only a year ago last January, on the occasion of the award to him of the Order of Lenin on his fiftieth birthday, he was called by Pravda Stalin's "coadviser."

Tonight Mr. Malenkov became the man who is picking up the torch of the Soviet State and the Communist party and leading the Government and party forward along the pathway laid out by Stalin.

The 51-year-old Malenkov thus becomes the custodian of the tradition of revolutionary Soviet leaders begun by Lenin and Stalin.

**Molotov Gets Back Old Job**

At the same time, it was announced, several veteran Stalinist colleagues—in particular Mr. Beria, Mr. Molotov and Marshal Bulganin—would assume direct charge of vital ministries.

Thus Mr. Beria becomes head of the Ministry of Internal Affairs, in which is combined the former ministries of Internal Affairs and State Security.

Mr. Molotov becomes once more the Foreign Minister, succeeding Andrei Y. Vishinsky, who becomes his First Deputy and permanent Soviet Representative at the United Nations. Jacob A. Malik also was named a First Deputy Minister, and V. Zuznetsov, former head of the trade unions, becomes Deputy Foreign Affairs Minister.

Marshal Bulganin resumes his former post as head of the War Ministry and has as his first deputies, Marshal Alexander M. Vassilevsky, who has been acting as War Minister, and Marshal Georgi A. Zhukov, famous Soviet commander in World War II.

Marshal Klimenti E. Voroshilov, Stalin's old civil war associate and close friend since the days when they fought together at Staritsyn, becomes President of the Presidium of the Supreme Soviet in place of Nikolai M. Shvernik, who is recommended to resume his old post as head of Soviet trade unions.

Nikolai M. Pegor, who was one of the Communist party's secretaries, was named as Secretary of the Presidium of the Supreme Soviet. Alexander F. Gorkin, who has held the secretary's post, becomes Deputy Secretary.

The Ministries of Foreign and Internal Trade were united with Anastas Mikoyan as Minister. Mr. Mikoyan's chief deputy will be I. G. Kabanov, who recently has been head of state supply and formerly was electrical minister. T. T. Kumykyn, who formerly was Minister of Foreign Trade, and V. G. Zhavoronkov were named as his deputies.

The Government announced that the Supreme Soviet, which is the highest legislative body in the Soviet Union, had been summoned to meet on March 14 to ratify the changes in Government.

The first and most important change in the party structure was the announcement of a new Presidium of the Central Committee, which comprises ten members and four alternates. This Presidium replaces the Presidium of twenty-five members and eleven candidate members named last October.

The new party Presidium comprises Malenkov, Beria, Molotov, Voroshilov, Khrushchev, Bulganin, Kaganovich, Mikoyon, Saburov and Pervukhin. The alternates are Shvernik, Ponamarenkro, L. G. Melnikov, who is the party leader in the Ukraine, and M. Bagirov, the leader in Azerbaijan.

In place of the ten-member secretariat of the party, which was named last October, a new three-member secretariat was named. The new secretariat comprises Semyon D. Ignatiev, Peter N. Pospelov and N. N. Shatalin.

Mr. Ignatiev, who was elected last October to the Presidium of the Central Committee, formerly was the Central Committee representative for Uzbekistan. He is a prominent new leading member of the central party and Government apparatus. Only last month he was elected to the Moscow City Soviet, having been nominated by workers of the former Ministry of State Security. In tonight's list of appointments, all the chief positions in the Government went to men whose names have been known for years as the closest collaborators of Stalin. The most interesting change was the concentration into a more compact body.

March 7, 1953

# MALENKOV RESULT OF POWER POLITICS

### Protege of Stalin, He Gained Top by Ruthless Drive and Ability to Accomplish

Georgi Maximilianovich Malenkov, new Premier of the Soviet Union in succession to the late Joseph Stalin, is a complete product of Russia's party, secret police and state bureaucracy.

He rose to the top as a protege of Stalin, almost by the same means Stalin had employed—building power within the totalitarian state where all power formally is concentrated in the hands of the "vozhd," or leader, by manipulating the personnel of the bureaucracy.

Called the man with the "card-index brain"—a tribute to his phenomenal memory, on which Stalin relied—he actually installed an elaborately cross-indexed dossier system recording in detail the careers of Russia's new aristocracy, the bureaucracy. He ran this department as Stalin's deputy.

He achieved the pinnacle by a ruthless drive for power combined with an ability to get political and industrial results under desperate conditions. He was only one of Stalin's proteges and he had to fend off or make alliances with the Premier's surviving allies. The fortuitous death of Andrei A. Zhdanov, another Stalin protege, in September, 1948, removed his last important rival.

Mr. Malenkov was born on Jan. 8, 1902, in Orenburg (now Chkalov), on Russia's former southeast border with Kazakhstan south of the Ural Mountains. Nothing is known of his parents or his early life, but the available evidence indicates he came from a bourgeois or land-owning family.

He was believed to have taken no part in the events of 1917 and 1918—he was hardly 15 years old at the start of the revolution. He joined the Red Army as a volunteer and became a political commissar of a squadron, rising to regimental and brigade commissar and finally to head of the political department of the Turkestan Army.

#### Joined Party in 1920

He joined the Communist party in April, 1920. Attracting the attention of the party department in Moscow concerned with the development of cadres, potential leadership material, he was called to the capital in 1922 to complete his education.

He attend the Higher Technical School, training ground for engineers and administrators, until 1925. While there he kept aloof from the first open fight between Premier Stalin and Leon Trotsky in 1923, keeping silent when most of his comrades plumped for Trotsky, but in 1924 he excelled in purging the school of anti-Stalinist elements.

He emerged as secretary of all the party cells at the school. This attracted Stalin's attention, possibly through Vyachislav M. Molotov, then a secretary of the central committee, and in 1925 Mr. Malenkov was called to the secretariat of the party. Stalin was engaged in the fight with old comrades in his coalition, chiefly Lev Kamenev and Gregori Zinoviev, and newcomers without an Old Bolshevik past were useful.

By 1930 Mr. Malenkov was a divisional chief of the central committee and a delegate to the Sixteenth Party Congress. He then was promoted to chief of the organizing department of the Moscow party, right-hand man of Lazar Kaganovich in stamping out the followers of Nikolai I. Bukharin, Alexei Rykov and Mikhail Tomsky.

After the Seventeenth Party Congress in 1934, Premier Stalin prepared the final purge of his enemies. Mr. Malenkov was named chief of the reorganized personnel departments of the secretariat, under Nokolai Yezhov, later head of the secret police. He, Yezhov and Andrei A. Vishinsky carried out the great purges of 1936-38. Only Yezhov failed to survive the "purge of the purgers."

In 1937 Mr. Malenkov became secretary of the central electoral commission, a post in which he was able to name governmental functionaries. By 1939 he was on the central committee and was made Premier Stalin's deputy as secretary of the organizational bureau. He was on the committee that revised the party program and statutes and was later appointed chief of the cadre administration.

The combination of posts put him in a key position to fill the party, secret police, state and industrial bureaucracies with his henchmen, loyal to him as well as Premier Stalin. In 1941 he was made a candidate member of the Poitburo after he delivered a speech that caused a shake-up in the government.

His first Politburo task was to step up airplane production on which he did an outstanding job. In 1942 Premier Stalin sent him to Stalingrad to serve as political commissar. Then he was put in charge of industrial rehabilitation. In 1946 he was named a full member of the Politburo.

Little is known of his personal life. He was married twice and has two children. The family lives in a Kremlin apartment and at a country house outside Moscow. Mr. Malenkov affects the military tunic and Russian cap that Premier Stalin wore. He is heavy, joweled, sallow and humorless.

March 7, 1953

# MALENKOV GIVES UP A TOP PARTY POST; KHRUSHCHEV NAMED

### Premier Yields His Secretariat Position but Retains Job in Communist Presidium

### FIVE-MAN GROUP CHOSEN

By HARRISON E. SALISBURY
Special to THE NEW YORK TIMES.

MOSCOW, Saturday, March 21—Premier Georgi M. Malenkov has relinquished, at his own request, his post as a secretary of the Communist party, and a plenary meeting of the party's Central Committee has elected a new five-member Secretariat.

Mr. Malenkov, in addition to continuing in his post as chairman of the Council of Ministers, which is the Premiership, remains as first member of the party's Presidium of ten members and four candidates.

Stalin before 1939 held only the post of secretary of the Communist party, but in the last fourteen years of his life he combined within his person the position of chairman of the Council of Ministers and the secretaryship of the party.

The action of the Central Committee is in line with what appears to be a tendency of the Government to make a clear-cut division of responsibilities and to give official titles to those individuals who exercise those responsibilities.

#### New Secretariat Listed

The new Secretariat comprises Nikita S. Khrushchev and Mikhail A. Suslov, both of whom were among the ten secretaries named at the party congress last October, and Peter N. Pospelov, Nikolai N. Shatalin and Semyon D. Ignatiev.

[Prior to this announcement, foreign observers generally believed that Premier Malenkov had succeeded Stalin as first secretary of the Communist party, although there had been no formal statement to this effect. The fact that Mr. Khrushchev's name appeared first, out of alphabetical order, on the new Secretariat list seemed to indicate that he was now actually first secretary of the Communist party, and therefore its administrative chief.

[In Washington, John Foster Dulles, Secretary of State, said Friday that the United States Government had received no "great comfort" from recent talk of peace by Mr. Malenkov and other Soviet leaders.]

Mr. Khrushchev has been a party secretary since 1949, and Mr. Suslov since 1947. Mr. Pospelov is a veteran party publicist and propagandist, best known for his annual delivery of the Lenin anniversary speech at the Bolshoi Theatre each Jan. 21, in recent times.

Associated Press
**RUSSIAN MOVES UP: Nikita S. Khrushchev, senior member of the five-man secretariat of the Central Committee of the Communist party in the Soviet Union.**

Mr. Shatalin is a new figure who has come up from the cadres department of the Central Committee, and Mr. Ignatiev is also relatively new, having most recently been elected to the Moscow City Council at the nomination of workers of the Ministry of State Security.

Responsibilities of very great importance were given to Mr. Khrushchev, who was listed first among the five secretaries. He is a veteran party leader, having carried out extremely important responsibilities in the Ukraine before coming to Moscow in late 1949 to join the party Secretariat and become first secretary of the Moscow party organization. Now he has relinquished the Moscow secretaryship to concentrate on the work of the Central Committee.

Mr. Malenkov had held his post as a secretary of the party since 1939. In recent years, he has carried very heavy responsibilities in the Secretariat.

The plenary meeting of the Central Committee that approved the changes in the Secretariat met a week ago today, the day before the Supreme Soviet met to ratify a sweeping series of changes in Government offices.

The action by the Central Committee completed the revision of the Secretariat that followed Stalin's death.

Previously, four other secretaries had been transferred to other duties. Thus, Nikolai M. Pegov was made secretary of the Presidium of the Supreme Soviet. Panteleimon K. Ponamarenko and N. G. Ignatov were released from secretarial duties in connection with their transfer to executive duties with the Council of Ministers—Mr. Ponamarenko in the role of Minister of Culture. L. I. Brezhnev was shifted to the political administration of the Navy.

The plenary session of the Central Committee dropped two others of the secretaries named last October. N. A. Mikhailov has become first secretary of the Moscow party organization, replacing Mr. Khrushchev in that capacity, and A. B. Aristov has been named to the Presidium of the Central Committee.

The plenary session advanced Mr. Shatalin from candidate membership in the Central Committee, to which he was elected last October, to full membership.

### Directorate Held Ruling

**By HARRY SCHWARTZ**

The announcement that Premier Malenkov is now no longer a secretary of the Communist party appears to be the strongest evidence yet available that he has not fully inherited the power held by Stalin, and that the Soviet Union is ruled today by a group of leaders rather than by Mr. Malenkov alone.

Where Stalin held three posts, Premier, head of the Communist party Presidium and head of the party Secretariat, Mr. Malenkov now holds only the first two, and Mr. Krushchev is first secretary of the party. Since the secretariat is the chief executive organ of the party and the prime body responsible for appointments and dismissals of personnel in the apparatus, it appears that now Mr. Khrushchev, and not Premier Malenkov, is the direct chief of the almost 7,000,000 Soviet Communists.

What appears to make this latest development particularly significant is the fact that, prior to Mr. Malenkov's departure from the Secretariat, Pravda, on March 11 and 12, referred editorially to him as both Premier of the Soviet Union and secretary of the party. This terminology was applied to Stalin during the latter's lifetime and its use with respect to Mr. Malenkov was interpreted earlier this month as indicating a Soviet effort to build him up as quickly as possible to a prestige position similar to that of his predecessors.

If, as now appears most likely, the Soviet Union is actually being ruled by a group directorate rather than by Mr. Malenkov alone, the leading members of the group, aside from the Premier, would seem to be the following: Lavrenti P. Beria, who is head of the secret police as Interior Minister; Marshal Nikolai A. Bulganin, who heads the armed forces as Minister of War; and Mr. Khrushchev, as chief of the party.

Although Foreign Minister Vyacheslav M. Molotov has appeared formally as one of the three top Soviet figures, along with Messrs. Malenkov and Beria, most foreign observers believe that his real power is now far less than that of the others listed above.

Mr. Khrushchev worked for many years as Communist party leader in the Ukraine, although he is himself believed to be of Russian origin. His rise has been particularly rapid since he moved from the Ukraine to Moscow in 1949 as head of the Moscow party organization, a post he relinquished two weeks ago to head the national party organization. His coming role as party chief was suggested at the nineteenth party congress last October, when he presented the main report on changes in the party's rules and regulations.

Mikhail A. Suslov, number two man on the Secretariat, is a former editor of Pravda and a leading party intellectual. Peter N. Pospelov is another former editor of Pravda who was until late last year the head of the Marx-Engels-Lenin Institute in Moscow. His major speech in January, 1951, was the signal for the intensified "Hate America" campaign in the Soviet press since that date.

Comparatively little is known about N. N. Shatalin and S. D. Ignatiev, although the records of both men suggest they have worked close with Mr. Malenkov in the party apparatus. Mr. Shatalin was elected to the party's Organization Bureau in 1946 and in 1950 was the Central Committee representative who purged the Communist party in the Moldavian Republic. Mr. Ignatiev has conducted similar purges in Uzbekistan for the Central Committee. Early this year, his connection with the secret police was suggested when he was nominated for the post of deputy in the Moscow Soviet by the central apparatus of the Ministry of State Security.

March 21, 1953

# SOVIET FREES 15 PHYSICIANS, ASSERTING NO PLOT EXISTED

## WHOLE CASE 'FALSE'

### ACCUSERS ARE ARRESTED

**By HARRISON E. SALISBURY**

Special to The New York Times.

MOSCOW, Saturday, April 4—The Ministry of Internal Affairs early this morning announced the release of the nine doctors arrested last January on charges of plotting to kill Soviet leaders. Six other doctors who had been detained also were said to have been freed.

The announcement said the evidence on which the doctors had been arrested was false and put the blame for the arrests on the former Ministry of State Security.

The announcement added that the persons who had been guilty of "incorrect conduct of the investigation" had been arrested and brought "to criminal responsibility."

It said that careful investigation by the new Ministry of Internal Affairs, which has been headed since the death of Stalin by Lavrenti P. Beria and which now incorporates both the old Ministry of Internal Affairs and the old Ministry of State Security, has shown that the case prepared against the doctors was false in its entirety.

#### Identity of Chief Hidden

[The identity of the Minister of State Security at the time of the arrest of the doctors last January is not known certainly. Mr. Beria was head of all Soviet security forces until 1946. Thereafter, until at least a year ago, the Minister of State Security was apparently Victor Abbakumov, but he has disappeared from the pages of the Soviet press in the last year and was not elected to the Central Committee of the Communist party last October.

[The suspicion has been widespread recently that S. D. Ignatiev may have been Minister of State Security last January, inasmuch as he was nominated then for a post in the Supreme Soviet by the central apparatus of the Ministry of State Security in Moscow. Within the past month however, Mr. Ignatiev was named a secretary of the Communist party. Mr. Beria is now a Deputy Premier as well as Minister of Internal Affairs.]

The announcement said that the evidence in the case was obtained by oppressive methods which are "impermissible and strictly forbidden by Soviet law."

This evidence, said the announcement, was obtained from the accused persons by former workers in the Ministry of State Security.

The announcement was published on the fourth page of all Moscow newspapers.

The announcement by the Ministry of Internal Affairs said that in all fifteen Soviet doctors, including the nine who were originally announced as having been arrested last January 13, had been released.

The fifteen doctors were given as: Prof. M. S. Vovsi, V. N. Vinogradov, M. B. Kogan, B. B. Kogan, P. I. Yagorov, A. I. Feldman, Y. A. Etinger, V. K. Vasilenko, A. M. Grinshtein, V. F. Zelenin, B. S. Preobrazhenski, N. A. Popova (a women), V. V. Sakusov, N. A. Sherevsky and G. I. Mairov, a surgeon.

The announcement declared that the inquiry disclosed that the original group of nine physicians were arrested "incorrectly, without any legal basis."

It added that the examination showed that the entire evidence was false and that the documentary data employed by workers in the investigation was "invalid."

April 4, 1953

# BERIA IS OUSTED AS 'ENEMY' OF SOVIET

## NO. 2 MAN PURGED

### Deputy Premier Accused of Seeking Power and Pushing Capitalism

By HARRISON E. SALISBURY
Special to THE NEW YORK TIMES.

MOSCOW, Friday, July 10 — Lavrenti P. Beria, a First Deputy Premier and Minister of Internal Affairs, has been dismissed from his Government and Communist party posts and handed over to the Soviet Supreme Court for criminal prosecution on charges of seeking to seize power and turn the Soviet Union back to capitalist paths.

The announcement of the downfall of the chief of the Soviet secret police was made in a declaration by the Central Committee of the Communist party, which revealed that Premier Georgi M. Malenkov had presented the report on which the action was based at a plenary session of the committee in the last few days.

### Deposed Red Leader and Successor

Sovfoto
**Lavrenti P. Beria, dismissed chief of the secret police.**

Associated Press
**Sergei Nikiforovich Kruglov, named as his successor.**

[Until the announcement of his dismissal, Mr. Beria was believed to be at least the second most important man in the Soviet Union. Premier Malenkov, Mr. Beria and Foreign Minister Vyacheslav M. Molotov, also a First Deputy Premier, formed what had been regarded as the country's ruling triumvirate.]

It was charged that Mr. Beria was not only "an agent" and "a hireling" of foreign imperialists but that he was also actively pursuing policies that would have led both to his own supremacy in the Soviet Union and to the restoration of capitalism in Russia.

Mr. Beria was accused of a variety of specific counts—of trying to place his Internal Affairs Ministry in a position of superiority to both the Government and the Communist party, of delaying important agricultural decisions to damage the collective farm system and weaken production of supplies for the Soviet state, and of sabotaging Government decisions to end all illegalities in dealing with civilians.

Mr. Beria was charged also with stirring up differences between various Soviet nationalities and with activating bourgeois nationalist elements.

Mr. Beria was accused of using the Interior Ministry as a springboard for personal ambitions and of grasping power in the Soviet Union for himself.

The announcement of the Central Committee said Mr. Beria's wrecking activity was directed against the Soviet state "and in the interests of foreign capital."

Mr. Malenkov continues, of course, in his position of Premier of the Government and Mr. Molotov continues as Foreign Minister.

Sergei Nikiforovich Kruglov was named Minister of Internal Affairs to succeed Mr. Beria. This is the post Mr. Kruglov had long held until Mr. Beria was named to the office last March.

July 10, 1953

# BERIA IS EXECUTED WITH SIX OF AIDES BY A FIRING SQUAD

## TRIAL ANNOUNCED

### Secret Supreme Court Hearings Said to Have Lasted Six Days

By The United Press.

MOSCOW, Dec. 23—Lavrenti P. Beria, former Soviet Deputy Premier, and six of his aides were shot today as traitors to the Soviet Union.

Izvestia, the Soviet Government newspaper, announced in tomorrow's edition that Beria and his co-defendants had confessed at their trial to the charges against them and that "the highest degree of capital punishment—shooting—was carried out."

The trial lasted six days. The seven were executed today, the announcement said. There had been no previous mention in the Soviet press that the trial was in progress. It started Dec. 18 and ended today.

The Government newspaper said Marshal Ivan S. Konev had served as chairman of the court. The prosecutor was not named.

Beria, former Interior Minister and head of the security police, was charged along with his aides with having tried to seize power in the Soviet Union and re-establish a capitalistic state.

The trial was held before a special judicial commission of the Soviet Supreme Court. All the defendants were present, Izvestia said. The trial was closed to the public.

**Text of the Sentence**

The official text of the sentence as carried by Izvestia said:

"The Special Judicial Commission of the Supreme Court of the U. S. S. R. decrees to sentence [Lavrenti P.] Beria, [Vsevolod N.] Merkulov, [Vladimir G.] Dekanozov, [Bogdan Z.] Kobulov, [Sergei A.] Goglidze, [Pavel Y.] Meshik, and [L. E.] Vlodzimirsky to the highest degree of criminal punishment—shooting—with confiscation of personal property and removal of military titles and decorations. The sentence is final and cannot be appealed."

Izvestia commented that the special commission "established the guilt of the accused L. P. Beria of high treason against his country, organization of anti-Soviet conspiratorial groups in order to seize power and restore the rule of the bourgeoisie, and committing acts of terror against political leaders who were devoted to the Communist party and the people of the Soviet Union."

The newspaper said Beria had been active in counter-revolutionary movements since 1919 and that he "continued and expanded his secret criminal ties with foreign intelligence services up to the moment of his exposure and arrest" last July.

Izvestia said "the guilt of all the accused on the charges brought against them was completely proved in court by original documents, material evidence, notes by the accused in their own handwriting and the evidence of numerous witnesses."

December 24, 1953

## Beria's Name Cut Out Of Soviet Encyclopedia

MOSCOW, Jan. 4 (UP)—The Soviet Union disclosed today another move to erase from the public records the name of Lavrenti P. Beria, former secret police chief executed for treason.

The State Scientific Publishing House is distributing with its latest volume of the Soviet Encyclopedia a four-page substitution for the article on Beria in Volume V. A notice with it said:

"The State Scientific Publishing House recommends that Pages 21, 22, 23 and 24 be removed from Volume V, as well as the portrait [of Beria] between Pages 22 and 23, to replace which the pages of a new text are enclosed."

On the substitute pages were an article on Friedrich Wilhelm Bergholtz and pictures of the Bering Sea.

January 5, 1954

## Soviet Party Rising To a Par With State

Special to The New York Times.

MOSCOW, May 26—Parity or duality of the Communist party and the state in the Soviet Union has been growing.

Observers in the foreign diplomatic corps note, for example, that at the recent session of the Supreme Soviet, two important addresses of equal importance were delivered.

The first was that of Premier Georgi M. Malenkov to the Council of Nationalities. The second was that of Nikita S. Khrushchev, first secretary of the Communist party, to the Council of Union.

Although the meeting of the Supreme Soviet is what might be called a "Government" occasion, none the less the party secretary, Mr. Khrushchev, spoke on a basis of full parity with Premier Malenkov.

This parallel role of party and Government, as exemplified in these two persons, was touched upon briefly by Lazar M. Kaganovich, a First Deputy Premier, in his address to Soviet railroad men a fortnight ago.

Referring to the meeting of the Supreme Soviet, he mentioned not just the Malenkov speech nor just the Khrushchev speech. He mentioned both speeches as of equal importance. In mentioning first the Khrushchev and then the Malenkov speech, he apparently sought to make it plain that party and Government were marching step and step together.

Visual demonstration of this shoulder-to-shoulder relationship of Mr. Khrushchev and Mr. Malenkov was given at the Dynamo Sports Stadium Sunday when they appeared together.

At the same time foreign observers have noted that as party secretary, Mr. Khruschev is playing a major role in many Government programs, most notably in connection with the agricultural program and particularly as it concerns an increase in grain production.

Mr. Khrushchev presented to the Central Committee of the Communist party a program for a sharp increase in the grain harvest by bringing under cultivation a vast area of previously untilled or idle lands in Siberia and Kazakhstan. He recently made a trip to Kazakhstan to see at first hand how the program was being carried out. Great hopes are riding on this program, and any shortcomings would have sharp repercussions.

The duality of party functions is being stressed in the 300th anniversary celebration of uniting the Ukraine to Russia. An anniversary meeting of the Ukrainian Supreme Soviet, which was held in Kiev to mark the occasion, had as its principal speaker the Ukrainian Communist party secretary, A. I. Kirichenko. The parallel meeting of the Russian Federated Republic Supreme Soviet will be held in Moscow Thursday.

May 27, 1954

## Malenkov Moves Out of Kremlin And the Government Will Follow

By HARRISON E. SALISBURY

Special to The New York Times.

MOSCOW, Aug. 26—Premier Georgi M. Malenkov and his Government colleagues have given up the Kremlin as a living place. They also are planning to give it up as the seat of Government.

Confirmation of reports circulating in Moscow for eighteen months that the new Government had decided to reopen the Kremlin to the public as a showplace and give it up as restricted Government quarters has been given by the Secretary of the Communist party, Nikita S. Khrushchev.

In the course of conversations at the time the British Labor party leader, Clement R. Attlee, was here, Mr. Khrushchev said the Government had decided to reopen the Kremlin to the public.

Exactly how soon the Kremlin will be opened is not certain. However, the Kremlin already has been given up as a living place by high Government officials.

Premier Malenkov and Mr. Khrushchev moved out of the Kremlin last winter into private residences.

Since the death of Premier Stalin more and more Government business has been transacted at offices elsewhere in the city. Foreign Minister Vyacheslav M. Molotov has retained his office suite at the Kremlin but in recent months he has received most of his visitors at his suite in the Foreign Office skyscraper on Smolenskaya Place.

It was believed the Kremlin would continue to be utilized for state receptions of ambassadors and diplomats presenting their credentials. These ceremonies are conducted by Chairman Kliment E. Voroshilov of the Presidium of the Supreme Soviet who acts as Soviet "President." It was thought that formal presentations of medals and awards which also are made by Mr. Voroshilov or one of his deputies, will continue to be made in the Kremlin.

The offices of the Presidium of the Supreme Soviet also may eventually be removed from the Kremlin, but perhaps not until the forty-six-story office building which is being built for the Government in the Zaradya area along the Moscow River just below the Red Square is completed. The steel work for the central part of this building is only up to about eight stories. It will be several years before the structure is finished.

It is understood that the Government decision to open up the Kremlin is one of principle. The numerous activities that have been held there in the past year—New Year's parties for young people, graduation dances for university students and conferences of various sorts—are believed to be part of the program that is designed to break down the aura of mystery and secrecy that has long surrounded the ancient, thick-walled citadel in the center of Moscow.

In Czarist days the Kremlin was open to the public. But in those times the seat of Government was in St. Petersburg.

August 27, 1954

# SOVIET STRESSING PARTY DEMOCRACY

### Communist Press Cites Need for Collective Leadership in Lower Echelons

By CLIFTON DANIEL

Special to The New York Times.

MOSCOW, Sept. 18—Throughout the Soviet Union, elections are now being held in the primary organizations of the Communist party, factory, farm and institutional units. In this connection party publications are conducting a vigorous campaign for "internal party democracy" and "collective leadership."

Those two principles, which are commonly referred to as among the highest in the party's plan of organization, are not new conceptions but they are now being re-emphasized and the sharpest criticism is directed at party members who violate them.

The general theme of the party publications is that with the present drive to increase industrial and agricultural production "internal party democracy" is needed to enlist the support, creative abilities and critical faculties of the party's 7,000,000 members.

Specific examples of "gross violations" of the party's principles and rules appear in the press from time to time. A recent one concerned a party secretary in Moldavia who repeatedly took decisions without consulting his colleagues. Another, reported to the magazine Party Life in a letter from a rank-and-file Communist, concerned the case of a man who had been summarily dismissed from the party by a district committee without investigation or explanation.

**Defects Are Listed**

The most exhaustive and authoritative exploration of this subject appeared in the August issue of the magazine Kommunist, theoretical and political journal of the Soviet party's Central Committee. It condemned certain "serious defects" in the activity of many party organizations, among which it mentioned the following:

¶"Uncalled-for regimentation," which inhibits the "creative forces and abilities" of Communists.

¶"Predeciding" the outcome of the party elections.

¶"Downright arbitrariness" in regulating and restricting speeches at party meetings.

¶The "harmful practice of indiscriminately imposing punishments on Communists."

¶The use of the "administrative fiat" rather than patiently training party members and failure to adopt the "individual approach to persons."

Kommunist cited as the "grossest violation of internal party democracy" the example of the district committee that attempted to dictate the election of a new party bureau for a collective farm, and, when it failed, prevented the elected bureau from meeting. The committee used the "crudest administrative fiat and coercion," the magazine declared.

Development of internal party democracy, Kommunist went on to say, does not mean that leadership can be relaxed. Such a conception, it said, "has nothing in common with democratic centralism, the guiding principle of the organizational structure of the Communist party."

"Democratic centralism" is one of those phrases in the Communist lexicon that is difficult for Westerners who have grown up with a different interpretation of democracy to understand.

As defined in the Communist party's rules "democratic centralism" involves (a) "election of all leading party bodies," (b) periodic reports by those bodies to their organizations, (c) "strict party discipline and subordination of the minority to the majority," and (d) "the absolutely binding character of the decisions of higher bodies upon lower bodies."

Thus, according to the article in Kommunist, "development of internal party democracy not only does not exclude but absolutely demands qualified leadership of the lower party organizations by the higher.

Such leadership to be correct must be "collegial," the magazine declared.

In the Great Soviet Encyclopedia "collegiality" is defined as a "method of leadership in which the leadership of one organ is carried on by a group of persons, a collegium."

Citing examples of violation of the collective leadership principle, Kommunist reported that in the Beloretsk city committee more than half of the members never spoke but only voted on "previously prepared decisions" and in some party bureaus decisions were taken in the absence of a quorum."

"Such cases are intolerable," the magazine declared "Collectivity of leadership is the highest principle of party leadership."

Internal party democracy, it added, "is the key to upsurgence of all party work."

September 19, 1954

# *Russia Re-Viewed:* The Prison Camps of Siberia

## *Grim M.V.D. Slave-Labor Empire Covers Major Part of Soviet Union*

*This is the ninth of a series of articles by a correspondent of The New York Times who has just returned to this country after five years in the Soviet Union. For the first time he is able to write without the restrictions of censorship or the fear of it.*

By HARRISON E. SALISBURY

Half a mile from the outskirts of Yakutsk, on a muddy road leading to the main channel of the River Lena there is a rather long building of log construction, about two and a half stories high.

Its walls have blank faces with no windows and it looks as if it might be a frontier fort or warehouse or, possibly, a place for storing ice.

The building is none of these things. It is, in fact, one of the most notorious prisons in the Soviet Union, a place of confinement for political prisoners who are regarded as being particularly dangerous.

This is the prison to which, it is said, Karl Radek, the writer and revolutionary who was known to many Westerners, was sent after he was convicted in one of the purge trials of the Nineteen Thirties. And here he is said to have died in the later years of World War II, the victim, so the story goes, of a fellow-prisoner who killed him in a rage or quarrel. Gregori Sokolnikov, the veteran Soviet diplomat who got ten years along with Radek in 1937, was another victim of this prison.

A glimpse of this prison was one of many terrible and chilling sights that this correspondent encountered in a trip to the Soviet North and Eastern Siberia. It was probably the most extensive survey of this grim region by an American since the journey in the late Eighteen Eighties of George Kennan, grand-uncle of George F. Kennan, former United States Ambassador to Moscow.

**Range of Inner Empire**

It is sometimes said that everything in Siberia is run by the M. V. D. This is not quite correct. Novosibirsk and Western Siberia are generally free of directly operated M. V. D. enterprises. On the other hand the M. V. D. runs most of the North and the Arctic and large areas of Central Asia, as well.

If you were to draw a map of M. V. D.-land, the capital would be at Khabarovsk, a grim, gray city on the Amur, six hours ahead of Moscow in time zone and nearly forty-eight hours distant by plane.

Khabarovsk is the administrative center of Russia's great empire-within-an-empire, the slave state of prison labor and forced-residence workers that extends 2,700 miles west to Novosibirsk, nearly 2,000 miles from the Arctic Ocean south to the Manchurian frontier, and 600 miles east to Sakhalin.

Great Central Asian areas also fall within M. V. D.-land—the coal basin and booming steel works of Karaganda, the copper mines of Balkhash, potash works in Uzbekistan, uranium mines in Tadzhikistan.

It is a fluid state and a superstate, imposed upon the ordinary civil apparatus with tentacles like those of an octopus, doubling back on itself and entwining half of Russia in its grasp.

The direction of this sinister super-state is housed in a great gray building of modernistic design that occupies a block or more of frontage on Volochayevskaya Street just off the main thoroughfare in Khabarovsk. This is the headquarters of the Eastern Administration of the M. V. D., the biggest and most powerful single administration in the Soviet Union and one of the biggest and most powerful in the world.

This correspondent, partly by chance and partly by management, happens to have traveled through more of this vast area of M. V. D.-land then any other foreigner.

There are vast areas still unvisited by any outsider—the Magadan gold field regions on the Sea of Okhotsk, Sakhalin with its oil fields and fisheries, Kamchatka, the Arctic fringe, the desert mining areas of Central Asia and scores of other areas, most of which are firmly closed to foreign visits.

**PRISON LABOR SITE: Board fence off the main street in Birobidzhan, Soviet Far East, hides a prison work gang. Corner hut is for M. V. D. soldiers who stand guard with submachine guns. Mr. Salisbury took this photograph during his survey of northern and eastern Siberia, probably the most extensive journey of its kind by an American in this century.**

**It is most difficult to generalize about conditions in an area so vast as this. It must also be re**membered that impressions of a traveler are a highly subjective thing. For example, the last two Americans to see Yakutsk before this correspondent were the late Wendell L. Willkie and Henry A. Wallace. Both were favorably impressed. Ten years later, in which time it may be deduced that such changes as occurred in Yakutsk were for the better, this correspondent got a decisively unfavorable impression.

Mr. Wallace's trip to Siberia in 1944 was one of the most unusual that ever occurred.

He saw things that no foreigners had seen before and few will ever see again — the Magadan gold fields for example; Yakutsk, as mentioned above; Karaganda, the Balkhash copper fields and a good many others. He was escorted from point to point by old Gen. Sergei A. Goglidze, whom Mr. Wallace praised for his gentleness and humanity.

But what Mr. Wallace did not realize until several years later was that good old Sergei Goglidze was the chief of the M. V. D. for all this enormous area. He was the biggest police boss in the world. He was the man who sat in those gray offices on Volochayevskaya Street and ran the whole thing. Mr. Wallace rode in General Goglidze's private railroad car and ate at his table every day. And never knew who his host was.

### Fate Tied to Beria's

General Goglidze is gone now. He went to his death with his boss, Lavrenti P. Beria, in December, 1953, presumably in one of the execution chambers under the old insurance building on Lubyanka Hill in Moscow, the main headquarters of the M. V. D., or possibly in some Army stronghold.

In any event, a new M. V. D. general runs the Volochayevskaya Street headquarters in General Goglidze's place. Some one else sits in his seat in the Supreme Soviet, representing the Jewish Autonomous Oblast, one of the minor dependencies in the M. V. D. empire. Another man holds General Goglidze's place on the Central Committee of the Uzbekistan Communist party.

There has been a big reshuffling of chairs since Beria's arrest at the end of June, 1953.

But nothing materially has changed on Volochayevskaya Street.

There is a special atmosphere in this gray prison land where the M. V. D. is master. This is not a subjective thing, nor do you have to be foreign to feel it. For instance, an airplane on which this correspondent was traveling had motor trouble and had to make an unscheduled landing at Karaganda, the big prison coal center in Kazakhstan. As the passengers walked from the runway to the airport buildings one Russian said to the stewardess, who had announced that we would have to stop overnight: "Please tell the local vlast [powers] that we are not staying here because we want to. I haven't any visa for Karaganda on my passport and I don't want to be rasstrelyan [executed by shooting]."

This was the passenger's idea of a joke. But a pretty serious joke, at that. Foreigners make plenty of remarks about persons being sent to Karaganda. But you don't often hear Russians making the same kind of remarks.

We spent about eight hours in Karaganda and the Russian passenger's fears were needless. No one, Russian or foreign, was allowed off the airport grounds. It was the first time an American had had a glimpse of Karaganda since Mr. Wallace was there. Without the advantages of a personal escort of top M. V. D. authorities, it was difficult to get more than a general impression of the place. But, even from the air, it was possible to ascertain that it had expanded enormously in recent years and a few more details could be garnered from the people at the airport.

At Yakutsk, the prison occupies a fairly extensive plot of land. It is surrounded by an eight-foot wooden fence, topped with four rows of barbed wire on stringers. At each corner and at intervals of about 200 feet on all sides are typical Russian wooden sentry towers, manned by M. V. D. soldiers with bayoneted rifles. A large searchlight on a swinging base is mounted at each tower.

The prison buildings themselves, like almost everything in Yakutsk, were of plain log construction with canted, tarpaper-covered roofs. The sides of the buildings were blank and windowless. Just below the eaves were long narrow slits, possibly a foot wide and three feet long, marked by a vertical row of bars. There was no other access for light or air. No door or entrance to the buildings was visible from the street.

Adjacent to the prison and also within the protective wooden fence and guard posts were wooden barracks for M. V. D. troops and smaller individual residences for M. V. D. officers and what apparently were office buildings.

### The Biggest Institution

This prison is the biggest single institution in Yakutsk. Its presence was not mentioned by local authorities, but, on the other hand, no special effort was made to keep it secret. Or at least there were no compunctions about driving past it with a visiting foreign correspondent. Possibly the authorities thought he wouldn't know what it was. But more likely they had just seen it so often it didn't register any more.

Prisons are an old, old institution in Northern and Eastern Siberia. In the Yakutsk local museum there are pictures of the ostrogi, or prisons, where the Czarist police used to keep their political captives. The buildings look very much like the long house in Yakutsk, but the modern prison has one refinement the Czar's jailers overlooked. The old Czarist jails had ordinary windows that let in light and air. The new Soviet jails keep light and air to a minimum.

In the days just after the 1917 Revolution the Bolsheviks had a poster they put to very effective use in Siberia and Central Asia and other backward areas. It showed an underground pit, in cross-section. At the bottom were

The New York Times Sept. 27, 1954

**M. V. D.-LAND: The empire ruled by the secret police is shown approximately by vertical shading. Its capital is Khabarovsk (1). Among the more notorious prison areas are those at Yakutsk (2), Magadan (3), Chita (4) and Karaganda and Balkhash (5).**

prisoners, shackled, working with bent backs in a cavern too low for upright posture. Just above them was another layer of workers with a little more shoulder room. Above them, petty officials with space for comfortable breathing. Above them, the clergy and nobles and at the top of the pyramid the Czar.

The poster is still to be seen in dim corners of dusty provincial museums—like that at Yakutsk. It has been many years since it had been posted on street walls or fences and probably just as well, so far as the regime is concerned. The public might see too plain a parallel with present conditions.

The fact is that when you get out into northern and eastern Siberia there is nothing very secret and nothing very much concealed about prisons, prisoners, labor camps, prison labor, forced residence, forced settlement and all the rest of the grim and horrible apparatus of the M. V. D.

**Little Difference Noted**

Prisoners and the police apparatus are so routine, common and ordinary a part of life in these regions that local residents seem not to have the slightest embarrassment about such phenomena.

Actually, there is so little difference between the life of prison labor and the life of "free" labor in the North and the East that the whole question of the labor camp and forced labor suddenly seems to be legalistic and scholastic.

Americans, in particular, and Western-oriented people in general would be quick to note that there is a spiritual difference between working under the ever-present muzzle of a tommygun in the hands of an M. V. D. guard and free labor; between going home at night to a barb-wire-encircled camp and to your own room.

Having seen the free workers and the slave workers, having seen them doing identical tasks, except for the presence of the guards; having seen the barracks in which the free labor for the most part lives, this correspondent has considerable doubts as to the existence of any great spiritual differences. In fact, the conditions of life are such as to leave very little room for things of the spirit, regardless of the technical status of the individual.

The editor of the Yakutsk paper felt no reluctance in showing the visiting correspondent from New York a new printing plant being built to house the two Yakutsk newspapers and the local publishing institution. The fact that the plant was being constructed by prison labor, working under guards carrying tommyguns, did not strike him as embarrassing or a circumstance that should be concealed.

Elsewhere in eastern Siberia the same attitude was apparent.

At Chita there is a prison camp not far from the airport. You can't drive from town to the flying field without going right past it. While not quite so grim a sight as Yakutsk's prison—it was composed of a series of one-story wooden barracks with typical barred, slit windows, just under the eaves—the Chita camp did not look like a health resort.

But I doubt that the Chita officials who drove me past the place four times even noticed it any more than they paid the slightest heed to gangs of women working in a near-by potato patch with the inevitable tommy-gunned M. V. D. escorts or the gangs of men in another field a little farther up the road where the M. V. D. tommygunners were mounted on Mongolian ponies, or the mixed gangs of men and women digging drainage ditches along the side of the highway while their guards lolled in the shade of a cottonwood clump, resting their chins on the stocks of their guns.

And, certainly, slave labor does not bring any blushes to the cheeks of the citizens of Khabarovsk, the great Far Eastern capital. The main street of Khabarovsk is Karl Marx Avenue and the principal square of the city is named for Lenin. In six blocks along this street five large construction projects are in progress—office buildings, dwellings and a hospital.

Each project is being built by prison labor. Each is surrounded by board fences with tommy-gunners of the M. V. D. mounted in guard towers at each corner. At one building the construction crew was almost entirely women, but the guard was just as large as at those buildings where the construction force was a mixed group of men and women or entirely masculine.

This correspondent drove a good many miles through the streets of Khabarovsk and was much impressed by the volume of new building going on, particularly of new apartment house construction.

**No Civil Construction**

He was even more impressed by the fact that every construction job he saw was being carried on by prison labor—except for a dozen or so buildings that were being put up by regular Soviet Army troops.

In the whole city of Khabarovsk, out of forty or fifty building projects *not one* was being carried out by ordinary free, civilian labor.

This correspondent stood for a while in Lenin Square, across the street from a fine-looking hospital to which a large addition was being constructed. The annex was being built, of course, by prison laborers, most of whom appeared to be women. There were M. V. D. tommygunners right beside the sidewalk at an entrance to the construction site for trucks, and hundreds of people, men and women, were strolling past.

The citizens of Khabarovsk

©1954, The New York Times Company The New York Times (by Harrison E. Salisbury)

**A MOSCOW PRISON: Another tower for guards overlooks a prison in the heart of Moscow, adjacent to the central market. Only one small window breaks massive stone wall.**

streamed steadily past the building site. No one averted his eyes. No one looked away. In ten minutes of watching I saw no sign of interest, no sign of curiosity in the faces of the passersby.

There is also a new type of mixed M. V. D. operation. In its vast construction operations, the M. V. D., over the years, has developed an expert engineering force, one of Russia's best in certain fields, such as for the construction of dams, canals and other hydro-installations.

Sometimes, in recent years, the M. V. D. technicians have been assigned to free or mixed construction projects. In the first type no prison labor is used. In the second, both free and prison workers are employed.

The great Volga-Don Canal is an example of such a project. The expert M. V. D. engineers who built the Moscow-Volga and White Sea Canals with prison labor built this new project, employing almost entirely free labor. M. V. D. engineers are associated with most of the large hydroelectric projects now under way in the Soviet Union. But only a few such operations use any prison labor and then largely on preliminary land-clearing and excavation tasks.

September 27, 1954

# *Russia Re-Viewed:* Censorship of News Is Erratic

## *Moscow Correspondents Regard Arrest for Taking Pictures as Routine*

By HARRISON E. SALISBURY

The last dispatch this correspondent filed before leaving Moscow was killed in entirety by the censorship. So was the next to the last.

On the other hand, the censors did not delete a single word from any of the first six dispatches sent to The New York Times by Clifton Daniel, its new Moscow correspondent.

This illustrates one of the difficulties of generalizing about the Moscow censorship. The most important single fact about the censorship, however, is that it exists and that every line filed from Moscow must go through the censor's hands.

One day the censor is light and passes a story. The next day he kills an almost identical dispatch. Sometimes, censorship is so erratic that only differences of individual taste seem to offer an explanation.

However, in general, Moscow censorship like most of the other restrictions and handicaps on correspondents in the Soviet Union is much lighter under the new Government than it was under Stalin.

The "lightness" of handicaps on Moscow correspondents, of course, is a relative matter.

A little more than fourteen months ago the new Soviet Government in one of a series of moves to remove irritating restrictions on foreign diplomats and correspondents greatly extended the area in which travel is permitted in the Soviet Union.

Some regions remain closed—notably the Baltic states, border areas, the great Urals industrial region, a few naval bases, and virtually all the principal cities of Siberia.

However, travelers may now visit most parts of European Russia, the Ukraine and the Caucasus. Large areas of Central Asia are open and certain delimited regions of Siberia, the Soviet Far North and Far East.

It so happens that this correspondent in recent months encountered unusual attention from the Ministry of Internal Affairs.

УДОСТОВЕРЕНИЕ

№ 72

Отдел печати Министерства Иностранных Дел СССР удостоверяет, что г-н Солсбери Гаррисон действительно зарегистрирован как корреспондент газеты „Нью-Йорк Таймс"

24 февраля 1954 г.

30 июня 1954 г.

SHEET XIII-14

Уполномоченный Главлита

26 VII 1954 г.

-4-

...anov, provincial mathema...
...ther of Vladimir Lenin. He di...
...sky cemetery; girl reading a...

6--Two views of main street in Ulyanovsk,
7--Three views of main street in Ulyanovs...
traffic.

9-Tugs, ships and shipping tied up at Uly...
10-Trinity cathedral in Saratov, a buildi...
Note the second story galleries which enc...
11-Portico of the Trinity cathedral. Hundr...

**CREDENTIALS AND CENSORSHIP: Below Mr. Salisbury's press card are two examples of censorship. At left, on a corner of a sheet of picture captions, is the censor's stamp with the date—July 26, 1954—written in ink. Farther down on the caption sheet, Item 8 has been entirely eliminated. Instead of using shears, censor has X'd out lines on his own typewriter.**

Possibly this attention was attributable to the fact that the correspondent in recent months had done much traveling, sometimes deep into territory run by the ministry. Perhaps is has been because he has gone armed with a camera and the Interior Ministry fears a camera like the devil fears holy water.

These attentions reached a peak on a trip to Siberia. On board a plane from Novosibirsk to Yakutsk a Security Police agent jimmied the lock of my suitcase, rifled through the contents, even going so far as to slit the linen inner lining, presumably hunting for concealed documents, and he exposed some rolls of unexposed film.

This was merely by way of introduction. There is nothing unusual in the Soviet Union to find yourself, from time to time, being followed by an agent of the Soviet Secret Police or the M. V. D. Sometimes United States military attachés are honored with an escort of as many as four.

**M. V. D. Always There**

Beginning in Yakutsk and continuing throughout northern and eastern Siberia (with the exception of Chita, which is clearly an Army rather than an M. V. D. town) this correspondent was never, so far as he could determine, out of sight of an M. V. D. agent with the exception of times which he was in his hotel room.

And, at times—notably in Birobidzhan—there were at least twenty agents on the job.

It was impressive, intimidating and, sometimes, almost terrifying. Eastern Siberia is not a place in which a lone United States correspondent is likely to feel very comfortable or secure even under the best of circumstances. Surrounded by M. V. D. agents, day and night, one found it difficult to maintain a consistently objective and impassive viewpoint.

There were numerous aspects, too. The Birobidzhan hotel has no interior plumbing facilities. There is, however, an outhouse in the backyard with two compartments. By what was clearly no coincidence this correspondent never found it possible to pay a solitary visit to this homely facility.

**Even as Taxi Driver**

When I rode the Trans-Siberian train from Khabarovsk to Birobijan, two M. V. D. agents occupied the compartment next to mine. Even after I had gone to bed they stayed awake and on watch. An M. V. D. officer drove my cab in Khabarovsk. He didn't bother to change his uniform trousers and boots. But he collected his 100-ruble fare, just like a real taxi driver.

Two M. V. D. cars followed me to the station. Agents sat outside the Khabarovsk Hotel and openly trailed behind each time I went walking.

They were so thick around the hotel in Birobidzhan that each time I emerged on the hotel steps with camera in hand I could see them scurrying in all directions to get behind posts and fences and trees so as not to have their photograph snapped. All I had to do was raise my camera to start a small stampede. It was funny. But it was also tragic and alarming.

A local M. V. D. official installed himself in the Birobidzhan hotel as the ostensible manager. Between keeping up his act as hotel manager and conducting all his routine M. V. D. business he was a busy man. When I walked in on him one day as two uniformed M. V. D. officers were reporting to him about a case of "speculation" on the local market he didn't even turn an eyebrow.

The custom of installing an M. V. D. officer in the local hotel as "manager" while foreign guests are in town is not confined to Birobidzhan. I first encountered it in Bukhara. As in Birobidzhan the agent was kept very busy, dividing his time between police headquarters and the hotel office. But it simplified the question of supervision.

Shadowing in Moscow (except for military personnel) is the exception rather than the rule, although many foreigners, conditioned by what they have heard about Moscow, tend to see little men following them wherever they go. Actually shadows are assigned to diplomats and correspondents usually only by way of occasional spot checks. If a correspondent should find himself constantly being shadowed it is almost a certain sign that he can expect very serious trouble from the M. V. D. That was why the amazing M. V. D. attention in Siberia was so alarming. However, no correspondent has gotten into serious trouble since Stalin's death, although several correspondents were expelled in the years between 1945 and 1953.

Ever since the assassination of the German Ambassador in Moscow, in the early days after the Revolution, a constant security guard had been assigned to the top Ambassadors in Moscow—the United States, British, French, German and Japanese. In other words, agents watched those diplomats whose assassination might provoke serious international difficulties for the Russians.

These security guards stayed so close to ambassadors that, for example, when Admiral Alan G. Kirk, former United States Ambassador once went rowing on Lake Baikal, the "boys" had to go along, too. If a United States Ambassador went to a football game, four M. V. D. men went along and sat next to him. If he went to the opera they went, too, and sat in the back of his box.

**Then They Depart**

The "security" was so close and so complete in recent years that the only Russians a United States Ambassador ever got to know outside of his own servants, were his "boys."

These guards, however, were withdrawn more than a year ago as one of the first of many acts of the new regime designed to eliminate minor annoyances from diplomatic life in Moscow.

However, the shadowing of foreigners on trips about the Soviet Union continues and even seems to have somewhat expanded during the summer. For example, every diplomat who travels (under the easing of travel restrictions) in his own car around the Soviet Union is closely followed by an M. V. D. escort car.

This correspondent in an automobile trip from Rostov-on-Don up through the Ukraine to Moscow was never outside the sight of an escort of four M. V. D. men in an automobile. And not infrequently two cars were assigned to him, particularly in cities such as Rostov or Kharkov or Dnepropetrovsk where it is more difficult to tail an automobile and through the Donbas industrial region where, presumably, there are more "sensitive" things from the security viewpoint.

Even a steamboat ride down the Volga warranted a four-man M. V. D. escort—two for day duty and two for night!

There were times since Stalin's death when it looked as if the censorship might have been quietly abolished without any word to the correspondents. However, each time this correspondent tested that theory by filing a dispatch on some known "forbidden" topic—such, for instance, as the secret police—he quickly found the blue-pencil wielders still on the job.

My last two dispatches that the Moscow censors killed dealt with that most touchy and forbidden topic of all—forced labor and the prison camp system. They were filed specifically with the purpose of testing the censorship, which had been extraordinarily light in previous weeks.

The easing of censorship is evidenced by the fact that no cuts had been made in Mr. Daniel's initial dispatches. In contrast to Mr. Daniel's experience, when this correspondent first arrived in Moscow in 1949 fully 50 per cent of his first fortnight's file from the Soviet capital was stopped dead by the censorship.

A progressive lightening of censorship has been observed since Stalin died.

Some very important restrictions have been eliminated. For instance, correspondents may now report retail prices of goods and describe their quality and make comparisons with United States products. This was completely banned before.

**Some Data Allowed**

Correspondents are allowed to write, fairly freely, about Soviet

# Samples of Censorship

Following are deletions typical of those made by Soviet censors in dispatches recounting a trip to Siberia and the Soviet Far East last summer.

The deleted material was varied—sometimes economic, sometimes political, sometimes quasi-military, sometimes sociological. The deleted sections are printed in bold-face type.

From a dispatch date-lined Novosibirsk: "The mighty Novosibirsk dam **which is scheduled to produce upward of 700,000 or 800,000 kilowatts of power** is the first effort to turn its [the River Ob's] vast energy to a useful purpose. * * *"

From dispatches from Yakutsk:

"They drink a special kind of brown vodka called hunter's vodka and also straight spirits with or without a beer chaser. **Drunkenness is a real problem. And not all residents of Yakutia are happy with their lot. To many this is an alien countryside and they would much prefer their native Kiev or Odessa or Tiflis. As is inevitable when a considerable fraction of the population has been directed to a particular region, not everyone adapts himself. And, there is plenty to adapt one's self to in Yakutia.**

"Housing is another problem. **Even miners get tired of barracks life and it is not suitable housing over the long term for families, especially with children. In work camps, of which Yakutia has many, of course this form of housing is normal.** But in Yakutsk a big drive is now being launched to provide better building * * *."

From a dispatch from Kirensk:

"This country virtually provided its own punishment although if the climate and living conditions were not enough the police were handy to make things worse for the prisoners. **It is easy to see why this region has an inevitable attraction for a police administration looking for a place to send persons from more civilized areas. While it seems doubtful that camps would hold any particular terror for local residents accustomed to a grim life already it would be a different matter to persons from Russia's more effete west.**"

From a dispatch from Chita (the introductory sentence):

"**Perhaps every third person you meet in the street in Chita is in uniform—the uniforms of the Soviet land forces, of the air force and civil air service and of the railroad enterprises and mining enterprises. This is natural because** Chita is one of Russia's eastern 'watchdogs.' * * *."

From a dispatch from Khabarovsk:

"'Of course we are a very young city and things are not as well fixed up as they will be later on.' This kind of remark is designed of course as an excuse for **all sorts of bad conditions and abuses—huts and barracks for housing, unpaved dirty streets, poor municipal facilities, inadequate sewers, almost any evil you can name.**"

By deleting unfavorable material and leaving the favorable material, the whole impression of the article often is changed and distorted.

economic production, making estimates of specific figures from Soviet percentages, comparing the output with previous Russian production and with production abroad. This was banned in previous years.

Correspondents are permitted to report wages paid Russian workers. But not all wages, and comparisons and analysis of Russian wages are still stricken from most dispatches.

Correspondents are allowed, quite often, to remark on poor Russian living conditions, poor consumer goods, poor services. However, if a great deal of such material is packed into one story there are usually cuts.

Considerably more freedom is allowed in discussing and analyzing Soviet foreign policy moves, although reports of outright criticism usually are killed.

Personality material about Soviet leaders may or may not be passed. The rule seems not to be hard and fast although, in general, small human interest details are likely to be deleted.

There also is a good deal more liberty in writing about military matters — characteristics and numbers of airplanes, and so forth. However, any mention of the Ministry of Interior is cut. Almost every mention of the police, or militia as it is called in Moscow, is cut.

However, compared to former conditions there is much greater elbow room. For purposes of contrast the tabulation of censorship kills this correspondent kept while in Moscow shows that in a fairly typical month, January, 1950, fourteen dispatches out of twenty-two that were filed were killed in their entirety. Eight of these stories were direct compilations from the Soviet press, dealing with a campaign then in progress against local graft and corruption. One dealt with Soviet population estimates, one dealt with reinstitution of the death penalty, one dealt with Soviet-Chinese negotiations and one dealt with new restrictions imposed on the then resident American priest, the Rev. John Brassard.

Two years later, in 1952, censorship was somewhat lighter, but in two months seven dispatches dealing with such topics as kidnapped brides and polygamy in Central Asia were killed outright.

In 1951 out of a group of dispatches dealing with a trip to Georgia in the Caucasus, three out of twelve articles were killed entirely. These articles touched on such varied topics as Stalin's youthful career as a poet, the position of the Georgian Jews, and greetings to The New York Times on its 100th anniversary from the editor of the local Tiflis newspaper.

#### Area of Sensitivity

In contrast with this, only one dispatch this correspondent wrote concerning his only trip to Siberia in June was killed outright—a dispatch describing the operations of the M. V. D. However, substantial cuts were made in the stories of any materials about police, surveillance or forced labor.

Censorship is only one of the hazards and restrictions on correspondents in the Soviet Union but it is one that every reader should always bear in mind when he sees the Moscow dateline.

©1954 The New York Times Company The New York Times (by Harrison E. Salisbury)

**TELEGRAPH OFFICE: Foreign correspondents in Moscow file their stories in the Central Telegraph Office, shown above. Offices of the press censors are also situated in the building.**

One of the biggest and most annoying handicaps currently encountered is being arrested for taking photographs. Since last autumn it has been theoretically possible to take pictures in the Soviet Union with full legal authority so long as the scenes, in general, were not of military or industrial objectives.

The Foreign Office even put out a circular stipulating that this was legal and proper under Soviet regulations and specifying just what could and could not be taken.

But try to make that stick in the provinces or even in Moscow. This correspondent was taken into custody within half a block of his apartment office in central Moscow a week before leaving the capital when he was snapping a simple street scene. It took fifteen minutes of argument to get free and then it probably would not have happened if the police officer on duty at the apartment had not come up and given the arresting officer the nod.

There is a policeman on the door of this building twenty-four hours a day—as at all buildings where foreigners live.

Arrest for picture-taking is so routine to Moscow correspondents that they count on an average of two or three arrests a day if they are going to be out taking pictures. One Canadian correspondent set a record by being arrested seven times in one day.

It is not always funny and it hardly ever is as light a matter as it sounds when put on paper. This correspondent has lost a substantial number of rolls of films he had to surrender to various officious individuals in Siberia and elsewhere.

#### Hazards Are Many

Once in a bazaar in Bukhara two native militiamen deliberately tried to arouse a crowd of natives against this correspondent in the course of arresting him for taking pictures of a local watermelon seller. At another bazaar on a remote mountain road en route to Frunze, in Kirgizhia, this correspondent was almost lodged in a local jail for no one knows how long. He was saved from this unlovely fate by a youngster whom he had been talking with on a bus who persuaded the militia to let him go by whispering that the correspondent was "an important foreign visitor." Moreover, the youngster's father was a local Communist party official.

There is no telling what you may get into trouble for if you are taking pictures. Once it was a monument beside which a colonel was standing. Apparently the colonel was regarded as a "military objective."

Another time it was an old, ruined church which happened to be across the road and up the block from a military office.

But the easiest and quickest way to the inside of a Soviet police station is to go to a local market and start snapping pictures. There are always plainclothesmen around whose duty is to stop "speculation" and they invariably take you in hand and march you off to the station.

Then there is the question of what is formally called "access to the news." This is much simplified in the Soviet Union because there is no "access to the news" unless you consider the privilege of getting a copy of Pravda such "access."

#### Farewells No Problem

When this correspondent left Moscow he had no problem of farewells as he would have had in any other country. He did not know a single Russian so there was not a single goodby to be said—except to other foreigners. When a Russian in the Foreign Office press department came to his apartment to attend a cocktail party for Mr. Daniel it was the first social visit a Russian had paid me in nearly six years!

It is not surprising in this atmosphere of suppression and censorship that rumors flourish and false reports often go unchallenged. Seldom do the authorities bother to deny these reports. Although last year when rumors in Moscow that the Government was planning a new currency "reform" reached the point of runs on the banks and a swarming into stores to buy "hard goods" as a hedge against inflation Arseny V. Zverev, Minister of Finance, did issue a denial. It is interesting that Mr. Zverev's denial was believed and brought the panic to an end, whereas in the previous three or four days Communist party meetings in shops and offices had failed to have any effect on the rumor and the public acceptance of it.

Very frequently, however, rumors that are in general circulation in Moscow (as distinguished from rumors circulating in the Moscow diplomatic corps) turn out to be correct. This is only natural since substantial numbers of Russians are likely to have access to information the Government may not desire to publish. The Moscow public always finds out in advance about impending price cuts and similar Government edicts. And the Moscow public knew about the removal of Lavrenti P. Beria, former chief of the Soviet Secret Police, days before the official announcement.

This last month a typical series of rumors has been circulating in Moscow. No one can tell whether they have any basis. One report is that there was a great explosion and fire in Stalingrad in a big oil refinery there. This correspondent was recently in Stalingrad and saw no sign of this, but the report is persistent. Another report says the drought in the Ukraine was so severe that the Volga-Don canal had to be closed for a time because of the low level of water in the Don.

The only way any Moscow correspondent has of verifying such tales is to try to go out and see for himself at first hand. Requests for information to the press department of the Foreign Office seldom bear any fruit and often do not even produce the courtesy of a reply—although recently there has been some improvement.

In March, 1949, this correspondent wrote the press department and requested permission to go on a trip to see the great Stalin auto works in Moscow, a sight that is shown to virtually every delegation of visitors that comes to the Russian capital. The request was renewed annually or semi-annually.

About a fortnight ago the press department telephoned and said a trip had been arranged to the Stalin plant for the next day if the correspondent was interested in going. Needless to say he went.

In March of 1949 and at frequent intervals thereafter this correspondent requested permission to visit a collective farm in the Moscow area. Years passed. He saw many collective farms in other regions. But nothing happened to the Moscow request.

The day before he left Moscow the press department took the local correspondents out to see not only a collective farm but a state farm and a machine tractor station. Maybe it's a trend.

October 2, 1954

# RUSSIAN ASSAILS SERIES ON SOVIET

### Writer for English-Language Magazine Calls Salisbury Reports Full of 'Untruths'

Special to The New York Times.

MOSCOW, Nov. 2—Harrison E. Salisbury's recent series of dispatches about the Soviet Union in The New York Times, were denounced today by News, monthly English-language review published in Moscow, as containing a "multitude of untruths."

The author of the News article, Pytor Nikitin, accused Mr. Salisbury, until recently New York Times correspondent in Moscow, of "piling invention upon invention and reproducing gossip," indulging in "unscrupulous journalism" and serving up "spurious concoctions" to his readers.

News, which is published by the trade union newspaper Trud (Labor) printed its article under the headline, "Mr. Salisbury's Turnabout." The article is the only comment on Mr. Salisbury's series that has so far been published in Moscow.

In the main, Mr. Salisbury's dispatches during the five years he was in Moscow "did not diverge from the facts," News said, but the fourteen articles written after he left the country refuted "everything he had written before."

If Mr. Salisbury wrote nothing but untruths for five years, the magazine asked, why were they not denied and why did The New York Times publish them? Perhaps, News suggested, he was told to "rectify" his former line for "some shady ends."

However, the thinking reader will have no difficulty in seeing through Mr. Salisbury's "far-fetched stories," the magazine said, for "Salisbury often contradicts himself."

The correspondent made up "absurd fabrications and speculation" about what happened inside the Soviet Government, News declared, and stuffed his articles with "obvious slander and scurrilous crude lies."

Mr. Salisbury reached the "amazing conclusion" that the successes of the present Soviet Government presented "new dangers" to the United States, News remarked.

He adduced the "astonishing argument" that retail price reductions in the Soviet Union had led to drunkenness, the commentator continued. In one passage he told of "vigorous young people" opening up new agricultural lands and in a later article he declared that "unhappiness, bitterness and suffering," had resulted from the land program.

It is not as if Mr. Salisbury had no chance to know the facts, Mr. Nikitin said, for he traveled widely and said that he was allowed to write about the Soviet economy, living conditions, quality of goods and military matters, the magazine stated.

Those whom Mr. Salisbury serves, Mr. Nikitin declared, want United States readers to see things in the Soviet Union not as they are but as the New York Times editorial office would like to see them. This, the writer said, is wishful thinking and Mr. Salisbury himself warned against that. His articles show "utter disrespect for the reader," News concluded, and the "reader will treat him accordingly."

November 3, 1954

# *BULGANIN IS PREMIER AS MALENKOV RESIGNS, BUT KHRUSHCHEV IS VIEWED AS REAL LEADER*

## MOSCOW SHAKE-UP

By CLIFTON DANIEL
Special to The New York Times.

MOSCOW, Feb. 8—On nomination by Nikita S. Khrushchev, first secretary of the Communist party, Marshal Nikolai A. Bulganin became head of the Soviet Government today. He replaced Georgi M. Malenkov, who had been Premier since the death of Stalin March 5, 1953.

Reproaching himself for inadequate leadership, Mr. Malenkov offered his resignation this afternoon to the Supreme Soviet, national legislature of the Soviet Union.

[News of the resignation was published in a Late City Extra of The New York Times on Tuesday.]

Mr. Malenkov said he would fulfill "with greatest scrupulousness" the duties that would now be assigned to him. Those duties were not stated at once.

In resigning Mr. Malenkov took on himself the "guilt and responsibility" for the present state of Soviet agriculture, which has been roundly criticized by Mr. Khrushchev.

**To Support Party Line**

Mr. Malenkov also proclaimed his understanding of the Communist party line that forced development of heavy industry must be the basis for increasing agricultural production and all other branches of the Soviet economy. That line has recently been re-emphasized with new firmness by the Central Committee of the party and its propaganda organs.

The Central Committee's decision, taken in the last days of January on the initiative of Mr. Khrushchev, gave orders for still further efforts to increase Soviet agricultural output and Mr. Malenkov said today the decision had revealed to him his shortcomings as an administrator.

The change in the Premiership, accomplished in barely ten minutes of swift political action, left two major questions unanswered for the moment:

What will be Mr. Malenkov's future position and who will be Defense Minister of the Soviet Union, a post now held by Marshal Bulganin?

This afternoon, on the platform of the Supreme Soviet, Mr. Malenkov continued to occupy his seat among members of the Presidium of the Central Committee of the Communist party. He sat at the left hand of Mr. Khrushchev and during a foreign policy speech delivered by Foreign Minister Vyacheslav M. Molotov the two of them chatted amiably with each other. Sometimes they exchanged jokes and laughed.

Behind Mr. Malenkov sat Anastas I. Mikoyan, who two weeks ago resigned from his post as Minister of Domestic Trade but retained his position as a Deputy Premier and member of the party presidium. Mr. Khrushchev once during the proceedings turned and talked over his shoulder with Mr. Mikoyan.

Having taken the post of Premier, Marshal Bulganin, a rotund and popular figure with a small white goatee and white hair, sat on the rostrum busying himself with some papers. But he did not immediately announce any changes in the Cabinet line-up. There was no Government job for Mr. Malenkov and no disclosure about the future of the Defense Ministry.

Popular speculation in Moscow was that the defense post would go to Marshals Georgi K. Zhukov or Alexander M. Vasilevsky, both professional soldiers and war heroes and both now Deputy Ministers of Defense. Alternative speculation was that an experienced Government administrator would get the job or that Marshal Bulganin would keep it himself.

**No Professional Soldier**

Although Marshal Bulganin bears a military rank and sat on the platform today wearing the green uniform of the Army, resplendent with medal ribbons, he is not a professional soldier but an old revolutionary Communist politician and administrator. He gained his military rank in World War II when he was a member of military councils on various fronts, what used to be called "political commissar" with the armed forces.

By contrast with Mr. Malenkov, the new Premier has had a long career as an administrator, and Mr. Malenkov gave as one reason for his resignation his lack of such experience.

February 9, 1955

# KREMLIN'S CABAL IS TRACED TO 1953

## Doctors' 'Plot' Is Viewed as Opening Move in Fight for Political Power

Yesterday's shifts in the Kremlin were the latest phase of a struggle that had raged for more than two years.

Georgi M. Malenkov first seemed to have all the trump cards and an unassailable advantage.

The first public indication of the struggle came shortly before Stalin's death. On Jan. 13, 1953, a group of Soviet doctors, mainly Jews, was accused of having murdered two high Soviet political figures and of having tried to murder high Soviet military figures.

It later appeared that the real target of these charges, however, was Lavrenti P. Beria. He had been the head of the secret police, charged with safeguarding the highest Soviet figures. He was consequently the seeming target of the Communist newspaper Pravda's editorial attack on the "negligence" of those who had permitted the "murders" to be committed.

There is evidence that Nikita S. Khrushchev, the party secretary, was one of the inspirers of these charges. It was his influence, apparently, that saved Semyon D. Ignatiev, the secret police chief under whom these charges were prepared. Mr. Ignatiev was removed as a Communist party secretary when Mr. Beria exposed the "doctor's plot" as a fabrication. Last year, Mr. Ignatiev reappeared as an important regional party leader under Mr. Khrushchev.

Stalin died before any high-level purge could be carried out.

**IT STARTED WITH HIM: Lavrenti P. Beria, former head of the secret police, who was executed by Soviet.**

Messrs. Malenkov and Beria, profited at first from his death. Mr. Khrushchev was set back. Mr. Malenkov became for nine days the key Soviet figure, occupying the posts of Premier, head of the Presidium of the Central Committee and, in effect, first secretary of the Communist party. Mr. Beria became First Deputy Premier and regained control of the secret police.

Mr. Khrushchev, on the other hand, was removed as Moscow party leader and given no new high-level post.

That the Premier fancied himself as Stalin's successor was indicated five days after the latter's death. On that day Pravda published a picture ostensibly showing the Premier, Stalin and Mao Tse-tung standing together. Foreign observers soon noted, however, that the picture had been altered. The original photograph had shown Stalin, the Chinese Communist leader and a group of other high Soviet figures, with Mr. Malenkov relatively distant from the two chief leaders.

This stratagem may have led to Mr. Malenkov's first major setback, the decisive one, it now appears. A secret meeting of the Communist party's Central Committee on March 14, 1954, accepted Mr. Malenkov's resignation as secretary. Mr. Khrushchev moved up automatically to become first secretary, leader of the party apparatus in fact though not yet in formal title.

The forces of Mr. Beria sought to undermine Mr. Khrushchev by attacking Soviet oppression of minorities in which the latter had played a major role. The height of this Beria bid for power came in early June, 1953, when Mr. Khrushchev's protégé, Leonid G. Melnikov, was ousted as party leader of the Ukraine, allegedly for oppressing the West Ukraine.

But Mr. Beria's very success caused all the others to combine against him. On June 26, 1953, Mr. Malenkov presented charges against Mr. Beria; he was purged and arrested; and his execution was announced six months later.

Premier Malenkov reached the peak of his public power in August, 1953. Then, addressing the Supreme Soviet, he laid down the line that the time had come to give consumer goods equal priority with heavy industry. His bid for power was on a platform of a better standard of living in the next "two to three years."

Mr. Khrushchev gained his first fruits of the victory over Mr. Beria a month later. A meeting of the Communist party's Central Committee in September, 1953, made him official first secretary of the party. It also accepted his ambitious program for raising meat, vegetable and potato production, the "stew program" as foreigners termed it.

More important, Mr. Khrushchev moved to solidify his control of the party apparatus by replacing the supporters of Mr. Beria or Mr. Malenkov. In Leningrad, Georgia, Azerbaijan and Moscow, his men became the party leaders. He wooed the army, too, seeing to it that Marshal Georgi K. Zhukov received Mr. Beria's seat in the Central Committee.

In February, 1954, Mr. Khrushchev's war against Mr. Malenkov progressed further. He espoused an ambitious program for raising grain production, which contested Mr. Malenkov's earlier public assurances that the Soviet Union had enough grain.

But the key to Mr. Malenkov's downfall apparently lies in large part in his misjudgment of the international situation. His August, 1953, program for raising the standard of living was based on the implicit premise that for the next two or three years the international situation would be less tense. This would permit the Soviet Union to reduce the proportion of capital investment in industry and increase the consumer goods industries' share.

As early as June, 1954, Mr. Khrushchev showed that he disagreed with Premier Malenkov's estimate. In a bellicose speech in Prague he went so far as to say that the Soviet Union had beaten the United States to the hydrogen bomb. As printed in the Soviet press the next day, Mr. Khrushchev's speech was toned down and his reference to hydrogen bomb priority removed.

Then, last fall, Mr. Khrushchev showed his prowess in the field of foreign policy. He headed the high-level Soviet delegation that visited Peiping. A new tightening of the Soviet-Chinese alliance resulted, though at the cost of Soviet concessions to Peiping.

February 9, 1955

# ZHUKOV IS SOVIET'S DEFENSE CHIEF

## Malenkov Made Deputy and Also Minister of Power Stations

By CLIFTON DANIEL

Special to The New York Times.

MOSCOW, Feb. 9—A professional soldier took command of the Soviet Union's defense establishment today. At the same time the nation's new Premier proclaimed defiance of United States "threats" and "aggression."

Marshal Georgi K. Zhukov, three times a Hero of the Soviet Union, a popular and influential personality in the Soviet Communist party and state, was appointed Minister of Defense in succession to Marshal Nikolai A. Bulganin, who became Premier yesterday.

Until today Marshal Zhukov, along with Marshal Alexander M. Vasilevsky, was a Deputy Minister of Defense.

With the appointment of Marshal Zhukov, Premier Bulganin named his predecessor, Georgi M. Malenkov, to the post of Deputy Premier and Minister of Electric Power Stations, a responsible but not a top-ranking position. Mr. Malenkov retained his seat in the Presidium of the Central Committee of the Communist party, the supreme leadership organization of the Soviet Union.

In the ministerial post, Mr. Malenkov replaced Andrei S. Pavlenko, a professional engineer known for his work on major canals.

No other changes in the Government were made by the new Premier, who, still wearing his khaki Army uniform with gleaming golden shoulder boards, stood in the floodlighted Supreme Soviet chamber today and proclaimed his loyalty to the fixed policy of the Communist leadership and his intention to carry it through.

No part of the new Premier's inauguration address was applauded more enthusiastically or longer than his declaration of the Soviet Union's solidarity with Communist China in its dispute with the United States over Formosa.

China "can count upon the help of its faithful friend, the great Soviet people," Premier Bulganin declared.

That declaration was underscored by vigorous handclapping. When the gust of applause seemed to be dying down, it was picked up and renewed and went on for half a minute.

The Soviet Army, the Premier declared, has shown its superiority in skill and weapons and will hold its supremacy. Army, Navy and Air Force, he added, are ready to fulfill any task given to them by the party and state.

February 10, 1955

# Secret Police Power Reduced by Moscow

By HARRISON E. SALISBURY

Information reaching the United States indicates that some key functions of the Soviet secret police have been sharply curtailed and others have been transferred to the Soviet Army.

A revealing picture of sweeping police and judicial changes in the Soviet Union is presented by information collected from several sources, including firsthand reports obtained in Moscow by Prof. Harold J. Berman of the Harvard Law School.

Professor Berman interviewed more than twenty high officials of the Soviet Ministry of Justice and obtained a mass of information hitherto unknown this side of the Iron Curtain.

The information obtained by Professor Berman on changes in the Soviet secret police system since the death of Stalin and the execution of Lavrenti P. Beria, former Minister of Interior, is supported by other reports from official and unofficial channels.

The information obtained by Professor Berman and others makes plain that the Soviet secret police continues to function; that arbitrary arrest of Soviet citizens is still possible and that the notorious forced labor and the exile systems still exist.

### Major Changes Listed

Radical changes, however, have been instituted and more are in the making, according to the data of Professor Berman and others.

The principal changes include the following:

¶The special M. V. D. (Ministry of Interior) troops that constituted a private army at the disposal of the police force have been abolished as such. Control of these units was shifted to the Soviet Army in September, 1953.

¶Three special three-man boards (troikas) of the M. V. D., which could sentence Soviet citizens to forced residence or forced labor terms on secret charges and without hearing the accused, have been abolished.

¶Conditions in the forced labor camps have been ameliorated and some camps are reported being liquidated. Soviet Army authorities have replaced M. V. D. officials in the direction of some camps.

¶Military tribunals are reviewing the cases of hundreds of thousands of citizens who were arbitrarily sent to exile or forced labor by the M. V. D. troikas. Many of these citizens have been released.

¶A new Soviet criminal code and code of procedure that substantially improves the legal rights of Soviet citizens is nearing completion and is expected to be placed in effect this winter.

¶It has been confirmed that the criminal penalties long imposed under Soviet law to enforce labor discipline and to prevent workers from changing jobs have been abolished.

### Effect of Shifts Unclear

The precise effect of many of these changes of procedure is still difficult to evaluate. Many of the legal rules have been changed secretly and without public knowledge.

The powers of the Soviet police remain much greater than would be tolerated in any Western state and such traditional Anglo-Saxon concepts as the right of habeas corpus are still unknown.

But the notable fact, as Professor Berman said, is that all of the changes are in the same direction, the direction of relaxing the severities of the police rule that was imposed under Stalin and carried out by Beria.

"The changes do not involve any really basic alteration of the structure of the Soviet state," Professor Berman noted. "The important thing as I was told in Moscow is the change in the climate."

One of the most curious aspects of the situation is the fact that most of the changes have not been mentioned in the public press of the Soviet Union. Soviet censorship has suppressed reports of foreign correspondents concerning some of the other curtailments imposed on the M. V. D.

Professor Berman was unable to obtain a copy of the Soviet decree abolishing the special boards of the M. V. D. Official reports of cases of the Soviet Supreme Court are not permitted to enter general circulation, apparently because of security considerations. Even the reports of some enactments of the Soviet Council of Ministers are unobtainable by foreigners.

But behind this facade of secrecy, profound changes, it is apparent, are going forward.

### Rise of Army's Power

The sharp curtailment of the powers of the M. V. D. and the transfer to the Army of many of its functions tends to support previous indications that the fall of Beria was accompanied by a profound rise in the influence of Army leaders such as Marshals Georgi K. Zhukov and Ivan S. Konev.

The extent to which the Army now controls M. V. D. troop formations is not precisely known. M. V. D. troops still parade past the reviewing stands in Red Square on the Soviet holidays with their distinguishing uniform pipings of red and their red-and-blue caps.

However, the green-capped Soviet border guards were said to have been transferred from police to Army direction in 1953.

The abolition of the special three-man M. V. D. boards is the single change apt to have the most consequence to the ordinary Soviet citizen.

These boards had existed since the purge days of the middle Nineteen Thirties. In practice, any three M. V. D. officers could sit as a tribunal and impose sentences for "counter-revolutionary" crimes. The accused did not need to be present, and in fact seldom was. Often he was not even told what he was accused of or the duration of his sentence until he arrived at the labor camp in Siberia or the Far North.

Such cases normally fall under Article 58 of the Soviet Criminal Code, which defines various "counter - revolutionary" crimes in terms so vague that almost any kind of conduct can come within its scope.

By placing such cases in the hands of the conventional Soviet military and civil courts the rights of Soviet citizens are considerably improved, in Professor Berman's opinion.

In the revision of the Soviet criminal code that is now in progress no substantial changes will be made in Article 58. Professor Berman asked Soviet legal authorities whether this did not, in fact, reduce the significance of other legal reforms designed to protect the rights of Soviet citizens. He was told that irrespective of changes in language the "change in the climate" was the most significant thing.

### Changes in Criminal Code

The new criminal code will make a number of similar changes.

¶Peasants will no longer be held criminally liable for failure to fulfill their labor requirements for work on collective farms.

¶Managers of factory enterprises will be permitted to sell surplus equipment and will be relieved of criminal responsibility for minor acts of negligence.

¶The notorious "doctrine of analogy" will be abolished. This allowed a court to convict a Soviet citizen for committing an act that was not prohibited by law but that the court held was "analogous" to a prohibited act.

¶The severity of punishments is being reduced in many instances. For example, the sentence for "counter-revolutionary propaganda" is being cut from a maximum of ten years to five years. The real meaning of such reductions, however, is obscure so long as the sweeping provisions of Article 58 remain in force.

One of the most important pending reforms places protective safeguards around the "investigatory" phase of Soviet detention. At present a Soviet citizen has no right to counsel until the trial stage of his case is reached. He may be held by the police up to six months and then for an indefinite period by a so-called judicial investigator.

It is now proposed to permit the intervention of counsel when the judicial investigator presents the first draft of an indictment to the accused.

Present Soviet law permits the Government to appeal an acquittal provided new evidence is discovered within a five-year period. This subjects Soviet citizens to double jeopardy. The new code will reduce the period in which such Government appeals may be taken to two years.

The Prosecutor's Office has been given new responsibilities with respect to preventing abuses in forced labor camps. While it had similar functions previously, under the new code prosecutors may be subjected to disciplinary or criminal punishment for failure to investigate or prosecute cases of camp abuses.

Professor Berman said he had been informed by Soviet legal authorities that it was a mistake to suppose that Soviet military tribunals dispensed a harsher kind of justice than normal civil courts.

The military tribunals are a permanent judiciary, Professor Berman noted, and are not to be confused with courts martial or the customary kind of Western military courts.

December 16, 1955

# RUSSIANS ASSAIL RULE BY ONE MAN

By WELLES HANGEN

Special to The New York Times.

MOSCOW, Feb. 16 — The Twentieth Communist party Congress, the first since Stalin's death, was told today that the "cult of personality" had wrought considerable harm to both the party and the Soviet Union.

Mikhail A. Suslov, who headed the party propaganda apparatus under Stalin, said the exaltation of an individual was alien to the Marxist-Leninist principles of "collective leadership."

He told the delegates in the Great Kremlin Palace that such practice belittled the role of the party and people, degraded collective leadership, undermined party "democracy," suppressed activity of party members and led to absence of control and responsibility.

Furthermore, Mr. Suslov said, the former system produced "arbitrariness" in the work of some party organs, obstructed development of criticism and self-criticism and gave birth to "one-sided and sometimes mistaken solutions of problems."

### Discussion Called Genuine

Mr. Suslov asserted that the principle of collective leadership had been "successfully re-established" in every party unit from the Central Committee down to the factory cell. He said this was particularly true of the Central Committee.

The collective leadership now practiced is reflected in "genuinely collective discussion and the settlement of the most important questions by party organs," Mr. Suslov told the Congress.

Party work must again be imbued with "Bolshevik fighting spirit and purposefulness," Mr. Suslov said. He declared this had been worked out by the party over a period of decades.

Anastas I. Mikoyan, a First Deputy Premier, also attacked the personality cult and strongly defended the type of leadership practiced here since 1953.

When members of the Presidium, led by Nikita S. Khrushchev, entered the Great Kremlin Palace this afternoon they were given the usual tumultuous ovation from the assembled delegates. Mr. Khrushchev, who is the party leader, then strolled to the microphone and announced that the Presidium had requested that they not be applauded every time they entered the room.

Mr. Suslov paid high tribute to Mr. Khrushchev's report as "concrete example of the creative use and development" of Marxist-Leninist theory. He said the party leader had generalized from new experience accumulated by the Soviet and foreign Communist parties as well as the "international workers' movement."

Mr. Suslov told the Congress: "It might be said without the smallest doubt that within the Central Committe the principle of collective leadership has been completely restored.

"The settlement of all the most important problems has passed into the jurisdiction of regularly convened plenary sessions of the Central Committee."

Mr. Suslov characterized the plenary session as "this broad collective body, the center of which is connected in the closest way with the decisive sectors of construction of the Communist society."

February 17, 1956

# MIKOYAN ATTACKS STALIN'S POLICIES

## Denounces Economic Theory, Handling of Foreign Affairs and Rewriting of History

By WELLES HANGEN
Special to The New York Times.

MOSCOW, Saturday, Feb. 18—The Twentieth Congress of the Communist party has heard a direct attack on Stalin's most important economic work as well as his handling of foreign policy.

In a lengthy speech delivered Thursday and published today in Pravda, the party newspaper, Anastas I. Mikoyan said some of the late Premier's basic economic theories were misleading and incorrect.

Mr. Mikoyan, a First Deputy Premier and one of Stalin's veteran collaborators, was especially critical of the ideas expounded in "Economic Problems of Socialism in the U. S. S. R." This main economic work by Stalin was published on the eve of the last party congress in 1952.

Turning to current foreign policy, Mr. Mikoyan hailed the introduction of a "fresh new stream." He said the party's Central Committee was now pursuing an "active, flexible foreign policy high in principle, restrained, calm in tone and without sharp words."

The Soviet Government, he said, has freely acknowledged "mistakes and shortcomings" in its foreign policy and has rectified them. He cited as an example the resumption of friendly relations with Yugoslavia.

Mr. Mikoyan said research, especially the writing of history, had been stifled in the period before 1952. He complained especially about Soviet histories of the Communist party in Transcaucus and Baku regions. Asserting that these works distorted facts, he said "some people were arbitrarily glorified while others were not mentioned at all."

The First Deputy Premier also implied that distorted versions of the Russian civil war of 1918-20 were also current.

In this connection, he said that "several complex and contradictory events" of that period were explained by Soviet historians, not by changes in the correlation of class forces at different periods "but by the alleged treacherous activity of individual party leaders of that time, who were unjustly declared enemies of the people many years after the events described."

Mr. Mikoyan gave no explicit indication of the persons to whom he was alluding.

February 18, 1956

# *Secret Khrushchev Talk On Stalin 'Phobia' Related*

By HARRISON E. SALISBURY

According to diplomatic reports, Nikita S. Khrushchev, Soviet Communist party secretary, made a secret address to the recent Twentieth Congress of the Communist party explaining why Stalin was being desanctified.

Mr. Khrushchev's address, according to information reaching the United States from Moscow, was made at a closed session of the party congress on the evening of Feb. 24. Delegates from foreign Communist parties were said to have been barred from this meeting.

Mr. Khrushchev was reported to have presented a sensational picture of events in the latter period of Stalin's regime. He touched on events surrounding the death of Lenin in January, 1924, and the party purges of the Nineteen Thirties.

It was understood Washington official quarters were aware of the reports about the Khrushchev speech and were giving them the closest study.

Mr. Khrushchev's address was said to have been comprehensive and forthright. It was said to make the speech in which Anastas I. Mikoyan, a leading party aide, criticized Stalin sound "like milk and water."

### Stalin 'Not Himself'

The picture painted by Mr. Khrushchev, according to these reports, was of a Stalin who was "not himself" in his late years and who through his career had been subject to phobias about the supposed treachery of his associates.

Possibly the most sensational revelation that Mr. Khrushchev is said to have placed before his colleagues was a declaration that the case of treason in 1937 against Marshal Mikhail N. Tukhachevsky and other high ranking Red Army men had been a fabrication.

As Mr. Khrushchev is said to have described the inner Kremlin scene, many of Stalin's closest associates were unaware of the fate of intimate friends and collaborators. The full story of what happened during Stalin's long years, Mr. Khrushchev was said to have indicated, became known only after Stalin's death.

According to the reports, Moscow, as Mr. Khrushchev described the atmosphere there in the late years of the Stalin regime, was a capital ridden by plots, counter-plots and intrigue, in which no one knew who might be the next victim.

Foreign diplomats in Moscow were said to be seeking official word on the precise contents of Mr. Khrushchev's address. The Moscow censorship has prevented foreign correspondents from cabling reports of the rumors circulating in the Soviet capital.

It was established that Mr. Khrushchev's speech was designed to tell the Soviet party members why the leadership had found it necessary to destroy Stalin's reputation for infallibility, wisdom and good works.

Party delegates are now spreading by word - of - mouth around the country the essence of Mr. Khrushchev's remarks. Some experts suggested that after Soviet public opinion had been prepared for the full shock the whole case against Stalin might be made public.

The execution of Marshal Tukhachevsky and seven other high Red Army commanders was announced in June, 1937. It occurred, according to an official statement, after a one-day trial before a military tribunal that convicted the men of treason.

Mr. Krushchev told his colleagues, it was reported, that there was no foundation for the charge against the Red Army leadership. The case was a fabrication and a "terrible mistake" that, he was said to have declared, led the Soviet Union "to the brink of disaster" when Germany attacked in 1941. The Red Army, deprived of its leadership, almost was overwhelmed by the German attack, Mr. Khrushchev is said to have declared.

### Army Influence Seen

It was believed by some specialists on Soviet affairs that the emphasis placed by Mr. Khrushchev on the Tukhachevsky case indicated strong Soviet Army influence in the present government, particularly that of Marshal Georgi K. Zhukov, Defense Minister.

Only one member of the tribunal that heard the Tukhachevsky case is known to survive. He is Marshal Semyon M. Budenny, an old associate of Stalin, who still is often seen in Moscow on official occasions.

Many of the announcements relative to Marshal Tukhachevsky and other cases involving Soviet defense forces, at that time were made by Marshal Kliment E. Voroshilov, then People's Commissar for Defense and now the titular chief of state.

The official charge against Marshal Tukhachevsky and his associates was treason. There was never any explanation of the charges, but it was widely whispered that the Red Army chiefs had plotted with Germany and Japan to overthrow Stalin with the aid of foreign military assistance. These charges were accepted even in Western circles.

The picture that Mr. Khrushchev was said to have painted in his address was said to bear a startling resemblance to the picture of the Moscow scene presented by this correspondent in a series of articles written on his return from Moscow in 1954.

Mr. Khrushchev was said to have asserted that even the members of Stalin's Politburo were often kept in ignorance of what was happening. An example was the disappearance of Nikolai A. Voznesensky, a Politburo member and head of the State Planning Commission, in March, 1949.

Mr. Khrushchev, it was reported, declared that the Politburo members did not know what had happened to Mr. Voznesensky at the time. No explanation was made to them by Stalin. Only later, Mr. Khrushchev said, was it learned that Mr. Voznesensky was arrested in March, 1949, and shot some time during the next twelve months.

It was reported that Mr. Khrushchev elucidated for the party members the details of the so-called Leningrad case, which has been frequently mentioned in Soviet circles.

The Leningrad case was first mentioned in December, 1954, at the time the execution of Victor S. Abakumov, former Minister of State Security, was announced. Mr. Abakumov was said to have falsely fabricated this case.

It has long been suspected that there was a connection between Mr. Voznesensky's fate and the Leningrad case, in which a number of former lieutenants of Andrei A. Zhdanov, a Politburo member who died in September, 1948, disappeared.

On the basis of Mr. Khrushchev's remarks it is now believed that these men, including Peter S. Popkov, former Mayor of Leningrad; A. A. Kuznetsov, a one-time Communist party secretary; Mikhail I. Rodionov, former Premier of the Russian Federated Republic, were all shot, either in 1949, the year of their disappearance, or in 1950.

March 16, 1956

# SOVIET TIGHTENS SECURITY IN WAKE OF STALIN EXPOSE

## Action Reported to Include Travel Curbs in Caucasus and Black Sea Areas

## MOSCOW CALLED TENSE

## Leaders Believed Confident Despite Disorder in Home Republic of Dictator

By **HARRISON E. SALISBURY**

Security measures, including travel controls, have been imposed in some areas of the Soviet Union because of repercussions from the attack on Stalin by the Soviet leadership, it was learned in diplomatic quarters yesterday.

Reports received by diplomats in the United States said the Soviet Government was exhibiting complete confidence in its ability to handle any flare-ups resulting from the Stalin exposure.

However, travel to some Soviet areas, including most of the Caucasus and some Black Sea areas, has been temporarily restricted.

It was also reported that the impact of the disclosures on ordinary Soviet citizens apparently was more extreme than the Government had expected.

Factory workers and office employes were said to be bewildered, dismayed or angered at the sudden destruction of the infallibility myth that had been painstakingly created around Stalin.

**Petitions Circulated**

Petitions were reported to be in circulation among Moscow workers asking the Government to remove Stalin's embalmed body from the mausoleum in Red Square, where it lies beside that of Lenin.

Other reports said many citizens were visiting Red Square daily, apparently to ascertain whether any move had been made to alter the mausoleum.

Other petitions were said to have been approved at mass meetings at which party workers discussed the revelations about Stalin. Some of these petitions requested that Stalin's name be removed from factories and other institutions. Among these petitions was reported to be one from the workers of the big Moscow automobile works, the city's largest industrial establishment, which has long borne Stalin's name.

Elsewhere, it was said, petitions have been sent to the Government asking for the removal of busts, statues and portraits of Stalin. In many places the images of Stalin were being taken down without awaiting formal Government action. Petitions of this type are, by Soviet custom, a usual preliminary to positive action.

**Reactions Said to Differ**

The reactions in Moscow, according to diplomatic advices, were not matched everywhere in the country.

Special precautions against any disorders or manifestations were said to have been ordered by the Government in the entire Caucasus area. The measures were understood to have been taken after the spontaneous outbreak of demonstrations in Stalin's home republic of Georgia.

Air travel was reported suspended to Tiflis, capital of Georgia; to Erivan, capital of Armenia; to Sochi, the famous Soviet resort on the Black Sea that was a favorite watering place for Stalin, and to Baku, the capital of Azerbaijan.

Diplomatic reports described Moscow as continuing to be in a state of considerable agitation. Among the unconfirmed reports current in the capital were said to be rumors that Soviet radio stations in some Volga River cities had suddenly halted transmission Saturday.

March 19, 1956

# PRAVDA CHARGES DISSIDENTS ABUSE ANTI-STALIN DRIVE

By **WELLES HANGEN**

Special to The New York Times.

MOSCOW, Thursday, April 5—Pravda today denounced "rotten elements" in the Communist party for using the campaign against Stalinism to attack the party's basic policies.

This was the first indication that the program enunciated by the party congress in February had opened the floodgates to criticism of the whole gamut of Communist policies. The denunciation was made in a 6,000-word editorial in the party newspaper.

Asserting that the party would never tolerate "anti-party statements" in its midst, Pravda declared:

"The party cannot permit that the freedom to discuss problems should be taken as a freedom to propagandize views alien to the spirit of Marxism-Leninism because this would contradict the party's rules and its principles."

Pravda said "rotten elements" within the party were rising to assail various aspects of the party's work under the guise of contributing to the campaign against the "cult of personality" [an allusion to Stalin's one-man rule].

**'Slanderous' Speeches Noted**

The paper cited an example of a meeting of party workers at an unidentified scientific laboratory at which four employes, who were party members, had made "slanderous" speeches "directed against the party's policy and its Leninist foundations."

Pravda complained that party leaders at the laboratory had failed to show "Bolshevik martial irreconcilability toward these anti-party sallies."

Another meeting of party members in the Moscow regional statistical bureau heard "provocative anti-party statements" from a Communist identified as L. Yaroshenka, Pravda reported. The editorial said such speeches were "a rehash from a fallen voice and a repetition of slanderous fabrications of fallen reactionary propaganda."

At a meeting in the Chkalov region, Pravda said, local leaders did nothing to stop an "exceptionally demogogic, incorrect" speech by a party member identified only as Ternovsky.

The party organ's unsigned editorial is considered by observers here the most significant indication of the difficulties encountered by the Soviet regime in winning acceptance for the new line adopted by the party congress.

April 5, 1956

# REDS NAME JEWS PURGED BY SOVIET

### Warsaw Yiddish Newspaper Confirms Execution Under Stalin—Blames Beria

By HARRISON E. SALISBURY

Polish Communist sources have confirmed that Soviet authorities liquidated a large number of Jews prominent in literary, cultural and political fields in the years before Stalin's death in 1953.

A similar purge was carried out during the Nineteen Thirties.

The description of the anti-Semitic excesses was given by the Warsaw Yiddish-language newspaper, Folksshtime, in its edition of April 4, which has just reached New York. Folksshtime is a Communist organ.

The Warsaw newspaper provided the first Communist confirmation of accounts previously published by The New York Times and The Jewish Daily Forward of New York.

The picture painted by the Warsaw report was one of excesses even more extensive than previously rumored. The list of Jewish victims published in Warsaw was longer than any that had been published by anti-Communist groups.

Publication of the Polish newspaper's account increased speculation that Moscow might be preparing to announce that the execution of the Polish Jewish labor leaders, Victor Alter and Henryk Erlich, carried out in December, 1942, was a result of charges that were without foundation in fact.

Mr. Alter and Mr. Erlich were arrested by the Russians when Poland was partitioned by the Soviet Union and Germany in 1939. According to the Soviet version the men were convicted of treason and executed.

The Polish account attributed all the anti-Semitic outrages to Lavrenti P. Beria, former Soviet secret police chief, executed in December, 1953. In fact the Jewish liquidations of the Nineteen Thirties occurred before Stalin brought Beria from Georgia to head the police apparatus in 1938.

Among those listed by Folksshtime as victims of the later Jewish purge of 1948-52 were the writers Itsik Feffer, David Bergelson, Perets Markish, Leib Kvitko, David Hofshtein, Isaac Nusinov, Elijah Spivak, Froyim Kahanovitch, S. Persov and Benjamin Suskin.

Only the first five of these writers had previously positively been known to have been executed in the purge.

The newspaper said that the Jewish Anti-Fascist Committee in Moscow had "suddenly without why or wherefore been liquidated and its leaders sentenced to destruction."

The committee was headed by the prominent Yiddish actor Solomon Mikhoels, whose death previously had been officially attributed to an "automobile accident." The newspaper account suggested that Mr. Mikhoels also was one of the victims of the anti-Semitic campaign.

Mr. Feffer, a poet loyal to the Stalin regime and a Red Army colonel during World War II, was one of the Anti-Fascist Committee leaders. He and Mr. Mikhoels toured the United States in behalf of the Soviet war effort during World War II.

**Victims of Thirties**

Among the Jewish victims of the Nineteen Thirties purges were listed S. Dimanshtein, Ester Frumkin, Rachmael Weinshtein, Moishe Litvakov, Izi Kharik, Moishe Kulbak, H. Duniets, Mikhail Levitan, Yankel Levin, Hershel Brill, Max Erik and Yasha Bronshtein.

Mr. Weinshtein and Mr. Levin were leaders of the Bund, a Jewish Social Democratic organization. Mr. Litvakov was a critic and editor of the Moscow Yiddish newspaper Emes (Truth). Mr. Erik was a leading Yiddish scholar in Kiev.

The Warsaw newspaper also listed a number of other "masters of Yiddish literature" who had been victims of anti-Semitic drives. One of the authors on this list, Samuel Halkin, has been reported recently to be alive in a Leningrad sanatorium.

Among the names on this list were those of Aaron Kushnirov, Lipe Reznik, Ezra Finenberg, Hersh Orland, Noah Lurie, Itsik Kipnis, and Note Lurie.

The text of the Folksshtime report was published by the New York Yiddish-language newspaper Freiheit, a Communist party organ. An extensive account was also published by the Jewish Daily Forward, strongly anti-Communist newspaper, which has long waged a campaign exposing the anti-Semitic excesses in the Soviet Union. The Forward published the confirmation of its charges with the comment "Communists in Warsaw and New York finally tell about Soviet pogrom on Yiddish writers."

April 12, 1956

# 9 EX-ARMY CHIEFS CLEARED IN SOVIET

### Yegorov and Bluecher Among Civil War Leaders Purged by Stalin and Now Cited

By WELLES HANGEN

Special to The New York Times.

MOSCOW, April 13 — The Soviet Union restored today the reputations of nine outstanding Red Army leaders of the civil war period who fell from grace under Stalin.

They included Marshals Aleksander I. Yegorov and Vasili K. Bluecher, known to have vanished in Stalin's purge of the Red Army in the Nineteen Thirties, and Jan B. Gamarnik, who committed suicide before his arrest.

The restoration of the nine to the honored status of "comrades" is the most drastic public step yet taken by the present Soviet leadership to exonerate victims of Stalinism.

All members of the group, except Andrei S. Bubnov, are thought to be dead. This former civil war commander was a member of the Soviet Communist party's first Politburo [top leadership group now known as the Presidium].

He was seen recently in Moscow, where he is thought to have returned from exile.

The others were listed as V. A. Antonov-Ovseyenko, Sergei S. Kamenev, M. S. Kedrov, Moissei L. Rukhimovich and I. S. Unschlicht.

The decision to exonerate the nine Army leaders was disclosed today in Voprosi Istorii, organ of the Institute of History of the Soviet Academy of Sciences. The journal is the official arbiter of Soviet history.

April 14, 1956

# SOVIET CONDEMNS PRACTICE OF TRIAL BY CONFESSIONS

By The Associated Press.

MOSCOW, April 22—The magazine Soviet State and Law denounced today the long prevalent Soviet practice of trial by confession. It criticized the late Andrei Y. Vishinsky for having developed the practice.

Mr. Vishinsky prosecuted the purge trials in the late Nineteen Thirties, at which many old Bolsheviks were convicted on their own confessions and executed. He later became Foreign Minister and chief Soviet delegate to the United Nations.

He died in New York in November, 1954, while attending a United Nations session. He received a hero's funeral in Red Square and his ashes were buried in the Kremlin wall, an honor accorded to top Soviet leaders.

[In contrast with the denunciation of Mr. Vishinsky, the rehabilitation of Alexei I. Rykov, former Soviet Premier and one of the executed Old Bolsheviks, was [illegible]dicated Sunday. Pravda, Sovi[illegible] Communist organ, printed a letter to Mr. Rykov from Leni[illegible] [illegible]itting the usual epithets that had accompanied the purged Premier's name in the past.]

The attack on trial confessions by Soviet State and Law is in keeping with policies laid down by Nikita S. Khrushchev, Soviet Communist party leader, at the party's recent Twentieth Congress. He called for an overhaul of the Soviet judicial system.

An unsigned article in the magazine, which is the leading Soviet law review, said Mr. Vishinsky's work had been turned into "unimpeachable dogma." It declared that persons in the field of jurisprudence must make a thorough study and throw light on the "questions of guarantees and the means of insuring legality in the matter of guarding the rights and interests of citizens of the U. S. S. R."

The article said Mr. Vishinsky's theory "denies the need for a court to establish the absolute truth in each case and permits the possibility of convicting a person on the basis only of the probability of some fact or other that is undergoing legal examination."

It called such procedure a "glaring violation of the principle of Socialist legality." The article added that the theory also was "at variance with the demands of the [Communist] party and Government for the strictest observance of legality by investigation courts and prosecuting organs."

April 23, 1956

# SOVIET ABOLISHES 3 PURGE ERA LAWS

By JACK RAYMOND

Special to The New York Times.

MOSCOW, May 4—A decree of the Supreme Soviet has abolished the special powers of Soviet security organs to deal with sabotage and terrorism.

These powers were introduced during the purges of the Nineteen Thirties. Some of them, it has lately been conceded, led to "impermissible" practices in the questioning of witnesses.

The decree was signed by Marshal Kliment E. Voroshilov, Chairman of the Presidium of the Supreme Soviet (Parliament). Investigations hereafter must be guided by the juridical standards established by law, the decree said. It was dated April 19 and appeared in The Journal of the Supreme Soviet, which became available today.

A group of French Socialists was received this afternoon by Anatoli Volin, President of the Soviet Supreme Court, who said that drafts had been prepared of new laws to modify investigation and trial practices.

**Lawyers Oppose Agency**

Mr. Volin told the visitors that Soviet lawyers were "profoundly opposed to such organs [as the since-liquidated Ossob of the old M. V. D., which could arrest or liquidate persons in extrajudicial proceedings] and it can be said that they will never be re-established." He referred to abolition of Ossob in 1953 shortly after Stalin's death.

The new Supreme Soviet decree abolished three decrees issued in 1934 and 1937 "which established a special method of investigation and court consideration" of certain crimes.

This was an evident allusion to techniques used to extract confessions from persons accused of counter-revolutionary efforts through sabotage of industry, transport, trade and money circulation as well as terroristic acts with counter-revolutionary aims.

It has since been conceded by Soviet leaders that charges of the Stalin period were often trumped up. The decrees now revoked demanded a full investigation within ten days. They made it possible for a defendant to be informed of the charges only one day before his trial. They made it possible for a defendant to be tried without being present. They provided for no appeal. They made mandatory immediate execution after imposition of the death penalty.

May 5, 1956

# LENIN TESTAMENT BARED IN MOSCOW

## Part of Document Warning Party to Remove Stalin as Secretary Is Quoted

By HARRISON E. SALISBURY

Lenin's warning to the Communist party against Stalin's personality was published in part in Moscow yesterday to explain to Soviet youth why the late dictator was being downgraded.

The Young Communist newspaper Komsomolskaya Pravda published what it called "A Child's Guide to Stalinism" to explain to puzzled Soviet youth just what was happening to the Stalin legend and why. It was the harshest denunciation of Stalin yet to appear in the Soviet press.

Lenin's warning was contained in his "last testament," a document that has never been published in the Soviet Union and that Stalin suppressed.

The newspaper did not identify Lenin's warning as coming from the "testament." Nor was there any reference to the testament in a dispatch from a New York Times correspondent in Moscow, apparently because of censorship deletions.

Komsomolskaya Pravda's quotation of the Lenin warning said:

"Lenin, in the last year of his life, pointed out that such negative features of Stalin's character as rudeness, lack of respect for working comrades, capriciousness and inclination toward abuse of power could lead to a violation of the rules of collective leadership.

"Unfortunately, it happened so."

The Soviet newspaper said it was publishing the "guide" in response to numerous inquiries from young persons wanting to know what was behind the attack on the "cult of the individual," the official terminology used in the downgrading of Stalin.

The essence of the article was that Stalin had made great contributions during the Bolshevik revolution and in the early days of his leadership but that in the later period he displayed all the qualities Lenin warned against and began to rule in an arbitrary, capricious, self-adulatory manner.

The Lenin document that Komsomolskaya Pravda paraphrased is one of the most famous in the history of Soviet communism, yet its very existence is still almost unknown to ordinary citizens of the Soviet Union.

In the early days Stalin admitted the existence of the Lenin testament and even quoted from it during his struggle with Leon Trotsky. But its text has been rigorously censored or excised.

The "testament" is actually a memorandum, dictated by Lenin in two installments, Dec. 25, 1922, and Jan. 4, 1923. He had had a paralytic stroke and the document was one of the last that he completed before his physical condition rendered work impossible.

It contained a brief characterization of the leading members of the party, Stalin, Trotsky, Gregory Zinoviev, Lev Kamenev, Nikolai Bukharin and Gregory Piatakov.

Lenin was concerned about the danger of a possibly fatal split in the party centered upon a conflict between Stalin and Trotsky.

The second section of the memorandum, which he added on Jan. 4, presumably after some personal disputes with Stalin, was devoted entirely to a negative assessment of the late dictator.

It concluded with a proposal to remove Stalin from his post as General Secretary and to replace him with another man "more patient, more loyal, more polite, more attentive to comrades, less capricious, etc."

In the intra-party struggle for power that broke out after Lenin's death in January, 1924 (between Stalin and Trotsky, as Lenin had feared) the testament became a key document.

Stalin succeeded in blocking proposals for its immediate publication on the ground that it would be disruptive of party unity. The behind-the-scenes struggle went on and as Stalin gradually gathered power into his hands the prospects of publication of the testament diminished.

The document was made public Oct. 18, 1926, in The New York Times by Max Eastman who had been associated in Moscow with Trotsky in the latter's fight against Stalin.

Its publication caused a sensation in Communist and other left-wing circles and it became a leading theme in the final stages of the Stalin-Trotsky fight.

Many Communists charged that it was a Trotskyite fabrication.

However, in the final showdown of the Trotsky-Stalin struggle Stalin himself acknowledged that the testament existed. He even permitted a reference to it to be published in Pravda, the official party newspaper, in November, 1927, in connection with the announcement of the ouster of Trotsky and Zinoviev from the Communist party.

This action had caused a sensation and Stalin published some remarks he had made in reply to allegations about the testament. He quoted Lenin's statement about his rudeness and lack of patience and Lenin's proposal to replace him with another man. He said he had submitted his resignation as General Secretary, but this had been refused. He acknowledged that he was rude, but said he was rude only "against those who try to split the party."

May 19, 1956

# KHRUSHCHEV TALK ON STALIN BARES DETAILS OF RULE BASED ON TERROR; CHARGES PLOT FOR KREMLIN PURGES

By HARRISON E. SALISBURY
Special to The New York Times.

WASHINGTON, June 4—The text of Nikita S. Khrushchev's secret speech attacking Stalin, as published by the State Department today, describes the late dictator as a savage, half-mad, power-crazed despot.

The speech shows that the old dictator utilized the Soviet and Communist apparatus to establish a rule based on terror, torture and brute force.

Stalin, as he is pictured by Mr. Khrushchev, turned the world about him into a miasma of treachery, treason and nightmarish plots. The picture was one that beggared the wildest surmise of political opponents of communism.

At the time of Stalin's death he was embarked upon a plot that, in Mr. Khrushchev's opinion, had as its objective the "wiping out" of all the older members of the top Kremlin leadership.

Mr. Khrushchev said Stalin apparently had determined to eliminate the older men and substitute younger Communists who would shower him with flattery and help erase the record of past crimes.

### Khrushchev Discusses Delay

Mr. Khrushchev himself posed the question of why he and his associates had not acted against Stalin or had not prevented Stalin from committing the grave crimes of which the old dictator was accused.

Mr. Khrushchev's answer was that he and his associates often had been divided in their views; that Stalin had deliberately withheld information; that he had terrorized anyone who opposed him; that he would brook no interference of any kind.

A flat assertion by Mr. Khrushchev that Stalin had planned the "annihilation" of the present group of older Soviet leaders seemed to leave the way open for some future declaration with regard to Stalin's death in the event it was shown that the dictator did not die naturally March 5, 1953, of cerebral hemorrhage, as was announced at the time.

So dark were the colors in which Mr. Khrushchev painted Stalin's deeds and records that it seemed inconceivable to specialists in Soviet affairs that the Soviet leaders would be able to halt their process of downgrading Stalin short of declaring him to have been one of the world's greatest criminals.

### Speech Adds Much Detail

Many details of the Khrushchev indictment were disclosed in earlier unofficial versions of the address published from March 16 onward.

The document released by the State Department was that of an address delivered by Mr. Khrushshev at a closed session of the Twentieth Congress of the Communist party. He began his speech Feb. 24 and concluded Feb. 25.

The document made public is not the text of this address as a whole but an edited version prepared for circulation to certain high Communist functionaries and groups.

The State Department did not indicate the source of its document. However, there was reason to believe that the text is that which Moscow is known to have sent to Belgrade, Yugoslavia, for the information of Marshal Tito and the Yugoslav Communist party about March 15.

Certain passages Mr. Khrushchev is understood to have delivered are omitted in this text. Apparently they will form the subject of later memorandums and releases.

While the present text is believed to have been circulated fairly widely within the Soviet Union for the information of top leaders and their guidance in informing the Soviet public, only the general outlines have been published by Pravda, Soviet Communist party newspaper, and many of the more horrible of Stalin's crimes are still not known by the Russian people.

A study of Mr. Khrushchev's purported speech suggests that it is only the opening general barrage on the subject of Stalin and his era.

Further detailed revelations, possibly of a very sensational nature, may be forthcoming, particularly in the field of Soviet foreign affairs.

Mr. Khrushchev's address touched in detail on only one foreign topic: relations with Yugoslavia. However, Mr. Khrushchev said that Stalin "threatened" Moscow's "peaceful relations with other nations." He added that "one-man decisions could cause, and often did cause, great complications."

The nature of these threats to Soviet peaceful relations is not spelled out in the present document.

### Korean War Data Awaited

However, it is believed by some who are familiar with the situation that a whole new dramatic chapter in "inside" Soviet history will be written if the Soviet leaders decide to make public the true story of relations with Communist China and particularly the real cause of the outbreak of the Korean war.

Other forthcoming revelations may touch on the Soviet incursion in Iran in 1945-46, the story of Soviet relations with Greece and Turkey in 1946, the real reason for the Soviet fiasco in the Finnish "winter" war of 1939-40, the circumstances of the onset of the Berlin blockade of 1948-49 and other Soviet aggressions of the post-war period.

Another notable omission in the Khrushchev document is the details of the liquidation of Marshal Mikhail Tukhachevsky and the other high leaders of the Red Army in June, 1937.

However, Mr. Khrushchev revealed that at the outbreak of World War II a number of high Soviet officers were in Siberian prison camps. These men were released and won great distinction in the war. Among those whom he named were Marshal Konstantin K. Rokossovsky, hero of the Battle of Moscow in 1941, who since has become Defense Minister of Poland; Marshal Alexander V. Gorbatov, former Soviet commander in Berlin; Marshal Kirill Meretskov, present commander of the Leningrad Military district and a number of others.

Most high Soviet officers with combat experience in the Spanish Civil War or in the Far East battle with Japan had been liquidated by the time World War II broke out, Mr. Khrushchev said.

Another subject not dealt with in Mr. Khrushchev's address is that of Stalin's periodic anti-Semitic drives. This has been discussed to some extent by the satellite press but apparently is scheduled for treatment only later within the Soviet Union itself.

It also is evident that a much more detailed account of the famous party purges of the mid-Nineteen Thirties will be forthcoming.

Contrary to previous indications. Mr. Khrushchev clearly laid the basis for the personal—as distinguished from the political—"rehabilitation" of such outstanding old Bolshevik leaders as Lev B. Kamenev, Grigory E. Zinoviev, Nikolai I. Bukharin and possibly even of Leon Trotsky.

Mr. Khrushchev declared that Lenin was often very critically at odds with such men as Kamenev and Zinoviev. He recalled that these men had opposed Lenin at the outbreak of the Bolshevik Revolution and that Lenin had considered them guilty of treason. Yet Lenin became reconciled with them and worked with them. Mr. Krushchev added.

Stalin, on the other hand, classfied them as "enemies of the state" and carried out his blood purges at a time when there was no threat whatsoever from such men, Mr. Khrushchev continued.

He said Stalin had carried out his attack on his old party associates under the pretext of a Trotskyite "threat." Yet, Mr. Khrushchev noted, the Trotskyites had practically vanished by this time.

Mr. Khrushchev indicated his belief that Stalin had been right in his political controversies with Kamenev, Zinoviev, Trotsky and the others. But he said he saw no reason for Stalin's demonstration of "brutal force."

Mr. Khrushchev was said to have opened his address with a dramatic gesture. He circulated among the delegates to the Congress a copy of Lenin's so-called last "testament."

This document, written by Lenin in December, 1922, and January, 1923 gave Lenin's personal assessment of the character of Stalin and other Bolshevik leaders of the time.

In it Lenin warned the party against Stalin and proposed to take steps to remove him as General Secretary. Because of illness Lenin was never able to carry out his intention.

The testament has never been published in full or generally circulated in the Soviet Union and for many years all reference to it was suppressed by Stalin. However, it has long been known outside the Soviet Union, having been first published by The New York Times in 1926 and reprinted May 19.

It has been evident in recent months that the Soviet leaders were preparing for general public presentation of the long-suppressed document.

The testament formed a cornerstone of Mr. Khrushchev's indictment against Stalin. He added to Lenin's "testament" two more documents. The existence of one, in which Lenin proposed to break off personal relations with Stalin, has been known. However, the full text presented by Mr. Khrushchev, in which Lenin accused Stalin of rudeness to his wife, Nadezhda Krupskaya, apparently had not been published before.

The revelation of this document was said to have caused a stir of excitement among the Communists at the party congress.

The second document was an appeal by Mme. Krupskaya for the protection of Kamenev against Stalin's "rude interference with my private life and from vile invectives and threats."

The existence of this document had been rumored, but it apparently had not been published previously. The appeal was made during Lenin's illness, when Mme. Krupskaya was devoting herself to his care.

Upon the basis of these documents dating from 1922 and 1923 Mr. Khrushchev built up a portrait of Stalin that, as he said, justified the worst of Lenin's apprehensions about him.

**Revelations by Khrushchev**

Among Mr. Khrushchev's revelations relative to the party purges of the Nineteen Thirties were the following:

¶The murder of Sergei M. Kirov on Dec. 1, 1934, is being carefully investigated because of suspicions of secret police complicity. The killing was used by Stalin to touch off the purges.

¶Stalin complained in 1936 that the secret police were "four years behind" their quota in making arrests. He dismissed Henry G. Yagoda, head of the secret police, and put in Nikolai Yezhov, who stepped up the purge.

¶Sergo Ordzhonikidze, a famous old Bolshevik, who was supposed to have died in 1937 of natural causes, actually shot himself under hounding from Stalin.

¶In 1937 and 1938 Stalin approved in advance the sentences to be imposed upon 383 lists of defendants against whom the police had prepared cases but had not tried them.

The revelations of Mr. Khrushchev provided a harsh but simple answer to the question that puzzled the whole world during the decade of the Nineteen Thirties—why did the old Bolsheviks confess?

The answer was elementary, Mr. Khrushchev said, "beat, beat and once again, beat."

"How is it possible that a person confesses to crimes which he has not committed?" Mr. Khrushchev asked. "Only in one way—because of the application of physical methods of pressuring him, tortures, bringing him to a state of unconsciousness, deprivation of his judgment, taking away of his human dignity."

Mr. Khrushchev illustrated his object lesson on the machinery of Stalin's dictatorship with letter after letter drawn from the state archives—the pathetic final appeals of old Bolsheviks, seeking clemency for crimes they had not committed.

Mr. Khrushchev cited the actual cases of several old Bolsheviks among the thousands who perished. One was an old friend of Lenin's named Mikhail Kedrov, who was arrested in the late Nineteen Thirties and convicted. He wrote a letter to Andrei Andreyev, then a Central Committee Secretary, appealing for mercy.

"I suffer innocently," Mr. Kedrov's letter read. "Please believe me. Time will testify to the truth."

Mr. Kedrov was found innocent by a military court. Nevertheless he was shot.

Another old Bolshevik, Robert I. Eikhe, a member of the Politburo of the party, appealed to Stalin, charging that the only crime of which he was guilty was that of having confessed crimes he had not committed "by not being able to suffer the tortures to which I was submitted."

In a final address to the court Feb. 2, 1940, Mr. Eikhe declared: "The most important thing for me is to tell the court, the party and Stalin that I am not guilty. I have never been guilty of any conspiracy. I will die believing in the truth of party policy as I have believed in it during my whole life."

Two days later he was shot.

Another last declaration was that of Jan E. Rudzutak, another Politburo member liquidated without public notice in 1938. He begged for permission to tell the Communist party Central Committee that:

"There is in the NKVD an as yet not liquidated center which is craftily manufacturing cases, which forces innocent persons to confess. The investigative methods are such that they force people to lie and to slander entirely innocent persons."

Mr. Khrushchev gave a case history of the precise methods used by the secret police to manufacture their cases. His explanation was identical with the allegations that long have been published abroad in countless "revelatory" books about the methods of the Soviet secret police in concocting evidence.

Mr. Khrushchev declared that Stalin's plot mania and his terrorism against his close associates rose to a peak after World War II.

**'Leningrad Affair' Recalled**

He confirmed previous reports that in the "Leningrad Affair" Stalin shot Nikolai Voznesensky, Chief of Soviet state planning, A. A. Kuznetzov, a Central Committee secretary and Leningrad Party chief, Mikhail Rodionov, chairman of the Russian Federated Republic and Petr S. Popkov, mayor of Leningrad and a Leningrad party leader and a number of others.

The executions apparently occurred in 1949-1950.

Stalin had launched on another and even more dangerous purge in the months just before his death, Mr. Khrushchev revealed. This apparently had its inception about the time of the Nineteenth Congress of the Communist party in October, 1952.

Prior to that time Stalin had forbidden Marshal Kliment E. Voroshilov, one of his oldest and closest cronies, to attend Politburo meetings because he suspected him of being a British spy. He also refused to allow Mr. Andreyev to participate in the sessions.

At the first Central Committee plenary meeting held after the Nineteenth Party Congress, Stalin made known his suspicions of Vyacheslav M. Molotov, Soviet Foreign Minister, and Anastas I. Mikoyan, Deputy Premier, according to Mr. Khrushchev.

Mr. Khruschc[illegible]v said Stalin evidently had pl[illegible]ns "to finish off" both these m[illegible]n as well as the other older members of the Politburo. This g[illegible] [illegible]resumably, including Mr. Khrushchev himself, Premier Nikolai A. Bulganin, Deputy Premier Lazar M. Kaganovich and possibly former Premier Georgi M. Malenkov.

Mr. Khrushchev said that Stalin often declared the older Politburo members should be replaced bw new ones and that he had deliberately increased the size of the party leadership group to twenty-five at the Nineteenth Party Congress as "a design for the future annihilation of the old Politburo members and in the way a cover for all the shameful acts of Stalin, acts we are now considering."

**'Doctors' Plot Laid to Stalin**

Mr. Khrushchev placed the full and complete blame for the so-called "Doctors' plot" on Stalin. In this "plot" a group of prominent physicians were charged in January, 1953, with a conspiracy against a number of high Kremlin individuals.

For the first time Mr. Khrushchev revelaed some extent of the population uprootings ordered by Stalin at the end of the war. He declared Stalin would have shipped all of the Ukranians away—if he had had a place for them.

Mr.. Khrushchev closed his report with a warning to his fellow Communist party members with regard to secrecy. He said that the exposé could not be permitted to get out of party circles or into the press.

On the other hand, he made it plain that whole new segments of the revision of history and the rehabilitation of mistreated Soviet citizens were at hand. He promised specifically a revision of World War II history.

A special commission under the Presidium of the Central Committee of the party has been set up to carry on the inquiry into the past, he revealed. Special courts are "rehabilitating" individuals. Up to the time of his speech 7,679 persons—many of them dead—had had their records cleared.

June 5, 1956

# WIDE SHAKE-UP IN KREMLIN OUSTS MOLOTOV, MALENKOV, KAGANOVICH AS KHRUSHCHEV TIGHTENS REINS

## 3 STALINISTS OUT

By WILLIAM J. JORDEN

Special to The New York Times.

MOSCOW, Thursday, July 4—The Soviet Communist party has accused Vyacheslav M. Molotov, Georgi M. Malenkov and Lazar M. Kaganovich of anti-party activities and has ousted them from the country's leadership.

They were removed both from the Presidium of the party's Central Committee and from the Central C[illegible]mmittee itself. However, they [illegible]emained as members of the party.

Dmitri T. [illegible]ov, who was said to have joined them in working against the majority, was also ousted from alternate membership in the Presidium, from the Central Committee and from his job as one of the party secretaries.

The three Communist leaders, all known for their connections with Stalin, were accused of having tried to restore "methods of leadership that were condemned by the Twentieth Party Congress," an allusion to the system prevailing in Stalin's time. They were said to have tried to form an anti-party faction to achieve their aims.

The action against them was

taken during an eight-day meeting of the Central Committee from June 22 through 29. The text of the committee's resolution was released by Tass, Soviet news agency, last night.

Of the former eleven members of the party Presidium only six remained. They are Nikita S. Khrushchev, Nikolai A. Bulganin, Kliment Y. Voroshilov, Anastas I. Mikoyan, Mikhail A. Suslov and Alexei I. Kirichenko.

**Zhukov Is Elevated**

Marshal Georgi K. Zhukov, the Defense Minister, and Miss Yekaterina A. Furtseva, the only woman on the Presidium, were among five alternate members who were raised to full rank. Four other regular members were newly added to the Presidium.

In addition to the four leading figures who were singled out for severe criticism and ousted from the Presidium, Mikhail G. Pervukhin and Maxim Z. Saburov also were dropped from the group.

Mr. Pervukhin was demoted to the position of alternate member of the Presidium, but nothing was known of Mr. Saburov's present position. He was not mentioned as having been dropped from the Central Committee itself.

Messrs. Molotov, Malenkov and Kaganovich were said to have opposed all the major policy moves of recent years that have come to be associated with the name of Mr. Khrushchev. The Central Committee's indictment specifically mentioned his plan for the reorganization of industrial management and expansion of agriculture.

The three, and especially Mr. Molotov, were said also to have opposed the current line of Soviet foreign policy. The former Foreign Minister was accused of "conservatism" and of hampering efforts to ease international tensions. His opposition to a rapprochement with Yugoslavia was picked out for special criticism.

The Central Committee disclosed that Mr. Molotov's stand on Yugoslavia had been unanimously condemned by the group at the plenary meeting in July, 1955, almost a year before he resigned from his post of Foreign Minister.

The New York Times
Vyacheslav M. Molotov

Associated Press
Georgi M. Malenkov

Mr. Molotov also was condemned for his opposition to the state treaty with Austria and restoration of normal relations with Japan. He also was said to have "denied the common sense" of the Khrushchev program of personal contacts with leaders of other countries.

**Pravda Hinted at Shake-Up**

The first hint that a major overhaul in the Communist party's leadership was about to take place appeared in the Communist party newspaper Pravda yesterday morning.

In its editorial and a long and more outspoken article, the party organ launched a bitter attack on Communists who refused to accept party discipline. The editorial and the article both emphasized that party leaders were in no special category and were as much subject to party discipline as rank-and-file members.

Pravda made a strong defense of all major policies advanced by Mr. Khrushchev since the twentieth party congress in February, 1956. It has been clear for some time that he has emerged as by far the most powerful figure in the Soviet hierarchy. Today's events further strengthened his authority and emphasized the fact that his policies were indeed the policies of the Soviet Union.

Messrs. Molotov, Malenkov and Kaganovich were accused of having opposed many measures that have struck a responsive chord among Soviet citizens. They were said, for example, to have worked against the program of granting more autonomy to the Soviet republics and to the local soviets.

The three formerly powerful figures were said to be opposed to the necessity of improving living standards and to have doubted the possibilities for rapid growth of the Soviet economy.

**Held Great Prestige**

All these charges presumably made the outster of the three more palatable to Soviet citizens who read of the widespread shake-up in their morning papers. This was a factor that could not be ignored by the Central Committee in its move against men who have enjoyed great prestige in the past.

Mr. Molotov, in particular, was not a person who could summarily be dismissed from party leadership without most important and convincing reasons. He was the only member of the leading group whose services in the upper echelons of the Soviet state dated from the Bolshevik Revolution forty years ago.

After its extensive attack on Mr. Molotov's views on both internal and foreign policy, the Central Committee's decision said the former Foreign Minister had been supported on "many of these questions" by Mr. Kaganovich and "in several cases" by Mr. Malenkov. It said the committee tried "to correct them patiently" but that the three "continued with their mistaken and anti-Leninist attitude."

"In the attitude of Comrades Malenkov, Kaganovich and Molotov, which differs from the party line," the Communist party group said, "the basic fact is that they were and still are being held captive by old ideas and methods, they lost contact with the party and the national life, they failed to see the new conditions, new situations and they display conservatism, stubbornly sticking to old forms and methods of work that do not exist any more and which do not correspond to the interests of the Communist movement."

**Dogmatism Charged**

In both internal and foreign policy, they were said to be "sectarians and dogmatists." In Communist parlance that means they were resisting change and were supporting methods and ideas that the present leadership considers outdated.

The party leadership decided "to condemn as incompatible with the Leninist principles of our party" the "factional activity" of the three and of Mr. Shepilov, "who joined them." This was the only mention of the man who succeeded Mr. Molotov in the Foreign Ministry post last year and then resigned last February to assume a leading propaganda post and supervision of intellectual currents.

The current party leadership said its action against the three leading officials and Mr. Shepilov would "further strengthen the unity of the party." Its decisions were said to have been adopted unanimously. There was one abstention in the voting, by Mr. Molotov.

In addition to Marshal Zhukov and Miss Furtseva, the alternate members of the Presidium who were raised to full membership were: Leonid I. Brezhnev, Frol R. Kozlov and Nikolai M. Shvernik.

The four other new regular Presidium members were Averky B. Aristov, Nikolai I. Belyayev, Nikolai G. Ignatov and Otto V. Kuusinen.

July 4, 1957

# BEHIND SOVIET POLITICS: THE SOURCES OF POWER

## Top Communist Bosses Rely on Army and Hierarchy of Officials

By HARRY SCHWARTZ

Who rules the Soviet Union now after the purge of Georgi M. Malenkov and his fellow victims? The news from Moscow this past week, with its outline of the machinations which led up to the final Malenkov defeat, gave valuable clues for anyone who would understand the present constellation of forces at the apex of the Moscow power structure.

One fact above all was clear from last week's news: Nikita S. Khrushchev is no Stalin. For all his free-wheeling speech making in Czechoslovakia and his exuberant cheer, Mr. Khrushchev was dependent upon the support of Marshal Georgi K. Zhukov and the Soviet armed forces for his victory. This implies a very great deal for the difference between the present Khrushchev era and the Stalin age.

Power in the Soviet Union, the present evidence suggests, is now a composite of many elements. Instead of one man's whim dictating policy, the interests of different groups interact and clash in the process of policy formation. The forums in which these clashes now take place are first the Presidium of the Communist party, the fifteen-member body elected after the Malenkov group's fall, and the Central Committee, the 133-member body whose prestige was tremendously enhanced by the latest events. It is in these bodies apparently that the direct and indirect representatives of different groups and currents in Soviet society now resolve their differences through argument and intrigue. At the top of the Soviet pyramid, something at least distantly resembling politics as we know it has begun to make an appearance.

### New Power Groups

Let us look more closely at the interacting groups involved:

*The Communist party*—This is the fundamental power mechanism of the Soviet Union, a fact emphasized more than ever by the latest events. For all practical purposes the party is the totality of the Soviet élite, since everybody who is of any importance in Russia's political life belongs to it and is subject to its discipline. That discipline is founded on the notion of "democratic centralism," that is, a decision by one party body is binding upon all subordinate party bodies. In the present situation, therefore, a decision by the Presidium or by the Central Committee of the party governs the expressed opinions and political actions of the party's more than 7,000,000 members.

Central in the Communist party is the small group of several hundred party leaders who run its apparatus throughout the country. This group, which is controlled by Nikita S. Khrushchev in his capacity as party First Secretary, makes up the largest single element in the Central Committee and undoubtedly contributed much to Mr. Khrushchev's victory. Most notable is the new rise in prestige of the party chiefs in different provinces and republics of the country away from Moscow. The new set-up of the party Presidium is such that these leaders outside Moscow may have more voice in national decisions than at any time in many years. At the same time the economic decentralization has given the party boss in each area a greatly increased degree of control over his own region's economic life.

*The military commanders*—Marshal Zhukov could not have been so helpful to Mr. Khrushchev if he did not speak as the representative of the leading commanders of the Soviet armed forces. The recent events provided this group with the second opportunity it has had in four years to exercise crucial political influence. Four years ago, the generals' part in arresting and deposing the late secret police chief, Lavrentia P. Beria, was also one of primary importance.

### Military Gain

One gain won by this group is already apparent. Marshal Zhukov has become the first professional military officer in Soviet history to sit in the Communist party's highest decision-making body, the Presidium. We may suspect with a high degree of probability that at least some, if not all, of the four vacancies in the Central Committee caused by the latest purge were filled with military men. But beyond all this is the chief gain: Since Mr. Khrushchev is at least in part indebted to the military commanders for his victory, he has assumed the implicit obligation of giving them at least some species of veto power over Soviet policy. Put another way, Marshal Zhukov now probably has more than the equivalent of one out of fifteen votes in the party Presidium.

*The central government bureaucracy*—This group has emerged shorn of much of its power and prestige from the latest battle, and many of its leaders—Malenkov, Vyacheslav M. Molotov, Lazar M. Kaganovich, Mikhail G. Pervukhin and others—have been either purged or very sharply demoted. This group's basic interest was to keep as much power as possible concentrated in its hands in Moscow, and for that reason the Khrushchev decentralization scheme posed the sharpest threat to its position and future. With the defeat this group has now suffered, it can offer little effective resistance to the plans of either the Communist party bureaucracy or the military commanders.

### Provincial Gain

*The provincial government bureaucracy*—This group has gained at the expense of the central bureaucracy, and some of these gains have been very great. The provincial representation in the new Presidium, especially among its alternate members, is up very sharply from the past. The Malenkov group has been officially condemned for opposing the transfer of powers and functions from the central to the republic and provincial governments. The industrial reorganization scheme gives persons such as the premiers of the union republics—the head of the Ukraine for example—and the chief executive officers of provinces far more real power and influence than they have ever had before. Not the least important aspect of this is the increased role it gives to non-Russian minority groups and their Communist leaders in different areas of the country.

*The secret police*—Perhaps the biggest difference between this latest Moscow struggle and those which have preceded it in recent years was the failure of the Soviet secret police to play any decisive role. This was interesting confirmation of the earlier indications that the secret police, while it still exists, is far reduced in power and prestige. One reason for the lack of prominence of the secret police in the latest conflict was the fact that the head of that organization, Gen. Ivan Serov, is of too low rank to be involved as a principle in any struggle for decisive power. This is a far cry from the situation in 1953 when Lavrentia Beria sought to use the secret police as the instrument by which he would become Stalin's successor.

* * *

### Far From a Democracy

All of these groups taken together, of course, constitute only an infinitesimal minority of the Soviet people. Yet the interplay among these groups and the resolution of that interplay determine policy, and therefore the extent to which the Soviet people's desires are served.

That the Soviet Union is very far from a democracy today was vividly shown in the nature of the latest power struggle and the means by which it was resolved. Yet to recognize this is not the same thing as to assert that the Soviet people played no part in the fight. On the contrary, the evidence suggests that the pressure of the Soviet people was very much on the minds of all the actual contestants.

The communiqué of the Communist party Central Committee announcing the purge of Mr. Malenkov and his associates reads in large part like an election platform for the Khrushchev party, a platform of peace and prosperity. That communiqué goes to great lengths to assure the Soviet people that the victors are against war and for rapid progress toward higher living standards and the like. One need not be over-cynical to see in this document that Mr. Khrushchev has taken over many slogans and emphases which four years ago were Mr. Malenkov's alone.

The communique was intended as progaganda, of course, yet it commits the Soviet government to certain specific domestic courses of action which are more than words. Thus the first Government decree issued after the resolution of the party struggle was that ending forced deliveries of produce from peasant gardens to the Government at very low prices.

The Soviet people are still not masters of their own fate. But their present masters cannot ignore their wishes entirely as Stalin once did. The latest struggle among Soviet hierarchs significantly widened the group of persons who had some say in the final outcome. If similar struggles recur in the future, there may be still further widening of that group.

Valtman in The Hartford Times

# ZHUKOV RELIEVED AS DEFENSE CHIEF; SOVIET GIVES NO CLUE TO HIS FUTURE; MALINOVSKY APPOINTED SUCCESSOR

## ACTION IS SUDDEN

### It Follows Marshal's Return From Albania and Yugoslavia

By MAX FRANKEL

Special to The New York Times.

MOSCOW, Oct. 26—Marshal Georgi K. Zhukov was relieved today as Minister of Defense.

The Government announcement was terse and without explanation. It named the new Defense Minister, Marshal Rodion Y. Malinovsky, but gave no clue as to Marshal Zhukov's future.

Marshal Zhukov, the Soviet Union's greatest living military hero, is believed to have attained great political prestige here in the last few months.

His growing prestige may be a reason why Marshal Zhukov has been removed from his Defense Ministry post. The combination of the power the military naturally presents and Marshal Zhukov's own widespread personal popularity among the masses may finally have loomed as too great a threat for the comfort of the Communist party leadership.

[Soviet correspondents in London expressed the belief that Marshal Zhukov would soon be named to "a high political post" in the Kremlin hierarchy, The Associated Press reported. The news of Marshal Zhukov's replacement surprised them, but they said any downgrading of the marshal would be unthinkable.]

**A Stalingrad Defender**

Marshal Malinovsky is known as one of the Soviet Union's best professional soldiers. He was in charge of vital rear-guard action against the invading German armies in World War II in the Ukraine and was one of the leading defenders of Stalingrad in 1942.

Marshal Georgi K. Zhukov

Associated Press

Marshal Rodion Y. Malinovsky

The announcement of Marshal Zhukov's replacement was made known here only about an hour after he returned to Moscow from an official visit to Albania and Yugoslavia. He had left the Soviet Union on Oct. 4 and the military press here each day carried generous accounts of his tour.

Thus the news came as a complete surprise to observers. It had been widely assumed that as Defense Minister Marshal Zhukov would preside over what promises to be the nation's most ambitious and grandiose military show—the display of armed might on Nov. 7, the fortieth anniversary of the Bolshevik revolution.

The Supreme Soviet meets on Nov. 6 in what has been billed here as a strictly ceremonial session for the anniversary celebration. Legally, however, it will be able to conduct business such as the confirmation of the replacement of Marshal Zhukov and any other government changes that may be considered desirable.

Since he became Defense Minister in 1955 Marshal Zhukov has regularly taken the salute in Red Square from atop the tomb of Lenin and Stalin and delivered major policy speeches about Soviet military power. This year it is now clear Moscow is planning to stage a monster parade of new ground weapons and machinery as well as short-range and perhaps medium-range atomic missiles.

Today's shift in personnel, of course, does not automatically bar Marshal Zhukov from an important assignment. Nothing at all was said about his future position in the Soviet hierarchy or whether he would have a future position.

**A Soldier Member of Premier**

He remains a full member of the Communist party's ruling Presidium, the most powerful body in the Soviet Union. He was elevated to that inner circle in last June's shake-up, which resulted in the ouster of former Premier Georgi M. Malenkov, former Foreign Minister Vyacheslav M. Molotov and Lazar M. Kaganovich.

Marshal Zhukov, who attained fame here in World War II comparable to that of President Eisenhower in the United States, became the first professional soldier to sit as a voting member of the party Presidium. He has been a full-fledged party worker most of his adult life as well as a professional soldier.

It was in the war that Marshal Zhukov became a personal friend of General Eisenhower and the two men conducted still undisclosed personal correspondence after the war. The Communist party leader, Nikita S. Khrushchev, and Premier Nikolai A. Bulganin took Marshal Zhukov to Geneva for the talks of the heads of government of the United States, Britain, France and the Soviet Union in the summer of 1955—presumably to deal personally with President Eisenhower.

But Marshal Zhukov and President Eisenhower slowly drifted apart. The possibility of their meeting again, however, to try on a personal level of mutual respect and one-time comradeship to solve some outstanding issues between the Soviet Union and the United States was regularly revived from time to time.

Last July President Eisenhower seemed to be suggesting that the marshal go to Washington for talks with his counterpart, then Secretary of Defense Charles E. Wilson. Mr. Khrushchev recently revealed that Moscow had shown interest in the possibility of such a trip for Marshal Zhukov but charged that Washington had backed down on its own proposal.

The party and Government shake-up last June was seen as a major triumph for Marshal Zhukov. He ostensibly had taken a strong stand on the side of Mr. Khrushchev against what was branded here as the "anti-party group" led by Messrs. Malenkov and Molotov.

Marshal Zhukov was immediately promoted from alternate to full member in the party Presidium and then began a round of speech-making in defense of the shake-up. In these speeches, he departed from strictly defense matters and dealt with domestic and foreign issues, publicly giving strong support to Mr. Khrushchev.

Before going to Belgrade three weeks ago Marshal Zhukov had stopped off in the Crimea to confer with Mr. Khrushchev, who was then vacationing in Yalta. There had been no indication here, however, of the impending change—ordered by the Presidium of the Supreme Soviet, the Soviet Union's version of a parliament.

**The Tass Announcement**

The announcement by Tass, the Soviet news agency, said:

"The Presidium of the U.S.S.R. Supreme Soviet has appointed Marshal of the Soviet Union Malinovsky Defense Minister of the U.S.S.R.

"The Presidium of the U.S.S.R. Supreme Soviet has relieved Marshal of the Soviet Union Zhukov of his duties as U.S.S.R. Minister of Defense."

There had been dozens of stories here in military newspapers in the last two weeks about the necessary subordination of the military to the Communist party. But this has been standard policy.

Marshal Malinovsky has performed successfully in diverse military assignments, but he has not achieved anything like the fame of his predecessor.

He, too, has a long record of loyal political as well as military work and at the Twentieth party Congress in February, 1956, he was promoted from alternate to full membership in the party Central Committee.

He first was identified here as a Deputy Minister of Defense in Krasnaya Zvezda, the army newspaper, in July of 1956.

Marshal Malinovsky, who is 57 years old, was corps commander at the outbreak of World War II.

He became a marshal late in the war. In 1944 he commanded a number of Ukrainian fronts and headed the Soviet armies that took Transylvania and Bucharest, the capital of Rumania, from the Germans. He was in France at the time of the Bolshevik revolution in 1917 but returned in the next year to join the Red Army as a machine gun instructor. He was graduated from the Frunze Military Academy here in 1930 and became a cavalry officer.

October 27, 1957

# KHRUSHCHEV TAKES FULL CONTROL, REPLACING BULGANIN AS PREMIER

## PARTY HELM KEPT

### Moscow Chief Thus Unites Jobs Stalin Once Combined

By MAX FRANKEL
Special to The New York Times.

MOSCOW, March 27—Nikita Sergeyevich Khrushchev became Premier of the Soviet Union today. Thus he has emerged as the undisputed leader and chief spokesman of this nation in name as well as fact.

The Soviet legislature, the Supreme Soviet, dutifully and unanimously elected Mr. Khrushchev chairman of the Council of Ministers—the Premier—to succeed Marshal Nikolai A. Bulganin, who submitted his resignation.

The Supreme Soviet was told at once that the new Premier would remain First Secretary and therefore leader of the ruling Communist party.

Associated Press Radiophoto

**VOTING FOR NEW SOVIET PREMIER: Raised hands in legislature signify approval of Nikita S. Khrushchev, head bowed, to replace Nikolai A. Bulganin, upper right, as Premier. Flanking Mr. Khrushchev are Anastas I. Mikoyan, left, and Marshal Kliment Y. Voroshilov. Others, from left, Averky B. Aristov, Nikolai I. Belyayev, Otto V. Kuusinen.**

Thus were joined again at the top the two hierarchies that direct the affairs of more than 200,000,000 Soviet citizens and lead the 1,000,000,000 persons of the Communist camp.

They were united in the ebullient and energetic person of Mr. Khrushchev, the 63-year-old former mine mechanic, who in the five years since Stalin's death has emerged from the collective leadership and advanced to overwhelming responsibility and power.

Mr. Khrushchev has now succeeded to the posts that Stalin had formally combined. He is not only the acknowledged architect of all Soviet foreign and domestic policies but the leader of the disciplined party ranks and the extensive ministerial apparatus that administers and enforces the policies.

The momentous change in the Government was effected quickly and in strict forms of parliamentary procedure. There was no debate on the move and even before the full weight of the switch was apparent Premier Khrushchev began a two-hour-and-forty-minute dissertation on agricultural reforms.

**Choked With Emotion**

He uttered only a few words of acceptance, words over which he appeared choked with emotion:

"With your decision," he told the 1,378 Deputies, "you have just expressed great confidence in me and have done me great honor. I shall do everything to justify your confidence and shall not spare strength, health or life to serve you."

His agricultural speech contained only one general comment that might be taken as an inaugural promise. "We shall conquer capitalism," Mr. Khrushchev declared, "with a high level of work and a higher standard of living."

Mr. Khrushchev was placed in nomination for the premiership by Marshal Kliment Y. Voroshilov only a few minutes after the marshal was elected to a second full term as titular chief of state.

The fate of Marshal Bulganin and the other ministers of the Government was not resolved at today's session. The ousted Premier had turned in a written resignation for the entire Cabinet. In short order this resignation was accepted and a resolution approving the Government's conduct over the last four years was adopted.

Marshal Bulganin, seated behind Mr. Khrushchev, applauded his successor generously. The retiring Premier was in the second row, among the lesser members of the party's Presidium.

As far as is known, Marshal Bulganin remains a member of the Presidium, the nation's policy-making body, but what Government job, if any, he will receive was not made known.

March 28, 1958

# BULGANIN ADMITS 'ANTI-PARTY' PLOT

## Ex-Premier Confesses Error at Kremlin Session—Hails 'Genius' of Khrushchev

By MAX FRANKEL

Special to The New York Times.

MOSCOW, Friday, Dec. 19—Former Premier Nikolai A. Bulganin has admitted all the charges brought against him by his former traveling companion and fellow member of the "collective" leadership, Premier Nikita S. Khrushchev.

The dapper goateed Marshal Bulganin, 63 years old, was a surprise speaker yesterday at the meeting of the Soviet Communist party's Central Committee. He confessed his errors and gave a glowing tribute to the "genius" of Mr. Khrushchev and the party.

The other members of the disgraced "anti-party group"—former Premier Georgi M. Malenkov, former party troubleshooted, Lazar M. Kaganovich and former Foreign Ministers Vyacheslav M. Molotov and Dmitri T. Shepilov—conspired against the party's domestic and foreign policies just as Mr. Khrushchev said they had, Marshal Bulganin declared.

"Everything is correct, everything corresponds fully to reality," he said.

Marshal Bulganin became Premier in February, 1955, succeeding Mr. Malenkov when Stalin's heir admitted his "inability" to run the Government. The so-called anti-party plotters were exposed and thrown out of the Communist heirarchy in June, 1957, but Marshal Bulganin remained as Premier until last March.

Marshal Bulganin, a Soviet Army officer and former Defense Minister, remained on the top-ranking party Presidium until September. He was not formally listed as a member of the "anti-party group" until a month ago.

According to Tass, the official Soviet press agency, Marshal Bulganin also described his precise relation to the anti-party group at yesterday's meeting.

In recent months Mr. Khrushchev has told correspondents that his predecessor as Premier was in poor health and was undergoing serious operations. The announcement of Marshal Bulganin's talk today identified him, however, as still the chairman of the economic council in Stavropol in southern European Russia.

This is one of more than 100 economic councils established after Mr. Khrushchev's reorganization of industrial management, which Marshal Bulganin apparently opposed. His work as a council chairman convinced him, Marshal Bulganin said, of the "full genius and wisdom" of party policy.

December 19, 1958

# KHRUSHCHEV SETS NEW SOVIET STYLE

## Policy Goals Are Unchanged but Mood Is Different—Initiative Is Stressed

By MAX FRANKEL

Special to The New York Times.

MOSCOW, Feb. 29—Soviet Communists are trying to commit to paper something they all know and feel but have never really defined: the new way—the Khrushchev way—of doing things.

The party leaders are drafting a new party program for proclamation at a party congress next year. They hope to offer more than a general statement of future plans.

They want to look over the years since Stalin's death in 1953 to discern the changes that they believe have again made the party a dynamic organization.

There is no way for a foreigner to know how the drafting committee is doing; things have not changed that much. But outsiders here also sense the changes and are trying to assess them in anticipation of the drift of events.

### Objectives Are Unchanged

The consensus is that Premier Khrushchev is trying to teach the country a new "style" of political life. He has not radically altered the objectives of foreign and domestic policy. The familiar institutions of party and government remain.

But the talk is becoming different: the way Comrade A talks to Comrade B and the way Ivan G. talks about "K." The mood is different: it is a mood of impatience with abstruse theorizing and a mood of respect for achievement.

Within the party, initiative, debate and new blood are wanted. And the public is being courted for sympathy and support.

These changes are far less dramatic than the visible improvements in Soviet living standards or successes in rocketry. They derive from the ebullient personality of Premier Khrushchev and his reforms, notably the inhibition of the nation's police apparatus.

It is not just that people now speak fearlessly about Nikita Kukuruznik, meaning Nikita Khrushchev, the Corn Man; it is that official party publications acknowledge and encourage such informality. It is not just that good party members are donning white shirts and ties; it is that substantial numbers of white-collar personnel, scientists and factory managers, appear to advance toward the decision-making center of the party apparatus.

The Communist party, of course, remains an instrument of centralized control over all facets of Soviet life. Its commitment to military order and obedience imposes a discipline unknown to political organizations elsewhere.

But it does not operate in a vacuum and it does not seem now to be just a lifeless transmission belt of orders from the top and news of disorder from below.

### Knowledge Now Expected

Increasingly, party officials are expected to combine authority with intimate knowledge of production and farming. Premier Khrushchev is warring, as he puts it, on those farm leaders whose familiarity with the subject derives only from the dinner table.

The consequences of failure are becoming no worse than in other political movements: demotion commensurate with the offense and removal from the center of power. The rewards of success and loyalty, on the other hand, are no longer just prestige and perquisites but opportunities to lead, to influence and to help decide.

New party members are being recruited into the 8,000,000-member organization at an apparently growing rate, now about 350,000 a year. They are ambitious and promising workers and farmers, effective administrators and respected specialists, and most of all young persons who, it is hoped, will be ready for responsible positions at the age of 35 and 40.

Somewhat surprisingly, the change in style is accompanied by an ever more noticeable build-up of Premier Khrushchev himself. Praise is being heaped upon the very man who is working to broaden the seat of power, to put some life into the old institutions and to rid the country of the worst evils of one-man rule and the "personality cult."

The reasons for this seem complex. There is, first, the Russians' quite evident appreciation of political symmetry; history seems to have conditioned them to prefer a clearly visible summit on the power pyramid.

Furthermore, much of the adulation of the Premier reflects a genuine gratitude for the better times over which he presides. And some aspects of the campaign, like the continuing celebration of Mr. Khrushchev's success in the United States, probably represent a deliberate effort to dramatize his claims of esteem for the Soviet Union abroad.

Another reason why the Premier probably permits the veneration of his person is that he wants to personify and thereby to dramatize the party's new spirit of vitality and arouse, in Communist terms, greater interest and participation in public affairs.

To lead efficiently while earning the people's respect and active cooperation is the essence of the Khrushchev program.

March 5, 1960

# PARTY'S RECRUITS DISPLEASE SOVIET

## Communists Voice Concern Over New Members' Weak Ideological Training

By MAX FRANKEL
Special to The New York Times.

MOSCOW, March 12 — The Soviet Communist party is concerned about the fitness and qualities of new members.

Membership is growing at an accelerating rate, partly because Premier Khrushchev wants to restore the majority of the proletariat — manual workers — among card-holders. But the party has found too many of the new young members ill prepared ideologically and organizationally for its exacting demands.

There is concern also that a diminishing number of new members is coming from the Komsomol, the Young Communist League. Women are said to be getting too few party cards.

### Greater Care Urged

In a mildly worded discussion of the recruiting problem this week, party headquarters demanded far greater care in the choice of new members and more diligent training of the youths accepted. The discussion, yielding a few new figures on party membership, appeared in the latest issue, No. 5, of Partinaya Zhizn, a journal for party workers.

On Jan. 1 this year, the article said, the party had 8,017,000 members and 691,000 candidates for membership. Candidates are on probation for one year, after which they must be admitted or dropped. In special cases the party charter permits a second year of candidacy.

For ambitious young Soviet citizens the big hurdle is achieving candidacy. Dedication and zeal, an avoidance of trouble and the passing of tests on Marxist theory are usually enough to receive full membership. Four of every five candidates appear to be reaching full membership these days.

### Gain Biggest Since Stalin

The number of members and candidates in January—8,708,000—was a net gain of 467,000, or 5.3 per cent, since the twenty-first party congress in January, 1959. It was the largest annual increase since Stalin's death in 1953.

The party admitted 224,000 candidates to full membership in 1955; 283,000 in 1956; 353,000 in 1957; 396,000 in 1958 and 488,000 last year.

The party's membership today is three and one-half times greater than in 1939. The nation's population in the same period increased by 12 per cent, from 190,000,000 to 212,000,000. About one of every twenty-five Soviet citizens today is a party member.

Until recently, however, manual workers were only 30 per cent of all members, half the percentage strength they had in the Nineteen Twenties. Premier Khrushchev wants to destroy the imbalance between officials and workers on party rolls.

For nearly two decades the party has not issued any breakdown of the social standing of its members and such data remain secret. This week's article spoke only of the growing proportion of workers and farmers among candidates for membership—59.5 per cent in 1956 and 65.4 per cent last year. The article complained that workers and farmers were still a majority of the candidates ultimately rejected from membership.

March 17, 1960

# SOVIET SHAKE-UP ELEVATES KOZLOV TO KEY PARTY JOB

## He Joins Central Committee Secretariat—5 Dropped —Kosygin Promoted

## 2 OUT OF THE PRESIDIUM

## Kirichenko and Belyayev Are Reduced—Mme. Furtseva Is Minister of Culture

By OSGOOD CARUTHERS
Special to The New York Times.

MOSCOW, Thursday, May 5—The Soviet Communist party and Government went through a major shake-up today.

Frol R. Kozlov was named to a reorganized secretariat of the party's powerful Central Committee, according to the official announcement, after having been released from his duties as a First Deputy Premier.

Named in his place as a First Deputy Premier is Aleksei N. Kosygin, w[illegible]s released from the chairmanship of the State Planning Committee. The other First Deputy is Anastas I. Mikoyan.

[The shake-up confirmed the control exercised by Premier Khrushchev on both party and Government. His own positions as party chief and head of government were not changed.]

### Principals in Soviet Union Shift

The New York Times
Frol R. Kozlov

Associated Press
Aleksei N. Kosygin

### 'Big Surprises' Promised

The Moscow radio was the first to report the decisions of the party hierarchy, under the chairmanship of Premier Khrushchev, who recently promised "big surprises" in preparation for a sweeping twenty-year development plan.

Major changes were made in the Presidium of the party, in the Council of Ministers, in the leadership of the state planning apparatus and in the party secretariat.

As had been expected, two men were ousted from the fourteen-man Presidium, but three new ones were added. This makes the strength of this body the greatest it has been under Mr. Khrushchev.

The two men ousted from the Presidium are Aleksei I. Kirichenko and Nikolai I. Belyayev. Elected as new members were Mr. Kosygin, Nikolai V. Podgorny and Dmitri S. Polyansky.

Vladimir N. Novikov was named as the new head of the all-important State Planning Committee.

The only woman member of the Presidium, Yekaterina A. Furtseva, was named Minister of Culture, replacing Nikolai A. Mikhailov. Mme. Furtseva was released from the secretariat of the party, as were Averky B. Aristov, who remains a Presidium member, and Pyotr N. Pospelov, a party historian and candidate member of the Presidium.

The latter two were released from the secretariat "to devote their energies to the work of the Central Committee" of the Russian Republic.

In the Council of Ministers, Nikolai G. Ignatov was named a Deputy Premier.

Mr. Kirichenko had been demoted to a lesser post as party chief in Rostov last January 13. There has been no explanation for the downgrading of a man who had succeeded Mr. Khrushchev in the party leadership in the Ukraine.

Mr. Belyayev whom Mr. Khrushchev sent to Kazakhstan as a trouble-shooter, was ousted from that post Jan. 20 after serious failures in the vast virgin-lands development project in that Far Eastern republic. He was made party chief in Stavropol.

Mr. Khrushchev was scheduled to speak later today at the opening session of the Supreme Soviet (parliament).

The decisions were announced after a one-day plenary session of the Central Committee in Moscow yesterday.

May 5, 1960

# Topics

**Names on Russia's Maps**

Pity the poor Soviet cartographers. It's name-changing time in the Soviet Union now for cities and towns, villages and hamlets, roads and streets. And every change means that hundreds, thousands, and perhaps in some cases millions of maps are out of date. The job of changing names on maps can hardly wait these days. After all, it's now practically subversive for anyone to refer to Volgograd as Stalingrad, Donetsk as Stalino, or Novokuznetsk as Stalinsk. It would seem a reasonable suspicion that the cartographers, the engravers, the printers and all the other skillful and industrious people who are needed to make new Soviet maps are working overtime these days.

**It Has Happened Before**

Fortunately for themselves, Soviet cartographers are more accustomed to this sort of thing than are, say, British and American mapmakers. Such changes are decreed by Moscow quite frequently, sometimes for political and sometimes for nonpolitical reasons. Only a few months ago the major city of Akmolinsk became Tselinograd and a whole raft of northern provinces in Kazakhstan became joined together in the new Tseliny Territory. And there have been earlier changes in recent years too. The city now called Perm was named Molotov for many years and was called Perm for many years before that. Similarly for the city of Lugansk, which had its own spell of being called Voroshilovgrad.

**Some Names Remain**

The reader should avoid jumping to the conclusion that all the names cities have been given during the Soviet period have been or are being changed. Quite the contrary, and there's a simple rule to clarify matters. The rule is that if a city was named for a man who has been dead over a decade it's likely to be permanent, otherwise not. Thus Leningrad seems in no danger of being renamed Petrograd or St. Petersburg. Gorky is still Gorky, and not Nizhny Novgorod. The city fathers of Sverdlovsk have shown no signs of ordering stationery referring to Yekaterinburg, and certainly there has been no suggestion that Kaliningrad be called Koenigsberg again. And admirers of "Appointment in Samara" should be reminded that the city of that title has been known for some time as Kuibyshev, and will apparently keep on being called that. Even those who are rusty on their Russian history don't have to be told who Lenin was, but they may be glad to have their memories refreshed on the fact that Gorky was the great Russian author, Jacob Sverdlov was a leading Communist who had the good fortune to die soon after the revolution, Mikhail Kalinin was the elder statesman who died shortly after World War II, and Comrade Kuibyshev used to be a top economic planner.

**Problems for the Children**

Children in many lands will undoubtedly complain loudly and often in future decades about this instability of Soviet place names. Consider a typical problem some young Johnny, Ivan or Miguel will face in the Nineteen Eighties or Nineteen Nineties. Did the decisive battle of World War II take place at Tsaritsyn, Stalingrad or Volgograd? The same city has borne one or another of these three names at different times in the past half-century. And by the time that the still-unborn youngsters we're concerned about here face the problem the city may have still another name. It will be confusion piled upon confusion.

**More Difficulties to Come**

We are obviously still only in mid-passage on this matter of name changing. One reason, of course, is that no city is yet named Khrushchevgrad, and the man who now rules in Moscow obviously expects the map to have some such name some day. One can imagine that he hopes the time will come when the Soviet map will show not only Khrushchevgrad, but also Khrushchevo, Khrushchevsk, Khrushchevabad, Khrushchevakan, and Mount Khrushchev, to name but a few. If there are any skeptics who think that the man who is getting Stalin's name, in its various forms, off the Soviet map is not interested in getting his name on instead, we suggest such skeptics follow the Soviet press. Once again we are reading in Pravda about one man's genius, one man's infallibility, and one man's brilliance. And once again we see pictures of one man surrounded by admiring collective farm peasants, by admiring American workers and by awe-struck Communist party officials. Khrushchev may have destroyed the Stalin cult, but the cult of Khrushchev isn't doing badly these days.

November 19, 1961

# KHRUSHCHEV ENCOURAGES DEBATE BUT—

## There Is a Limit to the Amount of Disagreement He'll Permit

By HARRISON E. SALISBURY

Special to The New York Times.

MOSCOW, Jan. 6—The Soviet Government — within definite limits—appears to be encouraging public discussion and debate of a kind unthinkable in Stalin's day or even in the fairly recent past.

In the last fortnight two extremely prominent scientists have politely but firmly taken public issue with one of Premier Khrushchev's pet policies—his dictum that youngsters should spend two or three years at a factory bench or farm field before going on to a university.

Two leading writers' journals have been laying down barrages, each complaining that the other is violating party precepts in literature. The leader of the Communist youth movement has called to account a leading youth magazine, but the magazine continues to publish the kind of material to which the party chief objects.

Soviet citizens often comment on the glowing year-end review of Soviet scientific achievements: "Surely we are proud of Gagarin and Titov, but it wouldn't hurt to get a little more meat in the shops and a lower price of butter."

Needless to say this kind of

Ivey in The San Francisco Examiner

"Tell me when I'm wrong!"

"thaw" in comment, criticism and discussion is not mere happenstance. It is the result of deliberate government policy which Mr. Khrushchev himself dramatically emphasized ten days ago with a public declaration that he is not infallible, that he can make mistakes and that it is the duty of scientists and good party members to call his errors to account. Mr. Khrushchev's statement did not touch off any national debate on fundamental policies of his Government. But it did give added impetus to a growing tendency toward freer talk and freer criticism.

There are varying theories among foreign observers as to why Mr. Khrushchev encourages this trend. But the most widely accepted explanation is that Mr. Khrushchev feels a certain amount of expression is a useful, healthy and desirable exhaust valve for public pressures.

That there are specific limits to such freedom is clearly evident. In the course of almost every speech he makes, Mr. Khrushchev engages in banter or serious argument with advisers or subordinates. There is no case yet recorded in the public prints, however, where an opponent successfully challenged a position the Soviet leader had put on record.

Nevertheless, it is evident to anyone who has seen much of the Soviet Union over recent years that there is more free talk and criticism at almost every level of society today than has existed since Stalin launched his first purges in late 1934 and early 1935. It is also evident that this kind of relaxation in comment, criticism and ordinary conversation is being deliberately and consciously encouraged by Mr. Khrushchev and his closest associates.

**His Aim**

Mr. Khrushchev's demand that he himself be subject to criticism when he made mistakes was probably deliberately aimed at further differentiating his position from that of Stalin's.

The question immediately arises as to how much criticism of the Soviet Government and its policies actually is going on and what weight should be given to it. In a month of considerable traveling in the Soviet Union, this correspondent has heard more frank and critical evaluations of policy by citizens than he would have heard in three years of Stalin's era.

This does not mean Soviet citizens are holding mass meeting or display hot indignation at Mr. Khrushchev's speeches. Far from it. Judging from private, informal talk the new element that has entered the picture is that a schoolteacher in Central Asia will say that she feels her Government's resumption of nuclear testing is a terrible thing; a Moscow newspaper man will say, "Well, privately, I think building the wall in Berlin was a most dreadful shock," and a casual airplane companion will offer a well-reasoned explanation why Russia fails to meet its goals — basically, he says, because the Government is prevented by ideology from giving the peasant the necessary monetary incentives.

**Talk Is Freer**

It is fair to conclude that if this kind of comment is being made repeatedly in casual conversation with a foreigner, Russians, among themselves, are talking things over with considerably more vigor. This impression is supported by the observations of many diplomats and by those foreigners resident in Moscow who have close contact with Soviet society. Here, too, it is worth noting that the diplomatic corps, which for years was almost isolated from Soviet citizenry, now notes a steady growth in its social contacts. Not a few diplomats, including those of Western countries, can honestly say that they possess several personal friends. It is also notable that not even the crisis that has marked so much of 1961 has had a measurable affect on these relations.

**Widespread**

Is this phenomenon confined to relations between Russians and foreigners? There is every evidence that it is not. It can be demonstrated from reading Premier Khrushchev's speeches and public discussions of questions of ideology and policy, which constantly fill the pages of Pravda and other newspapers, that violent and often savage exchanges on key issues occur in such forums as the Union of Soviet Writers and meetings of party propaganda workers, university faculties, and other bodies that bring together members of the élite.

There is probably no subject more constantly being analyzed by foreign observers in Moscow than the tendency of Soviet society to move from the harem-like security and harassed conditions of the late Stalin days to a rather breezy and free-wheeling atmosphere of the Khrushchev regime. So far, the main results of the process seem to be psychological. Russians feel more at ease with themselves and with foreigners and their conversations have begun to acquire the normal variations and contradictions which are found in any healthy social system. But so far nothing has happened to the basic elements of the system. The Government is still a dictatoship, albeit a far less harsh one than Stalin's.

There is gossip about the possibility of some kind of more realistic elections, at least at the lowest levels. It is noted that Mr. Khrushchev calls the Communist party now "all popular," which theoretically might blur the lines between party and non-party. Such a concept could lead to a gradual process of democratization. Some diplomats feel that this is the direction in which Mr. Khrushchev hopes to move. This is not impossible, but it is only realistic to emphasize that for all the unlimbering of the past eight years the Soviet regime is still one of the most authoritarian in the world.

January 7, 1962

# KHRUSHCHEV GIVES PARTY A NEW FACE

## Members Added Since 1957 Make Up 25% of Ranks

By HARRY SCHWARTZ

Official data on the Soviet Communist party's membership appear to suggest that Premier Khrushchev has used the period of his primacy to add a large new "Khrushchev" generation to the organization.

More than a quarter of the membership of the party consists of persons who became full members since Premier Khrushchev defeated the faction of former Foreign Minister Vyacheslav M. Molotov and purged it from high office in mid-1957. More than twice as many members have been admitted annually since then as were admitted yearly in the mid-Nineteen Fifties.

The indication of the change in admission policy was contained in data published in Partinaya Zhizn, a party organ, on the length of party membership. As of last Oct. 1 about 2,350,000 members had been in the party less than three years. This figure was almost twice as great as the 1,300,000 persons who had been in the same category on Jan. 1, 1956.

During 1955, 224,436 persons were accepted as full members of the party. In 1959, 488,174 members were added, in 1960, 545,000 members, and in the first nine months of 1961, 473,768.

The emphasis in the Khrushchev period, Partinaya Zhizn reports, has been on getting more manual workers and fewer white-collar workers into the party. In 1960, 43.1 per cent of all new candidate members were manual workers, 21.7 per cent were collective farmers and 34.3 per cent were white-collar employes. In 1955, 30.4 per cent were manual workers, 21.3 per cent were collective farmers, and 46.2 per cent were white-collar employes.

Despite this shift of emphasis, white-collar employes made up the largest single group, 48 per cent, of party members, while manual workers were 34.5 per cent of the total membership and collective farmers were 17.5 per cent. Collective farmers and their families make up almost half the population of the Soviet Union.

Premier Khrushchev apparently has tried to increase sharply the number of women party members, admitting 126,000 women in 1960 compared with 56,000 in 1955. But as of last October, women made up only one-fifth of all Soviet Communist party members.

Persons of Russian nationality make up almost two-thirds of the Communist party membership. Ukrainians account for 15 per cent. Other nationality groups having more than 100,000 party members include the Byelorussians, Georgians, Uzbeks, Kazakhs, Azerbaijanis and Armenians. The Soviet party's magazine Kommunist has printed material suggesting that there may be between 50,000 and 100,000 Jewish and Tatar members of the party.

The party ranks include a fairly large proportion of the highly trained persons in the Soviet Union. The official statistics report that as of Dec. 1, about 28.5 per cent of all Soviet economic specialists belonged to the party. The party membership as of July 1, 1961, included 55,090 persons who had degrees of doctor of science or candidate of science.

Total party membership as of last Oct. 1 was 9,716,005, a sharp rise from the 7,173,521 members enrolled in the party as of Jan. 1, 1956.

February 18, 1962

# Comrade of Khrushchev

## Leonid Ilyich Brezhnev

LEONID ILYICH BREZHNEV, whose attempt over the last 10 days to woo Yugoslavia back into Moscow's camp fell short of the mark, is one of Premier Khrushchev's oldest and closest associates. A prime beneficiary of the Premier's victory in the power rivalry after Stalin's death, he is an example of the Khrushchev "organization men" who now occupy a large percentage of the key posts of the Soviet Union.

**Man in the News**

A year ago, at the Soviet Communist party's 22d Congress, Mr. Brezhnev distinguished himself by delivering a speech extolling Mr. Khrushchev's "untiring energy and revolutionary passion" and was almost lyrical about his leader's "sincerity and straightforwardness." Mr. Brezhnev seemed determined to make clear that he, at least, was a faithful devotee of the cult of Khrushchev's personality.

Mr. Brezhnev's association with Mr. Khrushchev apparently began in the late Nineteen Thirties, when the latter was appointed political chief of the Ukraine and supervised there the great purges of that period. These purges opened up many high offices for ambitious young men, among them Mr. Brezhnev. He was shifted overnight in 1937 from his job as a metallurgical engineer to the post of Deputy Mayor of the city of Dneprodzerdzhinsk.

He apparently did well, for a year later he became a party leader in Dnepropetrovsk Province, thus beginning his political career alongside Mr. Khrushchev.

**Served as Commissar**

To satisfy Mr. Khrushchev's requirements, Mr. Brezhnev has had to prove himself in many different jobs. He was a leading political commissar with Ukrainian armies during World War II and attained the rank of major general in 1943.

After the war he resumed his career as a Ukrainian provincial party leader until he was shifted to be head of the Moldavian Republic's Communist party in 1950.

When Stalin died in 1953, Mr. Brezhnev was shifted again, becoming one of the political commissars overseeing the loyalty of the Soviet Army in the uneasy early post-Stalin period.

*Soviet organization man*

But it was between 1954 and 1956 that Mr. Brezhnev really endeared himself to Mr. Khrushchev, supervising the development of the huge virgin land area of Kazakhstan. He gained some early successes there for Mr. Khrushchev's cherished agricultural expansion program.

Like Premier Khrushchev Mr. Brezhnev cultivates the common touch and tries to show he is close to the concerns of the common man. At the party congress last year, he ridiculed bureaucrats. He cited a community where marriages could be registered only on Saturdays, a city that prohibited the sale of shashlik after 5 P.M., and a county where local officials passed an ordinance defining the precise times farmers had to go to work, have dinner and the like.

Born in 1906 in Dneprodzerzhinsk, Mr. Brezhnev was originally trained as a land-improvement specialist, but he later studied metallurgical engineering.

He is a member of the Presidium of the Central Committee of the Soviet Communist party and is chairman of the Presidium of Supreme Soviet (Parliament). The latter post makes him the titular head of state.

Mr. Brezhnev is married and has at least one child, an 18-year-old daughter, Galina, whose fashionable and expensive clothing was reported to have been one of the minor sensations in Yugoslavia as she toured that country with her father.

October 5, 1962

## STRIVING FOR ECONOMIC EFFICIENCY

# MALENKOV TO MAKE RADICAL REVISIONS IN SOVIET ECONOMY

### His Moscow Speech Admits Russian Consumer Suffered Under Policy of Stalin

### CAPITAL GOODS CUT IS DUE

### Emphasis to Be Put on Output of Basic Living Needs—Farming Changes Slated

By HARRISON E. SALISBURY

Special to THE NEW YORK TIMES.

MOSCOW, Aug. 9—For the first time since its Five-Year Plan was instituted in 1928 the Soviet Union is going to shift the weight of its economy from the production of capital goods to increasing the output of consumer goods, a study of the speech of Premier Georgi M. Malenkov to the Supreme Soviet Saturday clearly indicates.

Mr. Malenkov frankly acknowledged that for years the Soviet consumer had received the short end of the deal. He declared that the Government had decided to end this situation and was going to utilize some of the huge capital goods resources to produce more consumer goods and to give the peasants more incentive to turn out needed farm products.

Two other features of Mr. Malenkov's address attracted particular interest.

The first was the Soviet Premier's assertion that all conditions now existed for the restoration of normal Far Eastern relations and the picture he painted of what he called United States efforts to block the re-establishment of normal and friendly relations between Japan and the Soviet Union.

The second was Mr. Malenkov's strong new plea on behalf of Communist China. Diplomats thought his suggestion that the United States cease to "ignore" the Chinese Communists might be a bid for diplomatic recognition of the Peiping Government by Washington and a place for it in the United Nations.

**His View of the Far East**

Mr. Malenkov's remarks about the "normalizing" of Far Eastern relations caused considerable speculation about Indo-China, Malaya and other seats of Far Eastern warfare and semi-warfare. The Soviet leader did not mention Indo-China but he did not qualify his statement that objective conditions now existed to re-establish normal relations throughout the Far East.

Moscow diplomatic circles believed that Mr. Malenkov's bid to Japan would not go entirely unanswered, since they thought it certain that the Japanese, particularly the business men, desired to get relations back to normal with both the Soviet Union and Communist China.

[Some United States observers of Soviet affairs interpreted Mr. Malenkov's speech as an acknowledgment of domestic discontent with conditions in Russia. They cited especially his shift in emphasis from "guns" to "butter" and his virtual repudiation of several aspects of Stalinist policy. In effect, the speech was regarded as an effort to court popularity among the Soviet people for the new regime.]

In support of the new economic program, Mr. Malenkov presented figures that put into sharp relief the enormous emphasis long placed on the production of capital goods to the disparity of the output of consumer goods.

He said the output in capital goods was fifty times greater than it was twenty-eight years ago. While the production of consumer goods was only twelve times greater.

Comparative investments tell the story. Since 1929 638,000,000,000 rubles have been invested in heavy industry, and 193,000,000,000 in transportation, while 72,000,000,000 rubles have been spent in light industry and 94,000,000,000 in agriculture.

The Soviet Premier also said

that the peasants must get incentives to make the best possible use of their personal garden plots and to develop their ownership of livestock.

He revealed that a radical change would be made in the method of evaluating harvests and the collection of grain and other products.

He said that "it is essential to end the incorrect practice in which the result of the work of the collective farmers in producing grain and other products are evaluated not by factual collections but only by relative productivity."

Mr. Malenkov declared that what counted was grain in the warehouse not grain on the root.

It was thought Mr. Malenkov's remarks would end the long-established Soviet practice of calculating crops on the basis of what is called the "biological yield"; that is to say the estimated amount of grain or cotton standing in a field rather than the amount collected and put into a warehouse.

Mr. Malenkov said that the Government long had encouraged the production of technical crops such as cotton, sugarbeets and flax, by providing special incentives for farmers. But for livestock and vegetable production there have been no incentives but rather impediments to increased production by individual peasants, the Premier added.

He said the Government program was based on encouraging individual peasants to increase their own production.

Mr. Malenkov also revealed that the Government was going to take steps to see that the peasants got better prices for their livestock and vegetable products. The Government will continue its present policy of lowering retail prices but will pay higher prices in its general procurement program to provide an additional incentive for the peasants to increase their output, the Premier said.

Foreign diplomatic observers here expressed considerable interest in the implications of Mr. Malenkov's emphasis on the effect of a German settlement on France and Germany's other immediate neighbors.

The whole weight of Mr. Malenkov's discussion of the German question was on the threat to European peace that would arise from a remilitarized Germany.

Mr. Malenkov's remarks suggested that Soviet policy might have as its object now the organization of a strong European group directed against any revived militaristic threat from Germany.

August 10, 1953

# *Failure of Soviet Collective Farms Laid to Starved Peasants' Misery*

By DREW MIDDLETON
Special to THE NEW YORK TIMES.

LONDON, Jan. 6—"I have a cow, a lot of work, a lot of worries and I am hungry," a Russian peasant mother wrote to her soldier son to explain why she was selling her cow.

"Without a cow I will be equally hungry, but I will have less work and certainly fewer worries," she concluded.

This extract from the woman's letter has been used here to help explain the present agricultural crisis in the Soviet Union and one of its underlying causes, the surrender of the peasant in the face of insuperable obstacles.

Material of which this letter is a part has been gathered by Allied sources over the last three years from a number of former Soviet citizens who have left their homeland since World War II. Wherever possible, the information has been checked against existing records.

For more than a decade the Communist bureaucracy, adhering rigidly to a collective farm system that was falling apart before its eyes, punished with severity attempts to remedy the causes for the decline and to substitute individual ability for political orthodoxy in agriculture.

The Government of Premier Georgi M. Malenkov, with Nikita S. Khrushchev, first secretary of the Central Committee of the Communist party, in direct control, now is attempting to retrieve the situation. Yet the agricultural decay in fifteen Soviet provinces, as pictured by a number of Russians, is serious.

The testimony of many Russians, describing agricultural conditions since 1945 in provinces from Smolensk in the west to Tomsk in the east, indicates that the restoration of something approaching viable standards to rural Russia cannot be accomplished without major modifications of the collective farm system.

**Four situations have contributed largely to the present crisis:**

1. The shortage of manpower.
2. The poor condition of livestock.
3. The inefficiency of the Machine and Tractor Service Stations.
4. The burden of taxes and lack of incentives.

These situations, the sharp decline in living standards that accompanied them and the futile attempts to resist and to reform are described in the words of the Russians themselves.

The system, as it is now constituted, does not appear capable of raising enough food to feed either the growing population of the cities or the farmers themselves.

For instance, a collective farm in a part of the Ukraine, famous for its productivity since Czarist times, recently said it had fifty-two "grossly undernourished" horses and 120 oxen in "very poor condition" and was operated "by the work of women and oxen."

At another collective near Moscow a returning soldier found that "90 per cent of the farmers had no bread and lived on frozen potatoes and pancakes made of minced grass with a small addition of flour."

The manpower shortage appears to be general save in the autonomous republics of Soviet Central Asia.

Around Bryansk the male population, including youths of 17, formed only 10 per cent of the village population shortly after the war. The men available were not much help then or now, for it was reported recently that "the men have managed to secure for themselves various administrative jobs in the village and in the collective farm administration."

There and elsewhere the shortage of manpower was attributed to:

¶Arrests and deportations carried out among the men who had remained in the village under the German occupation and were charged with collaboration.

¶The movement of demobilized soldiers to factories in cities, where food and pay are better than on farms.

¶The severe losses during World War II.

To these causes might be added, it has been suggested, the demands of the topheavy Communist bureaucracy, which insists on at least fourteen officials for the administration of even the smallest collective farm.

In Stavropol Province the story was the same: The men working in the administration, the women in the fields.

In both areas and in Kursk Province eyewitnesses reported that men and women unable to get jobs in the bureaucracy, and therefore forced to work in the fields, were unwilling and inefficient workers.

"The foremen have to use persuasion and sometimes force to get the farmers out of the houses to attend to some urgent work," according to a report about conditions in Kursk.

### Ex-Soldiers Sent to Farms

Since 1950 the Soviet Government has ordered all soldiers demobilized after their military service to return to their native villages and has warned them that they will not be accepted as factory workers without a spravka (certificate) that they have been released by their collective farms.

The Soviet Government's admission last autumn that production of livestock was below that of Czarist times and that the number of draft animals was declining is borne out by reports from various parts of the Soviet Union.

In the Mari Autonomous Republic a former collective farmer did not remember a period in which at least two or three horses were not in a "suspended" state. This means that the animal "no longer has the strength to stand and is helped to do so by means of ropes fixed to the ceiling [of the stable] and fastened around its body."

In the Mordvinian Autonomous Republic the local authorities, it was said, have done their best to raise livestock production. But the increase "has not improved the food situation of the population, as the state deliveries of meat, milk and dairy produce were increased proportionally to the increase in the number of cattle."

Peasants may own a cow or a goat. The former is taxed, but the latter is not and consequently in the Mordvinia goats are known as "Stalin's cows."

In Chkalov Province and a number of other areas, it was noted, in the spring "much of the livestock dies from starvation due to the shortage of forage." This can be traced to the chronic shortage of storage facilities for any sort of food or other materials on collective farms.

The Machine and Tractor Service Stations were planned by the Bolsheviks of a generation ago as the political and mechanical color sergeants of the collective revolution.

Yet evidence of those who have had to work with them shows that, although the stations have remained centers of Communist indoctrination, they have failed in most areas to provide the kind of mechanical assistance required.

The collective farms pay a yearly rent for the use of the stations' tractors, combines and other machines and there are continued protests against the size of these payments.

"The M. T. S. machinery is old-fashioned, is in a poor state of repair and the work it performs is of little help to the collective farmer," one former resident of the Ukraine reported. He added that the payments to the stations were exorbitant.

"I have a very bad opinion of the work of the M. T. S.," a former collective farmer from Kharkov Province testified.

Even the introduction of new tractors, such as the ATZ, made by the Altai tractor works, has not silenced the peasants' resentment, which appears to be as sharp today as it was in the meager post-war years.

"I have often heard my fellow soldiers coming from other provinces resenting the fact that new Soviet tractors are sent for propaganda purposes to Germany, China and other satellite countries while the Soviet farmers have to use old wrecks," one Russian said.

Taxes and lack of incentive have played their part in reducing Soviet agricultural output since the war. Collective farmers in Russia pay income tax, cultural tax, agricultural tax and social insurance. Those who own small plots of land adjoining their cabins have to pay extra taxes in kind and in money.

The produce of these tiny garden plots is supposed to eke out the meager wages of the collective farmer. But after the payment of taxes they provide little with which to supplement his diet or sell at the nearest town for rubles.

Taxes and the annual subscription to various state loans leave the farmer little money. But even if he had plenty he would have no place to spend it. Without access to anything remotely resembling the American country store—one farmer complained that cosmetics were all he could buy in his village shop—the peasant is said to have spent his money on samogon (moonshine), the home-made spirit, which is cheaper and stronger than the vodka produced by the Government.

"In spite of the penalty of five years' imprisonment imposed for illegal distilling of spirits, this industry flourishes all over the Soviet Union," one Russian reported. Samogon and occasional dances are about the only entertainment available to most villages, it is reported.

Spasmodically there have been attempts to change the farming system and throw off the heavy hand of Communist orthodoxy in agriculture. Most of these attempts were by individuals or groups of five or six at the most.

When harvests were good in the Northern Ossetian Autonomous Republic, the chairmen of the collective farms were called together by the district party committee and "forced to pass a resolution" that because of the good harvest the collective farms had decided to raise the normal amount of deliveries to the state.

This, of course, robbed the collective farmers of the grain remaining after the normal deliveries had been made.

"Some of the chairmen who opposed this resolution were subsequently replaced, one of them was given ten years' imprisonment and another was deprived of his party ticket and had to work as a farmhand," the source said.

In Northern Ossetia about 2 per cent of the farmers are party members and as a rule they are "boycotted, unpopular and considered informers."

January 7, 1954

# VOLGA TOUR SHOWS LAND OF CONTRAST

## Jets and Plodding Oxcarts, Harvester Combines and Flails Are Found

By HARRISON E. SALISBURY
Special to The New York Times.

MOSCOW, July 27—Jet aircraft on training flights are a frequent sight over the Volga and Ukrainian cities. An equally frequent sight both in the cities and in the countryside is that of plodding ox-carts.

The Soviet Union has jet planes that can take off from a base in the southern Ukraine and fly to Moscow and back before a peasant on a near-by collective farm can drive his ox-team fifteen miles to town and back. This aspect cuts right down through the core of Soviet life.

In the rich grain fields of the central black-soil belt many fine modern-appearing combine harvesters may be seen rapidly chewing their way through the seemingly endless wheat fields. Within half a mile or a mile of these up-to-date farm machines there are peasant women flailing grain in the courtyards of their mud-walled izbas, or peasant huts, in the same manner their ancestors used 500 years ago.

In the upper Volga River regions there are fine hydroelectric stations generating quantities of power, good-looking plants that remind one of the Tennessee Valley Authority.

Just north of Orel in central Russia there is a fine truck garden that pumps water from the Oka River, using rotating high-level, high-pressure nozzles that sprinkle the garden in a manner reminiscent of Long Island or California. But women in the outskirts of Orel draw their household water from a hand-operated rope-and-bucket well and carry it home suspended from the traditional wooden shoulder yoke.

And there are equal contrasts from town to town. At several smaller Volga cities local residents swarm aboard the steamers from Moscow hoping to purchase cakes or cookies, beer or soft drinks or other delicacies that cannot be obtained in their town.

In some upper Volga towns, it is not usually possible to buy white bread. In some Ukrainian towns there is white bread for sale and dark bread is not to be had.

There is plenty of evidence to be seen in one city after another of determined and large-scale efforts to overcome the lag in civilian comforts and conveniences. In most cities primary concentration in this respect is in the construction of housing and the number of apartment houses that are being built in the Soviet Union today must run into five figures.

The conclusion is unavoidable that in rebuilding some of the Ukrainian and Central Russian cities local authorities after getting their industries going again —this task always had first priority—launched grandiose projects for building central squares, elaborately decorated government office structures, fancy promenades, much adorned by various kinds of statuary, and so forth.

Thus in not a few towns you will find hardly a trace of war damage visible in the central square. Industries will be running full blast, at or exceeding prewar capacity. But housing and such elementary facilities as sewage, water supply, electric lights, not to speak of such more advanced conveniences as telephones, laundries, dry-cleaning and even stores, will lag sadly behind.

In a big city of 600,000 persons like Rostov you see women taking their washing in baskets down to the muddy waters of the Don River to beat and pound it out as their ancestors did.

While most Volga cities have a number of new stores, it is notable that even such cities as Saratov and Ulyanovsk continue to rely for shopping facilities chiefly upon old trading arcades dating back to pre-revolutionary times. Stalingrad has its famous department store, a modern steel and concrete structure, but a peasant market, or bazaar, as it is more familiarly known in Russia, is in an open, dusty, wooden-fenced lot just a stone's throw away.

August 1, 1954

# SOVIET SETTLERS GET INDUCEMENTS

## Loans, Remissions of Taxes Offered for Development of Outlying Farm Areas

By CLIFTON DANIEL
Special to The New York Times.

MOSCOW, Oct. 17—In its drive for increased agricultural production, the Soviet Government today offered substantial inducements for new collective farm settlers, including those going to recently opened areas of Kazakhstan and Western Siberia.

The new settlers will receive loans and grants for housing, livestock and food, special tax concessions and in some cases outright cash grants.

The inducements were announced in the Government's

The New York Times Oct. 18, 1954

SETTLEMENT DRIVE: Moscow is offering inducements to farmers to go to areas underlined farm newspaper Selskoye Khozyaistvo (Agriculture) this morning. The newspaper published a table of loans and grants for various districts and told readers where they could obtain further detailed information.

A vast movement of population to agricultural areas, especially areas where great tracts of idle and virgin lands have been put to the plow, are planned for this winter and next spring. Widespread publicity is being given to the movement and posters have appeared throughout the country showing a happy citizen on a speeding train waving his arm and shouting "To the new lands."

**Transportation Is Provided**

Already 150,000 farmers and agricultural technicians have gone to the new areas and, according to Communist party and Government statements, this is only the beginning of a great migration.

Transportation is being provided for the new settlers and they are receiving special facilities for transporting their goods, chattels and livestock or obtaining these necessities on their arrival in the new areas.

Today's announcement from the Collective Farm and Settlers Departments of the Ministry of Agriculture said the settlers would receive loans of from 10,000 to 20,000 rubles each for home construction. They will begin to repay loans in the third year after houses and outbuildings are erected and will have ten years to pay.

[While the official exchange rate of the ruble is 25 cents, its actual value is considerably less for the Soviet consumer.]

In some regions from 35 to 50 per cent of the loans will be absorbed by the Government and will not have to be repaid.

On certain farms where the houses are already available settlers will have eight years to pay for their loans of up to 3,000 rubles for repairs repayable in three years.

**Bank to Give Loans**

The Agricultural Bank also will give livestock loans ranging from 1,500 to 3,000 rubles repayable in three years at 2 per cent interest.

Settlers will receive advances of food repayable in kind over a period of three years. There will be 150 kilograms (about 300 pounds) of grain or flour for each head of family and 50 kilograms for each additional family member.

For from two to five years settlers will be relieved of paying the agricultural tax and of making compulsory deliveries of produce to the Government, except for milk. The collective farm that takes in the new members will be relieved of income tax in proportion to the number of settlers for from two to five years.

Among the regions for which high inducements are being offered are the following: Sakhalin, Kamchatka, lower Amur, Khabarovsk, Magadan, Murmansk, Kaliningrad, Kuibyshev and Simferopol (former Crimea), Oblasts, the Jewish Autonomous Oblast, and the Armenian, Georgian and Azerbaijan republics.

October 18, 1954

# Visit to a Model Collective

**A reporter's inspection of the Pamyat Ilyicha farm near Moscow yields some facts and figures on how state agricultural communities in Russia operate.**

By CLIFTON DANIEL

*One of Russia's "showplace" collective farms is Pamyat Ilyicha, near Moscow. It is not a typical farm—in fact, it is exceptional, having won the Order of Lenin—but its methods of operation are typical in that they show how collectives throughout Russia produce goods, meet quotas and pay the men and women who work them.*

---

MOSCOW.

ON the Yaroslav highway about seventeen miles north of Moscow stands a wooden building with a façade of startling blue. Beside the building is a full-length statue of Nikolai Lenin (Vladimir Ilyich Ulianov), arm outstretched in an oratorical pose familiar all over the Soviet Union. Anyone who has ever traveled through rural America would recognize the building as a country store, with an apartment, a small meeting hall and an office on the second floor. In fact, the store is publicly owned, and the office is the headquarters of the Pamyat Ilyicha ("In Memory of Ilyich") collective farm founded twenty-four years ago on the anniversary of Lenin's death.

For twenty-two of those years, Osip Ruzin, a former bookkeeper whose parents were peasants in that vicinity, has been chairman of the collective. A man of 61 with a shaven head, horn-rimmed spectacles, and a typical Russian blouse under his blue serge suit. Ruzin receives visitors in his office, and, slapping his hand against the abacus that sits on his desk, rapidly rattles off facts and figures. They are the facts and figures of life and work on a Soviet collective, a Socialist institution that has been described, discussed and argued about for three decades. And now it is being subjected to severe new tests of practicality and productivity by the demand of the high authorities for greater farm output.

---

CLIFTON DANIEL is the correspondent of The New York Times in the Soviet Union.

THE chairman of Pamyat Ilyicha has the facts of collective agriculture at his fingertips, and with his fingers he deftly flicks the beads of the abacus as he recites the statistics. The staccato clacking of the beads puts an exclamation mark after every figure.

Size of the farm—700 hectares (1,730 acres). Clack! One hundred planted in vegetables. Clack! One-hundred-twenty in potatoes. Clack! And so on for fruit, fodder, turnips and beets, corn, cabbage, pasture and private gardens.

Population of the farm—about 1,000. Clack! Able-bodied adult workers—230 women (Clack!) and 140 men. Clack! The predominance of women, he explains, is due in part to losses of men in the war (Ruzin himself was a major in the supply services) and to the fact that some men who live on the farm work in near-by factories.

Specialized personnel—seventy, including five agronomists, two of them with university degrees; three animal husbandry experts; one veterinarian; six bookkeepers, fifteen drivers, one plumber and fitter, and, of course, the chairman himself.

Livestock—225 cattle, including 140 milk cows; 250 pigs, including fifty breeding sows; 2,500 chickens; 100 horses; 100 beehives.

Equipment—ten trucks; two small cars; repair shops; a new cow barn; seven greenhouses, including three big new ones; ten thousand new forcing frames; a potting shed; a steam generating plant for the greenhouses and forcing frames; and so on.

SOCIAL services—a kindergarten; a crèche for fifty children; a clinic with five doctors, who also serve the village; a school, with compulsory attendance for seven years; a club with dramatic circles and other recreational groups; a movie theatre; an orchestra; and a library with 10,000 books.

"We have educated our own intellectual specialists," Ruzin says.

Then he comes to methods of payment for the sale of produce and for sharing the proceeds among the members of the collective. One begins to understand why Ruzin needs the abacus, why there are six bookkeepers in the collective, why cartoons in Krokodil, the Soviet humor magazine, are always ridiculing farmers who are so busy shuffling papers that they have no time to dig potatoes.

The produce of the farm, Ruzin explains, is mar- (Continued)

**HEADQUARTERS** of the Pamyat Ilyicha collective farm (named for Lenin, whose statue is at left) is this building with bright blue front.

keted in three ways. There are, first, compulsory deliveries to the Government; second, additional voluntary sales to the Government; and, finally, free sales on the open market. This year, Pamyat Ilyicha sold approximately half of its output to the Government and half on the open market.

FOR compulsory deliveries, which have been drastically reduced since last year's agricultural decrees by the Soviet Council of Ministers and the Central Committee of the Communist party, there are fixed prices. For further voluntary sales to the Government, the farm now receives, instead of fixed prices, 75 per cent of the retail prices of the produce in state stores. These prices are generally, but not always, higher than the farm gets from compulsory sales. The highest rates of all come from sales in the open market, where the law of supply and demand and not official decrees govern the price level.

Just to take one staple product, in early September Pamyat Ilyicha was receiving 30 kopeks per kilogram (2.2 pounds) for compulsory deliveries of potatoes. The retail price in state stores was 50 kopeks, 75 per cent of which would be 37.50 kopeks. And the retail price in the open market was two rubles—that is, 200 kopeks.

When it comes to telling how the members of the collective are rewarded for their labor, Ruzin's abacus chatters louder and faster.

Workers at Pamyat Ilyicha, Ruzin says, have an average of 500 working day units a year. A working day unit is not a measure of time, but of output. For example, the working day unit for a dairymaid, a member of one of the cattle barn brigades, is fifty liters (13 gallons) of milk a day, the milk to have an average butter fat content of 3.8 per cent. If her section of the herd produces 100 liters a day, she gets credit for two working day units. A tractor driver who plows four hectares (10 acres) gets credit for three working days. And so on.

Every worker is required to fulfill a minimum of 150 working day units a year. If he (or she) does less, it is assumed that the worker is devoting too much time to his own personal garden plot, and he must pay double the annual tax of 300 rubles. For each working day unit, a worker at Pamyat Ilyicha received this year: 8.8 pounds of potatoes, 8.8 of vegetables, a pound of fruit, a pound of fodder and eight rubles in cash.

TAKING a representative list of farm products and their prices in state stores, one can calculate roughly that the cash value of a working day unit is 20 or more rubles, or 10,000 rubles a year for the average worker at Pamyat Ilyicha. (For foreign exchange purposes the ruble is valued by the Soviet Government at four to the dollar, but that rate does not necessarily reflect the relative domestic purchasing power of the two currencies.)

In addition to their shares from the collective, the workers each have, under the rules of that particular farm, a private plot of 300 square meters or three-quarters of an acre to use as the individual wishes. On that plot the worker has his own home, and may keep one milk cow, two calves, one sow, ten sheep, ten beehives and as much poultry as he likes. He may grow any crop he wishes or has room for.

The crops and the livestock on the individual plots are for personal use and may be either consumed or sold on the free market. The worker may also sell any surplus from his daily earnings of produce.

In addition, collective farmers may receive bonuses if, in the Soviet phrase, they "overfulfill their plan." Each farm and each brigade on the farm has a plan for the year—that is, a production quota. At the end of the year there is a general meeting of the collective to assess the farm's record.

IF the plan has been overfulfilled—and therefore more money earned—25 per cent of the extra earnings goes to the chairman and other executives and specialists. Brigades that have exceeded their quotas get the next bite. The rest is distributed among the rank and file in the form of increased pay.

Aside from bonuses, the chairman receives a salary of 500 rubles a month and gets credit for 100 working days a month. Ruzin says he owns a radio, a television set and a new Pobeda sedan, for which he paid 16,500 rubles last year.

The collective pays income tax at the rate of 8 per cent on its net earnings. Individual members pay the homestead tax and, if they earn enough to be in a tax bracket, the usual income tax. The collective pays 2 per cent of its income from state sales into the farm's mutual aid fund for pensions, disability benefits and relief. The individual also pays 2 per cent of his share from the collective. For each child who is cared for in the crèche while its parents are working there is a charge of 4 per cent of one parent's income from the collective. The fee is calculated on the higher income of the two.

NOW and then, as he runs through these complex figures, Ruzin changes pace to expound on the accomplishments of collective agriculture. He is not only a statistician, but a propagandist, an evangelist for the system in general, his farm in particular and especially for the aims and objects of the new Soviet agricultural drive.

Twenty-five years ago, he declaims dramatically, there were no buildings on the site of Pamyat Ilyicha except the homesteads of the peasants, including his own parents' home, and two country inns. Pamyat Ilyicha, he says, had twenty-seven founding members. In a glass case on his office wall is a book as broad as an atlas in which the deed to the farm is preserved. An imposing document adorned with flourishes of calligraphy, it conveys the land of Pamyat Ilyicha to its members in perpetuity.

Above Ruzin's head is another glass case, a tiny one, enclosing the medal and ribbon of the Order of Lenin, awarded to Pamyat Ilyicha for being represented three successive pre-war years in the great agricultural exhibition down the highway toward Moscow. Pamyat Ilyicha, whose products are in the fair again this year, is obviously an exceptional Soviet farm.

Ruzin leaves his desk, takes a pointer and goes to a multicolored map of the farm affixed to the opposite wall.

Chairman of the Pamyat Ilyicha collective farm: 61-year-old Osip Ruzin.

State farm—Women comprise 60 per cent of the workers at Lesniye Polyany, which compares to a U. S. agricultural experiment station.

Here, new greenhouses. There, new orchards. In that section, new forcing frames for vegetables. Over there, a new cow barn. Almost every operation on the farm is now mechanized, he says. The hundred horses? They are used in the long Russian winter when tractors and cars are snowbound. They are also lent to the workers to take their personal produce to market.

THE task of Pamyat Ilyicha under the new farm program is to double its production. In one year, Ruzin says, it has already achieved a 25 per cent increase. Its plan, he explains, calls for the creation of a group of agricultural "factories"—"a vegetable factory," "a milk factory," and so on. And in the fields, waving and pointing, the chairman shows where each new "factory" will be centered.

Across the fields and not far away is another type of farm, a state farm called Lesniye Polyany ("Forest Glades"), which breeds dairy cattle and horses, grows early vegetables and experiments with improving fodders. Its grounds are well kept and its central administrative building, yellow and white in the Russian style, is neat and clean.

In the assembly hall are rows of chairs with fresh linen covers, and around the walls photographs of the Soviet leaders. In one long narrow frame are the pictures of several farm employes who have been decorated as Heroes of Socialist Labor. One of them is Fyodor Ivanovitch Trizno, the present director of the farm, whose two immediate predecessors became deputy ministers in the Soviet Government.

STATE farms generally are engaged in one specialized type of production that the state wishes to promote. Lesniye Polyany's specialty is breeding Kholmogor cattle, a type that resembles the Holstein-Frisian, and raising the yield and quality of their milk. The average yield in its herd of 400 cows is 5,500 liters (1,453 gallons) a year, Trizno says. The milk is sold to state agencies, and the farm supplies breeding cattle to other state farms, collectives and institutions.

Lesniye Polyany also produces its own fodder and breeds both race horses and draft animals. In its stables is a famous Soviet racer, Godach, who once ran the 1,600 meters in 2 minutes 6 seconds, and is now retired to stud.

Unlike Pamyat Ilyicha, the state farm does not share out its produce. It operates on a state budget, like an agricultural experiment station in the United States, and its 300 workers receive cash wages. They live in two-family houses or in state-owned apartments with communal dining halls and five to six square yards of floor space per person.

SIXTY per cent of the workers are women and the average wage for a dairymaid, Trizno says, is 625 to 650 rubles a month. Workers who exceed their production norms get more pay and the best workers earn from 1,000 to 1,500 rubles a month. The director's salary is 2,400 rubles a month, and last year he received an extra 12,000 from the bonuses earned by Lesniye Polyany in "socialist competition" with other farms.

Ivan Markov, a 38-year-old tractor driver who lives in one of the two-family houses and has a broad smile for visitors, says he and his wife have a combined income of 1,500 to 2,000 rubles a month. Her earnings as a farm worker are actually larger than his.

As she is away at work, he is minding their month-and-a-half-old son, their third child. The child sleeps in his arms as he conducts his visitors through his three rooms and the kitchen that the Markovs share with another family. One of the Markovs' rooms is a glassed-in porch. The second is a sitting room with rough though clean embroidered cotton covers on tables and chairs. The third room is the bedroom. The kitchen has a wood stove built into the chimney in a way unfamiliar in the West and a one-ring electric hotplate that stands on a ledge covered with tough brown paper. Water is brought in from outside.

When Markov is asked about a refrigerator, he reports that they are building an underground storehouse for ice that will be cut from the ponds and will last all summer long. As for an automobile—well, he would rather have a television set, and is saving his money.

Back along the highway to Moscow is still another agricultural institution invented in Russia, a machine-tractor station (MTS) whose bright red brick buildings and walls and plots of flowers resemble the premises of a prosperous factory.

Machine-tractor stations provide mechanized plowing, cultivating, harvesting and construction services to state and collective farms, and this one, the Matishchin MTS, serves five farms. It has six tractor "brigades" and employs a total of about 100 persons, including "brigadiers" (brigade leaders), tractor drivers, combine operators and agricultural and animal husbandry experts who assist the farms. It has sixty tractors of various sizes, four grain combines, one hay combine and four potato combines.

The farms served by the MTS have a total area of 4,631 hectares (11,443 acres), of which 2,714 are plowed land. For tending these lands the station receives payment in kind—for example, one ton of potatoes for each hectare. The farm collects seventeen to eighteen tons, says the director. Nicholau Dimitry Akulinin. Construction work, such as the new greenhouses at Pamyat Ilyicha, is paid for in money.

HOWEVER, the MTS does not pocket the cash or sell the produce it collects. That goes to the state and the MTS operates on Government appropriations, like the state farm. Machine-tractor stations in grain regions pay their own way, Akulinin says, but this one, being in a vegetable region where the crops require more attention, does not meet expenses.

As elsewhere, workers at MTS are paid on a piece-work basis, which is complicated by a differential between the summer, when the tractors are busy, and the winter, when they are idle. The workers are paid in cash and in kind, receiving the same amount of produce as other workers on the collectives where they live.

The total value of the station, Akulinin says, is 2,500,000 rubles. The latest addition to its equipment is a large repair shop with machine tools, overhead cranes and a trolley line across its wood-block floor. It is one of eighty such shops erected in the Moscow region this year.

November 14, 1954

# Vast Drive in Soviet To Open East Urged

By CLIFTON DANIEL
Special to The New York Times.

MOSCOW, Jan. 7—A vast Soviet drive to the east to open up new land and expand power and population in this country was proposed here tonight by Nikita S. Khrushchev, Communist party leader.

He spoke at the Bolshoi Theatre to a mass meeting of Young Communists and other youths who have volunteered to go to the east this year and work on the virgin and idle land of Siberia, Kazakhstan and the Urals that is being put to the plow on a tremendous scale.

Also present at the meeting was Premier Georgi M. Malenkov, lending the prestige and influence of the Soviet Government as well as the Communist party to the current recruiting campaign for new land.

The campaign, which sent out 150,000 workers last year, is now gaining great momentum again. Many tens of thousands of young persons will be enlisted in the effort, Minister of Agriculture Ivan A. Benediktov said today in an article in Komsomolskaya Pravda.

Mr. Khrushchev, First Secretary of the Central Committee of the Soviet Communist party, made an extensive tour of the Far Eastern areas of the country toward the end of 1954. He told the young people at the Bolshoi that the cultivated area should be extended even farther than was now contemplated. The vast steppes beyond the Altai Krai (territory) should be plowed up, he said.

"People think of those lands as places of exile," he remarked. "But I have been there personally and there are too few people there."

He added forcefully: "The more people we have the stronger our country will be."

**Larger Population Urged**

Observing that the population of the Soviet Union is about 200,000,000, he declared that even if the country had 100,000,000 more there would still be too few.

The party secretary said it was well that youths were going to newly opened lands because it was easier for young unmarried persons than for large families to settle there.

However, he declared that the land was not to be abandoned after a year or two, but settled permanently, and the young pioneers should ge married there.

In that connection he identified himself as the originator of the Soviet Union's tax on unmarried persons and childless couples. He defended the object of the law.

"We must think about the development of society," he said. "Then we shall be strong. That is why we should have a family of at least three children and bring them up well."

The tax on those who have two children or less is justified, he declared, because those persons avail themselves of the benefits of Soviet society but then have no one to take care of them in old age.

**Riches of East Cited**

The party chief, who is in charge of the Soviet drive for a quick upsurge in farm production, expounded enthusiastically on the agricultural riches of the East.

He said new lands now being plowed up—17,400,000 hectares (42,007,000 acres) have already been plowed and the goal for 1956 is 30,000,000—were "much richer" than the renowned black earth of the Ukraine that he knew in childhood.

Yet, Mr. Khrushchev added, "on these lands goats and rabbits were living."

"The only thing they lack is population," he asserted.

However, some youths, often aided by doting parents, are resorting to tricks and dodges to escape assignments to far away places. Newspapers in all parts of the country have printed accounts of such cases.

The persuasive resources of the state and the Communist party machine are constantly being applied to the problem.

Young men and women who receive higher education at state expense are under obligation to give three years of service in any area to which they may be assigned.

A recently published complaint from Kaluga said that of twenty-six young doctors, dentists and other specialists assigned there in the last two years only nine had turned up and only seven stayed.

January 8, 1955

# SOVIET CONFIRMS INDUSTRIAL SHIFT

## Central Committee Endorses Stress on Heavy Goods—Sets New Farm Goals

By CLIFTON DANIEL
Special to The New York Times.

MOSCOW, Wednesday, Feb. 2—In a major statement published today the Central Committee of the Communist party confirmed that heavy industry would continue to have priority in the next stage of the country's development. At the same time it set new high goals for Soviet agriculture.

The declaration, which was partly foreshadowed last week, was adopted at the first announced plenary session of the committee in the last seven months. The session apparently was held in preparation for the important session of the Supreme Soviet of the U. S. S. R. that will be convened here on Thursday.

The Central Committee, evidently dissatisfied with the state of agriculture and particularly livestock breeding, called on the farms of the Soviet Union to produce not less than 10,000,000,000 poods (164,000,000 tons) of grain a year by 1960. More than 4,000,000,000 poods of that grain would be used for feeding livestock, according to the committee's calculations.

The committee also reaffirmed its intention to see 28,000,000 to 30,000,000 hectares (about 75,000,000 acres) of hitherto idle and virgin land plowed up on the Eastern Steppes by 1956.

For accomplishment of these tasks the committee summoned all organs of the party and state to major efforts to increase the knowledge and efficiency of the farmer, to strengthen the party and Government apparatus and to increase "mass political work in the countryside."

A number of ministries and state agencies were instructed to draw up plans for providing the necessary machines, tools and fertilizers for the new program and to present them to the Soviet Government next April 1.

Adoption of this declaration followed a speech by Nikita S. Khrushchev, rapporteur of the session and first secretary of the Communist party.

Yesterday, Mr. Khrushchev confirmed the meeting of the Central Committee, which lasted from last Friday until Monday, in a conversation with Marshall MacDuffie, New York lawyer.

The committee's statement said: "The Communist party guided by the teachings of the great Lenin on the parallel development of the heavy machine industries and the electrification of the country considers that, as before, the main task remains the expansion of heavy industry, which represents the foundation of our whole national economy, the unbreakable defense capacity of our country and the source of the continuing growth of the people's welfare."

That statement was foreshadowed eight days ago when Pravda, the party's chief newspaper, denounced those who would give equal or greater priority to consumer goods production and reaffirmed the party line that prevailed in Stalin's time of giving first consideration to heavy industry.

This decision followed a period in which considerable resources had been devoted to building up the food and light industries in an effort to achieve a rapid rise in the standard of living. Connected with that was a drive for "a sharp upsurge" in agricultural production, which obviously is to continue.

Feed for livestock is one of the main agricultural concerns of the Government and party, whose hopes for increasing livestock production in 1954 were not fully realized. The party statement said that the results were "unsatisfactory" in several areas and that many head of cattle had been lost because of poor feeding.

In October, 1953, according to the Government plan fulfillment report for 1954, the Soviet Union had 63,000,000 head of cattle. The Government goal for October, 1954, was 65,900,000. The actual figure achieved in October, 1954, according to the Government announcement, was 64,900,000, of which cows numbered 27,500,000.

The total number of cattle was still short of the figure for 1928, when the first five-year plan started, according to Mr. Khrushchev's figures, and the number of cows was short of the level for 1916, the year before the Bolshevik Revolution.

February 2, 1955

# MAGAZINE TRACES SOVIET SPENDING

## Moscow Publication Finds Most of Citizens' Money Goes for Food, Goods

Special to The New York Times.

MOSCOW, March 26 — Soviet citizens spend less than one-quarter of their incomes for rent, direct taxes, transportation, entertainment and other intangibles.

The rest of their money, in so far as it can be traced by Government researchers, goes for food and other goods purchased on the retail market.

These and other statistics on the spending habits of Soviet consumers, based on sales records of publicly owned and cooperative stores, appeared recently in Planovoe Khozhaistvo (Planned Economy), the magazine of the Soviet State Planning Commission.

Retail trade in the Soviet Union, where the Government is in business to an extent unknown in any other major state, is conducted almost entirely by Government departments and cooperatives of producers and consumers.

There is a small area of purely private trade, mostly in food. Collective farmers are permitted to sell their surplus produce directly to consumers in farmers' markets operated by the municipalities.

The extent of this trade has not been calculated for the country as a whole.

### Private Trading Decreases

Private trading has, of course, progressively decreased as socialization of the economy has been extended over the thirty-seven years since the Bolshevist revolution.

However, there has been an increase lately of food sales on the free market as farmers have been officially encouraged to sell more produce directly to consumers, who sometimes meet with shortages in state and cooperative shops.

### Statistics Reflect Trends

According to the Great Soviet Encyclopedia, consumers' cooperatives had more than 32,500,000 members in 1952 and more than 250,000 retail outlets. Only 10 per cent of the cooperatives in 1954 were producing goods for sale; the rest were trading cooperatives buying goods for resale.

Statistics published in Planovoe Kozhaistvo confirmed these prevalent impressions about retail trade in the Soviet Union:

¶That the volume of manufactured non-food goods in the Soviet Union has been increasing.

¶That expansion of shopping facilities has conspicuously failed to keep pace with the increase in production of consumer goods and the growth of the population.

¶That the purchasing power of the rural population is rising and the supply of consumer goods to country districts is increasing at rates greater than in towns and cities.

Between 1940 and 1953, according to Planovoe Khozhaistvo, the proportion of food products in the total trade turnover declined from 63 per cent to 55, indicating an increase in the availability of other types of goods.

By 1953 the retail trade turnover, compared to 1940, had increased 79 per cent. However, the number of trade outlets has grown only 14 per cent.

In an effort to correct this disparity a plan for "widening the trade network" was made in October, 1953. That plan, providing for 40,000 new stores and 11,000 new "social feeding establishments," is still in the process of being realized.

The magazine pointed out that all wages in the Soviet Union are derived from state or cooperative enterprises and are determined in advance. Therefore the planners can know what level of income to expect.

The incomes of collective farmers are derived from two sources—what they get from their domestic efforts and what they get from selling their individual private produce.

As the second of these factors is variable and unpredictable, planners must base their calculations on state procurements; that is, deliveries of produce that the collective farmers are scheduled to make to the state.

As the result of measures taken since 1945 the income of farmers from both sources—and their purchasing power—has notably increased.

March 27, 1955

# *Khrushchev Favors Revised Farm Policy*

By CLIFTON DANIEL

Special to The New York Times.

MOSCOW, June 17—Nikita S. Khrushchev, who was in charge of the 1950 program for consolidating Soviet collective farms, has suggested that some of them should be broken up.

The Communist party's First Secretary spoke yesterday at Riga, Latvia, at a conference of farmers, agricultural experts and officials of the three Baltic states that were incorporated into the Soviet Union fifteen years ago. His speech appeared today in the party newspaper Pravda.

Mr. Khrushchev remarked that when the farms were consolidated, some of the resulting units were difficult to manage. They did not have an exceptionally large amount of land, he said, but the land was widely scattered.

"One should think and take a sensible approach to this question," the party chief said, "and where it is necessary, agree upon breaking them up into smaller units."

As a result of the consolidation of farms started in 1950, the number of collectives had been reduced from 254,000 to 94,000 by 1953. Each unit then had an average of 1,693 hectares of cultivated land instead of 589. (A hectare is 2.471 acres.)

Meanwhile, it became known that a regional chief of the Communist party had been dismissed recently for poor leadership in agriculture. He is Gennadii A. Borkov, one of the 125 members of the Central Committee of the party and a member of the Supreme Soviet, the central legislature of the Soviet Union.

According to a recent issue of the party journal Partiinaya Zhizn, he was relieved in April of his duties as the party's first secretary in the Saratov region on the Volga.

### Baltic Milk Output Scored

In his Riga speech, Mr. Khrushchev disclosed that milk production on collectives in the Baltic republics had been falling recently and that the feeding of pigs was badly organized.

An article in the Government newspaper Izvestia this week also declared that the production of bacon in Latvia had been "undeservedly forgotten."

The decline in bacon production was first remarked in this year's order on decentralization of farm planning. The order noted that although Latvian farmers were experts in growing bacon, they had been unaccountably ordered by central authorities to feed their pigs to produce fat.

While criticizing the livestock situation in the Baltic states, Mr. Khrushchev declared that in the country as a whole, the plan for putting virgin and idle lands into production was proceeding ahead of schedule.

June 18, 1955

# COST CUTTING SET AS A SOVIET GOAL

## Coming 5-Year Plan to Aim for More Output and End of Unlimited Subsidies

By WELLES HANGEN

Special to The New York Times.

MOSCOW, Dec. 24—More production at lower cost is to be the keynote of the Soviet Union's sixth five-year plan, scheduled to begin early next year.

Heavy industry is still the favorite child of the Soviet regime, but it is no longer to be allowed the same prodigality in the consumption of resources as before.

The day of unlimited subsidies and blank checks for factory directors and farm chairmen appears to be over. The new five-year plan, according to authoritative information available here, will emphasize strict cost accounting and higher man-hour output.

State farms or other enterprises that consistently operate at a loss are to be subject to sanctions. Plans call for subsidies to be eliminated or sharply reduced and for individual managers to be held responsible for putting their concerns on a paying basis.

The outlines of the new project have emerged during recent conversations between Western experts, including those sent by the United Nations Economic Commission for Europe, and leading Soviet economic planners. These outlines are confirmed by statements by Soviet leaders.

The new program is due to step up the drive begun in 1954 to eliminate redundant administrative apparatus. It will seek to decentralize operations as much as possible by emphasizing local responsibility.

As in all previous five-year plans, heavy industry will receive the lion's share of materials, labor and managerial talent. Projected increases in output are expressed in the following table:

| | Present Annual Rate in Tons. | 1960. |
|---|---|---|
| Steel ........ | 45,000,000 | 60,000,000 |
| Pig Iron..... | 33,000,000 | 50,000,000 |
| Coal ......... | 390,000,000 | 500,000,000 |
| Oil .......... | 70,000,000 | ——— |

The projected increase in electric power output is from the current 166,000,000,000 kilowatt hours to 250,000,000,000 in 1960.

These goals, with the exception of the one for oil, correspond to the aims enunciated by Stalin in February, 1946. He predicted their attainment would require "three five-year plans or even more."

The output of crude petroleum has actually increased more rapidly than the Soviet Government expected. Rich new wells in Bashkir and the Tatar Republic have caused Soviet production to soar well beyond the capacity of refineries.

As Premier Nikolai A. Bulganin has said, this problem has been complicated by the "systematic failure" to increase refinery capacity adequately.

Steel production has risen sharply with the completion of such new integrated mills as the Rustavi plant in Soviet Georgia. A shortage of scrap metal has acted as a bottleneck to further expansion.

Although the level of mechanization is high in the coal industry, productivity has increased only slightly, and there are wide disparities in costs. It costs five times as much to dig a ton of coal in the old Donets Basin mines as in the Kuznetsk Basin of Western Siberia.

Geographical imbalance is especially acute in power production. The European area of the Soviet Union produces only 11 per cent of the country's power but consumes more than 77 per cent.

The aim is to create a unified power grid for the entire country, but Marshal Bulganin has conceded that this goal is still far from realization. Power output is due to jump dramatically next year with the completion of the large Kuibyshev, Gorky, Stalingrad and Kakhovka hydroelectric stations.

The new five-year plan, it appears, will seek to bring production facilities closer to sources of materials and power.

The relocation of industrial plants in the next five years is scheduled to emphasize development in the East. It is also to seek to limit further concentration in such congested urban areas as Moscow and Leningrad.

Despite the pressing need for more power, the Soviet Union does not contemplate any large-scale construction of atomic power stations in the period ending in 1960. One small 5,000-kilowatt station is already operating, and two larger stations are now under construction.

The campaign to raise productivity will call for a virtual revolution in the Soviet wage system, authorities here assert.

A committee is studying simplification of the wage and bonus system. New norms are being set up to encourage individual initiative.

A study of foreign machinery and technology is being intensively pursued in almost every Soviet industrial administration.

Agricultural output is to rise to between 200 and 250 per cent of the 1954 level, with emphasis on increased output of livestock.

Each collective farm, it is said, will be authorized to formulate its own production plan on the basis of 100-hectare units. (A hectare is nearly two and a half acres.)

Western diplomats here say the Soviet objective is to recapture a position in the international wheat market by 1960.

The emphasis in consumer goods industries is to be on standardization and improvement of quality.

The central G. U. M. department store in Moscow now carries neckties in 800 different patterns. The aim is to determine customers' preferences and reduce the bewildering variety of models and styles in neckties and other consumer items.

The new plan is also due to embrace a vast program of urban construction based on the use of standardized designs and prefabricated sections. Residential housing is to have priority.

Details of the next five-year plan are expected to be disclosed when the twentieth congress of the Soviet Communist party convenes here in February.

December 25, 1955

# SOVIET RESTRICTS SIBERIAN FARMING UNDER NEW PLAN

By WELLES HANGEN

Special to The New York Times.

MOSCOW, Jan. 15—It appears that further expansion of new farmland in the eastern part of the Soviet Union will virtually cease after this year.

The Government apparently plans to bring new soil under the plow only if it promises high stable harvests and requires relatively modest capital outlays.

These deductions emerge from the sixth Five-Year Plan announced today in the Soviet press. The plan's directives reaffirm that a total of 30,000,000 hectares (75,000,000 acres) of previously virgin or idle land are to be sown to crops by the end of 1956. Thereafter, they indicate, no further major expansion of the sown area is contemplated.

Assimilation of the empty steppe land of Western Siberia, Kazakhstan and the Volga region has run into difficulties since Nikita S. Khrushchev, Communist party secretary, visited these regions in 1954 and pronounced them cultivable.

In 1954 a bumper crop was obtained in the eastern lands but last year's harvest was severely cut by drought. There have been reports of lagging construction on newly created farms and tardy delivery of equipment, seed and fertilizer.

Since 1954, 560 new state farms have been set up, most of them in the once desolate eastern areas. Enormous amounts of agricultural equipment and construction materials were earmarked for the program.

Total investment in agriculture this year will amount to 21,300,000,000 rubles of which 8,000,000,000 rubles will be spent on financing state farms, especially those in the new lands. There are four rubles to the dollar at the official exchange rate.

The bearish tone adopted by the Five-Year Plan directives toward the new lands contrasts sharply with the optimistic utterances of Ivan S. Benediktov, Minister of State Farms, in September. Mr. Benediktov told diplomats and correspondents then that the Government was determined to push the program of exploiting the new territory far beyond the target of 30,000,000 hectares set for this year.

Emphasis in the new plan appears to have swung to improving the quality of agricultural output and yield per acre in lieu of further massive increases of the sown area.

Fertilizers, long a deficient item on Soviet farms, are scheduled to be more plentiful. The plan provides for the production "new kinds of concentrated mineral fertilizers and more effective insecticides and pesticides." Concentrated phosphate fertilizer output is to reach an annual rate of 1,000,000 tons by 1960.

Hybrid seed production is to be organized on a wide scale at state farm selection stations and collective farms.

A new time limit has been set for bringing in the grain harvest. It will be not more than ten working days in the European part of the Soviet Union and between seven and eight days in Siberia and the Far East. This, it is hoped, will reduce harvesting losses that Mr. Khrushchev has estimated as high as 25 per cent of the crop.

"Milk-vegetable zones are to be organized around all major cities and industrial centers to supply milk, potatoes and vegetables to the Soviet Union's rapidly growing urban population. New state farms are to be set up in these zones. In addition, city workers and collective farmers will be encouraged to garden on their private plots.

The influence of United States farm practices is clear in the plan directives. Hogs are expected to provide half of the Soviet Union's meat in the future and are to be raised for pork and bacon instead of lard. Cattle are to be initially raised on the dry pastures of Kazakhstan, Siberia and the Volga region and fattened at enterprises modeled on Iowa cattle finishing farms.

Mechanization is to advance another step with the provision of 1,650,000 tractors (in terms of fifteen-horsepower units) in the next five years. There will be strong emphasis on Diesel tractors and combines.

Major industrial goals announced in the new Five-Year Plan are given in the following table. (All units in million metric tons, except electric power in billion kilowatt-hours.)

| | 1955 | 1960 Plan |
|---|---|---|
| Pig iron | 33 | 53 |
| Steel | 45 | 68.3 |
| Coal | 390 | 593 |
| Oil | 70 | 135 |
| Electric power | 170 | 320 |

The five-year program also provides for atomic power stations with a total capacity of 2,000,000 to 2,500,000 kilowatts.

The directives for the new program were more detailed than the published goals of the fifth Five-Year Plan, which ended last year. The new plan, covering the period 1956-60, is to be approved by the twentieth congress of the Soviet Communist party, which convenes Feb. 14.

January 16, 1956

# *Soviet Plans to Reform Farming; Aims to Eliminate Private Plots*

By WELLES HANGEN
Special to The New York Times.

MOSCOW, March 9—The Soviet Union announced tonight a far-reaching program aimed at increasing farm production for the state and eventually eliminating privately owned plots on collective farms.

The members of the Soviet Union's 94,000 collective farms will henceforth receive the bulk of their income from work on the communally owned fields. The private plots and private livestock are to be progressively reduced to a point where they only "decorate" the life of the collective farmer.

The Communist party Central Committee and the Council of Ministers, two top policy-making agencies, issued 10,000 words of "recommendations" as the basis for drastic revision of the collective farm system. There was little doubt that the recommendations would be adopted in full throughout the country.

To make work on the collectives' lands more attractive the farms will be accorded wider initiative in planning production and establishing pay scales. The general meeting of each farm will henceforth have the final power to expel undesirable members and reduce the private plots of those who live on the farm but do not participate in the collective's work.

The farmers will receive monthly money advances up to one-half of the proceeds to be derived from their deliveries and sales to the state. Until now many farmers, especially on the poorer land, have had to wait till the end of the agricultural year before seeing the result of their work on collective fields.

The system of money advances is to be facilitated by the establishment of special transferable accounts with the State Bank of the Soviet Union and subordinate banks.

The practice of many farm members of consistently evading work on the collective fields is to stop. The farms are authorized to set a minimum number of days that every member must work on the collective land or with the collectively owned livestock.

The recommendations of the party and Government are addressed to the "honest collective farmer" who consistently fulfills his quota and enables the farm to meet its output goals for the state. The tone of the recommendations is conciliatory and even deferential.

It is clear that the new collective farm system will depend upon persuasion rather than compulsion. Instead of the farm having its economy regulated from Moscow or regional centers the farm will be allowed to set its own output norms and remuneration for labor.

The recommendations insist, however, that these norms must take account of any increased mechanization of the farm as well as special local conditions.

Incentive pay must act as a real spur to production and not be dispersed in accordance with outmoded standards, it was said.

The Central Committee and Council of Ministers concede that the present charter for collective farms adopted in the late Nineteen Twenties at the beginning of all-out forced collectivization no longer conforms to conditions in the Soviet countryside.

Private farming is now tolerated only on small plots of from one-quarter to one-half a hectare and privately owned livestock rarely consists of more than a pig, a cow and a few chickens to each family. A hectare is equal to 2.47 acres.

Even more important, the recommendations concede, is an increase in the "political consciousness" of the new generation of peasants that has grown up in the collective farm system. The farms themselves are now directed in most cases by trained party members, often recruited from urban and industrial areas.

The farms have achieved a certain degree of economic viability and "reliability" that permits the regime to grant them wider local autonomy.

The recommendations sadly chastise local officials for interfering in collective farm affairs. Such functionaries, the document says, consistently overrule decisions of farmers and obstruct the economic farm operations.

Henceforth the farmers themselves will have the unqualified right to expel members as well as to reduce their private holdings. The recommendations note that the allotments of livestock to a family are now no longer necessary for survival. In consequence, the document says, "there is no point in retaining the former amount of livestock for personal use because this livestock can now go into the general collective farm economy."

The new farm system is designed to satisfy virtually all the needs of farmers from collective production, according to the recommendations. The private plots should henceforth meet only the farmers' requirements for vegetables, fruits and berries with which "to decorate the life of the farmer."

The recommendations assert the communal output has already grown to such extent on many farms that the farmers "are not interested in having a personal subsidiary economy to the extent provided by the original charter."

Revision of the collective farm charter involves remolding one of the fundamental institutions of Soviet life. The charter has been the governing instrument for collective farms throughout the country for more than twenty years and has influenced the rural inhabitants more deeply than any other instrument of the Soviet regime.

March 10, 1956

# SIBERIA 'CAPITAL' LIVING IN FUTURE

## Novosibirsk Found to Be Raw Frontier Town With Dirt Roads and Log Huts

By WELLES HANGEN
Special to The New York Times.

NOVOSIBIRSK, U. S. S. R., Aug. 22—A group of Americans was admitted to this sprawling Siberian industrial metropolis today.

Three United States correspondents arrived here early today with eleven other foreign correspondents on a tour of Siberia arranged by the Soviet Foreign Ministry.

No amount of official arranging could prevent their seeing at once that Novosibirsk is a raw, rugged frontier town that lives in the future tense. It is a city of towering grain elevators, machinery plants, squat log cabins and unfinished office and apartment buildings.

The New York Times Aug. 23, 1956
'CAPITAL' OF SIBERIA: U. S. newsmen paid a visit to Novosibirsk (cross).

The Government's drive to make Siberia an agricultural and industrial bastion of the country has made Novosibirsk a boom town of 731,000 persons with more arriving with every train and plane. The influx of new residents has outstripped the capacity of the city authorities to provide them with adequate housing or municipal services.

The visitors were driven along miles of dirt road past an oppressive collection of shanty wood huts served by outhouses and roadside water pumps.

Although Novosibirsk may be uncongenial to Westerners today, city officials are optimistic about the future. Anatoli Y. Moskovshenko, a project engineer, told correspondents today that a new hydroelectric station on the near-by Ob River would have a capacity of 400,000 kilowatts of power for Novosibirsk when it is completed next year.

He said the vital river commerce on the Ob would be facilitated by an eight-and-one-half mile canal being constructed to enable river craft to pass the new dam. The flow of the river, frequently deficient in the summer, will henceforth be regulated with the help of a 2,600-square-mile artificial lake that will be created behind the dam and hydroelectric station.

Since the present project was conceived in 1950, almost all of the 26,000 residents of the town of Berdsk have been resettled thirty miles away to make place for the reservoir.

Since 1954, Novosibirsk has become a vital processing center for the products of a large part of the new lands developed under the program for expanding grain production.

According to Adam K. Chepikov director of an agricultural experiment station outside the city, strong efforts are also being made to provide fruits and vegetables for Siberian residents who must endure winter temperatures of 50 below zero.

Mr. Chepikov showed correspondents work being done in developing hardy Siberian strains of apples, pears, berries and other fruit from United States and Canadian varieties. The Siberians' diet has been notably lacking in such elements.

Tomorrow the correspondents will travel up the Ob on a river steamer to one of the new state farms in the Siberian steppes where they will spend the night.

August 23, 1956

# BLACK MARKETEER BUSY IN THE SOVIET

## 'Profiteering' Even Involves Leading Officials, Critical Reports Tell Public

By WILLIAM J. JORDEN
Special to The New York Times.

MOSCOW, Sept. 15—Everywhere in the world where there are shortage of the goods people want, speculators find a fertile field. The Soviet Union is no exception.

Newspapers and magazines here regularly describe activities of these "anti-social" operators and their "profiteering." Frequently high officials of the state trade organizations who cooperate with the speculators come in for criticism.

Apparently many persons including even the police and public prosecutors are inclined to take a rather lenient attitude toward these operators. Party and Government newspapers throughout the Soviet Union, which discuss the problem frequently, decry not only speculation itself but the way cases are handled by the courts and enforcement officials.

Speculators attract some sympathy because they often are able to do what normal trade channels cannot do—supply people with what they want. Of course, the speculators get handsome rewards for their prices are well above market levels.

### Extensive Speculations

A recent report from the Georgian Republic tells of extensive speculative operations in that area Stalin's home. The journal Soviet Trade told its readers that speculators in Tiflis, for example, were selling such items as pianos, refrigerators and furniture for as much as three times their regular prices. Nor are the black marketeers confining themselves to such large items. Apparently there is a thriving trade in such things as razor blades, wicks for kerosene lamps, vanilla and bluing.

The most common places picked by black marketeers for their operations are state commission stores, which are outlets for used clothing, kitchenware, furniture and almost everything else. Speculators pick likely prospects from among the customers who are unable to find what they want in the commission stores.

### The Typical Approach

"I have what you are interester in — just tell me the size and color you want," is the typical speculator's approach, according to Soviet Trade.

The customer usually is taken by automobile to the speculator's place of business in a remote area. There he finds a wide selection of goods—often just what he was looking for. Many Soviet citizens are willing to pay prices well above the normal market levels for scarce goods.

Speculators often range over a wide territory. One case recently disclosed involved a woman who made a practice of buying goods as soon as they appeared in Moscow stores and then selling them in remote provinces.

Soviet Trade complained that in many cases officials were content just with the individuals caught selling goods on the black market. Rarely is there any investigation of where the goods come from, who the speculators' accomplices are and the laxness of trade officials handling legal sales, the journal complained.

It noted that a Communist party member, recently arrested for speculation, had not even been dismissed from the party's ranks. At a meeting at which the case was discussed, fellow party members said that one had to feel sorry for the culprit and that she "had not done anything special."

September 16, 1956

# SOVIET TO SET UP 92 REGIONAL UNITS TO RULE INDUSTRY

## Khrushchev Plan Also Calls for Elimination of Most Economic Ministries

Associated Press Radiophoto

**PROPOSES REVISIONS IN SOVIET INDUSTRY: Nikita S. Khrushchev, Communist party chief, addressing session of the Supreme Soviet (legislature) yesterday in Moscow.**

By WILLIAM J. JORDEN
Special to The New York Times.

MOSCOW, May 7—Nikita S. Khrushchev proposed today that the Soviet Union's vast industrial empire be divided into ninety-two economic regions. He said most of the industrial ministries now running that empire should be abolished.

The sweeping revision of the Soviet system of industrial management was made public by the Communist party leader at a session of the Supreme Soviet, the national legislature.

In a three-and-a-quarter-hour speech Mr. Khrushchev provided additional details of the program announced in February and elaborated by him in a long report at the end of March.

[Mr. Khrushchev presented a less decentralized plan to the Supreme Soviet than he had proposed originally. His latest program provides for continued ministerial control over about ten heavy and defense industries.]

### Approval Expected Soon

The Supreme Soviet is expected to approve the plan in a few days. The program may be modified somewhat by a debate scheduled to begin tomorrow, but probably not in any extensive way.

The plan set forth by Mr. Khrushchev today would divide the Russian Republic, the largest in the Soviet Union, into sixty-eight economic units. The Ukraine would make up eleven regions. Each of the thirteen other Soviet Republics would be a separate economic region.

Economic councils will be established in each region to direct industrial production and construction. The Governments of the Soviet Republics are to be given broader control over industrial planning and financing than ever before.

Heretofore Soviet industry had been tightly controlled by the central Government through an elaborate system of ministries covering everything from textiles to electric power stations. Under the Khrushchev plan most of those ministries will be abolished.

### Some Ministries to Be Kept

The industrial ministries that are to be retained are those of obvious national concern, particularly from the point of view of national defense. They are aviation, shipbuilding, electronics, chemicals, transportation machinery, and medium machinery.

[Medium machinery is believed to be a cover name for nuclear weapons. Mikhail G. Pervukhin, a First Deputy Premier, was appointed to this ministry last Saturday.]

Mr. Khrushchev said the general machinery and defense industry ministries would be combined, as would those of electric power stations and power station construction.

He asserted that the ministries retained at the national level would be "radically reorganized." He said they would be relieved of direct management and would retain planning and technical control functions.

The party secretary said there was no necessity to have national ministries for such industries as coal, oil, ferrous and nonferrous metals. He proposed that republic ministries take charge of those industries in the republics directly concerned.

The Khrushchev plan is designed to stimulate production by giving heightened control and initiative to local areas. It is also designed to break the stranglehold the ministries have held over production, often to the detriment of efficiency and at the price of fantastic duplication.

May 8, 1957

# SOVIET SCRAPPING ITS 5-YEAR PLAN FOR A LONGER ONE

## 1959-65 Goals Will Reflect Recent Decentralization and New Mineral Finds

By WILLIAM J. JORDEN

Special to The New York Times.

MOSCOW, Sept. 25—The Soviet Union has found it necessary to undertake a major revision of its economic planning.

The Central Committee of the Communist party and the Government announced today that the present Five-Year Plan would be scrapped at the end of next year and would be supplanted by a new seven-year production schedule covering 1959 through 1965.

The recent decentralization of Soviet industrial management was said to have made necessary a "radical change in the system of current and future planning."

[The Soviet move is believed to presage cutbacks in the economy and to threaten the position of Nikita S. Khrushchev, Communist party chief.]

### New Minerals Discovered

The industrial decentralization involved elimination of ministries within the central Government and their replacement by regional economic councils. The country is in the process of carrying out that revision, with all its attendant stresses and adjustments.

Today's announcement said that, in addition to the recent reorganization, the new plan had been made necessary by the discovery of new deposits of mineral raw materials and sources of electric power.

The discoveries of raw materials and a newly formulated program for the development of plastics and synthetic fibers were said to have opened up unexpected industrial opportunities.

The announcement said that the old Five-Year Plan of 1956-1960 had not provided for these new developments and for the strain of shifting industrial management from Moscow to the 105 economic regions that have been established.

"In order to establish the new enterprises and centers," the joint party and Government announcement said, "the remaining three years of the current Five-Year Plan are not enough. To carry out such a big task it is necessary to have not less than from five to seven years."

The party and Government said that the present economic program would be abandoned at the end of 1958. By July of next year the new seven-year program is to be completed and submitted for the Government's approval. The task of drafting the new economic development program has been given to the State Planning Commission, the governments of the fifteen Soviet republics and the economic councils as well as the remaining ministries and agencies of the central Government.

Heavy industry is to retain its position of highest importance in the Soviet economic plan. The announcement said that the primary task of the economy still was to overtake the mostly highly developed capitalist countries in per capita production.

### Synthetics Are Stressed

In what amounts to a directive for the guidance of the economic planners, the announcement said that the highest possible development of the natural riches of Siberia should be part of the long-range economic program. It also called for rapid development of ferrous and nonferrous metals, chemicals, synthetic fibers, plastics, food substitutes, artificial leather and other synthetic materials.

Coal, oil and gas resources are supposed to be developed more intensively in the future. Electrification is to be pushed. Housing, one of the most troublesome problems for Soviet planners, received special attention.

The program of catching up with the United States in per capita production of meat, milk and butter was made still another important objective for the men who will organize the new economic plan. They were also told to increase the supply of consumer goods available to Soviet buyers.

Today's announcement said industrial output during the first eight months of this year had exceeded by more than 10 per cent that of the same period in 1956.

The current five-year plan was adopted in February, 1956, by the Twentieth Congress of the Soviet Communist party. Last December it was announced that the plan would be revised and that the new draft would be submitted to the Supreme Soviet in the second half of 1957. This has not been done.

Today's announcement of a complete scrapping of the current plan evidently is a further step in recent Soviet efforts to align the planning system with changed conditions.

September 26, 1957

# SOVIET MAY CLOSE TRACTOR STATIONS

## Khrushchev Urges Machines Go to Collective Farms, a Move Stalin Vetoed

By WILLIAM J. JORDEN

Special to The New York Times.

MOSCOW, Jan. 25—Nikita S. Khrushchev, Communist party leader, has proposed another major revision of the Soviet Union's economic system — elimination of the machine and tractor stations that have been an integral part of Soviet agriculture for many years.

It was a proposal Stalin once vigorously condemned as a step away from communism. Mr. Khrushchev defended his proposal by suggesting it would bring closer the day when the Soviet Union could move from Socialist to Communist principles.

State-run tractor stations have provided virtually all the tractors, combines, cultivators and other implements used on Soviet collective farms. They also have been an important instrument of political control in rural areas.

### Repair Role Urged

In a speech to agricultural specialists at Minsk last Wednesday, Mr. Khrushchev suggested that the machine and tractor stations gradually be eliminated and their implements sold to the collective farms. He said in the future stations should be operated merely for the repair of farm machinery and for the sale of spare parts and machines.

The Soviet leader, whose speech was published in Moscow today, said the stations had outlived their economic, technical and political usefulness. He said they represented duplication and economic waste in management and that many farms had reached a point where they could more advantageously own and operate their own machinery.

January 26, 1958

# MOSCOW REVISES PRICE PAID FARMS FOR THEIR OUTPUT

## Ends Compulsory Deliveries by Collectives for Fixed Token Payments

By MAX FRANKEL
Special to The New York Times.

MOSCOW, Friday, June 20—Premier Nikita S. Khrushchev has proclaimed "a new order" and new price and delivery schedules for Soviet collective farms. The full scope of the change probably will not be known until tomorrow.

The Soviet Communist party's Central Committee announced that it had decided at a meeting Tuesday and Wednesday to effect a radical change in the system under which the Government obtained produce from collective farms.

Until now collective farms had been required to sell a quota of their produce to the state at very low token prices in what was called "compulsory deliveries." An additional quota had to be sold to the state at higher prices, in what was known as "state purchases."

Under the new system, no more produce is to be collected from the farms in the form of "compulsory deliveries" at low prices. All farm produce is to be procured by the Government as "purchases" at higher prices.

In order to start the new plan with a clean slate, the party canceled all outstanding debts of the farms. Abolished were debts to the state for past failures to meet the compulsory delivery schedules and also debts in kind to tractor stations.

June 20, 1958

# KHRUSHCHEV BIDS SCHOOLS PREPARE PUPILS FOR LABOR

## Gives Party-Approved Plan to Limit Higher Learning to the Most Gifted

By MAX FRANKEL
Special to The New York Times.

MOSCOW, Sept. 21—Premier Nikita S. Khrushchev told the Soviet people today that their school system would be completely overhauled to teach youngsters respect for physical labor and to prepare them from the first grade for "useful work."

The Soviet leader published a long discourse on education that he said had been approved by the Communist party Presidium. It threw the party's support behind the plans of manpower experts who for months have been debating the reorganization of the schools with prominent educators.

Mr. Khrushchev's ideas were described as "proposals" for discussion and in some respects left it to others to decide the details of reorganization. But he left no doubt that within three or four years most Soviet youngsters would be sent to factories, farms and factory or farm schools at the age of 15 for "practical" training.

**Further Classes Urged**

They will be encouraged but not compelled to take further academic courses in the evenings or by mail.

Furthermore, admission to universities and other higher institutes will be made conditional on the recommendations of the Government trade unions and the Young Communist Leagues. Even students in the advanced five-year institutes will be required whenever possible to stay on the job during the first two or three years of higher education.

People all over Moscow were studying the Khrushchev discourse, which ran to more than a full page in the major papers. They know that in essence the Premier's "suggestions" will soon become the nation's laws. They read closely also because Mr. Khrushchev discussed publicly some current malpractices and shortcomings that they had experienced but not mentioned openly.

Three aspects of the present education system, the Premier said, have become "intolerable."

First, he said, the nation's elementary and high schools were producing graduates unfit for anything except more study, even though higher institutes and universities had room and use for only one in three or four of the graduates.

Second, he declared, the graduates of this system, and to an even larger extent their parents and families, have come to regard physical labor as the lot of failures and respect only those with a higher education.

Finally, he said, the combination of these circumstances has produced heated competition among applicants for higher schools, with the influence and standing of the parents often counting for more than the abilities of the students. Only 30 to 40 per cent of the students in advanced schools now are the children of workers and farmers, Mr. Khrushchev disclosed.

The heavy representation of children of office workers and intellectuals, he maintained, is "obviously abnormal."

**'Decisive' Change Planned**

These complaints against the Soviet school system are not altogether new. But the growing demands of the country's rapidly expanding industries have made their solution a pressing matter. Halfway measures, like the recent rule requiring two years of work experience for all college applicants, are to be scrapped, the Premier indicated, in favor of a "decisive" reorganization.

The Premier described the present situation as the school system's "separation from life." What is needed most to end the drift, he said, is a slogan, which he proposed as: "That all children must prepare for useful labor and participation in the building of Communist society."

As a general principle, Mr. Khrushchev offered his "opinion" that "all pupils without exception should be involved in socially useful labor in industry or on collective farms after they finish seven or eight grades of school."

Later in his discourse, the Premier did provide for some exceptions, especially the very gifted students of the theoretical sciences or of the arts. Apparently they will continue to go straight from elementary school to high school and then to the universities.

But his meaning was clear.

While some youngsters at the age of 14 or 15 will go straight to work with or without supplementary evening or correspondence training, and while others may go to the factory or farm "schools," the vast majority will at last have some job while studying the theory of their future professions.

At present, basic schooling in rural areas is compulsory for seven years. In recent years urban youngsters have been forced to go to school for ten years.

The Premier recommended a new system of basic training in two stages. The first will involve obligatory schooling for all for seven or eight years, with major emphasis on science, polytechnical training and labor education, education in "Communist morals," physical training and the development of good artistic taste.

Mr. Khrushchev said all additional training should be related to practical work physically in the factories and on the farms.

Young people who still want to study, he asserted, would have that opportunity, but only after they had proved themselves at work and had been tested by evening or correspondence schools.

September 22, 1958

# SOVIET PLANNING 80% INDUSTRY RISE IN NEXT 7 YEARS

By MAX FRANKEL

Special to The New York Times.

MOSCOW, Friday, Nov. 14—The Soviet Government announced today that it planned to increase gross industrial production by 80 per cent in the next seven years.

[News agencies said that according to Mr. Khrushchev the Communist bloc would account for more than half the world's industrial output by 1965.]

The new plan for 1959-65 was presented to a plenary meeting of the Central Committee of the Communist party Wednesday by Premier Nikita S. Khrushchev. The committee submitted it for nation-wide discussion prior to final adoption at a special party congress next January.

Priority will continue to go to heavy industry in the stepped-up production schedule. But the Government insisted also that its people would be treated to a better life. The Kremlin leaders promised that by 1970 the Soviet people would enjoy the highest standard of living in the world.

**School Reform Backed**

The Central Committee also resolved to revamp the Soviet school system, adopting the advice of Mr. Khrushchev and manpower specialists who want nearly all youngsters to be sent to work after eight years of basic education.

Mr. Khrushchev vowed that the Soviet Union would have the highest rate of per capita production in Europe by 1965 and in the world by 1970. Therefore, the Soviet leader said, the new plan is a challenge to the capitalist world for all-out economic competition.

To achieve the 80 per cent increase in industrial output, Mr. Khrushchev proposed a capital investment program in the next seven years that will "almost equal" investments since the Bolshevik Revolution forty-one years ago.

The 80 per cent increase in total production will be realized through an 85 to 88 per cent increase in heavy industry and a 62 to 65 per cent increase in the production of consumer goods.

Agricultural output is to increase by 70 per cent in the next seven years and national income will go up by 62 to 65 per cent, he said.

The goals for specific heavy industries allowed a margin of error. For instance, steel production in 1965 is to be 86,000,000 to 91,000,000 tons, an increase of about 56 to 65 per cent over 1958, Mr. Khrushchev said. The higher of the two figures will approach the goal originally intended for 1972.

Pig iron output in 1965 is to reach 65,000,000 to 70,000,000 tons, or 65 to 77 per cent more than in 1958.

Petroleum production is to reach 230,000,000 to 240,000,000 tons, or about twice as much as in 1958. Natural gas output is to rise to 150,000,000 cubic meters, compared with 30,000,000,000 in 1958.

The output of electric power in 1965 will reach 500,000,000,000 to 520,000,000,000 kilowatt-hours. That is 2 to 2.2 times the present output.

Coal production in 1965 is to reach 596,000,000 to 609,000,000 tons, or 20 to 23 per cent over 1958.

Lest this speed-up of heavy industry sound too severe, Mr. Khrushchev dwelt at length on the bright future awaiting Soviet workers and consumers.

**Shorter Work Day Due**

He promised to press on with the transition to the seven-hour work day in factories and offices and the six-hour day in mines and other special branches of industry. He said it had been "suggested" that the Government introduce a five-day work week but he made no commitment on this point.

Real income of factory and office workers are to go up an average of 40 per cent by 1965 and that of collective farmers by at least 40 per cent. The number of factory and office workers will increase to more than 66,000,000, the Premier said.

The Government promised to build 15,000,000 city apartments and 7,000,000 rural homes in the next seven years to alleviate the housing shortage. The Soviet population, estimated at 200,200,000 in April, 1956, is thought to be increasing at the rate of about 3,000,000 annually.

The school reform as previously outlined will require virtually all youngsters to seek work at the age of about 16.

Only highly gifted pupils in the arts and sciences are to continue through high school and advanced institutions without interruption. The rest will be encouraged to combine work with evening or correspondence school training.

**Specifically Related**

Together, the school and economic plans unquestionably are destined to have a profound effect on Soviet society. They are specifically related, since the success of the economic plan is likely to hinge in large measure on the availability of properly skilled workers and technicians at the right times in the years 1959-65.

November 14, 1958

# SOVIET ADOPTING A NEW ECONOMICS

By HARRY SCHWARTZ

Revolutionary changes are taking place in Soviet economic planning and thinking as a result of recent decisions to take over Western concepts and techniques. These innovations may substantially improve the operation of the Soviet economy.

The changes have been reported by Dr. Wassily Leontief, Professor of Economics at Harvard University, who recently returned from a visit of several weeks to the Soviet Union. Dr. Leontief has been one of the pioneers in the development of some of the techniques that are now being adopted in the Soviet Union, where they were long forbidden.

In terms of theory, Dr. Leontief reports, the most important change is a decision to plan Soviet capital investments by taking account of the interest cost over the lifetime of such investments.

Soviet economists formerly denied that interest on capital was a legitimate cost, since it did not seem to fit in with the Marxian theory that only direct labor produces economic value. The result was much misdirection of Soviet capital investment, usually taking the form of building projects that were far larger and more expensive than would have been built had interest costs been considered.

The first hint that Soviet planners were beginning to take account of interest costs came last August when Premier Nikita S. Khrushchev announced a cutback in the Soviet program of building hydroelectric plants.

Dr. Leontief's findings appear to confirm the suspicion of Western economists that the drastic change in plans resulted from the Soviet discovery that if interest costs are taken into account gigantic hydroelectric plants are, under Soviet conditions, frequently uneconomic compared with other means of generating electric power.

Dr. Leontief also found that Soviet economists had embarked upon a major effort to apply mathematics to Soviet economic problems. Earlier in the postwar period mathematical economics was denounced and virtually abandoned in the Soviet Union on the ground that it was anti-Marxist.

"An astounding amount of intellectual and material resources has been thrown in to assimilate the new principles and to introduce them with the least possible delay into practice," Dr. Leontief reports. He adds that professorial chairs of mathematical economics have been set up at Moscow and Leningrad universities, though the holders of these chairs had not yet been named at th tim h lft the Soviet Union.

Dr. Leontief says two branches of mathematical economics are receiving particular emphasis in the Soviet Union. They are input-output analysis, which Dr. Leontief pioneered in the United States several decades ago, and linear programming.

Input -output analysis is a technique for obtaining a complete mathematical description of an economy by a series of equations relating the output of industries with the resources needed to produce that output. Western economists have long been aware of the potential usefulness of this technique of economic planning, sinice equations describing the operation of an economy permit planners to study what would happen to that economy if changes were introduced into its operations.

Input-output analysis requires large-scale computation best done on high-speed electronic computers.

Dr. Leontief found that priority being given to this work in tne Soviet Union was sufficiently high so that Soviet computers, still in short supply, were being used for this work. By the end of this year, he reports, all input-output research will be centered at the new branch of the Soviet Academy of Sciences now being constructed in Novosibirsk.

Linear programming is a mathematical technique that permits the solution of involved problems of economic operation.

Such a problem might be how to operate an oil refinery most efficiently, taking into account the fact that the chemical composition of crude oil changes from time to time with resulting changes in the yield of gasoline, lubricating oil, fuel oil and other products.

Linear programming is being used by large concerns with complex problems of scheduling the use of manufacturing or transportation equipment.

One result of the new interest in mathematical economics in the Soviet Union, Dr. Leontief reports, is that a new generation of young mathematically trained economists is forging ahead of the old generation of Soviet economists.

Among the Soviet economists being trained in the new techniques, Dr. Leontief reports, are experts on under-developed countries. This raises the possibility that the Soviet Union will soon offer experts in these techniques to under-developed countries as one of the means of Soviet aid for economic development.

April 19, 1959

# CENSUS IN SOVIET, FIRST IN 20 YEARS, LISTS 208,800,000

## Excess of Women Reflects Huge Wartime Losses—Party to Meet in June

Special to The New York Times.

MOSCOW, May 10—A census report putting the Soviet population at 208,800,000 was issued here today.

At the same time the Communist party leadership called a meeting of the Central Committee for June 24 to consider key economic questions.

These include the integrated mechanization of agriculture, introduction of automation, production-line techniques, ration alization, wider use of synthetics and the miracle magic of modern chemical industry.

The long-awaited report of the Central Statistical Board covered the census taken last Jan. 15. This was the first Soviet census since Jan. 17, 1939.

**Low Death Rate Noted**

The census showed that the Statistical Board's estimate of April, 1956, which put the population at 200,200,000, was accurate.

The population has risen by 8,600,000 since the 1956 estimate, at a rate of about 3,000,000 a year.

The census takers placed Soviet marriages at 12 per 1,000 persons a year, births at 25 per 1,000, and deaths at 7.5 per 1,000. The report said the death rate was the lowest in the world. No figure on infant mortality was given.

The census report revealed the high mortality suffered by the Soviet population in World War II.

**Population Shifts to Cities**

The census also disclosed a shift from rural to urban population patterns. In the last twenty years the share of urban population rose from 32 per cent of the total to 48 per cent.

A swing to the eastern parts of the country has been shown by differential growth rates. The nation as a whole increased its population by 9.5 per cent from 1939. But the Urals grew by 32 per cent, Western Siberia by 24 per cent, Eastern Siberia by 34 per cent and the Soviet Far East by 70 per cent.

The war's effects are shown in the sex composition of the population, which gives 55 per cent women and 45 per cent men, compared with 48 per cent men and 52 per cent women in 1939. The imbalance in the older age groups is a result of wartime losses. Below the age of 32, however, there is balance between men and women.

Among the large cities, Moscow reported a population of 5,032,000 compared with 4,183,000 in 1939, and Leningrad, hard hit by the war, still showed a loss at 2,888,000 compared with 3,015,000 in 1939.

But other cities are booming, with increases of up to 250 per cent.

Gorky jumped from 644,000 to 942,000, Tashkent from 650,000 to 911,000, Novosibirsk from 404,000 to 887,000, Chelyabinsk from 273,000 to 688,000 and Erivan from 204,000 to 509,000.

It is the pattern of this population, its composition, its shifting movement, its increased urbanization and its gaps from wartime losses that provide the basic integers of the economic problems that the managers of the Soviet economy will be discussing in June.

In these discussions it may well turn out that Iosif I. Kuzmin, who was assigned to the new task of scientific-economic coordination, will play a leading role. The intimate integration of science and technology with industry is a prime requisite if the great pace of Soviet economic development is to be maintained.

Rationalization of production, increased labor efficiency, lower costs, lowered time lag from laboratory development to machine shop—these are the key questions that will be subjected to searching examination at the Central Committee meeting in June.

May 11, 1959

# *Soviet Revising Bonuses To Reward Cost Cutting*

By MAX FRANKEL
Special to The New York Times.

MOSCOW, Dec. 11—The Soviet Government has decreed a new formula for bonuses. In effect, the largest rewards will henceforth go to enterprises and workers who drive down production costs. This in most cases will supplant the system of rewarding quantitative output, often without regard to quality or cost.

The drive to fulfill and overfulfill production plans has hitherto dominated Soviet industry and proved an obsession to many skilled workers and administrators.

The change, therefore, is likely to affect the take-home pay of the overwhelming majority of employes. Plainly, the Government expects this in turn to change their approach to production.

**Inequality Heightened**

The new regulations were described in the latest issue of Sotsialisticheski Trud, the magazine of the Government's Committee for Labor and Wages. They will become effective Jan. 1.

Under the old system, a steel mill with a plan of 1,000,000 tons or a truck driver with a plan to move 1,000 tons of goods for 1,000 miles earns generous bonuses for meeting or exceeding those goals. So, usually, do the managers, bookkeepers and others related to the successful effort, and often also personnel not so obviously related.

For some the bonuses amount to twice the base pay or more. Since bonuses usually are related in size to base pay, the system tends to widen the gap between high-paid and low-paid workers.

What the Government now intends is that the cost of producing steel or moving goods become the factor controlling bonuses, and that bonus funds be distributed more equitably.

The old system worked well, the Government said, to spur rapid increases in production. Such rewards will be retained in industries marked for continued rapid growth, such as coal, oil and gas, metallurgy, chemistry, building materials, fishing, textiles and shoes.

Even here, however, new formulas will give weight to cost, quality and timely deliveries.

The old system was inadequate to a more economical development of industry, the Government said, and was susceptible to abuse. Factories engaged in periodic speed-ups and let-downs, tended to under-rate their capacities in drafting plans and at times spent more than they earned to increase output.

The new system will provide bonuses for the fulfillment of a cost-of-production index. In some industries, bonuses also will depend on improvements in quality, increases in labor productivity and meeting obligations to deliver goods to other economic regions.

The delivery requirement already applies in many situations to prevent "localism," or the tendency to supply local needs first.

To prevent disruption of the "rhythm" of work, bonuses henceforth are to be paid quarterly, instead of monthly. However, if the plans for any month within the quarter are not met, bonuses are to be reduced.

Limits on the size of bonuses, averaging about 50 per cent of base pay, are to be established. A revamping of the wage system in the next two years will follow the bonus changes, which makes it difficult now to estimate the effect of the new system on pay.

Workers and employes not directly involved in production successes will henceforth be subject to a separate bonus schedule, to prevent front-office expropriation of bonus funds intended for workers.

December 18, 1959

# U.S. Syndicate Will Equip Big Textile Plant in Soviet

## Group to Install Spinning and Weaving Machines Valued at $20,000,000—First Such Deal Since the War

By OSGOOD CARUTHERS

Special to The New York Times.

MOSCOW, Dec. 28—A consortium of more than forty American companies signed a contract with the Soviet Union today to provide the machinery for a new $30,000,000 textile plant.

The American group will also install the machinery in the projected 50,000-spindle plant. It will be one of the largest spinning and weaving mills erected anywhere since World War II.

It was understood that the cost of the machinery to be purchased from the American consortium would be about $20,000,000. The estimated total cost of $30,000,000 includes construction.

This was the first such agreement between the Soviet Union and American companies for construction of plants since the years before the war, when Ford and International Harvester set up factories in the Soviet Union and United States engineers helped build the first big hydroelectric power dam on the Dnieper River.

The contract was signed in Moscow after months of difficult negotiations and intensive competition with a British group.

The consortium is Intertex International, Inc., 270 Madison Avenue, New York. It agreed to furnish machinery and install it in the plant at Kalinin, half-way between Leningrad and Moscow.

Although the Soviet Union originally sought credits and had been offered them by the British group, the final deal called for cash payments. The American negotiators, headed by Sidney H. Scheuer, board chairman of Intertex, said shipments of equipment were expected to be completed during the first quarter of 1961.

The American group of fifteen sales executives and technicians who had conducted the negotiations were cautious about revealing details of the contract they signed today with representatives of the official Soviet organization called Techmachimport. It was believed, however, that actual construction of the plant would be carried out by Soviet workers, possibly with the Americans giving technical advice on the installation of machinery.

A statement issued by the consortium said the plant would represent "the most advanced technology in all departments."

A plant of this kind, which, according to the American representatives, would be able to spin, weave and finish cotton, worsted blends and synthetic fibers, will obviously give valuable assistance to Soviet textile production.

Less than a month ago the Government decreed a great expansion of the textile industry, including the building of new plants, renovation of old ones and streamlining of existing production lines. This was ordered as a measure to meet growing consumer demands for quality goods as well as quantity and to fit into Premier Khrushchev's elaborate seven-year economic plan for overtaking the United States.

The New York Times Dec. 29, 1959

PLANT TO BE BUILT: New Soviet textile mill is planned at Kalinin (cross).

Part of that plan calls for production of synthetic materials on an infinitely greater scale. The Soviet Union has already asked the United States for credits and approval of the purchase of whole chemical plants to produce them. Thus far, Washington has rejected such requests.

The Soviet Union has recently concluded contracts with Italian concerns to build a nylon plant. It is reported that this plant will also be near Kalinin, a city of 260,000, and that it no doubt will supply materials for the spinning and weaving plant.

Production from such plants will enable the Soviet Union to offer greater amounts of materials to the under-developed countries, where an all-out economic aid and trade offensive is going on.

There appeared to be political significance in the fact that the Soviet Union has been trying for more than a year to penetrate Washington's unwillingness to trade with the Communist world.

The contract signed today far exceeds the total value of United States exports to the Soviet Union in 1958. According to Soviet statistics, this trade amounted to 19,000,000 rubles or, at the official rate of four to a dollar, a little less than $5,000,000. Soviet-American trade showed a marked increase this year.

Among major companies associated with the transaction are the James Hunter Machine Company of North Adams, Mass.; Crompton & Knowles of Worcester, Mass., the Whitin Machine Works of Whitinsville, Mass.; the Rodney Hunt Machine Company of Orange, Mass.; the National Drying Machine Company of Philadelphia, and the Cocker Machine and Foundry Company of Gastonia, N. C.

Mr. Scheuer led the negotiations and was aided by Norman Garlington and T. D. Lewis Jr., vice presidents of Intertex.

The negotiations were based on a project outlined in April, 1958. Earlier this year they nearly broke down, but resumed at the beginning of this month.

### Earlier Deals Noted

Mr. Scheuer said here yesterday that Intertex had been selling complete textile plants to the Soviet Union for some time.

A knitting plant supplied by Intertex is operating and equipment is being shipped for a 15,000-spindle worsted spinning plant and a tufted-carpet mill.

Mr. Scheuer emphasized that the new contract was the first to provide also for American assistance in the installation of the plant equipment.

Intertex International is an affiliate of Scheuer & Co., a textile brokerage concern also of 270 Madison Avenue. The active phase of business relations between Intertex and the Soviet Union dates from April, 1958, when the New York concern invited a group of Soviet textile men to visit the United States.

The group, led by N. Y. Chesnokov, chief of the Light Industry Section of the Soviet Planning Committee, toured the plants of many of the textile-machinery manufacturers associated with the new contract.

December 29, 1959

# Soviet Consumers Becoming Choosier

By MAX FRANKEL

Special to The New York Times.

MOSCOW, March 3—Soviet planners warned today that the Soviet consumer was becoming choosy and increasingly unwilling to gobble up goods that happen to reach store shelves.

They said the country's consumer industries and retail networks were courting serious trouble if they continued to ignore shoppers' demands for good-quality and fashionable clothing and adequate stocks of durable goods.

Unwanted merchandise is piling up in warehouses and storerooms, the planners declared. They said such stocks demonstrated that volume increases in consumer-goods production no longer resulted automatically in increased sales.

The warning was issued by Planovoye Khozyaistvo, official magazine of the State Planning Committee. It recommended extensive and continuing studies of buying habits in place of the traditional gauging of demand by the amount of money in the hands of consumers.

The article did not intend to suggest that Soviet industry was overproducing or that there were not important shortages of consumer goods. But it warned that costly surpluses of some goods would develop if production schedules were not matched to scientific studies of demand.

The volume of retail trade last year increased by 8 per cent, but fell short of the planned volume by more than 1 per cent, the magazine said. This occurred despite an increase in consumer goods production of nearly 4 per cent above the plan. Inventory checks disclosed that warehouse stocks were increasing at an undesirable rate, the magazine added.

March 4, 1960

# PARTY IN SOVIET ACTS ON CHEATING

## Tightens Grip on Economy to Stop False Reports

By SEYMOUR TOPPING

Special to The New York Times.

MOSCOW, June 27 — The Communist party instructed its members today to tighten their control over the economy in order to curb the falsifying of records by state managers in agriculture and industry.

Party organizations were blamed in part for the recent scandals in agriculture. It was indicated that similar widespread cheating in reporting the fulfillment of economic plans had been uncovered in industrial enterprises.

In preparation for the twenty-second party congress in October, a discussion has begun in party publications and at meetings about new techniques of control to insure the proper reporting of economic data.

The problem is regarded here as fundamental to the question of whether the Soviet Union's planned economy can operate efficiently.

The party, through its nearly 9,000,000 members, already operates a pervasive inspectorate that oversees every phase of Soviet life.

Communist theory holds that official corruption will vanish once the vestiges of capitalism are eradicated. However, the Soviet Government found it necessary only last May to decree that persons could be imprisoned up to three years for "the padding of state reports and the deliberate distortion of reports on the fulfillment of plans."

Articles published in Kommunist, the party's chief theoretical journal, and Pravda, the party newspaper, have said that more control was the best answer to economic fakery.

Kommunist, in an article entitled "Deceit and Falsification," indicated that the party had been shocked into action by the fraudulent reporting in agriculture made public early this year.

**Deception Uncovered**

The journal reported that many instances of deceit had been uncovered at farms and industrial enterprises after they had been inspected and approved by party officials.

"In order that such phenomena are not repeated, leading party organs must establish permanent and efficient control over the manner of fulfillment of party and government directives," Kommunist said.

Writing in Pravda, Andrei A. Kirilenko, first secretary of the Sverdlovsk regional party committee, reported on new control techniques.

Mr. Kirilenko, a candidate member of the Presidium of the Central Committee, said that the party had taken more direct control of industry, building construction and the reorganization of agriculture. Top party members have been made responsible for the fulfillment of decisions.

The party secretary conceded, however, that in some districts of his region party control operated only on paper. This has encouraged falsifiers who "try to create illusions of success," he said.

Mr. Kirilenko asserted that his regional party had 3,328 inspection commissions operating to check on agricultural and industrial units.

June 28, 1961

# Huge Soviet Factories Rise in Siberian Cold

## *Hydroelectric Plants Are Built Despite Sub-Zero Climate*

By HARRISON E. SALISBURY

Special to The New York Times.

IRKUTSK, U. S. S. R., Dec. 15—At 45 or 50 degrees below zero the cold of the Siberian taiga or forest region cuts through heavy clothes, numbing hands, face and body. It can freeze a man to death almost before he realizes what is happening.

"We halt operations when the temperature drops to 40 below zero," said Alexander Zarudsky, deputy chief engineer of an enormous aluminum plant that sprawls over the taiga at Shelekhov, north of Irkutsk.

"If there is a strong wind we close down at 35 below zero," he added.

As he spoke the temperature stood a degree or two above 40-below in the unfinished electrolytic works of the vast aluminum enterprise.

Half the workmen were huddled around coal-oil or wood fires, trying to thaw some sensation into their hands. But the other half of the work force was on the job. A great overhead traveling crane moved swiftly from one end of the long hall to the other. The clang of fitters' hammers rang out in the murky shed.

**'A Little Frost'**

"We Siberians are used to the cold," said Mr. Zarudsky, a great hulk of a man bundled in sheepskins. "A little frost doesn't halt us."

All over eastern Siberia tremendous industrial enterprises are going forward in a program which, within the next twenty years, is designed to transform this desolate region into one of the world's great industrial areas. One day it may be comparable to the Ruhr or Pittsburgh or the Donets region of the Soviet Union itself.

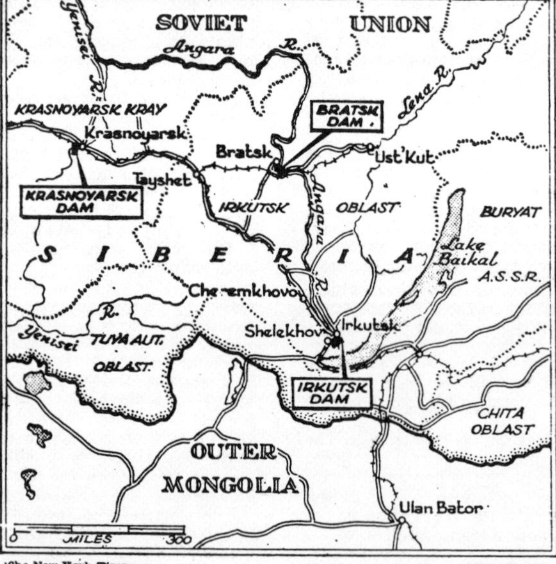


**The Soviet Union hopes to transform the desolate area of Eastern Siberia into a highly developed industrial region.**

The world's biggest power plants—both hydroelectric and thermal—are going up. The world's greatest open-cut coal mining operations are getting under way. At Shelekhov one of the world's biggest aluminum works is being built.

Everything in eastern Siberia seems to be a superlative—the biggest, the most distant, the most difficult, the coldest.

**Source of the Power**

This is the region of the Angara River—the world's largest single potential hydroelectric power source; of Lake Baikal, the world's deepest fresh-water lake where 1,800 kinds of plant and animal life are to be found, three-quarters of them not existing anywhere else in the world; of coal reserves of 6,800,000,000,000 tons; of the cheapest electric power in the world—less than a tenth of a cent for each kilowatt hour at the great Bratsk dam.

Bratsk, of course, will be the world's biggest hydroelectric producer when it is finished two years hence. It may have a rated capacity of 4,000,000 kilowatts or 21,000,000,000 kilowatt hours a year. Some say it will have a rated capacity of 4,500,000 kilowatts. But big as it is, Bratsk will reign supreme for only a short while. The even huger Wrasnoyarsk dam on the Yenisei River is planned to have a 5,000,0000 kilowatt capacity.

"Is it true," a group of excited young Bratsk workers asked an American visitor, "that Bratsk is bigger than any plant in America?"

They were told that this was true; that Bratsk was about twice as big as Grand Coulee Dam in Colorado, the biggest hydroelectric plant in the United States.

"And is it true that Russia is the biggest country in the world?" they asked.

Yes, the American said. That, too, was true.

The young people beamed at this evidence that they were really working on the biggest dam in the biggest country on earth.

"And," they continued, "does it ever get as cold as this in America?"

They were a little disappointed to learn that at some places and at some times in the United States Siberian cold could be matched—at least for a day or two.

The Shelekhov aluminum works is typical of the huge enterprises that are now beginning to rise upon the foundation of cheap power provided by the Angara River.

The first dam is already pouring power into the area. This is the Irkutsk station, which has been delivering power from its eight generators with a rated capacity of 660,000 kilowatts for three years. A good bit of the Irkutsk output is being fed over a 220,000-volt transmission line to Bratsk, which is about 350 miles to the north, to provide an energy source for that big project.

Precisely how big the Shelekhov works ultimately will be is a secret. It may not yet have been decided by the top Soviet planners. The initial electrolytic plant, which will begin preliminary operations sometime this winter, is expected to have a capacity of 50,000 tons a year. Two more units, presumably of similar capacity, are under construction. Beyond that there will be additional units—just how many no one at Shelekhov can or will say.

How big an enterprise this is can be judged by the fact that the area was laid out in 1953. In 1956 the building of a base for construction workers was started. Thousands of young Russians were drafted for duty on the site, then wilderness, meadow and Siberian forest land. The young people lived in barracks and tents through the first winter as they built facilities for the construction crews.

They had to build housing for thousands of workers, a filtration plant, a sewer system, a cement plant, a factory to produce prefabricated panels and dozens of other structures. Work on the aluminum plant itself did not start until more than a year later.

Today the Shelekhov construction site is a city of 25,000 persons, most of them living in apartment houses. It has its own stores, schools, a hospital, movie house and rapidly is acquiring the appearance of a permanent town. More than 14,000 of the 25,000 population are actively employed in construction of the aluminum works.

Construction at the Shelekhov works goes on winter and summer—as it does at all the great Siberian operations. Workers get premium pay—about 20 per cent over average—for working in the severe conditions of eastern Siberia. They are allowed fifteen minutes out of every hour to thaw out around stoves and open fires on the factory floor. Whether this is economic use of manpower no one on the Siberian construction sites seemed to know. Cost factors in Soviet construction operations are almost impossible to calculate.

What seemed to matter to everyone was that even in the most severe weather the construction projects advanced—even if slowly.

At Bratsk and the hydroelectric construction sites the pace of winter work is actually much brisker than at the complex aluminum factory installation where, some workmen said, operations really must be halted when the cold is severe because metal cannot be worked properly.

At Bratsk, Krasnoyarsk and Ust-Ilinsk where preliminary work on another huge Angara dam has started, much of the task involves earth fills, excavations and the pouring of concrete. It is not so difficult to go forward with such work even at 40 degrees below zero.

Masses of young people have been brought into the transformation of eastern Siberia. Many have volunteered under the emotional appeal of the Communist Youth Organization. Others have been directed by the Government to take jobs here on completion of their education. Others have been attracted by the comparatively higher pay.

Not all of them are happy about working in eastern Siberia. But on the Bratsk project, where about 40,000 persons are at work and the average age of thousands of them seems to be below 25, enthusiasm is more common than disaffection.

Alongside the industrial developments of eastern Siberia there is rising a great science center based on Irkutsk. This is the second of two big Siberian science centers. The other is in Novosibersk, the unofficial capital of western Siberia.

The principal units of the center here are Irkutsk University, which has 5,000 students, half of them correspondence and night students, and a branch of the Soviet Academy of Science, which is specially devoted to problems relative to eastern Siberian development. There are also half a dozen other institutes specializing in various fields with a total of 24,000 students.

December 28, 1961

# Burgeoning of Economic Crime One of Soviet's Major Worries

## Death Penalty and Long Prison Terms Decreed for Speculation Reflect Fear of Damage to System

By SEYMOUR TOPPING
Special to The New York Times.

MOSCOW, June 22—The Soviet press published today three typical news items that portrayed the nature of one of the most serious social problems confronting the Soviet Union. The problem is economic crimes and Soviet courts are combating it by meting out death sentences and lengthy prison terms.

One item was a report from Minsk, where eighteen men are on trial charged with speculation in foreign currency and gold worth millions of dollars.

From the Ukraine it was reported that the director of a china factory had been indicted for selling part of his output to illegal private dealers.

Near Moscow, the manager of a shop went on trial for having filled vodka bottles with water and selling them as the real article.

Over the last year the Soviet press nas burgeoned forth with numerous such articles detailing "crimes against the state" in the forms of speculation, embezzlement and misappropriation of state funds.

### Many Jews Involved

One of the objectives of the publicity, according to Soviet officials, is to deter would-be offenders. However, a by-product of the campaign has been to stir some apprehension of a revival of anti-Semitism, because a considerable number of Jews have been condemned in the campaign against currency and gold speculation.

Some Western observers trace the inspiration for the intensive drive against economic crimes to disclosures by Premier Khrushchev in 1960. The Soviet leader found then that one of the reasons for the Soviet Union's agriculture difficulties was widescale swindling.

Investigations that subsequently were extended to industry and commerce uncovered scandals that resulted in a decree authorizing the death penalty for major economic crimes.

By Western standards the punishments seem severe. They are not necessarily so by Soviet standards, which allow more tolerance for a murder committed under strong emotional impulse than for embezzlement of state property.

Economic crime is considered a more heinous offense here because its very nature threatens the foundations of Soviet society. The Communist system breaks down when citizens fail to respect the principle of public ownership or officials fail to provide the honest statistics required for efficient economic planning.

According to information reaching Western officials here, about 225 persons have been sentenced to death by Soviet courts over the last year. The majority of those shot are believed to have been convicted of economic crimes.

Jewish organizations abroad have focused foreign attention on the Jews among those executed for economic crimes.

This reflects the fear of some Jews in the Soviet Union that latent anti-Semitism among the population may be stirred up by the publicity given the economic crimes.

Among those defendants cited in the three cases reported today in the Soviet press, six of the eighteen persons charged in the Minsk speculation case appeared to have Jewish names.

**Jewish defendants have not been identified as such in Soviet press accounts of the trials except by implication in two known instances where religious associations were mentioned during the presentation of evidence.**

Anti-Semitic feeling has been suspected in a number of recent incidents. One such case was the burning of a synagogue by vandals in a small town in the Republic of Georgia. However, these incidents have not fallen into a pattern and Soviet authorities have intervened where violations of law have been apparent.

One Soviet Jew was able to provide specific information of an anti-Jewish manifestation resulting from the speculation cases. The Jew heard workers joking in his factory about the Jews in the speculation trials.

He protested to the shop chairman, who was a member of the Communist party, and subsequently received an apology and assurances that no anti-Semitic feeling was involved.

June 23, 1962

# MOSCOW SUSPENDS INCOME TAX CUTS

By THEODORE SHABAD
Special to The New York Times.

MOSCOW, Sept. 24 — The Soviet Government announced today that it was postponing scheduled income tax cuts to help pay for further economic development and increased defense preparedness.

A decree of the Presidium of the Supreme Soviet (Parliament) said the tax reduction phase that was scheduled to begin next Monday had been canceled "until further notice" because of "an increase in the aggressive schemes of imperialism."

The projected cuts were part of a program of a gradual abolition of the income tax that began two years ago and was to be completed by 1965. Two previous stages have already abolished the tax on incomes up to 60 rubles ($66.60) a month.

**Follows Price Increases**

Today's announcement, published on the front page of Izvestia, the Government newspaper, was the second major Soviet decision this year affecting the pocketbook of the ordinary citizen. Last June 1, meat and butter prices were raised by an average of 25 to 30 per cent to spur lagging farm output of livestock products.

The Government anticipated the undoubted disappointment of the Soviet people over the income tax change by printing an explanation that took up almost half a page in Izvestia. Having reviewed the program of social benefits, increasing world tension and the need for continued economic growth, the explanation said:

"There can be no doubt that the decree published today will be correctly understood and unanimously endorsed by the nation as a measure dictated by the interests of all working people and the interests of the security of our country."

September 25, 1962

# U.S. GETS REPORTS OF RIOTS IN SOVIET

## Experts Say Hundreds May Have Been Slain by Troops During Price Protests

By MAX FRANKEL
Special to The New York Times

WASHINGTON, Oct. 7 — A vivid description of protest rallies and riots that caused dozens and possibly hundreds of deaths in a southern Soviet industrial city last summer is being pieced together by Government analysts here.

The demonstrations, never directly reported by the Soviet press, apparently were touched off by sudden increases June 1 in the prices of meat and butter. But they are said also to have reflected deeper resentments over food shortages and work speed-ups.

The violence took place in Novocherkassk, an industrial center 20 miles northeast of Rostov. The city has a population of 94,000 and produces locomotives and farm and mining equipment and has several important technical schools.

It is nearly 600 miles south of Moscow and about 230 miles west of Stalingrad.

**Army Units Aid Militia**

Soviet army units are said to have been needed to help the local militia at the height of the unrest in early June. The entire region has been closed to foreign diplomats and newsmen. The regional party leader has been replaced and all young persons have been subjected to a strict curfew.

Reports from the area are necessarily second-hand, but Soviet specialists here give credence to the broad outlines of the reports they have heard. Word of the rioting is said to have spread quickly through the Soviet Union and was carried by some young Russians to the World Youth Festival in Helsinki in August.

Official accounts of Communist party and local government activity in the Rostov region since June are read here as circumstantial but corroborative evidence of the disorders.

Travelers through the Soviet Union also have heard that smaller disorders took place about the same time in smaller cities near Rostov as well as in Voronezh, 300 miles to the north, Krasnodar, 150 miles to the south, and Grozny, 400 miles to the southeast.

October 8, 1962

# *Soviet Revamps Controls On Industry and Farming*

By THEODORE SHABAD
Special to The New York Times

MOSCOW, Nov. 19—Premier Khrushchev announced today a sweeping reorganization of Soviet governmental administration and of the ruling Communist party to channel the country's efforts more effectively into development of industry and agriculture.

The reform will in effect divide virtually all national activity into two main sectors, industrial and agricultural, under a dual system of administration extending from the central authority to the local level.

It is as if each state in the United States were to be given two parallel governments, one administering all industrial activity and its manpower, and the other the entire sphere of agricultural production and all people connected with it.

In a five-and-a-half-hour speech on the opening day of a meeting of the Communist party's policy-making Central Committee, Mr. Krushchev also announced the following reforms in the Soviet Union's economic life:

¶Combination of the country's 100 industrial management regions into about 40 larger units. The merger is intended to overcome a tendency toward factionalism and regional deficiency at the expense of the national interest.

¶Decentralization of economic planning to bring "to a logical conclusion" the decentralization of economic management introduced five years ago."

¶Centralization of industrial construction and design under specialized state committees that will be given greatly expanded powers in planning, research and technical development in the various industries.

¶Establishment of advisory workers' committees in factories to confer with the plant management on planning, work norms and personnel assignments.

¶Introduction of a joint party-government control agency to check on implementation of party and government directives with the assistance of public-sipirited volunteer inspectors.

Associated Press Cablephoto
Premier Khrushchev speaking yesterday at party meeting

**Major Decision Postponed**

Mr. Khrushchev postponed a decision on a new system of economic planning procedures and production incentives and called on planners and economists to examine proposals made in the Soviet press on this subject during the last few months. However, he described the profit index proposed by Prof. Yevsey G. Liberman of Kharkov as having "great importance as an economic indicator" of efficient plant operation.

The gist of Mr. Khrushchev's proposals was made public in an 8,000-word summary distributed by Tass, the official Soviet press agency. The text of the Premier's speech is expected to be published in tomorrow's newspapers.

[Mr. Khrushchev said the Soviet Union should readily learn from the experiences of the capitalist countries and adopt whatever good ideas they had, United Press International reported. The Premier declared: "There was a time—I mean the period of the personality cult— when the idea was sedulously fostered that everything that is ours is unreservedly ideal and everything foreign is unreservedly bad. But the times of the personality cult have passed. We should remember Lenin's injunction to be able, if necessary, to learn from the capitalists, to imitate the good and profitable they have."]

In introducing the dual system of industrial and agricultural party organization, the Premier said "radical measures" were needed to bring the party structure into line with previous economic management reforms.

These were, in industry, the organization of about 100 regional management agencies in 1957, replacing central industrial ministries, and, in agriculture, the establishment last March of 1,500 producer administrations dealing directly with collectives and state farms.

Although the old party committees were expected to concern themselves with the economy, Mr. Khrushchev said, they often lacked the manpower for detailed supervision and were forced to resort to what he called "crash programs" to enforce Government policy.

**Dual Hierarchy Planned**

Under the new system, a dual hierarchy of industrial and agricultural party committees will replace the present sructure of single committees concerned with all aspects of the nation's life.

The split will be most sharply defined at the regional and local levels where the dual chain of command will also penetrate into Government administration.

Instead of the present regional (oblast) party committee, which has been in practice the highest authority on the regional level, there will henceforth be two party committees, one dealing with the industrial sector and the other with agriculture. Similarly, there will be two regional governments.

The regional agricultural body will administer county-like agencies known as agricultural producer administrations. The present rural districts (rayons) within the administration are to be abolished.

The regional industrial body will directly administer cities, industrial zones within a rural area and fairly large isolated industrial plants.

The dual structure is to be reflected in the central party committees of the Soviet Union's constituent republics and in the national Central Committee, where separate party bureaus or boards will be established to deal with industry and agriculture.

November 20, 1962

# Soviet Drops 7-Year Plan, Sets Up New Industry Rule

Special to The New York Times.

MOSCOW, March 13—The Soviet Union disclosed today that it was scrapping its seven-year plan, which it said was out of step with the times. A new plan, reflecting major changes in economic policy and technology, is to be drawn up for the last two years of the original period ending in 1965.

It was also announced that the Supreme Council of National Economy would be set up to coordinate the planning and management of industry and construction on a nationwide basis.

Dmitri F. Ustinov, 54-year-old administrator of the defense industries, was named chairman of the Council and a First Deputy Premier. Aleksandr M. Tarasov, 51, manager of tractor plants and lately head of industry in the Byelorussian Republic, was named Deputy Chairman.

These sweeping decisions, the latest in a wave of economic reorganizations set in motion last November, were taken at a joint meeting of the Communist party's ruling Presidium and the Government Council of Ministers, presided over by Premier Khrushchev.

The meeting also ordered the drafting of a new five-year plan for 1967-70, at the end of which, according to Communist reckonings, the Soviet Union is supposed to surpass the United States in per capita production.

The decision to draft a new two-year plan and the establishment of the industrial superagency seemed to implement policies adopted at the plenary meeting of the party's Central Committee in November.

The meeting split the nation into two independent administrative systems, focused on industry and agriculture. It also called for a greater allocation of resources to modern industrial sectors such as chemicals and electronics, at the expense of steel, as well as to consumer goods, housing and agriculture, which have been at levels far short of needs.

March 14, 1963

# KHRUSHCHEV SAYS HARVEST IS POOR

By THEODORE SHABAD
Special to The New York Times

MOSCOW, Sept. 30—Premier Khrushchev declared in a speech made public tonight that a poor harvest this year had placed the Soviet Union in a "difficult position."

He called for an expansion of irrigation and of the output of chemical fertilizers to insure the country against "all eventualities."

Serious crop failures have forced the Soviet Union, normally the world's largest grain producer, to make large wheat purchases abroad and to launch a campaign to cut down on the use of bread.

The Soviet leader spoke Friday in the southern Ukraine on a tour of farm areas that he hopes will be able to realize his latest agricultural goal. This goal calls for a "guaranteed" annual grain supply of 25 to 30 million tons from irrigated land in addition to the present fluctuating deliveries of 35 to 55 million tons from dry-farming regions.

Mr. Khrushchev made it clear that he had abandoned hope of curing the nation's agricultural ills through a vast expansion of crop acreages, such as the virgin lands project undertaken ten years ago.

October 1, 1963

# Soviet Setting Price Revisions To Take More Account of Costs

By THEODORE SHABAD
Special to The New York Times

MOSCOW, March 1 — Soviet planners have worked out a new system of industrial wholesale prices to go into effect next Jan. 1, according to the economic weekly Ekonomicheskaya Gazeta.

The price revision, the first in ten years, is intended both to reduce Government subsidies to industries operating at a loss and to stimulate the introduction of plastics, manmade fibers and other synthetic products into machine-building and consumer goods industries.

The reform will not fundamentally change the Soviet system of fixing prices. These are manipulated by Government planners as instruments to achieve economic goals and they do not reflect the supply and demand relationships of a free-enterprise economy.

The revision will introduce more reason into the price structure by reducing the number of products for which prices were kept artificially low.

Ekonomicheskaya Gazeta said that new prices would "reflect more accurately necessary production costs and at the same time insure profits." The Government-fixed profit mark-up, usually 5 per cent, is an important source of Government revenue.

With the introduction of higher prices for coal, iron ore, manganese ore and other ores and concentrates, the Soviet Union's coal and metal mining industries are expected to become profitable for the first time. They have been operating at deliberate losses and receiving Government subsidies.

Some Soviet economists have contended that because of excessively low steel prices, made prices, steel has appeared to be more profitable in the Government's calculations than new chemical products.

In a major shift of economic development, Soviet planners are now emphasizing the growth of the chemical industry, which has been lagging behind the levels achieved in the West.

Higher prices in the coal and metal industries, beginning next year, are expected to cut the number of industrial plants operating at a planned loss by at least half.

On the basis of planned reductions in production costs, prices will be cut in the machine-building, chemical and electric power industries.

According to the weekly, prices in heavy industry and freight rates were reviewed over the last two years and work on revisions of prices in consumer goods industries has begun.

New prices are to be used in planning and in the calculation of the gross industrial output index, the basic Soviet measurement of the industrial economy.

The authors of the article, V. Lipsits and Y. Danilevich, economists, urged that a system be devised for periodic revisions of industrial wholesale prices.

They said that in industries with a rapidly changing product assortment and a high rate of growth, such as machinery and chemicals, prices should be reviewed at least once every two to three years.

In comparison with the past rigidity of the price system, such an approach reflects a desire to introduce a more flexible and meaningful method of making the most efficient use possible by low coal and ore of resources.

March 2, 1964

# More Advertising Is Urged in Soviet

By THEODORE SHABAD

Special to The New York Times

MOSCOW, April 25 — Does the Soviet Union's planned economy need advertising? An emphatic yes has appeared in Izvestia, the Government newspaper.

Reporting on a survey of advertising needs and facilities, the newspaper called for a system of billboards, posters and other promotion methods to help the consumer make up his mind.

Izvestia said growing consumer choice in the Soviet Union pointed to the need for a Government-run advertising agency that would employ "not only artists and designers but market research economists who would study the ebb and flow of demand, its prospects, its characteristics, its geography."

Yevgeny G. Kriger, the author of the Izvestia report, conceded that he had found little enthusiasm among retail organizations for advertising.

"Advertising," he quoted one official as having said, "what for? We cannot get rid of customers as it is. Anyway, who says we need advertising under Socialism? We don't want any Broadway here."

Mr. Kriger said the contention that advertising had no place in an economy where there were still shortages of some consumer goods was fallacious. Even now, he said the Soviet consumer is confronted with a wide choice among durable goods and appliances such as watches, refrigerators and electric razors.

"Suppose you are in the market for a refrigerator but you do not know all the fine points of the refrigerator business", Kriger wrote." The names 'Zil', 'Dnieper,' 'Saratov' and other makes do not tell you anything. All you are told is the capacity."

"What you want to know" he added, "is whether this refrigerator suits your particular needs, the size of your family, your ideas of convenience and comfort. On that point you just encounter silence."

The Izvestia writer decried the type of general purpose advertising now common in the Soviet Union.

"Who wants to be told nowadays that tea is a useful and tasty drink or that money should be kept in a savings bank or that traffic regulations must be observed on the street?" he asked.

In the same category the writer added, is a huge sign on the Kursk railroad station, one of Moscow's busiest terminals, urging the commuter who is late for the 5:15, "Use the services of railroad transportation."

Opposition to advertising in the Soviet Union, Mr. Kriger continued, is based on a fear of "cheap temptations and evil influences supposedly engendered by the electric frenzy of Broadway," which is the Soviet propaganda stereotype of New York.

Assuring Russians that advertising could be used in moderation on Moscow thoroughfares, Mr. Kriger said: "Broadway is Broadway and Gorky Street is Gorky Street."

Nor is there any intention, he added, of restoring to what he called the 'nihilism' of one advertiser who paid for a full page carying only a small message in tiny print that this partcular concern did not advertise.

Mr. Kriger said tasteful advertising, billboards and window displays enhanced the appearance of cities and made them more pleasant places in which to live. In previous articles, he assailed the dullness and lack of inventiveness of store signs that announce, for example, "Meat" over a butcher shop or "Bread" over a bakery.

This concern for appearances in everyday Soviet life is part of a growing trend to pay more attention to esthetics, human relations and other intangibles after decades of emphasis on material aspects.

April 26, 1964

# SOVIET SCHOOLING CUT TO 10 YEARS

## Abandonment of 11th Term Aims at Speeding Pupils Into the Labor Force

By THEODORE SHABAD

Special to The New York Times

MOSCOW, Aug. 12—The Soviet Union announced today a reduction of its 11-year system of primary and secondary education to 10 years.

The change is part of a new educational policy intended to speed the entry of young people into the labor force. The Soviet Government announced earlier this year that the four-year to five-year period of higher education would be reduced by one year.

A decree of the Soviet Communist party and the Government, made public today, said the transition period to the new system was to be completed by the end of the 1965-66 school year. The decision meant in effect that the Soviet Union's long-range goal of achieving 11 years of universal compulsory schooling by 1970 had been dropped.

Since the school year 1962-63, the Soviet Union has had eight years of compulsory education, from age 7 to age 15.

About 40 per cent to 50 per cent of the graduates of eight-year schools have been taking full-time jobs and continuing their education at evening classes. The others have moved on for an additional three years in so-called polytechnic day schools in which a fourth to a third of the school time is devoted to shopwork and other forms of industrial training.

The one-year reduction was made in the period of polytechnic training.

Explaining the significance of the decree, the Education Minister of the Russian Republic, Yevgeny I. Afanasenko, said in an interview with the Tass press agency that the curriculum adjustments would involve mainly a reduction in the time spent in industrial training.

Soviet education has had a history of considerable experimentation.

Between 1919 and 1931, the basic school in the country provided nine years of noncompulsory polytechnic education, with stress on industrial training.

A reform in 1931 established 10-year schools, with seven years of attendance compulsory. Polytechnic training was deemphasized but never completely dropped.

Another education reform, in 1958, raised the compulsory schooling period to eight years from seven, with the transition to be completed by the fall of 1962, and extended the 10-year course to 11 years, with renewed emphasis on industrial training in the senior classes.

### System Was Criticized

MOSCOW, Aug. 12 (AP)—The Soviet decision to abandon the 11-year-school system follows several months of debate in the Soviet press over shortcomings in the industrial training program, introduced at Premier Khrushchev's insistence five years ago.

The Soviet leader pushed through a radical reform of the public education system under the slogan: "Strengthening the bonds between school and life."

Among criticisms of the 11-year system were these:

¶The students lost one year they could use to acquire a higher education or enter a profession.

¶Scholastic standards and educational levels decreased.

¶Vocational training was badly organized and students frequently stood around idly observing factory workers at the jobs.

¶The trades being taught were of no practical use or interest to the students and frequently too simple to justify three years of training.

August 13, 1964

# ENGINEERS MOVING TO TOP IN MOSCOW

## Future Leaders Expected to Be Industry Experts

MOSCOW, May 16 (AP)—The rule of self-made Communist party career men is ending in the Soviet Union and the country is moving toward an era of government by engineers.

The organization men of a new industrial society might provide a more technical, and therefore more reasonably stable, form of management for the Soviet Union.

The tendency in the past was toward expensive and often wasteful plunges toward officially favored solutions to economic problems. Those that succeeded made the nation strong, but some such as the effort to transform the semi-desert virgin lands into a breadbasket, involved enormous costs.

The next generation of leaders behind 70-year-old Premier Khrushchev is composed of technocrats, qualified as modern industrial managers, as well as Communist party organizers.

The two dozen men youner than Mr. Khrushchev who hold the most important positions in the nation today average 55 years of age. They have broad backgrounds of economic and party work plus foreign travel.

**New Leaders Better Educated**

This makes them a different breed from the Bolsheviks who created the Soviet Union almost half a century ago and their immediate successors, who were caught up in the early days of Communism and left with no time for formal education.

Mr. Khrushchev was one of those too absorbed in party work to acquire much book knowledge.

The new men were trained by the early leaders to build peasant Russia into a great industrial power.

There is a touch of the Western business man-politician about them, except for one thing: a cool reserve in personal manner. They lack Mr. Khrushchev's bouncy touch.

More than half the two dozen are engineers experienced in running factories or Government businesses. A professional soldier, a Communist party historian and three ideological journalists are included. Only five have had careers almost exclusively in party work. The usual career pattern for these men is:

Started work as an uneducated laborer, drawn into work for the new Communist regime in its tumultuous early days, joined the party, chosen by the party for technical education during the first five-year plan, graduated and rose to responsible industrial job, drawn increasingly into party duties, became full-time party official in middle age.

This sequence reverses a tendency in the early days of industrialization. Then, Stalin put party men in charge of technical operations—about which they knew nothing—to insure control.

Stalin kept his officials isolated from the world. The new men have traveled abroad on official missions to other Communist nations and to the Western world.

**Brezhnev Represents Change**

The most prominent example of the new men is Leonid I. Brezhnev, a 58-year-old metallurgical engineer by profession. He is chairman of the Presidium of the Supreme Soviet (Parliament), or chief of state.

More important, he is a member of the Central Committee's Presidium and its Secretariat, the seats of power.

Illness appears to have removed Frol R. Kozlov, 56, and also a metallurgical engineer, from the line of possible successors to Mr. Khrushchev.

Another strong contender is believed to be Nikolai V. Podgorny, 61, a sugar-plant engineer.

Beside Mr. Brezhnev, Mr. Podgorny and Mr. Kozlov, the only man younger than Mr. Khrushchev who belongs to both party Presidium and its Secretariat is Mikhail A. Suslov. This 62-year-old ideological specialist has made his career in party work.

May 17, 1964

LIFE UNDER KHRUSHCHEV

# SOVIET LEGALIZES ABORTIONS AGAIN

## Move After Twenty Years Viewed as Part of General Easing of Restrictions

Special to The New York Times.

MOSCOW, Nov. 30—The Soviet Union has legalized abortion for the first time in almost twenty years.

The step, announced today in the Government newspaper Izvestia, was interpreted as part of a general easing of restrictions on Soviet citizens. It was also linked with a net annual population increase of 3,000,000 persons that has more than offset the wartime depopulation.

The edict, passed last Wednesday by the presidium of the Supreme Soviet, says it is "possible to dispense at the present time with the prohibition of abortion carried out according to law."

Henceforth the state will rely on education and propaganda to encourage motherhood and prevent unnecessary abortions, the edict says.

It asserts that "unceasing awareness and the rising cultural level of women" in every walk of life have made it possible to abrogate Article 1 of the decree of June 27, 1936, prohibiting abortions.

**Relaxing Since 1954**

Under the Soviet criminal code, physicians were subject to one to two years' imprisonment if they carried out illegal abortions. An operation was authorized only when birth would be dangerous for the life or health of the mother or when it would make possible the inheritance of a serious illness.

Relaxation in the official attitude toward abortion began Aug. 5, 1954, with the issuance of a decree abolishing criminal responsibility for women who consented to abortions.

Provisions of the criminal code prescribing up to three years' imprisonment for unqualified persons who perform abortions, or physicians who perform the operation in unsanitary conditions, are maintained, today's edict declares. A penalty of two years in jail is still in effect for anyone who obliges a woman to have an abortion.

One clear aim of the new edict is to minimize the considerable number of abortions now carried out in the Soviet Union by quacks or other persons without access to medical institutions.

Abortion in the Soviet Union has had a checkered history. Between the Bolshevik Revolution and 1936 it was freely practiced, especially in major cities. With the onset of a more conservative trend, the legal ban was rigidly enforced.

By the end of 1955, the Government's drive to step up the birth rate through bachelor's taxes, family allotments and other devices appears to have met with signal success. Indeed, the population increase is far outstripping the Government's ability to provide more housing, schools and other facilities.

December 1, 1955

# Russian Journey: 'Sovietgrad' Is Not Moscow

**The Russian capital is one thing, but the typical provincial city is another, a tourist finds. Here is a composite picture of the places that lie beyond Moscow.**

By WELLES HANGEN

MOSCOW.

FOR the prospective traveler in the Soviet Union there is as yet no Baedecker guide to the country nor any equivalent of a Cook's tour of this enormous land. A month's rapid travel through the principal regions of the Soviet Union now open to foreigners is enough, however, to gather a few general impressions of use to the foreign visitor.

The first and inescapable conclusion is that Moscow is no more representative of the Soviet Union than Washington is of the United States or Paris of France.

The capital has its distinctive bustle, its Stalin-era skyscrapers, Red Square and the Kremlin, the foreign colony and many other adornments lacking in provincial Soviet cities. Moscow also boasts several reasonably comfortable hotels staffed with English and French speaking employes.

There is still no guidebook to the capital in English nor are maps of Moscow generally available. On the other hand, Intourist interpreters, private cars for hire and other tourist amenities are more readily obtainable here than in any outlying center.

Most important to the pleasure traveler, Moscow has an individuality and an atmosphere that set it apart from any other city. The same is true for Leningrad and Kiev, where the heritage of Czarist Russia has been only partially submerged.

But once the visitor leaves the three largest cities of the Soviet Union he must proceed slowly and with deliberation. Otherwise the provincial capitals and other outlying cities he visits will run together in the mental picture he takes home.

THE thing that most strikes the visitor from Western Europe or the United States is the depressing uniformity of Soviet cities. The sameness may be only brick-deep and easily discounted by the specialist in Russian affairs who knows the history of each town he visits. But for the uninitiate, Stalingrad, Rostov-on-Don, Dnepropetrovsk, Alma-Ata, Kuibyshev and most other cities of provincial Russia look as if they had been coined at the same mint.

Standardization is the rule everywhere—in the design of new buildings, in parks and playgrounds, in statues, on the main shopping street, in restaurants and hotels and, perhaps most of all, in the appearance of the people.

The visitor's first glimpse of Sovietgrad (a mythical composite of provincial cities) is uninspiring. His two-motored Aeroflot Ilyushin-14 lands on a sod strip and taxis to a low wooden terminal building. On the road into town the traveler passes squalid suburban slums made up of mud huts or log cabins as the climate of the region dictates. Moscow alone among Soviet cities has a sharp boundary marked by the city's outermost apartment buildings.

As he approaches Sovietgrad, the visitor beholds factories and barracks-like living quarters plastered with slogans exhorting the Soviet people to higher production or commanding, "Glory to the Builders of Communism!" In this respect, too, Moscow is exceptional; it has almost none of the propaganda posters that hang like barnacles on the walls of lesser cities.

Most of the anti-American posters that used to dot the countryside have now been supplanted by innocuous admonitions to promote peace or live in friendship with foreign peoples.

The center of Sovietgrad bears the unmistakable stamp of Soviet design. There is the familiar Park of Rest and Culture with its ornate archway entrance flanked by plaster busts of Lenin and Stalin. The same Communist luminaries, cast in the same or slightly different poses, inhabit practically every corner of the city.

THE main public buildings are grouped around a large open square, equipped with a public address system, where mass rallies are held. These buildings include the headquarters of the City Soviet (council), a massive concrete structure. The city theatre is patterned on Moscow's famous Bolshoi Theatre, with sturdy Greek columns at the entrance and a fancy baroque interior. An elaborate new railroad station surmounted by a luminous red star is another typical embellishment.

Sovietgrad, like other important provincial towns, has a hulking Univermag (department store) on the main shopping street. None of the dusty merchandise in its display windows would be likely to excite the enthusiasm of a New York department store shopper. Prices are high—more than 1,600 rubles for a cheap man's suit and 500 rubles for a rayon print dress. [The average monthly earnings of the Russian worker is estimated to be between 700 and 800 rubles.] But the windows aren't smudged enough to conceal the poor quality of the goods.

Smaller stores are equally unenticing. Food shops, called "gastronomes," have the habit of displaying plastic models of such products as cheese and salami. These are particularly unappetizing when they have become encrusted with dust and grime.

If the foreign visitor, or, for that matter, a Soviet citizen in Sovietgrad, makes a purchase at a state store it is because he needs something, not because anyone has cajoled him into buying by appealing to his ego or titillating his senses.

In contrast to Sovietgrad's somnolent state stores stands the city's turbulent free market. The free market is a vortex of trade and commerce while the state stores are a kind of commercial backwater. In the free market, peasant women from the surrounding countryside come to sell their produce at the best price they can obtain and artisans' cooperatives retail their manufactured goods.

Sovietgrad's apartment houses are typically formless products of Soviet architecture. Most are built of sandstone or other locally quarried rock. They seem to rise endlessly and almost every one is surmounted by two or three construction cranes. These solemn-

**STATE STORE**—A queue forms outside a confectionery store in Rostov.

**WELLES HANGEN**, a Times correspondent in Moscow, has traveled in the Soviet hinterland.

looking devices are as much a part of the Soviet urban landscape as television aerials are of the American city skyline.

CRANES and other evidences of construction are by no means confined to new buildings. Like the Pharoahs of ancient Egypt, the Soviet leaders believe in continuing the work of erecting monuments from generation to generation. Work is carried on sporadically on many buildings for years. Some are left only partially finished while construction equipment and manpower move to more urgent projects

Many apartment buildings have no facing over their basic brick construction. Girders rise abruptly from atop others where an additional story will someday be completed.

Hotels and restaurants in Sovietgrad are also products of the era of interchangeable parts. The newest and largest hostelry (frequently operated by Intourist, the official Government organization for foreign travel) is an ambitious structure with cavernous lobbies and great expanses of hallway. Electric lights blaze with naked fury along the main staircase which is laden with marble and mirrors to enhance the impression of spaciousness.

The visitor to Sovietgrad soon discovers that his hotel's newness does not guarantee the adequacy of its plumbing by American standards. Depreciation seems to set in almost at once on bathtubs, toilets and similar items.

When the visitor first enters his room, it is likely to be reverberating with the strains of Radio Moscow piped through a loudspeaker hooked into a central receiving set. The non-Russian-speaking guest can usually spare himself the lectures on veterinary science and related topics by yanking out the jackplug connecting his room loudspeaker. This is a much more difficult problem on Soviet trains and ships, where there is no getting away from the voice of Radio Moscow.

The same absence of individuality that characterizes Sovietgrad's hotels is apparent in its restaurants. These are grandiose high-ceilinged affairs with fancy draperies at the windows. The small, intimate restaurant seems to be a casualty of the Soviet system. The food is acceptable even for the foreigner unused to Russian specialties, but it lacks imagination and variety. Borsch, caviar, smoked salmon, lamb and veal recur with monotonous regularity.

THIS is not to say that regional dishes have disappeared. In the Ukraine the visitor will be welcomed with the traditional bread and salt and he will taste a delicious cherry dessert of local origin. In Soviet Central Asia he will find excellent shish-kebab and other Turkish preparations. In Tashkent he can sample some of the most delightful melons and grapes in the world. But the leitmotif of Soviet food remains stolidly Russian wherever one goes.

A walk through Sovietgrad's main square or *(Continued)* along its broad sun-drenched boulevards will convince the visitor that the city is surprisingly clean. Nor will he find beggars or evidence of professional prostitution in the areas frequented by foreigners.

Traffic is usually heavy in the downtown area but it thins out rapidly as one moves toward the outskirts of town. Sovietgrad's main street is noisy not only from honking horns but as a result of strategically located loudspeakers,

"Dress in Sovietgrad is shabby and standardized to the American eye."

through which music and the human voice pour relentlessly from 6 A. M. until midnight.

Sovietgrad and its sister cities show more evidence of town planning than most American urban areas. Factories are almost invariably on the outskirts of town, while the center is reserved for commercial and residential purposes. The streets are broader and there is more attention to planting trees and flower beds in the heart of town than there is in comparable American cities.

DRESS in Sovietgrad is shabby and standardized by comparison with American styles. The peasant women wear colored scarves and frayed wool coats and the men present themselves in ill-fitting double-breasted store suits. If Sovietgrad were in the Ukraine, many open-necked Ukrainian shirts with the embroidered stripe down the front would be in evidence. If it were in Central Asia, a large proportion of the men would be wearing the traditional Moslem tubeteka skullcap. Generally, however, the manufactured uniformity of Soviet clothing overshadows regional variations in dress.

Racial characteristics also seem to have taken on a common mold. The Slavic face and figure predominate even in the major cities of non-Slavic republics of the Soviet Union.

One of the most remarkable things about Sovietgrad is the way it seems to have severed its links with the Czarist past. The town is full of pre-revolutionary buildings, but history, as enshrined in monuments, statues and plaques on public places, starts with the October Revolution. This truncated past makes it more difficult for the foreign visitor to get his bearings in a Soviet city because he looks in vain for evidence of the Russian history he learned in school.

IN most Western European cities the traveler would find something familiar in the history of the town cathedral or the palace of a former ruling prince. In Sovietgrad this process of self-orientation is impossible. Those churches that have survived frequently serve as warehouses or museums and seem to offer little of the attraction of places of worship in other countries. Similarly, mosques in Soviet Central Asia are astonishingly difficult to find and once the visitor has sought them out he is disappointed by the evident neglect they have suffered.

Sovietgrad, as here described, would pass for almost any Soviet provincial center. It particularly fits such depressing urban agglomerations as Kuibyshev, Dnepropetrovsk, Kharkov, Krasnodar, Zaporozhe, Rostov-on-Don and Novorossiisk.

DESPITE the deadening influence of uniformity in Soviet city planning, the visitor will find many things to commend a trip into the provinces of the Soviet Union. For one thing, he will have an incomparable opportunity to observe the true friendliness of the Soviet people.

In Moscow and Leningrad the visitor will find himself restricted to a relatively small circle of Soviet citizens specially designated to cater to foreigners. But in outlying areas he will have an opportunity to mix with Soviet people of every description and observe how immune they have been to a decade of anti-American propaganda.

# The People of Russia

## *Moscow Bus Driver, a Georgian Doctor And a Writer Talk With U. S. Newsman*

By **WILLIAM J. JORDEN**
Special to The New York Times.

MOSCOW.

Vladimir Nikolayevich Lyutikov is a Soviet bus driver.

For the last twenty-two years he has been driving for Moscow's Bus Division No. 1. In all that time he has had no serious accidents. He has won two driving awards. His proudest possession is a gold watch that he won in a 300,000-mile driving competition based on low gasoline consumption, absence of major repairs and safety.

With his long experience and excellent record, Mr. Lyutikov could hardly be considered an average driver. But his way of life, his problems and his attitudes are not drastically different from those of thousands of his fellow-citizens who drive trucks, buses and taxis. His standard of living is higher than that of most drivers, but not so high as to make him exceptional.

Vladimir Nikolayevich, as he is known to his friends, is a small, slender man, about five feet six inches tall and weighing about 130 pounds. He has sandy hair, gray-blue eyes, and the muscular hands and arms of bus drivers the world over. He takes himself and his job seriously.

He talks about his work the way he would explain the functioning of an engine to a group of students—precisely, methodically, never moving on to a second part until the first ha[illegible]n completely and carefully described.

Vladimir was born in 1911 in the Vologda district of Northern European Russia. His father, Nikolai, was a forest warden. Early in life, Vladimir and his brother Pavel, seven years his junior, learned from their father the skills of hunting, fishing, skiing, and other outdoor activities.

Vladimir rarely gets a chance to go hunting now. But he still loves to tramp through the woods and to gather mushrooms for the family table. And in the winter, he takes his young son Boris skiing, as his father took him.

Vladimir Lyutikov had to go to work when he was still very young. His father was disabled during World War I, and died a few years later. The elder son was able to finish only four years in the village school. His mother died in 1929, and the following year he was one of thousands of young men recruited to help on construction projects in Moscow.

"I wanted more education," he said, "so I worked as a laborer during the day and went to school at night. I did it for seven years."

In 1934 he went to a school for drivers. In the Soviet Union, drivers learn much more than traffic signals, how to shift gears and otherwise drive a car. They learn how to take an engine apart and put it together again. A Soviet bus driver or truck driver is expected to be able to perform all but the most specialized repairs on his own vehicle.

### Drove Bus During War

When he finished drivers' school, Mr. Lyutikov was hired by Bus Division No. 1, one of six in Moscow. That was in 1935. He has been there ever since. Even during World War II, Mr. Lyutikov drove buses carrying soldiers and wounded during the defense of Moscow.

Bus drivers, like workers in most Soviet industries, operate in teams. Mr. Lyutikov and two other drivers make up such a team. They take turns driving the same bus. Safety and maintenance records are kept for the team, not for the individual. The team system is designed to stimulate competition for higher efficiency and lower maintenance costs.

One member of the team goes to work at 5:30 A. M. and drives until 3 P. M. The second driver takes over at 3 and works until 12:30 A. M. The third member has a day off. Mr. Lyutikov and the other drivers work the early shift two days in a row, have a day off, then work the late shift two days. When not actually driving, they are on stand-by duty or doing repair work in the bus garage. The drivers work an average of forty-four or forty-five hours a week.

Vladimir Nikolayevich and the members of his brigade drive a ZIS bus (the "S" stands for Stalin, but the factory has been renamed for the engineer Likhachev and the new buses and automobiles it produces are now called ZIL). It looks very much like the city buses in New York, except that it is smaller and the driver's compartment is separated from the passenger section by a partition. A girl conductor rides in the passenger section to collect fares and announce the stops.

The ZIS buses gradually are being replaced by new Model 158 ZIL's. These have glass for two-thirds of the roof area so that passengers can see the sights as they ride along. The old buses are being sent to the provinces.

Mr. Lyutikov said he drove about 110 miles a day and that he normally carried 800-900 passengers—more than 1,000 on Sundays and holidays, but fewer on Mondays when most stores are closed.

### Data on Earnings

Drivers earn 1,600 rubles a month ($400 at the official rate and $160 at the tourist rate of exchange). In addition, they are paid differentials according to their job rating; as a first class driver, Mr. Lyutikov receives 141 rubles. A seniority differential adds about 140 rubles. Bonuses and special awards further increase his income.

Mr. Lyutikov averaged 2,200 rubles a month last year. That is enough to buy a television set or a better-than-average Soviet suit of clothes. It is one-tenth of the purchase price of a Pobeda, the most popular Soviet automobile. It will buy eighty-eight bottles of the best vodka, or five pairs of shoes.

As a union member Mr. Lyutikov gets 90 per cent of his salary when he is on sick-leave; a non-member would get 60 per cent. All the drivers of Bus Division No. 1 belong to the union. If a member goes to a rest home or sanitarium for his vacation, the union pays part of the cost.

Mr. Lyutikov and his wife, Maria Aleksandrovna, and their two children live in a small apartment in a building completed only last year. It is situated in Rublevo, a suburb about twenty miles west of the center of Moscow. They have one room, about 15 by 25 feet, that serves as living room, dining room and bedroom. They have a small kitchen and their own bathroom. The apartment has steam heat.

Their rent is nominal, only 23 rubles a month or slightly more than 1 per cent of Mr. Lyutikov's salary. Their electricity bill is 25 to 30 rubles a month; water is 2 rubles. They have no gas supply. Cooking is done on a hot plate and water is heated for the bath by a wood stove in the bathroom. They have a television set with a nine-inch screen and an electric washing machine.

One of their family's major expenditures is for food, as it is in most Soviet families. Most or all of one average worker's income is required to feed a medium-sized family.

### Wife Works as a Nurse

As in most Soviet families, both husband and wife work. Maria Aleksandrovna is a nurse and works at a nursery near their home. She earns 700 rubles plus a 350-ruble seniority differential.

The Lyutikovs' daughter Alia, 17, has just finished high school and is preparing to enter a medical school this fall. She was visiting friends in Odessa the day I called on the parents, who showed me her graduation picture. Her parents want her to be an oculist.

"It is a good profession," her father said. "Lots of people have eye trouble."

Boris, 14, was at Pioneer camp for the summer. The Pioneer youth group is the training ground for the Komsomol (Young Communist League). His parents showed me examples of his woodworking skill—an elaborately cut picture frame, a butterfly and other objects.

"They make wonderful gifts for his friends," his mother said proudly, "and he does not have to spend money when he wants to give someone a present."

Mr. Lyutikov said he has a month's paid vacation each year. His wife gets the same length of vacation but they often do not go away together, if they go away.

"I like the Caucasus," he said, "and she likes the Crimea. In 1951 I went to Sochi and in 1954 I was near Sukhumi. My wife likes Yalta."

As we talked, Maria Aleksandrovna was busy in the kitchen. I soon learned why. She began to bring in dishes and soon the table was covered. It is an old rule of Russian hospitality that a guest shall not leave until he has had food and drink at the host's table.

I was told that everything on

## A Note by the Reporter

The articles in this series are an attempt to describe living conditions in the Soviet Union in human terms rather than statistically or ideologically.

As much as possible, I have written from the viewpoint of the Soviet people themselves. When a home or apartment is described as "comfortable," for example, it means that a Russian would consider it so. A "high" income is one that permits a man to live well by Soviet standards. Only one who has spent some time in the Soviet Union and has come to know the people can understand how completely cut off most of them are from any scale of measurement other than their own.

No attempt was made in these articles to explore the political attitudes of those who are described. The sources of information available to the Soviet people are severely restricted.

I would not feel free to repeat it if any of those interviewed had expressed opposition or complaints, for political opposition is still not welcome in the Soviet Union.

There are no eleven persons, or even eleven hundred for that matter, whose stories could tell the whole truth about their country and its life. But these eleven stories may make the Soviet people a bit more real and understandable.

the table had been produced in the Lyutikovs' own garden or kitchen. They have a garden plot about 200 square yards in area, which is their main hobby. All the raspberries, cherries, cucumbers, tomatoes and other fruits and vegetables on the table were their own. Maria Aleksandrovna had baked thick sweet rolls. Only the fish and vodka came from the store.

"I would like to make a toast," said Mr. Lyutikov. "We are glad to welcome a representative of the United States to our home. I hope you will write about us honestly and truthfully. I hope we can all understand each other better and that there never will be a war between us. To your health!"

I said, in response, that there were few people in the United States or any other country who would not subscribe to that wish, that no one in his right mind wanted war, and that talk about other countries' plotting to attack the Soviet Union was not true.

"I hope not," he said. "We have had enough of war. We want no more."

## A Georgian Physician

TIFLIS.

Leonid Grigorievich Dvali is a Soviet physician.

He was born here in the capital of Soviet Georgia, Stalin's homeland, thirty years ago. He is the only child of Grigori and Nina Dvali.

Young Leonid grew up in far more prosperous circumstances than the average young Soviet boy or girl. His father, a construction engineer, lectures in a technical school. He has been honored by the state for his teaching work. Leonid's mother, an attractive woman of 51, is a textile engineer who works for the Georgian Ministry of Local Industry.

### Medical Training Shorter

With their higher-than-average income and education the Dvalis were able to give their son encouragement and opportunities often denied young people. They exposed him to good music from his childhood. There were always plenty of books. Learning was encouraged and Leonid had excellent marks in school.

I asked him how he became a physician.

"We had several neighbors who were doctors," he said. "They used to take me to visit the clinics. I just fell in love with medicine and never wanted to be anything but a doctor."

When he finished the first ten years of school, Leonid passed the entrance examinations for the Tiflis Medical School. Unlike the United States, where would-be physicians must take pre-medical training in college before going on to medical school, the Soviet Union starts the professional training of physicians, lawyers and others after they have completed the equivalent of high school. A physician in the United States must spend nineteen years in school; his Soviet counterpart fifteen.

The medical course is five years and on completion the graduate is authorized to practice medicine. However, he must have additional training if he expects to specialize.

During his medical training, Leonid decided he wanted to become a chest surgeon. That meant additional study and work. When he finished medical school, he went to Moscow. There he worked for eight more years as an interne in clinics of Moscow medical schools.

Dr. Dvali performed his first operation, an appendectomy, during his first year at a Moscow clinic. He has been operating ever since. Before he could receive his certification as a surgeon, he had to pass four examinations—in surgery, physiology, a foreign language (he took German), and dialectical materialism (the "philosophy" of Marxism).

After his eight years in Moscow, Dr. Dvali returned to his home town to work as a chest surgeon in the First Polyclinic of Tiflis. He is also doing research for his thesis which, if approved, will make him a Candidate of Medical Science. Later, he hopes to become a Doctor of Medical Science, which will mean increased pay and prestige.

Physicians' salaries in the Soviet Union are rather low except for those who acquire advanced degrees. When he went to work in the Moscow clinics, Dr. Dvali received only 650 rubles a month. That is barely enough to buy food for the average couple. After five years, his pay was automatically increased to 850 rubles. Two years hence, he will receive his last automatic increase, to 1,150.

### Research Work Published

Like many Soviet physicians, Dr. Dvali supplements his income by publishing articles about his research work in medical journals. He has had four such articles published in the last year or so and each of them brought in 700 to 800 rubles. He has just finished a long article on "Principles of Post-Operative Treatment in Lung Surgery" for which he expects to be paid 1,200 rubles.

If a physician works in a particularly dangerous or potentially harmful field, such as X-rays or the treatment of infectious diseases, he receives additional payment equal to 15 per cent of his base pay.

Dr. Dvali is on duty six hours a day, six days a week at the surgical clinic. But he said that he usually operates on only three of those days and performs three or four operations in a day. His specialty as a chest surgeon does not keep him busy. He therefore performs other operations; in fact, he said, about one-half of his operations are appendectomies.

A person who gets sick in the Soviet Union usually goes to a clinic operated by the Ministry of Health. Cases requiring hospitalization or surgery are referred to a polyclinic or hospital. As a surgeon, Dr. Dvali sees only those patients assigned to him by other physicians.

In the Soviet Union, all costs of surgery and hospitalization are borne by the state. The patient pays nothing for his bed, food, nursing care or medicine. A patient who is not hospitalized does have to buy his own medicine. Persons suffering from diseases requiring lengthy treatment, such as tuberculosis, must also pay to stay at a sanitarium although they may get some union benefit.

Leonid Grigorievich is a rather tall, rugged and darkly handsome man. Like nearly all his fellow Georgians, he has dark hair and eyes, and a black mustache. His wife, Lia Nikolayevna, 27, is a Tiflis girl who met Leonid when they were both in school here. She is a dentist.

### Wife Away on Vacation

The Dvalis have a son, Merabi, who is 8 years old. He and his mother were away for a short vacation the day I talked with the doctor. Lia worked in a dental clinic of the Ministry of Construction in Moscow while her husband studied surgery. She brought her instruments with her when they returned to Georgia and expects to resume work here soon.

I noticed that Dr. Dvali smoked cigarettes and asked whether much work had been done in the Soviet Union on the possible connection between smoking and lung cancer.

"Some of our doctors are studying the problem now," he said, "They seem to think there is some connection, but it has not been proved. There have been a number of reports on the matter, but nothing conclusive. I still smoke."

Like all Soviet physicians, Leonid gets twenty-four days' paid vacation a year plus four Sundays. He, his wife and their son usually go to Gagra, a Black Sea resort. He plays tennis three or four times a week to keep in shape.

The Dvalis live with his parents in a pleasant and larger-than-average apartment. The parents have one bedroom; the young couple and their son another. There is a fairly large living room and a kitchen and bath. The rent is 50 rubles and 25 kopecks a month, including electricity and gas. The mother said the family spent 50 rubles a day for food.

### Proud of Refrigerator

One of the family's proudest possessions is a new refrigerator, and the doctor's mother served home-made ice cream from it as we talked. The doctor is saving his money to buy an automobile. At his present salary, it will take two years' worth of base pay.

But the total family income is high enough to enable him to save much of his earnings, and he will be able to save even more when his wife begins to work again. Until he buys a car, the doctor will continue to go to the clinic by trolley-bus.

Dr. Dvali said that medicine was one of the most popular professions in the Soviet Union.

"Students are eager to study medicine," he said. "They are not discouraged by the difficult entrance examinations to medical school. Here in Tiflis there are six candidates for every vacancy in the first-year class. But that does not stop them from applying."

Dr. Dvali is interested not only in practicing medicine but in passing on his skill to the next generation. He works now with young medical students in the clinic. And some day, he hopes, he will be a full-fledged teacher of surgery. On the basis of his record to date, he seems almost certain to attain that goal.

## A Leading Soviet Writer

MOSCOW.

Vsevolod Ivanov is a Soviet writer.

He is a chubby man of medium height, the kind doctors are inclined to advise to lose a few pounds. He has light blue, twinkling eyes and thinning white hair. If he had a beard, he would be a perfect Santa Claus.

As a writer, and one whose works have always found favor with the Communist party, Mr. Ivanov is a member of the Soviet élite. He recently completed a book on which he was paid 120,000 rubles for the magazine rights and another 120,000 as advance royalties for the book itself.

He gets 6 per cent of the receipts at the box office for a play of four acts, wherever or whenever the play is produced. He is still collecting royalties for his best-known play, "The Armored Train," written thirty years ago.

He is now working on the script for a motion picture for which he will be paid 80,000 rubles plus a percentage of the box-office receipts. Because the Soviet Government collects most of its revenue from the turnover tax on transactions, it collects a relatively small amount from income taxes. Despite his high income, Mr. Ivanov pays only 13 per cent tax.

### Life of An Adventurer

Mr. Ivanov's life has been as varied and interesting as many of the exciting stories he has written. One of his most widely read novels could well be the story of his life; it was called "Travels of An Adventurer." His life has been nothing if not adventurous.

Vsevolod was born in the small village of Lebyazhye on the Irtysh River in East Kazakhstan sixty-two years ago. His father was a village school teacher and, as the writer said, "a very poor man." But he remembers that his father loved to travel and that that love was instilled early in Vsevolod and his brother.

In his youth, the future writer did a variety of jobs. He worked as a printer's assistant, was a sailor, worked in a coal mine, and joined a circus. With the circus, Vsevolod took on all comers as a boxer; then, after being badly beaten by one of his challengers, he became a magician.

Not long ago, when he became head of the examination committee of the Literary Institute in Moscow, Mr. Ivanov had to give particulars of his own education. He simply wrote: "Three years of village school." Always an avid reader, he picked up his education as he went from job to job.

During the Civil War that raged through Russia in the wake of the Bolshevik Revolution of 1917, young Vsevolod commanded a machine-gun detachment of the Red Guard, the forerunner of the Red Army. He lived and fought in the underground and the experience inspired his first serious literary work, a short novel called "Partisan." It was published in 1921.

**An Interest in India**

His contact with magic in the circus promoted an interest in India. The result was a trek across Central Asia with some companions and later a book called "We Walked to India."

Altogether Mr. Ivanov has written about twenty-five books. He is the author of fifteen plays, twelve of which have been published and six actually produced. Five of his books are collections of stories. The rest are novels. He is busy preparing a collection of his works for publication.

In the Soviet Union, professional writers get their start in much the same way as in other countries. They write and try to interest a publisher. They usually have a full-time job in their early stages. Many are teachers or newspaper men; others, like Mr. Ivanov, may be doing odd jobs. He was a soldier when he wrote his first serious book.

There is a one big difference, of course, between the roads to a literary career in the Soviet Union and elsewhere. A Soviet writer must produce works that not only interest readers, but, more important, please the Communist party. Literary works are judged by their political flavor at least as much as by their literary merit.

Mr. Ivanov is not a party member. But like any successful Soviet writer he must walk the tightrope of acceptability laid down by the party for writers. In the past it was impossible and now it is only barely possible to get a work published if it deviates from official norms. It is even harder to get something published if a previous work has been criticized in the party press or literary journals.

The party formula for a successful work of art, be it a painting, a novel, or a piece of music, is called "Socialist realism." No one has ever defined that phrase very successfully. In general, it prescribes that art should be realistic, but at the same time hopeful and inspiring. Individuals can be criticized, but not the Communist party, the Government or the system as such.

**Sees Hopeful Trend**

Mr. Ivanov professes to find no objection to the system of judging literary and other art works from a political point of view. He feels, too, that the area of freedom within which Soviet writers work is gradually broadening. He is hopeful the trend will continue.

The Soviet writer has a large, six-room apartment in Moscow but he rarely stays there. It is used by his two sons. One of the sons is a physician, the other is at 30 one of the youngest and most promising Soviet classical scholars and a specialist in the extinct Hittite language of Asia Minor.

The Ivanovs also have a daughter, 18, who is studying foreign languages [illegible] the university. Mme. Ivanov knows French and has done translations.

Mr. Ivanov and his wife live in a country or dacha, about twenty miles from Moscow. Mme. Ivanov is a tall and stately woman. She has white hair now and must have been an extremely beautiful woman when she was younger. She still is striking-looking and has the grace and charm of the true aristocrat.

The urge to travel is still a driving force in Mr. Ivanov's make-up. Last year, to celebrate the news that his latest book was to be published, he got on a plane and flew to Chita. Then he traveled by car more than 3,000 miles through the Chita Region and Buryat-Mongolia.

He climbed mountains and engaged in his favorite hobby, the collection of unusual and semi-precious stones. His prize was a large piece of jade. He spent some time with fishermen along the shores of Lake Baikal.

**Impressed by Baikal**

"I have seen much of beauty in my life," the writer said, "but I was truly impressed by Baikal. It was the first time I had been there and it was lovely."

He traveled through Siberia for more than two months, then returned to Moscow for three days. He was off immediately for Czechoslovakia.

"I went there to cure all the ills I had picked up on my trip," he said with a laugh. "There was a big contrast between the Siberian forest and Czechoslovakia, from a completely wild area to civilization and culture."

It was after this trip that he decided to continue his work on "Travels of An Adventurer." He wrote the first volume thirty years ago. The second was finished last year. Now he is writing a third volume. The travels continue, the adventures go on, and books by Mr. Ivanov come from the presses.

But despite his vigor, and his love of travel, the 62-year-old author thinks more and more of rounding out his career. As we sat in his study at the dacha one bitterly cold day last winter, he leaned back in his chair and said:

"I began my writing with poetry and I will probably end with it. In youth and old age there is a strong feeling for life that is best expressed in verse. In between there is a certain pessimism."

We moved from the study to the dining-room. A chill north wind rattled the windows and swept the snow in small clouds. But inside the Ivanov dacha there was warmth, good talk and good food. There was the feeling, on both sides, I think, that more meetings of the kind we were having might slowly bring about understanding.

August 18, 1957

# The People of Russia

## *An Interview With the Communist Party Leader of a Moscow Borough*

By WILLIAM J. JORDEN
Special to The New York Times.

MOSCOW.

Aleksei Nikolayevich Nikiforov is a Communist party official.

He is one of that relatively small but highly disciplined minority that runs the Soviet Union. For, though only 7,200,000 Soviet citizens belong to the party, that 3½ per cent of the population wields virtually complete authority over every important phase of life in the country.

As secretary of the party committee in the Stalin Borough of Moscow, he is something of a city councilman, party boss, father confessor, dictator and public servant to 300,000 people.

Big problems and small, everything from the political orientation of the people in his borough to a factory worker's disagreement with his wife, are likely to come to Mr. Nikiforov's notice and demand his attention.

**It is up to him to listen to** the complaints of the people living in his borough and to try to do something about them. It is also his responsibility to transmit to those in his borough the plans and policies of the top level of the party, to explain them and to arouse some enthusiasm among the people in support of them.

His job is not unlike that of political workers in any country. There is at least one important and obvious difference, however. There is no opposition down the street competing with Mr. Nikiforov for the people's attention and support. The one-party system, the Communist system, takes care of that.

Aleksei Nikolayevich is a tense, voluble man. His sharp, piercing eyes move quickly behind rimmed glasses. He is high-strung and nervous, though probably more so in talking with a foreigner than he would be at a party meeting. His conversation is filled with the clichés that are the special vocabulary of communism.

He was born 52 years ago in what was then St. Petersburg, now Leningrad. His father, who died in 1920, used to make piano strings in a piano factory. Aleksei's mother was a textile worker. She died in 1941.

Aleksei completed nine years of school. At the age of 16, he went to work in a plant producing transformers and generators. In 1927, he served two years in the Red Army. After his stint in the army, Mr. Nikiforov came to Moscow and went to work in a Moscow electrical goods plant. He studied at night and became an electrician.

**Daughter in Aircraft Plant**

At the Moscow factory he met a young secretary named Ilyena and married her. That was twenty-five years ago. They have two children. Their daughter Valentina, 23, was graduated from an aeronautical school and is working as an engineer-designer in an aircraft plant. Their son Yevgeni, 15, enters the last year of school this year.

Mr. Nikiforov, like most Communist officials, was reluctant to talk much about his private life. When I asked whether I might visit his home and meet his family, he said they were at their country house (dacha) and, in any case, he was too busy. When I asked what kind of apartment he had, he described it as "average," then went into a lengthy discourse about what the Government and party were doing to alleviate the country's serious housing shortage.

Aleksei Nikolayevich joined the Communist party at a relatively late stage, when he was 35 years old. But once in the movement, he progressed rapidly. He joined the party cell at the Moscow plant in 1940. The following year he was chosen to be first secretary of the cell's executive committee. Because of the size of the cell, the job of secretary was a full-time post.

He joined the Communist party, as all its members must, through the recommendation of persons already in the movement. To join the party, you must have the endorsements of three persons who have been Communists for at least three years. They must have known the candidate for at least one year at his job and be familiar with him personally.

I asked Mr. Nikiforov why he had become a Communist.

"I decided to join the party as a matter of conscience," he replied. "I wanted to take part in the Communist construction of our country. Our party is and always will be in the vanguard of the workers' movement and of Communist construction. I wanted to be in it."

Mr. Nikiforov said he had had no theoretical training in communism before he joined the party. Since then, however, he has worked hard to make up for lost time. He said he read the works of Lenin and spent a good deal of time studying the party journals and the classic works of communism, even during the war. Later, he qualified for and was graduated from the Higher Party School run by the Communist party's Central Committee.

"Any person is eligible for membership in the party," Mr. Nikiforov said, "if he does not exploit labor, if he accepts the rules of the party and if he agrees to carry out party decisions. Admission is a highly individual matter. Not all who apply are admitted; only the best."

In small party cells, the members elect a secretary for one year. It is not a full-time job, however, and the man continues his regular work in addition to carrying out his party duties. In a large cell, such as an electrical goods plant, the membership picks a committee of from five to eleven members and that group in turn selects its own secretary.

The salary of a secretary of a party cell depends on the size of the cell and is fixed by the party's Central Committee. Mr. Nikiforov earned 1,400 rubles. He said he received 3,300 rubles as secretary of the Stalin Borough Committee. That is $330 at the tourist exchange rate, an extremely high salary by Soviet standards.

Salaries of full-time party employes are paid from the party treasury. Dues are paid by members according to their income. Mr. Nikiforov said party members earning less than 500 rubles pay one-half of 1 per cent as party dues. For those getting between 500 and 1,000 rubles, 1 per cent goes to the party. From 1,000 to 2,000, the rate is 2 per cent. And those earning more than 2,000 pay 3 per cent.

What does a full-time party worker do to earn his salary? According to Mr. Nikiforov, his main task is "the political education of members and candidate members." He must encourage the propagation of Marxist-Leninist theories. He must organize party work and enforce "standards of party behavior."

In a factory, he must be interested in production plans and do everything he can to encourage workers to fulfill their assigned norms. He must explain to them why they must work hard and what the ultimate goals of the party are.

During the recent upheaval in the upper echelons of the Communist party, when veteran leaders like Georgi M. Malenkov, Vyacheslav M. Molotov and Lazar M. Kaganovich were expelled from their positions of leadership, one of Mr. Nikiforov's jobs was to meet with party members and non-party workers to explain why the Communist party had acted as it had.

On a typical day recently, Mr. Nikiforov arrived at his office at 9 A. M., one hour earlier than usual, to meet with a delegation from a group of factories in his borough. The most important question they took up was the matter of releasing some factory labor temporarily to go to Siberia to help bring in the harvest on the newly developed grain lands.

Then he did some paper work and met a few callers from local party organizations. Later in the day, a secretary of the party cell and the deputy director of a factory came to ask him to appeal to the Moscow City Council to speed up the allocation of ground for new housing for workers. Mr. Nikiforov is a city councilman and also a member of the council's executive committee, which performs the functions of Mayor.

At 3 P. M. he went to a meeting of the city council, which discussed the problem of improving public transportation. The council members talked about measures to improve cleanliness in the city. The meeting lasted until 8 P. M.

Mr. Nikiforov said he rarely gets home early. Party officials from subordinate units in the borough frequently come to see him after the regular working day is over, at 6, 7 or even 8 P. M. There frequently are meetings at night.

In his spare time, when he can find it, the party official likes to go to the theatre or to hear good music. He is an avid reader.

"Even when I am very busy," he said, "I usually stay up reading until 2 o'clock in the morning."

He gets one full month of paid vacation. For the last two years he and his wife have gone to Carlsbad, Czechoslovakia, for their holiday.

August 20, 1957

# The People of Russia

## A School Teacher in Soviet Armenia Mingles Family Life With Her Work

By WILLIAM J. JORDEN

Special to The New York Times.

ERIVAN.

Siranush Martirosyan is a Soviet school teacher.

For more than thirty years, she has taught Armenian language and literature to students, first in a village school and then in the school system of Erivan, the Armenian capital. She became eligible for a pension five years ago, but she continues to work "because I cannot imagine doing anything else."

Miss Martirosyan—like many Soviet women, particularly in the professions, she retained her maiden name after her marriage—was born in 1902 in the Armenian village of Karaklis, now the town of Kirovakan. Her father was the village blacksmith. Her sister went to an agricultural school and now is an agronomist on a collective farm near Kirovakan.

Siranush attended four years of elementary school in the village and then came to Erivan for five more years of middle school. During her school years, she was influenced by one of her teachers, Derenik Demirchyan, a well-known figure in Armenian literature, and decided then to become a teacher.

In 1922, she was admitted to the State University in Erivan and four years later she was graduated from the Department of Philology with a certificate as a middle school instructor.

For two years, she taught Armenian to students in a village school at Nerkin Akhta, about twenty-five miles from Erivan. In 1928, she came to Erivan to teach. For the last twenty years she has worked at Public School 19, where I met and talked with her.

Siranush Martirosyan looks like a schoolteacher. She has a gentle and intelligent face. Her gray hair is combed straight back and rolled into a bun. She dresses plainly but neatly. Her dark eyes look serious but tolerant, and they twinkle when she smiles.

In the Soviet school system, teachers of outstanding ability receive the rating of Teacher of Merit. The teachers' union makes the recommendation and relays it to the school principal for approval. The principal's report is sent to the Ministry of Education of the republic, in this case Armenia, for final action. It was through this process that Miss Martirosyan became a Teacher of Merit.

When she began teaching, she received 700 rubles a month. At the time of her official retirement, she was getting 1,400 rubles. Now, for teaching fourteen hours a week instead of the usual eighteen, she receives 800 rubles. In addition, she gets 414 in pension payments. If she were not working at all, her pension would be 800 rubles. That is $80 at the tourist rate of exchange. It is enough to buy food for a couple for about a month, or two pairs of shoes, or an average dress.

### Two Shifts in School

At School No. 19, students have four hours of classwork in addition to exercise and sports. Because of a shortage of school space two shifts of students use the school. One group goes to school at 8:30 A. M. in the winter and half an hour earlier in summer and fall. The second shift starts at 2:30 P. M.

School is taught usually in the language of the given Soviet republic. Thus, in the schools of the Armenian Republic, teaching is done in Armenian. Russian is taught as a required second language. There also are schools where all instruction is in Russian for the children of Russians and any others who prefer to study in that language. In Russian-language schools in Armenia, the local language is a required subject.

Siranush teaches students of the eighth and ninth grades five hours each, two hours of language and three of Armenian literature. She teaches a class of tenth-year students four hours weekly. The size of the classes ranges from twenty to twenty-five students each.

Miss Martirosyan was married the year she finished her training at the university. Her husband was a classmate, Morus Khasratyan. He teaches history at a teachers' college in Erivan. His salary is a comfortable 3,500 rubles. University or college teachers receive two or three times as much as secondary school teachers.

The Khasratyans have two sons. The older, Bakur, was born in 1927 and he now is a boxing coach at the Institute for Physical Culture. He is married and has a daughter, Narin, 16 months.

The younger son, Murat, is 22 and is now in his fifth year at the Polytechnic Institute, where he is studying architecture. His mother said he was an excellent student and had won the coveted gold medal for excellence in secondary school. Murat lives at home with his parents.

Like virtually all Soviet citizens, the Khasratyans have a

housing problem, but it is far less acute than for most. They have a two-room apartment with their own kitchen and bath, far more space than the average family. They have steam heat and use electricity for cooking. Their rent is about 100 rubles a month in the winter and 70 to 80 in the summer. Their major outlays are for clothing and food.

"I love to cook," Siranush said, "and my husband often helps me with the marketing. Every Saturday night we get together at the home of one of the teachers for dinner. There is quite a competition to see who is the best cook."

Siranush plays the violin and her son Murat is a pianist, so there are frequent duets in the Khasratyan home. The whole family loves music. The father's favorite pastime is chess and his fellow teachers frequently drop in for a game. The father and son also play together often.

"My husband used to win every time," the mother said, "but now our son is a match for him. They are about equal."

As teachers, the Khasratyans get two full months' vacation each year. Two years ago they went with their son to Moscow, Leningrad and Riga. Siranush has a heart ailment and she went for treatment to a sanitarium in Georgia last year.

When Siranush is not talking about her family, she is happiest talking of the many students who have passed through her classes. She speaks of them with pride: the promising young physician, the candidate in mathematics, the lecturer in architectural history. She is probably proudest of those who have gone into teaching, like one of her students who recently joined the faculty at School 19, following in her footsteps.

August 21, 1957

# The People of Russia

## A Visit With a Stalingrad Steelmaker, Key Worker in High-Priority Industry

By WILLIAM J. JORDEN

Special to The New York Times.

STALINGRAD.

Ivan Vasilievich Gerasimenko is a Soviet steel worker.

I saw him first bathed in the red-orange light of an open-hearth furnace at the Red October steel plant in Stalingrad. He looked at the flame with a practiced eye, turned and picked up a shovel. Then, with the smooth motions and quick grace of stokers and steelmakers, he threw several shovelfuls of coke into the furnace.

He turned for a moment to rest his eyes from the blinding light of the fiery furnace. Then he signaled the crane operator to put another load of pig iron and scrap into one of the glowing openings. Ivan was busy at his trade; he was making steel.

Steelmaking is one of the most favored of industries in the Soviet Union. Probably only nuclear energy and arms producion have a higher priority. Heavy industry is the heart of the Communists' economic program, and steel is the basis of heavy industry. It is all part of the Kremlin's plan to catch up with and surpass the United States in industrial output. Ivan is playing a small but important part in that program.

### An Enthusiastic Worker

He plays his role eagerly, enthusiastically, as younger men play basketball or soccer. He has the same pride when his work team produces more steel than the others in his plant as a ballplayer on a winning team. The fact that he is earning far more money than most other Soviet industrial workers helps him to be enthusiastic.

Ivan was born thirty years ago in the village of Orekhovo near Stalingrad. His parents were peasants. His father, Vasili, was drafted into the Red Army during the war and was killed in 1942 in the Ukraine. Ivan's mother now lives with him and his wife. He has a younger brother, Feodor, 27, who also works at the Red October plant.

Ivan entered school in the village when he was 9 years old and he completed eight years. The following year, as soon as the war was over, he came to Stalingrad to find work.

"There was nothing but stones where the mill is now," he said, "and at first we were busy rebuilding. Not many people wanted to come here to work in those days and we received 30 per cent bonus pay."

While he was working, he was attending the factory school. There he completed the work of the last two years of secondary school. He also studied special subjects connected with steel production. When he finished his course, he went to work as an assistant steelmaker. Since 1950, Ivan has been rated as a steelmaker himself.

### Bonus Pay Eliminated

The 30 per cent bonus payment for workers who went to Stalingrad was gradually eliminated as the city returned to normal. But, though the bonus was eliminated at the Red October plant in 1950, premiums for the overfulfillment of quotas even now are figured on the basis of a worker's basic pay plus 30 per cent. That is one of the incentives designed to attract workers into the steel industry.

Ivan's fixed minimum pay is 46.80 rubles a day, but bonus payments raise it well above that figure. The smallest monthly payment he received in recent years was 2,550 rubles and the largest payment was 3,700. His average income of about 3,000 rubles ($300 at the tourist exchange rate) is more than double that of a schoolteacher with thirty years' experience and three times that of a physician his own age.

In addition to his regular pay and bonuses for quota fulfillment, Ivan and other workers at the Red October plant receive an annual lump-sum payment based on seniority. Last year, for example, he received 3,400 rubles, the equivalent of a month's pay.

Ivan and three other steelmakers make up a team that operates a bank of five open-hearth furnaces. There are two teams. Together they keep the furnaces operating around the clock. Bonus payments are based on their production and competition among the teams is fierce.

### Four Work Crews Planned

The steelworkers are on the job eight hours a day five days a week and six hours on the sixth day, a total of forty-six hours a week. Stand-by crews handle the furnaces when the regular shifts are off. Plans are now being made for four full-time crews on the furnaces, each working forty hours a week.

Ivan and his wife, Valentina, 24, live in a small house owned by the steel mill. They have electricity for their two rooms and are hopeful they will have gas soon. They have no refrigeration but are able to keep some vegetables in a cold cellar. They have no running water inside, but a faucet and an outhouse in the yard.

"Our only problem," said Ivan, "is that there is no television available now. We plan to buy a set by the end of the year when a TV station is supposed to begin operating."

Ivan met his wife through mutual friends. They were married three years ago. They have a 2-year-old daughter, Lyuda. Ivan's mother takes care of the baby and works in their small garden plot. Ivan said the garden did not produce much and that they bought most of their vegetables and other food.

Rent, including electricity, costs between 55 and 60 rubles a month. Food costs between 800 and 1,000 rubles. In the winter it drops to about 600 because there are few fresh vegetables or fruits available.

Valentina works in the long-distance department of the Stalingrad telephone office. She supervises the operation of current regulators. Her base pay is 610 rubles; she receives in addition a 15 per cent seniority differential.

### Relatively Big Income

Because of their relatively large income, the Gerasimenkos are able to live much better than most Soviet families. Ivan's hobby is photography and he has a camera that cost 705 rubles. He develops and prints his own pictures. They have not missed a new movie in recent years and they go as often as three times a week. With his mother living with them, they do not have to worry about a baby sitter.

Unlike most Soviet citizens, they also are able to save money. In June, for example, they were able to put 1,100 rubles into savings even though they had paid to send their daughter and her grandmother to the village for a visit. They are saving to buy a television set, and someday Ivan would like to have a car.

They received me hospitably and with kindness. I wondered at the time whether a Soviet newspaper man would receive as generous a reception if he were to drop in on an American family unexpectedly. I thought he probably would.

I thought, too, that he might hear precisely the same words I heard from Ivan Vasilievich.

"All we want," he said as he raised his vodka glass, "is to do our work and live our lives. We want peace for ourselves and our children. Let us hope we will have it."

August 22, 1957

# The People of Russia

## *Visits With an Engineer and a Colonel, And Impressions of a Correspondent*

By WILLIAM J. JORDEN
Special to The New York Times.

STALINGRAD.

Vasili Nikolayevich Baidalakov is a Soviet engineer.

He is helping to build the huge new Stanlingrad Dam and power station on the Volga River just north of Stalingrad. When it is finished he plans to go to work in one of the new industries that will be set up here to take advantage of the new power supply.

Mr. Baidalakov is typical of the new generation of Soviet engineers and technicians who have helped transform a once backward nation into the second largest industrial power in the world.

Some observers believe that the development of this group has already had considerable influence on the Soviet system. They believe that the technicians and engineers will play an increasingly important role in bringing that system down from the clouds of Marxist dialectics, in modifying it in ways as yet unforeseeable.

If Mr. Baidalakov shared that idea, he gave no hint of it in our talk. He was simply a man who believed in getting the job done and one who was searching for better ways of doing things. He seemed more concerned with laying a rail line and moving concrete than with abstract ideas.

### A Man of No Pretense

Vasili Nikolayevich is a quiet, intensely serious man. He is a person with few hobbies and one whose work is never long out of his mind. There is no sham or pretense about him. When I went to his apartment, I asked him if he would not like to go ahead and tell his wife that a visitor was coming. I was thinking how the average woman feels about unexpected callers. He replied:

"It is not necessary. You said you wanted to see how we live. You better see us as we are."

The engineer looks like the kind of person he is. His expression rarely changes; he smiles little. But he is not unfriendly, only careful, in the way of people who make friends slowly but keep them once they are made.

His features are finely chiseled, a straight nose, strong jaw and broad forehead. His eyes are deep-set and intense, changing with his mood and reflecting his thought while the rest of his face remains impassive. Vasili's weather-beaten skin and prematurely gray hair make him look older than his 39 years.

He was born in 1918 in Tsaritsyn, now Stalingrad, the second child and first son of a steelmaker at the Red October Steel Plant. His mother died the year after he was born and his father was killed in the Civil War the following year. Vasili and his sister were raised by an aunt who died during World War II. His sister died three years ago.

### He Studied at Night

When he was 17 years old and had completed seven years of school, young Vasili went to work in Stalingrad's tractor plant. He worked days as a metal cutter; at night he studied at the tractor plant's technical school. Between 1935 and 1940 he completed his secondary education and studied metallurgy. From 1938 to 1941, he worked on the repair of equipment and designed tools for the repair of metal working machinery.

When World War II began, the tractor plant was evacuated to Rubtsovsk in Siberia. Vasili Nikolayevich went along but found work at a defense plant in Novosibirsk. In 1944, he was drafted into the Army and saw action in the artillery. When he was discharged in 1945, he returned to Stalingrad.

The city was a battered ruin and the only jobs available were concerned with rebuilding. Vasili became a construction foreman. He also enrolled as a student in the engineering school at the tractor plant. He specialized in the cold treatment of metals and in 1951 received his diploma as an engineer

### Seeks Time-Saving Methods

In 1950, when construction began on the Stalingrad Dam, Vasili went to work there, helping to put up the first temporary buildings. He is one of the few people who have been on the project from the very beginning. Two concrete-making plants have been completed, and one of his principal jobs is supervising the delivery of their output to the dam and seeing that it is poured properly.

He is also what is known in Soviet parlance as an "innovator," a person who seeks to work out simplified methods and increase the efficiency of operations. The deputy chief engineer on the dam project said that Mr. Baidalakov had worked out dozens of "innovations" that had saved time and money.

"Even when I am at home, I'm trying to think of better ways of doing the job," the engineer said. "I always have my work with me."

Vasili works forty-six hours a week, six hours on Saturday and eight hours on other days. He receives 1,800 rubles basic pay plus a 270-ruble seniority differential. Overfulfillment of the quarterly plan brings a premium of 25 per cent of one month's pay, an average of 150 rubles a month.

His average monthly income is about 2,500 rubles ($250 at the tourist exchange rate). His rent (80 rubles a month) and utilities (electricity averages about 35 rubles) take about 5 per cent of his pay. Food takes 25 per cent.

His taxes are 13 per cent for income tax, the maximum rate, and 1 per cent because he has only one child. A voluntary subscription to the government loan brings his total regular outlays to 50 per cent of his salary. His wife said that all the rest went for clothing and a little entertainment. They said they had no savings.

### He Was Married in 1953

In 1953, Vasili visited some friends in Astrakhan. There, he met and fell in love with a 23-year-old girl named Dina Germanovna. They were married soon after and he took his bride back to Stalingrad. They have a daughter, Ilyena, 2½. In Astrakhan and then in Stalingrad, Dina worked as a bookkeeper. She stopped working when Ilyena was born.

They live in an apartment in the town of Volzhski, a new settlement built to house workers on the dam project. They have a two-room apartment, with a small balcony overlooking the courtyard. There is no gas supply and cooking is done with electricity.

They were offered a small garden plot where they could raise some of their own vegetables, but Vasili turned it down; he said it would "take too much time from my work." They raise a few flowers in window-boxes on their balcony.

The Baidalakovs go to the movies about three times a week. There is no restaurant yet in Volzhski, so they do not go out to eat.

"Anyway, it is not the custom here for families to go to restaurants," Vasili said a little defensively.

"That depends on your taste," said his wife, registering a minor dissent. Like most women, she rather looked with favor on a respite from her duties in the kitchen.

---

## Colonel Dislikes War

MOSCOW.

Georgi Ivanovich Pisarev is an officer in the Soviet Army.

He is a lieutenant colonel in the infantry and a battalion commander in the Moscow military district. He is a man who must be prepared to fight, but hopes he will not have to. It is his job to train men in skills he hopes they will never have to use. He is a man of war who loves peace.

"No one who has seen much of war," said this much-decorated veteran of many battles, "could want to see more of it. We will always be ready to fight if we have to, but we hope we will not have to."

Georgi Ivanovich was born in Siberia near Omsk, thirty-five years ago. His parents, Ivan and Anna, were peasants and they both now work on a collective farm in the Omsk region. His only brother, Vasili, lost both hands as a soldier in World War II. He is now deputy chairman of a collective farm.

Georgi attended school for seven years in his native village. Then he went to Omsk to complete the last three years of secondary school. After having finished his schooling, he went back to the collective to work as a farmer like the rest of his family. He had no thought of a military career, at least until he was drafted into the army in 1941 following the outbreak of war.

### Assigned to the Infantry

Georgi Ivanovich was assigned to the infantry. His ability and aptitude soon set him apart from the regular run of recruits. He passed the necessary tests and was assigned to an officer-training school. He completed the course in 1943 and received his commission as a lieutenant.

The young officer went into action for the first time in Byelorussia as the commander of an infantry platoon. A combination of his valor and skill and the high casualty rate among Soviet officers brought him rapid promotion.

Early in 1944 he became a senior lieutenant and was given command of a company. By the end of that year he was a captain and a deputy battalion

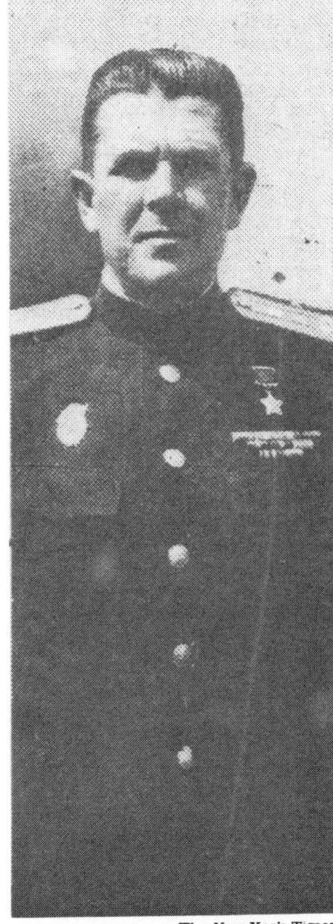

The New York Times

**ARMY MAN: Lieut. Col. Georgi Ivanovich Pisarev commands a battalion in Moscow military district. A combat veteran, he hopes that there will be no war.**

commander. At the war's end, he had the same job but had risen to the rank of major.

If promotions came fast during the war years, they have been exceedingly slow since then. Georgi Ivanovich was promoted three times during the last two years of the war. He moved up only one rung in the military ladder, to his present rank of lieutenant colonel, in the next twelve years.

**Picked for Advanced Study**

But it seems quite clear that he has been picked by his superiors as a man with a bright military future. In 1950, Colonel Pisarev was sent to the Frunze Military Academy for advanced studies. As he describes it, it resembles the United States Army's Command and General Staff School, where officers who demonstrate special ability receive special training. Colonel Pisarev was graduated from the Frunze Academy in 1953, and returned to his battalion.

I had asked to meet Colonel Pisarev both at work and at home, but that proved to be impossible. I was not permitted to visit the army camp where his battalion was stationed. Nor was I able to see his Moscow apartment. The colonel said his family was out of town.

We met at the Central House of the Soviet Army, an elaborate club for officers and their families.

The colonel was in his dress uniform, his chest ablaze with the many decorations he had won. Topping them all was the red ribbon and gold star of Hero of the Soviet Union, the country's highest military decoration, equivalent to the Congressional Medal. Among his other decorations were the Order of Lenin, two Orders of the Red Banner, two Orders of the Red Star, and the Medal for Distinguished Military Service.

Colonel Pisarev is about 5 feet 9 inches with the build of an athlete. His brown hair was cut short in the fashion of most Soviet officers. His grip was strong, his eyes were steady and clear. He was a man with a good physique who obviously was determined to keep it that way.

He was a bit stiff and somewhat ill at ease with a foreign newspaper man. He was nervous about any questions that dealt directly with military matters. Sensing that, I tried to ask only questions I thought he could answer.

**Shy About Experiences**

He was shy about discussing his war experiences. It was clear from what he did say that he had been in many battles and some of the toughest campaigns of the war. He was wounded four times, near Kursk, at Stalingrad, in the Baltic area and in the Crimea.

It was in the Crimea that Colonel Pisarev said he had won his highest award, the medal of Hero of the Soviet Union. He said that he and a group of his men had captured a village from the Germans and defended it until reinforcements

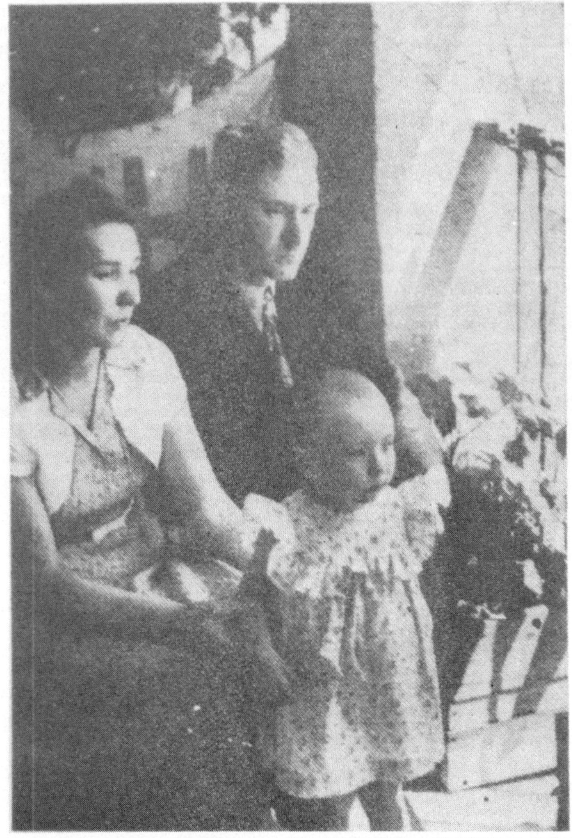

The New York Times (by William J. Jorden)

**ENGINEER: Vasili Nikolayevich Baidalakov with his wife and daughter, Ilyena, 2½, on the balcony of their home in Volzhski. He has worked on Stalingrad Dam and power station near Stalingrad since construction began.**

could arrive. I suspected there was more to it, but the officer would add no further details.

When the war ended, Colonel Pisarev and his battalion were in Rumania. They remained there until 1947. By the time they left, the Communist regime was firmly established in that country.

In 1946, Colonel Pisarev returned on leave to his home near Omsk. During his visit, he married a girl with whom he had gone to school before the war. She returned with him to Rumania. The colonel said that his wife, Tatyana Ivanovna, 33, had worked on a collective farm during the war years but was not working now.

**Pay Based on Type of Job**

The Pisarevs live in a two-room apartment in Moscow, the colonel said. That would indicate they are as crowded as many Soviet citizens, though not as much as most, for the Pisarevs have two sons, Viktor, 10, and Gennadi, 4. Two persons to a room is below average.

Their rent is 30 rubles, surprisingly low even in a land where rent is among the smallest items of living expense. They pay separately for gas, electricity, telephone and water.

The colonel's base pay is 2,000 rubles ($200 at the tourist exchange rate). He gets an **additional 200 rubles (10 per cent of base pay) for length of** service. The colonel said Army pay was based on a man's job, not on his rank. When he was promoted to the rank of major during the war, his pay was not increased, because, he continued in his post as deputy battalion commander.

The colonel works seven hours a day, six days a week. He is up at 7 A. M. and with his unit an hour later. His duties are finished at 3 P. M. Often, of course, administrative duties, night training and the like keep him at the camp.

"My main job is the training of soldiers," he said.

All Soviet young men are subject to compulsory military training for at least two years. They do not go to special camps for their basic training, but join regular units like Colonel Pisarev's battalion. The colonel estimated that it took six months to give a recruit the necessary training in fundamentals that would prepare him for combat.

The colonel gets one month's vacation plus travel time. Last year he went with his family to Yalta. The year before, they went to Sukhumi, another Black Sea resort. This year they plan to go to the colonel's home in Siberia to visit his family.

In the evening, when he gets home to his family, Colonel Pisarev frequently helps his older son with his homework. He said he likes to read and often writes to his parents. He and his wife enjoy watching television or the movies. On Sundays, the family likes to get out of Moscow and sometimes they go swimming. In the winter, the colonel likes to do some hunting, a sport he has enjoyed since his boyhood in Siberia.

As we said good-by, the colonel shook hands and, with a serious look, said: "We don't want another war. Our people have seen enough of it. I hope you understand."

I told him the feeling was not peculiar to the Soviet people, that his sentiments were shared by people in the United States and every other country. I said reports that the United States was planning to attack the Soviet Union were lies.

I don't know if he believed me. He looked as if he wanted to.

## Some General Impressions

MOSCOW.

The previous articles in this series have described eleven citizens of the Soviet Union. Some persons were selected at random as I traveled through the country. Others were introduced to me by Government agencies. They were selected to represent a variety of occupations, incomes and localities.

Some of them, like the bus driver, steelworker and farmer, work with their hands; others, like the Communist party official and novelists, with their heads.

Their base pay ranged from the physician's 850 rubles a month ($85 at the tourist rate **of exchange) to probably ten times that for the novelist. Their education ranged from three years of primary school (the novelist) to university and beyond (the physician, the school teacher and the actress). There was no correlation between education and income.**

**All were fairly well established in their jobs. I did not try to select persons who either had just started work or had retired. Most of them were well above average in terms of income and living standards compared with other persons doing the same kind of work. It proved impossible to gather material on a representative of the large mass of Russians who do common or semi-skilled labor.**

**All But One Married**

**The ages of the eleven ranged from 27 to 62. All but one were married, and they had from one to three children.**

**What impressions stand out as a result of my meetings with these Soviet citizens?**

**Most striking to a foreigner was that they all seemed fairly content with their living conditions. They were ill-informed about conditions in other countries. Most of them had no clear idea of how persons doing their kind of work lived in the United States or Western Europe. They thought in terms of what they themselves had one year, five years or fifteen years ago. By that standard they**

could see visible improvement.

The bus driver, for example, had only a one-room apartment, but he and his wife now have their own kitchen; a year ago they were sharing cooking facilities with others. Until two years ago, the farmer lived in a shack; now he has his own small home. The store section manager and her husband built a small house five years ago; now they are adding a porch and making other improvements.

Despite these signs of improvement, housing remains one of the most serious problems. Even persons living two or three to a room felt a bit cramped and yearned for more space and privacy. Most, however, live four and five to a room and share kitchen and bath with several other families.

If living space is limited, at least it is cheap. In most cases, rent took only 2 or 3 per cent of income.

If rent in the Soviet Union is low, utility costs are high, sometimes as much as the rent itself. All of the houses and apartments I visited had electricity, but six of the eleven had no cooking gas. None had hot running water and three of the families had no plumbing at all. They used outhouses.

Soviet housing is cheap, but food is exorbitant. Most persons said they spent 600 to 800 rubles a month to feed a small family, sometimes more. The physician's food bill, for example, was just about equal to his base pay of 850 rubles.

Food is not always in plentiful supply. In the winter there is a shortage of fresh vegetables and fruit because the Soviet food industry and transport system are not geared to high-speed, long-distance hauls of perishables. A foreigner is struck by the lack of variety of food, especially in the winter months, when potatoes, cabbage, carrots are almost the only vegetables available.

**Many Have Own Gardens**

Half the families I met had their own gardens, both for reasons of economy and for variety in diet. Some of the women canned fruits and vegetables for the winter.

Clothing is another high-cost item. A pair of women's shoes, good by Soviet standards, but only fair in quality and poor in style elsewhere, costs 400 rubles, and a dress costs twice that much. A man's suit, of fair material and badly tailored, costs from 1,400 to 2,000 rubles, or at least a month's pay. Not only is clothing expensive, but fabrics are drab and the designing and tailoring quite poor. Of all the persons interviewed, only the actress was fairly well dressed by Western standards.

Many items regarded as virtual necessities in the United States are still luxuries in the Soviet Union. Only one of the persons described in these articles had a car, for example. The four refrigerators I saw were small and outdated in design. Three persons had television sets, one of them with a "giant" twelve-inch screen. Most of them had radios, but only a few had electric washing machines or vacuum cleaners.

I was impressed by the number of persons in a Soviet family who work. One reason, of course, is that a single income is rarely enough to support a family. In all but three cases, the wives were working, and all of them had worked at some time.

In some families, the mother and father and at least one child were employed. In several cases, a grandmother or aunt lived with the family and took care of the house and children while both parents worked. Many industries provide nurseries and kindergartens for the children of working mothers.

**No Installment Buying**

Because there is no installment buying in the Soviet Union, though it has now been promised, everything has to be purchased with cash. Several persons were saving money. The physician hoped to buy a car, the store employe a piano and the steelworker a television set. Others said they spent everything they earned and had no savings.

Nearly all the persons I have described receive four weeks paid vacation (twenty-four working days plus four Sundays). Most visited rest homes operated by their trade unions, or sanitariums run by the Ministry of Health. Some visited their relatives.

The Soviet Government is making an impressive effort to provide medical and recreational facilities. Only a relatively small percentage of the population benefits as yet, but at least that group is getting reasonably good care. The cost is rather high—1,600 rubles for twenty-four days at a sanitarium—but many workers get some assistance from their unions.

**Adverse Effect on Quality**

It is difficult for foreigners to realize that in the Soviet Union all aspects of life, health, education, most housing, employment, food and clothing are the exclusive province of the Government. Nearly every one of the persons described is a Government employe. Possible exceptions are the collective farmer, the novelist and the Communist party official.

In a system where the Government provides employment and the goods and services, there is a kind of minimal security for all. There is no incentive for competition and a prevalence of mediocrity.

The Soviet system has tried to promote internal competition by setting individuals and work teams [illegible]st either production norms or against each other, with bonuses going to those who overfulfill their quotas or produce more than a competing group. But nearly everyone with whom I talked was overfulfilling his norm, and regarded production bonuses as a regular part of his income.

The emphasis on quantity production has had a devastating effect on quality. This is evidently not the case when it comes to aircraft or atomic bombs. But clothing and other consumer goods are poorly designed and produced. Standards in construction are low. The quality of carpentry, electrical wiring, plumbing, plastering or painting would usually be inadequate for a second-rate housing project in the United States or Western Europe.

Much of the material for this series was gathered in the course of a trip through the Ukraine, the Caucasus and southern European Russia. In most cases, I picked out the person with whom I wanted to talk. I found the farmer out in a field on a collective farm; the steelworker was tending a furnace at a steel mill I visited in Stalingrad; the engineer was working on the new Stalingrad Dam.

In Moscow, where contacts between foreigners and Russians are more restricted and carefully controlled, it was a different story. Applications to meet and talk with people are submitted to a Government agency in charge of relations with the foreign press. It took more than six months to arrange the interviews in the capital.

In general, I found that the persons I met outside Moscow were friendly and hospitable once they knew who I was and what I was trying to do. Their suspicion was never completely eliminated and there was always a certain amount of uneasiness in conversation. But by and large they received me warmly and they were frank in discussing their lives and their jobs. In Moscow, with the exception of the bus driver and the novelist, they were nervous and on the defensive.

**All But 3 Homes Visited**

With the exception of three, the actress, the Army officer, and the Communist party official, all persons interviewed invited me to their homes when I expressed an interest. I had the feeling that in refusing the actress was being temperamental, the officer was being careful and the party official was being a Communist.

The others impressed me with their warmth and their willingness to try to help a foreigner understand them and their country. Some of them were curious about the United States and about conditions there, but in general they were very careful about the questions they asked.

Most of the questions related to such matters as unemployment, treatment of Negroes and the possibility of war. The Russians' ideas of the United States and the rest of the world were usually warped and reflected the limited information available to them. But at least some of them were eager to hear more.

I finished gathering the material for this series with the feeling that if more Russians and Americans could get to know a little more about each other, it might help in some small way to ease the bitterness and suspicion that have dominated their relations in recent years. I was sure that a good many Russians would like that, if they had anything to say about it.

August 25, 1957

# U.S. MISSION FINDS SOVIET EDUCATION IS 'GRAND PASSION'

By FRED M. HECHINGER
Special to The New York Times.

WASHINGTON, Sept. 5—An American team of school experts has found the Russians to be a people with a "grand passion" for education.

According to the report of the first official United States education mission to the Soviet Union, the Russians' leading slogan is:

"Reach and over-reach America."

The report said the people of the Soviet Union "are convinced that time is on their side and that through education and hard work they can win their way to world acceptance of Communist ideology."

**Eleven on Month's Tour**

The report, a 135-page document, "Soviet Commitment to Education," was released by the United States Office of Education today. It covers a one-month tour, from May 8 to June 6, 1958, by an eleven-man team, headed by Lawrence G. Derthick, United States Commissioner of Education.

The tour included visits to about 100 schools and other educational institutions. The group traveled from Belorussia to the Urals and from the Chinese border to the Black and Baltic Seas.

In their joint report, the American educators said they were convinced that the Soviet Union regarded education "as one of the chief resources and techniques for achieving social, economic, cultural and scientific objectives in the national interest."

**Part-Time Study Sought**

They found the Soviet people not only crowding schools and

universities but also seeking part-time education by way of evening study and correspondence courses.

They were impressed by the national and personal sacrifices that the Russian people were willing to make for the sake of better schooling "because being well educated is the key to advancement."

They are convinced that the Russians are making those sacrifices because they consider the schools "as the necessities in their race for world supremacy."

Among the key observations of the mission are that:

¶The Soviet is channeling between 10 to 15 per cent of its national income into education, as compared with about 5 per cent in the United States.

¶The Soviet's 1,800,000 teachers are considered members of a privileged profession, paid roughly on the level of physicians.

¶Soviet teachers are subjected to far more intensive study of the subjects they teach than are American teachers.

¶In the preparation of elementary and secondary school teachers there appears to be an increasing emphasis on solid subject-matter content, with relatively less emphasis on pedagogy.

**Comparisons Avoided**

The report carefully avoids comparisons with the United States. But it warned that "we cannot afford to be apathetic about educational developments in the U. S. S. R."

It said that "clearly the Soviet Union is bent on overtaking and surpassing us as a world power, and it proposes to use education as one of the primary means of obtaining this objective."

Not everything the American observers encountered seemed to them admirable or superior. For example:

¶They were critical of the method of language instruction, although they admired the extent of the language requirement.

¶They questioned the uniformity of the curriculum in the ten-year schools of general education. Both as to content and method they found teachers subservient to the idea that "there is just one right way to do anything in the classroom."

¶They found little stress on the humanities, and while superior work in music, dance and art is being done by a small, selected group of youngsters in special schools, these areas are generally neglected in the mass-education schools.

¶They saw examinations used only to push students into habits of hard work, without any attempt to test aptitudes or to encourage the cultivation of special talents.

**Chance for Good Work**

But despite these limitations, the report warns, it would be wrong to conclude that many able students were not being given a chance to do outstanding work, even when their classroom requirements made no special allowance for this.

Students, it was found, have opportunities to work on independent projects and develop their creative ability through extra-curricular activities in carefully supervised circles.

Outstanding students often are given special, personal attention by their teachers. A variety of competitive devices are used to inspire students to give their all to their studies.

In one school a classroom was dedicated to two former pupils who had been killed in World War II. Each year the class judged to be the best in the school was given the privilege of using that classroom.

There seems to be no conscious attempt to separate children according to academic ability. But those who fall behind in their studies are frequently helped by their teachers or by outstanding fellow-students.

**Reform Plan Minimized**

The report includes an appendix on the recently announced school reform and an analysis of that reform by William K. Medlin, specialist for Eastern Europe of the United States Office of Education. But the members of the team found Soviet reform plans far less radical than had earlier been believed.

In a special news conference at the Department of Health, Education and Welfare yesterday, Dr. Derthick said that he and his staff had been startled by the original terms of the school reform.

"But after conferences with Soviet officials, we found that the changes are not going to alter the basic program substantially."

He emphatically denied that there was any reason to expect a watering down of the academic content of the Russian elementary and secondary school as a result of the reform.

**To Link Study and Work**

According to the report and to the more detailed study by experts at the United States Office of Education, the reform will increase the number of students who will combine study and work during the last three years of the ten-year school.

An indication that this is not expected to detract from academic goals is the announced intention to add an eleventh year to the secondary school.

At the same time, flexibility will be added by an option to continue on a work-study basis after grade seven or to leave school and continue academic work through correspondence courses.

Also, the ablest seventh-year students may continue the last three years much as in the pre-reform academic fashion. This would be closer to the American pattern than the Russian school had been in the past.

Actually, some members of the team feel, the major reason for the school reform is not educational. They say it is an attempt to stop the massive rush to the universities and to provide instead more skilled manpower for technology on a level that does not require university training.

**Rush to Universities**

In the last four years, the Russian ten year schools have been turning out about four times as many qualified university candidates as the universities were able to admit.

The key to Soviet education progress is probably the tough and demanding teacher training program. It is four years for elementary and five years for secondary school. However, many of the present teachers undoubtedly have less schooling.

Dr. Medlin estimated that five years of Russian teacher training add up to about twice the number of classroom and practice hours as a five-year course in the United States.

It is estimated that Soviet teacher trainees spend 40 per cent of their time on preparation of their major subject, 15 per cent on technological application of their specialty and 15 per cent on the specific method of teaching their major subject.

The remainder is divided among general pedagogy, psychology, foreign languages, physical education and political indoctrination.

**Relatively Well Paid**

The report summed up the Soviet teacher this way:

"In general, teachers appear to be relatively well paid; they have very good working conditions; as a group they appear to be highly motivated and well educated professionals who are happy in their work and proud of it.

"Teachers are not overburdened with extracurricular work. Their clerical duties are minimal. Extra teachers, or tutors, are available to work with slow learners, and to assist generally as teachers' aides. Although schools in the Soviet Union meet six days a week, each teacher has one work-day a week completely free."

There are striking contrasts on the Soviet education scene. There is no teacher shortage. On the contrary, too many young Russians want to enter the profession, which ranks high in esteem and equals the pay of physicians.

But because of the rapid growth of the system, there are still many double sessions. In Moscow, 27 per cent of the pupils were on two shifts last year.

**Hours Remain Long**

The double sessions, however, do not cut the number of school hours required. The morning shift runs from 8:30 A. M. to 2 P. M. and the afternoon shift from 2 P. M. to 7 P. M.

The Soviet problems, both real and imagined, seem to range wide. Anatol Shustov, Moscow's chief education officer, was asked about his problems. He included among them the question of general versus vocational education, as well as "the need to agitate for tennis courts; they are not in the standard plan."

Enrollment in 1957-58 in all elementary and secondary schools was 30,624,900 in 214,162 schools. This includes 104,500 pupils in 456 boarding schools, which are still considered somewhat experimental.

In 1957, about 1,500,000 pupils were graduated from secondary school and 686,000 finished the lower type of labor reserve schools. Enrollment in the United States for 1959-60 puts elementary and secondary totals at 42,700,000.

**Correspondence Courses**

About 2,000,000 Russians of varying ages are reported to be enrolled in correspondence courses that may lead to high school graduation as well as to admission to the universities.

Both correspondence courses and part-time study, often with released time from industry, are a very common Soviet practice, the report said.

There appears to be some conflict as to the need for such academic subjects as advanced mathematics.

"Soviet officials recognize that many pupils will never use the algebra and geometry they are required to learn, but they believe that such study is good discipline and has great transfer value," the report says.

There are, however, indications that in some of the new polytechnical courses, which combine industrial work with academic study, such subjects as mathematics are taught as applied, practical tools rather than as theoretical studies.

Along similar lines, the report states:

"Pupils without the ability or talent to become scientists use the science training they receive as a base for polytechnical education, which prepares them for industrial work."

In physics, along with the conventional idea of introducing pupils to the natural phenomena, the Soviet student must study "the basic principles of production processes."

**Stress on Technology**

Increasingly, the United States mission found, "the primary emphasis appears to be on the practical and technological aspects of science."

Even a state-wide competition for new science textbooks made it clear that the prizes would go to "works which have a bearing on the polytechnical training of the students and the formation among them of a materialistic world outlook."

About 45 per cent of the pupils required to learn a foreign language selected English. About 35 per cent study German and 20 per cent French. A substantial number of special students also are said to study such languages as Arabic, Chinese, and Hindi.

Soviet youngsters are required to do a fair, but not a staggering amount of homework. The daily assignments vary from one to four hours, but young children are given very little.

One Soviet school director said:

"The better the teacher, the less homework is required."

**No Corporal Punishment**

The Soviet school does not permit corporal punishment. Membership in the Young Pioneer organization is a matter of considerable status importance. So withdrawal of the student's membership is considered severe punishment.

But probably more important, the ever-present realization that education is the means toward a better and perhaps easier life is in itself both stick and carrot and decreases the customary discipline problem.

Dr. Derthick told the news conference, "Direct comparisons of the quality of education in two countries as different in goals and aspirations are difficult, if not impossible."

Soviet teaching methods and content, he said, are designed to insure that "every pupil passes." Since low marks are often considered a reflection on the teacher rather than on the pupil, teachers do their utmost to get pupils to pass, either by extensive drill or by special help.

The report dealt mainly with the ten-year school. But it also contains a brief section on the universities, some special schools and kindergartens.

**Stipends Are Cited**

"To provide the professions and trained manpower the Soviet Union needs, the state pays stipends to approximately 80 per cent of the 1,100,000 full-time students in institutions of higher education," Dr. Derthick said. None of these students pays tuition.

The American team explains its reluctance to compare the Soviet and the American education systems by stressing the difference of the roles given to education by a totalitarian and a free society.

Actually, it is known that there had been some disagreement on this point in the preparation of the report. Some team members felt that an attempt to relate the meaning of the Russian findings to the American school scene would have been a valuable service and a guide in the competition for world leadership.

**Common Aim Detected**

One team member noted that while the systems and the societies they serve differ greatly, the ultimate aim of survival is common to both. But since the document was a team report, it was ultimately agreed that, in the main, no comparisons were to be made.

Dr. Derthick said that while he was greatly reassured by progress made in recent years in the better American schools, he was "more disturbed than ever about this country's poorer schools when he saw the tremendous contest" in the Soviet Union.

"The American schools are doing a better job than ever before," he asserted, "but because of the explosion of knowledge we have to do much better than that."

"Soviet Commitment to Education" is part of a series of studies issued by the Office of Education. It was preceded in 1957 by "Education in the U. S. S. R."

The complete "Soviet Commitment to Education" is available for 70 cents from the Government Printing Office in Washington.

September 6, 1959

# *Khrushchev's Russia*

## *Anti-Semitism and Religious Upsurge Are Said to Baffle the Soviet Regime*

By HARRISON E. SALISBURY

The audience in the dingy hall of the Moscow Railroad Workers Club shifted forward on the hard seats. There was a hush as the buxom blonde announcer in her flowered silk dress came down to the footlights.

"The next number will be a song based on a poem by Itsik Fefer," she said. There were gasps and whispers. When the song was finished the applause went on and on.

Zinovi Shulman, flapping the coattails of his faded evening clothes, took bow after bow. He seemed a little embarrassed. Even he knew his voice at 60 was not that good.

**Martyr of Anti-Semitism**

The applause, of course, was not for Mr. Shulman. It was for a man seven years dead—Itsik S. Fefer, Yiddish poet, colonel in the Red Army, admirer of Stalin, Communist, martyr to the anti-Semitic mania that gripped the Soviet Union in the old dictator's last years.

The shabby little concert of Yiddish songs in a workingmen's hall in Komsomolskaya Square was in reality a small, almost grudging act of contrition for the horrors that Stalin visited on the Jews of Russia.

This concert like others that have been given in the Soviet Union in recent years was part of a halting effort to come to grips with one of the heritages of the Stalin days — government-directed anti-Semitism and persecution of Jews that cost thousands their homes and their jobs and sent thousands into exile and a number still unknown to death before firing squads.

**No Active Persecution**

Let us note immediately that active anti-Semitism or active persecution of Jews no longer is carried out by the Soviet Government. The situation of the Jew in Russia, like that of any Soviet citizen, is far better today than in the final years of Stalin's life.

But the consequences of official anti-Semitism and its widespread dissemination among the population are far from ended. Indeed, only fumbling and half-hearted efforts have been made by the government to face up to the reality of the problem. Anti-Semitic tendencies are still alive and powerful.

The Jewish problem is one of two connected with religion that confront the Soviet regime today. Perhaps, the other might be called the Christian problem.

It relates to the continuing and growing appeal of Christian faiths to the Soviet public, particularly the young people, despite forty-two years of atheistic propaganda and frequent persecution of organized faiths. The resurgence of the Christian faith has been met by a vigorous propaganda offensive against religion.

Both of these problems represent social questions for which the Khrushchev regime has found no ready answer. Both provide evidence of deep cleavage within Soviet society. Both touch on matters in which there is intense interest in the United States. In the course of his visit to the United States Nikita S. Khrushchev is certain to encounter frequent evidences of this interest.

The dimensions of the Jewish problem are possibly best indicated by examining what lay behind the applause that greeted the Fefer number at the Railroad Workers Club.

There were perhaps 1,200 people in the hall, a cross-section of Moscow's Jewish population, most of them people of the middle ranks of Soviet society. Many youths in their teens or early twenties accompanied their parents. The young people did not know Yiddish and the nature of the songs had to be explained to them. The audience was almost entirely Jewish. There were eight or ten foreigners, including three American tourists from Brooklyn.

**Thought Himself Russian**

"Before Stalin's last years," a Moscow Jew said, "many of these people would not have regarded themselves as Jewish. Take myself, for example. I grew up in the Nineteen Twenties and early Thirties. I thought of myself as a Russian, not a Jew. Then after the war I found that it did not make any difference what I thought about myself — I was a Jew on the books. I was a Jew to the director of the institute where I worked. Very well. I became a Jew to myself."

Persons who grew up in the Soviet Union in the first fifteen years or so after the Bolshevik Revolution believe that in few places in the world was there less anti-Semitism. The days of czarist pograms and of the Jewish Pale, an area where Jews were compelled to live, seemed far distant.

Even the purges of the Nineteen Thirties, in which many victims were Jews, failed to arouse general anti-Semitism. Indeed, a joke of the period was, "You're not a Trotskyite and you're not a Jew, so why were you arrested?"

Active anti-Semitism made its appearance in the Soviet Union early in World War II. Was it brought in by the Nazis? This is what Soviet authorities now like to say. If so, no effort was made by Stalin or his associates to halt its spread. The Ukraine, a hotbed of anti-Semitism under the czars, was most receptive.

**Wartime Anti-Semitism**

In Moscow anti-Semitism was rampant under pressure of the early German advance.

"The Jews are getting out," "The Jews are saving their skins," "The Jews are bribing the railroads and carting off their gold"—these were stories heard in Moscow in the days of evacuation in the autumn of 1941.

Did Stalin encourage this? It is hard to tell at this late date. Certainly, not much was done to discourage the anti-Jewish bias. After nearly two years, Moscow party workers were finally called in and informed that anti-Semitism was not the official line of the party.

"What everyone overlooks in discussing anti-Semitism under Stalin," said one man who has lived many years in Moscow, "is that anti-Semitism was popular. People liked to believe bad things about the Jews during the war. After the war even if Stalin had wanted to stop anti-Semitic sentiment it would not have been so easy."

But Stalin had no desire to halt it. Unknown to the outside world, anti-Semitism was adopted as an official policy of the Stalin Government in the autumn of 1948. It remained an official policy until Stalin's death.

"The difference between the terror of the Nineteen Thirties and that of the Forties was this," one man said. "In the Thirties you had to be important to be arrested or shot. In the Forties it made no difference. Anyone could be arrested, literally anyone. One day a little watch repairman was arrested. A few days later he was executed. Why? No one knows. I don't think the police knew. His name just happened to be on a list."

**'Doctors' Plot' Last Act**

Even today many people assume that an anti-Semitic insanity afflicted Stalin only in the last weeks of his life at the time of the so-called Kremlin doctors' plot. But Stalin had been carrying out secret persecution of Jews on a wide scale since 1948. Hundreds of prominent Jews underwent interrogation and torture in Lubyanka prison. When, in late autumn of 1952, Stalin set into motion the machinery of the "doctors' plot," he was merely preparing a new act in a Grand Guignol that had been preoccupying him for four years.

Only a few men lost their lives in the "doctors' plot." One of the accused doctors committed suicide. Another died of a heart attack. But the roll of victims between 1948 and 1952 included some of the most distinguished Jewish names in the Soviet Union.

This was the reason for the ovation that greeted Mr. Shulman when he sang Mr. Fefer's song at the Railroad Workers Club. Mr. Fefer was executed Aug. 12, 1952, on charges of Jewish nationalism and of conspiracy with foreign states to detach Soviet territory (the Crimea and Eastern Siberia) from the Soviet Union.

**One of 25 On Trial**

Mr. Fefer was one of twenty-five defendants in a secret trial of "Jewish nationalists" conducted in Moscow the previous July 11 to 18. All but one of the defendants were executed.

No one knows to this day how many persons died during the anti-Jewish campaign. A check of a list of twenty-four prominent Soviet Jews who on April 14, 1944, attended a meeting of the Jewish Anti-Fascist Committee, an organization set up in 1942 to conduct propaganda for the Soviet war effort, shows only two persons alive today. One of them is Ilya Ehrenburg, the writer. The other is Lina S. Shtern, a physiologist and member of the Soviet Academy of Sciences. She was the sole survivor of the 1952 trial, in which she received a life sentence.

It was not only in Moscow that the persecution of the Jews was carried on by Stalin. In far-off Birobidzhan, the ill-fated Jewish settlement area of the Far East, arrests struck in 1948 and 1949. There, too, prominent Jews were tried on charges of plots and conspiracy. Jews were arrested in the Ukraine and deported to Kazakhstan. Jews who had survived Nazi occupation in Byelorussia were shipped to Siberia.

**Jew 'Lost' Passport**

To this day an Eastern Siberian city such as Irkutsk has a far higher proportion of Jews in its population than Moscow, Leningrad or Kiev.

"No one who was not a Jew in Moscow in 1949 knows what it was like," one man said. The internal passport of each Soviet citizen specifies his nationality—Russian, Georgian, Ukrainian or Jewish. This man decided to "lose" his passport. He tore it up and flushed it down the toilet. Then he applied for a new one at the local police station. He put down his nationality as Russian. The passport was issued in that form.

"Many of us did that," he said. "It was a matter of self-preservation. The word Jew is not on my passport today. But I feel more Jewish than in the days when it was there."

**University Ousted Jews**

Many persons, however, could not protect themselves so simply. They were prominent and known as Jews. The more prominent they were the more quickly they lost their jobs, particularly in cultural and intellectual fields.

Moscow State University announced that it was a "Russian" citadel of culture. Not a Jewish professor was permitted to remain on the rolls. Even today only one full professor is a Jew. A similar situation existed in the Academy of Sciences except that in physics and higher mathematics Jewish predominance was so overwhelming that the worst effects of the purge were thwarted.

These years of terror, discrimination and hatred have provided a legacy of social ills for Mr. Khrushchev.

Neither he nor his associates seem to have found it possible to confront the problem candidly. Few facts of the Jewish persecution have been placed on public record, although Mr. Khrushchev and his associates sometimes discuss Jewish questions privately with foreign visitors.

The families of those Jews who were executed by Stalin have been given pensions. They have been advised that the executions were unjustified. Other victims have been released from prison or returned from exile.

Russian-language translations of the works of some of the executed Yiddish writers have been published. But none of the suppressed Jewish cultural institutions—the Yiddish publishing house, the Yiddish newspapers (except for one in Birobidzhan), the Yiddish theatres—has been revived.

Official tribute was paid to Sholem Aleichem, Yiddish writer, on the 100th anniversary of his birth last winter. His collected works are being published in Russian in an edition of 225,000. But a volume of his stories in Yiddish appeared only in a small edition that was sold out quickly in Moscow.

Jews are still barred from the higher military schools. They are not admitted to cadet schools. They are not admitted to the foreign service school. Their admission to universities is not always easy. No leading party editor is a Jew. No Jew has risen to high party position under Mr. Khrushchev.

In religious matters there is discrimination against Jews. Jews have fewer and poorer houses of worship compared with other faiths. They are permitted to train few rabbis. They have few printed materials. Jewish religious objects are scarce. Jews have difficulty obtaining appropriate foods for Jewish holidays. Kosher facilities are rare. But, in contrast to five years ago, two Moscow restaurants now serve traditional Jewish dishes.

A few months ago a rash of anti-Jewish articles appeared in Ukrainian provincial newspapers. Ukrainian authorities closed some Jewish houses of prayer in small communities and carried out other discriminations.

Why has Mr. Khrushchev failed to act in forthright and principled fashion against anti-Semitism? There are those who suggest that it is because he himself has inherited the anti-Jewish attitudes so common in the Ukraine, where he grew up.

Others suggest that Mr. Khrushchev fails to act because anti-Semitism, actively propagated for many years, has become a popular policy.

There is no official count of the number of Jews left in the Soviet Union. Mr. Khrushchev recently placed the figure at 2,000,000, possibly on the basis of the 1959 population census. There were 4,500,000 to 5,000,000 before the Germans invaded the Soviet Union, occupying the traditional areas of Jewish settlement.

There is no doubt that many Jews would leave the Soviet Union if given a chance. Emigration is not permitted now and there seems little likelihood that it will be, although Mr. Khrushchev said some weeks ago that the day might come when it would be possible.

Jews would leave because they have been treated as enemies of the Soviet state by the Government and as inferiors by their fellow citizens.

The fact is that the Khrushchev Government, like the Stalin Government, treats the Jewish population as a national security risk. There seems little prospect of any positive action by Mr. Khrushchev to correct this situation in the near future.

The Soviet Union has embarked on a foreign policy favorable to the Arab states and antagonistic to Israel. Jewish cultural and emotional ties to Israel have fed Soviet suspicions concerning Jewish loyalty to the Soviet Union.

Mr. Khrushchev's "Christian" problem is of a different order. It stems from the strong revival in religion that got under way in the Soviet Union during World War II and has continued to the present time.

Large numbers of Russian Orthodox churches have reopened since World War II. Many village churches that were commandeered, for use as granaries or office buildings, have been returned to the believers.

So long as most believers were middle-aged people, largely women, the state did not seem much concerned. In Stalin's last years and the first years after his death anti-religious propaganda was almost a dead letter.

However, the church began to attract more and more young people. Church marriages again became fashionable. Sometimes, Communist youths went to church en masse—"just to see what it was like."

As more churches opened and more people went to church the revenues of the Orthodox Church began to rise. Russians are generous people and the collections at Easter time are staggering. Priests use bushel baskets to hold the blizzard of ruble notes.

The funds have enabled the church to rehabilitate many old buildings. Onion domes again glitter in gold leaf.

Alarmed by the growing attraction of the church for young people the Communist party has lumbered out its old propaganda weapons. Atheistic literature is to be found on every bookstand. Atheistic lectures are delivered in neighborhood halls. Neighborhood atheist societies have been formed. And the Communist youth organization is devoting much energy to combatting the effects of religion on the young.

A leader in this campaign has been Aleksei I. Adzhubei, son-

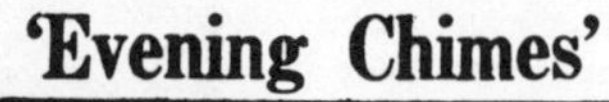

From Krokodil. English translation substituted for original Russian

**An example, from a humor magazine, of the anti-religion campaign. Atheistic literature is plentiful at bookstands, and atheistic lectures are given at neighborhood halls.**

in-law of Mr. Khrushchev and until recently editor of the Communist youth newspaper, Komsomolskaya Pravda. Mr. Adzhubei directed his fire not only at the Orthodox Church. He also singled out the Baptist Church, which has proved a great attraction for young people in recent years.

Mr. Adzhubei's speciality has been to publish articles of the "confession" type — "The Truth About the Baptist Cult" or "Why Grigory Ivanovich Left the Baptist Faith." Some articles tell about young university students who were doing well in their studies until they started going to church. Others seek to associate religious belief with superstition, selfishness or other character weaknesses. Much attention is paid to any evidence of luxurious living by the priests or pastors.

The campaign has involved no official pressures. No Orthodox or Baptist churches have been closed. Indeed, Baptist church leaders say their ranks have been swelled by youngsters who first read of the faith in Komsomolskaya Pravda. "It is good advertising," one young Baptist said.

The revived campaign against religion seems to have had little effect. Moscow's churches last Easter showed little change. There may have been fewer young people than usual. At the monastery of Zagorsk, forty miles from Moscow, the crowds were as great as ever. There was no reduction of crowds in village churches or of queues of women bringing their cakes and eggs to be blessed for the Easter feast by the priest.

What is interesting about the new concern of the state in religious matters is the insight it brings on two important questions.

The first is the inability of the Communist doctrine to stamp out or replace man's belief in religion. The second is the inability of Communist rulers to become reconciled to the existence in the minds of the people of any beliefs other than those emanating from communism.

September 12, 1959

## *Soviet Family Realizes Dream: A Room to Live In All by Itself*

By SEYMOUR TOPPING

Special to The New York Times.

**MOSCOW, Dec. 1—"You can't imagine how happy we are," said the Russian factory worker as he glanced around the room in which he lives with his wife, who is expecting a child, and their 5-year-old daughter.**

"It seems like a dream to me; we have a room of our own," he said with unabashed delight.

The room had a low ceiling, concrete walls and was just 162 square feet in size. It was in one of Moscow's newest housing developments.

Could a similar United States family be delighted with such housing? The question is not too pertinent in the Soviet Union, where people do not generally compare their living standards with those in the West. Many are content simply because they know things are better today than they were yesterday.

Before that gala day recently when the Russian worker moved into his new room, he lived with his immediate family, an ailing teen-age sister-in-law and his aged parents in a single ninety-seven square-foot bedroom.

**Family Given Priority**

When the construction of a highway compelled the demolition of their dwelling, the family received a Government priority enabling them to move into a three-room apartment. The sister-in-law now occupies one room of the apartment, the parents another and the worker and his family the largest room. They share a small kitchen and bathroom.

About 10 per cent of the worker's salary and his parents' pension goes to pay for the rent, central heating, hot water, gas and electricity.

This was a lucky Soviet family. Many Moscow families in similar circumstances have been waiting three to ten years to move into one of the new apartment houses four or five stories tall being erected here at an average rate of four a day, according to the city administration.

Throughout the Soviet Union this standardized-type apartment house, without elevators and made of prefabricated concrete slabs, is being thrown up on a crash basis.

There is criticism in the Soviet press of poor finishing of the houses, but the dwelling shortage is so great that building is going forward as planned on this mass production scale. Officials speak of every Soviet family possessing its own apartment in ten to twelve years.

Some of the most troublesome social problems confronting Soviet society stem from communal dwellings. Most Soviet families, in such crowded, fast-growing cities as Moscow, must share an apartment, usually with strangers.

Sometimes several families, obedient to tenets of "socialist brotherhood," live quite contentedly as one. Yet many cases exist where the agonizing lack of privacy creates an atmosphere of friction. Moscovites tell stories of families that have lived in a communal apartment for as long as ten years without speaking to one another.

In a typical communal apartment as many as five families will share a kitchen and bathroom. In the kitchen there will be a table for each, and in the toilet sometimes a detachable seat for each.

Quite often a family will share its single bedroom with relatives. This usually happens when a daughter or son brings a new spouse into the household. Another curtain is put up and that is the sum of privacy.

The corridor outside each room is staked out by the family for a chest or wardrobe that is kept locked. There is a common telephone and individual door bells. There are also individual gas and electricity meters.

**Quarrels Arbitrated**

When families in a communal apartment quarrel habitually, the Government housing management may appoint an arbitrator among the concerned families. There is a standing committee that checks on sanitary conditions.

Some disputes are settled in a Comrades' Court, which can be made up of respected laymen associated with the individuals involved. This court can issue reprimands, recommend to the police that an individual be banished from Moscow or refer the case to the regular People's Court.

Most quarrels in communal apartments are of a petty nature: a child or pet infringes on someone else's domain, a family neglects to do its part in cleaning, there is a dispute over use of kitchen or toilet.

The woes of communal living are often dealt with on the Soviet stage, in films, or in such satirical magazines as Krokodil. Muscovites recall a Hungarian film shown here on the subject of a communal flat in which an occupant, a retired judge, remarks:

"I sentenced people to prison and to exile, but never to death or life in a communal apartment."

December 11, 1960

# Challenge of the 'New Soviet Man'

**Thoroughly indoctrinated in Communist values and behavior, he is a confident breed. Here is how his character is built, from the cradle on.**

By URIE BRONFENBRENNER

WHATEVER course Mr. Khrushchev elects to follow in the development of world communism, its success or failure, so far as Russia is concerned, will depend on what Russian leaders call the "new Soviet man." Mr. Khrushchev has spoken about him in his speeches. We have seen his power reflected, so the Russian press tells us, in Soviet achievements in industry, athletics and science. And, of course, only recently the Russians introduced him to us in the flesh, in the persons of Major Gagarin and Major Titov.

The Soviet leaders give a double reason for their enthusiasm about the new Soviet man. They express pride not only in what he does, but also in what he is. For he is, as the Russians see it, a planned product of Communist society—the result of an explicit system of character training being employed daily in Soviet families, nurseries, schools and youth groups.

What is the nature of this system? One of the best ways to become acquainted with it is to examine some of the books and manuals for parents, teachers and youth workers that are published by the hundreds of thousands in the U. S. S. R. By far the most important of these are the works of

*URIE BRONFENBRENNER, a professor of psychology and child development at Cornell, traveled in the Soviet Union last summer, visiting laboratories and education centers.*

the Soviet educator, A. S. Makarenko.

In the early Nineteen Twenties, Makarenko, then a young school teacher and a devout Communist, was given the task of developing a rehabilitation program for some of the hundreds of homeless children who were roaming the Soviet Union after the civil wars. The first such group assigned to him consisted of boys about 18 years old with extensive court records of housebreaking, armed robbery and manslaughter. For the first few months, Makarenko's school—an isolated, ramshackle building—served simply as the headquarters for a band of highwaymen who were his legal wards.

BUT gradually, through development of his group-oriented discipline techniques, and through what can only be called the compelling power of his own moral convictions, Makarenko was able to create a sense of responsibility and commitment to the work program and code of conduct he had laid out. In the end, the so-called Gorky Commune became known throughout the Soviet Union for its high morale and discipline and for the productivity of its fields, farms and shops. And in the years that followed Makarenko's methods came to be widely adopted not only throughout the U. S. S. R. but also in the satellites, notably East Germany, and in Communist China.

To get some notion of Makarenko's ideas, we might look first at what is probably the most widely read of his works, "A Book for Parents." Here is an excerpt:

> Our [Soviet] family is not an accidental combination of members of society. The family is a natural collective body and, like everything natural, healthy and normal, it can only blossom forth in Socialist society, freed of those very curses from which both mankind as a whole and the individual are freeing themselves.
>
> The family becomes the natural primary cell of society, the place where the delight of human life is realized, where the triumphant forces of man are refreshed, where children—the chief joy of life—live and grow.
>
> Our parents are not without authority either, but this authority is only the reflection of societal authority. The duty of a father in our country toward his children is a particular form of his duty toward society. It is as if our society says to parents:
>
> "You have joined together in goodwill and love, rejoice in your children and expect to go on rejoicing in them. That is your personal affair and concerns your personal happiness. Within the course of this happy process you have given birth to new human beings. A time will come when these beings will cease to be solely the instruments of your happiness, and will step forth as independent members of society. For society, it is by no means a matter of indifference what kind of people they will become. In delegating to you a certain measure of societal authority, the Soviet state demands from you the correct upbringing of its future citizens. Particularly it relies on you to provide certain conditions arising naturally out of your union; namely, your parental love.
>
> "If you wish to give birth to a citizen while dispensing with parental love, then be so kind as to warn society that you intend to do such a filthy thing. Human beings who are brought up without parental love are often deformed human beings."

FROM this it can be seen that paramount in Makarenko's thinking is the thesis that the parent's authority over the child is delegated to him by the state, and that duty to one's children is merely a particular instance of one's broader duty toward society. A little later in the book he makes this point even more emphatically. After telling the story of a boy who ran away from home after some differences with his mother, he concludes by affirming: "I am a great admirer of optimism and I like very much young lads who have so much faith in the Soviet state that they are carried away and will not trust even their own mothers."

In other words, when the needs and values of the family conflict with those of society, there is no question about which gets priority. And society receives its concrete manifestation and embodiment in the collective, which is any organized group engaged in some socially useful enterprise.

THIS brings us to the second major theme in Makarenko's work—the focal role of the collective in the child's upbringing. In his view, only the collective can supply the necessary conditions for achieving what he describes as the main aim of Soviet education—that of developing persons who possess the ability, motivation and skill for working together to attain the goals set for Communist society by its leaders. Accordingly, in his voluminous writings, Makarenko devotes considerable attention to the principles and procedures that are best employed for building the collective and using it as an instrument for character education.

It is these same principles and practices which pervade the manuals outlining the procedures to be employed for the training of Soviet youth. The introduction to one typical example describes the work as a handbook for school directors, class supervisors, teachers and Young Pioneer (Communist youth organization) leaders.

The title gives one pause, for this book on how to conduct classroom activities is called "Socialist Competition in the Schools." And the same idea is echoed in the titles of individual chapters: "Competition in the Classroom," "Competition Between Classrooms," "Competition Between Schools," and so on. It is not difficult to see how the Russians are led to the notion of competition between nations and social systems.

To turn to the text itself: In an early chapter we find ourselves in the first grade on the first day of school. There is even a photograph of the teacher addressing the class. She is saying, "Let's see which row can sit the straightest!"

THIS approach, the book tells us, has certain important psychological advantages, for in response:

> The children not only try to do everything as well as possible themselves, but also take an evaluative attitude toward those who are undermining the achievement of the row * * *. Gradually the children themselves begin to monitor the behavior of their comrades and remind those of them who forget about the rules set by the teacher * * *. The teacher soon has helpers.

Nor is the emergence of such help left to chance, for the teacher appoints row monitors for each activity—for personal cleanliness, condition of desks, conduct in passing from one room to the other, quality of recitations in each subject, and so on. Following the teacher's example, the monitors are taught to evaluate the behavior and performance of their classmates and then to report their evaluations publicly or to "link" leaders.*

> Here is a typical picture [we read]. It is the beginning of the lesson. In the first row the link leader reports, basing his comments on information submitted by the sanitarian and other responsible monitors: "Today Valodya did the wrong problem. Masha didn't write neatly, and forgot to underline the right words in her lesson. Alyosha had a dirty shirt collar."
>
> The youngsters are not offended by this procedure; they understand that the link leaders are not just tattling but simply fulfilling their duty. It doesn't even occur to the monitors and sanitarians to conceal the shortcomings of their comrades. They feel they are doing their job well precisely when they notice one or another defect.

In the third grade, the teacher introduces a new wrinkle. She now proposes that the children compete with the monitors, and see if they can beat them at their own game through self-criticism. The results of this procedure are "spectacular," we are told. "When the monitor is able to talk only about four or five members of the row there are supplementary reports about their own short-

*A link is the smallest unit of the Communist youth organization, which reaches into every classroom, from the first grade on. Link members are commonly seated together and there are usually several links in each class.

comings from as many as eight or ten pupils."

Evaluations come not only from teachers and classmates but also from parents, who are asked to report grades for their children's behavior and performance of chores at home. But how can one depend on parents to turn in truthful reports? Part of the answer was supplied to me in a conversation with a Soviet agricultural expert.

He explained that, no matter what a person's job, the collective at his place of work always took an active interest in his family life. Thus a representative would come to the worker's home to observe and talk with his wife and children. And if any undesirable features were noted, these would be reported to the collective.

Asked for an example, my informant said: "Well, suppose the representative were to notice that my wife and I quarreled in front of the children. That would be bad. They would speak to me about it and remind me of my responsibilities for training my children to be good citizens."

He agreed that the situation was different in America, and said: "That's one of the strange things about your system in the West. The family is separated from the rest of society. That's not good."

He paused for a moment and then went on. "I suppose if my wife didn't want to let the representative in, she could ask him to leave. But then, at my place of work, I should feel ashamed—'Ivanov,' they would say, 'has an uncultured wife.'"

But it would be a mistake to conclude that Soviet methods of character education and social control are based primarily on negative criticism. On the contrary, there is as much of the carrot as the stick. However, the carrot is given not merely as a reward for individual performance but explicitly for the child's contribution to group achievement.

THE great charts emblazoned "Who Is Best?" which bedeck the walls of every classroom have as entries the names not of individual pupils but of rows and links. It is the winning unit that gets rewarded by a pennant, by a special privilege or by having its picture taken in parade uniforms.

Helping other members of one's collective and appreciating their contributions—themes that are much stressed in Soviet character training—become matters of enlightened self-interest, since the grade that each person receives depends on the over-all performance of his unit. Thus the good student finds it to his advantage to help the poor one. The same principle is carried over to the group level. There, champion rows and classes are made responsible for the performance of poorer ones.

THIS, then, is the process through which the Russians attempt to form the new Soviet man. Its aim is clear enough—to build a sense of commitment to and identity with the collective and, through it, with Communist society. How successful are the results of this massive endeavor? Here are some random impressions based on my own observations and those of other social scientists who have visited the U. S. S. R.

Like other observers, I was struck by the precociously adultlike behavior of Soviet children. By Western standards, they are remarkably well-mannered, industrious, serious and well-informed. But equally impressive to a social psychologist were certain aspects of the adult society. These features can be seen from two perspectives.

From one point of view, there is certainly, in the Soviet Union, a pervasive conformity to group norms, which is reinforced by social criticism—informal as well as formal. Deviant behavior, such as tossing a scrap of paper on the pavement, is promptly reprimanded by the nearest passer-by as *"nyekulturno"* (uncultured). And when one requests anything that is the least bit irregular, there is a ready answer: "It is impossible" or "It is not my affair." Individual needs have no status. To have a request granted, one has to appear as a member of one's collective.

BUT there is another view of this same picture. Along with conformity, there is a common commitment to values, goals and ways of life. As I observed, listened to, and talked with many Russians, I was surprised by the strength and pervasiveness of what appeared to be genuine pride and faith in their system.

What is more, the commitment extended beyond mere words. On every side people were busily engaged in some form of productive activity, and they spoke enthusiastically of the progress they were making. Not only the newspapers, but the man on the street would proclaim proudly, "In a few more years, we shall catch up to you." Then, with a grin of confidence: "And a few more years after that, we shall be way ahead of you!"

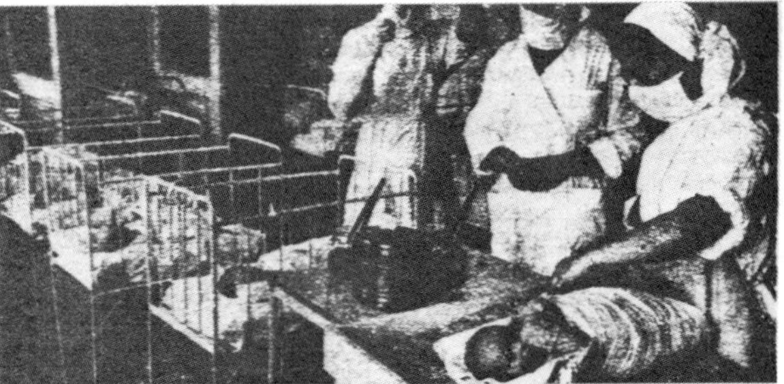

**SWADDLING CLOTHES**—A scene in a Moscow maternity hospital. Many Russian infants are boarded out at the age of three months.

Of course, not everything is going the Communists' way, even in the U. S. S. R. The apathy, corruption, disaffection and alcoholism which the Soviet leaders, in effect, acknowledge by their frequent denunciations are apparent to the visitor, especially if he takes the trouble to depart from the Intourist track and wander on his own.

In the face of such problems, the Soviet Government is placing more, rather than less, reliance on its methods of character education. A major aspect of the educational reform announced two years ago involves the development of several new types of educational institutions. The most important of these is the *internat* or boarding school, in which children are to be entered as early as three months of age, with parents visiting only on week-ends. (Surprising as it may seem to Americans, Russian infants are boarded out at this age.)

Recent statements in the Soviet press reveal that the Government is experiencing some difficulties with these schools. Construction is not proceeding according to plan and some parents object to sending their children to school in other cities or towns.

BUT the Government, apparently, has not modified its ultimate objective. Other types of schools will keep the youngsters from 8 in the morning until 8 at night. All types are designed not only to provide adequate care for children in a nation of working mothers, but also, in line with Makarenko's principles, to give maximum opportunity for training in practical education, character building and experience in collective living.

What are the implications of these developments for the West? Clearly, some central features of the Soviet approach, such as the denial of the right to deviate and the glorification of the "informer," are incompatible with what we regard as moral and right. But this does not mean that the Soviet methods are not effective. On the contrary, they may serve quite well for developing the motives and skills that make for progress and productivity in a Communist society.

Moreover, the Soviet social technology is exportable, and it *is* being exported on an extensive scale to other nations around the world. To cite but a minor example, a Russian educator told me that his latest book was the largest-selling psychology text in Mexico (and probably the cheapest in price). Finally, it is entirely possible that the recent Soviet achievements in industry, education, sports and science are merely the first fruits of an equally potent social technology which renovates not only things but men themselves.

WHAT does one do in the face of such a challenge? Clearly, there is no simple, quick countermeasure that will remove the threat and relieve our anxiety. In fact, we have yet to learn to become anxious, to appreciate the full extent and nature of the danger we face. For it is not what the Communist world can and will do, but what we can and will not do that carries the threat to our Western civilization.

Our civilization challenges the Communist world with the revolutionary proposition that responsibility is not incompatible with freedom, and that the welfare of society and the dignity of the individual are inseparable. But the question of which thesis will triumph clearly depends not on ideas alone but on the actions these ideas inspire.

In the realm of education the Communists are giving systematic attention and major emphasis to training in values and behavior consistent with their ideals. We can hardly claim we are doing as much or as well for our own value system. In American schools, training for action consistent with social responsibility and human dignity is at best an extra-curricular activity. Yet we are fond of saying that the American school is the bulwark of democracy. If this be true, we had better look to our defenses.

# Spiritual Key Is Hunted By Some in Soviet Science

By HARRISON E. SALISBURY

Within the most advanced echelon of Soviet science there is emerging a tendency to seek a nonmaterialist, spiritual concept of the universe. This startling development within the élite corps of Soviet society is closely related to two collateral tendencies—a new and vigorous Communist party drive against religious beliefs and a reform move within the Russian Orthodox Church to adapt itself to the modern technological society.

The fact that some of the most brilliant Soviet scientists suggest that there must exist in the universe a force or power that is superior to any possessed by man is said to have shocked conventionally minded Communist party functionaries.

How widespread this tendency is cannot be established. Names are not being given. But there is reason to believe that some of the most eminent figures in the galaxy of Soviet physicists, astronomers and mathematicians are involved.

### Tendency May Spread

They are men of great influence. It may be presumed that the tendency that they represent will not long be confined to the field of science. These men have not become believers in a formal religion or dogma. Their faith is more akin to that appearing among many of their Western scientific colleagues. But they are no longer atheists.

A succinct summary of the nature of this belief has been stated in fictional terms by V. Tendryakov, one of the younger generation of Soviet writers. There is reason to believe that Mr. Tendryakov's fictional statement is close to that embraced by a number of eminent scientists.

The author put it in these words:

"I do not imagine God as He is depicted on icons. To me God is a sort of spiritual principle, the stimulus to the emergence of the galaxies, the stars, the planets and of everything which lives and reproduces on these planets, from the most elementary cells up to man."

The Soviet Communist movement has traditionally opposed all religious faith. Atheism is supposed to be the party dogma.

The Russian Orthodox Church, the major Christian faith in Russia, has been dominated by a ritual and liturgy deeply rooted in the distant past. The typical Russian "believer" has long been an old and often superstitious woman whose visible evidence of faith was marked by prostrate prayer and reverential kissing of the icon.

### Young Priests Stressing Church Ties to Life

The relationship of the Orthodox Church to science, advanced technology or contemporary social problems has been slight. Now, however, concurrent with the emergence of religious faith in the high echelons of Soviet society, a new movement within the Orthodox Church, strongly backed by the young priesthood, has arisen.

A key figure in the new movement is Archbishop Nicodemus, a 32-year-old prelate who last year became head of the church's department of foreign affairs.

Archbishop Nicodemus, however, is merely symbolic of a new current that has emerged in the ancient church as a new generation of young priests, the first really new generation trained since the Bolshevik Revolution, has begun to assume important posts.

The new young men, all in their late twenties or early thirties, are seeking to break the image of the Orthodox Church as a fortress of superstition and backwardness. They seek to develop an appeal to youth. They are aware of the tendencies emerging among men of science and they hope to adapt the church to the complexity of the modern world. Like ministers in Western churches, they wish to relate the church to the life of the community.

This is not easy in ecclesiastic terms because the Orthodox Church never underwent a Reformation. Nevertheless, they are tackling the problem boldly and unconventionally.

One priest, for example, is presenting a series of sermons on topics of immediate and controversial interest. He announces the series in advance, like a lecture course, and encourages discussion after the sermon.

The priest chooses subjects that are of intellectual interest and he has found that more and more young people are now sprinkled among the old women who used to make up 80 per cent of the congregation.

Other churches are introducing activities especially interesting to young people, such as sports programs, football teams and hobby activities.

### Church Policy Reversed In International Field

In the international field, Archbishop Nicodemus has reversed the policy followed by the late Metropolitan Nikolai, whom he succeeded. The Metropolitan, a powerful man, sought to gather all the Orthodox churches of the world under the Moscow patriarchy. The policy of unification and Russian domination was roughly equivalent to the Stalinist foreign policy of that period.

Metropolitan Nikolai, as the foreign director of the church, worked closely and effectively with the late Georgi G. Karpov, state liaison man between the Orthodox Church and the Government. Before getting that post, Mr. Karpov was active in atheistic propaganda.

The new line of the Orthodox Church is for ecumenical relations and contacts as widespread and as close as possible with other churches. Thus, the Orthodox Church has now for the first time joined the World Council of Churches. It is active in seeking better fraternal relations with other Orthodox groups and with the Church of England.

This, in general, is felt to fit more closely with the Khrushchev foreign policy of widespread contacts throughout the world rather than the narrow type that prevailed under Stalin.

In the post-war years the Orthodox Church, largely unmolested by the party and often aided by the Government's liberality in returning churches to communities, enjoyed substantial growth both in membership and financial stability. New ecclesiastic schools were opened.

The number of believers was—and still is—estimated at about 50,000,000 in a total population of about 215,000,000.

However, the obvious signs of strength and vitality in the Orthodox Church have increasingly disturbed Communist activists, particularly the neo-Stalinist propaganda specialists. Youth leaders have become concerned, too, at evidence of the continuing attractive force of the church for young people.

The question has been raised repeatedly in party circles why, after more than forty years of party propaganda, repression and administrative action, the church still remains a powerful and vigorous force in Russian life.

With their passion for attacking any area of nonconformity, party activists have gradually stepped up their campaign against the Orthodox Church as part of a general drive against religious belief.

Recognizing that much party atheistic literature was primitive and useless, the propaganda department has turned to the production of a wide variety of new works on the subject. Party and political bookstores now offer a dozen or more anti-religious works at any moment. Anti-religious instruction in the schools has been invigorated and more public lectures are offered on anti-religious themes. Most of this is ignored by the Soviet public.

However, the party has not been content to confine itself to propaganda—although Premier Khrushchev has several times warned against utilizing "administrative" measures against the church.

For reasons that are not entirely clear—but may be related to the use of the area by both the Czarist and Stalin regimes as a dumping ground for political prisoners—all Orthodox sermons in Siberia must be submitted to civil authorities for censorship.

This is not true of sermons in European Russia. The regulation is sometimes evaded by Siberian priests by submitting their sermons to the Journal of the Patriarchy, a publication of the church. Once printed in the journal they may be freely delivered.

In the weeks just before the twenty-second party congress in October, local authorities in many places began to close churches. They had heard a rumor that the congress would ban churches throughout the country. In some areas of Siberia bands of Komsomol youths attacked churches, breaking windows, smashing altars and defacing icons.

This alarmed the Government, which is always sensitive to unauthorized or unorganized violence. The police and the quasi-official druzhina, or auxiliary police, were ordered to protect the churches and bring the violence to an end.

### Government Continuing Tactics of Harassment

However, the Government itself has not ceased its campaign of harassment. Three Orthodox seminaries have been closed, leaving five seminaries and two academies in operation. Two archbishops have been sent to prison on charges of misappropriation of funds, nonpayment of taxes and other fiscal irregularities.

There have been persistent rumors in the West that large numbers of Orthodox churches have been closed recently. However, there is little evidence either in the principal Soviet cities or the countryside of such action.

Estimates that 1,500 to 2,000 of the 20,000 to 22,000 churches have been closed do not seem to be borne out by information provided within the Soviet Union by Orthodox Church sources.

The other estimates, which seem to have had their origin in Orthodox Church sources in Paris, may relate to closings over several years, but this is not certain. Such closings as have been verified are largely confined to areas in western Russia, particularly regions incorporated into the Soviet Union in World War II.

The famous Pechersky monastery in Kiev has been closed. However, this is situated on the Dnieper River cliffs in the center of a large area that has been closed off since last spring. A section of the cliff had broken off and caused a disastrous mud slide in which there was a heavy loss of life.

Metropolitan Nikolai died last December and was buried with full honors of the church. A number of foreign clergymen were in Moscow at the time and attended the funeral.

One church official commented: "It is fortunate there were foreigners here. Otherwise there would have been rumors about Nikolai."

Despite the presence of the foreigners, rumors have circulated alleging that the Metropolitan received improper medical treatment and that in some manner his death was not natural. This has been related to his abrupt resignation last year and replacement by the youthful Archbishop Nicodemus, who had been his deputy.

However, persons close to the church insist that Metropolitan Nikolai had often offered his resignation in the past; that with a change in church foreign policy a change in personnel was dictated and that he was offered the metropolitanship of Leningrad but preferred to go into retirement.

If the Government campaign appears thus far to have caused little damage to the Orthodox Church, the same may also be said for the increased propaganda against the Baptists, the most rapidly growing faith in the Soviet Union.

Because of the vigor of the Baptist Church and particularly because of its demonstrated appeal to young people it has felt the weight of a very strong propaganda campaign.

### Denunciation of Baptists Affects Membership

Newspapers of the Communist Youth League are constantly publishing articles denigrating the Baptists. They are charged with diverting young people from their studies, with primitive superstition, with financial and moral abuses and with just about any kind of accusation that comes into the mind of party agitators.

This has not left the Baptist Church entirely unaffected. There has been a slight drop in the last year in the number of baptisms and weddings performed by the Baptists in Moscow and Leningrad. Some small communities in rural areas have lost their church facilities. Others have found it more difficult to operate. But in general the Baptists have weathered the storm.

The greatest wrath of the party is directed toward minor faiths such as the Jehovah's Witnesses and the Seventh Day Adventists, which are regarded as "alien" and "subversive."

One factor that militates against closing of Orthodox or Baptist churches is said to be a fear by the party that the church might go underground, where it would be even more difficult to combat.

Recently, court action was brought in the Soviet Republic of Kirghizia against three resettled Volga German families who were Seventh Day Adventists. They were deprived of parental rights over their children on the ground that they had refused to let the youngsters go to school on Saturdays or join the Pioneer youth organization.

The trial was conducted in typical Soviet fashion with audience participation and applause. A newspaper commented:

"Henceforth, Soviet parents will be the loving and caring educators of these children and the time will come when the children will cordially thank them for their trouble."

February 7, 1962

# *'Lost Generation' Baffles Soviet; Nihilistic Youths Shun Ideology*

By HARRISON E. SALISBURY

A "lost generation" has appeared in the Soviet Union, alienated from Soviet goals and strongly oriented toward almost anything Western—from a new hair-do to a belief in democratic freedoms.

These young people—raised entirely under communism, never having known life except in a Marxist environment and many of them barely old enough to remember World War II and Stalin—are the despair of the Communist party.

Some of the youngsters are hooligans and adolescent delinquents, the Soviet cousins of the shook-up generation of New York. Others are well-educated, cultured young people, sons and daughters of high party and Government officials. These are the counterparts of the beat generation of San Francisco or the existentialists of the Left Bank in Paris.

From the dark provinces to the neon lights of Moscow's Gorky Street (which the young people persist in calling Brodvay) the generation ranging in age from about 15 to 25 has risen in the same kind of nihilistic revolt as that of their coevals in the West.

Party agitators exhort them. Komsomol bully squads rout them out of the restaurants and cafes and send them home. Photographs of them are plastered on billboards under headings: "Parasites, Get Out!" They are shipped to the virgin lands or the construction sites of Siberia.

But nothing that the party has been able to devise wins back the loyalty or enthusiasm of the bored, nihilistic and disoriented generation.

"This is our greatest defeat," a middle-aged party man conceded. "The young people have deserted the cause. I do not know how we are going to get them back."

Not all the young people, of course, have turned their backs on communism. Enthusiasts are to be found in Siberia working with vigor even in temperatures of 40 degrees below zero. They are to be found in Moscow University and in the Communist Youth organization.

But the numbers of the internal rebels are great. They can be seen everywhere. They dance to Western music. They wear Western-style clothes. They act as much like Westerners as they are able.

American jazz has swept the field. The party no longer even attempts to keep up the barriers. Moscow bands play a solid repertory of Western numbers. When the bands stop playing they switch on tape recordings made from broadcasts of "Music, U. S. A.," a Voice of America program.

The rhumba, the samba, the mambo, the cha-cha-cha—every form of Latin-American dance —are now permitted. These are the "native folk dances" of Cuba, Russia's good friend, so how can they be banned? Party propagandists still inveigh against jitterbugging (which few of them have ever seen) and rock 'n' roll.

### Soviet Youngsters Eager To Learn the Twist

But Soviet young people have abandoned these dances for the Latin fad. Now they are eagerly awaiting the twist. They know of the twist craze and have seen blurry photographs of the dance accompanying propaganda attacks on it. But no one in Moscow, outside of a few diplomats, yet knows how to do the dance.

However, it will not be long before Moscow's young people are twisting with the rest of the world. The question they ask nearly every foreigner they meet now is: "Can you show us how to do the twist?"

In Moscow restaurants and theatres it is hard to distinguish between many Soviet young people and foreigners. The girls wear their hair in lovely blonde beehives or variants of the loose, flowing Italian and French hair-dos.

For evening wear they favor excellently cut, short cocktail dresses, often off the shoulder or with bare arms. Their nylons are as sleek as those of their Western friends. Many wear fine Italian spike heel shoes or perfect copies from Czechoslovakia or handmade Moscow imitations.

Others pattern themselves after Brigitte Bardot, the idol of their boy friends. No Bardot films have been publicly shown in Moscow. But some have had private screenings to selected audiences and most Soviet young people are familiar with her features from photographs in East European publications.

In cafes young girls with pony-tail hair-dos, black cotton stockings, flat-heeled shoes and the rest of the ballet-style get-up are not uncommon. Usually their escorts are young men with fringe beards and tan slacks whose prototypes are to be found on a hundred American campuses.

Party authorities hate the beards as much as they do the cha-cha-cha. But Premier Fidel Castro wears a beard so the fad is not attacked outright. However, lectures on the virtue of shaving every day are frequent.

On the stage and in cartoons the party still lampoons the so-called "stilyagi" with his long zoot-suit jacket, flamboyant painted tie (often sporting a nude) and long watchchain.

But even in the distant provinces this caricature has long since vanished.

The present-day young man dresses with quiet conservatism. He has a Princeton or Yale haircut instead of the floppy Tarzan trim of a few years ago. His suit is usually dark blue or Oxford gray. He wears a white shirt and narrow Italian-type tie with neat horizontal stripes or, sometimes, a dark solid-color shirt with a contrasting tie of solid yellow or powder blue. His trousers are no longer bell-bottomed. They are pencil slim.

Occasionally, the young man may sport a porkpie flat-top hat with slightly flaring brim and bluejeans, which are called either "kowbois" or "Texas trousers."

Nothing infuriates party propagandists more than the bluejean fad. They declare that this is a completely alien style. They note that blue denim material is not even produced in the Soviet Union. Where the bluejeans come from is not certain. But it is believed they are smuggled in from Berlin through Poland.

### Tourists Transmit Tastes And Fads to Russians

These youngsters make a fetish of reading Polish newspapers or Western Communist organs such as L'Unità of Italy, L'Humanité of France or The London Daily Worker. Non-Communist Western publications seldom circulate in the Soviet Union, but sometimes copies of Time, Life, or Vogue are obtained from tourists. The tourists, as well as students from Poland and Western Europe, are the principal transmission belt for Western tastes and fads.

Another source is the anti-Western movie. Youngsters turn these pictures upside down, glorifying what they are supposed to despise. Two such films are now being shown in the Soviet Union—"America Through the Eyes of the French" and "Multi-Storied America." Neither picture is by any means completely anti-United States, but they are shown for their negative bias.

Some of the typical reactions

The New York Times (by Harrison E. Salisbury)

**"PARASITES GET OUT OF MOSCOW" is the message on this sign in the Soviet capital. The "parasites," some of whose photos are displayed, are young people who are captivated by Western customs and ideas, and tend to scorn precepts of communism.**

of Soviet young people to the films are as follows:

"Have you seen 'America Through the Eyes of the French?' What a wonderful picture! Is life in America really so thrilling? Here things are so boring! Do you really have automobile graveyards in America? Are there really teen-age gangs? Do they fight each other? Do you really smash cars up by deliberately running them into each other? (the reference is to a county fair "wreck" sequence) How much does the cheapest car cost in America—not a new one but an old one?"

And so on. The conversation is punctuated with exclamations and is conducted almost entirely in an excited tone.

Like their counterparts in the United States the Soviet youngsters talk in a special jargon, comprehensible only to themselves. Many of the terms are the equivalent of Western expressions. The boys refer to each other as "zhentlmen." They pepper their conversations with words like "tip-top" and "okay."

A favorite phrase is "Don't be afraid, lads, keep your pistol in your belt." This apparently is derived from old Western films or smuggled-in comic books. The comic-book has a vogue even among boys who cannot read foreign languages.

The more sophisticated members of the "lost generation" prefer J. D. Salinger, whose works recently have appeared in translation. "Catcher in the Rye" has become almost a status symbol among the university generation. And they are beginning to take up John Cheever in translation.

What do these young people want?

### Writers Are Denounced For Studies of Youth

There have been several sensitive studies of the generation by sympathetic young writers. The writers have been promptly denounced by the party as being members of the lost generation themselves, a charge that is not entirely without foundation.

One youngster, in a play by Ivan Kupriyanov, put it like this:

"It's too boring, being one of the orthodox. You can't do this. You must not do that. I'm sick of it. Sick of it all. It doesn't take brains to blat out commonplace truths. If I had the power I would forbid bombast for good."

Another youngster, in a scenario by Viktor Rozov, retorted when his mother told him he should behave better:

"Should! Should! I've hardly entered the world and all I hear is 'You should do this. You should do that. You should . . .' There is nothing whatever that I should do."

When this youngster runs away his girl says to him:

"I understand you. You are offended now. It seems to you that you are the only one in the whole world. The only only one. It's been that way with me, too. Sometimes, all of a sudden I am so sad . . . so terribly sad. It seems that no one needs you. You even cry. I cry and cry . . ."

A ruder young man, a complete delinquent, is asked what he wants in life:

"My golden desire? Well, nobody wants a heart attack. What do I want? Drink . . . restaurants . . . jazz . . . money . . . women . . . a Volga [a Soviet car] . . . a country cottage . . . you know, the complete gentleman's selection."

This kind of reaction baffles the older generation. As a party chief accurately declares in one play:

"I cannot understand our young people. They have some kind of kink. They are growing up without ideals. They have lost their ideals."

But the reply is: "What kind of ideals were they—that they were so easy to lose?"

Many of the young people have plenty of money. Many are the sons and daughters of important Soviet officials, directors of enterprises, party men.

They spent their evenings at the National Hotel restaurant until a "hot" band there was moved by the authorities to the less prominent Budapest Restaurant. They tagged over there, constantly chevied by the young Komsomol "druzhina" patrols, individuals wearing red arm-bands who are quasi-official guardians of social conduct. Now they go to the Metropole Hotel, where there is a new "iron" band. "Iron" is a superlative adjective in their vocabulary.

A fringe of them was involved in black-market currency operations with foreigners. Some of them traded icons to tourists for foreign clothing. Now the Government's draconian measures—execution of illegal dealers in currency by firing squads—has brought this activity to a halt.

### Gangs Terrorize Towns And Attack Policemen

In provincial towns and Moscow's sprawling industrial suburbs the picture of the "young generation" is hardly attractive. The boys organize in tough gangs that often terrorize people on the streets. The newspapers constantly report that in Pskov, Saratov or Zagorsk bands of hooligans have taken control of the streets and ordinary citizens hardly dare venture out at night. The gangs amuse themselves by attacking police posts and beating up militia (police) officers.

At some Moscow railroad stations billboards have been put up with photographs of out-of-town rowdies and warnings: "You shall not pass. We have no place for hooligans in our society."

But the drunken brawls that burst out in Moscow restaurants, in queues waiting for taxis, in the subway stations or in the markets make it evident that what the Young Communist press calls the "bacilli" of hooliganism have deeply affected the capital city as well.

What do these youngsters think of communism?

One of them snatches a pack of cigarettes from a stand and slips away. His friend exclaims: "But you didn't pay!"

"I'm just anticipating the arrival of communism when everything will be free," the thief responds.

Another youth says: "We have heard how great life is and of all the sacrifices that have been made to build our society. Now it is time for us to enjoy it."

"Do I enjoy my work?" a youngster says. "Certainly I do. Every 1st and 15th of the month, when I get my pay envelope."

Truth—by this the Russian young person means sincerity and genuineness—is the great goal.

Those who are more serious, those who have not given themselves up completely to aimless chasing of Western fads and fancies, seek out Western individuals and question them endlessly.

They have little hope of finding their ideals in the gray and hypocritical world in which they live. They hope that "the truth" may exist in the West. Those who try to respond to their eager, feverish questions about life beyond the Soviet frontier can only hope that the West will not prove to be equally disappointing.

"Oh, if you only knew how I want to travel!" said a bright-eyed well-groomed young girl of 21 in Samarkand. She had gone there after graduation from a university in a Volga town "because at least Central Asia is different."

"I have been here a year," she said. "It is just as boring as the Volga. I must go abroad. I must. Even if only to Rumania. If you only knew how boring life is in Russia!"

## Slang of Soviet Teen-Agers

***Following is a glossary of current teen-age slang in the Soviet Union:***

| Russian | Literal Translation | Slang |
|---|---|---|
| Predki | ancestors | parent |
| Kon | chess knight | father |
| Khata | peasant cottage | pad |
| Zhelezny | iron | terrific, great |
| Kusok | piece | money, specifically, 1,000 old rubles |
| Chuvok | meaningless, possibly derived from chuvstvo (feeling) | boy |
| Chuvika | same as above | girl |
| Oryol | eagle | great, terrific |
| Zapravlyat | to mix or season | to tell a lie |
| Tachka | wheelbarrow | one's private car |
| Flesh-royal | royal flush | wonderful |
| Pizhon | fop | youngster |
| Malchishki | street urchins | shook-up kids |
| Milti or miltami | derisive diminutive form of militia, or police | policeman |

THOUGHT AND CULTURE

# Ehrenburg Lifts the Iron Curtain a Bit

**The Russian writer's recent story, 'The Thaw,' stirs controversy in the Soviet Union, and gives the West a vivid picture of conflicts in the Communist state.**

By THOMAS P. WHITNEY

DURING the last few days the Kremlin Palace in Moscow has been ringing with the words of a distinguished literary discussion. The Second Congress of Soviet Writers—the first such meeting in twenty years—was finally convened there on Dec. 15 after having been postponed twice this year while the Communist party made up its mind on the party line for literature. Present when the writers' session opened were Premier Georgi Malenkov, First Secretary of the Central Committee Nikita Khrushchev, and the other most important Soviet leaders.

It was appropriate that they were in the hall, for no activity has suffered so much from Kremlin tyranny as writing. The post-war U. S. S. R. possessed writers of talent and an enormous reading public with an insatiable thirst for works expressing the deep emotions of Soviet life. This could have been the beginning of a new creative period of Russian literature to rival that of the nineteenth century. But Stalin was determined that Soviet post-war literature must serve only to glorify himself and the Communist party. He was willing to go to any lengths to get what he wanted and to suppress anything else.

Moscow street scene—"Ehrenburg has put into the mouths of his characters some of the previously unsaid things that many Russians think."

As a result, the period from the end of the war to Stalin's death was almost totally barren of all creation. Purges of literary figures, promulgations and reversals of new party lines and critical standards, imprecations from the heights of the Central Committee, acrid group discussions of Soviet writers, and abject prostrations of authors charged with sins—these made up the post-war literary scene. They produced an appearance of vast activity—but no significant literature. The wisest men among Soviet writers, many of them, found ways of busying themselves with administrative problems and "safe" activities and subjects.

THUS when Stalin died, his erstwhile subordinates who became his heirs understood that here, as elsewhere in Soviet life, there must be changes.

The heavy hand of party control over literature was slightly lifted for a little more than a year after Stalin died. Fresh ideas began cautiously to appear in drama and in the literary magazines. To the Western mind these ideas did not appear to be revolutionary. But they were enough apparently to frighten the powers-that-be in Russia.

And so now, and since mid-1954, Messrs. Malenkov, Khrushchev and company are busily engaged in reasserting Communist party domination over literature. The editors of two of the most important Soviet literary magazines have been removed. Several writers have been charged with immoral conduct and booted out of the Soviet Writers' Union. Other prominent writers have been severely criticized.

But the Kremlin faces in the long run an insoluble dilemma: on the one hand, reimposition of strict party control in literature will frustrate all creative work—even production of good propaganda for the party; on the other hand, relaxation of such control means immediate expression of "dangerous ideas."

It is in this context that a close look at the most important piece of literature produced in the Soviet Union in 1954 is revealing. The work in question is a long short story by the well-known writer Ilya Ehrenburg published in the literary magazine, "The Banner." Its title is, significantly, "The Thaw."

"The Thaw" describes the emotions and reactions of Russians to the post-Stalin environment of the late winter of 1953-54. Its action takes place in an industrial settlement on the Volga River a long way from Moscow, near the city of Saratov. The big enterprise is a machine-tool plant. The characters of the story—of whom there are more than a dozen—come mostly from the local intelligentsia, in part from the top brackets of the factory administration.

LIKE most Soviet stories, "The Thaw" runs light on plot and heavy on conversations and monologues expressing the thoughts of its characters.

"The Thaw" is important because it is controversial. It has drawn heavy attack from critics in the Soviet Union. Ehrenburg has been severely criticized

THOMAS P. WHITNEY spent nine years in Russia as Associated Press correspondent. He is now editing A.P. foreign news in New York.

by the Communist Youth League paper and by one of the top men in the Writers' Union, Konstantine Simonov, himself a well-known writer and a member of the Central Committee of the Communist party.

"The Thaw" is controversial because of what it reveals about today's Russia. Much of it is quite ordinary and accepted by Soviet standards. But at the same time Ehrenburg has put into the mouths of some of his characters quite unorthodox remarks to which Soviet readers are unaccustomed and which express, as anyone who knows contemporary Russia can confirm, some of the previously unsaid things many Russians think.

Nor is it entirely what the characters say or think that is controversial; it is also the kind of people they are. Take, for instance, the engineer K., one of the most positive characters in the story. Says Ehrenburg in describing him:

"He was in the tenth class when he experienced his first great tribulation. In the autumn of 1936 his stepfather was arrested. The morning after, he met his best friend Misha near his home. K. called out to him—wanted to share his grief, ask him what to do. But Misha scowled and without saying anything to him crossed over to the other side of the street. Soon K. was expelled from the Komsomols. * * * He went to work in a factory."

This brief but frank mention of one of the more terrible things in Soviet life—the cruel visitation upon children of the misfortunes of their parents—is something which in previous years one could never have found in Soviet literature. It is a facet of Soviet life that everyone in the country knows about but that no one could write about.

In describing a Jewish woman doctor, Ehrenburg tells in her own words how she was mistreated by Russians in January and February, 1953, when the so-called "doctors' plot" hung over the Soviet Union with anti-Semitic sentiments being stirred up by the Soviet Government itself: "Sometimes after the communiqué [on the doctors' plot] I had to listen to such [cursing]."

The workers in the factory, as Ehrenburg describes them, live in damp, dark little houses, whose roofs come off and whose walls cave in when a strong windstorm blows up.

ONE of the women in the story goes about town searching for food for a birthday banquet. She "went through the entire city and just barely succeeded in getting together enough flour. She could not find a turkey nor a goose anywhere and there were no eggs at all, as if on purpose."

Ehrenburg has two artists—painters—in his story. One of them is a hack and a careerist. He starts off to a good career by painting an immense and bad painting entitled "The Collective Farm Feast." As a result he gets a studio in Moscow and a large fee for his work. But he is in trouble shortly thereafter—not for doing bad work as an artist but for criticizing some of the leading Moscow painters. Immediately he loses his studio.

He then begins in another direction, having understood his mistake. He repairs his relations with the big men of the Soviet art world by praising them on every occasion possible. As a result he is soon well on the way toward regaining his lost position. He is completely cynical about his work and frankly admits he is a hack. This, he says, is the only way to be a success in art in the Soviet Union.

The other painter in Ehrenburg's story is a true artist. He lives only for his painting. But he refuses to do what the party demands of artists. Instead of painting portraits of Soviet officials or propaganda pictures, he paints portraits of his crippled wife and landscapes which, according to Ehrenburg, are works of genius. But they find no appreciation; they gather dust in his closet.

The artist and his wife occupy one single room, dank and dismal. It is in a home which before the revolution was occupied by one petty merchant and now must house four entire families. He himself cannot even support himself and must live off the earnings of his wife.

And then there is the engineer S., who has been beaten, buffeted and humiliated year after year in an unending series of security checks. Why? Because his daughter lives outside the Soviet Union, in Belgium.

EHRENBURG makes many comments about the situation in Soviet art through the mouth of the cynical painter P., who stands out as one of the chief characters in his story. This painter says:

"They don't pay for ideas. With ideas you can only break your own neck. In a book there is supposed to be ideology. If there is, that's good. But only insane people have ideas."

"Nowadays they would not take Raphael into the Soviet Painters' Union!"

"Nowadays everyone shouts about art and no one loves it. Such is the epoch!"

"In Moscow, X, at the discussion of the painters' exhibition, scolded the painters for pessimism. He shouted: 'We need boldness!' and then became such a drunkard they had to take him to a hospital."

He declares of the poor but honest painter who is a friend of his: "S. lives poorly. * * * Well, one can reconcile one's self to that. But indeed no one even knows of his work. He told me I am the first artist who ever came to see him. * * * In the Painters' Union they consider him abnormal. And in fact it's true: one must be a schizophrenic to work as he does: not to give in, to do what one feels * * * yes, that sounds silly, but it's a fact. I envy him."

Ehrenburg also has his characters say things which perhaps have even broader meanings than is immediately apparent.

"One cannot trust anyone!" declares the factory director, a hard-working but tyrannical, Stalin-type boss.

EHRENBURG depicts this director as a person with many bad characteristics and guilty of gross negligence of the welfare of his workers. But, at the last minute, as he goes to Moscow where he is to receive the news of his dismissal—he is being "purged"—the writer takes some pity on him.

"Here am I, an honest Soviet person!" the director thinks to himself. "I have given my entire life to the state, but now I'm done for * * * and nobody gives a hoot!"

And, as Ehrenburg makes clear, no one really does.

"Where is Z.? What has happened to him? Not even one living soul remembers him."

The director Z. obviously here is more than just a character. He is a symbol. How broad a symbol?

Speaking of Z. and those like him—of whom, the story makes clear, there are still plenty in Russia—Ehrenburg has one of his characters declaim:

"People are sick of them, oh, how sick of them!"

The author expresses in a number of passages the deep longing for change, to be rid of people like Z.

One character says to himself: "Probably I've gotten used to remaining silent, to

Ilya Ehrenburg.

looking at garbage and not noticing it. That's what's bad. When we only began to build it was natural that there should be a lot of trash around. But now it's time to clean it out—the house is being lived in."

EHRENBURG expresses another thought through the words of the engineer whose daughter is in Belgium. It is the concept that the experiences of Soviet people have been so profound that only they themselves can understand themselves, that there is an impenetrable barrier between them and the outside world and the people from the outside world—even those who understand the language.

S. writes to his daughter Mary, who left Russia when she was a little girl and who now speaks of coming back for a short visit with her Belgian husband:

"Of course it will be interesting for you * * * to see another world. But don't think you will understand it easily, just because you were born in Moscow. I remember how you played in the sand on Gogol Boulevard. You had young friends there. They understand how we live and why: they grew up here, worked here, they had much grief and happiness and hope. You are not to blame that your mother took you to Belgium.

"But understand one thing, be serious: you will feel yourself here a tourist, a foreigner. You write yourself that you don't understand how we live. If you were to be here, were to see how I work, how my comrades work, what enrages us, what makes us glad, you would still not understand anything. It's a different world, completely different!"

But the story has even more than this. In its last pages there crops up repeatedly the concept of "sudden change."

Krokodil on writers—"What are you doing?"—"Observing life."

The actress Tanya says to the painter P:

"Don't lose heart. I am also often in this state. I let my hands fall by my sides. * * * But then I begin to think—everything can change suddenly. * * * Don't laugh. I am certain it happens. * * * Do you believe in miracles?"

"And what do you call a miracle?" he asks her.

"For example, when it's very bad and suddenly it becomes good, everything changes; that is, everything stays the same—the city, the people, the things—but everything is different * * * do you understand?"

"No, I'm not talking about the weather. Everything can be much more deep," she adds a moment later.

HOW are such phrases to be interpeted in the context of the story which Ehrenburg has produced? Is he suggesting the possibility of further important changes to come in Russia? If so, what kind of changes?

Ehrenburg has had a motley career. He was in the Bolshevik underground inside Russia before 1909, when he emigrated to France and lost interest in the revolution. He returned to Russia during the revolution only to write anti-Soviet verses. Later he swung back in the direction of the Soviets—but remained abroad.

Finally he returned to the U.S.S.R. for good and won the favor of Stalin, who liked his work. During the war, as Russia's most popular war correspondent, he led the hate campaign against the Germans.

Certainly no one outside of Russia can tell precisely what Ehrenburg was trying to do and say in "The Thaw." In attacking Ehrenburg for this story, Konstantine Simonov took the attitude that Ehrenburg was intentionally putting the entire Soviet Union in a negative light. Ehrenburg in a lengthy answer defended himself by claiming his artist's right to portray his characters through their own thoughts and statements even if these statements were untrue.

HE justly pointed out that his characters were almost all of them positive persons from the Communist point of view. He answered that he had made clear in his story that the Soviet Union is in a state of advance and a mood of optimism. And, indeed, in judging this story, one has to take into consideration that the over-all impression it makes is one which is in some respects quite favorable to the present post-Stalin Government.

Even after the opening of the writers' congress it was by no means clear just exactly what form the final verdict on "The Thaw" would take.

But the fact is that, whatever Ehrenburg himself may have meant, he has in any case opened a small—a very small, but a *new*—window into the minds and feelings of Russians.

Ehrenburg may have to issue repeated disclaimers that the feelings to which he gives expression are his own, but he has stated them so well one naturally suspects they are not entirely strange to him, even though he has been a loyal servant of the regime for so many years. One also suspects that if Ehrenburg gives voice to these ideas it is because he understands they will strike a chord in the mood of the Russians.

At one point, the story says: "In life there occur miracles, perhaps hidden beneath a shell. * * *"

And so it is perhaps with the whole story; there is, perhaps, meaning "hidden beneath a shell."

December 26, 1954

# 3 SOVIET WRITERS RETURN TO FAVOR

## Authors Formerly Criticized Named to Board of Union by Literary Congress

By CLIFTON DANIEL

Special to The New York Times.

MOSCOW, Dec. 26—At least three authors whose works had been severely criticized here in the past appeared today on the new board of directors elected by the Union of Soviet Writers.

The names of the 134 members of the directorate were announced this afternoon at the final session of the second All-Union Congress of Writers held in the Great Kremlin Palace. The congress, the first in twenty years, started Dec. 15.

Three board members whose names were of particular interest were Alexander Tvardovsky, poet, and Vera Panova and Vasily Grossman, novelists.

Last August, Mr. Tvardovsky was replaced as editor of Novy Mir, one of the organs of the Writers Union, after the magazine had published an article by Vladimir Pomerantsev saying that the only criterion of a writer's effort should be his sincerity.

**Forgiving Attitude Recalled**

That article was roundly denounced as an attempt to change the ideological basis of Soviet literature, which is supposed to serve the cause of communism consciously and actively.

Miss Panova was much criticized for her latest novel, "The Seasons," which was decried as being too "objective." Mr. Grossman came under attack from Mikhail Bubennov, a critic, for his novel on World War II, a work that is now in circulation and was praised during the congress by Alexei Surkov, secretary of the Writers Union.

The election of these three recalled speeches by Mr. Surkov and Alexander Korneichuk, prominent Ukrainian playwright, advocating a more forgiving attitude toward authors who, having been charged with ideological errors, recognize their mistakes and change their course.

Present at the congress and active in its proceedings was Anna Akhmatova, whose verses were partly responsible for the 1946 decree of the Central Committee of the Soviet Communist party laying down the law for Soviet writers.

**Love Poetry Unusual**

The Central Committee at that time abolished the magazine Leningrad, saying it had forgotten that magazines must not be "apolitical." Leningrad had published among other things poetry by Miss Akhmatova that the Central Committee described as "empty and idealistic, full of pessimism, decadence and bourgeois estheticism."

Miss Akhmatova wrote love poetry, an unusual thing in the Soviet Union, and slender volumes of her verse are still sought and treasured by young girls.

With the abolition of the magazine Leningrad, the Soviet

Union's second city, was left with only one literary journal, Zvezda (Star). During the writers' congress it was announced that the city would again have a second magazine to be called Neva, after the river that flows through Leningrad.

The congress began with a message from the Communist party's Central Committee laying down the line for Soviet literature. It ended with a message from the congress to the Central Committee pledging loyalty to the political directive. The writers promised to struggle for the building of communism, to expose capitalist prejudices, to eschew bourgeois "isms," to reflect the struggle between the old and the new in Soviet life, to fight for peace and against warmongers and to give all to the country in case of war.

Although subordination of art to politics was re-emphasized, some new trends appeared in the Congress debates.

One was the proclamation of a more forgiving attitude toward ideological backsliders.

Another was the declaration, frequently made, that Soviet writers should study the "progressive" literature of other countries and make use of it in perfecting their own technique.

The third was the idea mentioned in the message to the Central Committee today that the writer must not be afraid to present conflicts and contradictions that still exist in Soviet life.

There was a certain amount of give and take in the debates. Speakers from the floor challenged notions voiced from the platform and were in their turn challenged.

The speeches were generally moderate and no sensational or rude accusations were made. Strong political condemnation of this or that author was avoided.

December 27, 1954

# *Lysenko, Stalin's Protege, Out As Soviet's Scientific Chieftain*

By WELLES HANGEN
Special to The New York Times.

MOSCOW, April 9—Trofim D. Lysenko, who once wielded Stalin-like power over Soviet biological research, has resigned as head of the All-Union Academy of Agricultural Science. His successor is Pavel P. Lobanov, a Deputy Premier in charge of agriculture.

Vladimir V. Matskevich, hard-working Minister of Agriculture who led the Soviet farm delegation on a tour of the United States and Canada last summer, succeeds Mr. Lobanov as Deputy Premier. Mr. Matskevich is known as a strong supporter of Nikita S. Khrushchev's panaceas for the Soviet Union's farm problem.

Academician Lysenko's resignation and the two new appointments were announced tonight by Tass, official Soviet news agency.

Observers here drew the following conclusions from the changes:

¶Soviet scientific research is being progressively divested of the men whom Stalin designated to enforce paralyzing orthodoxy in all fields.

¶Mr. Khrushchev, the Communist party chief, is further consolidating the critical agricultural sector of the Soviet economy.

The three-paragraph Tass announcement gave no indication what position, if any, Professor Lysenko would now hold. It said merely the Council of Ministers had accepted his request to be relieved of his responsibilities as head of the Academy of Agricultural Sciences.

**Professor Lysenko won fame in the Stalin era as the exponent of the officially approved theory that acquired characteristics were hereditable. According to this theory, new plant species may be produced by subjecting the seed and later the plant itself to drastic environment changes.**

**Thus Professor Lysenko held that new varieties of corn, wheat or other crops could be evolved by climatic, nutritional and other environmental conditions. He asserted that changes produced in this way would be transmitted to subsequent plant generations.**

**Professor Lysenko's view was bitterly contested abroad. In the Stalin era, however, it was enshrined as the official Soviet doctrine.**

**Attacked by Scientists**

Following the dictator's death in March, 1953, Professor Lysenko was openly attacked. Several learned journals published articles disputing his views and presenting evidence to show that acquired characteristics are not inherited.

The United States farm delegation found last summer that most Soviet agricultural experiment stations were ignoring Professor Lysenko's dogmas. On the farms themselves the Americans found his injunctions had failed to yield tangible results and were being increasingly discarded.

His prestige was not enhanced when Mr. Khrushchev began to champion the widespread planting of hybrid corn as a means of meeting the Soviet Union's needs for human and animal feed.

It was recalled that increasingly sharp attacks had been launched on Stalinist methods in scientific research since the party congress in February. Stalin and his "toadies" have been accused of stifling free inquiry and causing Soviet research to stagnate in many fields.

April 10, 1956

# NEW SOVIET CULTURE IS DE-STALINIZED TOO

## But Writers and Others Are Warned They Serve the Communist State

By JACK RAYMOND
Special to The New York Times.

MOSCOW, July 28—A few lines in a single Soviet newspaper this week revived the official reputation of V. E. Meyerhold who was purged in the Nineteen Thirties and his imaginative ideas of modern theatrical productions condemned to the fires of Soviet realism.

A few days earlier two Yiddish writers were similarly posthumously rehabilitated. Six poems of Peretz Markish were published in a newspaper. Itsik Feffer was mentioned in a favorable light. They had been purged in 1948.

Thus in its offhand way did the regime seek to right wrongs against men of art which had been perpetrated during Stalin's reign. Other rehabilitations had taken place in the political field.

But what of art itself? Of the principles of cultural freedom in literature, theatre, music and painting which had become stultified? A new mood seems presaged although it cannot be said that the kind of ferment that has made itself visible in Poland and Hungary is indicated here.

Under Stalin idolatry of Stalin

'CRITERION OF GREAT ART'

Alexander in The Philadelphia Bulletin

himself was a primary consideration in the creative arts. The painter and sculptor were at a particular disadvantage since they had to devote themselves to reproducing his image or painting it into scenes where its relevance was political. However, artists in all fields had to attune their works to his tastes. He could close a play or keep it open by his personal reaction. A natural corollary was sycophancy.

V. Ermilov, the literary critic, referred in a recent book review to the "tendency to trite pompousness, the varnishing of reality and excessive praise and glorification" which featured literature under Stalin.

In a sense, however, these attributes were superficial. The real crime of repression of artistic values in the Soviet Union has been its almost morbid conservatism. The delights of imagination and spirit were forsaken for the safety of approval.

It is against this situation rather than the linking of culture to political ideals that men like Dmitri Shostakovich have lately spoken out. In a recent appeal the man who is regarded as the Soviet Union's greatest living composer assailed the "dogmatists" and hailed "bold innovation."

In 1948 Shostakovich was denounced by the Central Committee of the Soviet Communist party and accused of writing music that reflected "formalism with bourgeois influences directed against the people." Shostakovich apologized then. But now, citing the decisions of the party congress in February, he called for a new birth of creative liberty. Moreover, he made it clear that it was not he alone who was speaking. He cited the congress expressly to show that the present party leaders were behind him.

### System Not Attacked

At the same time too sharp a line should not be drawn between the attitude of the present regime and that of the past in terms of ideology. It should not be forgotten that de-Stalinization is essentially an assault on an individual and not on the existing system.

Recently the party theoretical organ Kommunist declared:

> There have been of late unhealthy tendencies among some politically immature writers and artists. There has been a conciliatory attitude toward bourgeois art—the outcome of a misguided attempt to extend the coexistence thesis to the plane of ideology. Certain writers and artists who in the past were rightly censured by Soviet society now seek revenge and there have been all sorts of attacks against party leadership in the fields of literature and the arts.

### Stalin's Role

This shows that the present leaders are not seeking to reverse entirely the development of Soviet culture during the three decades of Stalin's rule.

"There are people who call upon us to revert to the state of affairs in the early and middle Twenties and who affirm that everything was right and perhaps even ideal at that time," declared Literaturnaya Gazeta in an editorial making it clear that the editors did not agree with such people. Nevertheless the present arbiters of Soviet culture have undertaken to give the people a feeling of change in the arts as well as in politics.

The fundament of this program is, of course, the removal of the "cult of personality," that is, Stalin's personality.

They started removing Stalin's pictures and the first place they did so was from the wonderful Tretyakov Galleries. Distinctively Western art forms were revived, noticed and exhibited. An exhibit of modern French art and literature was rapturously received in Moscow.

### Successful Play

Vladimir Mayekofsky's play "Klop" ("The Bug") is enjoying a brilliant success. This alone is a great manifestation of a new era for it is staged in the free-wheeling spirit of Myerhold and appeared on the boards even before Meyerhold's formal rehabilitation.

Any discussion of the arts inevitably includes the question what Soviet artists did during Stalin's rule, just as the successors to Stalin were called upon recently to explain their own record.

The answer is that they have chosen to hail the future rather than explain the past. They have admitted "mistakes" but they have not gone so far in condemnation of the cultural record as has already been done by others in politics. Perhaps one reason is that Russian cultural life has not been completely unpraiseworthy, particularly in music. While Soviet leaders admit that Stalin's rule harmed literature, especially poetry, it is nevertheless asserted that many writers made "gigantic forward strides" despite Stalin.

Soviet cultural leaders have not shown any of the defensiveness about their past that many persons in the West would expect them to do. And their future is clearly marked in the Literaturnaya Gazeta editorial which says: "Soviet literature was, is and will remain powerful because of its commitment to the party, its direct link with the policy of the Communist party and the Soviet state."

This should make it clear that the new mood of tolerance toward inventiveness and imagination in the cultural arts by no means implies acceptance of the idea of art for art's sake.

July 29, 1956

# At the Root Of It All

**NOT BY BREAD ALONE. By Vladimir Dudintsev. Translated from the Russian by Edith Bone. 512 pp. New York: E. P. Dutton & Co. $4.95.**

**By MARC SLONIM**

IN the preface written for the English version of his novel Vladimir Dudintsev complains of the articles with "strident headlines" and the "fuss" made in Europe and America about "Not by Bread Alone." What he fails to mention, however, is that since the fall of 1956, when it was serialized in the Moscow magazine Novy Mir, his book has been a real sensation in the U. S. S. R. It provoked riotous discussions and hundreds of articles with more than "strident" headlines all over Russia. It has been attacked and defended in special sessions of the Union of Soviet Writers, and it was talked about in party councils and government meetings.

Party Secretary, Nikita Khrushchev, in his speeches on art and literature, summarized in August in the twelfth issue of The Communist, singled out Dudintsev as a "calumniator who took a malicious joy in describing the negative sides of Soviet life" and tagged his novel "unhealthy, tendentious and obnoxious." While affirming that "reactionary forces abroad attempt at using this book against us," Khrushchev failed to explain the reasons for its smashing success at home. Neither the party leader nor the numerous Communist critics who accused Dudintsev of all mortal sins, ever dared to answer a very legitimate, natural question: Why has this novel, which certainly does not shine with any particular artistic merits, become such an important and central phenomenon of Russia's literary life? And why does it possess such an emotional appeal for its readers?

Before "Not by Bread Alone" was released in book form, the issues of Novy Mir in which it appeared commanded three times their normal price, and huge crowds gathered outside the jammed halls where panels on the novel were held. At one of these panels at the Central House of Writers in Moscow last October, the chairman, Vsevolod Ivanov, himself a well-known author, remarked that he had not seen such passionate debate since the Twenties.

THE novel that aroused such a genuine and unusually strong response has a complicated plot, with various twists and ramifications, but its main line is rather simple. It revolves around Lopatkin, a former physics and mathematics teacher who became an inventor after the war and worked on a machine for the centrifugal casting of iron drain pipes. A single-minded man, he devotes all his time and energy to the promotion of his project but falls victim to red tape, disloyal competition and intrigues. He does not belong to the "gang," lacks the "right connections" and seems a dull nuisance to experts and ministry functionaries. His invention rejected, Lopatkin is reduced to poverty and starvation.

He takes refuge with an old professor, Busko, also an inventor and an eccentric who has been defeated in his fight against the alliance of Communist bosses, powerful technicians and secret police officials. The only person who helps Lopatkin is Nadia, the wife of Drosdov, a prominent executive and the inventor's chief enemy. Nadia leaves her husband and tries to gain Lopatkin's love. At one moment the inventor succeeds in finding some support among the military who give him the means for building his model, but competitors accuse him of "divulging State secrets," and Lopatkin is arrested, tried and sent to a concentration camp in the Arctic.

The intervention of a trial judge dissatisfied with some legal aspects of the case, brings about its revision; and after Stalin's death Lopatkin returns to Moscow, is rehabilitated, is again helped by the military obviously interested in the use of his machine for the army, and finally emerges as a victor. Yet all the "big shots" who snubbed or crushed him, are still there, and Drosdov is about to become deputy minister. The evil is unpunished, the struggle goes on, and the "happy ending" is by no means a satisfactory and terminal solution.

While Lopatkin and Busko represent the lonely individual pitted against the collective, Drosdov and his friends embody the very forces Dudintsev is hitting at in his exposé of Soviet society. Unlike other negative characters in contemporary Russian fiction, Drosdov is neither a villain nor a paid "agent of American imperial-

*Mr. Slonim is the author of "The Epic of Russian Literature" and other books.*

ism." He is a solid citizen and a first-class business man.

"I belong to the producers of material values," he says to Nadia. "The main spiritual value of our time is the ability to work well and to create the greatest possible amount of necessary things. We are working for the basis." And when Nadia mentions the relationships between people, he retorts that "matter comes first. Let us have things, we do not need to worry about relationships in connection with them * * * You won't find it in Turgenev * * * What you say is nineteenth century * * * The whole truth is in my hands. I am a carpenter, I will build the house and then you will begin to hang little pictures and china plates on the walls." He dismisses all the "ornaments," all the "superfluous rubbish," and he sees in Lopatkin one of those undisciplined idealists who mumble "not by bread alone," take fantasy for reality and prefer individual effort to teamwork.

BEHIND Drosdov stands a whole army of party leaders, academicians, generals, experts, government employes—all that "apparatus of the State" which has replaced the Old Guard of Communist intellectuals. In a series of well portrayed minor characters, Dudintsev paints the officialdom of his country as "monopolists," "monopoly" being the term used by Lopatkin. And this means that Dudintsev has bluntly asserted what many of his readers thought or guessed but he did not dare to say: the ruling class of the Communist society has the same kind of vested interests, methods and mentality as those very American executives or European industrial managers who are pilloried by official Moscow propaganda as "sharks" and fiends preying on the working man.

The monopolists form a sort of pale or restricted area within which they move and use their influence; they all are one happy family, separated from the rest of the nation, and when a lonely talented non-conformist such as Lopatkin, challenges them, they all unite in curbing him. Non-conformism in Russia is another problem raised by the author, and its treatment surely touched off many responsive chords.

If Drosdovs are the end result of the Communist regime, then Dudintsev's social novel is more than a customary denunciation of the "little defects of the mechanism." In fact, it questions the basic structure of the system—of course within the limits that one can do such a thing in Russia—and therein lies the difference between "Not by Bread Alone" and other works that contain critical thrusts against the bureaucrats. This is also the cause of its drawing power for the Russians. At a discussion of the novel among Soviet writers, Konstantin Paustovsky, a prominent author, declared the Dudintsev book was a first round in the battle against the Drosdovs "whom literaturé should fight until their complete extermination." "The book expresses the anxiety we all feel about the moral aspect and purity of the Soviet man and our culture," said Paustovsky.

Apart from its outspokenness in depicting evil as a commonplace, Dudintsev's work is notable also for its serious preoccupation with realism. After the end of the war and the tightening of controls in 1946, the cliché reigned supreme in Soviet letters. Instead of representing reality, fiction had tended to "varnish it"—to use the current Muscovite expression. Writers followed a pattern of cinemascopic vision in pseudo-Marxist technicolor in which faultless secretaries of local party organizations exposed and punished traitors, and buxom *kolkhoze* girls breathed optimism and devotion to the Communist cause.

No real conflicts were allowed in these artificial and dull compositions; and what semblances of conflict did appear were promptly solved by the wise leaders or resolutions of party conventions. Such annoying phenomena as arrests, exile, purge —or, on the family level, failure, weakness or adultery were simply dismissed. This literature of ready-made formulas of Communist cheesecake and deliberate distortion proved to be as sterile as it was untrue, and its artistic level sank with each year.

AFTER the death of Stalin, the reaction against this degradation of art took different forms, from the mild mention of "facts of life," such as the purge of an innocent in "The Thaw" by Ilya Ehrenburg, to direct accusation of the power-hungry dignitaries in "Volga Mother River" by Fedor Panferov (the second volume of which was never published). From 1954 to 1957 numerous authors depicted defects and abuses of Russian life in plays, short stories and novels which marked the rejection of the official mold. Dudintsev epitomized this veering from socialist to critical realism: he reflected in his novel all the shifts of the post-Stalin era.

The book does not rate high from a purely esthetic standpoint. Its structure is loose; its exposition often heavy or verbose; its style pedestrian; its feminine characters pale. Lopatkin does not always come to life and the writer usually respects dated literary conventions. But the sad odyssey of the inventor and his search for truth and justice is depicted with such intensity, the ruling class of the Soviet Union is exposed with such sharpness, and the worries of a whole generation are interpreted with such convincingness that the work, despite its literary shortcomings, becomes a document of an epoch and allows a glimpse into thoughts and moods of Russian intelligentsia. It sums up the whole literary and social movement of recent years, and offers to the Western reader a picture of Russia far different from official statements and hasty reports by travelers.

THERE is no doubt that Dudintsev's extraordinary success was one of the factors in the new strengthening of censorship by the party last summer. Criticism of realities, denunciation of social ills, political shortcomings and ideological ineptitudes as well as "deviations" from the pattern of "Socialist realism" went so far and produced such dangerous manifestations not only in satellite states but within the Soviet Union itself that a counter-offensive was recently ordered by the Party Central Committee, and new restrictive measures were adopted in the arts and letters.

It is too early to predict whether this reactionary step marks the end of a relatively liberal period during which the publication of a Dudintsev was possible. In any case, for the moment "Not by Bread Alone" remains the high point in the effort of Soviet writers to speak boldly and frankly about the burning problems of their country.

October 20, 1957

# RUSSIAN REGRETS STORM OVER BOOK

## Pasternak, in Interview, Says Novel Barred by Moscow Reflects Trend of Times

By MAX FRANKEL
Special to The New York Times.

MOSCOW, Dec. 16—Boris Leonidovich Pasternak is a Soviet poet and translator, whose major work, though kept from his countrymen, will soon be well known in the rest of the world.

His novel, "Doctor Zhivago," is the story of two families caught in the Bolshevik Revolution and the early Soviet period.

An Italiian publisher, refusing the request of the Soviet Writers' Union and of the Italian Communist party to return the manuscript and agree to a postponement of the publication date so revisions could be made, published it last month. West German, British and United States editions will follow in the Spring.

Mr. Pasternak, who in an interview yesterday said he wrote the novel in his sixties in an effort to merit his previously high reputation abroad, is unhappy. He is unhappy about the storm raging around the book, which contains a number of anti-Marxist passages. And he is unhappy that his fellow Russians, for whom the book was intended, apparently will not have a chance to read it for some time.

### Reviser Was Appointed

He had already accepted the appointment of a "young and enthusiastic Communist" to help him with the "improvement" of the book, confident that the deletion of a few pages would not alter its meaning and significance, but even this concession fails to bring it closer to publication here.

The book, 700 pages long, attempts to capture the sweep of recent Russian history through the lives of its characters between the years 1903 and 1929. Mr. Pasternak began the work before the death of Stalin but wrote it, he said, because he was confident that "times were changing."

"Doctor Zhivago" is tragic in incident but leaps forward at the end to an optimistic appraisal of the world after World War II.

It appears therefore to be the embodiment of Mr. Pasternak's current belief: that the Marxist revolution in the Soviet Union has served its purpose and made great contributions to history and that "a new epoch, a new era is being born in silence, being born and growing like grass, like plants, all around; it is being born in children and in everything else; it will not be proclaimed, but it is coming, evolving."

### Idea Echoed in Novel

These are Mr. Pasternak's thoughts as expressed during yesterday's interview, which lasted five hours. This is also how his novel ends as he discusses the return of two young men from World War II:

"Though the clarification and freedom they had expected after the war had not come with victory, as they had hoped, that did not matter. A foreboding of freedom was in the air in the years after the war and was their only historical content."

"This is not politics," Mr. Pasternak said yesterday. "I am not a politician. But every poet, every artist must somehow grope for the trends of his age." He said it was the duty of a writer to testify to his experience.

Though based upon the experience of his large circle of friends among the Russian intelligentsia, Mr. Pasternak's book is not autobiographical, he said. A work of art, he believes, is not a single thing, like a mathematical treatise or an earth satellite, it has many sides and a life of its own and its relation to the precise thoughts of its author is never easy to determine.

What then about the anti-Communist expression in the book? These are passages in which various characters deny that Marxism is a science, oppose the Soviet collectivization of farms and deplore what they portray as the corruption of the Russian enlightenment into the Russian revolution.

Three or four pages out of 700, Mr. Pasternak said, do not represent a work of art. "They are not typical of it," he said. "The book has many sides, characters say the right things and wrong things and partial things. You have a right to ask, Do I believe what I wrote? Naturally I do. But this book is not a judgment or indictment of Soviet society. It is an exposition and an episode in a great evolution."

Mr. Pasternak, a slight but energetic man, was speaking to a group of Western correspondents in the sparsely furnished study of his home at Peredelkino, a writers' colony fifteen miles southwest of Moscow. He lives there the year round with his wife.

Spry at the age of 67 and conversant in English, German and French in addition to Russian, he gesticulated and contorted his sharp features through an unending monologue, rarely interrupted by questions.

"Doctor Zhivago" was completed two years ago and was sent to several Soviet book and magazine publishers. It was scheduled for publication at the end of 1956 and Mr. Pasternak arranged for the book's simultaneous appearance in Italy.

Then came the first indication of doubt among authorities here. The book had been completed in a period of general loosening of reins here, but after the Hungarian revolt the Communist party felt that breaches of discipline had gone too far.

"They" first suggested, Mr. Pasternak recalled, that he obtain a six-month delay in publication abroad so that certain objectionable passages might be deleted from the book. Both Mr. Pasternak and the Italian publisher agreed.

But the deletions were never made because, Mr. Pasternak said, "they" seemed to feel the decisions had to be made by someone "big" and no one along the line felt himself "big" enough. At the end of the half-year he was asked to urge the Italian publisher to return the manuscript but Mr. Pasternak told his Soviet advisers that he doubted this maneuver would succeed.

The efforts failed as he had predicted. Is he sorry? He is sorry, he said, about the "noise" about the novel and that it was not published here, in full or with the once-planned deletions.

Now, Mr. Pasternak said, he has been asked to write a treatise on "peace." This is such a simple and appealing idea, he remarked, but simple ideas in literature usually come out as "affected" prose. He agreed to work on the article but warned that it would not be as expected, that he would have to write it in his own way, in human terms.

Then at the dinner table Mr. Pasternak toasted peace and finally proposed a really "patriotic toast." He used to be condemned for being an esoteric and a symbolist, he said. "They" never made him into a "Socialist realist." But he is grateful to Socialist realism because it made him a realist and he is grateful to his epoch and country for everything he is.

December 17, 1957

# Clamor Grows in Moscow For Exiling of Pasternak

By MAX FRANKEL
Special to The New York Times.

MOSCOW, Oct. 31—The Moscow section of the Soviet Union of Writers has petitioned the Government to strip "the traitor Pasternak" of his citizenship and expel him from the country. This formal action, taken today, was the second step in what appeared to be a determined campaign designed at the least to drive Boris L. Pasternak from his native soil.

Mr. Pasternak, author of the novel "Doctor Zhivago," who this week won and declined the Nobel Prize, was openly invited to leave by a high Communist party official two days ago.

The writers' meeting was only one of a series being called here to take up the Pasternak affair. Eight hundred critics and writers were said to have approved the petition unanimously.

### Reviled as Betrayer

Among other things they said: "No honest person, no writer, none who are loyal to the ideals of peace and progress will ever shake the hand of him who has betrayed his homeland and his people."

The writers said Mr. Pasternak had committed "a treasonable act with reference to Soviet literature and the Soviet country."

Thus far the Government has studiously remained aloof from the Pasternak storm raging here. But the Union of Writers, the Communist party and the Young Communist League have spoken in most outraged terms. The poet has been expelled from the Writers Union and has been called a "Judas" and a "pig."

Mr. Pasternak's rejection of the Nobel Prize for Literature has not tempered the campaign against him or the tone of the denunciations. The fact that he has renounced the prize because of "the meaning attached to it in the society in which I live" has still not been published here.

### Rejection Is Ignored

On the contrary, the writers' resolution today cited only Mr. Pasternak's first telegram to Stockholm last Friday, in which he accepted the award gratefully. The writers said: "He not only did not reject the prize but even sent a telegram to the enemy for this handout."

Sergei S. Smirnov, chairman of the board of the Moscow section, presided at the five-hour meeting. All the speakers supported the move to strip Mr. Pasternak of citizenship, urging that he be left out of the forthcoming Soviet census and forbidden to breathe the air of the Soviet Union.

Throughout the meeting the poet was referred to as "Gospodin Pasternak" (Mr. Pasternak), an insult among Russians who normally address each other as tovarishch, or comrade.

Mr. Pasternak was invited to attend the meeting, but pleaded illness. He was reported to have sent a letter to the meeting trying to justify his position. When someone mentioned the report that Mr. Pasternak had renounced the Nobel Prize, the chairman is said to have ruled that this was not official information and was therefore inadmissible in the discussion.

One by one the organizations of creative professions are being called into special session to endorse the attack and to brand him a traitor. The cinema workers met here yesterday and members of Moscow writers' organizations jammed into a movie house to do their duty today. Many other meetings have been called for tomorrow and next week.

One of the most persistent charges against the poet has been that for a long time he has lived here like an "internal immigrant." He is called not only a traitor but a man who turned his back on the Communist revolution and his people.

However, none of the charges had been made against him before last week's announcement that he had won the Nobel Prize. Among the vehement denunciations that followed were clear signs that the poet would have been permitted to go to Stockholm to accept the award. There were suggestions also that he would not be missed if he failed to return.

Wednesday evening Vladimir Y. Semichastny, chief of the Young Communist League, urged Mr. Pasternak to resettle in "his capitalist paradise." Premier Nikita S. Khrushchev and most other prominent Soviet leaders sat on the platform from which the youth leader spoke.

It had been doubted here, however, that Mr. Pasternak would ever leave the Soviet Union voluntarily. He is deeply attached to Russian soil and has endowed his unhappy hero, Dr. Zhivago, with the same attachment.

The writers' request that the poet be deprived of citizenship probably will be followed by similar petitions from the other meetings of intellectuals now scheduled. This would give the Government a clear chance to step into the case and to honor the request if it intends to expel Mr. Pasternak.

Mr. Pasternak's father, Leonid, a famous artist, left the Soviet Union voluntarily and died in exile.

What Mr. Pasternak himself thinks of the developing campaign against him probably will not be known for some time unless he is deported. Mr. Pasternak's wife told a visitor to their country home in Peredelkino, near Moscow, this afternoon that the poet planned to live quietly for at least a year without seeing anyone and without making any statements.

November 1, 1958

# Khrushchev's Russia

## *Premier Tries a Pragmatic Approach Toward Soviet Arts and Literature*

By HARRISON E. SALISBURY

Some people in Moscow are convinced that there was a plot last autumn in which a group of writers and editors allied themselves with powerful Communist party forces in an attempt to turn the ideological clock back to Stalin.

This, it is said, was an underlying reason for the savagery with which Boris Pasternak, Nobel Prize winner, and his novel "Doctor Zhivago" were attacked.

In the end Nikita S. Khrushchev turned against the cabal and repudiated the Stalinist implications of the literary-political intrigue and a new era of toleration in creative matters was decreed.

The Pasternak affair and its ramifications illustrate the dilemma of the Khrushchev regime in dealing with the intellectual. Mr. Khrushchev is deeply committed to greater creative freedoms. But Soviet writers, artists, musicians and poets move faster than the Communist party is prepared to go.

The ideological difficulties have been most severe in the realm of the printed word. In some artistic fields a quiet revolution has occurred with the aid and encouragement of Mr. Khrushchev. This is notably the case in architecture. Music is not far behind. Painting and sculpture are rapidly moving toward more modern Western concepts. Ballet stands on the threshold of new experimentation.

Only occasional echoes of the battles on the artistic front are heard in the West because the Soviet censorship often refuses to pass dispatches that touch on vital aspects of the controversies.

For example, the censors consistently eliminated all references to the fact that Mr. Khrushchev had sober second thoughts about the Pasternak case. The censorship also suppressed any reference to a collateral literary controversy—that over the tragic ending Mikhail A. Sholokhov gave to the thus far unpublished sequel to his Don country novel "The Virgin Soil Upturned."

It seems apparent that Mr. Sholokhov's novel is now going to be published after a year's delay, and in a form presumably satisfactory not only to Mr. Sholokhov but to Mr. Khrushchev.

There are many people in Moscow who are convinced that "Doctor Zhivago" will also be published eventually in the Soviet Union, possibly two years hence with some slight excisions. This turn of events has followed a re-evaluation by Mr. Khrushchev himself.

### 'Zhivago' Reconsidered

The Soviet Premier sat on the platform last October and listened impassively when Vladimir Y. Semichastny, then head of the Young Communists, denounced Mr. Pasternak and demanded that the writer be driven from the country.

But Mr. Khrushchev is a shrewd man. He had not then read "Doctor Zhivago." He still has not. But as tidal waves of world reaction arose about the Pasternak case he began to wonder. Was the book as bad as it was painted? Did it really justify such a loss of face, a propaganda defeat of global dimension?

Mr. Khrushchev turned to a trusted aide—Aleksei I. Adzhubei, his son-in-law and then editor of the newspaper Komsomolskaya Pravda. He asked Mr. Adzhubei to read "Doctor Zhivago" and give him a report.

Mr. Adzhubei read the book. He reported, or so Moscow believes, along these lines:

It is true that the book adopts a negative attitude toward the Bolshevik Revolution and, in general, toward Communist society. However, these attitudes are those of the book's hero and are consistent with his character and the plot of the book.

### Khrushchev Takes Steps

It is not a book that would cause a good Young Communist to toss his cap in the air. But it is not a book that would touch off counter - revolution. Mr. Adzhubei's verdict: the book could well have been published with the deletion of, perhaps, 300 or 400 words.

Mr. Khruschchev exploded. The Pasternak furor, he became convinced, was unnecessary, stupid and damaging to the Soviet state. It had its source, he concluded, in a struggle for power within literary circles in Moscow and ideological circles in the Government.

According to the version current in Moscow, Mr. Khrushchev did what he could to repair the damage and make certain that the Pasternak case would not be repeated. He removed Mr. Semichastny from direction of the Young Communist League. The secretary of the writers' union and the editor of the newspaper Literaturnaya Gazeta were dismissed. Reprimands were widely distributed.

### Orders to Pasternak

When the writers union convened, Mr. Khrushchev went before the meeting and laid down the new line. The essence of it was: no more feuds. It is time, he said, to let the angels of reconciliation descend on the battlefield.

A formula was reached to liquidate the worst consequences of the Pasternak case. There were to be no more attacks and no more public discussion of the case. Mr. Pasternak was to be on his good behavior and to discourage the pilgrimage of foreign visitors to his country home at Peredelkino.

After a decent interlude Mr. Pasternak would write a simple letter to the writers' union, expressing regret at the storm raised over "Doctor Zhivago" and disassociating himself from it. He would ask readmittance to the union. This would be quietly granted. There would be no publicity—or a minimum of publicity.

The first evidence that Mr. Pasternak was returning to a normal place in Moscow's artistic life was his appearance Friday at the final concert of the New York Philharmonic in Moscow. He appeared on the invitation of Leonard Bernstein, conductor of the orchestra.

### Struggle Is Fundamental

The literary struggle exemplified by the Pasternak case is a fundamental one for creative freedom. Young Soviet writers and poets tend to follow the path trod, for instance, by young Polish poets and writers. The Russians want to write about their country and their life as they experience it.

They are tired of being cut off from the main stream of world literary trends. More and more they are reading, in the original or in unofficial mimeographed translations, the works of avant-garde writers of the West.

They have read such realistic contemporary novelists as Marek Hlasko of Poland. They are interested in the post-existentialist movement in France. They know the name of Jack Kerouac and have heard of the rise of the "beat generation" literature in the United States.

Some of the younger writers, such as Yevgeni Yevtushenko, a talented poet, attract small circles of writers who wish to experiment with new forms and new ideas and write poems and short stories that no Soviet publication would dare to print.

Today such activity, while not encouraged, is not interfered with.

Last autumn there was real cause for alarm. The hue and cry over Mr. Pasternak was linked with what some Muscovites believe was a political conspiracy. A central role in the conspiracy was played by a novel called "The Yershov Brothers" written by Valentin Kochetov, then editor of Literaturnaya Gazeta and a leader of the anti-Pasternak forces.

The "Yershov" book was a literary tract. Its theme was that "revisionist" writers who were breaking with the old party line were agents of Western imperialism and traitors to the Soviet state. It suggested that the real aim of the writers was to carry out a revolution in the Soviet Union.

Loyal workers in the industrial proletariat, said the book, must rise in defense of the revolution and smash the plot of the intellectuals. The book warned that no intellectual could be trusted and that all were suspect.

### Personalities Cited

The book mentioned many actual personalities in Moscow.

Some Moscow observers believe this was part of a deliberate attempt to turn the Soviet Union back to the Stalinist line, to raise anew the threat of terror and the threat of fear and to divide workers from the intelligentsia.

The attempt had backing within the Central Committee and the party's Presidium. Who the backers were and what their motivations were, it is not possible to say precisely.

In any event the plot failed. Mr. Khrushchev sensed what was going on. He reversed the field on the Pasternak case. He repudiated the Yershov line. When the book appeared in the form of a play recently its entire political content had vanished.

Mr. Khrushchev's taste is not avant-garde. But he has not set his face against experimentation and modernism. He is willing to go along with the forces striving for greater creative liberty, provided the pace is not too fast. This means that it is still a case of two steps forward and one step back.

### A Pragmatic Approach

The fact is that Mr. Khrushchev's approach to literary matters is almost as pragmatic as it is to questions such as substituting corn for wheat or introducing silage trenches in place of costly silos.

When he was first told that Mr. Pasternak had written a "bad book" he threw up his hands. The author has been away from the people too long, Mr. Khrushchev is said to have exclaimed. Let us send him on a trip to see what the Soviet people are building, the Premier is said to have added, let him go to the Bashkir oil fields or out to Siberia. That will give him something to write about.

It took Mr. Khrushchev some time to realize that his customary prescription of "getting close to the people" might not work in the case of a poet like Mr. Pasternak.

But Mr. Khrushchev has not given up. The entourage that is coming with him to the United States includes not only official advisers and regular foreign correspondents.

Mr. Khrushchev has invited Mr. Sholokhov and other writers, including Alexsandr Tvardovsky, the poet; Aleksandr Y. Korneichuk, Ukranian playwright known for the topicality of his dramas, and Ilya Ehrenburg, who has become increasingly nonconformist in his literary opinions since Stalin's death.

Mr. Khrushchev almost certainly has invited these writers to introduce them to fresh themes and expose them to unusual stimuli in the hope that they will bring new currents into turgid waters of the Soviet literary stream.

**Other Fields Advance**

While Soviet writers are still fighting to break through the party's ideological barriers, other Soviet creative artists have already overturned the barricades.

The greatest revolution has occurred in the field of architecture and design. In this the artists have had the support of Mr. Khrushchev himself.

With Mr. Khrushchev it may be more a matter of economy than a matter of taste. But the result works out the same. Moscow has gone Park Avenue modern so far as architecture is concerned.

**Functional Designs Gaining**

Thus far only a few examples of the clean functional buildings have been erected. Two or three of them are on the grounds of the permanent Soviet industrial and agricultural exposition in Moscow.

But the shape of things to come is clearly seen in the plans for new buildings. Stalinesque wedding-cake towers have been tossed into the garbage can. The most dramatic example is provided by the architectural competition for the new Palace of Soviets. Before the war Stalin planned to erect a 100-story building topped by a 200-foot statue of Lenin, just tall enough to beat the Empire State Building.

World War II thwarted Stalin's ambition. But his heirs still want a Palace of Soviets. An architectural competition was opened four years ago. The designs in the first round would have delighted Stalin's heart—masses of gingerbread, grandiose imitations of the Kremlin's Spassky Tower.

The other day the second-round projects were exposed to view. Gone was the gingerbread. In its place were imitations of Lever House and the United Nations building.

Naturally this was no accident. A few days later plans were published for a new All-Union Palace of Books. They follow the same trim functional rectangular lines. Not since Le Corbusier was permitted to experiment in Moscow in the early Nineteen Thirties have buildings like this been seen in the Soviet Union.

**Economy Is a Factor**

Mr. Khrushchev has given the architects his blessing for the most practical of reasons. He wants buildings that are simple in design and economical in construction. Stalinesque was one of the most costly and wasteful extravagances of the old regime.

The same patronage has given Soviet designers an opportunity to attack the nightmare of Russian décor. Simple Scandinavian designs are being introduced in furniture and textiles. Pravda has denounced orange tasseled lamp shades, a Soviet standard. A ban has been placed on construction of heavy wardrobes.

Thus far only a dent has been made, but the first blows are being struck.

**New Freedom in Music**

In music the revolution is also triumphing. Serious Soviet composers are writing what they wish. The movement toward modernity is gathering speed. But it is plain that Western modes will undergo substantial modification to suit the more flamboyant Russian taste. Ideological polemics over atonal music and mechanistic Western composers have been muted.

In popular music tides of Western jazz are choking the party's sentinels who still attempt to defend the Soviet ramparts. The published line is maintained. But in practice Soviet youth sings, dances and listens to the Western beat.

There is no possible way in which party propagandists can reverse the trend. Youngsters smash the doors of a Gorky park restaurant to hear a good Czech combo. They turn a West German jazz concert into a riot.

In painting and sculpture the breakthrough of modern form and modern style is perhaps two years distant. Hardly a day goes by when the "reserve" collections in Moscow's Tretyakov Gallery and Leningrad's Hermitage are not viewed by more visitors.

The reserve collections consist of works by Russian modernistic and abstract painters of the period ending in the early Nineteen Twenties. There are many works by Marc Chagall, Vasily Kandinsky, Kazimir Malevich and Pyotr Konchalovsky done before Russian painters were cut off from the mainstream of artistic creation.

The intense interest of Soviet painters in Western form and style has produced a whole school of "closet" painters, artists who paint in modern, abstractionist style but are unable to exhibit their works.

Once this kind of painting and sculpture was entirely secret. The penalties for deviation in the Stalinist period could be most severe. Today, however, it is completely open. Many Soviet intellectuals collect the abstract works of the "closet" school.

None of these paintings has yet been shown in public. But such exhibitions will not be long delayed. A show of young Moscow painters that included the work of many artists who privately paint with advanced techniques was held this year.

In the Soviet theatre no strong movement toward new form has yet appeared. However, the Soviet theatre is increasingly under the influence of the great innovators of the past. The traditions of Vsevolod Meyerhold, theatre director purged by Stalin, have been revived. The techniques of Vladimir Mayakovsky, the revolutionary poet who committed suicide in 1930, are being tried again.

But ballet stands on the threshold of bold change. The contact with the West experienced by the Moiseyev dance company and the Bolshoi Ballet has provided a creative stimulus.

Leningrad, always a leader in experimentation and never a victim of Stalin's most leaden taste, is setting a pace in introducing new ballet forms. These lean heavily toward the abstract and symbolic ballet of the West.

Igor Moiseyev, the folk-dance director, is experimenting too. He has created some numbers that incorporate both folk and contemporary American themes. But he has not yet been able to show them publicly. His latest ensemble is a mishmash of stereotypes. Here too it will take a year or two for the breakthrough.

September 14, 1959

# *Moscow Paper Assails Writer For Criticism of Anti-Semites*

## *Popular Poet Is Accused of Slandering Russians by Hint That Bigotry Continues in Soviet Union*

By HARRY SCHWARTZ

A popular young Soviet poet has come under severe attack in Moscow for having published a poem denouncing anti-Semitism and hinting that it still existed in the Soviet Union.

The poem, "Babi Yar," by Yevgeny Yevtushenko, was published in Literaturnaya Gazeta, organ of the Soviet Writers' Union, Sept. 19, the eve of Yom Kippur, the Jewish Day of Atonement. The poem reads as though it were intended to be Mr. Yevtushenko's confession of Russian guilt for anti-Semitic outrages. On Yom Kippur Jews confess their sins and pray for forgiveness.

Observers here of Soviet affairs could not recall any piece of literature of similar emotional intensity on the subject of anti-Semitism by a non-Jew that had ever been published in the Soviet press.

Two articles published in the last week in Literatura i Zhizn, another literary journal, bitterly denounced Mr. Yevtushenko for allegedly slandering the Russian people in his poem and for ignoring the Communist party's alleged opposition to anti-Semitism.

**Called 'Pigmy Cosmopolitan'**

One of the articles termed Mr. Yevtushenko a "pigmy cosmopolitan" for his "slander," thus employing an epithet that was used widely against Jewish intellectuals in the bitter anti-Semitic campaign of early 1949.

Mr. Yevtushenko, who is 28 years old, is the idol of many thousands of Soviet young people. They flock in large numbers to his poetry reading sessions and have created such a demand for his collected poems that volumes containing his writings quickly become collectors' items.

The title of the poem is taken from Babi Yar, a ravine near Kiev where the Germans in 1941 machine gunned to death an estimated 40,000 Jews.

Mr. Yevtushenko's poem begins with the complaint that there is no memorial at Babi Yar to this tragedy and he adds, "To me this is terrible." To describe his feelings of remorse he writes that he feels as old as the Jewish people and he feels that he is a Jew, one who tramps through ancient Egypt, who is crucified on the cross.

In the poem Mr. Yevtushenko identifies himself with Anne Frank and with Alfred Dreyfus, two of the most publicized individual victims of anti-Semitism in the last 100 years. He denounces the Russian anti-Semites who carried out pogroms under a slogan that originated in Czarist times but has been clandestinely spread by anti-Semitic groups in the Soviet Union in recent years.

He denounces those who defame the word "Russian" by using it to advance anti-Semitism and declares that he is like a Jew in hating anti-Semites "because I am a real Russian." He makes it clear that he has no Jewish ancestors.

Some excerpts from a rough English translation of the poem follow:

* * * It seems to me that I am as old
As the Jewish people itself.
It seems to me that I am a Jew.
I am tramping through ancient Egypt
I am dying, crucified on the cross
And till this time I have traces of the nails.
It seems to me that I am Dreyfus * * *.
It seems to me that I am a youngster in Bialystok
Whose blood is running over the floors
The victim of the hooliganism of

the leaders from the saloons * * *.
Oh my Russian people, I know that you
Are in essence internationalists
But often those whose hands are unclean
Brandish your purest of names
How base that the anti-Semites
dare to call
Themselves the "Union of the Russian people."
It seems to me that I am Anne Frank * * *.
Over Babi Yar there is the hum of the thick grass
The trees look powerful, like judges
Everything screams silently here,
and, removing my hat,
I feel that I am growing gray slowly
And that I am myself a totally soundless shriek
Over the thousands of thousands who are buried.
I am each old man that was slaughtered here
I am each child that was slaughtered here.
Nothing in me can forget this.
Let the "Internationale" sound out joyously
When the last anti-Semite on earth will be buried * * *.

September 28, 1961

# 'THAW' FOR ARTS HINTED IN RUSSIA

## Stravinsky Visit Yields Clue of 'Liberalizing Trend'

Special to The New York Times

LENINGRAD, Oct. 9—When Igor Stravinsky came to Leningrad this week, the intellectuals spoke of the visit as another manifestation of "podsherstok" in Soviet art. Podsherstok is the fine underhair of an animal's coat that sustains it in cold climates yet cannot be seen.

Soviet art in many respects still displays the face of the Stalin era. Yet there is evidence of an underlying trend of liberalization and this is what the return of Stravinsky and his music signifies to the Leningrad intellectuals.

The arbitrary rule of Socialist realism, a dogma that insists on propagandistic expression, is also being challenged in the other arts. In the studios of Leningrad and Moscow, painters and sculptors are doing abstracts and nonobjective works without fear of police interference. Their art cannot be shown publicily as yet.

However, senior Soviet officials privately are viewing these works. The ideological debate as to whether the nonobjective works should be exhibited has not discouraged leading Soviet personalities from acquiring pieces for their personal

The Leningrad theater also reflects the mood of change in the arts. The most popular play is "The Dragon," which is on the boards in the Nikolai Akimov Comedy Theater.

The dragon, which is the symbol of tyranny, is slain but its influence persists in the town. The message of the allegory is that it is not enough to topple tyranny but one must continue to struggle against it. While some Russians accept the allegory as applying to West Germany today, there are others who see it as a call to struggle against the remnants of Stalinism.

The presence here of Stravinsky on the invitation of the Soviet Government has encouraged Leningrad intellectuals to hope that a new era of freedom is at hand that will permit a renaissance of Russian art. They say that the time of podsherstok will be over when the official signal is given for what has been created privately on the piano and with the paint brush to be exhibited publicly.

Stravinsky, returning to his native Leningrad, after an absence of 52 years has found that Russian art lags many years behind the West, but he also has been exhilarated by the signs of change.

Stravinsky's discussions with the musicians of Leningrad have stirred more excitement here than his two concerts. At a meeting with the local Union of Composers and in a lecture before students after a concert rehearsal, Stravinsky pleaded for tolerance and respect for modern Western music. With Soviet officials listening, he defended the work of such moderns as Schönberg, the father of serial music, and Webern, who projected the technique into still newer ways of ordering musical relationships. By the usual Soviet ideological standards, Stravinsky preached heresy.

October 11, 1962

# *Soviet Orders Disciplining For Cultural Avant-Garde*

By SEYMOUR TOPPING

Special to The New York Times

MOSCOW, Dec. 3 — The Soviet Communist party ordered today the disciplining of artists, writers and composers who had "betrayed" socialist realism under the influence of modern Western trends.

Members of the avant-garde of the Soviet cultural world were accused of having become subject to "all-forgiving liberalism or rotten sentimental complacency."

A front-page editorial in Pravda demanded that organizations of the party, professional unions, the press and the public join in fighting uncompromisingly against any deviation from the Soviet concept of art as a propaganda vehicle for the Communist party and state.

The editorial and two other articles in Pravda, the newspaper of the Communist party, indicated that the bravado shown recently by Soviet abstractionists, individualistic writers and the composers of 12-tone and similar music had induced one of the recurring cultural repressions.

### Curbs Imposed Previously

Similar curbs were imposed in 1954 after the initial upsurge of the arts following the death of Stalin, in the wake of the Hungarian revolt in 1956, and about two years later after the denunciation of Boris Pasternak, the author of "Doctor Zhivago."

Soviet intellectuals, shocked by the abrupt setback to their hopes for freer expression, were waiting for the appearance of the official cultural publications, which were expected to contain a more precise delineation of the new line.

While attacking the "incorrect tendencies" of some writers, Pravda strongly endorsed the de-Stalinization trend in literature. Writers were given license this month by Premier Khrushchev to undertake their boldest exposés of the so-called cult of personality.

The Pravda editorial asserted that de-Stalinization had removed everything that had "hindered the bright and original display of talent and creative individuality of the artists."

Soviet writers privately were interpreting the party injunction as meaning that they would continue to enjoy freer expression within the framework of realism. However, it was predicted that experimentation in the modern literary forms and styles common in the West would be frowned upon.

It was the new de-Stalinization trend, symbolized by the publication this month of an anti-Stalin novel, "One Day in the Life of Ivan Denisovich" by Aleksandr Solzhenitsin, that had encouraged Soviet painters and sculptors to display their avant-garde works.

The Pravda denunciation fell most heavily on these artists. The editorial declared: "Our people resolutely reject abstractionism, which has suddenly begun to be imitated by a few persons who do not care to notice its frankly reactionary and antipopular essence."

Some of the obviously bewildered artists, who had gained the impression from cultural officials that their works might be tolerated, trace the origin of the campaign against them to Premier Khrushchev's condemnation of abstract art.

Mr. Khrushchev, accompanied by other party and Government leaders, toured the official exhibition of Moscow painters in the Menezh Hall on Saturday.

Soviet sources said that the Premier, apparently unexpectedly, was taken to a private exhibition of abstract works in three small rooms of the hall. Officials evidently wanted Mr. Khrushchev's reaction.

It was the first time that Mr. Khrushchev had been confronted by a Soviet exhibition of abstract works and he was reported to have become enraged. He told the assembled artists that their paintings looked as if they could have been "daubed by the tail of a donkey."

Pravda published today a cartoon illustrating Mr. Khrushchev's remark. The Premier's outburst seemed to have come as a surprise to some Soviet officials who had been quietly condoning production of abstract painting and sculpture on an experimental basis.

Moscow intellectual circles were buzzing with excitement and ferment tonight over the art controversy. Crowds gathered within and before the Menezh Hall near the Kremlin to debate the issues. Most arguments heard were in favor of the painters.

In the public exhibition of Moscow painters, several nonabstract paintings and sculpture—also criticized by Mr. Khrushchev as having strayed too far from Socialist realism—still were on display. Crowds poured into the gallery to view and discuss the works.

In its attack on modern music, Pravda said: "Socialist art resolutely and firmly rejects the unjustified imitation by a few of our musicians of low-quality bourgeois musical composers who are ready to make the whole of Soviet music sound like thundering jazz."

December 4, 1962

# *Shostakovich's 13th Is Silenced In Moscow for Ideological Taint*

### *Composer Is Rebuked for Use of Poem on Jews as Theme for His Latest Work*

By SEYMOUR TOPPING
Special to The New York Times.

MOSCOW, Jan. 11—Dmitri Shostakovich, Russia's best known composer, has demonstrated once again that he is more a master of music than of Communist ideological tastes.

Popular cheers that sounded here recently in Tchaikovsky Hall for Mr. Shostakovich's new 13th Symphony have not been echoed by the official overseers of Soviet culture.

The symphony has been ignored by the Soviet press since its premiere Dec. 18. It has also been quietly withdrawn from the program of a festival of Soviet music scheduled to be held in London next September.

It was understood that Mr. Shostakovich had been privately rebuked for his selection of the verses that are sung during the symphony by a choir.

The verses are drawn from poems of the young Soviet poet, Yevgeny Yevtushenko.

Communist ideologists have objected to verses based upon "Babi Yar", a controversial poem which has been taken to imply that anti-Semitism persists in the Soviet Union.

The poem takes its name from a ravine near Kiev, the capital of the Ukraine, where thousands of Jews were slaughtered by the Nazis during World War II. The poem protests that no memorial has been erected at Babi Yar.

Mr. Yevtushenko, who survived criticism in 1961 of the widely discussed poem to become a favorite of the Communist party, has said that the poem was directed against the Nazi executioners.

An informed source said inclusion of the Babi Yar verses in Mr. Shostakovich's symphony was criticized Dec. 17 at a private meeting between Premier Khrushchev and other members of the Presidium with several hundred prominent intellectuals and avant garde writers and artists.

Associated Press
**Dmitri Shostakovich**

The meeting was arranged so that the leadership could explain to the restive intelligentsia the reason for the ideological campaign that had just been launched against abstract painting and other deviations from socialist realism in literature and art.

The complaint was made that the Babi Yar verses in the 13th Symphony would be cited by enemies of the Soviet Union in support of their contentions that anti-Semitism was prevalent in the country.

Mr. Khrushchev had taken the position earlier that there was no special need for a membrial to the Jews at Babi Yar because persons of other nationalities had also been murdered there.

Nevertheless, Mr. Shostakovich and Mr. Yevtushenko, who spoke at the meeting, decided to go ahead with the symphony premiere on the following evening. The popular reception was tumultuous, but officially it was ignored and frowned upon.

Aside from the Babi Yar verses, there were objections to the tragic overtones of the symphony, which was said not to be in keeping with the note of joyous confidence required by socialist realism.

January 12, 1963

CHAPTER 3

# Bureaucratic Modernization

Workers erect a giant portrait of Soviet President, Leonid Brezhnev on the Kremlin wall in preparation for the 60th anniversary of the Russian Revolution.
UNITED PRESS INTERNATIONAL

# KHRUSHCHEV OUSTED FROM TOP POSTS; BREZHNEV GETS CHIEF PARTY POSITION AND KOSYGIN IS NAMED NEW PREMIER

## MOSCOW IS QUIET

### Pravda Says Change Won't Bring Return of Harsh Policies

By HENRY TANNER
Special to The New York Times

MOSCOW, Friday, Oct. 16 — Premier Khrushchev has been deprived of political power in the Soviet Union.

He was replaced by Leonid I. Brezhnev, 57 years old, as First Secretary of the Communist party and by Aleksei N. Kosygin, 60, as Premier.

Mr. Khrushchev, who is 70, even lost his seat in the Presidium of the Central Committee of the party, the third most important position he held in the leadership.

This indicated that he had fallen into disgrace.

[Dispatches did not mention if Mr. Khrushchev had been removed from the Central Committee itself. Under normal procedure such action would come at a meeting of the Soviet Communist party Congress.]

**Adzhubei Reported Ousted**

The changes were announced by Tass, the Soviet press agency, a few minutes after midnight.

The Tass statement did not contain a single word of praise for the ousted leader.

Unofficial but reliable sources later reported that Aleksei I. Adzhubei, Mr. Khrushchev's son-in-law, had been deposed as chief editor of the Government newspaper Izvestia.

Mr. Khrushchev's whereabouts was not known. Nor was it known whether he was at liberty or under surveillance. Western diplomats assumed, however, that the changeover had been made peacefully.

**Diplomats Voice Assurance**

Moscow's streets were quiet. There were no signs of movements by either the army or police. Some of the smaller Western embassies, which had been without a police guard for the last several months, reported yesterday that the policemen were back in front of the gates.

Western diplomats said they did not expect the new leaders to change basic Soviet policy toward the West.

Mr. Brezhnev and Mr. Kosygin can be expected to continue Mr. Khrushchev's policy of "peaceful coexistence" with the United States, the diplomats said.

The Soviet Communist party newspaper Pravda indicated today that the party would continue to carry out policies of de-Stalinization and economic improvements under its new leadership.

The paper printed the same bare announcement that had been carried in the English-language version of Tass. There were one-column pictures of Mr. Kosygin and Mr. Brezhnev but no comment.

Pravda printed the following statement:

"The Communist party of the Soviet Union firmly and positively translates into reality the Leninist general line worked out at the 20th and 22d congresses of the party."

This could be construed as an assurance that there would be no return to Stalin's dictatorial policies.

Informed sources expressed the conviction that it was the Chinese-Soviet conflict that had led to Mr. Khrushchev's fall.

Mr. Brezhnev and Mr. Kosygin can be expected to put an end to the drive toward a showdown with the Chinese Communists, which has been the foremost trait of the last few months of the Khrushchev regime, the sources said.

**December Meeting in Doubt**

The sources said the new leadership might well have decided, even before coming to power, to call off the meeting of 26 Communist parties that was to begin here Dec. 15.

The meeting was to make preparations for a full-scale conference of the world Communist parties.

**Leonid I. Brezhnev**
*Named as the leader of the party*

Associated Press

**Aleksei N. Kosygin**
*Appointed as the Soviet Premier*

Mr. Khrushchev had staked his own prestige and that of the Communist party of the Soviet Union and the Soviet Government on this project for a conference.

But the response of the invited parties had been deeply disappointing. With Mr. Khrushchev's continued presence at the helm, the sources said, the Soviet leadership would have been committed to go through with a potentially disastrous project, while without him it would feel free to change plans and avoid a showdown.

Mr. Khrushchev has been under vitriolic personal attack by the Chinese leaders.

The two new Soviet leaders have consistently echoed the Khrushchev line on the Chinese-Soviet conflict and other issues. But this was not regarded as preventing them from adopting different policies now.

In the past Mr. Khrushchev had also been under attack for his agricultural policies. But this was not thought to have been a central issue in his fall.

This year's crop has been good, especially in the virgin lands, which was Mr. Khrushchev's special pride.

**Removal Took Two Days**

The maneuvering to bring about Mr. Khrushchev's fall from power covered two days, according to Tass. The meeting of the Central Committee, which took the party leadership from him Wednesday, was followed by a meeting of the Presidium of the Supreme Soviet (Parliament), which stripped him of the Premiership yesterday, the press agency reported.

Mikhail A. Suslov, a spokesman in the Kremlin's dispute with Communist China, was reported to have delivered the key address. Mr. Suslov had appeared at times to be lukewarm in his support of Mr. Khrushchev.

It was President Anastas I. Mikoyan, Mr. Khrushchev's closest and oldest friend in the leadership, who presided over the session of the Presidium.

Mr. Mikoyan lived up to his reputation of being adept at surviving political upheavals. He is the only man left who has been near the center of Soviet power continuously since the middle nineteen-twenties and all through Stalin's rule.

The Tass announcement emphasized that Mr. Khrushchev had been relieved of his duties at his own "request." If that was true he was the first Soviet leader since the revolution to have taken such a step.

October 16, 1964

# PRAVDA SAYS KHRUSHCHEV IS HAREBRAINED SCHEMER; GIVES WEST PEACE PLEDGE

## POLICIES OUTLINED

### New Chiefs Promise to Continue Efforts for 'Coexistence'

By HENRY TANNER

Special to The New York Times

MOSCOW, Saturday, Oct. 17—Without naming the deposed Soviet leader, Nikita S. Khrushchev, the new regime accused him today of "harebrained scheming," "bragging and phrase-mongering" and "armchair methods."

In its first declaration of a program the Soviet leadership at the same time pledged to continue its policy of peaceful coexistence with the West.

The new leadership, headed by Leonid I. Brezhnev and Aleksei N. Kosygin, said that it would press for a conference of world Communist parties next year to deal with the ideological challenge of the Chinese Communists.

In the ouster of Mr. Khrushchev, announced yesterday, Mr. Brezhnev took over the post of party First Secretary and Mr. Kosygin became Premier.

The program was defined in an editorial in Pravda, the party newspaper. A text of the editorial was made public by Tass, the Soviet press agency.

The Pravda editorial was clearly a devastating attack on Mr. Khrushchev by his former associates.

**Pretenses Removed**

Western observers felt that it did away with any pretense that Mr. Khrushchev's departure might have been voluntary on the grounds of old age and health, as yesterday's official announcement said.

The charges against Mr. Khrushchev seemed to center on his domestic economic policies.

This was contrary to the expectations of Western diplomats who had been convinced that the Soviet-Chinese conflict was the pivotal issue in his downfall. They still did not rule out the possibility that Mr. Khrushchev would be castigated on this issue later.

The editorial said:

"The Leninist party is an enemy of subjectivism and drifting in Communist construction.

"Harebrained scheming, immature conclusions and hasty decisions and actions divorced from reality, bragging and phrase - mongering, commandism, unwillingness to take into account the achievements of science and practical experience are alien to it.

"The construction of Communism is a live, creative undertaking that does not tolerate armchair methods, personal decisions and disregard for the practical experience of the masses."

**'Cult of Personality'**

These accusations appeared to include the charge that Mr. Khrushchev had been guilty of building up a "cult of personality" of his own while attacking similar practices of Stalin.

This impression was heightened by the fact that the editorial declared that "collective leadership" was the "most important Leninist principle of the life and activity of the party" and the "greatest political asset" of the Soviet Communist party.

What the new leaders and the others seemed to say in today's editorial, in other words, was that Mr. Khrushchev had departed from the principle of "collective leadership" instituted after Stalin's death.

The implication was that his successors would restore true "collective leadership."

The Communist party is irreconcilably opposed to the "ideology and practice of the personality cult," the editorial said.

**Parley May Be Broadened**

After having reiterated the Soviet leadership's determination to call for an international conference of Communist parties, the editorial said this conference should discuss "problems of peace" and of "national independence" as well as those of the unity of the international Communist movement.

This appeared to give the proposed conference a broader frame of reference than it had under the plans worked out by the Khrushchev regime. Such a broadening might serve to reduce opposition to the conference by other parties.

The Chinese Communists were not specifically named in the editorial.

Last Aug. 10 the Soviet leadership sent out invitations for a preliminary meeting of 26 Communist parties to begin here Dec. 15. The preliminary meetings would have the task of preparing for a full conference of all the parties some time next year.

This Soviet project ran into strong opposition from many foreign Communist parties. Even some of the Kremlin's closest allies, such as the Polish and Italian Communists, declared they would accept the invitation only with great misgivings.

The new leadership made its first public appearance at a Kremlin reception while Mr. Khrushchev was being pushed into oblivion.

The Government newspaper Izvestia failed to mention the former Premier's name in a long article on the liberation of the Ukraine from Nazi occupation 20 years ago.

This was in sharp contrast with the way Ukrainian history had been written while Mr. Khrushchev was in power. he had invariably been described as having played a heroic, indispensable role.

Shoppers who bought a portfolio of photographs of Soviet leaders early this morning found that Mr. Khrushchev's picture had already been removed.

**Close Associates Ousted**

At least four close associates of the deposed Premier are known to have been removed from their posts.

They are Mikhail A. Kharlamov, who was head of Soviet radio and television; Vladimir S Lebedev, Grigori T. Shuisky and Oleg A. Troyanovsky. The latter three were personal aides to Mr. Khrushchev.

These men along with Aleksei I. Adzhubei, Mr. Khrushchev's son-in-law who was the editor of Izvestia, were the key members of the "brain trust" of the former Premier.

Pravda was believed to be under new editorial direction.

Pavel A. Satyukov, editor of the newspaper during Mr. Khrushchev's rule, was unofficially reported yesterday as having been ousted. Today this report was amended to the effect that Mr. Satyukov was in Paris, would return to Moscow today and would "probably" be dismissed.

The scene at the big Kremlin reception given by the new leadership President Osvaldo Dorticos Torrado of Cuba was almost exactly the same as at all similar receptions in the past. The only difference was that Mr. Khrushchev was absent.

Among those at the reception was Mikhail A. Suslov, who was reliably reported to have played a key role in the crucial session of the Communist party's Central Committee that deposed Mr. Khrushchev.

It was he, according to authoritative sources, who delivered the principal accusing speech against Mr. Khrushchev.

Specialists explained that this did not necessarily mean that Mr. Suslov, a party secretary, had been the principal instigator and engineer of Mr. Khrushchev's overthrow. It was possible that he had been chosen merely as a spokesman by the anti-Khrushchev majority and assigned the most unpleasant part of the task.

Mr. Suslov charged that Mr. Khrushchev had made grave errors in the Chinese-Soviet conflict, that he had mishandled Soviet agriculture and that he was guilty of nepotism and of creating a "cult of personality," the sources said.

**Brezhnev Absent**

Mr. Brezhnev, the man believed to be the strongest figure in the new leadership, at least for the time being, was not at the reception. Officials said he was too busy to attend.

Anastas I. Mikoyan, the 69-year-old chief of state who had been Mr. Khrushchev's close personal friend, acted as host.

If Mr. Mikoyan's emotions had been touched at all by the events of the last few days, it did not register on his dark face. His voice was firm and controlled as he proposed a toast for President Dorticós Mr. Mikoyan ate heartily and conversed with gusto with his guests.

Premier Kosygin looked wan. his face more deeply lined than usual.

The most poignant moment was at the very beginning. About 10 of the leading members of the party and Government were standing in two rows waiting for President Mikoyan to bring President Dorticós up to them.

Then the orchestra struck up the Cuban anthem and all movement stopped.

The 10 men did not look like conquering heroes who had just taken over one of the world's most powerful governments.

They looked drab, tired and pensive as they stood rigidly staring into space, each alone with his thoughts.

Then the orchestra stopped abruptly and they burst into seemingly forced activity, smiling and shaking the hands of their Cuban guest.

Mr. Khrushchev was present

at the Central Committee meeting and defended himself in a lengthy speech, sources said.

Western observers noted that yesterday's Tass announcement, which is still the only official expalanation of the shake-up, did not say that the Central Committee had been unanimous in its decision to oust Mr. Khrushchev.

It was widely concluded from this that there had been discussion and probably dissension. The announcement mentioned, by contrast, that the action of the Presidium of the Supreme Soviet (Parliament) to depose Mr. Khrushchev as Premier had been unanimous.

The whereabouts of Mr. Khrushchev was not known today.

Soviet officials who were asked this question at the Kremlin reception answered either abruptly or in embarassment that they did not know.

In the Western community here, it was assumed that he and his family were at home in a building near the center of the city where many members of the regime, past and present, have apartments.

Ironically, the same building is also home to Vyacheslav M. Molotov, the former Foreign Minister whom Mr. Khrushchev ousted from power seven years ago.

Like Mr. Molotov, Mr. Khrushchev is believed to be an ordinary private citizen now.

By depriving him of his seat in the Presidium of the Central Committee of the party, as well as of his key positions as Government and party leader, his successors have removed from him a chance to continue in the role of an honored if inactive elder statesman.

October 17, 1964

# KREMLIN CURBING THE PARTY'S ROLE

## Pravda Asserts Legislatures and Plant Managers Will Be Given More Authority

By THEODORE SHABAD
Special to The New York Times

MOSCOW, Dec. 6—The new leadership of the Soviet Union, in a major statement of its program, made public today its principle for the political organization of Soviet society in the post-Khrushchev period.

An editorial in Pravda, the Communist party newspaper, said that the party's role would be limited in the future to "political guidance" and that its leaders would no longer try to "play all the instruments" in the "orchestra."

In an evident allusion to the highly personal style used by the former Premier, Nikita S. Khrushchev, in running the country, Pravda said:

"This not only spoils the music and opens the way for errors and one-sided decisions, but it paralyzes the work of officials who are fully empowered and competent to solve concrete questions."

**More Power for Soviets**

In the governmental sphere, local Soviets (legislative assemblies), until now largely rubber-stamp bodies, are to be given increasing powers and "will ultimately decide all local issues," according to the Pravda editorial.

In the economic field, the newspaper reiterated widely publicized plans for giving factory managers authority to set some production goals, wages and prices under the over-all guidance of the central planners.

Pravda called for the "correct selection, promotion and disposition" of personnel competent to make detailed decisions while high party and Government leaders dealt with major political problems.

December 7, 1964

# BREZHNEV GETS PRESIDIUM POST IN SOVIET SHIFTS

## Party Chief's Power Grows —Premiers Are Shuffled —Industry Aides Named

By THEODORE SHABAD

Special to The New York Times

MOSCOW, Oct. 3 — Leonid I. Brezhnev, Soviet Communist party leader, strengthened his position in the Kremlin leadership yesterday as the Supreme Soviet (Parliament) shuffled deputy premiers and appointed a powerful new hierarchy to run the nation's industries.

The 58-year-old party chief enhanced his authority by being appointed a member of the 30-man Presidium of the Supreme Soviet, nominally the highest state body in the Soviet Governmental system.

This gives him a high official post in the state system, in addition to the leading party role he plays as First Secretary.

**Polyansky Promoted**

The shuffle of high Government posts announced at the end of a two-day session of the Supreme Soviet affected the level of deputy premiers under Premier Aleksei N. Kosygin.

One of the youngest members of the Soviet leadership, Dmitri S. Polyansky, 57, was appointed a First Deputy Premier, joining Kirill Mazurov, 51, who was appointed to that level last March. Mr. Polyansky was an ordinary Deputy Premier since 1962 with supervisory powers over agriculture.

Two other deputy premiers lost their positions, Konstantin N. Rudnev, who headed the high-level State Committee for Coordination of Scientific Research, and Pyotr Lomako, who was also removed from the chairmanship of the State Planning Committee.

Mr. Rudnev, who is 53, and Mr. Lomako, 61, gained high Government posts under former Premier Nikita S. Khrushchev three to four years ago. They were relegated to head two of the 28 industrial ministries established yesterday, Mr. Rudnev, the Manufacture of Automatic Controls and Mr. Lomako Nonferrous Metals Production, his old field.

**State Planning Committee**

The new chairman of the State Planning Committee, which has been endowed with broader powers in planning of the Soviet economy, is Nikolai K. Baibakov, a 53-year-old oil administrator, who briefly held the planning job 10 years ago.

Mr. Rudnev's Research Coordinating Committee, renamed the State Committee for Science and Technology, is being taken over by Vladimir A. Kirillin, a 51-year-old heating engineer and vice-president of the Academy of Sciences. He is one of the rare academicians appointed to a high Government administrative position.

October 4, 1965

# MIKOYAN RESIGNS, PODGORNY NAMED SOVIET PRESIDENT

By PETER GROSE
Special to The New York Times

MOSCOW, Dec. 9—Anastas I. Mikoyan, who is among the last of the Old Bolsheviks, stepped down today as the Soviet chief of state. His resignation led to the most significant Kremlin shuffle since the downfall of Nikita S. Khrushchev 14 months ago.

Succeeding the 70-year-old Mr. Mikoyan as chairman of the Presidium of the Supreme Soviet or Parliament is Nikolai V. Podgorny, 62, a top party leader. A product of Mr. Khrushchev's Ukrainian party machine, he is considered a moderate in the Kremlin's political spectrum.

A controversial younger member of the party hierarchy, Aleksandr N. Shelepin, 47, was formally ousted from his posts in the Government.

Until today, he was a Deputy Premier. He was also chairman of the now-defunct Party-State Control Committee, which supervised the internal security machinery.

**Shelepin Still in Presidium**

Mr. Shelepin apparently retained his powerful job in the Communist party Presidium and Secretariat of the Central Committee, from which he could still operate to enlarge personal power.

But the weight of evidence as interpreted by Western analysts is that Mr. Shelepin, who has sounded a tough note on both foreign and domestic issues, has suffered a check to his ambitions.

The position of Aleksei N. Kosygin as Premier is unchanged, but today's shift suggests that the influence of Leonid I. Brezhnev, First Secretary or chief of the party, has been solidified as the nation's ultimate policy-maker.

December 10, 1965

# Soviet Endorses Relaxing Of De-Stalinization Policy

By PETER GROSE

Special to The New York Times

MOSCOW, March 30—The Soviet Communist party endorsed at a high level today moves to dismantle the de-Stalinization policy introduced 10 years ago by Nikita S. Khrushchev. The party hierarchy came to grips with the Stalin issue on the second day of the 23rd party congress.

The Soviet leaders shunned any suggestion of a personal rehabilitation of the reviled dictator and firmly rejected the possibility of a return to despotic one-man rule.

The problem was presented to the Communist assembly as a simple one of history:

How are citizens of the Soviet Union to assess the 29 years of history in which Stalin dominated the country and the entire Communist movement?

### Title to Be Revived

The direct and implied answers given to that question at today's session indicated the halting of de-Stalinization, a process in which everything associated with Stalin's rule was represented as an awkward aberration that modern Communists condemned.

First came an unexpected proposal to restore the title of "general secretary" for the head of the party, now called First Secretary. This is the title Stalin assumed in 1922 and made so much the symbol of his rule that no man since him has used it.

The proposal was made, evidently with higher-level inspiration, by Nikolai G. Yegorychev, secretary of the party's Moscow city committee.

Then Mr. Yegorychev went on to raise the Stalin issue which the party leader, Leonid I. Brezhnev, delicately skirted in his otherwise comprehensive report yesterday.

"It has recently become fashionable abroad to search our country's political life for some elements of so-called Stalinism, as a bogey to intimidate public opinion, especially the intelligentsia," Mr. Yegorychev said.

"We tell them: It won't work Gentlemen. No one will succeed in smearing the vanguard of the international Communist movement, the Communist party of the Soviet Union founded by the great Lenin.

"The cult of personality, the breach of Leninist norms and principles of party life, of socialist legality, everything that hindered our movement forward has been decisively rejected by the party, and there will never be any return to that past."

Mr. Yegorychev said the decisions of the 20th party congress, where Mr. Khrushchev first denounced Stalin in a secret speech, and the plenary meeting of the Soviet Central Committee of October, 1964, which toppled Mr. Khrushchev from power, were "reliable guarantees" against such a return to the past.

The Moscow party leader then added:

"At the same time the party also resolutely rejects every attempt to cancel out the heroic history of our people, which under the party's leadership has trod the hard but glorious path of struggle and victories for almost half a century.

"Now we see that some things could have been done better. Indeed 50 years have taught us much. But what has been done fills the hearts of the Soviet people with pride and is admired by our friends throughout the world."

Buried in this rhetoric was the assertion that though Stalin himself was condemned, good things had been accomplished under his leadership.

### Intellectuals Worried

Though Soviet authorities insisted that the official thinking would go no further, some foreign analysts felt this line of reasoning could be the thin edge of a wedge for hard-line bureaucrats to insist on tighter party control over society.

A group of 25 Soviet intellectuals warned the party leadership last month that the Soviet people "will never understand or accept any deviation, even in part, from the condemnation of Stalin's personality cult in 1956."

They went on, in a personal letter to Mr. Brezhnev, "any step toward rehabilitation [of Stalin] would lead to a new split in Communist ranks."

They specified the Communist parties of Western Europe, many of which, to enlarge their appeal in non-Communist societies, have been relieved to be able to dissociate themselves from Stalinist connections.

Equally, the East European Communist parties have expressed guarded doubts about any reversal of the de-Stalinization process, for it was Mr. Khrushchev's secret denunciation of Stalin in 1956 that opened the path to the larger autonomy of the one-time satellite countries.

Pyotr Y. Shelest, Ukrainian party leader and a member of the party's ruling Presidium, endorsed the proposals to reinstate the title of general secretary. The Presidium itself is to be renamed the Politburo, according to a proposal by Mr. Brezhnev.

Soviet sources said these were mere changes of nomenclature. They noted, however, that when the Presidium-Politburo change was enacted the membership of the new ruling body might be somewhat different from the present unit, and possibly fewer in number. The Presidium now has 12 members.

Both terms, general secretary and politburo, hearken back in the Soviet mind to the Stalin era, though the advocates of the change in terminology are careful to trace their ancestry to Lenin.

March 31, 1966

# Brezhnev Given Wide Publicity Again

By BERNARD GWERTZMAN

Special to The New York Times

MOSCOW, Sept. 5—Leonid I. Brezhnev's pre-eminence in the Soviet leadership was further underscored this week by what appeared to be an effort to add some color to his rather stiff public image.

During a week-long trip to the Central Asian republics of Kazakhstan, Turkmenia, Tadzhikistan, and Kirghizia, Mr. Brezhnev's picture was on the front pages of the major central papers almost every day in a variety of shirt-sleeve poses.

He was shown, without his jacket, inspecting a construction site for a hydroelectric plant, with a white straw hat against the heat walking past a new apartment house, and being cheered by workers. The impression given the reader was of a hard-working party leader out seeing what is going on.

In most countries, there is nothing unusual when the nation's most important figure is given front-page publicity while on a tour of the provinces. But the attention aroused interest here because ever since Mr. Brezhnev and his Politburo colleagues ousted Nikita S. Khrushchev in October, 1964, there has been a deliberate effort to avoid such personal publicity.

Mr. Khrushchev had his picture in the paper very often, and to re-establish collective leadership, the new leaders often went weeks without allowing anyone's picture in the newspaper. But this year, Mr. Brezhnev has received more publicity than his fellows on the Politburo, although he is far from matching Mr. Khrushchev's.

For instance, when Mr. Khrushchev toured the provinces his words of advice to farmers and workers were often reprinted in their entirety in the central press. But most of Mr. Brezhnev's speeches are not published.

Another sign of the publicity was an article by Veniamin E. Dymshits, a Deputy Premier, who wrote in the weekly magazine Ogonyok today his reminiscences about being head of the iron and steel plant in Zaporozhye in the Ukraine after the war. Mr. Brezhnev was party secretary there in 1946-47 and Mr. Dymshits gives unusual personal touches about the party leader.

"His knowledge of life and deep understanding of the situation, his great humanity, public spirit and kindness to people created an atmosphere of confidence at the construction sites," Mr. Dymshits said of Mr. Brezhnev.

Mr. Brezhnev's status as "first among equals," has gone through various periods when he was more the "first" and other times when he was more "equal." In April, in connection with the 100th anniversary of Lenin's birth, he virtually stole the limelight with four nationally televised speeches while his colleagues had none.

Following that, a two-volume collection of his speeches was published, and given extensive reviews in party publications. But the tone of the reviews was more restrained than those for similar collections of Mr. Khrushchev. A deliberate effort seems to have been made to avoid giving the people the impression that another personality cult was being developed, while at the same time stressing Mr. Brezhnev's pre-eminence.

Western diplomats tend to regard the upsurge in publicity about the party leader as part of an effort to stress the dominant role of the party with a new congress due in March. Mr. Brezhnev has seemed eager to convey the impression of an active party working energetically to overcome problems in society.

Others see last week's tour, for instance, as a signal by Mr. Brezhnev to party workers that he is the top man and there should be no questioning this in coming months when new party leaders are to be selected throughout the country for next March's party congress.

September 6, 1970

# Khrushchev Is Dead at 77

By BERNARD GWERTZMAN
Special to the New York Times

MOSCOW, Sept. 11—Nikita S. Khruschchev, who ruled the Soviet Union with a dramatic flair for more than a decade before his ouster seven years ago by the current, more conservative Kremlin leaders, died today of a heart attack. He was 77 years old.

Word of Mr. Khrushchev's death in a Kremlin hospital about noon was relayed to Western newsmen by friends of his family and confirmed informally by the Foreign Ministry in reply to queries.

As of 9 P.M. Moscow time —some nine hours later—there had been no official announcement of the death of the stocky man who became the head of the Soviet Communist party after Stalin's death in 1953 and who spent the next 11 years seeking to blacken the reputation and expose the crimes of the former dictator.

Associated Press
Nikita S. Khrushchev about to vote in national elections in Moscow on June 13 during his last public appearance.

### Stricken 4 Days Ago

Friends said that Mr. Khrushchev, who had a sclerotic condition for many years and who had been in and out of hospitals recently, suffered a heart attack about four days ago. He apparently was feeling better this morning, but about noon died in his sleep, the friends said.

His wife, Nina, and one of his daughters, Rada, were at his bedside, the friends said.

Because of the news blackout, ordinary Russians had no knowledge of the death of the man who made "peaceful coexistence" part of the world vocabulary. When told by newsmen, the reaction was much the same.

One woman said, "My God," but then continued on her business. Another woman said, "That's sad." In 24 hours, the word, however, will have spread throughout Moscow as people with short-wave radios tell their friends the news being reported from abroad.

The family said through friends that Mr. Khrushchev would be buried Monday in the Novodevichy Cemetery in Moscow, where many famous Russians, including Stalin's wife, have been interred.

As a former party and Government leader, Mr. Khrushchev would have been eligible for a full-scale state funeral, including a ceremony in Red Square and interment in the Kremlin wall.

After his forced resignation in what amounted to a Kremlin coup in October, 1964, Mr. Khrushchev lived in virtual isolation and was rarely mentioned in Soviet publications. His record was often criticized by current leaders who found him too erratic in his work and too domineering in his style of leadership.

He lived most of the last seven years in a fenced-in estate at Petrovo-Dalneye, a pine-studded village some 15 miles west of Moscow. He also maintained an apartment in an old part of the capital. But in recent years, because of his poor health, he rarely came into the city.

His living expenses were paid by the state, and he had a full retinue of security guards. His actions were limited and he was not usually permitted to go freely into public places.

The last time he was seen by Western newsmen was on June 13, when he and his wife arrived at their polling place in Moscow to cast their obligatory votes for the local candidate to the Supreme Soviet of the Russian Republic. Asked how he felt, he replied, "Good." Asked what he was doing these days, he said:

"I'm a pensioner. What do pensioners do?"

His death poses something of a problem to Leonid I. Brezhnev, who replaced him as party leader; Aleksei N. Kosygin, who took over as Premier, and the other members of the 15-man Politburo.

They must decide whether to allow Mr. Khrushchev to be eulogized for his past work or to maintain their virtual silence about him. The plans for a private funeral indicate that the current leaders have decided against any radical move to rehabilitate him.

Moreover, Mr. Khrushchev lived under something of a cloud, after the publication abroad last year of "Khrushchev Remembers," which is said to contain Mr. Khrushchev's own recollections about certain incidents in his life. The Soviet Union has officially repudiated the book, and Mr. Khrushchev last November was obliged to sign a statement terming it "a fabrication."

The appearance of that book, however, forced authorities here to lift temporarily the ban on the use of Mr. Khrushchev's name in the press and on the air. Tass, the Soviet press agency, distributed his short statement, and the Moscow radio broadcast it—the first time his name had been heard in a broadcast since his ouster.

But Mr. Khrushchev's name has not been eliminated completely. Official party histories still note that "N.S. Khrushchev" was First Secretary from 1953 to 1964. Records of World War II take note of his participation in the Ukrainian front.

He is still regarded ambiguously by Soviet intellectuals. They praise him for his anti-Stalin campaign and his efforts to rehabilitate those wrongly condemned. But they criticized him for vulgarity, boorishness, and meddling in the arts and sciences, which were considered beyond his competence.

When he was ousted in 1964, many liberal intellectuals believed that the new leadership would improve the climate. But since Mr. Brezhnev has partly rehabilitated Stalin as a wartime leader and has not given intellectuals the freedom they sought, Mr. Khrushchev in retrospect has gained more respect.

September 12, 1971

# Prestige of Stalin Now Reviving

By HEDRICK SMITH
Special to The New York Times

MOSCOW, March 4 — Two decades after his death on March 5, 1953, Stalin enjoys great latent prestige among the Soviet people and a much more favorable popular reputation than Nikita S. Khrushchev, the man who dared denounce him for his vast political purges.

Not only has Stalin been officially rehabilitated to a modest role in Soviet history, but there is an undercurrent of nostalgia for what many people now feel were in some ways the good old days of Stalin's rule, from 1924 to 1953.

This is a far cry, of course, from the outpouring of praise and adulation heaped upon Stalin during his lifetime. But it represents a distinct comeback from the Khrushchev era when he was either denounced or treated as a nonperson.

Today, approval is far from universal, and Stalin's excesses are on occasion obliquely criticized. But there is clear sympathy for crediting the former "friend and teacher" of the Soviet people with achievements of the past as well as a tendency in many quarters to idealize his leadership style.

With Stalin clearly in mind, many Russians comment privately that what the country needs is a "krepky khozyain" — a strong master.

A factory director, bedeviled by problems of labor turnover, alcoholism and absenteeism, will wistfully recall to friends the tight discipline maintained under Stalin when a worker could be harshly penalized, even jailed, for showing up 10 minutes late.

Older people, political conservatives, militia officers — irritated by the miniskirts, jeans, long hair, rock music and other fashions that trickle in from outside — hanker for the "order" of the Stalinist days when youth was more manageable.

Many ordinary people, grumbling about rising prices or never-ending shortages, remember Stalin's annual and highly publicized practice of reducing prices on a few items, though they usually forget that there were often hidden increases on others.

### A Longing to Be Awed

Still other people, criticizing Khrushchev as a bungler who tinkered unsuccessfully with the Soviet system, and dissatisfied with what they describe as the grayness of the present leadership, long to be awed once more by a ruler of Stalin's imposing mysteries and terrible presence.

"The present leadership has no sense of decorum or ceremony, but Stalin knew how to impress people," commented an Establishment intellectual. "People now feel that when he was alive, other countries respected and feared us more."

Sympathies for Stalin often emerge spontaneously. Sometimes when he appears in a documentary movie or fictionalized film history of World War II, an audience will break into applause. Not long ago, a West European diplomat was surprised to find himself at a small party with a group of middle-aged, middle-level Russian officials who toasted Stalin's health more than half a dozen times with no more pretext than that they were drinking one of Stalin's favorite Georgian wines.

### Purges Are Defended

In random conversations with foreigners, many ordinary Russians will excuse or even defend Stalin on the issue of the purges. Some months ago, an engineer explained that Stalin was a great man but that others committed mistakes in his name. A teacher in her late 20's said that people generally remembered him well "in spite of the fact that he was a hard man."

"Maybe he had to be a hard man at that time, maybe it was necessary," she said.

Liberal urban intellectuals and outright dissidents, who personally oppose and vehemently criticize Stalin and neo-Stalinism, acknowledge that the general opinion of Stalin is improving, and is especially strong in the countryside.

"Out there," said a writer in his 60's who spent years in a Stalinist labor camp, "Stalin has a real hold on the people. They feel that he built the country and he won the war. Now they see disorder in agriculture, disorder in industry, disorder everywhere in the economy and they see no end to it. They think that when there was a tough ruler, we did not have such troubles. People forget that things were bad then, too, and they forget the terrible price that we paid."

Politically minded Soviet citizens offer several explanations for the resurgence of Stalin's reputation. In part, they say, it is a reaction against Khrushchev and dissatisfaction with the present. With his de-Stalinization campaign and other programs, Khrushchev offended the vested interests of powerful segments in the Communist party, the military, and the police system. Some, it is said, are inclined to glorify Stalin precisely because Khrushchev attacked him so sharply.

### Rhythm of History

In part, Stalin's improved image reflects the passage of time, some say. In the two decades since his death, many of those who lived through the worst Stalinist purges of the nineteen-thirties have died and the memories of millions of others have mellowed.

One dissident suggested that the resurgence of Stalin's popularity reflected the natural rhythms of history. When thousands were rehabilitated and returning from Stalinist camps there was a revulsion toward Stalin. With the passing of a generation, the counterreaction began, the dissident reasoned.

"After all," he said, "it took about 30 years after Napoleon's exile from France in 1815 for his nephew to come to power as emperor but Bonapartism as a political movement emerged after only about 20 years. So, it is not so unnatural for there to be an upsurge of neo-Stalinist sentiment here now."

Roy Medvedev, a dissident who chronicled the Stalinist purges in his major work, "Let Hustory Judge," observed in 1968 that not only was Stalin's official public image refurbished, but that "some party officials openly and proudly call themselves Stalinists, without risking expulsion from the party."

Other noncomformist thinkers are concerned that the vigorous campaign of suppression against dissident activists in the last 18 months is evidence of a neo-Stalinist mood in the party. None, however, suggests that the latest campaign remotely compares to the Stalinist repressions in either numbers or methods.

Another reason for what might be termed Stalin's comeback is his improved treatment in the press.

In the first years after his death, the glorification of Stalin was gradually downgraded by his successors preparing the way for Khrushchev's stunning and aggressive de-Stalinization program.

### Famous 'Secret Speech'

This began sensationally with the famous "secret speech" at the 20th Communist party Congress in 1956 when Khrushchev condemned the Stalinist purges and "the cult of Stalin's personality." Thousands of his victims were freed from camps and cleared of charges.

Hundreds of towns, streets and sites bearing Stalin's name were renamed, including Stalingrad, where the battle the Russians consider the turning point of the war was fought. The city became Volgograd and the battle became the Battle on the Volga.

Stalin was derided as an ineffective wartime leader who had failed to anticipate the Nazi attack in 1941, had not prepared the country for war and had panicked when the attack came. As a peacetime leader, he was held to have made some contributions until 1934 and after that pictured as a suspicious power-mad leader who decimated a generation with his purges. To underscore his fall from grace, his body was removed from the Lenin Mausoleum on Red Square. Anti-Stalinist poems and prose began appearing.

After Khrushchev was ousted in 1964, his successors reversed the trend. They signaled the end of de-Stalinization in May, 1965, during celebrations of the 20th anniversary of the allied victory over Germany. The blackout on Stalin was lifted, Stalin appeared for the first time on television screens as a wartime leader and father figure for the Soviet people. The battle of Stalingrad regained its original name.

### More Public Honors

Increasingly after 1966, his wartime leadership was praised. In 1967, a handbook for Communist party officials called him an economic leader in peacetime and asserted that he had "made a serious contribution to the development of the world Communist and liberation movement."

In 1969, the leadership formally celebrated the 90th anniversary of Stalin's birth, praising him for "the gigantic transformation," as well as for his wartime leadership and for having fought such maverick Communists as Trotsky, though his "unjustified repressions" of the nineteen-thirties were criticized.

In June, 1970, a bust of Stalin was placed over what had been his virtually unmarked grave behind the Lenin Mausoleum. Last year, the 50th anniversary of the formation of the Soviet Union was commemorated on Stalin's birthday, Dec. 21, rather than on the proper date nine days later—a subtle acknowledgement of his role in Soviet history.

The current leadership has walked a careful, balanced line. It has restored much of Stalin's historical importance but rejected his methods. It has not forgiven Stalin's faults, but it has generally barred publication of works that expose them.

The result is that Soviet citizens know far less about Stalinist repressions than many people abroad. The famous "secret speech" has never been published here. Even allusions to it are rare.

Moreover, though the press continues to print ritual memorials to the most famous victims of Stalin's purges on anniversaries of their birth, it does so without any indication of how they died. This happened most recently with Marshal Mikhail Tukhachevsky, shot in June, 1937, along with other generals during the army purge.

Although an article in the Krushchev era on the 70th anniversary of Marshal Tukhachevsky's birthday described these events in detail, this year's article simply stopped recounting his career when it reached 1935.

### Poised and Dignified

Mention of Stalin in the press, books, magazines or television is limited, though generally sympathetic. He usually appears in the memoirs of retired generals or documentary or fictionalized movies about World War II — a man of great poise and dignity, decisive and respected but neither imperious nor threatening.

He is portrayed as a wise, kindly and reasonable military leader, accessible to his subordinates and tireless in his service to the country.

The latest installment of a serialized World War II novel, "Blockade" by Aleksandr Chakovsky, editor of the Writers Union weekly, Literaturnaya Gazeta, pictures Stalin as a masterful statesman struggling with the lonely decisions of supreme command, acknowledging only in the most minimal way that there were some "mistakes, miscalculations" at the start of World War II.

Moreover, "Blockade" contains only the gentlest possible allusion to the bloody purges —by merely mentioning the year 1937, when the purges were at their peak—and implies that it was the secret police chiefs, not Stalin, who were responsible.

Typically, the account omits any reference to Stalin's fierce temper or any hint of his fears of conspiracies that inspired extreme security measures in his later years.

### Play Upon Patriotism

Such accounts, although low key, play upon the naturally strong feelings of patriotism and thereby improve his popular image by linking him with the successful, if painful, war effort.

On occasion, either direct or implied criticism of Stalinist repressions emerges. The most striking current example is a play, "The Ascent of Mount Fuji," the story of four middle-aged men arguing over their guilt in the secret denunciation of a close friend for writing a pacifist poem during World War II.

Stalin is never mentioned. Nor are the secret police or the purges generally. But the play dramatizes forcibly for the first time since the Khrushchev era not only the problem of the Stalinist repressions but also the hypocrisy of the current silence about them.

"It's true," explained a leading Soviet poet, "a few people do want to bring up that issue and face it. But the great majority—the great majority—want to forget about it."

Similarly, very little is said or written about Stalin's role in the forced collectivization of agriculture in the late nineteen-twenties or his role as prime mover in the industrialization of the country.

**Anthem Without Words**

The result is a distinct gap in Soviet history-writing and some peculiar social anachronisms. Because the words to the Soviet national anthem mentioned Stalin in a flattering way, Khrushchev decreed that the words would no longer be sung. A commission was to be appointed to produce new lyrics, but none have ever been accepted. So, at major public events, Soviet citizens stand in silence while their national anthem is played. On Soviet calendars, which honor the birthdays of much lesser figures, Stalin is unmentioned.

More significant, some Soviet parents think, is the fact that a generation of young people is growing up without learning much about a long and crucial period of the country's history.

Some parents and teachers in higher educational institutions assert that there is a sharp polarization among today's young —a minority that consider the Stalinist purges an unforgivable black mark in Soviet history. Evidently a larger minority feel that the achievements of the Stalinist period far outweigh, and perhaps even justify the repressions.

"The issue for most of these young people is not whether they are for Stalin or against him, not whether the Stalinist period was a good thing for the country or a bad thing," said a man with a daughter studying at Moscow State University. "What my daughter's friends want to know is simply what happened. They feel as though it is part of the country's history and it should not be kept from them."

**A Contrast of Eras**

Others draw a contrast between today's youth, which seems relatively unconcerned with Stalinism as an issue, with the youth of a decade ago when university students were sharply challenging their parents about it.

One middle-aged woman expressed shock when a boy of 16 was unable even to identity Iosif Dzhugashvili, using Stalin's original Georgian name. (He took the name Stalin when he became a Bolshevik revolutionary.) It would be roughly equivalent for an American teen-ager not to be able to identify "Ike" as President Eisenhower.

Few things illustrate the gap between Soviet generations more starkly than the relative ignorance of youth about Stalin.

People in their 50's and 60's tend to recall the purges when talking with friends in private, and argue pro or con. Those in their late 30's and early 40's recall the jolt of disillusion at learning what had gone on under Stalin.

"Our generation was the hardest hit," said one white-collar worker. "When Stalin died, we were in university, and we thought it was the end of the universe. But we found out that we could go on even without Stalin."

"Then, we were terribly disillusioned to find out that so many innocent people had been killed and so much history had been falsified," he said. "Ours was the generation of fathers and sons, when sons asked their parents, 'Where were you when so-and-so was killed and you knew he was a good man and innocent?' or 'Why were you silent?' Now that's all over. You don't hear that much any more."

Still others vividly recall rushing out to the Kremlin to try to see the body of Stalin, the man who had been the center of the world, when they heard the news of his death, only to be caught up in riots that left hundreds dead and injured in the streets, crushed in the struggle between people and the police. His end was as stormy as his life, they say.

Many recount the surprising re-emergence of the invisible imprints of his rule, attitudes he encouraged toward previous iron-handed Russian rulers, like Ivan the Terrible, or fragments of memorized praise of Stalin.

"Not long ago, I was visiting with friends and we started singing," the white-collar worker recalled. "The next thing we knew we were singing a song about Stalin that we had memorized in school. We were surprised that we knew almost all the words. It was shocking to hear all those glorious words of praise coming out, as if our minds had been tape-recorders."

Opinions about Stalin differ not only from generation to generation but also from region to region. Although few generalizations will hold up completely, few dispute that Stalin is still regarded as a saint in his native Georgia and very fondly remembered in the Central Asian republics, but strongly disliked in the Baltic republic and in part of the Ukraine.

So far at least, opinion appears to be generally united on only one issue: whatever respect has been restored to Stalin as a leader who forced achievements upon the country and led the nation to victory in war, no one openly advocates a return to his devastating methods of political control.

March 5, 1973

# SOVIET REDS SEEK WORKER MEMBERS

## Recruitment Drive Is On to Reduce White-Collar Share in Party Cells

**By HEDRICK SMITH**
Special to The New York Times

MOSCOW, Nov. 9—A new internal directive of the Soviet Communist party has called for intensifying the drive to recruit new members among blue-collar workers, especially in the younger generation, according to Soviet sources.

The party leadership is reportedly concerned by the fact that intellectuals, administrative leaders and white-collar workers outnumber the blue-collar membership and by ideological apathy and skepticism among some of the educated young people who join the party.

For several years, party organizers have waged a recruiting campaign to make the party once again what the Soviet press calls "the party of the working class" but this has evidently still not borne sufficient fruit.

A directive issued in September by the Central Committee, Soviet sources disclosed, requires district party committees to take in four or five workers for each intellectual or white-collar worker, even in districts with a preponderance of intellectuals in educational or research establishments.

**Curbs on Students**

Party units were also reportedly given new instructions to step up their efforts to recruit members from the under-30 age group.

The redoubled emphasis on workers, young Moscow intellectuals say, has made it difficult for most undergraduates, graduate students and young scholars to join. In some institutes, waiting lists have accumulated among young people who regard party membership as the key to advancement or to jobs that would allow coveted travel in the West.

Some young people have been known, according to Soviet sources, to take temporary blue-collar jobs in factories to increase their opportunities for joining the party or have joined while serving in the armed forces where induction into the party is said to be easier.

In October, 1973, the party daily, Pravda, reported that 44.6 per cent of the party's 15 million members fell into the white-collar, administrative or intellectual category; 40.7 per cent were considered blue-collar workers, and 14.7 per cent were from the collective-farmer class. This followed a vigorous recruitment of blue-collar workers into the party.

**Statistics Are Misleading**

Soviet sources say the breakdown of party membership by social class is often misleading because the statistics go by the status of individuals at the time they join the party and in most cases do not change as the people change social class through education and advancement.

The result, they say, is that the working-class membership is probably statistically overstated and the administrative and managerial share of the membership is probably understated. For example, most of the leadership of the party is said to be listed still as worker or peasant members of the party because this was their category when they joined 40 or 50 years ago.

It is particularly fashionable among the leadership and activists in the party apparatus to emphasize working-class or peasant background.

For this reason, some Soviet scholars voice belief privately that the white-collar category probably represents an actual majority of party membership, something that the leadership is eager to hide from the public as well as to combat by recruiting campaigns.

November 10, 1974

# Soviet Agriculture Chief Is Ousted From Politburo

By CHRISTOPHER S. WREN
Special to The New York Times

MOSCOW, March 5 — The Soviet Minister of Agriculture was abruptly dropped from the ruling Politburo today apparently as punishment for the disastrous grain failure last year.

At the same time Leonid I. Brezhnev, riding a new crest of prestige in his leadership career, was formally reappointed as secretary general to head the Communist Party.

The name of the Minister of Agriculture, Dmitri S. Polyansky, was conspicuously absent from the list of the newly elected Politburo members that Mr. Brezhnev read to the nearly 5,000 delegates assembled for the closing session of the 25th Communist Party Congress.

Mr. Polyansky's future had become a subject of speculation after a drought last summer left a grain harvest of only 140 million tons, more than a third below the goal. But it was widely doubted he would be made a scapegoat because such a move would draw attention to the extent of the harvest failure and thus call Mr. Brezhnev's basic agricultural policy into question.

However, the Ministry of Agriculture was subjected at the congress to harsh criticism, aimed at showing that the carrying out of the policy was at fault rather than the policy itself.

Fyodor D. Kulakov, the party secretary for agriculture, has not been disciplined.

Two prominent party figures, Grigory V. Romanov and Dmitri F. Ustinov, were promoted to full members of the Politburo. Mr. Romanov, the Leningrad Region party chief and Mr. Ustinov, who heads the Soviet defense industry complex, were formerly alternate, or nonvoting, members.

In another surprise, Geidar A. Aliyev, the party chief of Azerbaijan in the Caucasus, was elevated to alternate membership in the Politburo past several more promising contenders who had prompted greater speculation.

March 6, 1976

# The Soviet Leadership: It's Unanimous

By DAVID K. SHIPLER

MOSCOW—The riddles of Kremlin politics have rarely been deciphered by outsiders except in retrospect, long after the denouément of some mysterious struggle behind the high brick walls that surround the seat of Soviet power. Then, looking back, it all becomes clear. A certain Politburo member saw leaders off at the airport only nine out of 28 times, his speech appeared only in Latvian newspapers, he signed only six of the 32 decrees issued in the absence of the Prime Minister, and so on.

Such Kreminology has gone out of fashion, but not out of existence. Radio Liberty, the American-financed station that broadcasts from Munich, made the airport and decree observations about Dmitri S. Polyansky after he was demoted in 1973 from First Deputy Prime Minister to Agriculture Minister. At the 25th Party Congress that ended March 5, he was dropped from the ruling Politburo as an apparent scapegoat for the Soviet Union's failures in agriculture. Perhaps the infrequency of his trips to the airport had meant something after all.

It is relatively easy to document the vulnerability of a junior member of the Politburo who is responsible for the weakest sector of the Soviet economy; it is quite another matter to catch glimpses of the more important dynamics of high-level maneuvering on issues such as détente, strategic weapons, military intervention, foreign trade and domestic economic priorities.

Under Leonid I. Brezhnev, the party has succeeded in masking differences within the leadership on such questions. Wrapped in collection unanimity, the Politburo conveys an image of conservative serenity and collegial decision-making, with little of the acrimonious infighting and sudden shifts of policy that characterized the Khrushchev era.

Many Western diplomats and experts who analyze Soviet affairs accept this image as representing reality. They see the present Politburo as cautious, perhaps inflexible. It is an old and nearly homogeneous group of men that seems to favor promotion on the basis of bureaucratic performance. The average age of the 16 members is just over 66, making it the oldest leadership in Soviet history. All but two have been educated as technicians: Mr. Brezhnev was a metallurgist, for example, and Prime Minister Aleksei N. Kosygin a textile engineer. The exceptions are Mikhail A. Suslov, an economist, and Arvid Y. Pelshe, a historian.

Analysts in Moscow cannot discern any strong disagreements within this group over key issues. They see no serious opposition to détente with the United States, and they believe that those American experts who see Mr. Brezhnev pitted against the "hawks" of the military establishment are making the error of projecting the configurations of American politics onto Soviet political life.

Writing in the magazine Foreign Policy last year, Lieut. Col. William E. Odom, of the United States Army, a former military attaché, in Moscow, even argued that the Soviet military probably favored détente for the benefits it could bring in Western technology. Since the entire Soviet economy is aimed at producing military power, Colonel Odom reasoned, and since the economy is suffering from stagnation and technology gaps, outside help would enable the Kremlin to avoid basic reforms that might alter what is now a "war-mobilization economy."

"Without peace and Western credits," Colonel Odom said, "the [Soviet] armed forces obviously cannot be strengthened as rapidly."

## Constituents and Old Associations

The Odom argument hints at the complexity of Soviet politics. Most Politburo members come to the high ranks of power through the party and governmental bureaucracy, bringing with them what some analysts call "tails" of constituents and old associations that can reach deeply into the ministries and state agencies and thereby influence the Politburo member's outlook and sense of obligation.

Thus, the two newest members, named March 5, look at first glance like men who will support continued investment in heavy industry as opposed to consumer goods. Grigory V. Romanov, the party chief of Leningrad, comes from a district rich in heavy manufacturing. Dmitri F. Ustinov made a lifetime career in the military industrial field.

Existing members have similar ties to organizational interests. Marshal Andrei A. Grechko, the Minister of Defense, can be expected to take a military point of view. Yuri V. Amdropov, head of the Committee for State Security (K.G.B.), is likely to want vigilance with respect to internal dissent. Fyodor D. Kulakov, an agronomist and party secretary in charge of agriculture, probably represents the view of the agricultural establishment on questions of allocating resources.

But not always. Analysts who have tried to diagram the leaders' attitude from their speeches have found "no tidy correspondence between policy positions, on the one hand, and organizational, functional, or even fractional (e.g. 'Brezhnevite') affiliations," wrote Grey Hodnett a year ago in the journal Problems of Communism.

Mr. Hodnett, an associate professor of political science at York University in Toronto, made a table of views that showed all but five of the present Politburo members favoring détente, all but two favoring Mr. Brezhnev as party chief, all but four favoring an effort to increase consumer goods and all but three for a policy of homogenizing the diverse national groups of the country.

The fluidity of Soviet politics derives partly from the role of issues as vehicles for a politician's success or demise. The smart politician with a durable career is usually one who can smell a change coming and make a timely jump onto the right side of the question. He who opposes a policy and doesn't swing the Politburo with him may find himself out of a job.

The most vivid recent case was that of Pyotr Y. Shelest, an advocate of the 1968 invasion of Czechoslovakia who lost his Politburo seat after he reportedly opposed the Nixon visit to the Soviet Union in 1972 apparently on the ground of American involvement in Vietnam.

In the last five years, Mr. Brezhnev has deftly removed other potential opponents and brought onto the Politburo men who seem to share his basic positions. Simultaneously, however, he has stacked the top ranks with men too old to succeed him, thereby reducing the chance of a power-grab, but also deferring decisions that will ultimately have to be made on who is to take power.

The result has been either stability or stagnation, depending on one's perspective. In Mr. Hodnett's view, Mr. Brezhnev has achieved both one-man rule and collective rule simultaneously; his policies become Soviet policies, but with a broad consensus that seems to guarantee continuity, at least until death, retirement or ouster forces change at the top.

*David K. Shipler is a correspondent in Moscow for The New York Times.*

March 14, 1976

# PODGORNY IS OUSTED BY SOVIET POLITBURO IN A SURPRISE MOVE

## LINK TO CONSTITUTION IS SEEN

### Diplomats in Moscow Believe New Charter May Be Issue That Led to Removal of President

By CHRISTOPHER S. WREN

Special to The New York Times

MOSCOW, May 24—President Nikolai V. Podgorny of the Soviet Union was dropped from the Communist Party's ruling Politburo today in a Kremlin move that is expected to spell the end of his political career.

It was the first such shift at the very top of the Soviet hierarchy since Nikita S. Khrushchev was ousted from power 13 years ago. Mr. Podgorny is expected to be removed from the post of President at the next session of the Supreme Soviet, the nominal Parliament, opening June 16.

No explanation was officially given for Mr. Podgorny's ouster, which was voted by the party's Central Committee in a plenary session today. A few Russians concluded that it was because of age; the President is 74 years old. But his peers at the Kremlin are hardly any younger.

**New Constitution May Be a Factor**

Another theory advanced by diplomats was that a power play was connected with the new Constitution, which was the main subject at today's session. The diplomats said that either Mr. Podgorny had objected to revisions or that the Constitution, a project of the party chief, Leonid I. Brezhnev, did not provide for Mr. Podgorny's continuation in the Presidency. If so, the title might conceivably be conferred on Mr. Brezhnev himself.

Mr. Podgorny's removal caught both diplomats and Russians by surprise. The baldish, button-nosed President had ranked in protocol second to Mr. Brezhnev, whose authority seems strengthened by the change.

Only this morning, the party newspaper Pravda published on its front page a decree signed by Mr. Podgorny giving President Tito of Yugoslavia the Order of the October Revolution in connection with his 85th birthday. And last month, Mr. Podgorny concluded a publicized trip through Africa that had suggested increased responsibilities.

The post of President in the Soviet Union is largely a ceremonial one, entailing the signing of decrees and the accreditation of foreign envoys. Mr. Podgorny's departure was not expected to produce any immediate changes in policies at home or abroad.

The Central Committee also confirmed the demotion of Konstantin F. Katushev by removing him from the post of party secretary responsible for relations with ruling Communist parties. In March he was appointed a Deputy Prime Minister under Aleksei N. Kosygin, with responsi-

Sovfoto

**In 1960, Mr. Podgorny—then head of the Ukrainian delegation to the United Nations—escorted Nikita S. Khrushchev, the Soviet Prime Minister, to the General Assembly. Mr. Podgorny's removal from the Politburo is the first top-level reshuffling at the Kremlin since Mr. Khrushchev's ouster.**

## At the Center of Power Since 1963

Nikolai Viktorovich Podgorny, once named by Nikita S. Khrushchev as possible successor, was born 74 years ago in Karlovka, the Ukraine. . . After eight years in engineering jobs at sugar-beet refineries, became a deputy commisar of Ukrainian food industry. . . Named party chief of Kharkov Province in 1950 and of the entire Ukrain in 1957 . . . Moved into higher echelons of the party on the basis of ties with Khrushchev, becoming alternate member of the ruling Politburo in 1958 and full voting member in 1960. . . Transferred to center of power structure in 1963 when he moved from Ukrainian party leadership to the post of a national party secretary. . . After ouster of Khrushchev in 1964, joined Leonid I. Brezhnev and Aleksei N. Kosygin in top levels of Soviet leadership and was appointed President—formal title is Chairman of Presidium of Supreme Soviet. . .Has represented the Soviet Union on foreign journeys, most recently to Africa. . . Is understood to have a wife, two daughters and a son.

bilities for economic relations within the Soviet bloc. In the Soviet political system, the governmental position is less authoritative than the corresponding party post.

Today, Konstantin V. Rusakov, a close associate of Mr. Brezhnev, succeeded Mr. Katushev as a national party secretary.

The official press agency Tass reported Mr. Podgorny's dismissal and the two other personnel changes as part of a larger report on the plenary meeting. With regard to Mr. Podgorny, Tass left out the phrase "at his own request," which is sometimes used to soften the retirement of officials.

With one swift stroke, Mr. Podgorny, a Ukrainian who started out as an engineer before switching over to the party apparatus in 1950, has thus been consigned to a future of official obscurity. "He will go and sit in a dacha," one Western diplomat remarked. "I can't see him getting another job."

Mr. Podgorny becomes the fifth Politburo member to lose his full position since the current regime took over in late 1964 and he is undoubtedly the most important. Others were Gennadi I. Voronov in 1971, Pyotr Y. Shelest in 1972, Aleksandr N. Shelepin in 1975 and Dmitri S. Polyansky last year.

### Position Had Been Thought Secure

There were rumors in Soviet circles that Mr. Podgorny was asked to step down about the time of the 25th party congress in February 1976 because of diminishing work capacity but had refused. Since then, it was generally assumed that his position was secure.

Though Mr. Podgorny is 74, Western diplomats say that he seems well enough. In the present Politburo, age itself would not be reason for retirement. Mr. Kosygin, who has ranked third in the hierarchy, is 73, and the leading ideologist, Mikhail A. Suslov, will be 75 in November. Arvid N. Pelshe, at 78, continues as the oldest member. Mr. Brezhnev himself is 70 years old.

Consequently, there was diplomatic speculation that the President might have resisted the new Constitution if it curtailed his role or eliminated it altogether. Mr. Brezhnev has been trying to introduce a Constitution of his own making that would replace one introduced under Stalin in 1936.

May 25, 1977

# Brezhnev Is Made Soviet President, First Party Chief to Take the Title

By CHRISTOPHER S. WREN

Special to The New York Times

MOSCOW, June 16—Leonid I. Brezhnev, the head of the Soviet Communist Party, was also named chief of state today, becoming the first person in his country to hold both posts simultaneously.

His election by the Supreme Soviet, the nominal Parliament, came at the outset of a two-day session. The move had been expected following the removal last month of President Nikolai V. Podgorny from the party's ruling Politburo, the main policy-making body, and the creation of a new post of First Vice President under the proposed new constitution.

The conferring of the Presidency on the 70-year-old Mr. Brezhnev appeared to confirm his political power. The honor also seemed calculated to add luster to his reputation as a statesman at a time when he has been the subject of increasing adulation at home.

While he had seemed content earlier to confine himself to his politically more significant party role, he may have felt that by assuming the Presidency as well he would enhance his prestige as an architect of East-West détente. He is scheduled to visit France and West Germany this year.

Mr. Brezhnev previously served as President under Nikita S. Khrushchev, from May 1960 to June 1964. Because the post is largely ceremonial, it then represented something of a setback since he had been closer to the seat of power in the previous four years as one of Khrushchev's national party secretaries. When Khrushchev was overthrown in October 1964, Mr. Brezhnev assumed the party leadership.

With his authority now at its apogee, Mr. Brezhnev has sought to avoid comparisons with the personality cults surrounding Stalin and Khrushchev. Even now, he is likely to maintain a semblance of consensus in the decisions made in the Politburo.

In accepting the post of President, known officially as Chairman of the Presidium of the Supreme Soviet, Mr. Brezhnev:

"The discharge of the lofty and responsible state functions connected with this, parallel with the duties of General Secretary of our party's Central Committee, is, of course, no easy matter. But the will of the party, the will of the Soviet people, the interests of our socialist homeland have always been for me the supreme law to which I subordinated and subordinate my entire life."

The newly created post of First Vice President cannot technically be filled until the constitution is approved at another session of the Supreme Soviet, in October. The job is expected to include some of the President's chores, such as meeting visitors and awarding decorations, freeing Mr. Brezhnev for his more important party leadership duties.

The final exit of Mr. Podgorny from the political scene today was handled speedily. Aleksei P. Shitikov, chairman of the Soviet of the Union, one of the two chambers in the Supreme Soviet, announced at a joint session that Mr. Podgorny had asked to be relieved of his duties "in connection with his retirement on pension." His final slide into obscurity was settled in less than a minute by a vote of the dispassionate delegates.

The only surprise came when the Politburo members, with Mr. Podgorny absent, filed onto the dais of the Supreme Soviet chamber inside the Kremlin. Fyodor D. Kulakov, the party secretary responsible for agriculture, moved into the front row next to, in ascending order, two other national party secretaries, Andrei P. Kirilenko and Mikhail A. Suslov; Prime Minister Aleksei N. Kosygin and Mr. Brezhnev.

Because the Politburo lineup is usually ranked at public events, this seemed to signal a rise in the stature of the 59-year-old Mr. Kulakov, who was left unscathed by the 1975 harvest disaster. His position today prompted speculation that he might be emerging as one of the successors to the present aging leadership.

Mr. Suslov, the ideologist, formally proposed Mr. Brezhnev for the Presidency in what was interpreted as a gesture of solidarity. The two men have been rumored to hold divergent views on some issues.

Although several East European party leaders have already assumed presidential functions as well, no precedent exists in the Soviet Union. Stalin and Khrushchev combined the jobs of party chief and Prime Minister. After Khrushchev was toppled in 1964, the party resolved that the two posts could not be held simultaneously but the restriction was not extended to the Presidency.

By also holding the post of President, Mr. Brezhnev resolves his protocol problems with elected Western leaders. He is expected to wield his new title when he visits France next week. Until now, he has had to sign international treaties with his party title, which has no counterpart in the West.

Confirming this motive, Mr. Suslov noted that Mr. Brezhnev had been signing "vitally important" international agreement and had served for many years as "the most authoritative representative of the Communist Party and the state."

Even without a formal state title, Mr. Brezhnev emerged as clearly the power in the Kremlin and now his authority appears unchallenged. Of his former rivals, only Mr. Kosygin remains in the top ranks of the Politburo and he never posed a serious threat in the jockeying that followed the removal of Khrushchev.

### Podgorny and Mikoyan Contrasted

Ironically, it was Mr. Brezhnev as party chief who nominated Mr. Podgorny to replace Anastas I. Mikoyan as President in December 1965, praising Mr. Podgorny as "one of the prominent party leaders and statesmen of our country." On that occasion, Mr. Mikoyan had bowed out gracefully on the pretext of age and ill health and was rewarded with an Order of Lenin. By contrast, a conspicuous silence met Mr. Podgorny's departure.

Western diplomats tend to feel that Mr. Podgorny was dismissed because he resisted yielding the Presidency to Mr. Brezhnev and accepting honorable retirement. Unlike Mr. Mikoyan, Mr. Podgorny was not present today to step down with his reputation intact.

Mr. Brezhnev was elected President with a predictably unanimous vote and a standing ovation from the delegates at the Supreme Soviet session. Mr. Suslov, setting the tone of subsequent compliments, declared;

"Throughout his life, Leonid Ilyich Brezhnev has dedicated his outstanding talent as organizer, far-sighted politician and leader of the Leninist type to selfless service to the working class, the peasantry and the intelligentsia, to constant concern for improving the life of the people, to the great cause of building communism."

June 17, 1977

# Soviet Adopts a New Constitution With Little Change

By DAVID K. SHIPLER
Special to The New York Times

MOSCOW, Oct. 7—The Soviet Union today adopted a new Constitution, which, apart from minor changes in language, is essentially the same as the draft made public in June. The subsequent months of a carefully orchestrated discussion in the controlled press appear to have made little substantive difference in the final adopted version.

Approved unanimously by about 1,500 members of the Supreme Soviet, or Parliament, the document puts particular stress on economic guarantees, such as rights to housing, education, employment and medical care. But like the three previous Soviet constitutions, the new one provides no mechanism for judicial review by which a citizen can challenge a law's constitutionality.

The new charter, replacing the one enacted under Stalin in 1936, makes no basic changes in the relationship between the individual and the state. It does not begin with the assumption, as does the American Constitution, that men are born with rights that government must not infringe. Rather, it operates on the principle that rights are granted by the state to its citizens, and therefore may be defined, limited or suspended by the state.

It was approved in 22 votes, linked to various sections of the document, taken in a hall of the Great Kremlin Palace, where both houses of the Supreme Soviet were in joint session. After the voting, there was prolonged applause laced with shouts of "Glory to the Communist Party!" "Glory! Glory!"

The new Constitution is a culmination of legal reforms begun under Nikita S. Khrushchev in the late 1950's and many of its concepts are contained in the revised civil and criminal codes.

The Soviet charter codifies the role of the Communist Party as "the leading and guiding force of Soviet society and the nucleus of its political system," thereby eliminating the anomaly of having the country's source of political power unmentioned in its basic law.

It contains a strong section on women's rights, calling for equal access to education, jobs, promotions and the like, as well as paid maternity leave. And in a clause added to the original draft it advocates the "gradual reduction of working hours for women with small children."

Apparently in response to some of the public discussion, the document strengthens a section on the right to criticize state bodies and other organizations. "Persecution for criticism is prohibited," the Constitution declares, and then adds a sentence not in the draft. "Persons guilty of such persecution shall be called to account."

In addition, the article barring "misappropriation and squandering of state and commonly owned property" is worded slightly more strongly than in the draft, perhaps as a result of many letters published last summer in the press from people who complained of theft and laziness on the job.

The public discussion of the Constitution, as controlled and censored as it was, produced some insight into the crosscurrents of opinion in Soviet society. Robert Sharlet, a political science professor at Union College in Schenectady, N.Y., identified several main issues of broad concern. He has written of his findings for an upcoming issue of the Washington journal Problems of Communism.

The most commonly discussed concerns were labor productivity and worker participation in management, he said. There were calls for greater involvement by ordinary people in enacting policy and suggestions for more moral incentives to stimulate better work. At the same time, Professor Sharlet observed an "illiberal" strain running through many letters and articles, calling for tough action against slackers and "parasites" who don't work.

In presenting the Constitution to the Supreme Soviet on Monday, Leonid I. Brezhnev, the Communist Party leader and chief of state, highlighted these concerns:

"Some letters report revolting facts of abuse by some persons in office of their position, facts of deception of the state by means of records doctoring and cheating, of bribe taking, of indifference and a superficial approach to the working people's requirements, of instances of harassment for criticism."

Mr. Brezhnev threatened punishment "with full severity of the law."

Intense "law and order" sentiments were apparent among a broad spectrum of letter writers, Professor Sharlet found, and their views resembled those of "law and order" advocates in the United States in support of stiff criminal penalties and tougher action against wrongdoers.

On the other side was a smaller voice on behalf of enhanced civil liberties, mostly from Soviet judges and lawyers. They used the opportunity to revive a debate of the late 1950's, when the country's criminal codes were being revised in the post-Stalin era.

For example, they called for earlier entrance of defense counsel into cases—now they are allowed to see the accused only after the police investigation has been completed—and they argued that the law should contain a presumption of innocence.

Some supported giving citizens the right to go to court to settle administrative differences. None of these liberal suggestions was reflected either in Mr. Brezhnev's speech or the final version of the Constitution.

In that sense, the document is a reflection of existing legal reality rather than a change of law. Balancing rights and duties, for example, is a principle found already in much of the revised Soviet law, including both civil and criminal statutes, land law and the like.

"Citizens' exercise of their rights and freedoms is inseparable from the performance of their duties and obligations," Article 59 declares. Later, the charter warns that citizens "are obliged to safeguard the interests of the Soviet state and to enhance its power and prestige."

In a section purportedly guaranteeing "freedom of speech, of the press, and of assembly, meetings, street processions and demonstrations," the Constitution says that such activities may be carried out only "in order to strengthen and develop the Socialist system."

This week, while the document was being discussed and approved, policemen kept about 20 Jewish dissidents in their Moscow apartments to prevent them from assembling at the Supreme Soviet's reception room, as they had planned, to ask for written explanations of the Government's refusal to let them emigrate to Israel.

October 8, 1977

# Soviet Encyclopedia Restores Khrushchev

MOSCOW, March 25 (Reuters)—Nikita S. Khrushchev, whose name was removed from official reference works after his fall from power in 1964, has been accorded a brief entry and a small portrait in the latest volume of the Great Soviet Encyclopedia.

The sketch, covering less space than that for President John F. Kennedy, calls Mr. Khrushchev a state and party figure and ascribes his fall to impetuousness and a failure to adhere to collective decisions.

The new volume, issued this month as the 27th in the 50-volume official reference work, replaces an edition issued in 1957 during Mr. Khrushchev's tenure as party and government chief. The entry in that version gave him a full-page portrait and praise as "the outstanding figure of the Communist Party and the Soviet state, a true disciple of Lenin."

Mr. Khrushchev, who died in 1971 in relative obscurity, is rarely mentioned. Last year Soviet television showed him briefly in a documentary about the year 1957.

AN ECONOMIC GIANT

# Moscow, Reversing Policy, Will Spur Private Farming

By THEODORE SHABAD
Special to The New York Times

MOSCOW, Nov. 6—The new Kremlin leadership, in its first reversal of a specific policy of Nikita S. Khrushchev, has moved to enhance the importance of private farming as a means of increasing agricultural output.

The ruling group also decided to continue increased capital investment in agriculture and fertilizer and farm-implement factories as well as in retail trade and consumer services, long a neglected area of the Soviet economy.

These policy decisions emerged tonight from a speech by Leonid I. Brezhnev, First Secretary of the Soviet Communist party, at a celebration of the anniversary of the 1917 Bolshevik Revolution.

Mr. Brezhnev acknowledged that "farm production still falls short of the growing requirements of our society."

**Barriers 'Now Removed'**

"It would be wrong," he added, "to disregard the potential of private plots cultivated by collective farmers, industrial workers and office employes to satisfy their personal requirements. Unwarranted limitations have been imposed in this sphere in recent years, despite the fact that economic conditions have not been ripe for such a step. These limitations have now been removed."

Thus Mr. Brezhnev acknowledged the productivity of the private sector, which is especially high in potatoes, vegetables and animal products. Although small privately owned garden plots once accounted for 3 per cent of the cultivated land, they account for about 33 per cent of gross agricultural output, including almost 50 per cent of the total output of livestock products.

Details of the Government's new policy toward private farming were becoming available even before Mr. Brezhnev announced the over-all decision. Newspapers arriving from the Ukraine and Estonia carried decrees canceling past limitations on the sizes of private plots and on livestock holdings.

One decree, printed in the Kiev newspaper Pravda Ukrainy, restored holdings that were permitted before 1956, when a campaign was begun to reduce the importance of the private sector. The decree called on collective farms and on local authorities to help supply pasture land and feed to owners of private livestock.

The Estonian law annulled decrees, adopted in May and June, 1963, that placed restraints on livestock holdings of city dwellers. Authorities were urged to make sure that such holdings would not be used for personal enrichment at the expense of other citizens or of the state.

Similar decrees are expected to be adopted in the 13 other republics that make up the Soviet Union.

Although Mr. Brezhnev said this year's grain-production goals had been overfulfilled, he made litle of the fact that deliveries to the Government, according to official announcements, established a record — about 10 million metric tons above the previous high, 56.6 million tons.

Mr. Brezhnev emphasized that increases in consumption confronted the leadership with the task of overcoming "the lag in agricultural output."

"We will have to continue to increase capital investments in agriculture and in the industries that supply it with machines and fertilizers," he said.

Alluding to suggestions that there should be greater freedom of action for collective and state farms in organizing and planning their output, Mr. Brezhnev said this must be done "not in words but in deeds."

The First Secretary also criticized "unjustified past neglect" of shopping facilities and consumer services and the apathy or even rudeness of sales personnel.

**Change Held Significant**

"We must, comrades, change our whole attitude toward the service sector and its employes," he said.

Encouragement of private farming is regarded here as the most significant policy reversal in the Soviet economy since Mr. Khrushchev's downfall as Premier and First Secretary, even if it is a tactical move rather than a long-term change of Communist aims.

Since the collectivization of agriculture in the early nineteen-thirties, the small private sector has been regarded ideologically as a temporary appendage to the collective-farm economy. The Socialist sector has been expected ultimately to provate adequate agricultural products, and the private sector to wither away.

Before the restrictions of recent years, every household was permitted to maintain for its own use one cow, one or two calves, one sow and a litter, sheep, goats, poultry, rabbits and 20 hives of bees. These were to be accommodated on the private-plot allotment, which in most cases did not exceed an acre.

Yet private farming, linked with the institution of farmers' markets, has played a significant role in the national food supply. It accounts for slightly more than 60 per cent of the nation's potatoes, 45 per cent of its vegetables, 41 per cent of its meat and 47 per cent of its milk.

Historically Soviet policy toward private farming has fluctuated. When food conditions improve, there is mere toleration or even hostility. When the food situation is especially difficult, there is encouragement.

November 7, 1964

# SOVIET FARM PLAN AIMS TO ELEVATE PEASANTS' STATUS

## It Includes More Investment in Agriculture and Lower Rural Costs and Taxes

By THEODORE SHABAD
Special to The New York Times

MOSCOW, March 27 — The Soviet Union announced today sweeping agricultural reforms that were interpreted as marking a major shift in the regime's attitude toward peasants, long treated virtually as second-class citizens.

The program, providing for more investment in agriculture, higher farm prices, lower prices paid by peasants for consumer goods and lower rural taxes, is expected to raise the farmers' purchasing power and to help reduce the sharp differences in living standards between town and countryside.

Details were disclosed with the publication of a speech made Wednesday by Leonid I. Brezhnev, First Secretary or chief of the Communist party, at a three-day meeting of the party's Central Committee, which ended yesterday.

**Economic Levers Stressed**

The farm program was the first major reform adopted by the new Soviet leadership since the reunification last November of the party structure. Former Premier Nikita S. Khrushchev, who was deposed last October, had divided the structure into urban and rural hierarchies.

The reform represents a major shift from the deposed leader's approach to the Soviet farm problem by emphasizing the economic levers of prices and costs rather than the use of farm techniques and cropping systems dictated from above.

The shuffle of technicians in the top echelons of the Soviet leadership that accompanied the adoption of the farm program is regarded as a move to place efficient managers in key positions rather than as evidence of a power struggle among politicians.

**Role for Mazurov Seen**

Kirill T. Mazurov, 50-year-old Byelorussian who was appointed First Deputy Premier under Premier Aleksei N. Kosygin and was made a full member of the party's ruling Presidium, is thought to be slated for a key role in implementing the agricultural reforms discussed by Mr. Brezhnev.

The heart of the reforms is the decision to more than double the investment in agriculture in the five-year plan of 1966-70 over the previous plan.

Mr. Brezhnev said the total investment from the Government budget and from the funds of the collective and state farms would be 71 billion rubles (about $78 billion). The comparable figure for 1960-64 period was about 33 billion rubles.

The party chief said that the plan for compulsory grain collections would be cut this year from 65.5 million tons to 55.7

million and that the new annual level would be maintained until 1970.

This meant not only that a greater share of grain would be retained by the farms for their own needs but also that they would be able to plan crops over a long range instead of having to depend on annual changes in Government requirements.

Mr. Brezhnev said price increases on compulsory grain deliveries would range as high as 100 per cent, with similar price rises set for animal products. These increases, he added, will be absorbed by the Government and will not entail rises in the retail prices of bread, meat or milk.

Mr. Brezhnev conceded that the lower level of Government purchases planned over the next six years would be inadequate to meet its needs. To supplement compulsory deliveries, he proposed paying a 50 per cent premium for surplus grain siphoned off large grain producers in excess of planned quotas.

### Weather Factor Cited

Whether grain purchases above the plan will be sufficient for domestic utilization, stockpiles and export commitments will depend to a large extent on the weather, a key factor in determining the size of the Soviet crop.

Some observers did not rule out the possibility that the Soviet Union might resort to wheat imports in lean years rather than revert to former high delivery quotas of past.

These often had the effect of depriving farms of part of their seed stocks so that the Government had to return collected grain to producers. Mr. Brezhnev said two million tons of seed had to be returned to farms by the Government this year.

Among other farm-aid measures Mr. Brezhnev listed a plan to bring the prices of food and manufactured goods in rural areas down to the lower levels in effect in cities. The cuts are scheduled to be made next May except for a delay for some unspecified goods until Jan. 1.

The party leader said the Government also hoped to be able next year to reduce electric power rates in rural areas to industrial-city levels to spur farm electrification. He said 12 per cent of the country's 40,000 collective farms still had no electricity even for lighting.

The income-tax load on collective farms is to be reduced by applying tax rates to net rather than gross income as in past years.

Mr. Brezhnev said the present Soviet system of state farms, owned and operated by the Government on a wage system, and collective farms, operated on a cooperative basis, would be maintained for the foreseeable future. He criticized the trend in recent years of encouraging the conversion of collective into state farms.

He also charged that the farm-merger policy favored by Mr. Khrushchev had resulted in farm units of "unmanageable" size, but he warned at the same time against hasty decisions to break up large farms.

A major factor in agricultural performance, in Mr. Brezhnev's view, is the right of the farms to plan crops in accordance with local soils and climate, provided state delivery plans are met.

Although the reforms are nominally restricted to agriculture, they have wide-ranging implications that may affect the entire economy.

Mr. Brezhnev gave no hint as to where the Government planned to obtain the additional billions to be invested in farming except to say the "budget will be redistributed."

Observers differed on whether investment funds would be trimmed from sectors of industry or from defense or space programs.

March 28, 1965

# 'NEW' ECONOMISTS HONORED IN SOVIET

## Lenin Award to 3 Viewed as Blow to Old-Line Marxists

By THEODORE SHABAD

Special to The New York Times

MOSCOW, April 22—The Soviet Union's orthodox Marxist economists have suffered a severe setback as a result of the awarding of the Lenin Prize to a group of reformers they opposed.

The award, among 40 Lenin Prizes announced early today, suggests that the new Soviet leadership is now fully committed to a radical change in economic theory and practice based on the interplay of supply and demand and other innovations in the past considered incompatible with Marxist theory.

The controversial award was given to three "reform" economists—Leonid S. Kantorovich, Viktor V. Novozhilov and the late Vasily S. Nemchinov—for their work in developing mathematical techniques in economics.

In the last decade, the three have been key figures in a drive for the adoption of economic methods outlawed under Stalin but widely used in the West.

Professor Kantorovich, the chief figure of the three, is the inventor of linear programing. This is a mathematical technique that can be used to solve such complex economic problems as how to set up most efficient airline or railroad schedules or how to operate oil refineries most profitably.

### Abstract Concepts Opposed

During the public discussion that preceded the Lenin Prize awards, orthodox economists spoke out strongly against giving the top intellectual prize of the Soviet Union to the three nominees.

The opposition was not so much against the mathematical technique itself as against the abstract concepts favored by the group.

Powerful opponents, headed by Academician Konstantin V. Ostrovityanov, accused Professor Kantorovich of ignoring Marx's labor theory of value and of favoring ideas of Western economic theorists such as the usefulness of marginal analysis.

According to Marxist doctrine, the ultimate value of goods is determined by the amount of socially necessary labor time incorporated into producing them.

The Western view is that the value depends on the relative scarcity of goods as reflected in the supply-demand relationship, which determines price on a freely competitive market.

Orthodox Marxists have also disdained Western marginal analysis, in which the producer would decide, for example, the wisdom of increasing output by comparing the extra, or marginal, cost of producing one more unit with the extra income to be received from selling that unit.

Marginal analysis is particularly applicable to an economy like the Soviet Union's, which still operates with limited resources and is essentially an economy of scarcities.

### Liberman's Ideas Fought

In a recent discussion, Academician Ostrovityanov said Professor Kantorovich's ideas had no application in the Soviet Union on the ground that the country was "advancing toward an abundance of products" under the promised Communism.

Orthodox economists are generally believed to have opposed, and in some cases to be still opposed to, the ideas of Prof. Yevsei G. Liberman, the economist who has proposed that Soviet managers be given greater freedom to plan production on the basis of consumer demand.

Four hundred plants in the textile, leather, garment and shoe industries are scheduled to go over to that system this year.

The evident espousal by the Soviet leadership of Professor Kantorovich's work is regarded here as even more significant than the shift to demand-based production because the economist has sought to provide central planners with better theoretical concepts and tools.

The Kremlin has insisted that planning would not be abandoned even if more attention was paid to consumer needs.

In the last few years, the 53-year-old professor has been deputy director of the Institute of Mathematics in the science community of Novosibirsk.

The new honor raises the question whether he may now be shifted to a more responsible position in Moscow.

April 23, 1965

# RUSSIANS URGED TO GO TO SIBERIA

By HARRY SCHWARTZ

The Soviet leaders appear to be planning to avoid a serious unemployment problem in the years ahead by a major campaign to encourage the migration of surplus workers from European Russia to Siberia and the Far East.

The possibility of serious unemployment problems has been posed by the fact that sharply larger numbers of young people will be entering the Soviet labor market in the years ahead. These will be young people born during the birth-rate boom of the late nineteen-forties and the early nineteen-fifties after large-scale demobilization of the Soviet Union's huge World War II armies.

They will be looking for jobs at a time when increasing automation and mechanization are planned to permit greater industrial and farm output with fewer workers.

Now hints have begun appearing in the Soviet press that jobs can be provided for large numbers of these young workers if they can be induced to move to the labor-short areas of distant Siberia and the Pacific coastal regions.

The magnitude of the problem of providing jobs for youngsters leaving Soviet schools during the late nineteen-sixties and early nineteen-seventies has been made vividly apparent by enrollment statistics recently published in the magazine Vestnik Statistiki (Journal of Statistics).

In 1958-59, all Soviet elementary and secondary schools enrolled 29,567,000 pupils, but in 1964-65 Soviet schools enrolled 42,000,000 students, an increase of more than 12,000,000 — or 40 per cent. The problem is even more acute in Soviet cities, where the enrollment increase has exceeded 50 per cent.

At the same time, the problem of people deserting Siberia to return to European Russia has been highlighted by the appearance of two books giving the reports of scientific studies of migration to and from Siberia.

One study, by V. I. Perevedentsev, has found that between 1959 and 1963 230,000 more people left western Siberia than arrived there.

As a result of this flight, the new cities and industries of the area have been staffed primarily by workers coming from the area's farms, though the region is relatively poorly supplied with workers compared with other Soviet areas. In western Siberia, for example, there is five times as much agricultural land available per collective farmer as in Byelorussia.

Mr. Perevedentsev's study emphasizes that other factors beside the extreme cold of Siberia help explain the eagerness of workers in Siberia to leave the area for other regions.

He notes that in western Siberia, the average pay of workers in transportation, trade, and other nonindustrial branches of the economy is lower than the national average. There is less housing per worker in western Siberia than the national average and its quality is poorer.

Transportation not only is poorer in the area but also is more expensive than elsewhere in the Soviet Union.

The scholar suggests in an interview, appearing in the literary newspaper Literaturnaya Gazeta, that migration to Siberia be stimulated by compensatory payments and other incentives.

September 12, 1965

# *Soviet Reforms Industrial Code; Gives Managers Profit Incentive*

By THEODORE SHABAD

Special to The New York Times

MOSCOW, Sept. 28—A new industrial "bill of rights" announced here today was expected to transform the Soviet factory manager from a virtual ward of the state to a more responsible, thinking executive of the Western type.

Under the new code described by Premier Aleksei N. Kosygin in a speech to the Communist party's Central Committee, directors of Government enterprises will have far greater room for initiative in running day-to-day operations of their concerns.

They will be less restricted by the maze of directives and regulations handed down by central planners and they will be encouraged to show their ability by aiming at ever higher sales and profits.

No longer will a factory executive be able to draw on unlimited Government funds for plant expansion and working capital. Budgetary allocations for this purpose are to be replaced by a system of long-term loans. Plant directors will also administer greatly expanded funds for the purchase of new equipment, payment of bonuses and provision of social benefits and housing to workers.

These and other details of new prerogatives of industrial executives emerged from the text of a speech delivered yesterday by Mr. Kosygin at the opening session of the Central Committee meeting on reforms in planning and management of industry. The text filled virtually the entire four-page editions of today's Soviet newspapers.

Mr. Kosygin also announced far-ranging changes in the structure of industrial management, replacing decentralized regional councils established by former Premier Nikita S. Khrushchev in 1957 with a new system of industrial ministries. The changeover is to be gradual, possibly extending over several months.

The Central Committee meeting, which will also hear a report by Leonid I. Brezhnev, Communist party leader, setting the date for the next party congress next spring, will be followed on Friday by a session of the Supreme Soviet (Parliament). The session will ratify Government changes that stem from the announced reforms.

Mr. Kosygin made it plain that the new "bill of rights" of factory managers would be combined with continued centralized controls. However in contrast to dozens of past assignments that left virtually no leeway for managers' judgment, Government directives will be substantially reduced in the future.

September 29, 1965

# SOVIET DISCLOSES NEW 5-YEAR PLAN; BETTER LIVING AIM

## '66-70 Economic Blueprint Assumes Period of Peace to Benefit Consumer

By PETER GROSE

Special to The New York Times

MOSCOW, Sunday, Feb. 20—The Soviet leadership disclosed its blueprint today for giving its citizens a better material life by 1970. It based its plans for economic growth on a five-year period of world peace.

Premier Aleksei N. Kosygin's long-awaited five-year plan for the second half of the nineteen-sixties acknowledges that certain long-range production goals set in 1961 were too ambitious.

Yet, by realigning priorities to emphasize consumer goods and agricultural production, the Soviet leaders are promising their citizens more wages, more automobiles and more and better food in the five years to come.

### Income Rise Projected

By 1970, according to the plan, the national income of the Soviet Union is to increase by 38 to 41 per cent, industrial output by about 50 per cent, per capita income by about 30 per cent.

Special measures are envisaged in the plan to narrow the gap in living standards between Soviet city dwellers and the rural population.

The draft directives for the 1966-1970 five-year plan were approved yesterday in a plenary meeting of the Communist party's ruling Central Committee. Down to minute details of economic targets, they were splashed over the pages of the party newspaper Pravda this morning.

### War Blamed for Flaws

A summary distributed by Tass, the official press agency, gave a hint that the Soviet leaders would blame the Vietnamese war and other United States military actions for many of the shortcomings in the national economy in the preceding seven-year period, covered by the previous economic plan.

"The closing years of the seven-year plan coincided with an aggravation of international tension, caused by American imperialism's aggression in different areas of the world," the Tass summary said.

"This required additional allocations to insure the country's defense capacity," Tass said.

Looking ahead now, the leaders said defense capacity would still have to be maintained, but they stated "the most vital task is not to allow a new world war to break out." The picture of the Soviet Union in 1970 given in the plan is one of a nation at peace, where its citizens can derive fuller individual benefits from the economic growth the planners are promising.

By setting this example of prosperity, the Central Committee said in its draft plan that the Soviet Union would be fulfilling its duty to the international Communist movement, would "attain new heights in the economic competition with capitalism," and thus would offer added attraction to newly independent nations that chose their own path of economic development.

This is a defiant challenge to the Chinese Communist criticism that the Soviet Union is striving too much to enrich itself and its citizens, in effect deserting the world revolutionary movement.

By 1970, the plan said, the national income of the Soviet Union is to increase by 38 to 41 per cent, industrial output by about 50 per cent, per capita incomes by about 30 per cent.

Special measures are envisaged in the plan to narrow the gap in living standards between Soviet city dwellers and the rural population.

Breaking down the industrial-growth goal, the plans calls for increases of 49 to 52 per cent in the production of capital goods, and 43 to 46 per cent in consumer goods. In the consumer area, the light industries and food producers are to increase their output by 40 per cent.

More than twice the present number of television sets produced, for example, is to come out of the factories by 1970. The output of home refrigerators is to increase more than three times.

Consumption of meat, per capita, is to increase 20 to 25 per cent, milk 15 to 18 per cent, vegetables 35 to 40 per cent, fruit 45 to 50 per cent and fish 50 to 60 per cent.

The most spectacular benefit to the Soviet consumer comes in the promise of sharply increased production of automobiles. Passenger-car production by 1970 is to be about four times greater than it is today. The total motor-vehicle production is to rise from the 1965 output, 616,400, to the maximum target, a million and a half, in 1970.

This promise—with broad sociological implications and the impetus it will give to related industries such as fuel, accessories, roads and service stations—is perhaps Mr. Kosygin's single most striking reversal of the economic theories of former Premier Nikita S. Khrushchev, who tried to discourage private-car ownership.

On some basic commodities, the Kosygin Five-Year Plan reduces the 1970 production goals given in the 22d party congress in 1961. Western experts consider the new aims a more realistic recognition of the economy's capabilities.

Oil production, originally aimed toward 390 million metric tons in 1970, is now intended to reach 345 million to 355 million metric tons. This figure represents an increase of 40 per cent over the 1965 total and is in line with actual yearly growth over the last five years.

Steel production, formerly aiming at 130 million to 135 million short tons, is to reach 124 million to 129 million short tons. The 1965 production was 91 million short tons.

February 20, 1966

# CREDIT IN SOVIET: A COLLECTIVE RISK

## Nonpayment by One Worker Halts Transactions for All

By HENRY KAMM

Special to The New York Times

MOSCOW, Aug. 26—If only the Echmiadzinsky agricultural machinery factory would make the payments on the refrigerators and overcoats that its workers have bought, the man from the tractor division could buy a piano.

In Soviet society, where the individual surrenders a great deal of his private business to the collective, buying on the installment plan is no exception. The purchase is not simply a transaction between store and customer but between two collectives: the organization of stores and the buyer's place of work.

The man who buys his living-room furniture on credit does not make payments to the store where he bought it. His employer deducts each installment from his monthly pay and sends it, not to the furniture store, but to the organization of all the stores in the city or region that sell on credit.

Often, apparently, the complexity of these transactions overwhelms one or the other of the organizations involved, and the buyer's payment does not reach the seller. In a collective society, all then suffer for the one member's fault, even when it isn't his fault.

### All Credit Halted

If a worker at a factory is in arrears on his television set, no other employe of the same concern can buy a watch or a washing machine on credit.

The problem has become serious in Erivan, the capital of Soviet Armenia. Kommunist, the newspaper of the Armenian Government and Communist party, reported the other day that 1,246 enterprises and institutions were delinquent in their payments to the Erivan Union of Installment Buying Stores.

The total they owe for this month, 53,000 rubles, or $58,300, is not big in view of the fact that a number of major enterprises are on the delinquent list. But even the smallest debt anywhere is enough to disqualify all.

A man walked into the Erivan musical-instrument store recently to buy a piano. He had the required 25 per cent of the purchase price in cash. The rest he wanted to pay on time.

He brought along, in addition to the usual documents to prove his identity, a certificate attesting to his fixed residence and another to his fixed employment. As is the case with all documents required for ordinary living in the Soviet Union, the prospective piano buyer had invested a great deal of time in obtaining them. The investment did not pay off.

### Offer for Colleague

His employer owed 20 rubles for someone's earlier purchase of something somewhere else. No cash, no piano, the man was told. He offered to pay the 20 rubles on behalf of his unknown colleague. This bit of typical American business acumen was taken under study, but its originality proved too great. The piano is still in the Erivan store, Kommunist reported.

The party and Government daily paper suggested that companies not meeting their payments on time be fined the same as nonworking individuals who miss a payment—a tenth of a per cent per day.

The paper also criticized the incomplete selection of goods available for purchase on credit. Of 19 items on the list, half are not available in the credit-buying stores in Erivan.

The Soviet Union did not overcome its ideological objections to installment buying until 1959, when Nikita S. Khrushchev put the economy on a more consumer-oriented basis. Since then the habit has taken hold and is believed to be reaching the $4-billion a year level.

Length of credit depends on the price of the goods, with two years as the maximum. The amount of credit is limited by the buyer's earnings. A two-year credit term must not exceed the purchaser's wages for eight months. Credit charges range from 1 to 2.5 per cent.

August 27, 1967

# RUSSIANS REDUCE INEQUITIES IN PAY

## Wide Extremes of Stalinist Era Appreciably Narrowed

By HARRY SCHWARTZ

Soviet executives and specialists are still paid much better than ordinary workers, but post-Stalin Soviet policy has lessened appreciably the former extreme income inequalities in that country.

Inequalities of earnings and living standards in the Soviet Union have been sharply criticized in recent years by both Chinese and Cuban spokesmen, who have contrasted Soviet reality with the Communist ideal of equality. New data recently released by the Soviet regime show that this inequality reached its peak under Stalin, but is now less extreme.

At the end of 1945, these data reveal, engineers and other executives and specialists in Soviet industry earned on the average about 2.3 times as much as manual laborers. In 1966, however, the higher paid group earned less than 50 per cent more than the manual workers.

### Some Wages Doubled

The discrepancy was narrowed by permitting manual workers' earnings to increase by more than 100 per cent between 1945 and 1966, while the increase in the higher paid group's salaries was kept down to less than 50 per cent in the same period.

Data on these differences in earnings have been hitherto considered so sensitive that they had not been published for roughly three decades, or well before the 1941 German invasion of the Soviet Union. In 1966, the average Soviet manual laborer earned 104.4 rubles a month—about $115 at the official exchange rate—the average Soviet engineer or other executive or technical specialist 150 rubles a month—$165—and the average clerical employe 88.2 rubles, or $97.

These wage data are not strictly comparable with American wages because of the low rents Soviet workers pay for their small dwellings, and because of the extensive socialized medicine and related welfare systems of the Soviet Union.

### Differences Remain

Even now, however, the Soviet Union has very extensive earnings differences among different industries, apparently a reflection of the difficulty of attracting workers to different occupations.

The best paid industries in the Soviet Union in 1966 were coal mining, where the average monthly earnings were 195.3 rubles; fishing, average earnings 181.2 rubles, and water transportation, average earnings 142.5 rubles.

The poorest paid industries in 1966 were the needle trades where the average monthly earnings were 76.1 rubles, agriculture where state farm monthly earnings averaged 79.8 rubles, and sugar refining where earnings average 81.1 rubles.

August 12, 1968

# SOVIET INCREASES BONUSES TO RAISE FARM PRODUCTION

## Action Is Part of a Program to Provide More Meat and Dairy Products

## BREZHNEV SPURS DRIVE

## Effort to Help Consumers Follows His Criticism of Food Shortages

By JAMES F. CLARITY

Special to The New York Times

MOSCOW, July 19—The Soviet Union has initiated a broad program to put more meat and dairy products on the tables of this country's 240 million consumers.

The program, part of an overall plan to increase the productivity of Soviet agriculture, is apparently aimed at meeting increasing consumer demands for more, and higher quality, meat, eggs, milk and other livestock products.

The present supply of such products is limited and Soviet housewives complain wearily about relatively expensive beef that is good only for stew, scrawny chickens that cost as much as $1.50 a pound, and the lack of salami that is not heavy with fat.

**Better Prices for Products**

Yesterday the newspapers announced that the party and the Government, following the plan approved by the Central Committee earlier in the month, would increase the prices the state pays for meat and dairy products to collective and state farms, and to individuals.

Today, the papers printed a Government directive providing increased bonuses to workers on state farms.

Collective farm workers get bonuses based on production above set plans. State farm workers, who are paid salaries, receive cash premiums. Individual producers may sell their products to the state, or on the free market, after they have fulfilled their state quotas.

**Brezhnev Gives Speech**

The drive to solve the meat problem was signaled on July 2, when the Communist party chief, Leonid I. Brezhnev, told the party's Central Committee that "as we all know, the demand of the population for livestock produce, especially meat, is not being satisfied by far."

Mr. Brezhnev said that by 1975, the nation should be producing an average of 15.6 million tons of meat a year, compared with an average of 11.4 million tons in the last five years.

His report to the committee also included admissions of inadequate production of grain and other foodstuffs, and said that agricultural investment would be increased 70 per cent, or $85-billion, in the five-year plan scheduled to begin in January.

The increase in the agricultural budget, according to Western analysts, is probably one of the reasons for the delay in the disclosure of the final 1971-75 economic plan, and led to the postponement to March of the party's 24th Congress, which must approve the plan.

The agricultural increase presumably means that other areas of the economy will have to be cut.

How much of the increased spending on agriculture will go to improve livestock breeding has not been disclosed. But in recent days it has become clear that the Kremlin was eager to convince the public that action was being taken to solve the meat problem.

The Government directive said that, retroactive to last May, the state would pay an average of 20 per cent more for milk and cream. Prices paid to raisers of young cattle would be increased on a scale of 35 to 50 per cent.

In addition, producers will be paid 50 per cent more for cattle, poultry, milk, wool and eggs produced in excess of plan quotas.

The increased payments, according to official announcements, would not be accompanied by retail price rises.

Particular emphasis in the increased incentive plans appears to be directed at the private breeders of livestock and producers of related products. The private producers provide, according to Western analysts, about 40 per cent of the Soviet Union's meat products.

Mr. Brezhnev indicated in his report that the private producers were not being given adequate incentives. "When we speak of livestock breeding," the party chief said, "we mean not only collective farms and state farms. Often local cadres, as they assess the situation in this area, are satisfied merely with the growth of publicly owned herds. Other areas of the economy do not bother them."

"We must take a realistic view of things," Mr. Brezhnev said. "Many agriculturists have livestock and poultry of their own, and due care should be shown so that they can purchase young stock and prepare fodder for their livestock."

July 20, 1970

# MOSCOW UNVEILS NEW 5-YEAR PLAN AIDING CONSUMER

## '71-'75 Economic Program Stresses Light Industry and Food Production

## DEFENSE OUTLAY RISES

By BERNARD GWERTZMAN

Special to The New York Times

MOSCOW, Sunday, Feb. 14—The Soviet Union made public today its new five-year plan, which aims at using modern technology, greater efficiency and better management to raise substantially the living standards of its people by 1975.

Tass, the official press agency, distributed early this morning a summary of the 1971-75 plan, which was formally approved in draft form by the Communist party's Central Committee yesterday. It will be published in all central newspapers today and discussed and publicized throughout the country in advance of the party's 24th Congress, which opens on March 30.

Premier Aleksei N. Kosygin, who was largely responsible for organizing the plan, will offer it for approval of the Congress and it eventually will become a law of the land.

**Debate in High Circles**

The plan's outlines reflect the result of months of debate within high leadership circles on what direction the country should follow, what branches should get priority, and how much should be allocated to defense and how much to the consumer.

The draft plan said that "the main task of the five-year plan is to ensure a considerable growth of the people's living and cultural standards on the basis of a high pace of development of production, the raising of its efficiency, scientific and technical progress and accelerated growth of labor productivity."

The Soviet leaders apparently decided that steps must be taken to meet the complaints of the Soviet consumer, whose expectations of a better life have been frustrated in recent years by recurring shortages of meat, vegetables, fruits, and a whole range of consumer goods.

But the defense sector was assured continuing growth to protect the Soviet Union. The plan calls for significant increase in the fuel and power sectors, indicating the decision to go ahead with ambitious projects to develop the oil and natural gas reserves of western Siberia and to harness the rivers of the country.

The growth figures projected for 1975 appear for the most part quite modest in comparison with the often-inflated figures of past five-year plans. This sober look at the future reflects a desire by the leadership to have a more precise system of planning as well as the strains in the economy, caused by tight labor and capital supplies.

In comparison with the 50 per cent growth in industry claimed for the last five-year plan, which ended Dec. 31, the new blueprint asks for a rise of between 42 and 46 per cent over the five-year period. Significantly, the light sector of industry, known as Group B, is to rise by 44 to 48 per cent, whereas the heavy industry sector, Group A, by 41 to 45 per cent.

The edge given light industry's rate of growth continues a trend of recent years, and is the first time that a five-year plan actually called for Group B to have priority. But in actual ruble figures, the amount of money spent in the heavy-industry sector is considerably higher.

But the decision to allow the light-industry sector to show a higher rate of projected growth is thought to represent a victory of sorts for those in the leadership who have pressed for a quicker rise in living standards.

It is thought here that the delay in releasing the plan, originally set for publication in January, was due to a desire to increase allocations to the consumer in light of the stormy events in Poland, in which worker unrest led to riots and the downfall of the Gomulka regime.

The plan said that its "main tack" was to "ensure high rates of growth and proportional development of social production, especially agriculture, light and food industry, to raise considerably the efficiency of all branches of the national economy."

It called for an acceleration in the pace of scientific and technical progress and for continued work in "the improvement of management, planning and economic stimulation of production."

As part of the need to increase labor productivity, the plan called for a rise of between 36 and 40 per cent over the five-year period. These savings were to secure 87 to 90 per cent of the rise in industrial output, a sign that investment funds were scarce.

Reflecting Soviet desire to prevent inflation, the plan called for only modest salary gains in the next five years. The projected rise was for 20 to 22 per cent for workers and office employes and 30 to 35 per cent for farmers, who are usually less well off than urban dwellers.

One of the main complaints of Soviet people has been the uneven and often low quality of the supply of meats and other foods.

The new plan said 82.2 billion rubles would be channeled into investment in agriculture. "The task is to meet more fully the population's growing demand for foodstuffs and industry's for raw materials."

Grain production is to rise to a level of about 195 million tons a year, an extremely high figure since the previous record was 171 million tons and in 1970, with very favorable climate, it is believed that the figure reached 185 million tons.

Recognizing that meat production takes a long time to develop, the plan calls for a rather modest target of an average of 14.3 million tons a year for the five-year period. Last year, the figure was 12.3 million tons.

The new plan sets a target of billion kilowatt hours of electricity by 1975. Last year the figure was only 740 billion.

Oil output is slated to rise to 480-million or 500 million tons by 1975 in comparison with the 1970 total of 353 million. Natural gas, the fuel of the Soviet future, is to rise to 300 billion or 320 billion cubic meters by 1975, a 50 per cent rise over the 200 billion of 1970.

Steel is targeted to rise by 142 to 150 million tons by 1975, in comparison with the 1970 figure of 116 million tons.

By 1975, it is hoped that between 2 million and 2.1 million motor vehicles—trucks and cars—will be produced, in comparison with the 916,000 last year.

The national income of the country is planned to rise by 37 to 40 per cent, about the level that it rose in the preceding plan. The per capita rise will be 30 per cent over that period, the plan said, a 3 per cent drop from the somewhat inflation-aided rise of the 1966-70 period.

Housing, a perennial complaint, is to be enlarged at about the same rate as in the past plan—some 533 million square meters for the next five years.

February 14, 1971

## Soviet Passes U.S. In Steel Output For the First Time

By HARRY SCHWARTZ

The Soviet Union realized an old ambition for the first time last year by exceeding United States steel production and becoming the largest steel producing nation in the world.

A spokesman for the American Iron and Steel Institute attributed the American loss of steel primacy last year to the combined effects of the economic recession and record or near-record imports of foreign steel.

The institute's estimate of 1971 United States steel production is 120.2 million tons. Official Soviet data released last weekend put the Soviet steel output at about 133 million tons. Both figures are in tons of 2,000 pounds each.

In 1969 the United States produced about 141 million tons of steel, or substantially more than the Soviet Union manufactured last year. In that same year the Soviet output was about 121 million tons. The American edge was then narrowed in 1970 when United States production fell to 131.5 million tons and Soviet output rose to about 128 million tons.

In the last half of last year United States steel output was ahead of the Soviet Union as mills in this country operated at a high level to satisfy the demands of buyers who feared a steel strike. "Hedge-buying" against the danger of a strike was responsible for imports of about 18,000,000 tons last year. But when the strike did not take place, American steel output fell sharply last summer and in August American steel mills turned out less than half as much steel as they had the previous May.

January 27, 1972

# Siberia Still Has Hazards and Terrors, but Many Love It and It Is Growing

By HEDRICK SMITH
Special to The New York Times

NOVOSIBIRSK, U.S.S.R. — Maxim Gorky once called it "a land of death and chains." The 18th-century scientist Mikhail Lomonosov glowingly predicted that it would eventually become a source of Russian might.

Today the reality of Siberia lies somewhere in between—neither so terrifying as the boundless prison without bars used by the czarist and Stalinist Governments nor so romantically productive as Lomonosov dreamed.

Even now university students in Moscow and Leningrad shudder at the thought of their two to three years of compulsory labor for the state on some new project in the remote, desolate territory, which stretches 3,400 miles from the Urals to the Pacific, across nine time zones.

But a visitor to Siberia encounters people who firmly proclaim their devotion to the beckoning solitude of the taiga (pine forest) and who vow they would never trade their stern existence or the outdoor freshness for the overcivilized, overcrowded, overbureaucratized life of European Russia.

### 'People Are More Friendly'

"I don't like the west," said a young professional woman in Irkutsk, not meaning London, Paris or New York but Moscow. "I have a lot of friends there, but I don't like it. The people are rude. They are in too much of a hurry. They are too tense. Out here people are more friendly. They have that broad Siberian spirit."

For the loyal Siberyak, his is the land of manifest destiny, filling up with strong young people throwing hydroelectric dams across great rivers, planting mighty construction projects in the rich but untapped wilderness, building a new civilization. The unquestioning faith in economic growth is usually expressed in superlatives.

"This is all virgin territory," a journalist in the far-off Yakut region said with the kind of pioneer spirit that would have warmed the heart of Horace Greeley. "People here have much more opportunity than they do back in the west."

"Back there they are bureaucrats," a blunt-spoken Bratsk engineer commented disdainfully. "Out here we are democrats, working together."

### Some Striking Results

Through just such dedication and will power, the settlers have achieved some striking results over 25 years, often in latitudes as far north as Alaska and the Canadian Yukon. The hydroelectric dams at Bratsk and Krasnoyarsk, already world-famous, are to be joined by massive power projects at Ust-Ilimsk and Sayan. At Norilsk, in the far north, a mining-industrial complex is refining copper, nickel and platinum. Other metals are being produced at Bratsk, Krasnoyarsk and a cluster of satellite cities around Irkutsk. Pipelines and power lines crisscross the frozen wastes.

The messianic enthusiasm of those who have settled here belies the problems, overlooking the fact that roughly as many people are moving out as in except in certain high-priority areas. The acute shortage of skilled labor has put a crimp on the growth that Siberia's proponents want.

The heyday of Siberia's development came during World War II, when it was a refuge for industry, and again in the

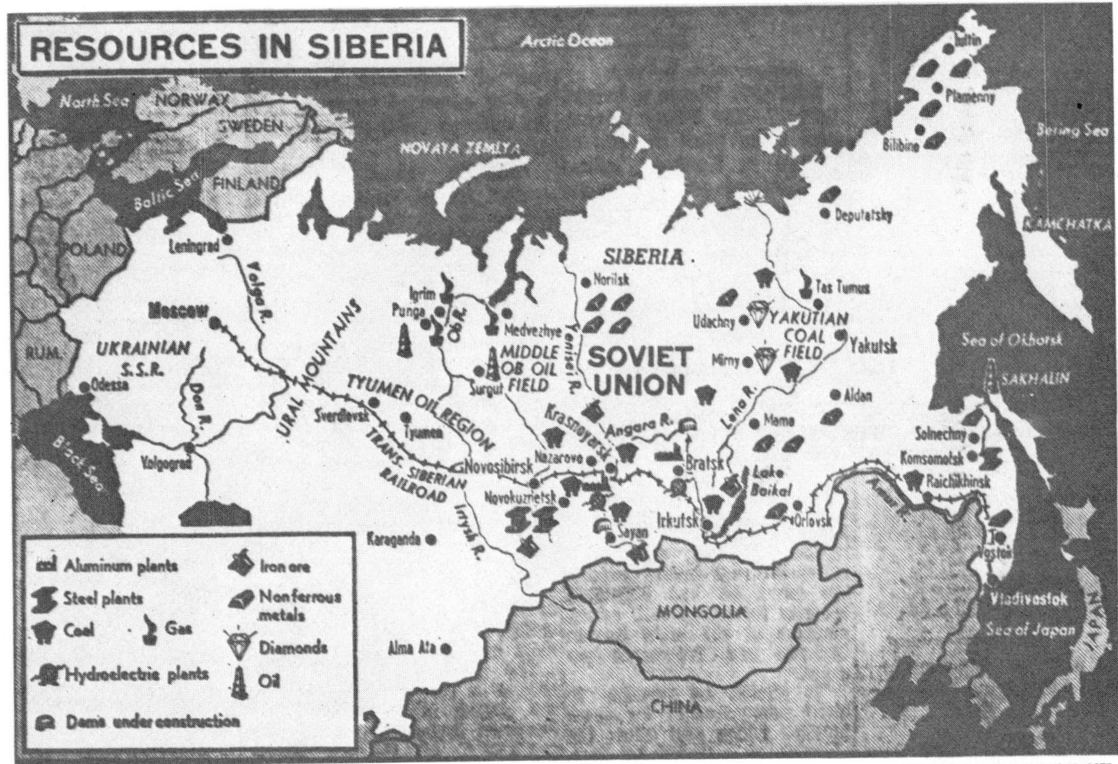


The New York Times/April 28, 1972

**Siberia, stretching from the Urals to the Pacific, has 60 per cent of Soviet Union's timber, 60 per cent of its coal reserves and 80 per cent of its water power. There are large deposits of diamonds, of gold and other metals plus vast quantities of other resources. Stress is on basic industries—coal, iron, steel, timber, power.**

early nineteen-sixties. Now, however, ruble-conscious central planners in Moscow have discovered that while the plentiful Siberian mineral resources are relatively cheap to develop, the costs of getting and holding the necessary work force are often prohibitively high.

Siberia's rate of production growth, about 8 per cent a year, is better than the national average. But even Siberian economists have observed that their region is building up relatively old-fashioned basic industries like coal, iron and steel, timber and power while European Russia is moving into modern fields like electronics, synthetic chemicals, computers and precision instruments.

The development of industry is pushed hardest where it is easiest—in or near established cities on the Trans-Siberian Railroad or in southern regions like the new Sayan complex south of Krasnoyarsk, where the climate is not so forbidding. When new towns sprout in the severe conditions of the north, it is because that is where vital mineral resources are.

Those resources are staggering. Known iron-ore reserves are greater than those of the United States, Britain and France combined. The natural-gas fields of western Siberia are said to be the largest in the world, with bigger reserves than in the United States. Recently discovered oil fields in the Tyumen region, also in western Siberia, are the biggest in the Soviet Union.

In an area the size of the United States plus half of Canada, Siberia holds 60 per cent of the timber of the Soviet Union, 60 per cent of its coal reserves and 80 per cent of its water power, on giant rivers that, if linked, would circle the globe 25 times. There are large gold and diamond deposits — Moscow will not say how large —in the Yakut region and the Far East. Elsewhere are rare metals like platinum, molybdenum and wolfram—in fact, just about every element.

**A Rebuff to the Cassandras**

So vast are the reserves that Soviet economists and engineers wave away the Cassandra-like warnings of Western scholars that mankind is recklessly exhausting the world's natural wealth. "We have only begun to tap the resources of Siberia—let's say 5 per cent," a university lecturer in Bratsk explained. "We could work it for 1,000 years."

Only a few years back the region's most enthusiastic boosters were predicting that its dazzling prospects would lure a population of 60 million to Siberia and the Soviet Far East by the year 2000. The figure was 22.6 million in 1959 and only 25.5 million in 1971; at that rate it would be 33 million by 2000.

The dream of the great frontier has become tarnished now. It is not just that the population has been growing more slowly than that of the nation as a whole. Even more of a shock was the finding that since 1966 western Siberia had suffered a net loss and that eastern Siberia and the Far East had not kept pace even with natural population growth.

Recently economists have reported that labor turnover in places like the western Siberian oilfields is disastrously high and that the "labor deficit" is growing. For every 100 new laborers in the Ob River oilfields, according to one report, 70 leave.

"The exodus from Siberia is increasing," the journal Voprosi Ekonomiki warned in late 1970. "This is because Siberia lags behind the other regions in the living standards of the population."

**'The Long Ruble' Helps**

The big lure for most workers is what the Siberians call "the long ruble"—the pay bonus that ranges from a minimum of 15 per cent in the established cities of "soft" southern Siberia to nearly triple pay in the "hard" Arctic Circle outposts.

In addition to hardship pay, workers north of the main line of the Trans-Siberian generally get a 36-day annual vacation instead of 24 days, a fully paid trip to any place in the Soviet Union once every three years and retirement five years ahead of normal.

Increasingly, the economic planners are finding that even big paychecks will not hold enough people in northern cities. Last summer Literaturnaya Gazeta, the publication of the Writers Union, commented that many people in Siberia were in a "suitcase mood"—not planning to settle down but only here to make quick cash. It said that because they were frustrated by poor living conditions and overwhelmed by having to endure temporary housing and other discomforts, they were dreaming of the time when they could return to "the mainland."

One reason, a Novosibirsk economist suggested, is that the pay differentials are misleading because living costs are so much greater.

**Higher Standards Urged**

The remedy long advocated by Siberian officials is to raise living standards to levels higher than in European Russia. Despite major efforts in that direction, much of Siberia seems to fall further behind. Stores are not well stocked with clothing or consumers goods and fresh fruits and vegetables virtually disappear in winter.

People in Novosibirsk complain that the buses break down and that even when they run they are too cold. A writer contends that in the Irkutsk region leisure-time activities are dull and civic centers inadequate. In

Bratsk a teacher confesses that she could not endure Siberia were it not for her annual trip to the Ukraine. Professional women say they count on a yearly shopping expedition to Moscow for essential clothing.

What is most needed, Siberian officials explain, is better housing with more modern conveniences—which they are throwing up all over Siberia. But if electricity has long since been taken for granted even in the villages, indoor plumbing is still a privilege even in the cities. All across Siberia people line up for water at outdoor spigots and they use outhouses in the dead of winter.

The answer, according to such modern-minded scholars as Abel G. Aganbegyan, director of the Economics Institute here, is not a great new influx of immigrants but rapid and extensive mechanization of mining and industry and far more systematic development of selected areas to insure that housing and services are installed along with dams and factories.

April 28, 1972

# Soviet Population Is Put At 241.7 Million in Census

By BERNARD GWERTZMAN
Special to The New York Times

MOSCOW, April 18—The Soviet Union's population, on the basis of preliminary 1970 census figures issued today, stood at 241,748,000 last Jan. 15, with the most significant increases in all urban areas and in the Asian and Caucasian regions.

The population figure was somewhat more than the precensal estimate of 241 million as of the beginning of the year, following an average annual growth of about 2 million in recent years.

Izvestia, the Government newspaper, provided the first official report on the census, the first in 11 years. The population grew by 15.8 per cent during this period, with a rise lower in the European Russian-populated parts, and higher in some Asian ethnic minority areas.

The preliminary figures did not provide the results on the size of ethnic groups, education, migration, family size or occupations. These will be correlated and published later, the report by the Central Statistical Administration said.

### Moscow Size Is Larger

The Moscow City Council, which had based its projections of housing and transportation on an estimated population of 6.7 million, was reported by a reliable source to have been astonished when told that Moscow's population was actually 7,061,000, according to the census.

The Soviet authorities, through residence restrictions and other administrative measures, have sought to limit what they consider an unhealthy excessive growth of very large cities.

Despite existing curbs, big cities showed steady increases, reflecting the attractiveness of existing urban complexes for industrial expansion and the desire of people to seek the relative comforts and richer cultural life of the urban areas.

The statistics confirmed what demographers had seen as a trend in recent years, namely a high birth rate in the Central Asian and some Caucasian republics with their non-Russian indigenous groups, and a slowdown in the rate of natural increase among the Slav and Baltic peoples of the European areas.

The growth rate for the Russian Federation, the largest and most important republic, was only 11 per cent in the 11-year period, nearly 5 per cent less than the country as a whole. Moreover, in less desirable parts of the Russian Federation, such as in Western Siberia, the growth was less than that. One of the problems facing Soviet leaders is to persuade workers to move to places rich in resources, such as Siberia, but with less desirable climate and living conditions.

The Ukraine showed a 13 per cent rise and Byelorussia an increase of 12 per cent. The three Baltic republics, Latvia, Lithuania and Estonia, also recorded growth figures less than the national increase.

In Asian areas, the picture was different. The population of Uzbekistan rose by 45 per cent in the 11-year period, Kazakhstan by 40 per cent, Kirgizia by 42 per cent, Tadzhikistan by 46 per cent, and Turkmenia by 42 per cent.

Moreover, Armenia recorded a rise of 41 per cent and Azerbaijan, also in the Caucasus, an increase of 38 per cent. Georgia, the largest of the three Caucasian republics, had only a 16 per cent rise.

### Slavs Still in Majority

Despite the high growth rates in those areas, the three Slavic republics, Russia, Byelorussia, and the Ukraine, still accounted for about 70 per cent of the population. Moreover, as the country's most mobile population group, Russians are found in large numbers in most other republics as well.

The figures confirmed the urbanization trend. Whereas in 1959, most of the country still lived in rural areas, the latest figures show 56 per cent, or 136 million, in urban areas, and 44 percent, or 105.7 million, in the countryside.

In 1959, there were only three cities with populations of more than a million: Moscow, Leningrad and Kiev. Seven more have been added in the 11-year period: Tashkent, Baku, Kharkov, Gorky, Novosibirsk, Kuibyshev and Sverdlovsk.

April 19, 1970

# Soviet Announces Program to Combat Pollution and Conserve the Nation's Water Supply

By JAMES F. CLARITY
Special to The New York Times

MOSCOW, April 27 — The Soviet Union announced a comprehensive legislative program today to conserve water and curb increasing pollution.

The legislation, which covers industrial pollution, sewage disposal and the contamination and dehydration of lakes, proposes criminal and administrative penalties.

It forbids the disposal of waste materials, with the exception of treated sewage, in any body of water. It also applies to research operations for new resources, such as oil, in lakes.

Individual enterprises found guilty of polluting the water with fertilizers or chemical insecticides can be closed down and the water supply of offending enterprises can be curtailed.

Enterprises found guilty of violating the law would be required to repay for the damages incurred. The draft law does not specify scale of fines, nor does it say for what period the water supply might be shut off.

### Victory for the Critics

The need for conserving water for human consumption and for the breeding of fish is underlined in the program, which provides also for local sanitation organizations in each of the 15 union republics, giving them the authority to supervise conservation and implement antipollution measures.

No industry, agricultural enterprise or individual would be immune from the law's provisions.

The program appeared to be a victory for conservationists, who had complained that the government's piecemeal handling of the problem was inadequate.

Izvestia, the Government newspaper, devoted an entire page to the law, which the Supreme Soviet (parliament) is to consider at its next session. In Soviet practice, the statement was tantamount to an announcement that the law would be enacted.

It has been estimated that water pollution costs the Soviet Union the equivalent of $6-billion a year.

The legislation was not accompanied by a commentary on the damage being done by polluted waters and shrinking lakes, but the gravity of the situation was implicit in its provisions.

Pollution and the need for saving water have become a matter of urgent concern among Soviet conservationists in recent years. Public awareness of the problem has been stimulated by numerous articles and by personal experience.

The Moscow River, which flows through the capital, is polluted, although Muscovites swim in it several miles outside of the city. A woman who read the text of the law said that it was needed since "every few days I have to wash out my teapot because of the sand that comes in with the ap water."

Articles in national and local publications have warned of increasing pollution of the Volga and other rivers, Lake Baikal and the Caspian Sea, and of the slow drying up of the Aral and Azov Seas.

A recently released film, "At the Lake" dramatizes the conflict between a determined conservationist and a dedicated industrial manager regarding the pollution of Lake Baikal, the the world's deepest lake.

The declining water level of lakes, according to scientists, is caused largely by the diversion of the rivers that feed them to provide water for irrigation and for hydroelectric stations. The result has often been higher salinity and the destruction of the plant life that sustains fish.

Particular note has been made of the declining water level of the Caspian Sea and its pollution by the oil industry at Baku. The shrinkage and pollution have adversely affected sturgeon in the lake and reduced the supply of caviar.

April 28, 1970

## Soviet Schools:

# A New Emphasis On an Old Approach

**MOSCOW**—Economic conditions in the Soviet Union are forcing the Russians to realign their educational priorities, and the effects are not likely to be greeted with universal enthusiasm.

The economic problem: a shortage of semi-skilled workers to meet the needs of a growing Soviet industry and a declining manpower pool to work the farms. The difficulty has been aggravated by the Government's goal of a high school education for all young people—which diverts potential workers away from jobs—and the traditional desire, among youths from prosperous families in particular, for an academic education leading to college and white-collar jobs. Industrial managers have raised an alarm that many youths are loath to take manual jobs.

The proposed solution: an increase in vocational training at the high school level.

The Soviet Government and the Communist party recently announced a new program of school reforms. The program emphasized wider use of modern teaching techniques, radio and television and counseling that would seek to stimulate more student interest in factory and farm careers.

The combined elementary and secondary education for Russian children lasts 10 years, compared to the usual 12 years in the United States. While school attendance has been compulsory—on paper at least—until completion of eight grades since 1958, there has been a high dropout rate in many areas. In the central Asian republic of Turkmenia, for example, only 81 per cent of the students who started first grade in 1963 completed eighth grade last year.

To work toward universal high school education and then to channel a greater portion of high school graduates into industry and farming instead of higher education, the present plan is ultimately to provide a secondary education through four distinctive channels:

● *Regular day high schools.* These have been traditionally the channel to higher education, although those who fail the highly competitive entrance examinations to college end up going to work or into the army. The tenor of the current educational debate suggests that even in these schools, greater stress will henceforth be placed on career counseling and work-oriented activities to stimulate interest in blue-collar jobs. Educational authorities estimate that about 65 per cent of those receiving a secondary education in the mid-1970's will obtain it in this type of school.

● *Evening high schools.* These will be for young people who go to work after completing the eighth grade but will be expected to complete their secondary education in the evening after work. Between 10 and 15 per cent of high school students attend these schools, which also focus on academic subjects but have lower standards than the day schools. The authorities have met resistance in the past in inducing young workers to go to night school. Many of those who are coaxed into resuming their studies soon drop out. In a play now on the Moscow stage, such a dropout contends he is making more money on his job than friends who spend their time studying.

● *Technical high schools.* These schools, known here as technicums, will provide medium-level specialized training in such fields as textiles, forestry and nursing. They now turn out about 1.1 million such specialists a year in all walks of life. Between 10 and 15 per cent of high school youths study at the technical schools.

● *Vocational schools.* Significant expansion is planned over the next few years in the network of these schools, many of them attached directly to industrial establishments or farms and training skilled workers specifically for jobs such as lathe operator and tractor driver. Few of these factory schools offered a secondary education in the past, but under the current program their standards are to be raised and an increasing number is expected to provide the required academic subjects in addition to purely vocational training.

—THEODORE SHABAD

July 16, 1972

# *U.S. to Let Russians Buy 136-Million in Feed Grain*

By WILLIAM M. BLAIR

Special to The New York Times

WASHINGTON, Nov. 5 — The Nixon Administration announced arrangements today for the commercial sale of nearly $136-million worth of corn and other livestock feed grains to the Soviet Union.

Nixon Administration officials termed the planned sale by two United States grain companies "the first step in the expansion of trade with the Soviet Union," and said that the impetus had been generated for more sales in the future. But they declined to speculate on whether such sales would extend to China in the near future. President Nixon will visit China after the first of the year.

According to Administration officials, the key to the sale was a waiver of American maritime unions' long-time demand that at least 50 per cent of grain shipments to the Soviet Union be carried in American ships.

The officials attributed the maritime unions' action to the Administration's efforts to revitalize American merchant shipping, which include a 10-year program of subsidies to enable domestic shipping to compete with foreign-flag ships.

The sale was expected to have a significant political effect in the big mid-Western corn states. Farmers have complained of depressed prices caused by increasing stocks of grain, including wheat.

There has been a record corn crop this year, and The Administration recently announced a program to combat the price slump — it was also designed to offset political unrest — by paying farmers $600-million more in subsidies to take more acres out of production next year.

The pending sale to the Soviet Union is the first since President Kennedy authorized a $100-million wheat sale to Russia in 1964, a move that stirred controversy.

The new sale will be made by the Continental Grain Company and Cargill, Inc. Spokesmen for the companies declined, for competitive reasons, to disclose how much of the total sale each company would handle. The sale covers 80 million bushels of corn, 28 million bushels of barley and 21 million bushels of oats.

Officials said that the shipments could start immediately, mainly from Great Lakes ports.

The grain deal was described as an indication of an improved climate of relations with the Russians, who were reported to want more trade with the United States to help overcome consumer problems, including the need for higher-protein foods.

The Russians are expected to use the grains particularly for greater pork and poultry production. The $136-million worth of grain exceeds by $18-million the total of $118-million representing all commodities exported to the Soviet Union last year.

November 6, 1971

# SOVIET PURCHASE OF GRAIN FROM U.S. MAY TOTAL BILLION

## Estimate by the Agriculture Department Points to New One-Year Trade Peak

## BAD HARVEST REPORTED

## Brezhnev and Aides Meet on Farm Issues—Attempts to Spur Output Indicated

By BERNARD GWERTZMAN
Special to The New York Times

WASHINGTON, Aug. 9—The Agriculture Department estimated today that the Soviet Union would purchase a billion dollars worth of farm products from the United States over the next 12 months. This would raise Soviet-American trade to unprecedented heights.

The forecast was compiled by leading department officials on the basis of recent talks with private commercial dealers negotiating with the Russians and of reports from Moscow indicating a bad Soviet harvest this fall.

The spring harvest was called a "disaster" by many officials and it was reported from Moscow today that Leonid I. Brezhnev, the Soviet Communist party leader, had held a new high-level meeting on farm issues, evidently in an effort to spur the harvest.

**$500-Million in Wheat**

The Agriculture Department's projection of a billion dollars in sales goes far beyond the $200-million in grains that Moscow agreed to purchase as part of a $750-million, three-year deal announced July 8.

Department officials said that about $500-million of the billion-dollar sales would probably be in wheat. This indicates that Moscow is anticipating shortfalls in its chief crop, vital to the bread supply that is a staple of the Soviet diet.

The rest of the total will probably be in corn, sorghum, rye, barley, oats and soybeans, the Agriculture Department estimated.

Department officials said that an American company, Cook Grains of Memphis, had just about completed arrangements for the first sale of soybeans to the Russians—one million tons, valued at about $100-million.

These products are used in producing animal feed. Soybeans in particular are valued for their high protein content, useful for the growth of cattle. Under the current Soviet five-year economic plan, Moscow is committed to a 25 per cent increase in protein consumption, to be achieved principally through an increase in the amount of meat and dairy products in the Soviet diet.

The large sales to the Soviet Union will cause a severe imbalance in trade between the two countries. Last year, the United States exported about $125-million worth of goods to the Soviet Union and imported about half that amount. The disproportion will grow with the extensive agricultural purchases as well as with a step-up in Soviet purchases of American industrial equipment for a truck factory on the Kama River.

**Gold Sales Possible**

Because of this anticipated trade imbalance, Moscow will have to find ways of paying for its purchases. Under the original $750-million three-year deal, the Administration, through the Commodity Credit Corporation, had agreed to extend a maximum of $500-million in credit.

Agriculture Department officials said that the additional purchases would be paid for "privately," meaning, in most cases, by cash.

Some officials here believe that the Russians may have to sell gold on the world market to cover the heavy agricultural purchases.

It is believed that under the terms of the deals, some of the farm products will be delivered by third-country ships and the rest by Soviet and American ships.

The Russians, aware of the trade imbalance, have been seeking to persuade the United States to participate in joint efforts to exploit the untapped oil, gas and metal resources of Siberia.

This was a major topic discussed by Commerce Secretary Peter G. Peterson and Mr. Brezhnev when they met two weeks ago in the Soviet Union.

Mr. Peterson was there as head of the American delegation to the first session of the newly created Soviet-American commercial commission.

So far, American companies have expressed an interest in such joint ventures, but the Government has been wary of a drain on Government credits that would be needed for such large undertakings.

The Soviet Union would probably be able to sell its products more successfully in the United States if a trade agreement is signed and it receives regular tariff treatment. But such an accord has been help up pending resolution of the lend-lease negotiations to settle the Soviet Union's World War II debts.

The Soviet Union and other Communist countries, except Poland and Yugoslavia, are barred from receiving what is known as "most favored nation" treatment. This means that goods from those countries are taxed at a higher rate than those from the rest of the world—the most favored nations. The Russians have been pressing to receive most-favored-nation treatment.

August 10, 1972

# SOVIET ORDERING INDUSTRY REFORM OVER THREE YEARS

## Plan, Most Comprehensive Since '65, to Spread Out Operations of Plants

## 50,000 UNITS INVOLVED

By THEODORE SHABAD
Special to The New York Times

MOSCOW, April 2 — The Kremlin ordered today a reorganization of this nation's industry as part of a continuing search for an efficient system of managing the vast Government-run Soviet economy.

The reforms, the most comprehensive since 1965, will be carried out over a three-year period and will have the effect of consolidating day-to-day operation of the country's 50,000 industrial plants into a system of large Government corporations combining related factories.

The corporations, known as "production associations," are designed to focus industrial management at a middle level between the supervisory ministry and the individual plant. The role of ministries will be limited to formulation of overall policy in planning, investment and much-needed technological improvement.

**Compromise Is Apparent**

Most individual plants will become simple operating divisions of corporations, and the decision-making powers granted to factory managers in the 1965 reform will be assumed by the corporations.

In seeking to cope with the huge job of managing the Soviet Union's economy, second only to that of the United States, the Kremlin has been vacillating between two basic approaches: All-out centralization at the ministry level, which was the main approach during the Stalin era, and regional decentralization, attempted by Premier Nikita S. Khrushchev from 1957 until his downfall in 1964.

The new system of middle-level corporations, which will control not only production but also research and development, appears to be a compromise between the previous extremes.

The reorganization comes at a time when the Soviet Government is struggling to get more steam behind a sluggish economy after a poor crop year that required heavy food purchases abroad, mostly in the United States.

After a disappointingly slow start in the current five-year plan, running from 1971 to 1975, the year 1973 has been proclaimed, in a widely used slogan, to be the "third and decisive year" that may make or break ultimate fulfillment of the economic program."

Sketchy details of the industrial reform were published tonight in a summary of a joint Government and Communist party decree distributed by Tass, the official press agency. The detailed text will appear tomorrow on the front pages of the nation's controlled newspapers.

**1975 Deadline Is Set**

According to the Tass summary, all of Soviet industry is to be converted to the new system by the end of 1975. Middle-level corporations of the type that will now be the key units in Soviet industry began to be introduced on an experimental basis in the late nineteen-sixties, and about 1,000 are already believed to be in operation.

The decree called on each of the 30-odd industrial ministries, ranging from coal mining to meat and dairy products, to prepare a reorganization plan and to present it to the Government for approval within six months.

Corporations will be essentially of two types. In industries with a relatively small number of plants—for example, the rubber-tire industry — a single national corporation will be set up under the ministry, which in this case is the Ministry of Petroleum Refining and Petrochemicals.

On the other hand, in industries with a large number of production units, say, the coal-mining industry or the crude-oil industry, regional corporations will be established in producing areas.

**Coordination Lack Cited**

By incorporating research and development into the corporations, the Soviet Government hopes to bring industrial research closer to actual application. A lack of coordination between research and production has tended to slow technological progress in the past.

The latest reorganization is part of a long effort aimed at finding the most effective system of running a vast centrally planned economy. Under Stalin, absolute powers entrusted to ministries tended to give rise to separate industrial empires with little coordination among industries.

Premier Khrushchev sought to achieve coordination by abolishing the national ministries in 1957 and shifting control to about a hundred regional management agencies that were responsible for all industries within a particular region. This was found to give rise to a tendency to place regional interests above national.

A profit-oriented economic reform in 1965 returned to the ministerial system but also granted broader rights to the managers of individual plants. Experience showed, however, that many factories were too small to effectively exercise the powers given to them and that there was need for larger integrated production units combining several related plants.

April 3, 1973

# Soviet Is Regrouping Its 15 Republics Into 7 Big Planning Regions

The New York Times/May 4, 1973

**By THEODORE SHABAD**
Special to The New York Times

MOSCOW, May 3—The Soviet Union has quietly begun a controversial consolidation of its national planning regions that may ultimately erode the significance of individual Soviet ethnic republics as economic planning and management areas.

A new seven-region system grouping republics into larger planning units has been adopted in connection with the drafting of an ambitious 15-year plan that will outline basic investment and development policies for the Soviet Union until 1990.

The consolidated regional system, which is being introduced in the face of persistent nationalistic sensibilities, is part of a growing trend to ignore particular interests of the republics in an effort to achieve more efficient coordination and long-term planning of the complex Government-run economy.

The detailed local planning of economic development will, at least for the immediate future, continue at the republic level. But the basic, over-all national development policies will in future be based on the new regional planning units.

The regional reform was foreshadowed last December by Leonid I. Brezhnev, the Soviet party leader, in a keynote speech marking the 50th anniversary of the formation of the Soviet Union as a nominal federation of republics.

Now that a relatively common level of development has been reached by the various republics, Mr. Brezhnev said, future economic decision-making in the 15-year plan should be for the good of the country as a whole rather than focus on the interests of individual republics.

Mr. Brezhnev's broad policy statement was amplified by more detailed proposals in economic and technical journals, some of which went so far as to suggest that the boundaries of some of the Soviet Union's 15 republics might be modified if they were not in keeping with efficient economic regions.

In an effort to shift the focus from the political sensibilities of the various ethnic areas to one of national efficiency, Soviet information media have also been working hard to generate an over-all "Soviet" nationalism and a national pride in economic achievements to replace the fragmented ethnic loyalties among the country's hundred-odd nationalities.

**Republics Jealous of Rights**

The new regional planning program is an attempt to depart from existing republic boundaries in allocating capital investment to the development of the Soviet economy. In the past the various republics have been jealous of their prerogatives as integral economic regions within the Soviet Union.

The potentially far-reaching decision to establish the new consolidated national planning regions was disclosed in the April issue of the Government's planning journal, Planovoye Khozyaistvo (Planned Economy).

A progress report on the drafting of the 15-year plan said that the existing system of 18 planning regions, which followed republic boundaries, had been revised into a set of seven consolidated regions — three in the European part of the Soviet Union and four in the Asian part.

The three European regions that figure in the 1975-90 plan are a combined north-central region, a southern region, and a combined Volga-Urals region. The four Asian regions are Siberia, the Far East, Kazakhstan and Central Asia.

In reducing the existing 18 planning regions to seven, Soviet planners were evidently concerned with producing a system of planning areas that would be of roughly similar economic potential and area. The existing system includes both small, densely settled regions of European Russia and the vast, virtually undeveloped expanses of Siberia.

In allocating four regions to the Asian part of the Soviet Union and only three regions to the developed European portion, the economic planners appeared to focus on the future development of the Asian potential.

The consolidation of planning regions has affected the interests of individual republics, especially in the European west. For example, the Baltic republics and the Byelorussian Republic have been combined with the adjoining Leningrad and Moscow regions of the Russian Republic in the new north-central region.

Similarly the new southern region combines five republics —Moldavia, the Ukraine, Georgia, Armenia and Azerbaijan —with the northern Caucasus portion of the Russian Republic.

The now separate Volga and Urals regions are being combined into a Volga-Urals region to point up common problems of development. The Volga-Urals has been one of the most rapidly growing sections of the Soviet Union in recent decades.

May 4, 1973

# BECHTEL COMPANY SIGNS SOVIET PACT

### Accord Calls for Exchange of Technological Data

Special to The New York Times

MOSCOW, July 2 — One of America's leading engineering and construction concerns, the Bechtel Corporation of San Francisco, today signed a broad agreement on technology transfer with the Soviet Government.

The agreement, which follows similar Soviet pacts with American corporations, is believed to be of particular interest to Moscow because of Bechtel's involvement in key industrial projects in the United States, especially in the energy field.

Bechtel has been looking into pipeline projects for Alaskan oil, into the feasibility of building nuclear plants on artificial islands off New York City and into the prospect of building and operating a commercial uranium enrichment plant.

The accord with the Soviet Union ranges over cooperation in virtually all branches of heavy industry, from the use of managerial techniques in construction to metals and petrochemicals and the pipeline transportation of oil and gas.

Jerome W. Komes, Bechtel president, signed for the West Coast concern, and Dzherman M. Gvishiani for the Soviet Government.

Mr. Gvishiani, a dynamic, 44-year-old sociologist and management expert, has been spearheading the Soviet drive for Western technology in his capacity of deputy chairman of the Government's State Committee for Science and Technology. He is a son-in-law of Premier Aleksei N. Kosygin.

Ivan A. Ganichev, a Deputy Chairman of the State Committee for Construction Affairs, which is a powerful policy-making and co-ordinating body, also signed for the Soviet Union.

News about the Bechtel agreement was made public through the Soviet press agency, Tass, after the closing of business today. Neither Soviet officials nor Mr. Komes was available for comment.

Although some American corporations have made an effort to brief American newsmen here directly on their activities, other concerns have preferred to rely on the restrictive press relations of their Soviet hosts and have avoided contact with representatives of United States news organizations. This information policy has made it difficult to verify details of Soviet-American accords.

July 3, 1973

## Soviet and France in Agreement

Special to The New York Times

MOSCOW, July 10—The Soviet Union and France today adopted a 10-year program of cooperation in industry, providing for the construction of industrial complexes in the two countries.

The program, which also calls for long-term French-supported development projects in the Soviet Union, is an outgrowth of a 10-year economic agreement signed by Leonid I. Brezhnev, the Soviet leader, during a visit to France in October, 1971.

No details of today's implementation accord were made public, but Valéry Giscard d'Estaing, France's Minister for Economy and Finance, said he had offered $1.3-billion to $1.8-billion worth of new deals to the Soviet Union. Last year's trade between the two countries totaled $700-million.

July 11, 1973

# *Soviet Is Reconciling Its Quest for Modernization With Communist Ideology*

By HENRY R. LIEBERMAN

Ever since the Bolshevik Revolution, the Soviet Union—now a superpower with great enterprises and a higher living standard to point to—has focused on science and technology as prime levers for rational development of a Communist society.

The emphasis is especially heavy now that the country is seeking to modernize its bulky planning apparatus and trying to get maximum efficiency out of its centralized economy in pursuit of specific goals.

Much seems to depend on the extent to which new techniques, methods, systems and even habits of thought can be reconciled with what has evolved in the 56 years since the Bolshevik Revolution. There are both rigidities and impressive achievements.

On the one hand is institutional inertia, bureaucratic vested interest and dogma; on the other, the quest for modern management and the drive for greater productivity in a "post-industrial" age symbolized by the computer rather than the blast furnace.

The ninth five-year plan, which began in 1971, envisages a "major step in realizing the achievements of the scientific and technological revolution." This theme, binding the past to the present is expressed in blue and white by a large sign on the road to Akademgorodok (academic city) in Siberia: "To manage the economy in Lenin's way means to base oneself on science."

The term science (nauka in Russian) is an all-embracing concept in the Soviet Union. It encompasses the social and behavioral sciences and the humanities as well as the physical sciences and mathematics. Even engineering is often included in the concept of science, which is really a broad appreciation and respect for highly developed minds and skills.

Status and material rewards for the scientist rise as he progresses through the hierarchy from the lower reaches to candidate of science (roughly Ph.D.), then to doctor of science (postdoctoral level), then to corresponding member and ultimately to full-fledged academician in the Soviet Academy of Sciences. There are now about 225 academicians and twice as many corresponding members.

While engineering salaries are low by American standards —200 to 300 rubles ($280 to $420) a month—an active academician who also teaches, writes and serves as a consultant is said to earn as much as 2,000 rubles ($2,800) a month. The average industrial worker's gross monthly pay, according to a United States Congressional study, is about 135 rubles ($190).

Large resources are going into Soviet research and development. The 1971 expenditures are listed at 13 billion rubles ($18.2-billion), 1972 expenses at $14.4 billion rubles ($20.1-billion), and the 1973 plan called for an outlay of 15.5 billion rubles ($21.7-billion), including capital expenditures. In 1971 about three million people, including engineers, technicians and auxiliary personnel, were said to be employed in the "field of science."

**Comparisons Are Difficult**

As defined by educational background and the kind of work actually done, about a million are believed by an American specialist to be engaged in research and development—roughly 20 per cent being doctors and candidates of science. The American estimated that it would cost $40-billion annually to support such an establishment in the United States.

About 425,000 Americans are listed as having engaged last year in total research and development activities at a cost of $28.9-billion. But different systems, different definitions, and different output efficiencies make accurate comparisons impossible.

Soviet science at the top level is generally recognized to be of very high quality and there is much evidence of top-grade engineering talent and skills. At the lower levels, however, a number of Soviet engineers have complained that they received inadequate training in mathematics.

More important, as Western specialists see it, is the organizational inertia that has slowed technological innovation. Dr. Dzhermen M. Gvishiani, deputy chairman of the State Committee for Science and Technology, says that a number of technological breakthroughs were not pursued because "for us there is always the question of whether to do research for immediate needs or look to the long term."

**Party Is a Major Pillar**

Throughout the years research institutes have proliferated in the Soviet Union under multiple auspices. Now research and development are being pushed even at the factory level.

Major pillars in the science-technology structure are the Communist party, the State Committee for Science and Technology and the Soviet Academy of Sciences. The State Committee, set up in 1965, has emerged as the primary coordinating force in research and development and in "scientific and technical collaboration" with foreign countries.

The Soviet Academy is concerned with basic research, but its institutes are also engaged in priority applied research and do work for industry that supplements their budgetary allotments. At Akademgorodok, the main center of the Siberian Academy of Sciences, the annual budget of 100 million rubles ($140-million) is supplemented by outside income of 20 million rubles ($28-million).

Akademgorodok, situated in a pine-and-birch forest just 18 miles south of Novosibirsk, is one of the most prestigious of the Soviet Academy's centers.

Set up just 15 years ago with an initial outlay of $280-million and a relatively free hand for its leadership, the city is a virtually self-contained community of 56,000 whose only "industry" is science. Twenty-one thousand people are involved in a research effort encompassing 22 institutes, four in Novosibirsk and the rest in Akademgorodok.

The physicist Gersh I. Budker is at Akademgorodok, still concentrating on building bigger colliding-beam accelerators to produce incredible energies. But broad-based research is also going on in thermodynamics, hydrodynamics, atmosphere and ocean physics, chemistry, biology, geology, automation and electrometrics, mathematics, mathematical economics, and computer science.

**Research in Junior Year**

Novosibirsk University, with 3,800 students, and a preparatory school is also part of the Akademgorodok complex. Ninety per cent of the university's faculty is said to consist of scientists from the institutes, and when a science student reaches his junior year, he starts doing research at an institute.

Akademgorodok combs Siberia systematically for scientific and mathematical talent. For some years now it has sponsored a different kind of Olympiad, a Siberia-wide hunt for young wizards in the 15-to-17 age group.

In December local newspapers publish a list of problems in mathematics, physics and chemistry. The young people who submit solutions are graded for originality as well as accuracy, and those considered outstanding are invited to regional centers, at Akademgorodok's expense, to take an examination.

About 600 who excel are then enrolled in a boarding school at Akademgorodok, from where they go to the university. If a young Yakut genius cannot meet the entrance requirement for an acceptable composition in Russian, he is permitted to write in Yakut.

Founder and leader of Akademgorodok is Mikhail Y. Lavrentyev, 72, a mathematician who is also head of the Siberian Academy of Sciences. He is an open, rugged, big bear of a man. His aim is to create more opportunities for young scientists, to teach the young "to think" and to develop fresh talent for the next generation of Soviet scientists.

**Basic Issues Unsettled**

Academician Lavrentyev acknowledges the value of sophisticated automation. But he said there were more fundamental unsettled problems: the nature of life, the environment, the mysteries of ocean phenomena, more accurate weather prediction.

"The greatest achievements will not be made by cybernetic machines, but by the cybernetics of the brain," he said.

At the Soviet Union's prestigious Steklov Institute of Mathematics in Moscow, 82-year-old Ivan M. Vinogradov, the director, said he was also interested in finding top mathematical talent. Even the quality of Moscow University mathematics does not satisfy him. "They prepare too many people and don't separate the weak from the strong," he said.

The Steklov Institute concentrates on pure mathematics and its main goal, according to Academician Vinogradov, is to keep the institute small, pursue only the highest quality and forgo certain areas of research, even when they are important, if top-flight people are not available. Only about 20 new postgraduates a year are accepted at the institute, which now has about 100 "scientific workers" and 50 postgraduates.

Academician Vinogradov, himself a specialist in number theory, noted that both Mr. Lavrentyev and Mstislav V. Keldysh, head of the Soviet Academy, had once worked at the Steklov Institute. "It is impossible to create a good applied research center if it is not also a good theoretical center," he said.

Akademgorodok is both—and there is a much more relaxed feel about the place than there is in Moscow.

At Akademgorodok, Yuri A. Nesterichin, head of the city's automation institute, and Andrei P. Yershov, head of the main computing center's Department of Computer Science—both of whom are 43—displayed their computers and talked about their problems.

The computing center has six Soviet computers—three BESM-6's, two M-220's and a Minsk-22—and a heterogeneous assortment of peripheral equipment manufactured in the Soviet Union, Eastern Europe and the West. The equipment is not as impressive as in big Western computing centers, but Mr. Yershov said he was getting computers to do his work and had a "comfortable feeling."

"We have many problems—organizational, technical, getting people and good quality, but we are making strides," he said. As to Western criticisms of Soviet computer operations, he said there was some "underestimating" and added: "There was also speculation about when would the Soviet Union make an atomic bomb."

One of Akademgorodok's prominent figures is Abel G. Aganbegyan, a mathematical economist whose world is now filled with computerized models projecting the Soviet Union's next 10 years and beyond. A 15-year future is often cited in discussing changes in the Soviet planning approach.

A tall, heavy set man of Armenian descent, the 41-year-old Mr. Aganbegyan heads the Institute of Economics and Organization of Industrial Production.

"By using models, we can make predictions in a more reliable way," he said in an interview. "We make three-year models of the United States economy as well as predictions about the Soviet economy."

Any model—a map, for example—is a representation of reality. A mathematical model seeks to represent a real process by means of equations into which different assumed numbers are plugged to compare alternative situations.

Mr. Aganbegyan said he was devoting about two-thirds of his time to national models, but was also working on branch models of different sectors of industry and on regional models. He said use of models could lead to a 5 to 10 per cent saving in costs.

Many of the technical pitfalls of economic forecasting were detailed by Mr. Aganbegyan last year in a speech on an "optimal approach to long-range planning." Nevertheless, he said, it is necessary to look 10 to 15 years ahead because of scientific, technological and socio-economic development. For example, he said, it takes 10 years to develop and test a supersonic transport system and five years "for serial production and introduction."

**Planning Is Stressed**

At the Soviet Academy's Institute of Mathematical Economics in Moscow, Academician Nikolai P. Fedorenko, the director, also emphasized the need for long-term planning within the framework of the state's social and economic aims. He said that while a truly optimal plan for economic efficiency could not be realized even in theory, the main task was to come as close as possible. "The cost of not achieving the best solution has become more and more expensive," he said.

Academician Fedorenko was flanked by three of his aides while being interviewed in his office in one of the yellow buildings clustered on the oasis of the Soviet Academy in Moscow. The 56-year-old academician, who described himself as an economist-chemical engineer-mathematician, directs a staff of about 1,000.

"Until a few years ago, we dealt with static models," he said. "Now we use dynamic models, introducing the factor of technological change. Also, we can say now: you must do better, and we can use computers for this purpose. But there are drawbacks even here. It is not sufficient to have a balanced plan. We must be sure it is the best plan."

It is "stupid" to think that all this can be solved by the computer, he went on. "There is the problem of functioning—of economic management."

Conceding the possibility of mistakes in simplifying complex aggregates, he said there were, in addition, questions of incentives and such questions as to what extent there should be decentralization.

Valued though they now are for their ability to help the economy achieve maximum current efficiency, and as long-forecasters, Soviet mathematical economists are not in a particularly enviable position. The technical problems are especially great in the Soviet Union, it is acknowledged, and there is frequently inadequate statistical and planning information. In addition, bureaucrats and ideologues keep nipping at the mathematical economists' heels.

Regarded with suspicion in Stalin's day, when economics was saturated with orthodoxy, mathematical economics has made considerable headway since the organization in 1963 of the Soviet Academy's Institute of Mathematical Economics. "Libermanism" — named for Yevzei G. Liberman, the Kharkov economist who stressed profitability as the main success criterion for an enterprise—sprang up at about the same time in the prelude to the 1965 economic reforms.

But criticism of intrusive "bourgeois ideas" still crops up. In October the journal Planovoye Khozyaistvo (Planned Economy), which is published by Gosplan, the State Planning Committee, reported a June meeting of the publication's editorial board, various economists and others who had gathered to criticize the advocates of the system for optimal functioning of the economy.

Mathematical economics as a field was not attacked. However, the unnamed economists, who did not seem to have been present, were accused by one speaker of borrowing concepts "peculiar to bourgeois theory—the theory of marginal utility factors in production, market socialism, automatic regulation of prices."

Another speaker, described as a deputy division chief in Gosplan, was quoted as having said:

"Recently the center of the ideological struggle has noticeably shifted into the field of economic science. Bourgeois ideologists are trying to show the commonality of the character of the development of contemporary industrial society independent of government or social structure, to draw a parallel between socialism and capitalism."

Clearly, there are fundamental diferences between the socialist Soviet Union and the capitalist United States. But they share some important things, including the "scientific-technological revolution.'

This revolution promises to leave a deep imprint on both.

December 14, 1973

# Arthur Andersen Office Due in Moscow

By THEODORE SHABAD

One of the largest accounting firms in the United States is expected to open an office in Moscow soon as part of a broad-ranging agreement with the Soviet Government in auditing, international taxation and management services.

The firm, Arthur Andersen & Co. of Chicago, will become the first American company to work closely with the Russians in the field of Western management techniques as the Soviet Union expands its worldwide commitments. A final accord is expected next month, according to American business sources.

Harvey E. Kapnick Jr., chairman of Andersen, declined to disclose details of the negotiations pending an agreement.

"We are moving along on schedule," he said by telephone from Chicago, "and hope that the talks will culminate in our presence in Moscow in the near future."

Describing the prospective arrangement as an "exciting challenge in East-West economic relations," the 48-year-old Mr. Kapnick said:

"We believe that our cooperation with the Soviet Union will help foster East-West trade by helping each side understand the business practices and philosophy of the other."

Mr. Kapnick, who became chief executive in 1970, has been described as something of a "whiz kid" at Andersen. Raised on a Michigan farm, he went to work in the firm's Chicago office in 1948, rising to the rank of partner in eight years; ordinarily it takes about a dozen years to get that far.

On the Soviet side, too, a "whiz kid" has been the moving force behind the project. He is Dzhermen M. Gvishiani, the 45-year-old deputy chairman of the State Committee for Science and Technology, who has been in the forefront of Soviet efforts to use Western management techniques to the extent that they are compatible with Marxist ideology.

Only last week, Pravda, the Communist party newspaper, stressed the need for a psychological reorientation in economic management. In an editorial criticizing delays in establishing a new system of Soviet state corporations known as production associations, it said:

"The modern executive must be familiar with the science of management, broaden his horizons, be able to improve the planning and organization of production, and adopt a party-oriented approach to any problem."

Mr. Gvishiani, who is Premier Aleksei N. Kosygin's son-in-law, has long favored economic reforms that would shift short-term decision-making from central ministries to the new state corporations.

Mr. Gvishiani played a key role in the organization in 1972 of the International Institute of Applied Systems Analysis in Laxenburg, Austria. The institute, an international "think tank" sponsored by a dozen nations, will study pollution control, urban growth and other problems of industrial countries.

A specialist in American management science, Mr. Gvishiani has also led a drive for training Soviet economic executives in modern management information and control systems. A high-level business administration school, known as the Institute for Management of the National Economy, opened in Moscow in February, 1971.

In Arthur Andersen, the Soviet Government will have the services of an accounting firm that serves more companies listed on the New York Stock Exchange than do any of its rivals. Among the companies served by Andersen are Tenneco, Inc., and the Occidental Petroleum Corporation, which have plans for bringing Soviet liquefied natural gas to the United States, and the General Dynamics Corporation, which builds ships for the transportation of liquefied gas.

Another Andersen client is Combustion Engineering, Inc., whose Lummus unit is doing engineering and construction for the Soviet chemical industry.

The accounting firm is expected to advise its American clients on the Soviet Union's industrial and trade program and to assist Soviet officials in dealing with the wide range of business procedures and practices encountered in expanding foreign operations.

The Soviet Union is also expected to benefit from Andersen's personnel-training program, which has made use of advanced audio-visual techniques for instruction in the firm's worldwide network of offices. Soviet officials may also attend the firm's training center, with accommodations for 600 people, at St. Charles, Ill., west of Chicago.

The firm's approaches to the Soviet Union began in 1972 when it filed an application for permission to establish an office in Moscow.

Last May, Mr. Kapnick and Robert I. Jones, vice chairman for international operations, visited Moscow and signed a preliminary agreement.

March 19, 1974

# Japan and Soviet Plan Siberian Loan

Special to The New York Times

TOKYO, April 22 — Japan agreed tentatively today to lend the Soviet Union $1-billion at relatively low interest to finance three projects involving the development of coal, gas and forestry resources in Siberia.

Satoshi Sumida, president of the Japan Export-Import Bank, and Vladimir Aikhimov, the Soviet Deputy Minister of Foreign Trade, signed the agreement here on the assumption that negotiations on other details of the projects would be completed within six months.

The deal would pour Japanese funds into the extraction of coal and gas resources in Yakutia and into felling timber from the forests of Far Eastern Siberia. Japan, which is poor in natural resources, is scheduled to share some of the output.

The agreement appeared to be a breakthrough for Japanese and Russian negotiators, who have been in the midst of intensive new discussions over joint development of the Siberian resources after a decade of sporadic bargaining marred by deep mutual suspicion.

Among the major issues to be decided in reaching final agreement on the Siberian project is how much of the coal, gas and timber would be shipped to Japan. Japanese and Soviet negotiators must also agree on how to price the products, a fundamentally difficult question because Soviet prices are determined by the state and

Japanese prices largely by market forces.

A team of Soviet economic specialists arrived here three weeks ago to continue negotiation over five Siberian projects that would probably require more than $7-billion in Japanese credits and equipments.

Japanese officials familiar with the negotiations said that, as in the past, there were serious arguments over prices and terms of the Japanese loans. The Russians are reported to have wanted concessionary terms, like those granted a developing country, while the Japanese were insisting on commercial rates. Today's agreement, which calls for an interest rate of 6.375 per cent appeared to have been a compromise weighted toward the Russian side. But one official said the discussions had been "more businesslike" than in previous years. Among the other proposals are exploration for oil off the island of Sakhalin, east of Siberia and north of Japan, and development of oil from Tyumen in Western Siberia, but Japanese participation in this project appears to be in abeyance. There are many complexities because the Japanese insist that American participation is required in at least some projects.

### American Role in Doubt

The American role has been thrown into doubt in recent weeks because of mounting Congressional opposition to Export-Import Bank loans for the Soviet Union. Japanese businessmen and Government officials have wanted the American participation, both as a guarantee of Soviet deliveries and as an essential added source of capital and technology.

Officials at Keidanren, the influential federation of economic organizations that has played a major role in the discussions with the Russians, say they are still confident the American companies will be able to join them, even if the Export-Import Bank is restricted in granting credit to the Soviet Union. The American concerns would be El Paso Natural Gas and Occidental Petroleum in the Yakutsk gas deal and Atlantic-Richfield in the Sakhalin oil-exploration project.

Whatever any eventual American role, both the Japanese and the Russians, spurred by the energy crisis, appear more anxious now than in earlier years of the negotiations to reach some practical result. The talks began in 1965.

### Meeting With Tanaka

Apparently as an indication of this seriousness, Mr. Alkhimov, the Soviet Deputy Minister of Foreign Trade, met with Premier Kakuei Tanaka earlier this month to deliver a personal letter from Leonid I. Brezhnev, the Soviet Communist party leader. The contents of the letter have not been disclosed, but it was reported to have contained a plea for speedy agreement on some of the projects.

However, despite this new sense of purpose, the obstacles to any final agreement remain formidable.

The most basic of these, stemming from the first time the Russians and Japanese came into contact with each other in Siberia in the early 19th century, is their deep mutual hostility and distrust. They have always been bitter rivals, for Siberia and Manchuria, and the history of their relations has been punctuated with violence, such as the Russo-Japanese War of 1904-05, Japan's unsuccessful Siberian expedition at a time of the Russian Revolution, the Soviet Union's last-minute attack on Japan at the end of World War II despite a nonaggression pact, the Soviet retention of four Japanese islands off Hokkaido and continued Russian seizure of Japanese fishermen.

### Japanese Doubt Results

While American policy makers often like to say that increased contact and trade with the Soviet Union should lead to better relations and possibly even moderation in Soviet domestic policies, few Japanese believe their participation in Siberian development would have any effect on their relations with the Soviet Union.

"We are not so naïve," a senior Japanese diplomat remarked. "Even if we agree on all these projects, that is not going to change the hostility between us."

Agreement on the Siberian projects was also delayed by widely divergent demands on prices for the Siberian resources and terms for the Japanese credit.

According to Japanese officials, the Russians insisted on prices above those paid by the Japanese for Australian coal or Middle Eastern oil, while also demanding loans at low interest rates, comparable to those given developing nations.

In the coal negotiations, for example, the Russians were reported to have sought a $450-million credit at 6 per cent interest. The Japanese demanded at least 6.5 per cent, noting that the United States Export-Import Bank now required 7 per cent.

The northern Yakutian natural gas project could eventually involve $3.5-billion in Japanese and possibly American capital.

The Japanese hope to press on with exploration work to determine whether the area contains at least one trillion cubic meters (35.3 trillion cubic feet) of natural gas, the minimum the Japanese believe is necessary to justify full-scale work on the project. The initial exploration is expected to cost $150-million.

The Sakhalin offshore oil-exploration project, which oil-industry officials here say holds great promise, would involve about $200-million in American and Japanese credits, with much of the drilling to utilize American and Japanese rigs.

The timber project calls for a Japanese credit of $500-million in exchange for 16.6 milion cubic meters (585 million cubic feet) of Siberian logs over five years. It is a continuation of an earlier timber project worked out in the late nineteen-sixties, one of the two development deals on which the Japanese and the Russians have managed to agree.

The other was an $80-million Japanese loan to help in the development of a new port at Wrangel near Nahodka facing the Japan Sea.

April 23, 1974

# *Soviet Far East Turning to Trade With Pacific Basin*

By CHRISTOPHER S. WREN

Special to The New York Times

KHABAROVSK, U.S.S.R.—The Soviet Far East, an area ranging from mosquito - ridden swamps to permanently frozen wastelands and encompassing the sprawling Pacific territories of the Soviet Union, is quietly shaking off long years of geographical and economic isolation. Hydroelectric dams and railways are being built, and, with Japanese help, the Russians are developing timber and paper industries, constructing a deep water port and prospecting and drilling for oil and gas.

Perhaps the most dramatic venture is the 2,000-mile Baikal-Amur Mainline railway being laid north of the Trans-Siberian. Once commissioned in 1983, it will lay open inaccessible regions to economic exploitation, with the raw materials dispatched to the growing network of Pacific ports.

Elsewhere in the Far East, dogged development efforts have given cities like Khabarovsk an industrial growth rate running well above the national average.

### Most of Area Is Closed

The difficulties of development have been psychological as well as physical, for the Soviet Far East remains a distant land even to most Russians. In fact, it looms geographically larger than Western Europe, with a ragged coastline stretching nearly 3,000 miles from Bering Strait to North Korea. By contrast, its population runs about six million, little more than that of Massachusetts.

Foreigners consider the Far East as the easternmost part of Siberia, which Western usage defines as extending from the Urals all the way to the Pacific Coast. But in the Soviet Union, the area is broken down into three components—West Siberia, East Siberia and the Far East.

The Far East is almost entirely closed to foreign visitors, in part for military reasons. Only Khabarovsk accommodates Western tourists though a traveler may ride a night train that skirts the Chinese border to the port of Nakhodka and a waiting steamer.

The Far East offers more than its share of paradoxes. Geographically it is Asian, yet in culture and outlook it is European.

### Economy Being Reoriented

Despite the fighting between Soviet and Chinese troops on the Ussuri River six years ago, Far Easterners act far more casual about their Chinese neighbors than other Russians. And though the Far East leans on Moscow, it has been reorienting its economy gradually toward the Pacific Ocean.

The more temperate regions resemble the Pacific Northwest or, perhaps, Alaska, though they are visited by bitter winds in winter and sometimes devastating floods in summer. To the north, the climate grows so harsh that animals struggle to survive and men must be lured by the promise of double wages.

Yet the natural riches abound, from gold in Magadah to reports of oil off Sakhalin. "They say that when God was flying over Russia distributing the world's wealth, his bag broke over the Far East," a Soviet journalist related. "Our geologists tell us we have every mineral found in the Mendeleyev table of chemical elements."

To tap such resources, Moscow has sought Japanese cooperation on some projects. These include the timber and paper industry, construction of the deep-water port of Vostochny, near Nakhodka, prospecting and drilling for oil and gas in the Sakhalin waters and extraction of natural gas and coal in Yakutia.

Signs of progress are becoming apparent. With one-sixth of Soviet timber reserves in the Far East, major timber-processing complexes are springing up like that at the Pacific port of Vanino, which employs Japanese tecnology.

In September, a new railroad bridge across the mile-wide Amur River at Komsomolsk was put into operation, opening up a through route from the Trans-Siberian to Vanino. Previously railroad cars had to be ferried across the river in summer or used temporary rails laid across the ice in winter.

The Far East will also assume increasing economic importance as container traffic grows across the Trans-Siberian "land bridge" between Japan and Western Europe.

On the Zeya River, the Far East's first hydroelectric station, with a planned capacity of 1.2 million kilowatts, is about to begin operating. Two more hydroelectric stations are planned on the turbulent Bureya River and yet another on the Kolyma. On the peninsula of Kamchatka, underground steam has even been tapped to provide geothermal power.

Though Khabarovsk itself lies directly north of Japan, its residents have not taken on an Asian identity.

"It's a question we don't ask ourselves", explains one man. "Of course we are near other Asian nations and can feel them. But we live in the Soviet Union."

The thousands of Japanese tourists who visit Khabarovsk annually in hopes of glimpsing the real Soviet Union are not disappointed. Khabarovsk, with its 500,000 mostly Slavic residents, looks the typical European Russian city, from the commanding statue of Lenin in the main square to the rows of new prefabricated apartments on the city outskirts.

**Shops on Karl Marx Street**

The stores along Karl Marx

The New York Times/Nov. 25, 1975

**Khabarovsk area has labor shortage, officials complain**

Street are stocked with Soviet goods hauled over the Trans-Siberian railroad. Shoppers queue under the poplars for luxuries like fresh grapes. Along the sandy banks of the Amur, fishermen stand motionless as they do on the Volga. Still, geographical realities do intrude, as when the local newspaper recently advertised for "smoke-jumpers" to be trained to fight fires out in the forest.

The exotic quality of Khabarovsk is its location—fewer than 40 miles from the city center to the border with China. A view of the border itself is obscured by the triangular green Kazakevich Island, formed by the confluence of the Amur and Ussuri rivers.

The lush island is Soviet, though the Chinese claim it, and its significance is minimized by guides as an urban "green belt." Whatever Soviet troop units there are have been tactfully tucked from sight, and soldiers in Khabarovsk look no more conspicuous or numerous than they would be in any other Soviet city.

Khabarovsk appears unruffled by its proximity to China.

"It doesn't make any difference for us in the life of the city," said Mayor Pavel L. Morozov, who noted that "the farther from Khabarovsk, the more the question is asked."

Some locals become alternately amused and annoyed by what they consider a tourist preoccupation with the border.

"If people were nervous, they would be stocking up on staples like sugar and flour," said one Khabarovsk journalist. "Go into a store and you don't see that, do you? Also, if people were alarmed, they would be leaving. Instead, they are moving in."

"Of course, it would be more pleasant if relations were like before, when the frontier was symbolic," added his colleague. "The Chinese would come over to trade and shop and even use our hospitals when they were sick."

"But," he added hopefully, "it's only a temporary situation."

**Some Local Trade**

Nonetheless, the Soviet Far East has drawn deliberately closer to its other Asian neighbors. To alleviate the dependence on European Russia, the region has been permitted to develop its own independent trade ties. The system, called coastal trade, follows a similar arrangement that Leningrad enjoys with Finland.

The Far East's coastal trade mostly involves about 100 Japanese companies though there is some exchange with North Korea.

The total turnover, conducted since 1964 through a regional organization called Dalintorg in the port of Nakhodka, now runs a modest $40 million a year. Its scope is limited compared with Moscow-supervised trade with Japan, which last year was $2.2-billion.

As Vyacheslav V. Burenkov, the Khabarovsk area's coastal trade representative, explained the arrangement, Dalintorg exports regional raw materials like timber and coal and foodstuffs like fish. In return, it receives light machinery and technology, medicine and popular consumer goods. One of the hottest items, he reported, has been the Japanese pocket calculator, which is becoming a prestige symbol for local businessmen.

**Some Product Sidelines**

There are other attempts toward self-sufficiency. As happens elsewhere in the Soviet Union, Far Eastern industries are encouraged to develop consumer product sidelines. For instance, the Energomash turbine and generator plant in Khabarovsk is also turning out baby carriages.

Local industrial growth is expected to rise 50 per cent during the five-year plan ending this year. "What we really have to think about is agricultural development, particularly fertilizers," said Iosif K. Mikhailov, deputy chief of planning for the Khabarovsk area.

More staples like potatoes and cabbage are being grown but poor soil conditions still require the import of grain. Two pig and poultry complexes have been built with East German technology to cut the Trans-Siberian imports of meat and eggs. A champagne and wine factory is planned, though Mr. Mikhailov said the grapes would probably come from Moldavia, at the opposite end of the Soviet Union.

**Big Shortage of Labor**

In interviews, officials agreed that the biggest problem is still a shortage of labor. Incentives to attract workers include private livestock for farmers and bonuses for industrial specielists and their families as well.

"We have work to do and not enough hands, "Mr. Morozov said. "We want people not only to come and see this place but to settle down. That's why wages are 20 per cent higher here."

Last July, the Communist party newspaper Pravda complained that "romantics" from the western Soviet Union were taking advantage of free fares to visit the Far East and then pull out before their contracts expired. In the first five months this year, it revealed, 330 of 477 dockworkers whose travel expenses were paid to the fishing port of Nakhodka either left early or never began work.

On the other hand, there have been those like Pavel Morozov, who came out on contract as an engineer more than 20 years ago and stayed on to become Mayor of Khabarovsk. He reported that he had recently turned down a "lucrative" executive job back near Moscow.

"Every bird sings for its own forest," he said, "and we like our city best."

**3 New Year's Celebrations**

Since it is already 4 P.M. in Khabarovsk when offices open at 9 A.M. in Moscow, local officials say their biggest problem is the jet lag they incur when they fly back to the capital on business. A journalist, too, recalled coming home not long ago and going swimming at 4 A.M. because he could not sleep.

The supersonic TU-144 jetliner is eventually expected to

go into service between Khabarovsk and Moscow, cutting flying time from eight to four hours.

"We will be able to leave Khabarovsk today and arrive in Moscow yesterday," a Far Easterner quipped.

The newspaper Komsomolskaya Pravda buttressed his assertion by noting that the TU-144 would make it possible to celebrate New Year's in both Khabarovsk and Moscow. But that problem already appears to be solved.

"We start greeting the New Year when it arrives in Chukotka three time zones away," a Khabarovsk resident said. "Then we celebrate our own New Year here at midnight. And when the Kremlin's chimes ring in the New Year in Moscow, it is 7 A.M. here and we are still celebrating."

November 25, 1975

# SOVIET DISCLOSES NEW 5-YEAR PLAN WITH LOWER GOAL

## Economic Growth Cut Back and Heavy Industry Is Favored Over Consumer

## VAST OUTLAY ON FARMS

By CHRISTOPHER S. WREN
Special to The New York Times

MOSCOW, Dec. 14—The Soviet Union today publicly outlined its new five-year plan, with more modest hopes for economic growth and a return to the traditional reliance on heavy industry.

The message inherent in the directives of the 1976-80 plan was that Moscow had scrapped for the rest of the decade its previous efforts to redirect the economy in favor of the long-neglected consumer. The leadership had promised to raise living standards substantially in the 1971-75 plan but acknowledged last year its failure to meet the ambitious targets.

Today's directives also tacitly confirmed earlier indications of a 1975 harvest disaster by hinting that the grain yield might be even slightly less than the 137 million tons extrapolated from an official speeech earlier this month. The report today said that the average harvest in the current five-year period would "exceed" 180 million tons; this suggested a figure of 133 million tons or more, taking into account the four earlier harvests.

### Farm Spending on the Rise

As part of its continuing battle against agricultural setbacks, Moscow announced in the plan that expenditures on agriculture would be increased nearly a third over the next five years, injecting new momentum into the drive for self-sufficiency that was started by the Soviet party leader, Leonid I. Brezhnev, just over a decade ago.

The proposed new rise of 35 to 39 percent in over-all industrial production was substantially less than the 43 percent achieved in the current five-year period, as well as the 47 percent originally planned.

The lower new target, which was generally reflected in other areas, pointed to a slowdown in economic growth as Soviet industry sought to trim its extensive capital investment in favor of getting more quality and efficiency on the job. The directives, in setting growth of 30 to 34 percent in industrial labor productivity, looked for this to be a major source of growth in both industry and agriculture.

With the over-all goals set at a more realistic level, it seemed less likely that Moscow would have to scale its new plan downward as it did in the current period after the 1972 harvest failure.

Elsewhere, in the critical energy field, Moscow signaled a slight policy shift by emphasizing increased production of coal and building of more nuclear power stations to conserve on domestic demands for oil and natural gas.

Since oil is the Soviet Union's largest earner of foreign currency, which has reportedly been hit hard by purchases of Western technology and grain, it appeared that Moscow intended to hold back on the use of oil and gas at home in order to be able to sell more abroad. The new plan called for an increase of 25 to 30 percent in oil production, with a planned yield of 620 to 640 million tons by 1980. This year's output is expected to be about 490 million tons.

The economic blueprint also proposed that the extraction of natural gas, another hard-currency earner, be increased to 400 billion to 435 billion cubic meters, with nearly 22,000 miles of gas pipeline put into operation by 1980.

### 6 Pages in Pravda

The draft outline of the new plan covered six pages in Pravda and other principal newspapers today. It was issued by the Communist Party's central committee but signed, as in 1971, by Mr. Brezhnev, underscoring his continuing leadership of the Politburo.

The 1976-80 plan was arrived at after months of closed economic study and debate within the Soviet bureaucracy and will be discussed further in the Soviet press before it is fine-tuned and formally adopted at the 25th Party congress in February.

Briefly, it represents the basic working document of the state-controlled economy, setting forth priorities for expenditure and development as well as the return anticipated over a five-year period. The details extend to science, education and social welfare and the plan itself is studied by Western analysts to determine trends on such matters as defense or energy. The current plan suggested that both would continue to receive strong support.

The document stated: "The main task of the 10th five-year plan is consistent implementation of the Communist Party's course for raising the material and cultural standards of the people on the basis of dynamic and well-balanced development of social production and raising its efficiency, accelerated scientific-technical progress, higher labor productivity and an all-out effort to improve quality of work at all levels of the national economy."

The Soviet press gave prominent attention to this passage, apparently to reassure citizens of the Government's continuing concern for their welfare. The plan itself promised that prices would generally remain stable, while industrial and office salaries rose 16 to 18 percent to reach an average 170 rubles a month, roughly the equivalent of $225, at the end of five years. Incomes of collective farmers, who earn considerably less, are scheduled to rise 24 to 27 percent though no precise figures were given.

But in calling for a rise in production of up to 39 percent, the draft plan reported that the heavy industry sector would rise only 26 percent.

At the same time, the plan said that production of consumer goods would rise 30 to 32 percent. The somewhat higher figure is believed to reflect foodstuffs and consumer durable items produced as a sideline at many heavy industrial enterprises.

By contrast, the 1971-75 plan sought to reverse traditional priorities and give the consumer sector a faster rate of growth. But last December, Nikolai K. Baibakov, who heads the state planning organization Gosplan, said that the consumer targets had proven unreachable.

It was not known why Moscow was unwilling to try again, though perhaps its resources were stretched by this year's harvest disaster and by such perennial industrial problems as lagging in the building of new factories. The directive today conceded that some goals in the concluding five-year plan "have not been met in full."

The new plan called for an annual increase of 14 to 17 percent in agricultural output and stressed that "the most important task is the utmost raising of grain production." It said that average yearly grain yields should rise to 215 or 220 million tons, which approaches the 222.5-million-ton record crop in 1973.

### Outlay for Agriculture

It reported that the equivalent of about $225 billion, the bulk of it capital investment by the state, would be plowed into agriculture over the next five years, largely to improve land and modernize machinery and technology. The push seems likely to be focused on the European part of the Soviet Union, where a campaign has already been announced to upgrade the regions where the soil is less rich.

It was also announced that growth of industry in the European part of the country would be accomplished by re-equipping and modernizing existing facilities, a cheaper process than building new ones. It was indicated that construction of new energy-intensive and water-intensive industries would be restricted to Siberia and the Far East.

The plan envisioned an increase of coal production to 790 million or 810 million tons by 1980 to meet rising energy needs. The plan set a target of 1.34 trillion kilowatts to be generated by 1980. Of 67 million to 70 million kilowatts in new capacities, it said, a fifth would come from nuclear power through the increased building of atomic power stations, including fast breeder reactors.

The volume of foreign trade is expected to grow 30 to 35 percent by 1980, the draft plan reported.

December 15, 1975

# SOVIET CONFIRMS POOR '75 HARVEST, LOWEST IN DECADE

## Year-End Report Reveals Failure to Meet Several Five-Year-Plan Goals

## CONSUMER GOODS LAG

## Grain Crop, Which Required Large Purchases Abroad, Put at 140 Million Tons

By DAVID K. SHIPLER
Special to The New York Times

MOSCOW, Jan. 31 — The Soviet Union today issued its final economic figures for 1975, confirming earlier estimates of a serious decline in agricultural output and revealing a failure to meet many of the goals of the last five-year plan.

Today's statistics completed the economic picture for the last five years, showing steady growth in most key sectors except agriculture. But the rates of increase in most cases did not keep pace with the targets of the original plan for 1971-75.

Planners' priorities for consumer goods were not realized, and contrary to the objectives put forth five years ago, heavy industry continued to grow more quickly than consumer goods production.

**Downturn in Farming**

The most dramatic failure was agriculture, which dropped in output by 6 percent below 1974, which in turn was 3.7 percent below the extremely good year of 1973.

Most of the 1975 farm setback was attributable to the bad grain harvest, which today's figures put at 140 million tons, 3 million tons above estimates of December, but still less than two-thirds of the planned 215.7 million tons. It was the worst grain harvest in a decade.

The grain failure has forced the Soviet Union to buy about 25 million tons abroad, mostly from the United States, Canada and Australia, and to cut the size of livestock herds by increased slaughtering. The statistical report, using a phrase that appears annually, blamed "unfavorable weather." The Soviet press has also blamed the poor quality of farm machinery, a lack of spare parts and other managerial problems.

The figures show that labor productivity, a key element of industrial growth, grew by 5.9 percent last year, down from 6.5 percent in 1974. Over-all industrial output was up by 7.5 percent compared with an 8 percent increase the previous year.

The report compared this with a planned increase of 6.7 percent, but did not mention that the goal had been revised downward. The original five-year plan called for industrial growth of 42 to 46 percent while the actual growth over the five years was 37.2 percent.

Under the five-year plan, heavy industry was scheduled to grow by 41 to 45 percent and consumer goods by 44 to 48 percent. The actual growth rates were 38.9 percent for heavy industry and 33.5 percent for consumer goods. The production in both categories rose more slowly in 1975 than during the previous. year.

This slowdown has not surprised Western analysts, who noted at the beginning of the five-year period that to increase production, Moscow was planning to rely more heavily than in the past on increasing the efficiency of the labor force, and less on increasing the number of workers or the input of capital. Evidently, the efficiency did not improve as much as the planners had hoped.

The 1975 figures showed strong increases in the traditional, key indices of primary industry.

**Leading Oil Producers**

The Soviet Union remained the world's leading producer of oil, extracting 491 million tons last year, a substantial increase over the 459 million tons of the previous year and a 32 per cent growth from 1971. The five-year plan goal of oil production was 480 to 500 million tons by 1975.

Similarly, electric power output exceeded one trillion kilowatt-hours last year, meeting the plan's target and representing a 30 percent rise over 1971. Some 289 billion cubic meters of natural gas was produced, 36 percent above the 1971 figure, but short of the goal of 300 to 320 billion.

The goal for steel production was nearly met—141 million tons in 1975 compared with the target of 142 to 150 million tons.

Individual consumer items showed less growth, and in some cases decline. The production of new housing remained approximately steady during the five-year period, hovering between 2.2 and 2.3 million units a year.

The output of fabrics grew slightly, but ready-made clothing rose by a bare 11 percent from 1971, leather footwear by only 2.7 percent, refrigerators by 21.7 percent and television sets by 20.6 percent.

The production of radios fell last year, to 8.4 million units, from 8.8 million the year before. And butter production was less—1.2 million tons compared with 1.26 million in 1974.

The figures, issued by the Soviet Union's Central Statistical Board, showed an average industrial wage of 146 rubles ($193). This compared with 141 rubles the previous year and 126 rubles in 1971.

Per capita income, the report said, rose by 4.2 percent year, and by a total of 21.6 percent over the five years, considerably less than the 30 percent originally planned.

February 1, 1976

# *Moscow Will Slow Industry Expansion Following Setbacks*

By DAVID K. SHIPLER
Special to The New York Times

MOSCOW, Dec. 14—The Soviet Union announced plans today for low growth rates in key sectors of its economy during 1978, including the smallest increase in heavy industrial production since World War II.

In a fairly gloomy speech filled with criticism of poor performance, Nikolai K. Baibakov, the economic planning chief, listed goals that will virtually level off steel output, breaking a pattern of the last 30 years. A slowdown in growth was also forecast for consumer goods.

A reduction of growth was also evident in energy. Now the world's largest oil producer, the Soviet Union plans a yield next year of 575 million metric tons, the equivalent of 11.5 million barrels a day, up from the 1977 goal of 550 million tons. This is not enough to keep up with the five-year plan, which calls for an annual increase of 30 million tons from 1976 to 1980.

**Brezhnev Absent From Session**

Natural gas production is to rise from 12,000 billion cubic feet planned for this year to 13,000 billion in 1978. About 746 million tons of coal is to be mined next year, compared with 711.5 million in 1976.

Mr. Baibakov spoke in the Supreme Soviet, the nominal parliament, which is to approve the economic plan and the 1978 budget this week. Leonid I. Brezhnev, the Soviet leader, was not at the session, which was held in the Great Kremlin Palace. No explanation was given for his absence.

Vasily F. Garbuzov, the Finance Minister, in outlining the 1978 budget, said defense spending would be 17.2 billion rubles ($23.7 billion), the same as this year. The published defense figure is regarded by Western experts as indicative of climate rather than of actual spending, which the United States Defense Intelligence Agency recently put at the equivalent of $118 billion, compared with American spending of $84 billion.

The low economic goals make it likely that the Soviet Union will fall short of its five-year plan, which envisions a 36 percent industrial growth from 1976 to 1980. The planned growth for next year is 4.5 percent compared with a 1977 plan of 5.6 percent.

The 1978 goal for growth in heavy industry is set at 4.7 percent, the lowest since the war. The consumer sector, including light manufacturing and food processing, is to grow at 3.7 percent, with 4.3 percent in light manufacturing and 3.2 percent in the food industry.

Although no reason was given for the low gain in heavy industry—especially in steel, which is to go from this year's planned 152.3 million tons to 152.6 million tons in 1978—Marshall I. Goldman, a visiting economics professor from Wellesley and a specialist on the Soviet economy, said he thought it was due in large measure to an energy squeeze.

The Russians must export oil, he said, to supply their allies in Eastern Europe and to earn hard currency in the West. Since even their growing oil production is inadequate to meet both export requirements and expanding consumption, Professor Goldman said, the Russians have chosen to hold down domestic consumption. This rose by only 2.9 percent in 1976 compared with 5.7 percent the previous year, he said.

"The Soviets aren't having recession," Professor Goldman observed, "nothing close or comparable to that." But he said the low growth of oil production was bound to have an impact on the domestic economy just as it has in the United States.

Other impediments to economic growth, mentioned by Professor Goldman, Mr. Baibakov and the official press in recent weeks, include construction delays, transportation deficiencies and the counterproductive nature of incentives and bonuses that are supposed to induce factories and workers to do more faster, but often have the opposite effect.

Furthermore, the low anticipated increase in the food sector is partly the result of a bad grain harvest this year of 195.5 million tons—a revised figure given today by Mr. Garbuzov, the Finance Minister — compared with last year's record of 224 million tons.

Dale Hathaway, a United States Assistant Secretary of Agriculture, said at a news conference that the Russians had indicated that they would buy "substantially more than 8 million tons" of American grain in the year running from October 1977 to October 1978, but not more than 15 million tons.

According to Mr. Baibakov, the average monthly industrial and office wage will rise to 159 rubles ($219) by the end of 1978, compared with 155 rubles at present. The average farm wage is to go to 107 rubles a month, or $145.

December 15, 1977

# *New Rail Project Dramatizes Soviet Power*

**By DAVID K. SHIPLER**

**Special to The New York Times**

BAIKAL TUNNEL, U.S.S.R.—Beneath the remote, forested mountains of Siberia, small teams of tunnelers work in dim light against a gray face of granite.

In rough clothes the color of stone, they melt into the subterranean dusk, their chalky faces and plastic construction helmets bobbing, weaving as they heave jagged rocks broken by the last blast of dynamite, their shouts rising above the roar and whine of compressors and drills like the shouts of men in a storm.

This will be a four-mile railroad tunnel, the second longest of seven tunnels in the most difficult stretch of what the Russians call "the construction project of the century"—a 2,000-mile railroad across the sparsely populated wilds of Siberia to the Pacific.

**Antidote to a Stereotype**

It is a dramatic illustration of the immense power of the Soviet Union's economy and political system to focus huge resources on a single effort, to invest enormous labor and capital in a formidable task that will produce substantial returns no earlier than a decade from now.

The project is an important antidote to the Western stereotype of a Soviet economy muddled with bumbling performance, shoddiness and waste. That is a valid image as far as it goes, but overlooks the Russians' passion for bigness and their ability to overcome inefficiency by the sheer size of a commitment.

**Seven Mountains to Cross**

The new line has seven mountain ridges to cross and miles of untracked forest to penetrate. It will require 3,700 bridges and culverts, 200 stations and sidings (including 64 urban settlements), 70 million square feet of housing and work space and a billion cubic feet of earth-moving.

Paralleling the famous Trans-Siberian Railroad on the north, the new track, known as the Baikal-Amur Mainline, is designed to unlock some of the world's richest deposits of minerals and timber and to settle a frontier no less imposing than the American West of a century and a half ago.

According to geologists and other official sources, the region is estimated to have 17.5 billion cubic feet of timber growing in an area of 173 million acres, copper deposits totaling 1.2 billion tons, extensive coal basins, including one in South Yakutia with 500 billion tons, and deposits of iron ore, zinc, gold, nickel, tin, molybdenum, asbestos and various building materials.

"There is probably a lot more," a geologist said. "This area hasn't been studied very well." Much of the coal, originating at the northern end of a spur already completed, will be exported to Japan, and Japanese and American equipment is being used in the construction.

The new line, known by its acronym BAM, will also have military significance, providing an alternate east-west route to the Trans-Siberian, which lies closer to the Chinese border.

Army railroad troops are working on its eastern sections, said Nikolai I. Kryuchkov, the Communist Party secretary for Severobaikalsk District, where the tunnel is situated.

They are supplemented by highly skilled specialists such as the tunnel crews, who have come from building subways in Moscow, Leningrad and other cities, and by thousands of members of Komsomol, the Young Communist League, assigned to the project or drawn by extra pay and the romance of struggling against the elements. Dissidents in Moscow say prisoners are also used as forced labor on the line, but Mr. Kryuchkov denied it.

Official outlets, from television to pop music, have glorified BAM, surrounding its workers with an aura of heroism and patriotism as glamorous as any accorded frontline troops in wartime.

Most of those who began the construction in 1974 had to go to the sites by helicopter and live in tents. Then, as nearly 2,000 miles of rough roads were bulldozed through the forest, prefabricated vans were brought in for housing, log cabins were built and corrugated metal quonset huts were assembled, lined with wood-paneled interiors and used as schools, stores and community centers.

At Severobaikalsk, where nothing but forest existed three years ago, 8,500 people live in one-story wooden dormitories and apartment houses spread among the trees. The population is to reach 60,000 in the next few years as the town becomes a permanent city.

**Privileges for Tunnel Workers**

Up the road, a few miles from the eastern and western portals of the Baikal Tunnel, and at other sites, smaller temporary settlements of wooden buildings have been placed neatly along the bumpy bulldozer track. These house the tunnel workers, their wives and children.

Special efforts are reportedly made to keep the stores here steadily supplied with red meat, a scarcity in most of the country, and with fruit, milk and eggs brought in by air. As a result, the store at one remote workers' settlement near the tunnel's eastern end has gained the reputation of being a better place to shop than even the district seat at Nizhneangarsk, where local party officials and administrative personnel live.

Those who work here are paid 1.7

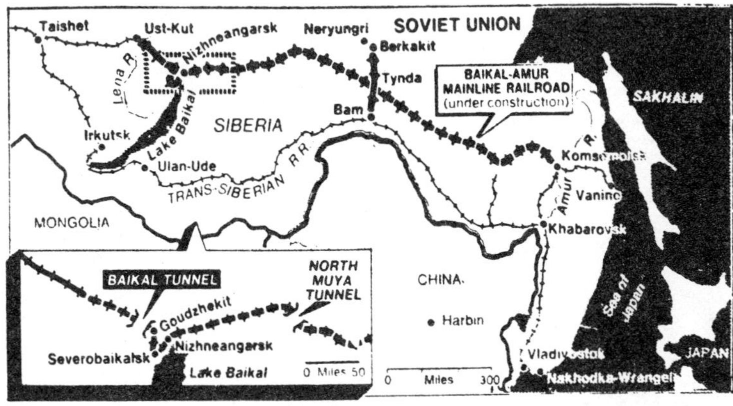


**The Baikal tunnel, which is to be four miles long, is being built as part of a new 2,000-mile rail line in Siberia.**

times the normal pay rate for their work plus an additional 10 percent for each year on the job up to five years. Twelve days a year are added to the normal vacations, and free tickets are given for trips to any place in the Soviet Union.

Anyone signing a three-year contract receives an immediate bonus equal to twice his pay for a month, and after the three years he has the right to buy a small Soviet-made car, for which there are normally long waiting lists.

Construction of the line has been complicated by severe weather and geography. The winters are long and harsh, with temperatures often dropping to 60 or 70 below, and the summers are hot and mosquito-ridden.

"The work is extremely difficult because of swamps, taiga and permafrost and high seismic conditions," Mr. Kryuchkov said.

**No Work at 49 Below**

When the temperature hits 49 below or lower, work is halted, and 12 or more days are lost each winter. Overall productivity, he said, drops by 25 percent in the winter months.

Because of the high probability of earthquakes in the Lake Baikal region, special reinforcement is required. And to avoid thawing the permafrost, which would cause buckling, roadbeds must be built high and rails insulated.

The completion date for the line is 1983, to be followed by two years of test runs. Commercial freight is to be shipped beginning in 1985, according to officials in Moscow.

As of now, 683 miles, or about one-third of the track, have been laid, mostly in the eastern section. The going is considerably slower in this western segment, known as "the barrier section" with its 18.1 miles of tunnels. A little over two-thirds of a mile of tunnel has been dug.

**Cost Put at $8 Billion**

"It is one-sixth of the length, but one-third of the cost," a construction official said of the western section. He put the total cost of the line at 6 billion rubles, or $8.46 billion. Some Western experts have projected the cost, including ancillary construction of roads and buildings, at $15 billion.

One problem here is that the tunnel-building delays the advance of new track, complicating transportation. Materials must be shipped by freight from Irkutsk up the 400-mile length of Lake Baikal, or by road, in the winter by an "ice road" on the frozen lake.

This has entailed a large investment in ships and port facilities, and the Communist Party newspaper Pravda has complained of bad coordination and snarled deliveries, which have cost time.

To ease transportation, planners have decided to build temporary rail by-passes around the Baikal tunnel, where 460 yards of its total 4.16 miles have been dug, and around four lakeside tunnels totalling 3.23 miles.

But Ivan A. Salopikin, chief of tunnel construction, said that rugged terrain made it impossible to do the same at the 9.5-mile tunnel through the North Muya Mountains, where construction has just begun. This means that operation of the full line will have to await the tunnel's completion.

"I want to thank all the American specialists who came here " Mr. Salopikin told an American correspondent, referring to the men from private concerns that sold equipment for the project.

He said that his General Motors, Caterpillar and Ingersoll-Rand machinery was working well. "It is very good equipment, and we are very happy with it," he said.

March 9, 1978

## SCIENTIFIC AND MEDICAL ACHIEVEMENTS

# SOVIET USES SCIENCES TO ADVANCE THE STATE

## Groups Those With Related Aims to Save Repetition, Making A System That May Prove Powerful—Striking Results of New Researches

By J. G. CROWTHER.

WILL Soviet Russia become not the richest but the most powerful country in the world within the next twenty years? A tour of the scientific institutions in Leningrad and Moscow inspires this question. It is impossible to visit many laboratories there without realizing that all scientific work in the Soviet Union is planned from above.

This planning of the whole of the nation's scientific work arises quite naturally from the fact that nearly all of the nation's wealth is owned by the State. The capital necessary for the foundation of scientific laboratories is owned by the State. Since the State has to pay for this institution and takes into consideration the condition of all institutions doing the same kind of work, it tends to group them together and see that each receives its fair share of the available money.

In American and Western European countries scientific institutions are not grouped and planned to work together by an all-powerful State authority; they tend to be independent and follow those lines of work in which they are interested, irrespective of whether other institutions are doing the same kind of work. This independence leads to repetition; half-a-dozen laboratories may all be trying to solve one problem in the same way, instead of tackling the problem in six different ways. In Russia the State-planning departments would try to re-arrange this and save the waste of repetition.

This State planning of scientific research may perhaps prove very powerful. After a number of years the Soviet may be able to organize the country and scientific research into one huge integrated unit. It may be that no one will become rich, but the whole country may make up by organization what it lacks in wealth. Marshal Foch said that morale is the most powerful factor in establishing a nation's might. It appears to me that the Soviet may produce by organization a very high morale, even if it does not produce great wealth.

**Generous to Science.**

Next to the all-embracing system of scientific research, the most noticeable thing to a visiting scientist is the astonishing sums the Soviet is spending on science. Soviet Russia is at present a poor country, but her expenditure in this direction compares favorably with that of rich countries such as America and Britain. She probably spends a much greater percentage of her surplus wealth on science than any other country. For instance, she spends $1,500,000 a year on research in applied botany. On seismology she is spending $250,000 next year. An experimental electrical laboratory in Moscow is being erected at a cost of $7,500,000. If Soviet Russia can make efforts such as these now, when the country is still very poor, what sort of efforts will she make when she becomes more prosperous?

The next point observed was that scientists have great prestige in Soviet Russia. They are better paid and more respected than nearly all other citizens. A good scientist receives about $2,500 a year. A very good one may receive $5,000. Some engineers receive as much as $17,500 a year. These salaries may appear small, but they are larger than those of other people. Business men usually receive less; in fact, there are very few business men in Russia. There are experts who run factories, but all factories are owned by the State.

The researches on applied botany are among the most remarkable in progress in Russia. As Russia is predominantly an agricultural country this is not unexpected. The department of applied botany organizes and plans the applied botanical research done everywhere in the country. For instance, the study of plant breeding is directed by Professor Vavilov. The whole world is ransacked for new specimens of wild oats and other cereals. A new specimen is discovered, say, by a Russian expedition in Abyssinia. It is brought back to Russia, and plants of the new species are sent to plant-breeding grounds in different parts of the Union.

In this way the reactions of a plant to a variety of environments are discovered. The plants grown in the different parts of Russia are then sent to Leningrad, where they are placed in a huge herbarium of cultivated plants. In this herbarium there are from 10,000 to 20,000 specimens of each of the chief cereals—oats, wheat and barley. Immense numbers of specimens of cabbages, peas, beans, fruits, &c., are also filed. In the station for the study of plant genetics at Detskoi Selo, formerly the Czar's villa near Leningrad, some extraordinary plant-breeding experiments are in progress.

**New Vegetables Produced.**

It will be remembered that plants of different species do not in general give fertile crosses, that is, the offspring of such crosses are sterile. Professor Vavilov's workers have produced fertile crosses between entirely different species; for instance, between the cabbage and the radish. This new plant is quite distinct and produces offspring like itself. An other plant crosses cabbage, radish and mustard. It also breeds true. So the Russian plant geneticists are inventing entirely new strains of vegetables.

Not only can they produce new species of plants, they can explain how they arise on the modern chromosome theories of heredity. They are much interested in plant physiology. Sometimes plants occur whose cells contain twice the normal number of chromosomes. When this occurs, the plant is often a giant, twice the normal size. It may also breed true. The Russian geneticists are trying to discover cabbages with double chromosome numbers so as to produce new species of cabbage double the normal size. This problem particularly interests the Russians, because the cabbage is used in many dishes, cabbage soup being a staple in Russian cookery.

In another palace at Detskoi Selo, once owned by Prince Yusupoff—in whose Leningrad palace Rasputin was murdered—there is a laboratory for testing the baking qualities of flour. Specimens of corn are sent there from all parts of the Union and milled into flour which is baked into loaves. In this way the food qualities of new races of wheat and corn can be studied and also the qualities of flour made from mixtures of various corns.

In the Biochemical Institute in Moscow experiments are being conducted on injections and immunity. It has been found that if eggs are injected at a certain spot with certain amino-acids, they hatch out large chickens which grow into giant fowls. If injected at another spot, the chickens are dwarf, and grow into dwarf fowls. The Soviet Department of Agriculture is endowing further research on this discovery. In the same institute an investigator has found that certain pure amino-acids when injected into an animal confer on it some degree of immunity from certain diseases.

**Work in Biophysics.**

Work is being done in biophysics. Professor Lasareff, who directs the Institute of Biophysics in Moscow, has worked out a mathematical theory of biological stimulation. When a piece of living matter, such as a finger or the eye, is stimulated, chemical changes occur in it. Now chemical changes do not happen anyhow. They proceed at rates governed by mathematical laws and the quantities and qualities of the substances engaged in the reaction. Professor Lasareff considers he has shown that the rate of change in living cells, after they have been stimulated, must follow certain mathematical laws. He can show further that the sensitivity of living matter must change according to its age.

On his theory, the brain of man is most sensitive at the age of about 21. It increases up to that age and then declines steadily until it is normally non-existent at 80 or 90 years of age. Now it is possible to measure by experiments on the eye and ear the sensitivity of those parts of the brain associated with these organs. Professor Lasareff states that these experiments have been made, and shows that the sensitivity of the brain normally changes, as his theory would indicate. In fact, by experiments on a healthy person's eye or ear he can deduce their age to within a year or two; he can detect persons who conceal their age.

But he finds, he says, that persons in ill health depart from the normal curve. If he is told a person's age and finds that his brain sensitivity does not correspond to his age, Lasareff can predict with some confidence that that person is ill, even if he shows no other symptoms. So he appears to have discovered an additional method of diagnosis. Professor Lasareff asserts that his results have been confirmed by direct experiment on brain centres during operations on the brains of living persons. Apart from the general level of sensitivity of the brain, there are various secondary changes in its sensitivity.

**Sensitivity of the Eye.**

For instance, the eye is most sensitive at about 2 A. M., and least at about 2 P. M. This is to be expected, since the exposure of the eye during the morning must fatigue it. He also finds that the brain-centres connected with the eyes in Indians are less sensitive than those in Russians, but if the Indian settles in Russia, the sensitivity of his brain centres gradually rises to the Russian level. This obviously would appear to be connected with the fact that the sun's glare in India is much greater than in Russia.

To turn to the physical sciences. Russia has always been eminent in the study of earthquakes. One of the pioneers of this subject was Prince Galitzin, and his successors are carrying on his work energetically. Until recently, seismology was only one of the subsections of the mathematical and physical department of the Academy of Sciences. Now it has been given a special department of its own and a new institute is being built for it. The work is directed by Professor Nikiforoff. The activity in seismology considerably surprised me. Why should Bolshevik Russia spend money on earthquake study when there are so many other things to be done?

This question leads immediately to the five-year industrialization plan. The rulers of Russia are trying to carry out the first instalment of the industrialization of Russia during the passing five years. The study of mining is becoming important. Seismology now has considerable importance in mineral prospecting. The Soviet desires to prospect Russia thoroughly. So the seismological department receives money to research on apparatus for mining prospecting. They have already invented and manufactured improved field seismographs and Etvos balances.

The latter are used for detecting local changes in the strength of gravity. When there are deposits of certain minerals in any district, the value of gravity, i. e., the weight of a pound, departs from the normal. These sensitive instruments can detect very slight changes in the weight of a pound, and hence the presence of the minerals.

Another seismological study of importance is concerned with the effect of vibrations on buildings. The vibrations caused by heavy traffic are like tiny earthquakes. This research provides data which help to design buildings immune from the disintegrating effects of earthquakes and heavy traffic. Models of buildings and embankments are mounted on platforms caused to tremble as if they were having earthquakes. The effects of the tremblings can be measured experimentally, then the theory of them can be worked out and applied to buildings to be erected in earthquake zones.

Earthquake waves are utilized in warfare. When a gun is fired, it gives a shock to the ground which travels as a small earthquake. If the time the shock takes to reach two observation stations is measured, it is easy to calculate how far the waves have traveled and hence the whereabouts of the gun. The development of instruments for this purpose is the job of one subsection of the seismological department.

**Electrical Development.**

Perhaps the most remarkable of the new Russian scientific developments are those in electrical engineering. The Soviet is building many large hydroelectric plants in various parts of Russia, in the mountains of the Caucasus and on the rapids of the great rivers. The river Dneiper rapids are being harnessed to a 700,000 horsepower hydroelectric plant now under construction. In light engineering, the telephone and radio are being rapidly developed. This extension of electrical service is creating a demand for electrical engineers, and laboratories where electrical engineering problems can be studied.

The Soviet Government has met the demand. It is building a vast experimental institute in Moscow in which all the main branches of electrical engineering—dynamos, radio, telephones, X-ray apparatus—can be studied and tested. The first installation is costing $7,500,000. There is an immense laboratory for a 1,500,-000-volt transformer. This apparatus will be used for studying the properties of the insulators used in the transmission lines which will spread the electricity generated in the new power plants to the surrounding districts.

December 29, 1929

# SOVIET FIRES EARTH SATELLITE INTO SPACE; IT IS CIRCLING THE GLOBE AT 18,000 M. P. H.; SPHERE TRACKED IN 4 CROSSINGS OVER U. S.

## 560 MILES HIGH

By **WILLIAM J. JORDEN**

Special to The New York Times.

MOSCOW, Saturday, Oct. 5— The Soviet Union announced this morning that it successfully launched a man-made earth satellite into space yesterday.

The Russians calculated the satellite's orbit at a maximum of 560 miles above the earth and its speed at 18,000 miles an hour.

The official Soviet news agency Tass said the artificial moon, with a diameter of twenty-two inches and a weight of 184 pounds, was circling the earth once every hour and thirty-five minutes. This means more than fifteen times a day.

Two radio transmitters, Tass said, are sending signals continuously on frequencies of 20.005 and 40.002 megacycles. These signals were said to be strong enough to be picked up by amateur radio operators. The trajectory of the satellite is being tracked by numerous scientific stations.

**Due Over Moscow Today**

Tass said the satellite was moving at an angle of 65 degrees to the equatorial plane and would pass over the Moscow area twice today.

"Its flight," the announcement added, "will be observed in the rays of the rising and setting sun with the aid of the simplest optical instruments, such as binoculars and spyglasses."

The Soviet Union said the world's first satellite was "successfully launched" yesterday. Thus it asserted that it had put a scientific instrument into space before the United States. Washington has disclosed plans to launch a satellite next spring. Oct. 4."

The Moscow announcement said the Soviet Union planned to send up more and bigger and heavier artificial satellites during the current International Geophysical Year, an eighteen-month period of study of the earth, its crust and the space surrounding it.

The rocket that carried the satellite into space left the earth at a rate of five miles a second, the Tass announcement said. Nothing was revealed, however, concerning the material of which the man-made moon was constructed or the site in the Soviet Union where the sphere was launched.

The Soviet Union said its sphere circling the earth had opened the way to interplanetary travel.

It did not pass up the opportunity to use the launching for propaganda purposes. It said in its announcement that people now could see how "the new socialist society" had turned the boldest dreams of mankind into reality.

Moscow said the satellite was the result of years of study and research on the part of Soviet scientists.

**Several Years of Study**

Tass said:

"For several years the research and experimental designing work has been under way in the Soviet Union to create artificial satellites of the earth. It has already been reported in the press that the launching of the earth satellites in the U. S. S. R. had been planned in accordance with the program of International Geophysical Year research.

"As a result of intensive work by the research institutes and design bureaus, the first artificial earth satellite in the world has now been created. This first satellite was successfully launched in the U. S. S. R. October four."

The Soviet announcement said that as a result of the tremendous speed at which the satellite was moving it would burn up as soon as it reached the denser layers of the atmosphere. It gave no indication how soon that would be.

Military experts have said that the satellites would have no practicable military application in the foreseeable future. They said, however, that study of such satellites could provide valuable information that might be applied to flight studies for intercontinental ballistic missiles.

The satellites could not be used to drop atomic or hydrogen bombs or anything else on the earth, scientists have said. Nor could they be used in connection with the proposed plan for aerial inspection of military forces around the world.

**An Aid to Scientists**

Their real significance would be in providing scientists with important new information concerning the nature of the sun, cosmic radiation, solar radio interference and static-producing phenomena radiating from the north and south magnetic poles. All this information would be of inestimable value for those who are working on the problem of sending missiles and eventually men into the vast reaches of the solar system.

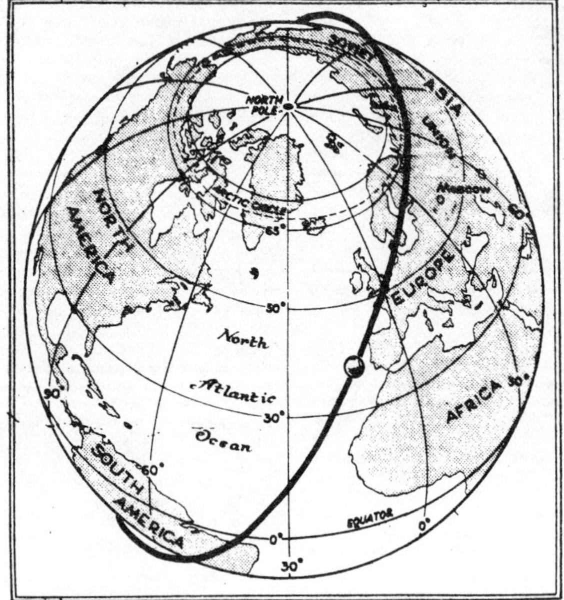


The New York Times Oct. 5, 1957

**The approximate orbit of the Russian earth satellite is shown by black line. The rotation of the earth will bring the United States under the orbit of Soviet-made moon.**

Publicly, Soviet scientists have approached the launching of the satellite with modesty and caution. On the advent of the International Geophysical Year last June they specifically disclaimed a desire to "race" the United States into the atmosphere with the little sphere.

The scientists spoke understandingly of "difficulties" they had heard described by their American counterparts. They refused several invitations to give any details about their own problems in designing the satellite and gave even less information than had been generally published about their work in the Soviet press.

**Hinted of Launching**

Concerning the launching of their first satellite, they said only that it would come "before the end of the geophysical year"—by the end of 1958.

Several weeks earlier, however, in a guarded interview given only to the Soviet press, Alexander N. Nesmeyanov, head of the Soviet Academy of Science, dropped a hint that the first launching would occur "within the next few months."

But generally Soviet scientists consistently refused to boast about their project or to give the public or other scientists much information about their progress. Key essentials concerning the design of their satellites, their planned altitude, speed and instruments to be carried in the small sphere, were carefully guarded secrets.

October 5, 1957

# SOVIET ORBITS MAN AND RECOVERS HIM

## 187-MILE HEIGHT

## Yuri Gagarin, a Major, Makes the Flight in 5-Ton Vehicle

By United Press International.

MOSCOW, Wednesday, April 12—The Soviet Union announced today it had won the race to put a man into space. The official press agency, Tass, said a man had orbited the earth in a spaceship and had been brought back alive and safe.

A brief announcement said the first reported space man had landed in what was described as the "prescribed area" of the Soviet Union after a historic flight.

A Moscow radio announcer broke into a program and said in emotional tones:

"Russia has successfully launched a man into space. His name is Yuri Gagarin. He was launched in a sputnik named Vostok, which means "East."

**Reports on Landing**

Tass said that, on landing, Major Gagarin said: "Please report to the party and Government, and personally to Nikita Sergyevich Khrushchev, that the landing was normal, I feel well, have no injuries or bruises."

He landed at 10:55 A. M. Moscow time [2:55 A. M. New York time].

Earlier, the major reported: "Flight is proceeding normally, I feel well."

After orbiting the earth the major applied a braking device, and the vehicle space landed in the Soviet Union, Tass said.

Major Gagarin, 27 years old, is an industrial technician, and married. He was reported to have received pre-flight training similar to that of the astronauts who will man the United States' first space ships.

**Soared to 187 Miles**

The announcer said the Sputnik reached a minimum altitude of 175 kilometers (109½ miles) and a maximum altitude of 302 kilometers (187¾ miles).

He said the weight of the Sputnik was 10,395 pounds, or slightly over five tons.

The announcement of the launching came at 2 A. M. New York time.

It said everything functioned normally during the flight.

Constant radio contact was maintained between earth and the sputnik, the Moscow radio said.

The announcer said the duration of each revolution around the earth was 89.1 minutes.

The title of the announcement was "The First Human Flight into the Cosmos."

The radio, which was quoting a Tass press agency statement on the launching, said that Maj. Gagarin "is feeling well" and

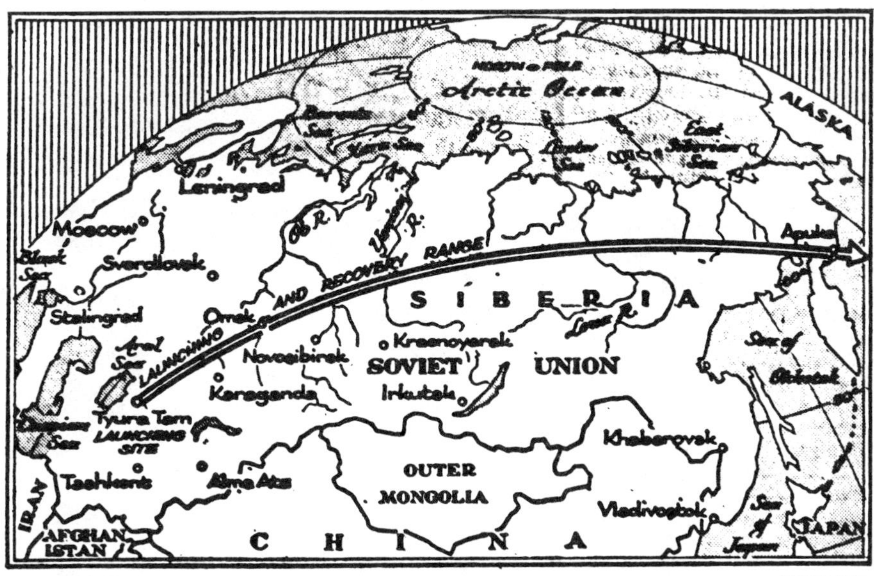


The New York Times April 12, 1961

**PROBABLE TRACK: Reported path of astronaut's flight from launch site at Tyura Tam.**

that "conditions in the cabin are normal."

As soon as the Moscow announcement was made, Russians began to telephone congratulations to each other.

The first astronaut is a major in the Soviet Air Force and is believed to be a test pilot.

The Tass announcement said that the launching of the multi-stage space rocket, which carried the Sputnik into orbit, was successful.

After attaining the first escape velocity, it said, and the separation of the last stage of the carrier rocket, the space ship went into free flight on a round-the-earth orbit.

Reports of the launching of a Soviet space man had been reported repeatedly in Moscow for the last twenty-four hours.

The London Daily Worker and other sources had said the Soviet Union had sent a man into space last Friday and had brought him back alive.

Many persons in Moscow were convinced after today's announcement that another flight into space was attempted on Friday and there was speculation that something might have gone wrong.

The announcement of the first flight into space was repeated three times, after which the normal radio program of music was resumed.

The radio also broadcast patriotic songs.

The announcement said the condition of the navigator was being observed by means of radio telemetering devices and television.

Major Gagarin, the announcement went on, withstood satisfactorily the placing of the satellite ship into orbit.

April 12, 1959

# SOVIET ROCKET HITS MOON AFTER 35 HOURS; ARRIVAL IS CALCULATED WITHIN 84 SECONDS; SIGNALS RECEIVED TILL MOMENT OF IMPACT

## FLAGS IN VEHICLE

### Sphere Rams Surface at 7,500 M.P.H.— Moscow Jubilant

By MAX FRANKEL

Special to The New York Times.

MOSCOW, Monday, Sept. 14 —The Soviet Union hit the moon with a space rocket early this morning.

The first object sent by man from one cosmic body to another bore pennants and the hammer-and-sickle emblem of the Soviet Government.

The announcement said steps had been taken to prevent the destruction of the pennants by the impact.

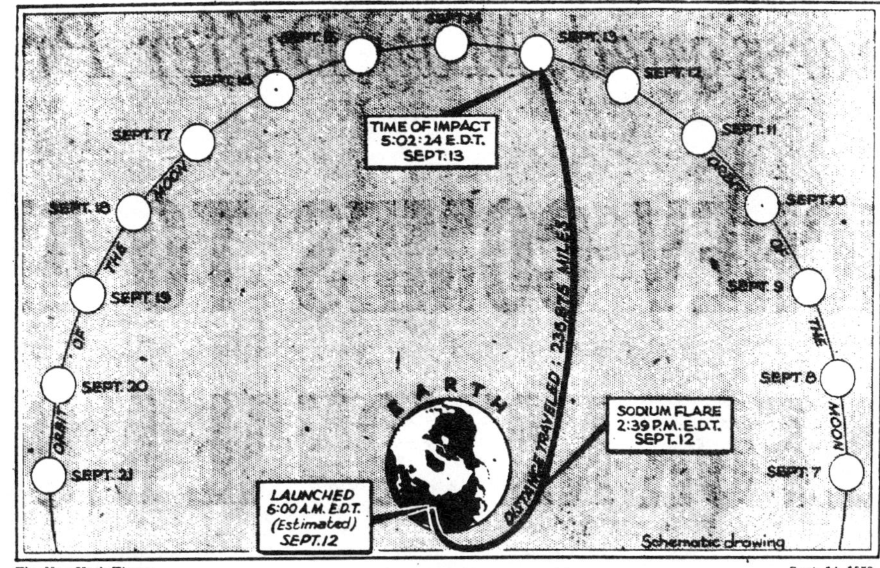


The New York Times Sept. 14, 1959

PATH TO THE MOON: Solid line shows path traveled by the Soviet rocket to the moon.

The object was a sphere of unknown size weighing 858.4 pounds. It crashed into the moon at a speed of about 7,500 miles an hour at 2 minutes and 24 seconds after midnight Moscow time. This was 5:02:24 P. M. Sunday in New York.

The time of impact was only 84 seconds later than Soviet scientists had predicted.

The success of the Soviet's moon shot was made known in a jubilant Government announcement at 35 minutes after midnight over the Moscow radio.

The sphere was a hermetically sealed instrument container that had been ejected from the last stage of a multi-stage rocket.

The rocket was launched from Soviet territory at about one o'clock Saturday afternoon Moscow time (6 A. M. in New York).

The container covered a distance of 236,875 miles in about 35 hours.

The New York Times

Sept. 14, 1959

**AREA OF IMPACT:** Cross near right center shows area where Soviet rocket hit surface of moon. Photograph is a composite picture of face of moon taken by camera of Lick Observatory near San José, Calif. Labeled are craters such as Copernicus at left center and three seas in area of the landing, Tranquillity, Serenity and Vapors.

The impact was not visible from the earth, but the strike was signaled by the sudden end to radio transmissions that were being received here from the container during its space voyage.

[Jodrell Bank in England reported that it had received the signals up to the time the rocket hit the moon.]

The sphere was able to reach the moon's surface because there is little or no atmosphere that would produce friction and burn it up.

It is not known whether it shattered on impact or penetrated the dust that is thought to blanket much of the moon's surface.

Soviet scientists had estimated before the final announcement that the container would hit at a point about 270 miles from the center of the face among three large depressions in the moon's surface known as the Seas of Tranquillity, Serenity and Vapors.

There was no word here on the fate of the last stage of the rocket, which had been flying in space near the container. The container was separated from the rocket segment after they had safely escaped from the earth's gravitational pull in the first hour of flight on Saturday.

The rocket section, which weighed 3,324 pounds without fuel, had been described here as "guided." One scientist said that Soviet experts thus had had "the possibility of correcting its flight."

But there was no official word on whether this actually had been done or how it was to have been done.

The rocket and the container flew at slightly different speeds and in slightly different trajectories toward the moon, according to bulletins issued here yesterday evening.

The rocket, it was disclosed, carried its own radio transmitter. But signals from it, on two frequencies, were reported getting steadily weaker five hours before the moon strike.

Soviet scientists took special measures before the launching to prevent the sphere from contaminating the moon's surface with terrestrial micro-organisms. They did not describe the measures.

**Urged by Scientist**

Such precautions have been urged repeatedly by scientists so that future studies of the moon will not be thrown off by elements that might have been imported from the earth.

The announcement this morning said special but unspecified measures also had been taken to "preserve" the pennant carried by the container, which bore the inscriptions "Salute to the Union of Soviet Socialist Republics" on one side and the Soviet insignia of a hammer and sickle inside a garland and "September 1959" on the other.

A somber-voiced announcer for the Moscow radio shouted the word "Attention" at thirty-five minutes after midnight, interrupting a program of classical music.

"Moscow speaking," he said and proceeded to read a bulletin from Tass, the official Soviet press agency.

It said the container had made history's first flight from the earth to another cosmic body. The moon strike was an outstanding achievement of Soviet science and engineering and had opened a new page in space research, the announcement added.

The bulletin was read three times. A scientific worker then vaguely described the importance of preventing micro-organisms from the earth from reaching the moon and the program of classical music was resumed.

The moment of impact with the moon was 2 minutes and 30 seconds earlier than Soviet scientists had predicted on Saturday shortly after the rocket was launched.

At 7 P.M. yesterday, five hours before the strike, they forecast the impact for one minute after midnight. This turned out to be a minute and twenty-four seconds too soon.

These projections as well as the entire moon shot operation were evidence of the high degree of accuracy achieved by Soviet rocket experts.

As one scientist pointed out here this morning, the moon shot required infinite care. Although the moon is 2,160 miles in diameter the problem of hitting it with a rocket is equivalent to firing from a moving and rotating platform, the earth, at a moving target, the moon.

The Soviet press and proclamations issued both at home and for abroad were quick to restate the claim of superiority for Soviet science and by extension the superiority of the Communist system that has supported it.

**U. S. Failures Recalled**

Some statements also compared the Soviet achievement to last year's moon-shot failures in the United States. Still other commentators contended that the Soviet feat was made possible by rocket fuels and equipment superior to those of the United States.

But most of all, Soviet propaganda seized upon the event as being of special significance to the forthcoming Eisenhower-Khrushchev talks. The Soviet leader will arrive in Washington tomorrow at the dramatic height of world attention to the Soviet moon strike.

The Premier is certain to offer the event as proof of Soviet might, skill and determination to surpass the United States in all other fields of production and technology.

A few minutes before the container struck the moon a special altimeter went into operation inside the sphere. It radioed back data on the angle and speed of approach to the moon, providing a kind of countdown to the moment of impact.

**Altimeter Data Sent**

Signals from the altimeter were transmitted on a frequency of 183.6 megacycles from one of two radio transmitters in the container.

A second radio also was working well on a frequency of 39.986 megacycles but the impulses it sent on the frequency of 19.993 had become considerably weakened five hours before the impact.

Reception from the radio aboard the last stage of the rocket also had weakened by that time. Its frequencies were 20.003 and 19.997 megacycles.

The fact that one of the radios sent toward the moon was in the last stage of the rocket was made clear in communiqués here only last evening. It also had not been previously clear whether the instrument container was flying in front of or behind the last stage of the rocket.

All communiqués until last evening had spoken only of the rocket. When the final impact was predicted at 7 P. M. yesterday, scientists said they were really talking about the sphere carrying the instruments.

**No Photographs**

Thus far no pictures or detailed descriptions of either object have been released.

A cartoon in Izvestia pictured a round sphere flying ahead of a blunted rocket section. But the drawings in other papers portrayed pointed rockets streaking into the sky.

The only description of the instrument container offered here has been the statement that it carried pennants, the date of launching and the Soviet Union's insignia.

If it resembles the container sent past the moon by Soviet scientists last January—and apparently it does—then a photograph published by Pravda in January is the best image of the object available thus far.

If they are similar, then the container that struck the moon had a surface of pentagonal stainless steel plates, most of which bore inscriptions that read either "U.S.S.R. September 1959," or simply "U.S.S.R.," with an etching of the Soviet seal, a crosed hammer and sickle surounded by a garland.

**Had Inscribed Plate**

The final rocket stage of the January shot had also carried a plate reading "Union of Soviet Socialistic Republics" on one side and the seal and date on the other.

The pentagonal segments gave that instrument container the appearance of a seamed volleyball.

The container that hit the moon yesterday was hermetically sealed and filled with an unidentified gas.

The instruments inside were connected with the two radios. They gathered information on the magnetic field of the earth and whether the moon has a magnetic field, the belts of radiation around the earth, the intensity and variation of cosmic rays, the heavy nuclei of cosmic rays, the density of matter in space, and on the number of meteoric particles encountered.

Soviet scientists looked forward especially to the answer on the question of a magnetic field around the moon and on the moon's gravitational pull and therefore its mass.

A leading Soviet space expert, Yevgeni K. Fedorov, said the study of cosmic ray protons and of corpuscular radiation of the sun had been dropped after the January shot because they were of less interest now than radiation zones around the earth.

A study of the radiation belts is crucial to the working out of safety measures to protect future space travelers.

A number of writers in the Soviet press this morning said that it was now clear that the day was not far off when man could be flying toward the moon.

Mr. Fedorov, as well as several other top Soviet scientists, wrote in the newspapers that it was now "especially important to insure extensive international cooperation of scientists, especially the scientists of the Soviet Union and the United States."

There was some speculation here that Premier Khrushchev would bring to the United States some specific proposals for cooperation if not joint ventures into space.

The excitement over the Soviet achievement built up slowly on what was an unseasonably warm and sunny Sunday afternoon in Moscow.

The moon itself, which will be full on Thursday, was easily visible last evening through a partially cloudy sky over the capital.

But there were not many moon gazers in the streets at midnight. Several articles in the papers yesterday had indicated that the moon strike could not be seen from the earth.

Shortly after launching of the multistage rocket on Saturday its final stage achieved a speed of seven miles a second to escape the earth's gravitational pull.

Then the rocket and the container, which was separated from it, slowed down as they coasted toward the moon.

At 7 P. M. last night, Moscow time, they entered the gravitational field of the moon at a speed of 1.44 miles a second. As they approached the moon it exerted an increasing pull and their speed was 2.06 miles a second at the moment of impact.

**Log of Moon Trip**

The Soviet space vehicles were 95,000 miles from the earth at 10 P. M. Saturday, Moscow time (3 P. M. New York time). At 10 o'clock yesterday morning (3 A. M. in New York) they were 161,250 miles away and at 7 P. M. last night (noon Sunday in New York) they were

201,250 miles from the earth.

Soviet tracking of the last rocket stage was based on radio signals as well as direct observation at one short minute during the flight. This was made possible by the emission from the rocket of a bright yellow sodium cloud at 9:40 P. M. Saturday, Moscow time.

The cloud was not visible in Moscow because of overcast skies, but it was photographed by at least two Soviet observatories, in the Caucasus and in Uzbekistan in Central Asia.

September 14, 1959

*1917—The Russian Revolution—1967*

# Soviet Union's 'Academic Cities' Symbolize New Efforts in Scientific Research

By WALTER SULLIVAN

IN the 50th year of the Soviet state bulldozers are pushng through virgin forests of spruce and birch, clearing sites for "academic cities" in remote Siberia and in the depths of old Russia, symbolizing the new Soviet science.

The new cites, hacked out of the raw taiga, crammed with complex and exotic scientific equipment and staffed with young science sophisticates who love Western music and British detective stories, constitute the capitals of the Soviet "takeover" generation.

After 50 years of revolution, civil war, ideological struggle, global conflict, military devastation and Stalinism, Soviet scientists and their technological associates are moving to the helm of Soviet power.

In the academic cities ("akademgorodki") the shackles that Stalin fastened onto scientific inquiry have been struck off. Here some of the most far-out experiments in the world today are in process. Here the ancient heritage of ignorant, peasant Russia is being obliterated and the new Russia of the 21st century is being created.

The New York Times Oct. 16, 1967

**ACADEMIC CITIES: The rise of Soviet science parallels the growing number of scientific communities in the nation.**

### First Community Completed

The first of these communities near Novosibirsk in the heart of western Siberia has risen near a huge lake formed by damming the Ob River, which flows into the Arctic Ocean. The community is the kind of place in which a man from Cambridge (either England or Massachusetts) would feel at home. Or from Oak Ridge, Tenn., or the Brookhaven National Laboratory in the piney woods of Long Island for that matter.

The "akademgorodok" at Novosibirsk possesses a different atmosphere from the big academies and institutes of Moscow and Leningrad, close to the watchful eyes of the Communist party and the government hierarchy. The population in Siberia is young. It prides itself on its freedom. An American visitor to the Integral, a student club, confronts a bearded young man, guitar in his lap, strumming an American folk-rock song of protest. For a moment the visitor thinks he is back in Berkeley.

Scientifically the akademgorodok has stimulated new lines of experiment. Not the least notable is the remarkable nuclear research device, the Alice-in-Wonderland machine, being built at Novosibirsk by Gersh I. Budker.

If one man can be credited with originating the idea of the akademgorodok it is Mikhail A. Lavrentyev, an authority on complex variables in mathematics. Sitting in his office in Novosibirsk, Mr. Lavrentyev told how the center there had come into being.

From the days of Peter the Great, Russian science had evolved chiefly around St. Petersburg. When the capital shifted to Moscow after the Bolshevik Revolution, many insitutions and scientists followed the move. In some fields, such as mathematics, Soviet talent became as much concentrated in Moscow as French mathematics is centered in Paris.

### Decentralization Attempted

"There were attempts at decentralization here and in France," said Mr. Lavrentyev, "but they were small-scale and never came off. The best people always came back to Moscow or Paris. It is said that the first man sent to the moon should be a Muscovite, because then we can be sure he'll come back!

"What we needed, therefore, was a critical mass, so to speak. We had to get something going that was big enough and attractive enough to hold the best people. We looked around for good men with an entourage of young scientists who could not find a home in any Moscow institute.

"Ten and a half years ago I flew alone to Novosibirsk and Irkutsk. I spoke to the savants. It was obvious that our center should not be inside an industrial city. We wanted an attractive site, railroad connections, and plenty of electric power. Up the Ob River from Novosibirsk a big hydroelectric dam was being built.

"It would offer ample power and the dam was impounding what is now the Ob Sea [a lake 125 miles long set in low rolling country of heavy pine and birch]. Sobolev [Sergei L. Sobolev, a fellow mathematician] and I called on the Government with our scheme and won all-out backing for it."

In recent years Soviet education and research have been almost completely isolated from one another. Universities were for teaching, institutes were for research. There was little or no interchange of faculty or young researchers. Mr. Lavrentyev demanded a free hand to experiment in education and in organization.

Spartak T. Belyayev, the dynamic 43-year-old rector of Novosibirsk University, forming part of the akademgorodok complex, told this writer that of 80 or 90 professors on his faculty, only six were full-time men. The rest divide their time between the university and one of the many research institutes. The students spend much time in the institutes, helping in real research instead of dabbling in instructional laboratories.

"We have three tasks here of equal importance—un ménage à trois," said Mr. Lavrentyev, "education, research, and help to industry." Experimental factories have already been set up near other centers of research in cybernetics and automation, as in Kiev. Mr. Lavrentyev said he hoped the same could be done near his center. The evolving pattern is much like the cluster of electronics laboratories and research industry that has sprung up around the California Institute of Technology, Stanford University and the Massachusetts Institute of Technology.

### Recruiting Plan Described

Mr. Lavrentyev is proud of the recruiting program, called an Olympiad, that he has organized in Siberia, the best known of such programs in the Soviet Union. Each October, youth magazines, newspapers, and posters display a list of problems in mathematics, physics, and chemistry. Those who send in the best, most "original," answers are invited in the spring to visit one of 20 or 30 centers east of the Urals for interviews and examination.

About 700 students are chosen to spend the month of August at the akademgorodok. The way is paid to the campus. In the morning they hear lectures, take part in seminars, and visit the laboratories. In the afternoon they engage in sports, hike, or swim at the newly made beach on the Ob Sea, a few minutes from the campus.

Approximately 250 students are chosen from these and other candidates to take the intensive preparatory course at the Physical-Mathematical School on the campus.

The avenue of institutes at Novosibirsk is dominated by the Institute of Nuclear Physics. Other institutes deal with genetics, cytology and geology. Nearby is Mr. Lavrentyev's own Institute of Hydrodynamics, where work is being done, for example, on the use of computers to predict river floods.

One of the most important units is the Computing Center, headed by Guri I. Marchuk, a well-known specialist. The center performs two functions: it is a research institute and it serves as a "computing factory" for Siberian industry. The industrial work is done for a fee, which helps sustain the institute's budget.

The center is four years old, and its staff has grown to 400, including 30 "candidates" (equivalent to Americans with doctorates) and eight "doctors" (a higher academic rank with no American counterpart). There are five computers: three old-fashioned vacuum-tube types, the fourth a Minsk-22 with some semiconductors, and the fifth a BESM-6, the most advanced model now in general use in the Soviet Union.

Soviet specialists seem to agree with their American counterparts that Soviet computer technology is 5 to 10 years behind that of the United States. However, the Russians have a special mathematical genius (which helps to account for their leadership in chess), and they make good use of the machines they have.

Mr. Marchuk said his BESM-6 handles a million operations a second. This, he added, puts it between the 3600 and 6600 computers of the Control Data Corporation in the United States.

Because of Mr. Marchuk's interest in meteorology, one of the chief lines of research at the center is in numerical weather forecasting and analysis.

As observational techniques, with rockets, weather balloons, earth satellites and other devices, have improved, so have the chances that weather phenomena can be described, understood—and predicted.

The New York Times (by Walter Sullivan)

**DYNAMIC: Spartak T. Belyayev, 43, rector of the Novosibirsk University, a center in Siberia.**

The Novosibirsk center studies tornadoes and localized phenomena. It analyzes weather reports from 2,000 stations in an effort to produce three-day forecasts for the region from Moscow to Tokyo. Mr. Marchuk said his computer method had now been adopted by the central weather bureau in Moscow.

### Computer Analysis Done

The Novosibirsk center does computer analysis for other research institutes. It was trying to fit into a comprehensive picture the observations—magnetic, seismic, and gravitational—made by an expedition surveying the top three or four miles of the earth's crust in Kazakhstan. It was also developing methods for quantitative solution of catalysis problems in industrial chemistry, previously solved only qualitatively.

Industrial representatives are taught, at no cost, how to program problems themselves. The center charges for punching the business-machine cards as well as for time on the computers. So far there is no time-sharing system whereby other institutions, via a land line, can feed their problems into the computer. However, Mr. Marchuk said the BESM-6 could handle such traffic.

While the BESM-6 displayed the banks of flashing lights, spinning wheels of magnetic tape and neatly packaged electronic units typical of a modern computer, the electronic memory units not in current use were stored on the floor in rough wooden boxes. It is, of course, results and not frills that count, and memory stacks in wooden crates are not necessarily an index of competence.

Nevertheless, modern computers seem much scarcer in the Soviet Union than in the United States, particularly those used for research.

Mr. Lavrentyev spoke with pride of the way in which his academic city was being imitated in other parts of the Soviet Union and of plans for more centers in his own region. The Ukrainian Academy of Sciences has set one up at Donetsk, in the Donets Basin. Its university is two years old, and research institutes are being built.

### Earth Sciences Stressed

The akademgorodok across the Angara River from Irkutsk is in a region that is booming because of huge hydroelectric projects. The institutes of this center specialize in subjects that are closer to the earth than those of Novosibirsk: study of the earth's crust, geochemistry, the physiology and biochemistry of plants. The community is being built on the edge of the city's industrial belt and lacks the scenic beauty of Novosibirsk. The university at Irkutsk is slated to move to the new site, as is an institute of mining technology now in the city, but promoters of the new, young look in academic communities are confronted with the fact that the University of Irkutsk is old, set in its traditional ways and committed to a well-established hierarchy. The University of Novosibirsk was built from scratch.

Other science centers are projected for Omsk and Krasnoyarsk and there is talk of moving an oceanographic institute to Vladivostok on the Pacific coast. Mr. Lavrentyev spoke with special enthusiasm of plans for a new Akademgorodok at Shushenskoye, a village near the Mongolian border. It lies south of Abakan on the rushing Yenisei River. Lenin was exiled there as a young man and wrote that it was "not a bad place." Impounding of the river will furnish 6,000,000 kilowatts of power within a few years, and a new rail line to Taishet, on the Trans-Siberian Railway, provides a transport link.

### Centers Near Moscow Listed

A number of new science centers are within 70 miles of Moscow. They include:

¶Serpukhov, site of an atom smasher that promises to dominate the world's big machines for a number of years to come. It is designed to generate protons with 70 billion electron volts of energy. The machine is more than 1,000 yards in diameter.

¶Dubna, site of the Joint Institute for Nuclear Research operated on the banks of the Volga as an international center primarily for scientists from Soviet bloc countries.

¶Obninsk, home of research centers in radio biology, atomic reactor development, meteorology and seismology.

¶Pushchino, site of a new complex of biological research institutes.

¶Krasnaya Pakhra, long the seat of a research center in radio wave propagation, now being expanded to include institutes dealing with other aspects of earth physics.

¶Chernogolovka, site of the new Institute of Theoretical Physics that has attracted some of the Soviet Union's brightest young physicists. It is off limits to foreigners.

The new feelings of freedom are not limited to outlying centers. In the Moscow institutes, where pictures of Marx and Lenin seem to hang on every wall, one can also find a picture of John F. Kennedy tucked away in an inconspicuous corner. He is a hero because he is associated with a relaxation of international tensions that led to a loosening of restrictions at home.

The staff club of one Moscow institute is giving twist lessons (they have not yet come to the frug). A midnight stroller along the Neva River in Leningrad encountered a tight crowd of sailors, naval cadets and students around a guitar player. They were bobbing up and down singing in a strange tongue.

Closer listening revealed that the tongue was English. The words had been tape recorded from a foreign radio broadcast and then rerecorded on countless other tapes. It was one of the Beatle hits.

October 16, 1967

*1917—The Russian Revolution—1967*

# Soviet Genetics Reborn After Lysenko Period

**By WALTER SULLIVAN**

LAST spring a delegation from the National Academy of Sciences went to Moscow to present the Kimber Genetics Award to Nikolai V. Timofeyev-Ressovsky.

George B. Kistiakowsky, Harvard chemist, designer of the explosion that fired the first atomic bomb, former adviser to President Eisenhower and former member of the White Russian army, read the citation, a bouquet was thrust into Timofeyev-Ressovsky's arms and Nikolai N. Blokhin, president of the Soviet Academy of Medical Sciences, was about to end the ceremony when a woman pressed forward.

She had come up from Timofeyev-Ressovsky's institute, at near-by Obninsk, to witness the presentation and now she launched into a eulogy of the old geneticist, who left the Soviet Union in the nineteen-twenties to become a leading figure at the Max Planck Institute for Brain Research in Berlin. When the Red Army took Berlin he was arrested and sent to Siberia, but later he was rehabilitated.

### Tears Hidden Behind Champagne

Suddenly the Americans saw that tears were running down the cheeks of some of the Russians facing them. A tray of champagne glasses was brought in and the tears were quickly hidden behind the bubbling wine.

Why the tears? They were shed both for the personal tragedy of Timofeyev-Ressovsky and for the national tragedy of Soviet genetics. They were also tears of joy at the renaissance in the Soviet Union of this science, so vital to the relief of human suffering, to the conquest of cancer, to agriculture and to the future of the human race.

A one-month tour of Soviet laboratories and consultations with a number of leading American specialists showed that, after years of suppression during the rule of Stalin and his protégé, Trofim D. Lysenko, Soviet genetics and molecular biology are making a swift comeback. In some areas the work has already reached parity with research in American, British and West European laboratories.

The speed of recovery can be attributed in part to the existence of a strong genetics tradition. So discredited did Russian genetics become, when it was dominated by Lysenko, that many have forgotten the surge of intensive genetics research during the early years of the Soviet regime.

Many in the West fail to realize that science had deep and rigorous traditions in Russia long before the Bolshevik coup d'état of 1917 put the Communists in command.

The early years of Communism in Russia were marked by an explosion of talent in many scientific fields, including genetics.

Some enthusiastic Soviet geneticists of the nineteen twenties saw in their science the possibility of improving the inherited qualities of mankind. Soon after the Revolution a Bureau of Eugenics was formed and genealogical studies of the intelligentsia were made in search of material for improving the breed of man.

### Emphasis on Agriculture

Then famine hit Russia and the emphasis shifted to agriculture. A young man named Nikolai I. Vavilov was chosen to lead an effort to improve food production through the development of better strains of crops and livestock.

Vavilov, a student of William Bateson in England, the man who gave genetics its name, believed that the great food crops—wheat, potatoes, corn and barley—could be invigorated if crossbred with strains obtained from regions where those crops originated. He traveled to all parts of the world. He and his colleagues brought home 25,000 living samples of wheat.

Despite these efforts food production by Stalin's new collective farms was disastrously low. The stage was set for a man who made extravagant promises —Trofim Lysenko, who with his deep-set, burning eyes and almost religious fervor has been called the "Savonarola of Soviet science." He was a plant-breeder from the Ukraine who said he had a method of treating the seeds of winter wheat so that they could be planted in the spring and produce a heavy crop. This would open vast eastern regions in Siberia to productive farming.

Lysenko said characteristics acquired by an organism in its lifetime could be passed on to future generations. This had ideological appeal. Charles Darwin had believed it and the fathers of Communism, Marx and Engels, had been ardent admirers of Darwin.

### Ridiculed Hybrid Corn Work

Modern genetics had shown that Darwin was wrong. But Lysenko contended that genetics "is merely an amusement, like chess or football" and ridiculed efforts to seek the basic principles of heredity through studies of the fast-breeding fruit fly, work that led to several Nobel Prizes.

Lysenko denounced the American method of breeding hybrid corn, which was based on classical genetics. He ignored evidence that the blight that affected potatoes was a virus disease. His policies produced disasters in food production, but by this time Lysenko's drive against genetics had put Vavilov in jail. He was sent to Siberia where he died in 1943.

Despite the rise of Lysenko as a virtual czar of science there was a move within the Soviet Academy of Sciences after World War II to create an institute that would revive classical genetics. It was to be headed by a man named Nikolai P. Dubinin, whose work in cytogenetics had excited interest abroad. The plan was blocked and in 1948 a conference was organized by the Academy of Agricultural Sciences to assess the rival claims of the geneticists and the followers of Lysenko.

The geneticists leaned over backwards to compromise and appease their opponents, but they were doomed. Lysenko waited until the end to announce that Stalin had officially endorsed his theories.

Some of the geneticists rose and recanted as Galileo had done before the Inquisition. The Academy of Sciences published a letter to Stalin pledging to abolish the institutes doing work in classical genetics, including the one where Dubinin was working. It promised to purge from the field of biology all those adhering to heretical (non-Lysenko) views.

That was the low point in Soviet biology. Today the situation has altered completely. Dubinin and his colleagues are on top. Lysenko is living in relative obscurity near Moscow.

### Dubinin Heads Genetics Research

Why have the tables turned so completely? What has restored freedom of inquiry to Soviet genetics and biology? A number of those involved in the turnabout told their stories to this correspondent.

Dubinin is installed as head of a new Institute of General Genetics much like the one envisioned for him by the Academy of Sciences 20 years earlier. The temporary quarters of his new institute, barely a year old, is in a suburb of Moscow torn up by the construction of new apartments and laboratories.

His conference table was heaped with current issues of the American journal Science and other American, European and Soviet magazines. He ticked off the recent developments. He knew them well, for he is now president of the Scientific Council on Genetic Problems of the Academy of Sciences, a coordinating panel on which various research and public health agencies are represented.

He pointed to a new Soviet journal, Genetika.

"It is our first review on genetic questions," he said. "We began monthly publication in 1965. During the last two years, 10 new laboratories have been organized in the Institute of Biological Problems.

"In the Byelorussian Academy of Sciences at Minsk, an Institute of Genetics was formed a year and a half ago under Turbin, who is working on hybrids of corn and wheat. In Kiev, at the Ukrainian Academy of Sciences, there is a department of genetics with several new laboratories doing experimental work on mutagenesis and radiation chemistry.

"In the Academy of Medical Sciences there will soon be an Institute of Human Genetics. And in Obninsk there is Timofeyev-Ressovsky. He heads the department of radiation genetics in the new Institute of Radiobiology."

A special source of pride to Dubinin is the Institute of Cytology and Genetics that he himself established near Novosibirsk, in the heart of Siberia. At the time when Nikita S. Khrushchev still retained some loyalty to Lysenko, he is reported to hav easked why, if Dubinin was a "bad scientist" in Moscow, he was not also a bad scientist in Novosibirsk.

The first public criticism of Lysenko came in 1952, close to the end of the Stalin era. But it was the death of Lysenko's chief sponsor, Stalin himself, that turned the tide. The next year, 1954, the party organ, Kommunist, encouraged free scientific discussion (although calling for it to be based on dialectical materialism) and it opposed the suppression of divergent views.

It was evident to the new leader, Khrushchev, that Soviet agriculture was in a sorry state. The Central Committee of the Communist party decreed the intensive development of hybrid corn, and this offered to the bolder geneticists a chance to strike back.

Foremost among them was Dubinin, who had been out of sight since 1948. In a 1955 article he wrote:

"T. D. Lysenko caused the stoppage of work at the critical moment when hybrid corn began to emerge from the experiments in the fields of our kolkhozes and sovkhoses [collective farms and state farms]. Now 20 years later, after the United States, using the very same methods which were worked out in our country, has achieved the introduction of hybrid corn and the establishment of the foundation for production of animal fodder, the U.S.S.R. faces the problem of catching up in a very short space of time on that which we let slip."

### Kurchatov Aided Geneticists

The word began to get around that the Soviet Union's leading nuclear physicists had helped keep genetics alive by quietly sheltering some of its most able practitioners. The great physicist Igor V. Kurchatov (who died in 1960) played a central role in providing the Soviet Union with its first atomic weapons. His Institute of Theoretical Physics in Moscow was almost sacrosanct, as far as government interference was concerned.

Since radiation, such as that from X-rays or radioactive materials, can cause hereditary changes, there was some logic to the conduct of genetic research at the institute.

Thus in the nineteen-fifties there was a large department of genetics in the Kurchatov Institute, and a Laboratory of Radiation Genetics was quietly organized by Dubinin at the Institute of Biophysics of the Academy of Sciences in 1958. It was this laboratory which evolved into a the full-fledged institute that he now heads—an institute that itself has a dozen laboratories devoted to such problems as evolutionary genetics, space genetics, viral genetics, immunogenetics, and so forth.

A sampling showed that research at one laboratory has, as its starting point, discoveries reported by Richard F. Kimball at the Oak Ridge National Laboratory in Tennessee. Kimball has been studying the manner in which the living cell can sometimes repair genetic damage caused by radiation. In Moscow the work is concentrated on repair processes where the genetic damage, or mutation, has been caused by a chemical, such as mustard gas or ethylenimine.

In another sophisticated line of research, David M. Goldfarb is investigating the manner in which bacterial cells protect themselves against incorrect genetic information that might be infiltrated into them by foreign DNA.

DNA, or deoxyribonucleic acid, is the long, twisted molecule that carries the hereditary information needed for the continuity of life, much as magnetic tape can store an entire television program. Apparently the enzymes that unwind the DNA molecule, making it active, "know" the DNA native to that cell and do not act on foreign DNA.

### Strong Practical Element in Research

There remains a strong practical element in Soviet genetic research. On a visit to the Institute of Cytology and Genetics near Novosibirsk, its director, Dmitri K. Belyayev, stressed the economic benefits deriving from the work there, much as an American scientist might do in testifying before Congress on behalf of his program.

Belyayev said it had been found that, contrary to earlier belief, mutations or heredity changes induced by radiation were not always predominantly harmful. In fact, with some plants there seems to be an optimum dosage that produces many beneficial mutations. He cited wheat, for which the best dosage lies between 5000 and 10,000 roentgens. Treatment with such dosages has generated strains that have short, thick stems, making them resistant to wind, yet have good baking qualities.

At the institute there is a Laboratory of Polyploidy, a field that was anathema to the Lysenkoists, because it was firmly rooted in classical genetics. Polyploidy is the occurrence of plants (and in some cases animals) whose cells have unusual multiples of a basic number of chromosomes. The latter are the bundles of genetic material visible during cell division.

The sugar beet normally has 18 chromosomes (nine kinds, occurring in pairs, one set contributed by each parent plant). But by treatment with a chemical, colchicine, it is possible to produce plants that have four of each kind, instead of two: that is 36 chromosomes. These are "tetraploids." By crossing them with ordinary sugar beets it is possible to obtain an odd strain—a "triploid"—with three of each chromosome type: that is, with a total of 27.

Such a strain, according to Belyayev and his colleagues, has been developed with dramatic results. Sugar production per acre, they say, is 15 per cent higher than with ordinary beets. The new strain has been in use for three years and is now growing on many farms in southern regions of the U.S.S.R.

Belyayev has been interested in the fact that female silver foxes on fur farms have several periods of heat in a year whereas wild foxes have only one. He has found evidence of a genetic relationship between multiple periods of heat and docility.

Foxes that are docile are the most likely to be caught and the least likely to escape or die young in captivity. This has led to a fox-farm population that has the twin characteristics of docility and multiple periods of heat.

Belyayev predicted that in the near future scientists would decipher the manner in which genetic information wrapped up in the nucleus of the cell actually controls development. "We are trying to direct as much as possible of the work in our laboratories toward that goal," he said.

Soviet science has largely shaken off the shackles of Lysenkoism, although the final step was taken only three years ago, when Lysenko was ousted as head of the old Institute of Genetics. Could it happen again, could another Savonarola, another man of passionate, arrogant and intolerant views impose his will on science in the Soviet Union?

### Causes of Lysenko's Rise

To assess this possibility one must examine the causes of the past episode. A number of factors were involved:

1. The ideological attraction of Lysenko's ideas as presented by his more rhetorical backers.

2. The existence of a strong national tradition in empirical plant breeding.

3. The agricultural crisis of the nineteen-thirties that made the party and government responsive to extravagant promises.

4. The existence of a dictator deaf to the logic of Lysenko's opponents and powerful enough to impose his will without challenge.

In talking to those in the current mainstream of Soviet science one is reminded at every hand of their awareness of the disastrous sequence of events behind them. As early as 1957 this was related by Aleksandr N. Nesmeyanov, then president of the Academy of Sciences, when he said:

"We must frankly state that our biology had been acquiring the bad habit of solving debated scientific problems through the pressuring and suppression of scientific opponents, the use of disparaging labels, and other unscientific means. All this has had a negative effect on the development of a number of branches of biological science. . . . In general, it must be stated that one-sided evaluation and attempts at arriving at official evaluations in science by a majority of votes or more vocal behavior are not fruitful."

Such candor is now commonplace. One is left with the impression that the Soviet establishment has learned its lesson and that a recurrence of suppressive tyranny in the physical or biological sciences is unlikely.

### Advances in Molecular Biology

Closely linked to the new genetic research has been the explosive growth of molecular biology. As with genetics, this revival had its birth in the concern of Soviet nuclear physicists with the deplorable state of biology. The extent to which the country had fallen behind became evident as windows to the West were opened after Stalin's death in 1953.

The situation was a frequent subject of discussion at the weekly seminars known as "Kapishniks" because Peter

Kapitsa was their central figure. Kapitsa had been one of the most brilliant pupils of Ernest Rutherford, the British physicist.

In 1934 Kapitsa made a visit to his Soviet homeland and was told he could not return to England. Not until 1966 was he allowed to do so and he promptly returned to Russia, where he had become a spokesman for freedom of scientific discussion.

It was this freedom that dominated the Kapishniks. The participants included such figures as Igor E. Tamm and Lev D. Landau, both Nobel laureates in physics. Tamm, a robust figure who wore the emblem of Master of Sport in mountaineering, gave a lecture about 1956 that added fuel to the fire.

Speaking in the biology department of the Kurchatov Institute, he told of exciting new developments in Britain and the United States. It was evident that by analysis of DNA (deoxyribonucleic acid) Western scientists were zeroing in on the chemical mechanism of heredity.

The prospects for genetics, for biology, for the future of mankind were awesome, for there now loomed the possibility of engineering heredity, not by Lysenko's manipulation of the environment but by ingeniously controlled mutations. It was obvious to Tamm that Soviet science was in danger of being hopelessly left behind.

## A Pioneer in Muscle Chemistry

One of the more venerable opponents of Lysenkoism had quietly moved into the field. He was Vladimir A. Engelgardt, who, in the nineteen-thirties pioneered in muscle chemistry. His interest has shifted to the nucleic acids (such as DNA) and their role in genetics.

About 1958 (which seems to have been a critical turning point) it was decided to form an Institute of Radiational and Physical-Chemical Biology, with Engelgardt as director. This cumbersome title served as a camouflage for the real thrust of the work there.

A visit to his institute found him overflowing with enthusiasm despite his 72 years. He explained that at his request the name of his establishment had been changed to the Institute of Molecular Biology, which more accurately reflects the nature of its research.

At his side was Aleksandr Y. Braunshtein, his prize pupil and perhaps the best-known biochemist in the Soviet Union. Braunshtein told of his current studies of vitamin $B_6$ chemistry, an enormously complicated — and vital — problem. The vitamin, in its various forms, joins with more than 60 enzymes to catalyze, or stimulate, reactions in the life process.

Some of the antibiotics inhibit certain of these reactions, and so a three-dimensional understanding of how the molecules twist and turn in their interactions with one another has important medical implications. To achieve this understanding, Braunshtein is using ultraviolet, visible, and fluorescence spectra.

One of the men at Engelgardt's institute, A. A. Bayev, had recently deciphered the structure of another key substance — the transfer-RNA (ribonucleic acid) that is responsible for the destiny of valine. The latter is one of the 20 components (amino acids) that are linked in an almost infinite variety of sequences to form the giant protein molecules.

The role of the transfer-RNA is to pick up a molecule of valine and see to it that it slips into the correct slot in the formation of a protein. The only other transfer-RNA charted so far is that for alanine, a feat completed in 1965 by Robert W. Holley, at Cornell University. It involved charting the correct sequence of the 77 chemical units forming that molecule.

It took Bayev five years to do the job, Engelgardt said. Now, he added, Bayev is seeking out the structural features common to all the transfer-RNA's (about 50 in number).

American specialists who have toured Engelgardt's institute consider it well equipped by Western standards, with automatic spectrophotometers, ultracentrifuges, and other analytical devices. They have also remarked on a practice that they found somewhat quaint and that is based on the belief that those working with poisonous or radioactive substances should drink milk. Every day there is a pause while milk is taken from the laboratory refrigerators and distributed to the researchers—a half-liter apiece.

Engelhardt said that, as in genetics, there is a new journal, Molekularnaya Biologiya, whose first issue came out early in 1967, and an interdepartmental council has been formed to coordinate research in this field. In a crash training program, he added, a "winter school" is held each January at Dubna, the atomic research center on the Volga River. About 200 promising youngsters are brought together to hear talks by leading men in the field. "Actually," he said, "there is more discussion than lecturing. And after the sessions they go skiing."

## Physicists Drawn In

"I tried to get physicists and biologists into the program to avoid compartmentalization, although at first the physicists were not very enthusiastic," he said.

He added that a new brand of scientist was appearing on the scene — a sort of Renaissance man in the scientific sense, grounded in many fields: chemistry, physics, biology, statistics.

A major source of such talent is the new Physical-Technical Institute, established near Moscow by a group of leading scientists including Kapitsa and Nikolai N. Semenov, a Nobel laureate in chemistry.

A visit to Semenov's department in the Academy of Sciences and to various Moscow institutes showed many signs of the Soviet race to catch up with the West in genetics, molecular biology and biochemistry.

Semenov explained that the Academy of Sciences, a giant organization that towers over Soviet science, was now divided into three sections, one of which, dealing with chemistry and biology, was under his direction. Another deals with the physical and mathematical sciences, and the third is concerned with the social sciences.

Semenov, at 71, was full of energy and humor. In founding the Institute of Chemical Physics in 1931 he had brought about a certain synthesis of chemistry and physics, emphasizing application of the new discoveries in physics to the construction of theories to account for chemical reaction rates and energy releases, including those of explosions. It was for such work that he won his Nobel Prize.

"My goal, since 1950, has been to achieve a marriage between biology and chemistry," he said. "At first it was slowed by the difficulties of the time—the Lysenko problem. However, five years ago [in 1962] I was able to form a new Division of Biophysics, Biochemistry and Physiologically Active Compounds within the Academy."

He found, as Engelgardt had, that physicists, biologists and chemists, trained to limited fields of interest, did not mix easily. Of this new unit in the institute he said with a grin: "At first it was a mechanical mixture, but now it is nearly a chemical compound!"

He told of a proliferation of new institutes in the field. One of them, to study the manner in which proteins are formed, is being organized by Aleksandr S. Spirin at the new "science city" of Pushchino.

"He has invited four or five colleagues, young men of 35 and 36 years, to join him there," Semenov said. "He is a biologist and his associates will be physicists and chemists."

American scientists speak of Spirin as one of the most promising young biochemists in the Soviet Union. He works at the Bakh Institute of Biochemistry, headed by Aleksandr I. Oparin, father of modern scientific thinking on the origin of life.

Spirin is a dark-haired, diminutive man who looks a little like Frank Sinatra. He told of his efforts to dissect and reconstruct ribosomes. These are tiny structures within the cell, so small that they cannot be studied in any detail even under the most powerful electron microscope.

The ribosomes are thought to be the site where the essence of the life process, the assembly of amino acids into proteins, is carried out, following genetic instructions stored in the DNA of the nucleus and carried to the ribosomes by RNA.

## Medical Implications Seen

Spirin explained that knowledge of ribosome structure could be of major medical importance because many antibiotics, such as the tetracyclines, alter the mechanism of protein synthesis in the ribosomes of bacteria, thus interfering with their life process. Such drugs can be used to fight bacteria because they affect bacterial ribosomes, but, apparently, not those of human cells. Intimate knowledge of this process and of ribosomal structure could make it possible to design antibiotics against ailments now beyond reach—even, Spirin said, against cancer.

Each ribosome is formed of two rounded structures of unequal size. These were separated by American researchers in the late nineteen-fifties, and then Spirin, in 1963, managed to unfold both the large and small component into a tiny filament.

It was then possible to do what he called in English a "strip tease" of each filament, to see what it was made of. It turned out that the large component consisted of an RNA molecule enveloped in 30 protein molecules, whereas the other was an RNA molecule wrapped in 15 proteins.

In 1966 the components were reassembled into ribosomes by both his laboratory and American workers. Now he is trying other ways to reassemble the ribosomes into bodies that act normally in the life process. In this way it may be possible to learn more about details of their invisible structure.

To what extent have government and party interference handicapped the development of Soviet science outside of genetics? What about physics, chemistry and other fields?

The most serious ideological invasions date from a speech given by Andrei A. Zhdanov of the Politburo on June 24, 1947. This policy statement, part of a period of repression known as the "Zhdanovshchina," set the tone for what followed, including the grim meeting of 1948 at which Trofim D. Lysenko delivered the coup de grace to his adversaries in genetics.

It is ironic that two of the most prominent Western scientists denounced as corrupting modern, materialist science with bourgeois "idealism" were Bertrand Russell and Linus Pauling, who were later to champion the Soviet point of view on such questions as the Vietnam war and nuclear-weapons testing.

Early in 1950 Russell and his coworker Alfred North Whitehead were denounced for their trail-blazing role in the development of symbolic logic. Pauling was found guilty of inventing the resonance theory of chemical bonds.

In both cases those attacked had made use of symbols or descriptions of things that did not necessarily exist. This was heretical to adherents of Lenin's teaching. Lenin had written an entire book to rebut what he considered errors in the physics of his day, particularly the ideas of Ernst Mach, an Austrian physicist and philosopher.

Although Mach did most of his important work late in the 19th century, his influence on contemporary science has only recently been widely recognized. In fact, to laymen his name is still chiefly familiar because of its use in expressing the speed of a supersonic aircraft: a vehicle flying at Mach 2 is traveling at twice the speed of sound in that medium.

Mach demanded the most rigorous experimental criteria in determining the reality of what he considered abstract concepts, such as "atoms," "molecules," "space," and "time." He thus brushed cobwebby concepts from the minds of scientists and helped clear the way for Einstein's relativity theory. His parallel belief that all existence is sensation led to Lenin's rebuttal in 1909.

Lenin dismissed this view as idealism and said that concepts were meaningful only if they represented something with a material existence. Furthermore, he said, matter can exist quite independently from mental processes.

### Ideological Diseases of Chemistry

In 1951, a conference was held to diagnose the "ideological diseases" of Soviet chemistry. Gennadi V. Chelintsev, a professor of chemical warfare at the Voroshilov Military Academy, tried to play the role in chemistry that Lysenko had performed in biology, but failed.

The leaders of Soviet chemistry, including the Academy of Sciences president, Aleksandr N. Nesmeyanov, devised a theory similar to that of Pauling, but without its emphasis on artificiality. By 1961 Pauling was lecturing on his theory in Moscow although the subject of resonance was still handled gingerly in the Soviet literature.

The controversy in physics has followed parallel lines, but it has also been intertwined with a worldwide debate on the meaning of quantum theory, with roots in one of the basic paradoxes of science: the seemingly contradictory evidence that light consists of waves and that it is formed of discrete particles.

A mathematical method, known as quantum mechanics, has been devised to account for the behavior of light and atomic particles, but what is its meaning with regard to the actual nature of those phenomena?

Twin concepts, advanced by Niels Bohr, of Denmark, and Werner Heisenberg, of Germany, prior to World War II, sought to resolve the problem. They said that no observable property of a particle, whether it refers to its wave-like characteristics or its manifestations as a particle, has any reality until that property is measured. This came to be called "complementarity."

### Uncertainty Principle Stated

Likewise, Heisenberg's uncertainty principle said that any such measurement intruded into the situation in a manner that made it possible to measure, with precision, only one property of the particle.

This "Copenhagen interpretation" of quantum theory had been accepted by a number of Soviet physicists by the time Zhdanov made the 1947 speech, in which he said: "The Kantian vagaries of modern bourgeois atomic physicists lead them to inferences about the electron's possessing 'free will,' to attempts to describe matter as only a certain conjunction of waves, and to other devilish tricks."

Like symbolic logic and the resonance theory, the Copenhagen interpretation seemed inconsistent with Lenin's view that ideas were valid only if they had a clear material base. The effects of the Zhdanov speech endured until about 1960.

Today the debates in Russia on quantum theory largely parallel those in the West. Furthermore it is clear that ideological issues have not handicapped Soviet physics in any manner comparable to the throttling of biology by the Lysenko affair.

The most dramatic product of quantum electronics is the laser, a device that produces an intense and narrow beam of light and has already figured as a weapon in a James Bond moving picture. It is noteworthy that the Nobel Prize given in 1964 to the inventors of this device was shared by one American and two Russians.

### Advances in Cybernetics Made

One of the most remarkable developments in Soviet science is the current vogue for cybernetics, the science of control systems in machines and living organisms. In the early postwar years Soviet theoreticians dismissed cybernetics as a capitalist scheme to replace troublesome workers with machines.

There was also objection to the concept of Norbert Wiener, father of cybernetics, that it could become a universal science, helping man solve his social as well as his material problems. This was seen by Communist theoreticians as a new ideology, attempting to usurp the role of the Communist dogma, dialectical materialism.

But by the nineteen-fifties it became apparent that unless the Soviet Union delegated some of its control operations to machines, it would be paralyzed by its own bureaucracy. An academician in Moscow predicted that if the then current trend continued, by 1980 the entire population of the Soviet Union would be involved in planning and administration.

However, a major obstacle to rapid development of cybernetics in the Soviet Union has been the absence of an electronics industry as broadly based, competitive and diversified as that of the United States. The Russians' successes in the launching and control of spacecraft and missiles have shown that they can perform in a first-rate manner with computers, but, as with many aspects of the Soviet scientific and technological scene, they have had to ration their resources and only activities with top priority have the benefit of such sophisticated aids.

October 17, 1967

*1917—The Russian Revolution—1967*

# Soviet Medicine Combines Old-Fashioned Methods and Ultramodern Techniques

By WALTER SULLIVAN

**THE surgeon was a woman and she worked with skill and speed. Yet the visiting American surgeon at her elbow was less fascinated by her performance than by her earrings.**

**They stuck through her sterile cap and mask, wiggling with each movement. As he watched them dangle perilously over the gaping body cavity he thought, "What if one of them drops!"**

**The same surgeon saw flies in a "sterile" operating theater in a good Moscow hospital. Yet he spoke with admiration of the new Soviet surgical tools—instruments that quickly staple two severed blood vessels together or repair a damaged eye.**

**Soviet medicine is marked by contrast. On three trips to the Soviet Union in recent years it has been possible to watch the blood being drained from a newly deceased woman for use in living patients.**

One biologist told how he had developed a technique whereby human muscle tissue is minced and then stuffed into wounds, where it allegedly reorganizes itself into new muscle of the proper configuration. Such procedures are typical of dramatic developments in Soviet medical practice.

### Facilities Lacking in Past

Soviet medicine of today is meaningful only when viewed against the backdrop of the past. When the Soviet state was formed in 1917 there was a gross lack of public health facilities. The need to develop a health service that would bring at least moderately professional care to a vast country demanded special measures, such as the training of feldshers—men and women with less than a full medical education to deal with routine problems.

World War II has left its mark in the dominance of Soviet medicine by women. The war decimated the male population and diverted from medicine the men who today would have been experienced physicians and surgeons.

The organization of medicine still reflects its early goal of broad service. The basic treatment center is the polyclinic. It may be in a factory, a school, or a large block of apartment houses. Every citizen, from birth, has a medical card and is assigned a physician at his local polyclinic.

He can change doctors if he wishes, but must submit a request in writing. The more well-to-do can seek out a physician of high repute and pay him a private fee. Otherwise medical care is free, apart from drugs purchased for home use from the drugstores.

Up to 16, the resident of a large city goes to a pediatric clinic. Then he is issued a new medical card and is referred to an adult polyclinic. The staff of a city polyclinic consists, typically, of four specialists in internal medicine, two surgeons, two gynecologists, a pathologist, a radiologist, and a specialist in disorders of eyes, ears, nose, throat and skin, plus various auxiliaries. There are no hospital beds. If a patient needs bed care he is sent to a hospital or specialized institute.

Hospitals, unlike those in the West, do not usually handle outpatients. Once someone has been discharged from a hospital he is referred to his local polyclinic. While general hospitals handle all types of cases, the remarkable feature of the Soviet system is the emphasis on specialized institutes and on specialization in medical practice.

### Specialized Treatment Is Centralized

According to Dr. Aleksandr R. Luria, the internationally known researcher on brain function, his research has been made possible by the fact that brain tumor cases from all over the Soviet Union are flown to Moscow for treatment at a specialized institute there.

The Russians have a program of "sanitary aviation" to bring patients to the doctor or vice versa. At the Moscow institute several brain tumors are removed each day. Such operations are comparatively rare in any single American institution.

Dr. Luria has been exploring the detailed function of various parts of the brain by systematically testing patients before the operation to bring to light abnormal aspects of brain function. He then makes careful note, from the surgical results, of that part of the brain affected by the tumor.

In Survey, a British journal of Soviet and East European studies, Dr. Robert Roaf, Professor of Orthopedic Surgery at the University of Liverpool, tells of visiting the Central Institute for Trauma and Orthopedics in Moscow. Trauma is injury of the body, as by an accident. Orthopedics is the correction of deformities.

In a single room he found seven patients with a rare congenital condition, the absence of the radius, or heavy bone of the forearm.

The 10 departments of the institute's hospital are a commentary on the hazards of Soviet life. They handle sport trauma, ballet trauma, electric burns, tumors, arthritis, hand surgery, neurosurgery, and children's orthopedics.

Each has its own corridor with small wards of three to six beds each. Some of the beds are equipped with earphones (presumably for music and radio programs) and a bell to summon aid. There are six operating theaters in the building.

"We saw many cases of difficult tumors treated by widespread resection [removal] of bone and replacement by whole sections of preserved frozen cadaveric bone," Dr. Roaf reported. Like live bone transplants, the inserted bone serves as a matrix that is gradually replaced by the patient's own bone tissue.

### High Ratio of Doctors to Patients

In larger cities there are specialized institutes in cancer and neurosurgery. In the whole of the Soviet Union, for example, there are 18 institutes of orthopedics and traumatology, all under the central one in Moscow.

The Moscow institute renders advice and relays new techniques to the provincial institutes, which help out the general hospitals of their region.

Many foreigners find the wards crowded by Western standards, but they are amazed at the high ratio of doctors and nurses to patients. Dr. Roaf tells of an adult polyclinic with 45 doctors for a population of 100,000 (one for every 222 people compared with one per 630 in the United States as a whole). At a 1,300-bed children's polyclinic in Tbilisi there are 250 doctors and 600 nurses.

The large rosters may, in part, be related to short working hours. Some physicians do a four-hour shift, then work four hours at another clinic. The pay for ordinary practitioners is low, comparable to that of a moderately skilled worker. Student nurses are taken on at the age of 17 or 18 and live at home.

Because Russia came out of the war with large numbers of maimed citizens, it has emphasized the development of artificial limbs. The best known is an arm attached in such a manner that electrical impulses are picked up from the patient's own muscles. These are amplified by a tiny transistorized unit, and a small electric motor responds to the impulses by moving forearm and hand.

More than 150 of these limbs are in use. Electrically controlled hands, driven by electric power or compressed carbon dioxide, have been tried in the United States, but American specialists believe they are too difficult to maintain for general use. The conventional hook-like device is far simpler.

### Cancer Treatment Is Organized

The treatment of cancer in the Soviet Union has been organized on a national scale. Known as the Oncology Service, it comes directly under the Ministry of Health in Moscow and is responsible for cancer treatment and for treatment of all tumors, benign or malignant, and for propaganda—by posters, briefings of physicians and health lectures—designed to achieve early diagnosis.

A special role is played by the Herzen Institute. It gives postgraduate training and directs more than 200 oncological (tumor-treating) clinics.

Those wishing to join the Oncology Service usually must have spent three years in general practice. Competition is keen for posts in the research institutes, particularly those in Moscow and Leningrad. The top-ranking trainees get these jobs.

Statistical studies of cancer incidence have shown regional differences that could throw light on causes of the disease. Hence the Herzen Institute is conducting a demographic tumor survey through its dispensaries, some in areas with unusual environmental conditions. In some regions it has been found that the rates of primary liver tumors or tumors of the upper digestive tract are unusually high.

In big cities, such as Moscow, there is a central registry of tumor cases. Whenever a research institute needs cases of a special type, it can seek them out through this registry.

How are new medical procedures tested in the Soviet Union? The rate at which new drugs are introduced seems considerably lower than in the United States and Western Europe.

According to officials at the Ministry of Health drug screening and approval are the responsibility of the ministry's State Committee on the Pharmacopeia. To achieve objectivity, a drug developed by one institute is allocated to another for testing, and the State Committee decides, on the basis of the reported results, whether or not to include it in the next list of approved treatments.

One drug widely used in the West is not approved for general use in the Soviet Union. That is "the pill," which serves as a female contraceptive. Dr. Lidiya K. Skornyakova, who heads the Department of Maternal and Child Care in the Ministry of Health, said there was concern about the cumulative effect of its use throughout a woman's child-bearing period of life.

### 'The Pill' Not in General Use

However, among Soviet students and members of the intelligentsia, there is clamor for the pill. They complain that mechanical birth control devices are expensive, ill-fitting and poorly made. Devices inserted into the uterus by a clinician normally provide protection as long as they are in place, but unwed girls are hesitant to apply to their polyclinic in what is still a rather puritanical society.

A measure of the problem is the high rate of abortions. The number of criminal abortions became so large that abortions were legalized in 1956. Now a girl need only obtain the approval of a responsible physician.

Nevertheless "black market" abortions persist. Unwed girls fear that a record of one or more abortions on their medical cards will stand in the way of their careers.

An active area of Soviet medical research is in regeneration. When a claw is torn from a crab it can grow a new one. When a salamander or its larval form (an axolotl) loses a leg, a new one sprouts in its place. What prevents a higher animal from doing the same, and can the impediment be overcome, enabling a man to grow a new leg or a new kidney?

One of those working in this field is Dr. Aleksandr N. Studitsky, at the Institute of Animal Morphology in Moscow. It is he who has been experimenting with the use of minced muscle to replace tissue lost in accidents.

### Muscle Does Not Regenerate

Muscle tissue does not regenerate to any extent. If an alligator bites a piece from someone's thigh, the lost muscle is replaced by scar tissue and other nonfunctional material, leaving an unsightly cavity. In his experiments Dr. Studitsky takes the thigh muscle of a rat, chops it fine, and puts it back in the rat's leg, coupling it with the nerves and blood vessels of the leg.

"Within three weeks," he said in a recent interview, "there is a normal muscle with its net of capillaries, nerve endings and functional activity."

The technique has also been successfully tried in human beings, he said, with muscle taken from one part of the body, minced, and stuffed into a wound elsewhere in the same individual.

He said he is now experimenting with the transplantation of intact muscle. However, he believes that the muscle must be coaxed—or shocked—into a "plastic" state (comparable to the disorganization of minced muscle) before, under the influence of neighboring tissues, it adapts itself to its new role in the body.

Dr. Studitsky's muscle-mincing technique is not yet in general clinical use. He has raised scientific eyebrows with a variety of unorthodox proposals. He contends that the higher animals, including man, are more efficient at regeneration than lower animals such as crabs, salamanders and axolotls.

The latter have evolved an ability to grow new appendages because they keep losing them, but they cannot regenerate internal organs. On the other hand, man, according to Dr. Studitsky, can grow a new liver even if 90 per cent of the existing one is removed. Furthermore, he believes, one's ability to regenerate increases with age.

Since advancing years carry us further and further from the time when we first grew our arms, legs and other organs, most researchers in the field believe the ability to replace lost tissue declines with age.

Dr. Studitsky says the growth and health of muscle and bone are dependent on their interactions with neighboring tissue. In this, too, he is unorthodox. Most biologists believe the development of a cell is essentially governed by its own genetic information—its store of DNA.

Dr. Studitsky has interposed barriers of cellophane or metal foil between muscle and neighboring tissue and finds that tumors develop in the muscle even though, so far as he can tell, there has been no interference with blood and nerve connections.

He believes that in the healing of bone an esssential role is played by interactions between the "skin" of the bone, or periosteum, the cartilage, and the ends of the bone. He has repeatedly removed, from a living animal, all of a leg bone except its ends, its cartilage, and its periosteum and has found that the bone regenerates promptly.

### A Three-Legged Axolotl

During an interview Dr. Studitsky reached into a cabinet and pulled out a large, liquid-filled jar containing a preserved axolotl with three legs. The animal had been white, but the leg of a dark axolotl had been grafted onto it. At the time of its death and preservation its other legs had begun to turn dark, too, demonstrating, Dr. Studitsky said, the exchange of "genetic" or control information between organs of the body.

Dr. Bruce Carlson, at the University of Michigan Medical School, has verified some of Dr. Studitsky's findings with minced muscle and has himself been exploring the mechanisms of regeneration. He points out that most of Dr. Studitsky's work has been with small volumes of muscle. If his mincing technique (which seems to work better than an intact transplant) is to replace large chunks of muscle, a way must be found to restore the main blood vessels needed to supply such tissue.

Dr. Carlson worked for five months in the laboratory of Dr. L. V. Polezhayev, who for more than 35 years has been trying to stimulate regeneration in various kinds of tissue. This research, which like that of Dr. Studitsky is at the Institute of Animal Morphology, is currently focused on heart muscle.

### Heart Attack Is Analyzed

When a person has a "heart attack," it typically involves the blocking of blood flow through a coronary artery that supplies the heart muscle. As a result, part of the muscle "dies"—what is known as an infarct. If the person survives the attack, he is handicapped for life to a degree dependent on the extent of the damage. If a way could be found to stimulate regeneration of the heart muscle, it would become possible to rehabilitate such cases.

Dr. Polezhayev's experiments with rats, dogs and rabbits involve the inducing of artificial "heart attacks" followed by the injection of substances to stimulate muscle fiber growth and inhibit the formation of scar tissue. So far, although there has been some regeneration, the scar tissue has always won out.

To compare Soviet medicine and medical research with those of an affluent society like the United States is difficult. Even when the assessments of specialists who have visited a dozen hospitals are available, one must remember that they have seen only a small sample of the whole, and probably the best sample, at that.

The best of Soviet surgeons are virtuosos on a par with some of the best in the West. But on the average Soviet medicine is probably well below American standards. It also seems likely that it is providing better medical care to the lowest strata of its society than is the case in a number of countries in the West.

October 18, 1967

# SOVIET SAYS CRAFT LANDED ON VENUS AND RADIOED DATA

## Unmanned Ship Reportedly Touched Down on Dec. 15 After 120-Day Journey

By BERNARD GWERTZMAN

Special to The New York Times

MOSCOW, Jan. 26—The Soviet Union announced today that its unmanned Venera 7 last month made the first soft landing on Venus's torrid surface and sent back data for more than 20 minutes.

A report published in Izvestia, the Government newspaper, and a summary issued by Tass, the official Soviet press agency, broke a six-week silence on the results of the Soviet Union's latest and most successful Venus probe.

Preliminary data released by Tass on Dec. 15 said nothing about a soft landing and left the impression that Venera 7 had been no more successful than the previous Venera craft that had failed to endure the extreme heat and high pressure of Venus's cloud-shrouded atmosphere, which has a great deal of carbon dioxide.

But today's official report said that "it was the first time that scientific information was relayed directly from the surface of another planet in the solar system."

### Another Achievement

Venera 7 clearly was another technological achievement for the Russians, who have recently put the stress in their space program on unmanned projects. It contrasts with the emphasis placed by the United States on its Apollo program and putting men on the moon. Apollo 14 is scheduled to be launched on Sunday.

The scientific information sent back to earth by Venera 7's instrument capsule caused no surprises and tended to fortify the general consensus held by scientists since the Soviet Venera craft and the American Mariner 5 sent back data in recent years on missions that fell short of soft landings.

According to the Soviet report, Venera 7's instruments reported that the surface temperature on Venus was as hot as scientists had been predicting. It was 475 degrees Centigrade, with a margin of error of 20 degrees in either direction. In Fahrenheit, this means that the surface of Venus at the point where Venera 7's instruments lay ranged from 847 to 923 degrees above zero.

This is more than four times the temperature at which water

boils and means that it is impossible for oxygen to exist in any quantity on the planet's surface.

Venera 7's instruments also reported that the atmospheric pressure on the surface was equivalent to 90 atmospheres—or 90 times that of earth at sea level—with a margin of error of 15 atmospheres in either direction.

Because more than 90 per cent of the atmosphere is carbon dioxide, the density of the atmosphere at the surface was about 60 times greater than that of earth, the report said.

The combination of scorching heat, crushing pressure and dense air makes it highly unlikely that any human could long endure on the surface, even in the most technologically advanced life-support systems, experts here said.

Because of the thick, dense clouds that surround the planet, it is impossible to see the surface from earth. And because the space capsule must land on the "night" side—facing earth—to facilitate radio communication, no television pictures were possible.

The chief designer of the Venera series said in May, 1969, after the descent of Venera 5 and 6 into the atmosphere, "I am not confident that in the near future it will be possible to receive television pictures of the planet's surface."

Venera 7 was launched on Aug. 17 on its 120-day journey to Venus, the closest planet to earth, and the second closest planet to the sun. On Dec. 15, Tass announced that the 2,590-pound craft had completed its mission and that it transmitted information for 35 minutes as its instrument capsule floated by parachute through the Venusian atmosphere.

Nothing was said, even in subsequent days, about a soft landing, and it was assumed here that Venera 7 had followed the pattern of Venera 4, 5 and 6—all of which sent data while descending but apparently either burned up or failed to communicate from the surface.

There was no explanation given today as to why the Soviet Union had not announced its latest technological achievement earlier.

The report said it had been ascertained that the craft's capsule had landed on the surface when the radio signal frequency stopped changing.

"The signals from the descending probe were received for another 23 minutes after landing," Tass said. "Here the voume of the signal was about a hundred times less than during the descent."

The report said that "a special method" using computers had detected "this weak signal" and allowed it to be deciphered.

The temperature outside the capsule increased as it penetrated the atmosphere, starting about 40 miles from the surface, the report said. At the time of landing, the distance between Venus and the earth was about 36.3 million miles, while the radio signals took 3 minutes 22 seconds to reach the earth.

According to the report, Venera 7's design was similar to that of the last three Venera craft. But it was heavier, to withstand pressures of up to 180 atmospheres and temperatures of up to 530 degrees Centigrade.

Tass called the latest achievement "a successful implementation of the Soviet program" and said it "has pushed back the frontiers of man's knowledge of the nature of this planet which lies closest to earth."

The Venera 7 was on the surface of the planet at the same time as the Soviet moon rover, Lunokhod 1, was sending back information from the lunar surface. This was the first time, the report said, that "earth was receiving information simultaneously from two celestial bodies."

The recent successes of the Soviet Union in unmanned craft—the Luna 16, which brought back lunar samples to earth in September, Luna 17, which deposited the still active Lunokhod on the moon in November, and Venera 7—underscore the determined thrust of Soviet space research toward unmanned vehicles with manned flight only being used around the earth in preparation for an orbiting space station.

Venera 7 did not receive unusual publicity in the Soviet media tonight. Television did not do more than report the Tass summary. For most Russians, the latest achievement does not arouse any particular interest. Russians by and large are much more interested in the drama of manned flight.

January 27, 1971

## A SOCIALIST SOCIETY?

### The Party Zealots Ask: Za Chto Borolis'? (Is *This* What We Fought For?)

# Russia's New Bourgeois Grows Fat

By ALBERT PARRY

AT the recent 23d Party Congress in Moscow, the Soviet leaders, in lieu of calls to the barricades, promised their people for the next four years: four times as many refrigerators, nearly twice as many washing machines and more than twice the number of television sets as in 1961-65, an increase in automobile production from 200,000 to 800,000, and lower prices, more housing, higher wages and a shorter work-week. In short, a continued middle-class existence.

Their official line of course denies that there is today in the Soviet Union either the upper "New Class" condemned by Milovan Djilas or any middle class such as the West knows. Yet we can plainly see that Russia's industrialization, its peasant past and the ordinary laws of human nature have indeed created these two classes, the upper and the middle. My guess is that these bureaucrats, technocrats, managers, men of the arts and other professionals, together with their families, are at least 10 per cent of the Soviet population, or nearly 23 million men, women and children out of a total of some 233 million.

Red Chinese leaders also note this *embourgeoisement*, though far less happily or hopefully than we do, and in great ire accuse Moscow of going to the revisionist dogs. But Moscow's leaders insist that Peking is wrong, that all this bounty does not and will not make the Soviet man a neo-bourgeois. In effect, they echo Khrushchev's line that an extra pound of butter helps, not hinders, the making of a better Marxist. As a writer in Komsomolskaya Pravda declared: "We are not hypocrites nor ascetics. We wish everyone to have a good apartment, handsome clothes, graceful furniture, just as the party program says. But we want our youth to walk toward it by the same honest path that their fathers used. So there won't be any backstairs to it." And an Izvestia journalist pontificated: "In our society, material things do not dominate man. Man is above material things."

THE trouble, though, is that things material do become paramount with the middle- and upper-class man and his family in the Soviet Union. Backstairs deals, dishonesty and corruption, as well as legitimately high incomes in this unequal society, do

**ALBERT PARRY** is professor of Russian civilization and language and head of Russian studies at Colgate. His most recent book is "The New Class Divided."

constitute a way to individual prosperity. With comforts and conveniences, with elevated stations in life, emerges a new psychology quite at variance with the stern Marxist-Leninist precepts.

Not only in the fact of his possession of worldly goods and social prestige, but even more in the attitude to this possession, the new élite man is indeed bourgeois. For his attitude is that the possession and its enjoyment is an aim in itself, not a mere unstressable consequence of his progress.

This new bourgeois grows fat and gathers goods, however, with a semi-cautious eye over his shoulder. For he knows that his style of thinking and living is not what the republic's founding fathers had in their minds and holy writ.

Not that the holy writ is too explicit on the subject. Marx and Lenin were marvelously adept at calling for a revolution, yet rather vague in spelling out the glorious morning after. But both were surely against the mode and the mood of acquiring property by individuals and classes at the expense and grievance of the masses. In general terms, both said that, comes the revolution, every citizen will have no more and no less than any other citizen. Higher pay for professionals and bureaucrats, leading to the rise of the new middle and upper classes, was not in the original Marx-Lenin preachment.

As early as 1903, in "To the Rural Poor," Lenin had given his brutally simple definition of "bourgeois": "Bourgeois means an owner of property. The bourgeoisie are all the owners of property taken together. A big bourgeois is the owner of big property. A petit bourgeois is the owner of small property." In 1917 he was even more blunt: *"Grab' nagrablennoye!"* "Steal that which has been stolen from you!" was a wonderfully effective Leninist slogan, promptly and widely practiced by the erstwhile suppressed, oppressed and depressed masses of Russia.

In the distribution of the sequestered property the regime meant to be strictly egalitarian. Just before the November revolution, at one of the frequent impromptu street huddles of citizens in my home city of Rostov on the Don, I heard a heated argument as to precisely how many pairs of trousers each man should have after the oncoming Socialist takeover. To a group of doubters one Bolshevik insisted that one pair should suffice until worn ragged. "Why not split a pair between two men?" was a sarcastic rejoinder from the crowd.

During the ensuing civil war a report was circulated that in a Volga city, freshly captured by the Reds from the Whites, a unit of revolutionary sailors confiscated most of a scholar's library and one of his twin beds. Their spartan point was that these were too many books for one man, and that surely the professor and his wife could sleep in one bed. The story was that the deprived scholar complained to Lenin himself, and that Lenin ordered an exception to be made in this case.

Theoretically, of course, the neo-bourgeois should not have at all resulted from all this. But he is the fact of Soviet life. And he forges on, confident that the future even more than the present belongs to him. The rapidly fading zealots of The Cause are bitter as they helplessly ask one another their favorite and now-famous question:

*"Za chto borolis'?"*—"Is *this* what we fought for?"

In today's Soviet Russia the new middle-class man, reaching out to grasp the lower rungs of the upper class, is neither the merchant nor the peasant but the peasant's and worker's descendant—the engineer. Engineers earn enough to have apartments or houses of their own and to buy goods of wider variety and better quality. They—especially their women—are foremost among style-choosers: fashion-setters for the lower classes.

Other professionals—scientists, top managers, high military men, writers, theatrical folk—are more prominent and more prosperous, but they are not as numerous as engineers nor as close to the classes below in their daily contacts. Fashions that scientists or marshals would set are entirely too expensive for the masses even to aspire to—and often seem too ridiculous. An upper-class family these days will, for instance, vacation on the cool piny Baltic shore—to get away from the crowd, of course. The middle class still chooses the warmer, palm-fringed Sochi, even if it is thronged.

Fiction increasingly features engineers rather than either men of the higher strata or those Soviet heroes of yesteryear, the peasants and the workers. Recently a journalist in Komsomolskaya Pravda confirmed that it is "the stylish thing to vent one's irony on an agricultural novelette." Two days earlier, in Sovetskaya Rossiya, another complained that "not many books in recent years have reached the Soviet reader which present the worker as the chief and artistically interesting image."

Daniil Granin, one of the best writers on the country's scientific and engineering élite, points out that one of the main reasons for the worker's recession in stories is the socio-technical transformation of the Soviet Union: in Leningrad, the city of precision-tool making, there are 800,000 workers and 300,000 engineers and technicians. Elsewhere this élite's proportion is smaller, but it is steadily growing everywhere in Russia.

It may be difficult for a Westerner to understand just how a lower technician's or executive's family can legitimately graduate to a higher stratum of Soviet society. There is, of course, the common expedient of both husband and wife working for far longer hours than Western families would consider in view of the hardship imposed on their children. One can also educate oneself into a higher technical or engineering class, and thus a better salary. But this takes brains, effort and many years of evening school.

A quicker way is to sacrifice a few years on almost any job in the pioneering North or East, where bonuses are hefty. Explaining her husband's decision to move to the Okhotsk seashore, a young woman wrote to her mother: "A couple my Misha knows have returned from Chukotka. In a mere three years they brought back with them a television set, a refrigerator, rugs and a complete change of furniture." For themselves, Misha and his wife decided to stay in Northeastern Siberia long enough to buy not only rugs and a television set, but also a Moskvich or even a Volga car.

The Western influence is marked. It is the engineer, the technician, the young scientist or the manager who is fascinated by things Western, and has a chance to bring them back from missions or tours abroad, for himself and his women: brightly colored pull-over sweaters and scuba diving equipment, nylon stockings and spike-heel shoes, instant coffee and transistor radios.

He has a sharp hankering for the color of the Western street scene, particularly Western cafes and civilized conversation over coffee and apéritifs. So far, most of the efforts by the Soviet young to create such centers in big cities have lasted but briefly; the best of the cafes, "The Restless Hearts" in Leningrad, passed away after a few months of some success. The fault is usually in the desperate effort of the party or Komsomol authorities to supervise such cafes, to see to the orthodoxy of poetry readings and philosophical or political discussions at the tables. The "youth cafes" die of over-organization by the powers that be.

Party preachers still attack certain writers and poets for their "bourgeois" or "petit bourgeois" spirit—their total avoidance of revolutionary or Five-Year-Plan themes in favor of love, love, love. And yet in his recent short story, "By the Campfire," the writer N. Pochivalin stubbornly presented a 19-year-old engineering college student as a positive character despite his Western clothes and nonconformist views. The lad is dressed in American-style *jeans-y*, and his ultra-bright American-imitation shirt is ornamented with pictures of monkeys and parrots. He believes in nothing "except cybernetics and conditioned reflexes." He is annoyed by his father's conversation with his middle-aged friends about crops—"boring!" But the lad knows his science and generally "is not a bad one."

The neo-bourgeois of Russia longs for more elegance, better pastimes and better manners. The new intellectual now goes for a hobby that is above both the party's trite prescription of more Marxist reading and the peasantry's simple games. (There is no Russian word for "hobby," so the intellectuals have coined *khobbi.*) A movement is afoot in the large cities to discard the colorless greeting "comrade" or the officious "citizen" for "sir" and "madame" (the old-fashioned, pre-revolutionary *suдar'* and *sudarynia*). In Leningrad, last month, the first *literaturnyi salon* was opened in a Nevsky Prospect bookstore; "literary salons," mused a Soviet journalist approvingly—"such gentility, such patina of aristocracy."

WESTERN journals have recently given an ample account of the tremendous hunger for cars on the part of those Russians who can afford them. But the greatest passion of a middle-class family is to own a house of its own.

Soviet law says that you cannot own any *lot* (since all land belongs to the state), but a *house* can be privately owned—if it does not exceed five rooms and a total living space of 645 square feet. Wonders can be done even within these limits. An aroused correspondent described in Izvestia "a kingdom of private enterprisers"—a bourgeois suburb of a new West Siberian industrial town:

"Solid-looking, thoroughly built cottages and houses, some two-storied, their roofs of slate or even iron. Each has its own steam-heating, also verandas, with or without mansard attics, with barns made of slag-blocks and basements of reinforced concrete. As we pass, people are on guard as they stare at us from their windows with curiosity, and angry watchdogs bark."

Watchdogs, ever-present in such communities, are denounced by Communist propagandists no less than the high fences around these private houses, the scarce and high-quality materials going into such construction and the speed with which the buildings—in groups or singly—are erected. Some houses acquire yet more singular guardians. In Kiev a scientist bought a bear to waddle and growl along a wire between his gate and his house. In Magnitogorsk a metallurgical engineer planted a mine under his apple trees, and elsewhere a major of engineering troops rigged up a detonating device at his private garage door. The gadgets received unexpected publicity when both owners accidentally exploded the devices and injured themselves. More frequent are court trials of the owners who patrol their houses and orchards with guns and have shot trespassing fruit-pickers, usually young men or boys, sometimes fatally.

In addition to protective devices, Russian houses have other bourgeois features. Near Moscow, the two-story *dacha* of a senior salesman in a food store was found by the investigating authorities to have a swimming pool, a rarity for the Soviet middle-rank élite. In the same area, an executive in charge of building materials illegally erected two houses for himself and his family, one of which had a reinforced-concrete bomb shelter, even rarer in the Soviet Union than in the United States.

**KEEP OUT!—A Soviet cartoonist satirizes the bourgeois passion for fencing off public land to create private gardens in violation of collectivist ideals.**

STILL sharper is the middle-class man's hunger for land of his own. Land cannot be bought or sold, of course, but it can be used. The state has allowed Soviet citizens to use suburban land for orchards or summer rest and every city is ringed by numerous such "plots-for-use."

Usually these plots are held in cooperative groups, but the cooperation does not last. Its dissolution begins with each family clearing stumps separately, building first shacks and then solid houses individually and then planting its own fruit trees and berry bushes. Fences go up, doghouses appear, finally one-car garages are built. And from summer settlements the homes are transformed into year-round dwellings.

At meetings of the cooperatives, high-sounding phrases about Socialism and Communism reverberate, but, as a woman journalist asked bitterly in Literaturnaya Gazeta:

"What worth have these phrases . . . side by side with this real phenomenon of one's own plot of land, this sharply felt matter of one's own irrigation ditch behind the fence, this asphalt-paved path to one's own privy? . . . This is real, this can be touched and felt with one's own hands, and it is precious also because it can become a durable guaranty of some future prosperity, such as one's own car . . . and you can never tell what else may yet be installed on one's own land."

Often parts of collective farm land are illegally divided into private plots. In Volgograd the manager of a suburban state farm was approached by the manager of a building trust. In exchange for lumber needed for the farm manager's new house, he gave the trust manager a thriving garden, which the latter at once distributed among his staff, preserving the staff's pecking order: thirteen trees to a submanager, eight to an engineer, seven and six to yet others. An Izvestia correspondent complained: "With the help of mutual bribery, in essence a purchase-and-sale of state land was committed." Some such wheeler-dealers even issue to one another deeds and other land-sale documents, completely illegal and sternly punishable in the eyes of the Soviet law, but circulating in secret and having a quasi-legal effect in that tight law-breaking circle.

When a party zealot got up at one meeting of a gardeners' cooperative and urged that the cooperative ideal be restored by taking down all the fences and merging all the gardens and berry patches into one big commune, the answering cry (as reported in the Soviet press) was: "Burn it! We'd rather burn everything! So that nobody would get it!"

And they mean it. In Ashkhabad a professional couple, on being transferred to Voronezh, tried to sell their house and garden but for some reason could not. Rather than give up the property to the state, the man and his wife (she an assistant professor) in cold fury, just before departure, chopped down every tree and every grapevine, right at the roots.

It is clear that the Soviet bourgeois is frankly out for himself and does not care two kopeks for the party-decreed collective. This spring, at Cheboksary on the Volga, an outspoken student was expelled from a teachers' college dormitory by the local Komsomol. His schoolmates, feeling the punishment was undeserved, protested, and two groups of students refused to take an examination. A regional Komsomol secretary shouted at the protesters: "Why is this all happening? It's all because you spend so much time defending individuals when you should defend the collective!" It did not apparently dawn upon him that the students *were* a collective, albeit banding together to oppose the state and its official collective.

For students, technicians and other middle-class professionals do have their own "collectives" which quite often operate apart from the state's effort to herd them into supervised groups. Family merriment and friends' gatherings are the envy of party organizers. Last New Year's Eve a Soviet journalist wondered why there are no spontaneous street festivals in Russia, such as Soviet travelers have recently seen on their foreign visits. The answer is that everyone hastens to a private home "collective" to have a good time by shutting off himself and his kin and his friends from the rest of the world.

There is also often an office collective where engineers or other specialists pit their group against the rest of the Soviet world. A defector, a former Soviet naval officer specializing in geodesy and radar, told me:

"Take a typical engineering planning office, such as where I worked before defection. It's a closed-in beehive all its own, fiercely selfish, ferociously self-protective against anyone that may try to interfere from outside. Such an office is a collective, all right. To the men and women in it, the interests of this group are second only to the members' individual self-interest. This group, this team, fights for its interests—and each member expects its total benefits to be distributed among the members. And they usually are distributed, once these benefits are won. To be sure, there are petty differences and jealousies and intrigues within this engineering collective, there are in-fights, but the ranks are closed when the team faces the outside world, which means also its employer—the state, the party."

The party's hierarchs, by far no fools, know what is happening. They take lightly their propagandists' denial of the very existence of the middle and upper classes in the new Russia. They try to halt the aspirations of this new élite, to thwart its influences when they find them excessive or dangerous to party control. They impose limits on literary expression and real-estate ownership or use, foreign travel and other means of getting to know the West, consumer pressures and non-party pleasures. But, obviously, without much success.

Some party leaders, knowing that they really cannot buck the tide, explain away the discrepancy between the Communist ideal and the bourgeois reality by saying that the founding comrades never actually opposed *personal* property, that what they forbade was *private* property. Ah, but *property*, the neo-bourgeois says triumphantly, so I will continue to collect it and it will be I—not you, comrades—who will decide where "personal" stops and "private" begins.

For life is stronger than dogma. History teaches us that when a class, or a cluster of classes, wins economic strength and social prestige, inevitably it reaches out for yet more strength—for some political say-so, for political power. In ways that are gradual and sometimes unnoticed by the power-seekers themselves, the new experts —the Soviet neo-bourgeois—have already begun to nudge the rulers into a different political stance, a live-and-let-live attitude entirely unlike the will of Marx, Lenin and Stalin.

The Soviet rulers are now heirs not so much to Marx and Lenin as to King Canute.

June 5, 1966

# Soviet Urban Sprawl Defies Official Efforts to Curb the Growth of Cities

By RAYMOND H. ANDERSON
Special to The New York Times

MOSCOW — The blandishments of urban living have frustrated carefully laid plans of Soviet authorities to freeze the growth of large cities.

Hopeful of escaping the problems plaguing metropolitan centers the world around, the Soviet Union prohibits the construction of new industries in its larger cities and hampers changes of residence through a rigid passport-registration system.

But the cities are continuing to expand in population and in recent years have begun to sprawl relentlessly over their borders into surrounding fields and forests.

The urban influx is producing the irritations so familiar to residents of New York, London and other large cities: congestion, transit pains, air pollution, dirt and din.

Inadequate planning and zoning controls have added to the normal problems of growth as factories and housing are intermingled on available sites without consideration of the consequences. One industrial city near the Urals has been forced to abandon its residential quarters, at a cost of many millions of rubles, because the smoke and fumes of factories had become hazardous to health.

The difficulties confronting Soviet authorities as a result of the inexorable growth of cities are described in Oktyabr, a monthly journal, by Boris Y. Svetlichny, a Soviet architect and specialist in city planning.

"Our cities are continuing to grow despite all the theories of our city planners, who long ago declared a verbal war against giant cities, and despite a ban on constructing new industries in large cities," he complained.

Half a century ago, 18 per cent of this country's population lived in cities. Today urban residents account for 54 per cent of the population and the ratio is changing fast as young people quit farm villages for factories.

As recently as seven years ago, only three Soviet cities, Moscow, Leningrad and Kiev, had populations of more than one million. Since then, five more cities, Baku, Tashkent, Gorky, Kharkov and Novosibirsk, have passed the million mark.

This total is expected to double in the next few years as major industrial cities already pressing the million figure, among them Kuibyshev, Sverdlovsk, Chelyabinsk, Kazan and Minsk, continue their growth.

Besides the lure of urban comforts in a country where life in farm villages is still isolated and hard, the economic exigencies of an industrializing society draw people into the cities.

Planners find it much cheaper and more efficient to build factories in large cities already supplied with transit, housing, electrical power, shopping facilities and other community needs.

"For these reasons, the human stream is continuing to flow into our cities," Mr. Svetlichny wrote. "And local measures to stem the flow—restrictions on residence registration, the drawing of hard city boundaries and the creation of barriers such as green belts and surrounding parks—have proved futile."

In the 1930's, the ruling Communist party decreed that a lid be put on the size of Soviet cities and that new industries should be constructed in small towns or undeveloped areas.

The failure of this plan is best illustrated by Moscow, which mushroomed in the three decades from a population of 3.6 million to almost 6.5 million today.

Moscow authorities are determined to hold the line now and block any further expansion in population or size, but the battle is made difficult by the traditional fascination Moscow holds for most Russians.

Mr. Svetlichny said that recent attempts to curb the growth of major urban centers through the construction of satellite cities had proved unsuccessful.

"Life has demonstrated that these separate, deliberately designed annexes are soon transformed into new cities with their own independent existence," he wrote.

"Life in the city from which they were detached becomes neither better nor more comfortable."

The architect protested that bad planning or, in some cases, no planning had spoiled Soviet cities by permitting unwise construction of industrial plants in residential areas.

Worse, he added, widespread evasions of regulations on filtering equipment have led to the choking of some areas on their own fumes and smoke.

Another result of inadequate urban controls and planning, the architect said, is industrial fouling of formerly clear rivers, depriving cities of water sources and destroying millions of fish.

November 13, 1966

## *Soviet Study Finds Prosperity On Farms Is Lowering Morality*

By RAYMOND H. ANDERSON
Special to The New York Times

MOSCOW, March 15—A new problem is arising on the Soviet Union's collective farms—the blight of prosperity.

According to a sociological study published today, the rapid improvement in the condition of farmers is being accompanied by a deterioration of moral integrity and work discipline and an undermining of the development of a "Communist psychology."

The study concentrated on the collective farm at Kazminskoye in the fertile Stavropol region north of the Caucasus.

The writers noted that earnings on the farm more than doubled in the last six years.

At the same time, the sale of vodka in the village stores also doubled. This was eloquently evident, they said, from the number of drunken people stumbling along the village streets in broad daylight.

The results of the study were printed in Komsolskaya Pravda, newspaper of the Komsomol (Young Communist League).

The writers, Vladimir Logvinov and Aleksandr Yanov, protested that farm leaders were neglecting the "moral education" urgently needed as farmers found themselves with money to burn.

Instead of organizing discussions of local social problems, they said, the farm officials dream up lectures on subjects such as "Space and International Relations" and "The World of the Future in Science Fiction".

Farm family earnings have risen sharply in the last few years as a result of reforms allowing larger personal plots and higher prices for produce. Guaranteed wages and pension systems also have been introduced in the countryside.

The Komsomolskaya Pravda article laid a large share of the responsibility for an erosion of rectitude on the Kazminskoye farm to arbitrary one-man rule of the director. The farm members have lost interest in the collective fields and barns because their views and proposals for improvements are overridden or ignored, the sociologists said.

As a result, they added, the farm families are giving more time to their private plots and animals and have become increasingly involved in shady manipulations to increase their wealth at the expense of the collective farm.

An indifference to theft on the farm was assailed by the two sociologists, who described the following scene with dismay:

"On the farm sector operated by the fourth brigade, women were stuffing bags full of cornstalks before our eyes and those of the director, A. I. Rudenko. They were dragging the bags home and returning for more.

"'You don't really think that is stealing, do you?' Rudenko said, shrugging his shoulders, 'after all, a team driver will load up a whole wagon and dump it in his yard. And you should see what the tractor drivers take.

March 16, 1967

# *In Soviet Nurseries, the Parents Are Punished for Bad Children*

By CHARLOTTE CURTIS
Special to The New York Times

MOSCOW—When the littlest Communists are naughty in the nursery schools or kindergartens, where a lot of them spend most of their days, they're neither stood in a corner, spanked nor sent to bed without any dinner. It's against the law.

Instead, they're deprived of the candies and plastic toys used to reward good children or made to sit in a room all by themselves. But if they're really bad, which is to say somewhere near incorrigible, their parents are the ones who are punished.

"Children are not bad by themselves," said Mrs. Evgenia Sizova, director of a combination nursery and kindergarten in a leafy green Moscow suburb. "They act the way they do because of the conditions around them. There must be something wrong with the family."

In these sentences, Mrs. Sizova, a blond Russian who has grown children of her own, revealed herself as a Marxist who believes in Pavlovian psychology—a point of view she later confirmed. Marx believed that man was a product of his environment and that to change man, one had to change the environment.

Pavlov, the psychologist best remembered for conditioning dogs' reflexes, believed that an individual's personality was conditioned by stimuli and that his patterns of behavior could be changed not by dealing with him directly but only by changing his environment.

This is why Mrs. Sizova is more concerned with a child's parents and the home situation than with the child himself.

She sends a kindergarten teacher or nurse to the homes of problem children for talks with the parents. And if this doesn't work, she writes to the parents' factories or offices, a common Soviet device for putting on the pressure.

"I suppose children are put in the corner at home," she said, "but we don't approve of that."

What Mrs. Sizova and others who work with children do approve of is positive programs—keeping the 3-to-7-year-olds so busy they don't have time to get into mischief. And at her kindergarten-nursery, a simple white building surrounded by informal gardens, playgrounds and pools, where little boys float their toy boats, that's the kind of program the children get.

The 12-hour, six-day program, which costs parents up to $13.20 a month depending upon their salaries, begins at 7 A.M. It includes three meals, lessons in such subjects as music, dancing, reading, writing, drawing and art, afternoon naps, work sessions and organized play.

By the time he is 2½, a Soviet child is expected to dress and undress himself and make his own bed. At 3, he begins to count, and he is considered old enough for a 15-minute lesson in a class whose primary aim is to accustom him to sitting quietly in one place. When he is 4, he is given an apron, a little broom and a dustpan, and expected to take his turn on the clean-up squad. And he is only as good as his group.

### No "Skipping"

"We try not to distinguish the wunderkind from the other children because it would spoil his character," Mrs. Sizova said. "If he were praised, he might become proud. We are more concerned with the slower children.

"In either case, we shall keep children of the same age together. A child who is slow stays with his age group. We do not have what you call 'skipping.'"

Individualism is not an anathema, but it is not encouraged. Children are given group projects for which they receive group grades. Instead of drawing what they will in art classes or selecting their own subjects for compositions, the whole class will be assigned the same project.

Fast learners are praised more for what they do to help slow learners. And slow learners are praised if they raise their standards. The best student, therefore, is the average student.

"All our children work," Mrs. Sizova said. "They help with everything."

As she talked, a troop of 6 year olds was busily brushing off the flower-edged sidewalks. Another group had already weeded its vegetable garden. And upstairs, there were the modeling-clay fruits the children had made to play store.

Playing store, like playing at being a doctor, a nurse or a railroad engineer, is supposed to help prepare a child for his role in an adult society that thinks all people should have a job.

"The boys want to be Cosmonauts," Mrs. Sizova said. "They love it when they can dress up in their silver suits."

**By Age Groups**

The little suits, sometimes accompanied by big round plastic helmets, appear when it's time for the children to move into a playground equipped with slides. The top of the slide is designed to look like a rocket. Swooshing down the metal runway is supposed to simulate taking off.

Each age group has its own lockers, bathrooms, nap area and main room. And each main room is stocked with an aquarium, potted plants and a bird in a cage—all of which are the children's responsibility. There also are masses of plastic toys, although the Soviet Union has never been able to keep up with the demand for them.

"The children grew these flowers," Mrs. Sizova said, pointing at vases of red and pink sweet williams on the little dining tables. "If they have bad manners, we take the flowers away."

What she meant was that if one of the four children at a table has bad manners, the whole table loses its flowers. This sharing of blame, typical of the collective approach to life that permeates all of Soviet society, produces a group response from the offender's peers. And the pressure, like the co-workers' pressure on a parent whose employer has been notified of a child's misbehavior, often works.

"Nobody wants his friends mad at him," Mrs. Sizova said.

August 7, 1967

# Television Alters Living Habits

Nothing in recent social history, not even the coming of the automobile, has done more to change Soviet living patterns than television.

Antennas spring from the roofs of wood or mud houses that have no running water, from the tops of newly built apartment buildings and from palaces within the Kremlin walls.

Tour leaders on sightseeing buses point with pride to the new television towers in city after city. Big city hotels, which have not yet come to terms with the mechanics of the flush toilet, are quick to announce that guests may rent television sets for their rooms. But for most families, the first problem in crowded living quarters is where to put this marvelous toy.

Television sets in the Soviet Union cost anywhere from 200 to 400 rubles ($220 to $440), depending on screen size and quality. This is the equivalent of two to four months' salary of the average Soviet wage-earner.

For centuries, life has revolved around the kitchen. Dining rooms were and generally are nonexistent. Parlors, when they were to be had, were for family celebrations. At night, most parlors became bedrooms. The only other rooms were bedrooms for two or more, bathrooms and toilets.

Meals were served in the kitchen, and that is where the dining table was kept. So some television sets went immediately into the kitchen.

"Everybody I know gathers in the kitchen," said a Moscow journalist whose friends must be reasonably affluent, "because the television and the refrigerator are there."

But some television sets went into what passed for the living room. And when it did, a second dining table and some of the meals went with it.

After a while, babushkas (grandmothers) had to be reminded that their evening television-watching stints were disturbing the children's homework. Fathers complained that mothers appeared to care more for television than the upkeep of the household.

And youngsters arranged their lives so they could see "Good Night, Children," an evening broadcast of fairy tales and entertainment.

In Moscow a woman said she stopped reading (a common complaint) after she and her husband got their television set and that they are now forcing themselves to leave their apartment for walks just to escape it.

A former woman deputy in the national Supreme Soviet—a vigorous athlete who plays volley ball, skis and ice-skates—used to join the thousands of spectators at sports events. Sometimes she still does. But she is more likely to stay home and watch them from her easy chair.

"Why should I go out," she asked rhetorically, "when I can see them at home?"

Moscow has two news and entertainment channels and one devoted to education. The stations are on the air for about two hours around noon and off again until 5 P.M. Then the broadcasts begin again and last until midnight. Other cities have only one channel.

The state-controlled television covers the news as the Government sees it and sports events. It takes viewers into restaurants for interviews and features movies and drama. Programs also take up the problems of the family, youth, home and health and teach foreign languages.

October 9, 1967

*1917—The Russian Revolution—1967*

# Soviet Union's Sports Follow Purposeful Course Under Government Direction

By ROBERT LIPSYTE

IN 50 years, from nearly a standing start, the Soviet Union has increased sports participation from 50,000 to 50 million and has become a leading athletic power in the world. From the ranks of its organized physical culturists will spring the teams to beat in the 1968 Olympic Games.

There are no professional teams in the Soviet Union to skim the athletic cream, no factions struggling for control of amateur sports. A central system spends more than $2.2-billion annually to fulfill an axiom attributed to Lenin that a nation cannot be strong unless it is strong in sports.

Even now, a year before the world meets in Mexico City, Soviet Olympians are honing their talents in competitions throughout the world, as individuals and as members of national teams. But Soviet officials will say that preparation for next October's Olympics began many years ago, even as youngsters right now are being groomed for the Olympics of 1984.

A visitor to the Soviet Union last summer saw sport begin in earnest when he stood on a misty, wind-swept bluff overlooking the Gulf of Finland.

**11-Year-Olds Being Groomed**

A dozen 11-year-old boys, damp-faced and red-kneed, churned over a lumpy cinder field, scrabbling to kick a brown ball at a splintery wooden goal. They might be small boys at play anywhere, except for their intensity and their silence. From a corner of the field, a middle-aged man studied them relentlessly.

He had been watching them since January, when they trooped through the snow, nervous and chattery, to a drafty gymnasium owned by a trade union sports society called Spartak. Beneath crimson banners that read "Mass and Quality is the Slogan of Soviet Sport" and "Glory to the Communist Party," the boys had been examined by doctors, interviewed by teachers and handed soccer balls.

There were 512 boys in January, the oldest 16, the youngest 10. By late March there were 100, ready for the cinder field.

The middle-aged man divided them into groups, by age. The 11-year-olds would practice from 4 to 5 P.M., twice a week, until school let out in June. Then it would be three times a week, from 11 A.M. to 1 P.M.

He told them, quite sternly, about the importance of sleep, proper eating habits, moral quality and collective play. They had heard it all before, but they listened carefully. They knew that the middle-aged man, Boris Oreshkin, had once played for the national soccer team.

He also told them, gently and with laughter, to forget the little mannerisms, the swaggers and the shoulder rolls they had picked up watching Class A games on television. There would be time enough for such things when they got to the Lenin Stadium in Moscow and played to the roar of 100,000.

**Not So Wild a Dream**

It was not so wild a dream, even for 11-year-old Leningrad boys in sneakers and hand-me-down spikes racing through a practice period in the 50th year of Soviet rule.

If they did well here, if Boris Oreshkin thought he saw something in the snap of their head shots, the drive in their legs, the world's most structured and supervised sports system would find hands to lift them up.

There would be special summer sports camps and "comradely matches" against the youth teams of other trade union societies. There would be opportunities to represent the society in district, city, republican and even national tournaments, opportunities to represent the city in a Spartakiad, the quadrennial internal Olympic Games.

A team of cyclists, hunch-backed on their frail machines, eerily buzzed out of the mist, circled the cinder field and disappeared. None of Boris Oreshkin's 11-year-olds looked up. Thirty women in bulging jerseys, their gray-haired heads wrapped in white kerchiefs trotted unsteadily behind a physical culture instructor.

Somewhere beyond the trees, a basketball slammed against a backboard, then skittered along a concrete, winter-cracked court.

Far below the wind-swept bluff, children were scrambling into the little wooden sailboats of the Central Yacht Club. Like the silent soccer players, they were students in a sports school, one of 2,500 in the country. Their Boris Oreshkin, once an M Class sailing champion, was another of the country's 175,000 sports and recreation teachers.

**Facilities Are Improving**

The Soviet Union's sports advances have been made on facilities that are rapidly improving but are still inferior by Western standards, and by a population that only in the last generation has been eating beef and greens in quantity.

The system works because the government ultimately controls the construction of paddle-ball courts and 100,000-seat stadiums, the transportation of teams, the curriculum in physical culture institutes and the production of table-tennis balls.

For the common man, sports participation is inexpensive, easily accessible and sometimes obligatory. It is also, he is told, in the interests of national purpose, essential for his health, for productivity, for progress toward Communism.

The star athlete gets subsidization, material rewards and an avenue for the self-expression that is not always easy in a controlled society. There are no professional athletes in the Soviet Union, but the champion amateur can remain in school or at a nominal job that does not interfere wth his training as long as his legs can carry his weight.

"The games and the equipment are the same the whole world over," says Stanislav Yananis, head of the chair of Sports Theory and History at the Lesgaft Institute in Leningrad, the first and most prestigious of the Soviet Union's 16 physical culture institutes of higher education.

"But there is a difference between sports here and in a bourgeois society. Our system is directed by a socialist state and sports is not an end in itself. We are creating a new man, physically, mentally, morally."

Soviet sport is not always grim, but it is always serious. Because an important athlete is required to be an example to youth and a reflection, to the world, of socialist vitality, his attitude is under constant scrutiny. The sports columns of Pravda reserve their strongest scorn for the athlete who lost through "moral weakness."

Before the revolution, sports was an upper-class activity. Aristocrats hunted, rowed, raced horses and sailed at the Imperial Yacht Club. Merchants' sons skated and worked out in athletic clubs inspired by German traders.

The ineffectual teams that Russia sent to the Olympic Games of 1908 and 1912 were selected to balance club representation and skirt the traditional St. Petersburg-Moscow rivalry. Russian athletes won few medals at the Olympics, but competitors found them an extremely genial, relaxed and well-tailored group.

It was 40 years before a Russian again participated in the Olympics. In 1952, in neighboring Helsinki, the Soviet team nearly won the unofficial championship, losing in the last day to an American surge.

The impact of the Soviet effort upon international sports was tremendous. The Olympics, which have always been subtly merchandized as a kind of moral equivalent to war, became an arena for the muscle of ideology.

In the years to come, as both East and West charged each other with hypocrisy and professionalism and the use of sports as a political tool, always with some justification, controversy obscured what to the Russians was the crucial issue. For the infant Soviet state, sports had been an element in survival.

The physical culture movement, at first an amalgam of Swedish, Czech and German mass exercises, was begun in the Red Army in 1918 to improve the fitness of recruits. It grew and spread, particularly among workers' groups, military units and the internal security forces.

Although Lenin is now said to have been a hunter, hiker, skater and cyclist, the Communist party took only an encouraging, advisory role until 1929 when it established a single central government agency to direct all physical culture and sports.

The sports organization remained essentially the same until the creation of the present Union of Sports Societies and Organizations in 1959. The Moscow-based union directly controls 44 of the 59 types of sports played in the Soviet Union.

The 15 so-called "technical" or paramilitary sports, such as parachute-jumping, automobile racing and gliding, are supervised by the Voluntary Society for Assistance to the Army, Air Force and Navy, a group known by its initials, DOSAAF.

The development of Soviet sports between the revolution and World War II was marked by the methodical introduction and encouragement of particular sports at particular times in a pragmatic attack on poor health, faltering production, boredom and political ignorance.

**Master of Sports Introduced**

Organized sports provided exercise, increased efficiency, easy amusement, emotional release, and a handy network of clubs for the dissemination of Communist thought. Even now, the prime mover in Soviet sports is the Komsomol, the Young Communist League of 15-to-28-year-olds.

After the war, the sports classification standards leading to the Master of Sports medal were introduced, causing a new surge in the program. The bronze, rectangular medal symbolized championship class proficiency for massive weight lifters, willowy girl runners and pale, concave-chested checker players.

Despite party boasts on Physical Culture Day and American exaggeration during Olympic fund drives, the Soviet Union does not spring up at dawn for push-ups and a cold shower. The radio broadcasts 15 minutes of setting-up exercises, but even Soviet radios have to be turned on.

The sports hierarchy has been trying for years to increase the number of gym periods for schoolchildren, but the science and math teachers feel that two hours a week are sufficient. And, though not yet in the Western-style epidemic stage, "spectatoritis" is on the rise.

Except at the racetrack, where his conduct is deplorably universal, the Soviet sports fan is enthusiastic, knowledgeable and among the best behaved in the world. Once, his enthusiasm could be solely attributed to hunger for entertainment, but now it is more an outgrowth of early exposure to sports.

Hundreds are still turned away from volleyball games between Moscow girls' teams, and on a night when several thousand climbed a muddy, construction-littered hill in Kiev to see a Greco-Roman wrestling match, there were dances, jazz concerts and lectures in the public parks, the movie houses and television stations were offering a full and varied program, and a lover's moon hung over the Dnieper River.

The sports fan is never more visible

or vocal than when the soccer season is stoking up. Usually the blue-and-white-clad squads of Moscow's Dynamo lead the two-conference, 39-team Class A division, the major league. Formed in 1923 to represent the internal security forces and strengthened later by the interest of Lavrenti P. Beria, Stalin's internal security chief, Dynamo is the oldest, richest and best equipped of the nationwide sports societies. Dynamo has lost its secret police image, but not the early advantage that enabled it to build and collect rentals from the first stadiums, establish sports equipment outlets and recruit the best young players.

Much of the intense rivalry between cities and regions is historical, some of it is ethnic, but, in sports, a great deal of it developed during the long period of Soviet isolation. Between the revolution and World War II, under pressure from governments that did not recognize the new regime, international sports federations would not admit Soviet teams or sanction Soviet records.

"It was a sports blockade," says 70-year-old Aleksander Toivonen, one of the early wrestling coaches.

"We sportsmen only waited for the day when we could compete internationally. We felt that we would never really grow until then. But, perhaps in the long run, we ended up stronger because we had to turn inward into ourselves."

This turning inward involved the creation of elaborate calendars of internal competitions culminating in the Spartakiad, first held in 1928, and the encouragement of intramural sports rivalries not very different from the quota competitions among factories. Teams and individual athletes receive cash bonuses and free vacation trips.

The Soviet approach to sports became — and still is — painstakingly academic. Foreign books and photographs were reproduced and studied, observers were sent when possible to shoot movies of champions in action. Esoteric monographs were prepared on sports minutiae. Valery Brumel's 1963 world record was credited, in part, to a 300-page Soviet high-jumping manual 30 years in preparation.

This academic approach, consonant with Marxist science and reason, reaches its peak in the higher education of athletes. There is a medical school in Estonia offering a six-year course leading to a doctor-coach certificate. The doctor-coach, it is said, will be able, among other things, to integrate the technical training of an athlete with his individual hormonal development.

There are two sports-science research institutes where complex machines are being developed to measure the energy patterns of runners and swimmers.

Igor Ter-Ovanesyan, the long-jumper, has been working for several years on his post-graduate dissertation, "The influence of different rhythms upon the speed at which certain movements, in jumping and throwing, are executed."

Yuri Vlasov, the weight-lifter, a former engineering student, has created a rack-like machine to develop certain leg muscles that most people never use.

The Soviet Union did not enter the International sports arena until 1946 and the Russians quickly became box-office, an important consideration in the frequently shoestring world of international sports.

The great Soviet triumphs in European and world championships and in the 1956 and 1960 Olympic Games encouraged and glamourized sports activity at home. Society membership rose, budget strings loosened, and new facilities were built. The pride of Soviet sports complexes, built in 1955 on a swamp in Moscow called Luzhniki, is a 17,000-acre microcosm of the entire nation at play.

### Central Stadium Seats 100,000

The focal point of Luzhniki is the Central Lenin Stadium, built with the help of volunteer labor in time for the World Youth Festival. The haste in which it was built is reflected in the somewhat crumbly appearance of its yellowing stone façade, but the oval arena, nearly a mile around, holds 100,000 for an important soccer game or track meet.

On a day when the Stadium was being prepared for the 1967 Spartakiad, the Soviet Davis Cup team was playing Chile in the 14,000-seat secondary stadium. Admission to the tennis match ranged from $1 to $1.50. Outdoor volleyball and basketball games are also staged there.

On nearby indoor courts, Anna Dmitriyeva, a pert-faced teacher of French and the country's top woman player, was rallying with Galina Baksheyeva, a redhead with long false eyelashes, who is No. 2 and a university student. Anna's year-old daughter watched the two women in their last practice before they were to leave on a European tour.

In the 12,000-seat outdoor heated pool the Astrakhan water-polo team was working out with Moscow University, and 8-year-old divers were hurtling off high boards in a sports school session. A squealing pack of Young Pioneers, their red neckerchiefs askew, were waiting their turn outside the locker-rooms. They would change into bathing suits, jump into indoor pools, and swim along a waterway corridor into the main outdoor pool.

In the Palace of Sports, the 15,000-seat main indoor arena, an Austrian ice revue was practicing for an evening performance. The arena also is used for basketball, volleyball, indoor track and field, and boxing matches. On a secondary ice-skating rink, Moscow mothers in the ubiquitous thin blue raincoats were anxiously watching 6-year-old daughters who would all grow up to be Lidiya Skoblikova, the champion speed skater.

There are 28 gymnasiums in Luzhniki and most were occupied, mostly on a rental basis, by sports schools. Lithe young girls spun over Turkoman carpets, weight-lifters heaved and boxers sparred cautiously. Soviet boxers are quite cautious, partly out of "science," partly because a knockout is followed by a 3-month suspension, a third knockout in a career means banishment from the ring.

On well-tended fields around the main buildings, students played tennis, badminton and soccer. The health clubs, hundreds of women on their lunch hours or after early factory shifts, touched toes and waved small dumbbells.

The Luzhniki complex, which officials hope will some day host an Olympics, is owned by the Moscow City Council. Like many other municipal facilities, it is on a self-supporting basis. It is an example of sports as big business.

Once isolated internationally, the Soviet Union now maintains sports relations with some 80 countries, and receives some 10,000 foreign athletes a year, mainly from the Communist bloc and from Scandinavian countries. More than 10,000 Soviet athletes go abroad each year.

In sports, at least, the Soviet Union has made almost incredible advances since the days when Pravda called tennis "decadent and bourgeois." The statement is now denied and scorned as "Chinese thinking."

"You must understand this," says Gavriil Korobkov, the national track and field coach. "We had many problems. We didn't have enough food and tens of millions were living in holes in the ground. Houses come before swimming pools and potato fields before tennis courts. Now we are building those tennis courts and those swimming pools. It's as simple as that. And someday we might build a golf course. Why not?"

November 2, 1967

# RISING DRUG USE A SOVIET PROBLEM

### Decree Increasing Penalties Published in Republic

MOSCOW July 26 (Reuters) —An admission that the Soviet Union is facing a growing "bourgeois" problem of drug addiction appeared recently in a local newspaper in the Georgian Republic.

The newspaper, Vecherny Tbilisi, published a decree issued by the Soviet Republic of Georgia that virtually doubled the possible sentences for taking or peddling drugs.

The decree increased the sentences for using drugs without medical permission to 10 to 15 days compulsory treatment, and for second offenders up to a year in a special camp for drug victims. It also increased to 15 years the maximum sentence for persons who operate places where narcotics are used or who grow or process them.

Persons inducing others to take drugs can now be imprisoned for up to 10 years. This provision previously applied only to persons supplying drugs to adolescents and provided a maximum sentence of five years.

The Georgian decree is

based upon a series of laws enacted in 1965 for the entire Soviet Union, but it was not immediately determined whether the same increases in penalties have been applied to the rest of the Soviet Union.

Informed sources said drug-taking was a more serious problem in Georgia than in many other parts of the Soviet Union because plants from which drugs come grow more easily in the republic's warm and fertile soil.

Alongside the decree, the newspaper printed an explanatory article that said:

"The people's lawmaking organs cannot reconcile themselves to a spread of this terrible evil.

"The capitalist world has for long been in the fever of narcomania. Unfortunately, here and there we, too, have a few young people who blindly follow the bourgeois example, lose their human feelings, substitute socially useful work and study with idleness and drug-taking, thus harming themselves, their families and the interests of the whole nation.

"It is clear to all that drug-taking is not characteristic of the Soviet way of life and is a foreign bacteria that has penetrated the healthy body of our society," the article said. "But, however small the bacteria is, it is extremely dangerous."

July 27, 1969

# SCHOOLS IN SOVIET REVISE PROGRAMS

## Seek to Stimulate Pupils to Creative Thought

By JAMES F. CLARITY

Special to The New York Times

MOSCOW, Aug. 30—Carrying flowers for the teachers, wearing traditionally somber-colored suits and jumpers, and facing—whether they know it or not—a nationally revised curriculum, some 45 million Soviet boys and girls will begin the fall school term Monday.

The demand for flowers has driven the free-market price up to more than $1 for a small bouquet of phlox. Patient mothers have been waiting for hours in department-store lines to buy clothes for their restless young.

The curriculum revision is designed, according to Soviet educators, to stimulate the pupils to creative rather than stereotyped thought.

The revision includes the condensation of the first four years of the old curriculum into three and the teaching of basic algebra in first grade. Learning by rote, without explanation and discussion, is to be reduced.

The condensation and revision are expected to prepare the children for more advanced work in the last seven of their 10 years of combined primary and secondary education.

**2,072 Textbooks Used**

In preparation for the new school year the Ministry of Education reported that 292 million copies of 2,072 textbooks, including 20 completely new ones, have been printed. For the teachers who must transmit the new curriculum the ministry has published 39 guideline books.

While the curriculum will be new, the youngsters will be wearing virtually the same style clothes their parents wore to school. Girls wear black jumpers over brown dresses with white collars, as they did before the Bolshevik Revolution in 1917. Boys wear dark suits, usually gray, but are not required to have ties.

In the last days before the opening of school. Moscow department stores specializing in youthware provided commercial torture equal in degree but different in kind, to that found in Macys, Gimbels or Korvette's in December in Manhattan.

At Detsky Mir (Children's World), a large department store in downtown Moscow, the abacuses clacked constantly the other day as salesgirls sold schoolbags of synthetic materials for as much as the ruble equivalent of $4, foot-long violins for $10, girls gym-suits for $1.50 and outfits for Young Pioneers, as the Government-organized scouts are called, for as much as $12 (cap, shirt, walking shorts or skirt and red neckerchief).

**'It Fits,' Mother Says**

One pioneer, a blond boy of 8 or 9, smiled broadly at a counter as a salesgirl reached into stacks of caps, shirts and pants. A red and gold profile of Lenin and the motto "Always Prepared" was on the wall above her.

The boy's mother slapped a cloth cap on his head and he raised his hands as if to feel it. "It fits," his mother said abruptly, tossing it on the counter. The boy seemed to want to touch his new pants as well, but after pressing them against his waist for an instant, his mother said, "It fits." An older woman, perhaps his grandmother, fingered the price tags and said, "It's a lot of money."

"They fit—we'll take them," said the mother, hurrying toward the cashier's booth with her order slips.

Judging from the movement of the line to the uniform counter, the woman had waited at least 30 minutes to place her order. She faced another 10 minutes' wait to pay the cashier, who rang up sales on a cash register but had an abacus at her elbow for emergencies.

The two-line wait in Moscow stores is the heart of the commercial malaise. Detsky Mir is scheduled to stay open specially tomorrow from 7:30 A.M. to 7 P.M., for last-minute customers.

August 31, 1969

# *Woman's Role in Society Is Troubling Soviet, Too*

By BERNARD GWERTZMAN

Special to The New York Times

MOSCOW, Jan. 24—Soviet women, who are expected to do everything, from digging ditches to producing babies, are grumbling these days about job discrimination, male chauvinism and lack of concern by Soviet authorities.

The result, according to one demographer, is the development of a "women's question" in the Soviet Union:

"Why has the idea of real emancipation of women still not emerged victorious in the public consciousness of both men and women?"

Sociologists are warning the authorities that the dissatisfaction of many women with their status in society is a contributing cause, if not the major one, for the sharp drop in the birth rate—from 24.9 per thousand in 1960 to 17 in 1969, the last year for which statistics are available.

Newspapers and magazines regularly print letters and articles related to the "women's question."

One woman writes that there must be 24-hour nurseries so that women can hold on to jobs. Another says bonuses should be paid women with children to allow them to quit work. A man from Kharkov complains that because his wife is so busy with the household chores and her job, she cannot make him a meal, so he has become an alcoholic.

"The revolution freed us," a middle-aged woman said, "so that we can work harder than men."

Many of the problems are similar to those faced by women in the United States and other Western countries where the women's liberation movement is active. But there is no comparable organized movement in the Soviet Union and, indeed, some of the problems are different.

For instance, Soviet women have no quarrel with the present rules on voluntary abortion, which is the main birth control method. They do complain about preference given to men in many fields of work and the paradox of public thinking as a result of which women are considered men's equals in doing heavy manual work but men generally refuse to do an equal share of household chores.

Sociologists report the difficulties that a woman faces in holding a fulltime job, running a household and having a family. The pressures often result in family disputes, a growing number of divorces and the birthrate problem.

Despite recommendations by scholars and by the women themselves, nothing seems to be done to ease the problem.

There are probably no easy answers. Women make up 50 per cent of the work force. Many typically female jobs are the least attractive: paving streets, picking up garbage, digging holes. Others, such as teaching, medicine and scientific work, are more gratifying, but even where women make up most of the workers, a man is usually in charge.

Lidiya T. Litvinenko, a demographer interviewed in the latest issue of Zhurnalist, the journalists' magazine, says it is no secret that factory directors prefer to give better jobs to men, out of concern that women often have to leave to take care of children. Women, she says, are faced with a choice —either to have a child or have a career — and most these days choose the latter.

Many men would like to put the women back in the kitchen and restore an old-fashioned family environment. But, Miss Litvinenko says, this is not acceptable to women. They want jobs that interest them and they do not want to be dependent on their husbands' salaries.

She acknowledges that some women share the prevailing male outlook on a women's role, but she maintains that they are either naive or hypocritical.

Moreover, sociologists point out that the Soviet economy, already short of workers, could not function if a substantial number of women quit the work force. They also say that a husband's salary alone is often not enough to make ends meet.

One of the most-talked-about pieces of writing in the last year is a short story, "A Week Like Any Other," written by Natalya Baranskaya, a laboratory worker, who relates the crisis of a young married woman driven to nervous exhaustion by the burdens of keeping a job, taking care of two small children and remaining attractive to her husband.

Her heroine, like many women in real life, is constantly tired and rarely gets time to see a movie or read a book. She is teased by her coworkers because she has two children while virtually none of her friends have more than one.

The trend toward a one-child family is so common now in the European parts of the Soviet Union that it is the prime concern of the demographers.

A sociologist, writing in the youth newspaper Komsomolskaya Pravda, said he was upset by the view of many youths who, he said, are opposed to having children because they regard them as a burden.

He reminded his readers that unless many families had at least two children—and many three children—society would not reproduce itself and the country would face more severe manpower shortages.

There already is a labor shortage in big cities and in areas with an inhospitable environment, such as Siberia.

Zoya A. Yankova, a sociologist working for the Academy of Sciences Institute of Social Research, is a specialist on women's problems, and her findings, as published recently by the academy, seem to verify what most Russians believe is the case.

On the basis of interviews in Moscow, Leningrad and Penza, she said that the Soviet woman, on the average, has to spend more time—six hours — on household chores than she did 40 years ago; the figure was four hours then.

Much of the extra work, she said, is the result of an almost complete abdication of men from household work and a discernible switch in Soviet families from patriarchal to matriarchal.

"If, earlier, the obligations of women in the home were limited mainly to preparing meals, housecleaning, and laundry, etc.," she said, "now their basic duties have also become the upbringing of children, supervising their activities, visiting children's institutions, shopping for the home, including major purchases, organizing the leisure time of the family and other not specifically women's obligations in the old, patriarchal family.

"Women, in other words, not only have to fulfill their traditional obligations, but have new ones, demanding extra energy and increasing the amount of time spent on work outside of their jobs."

Part of the extra energy is spent traveling between home and job. Because so much of the new housing available to new families is on the outskirts of urban areas, many women travel as much as an hour and a half each way, with additional time spent in shopping along the way.

In the past, Miss Yankova said, women could count on their mothers or mothers-in-law to help out with children and household work. But the improvement in housing conditions has allowed the two generations to live apart, and many grandmothers are no longer eager to work fulltime as babysitters and cleaning women at home.

Maids and regular baby sitters are difficult to find because factories and stores offer better wages—as much as 80 to 90 rubles a month for unskilled help — compared with the 50 rubles that a maid might receive. A ruble is $1.10 at the official rate.

Despite promises of expanded services, Miss Yankova found, only a third of the women in the survey ever sent clothes to the dry cleaner and then only two or three times a year.

In Moscow, where the standard of living is higher than in the rest of the country, only 15 per cent of the women have washing machines, 37 per cent refrigerators and 20 per cent vacuum cleaners, the survey showed.

Because of the lack of human or mechanical help, Miss Yankova said, "a significant part" of those polled replied, "Often" to the question, "Are you often tired?" Eighty per cent of those polled said their free time was limited to watching television or sleeping. Only 20 per cent said they went to the movies or the theater or entertained on a regular basis.

Many women said their lives would be easier if there were better nursery centers. About half of those polled said they were dissatisfied with the nurseries. A major complaint is the rule that if a child catches a cold or some other illness he must go home, and this means the mother must take sick leave to care for the child.

Miss Litvinenko said places of employment should provide nurseries and day schools that would keep sick children, thereby allowing the mother to stay at work and encourage her to have more children.

About 80 per cent of the women questioned by Miss Yankova said a woman should take care of children up to the age of 3, "since in the nurseries they often get sick." But Soviet law provides only one year's leave of absence.

Many women would also like to work part time to allow more time with children, Miss Yankova said, but Miss Litvinenko said in fact most women do not want to work less than full time.

Many sociologists seem to recognize that their rather frank criticisms of the status of women in Soviet society run counter to the frequent official boasts that women have equality under Communism.

To give the complaints ideological justification, some sociologists have quoted freely from Lenin's comments on the subject. Miss Yankova reminded her readers that he said:

"Very few men, even those from the proletariat, have considered how much they would lighten the burdens and cares of their wives — or even to relieve them of them completely — if they would help in 'women's work.' But no, this would be against 'the rights and dignity of man.' He demands that he has his rest and comfort. The household life of the woman is a daily sacrifice of herself as a victim to thousands of petty things. The old right of male supremacy continues to exist in concealed forms."

January 25, 1971

# *Sales of Vodka Cut Sharply by Soviet*

By THEODORE SHABAD
Special to The New York Times

MOSCOW, June 16—The Soviet Government ordered a sharp reduction today in the sale of vodka, and expanded the output of soft drinks in an intensified drive against heavy drinking.

The Government acted promptly to curb liquor sales after the ruling Communist party, in a decree by its Central Committee, acknowledged that alcoholism was causing "tremendous harm to the entire Soviet society."

The tougher actions by the authorities, which fall short of outright prohibition, reflected concern over growing drinking habits among young people and the impact of alcoholism on the productivity of labor, which is fast becoming a crucial index of economic progress in the Soviet Union.

A Government decree published today on the front pages of all daily newspapers called for reduction in the number of vodka retailing outlets, prohibiting sales altogether near industrial plants, schools, hospitals, theaters, railroad stations, recreational facilities and other heavily frequented places.

The sale of vodka is to be entirely banned on weekends and holidays, and the limitation of retailing hours from 11 A.M. to 7 P.M. is to be rigorously enforced. Retailing, like most other sectors of the Soviet economy, is operated by the Government.

Published analyses of drinking patterns have shown that absenteeism in industry after holidays and paydays is seriously hurting economic growth. In some factories, 10 to 30 per cent of the workers are said to spend at least one night at a sobering-up station during the year.

Alcoholism appears to have been fostered by the advent of a five-day work week in 1967 without provision for adequate recreational activities to reduce boredom and absorb surplus energy on the two days off.

A rise in vodka prices in 1970, episodic antidrinking drives in the press and the public exposure of habitual drunkards on posted "rolls of dishonor" appear to have had little effect.

The current campaign was set in motion Tuesday with publication of a party decree that appeared to focus on an evident increase in the consumption of alcohol among young people.

It called on press, radio and television as well as on motion pictures and the national public-lecture system to "intensify antialcohol propaganda and to make clear the tremendous harm caused by drinking to public health, the rearing of children and teen-agers and to the entire Soviet Society."

Educators, trade unions and the Communist youth organizations were instructed to "make recommendations for a system of antialcohol propaganda and the indroctrination of students and working youths and to insure implementation."

It is not unusual to see a Muscovite come reeling down a street with his body swaying at angles that seem to defy the law of gravity. The practice of a threesome sharing the cost of a bottle and finishing it off in a quiet corner has become a byword in the Russian language.

Although the social evils of drinking have long been publicized in the Soviet Union, the focus now appears to be shifting to the economic harm caused by alcoholism by reducing the productivity of labor.

The gradual depletion of the available manpower pool has ended the practice of expanding production through simple additions to the labor force. For further gains in output, Soviet industry must now rely on greater production per worker.

A young woman economist, Raisa D. Savranskaya, reported recently that even moderate drinking tended to reduce labor productivity the next day by 4 to 5 per cent, and heavier use of alcohol by as much as 30 per cent.

Writing in the industrial daily Sotsialisticheskaya Industriya, she said a high percentage of below-standard products, idleness of costly equipment and disorganization of the entire process of production, especially in assembly-line operations, posed serious problems after paydays and holidays.

Reporting on another study, Miss Savranskaya stressed the impact of habitual heavy drinking on labor turnover and the loss of work skills. A survey of a group of alcoholics, she said, had shown that 12 per cent were shifted to lower skill categories and about the same percentage frequently changed places of employment.

June 17, 1972

# SOVIET COVERAGE OF CRASH SKIMPY

## Domestic Catastrophes Get Little Media Attention

By HEDRICK SMITH
Special to The New York Times

MOSCOW, Oct. 16—For the discerning reader, there was no more to arouse attention than five husband-and-wife obituary notices in the Moscow press recording their "untimely" deaths.

At Moscow State University, a plaque suddenly appeared honoring a psychology professor, noting his "tragic" death. The only clue to how it happened was that it occurred Oct. 3—the day that an Aeroflot Ilyushin-18 airliner crashed near the Black Sea resort of Sochi, carrying 100 people to their deaths.

In this instance, as in other cases of domestic catastrophes, the Soviet press adapted in its own way the Western saying that no news is good news — bad news is no news.

The disastrous crash of an Ilyushin-62 airliner near Moscow on Friday night was a part exception because more than 50 foreigners were involved—Chileans, Algerians, a Frenchman and an Englishman.

A day later, after foreign news agencies had learned of the crash unofficially, the Soviet media carried a 52-word item on the accident. But they did not give the casualty toll, nor did they indicate that the crash had involved a Soviet plane, nor did they say that it was the worst crash in civil-aviation history. Unofficially, Soviet sources have disclosed that 176 persons perished. The affected foreign embassies were told of the deaths of their citizens but the Soviet public was left in the dark on that point.

**Phraseology**

Soviet newspaper readers have taken to interpreting phrases like "untimely" or "tragic" death as confirmation of rumored crashes. In instances of death from illness, other phrases are used in obituaries. Although the media are able to ignore the accidents themselves, the authorities are unwilling to overlook the deaths of certain members of society.

In the fall of 1971, a Hungarian airliner crashed near Kiev, in the Ukraine, killing 49 persons, and the Soviet press left the event unrecorded until four days later when it printed a telegram of condolence from Premier Aleksei N. Kosygin to the Hungarian Government.

No one here thought it unusual that the telegram asked that condolences be conveyed "to the families of the crash victims" without mentioning the crash and where, when or even that an airliner was involved.

The practice of ignoring untoward events extends to other fields as well. Although the Soviet Union is now energetically pushing into the automobile era, statistics on traffic fatalities are published erratically. But there are some signs that some officials think it would be wise to publicize the rising toll more to frighten people into driving more safely.

Soviet officials say privately they see no point in sensationalizing bad news as is done in Western media. But Western diplomats note that not even dry, factual accounts appear, and some suspect that the authorities are wary of reporting alarming death statistics that might reflect badly on Soviet roads or the state of repair of Soviet cars, both of which are generally considered to be far below standards in Western Europe or North America.

In particular, Western specialists gleaning a few statistics from various Soviet publications suggest that the traffic-fatality rates may be rising at alarming proportions. Articles last summer disclosed 8,797 fatalities in the Ukraine and Kazakhstan in 1971 — twice as many as in California although that state is estimated to have four or five times as many vehicles.

In some unusual cases, the media have taken the initiative in reporting catastrophes, though they have withheld the extent of the disasters.

After an industrial explosion in Minsk in March, the media reported the appointment of a high-level Government investigation commission and subsequently the punishment of several high officials for negligence.

But the media did not disclose how many people had died in the explosion and fire at the Minsk television and radio plant. Subsequently, unofficial sources said that as a result of briefings to Moscow fire-fighting units, they had heard 270 persons were killed.

In some instances, when continuing disasters have more immediate impact on public welfare, the media are notably slow in providing basic information.

Last summer, when there were vast forest and peat fires in central Russia covering thousands of acres and some even edging close to Moscow, the controlled press and radio ignored the fires until they were public knowledge.

October 17, 1972

# Religion Still Deeply Embedded in Soviet

By HEDRICK SMITH
Special to The New York Times

MOSCOW, Sunday, April 14—To the world the Soviet Union is the nation that marks its main national holiday, the anniversary of the Bolshevik Revolution, with a military parade through Red Square.

Yet across this vast land thousands of candlelight processions circling churches at midnight attracted millions of people to witness the traditional Russian celebration of Easter—their numbers testimony to the modest religious revival here in recent years.

Over half a century after the Revolution, religious tradition and belief remain deeply embedded in the life of this officially atheistic nation. Churches claim more than twice as many followers as the Soviet Communist party does members.

What strikes many people most sharply in the reawakened interest in religion in recent years is the crowds of curious young people who cram the courtyards outside onion-domed churches at Easter time to glimpse the gilded robes of priests, the ornate church interiors and the colorful rituals and to catch an exotic whiff of incense or to hear the chanting of the choir. However, a large majority of church-going Christians are older people, especially women.

Among all religious holidays in this country Easter, with its onion-dyed eggs, its sweet, curdled cream cheese, its raisin cake, its family gatherings and religious pageantry, has the most meaning and magnetism.

"Everyone celebrates Easter—believers and nonbelievers alike," commented a middle-aged Communist party member who finds visits to churches one of his favorite vacation pastimes. A 30-year-old engineer who keeps an icon in the corner of his room, the traditional place of prayer, qualified that observation: "Not everyone—but very, very many."

Pravda and other party publications acknowledged their concern over what Kommunist, the party's ideological publication, termed "the vitality and tenacity" of religion.

Just a few weeks ago Pravda carried a long article calling for stepped-up atheistic indoctrination among the young because of "a notable increase" in religious interest among young men and women, coupled with disturbing "indifference toward issues of atheism."

"The dying off of religion under socialism is not an automatic process," the party newspaper said, but requires increasingly sophisticated antireligious propaganda.

### Busy With Baptisms

Foreigners run into evidence of aroused interest in religion in many places. A foreign churchman is told by a Moscow priest that he has little time to counsel young people because he is so busy doing a thousand baptisms a year, like many other priests. An Intourist guide asks an American businessman for a Bible. Another young guide joins a foreign group in lighting a candle at the Zagorsk monastery.

An athletic coach laments to foreign visitors that his school has been built on the site of one of the most beautiful churches of his city, demolished a few years ago. A young woman, with great curiosity, draws out a visiting Roman Catholic priest to give an explanation of his religion and then, when he observes that she has her own ideology, responds, "But not like yours."

Two of the most striking Soviet films of recent years, "Andrei Rublev" and "The Red Snowball Bush," have religious overtones and sympathetic portraits of the tribulations of the church in Russian history.

Composers and musicologists have been deciphering the chants and canticles that were sung after the coming of Christianity from Byzantium in the 10th century. Some religious music has found its way into repertories of choral groups.

Millions of rubles have been expended in tourist cities like Leningrad, Moscow, Vladimir, Yaroslavl and Rostov-the-Great to restore abandoned cathedrals to their former glory, prompting some Communist propagandists to warn that people were "idealizing the life of the church."

### Other Churches Benefit

Not only the Russian Orthodox Church but others as well have benefited from the restoration work. The main cathedral of the Armenian Orthodox Church at Echmiadzin, outside Erivan, has been lavishly refurbished through foreign contributions. Millions of rubles have been spent restoring the tomb of Tamerlane in Samarkand, allegedly increasing its popularity as a shrine among the Moslems of Soviet Central Asia as well as an attraction for tourists.

At Saturday-night services in Orthodox churches and on Sunday mornings in the Central Evangelical Christian Baptist Church, which President Nixon attended during his 1972 visit, young people can be seen recording church music or taking notes on sermons. Many more watch for a few minutes and then depart.

Periodically, Communist publications chastise party members or members of the Young Communist League for participating in weddings, baptisms, funerals and other religious ceremonies. Pravda Ukrainy reported last year that while a Communist party official was lecturing on atheism, his children were being taken by his wife and mother-in-law to be baptized.

### From Dissidence to Faith

Some of the more sensational incidents are hushed up. Last year Alla Tarasova, a world-famous actress at the Moscow Art Theatre, member of the Communist party for 19 years and deputy in the Supreme Soviet (parliament) for 12 years, reportedly shocked party officials and friends by leaving a will demanding that she be given a religious funeral. So offended were the officials that she was not granted the expected honor of burial in the cemetery for notables.

Leonid M. Leonov, a well-established writer and Writers Union secretary as well as a Supreme Soviet Deputy for more than two decades, was said by other writers to have confessed religious belief and to have been dropped from nomination for the current elections to the Supreme Soviet.

A number of dissident intellectuals, disillusioned with what they regarded as fruitless protest in the late nineteen sixties, turned to the church in the early seventies.

The most prominent dissident and believer is Aleksandr I. Solzhenitsyn, the exiled novelist, whose final manifesto, sent to Soviet leaders last year, urged that the Russian Orthodox Church be permitted to operate without official harassment and that it be restored as the leading source of moral values—in place of Communism.

Even the Orthodox Church, largest of all religious institutions here, has its dissidents some of whom, according to religious sources, operate "underground monasteries" led by dissenting or defrocked priests opposed to the accomodation reached by the established church with the Communist authorities.

Undeterred by official criticism, many other members of the intelligentsia and the cultural élite, while far from being dissidents or believers, have taken up the fad of decorating their homes with religious icons and wearing crosses and other religious symbols as jewelry.

### Orthodox Put at 30 Million

The Communist party has 14 million members out of a population of 250 million. By Western estimates the Russian Orthodox Church has 30 million followers, the Roman Catholic and Lutheran churches of the Baltic republics have five million and the authorized Baptists about a million. There are also sizable followings for Islam and Judaism; smaller Christian groups such as Jehovah's Witnesses and dissident Baptists, who are not officially recognized, and small number of Buddhists.

The figures have limited significance. All churches are in a defensive, ambivalent position, at the mercy of the Communist party, which runs the country and sets the terms under which churches can survive.

Over the last decade the party leaders have tolerated a modest revival of church activity. Under Stalin in the thirties religion faced vigorous repression, with many churches closed and priests arrested. During World War II, however, Stalin allowed the Orthodox Church to revive as a rallying point for Russian patriotism.

After the war the Communist leaders, alarmed, restricted the church again. Under Nikita S. Khrushchev the campaign against the church was particularly severe, with up to 10,000 Orthodox churches reported closed.

The leadership that displaced Mr. Khruschev in 1964 has seemed divided in its attitude toward Orthodox elements in the ideological apparatus and in certain parts of the country such as the Western Ukraine, where large numbers of churches exist, have favored tighter controls. Other elements, evidently approving the restoration of Russian national culture, from which the Orthodox Church has benefited, have taken a more live-and-let-live position as long as the church hierarchy has subordinated itself to the Communist party and the Government.

### Restrictions and Pressures

The result is that the Orthodox Church maintains a dozen monasteries, has about 1,000 young men studying at seminaries in Zagorsk, Leningrad and Odessa, plus theological academies in Zagorsk and Leningrad, and, by one knowledgeable estimate, has about 7,500 parishes in 73 dioceses.

The church must function under a number of restrictions and official pressures. In the new industrial cities of Siberia and elsewhere in the country, the authorities do not permit church construction. In areas of traditional religious strength, congregations are pressed to close.

To deter young couples from having their children baptized, the authorities have required priests to demand domestic passports from the parents. The press later reported that the requirement was circumvented by having out-of-town baptisms on using rented documents.

On broader issues some churches have reportedly had difficulty obtaining religious literature in Russian, vestments and holy materials. The law strictly forbids organized religious instruction for children, especially Sunday schools, and priests, in areas like Lithuania, are regularly prosecuted for teaching children.

The Council for Religious Affairs, which has jurisdiction over all church matters, effectively bars some of the most intellectually qualified candidates for seminaries with the result, according to Russian church sources, that the great majority of seminarians are from rural areas.

Priests tempted to range beyond a narrowly prescribed set of sermon topics have reportedly been warned.

In some cases punishment has been meted out. Former Archbishop Yermogen of Kaluga, described in Orthodox circles as a leading dissenter in the church for his outspoken criticism of the hierarchy, was reportedly sent to a remote monastery a few years ago.

Last year Archbishop Filaret Vokrameyev, former rector of the theological seminary at Zagorsk with a reputation as a vigorous, rising young prelate, was transferred to Berlin to be the Exarch of Central Europe, an important post but well away from Moscow.

### Collaboration With Atheism

By and large the Orthodox hierarchy, traditionally a conservative force, has avoided clashes with secular authority — much as it did under the czars. Patriarch Pimen and other leaders give sermons endorsing or praising social and political policies, and they have defended the Soviet Government against accusations from abroad of suppression of religion and of civil rights.

Dissidents have accused the religious establishment of "collaboration with atheism." Mr. Solzhenitsyn, in an open Lenten letter to Patriarch Pimen two years ago, declared that "a church dictatorially directed by atheists is a sight not seen for 2,000 years." This was an allusion to the fact that the main overseers—the chairman of the Council for Religious Affairs, Vladimir A. Kuroyedov, and his three deputies — are Communists.

Nonetheless, such liberal-minded prelates as the Rev. Dmitri Dutko, once Mr. Solzhenitsyn's priest, who has gathered a following among Moscow intellectuals, have contended that the main achievement of the church over 56 years has been to endure.

Such churchmen have taken heart from the new interest of the young, especially in large cities. Many Russians, including occasional churchgoers, consider this an unimportant phenomenon, explaining that it represents no more than youthful curiosity about a long-forbidden realm as well as the attraction of pageantry in a country where civil ceremonies are drab and unappealing.

However, older churchgoers contend that something deeper is involved—that a segment of modern Soviet youth is not satisfied by Communist ideology and is groping for a new source of moral values. Some, they say, are protesting against the system, but in a way that stops short of outright dissent.

**Link to Russian Past**

Another broad motivation for interest in religion is nostalgia for the Russian past—the attempt to find a cultural identity and recover a cultural heritage. It is the link between religion and the Russian past that has apparently most troubled Communist ideologists. As Pravda observed in a lengthy commentary:

"Young people, gaining acquaintance with their cultural heritage, run into the fact that before the Revolution many writers, composers and artists created work on religious themes and were believers. They see church shrines, maintained by the Soviet state as monuments of history and culture. Icons are conceived by them as outstanding works of art, and religious ceremonies seem beautiful to some people.

"As a result, a part of our youth adopts an incomplete and thus simply incorrect notion about religion, deprived of class and social evaluation. Also, with these circumstances, one must not fail to consider the influence on young people of various works of literature in which the role of religion and the church in the cultural heritage of the past is incorrectly evaluated.

"In addition, some church officials and church workers try to play on the growing interest of the Soviet people in their history and cultural heritage. They want to represent the church as the guardian of the 'National Spirit,' eternal for all times."

Pravda urged Communist writers, artists and thinkers to combat this tactic with intelligent dissuasion rather than suppression, in the evident conviction that the current fascination with religion will pass. But some churchmen, who believe religious feeling is deeply rooted in the Russian character, think the modest revival will continue.

April 14, 1974

# In Soviet, Ingenuity Is Needed to Find an Apartment

**By HEDRICK SMITH**

Special to The New York Times

MOSCOW, Nov. 10—Just off Prospekt Mira in one of the older sections of Moscow, people gather on gray fall afternoons near the Rzhevsky bathhouse, milling around for hours like pickets outside a factory on strike.

On Sundays, hundreds of people, hands thrust into their pockets and scarves wound tightly against the cold, carry placards around their necks or hand-scrawled signs pinned to their sturdy cloth coats. Occasionally, they pause to converse quietly in twos and threes and then walk on.

But these are not Soviet strikers, they are walking want ads: Muscovites advertising apartments for exchange, eager to improve their living quarters.

A modish young couple offers an attractive "split" —the exchange of a four-room apartment, large by Soviet standards, for two smaller ones because the newlyweds want to escape living with in-laws and are eager for a place of their own. An elderly woman tries to coax a man in a dark fedora to take single rooms in two different communal apartments in return for his separate one-room flat with kitchen, bath and phone.

At the far end of the lane, students and officers swarm around a few landlords offering a room, a bed, or a small apartment for rent. Some students turn up their noses at a two-room unit in an old building with gas heat but no indoor plumbing. But a middle-aged woman and a married couple, less fussy, compete for it. In minutes, the apartment is gone for fifty rubles ($66.50) monthly, paid a year in advance.

The housing exchange and 29 other exchanges in Moscow plus many more in cities across this land of 250 million people, are reminders that despite tremendous gains in housing construction in recent years, adequate accommodation remains a central and acute problem for millions of Soviet citizens, far more essential than the fuss of a tiny minority over getting a car.

Paradoxically, housing is a realm of both triumph and of tragedy for the Soviet leadership.

The achievements have been staggering. Since 1956, roughly 42 million new units of housing have been built by the state, private and cooperative builders — more than any other country of the world, according to Henry W. Morton, a housing expert at Queens College in New York.

In the 1971-75 Five-Year Plan, Finance Minister Vasily F. Garbuzov said last year, the state is allocating 35 billion rubles ($48-billion) for housing construction. This year alone, he forecast, more than 11,000,000 people will improve their quarters. More than half are supposed to get new dwellings.

**Rows of Buildings Impressive**

The visible impact of the Soviet housing program is striking to foreigners returning after a decade of absence. They are impressed by the rows of prefabricated 9-story, 11-story and 14-story apartment houses dominating the outskirts of Moscow and other Soviet cities.

Almost anywhere the traveler goes, he encounters scholars, engineers and workmen boasting of new apartments, however modest by Western standards, that have provided the key to a new standard of living for their families—a break from the cramped conditions of the late nineteen-fifties or early nineteen-sixties when they were jammed into communal flats, sharing kitchen, bath and toilet with other families.

Yet so massive and aching is the Soviet housing problem that Gertrude Schroeder, an American economist who specializes in Soviet affairs, wrote earlier this year that this country remained "the most poorly housed of any major country in Europe — and poorly housed also by comparison with the [Soviet] Government's minimum standard for health and decency."

The Soviet "sanitary housing norm" was set back in 1920 by the Russian Government. It decided that nine square meters of living space to a person—equal to 10 feet by 10 feet—was the minimum target. And yet, more than half a century later, Mr. Morton wrote in a new study, "the great majority of Soviet people in urban areas have not reached the 1920 minimum level."

**Many in Communal Housing**

By Soviet accounts, somewhat over 25 per cent of urban dwellers still live in communal apartments and some Western scholars suspect that a third or more of this country's city dwellers still live communally.

In 1972, the last year for which figures are available, the national average was about 7.6 square meters of living space per person in Soviet urban areas—roughly half the average in Western Europe and one-third that in the United States.

But the problem is more human than statistical, as a number of Soviet writers have shown. Yuri Trifonov, a well known fiction writer, published a story, "Exchange," in which a son and daughter-in-law callously played on the housing space of a dying mother to expand their quarters before she died and her flat reverted to the state.

Playwrights have portrayed families crumbling into divorce —and still forced to live in the same room after divorce—for lack of alternative housing, or have shown frustrated young people unable to marry because they cannot get an apartment and their parents have no room to spare.

**Marriage for Apartments**

Individuals tell of cases of people marrying to get better apartments or to be registered as residents in a favored city like Moscow. One couple from out of town divorced, married persons who lived in Moscow, later divorced them and remarried once they had obtained their Moscow housing—a process that took several years, a Moscow intellectual reported.

Russian demographers, concerned by the falling birthrate among ethnic Russians, in contrast with other Soviet nationalities, put part of the fault on tight housing space and inadequate room to raise more than one child in a family. Komsomolskaya Pravda, the youth paper, carried an article in February, 1973, reporting on extensive research that families in the industrial town of Vyshny Volochek were forced to keep families small and some women preferred abortions because they lacked space for children. When they get an apartment, many have reached the age of 30 and feel it is too late to have children.

Several Soviet publications have attributed high labor turnover in Soviet industry to the failure of enterprises or construction projects to provide housing.

**Priority in Heavy Industry**

The housing situation differs markedly from city to city and factory to factory. A series of articles by the weekly Literaturnaya Gazeta in late 1972, comparing heavy industrial plants and consumer goods factories in a dozen cities, showed that workers in the heavy-industry factories consistently received more housing than those in the consumer sector.

Professor Morton of Queens College developed a series of comparisons from Soviet statistics that showed not only that Moscow was favored far above all other Soviet cities in housing investments but also that the average housing space per person in the "European" group of cities like Moscow, Kiev, Riga, Tallinn, Vilnius and Minsk was a third more than in the Central Asian group including Tashkent, Baku, Yerevan, Alma Ata, Frunze, Dushanbe and Ashkhabad.

The main reason for the continuing squeeze, in spite of the construction program under Nikita S. Khruschev and Leonid I. Brezhnev, is the appalling legacy of the Stalin period, when housing got very low priority. Much housing was destroyed in World War II.

**Population Increasing, Too**

Moreover, much effort has gone into merely keeping up with population growth and migration. While 42 million new housing units have been built since 1956, the population has increased by 42 million. Millions have moved into cities from the countryside, multiplying pressures on urban housing.

Demand for housing also remains heavy because Soviet rents, heavily subsidized by the Government, are very low. A modest two-room apartment will go for 6 to 8 rubles ($8 to $11.30) a month, including some utilities. A four-room apartment wil rent for 14 to 16 rubles ($18.20 to $22.30). Apartments in more modern buildings cost more because of additional services.

The result is that despite impressive statistics on housing construction, the backlog of applications for new apartments is tremendous. A five-to-seven year wait is still not considered uncommon. "It takes two to three years at one of the best factories around Moscow, which has a very substantial housing program for its workers," a young worker said. "It is worse in other places."

Not surprisingly, the Soviet press occasionally reports cases of bribery and "hard-core profiteering" by housing officials. In September, Pravda the Communist party daily, reported that A. A. Konstantinov, chairman of the housing committee in the Frunze District of Moscow, had taken 17 bribes totaling 2,517 rubles ($3,498) in a short period, and that several of his aides had been discovered taking thousands more in bribes.

Another problem, cited last year by Pravda, is line-jumping and influence-peddling by people in public posts, athletes, entertainers and various minor authorities.

"Too often the decisive factor is not the waiting list," Pravda remarked in February, 1973, "but a sudden telephone call. At one place, they suddenly give apartments to families of 'prospective' football players and the whole queue is forced back. At another, they decide to award apartments to 'activists' working on a so-called altruistic basis, and the line is pushed back again.

In some cases, apartment hunters are encouraged either to take temporary jobs in housing offices or actually to participate in the construction of new apartment buildings.

In one case an engineer-physicist reported having quit his regular job for a year and a half to help build a new apartment building outside Moscow to escape the communal apartment where his family of three was sharing a nine-room apartment with 54 other people.

Eventually, the family got their two-room apartment with a modest kitchen, bath and toilet. But they found the new housing area largely bereft of stores and convenient public transportation. A daily commute to old jobs near the city center took nearly two hours each way. Because of such inconveniences, the family gave up after a couple of years and moved back to their old communal apartment near the center. By then the number of people in the communal apartment was down to roughly half the former number.

**Housing Quality Deplored**

Complaints about the quality of Soviet construction are common in the press. Two years ago, Pravda carried a bitter article from the Armenian capital of Yerevan camplaining that construction agencies were in such a hurry to fulfill quotas, based on floor space, that new tenants had to spend much of their own time and money repairing taps, burners and switches, rehanging doors, fixing plumbing, installing light switches, fixing windows or doing plastering that was all supposed to have been done by the construction teams.

One outlet for more affluent families in the last decade has been the development since 1962 of cooperative apartment groups at governmental agencies, enterprises, scientific institutes, writers' organizations and other work collectives. Normally, Soviet practice requires a 40 percent downpayment and then 15 years to pay the balance.

But as demand has risen, along with construction costs, so have prices. Muscovites complain that an apartment of three rooms with kitchen, toilet, bath and hall—comfortable and large by Soviet standards—that used to cost 6,000 to 6,500 rubles in an outlying southwest region of Moscow in 1966, now costs from 8,500 to 10,000 rubles in a new cooperative.

Even within cooperative groups, the wait can be tedious. One novelist got a new two-room flat this year after waiting for five years in a one-room flat. Moreover, cooperatives provide an outlet only for more affluent members of society. They account for only about 3 per cent of all urban housing.

**Private Building Dominant**

Nonetheless, private construction generally has been far more crucial for coping with the housing squeeze than most foreigners, or Russians, realize. Professor Morton, developing estimates from Soviet statistics, has written that since the Bolshevik Revolution in 1917, more housing space has been provided by private and cooperative construction than by state programs. This is essentially because of the relative neglect by the state before the nineteen-fifties.

New restrictions on private construction in cities and the frustrations of long waits for new public housing are what push hundreds of thousands of people annually into the housing exchanges. So huge is that market that Moscow prints a 64-page weekly booklet "Rooms and Apartments for Exchange." Many other people prefer to go to the exchange to negotiate directly.

Even a "find" however, does not always provide quick results because the finder must work out an intricate or contorted exchange involving three, four, five, eight or even twelve others.

In a recent "musical chairs" exchange, a couple with a two-room apartment wanted more space because of a new baby. They had no luck so they persuaded the parents of one to throw their four room apartment into the bargain, in hopes of getting two three-room apartments.

That, too, fell through but they did find a desirable three-room apartment for one family. The problem was that it was then being used as a communal dwelling by two families and a single elderly man. So the young couple set out to help these people find suitable dwellings. When they finished, the exchange involved six apartments and eight families. The elderly man, not entirely happy, had to be paid 500 rubles to agree to move.

Then the entire arrangement had to be registered with city authorities who scrutinized each move to insure that no one was violating the Byzantine restrictions of maximum and minimum living space for different categories of people and the police rules that all be legally registered Moscow residents.

"It took an enormous amount of time and effort," the young husband told friends. "But it was worth it in the end. We got a very nice apartment."

November 11, 1974

# Low Living Standard in Soviet Rural Areas Drives Youths to Cities

By DAVID K. SHIPLER
Special to The New York Times

MOSCOW, April 19—The sleek train from Moscow to Warsaw glided through the Russian countryside and eased to a stop at the town of Vyazma, 125 miles west of the Soviet capital.

Suddenly, a dozen or so woman in coarse peasant dress, bundled in rough, heavily padded jackets against the cold, pushed their way onto the train and into the dining car where they lined up at two of the tables. At one, a waitress sold them bags of oranges, apples and candy and at the other bottles of fermented mare's milk — all delicacies rarely found outside the major cities.

The transactions were made with practiced swiftness, and the women—looking as if they had just left a supermarket—were back on the platform as the train began to move.

Buying from trains is a common feature of rural life in the Soviet Union, testimony to the great contrasts in living standards that exist between the cities and the countryside. One Russian recalls a summer's work on a collective farm where the manager, eager to keep his workers healthy and content, gave them a truck, and sometimes even money, so they could drive to a nearby town periodically and buy beer, fruit and vegetables from the passing trains. The farm grew only grain.

### Migration to the Cities

The differences between the material conditions of urban and rural life have contributed to a sharp growth in migration from the farms to the cities, especially from grain-growing areas of the Russian Republic and the Ukraine.

The increased flow has stimulated expressions of concern among some Soviet demographers and economists, prompting calls for even stricter Government regulation of population movement than at present.

Narrowing the gap in living standards has been a professed goal of Soviet economic planners for some time, and it is repeated in the five-year plan approved last month by the 25th Communist Party Congress.

But rural deficiencies remain. Much rural housing is still characterized by wooden izbas, cabins without running water or central heating. Many of the roads, unpaved, turn to mud in the spring thaw. Boredom is heavy.

A group of schoolchildren in the village of Ternovoye, 300 miles southeast of Moscow, wrote to the Government newspaper Izvestia in 1972:

"Dear Editor: Advise us how to occupy ourselves. It is dull and uninteresting in our village, especially in the summer. The river is far from Ternovoye. There are no sports facilities. The club has only dances and films for adults. Even when he is sober, the projectionist does not consider us an audience."

### Diets Reflect Shortages

Often there is just not enough to buy, and diets reflect the shortages. Official statistics show that in 1970, only 57 pounds of meat per capita were consumed in Azerbaijan, one of the more rural republics, compared with 160 pounds in Estonia, the country's most urbanized republic.

Consumption of milk and dairy products amounted to 500 pounds a person in Azerbaijan as opposed to 924 pounds in Estonia; of fish, 6.6 pounds compared with 66; of vegetables, 103 pounds versus 176, and so on.

Throughout the country in 1968, collective farmers were eating only 73 percent as much meat per capita as that consumed by industrial workers and office employees of Government agencies. This was just 5 percentage points higher than in 1960.

About 80 percent of the country's urban families have refrigerators but only a third of the rural families do, a planning official said recently.

### Unrest on the Farms

The Soviet press has attributed much of the urbanization of recent years to the dissatisfaction of rural residents, especially the young, with the deprivations of farm life.

In 1959, there were only three Soviet cities with a population of one million or more: Moscow, Leningrad and Kiev. By the 1970 census, there were nine. In 1959, most of the population—52 percent—was still rural, by 1975, the balance had shifted, and 60 percent of the 253 million Soviet people lived in cities. In 1973 alone, analysts found, approximately 3.6 million people moved into the cities and 1.7 million moved out.

Some Soviet sociologists and economists have deplored the flight of the young from the farms, noting that it leaves an aging work force behind, depriving agricultural areas of some of their best laborers at a time when food production has failed to keep pace with rising aspirations.

Such migration might be welcomed from rural areas with a labor surplus, such as Central Asia. But Viktor Perevedentsev, a noted Soviet demographer, has observed: "The problem is that the population mostly leaves places with a shortage of labor and hardly ever leaves districts with labor surpluses."

### Passports Control Movement

This has meant the greatest migration in the European part of the Soviet Union and the least in Central Asia. Mr. Perevedentsev has made vague suggestions in some recent articles for more Government control over population movement, and he has called for measures to stimulate the exodus of surplus rural population from the countryside into Central Asian cities.

At present, the Government controls migration and population distribution through a system of internal passports. Every citizen must present his passport when registering with local authorities for residence in a city, and some relatively popular cities such as Moscow, Leningrad and Kiev are closed to newcomers unless they have guaranteed jobs and housing.

Until recently, collective farmers were not issued passports automatically and could therefore move from the farms only with special permission. Last Jan. 1, a new system took affect under which farmers are to receive passports. But it is not clear whether this will actually facilitate their departure for the cities.

Aside from attempting to distribute the labor force as the economic need dictates, the Government has imposed restrictions on migration to some urban areas to limit crowding amid an acute shortage of decent housing and strains on various municipal services such as transportation and schools.

### Housing Is Crowded

Even though Moscow needs workers and is erecting 120,000 new apartments annually, many Muscovites still live in communal apartments, with several families sharing kitchen anl bathroom. Young married couples usually find it difficult to get their own places and often end up living with their parents.

The corollaries of urbanization—crowding, lack of privacy, the financial need for women to work, the growing instability of the family and a changing system of values—have all contributed to a declining birthrate in the European and most heavily urbanized parts of the Soviet Union.

"The one-child family is characteristic for residents of big cities," Mr. Perevedentsev wrote in Literaturnaya Gazeta last August.

This would be hailed in most parts of the West, but in a country whose sense of its own power has long been based on its economic prowess, the specter of a labor force without swift growth is regarded with apprehension.

### Russians Becoming Minority

Labor shortages already exist in many areas, and there is scarcely a factory manager who will not talk candidly of his need for more workers. But increased industrial production, once accomplished by heavy inputs of capital and labor, must now be created by automation and efficiency.

traits notably lacking in the Soviet economy.

Furthermore, differences in birth rates between ethnic Russians and minorities in Central Asia and elsewhere promise to make the Russians a minority in the Soviet population, possibly by the next census in 1979. In 1970, Russians made up 53.4 percent of the population.

Mr. Perevedentsev calculated that Central Asia, with 9 percent of the country's people, now contributes more than a fourth of the entire population growth, and will make up half the growth between 1970 and 2000.

Given the ethnocentrism of Great Russians, this phenomenon is sometimes seen as threatening. It also raises what some Western specialists believe are serious future problems of labor maldistribution since the heaviest labor requirements lie outside Central Asia.

In a January article, Mr. Perevedentsev put a positive face on the problem by suggesting that Central Asia contained great potential for rapid industrial expansion.

But he mixed this with a warning that the excessive growth of big cities should be avoided by building more new town clusters of new communities in the countryside. So far, he said, the new towns have contained standard low-ceiling apartments—not likely to attract the Central Asians used to more spacious and traditional living.

April 20, 1976

# Sexual Revolution in Soviet Straining Strict Morality

**By CHRISTOPHER S. WREN**

Special to The New York Times

MOSCOW, Sept. 24—The leading Soviet literary weekly suggested last spring that an increase in the number of children born out of wedlock not only might improve the country's sagging birthrate but also might allow women who do not marry to have families.

"Morality should not stand in the way of human happiness," wrote Leonid Zhukhovitsky in Literaturnaya Gazeta. "After all, its inherent obligation is to protect the human being and not itself."

Such frankness in the pages of the publication of the Writers Union can be attributed in part to the Kremlin's concern over a birthrate that has hovered near 18 per 1,000 of population for a decade. It also highlights changing attitudes toward the long-taboo subject of sex.

**A Puritanical Facade Maintained**

Since the Bolshevik Revolution, which was followed by a hedonistic period until Lenin attempted to squelch it, the Soviet Union has maintained a puritanical facade. Its citizens have been insulated from the pornography that assaults the West, and Soviet films and magazines are generally demure.

That facade does not reflect the realities in a country where one new mother in 10 is unmarried, where almost a third of marriages break up and where sexual encounters have become commonplace. The leadership has seemed ambivalent about how to respond.

The shift in moral values evokes the sexual revolution that hit the West some years ago, but a Russian contends that it results from a dissipation of faith. "We don't have anything to believe in," he said. "Either you believe in God or in the man who is leading you. Without either, it is hard to have morality."

A tolerance for sexual relations outside marriage has become most noticeable in the major cities. Viktor I. Perevedentsev, a leading social demographer, reported two years ago that nearly half of a sample of happily married women in Leningrad believed that they were entitled to extramarital affairs. Another researcher in Moscow privately recounted details of an unpublished survey of young unmarried women in which two-thirds condoned premarital sex and the rest were mostly indifferent.

A study of Leningrad students several years ago disclosed that 85 percent of the men and 64 percent of the women had had sexual relations before they were 21 years old. A few confessions have even emerged in the controlled press. "For goodness sake, don't think that some immoral woman is writing you," a 34-year-old Kiev housewife recently told the weekly supplement Nedelya in revealing details of an affair she had carried on for five years.

According to published statistics, over 400,000 babies a year are born out of wedlock despite the availability of birth-control devices and a national network of abortion clinics that charge less than $7 for a visit. A Leningrad study disclosed that one of 14 young brides questioned cited pregnancy as the motive for getting married.

The premarital pregnancy rate seems to be due not only to nonchalance among young men but also to sporadic shortages of the birth-control devices. Speaking of condoms, a young father said, "You don't always find them available." While Soviet brands sell in packets of five for 35 cents, foreign-made ones bring a ruble apiece, or $1.40, on the black market.

**Pills, Loops, Vasectomies**

The birth-control pill is less popular than in the United States or Europe because of side effects like weight gain. Soviet-made diaphragms are considered unreliable, with loops or cervical caps more widely preferred. A Moscow physician said that vasectomies had caught on only among Government or party officials who wanted to eliminate risk of blackmail if they engaged in extramarital affairs.

Though "gigantic shifts in society's approach to extramarital and premarital sex" were noted by Dr. Perevedentsev, the social demographer, more than two years ago, the authorities long refused to acknowledge that a problem existed. A researcher told of a censor who refused to approve a study of frigidity among women until the figures were lowered; a 1974 manual announced that 100 percent of Soviet men in a study reported achieving orgasm, though articles have since hinted otherwise.

One consequence is that schools have virtually ignored sex education, except for the Baltic republic of Latvia, which allots 12 hours a year. "We had no classes in it so we learned about sex ourselves," a Moscow member of Komsomol, the Communist youth organization, recalled. "In our school everybody slept around by the time we had finished the eighth grade. By the 10th grade one girl was already pregnant. But when I look at the kids today, I think we were quite moral."

Articles have dramatically limned the horrors of premarital sex. Zdorovye, a widely read health magazine, warned young men a couple of years ogo that intimacy before marriage "can cause fluctuations of potency that become the source of doubt, lack of confidence and sometimes even neurotic reactions." Young women, it said, usually encounter disillusionment and a conviction of frigidity.

**The Advice Is Sometimes Dated**

Zdorovye has taken the lead in telling Russians what they want to learn about sex, including how long intercourse should last—two minutes, it advised. It sometimes sounds dated for it says, among other things, that women have less interest in sex than men. "The most common male mistake is the tendency to overestimate the sexual aspirations of women," explained A. I. Belkin, a physician, in a 1975 article. "The coldness of a young wife becomes an unexpected and unpleasant discovery for the husband. Yet it is quite natural."

The cautious trend toward more candor has prompted a number of readers to share their experiences. "He swooped down like a kite and afterwards he fell fast asleep," a young bride complained, describing her wedding night. "In the morning when he woke up he was surprised to see my tear-swollen eyes." Zdorovye urged more tenderness from the bridegroom because "nature isn't on her side at this difficult moment."

Despite widespread interest, specialists still complain about a lack of literature on sexual subjects. A book on venereal disease for adolescents, "I Will Speak Frankly," was praised by critics but printed in only 30,000 copies.

Perhaps the biggest stride has been the creation of marriage clinics, first in Riga and then in Leningrad and Moscow. Cheslovas S. Grizitskas, a neuropathologist who runs the program in Riga, told a Soviet interviewer last year: "We simply prepare our young people very badly for marriage, and they enter adulthood considering that love is only enjoyment. But love is also responsibility."

Disenchantment is reflected in the divorce statistics, which last showed 27 divorces for 100 marriages. Dr. Perevedentsev, calling this figure low because it included only officially registered divorces, estimated that up to a third of the marriages might have ended. In cities like Moscow and Kiev the divorce rate is approaching 50 percent of marriages.

A Leningrad survey of 1,000 divorced people reported that 244 cited infidelity among the reasons why their marriages broke up while 215 mentioned drunkenness; these could be symptoms rather than causes, of course. The continuing housing shortage, which forces many newlyweds to squeeze in with relatives, has also contributed to the toll; another Leningrad study found that 79 percent of divorced couples polled did not have their own accommodations when they married.

The lack of apartments has apparently discouraged some couples from matrimony though not from love affairs. A popular trysting place for unmarried students in Moscow has been the cramped compartments of the overnight train to Leningrad.

**System 'Encourages' Affairs**

A divorced Muscovite contended that the rising statistics did not reflect the extent of failed marriages. "If you join the Communist Party or become an official, a divorce would look bad on your record," he said. "But the higher you go, the easier it becomes to acquire a mistress. The system encourages extramarital affairs." He reported that some young women at his office got promoted by sleeping with the manager.

The most recent census has shown 1.5 million more married women than men. Sociologists attribute the discrepancy in part to unwed mothers who list themselves as married. One in Sverdlovsk who is 46 wrote Literaturnaya Gazeta to plead for more understanding. "I am not a single mother at all," she said. "I don't feel alone because I have a son."

In the controversial article in Literaturnaya Gazeta suggesting more children out of wedlock Mr. Zhukhovitsky argued that an increase in extramarital affairs and illegitimate births should not be ascribed simply to promiscuity. "If many, many unmarried women did not become mothers, society today would be short many, many children. And children are the country's future." He concluded: "After all, what is really bitter is not life without a husband but life without love."

September 25, 1977

# *Rising Youth Crime in Soviet Troubles Regime and Public*

**By DAVID K. SHIPLER**

Special to The New York Times

MOSCOW, March 4—Quietly, and with much of the same anguish and bewilderment that Americans feel, the Soviet Union is struggling with the problems of street crime, teen-age gangs and juvenile delinquency.

Murders, rapes, beatings, muggings and burglaries now occur in Moscow and other cities with a frequency that arouses concern among some officials and ordinary citizens.

In parent-teacher associations, in neighborhood Communist Party meetings, in high schools, on the stage and even in the press to some degree, the baffling and often unanswerable question of why some youths engage in violence is receiving attention as the population becomes increasingly urban and mobile.

Because the violence is rarely publicized, the level of fear remains far below that of New York. Except in some working-class neighborhoods and notorious parks, Muscovites generally show little hesitation in walking alone at night or letting their small children run out of sight in playgrounds.

The evidence suggests that some of the fearlessness stems from ignorance, just as some of the fear in New York may be exaggerated by detailed reporting by radio, television and the press.

The scope of the problem is difficult to measure because crime rates are secret. But despite the Government's efforts to hide its difficulties and officials' refusals to discuss the matter with a foreign reporter, a picture of violent crime and some of its sociological foundations has emerged after months of interviews and conversations with a wide variety of Russians as well as a culling of Soviet publications.

Much of the violence, perhaps most of it, is the work of young people aged 14 to 18. Many of them are school dropouts without jobs who drink heavily, come from problem homes and roam in gangs that are sometimes led by older youths with previous convictions.

Others attend school and lead outwardly normal lives, and their crimes come as a shock to teachers, parents and friends. At both extremes, society seems at a loss about how to deal with the issue.

"If we wrote about crime in Moscow every day," said a staff member of the Government newspaper Izvestia, "there would be as much fear as there is in New York."

**Crime News Generally Suppressed**

Government policy keeps almost all reports of unsolved crime out of newspapers and off radio and television in a deliberate effort to contain fear and prevent what some Soviet journalists believe would be the rapid spread of violence if it was publicized.

For example, when Izvestia learned of a gang rape by 10 young men, the editors published nothing. "We referred it to the party and the police for investigation," a reporter said. As a rule, only solved cases are discussed in the press to make a sociological or moral point.

Occasionally the absence of information leads to rumor, as some years ago when there were stories in Moscow about a deranged man said to be murdering women in red coats. "A hundred people could be killed in Moscow tonight and we would never know it," said a young intellectual. "We are afraid because we do not know."

**False Sense of Security Seen**

More common is a sense of security so false that it can be dangerous. Not long ago, a boy of 14, walking alone down a Moscow street, was approached by four or five youths his age asking for money. In his innocence he thought they were joking, according to one of his friends. But when he tried to walk past, one of the youths attacked him with homemade brass knuckles, beating him so badly around the head that he was out of school for a month.

Similarly, a young woman student, alone in wooded Sokolniki Park, asked a man for directions to the subway. It was late afternoon, and the park was almost deserted. The man attacked her, tried to rape her and beat her severely.

Russians who have had trouble themselves, or who know about the problems of others, tend to be nearly as cautious as New Yorkers.

**Vandalism by Workers Feared**

One young Moscow resident, who was once followed into her apartment house by a young tough who cornered her in a corridor and stole her bracelet, now says she always takes off her jewelry when riding the bus at night, just to avoid attracting attention. She advises her teen-age sister to make sure anyone taking her home sees her all the way into the elevator before leaving.

Another woman, with a husband and a small daughter, refuses to live in a new four-room apartment on the ground floor, preferring three rooms above because she fears vandalism and burglary by young construction workers from Kazakhstan housed in a nearby dormitory.

A third woman who works for the police expressed amazement, when moving into a ground-floor apartment, that the windows had no bars.

Parts of some cities are considered unsafe at night. In Kiev, a visiting American was advised to avoid a major park because, his Soviet guide revealed, a woman had recently been murdered there. A policeman, asked about the report, said the woman was still alive.

Some well-educated Muscovites regard workers' neighborhoods such as Taganka in the southeast and Chertanovo in the south as dangerous because of heavy drinking that leads to violence. Another neighborhood, Marina Roshcha, in the north, is called "bandit's nest" by some.

And of nearby Timiryazev Park, one Russian remarked, "You wouldn't want to go there at night. You wouldn't be killed, but you would be beaten up."

The Ministry of Culture's paper, Sovetskaya Kultura, reported "an alarming increase in juvenile delinquency" in the Timiryazev neighborhood.

**Sale of Handguns Banned**

One of the greatest deterrents to violence is a ban on the sale of handguns and strict control of hunting rifles. Crimes involving firearms seem rare, although they occur occasionally when soldiers are involved. A taxi driver in Novosibirsk told foreign passengers recently of a fellow driver killed with a handgun last year.

Youth gangs in Moscow reportedly manufacture a variety of weapons, including long knives and zip guns.

Even the Soviet authorities may not know the full extent of juvenile crime, for lower officials often conceal negative information to avoid bringing criticism on themselves.

A teachers' journal, for example, reported that after two boys in Irkutsk had raped a girl, the high school's principal and teachers tried to hush up the incident by dismissing it as a "childish prank" and urging the victim and her parents to drop charges.

A former party member who served on a crime task force in Moscow's Chertanovo district told interviewers after he had emigrated that the commander of

Krokodil, 1974

**A cartoon in Krokodil, Soviet humor magazine, depicted a woman running from a mugger. At top, she cries out to people at a phone booth, "Citizens, please let me use the phone—a hooligan is chasing me!" At bottom, as they all crowd into the booth for protection, one says "Certainly."**

the local police precinct had admitted suppressing crime statistics.

"If I were to send in to police headquarters the genuine figures about juvenile crime in my precinct," the commander was quoted as having said, "I would not last a day in my job. This is what they all do; I am not the only one. Juvenile crime is a scourge in Moscow and in other cities as well."

The émigré, whose account was provided by a Western embassy here, said his task force had found that many crimes were covered up by schools. One involved a girl of 13 who had sexual relations with her stepfather, then tried to slash his throat when he took up with her girlfriend.

Another concerned a 13-year-old boy whose parents were invalids trying to live on 60 rubles ($84) a month in disability and pension payments. One day the boy began gathering up some bread that an elderly woman had sprinkled around for the birds.

"The neighbor rushed at him with a stick, which he tore from her," the émigré's account said. "He started beating her savagely, causing her severe injuries."

At the same time, the local precinct had some bizarre crimes on its books. A group of youths, 14 and 15, had been charged with murder after they had sharpened the points of umbrellas and spent evenings attacking lone pedestrians, swooping down on them, yelling, all stabbing at once, then pulling back and running off.

### Slain for Shearing Long Hair

Another teen-ager, with some friends, was accused of having murdered his mother, a party member, after she cut short his shoulder-length hair while he was sleeping.

When the special task force sent its report to the party's Central Committee, with the finging that up to 70 percent of criminal offenses were not reflected in police records, it drew only a rebuff and a reprimand from a high official who called it an exaggeration.

Visiting American jurists have been told officially that about 80 percent of murders are committed in the midst of drunkenness, and usually against relatives, neighbors or friends of the assailant.

### Case of a Matricide Reported

One foreign visitor to a juvenile reformatory near Moscow encountered a 15-year-old who said he and some other boys had beaten his mother to death while they were drunk because she had refused to give them money.

A Soviet magazine, Ogonyok, reported the murder of Viktor M. Fedotov by his son, Igor, 14, in the town of Uglovka, in the Novgorod region. The father, a former convict, was portrayed as a drunkard who beat his wife to the point where the boy and his mother sometimes had to spend the night in the hall or with a neighbor. Once, coming home to find his father at the table drinking, Igor stabbed him in the chest.

Society is ambivalent about opening such problems to extensive public discussion, and even lengthy case studies in the press often contain compromises.

The weekly Literaturnaya Gazeta published a series of articles titled "The Lesson" about a gang of eighth-grade girls who severely beat a classmate, Larisa Panteleyeva, while some 20 boys stood by watching. "Kick her! Kick her!" one of the boys shouted, and the girls kicked her.

What the paper did not say, according to a professional familiar with the case, was that Larisa had been attacked because she wanted to drop out of group sex that had been taking place, and the girls were afraid she would betray them.

"What a bunch!" the paper quoted one of the girls as having said to the boys after it was all over. "You watched as if you were in a zoo."

"We watched because you were beating her," one boy said.

"And we were beating her because you were watching," a girl replied.

### Controversial Play Discussed

One of the most controversial efforts at open discussion is a play called "Stop Malakhov" being performed nearly every Sunday at the Young Spectator's Theater here.

Based on a true story of a 15-year-old youth who mugged and robbed a woman, it explores the roots of his act. Performances are followed by discussion sessions among students, parents and teachers in the audience.

"Who is to blame?" the narrator on stage asks. "Who is to blame?"

Based on a book by a journalist who investigated the incident, the play is a harsh portrayal of nearly every element of Soviet society. The boy, Malakhov, falls in with a gang of thugs led by a man who, by day, is one of the star workers in a factory and an auxiliary policeman.

### Police Portrayed as Blind

The regular policemen are blind and bureaucratic. The parents, outwardly well adjusted and successful, are insensitive, the father is cruel. They blame the school, and the school blames them.

"You talk as if I had only 10 in my class," the boy's teacher shrieks. "I have 40. What else can I do? What else? We are powerless, absolutely powerless."

The play reportedly met opposition from teachers and party officials who thought it would convey the impression that parents, teachers and other adults and not the perpetrators themselves were responsible for juvenile crime.

The police, the Young Communist League and others of influence supported the production. They won their case when the Ministry of Internal Affairs, which oversees the police, distributed questionnaires among the audiences and got surprising results.

The survey found that most adults thought teen-agers would judge Malakhov innocent. Actually 90 percent of the young people saw him as guilty. "It's the generation gap," one Muscovite said. "Kids everywhere are always better than their parents think."

### Debate in the Theater Lobby

One evening after the final curtain, a large part of the audience from two high schools, together with parents and teachers, gathered with several of the actors in the theater lobby.

The discussion was slow to get going. "What is there to say?" one member of the audience murmured. Another offered formal thanks to the cast. Then, little by little, a debate developed, between advocates of punishment and of leniency, between those who believe in the individual's responsibility for a crime and those who blame society.

A well-dressed man expressed doubts that such crime was widespread and said the play had magnified "a statistically isolated case." There was derisive laughter. "That's what you think!" shouted a woman who headed a school parents' committee.

"You don't understand anything at all," another declared. And finally, as the talk moved into a search for the causes of such troubles, a young woman spoke up.

"Just look around you in streetcars and buses," she said, "We have become indifferent to one another."

March 5, 1978

# Soviet Crime Problem Tied To City Life and Social Ills

By DAVID K. SHIPLER

Special to The New York Times

MOSCOW, March 5—At the age of 14, Aleksandr Mikhailov dropped out of school and began to hang around the streets and staircases of his neighborhood in Gorky, an industrial city 250 miles east of here.

He had no job, and almost no relationship with his parents; they receded into the background of his world. The most important figure for him became another boy who taught him how to rob kiosks and streetcar coin boxes and stores. The money went for liquor.

By the time he was 17, Aleksandr had served two workhouse terms, of 10 and 15 days, and was facing a full-scale trial on charges of "cynical acts of brazen hooligan behavior."

The roots of crime in the Soviet Union are no easier to trace than in the United States, but the search goes on in similar areas.

**Rapid Urbanization a Factor**

Rapid urbanization has brought a breakdown of family and social ties, magnifying the impact of peer pressure on young people. Working parents have too little time for their children. School classes are too large to permit individual attention, and schools tend to encourage "difficult" youngsters to leave after the eighth grade.

As in the case of Aleksandr, whose story was reported in the official press, school dropouts without work appear prominently in the Soviet picture of vandalism, burglary and violent crime.

It is a problem causing increased worry and is becoming a subject for professional analysis. A special institute investigates the causes of crime. The Ministry of Internal Affairs, which supervises the police, operates a psychology department delving into motives and attitudes, especially among young people.

Both these agencies declined to discuss the problem with a foreign reporter. But a continuing debate about the causes of crime is evident among criminologists, sociologists, prosecutors, police officials, judges and others who write for specialized journals or who are ready to talk informally about the issues.

Juvenile crime is portrayed as a function of economic class, parental neglect, the abundance of alcohol, narcotics addiction, youthful boredom and what some Russians see as a profound amorality among the young, a lack of acceptance of either Mary or Jesus, or other higher values.

"Nobody believes in anything anymore," said the 17-year-old daughter of a scientist.

"There are no heroes," said a writer. "Who is your hero?" he asked his son, 14. The boy shrugged in silence. "You see? No heroes, just as in the West."

Crime rates are higher in cities than in rural areas, Soviet sociologists have noted, even though the Government controls the composition of the urban population enough to avoid the Western problem of impoverished city neighborhoods.

But urbanization has been swift as industrial towns have mushroomed into cities, and cities have spread outward in forests of prefabricated high-rises. Urban life has corroded the old values and the traditional, stabilizing relationships of the village. Divorce rates are high, family control is weak.

Not long ago, a law journal published findings that newcomers in cities were more vulnerable than longtime residents to the anonymity and disorientation of city life.

"Deformed or totally disintegrated family and kinship ties are much more common among migrants than among people who have always lived in the city," said the law-institute journal, Sovetskoye Gosudarstvo i Pravo, "A distinctive kind of 'vacuum' forms around such individuals and is often filled by people whose influence is very harmful."

A sample of lawbreakers showed that twice as many new arrivals as longtime residents spent their free time with former convicts, and the percentage of offenders was higher among newcomers.

"As a rule," the journal said, "the cultural level of these people is low, their needs are primitive and their interests are restricted to their immediate environment."

Another study of juvenile prisoners showed that most had spent their leisure time drinking and idling in public places.

Krokodil

**In a comment on class distinctions in the disciplining of children, a Soviet cartoon set in the children's room of a militia station had the caption: "Hey, take it easy! Don't forget whose son you are talking to!"**

"Only 15 percent of urban couples with children live with any of their parents," the magazine reported. "Since in nuclear families the parents both work, as a rule, and there are no other adult relatives in the family, teen-agers and young people often spend a good part of the day on their own. This is a contributing factor in the higher level of juvenile crime in cities compared to rural localities."

The strictest ideologists see crime as a holdover or infection from "bourgeois culture" and declare, in the words of one newspaper, "There are no socio-economic causes of crime in our country." The class conflict and exploitation that supposedly give rise to criminal behavior are supposedly absent in the Soviet Union, and crime rates, which are secret, are supposed to be falling.

Couched in Marxist ideology, such contentions inhibit debate, but not enough to prevent sociologists from doing their work. They may avoid the word "class," but the results are the same.

**Crime Grows With Lack of Skills**

A sociology journal reported a year ago that the higher the vocational skills, the lower the crime rate. For those in the machine-building industry, for example, the level is one-tenth of that among construction workers.

An official of a juvenile penal colony told a Soviet interviewer that many his wards has been school dropouts without work. Sergei I. Gusev, a Deputy Prosecutor General, wrote recently that the crime rate among dropouts was 24 times the rate of those attending school.

Children whose parents have a secondary or higher education, he said, are only half as likely to break the law as those whose parents went only to elementary school. About 70 to 80 percent of juvenile offenders come from problem homes, Mr. Gusev reported, and although parental difficulties cut across socio-economic lines, they are exacerbated in families with low educational levels.

A hint of the alienation between children and parents of higher status was given in a study of students at Tartu Unversity in Estonia. Seventy-five percent felt they had unsatisfactory relations with their fathers, 60 percent with their mothers, and only 10 percent were judged to have real emotional contact with their parents.

Other surveys have measured the correlation between crime and family problems. "Ten times as many juvenile delinquents come from an atmosphere of vulgarity or heavy drinking as from a normal environment," one criminologist said.

An example was reported by the Government newspaper Izvestia. Sergei Shubnikov, a schoolboy with an alcoholic mother, was sentenced to two years in a reformatory for hooliganism and brawling, was released in an amnesty three months later, started drinking and led a group of teen-agers in an assault on a 19-year-old stranger, who died.

The case was cited as an argument for sterner punishment, part of a continuing debate that parallels the American dispute between those who favor social remedies and those who advocate stronger deterrents to crime.

**Debate in Professional Journals**

Professional journals for teachers, jurists and sociologists often publish various sides of the question. Among the magazines are Sotsiologicheskiye Issledovaniya, published by the Institute for Sociological Research; Sotsialisticheskaya Zakonnost, of the Ministry of Justice; Uchitelskaya Gazeta, the teachers' daily, and Sovetskoye Gosudarstvo i Pravo, published by the law institute.

Soviet law-and-order advocates often report in the mass-circulation press examples of leniency leading to more serious crime. In Nizhnekamsk, a petrochemical center 500 miles east of Moscow, the police did nothing but warn two boys, 15 and 16, who had beaten up a classmate. A few days later they killed him.

**Criminals Are Often Executed**

In another incident, no action was taken when two eighth-grade boys repeatedly threatened a ninth-grade girl. Her body was later found, hacked and mutilated. In Petrozavodsk, in northern Russia, a 22-year-old man with four previous convictions committed rape and murder, for which he received a 15-year sentence, the maximum jail term.

"Humaneness toward criminals leads to cruelty toward their victims," a Leningrad man wrote indignantly.

The Soviet Union executes criminals regularly, and usually publicizes the sentences as a deterrent. Last November a Moscow factory worker was put before a firing squad for the rape and murder of a 12-year-old and on other counts of rape and attempted rape.

But police officials, prosecutors and others often express concern about placing youngsters in prison, which one specialist described recently as "universities of crime."

Recidivism accounts for a high proportion of crime—one source put it at 23 percent, but other estimates are higher—and criminologists have written of the damage imprisonment does to the structure of family and other relationships that can offer support.

An older inmate wrote in the Justice Ministry journal Sotsialisticheskaya Zakonnost of his distress at seeing youngsters enter prison. "Many of them lost the good qualities they had," he said. "Imprisonment can totally corrupt a teenager by teaching him the bad unwritten laws that still survive in prison."

Juveniles are usually sent to special low-security penal colonies separate from the hardened adult prison population. A year ago, the criminal code was revised to allow the substitution of work assignments and fines for imprisonment in juvenile cases.

**Juvenile Divisions in Precincts**

Police precincts have juvenile divisions handling teen-agers and registering them if they look like troublemakers. Committees of teachers, union representatives and police and party officials often deal with juvenile cases out of court.

But the system often fails to identify problem youths early enough, according to T. Firsova, head of the juvenile division of the Moscow prosecutor's office.

She wrote recently that only one-third of teen-age offenders were registered before their crimes, that police agencies make only perfunctory inquiries into the causes of crime and that communications among precincts and with the prosecutor's office are poor.

She said bad coordination reduced police effectiveness against youth gangs, 95 percent of which form near teen-agers' homes and then go into other precincts to commit their crimes. Furthermore, she wrote, some vocational boarding schools tolerate class-cutting, leaving teen-agers on their own. Health agencies fail to notify the police about teen-age alcoholism or drug addiction, which usually involves smoking hashish or injecting morphine.

**Child-Labor Laws a Factor**

Some have suggested relaxing child-labor laws, which prohibit anyone under 16 from working full time, to allow dropouts a steady occupation. There has been no move to increase the drinking age, which is now 16, even, even though alcohol figures in most offenses.

The most visible devices used to combat juvenile crime are propaganda and education. Television documentaries occasionally show a supremely efficient police force tracking down an offender. Moralistic novels for teen-agers dramatize the futility of crime.

High schools conduct required courses on the law, with detailed explanations of what constitutes criminal behavior and what punishments can be expected.

At one school in the Siberian city of Irkutsk, the course was taught so dryly, a newspaper said, that no sooner was it over than two boys raped a girl, and another group clashed with students from another school; in the fight one youth died.

So the problems remain stubborn, intractable. In a public discussion after a Moscow stage play about teen-age crime recently, the head of a school parents' committee expressed sorrow and frustration that parents who needed counseling almost never came to meetings. Someone noted that they had not come to the play either.

"Who is to blame?" one of the actors said during the discussion after the performance.. "I, you, everyone."

The cast visited a reformatory before putting the play on the stage, he said. "They were children, children," he said. "When I saw those children the first time, they all seemed innocent."

March 6, 1978

# *Soviet Reporters Investigate, Too, But Only Within Limits Set at Top*

By CRAIG R. WHITNEY
Special to The New York Times

MOSCOW, March 26—An alert worker catches the director of a state auto repair shop bribing city officials by servicing and repairing their cars free. When he tries to blow the whistle he is ignored and eased out of his job. In frustration he writes to a powerful newspaper. The paper vindicates him with an exposé that leads to a criminal investigation, reprimands and, possibly, the dismissal of the corrupt officials.

All this has happened in the town of Kuibyshev after revelations in Pravda, the newspaper of the Soviet Communist Party. Though the prosecutors have not finished their investigation, Boris F. Tretyachenko, the editor who oversaw the Pravda article, said, "I think many people are going to be punished by the time this is over."

Investigative journalism exists in the Soviet Union, but within carefully circumscribed and controlled limits. The press is constantly exposing wrongdoing and criticizing shortcomings in almost every area of national life. However, some matters are clearly excluded: the system itself, the policies handed down by the leadership, the correctness of the party's course.

**Consequences of Exposure**

In a series of interviews around the country Soviet editors have described some of the inner workings of the press—how reporters come to have almost as much authority as prosecutors, who authorizes them to investigate, what the consequences of exposure are.

Soviet "muckraking" is a carefully controlled, officially sanctioned process that has little in common with its counterpart in the United States. It starts with broad directives and sweeping authority—sometimes even commands—from the top levels of party and government. The press, actually an essential part of the apparatus of control, serves that aim by exposing shortcomings, following Lenin's dictum that the press should be "collective organizer" as well as "collective propagandist and agitator."

**Inefficiency, Corruption, Mistakes**

This year the central theme in the press is the necessity of increasing cost-effectiveness, from auto repair shops to the biggest industrial complexes. Andrei P. Kirilenko, a close associate of Leonid I. Brezhnev, the party chief and President, laid out that policy at a meeting of high officials of the press in January. "At the center of attention of the press," Pravda reported, "should be the struggle for all possible increases in the efficiency of collective production and in the quality of work done, the achievement of the highest possible productivity of labor and the lowering of the costs of production."

Since then article after article has focused on economic inefficiency, petty corruption and the costly mistakes of central planners. The report on the waste and corruption in the repair shop in Kuibyshev was displayed on Pravda's People's Control Page, which usually appears twice a month and carries many letters from "people's con trol committees" all over the country. These watchdog groups have long played a role in the Soviet system as a way of trying to reduce inefficiency and cor ruption. Reading between the lines of their forum, it seems that they have been less than successful.

N. Kravchenko, head of the committee in the Kuibyshev repair shop, wrote that he had been eased out of his regular job for complaining about the corrupt management of the director, Z. Kiriya. The editor of the page, Mr. Tretyachenko, said he sent Pravda's correspondent in Kuibyshev, Nikolai Mironov, to investigate. What was reported in Pravda in January was that Mr. Kiriya was doing illegal repairs for city officials to the tune of as much as 142,000 rubles—$213,000—a year. "He allocated spare parts the way he wanted" to a whole list of "useful people," the article said. It also criticized local agencies for not checking the control committee's complaints and denounced the prosecutor for not taking action.

Pravda's responsibility does not stop at exposing corruption, Mr. Tretyachenko said. After publication, Soviet law requires the officials directly involved to provide the paper with a reply. Mr. Tretyachenko sent copies of the Kuibyshev article, titled "Compromise," to the local authorities and to the prosecutor, who began a criminal investigation. The results, he said, are not in yet.

**The Authority of the Party**

When a Pravda correspondent writes, it is with "great authority," the chief editor, Viktor G. Afanasyev, said at a meeting with Western correspondents—all the authority of the Communist Party, which is where power really lies. When Pravda's correspondents appear on the scene, according to officials who have come under their scrutiny, it is with everything but the power of subpoena.

Last summer, when a Pravda team investigated progress on the Baikal-Amur Mainline, the 2,000-mile railroad being built across eastern Siberia to the Pacific, it was given official helicopters and full briefings everywhere it went. When the paper sniffs out evidence of law-breaking, Mr. Afanasyev said, correspondents may work with prosecutors or the police to make their investigations—apparently with equal power. Other editors suggested that the K.G.B., the security police, was sometimes consulted also, though Mr. Afanasyev denied that K.G.B. agents worked under the cover of the Pravda staff.

How a subject is chosen and cleared for investigation is a key to understanding the way the system works, and like almost everything else it is usually shrouded in secrecy.

In Kiev, Vladimir Y. Serobaba, editor of Radyanska Ukraina, the main Ukrainian-language newspaper, said in an interview that the Central Committee of the Ukrainian party must authorize the publication's most sensitive projects. "We get suggestions for situations that ought to be investigated from our local correspondents," he explained, "and most of the questions we can decide for ourselves, of course. We are aware of what questions we cannot decide, and then we inform the Central Committee." The subjects pursued seem to be those that are ideologically neutral.

Mr. Serobaba is proudest of his paper's exposure of pollution in the Dnieper River in 1977 and of the failure of officials and economic enterprises to obey party decisions to clean it up.

Sometimes the party tells the press what to do. In Novosibirsk, in the heart of western Siberia, Nikolai V. Bezryadin of the local paper, Sovetskaya Sibir, said: "The party can decide what should get the most emphasis. Last year, we were asked to publish an article about shortcomings in housing construction in this district so they wouldn't be repeat-ed in other areas." Investigations by the newspaper's staff, three-quarters of whom are party members, reevaled that construction officials were building fast and sloppily to overfulfill their plans, which seldom take account of quality. The crumbling construction was revealed.

Systematic errors such as faulty criteria in plans usually go unmentioned, but not always. On rare occasions more broad-ranged ills can be exposed and corrected. Dmitri V. Valovoi, a deputy chief editor of Pravda and an economist, wrote a widely discussed series condemning economic failures that ran last November, just before Mr. Brezhnev met with the Central Committee in secret session and criticized economic shortcomings.

One of the problems Mr. Valovoi noted was that there was no incentive in the production system for enterprises to fill specific orders from industrial customers. The system encourages them to meet the ruble totals of their plans without regard to where the products go, he found. On Jan. 1 a law went into effect requiring that contract terms be fulfilled before factory officials can be granted production bonuses.

Mr. Valovoi's series was said to have been carried out on his own initiative, not cleared by the Central Committee. Pravda, sitting, as it were, at the right hand of Mr. Brezhnev, is almost the only publication that can allow itself such freedom.

In the provinces things work differently. Nikolai Timofeyev, editor of Pravda Vostoka, published in Tashkent, said that most investigations it conducts start with letters from readers. "Our reporters," he said, "can go to the people's control committees if they need data for an investigation or can commission a government lawyer or accountant to help. We publish lots of articles with criticism of shortcomings, and sometimes they lead to criminal prosecutions." He added that journalists who distorted the facts could be taken to court, too.

Lenin is supposed to have ordained that even a one percent error was too much for the Soviet press, and by might or main his followers try to stay within that limit. The press seldom admits to being wrong—something individuals who complain find out the hard way.

Vladimir I. Bakharev, a former professor of conducting in the Gnesin Music Institute in Moscow, was denounced in Pravda a year ago as an inconsiderate, incompetent teacher who had spoiled conducting for hundreds of students. Mr. Bakharev, who has had ideological disputes with the authorities and who insists that a Pravda reporter never spoke with him and based his article on hearsay, complained and even went to court. "All I got," he said, "was a note from the paper that I had failed to refute any of their charges." When he carried his case to a party official, he related, he was offered a good review as amends because "Pravda will print whatever we tell them to."

Valentin I. Poplavsky, an employee of a maintenance factory for workers' housing in Klimovsk, near Moscow lost his job for refusing to sign falsified documents criticizing another employee for exposing embezzlement by officials higher up. When he tried to take his case to a reporter for the Moscow regional newspaper, Leninskoye Znamya, he said, he was rebuffed. "I made an appointment with a reporter I knew there," he said, "but he did not show up. He told me later his editor had told him not to bother with me if he valued his job."

Criticisms in the official press, Mr. Poplavsky believes, are nothing but "exceptions to the rule." Many ordinary citizens like him distrust the press out of deep-rooted cynicism. "They write 'exposés,'" he said, "only so that people will believe the propaganda that fills the rest of the space."

March 27, 1978

# In Soviet, Widespread Practice of Bribery Helps One Get a Car, Get an Apartment and Get Ahead

**By CRAIG R. WHITNEY**
Special to The New York Times

MOSCOW, May 6—The Soviet Union is a society of pervasive governmental control, where the state runs everything and the police have almost unlimited power

It is also a society of pervasive corruption, where officials embezzle hundreds of millions of dollars a year from state enterprises and where a policeman is willing to look the other way if the bribe is right.

Lenin called bribery "the worst enemy of the revolution."

Almost 50 years later, Nikita S. Khrushchev tried to stamp out corruption —"this disgraceful survival of the past" —by ordering the death penalty for serious bribery.

Today, corruption remains an inescapable fact of daily life throughout the Soviet Union.

A ruble or two will persuade a uniformed Moscow traffic policeman to forget that he saw the driver jump a red light.

For 80 rubles (somewhat more than $100), a clerk in the neighborhood department store will sell a pair of imported shoes under the counter, after everyone has been told the shoes have been sold out.

For 300 rubles ($435) "00" license plates, a status symbol normally reserved for the powerful and privileged, have been issued to people with the right connections.

For 2,000 rubles ($2,900) above the regular $11,000 purchase price, one can get a new Zhiguli, a Soviet-built Fiat, without having to wait the usual year or more.

And for 5,000 to 10,000 rubles an influence peddler will try to persuade a member of a local City Council to grant a permit for someone to live in Moscow. The privilege is worth the price to thousands of people in remote provincial cities where there is not even fresh meat in the markets.

"For bribes," Mr. Khrushchev said in a speech in 1962, "state funds are squandered, housing accommodations are granted unlawfully, plots of land are allotted, pensions are granted, students are admitted to colleges and even diplomas are issued."

"We can and must put an end forever to bribery and other disgraceful phenomena," he declared.

**A Call That Went Unanswered**

But recent interviews with scores of Soviet citizens and a daily flow of revelations of corruption in the official press leave little doubt that Mr. Khrushchev's call for reform was not answered. All the abuses he mentioned continue today. But by now a suggestion of helplessness runs through the leadership's calls.

The scale of crimes of embezzlement is a carefully guarded secret today. Only once, in a speech by Mr. Khrushchev in 1962, were the dimensions of the problem disclosed. He revealed that 56 million rubles (the equivalent of $81 million now) had been swindled from state enterprises, just in the cases prosecuted before the courts in the first half of that year.

Sixteen years later, crimes involving hundreds of thousands of rubles are being reported every week in the press, in Pravda, Izvestia and local papers from one end of the country to the other.

The reasons for corruption and bribery in the Soviet Union cover the spectrum of human weakness. But there is one underlying cause: This is a society of shortages caused by an inefficient bureaucracy. And bribery and corruption are sometimes the only way to get something. But the practices corrode public respect and ideological confidence in the system.

**'This Is a Society in Deep Crisis'**

"This is a society in deep crisis," said Lev Kopelev, a former Marxist whose belief in the system was shattered when he emerged from nine years in Stalin's prison camps. "It is part of a general collapse of all our ideological and moral values."

A Soviet journalist loyal to the system said: "There isn't much the leadership can say about corruption today because everybody at the top is raking off whatever he can. To admit that corruption is widespread would be to admit that the country has stopped being revolutionary."

Corruption and bribery were almost universal in czarist times—tolerated by Peter the Great, satirized by Gogol, firmly entrenched by the end of the 19th century. The Bolsheviks set out in 1917 to sweep it away.

But after a brief period of revolutionary purity, the Communists themselves succumbed to the blandishments of absolute power. Bribery at all levels, and skimming off the top for those in positions of authority, became firmly entrenched under Stalin, who came from what most Russians still regard as the "capital of corruption"—the Caucasian Republic of Georgia.

The national economy suffers hundreds

Sovfoto

**In a cartoon published in 1976 in Krokodil, the Soviet humor magazine, a man addresses an official, saying "I come to you with an open heart!"**

of millions of dollars every year in losses from embezzlement. But it is the everyday practice of bribery in its various forms that causes the real damage—to standards of decency, civility, the Communist ideal of "the new Soviet man."

**Evading the Rules Can Be Profitable**

There is such a welter of bureaucratic rules and restrictions in Soviet life that any lowly official is often in a position to mete out punishment or withhold some necessary permission or document from citizens with nowhere else to turn. What the regulations won't allow suddenly becomes possible for a little money under the table.

Like their colleagues in many American cities, Russian policemen, who make as little as $140 a month, are sometimes unable to resist the temptation to supplement their income with bribes.

Doctors and medical workers, whose average wage is 104 rubles a month ($151) are not averse to extra money. And the better the doctor the more willing are the patients to insure good treatment by giving a "present."

Sometimes it goes beyond that. The Azerbaijani newspaper Bakinski Rabochii, for example, reported a case in March that started when a truck driver hit a motorcycle rider near the Caspian Sea town of Alyat.

He took the injured man to a clinic and paid the doctor 300 rubles not to report the cause of the accident to the police. But they found out about it, and a captain and a major agreed to forget the case if the driver would give them 1,000 rubles.

The man, identified by the paper as Shakhker Kyamalov, tried desperately to raise the money but without success. Finally, he confessed to higher authorities about the bribes, hoping to escape prosecution.

**Bribery Part of Daily Life**

In 1962, part of Mr. Khrushchev's attempt to stamp out bribery was a change in the laws to let people who give bribes escape punishment if they informed the authorities that they had been solicited. Taking bribes was made punishable by as much as 15 years in prison and by death in extreme cases.

The doctor was sentenced to seven years in jail and the loss of all property; the two policemen got 8 to 10 years. Mr. Kyamalov was found not guilty, even of responsibility for the motorcyclist's injuries.

But bribery does not usually take such classic forms in the Soviet Union. Every sales clerk is a Government employee, for instance. Bribing one to avoid standing in line for scarce items, or just to find out when a shipment of oranges or imported Western shoes will go on sale, is established practice.

"I know a doctor who just took a high-paying job as a senior researcher in a medical laboratory," a Soviet journalist said recently. "But she wanted to go back to her old job as a general practitioner. She was making a better living then, even with $150 a month less in salary, because it went further—her patients who were sales clerks would sell her boots or cotton blouses for the normal price. Now, she says, she has to pay the clerks double to get them, just like everybody else."

Clerks make small salaries, averaging the equivalent of $110 to $125 a month.

"Money has no real value here," a social scientist said. "Even a bottle of good vodka is more of a convertible currency than the ruble."

One of the first surprises for any newcomer to the Soviet Union is learning how much influence he can have with a bottle of vodka.

A plumber will drop whatever he is doing to fix a leaking faucet and an overburdened repairman will find time to take on one more job. Even customs officials will sometimes be lenient for a bottle of premium Stolichnaya, which is sold for foreign currency here but is no longer available for ordinary rubles.

The special ruble coupons that foreigners and some privileged Soviet citizens get can be used in special stores to buy things like imported foods, sheepskin coats from Finland and shoes from France and West Germany. The coupons are among the most desirable black-market items in Moscow because they buy four to five times more than ordinary rubles.

Russians are not normally allowed to have the foreigners' coupons, and U.P.D.K., the state agency in charge of services for foreigners, will not allow its employees to sign contracts specifying part of their salaries in coupons.

A correspondent who arrived here last fall spent months trying to hire a local staff of interpreters and household help but all the prospective employees insisted on being paid partly in coupons. When he complained to the agency about this, he was told that it was his problem, not that of the service agency.

One of the scarcest necessities of life here is decent furniture. Bribery is frequently a quick way of getting it. A young Russian couple in Moscow said they could find nothing in the state stores for the three-room apartment they recently had redecorated but they were lucky. A friend who works in an embassy bought furnishings from the diplomatic agency and sold it to them "na levo," a Russian expression for "on the sly."

"We have the money," the young father said, "but even for a tip there was nothing to buy in the state stores."

Official permits are required for so many things that some minor official with power of approval is always in a position to ask for or take a bribe.

Vladimir I. Bakharev, a musician, said that when he was working as an orchestra conductor during the 1960's he had to agree to pay off the director of the State Concert Agency to get any engagements.

"It was made clear to me that if I didn't give him half my fee, I wouldn't get the work," he said. "Singers and players had to do the same thing."

He was given 10 engagements in 10 years and made a total of only 375 rubles [$544].

This sort of buying of privilege is not necessary for those who occupy high party or governmental positions or have "blat" ("pull") with friends in such positions.

Mr. Bakharev said, for example, that as a teacher in a music institute here he often came into contact with pupils whose parents were high up in the party elite. "Teachers were simply expected to help these students through their studies," he said. "And we did."

**Corruption at Top Rarely Divulged**

At such high levels it is not necessary to pay off grocery clerks for special merchandise or to find a foreign friend with currency coupons. The party elite has its own special stores, with all the best imported and domestic food and other luxuries.

"That's corruption in itself," a resentful young party member said. "It's why the leadership doesn't talk much about corruption anymore since Khrushchev failed. They're silent because they're all involved."

The press frequently exposes official corruption and cases of large-scale embezzlement involving party officials, but almost never at the very top levels in Moscow.

The last time any top Soviet official in Moscow came close to being officially accused of corruption was in May 1974, when Yekaterina A. Furtseva, Minister of Culture, was reportedly reprimanded by the party for having built a $170,000 dacha outside Moscow with state-owned materials obtained through fraud.

She did not lose her post, however, keeping it until she died of a heart attack later that year.

Enough is reported about misdeeds at the top in the 15 republics to suggest that corruption is continuing at high levels.

Georgia, where bribery and profiteering are not so much vices as local customs, is often singled out in press reports. The Georgian party chief, Vasily P. Mzhavanadze, was forced into retirement in September 1972 for allowing corruption in his republic to become a nationwide embarrassment. His successor, Eduard A. Shevardnadze, has been struggling with it ever since and scores of officials have lost their jobs.

None of the embezzlement cases disclosed in the press seem unique to Georgia but the scale is sometimes grandiose, even by Western standards.

The director of the medical institute in Tbilisi, the Georgian capital, for instance, was sentenced to 15 years in prison in 1976 after investigators discovered that no fewer than 170 of the 200 students had been admitted not for their qualifications but for bribes.

One father had to pay 10,000 rubles to arrange enrollment of his daughter, according to the Georgian Communist Party paper Zarya Vostoka. Russians say the practice is common everywhere, since there are frequently 10 applicants for every available place in the university system.

Despite six years of purges, Mr. Shevardnadze recently told the Georgian legislature that much remained to be done. "Taking of bribes, private profiteering, extortion and similar phenomena brought all ideological work to nought," he lamented in a speech April 15.

Another southern Soviet republic, Azerbaijan, also comes up frequently in Soviet articles about corruption.

The Soviet system of state enterprise and the fact that virtually everybody who works here is a state employee make embezzlement possible on a grand scale.

Recently, the publication Bakinski Rabochii reported the case of a local state farm director, who with 12 other workers filled out and stamped the documents for the purchase of 169,770 rubles' worth of nonexistent grapes. They pocketed the money, the equivalent of a quarter of a million dollars.

The most unusual feature of the case seems to be that they were caught. The director was given a maximum sentence of 15 years in a strict-regime prison and the local Communist Party secretary lost his job.

Two years ago, the entire field inspection team of the Azerbaijani Trade Ministry—24 persons—were thrown in jail for extortion. In just eight months, they had extorted 200 bribes worth 94,000 rubles from managers of shops and restaurants, threatening them with prosecution for sometimes imaginary offenses unless they paid off.

Such things, of course, are not unknown in New York. They existed in China in the last days before the collapse of the rule of Chiang Kai-shek, and in South Vietnam before its collapse in 1975.

The comparisons are invidious, but it was a Soviet journalist who made them; and for him the damage that is done is to Communist ideals.

Last year, the chief Soviet prosecutor, Roman A. Rudenko, wrote in the journal Kommunist about "embezzlement on a significant scale" not only in Azerbaijan but also in Uzbekistan, the Ukraine, the Russian Republic and "a number of other places."

"The necessary measures," he said, "have not been taken everywhere to intensify the struggle with embezzlement and other encroachments on the public weal."

"You can't cure corruption without eliminating what causes it," a Soviet critic said. "And they're a long way from being able to do that yet."

May 7, 1978

## NEW PRESSURES ON ARTISTIC FREEDOM

### *Kremlin Rules Out Easing of Arts Curb*

Special to The New York Times

MOSCOW, Jan. 9—The new Soviet regime served notice today in effect that it would not give artists and writers greater freedom of expression.

The message was contained in an editorial in Pravda, the Communist party newspaper, that called for greater ideological purity.

It was the first major pronouncement on Soviet arts and literature by the leadership since the removal of Nikita S. Khrushchev in October.

The move appeared to destroy the hopes, nourished through the last three months by some intellectuals, that the new regime's willingness to permit fresh approaches in the economic fields and education would also be extended to the arts.

The editorial warned against "so-called progressive" trends in art, against "formalism" and "digressions from realism."

It declared that "imperialist reaction does not stop its ideological subversion of Communism for a minute [and therefore] we have no right to a breathing spell in our ideological struggle."

"There cannot be any peaceful coexistence" in the field of ideology, the editorial said, echoing a phrase that Mr. Khrushchev used frequently in explaining his thesis that "peaceful coexistence" with the West applied only to the political and military spheres and not to the ideological contest between Communism and capitalism.

The Pravda editorial said the decisions adopted by the Central Committee of the Communist party at its session in June, 1963, remained the guidelines for the Soviet creative intelligentsia.

The 1963 meeting came toward the end of a six-month period of strong pressure exerted by the Khrushchev regime against young and unorthodox writers, painters and poets who experimented with new forms.

#### Campaign Was Muted

Leonid F. Ilyichev, one of the party's principal ideologists, summarized the position on art and literature at that meeting by calling for a campaign against "formalistic stunts." He declared that art had to be a "sharp weapon in the struggle against alien bourgeois ideology" and warned that the party "will not allow even the tiniest cracks to open through which our enemies could rush."

Shortly after the Central Committee meeting, the Soviet leadership began to play down its conflict with the young artists. This remained true through the remaining months of 1963 and most of 1964. While not making any concessions in official statements, the regime appeared to be willing to give gradually a little more leeway to the artists.

Against this background, it was felt that today's pointed reference to the 1963 party decisions would be regarded by many artists as a veiled warning.

#### Criticism of Behavior

Some specialists also drew the conclusion from the Pravda editorial that Mr. Ilyichev apparently still had the position of the party's watchdog on the arts. Until now there has been no conclusive indication on his standing in the new regime. He had been a close associate of Mr. Khrushchev.

Observers also noted a passage in today's editorial that could be interpreted as criticism of Mr. Khrushchev's behavior, as distinct from his policy, in dealing with artists and intellectuals.

While there can be "no concessions or compromises" with respect to "ideological errors" in art, the editorial said, the party will be "careful" in its attitude toward "talented people" and will not condemn the entire work of an artist for an ideological mistake that occurs in one poem or one painting.

Western observers felt that the editorial marked the end of a period of uncertainty about the new regime's intention toward intellectuals.

Editorials and articles that had appeared on the subject during the weeks following Mr. Khrushchev's ouster were vague and did not permit any conclusions.

It is felt that the subject apparently was discussed at length within the leadership and that a decision was reached that there should be no liberalization of the issue of party control over artists and intellectuals.

January 10, 1965

1917—The Russian Revolution—1967

### *Soviet Theater in Forefront of Creativity*

By HARRISON E. SALISBURY

OUTSIDE the Taganka Theater on the evening of July 2, 1967, the narrow sidewalk swarmed with eager young men and women, expectantly murmuring to passersby: "Lishni bilet yest?" (Got an extra ticket?).

Inside the theater, the excitement was electric. Every seat in the small, sparsely decorated house was filled. There were two or three diplomats in the audience, a rare sight in this most off-Broadway of Moscow theaters, several foreign correspondents and many of those who in Moscow constitute the liberal element in writing, in painting, in music. Obviously, an event was about to take place.

The event was the 200th performance of a theatrical spectacle that had been fashioned from a slender book of poems by Andrei Voznesensky called "Antimiry" (Antiworlds).

The performance came at a moment when Voznesensky was deeply troubled. He had been in the United States a month or so earlier and, on his return, had been subjected to more than the usual criticism from the party. In part this reflected tension in the international scene. In part it reflected the courage and candor of Voznesensky.

Always reserved and correct in his statements while abroad he had spoken out frankly on his return to Moscow. He had sent a strong letter to the Union of Soviet Writers, supporting the demand that Aleksandr Solzhenitsyn, author of "One Day in the Life of Ivan Denisovich," had made for the abolition of the censorship.

The cold warriors on the Soviet cultural front quickly retaliated. Amid much wrangling, permission for Voznesensky to go to New York to make a previously approved appearance at a Lincoln Center poetry festival was canceled.

Voznesensky was incensed at the party tactics.

"The worst part about this thing," he said, "is the uncertainty, the indecision. You do not know whether you will go or not and the decision comes at the last moment. Or is changed at the last moment. It is so boring in this day and age to have people act like this, always mixing politics into whatever you do."

Knowledge of Voznesensky's conflict with authority and the reputation of the Taganka Theater for controversy and courage had drawn a full house. Voznesensky himself, it was said, would appear. What would he say?

The play began in the Taganka tradition. Yuri Lyubimov, director of the theater, has perfected an exciting contemporary technique, the most exciting that Russia has seen since the great days of Vsevolod Meyerhold and Aleksandr Tairov. Lyubimov does not present plays. He presents spectacles, a montage of sight, sound, color, shadow, substance, words, emotion and music.

The Voznesensky spectacle opened with a number called "Rock 'n' Roll", splashy music, splashy movement, young people frugging and twisting across the stage. Next came a satire called "Strip Tease." A sinuous girl simulated Gypsy Rose Lee. Lights flashed. Electronic music assaulted the ears. The performance went on in the Lyubimov style. No intermission. Tension built higher and higher.

### Poet Speaks From the Stage

Finally it ended. Voznesensky emerged looking like a worn teen-ager — hair rumpled, face serious, hands thrust deeply in his houndstooth sport jacket. The crowd quieted and he began to recite. First, a conventional attack on China and the Cultural Revolution. Then he denounced "khamstvo" — Russia's traditional boorishness. He read a poem called "Revolt of the Strip Teasers" and another about the death of poetry, the death of Copernicus, the death of Dante. These great men died. But their truth lived on.

Again and again he spoke of truth. Nothing else mattered. Truth in life. Truth in art. Truth in politics. Each time he finished a poem, he ducked back into the stage wings only to return when the audience in the now darkened auditorium refused to leave. Finally he delivered a poem simply called "Monologue." We must bring hypocrisy to an end, he said. No more lies. Just speak the truth.

He spoke of things of which Russia might be proud and things for which she must be ashamed. Shame was not an emotion to be concealed. A face was not just for shaving. It was for blushing, too. He spoke of those who banged their shoes on the table of the United Nations and worried not about what they did, but whether their feet smelled. And he spoke with contempt of those who played with Vietnam as though it were a toy. Vietnam, he said, is not a game of lotto with which to amuse an idle afternoon. Today, said Voznesensky, the people have no need for fig leaves. They ask and need the naked truth.

The audience did not leave when he had finished. People stood and applauded. Voznesensky called for quiet. He spoke of Lvubimov, ill in a hospital. "He is a brave man," said Voznesensky. "He wants and needs your support." He passed out get-well cards — photoreproductions of verses from "Antiworlds" and asked everyone to send them to the director.

A youngster reminded Voznesensky of the violent attacks launched on him by Nikita S. Khrushchev in 1963. "That was a difficult time, too," Voznesensky recalled, "but we came through it." Curious things had happened then. Two young sailors had appeared at Voznesensky's apartment in Moscow. They had come to present him with a flag from their cutter. "If you're in trouble," they said, "just call on us. We'll come down and support you, just as the sailors did in 1917."

Voznesensky smiled sadly. He did not think he would need the help of the sailors. But he was pleased that it had been offered.

The 200th performance of "Antiworlds" was an event of major consequence in the Soviet theater. Not since the last public speech of the great director, Meyerhold, in 1939, had the Moscow stage resounded with words so strong, so forceful, so uncompromising in support of honesty and creativity, the freedom of the poet to write, of the painter to paint, of the stage to protray reality as it was perceived by the artistic conscience.

### Early Talents Extinguished by Stalin

The Russian stage at the time of the Bolshevik Revolution and the years just after had been dazzling. Those were the days of the glory of the Moscow Art Theater under the direction of Konstantin Stanislavsky and Vladimir Nemirovich-Danchenko; the explosion of talents of Meyerhold, which set the pace for the theatrical world far beyond Russia's borders, the flowering of Tairov, and the young Nikolai Okhlopkov with his revolutionary stage.

In those days the poet-playright-artist Vladimir Mayakovsky was creating new forms, breaking every ikon, smashing every tradition.

The Revolution raced like fire through the arts—ballet was transformed by Diaghilev, Bakst, Nijinsky and Stravinsky, art by Kandinsky, Malevich, Tatlin, Chagall. The world of films was electrified by the work of Eisenstein, Pudovkin, Dovzhenko.

Many of these talents were extinguished by Stalin. Meyerhold's theater was liquidated Jan. 8, 1938. The director himself survived a bit longer. In the spring of 1939 there was even a rumor in Moscow that Meyerhold might be given another theater. In June he was invited to address a conference of theatrical directors. On June 15, he spoke:

"Without art, there is no theater! Go visiting the theaters of Moscow. Look at their drab and boring presentations that resemble each other and are each worse than the others. . . . Everything is gloomily well-regulated, averagely arithmetical, stupefying and murderous in its lack of talent. Is that your aim? If it is—oh! you have done something monstrous! You have thrown out the baby along with bathwater. In hunting down formalism you have eliminated art."

Two days later a knock came at Meyerhold's door. The secret police led him away to die in one of Stalin's concentration camps in 1942. A few days after his arrest his wife, Zinaida Raikh, was murdered in their apartment, whether by police agents or casual murderers has not been disclosed.

For years Meyerhold's critique of the Soviet theater held true. The Art Theater survived as a kind of historical curiosity, a fly trapped in amber. It still presented Chekhov, but almost in caricature. Even "The Sea Gull" — the bird served as the emblem of the Art Theater — vanished from the repertoire.

Dramatists like Isaak Babel, Artem Vesely, Vladimir Kirshon and Sergei Tretyakov were arrested and died in Stalin's camps.

Tairov tried to carry on with his Kamerny Theater, but it was hopeless. In the "anticosmopolitanism" drive of 1948 and 1949 the theater was closed and Tairov died a premature death.

Slowly and painfully the Soviet theater began to revive after Stalin's death. One of the first innovators was Nikolai Okhlopkov. He had been one of Meyerhold's most promising protégés. Now, in his new Mayakovsky Theater, Okhlopkov began to experiment with some of Meyerhold's old excitements. He staged a dramatic "Hamlet" and an interesting "Mother Courage," the first Brecht play to be performed in Moscow. His production of Euripides' "Medea" with a choir of 100 voices and a Greek chorus of 40 women became a theatrical commentary upon the prison camp of spirit and body created in Russia by Stalin.

Okhlopkov died last year, his visions as a director still unfulfilled and his dream of a new experimental theater, a circular playhouse with 3,000 seats arranged in tiers and a plexiglass roof that could be opened on summer nights, unbuilt.

Valentin Pluchek, director of Moscow's Satire Theater, was the first to restore to the Russian stage the great satires of Mayakovsky — "The Bedbug," "The Bathhouse" and "Mystère-Bouffe" — all banned for years by Stalin. But Moscow still has a long way to go, in his opinion.

"We have no theater of the absurd here," he said. "Indeed, we have no young playwrights, nor old playwrights, writing in that genre. Ionesco is unknown to Russian audiences. A couple of years ago 'Rhinoceros' was prepared for presentation, but it was not put on. I don't know why."

The answer was official conservatism, a reluctance of the censors to permit the stage to present any spectacle that might be seen by the audience as implying some criticism, however oblique, of the party's state dictatorship.

Even Brecht is not yet widely played in Russia, except for "The Threepenny Opera," which has gone into the repertoire and can be found in provincial houses. The Lenin Komsomol Theater in Leningrad was presenting "The Threepenny Opera" this year in a production that was staged with boldness and imagination. For the first time in the experience of many members of the audience, words like "whorehouse" and "prostitute" were bandied across the stage, and blowzy prostitutes, breasts bulging and hips swaying, made their appearance before the spectators.

"We don't do Brecht very well here," Pluchek admitted. He thought the reason lay in the Stanislavsky tradition of realism. Whereas in the United States Stanislavsky ("The Method") had come to represent progressive theatrical art, in Russia it had become a brake upon imaginative techniques.

Not that the Moscow theater is ignorant of foreign plays and playwrights. John Osborne, Arthur Miller and Lillian Hellman have been presented. People know Edward Albee, Harold Pinter and LeRoi Jones. Albee's "Ballad of the Sad Cafe" was presented in 1967 by the Sovremennik (Contemporary) Theater, but, in general, a Moscow director said, "Homosexuality doesn't seem to us to be such a pressing problem and Albee's plays appear to be remote from our reality."

The playwright who interested Soviet directors most was Peter Weiss. "Peter Weiss is a genius of the first order," Pluchek said. "Marat/Sade is amazing."

He was asked whether he was going to put on this play.

"I don't think we can put on a play in which a revolution occurs in a madhouse in the jubilee year of the Revolution," he said.

Grigory Kozintsev, brother-in-law of the late Ilya Ehrenburg, is a Soviet film director who survived the harshest repressions of the Stalin days to win a prize for his film "Hamlet" in the post-Stalin era. He lives in Leningrad with a beautiful wife and 17-year-old son in a fine apartment, decorated with French abstract art, an Italian renaissance angel, No masks from Japan and pre-revolutionary cartoons by Mayakovsky. On a table overflowing with books is a big new volume called "Meetings with Meyerhold."

"Meyerhold is the great influence today," Kozintsev said. In films the influence of Eisenstein is supreme. Eisenstein escaped Meyerhold's fate by a heart beat. He died of a heart attack in 1948. Had he not been stricken he would certainly have been arrested in the "cosmopolitanism" drive.

Kozintsev was deep in preparation for a film of "King Lear," which he hoped to start in December. In his view, Shakespeare was a man with a remarkable contemporary spirit whose understanding of the universality of human character enabled him to foresee the future. Kozintsev's plans for the treatment of Lear revolved about this concept. Lear would be a universal, modern figure. He would come to life in contemporary terms.

Such an approach, Kozintsev was told, inevitably recalled Stalin. "Naturally," he smiled.

The younger Soviet film directors were beginning to move in the direction of Michelangelo Antonioni, who they felt was the most talented innovator of contemporary film making. They particularly liked Antonioni's "Blow-Up." Many Soviet film workers had seen "Doctor Zhivago" in the course of their trips abroad. Most of them liked it although some, like Kozintsev, were not impressed.

The 50th anniversary affected the Soviet film world as it did all fields of artistic and cultural endeavor. More than a dozen excellent films were said to be held up, awaiting the passage of the Nov. 7 celebrations before being released. Three of these were important pictures. These were a filming of Dostoyevsky's "A Boring Tale", a film of rural life called "Asya Khromonozhka" and the "Passion of Andrei Rublov," a story of Russia's famous medieval painter of ikons.

The pictures shared certain common characteristics. Each was harshly realistic in the Ingmar Bergman style, each contained grim, pathological, sadistic sequences. Because they broke with tradition and aroused controversy, they were put on the shelf, not to be released until after the holiday. In their place bland, slick films like "Zhurnalist" and a co-production with the Poles called "Zosya" were given the place of honor at the Moscow film festival in the summer.

The negative influence of the anniversary was to be seen in the theater as well. Directors of theaters like the Satire, the Sovremennik and the Taganka had increasing difficulty in getting clearance for new productions except of the conventional type.

The Taganka and its gifted director Lyubimov spent six months fighting for permission for a production about Mayakovsky called "Poslushaite!" (Listen!) It was given a preview in the spring of 1967 to a stony-faced audience of party workers and propagandists who stalked out with a mien so angry that many thought the play would never be released for general showing.

But Soviet cultural policy takes surprising turns. Permission to present "Poslushaite!" was given in the summer of 1967 and, instantly, the play became the most popular in Moscow. To create "Poslushaite!" Lyubimov ripped apart quotations from Mayakovsky, about Mayakovsky, poems by Mayakovsky, posters by Mayakovsky and declarations to Mayakovsky. He fashioned a scenic collage, mounting it against a battery of lights, noises, music, sound, pictures, posters and sensations that battered at the minds of spectators and the nerves of the actors.

The pace was so swift that the audience gripped the seats of its chairs. Spotlights jabbed through the auditorium; reversed footlights created a curtain of light through which actors appeared and disappeared. Out of this melange of sensation the portrait of Mayakovsky, human but heroic, emerged greater than life-size. The play turned into a raging debate between Mayakovsky, the free, iconoclastic artist, and the servile, sterile forces of party bureaucracy. A party meeting is summoned to denounce Mayakovsky for his unconventionality.

"Why don't you make everything beautiful the way they do at the Bolshoi Theater?" a woman party member asks. "You must write so that the workers and peasants can understand you," a party secretary insists. One critic appeals to the party group: "Am I right? Da ili nyet — yes or no." All shout: "Da". Only Mayakovsky says: "Nyet". Finally, Mayakovsky, tormented by the banality of his critics, flees the stage.

The final scene is a funeral. Mayakovsky has died. There are ikon-like portraits of him. The funeral oration hails the poet-playwright for his originality, his independence, his dedication to truth. Only the artist knows what the truth is in his own terms and only the truth is important.

The Taganka audience burst into applause at the oration and the question sprang to mind: Was Lyubimov suggesting that Mayakovsky had been driven to his death by suicide in 1930 by party demands for conformity? Was the director presenting a parallel between Mayakovsky and the struggle that raged around the role of Voznesensky, Yevgeny Yevtushenko and the pleiad of new Soviet writers, the new talents whose genius has burst upon the Soviet stage?

The Soviet theater has not yet regained the brilliance it displayed in the first years of the Revolution. "We haven't yet developed any productions which can hold their own with the best of the avant-garde in the West," Pluchek concedes. But unless the reactionary forces on the Soviet cultural front succeed in snuffing out the shooting stars of the Taganka, the Sovremennik and the Satire theaters in Moscow and those of Nikolai Akimov's effervescent Comedy Theater in Leningrad, a Russian "new wave" may soon splash over the stages of Berlin, Paris, London and New York.

October 24, 1967

# *Soviet Editor, a Liberal, Said to Resign in Protest*

By BERNARD GWERTZMAN
Special to The New York Times

MOSCOW, Feb. 14—Aleksandr T. Tvardovsky, the chief editor of Novy Mir, a liberal literary journal, was reported today to have resigned in protest over a shake-up in his editorial board. He contended it undermined his authority and would change the character of the magazine.

His reported resignation, not yet officially announced here, follows a dispute between Mr. Tvardovsky and his conservative antagonists over the contents of Novy Mir. He contended that the journal should publish high-quality works even if they exposed shortcomings in Soviet society.

His opponents said Mr. Tvardovsky failed to show awareness of an ideological threat from the West and often lent his journal's pages to articles that could be used for anti-Soviet purposes.

Mr. Tvardovsky's reported departure has already stirred emotional reactions among the few people who have heard the news.

Reliable sources said Mr. Tvardovsky tendered his resignation yesterday on the ground that it was useless for him to continue in a situation where conservatives opposed to his views had been named to the editorial board and liberals supporting him had been forced out.

He was referring to the decision announced last week by the secretariat of the Union of Writers—over Mr. Tvardovsky's vote—to dismiss four members of Novy Mir's board of editors, including Mr. Tvardovsky's deputy editor, A. I. Kondratovich.

They were replaced by men whose views were said to be more in keeping with the ideological orthodoxy advocated by the conservative leadership of the writers union and the party.

It was reported that Mr. Tvardovsky's successor is Vasily A. Kosolapov, a moderate, who was one of those named to the board.

He is thought to be a compromise choice—neither so conservative as to completely antagonize Novy Mir's readers nor so liberal as to defeat the purpose of the shake-up.

Mr. Kosolapov was the chief editor of Literaturnaya Gazeta, the newspaper of the writers union, from 1960 to 1962, before Aleksandr B. Chakovsky, the present editor, took over.

Under Mr. Kosolapov's leadership, the paper printed several controversial works, including Yevgeny Yevtushenko's poem "Babi Yar" in 1961. That poem created a stir for suggesting that a memorial had not been built to Jews killed at Babi Yar in Kiev because of lingering Russian anti-Semitism.

In recent years, Mr. Kosolapov had been a member of the editorial board of Voprosy Literatury, a middle-of-the-road journal aimed at specialists in literature.

Mr. Tvardovsky, who is 59 years old, was under pressure rom the writers' union leadership last summer to resign, but he refused. Because of his eminence as a poet and his lengthy history of party membership, including a one-time candidate membership in the Central Committee, he could probably resist being dismissed.

He was said to have decided to resign to show his resentment at the replacement of Mr. Kondratovich and other members of the board, Igor I. Vinogradov, Vladimir Y. Lakshin and Igor A. Sats.

Mr. Lakshin, 36, is regarded by many Soviet intellectuals as the most prominent literary critic in the Soviet Union, but conservatives have continually attacked him for his support of Aleksandr I. Solzhenitsyn and other writers disapproved by them.

**New Members Listed**

Mr. Tvardovsky was also said to believe that the men named to the board would try to undermine his policy. The most prominent newcomer is Dmitri G. Bolshov who was given the title of first deputy editor. Mr. Bolshov is regarded as an ideological conservative.

His last position was as a member of the State Committee for Radio and Television. Previously he served for six years as editor of the newspaper Sovetskaya Kultura and from 1947 to 1957, his biography lists him as a member of the leadership of the Young Communist League.

Others named to the board were Oleg P. Smirnov, Aleksandr Y. Rekemchuk, and Aleksandr I. Ovcharenko.

The latest campaign against Mr. Tvardovsky began last summer when the conservative magazine Ogonyok accused Novy Mir of harboring "cosmopolitans," a particularly odious term of attack since it was used by Stalin against his opponents. This attack was echoed by other newspapers and Mr. Tvardovsky himself was criticized.

Last fall, Mr. Tvardovsky replied to his critics and said that Novy Mir did not have to convince Soviet readers of its patriotism and did not have to put up with the "crude demogogy" leveled against it.

This seemed to end the polemics for a while, indicating that the party for the moment did not want to upset the balance between conservatives and liberals. But the expulsion of Mr. Solzhenitsyn from the writers union last November and the appearance of an openly pro-Stalinist book in the conservative journal Oktyabr written by its editor, Vsevolod Kochetov, led to concern that the balance had shifted to the side of the conservatives.

Mr. Solzhenitsyn was accused of not taking strong enough measures against publication of his works abroad, and apparently the same attack was later made against Mr. Tvardovsky.

Last Wednesday, in the same issue of Literaturnaya Gazeta that announced changes in Novy Mir's board, Mr. Tvardovsky printed a short letter saying that an anti-Stalinist poem of his had been published in the West without his knowledge. Soviet readers recognized the letter as having been written under pressure from the writers union.

The same issue of the newspaper contained criticism of Mr. Kochetov's novel, "What Do You Want?" Although the book, with its open calls for a return to the discipline of the Stalinist days, had alienated and angered many Russians, the criticism was rather mild.

This has reinforced the view that at the present time, with the Soviet Union preparing for Lenin's centenary on April 22, ideological orthodoxy is clearly in the ascendency.

Mr. Tvardovsky was first named editor of Novy Mir in 1950 but was dismissed in 1954 for publication in 1953 of an article by Vladimir N. Pomerantsev that was the first anti-Stalinist article to appear in the Soviet press calling for freer discussion of issues.

His successor as editor, Konstantin Simonov, was forced to resign in 1957 following a dispute over the novel "Not by Bread Alone" by Vladimir D. Dudintsev, which was published in Novy Mir. Mr. Tvardovsky assumed the chief editorship again in 1958.

February 15, 1970

# Soviet Poet Is Reported Going to U.S.

By HEDRICK SMITH

Special to The New York Times

MOSCOW, June 7—Iosif A. Brodsky, who is regarded by some liberal Soviet intellectuals and Western scholars as the most talented living Russian poet, has left the Soviet Union for the United States, reliable sources reported today.

The sources said that shortly before President Nixon's arrival on May 22, Mr. Brodsky, who had been trying to emigrate because he found it impossible to publish his works here, was summoned by the secret police and offered an opportunity to obtain an exit visa to Israel. However, the sources said they were certain that the United States was his destination.

Iosif A. Brodsky

The 32-year-old poet and translator, who is a Jew, was said to have flown to Vienna on Monday. American scholars were understood to be trying to arrange for him to become poet in residence at an American school, possibly the University of Michigan.

Mr. Brodsky's poetry, dealing in large part with philosophical and religious themes, is in a style that does not conform to the socialist realism promoted by the Communist authorities. He has appeared occasionally in underground journals here and in foreign anthologies of iconoclastic Soviet poets such as "Russia's Other Poets," published by Longmans in 1968. A Penguin volume of his poetry in English is due soon.

In the early nineteen-sixties he wrote verse that contained anti-Soviet themes, but in recent years his work has had little political content.

An American scholar termed him a master of the instrumentation of sound, rhythm and syntax who uses his religious and philosophical themes to convey his own moral viewpoint.

Anna Akhmatova, widely regarded as one of the great poets of the Soviet era, with whom Mr. Brodsky worked before she died, is reported to have called him the most talented poet of his generation. Nonetheless, he remains virtually unknown here compared with, say, Andrei Voznesensky and Yevgeny Yevtushenko.

His sentencing early in 1964 to a five-year term at forced labor for being "an idler and parasite" without "any socially useful work" stirred wide protests in the West and, to a lesser degree, here as well. He was released in September, 1965, and allowed to return to work as a translator.

He has been working on extensive translations into Russian of the English metaphysical poets and has also translated modern American and Irish poetry. He is known to have received only a modest income and to have lived in very modest circumstances.

June 8, 1972

# RUSSIANS DISRUPT MODERN ART SHOW WITH BULLDOZERS

## Unofficial Outside Exhibition Dispersed—Bystanders Hit and Paintings Confiscated

**By CHRISTOPHER S. WREN**
Special to The New York Times

MOSCOW, Sept. 15—In a dramatic confrontation over nonconformist art, Soviet authorities used bulldozers, dump trucks and water-spraying trucks today to break up an outdoor exhibition of unofficial art as it was being set up in a vacant lot.

A crowd of several hundred people, among them artists, Western diplomats, correspondents and curious neighborhood residents, scattered when dump trucks and a pair of bulldozers overran what the artists had billed as the first autumn outdoor art show in the Soviet Union.

Two water trucks, normally used for street-cleaning, pursued the fleeing crowds across the street. A handful of people pelted the trucks with clods of dirt.

**Three Americans Struck**

Three American correspondents—two men and a woman—were beaten by young vigilantes who roamed the scene intimidating people to move on. Several uniformed police looked on impassively and made no effort to stop the violence.

The young men who appeared to be organized into teams, ripped up, trampled and threw more than a dozen paintings into a dump truck to be covered with mud and driven away. Artists who protested were roughed up and at least five were arrested. An unknown number of angry spectators were taken to a nearby police station.

Later, one spectator who was released, Aleksei Tyapushkin, reportedly a member of the official Union of Artists and a decorated World War II veteran, said the police had told him that all the confiscated paintings had been burned.

Thirteen organizers of the exhibition sent a written protest to the Communist party Politburo protesting lawlessness, arbitrary misuse of force and violation of constitutional rights. They demanded an investigation, the return of their works and the punishment of those responsible.

A man in a trenchcoat who supervised the operation identified himself as an official of the Executive Committee of the city's southwest district. He asserted that the art exhibit was being broken up because workers had volunteered their Sundays to convert the empty lot into a "park of culture." He gave his name as Ivan Ivanovich Ivanov, a Russian equivalent of John Doe.

Witnesses reported, however, that no work was undertaken at the lot after the exhibition had been disrupted. The young men who had intimidated the exhibitors and spectators assembled afterwards and, upon instruction, left in a group, according to a person who remained at the site.

The American correspondents were assaulted after they had left the lot and were standing on a street near their automobile, watching the water trucks spraying the spectators.

**Camera Chips a Tooth**

An attempt to photograph a water truck as it drove over the curb to pursue one group caused a group of vigilantes to come up and smash the camera into this correspondent's face, chipping a front tooth. After this, the vigilantes' leader administered a blow in the stomach while the others seized and held his arms and torso.

Lynne Olson of The Associated Press rushed over and shouted at the vigilantes to stop and the leader turned around and hit her in the stomach with the same force, sending her sprawling.

Michael Parks of the Baltimore Sun was hit in the stomach by another young man while a policeman five feet away looked on.

When Russell Jones of the American Broadcasting Company protested, he was briefly manhandled but was not struck.

About two dozen artists, some from as far as Leningrad, Pskov and Vladimir, had come to exhibit their works at the show, which the organizers said was unofficial but not prohibited.

Some of the artists, the organizers said, have had works displayed in New York, San Francisco, London, Paris and Rome. But they have not been allowed to exhibit formally here and have not been accepted for membership in the Union of Artists because their styles do not conform with Moscows art doctrine, socialist realism.

**Officials Advised of Plans**

Two weeks ago, the organizing group of artists informed the Moscow City Council that they intended to hold an outdoor art show and asked to be informed within a week if there were objections.

At the council's request, the artists took their works for inspection by Communist party officials on Wednesday. On Friday, they said, a City Council official told them the vacant lot was available and that the exhibition would be neither encouraged nor forbidden.

But when the artists began setting up their works today on the lot, off Profsoyuznaya Street, they were immediately confronted by the trucks, bulldozers and water trucks and were ordered to leave.

The violence erupted too quickly to determine who had given the orders, although a few bystanders attributed them to a Mr. Knigin, who heads the local Communist party's ideological section.

Underground art has always encountered difficulties in the Soviet Union. In 1962, Nikita S. Khrushchev, then Premier, in a famous showdown with nonconformist artists, condemned as "filth" an officially organized exhibition that contained some works in abstract and other modern styles. Attempted unofficial exhibitions here in 1967, 1969 and 1971 were closed quickly by authorities, although without violence.

**'Heroic Optimism' Demanded**

Today, the paintings were seized too swiftly for spectators to get any idea of their content. But many of the artists are known for their modernism, abstractions and fantasies, pop art and nudes, as well as somber street scenes and landscapes that do not fit into the mold of heroic optimism demanded of art by Soviet authorities.

However, Oskar Rabin, an artist known abroad and an organizer of the exhibition, said earlier that the artists would not bring any works that would be considered anti-Soviet or pornographic.

The exhibition attracted diplomats from the United States, Western Europe, Asia and Latin America. They ended up running for safety.

Those arrested today were identified as Oskar Rabin, his son Aleksandr, Nadezhda Elskaya, Yevgeny Rukhin and Valentin Vorobyov.

Other artists who were expected to exhibit included Vladimir Nemukhin, Lidiya Masterovka, Boris Shteinberg, Aleksandr Malamid, Vasily Sitnikov and Igor Kholin.

September 16, 1974

# Excited Russians Crowd Modern Art Show

By [illegible]
Special to The New York Times

MOSCOW, Sept. 29—More than 10,000 people flocked today to the biggest officially [illegible] show of modern and unorthodox art by Soviet painters since the avant-garde movement in this country in the nineteen-twenties.

Packed five, six and even ten deep, they gathered in a huge open field on a sunny fall afternoon, scrambled up and down ditches, and held children aloft on their shoulders to get a glimpse of paintings by about 65 artists offering styles from whimsical realism or religious symbolism to surrealism, pop art, coloristic abstractions or the acid art of the psychedelic era.

Four members of the Union of Artists, which follows official doctrine on art style, defied warnings not to take part in the show because it [illegible] "anti-Soviet art." At least two who exhibited previously forbidden works said they expected to lose their jobs. Many of the other artists were members of a graphic artists organization.

After a decade in which Soviet authorities have increasingly tightened controls over culture, the show was an extraordinary event.

A French diplomat called it a Russian Woodstock." A Russian said it seemed more like Paris than Moscow—"abstract art but no drunks and no police."

Despite some apprehension, it went off without incident or any intervention by authorities, who kept a discreet watch.

After the violent disruption and repression two weeks ago of a similar but much smaller outdoor show by some of the same artists, the exhibition was probably more important politi-

[illegible] it was decidedly less daring than what Vasily Kandinsky, Kazimir Malevich, Vladimir Tatlin and others were painting half a century ago, work that is still not publicly exhibited in this country.

"This is a classic example of the influence of detente," said Aleksandr Goldfarb, a young scientist and friend of many of the artists. "This never would have taken place without the pressure of the West, and hard pressure at that."

And there were indications that the mere appearance of so much unorthodox art and the fact that authorities had been forced reluctantly to allow the show to take place, had sown seeds of ferment.

Some iconoclastic poets were talking about asking for permission for an outdoor reading of their works. The unofficial artists who organized today's show said they would press for an indoor exhibition as well as future outdoor shows.

And long after the 200 or so canvases had been taken off easels and carted away by the official 4 P.M. deadline, large knots of people, young and old, were quietly arguing the merits and demerits of modern art—an almost unprecedented public event in Soviet life.

"It's the first time in half a century we have had such a show," said a Moscow literary critic, "It's remarkable, tremendous."

"This must be a beginning and not an end," a Moscow student said in excitement as he approached a foreign correspondent. "We may not agree with all the art we have seen today, but it does exist and it is a possible course for our young artists. Thanks to your foreign broadcasts and foreign press articles, people found out where to come to see this art."

The mood of those who came, despite the lack of any local publicity, was a dramatic contrast with the atmosphere two weeks ago when bands of young vigilantes used bulldozers, dump trucks and water-spraying street cleaners to break up the first show.

After a backlash of foreign criticism, Moscow City Council authorities, on higher instructions, granted a group of 24 artists, led by Oskar Rabin and an art collector, Alexsandr Glazer, permission for today's show. The artists, with a touch of irony, termed it the "Second Fall Outdoor Art Show" on their typed invitations.

**Russians Are Photographed**

There was some concern that admission would be restricted to people with invitations, but no effort was made to curtail the crowd although plainclothes men with foreign movie cameras photographed Russians who talked with foreign correspondents and diplomats.

No preview of the art was undertaken by the authorities, but the artists refrained from showing paintings with political themes.

The visitors at the exhibition, mostly young and well-educated, were sometimes hippies and definitely in a holiday mood. They were friendly, respectful and curious about the art. For four hours, they inched along a thin string that stretched several hundred yards across the field, near Izmailovo Park on the eastern edge of Moscow.

Many took snapshots. Often there were calls for artists or paintings to be held aloft because the crowds were so thick it was impossible to see. On occasion, there was spontaneous applause.

Probably the most popular artist was Vladislav Zhdan, a balding 27-year-old painter, who created a sensation with a surrealistic still life of Boris Pasternak, the late Soviet poet. It showed an impressionistic portrait of Pasternak over a skull on a table. A tree of life grew from the skull and entwined the Pasternak portrait.

The crowd also liked Mr. Zhdan's blue fantasy of Ophelia drowning, her hair and limbs merging into the waves, his mauve painting, "Village Cemetery" from which an almost geometric stand of tall, straight birches rose, and another impressionistic, all-blue fantasy, titled "Dusk," of a girl in a kerchief emerginng from a forest."

"That's the new word, completely new," exclaimed one visitor. "Hold it up," shouted another voice. "Move a bit, young man, so I can get a picture," commanded a third.

"I never expected such a reaction," said Mr. Zhdan, a modest man in a black turtleneck and black leather jacket, who illustrates popular science magazines for a living.

Another success was Dima Gordeyev, a young dark-haired painter, whose whimsical realism poked fun at the prudishness and formality of Soviet public life. People laughingly called for his painting of a young couple kissing in the sky above a drab cityscrape, or his amusing park scenes with slouching, writhing statues and mildly grotesque figures.

Among the more far-out works was a collage by Svetlana Markova of a globe-head with real hair on each side, a real syringe giving the world a fix near the equator, five daisies growing out of the North Pole and a legend, in English, "Love and Peace."

Next to her Aleksandr Pennanen, a young artist with hair that fell in all directions to his waist, had a psychedelic head upon head upon head of Jesus—the nearest thing to acid art in the show.

Leonid Lamm, a well-known book illustrator arrested last December shortly after he had applied to emigrate to Israel, had three pastel fantasies done by needle scratchings in chalk; Nikolai Chernyshev offered bright Kandinsky-like geometric abstractions; V. E. Kropivitskaya had several animal fantasies, based on Russian folk themes, with rabbit-like figures in human poses and Mikhail Odnoralov exhibited two surrealistic still lifes with religious symbolism.

The four Union of Artists members who took part were Mr. Lamm, whose wife showed his works, Mr. Odnoralov, Viktor Skalkin and Aleksei Tyapushkin. Mr. Odnoralov said the four had been warned, under threat of reprisal, not to participate.

A young woman said she had come about 175 miles from Yaroslavl when she heard of the show via "the grapevine." In Moscow, the information passed by word of mouth in intellectual circles, but many people said they had heard of it from foreign radio broadcasts.

Not all the reactions to the art were approving. One middle-aged man pointed a finger at an expressionistic oil by Oskar Rabin and declared, "Under Iosif [Stalin] you could have been shot for that one painting."

A prim young man in a gray suit and wide tie challenged Aleksandr Yulikov, whose flowing hair and mustache make him look like Buffalo Bill, to explain why he painted incomprehensible works of art.

"I paint for those who understand them," the artist replied.

"No one will ever understand you," the young man insisted. But other onlookers quickly shushed him.

A white-haired woman complained that some of the art was too morose, too somber, too dark and gloomy. "Well," rebutted a man in a suede jacket, "the artist was in a dark, gloomy mood. When the sun comes out and his mood changes, he'll use other colors."

Theoretically, the paintings of most artists were for sale, but none were known to have been sold on the scene today.

Not all known modern Soviet painters took part today. Among those notably absent were Ernst Neizvestny, Vasily Sitnikov and Anatoly Zverev.

sometimes controversial Soviet poet, visited the art exhibition today and said after viewing the paintings: "I see some good pictures, some bad ones and some mediocre ones, but the most important fact is that they are here in the first place."

September 30, 1974

# Soviet Allows an Avant-Garde Show, Partly Censored

By CRAIG R. WHITNEY
Special to The New York Times

MOSCOW, March 7 — An officially sanctioned exhibition of 20 Soviet avant-garde painters opened today after the authorities had removed a score of paintings for ideological reasons.

Some of the artists who had fought with the censors for the right to show more of their works said they had agreed reluctantly to go ahead with the exhibition anyway.

"The chance to exhibit anything at all under the conditions in our country is something we simply couldn't afford to refuse," said one of them, Vladislav A. Provotorov.

The opening of the show in the headquarters of the Moscow city committee of the Graphic Artists Union was crowded. One man said, after having managed to get past a police cordon, "I don't know whether I liked it, but I'm thankful to have lived long enough to see the day."

**For Moscow, a Spectacular Show**

The show, scheduled to run a week, includes the kind of art that the police used bulldozers to scatter at an unofficial outdoor exhibition in 1974. After the embarrassment caused by that police action, official tactics changed and the artists have been tolerated.

What the artists do would not raise an eyebrow in New York or Paris, but in Moscow it is spectacular. It includes:

¶A 12-part work titled "Apocalypse," by Vitaly Linitsky, filling a whole room with Orthodox crosses, brilliantly colored images of Christ, futuristic visions of the crucifixion and of decay.

¶An image like a photograph of a bulletin board called "Books," by Nikolai N. Smirnov, showing collections of verse by Osip Mandelshtam, who died in a

Stalinist prison camp, and booklets about the work of Kandinsky, Chagall and other early 20th-century Russian artists whose works were later banned.

¶And Mr. Provotorov's three big Dali-like canvases of tortured decaying flesh, one of them titled "Inquisition."

**Direct Affronts Eliminated**

What the crowds that jammed the four rooms of the 120-canvas exhibition did not get to see were more direct affronts to the canons of atheistic Communism. They included a pointillist representation of the Virgin with the Christ child's arms around her neck, called "Our Lady of Tenderness," by Vladimir N. Petrov-Gladki, and a triptych by Nikolai N. Rumyantsev, showing the living among wraithlike visions of the souls of the dead.

Mr. Rumyantsev was allowed to show two works, one a self-portrait showing his mustached figure in a geometric pattern resembling cobwebs.

"Of course I'm not happy about it," he said of the partial ban as plainclothesmen, diplomats and invited friends of the artists milled about. "The other artists wouldn't agree to a walkout over the exclusions, and we all agreed to follow the will of the majority."

The line of about 300 people that formed behind the police barricades as soon as the show opened was one reason they agreed to compromise.

Mr. Smirnov, whose bulletin-board pictures resemble those of the American painter John Haberle, said he was afraid that the fight over censorship could still lead to punishment. "They threatened at one point to dissolve the union," he said, "and that question is still open."

"They" are the Culture Ministry and party officials who issue permits for art shows. "The union" is the special section of the Moscow city committee of the Graphic Artists' Union that officials set up for avant-garde painters after the 1974 fracas. Without the union, they could be arrested for "parasitism," or failure to hold legitimate employment, and could be forbidden to exhibit.

Public showings since 1974, even under difficult conditions, have made these artists popular. The last show in the union hall attracted thousands every day until it closed Jan. 27.

"Their art is clearly derivative and narrow when you consider the contemporary movements in Western Europe," an Austrian connoisseur said. "But an artist who might just be a little count anywhere else can become a king here."

March 8, 1978



***The new trials in Russia stir memories of Stalin's days***

# This Is the Winter Of Moscow's Dissent

By **PATRICIA BLAKE**

MOSCOW has just experienced an unusually fierce winter, many smaller towns were snowbound, and grave concern is being expressed in the press about air pollution—all of which is very convenient for Russian intellectuals, who commonly characterize their condition in meteorological images.

For example, Vladimir Bukovsky, who was sentenced last September to three years in prison for having organized a demonstration protesting the arrest of writers, has offered a comment on the miasma of intellectual life. In a sketch called "A Stupid Question," which appeared before his arrest in the underground magazine Phoenix, Bukovsky complained to a physician: "I just can't stand it any longer. I tried at first to ignore it but I couldn't . . . I can't, you see, take a really deep breath. . . . The doctors can't help me. . . . But I do so want to take a deep breath sometimes, you know, with all my lungs —especially in the spring. . . . There seems to be some obstruction to breathing. Or isn't there enough air?"

Recently, Yevgeni Yevtushenko complained of the same trouble. In "Smog," a poem datelined Moscow-New York, published in the Soviet magazine Znamya in January of this year, he writes that he is gasping for air. The locale is purportedly New York, but the weather conditions are Russian and clearly recognizable as such by the Soviet reader. Notices have been posted in bars, the poet says, which read: "You can breathe easily only through vodka."

Yevtushenko uses the device of putting words in the mouths of American writers. Allen Ginsberg is made to say: "Darkness is descending,/ darkness!/ This is the smell of outer hell./ There is no excuse for those/ who can breathe in this stench! In a world of moral vacuum/, in a world of fog and chaos/ the only halfway decent person/ is he who suffocates." In the same poem, Arthur Miller (who has publicly spoken out against the trials of writers in Russia) is described as "stern in his terrible prophecy." Miller supposedly says: "There will be still more burnings at the stake/ by Inquisitions./ Smog/ is the smoke of these stakes to come."

The atmosphere is indeed heavy with menace. Not since 1963, when Khrushchev carried on a ferocious campaign against the liberal intelligentsia, has creative life in Russia seemed in such jeopardy. The two recent trials of writers in Moscow represent only the most visible surface of what is actually taking place. The arrests of hundreds of intellectuals, for offenses ranging from the distribution of anti-Soviet propaganda to armed conspiracy, and other sinister signals suggest that a policy decision has been made, at the highest level, to reintroduce terroristic methods to stifle dissent.

These attempts at coercion have produced, not submission, but defiance more open and more widespread than at any time in the Soviet Union's entire history of persecution of intellectuals. The Communist leadership in Russia, and in parts of Eastern Europe as well, is being confronted with such spectacles as street demonstrations in Moscow, student riots in Warsaw and, in Prague, a

**PATRICIA BLAKE**, formerly a correspondent in Moscow, has edited four collections of Russian writing in translation.

resistance among intellectuals so massive that, in Czechoslovakia's newly favorable political climate, it appears to have succeeded in obtaining a reversal of cultural policy.

THE pattern of repression, as it has evolved under Brezhnev and Kosygin, is not so easily charted as it was under Khrushchev. For one thing, the style of new leadership in dealing with the unruly intelligentsia is more subdued. No longer is the chief of state heard denouncing abstract painters as homosexuals who (in Khrushchev's words) use human excrement instead of paint. There are no more mass meetings with writers and artists in the Kremlin, no more vast campaigns in the press against internationally known literary figures like Voznesensky and Yevtushenko.

Aims and methods have changed as well. Khrushchev believed for a time that he could turn the aspirations of the liberal intellectuals to his own political purposes; he attempted to gain their support by offering them a measure of freedom, but when they responded, not with gratitude but with ever greater demands, he turned on them with the full range of his celebrated invective. These repeated attempts to woo, then subdue, the intelligentsia produced the seasonal "thaws" and "freezes" that characterized cultural life under Khrushchev.

In contrast, the new leaders have always shown a determination not to allow the intelligentsia to play any sort of political role. Plagued with other problems inherited from Khrushchev, they at first seemed merely to be trying (with little success) to contain the most vociferous libertarians among the intellectuals. Now, however, they have been compelled to take notice of three problems that have strikingly intensified in the post-Khrushchev era: (1) the spread of dissent; (2) the breakdown of controls over the intelligentsia; (3) the publication abroad of suppressed works by Russian writers, much of which is damaging to the prestige of the Soviet leadership, the system and the ideology.

Thus, while Khrushchev relied largely on bombast and threats against dissidents (which he was unwilling or unable to carry out) the present leaders have introduced the technique of staging political trials of intellectuals, while at the same time giving the K.G.B. (Committee for State Security—the secret police) far greater powers in dealing with the intelligentsia than at any time since Stalin's death.

THE fact that this policy of selective terror was applied with increasing intensity in 1967, the year of the 50th anniversary of the Bolshevik Revolution, is a measure of the leadership's alarm over large-scale and unrestrained expressions of dissent. The crackdown has, in fact, come as a surprise to Western observers, and to many people in Russian literary circles who believed that the Soviet leadership would make no move to repress the intellectuals until after the anniversary celebrations last November. The existence of dissent would be played down, they said; an appearance of national unity had to be maintained, as well as a semblance of solidarity among the foreign Communist parties still more or less loyal to Moscow. The trial of the writers Andrei Sinyavsky and Yuli Daniel in 1966 had provoked such vehement opposition among foreign Communist leaders that it seemed unlikely the Soviet authorities would invite further embarrassment along these lines.

A number of officially inspired attempts were made before the anniversary to still the continued reverberations of that trial. Many newsmen in Moscow, and visitors from abroad, were systematically informed that Sinyavsky and Daniel would be released on the occasion of the general amnesty in November, provided the Western press would stop reporting the plight of the two writers and left-wing intellectuals would stop agitating about the case. "Dr. Zhivago," the recent writings of Alexander Solzhenitsyn and other suppressed works would soon be published, they were told. It was even suggested that censorship was about to be abolished, the only impediment to complete cultural freedom in the Soviet Union being the meddlesomeness of foreigners.

Nothing of the sort, of course, took place. Instead, the dawn of the anniversary year 1967 was marked by the arrest of a large group of intellectuals in Leningrad whose number has been estimated at from 150 to 300 persons. Precautions were taken by the authorities to prevent this action from causing an international sensation. The arrests were made among obscure persons, in a city where foreign journalists are not stationed. No mention of the arrests was made in the Soviet press. It is only recently, therefore, that some details of the Leningrad case have become known.

The roundup took place in late February or early March, 1967. Among those arrested were a number of Leningrad University professors, law and philosophy students at the university, poets, literary critics and magazine editors. At least one closed trial of four persons is known to have been held, and another is said to be in preparation now. Among those already tried, one is a Professor Ogurtsov, a specialist on Tibet at the university, who was condemned to 15 years at hard labor—the maximum sentence, short of death. A second, Yevgeni Vagin, an editor of a multivolume edition of Dostoyevsky, was sentenced to 13 years.

Those arrested were charged with conspiracy to armed rebellion. It was alleged that they were members of a terrorist network, with contacts abroad, which operated under the guise of various philosophical societies, including a "Berdyayev Circle," named after Nikolai Berdyayev, the Christian philosopher who was an opponent of the Soviet regime because of its suppression of freedom. Members of similar groups, said to be linked with the Leningrad organizations, have reportedly been arrested in Sverdlovsk and in several towns in the Ukraine.

THE Leningrad arrests are clearly the most menacing of the coercive actions against intellectuals that have been undertaken in the post-Khrushchev period. This is the first time in Soviet history that intellectuals are known to have been arrested and tried for possession of arms for the purpose of rebellion against the state. The charge is indeed so grave that it irresistibly raises the question of whether the arms case was not fabricated by the K.G.B. The purpose of such a provocation would be to smear the whole liberal intelligentsia, which, it might now be alleged, is so disaffected as to be capable of armed rebellion — thus opening the way to arrests on a much larger scale. The attempt by the K.G.B. to connect the Leningrad organizations with groups in other parts of the country suggests that something along these lines is in progress. Moreover, the possession of small arms, of which the Leningrad intellectuals are accused (in Sverdlovsk, they allegedly acquired machine guns), appears preposterous. Under peacetime conditions it would be extremely difficult to smuggle arms into the Soviet Union, and the rigid system of arms control in the police and armed forces requires the strictest accountability for every weapon and every bullet.

Although the arms case in Leningrad carries with it the most fearful implications, the area where selective terror has been applied most intensively under Brezhnev and Kosygin has been the Ukraine. Here, aspirations for intellectual freedom are mixed with demands for cultural autonomy, sometimes shading into Ukrainian nationalism. The wave of arrests began in January, 1966, when more than 200 university professors, students, journalists, writers and scientists were secretly tried for having distributed pamphlets in defense of Ukrainian culture and of the use of the Ukrainian language in the Ukrainian Republic. Public protest demonstrations took place in various cities in the wake of these trials. In Lvov, a crowd outside the courtroom showered the van carrying the prisoners with flowers.

The main point made in one letter of protest by a Ukrainian intellectual, Vyacheslav Chernovil, was to be echoed later by defendants at the Moscow trials — i.e., that the freedoms guaranteed by the Soviet Constitution are precisely those that are held to be criminal offenses in court: freedom of press and assembly, and freedom to hold demonstrations. Of judicial procedure, Chernovil wrote: "The secret trial reminds one of a boa constrictor to which a rabbit is thrown for the boa's breakfast, the rabbit having first been granted permission to present the hungry beast with arguments to prove his innocence."

THE K.G.B.'s far greater freedom of action in dealing with intellectuals, as evidenced by these cases, appears all the more remarkable in view of the sharp limitation of police power that was established after Stalin's death. No longer does the secret police penetrate all governing institutions and wield extraordinary political power. Mass police terror exists no more. At the same time, however, the Second Chief Directorate of the K.G.B. has a continuity of function that goes back to the old Cheka, the first Soviet secret police, of which it is the direct descendant. It gathers information and prepares dossiers on individuals, regardless of the political climate and of reforms in the society.

Built into the K.G.B., then, is a potential of extreme, oppressive action. It is a ready tool, when a political decision is made to use it, as has apparently happened now, to a still limited but highly suggestive degree. It is significant that the K.G.B. has been unleashed on two groups alone, where dissent runs high: the liberal intelligentsia and Russia's Protestants (particularly the Evangelical Christians and the Reform Baptists), who have been suffering from greatly intensified repression since 1966.

**ALEXANDER SOLZHENITSYN—His 1962 concentration-camp novel, "Ivan Denisovich," raised hopes of freer expression.**

The year 1967 saw a major attempt to rehabilitate the secret service, which, for the Soviet people, is quite properly associated with revolutionary violence, the bloody horror of the great purges, and the 20-year Stalinist terror. All the vast propaganda resources of the Soviet state were mobilized for this purpose. Countless books and articles glorifying the exploits of secret-service agents were cranked out by the state publishing houses during the past year. If this campaign was intended to popularize the K.G.B., it was naive, to say the least. Its main purpose appeared, rather, to rebuild the morale of the secret service and thus increase its efficiency.

The climax of this operation came in December, on the 50th anniversary of the founding of the Cheka, when Yuri Andropov, the head of the K.G.B., addressed Government and K.G.B. leaders in the Kremlin. Andropov assured his listeners that "in recent years our party has done an enormous amount of work to strengthen Socialist legality. . . . Thus our party has shown that there is and can be no reversion in any violation of Socialist legality whatsoever."

HOW this new Socialist legality actually works has perhaps never been better exemplified in the post-Khrushchev period than by the trial of Sinyavsky and Daniel for having circulated "anti-Soviet" works that were published abroad. A patently prejudicial press campaign took place before and during the trial. The presiding judge, Lev Smirnov, continuously interrupted the proceedings with grossly insulting or ironic interjections about the accused. As scores of Soviet intellectuals have pointed out, the verdict of guilty was clearly prearranged.

Having manufactured the case against Sinyavsky and Daniel, and persuaded the political leadership to make it a show trial, the K.G.B. proceeded to attempt to deal with the consequences. Sergei Bannikov, the general of state security in charge of the intelligentsia, called meetings at which he warned writers in the strongest terms against protesting about the trial. Then, on the eve of the anniversary of the revolution, it was officially announced that two K.G.B. generals had been named to the U.S.S.R. Supreme Court. One was a Maj. Gen. Nikolai Chestyakov. The other was Bannikov, who was designated vice president—one of the three top positions on the court.

Such K.G.B. appointments were unprecedented since Stalin's time; until now the court has maintained a semblance, at least, of judicial objectivity. Certainly the meaning of Bannikov's appointment was not lost on the public: more trials on the Sinyavsky-Daniel model could be expected. In case anyone missed the point, it was made abundantly clear when the Order of Lenin was bestowed on Smirnov, the judge at the Sinyavsky-Daniel trial, "for his services in strengthening Socialist legality."

THE most striking aspect of these coercive tactics is that they are not producing the desired results. The simple fact is that the Russian intellectual has, by and large, ceased to be afraid. The old, fearful sense of isolation from which writers and readers, teachers and students, scholars, scientists and artists suffered under Stalin has gradually been replaced by a sense of community that now gives them the courage to risk prison for the sake of commonly shared principle. This change seems very nearly miraculous when one considers how intellectually, artistically and morally stupefying was Stalin's terror. "They only ask you," said Boris Pasternak of the Soviet authorities, "to praise what you hate most and grovel before what makes you most unhappy."

Today intellectuals of all ages are openly calling, not only for greater intellectual and artistic freedom, but, increasingly, for fundamental changes in Soviet society. They are fighting for their beliefs from the prisoner's dock, on the streets, in underground books and magazines and, indeed, on any tribune they can find—including the foreign press. They throw flowers on paddy wagons, demonstrate outside courtrooms, and assemble in public squares carrying placards calling for adherence to the Constitution. They hold illegal press conferences for Western newsmen where they accuse Soviet newspapers of slander, and threaten to sue. They draft letters, signed by a who's who of Soviet literature, science and scholarship, demanding an end to violations of the law, and address them to Brezhnev and Kosygin, the Politiburo, the Supreme Court, Pravda and Izvestia, and circulate them all over Moscow. In short, the liberal intelligentsia is confronting the Soviet leadership with its own myths.

THE evolution of courage and conscience that has made these events possible in the present period of severe repression began much earlier in the post-Stalin era. The most obvious, and crucial, precondition was, of course, the elimination of mass police terror after Stalin's death. This, however, did not immediately lift the pall on the Soviet people; terror had been internalized far too long. For those intellectuals who had survived the purges, the reflex of distrust and deception was not easy to master. Soon, however, there were some stirrings of dissatisfaction—but these were limited to the cultural sphere, to censorship and other forms of artistic control. Skepticism about the basic values of the system began to become apparent only after Khrushchev's revelations of Stalin's crimes in 1956.

The scope of the reaction among intellectuals—and, indeed, among the public at large — may be appreciated when one considers that the whole ideological schema of Communism and the entire political and economic system had been for 30 years inextricably linked with the person of Stalin. The destruction of the Stalin myth put into question the legitimacy of the new leadership and, in fact, nothing less than the *raison d'être* of the Soviet system.

At this juncture, writers and poets began to command considerable influence over public opinion. A policy of relative permissiveness from 1956 to the end of 1962 (with some seasonal setbacks) resulted in the appearance of a mass of books and articles which criticized, in scarcely veiled terms, virtually every aspect of Soviet society, and which attracted a mass readership running into the millions. The publication in November, 1962, of Alexander Solzhenitsyn's harrowing novel of a Stalinist concentration camp, "One Day in the Life of Ivan Denisovich," led writers and readers to believe that the whole bloody history of the Stalin era could at last be publicly ventilated, and the most wicked of Stalin's accomplices purged from the governing bureaucracies.

Khrushchev, alarmed by the scope of expectations of the intellectuals, reversed himself in 1963. There followed a seven-month press campaign which excoriated intellectuals, and which was accompanied by censure meetings held all over the country. Liberals who had captured positions of influence in the cultural organizations (like the Writers Unions) were replaced by diehard Stalinists, and all references to Stalin's crimes were banned from literature. It was then, in response to Khrushchev's offensive, that intellectuals began to develop the sense of common cause they are so dramatically demonstrating today. The writers and other intellectuals under fire in 1963 steadfastly refused to recant, despite fearful pressures. Some remained silent; others counterattacked and defended one another.

During the first year after Khrushchev's fall in 1964, it became clear that administrative controls were inadequate to contain public expressions of dissent. Literary works of a highly unorthodox and critical nature were slipping past the censorship, and selling out at once, often in editions of 100,000 copies.

The distribution of mimeographed underground magazines and books had reached such proportions that the great Russian poet Anna Akhmatova, before her death in 1966, could airily say on a visit to Europe that "our literature has no need of Gutenberg's invention." Perhaps most galling of all, works unpublished in Russia, like those of Abram Tertz and Nikolai Arzhak, were reaching Western publishers almost as fast as they were being written.

The turning point of cultural policy under Brezhnev and Kosygin came in February, 1966, when the leadership gave the K.G.B. license to step in where nonterroristic controls had failed. The show trial of Sinyavsky and Daniel was the immediate consequence. All the subsequent arrests and trials of writers and intellectuals in Moscow in 1967 and 1968 proceed directly from this case.

THE trial of Sinyavsky and Daniel was an event equivalent in its divisive impact on Soviet society to that of the Dreyfus case on France in the eighteen-nineties. The reaction to it both reflected and intensified the struggle between the liberal intellectuals and other people of conscience and vested authority. It served to mobilize the intelligentsia, already united by the onslaughts of 1963, into expressing its indignation almost with a single voice. It made many older intellectuals, silent until then with their fearful memories of Stalinism, openly commit themselves to the liberal camp. And it raised the issue, in the most compelling public fashion, of the contradiction between "Socialist justice" and brutal reality.

The significant fact about the trial is that the two writers, charged with circulating "anti-Soviet" writings, readily admitted that they were the pseudonymous authors of the works in question, but denied that they were guilty of a crime. Their testimony and final pleas constitute a defense less of themselves than of literature itself, and a condemnation, in overwhelmingly eloquent terms, of the grossly simplistic and Philistine criteria applied to literature by the Soviet authorities for the past 30 years. Had they pleaded guilty, as the court evidently expected, they would have got off with lighter sentences. (Sinyavsky was condemned to seven years of hard labor and Daniel to five.)

It was clear that they wished to make examples of themselves, so that others might carry on after them. This hope was completely realized. The trial utterly failed in its purpose of terrorizing intellectuals. On the contrary, the behavior of the defendants infused the liberal intellectual community with a new sense of pride and honor. Sinyavsky and Daniel had established a standard of conduct which henceforth others would strive to meet. In sum, the moral quality of intellectual life in Russia was immeasurably raised by their action.

Not one prominent writer in Russia, except Mikhail Sholokhov, could be found to endorse the trial, while protests signed by hundreds of famous writers, scholars and scientists poured into Government agencies and newspapers. Opposition to the trial by European Communists became so strident that foreign Communist newspapers were banned for a time from Soviet newsstands. But, substituting for a free press, the foreign shortwave radio stations, the Voice of America, Radio Liberty, the B.B.C. and Deutsche Welle repeatedly beamed the trial transcript (which had been smuggled abroad) and the text of all the protests to their millions of listeners in Russia.

Thus the Sinyavsky - Daniel trial boomeranged by causing a national and international scandal, as well as by stiffening the intelligentsia's resistance. In May, the Congress of the Stalinist-dominated Soviet Writers Union was boycotted by leading liberals, and Alexander Solzhenitsyn, Russia's finest living prose writer, addressed his now-famous letter to the congress demanding the abolition of censorship. He charged that the K.G.B. had confiscated his manuscripts and that the leadership of the Writers Union, far from defending authors from such outrages, had a long history of being "always first among the persecutors" of writers who were slandered, exiled, imprisoned and executed. The reaction of the authorities was simply to hit harder—in Moscow, at the heart of resistance.

The first of the Moscow trials, in September, 1967, involved three young men charged with organizing a demonstration on Pushkin Square against the arrest of some literary figures a few days earlier. In the second trial, at the beginning of January, 1968, four young people, including two underground writers, Alexander Ginzburg and Yuri Galanskov, were accused of circulating an underground magazine, Phoenix '66.

Galanskov was said to have privately drafted a new constitution for the Soviet Union and distributed it among his friends. Ginzburg was also charged with editing and circulating a "White Book" on the Sinyavsky-Daniel case, consisting of the trial transcript, protests by Soviet intellectuals and a letter of his own to Kosygin in which he said: "I love my country and I do not wish to see its reputation damaged by the latest uncontrolled activities of the K.G.B. I love Russian literature and I do not wish to see two more of its representatives sent off to fell trees under police guard."

Ginzburg was sentenced to five years and Galanskov to seven. The third defendant, who turned state's evidence, was let off with two years, while the fourth, who was accused merely of typing manuscripts for the others, received a one-year suspended sentence.

In these trials, the authorities made determined efforts to seal off the proceedings so that any resistance on the part of the defendants would not become public. Except for a handful of relatives of the accused, the courtrooms were packed with preselected persons, who, according to one witness, read magazines or dozed during the trials, rousing themselves from time to time to utter "animal-like hoots and cries for severe penalties." The September trial received a brief mention in a Moscow newspaper, which stated that the accused had confessed their crime.

Thereupon, a 30-year-old physicist, Pavel Litvinov, the grandson of the late Foreign Minister Maxim Litvinov, saw to it that the actual testimony of one defendant was communicated to the foreign press.

It showed that the defendant, the 25-year-old writer Vladimir Bukovsky, not only had pleaded not guilty but had defended his right to demonstrate publicly under the Soviet Constitution. He protested that the investigation of his case had been conducted, not by the prosecutor's office, but by the K.G.B., in violation of the law. Bukovsky, who was sentenced to three years, ended his plea as follows: "I absolutely do not repent for organizing the demonstration. I find that it accomplished what it had to accomplish, and when I am free again, I shall again organize demonstrations —of course, in complete observance of the law, as before."

Litvinov further made public the record of his interrogation by a K.G.B. officer in which he defied a threat to arrest him if he circulated the Bukovsky transcript. After it was sent abroad, Litvinov told an American newsman that he had not been bothered since by the K.G.B. "When the K.G.B. sees that a man is not afraid of them, they do not call him in any more for more conversation. When they call him again, it's for good." Litvinov was immediately fired from his teaching job.

Ginzburg and Galanskov pleaded not guilty at the five-day trial in January. Said Ginzburg of the contents of his White Book. "Any patriot is obliged to give up his life for his country—but not to lie for it."

NEWS of the defendants' resistance quickly leaked out to the crowd of some 200 sympathizers who gathered on the street, in freezing weather, outside the courtroom. What took place was tantamount to a five-day press conference by friends of the accused with foreign journalists. K.G.B. men continuously mingled in the crowd, taking pictures of the protesters. Shouted a former major general, Pyotr Grigorenko: "You can't intimidate me. I bled for this country!" As the defense lawyers filed out of the courtroom, they were given red carnations by persons in the crowd.

Among those who kept a vigil outside the courtroom were Alexander Yesenin-Volpin, the son of the famous poet Sergei Yesenin, who committed suicide in 1925 and Pyotr Yakir, the son of Maj. Gen. Iona Yakir, who was executed during the purges of the Red Army in 1937, then "posthumously rehabilitated" after Stalin's death. Yakir distributed an appeal saying that the trial "has gone beyond all bounds in suppressing human rights. Even Andrei Vyshinsky would have envied the organization of this trial."

Shortly before the court sentenced the defendants, Pavel Litvinov and Mrs. Yuli Daniel issued a statement to foreign journalists, asking that it be published and broadcast as soon as possible. "We are not sending this request to Soviet newspapers because that is hopeless," they said. They called the trial "a wild mockery of justice . . . no better than the celebrated trials of the nineteen-thirties, which involved us in so much blood that we still have not recovered from them." The judge, they said, allowed only evidence "which fits in the program already prepared by the K.G.B."

Following this, 12 intellectuals, including Litvinov, Yesenin-Volpin, Yakir and Grigorenko addressed a similar statement about the trial to the Presidium of the conference of 66 Communist parties that opened at the end of February in Budapest for the purpose of strengthening their unity. One can imagine the reaction of the Soviet authorities on learning that the first news to reach the world of this parley consisted in front-page stories in The New York Times and other Western papers of an appeal by 12 Russian intellectuals to the conference's participants "to consider fully the perils caused by the trampling of man in our country."

One consequence of the Moscow trials was that the convicted writers gathered support from persons completely outside Moscow literary and intellectual circles, and for entirely extra-literary reasons. For example, among the signers of the appeal to the Budapest Conference were a former major general, the son of a general and the son of a Foreign Minister, a leader of the Crimean Tartar minority and a Russian Orthodox priest.

From as far away as Latvia came a letter to Mikhail Suslov, the Politburo member and party ideologist, from the chairman of a model collective farm who, in 1964, had been highly praised in the Soviet press. This letter, which was published, not in Russia but in The New York Times, called on the party to reach an understanding with the young rebels, rather than put them on trial. "Such dissenters will," the writer predicted, "inevitably create a new party. Ideas cannot be murdered with bullets, prison or exile." After describing the remoteness of the countryside where he lives, he said, addressing the Central Committee of the party, "If information has reached us on the broadest scale, you can well imagine what kind of seeds you have sown throughout the country. Have the courage to correct the mistakes that have been made, before the workers and peasants take a hand in this affair."

Protest against the trial also brought together two formerly distinct and antithetical groups within the intelligentsia itself. Until now, only one group, the "loyal opposition" — well-known published writers and respected scholars and scientists — had publicly expressed resistance, in relatively moderate terms, against attempts at coercion by the authorities. Now another group, "the underground"—dissidents who despair of effecting change through established channels —was making itself heard with unprecedented boldness in response to the persecution of Ginzburg and others among their members.

These two groups were first seen to join forces when 31 leading writers, scholars and scientists (including three members of the Academy of Sciences) addressed a protest against the Ginzburg trial to the Moscow City Court. Later appeals by loyal oppositionists included one signed by 80 more prominent intellectuals, and another signed by 220 top scientists and artists, from Moscow, Leningrad, Kharkov, Magadan and Dubna, the Soviet atomic center. In mid-March, 99 mathematicians, including seven Lenin Prize winners, rallied around Yesenin-Volpin (who is both an underground poet and a mathematician) in a protest against his forcible confinement in a lunatic asylum after he had participated in the demonstration outside the courtroom at the Ginzburg trial.

The central issue raised by all these protests (none of which was even mentioned in the Soviet press) was perhaps most eloquently defined by Pyotr Yakir in an appeal which is now being widely circulated in Moscow. "The inhuman punishment of members of the intelligentsia is a logical extension of the atmosphere of public life in recent years," he wrote. "The process of the restoration of Stalinism is going on — slowly but remorselessly." "The naive hopes" encouraged by de-Stalinization in 1956 and 1961 have not been realized. On the contrary, "the name of Stalin is being pronounced from the highest platforms in an entirely positive context."

Yakir, who spent 17 years in a Stalinist camp, deplores the fact that 10th-rate books praising Stalin are being published, while those that describe his crimes are being suppressed. His statement ends with an appeal to creative people in Russia to "raise your voices against the impending danger of new Stalins and Yezhovs. . . . We remind you that people who dared to think are now languishing in harsh forced-labor camps. Every time you are silent, another stepping-stone is added, leading to new trials of a Daniel or a Ginzburg. Little by little, with your acquiescence, a new 1937 may come upon us."

DOES the future hold a return to terror on the scale of the great purges of 1937-38? Clearly, the Soviet leadership finds itself in an impossible dilemma. On the one hand, it must now be clear that much larger doses of terror must be administered if the intelligentsia is to be silenced, and its influence on public opinion curbed. One sinister omen was contained in an article in Pravda last March 3, in which the recent Moscow trials were said to be as justified as the purge trials of the thirties—trials that have scarcely been mentioned favorably in the Soviet press since Khrushchev's de-Stalinization speech in 1956. On the other hand, the cost of a return to mass police terror would be incalculably high. It would reverse the effect of all Soviet policies designed to bring Russia into competition with the modern world, including those that offer individual incentives for industrial production and technological and scientific creativity. Moreover, the internal dynamic of the Stalinist police state, once provided by the myth of Stalin and by ideology, could not be restored in a society now rent by scepticism and dissent. Finally, a powerful secret police apparatus on the Stalinist model might well devour the political leaders who had revived it.

How Brezhnev and Kosygin will deal with this critical situation is still unclear. On the surface it would seem that a brutal showdown is at hand. Yet the Soviet leaders may be borne by the force of inertia and indecision that has determined their handling of other crises, both domestic and foreign. If so, we may be certain that the aspirations of the liberal intelligentsia, rising now for more than a decade, will continue to confront the leadership in irreversible and irremediable conflict. ■

March 24, 1968

# Soviet Expert Asks Intellectual Liberty

By RAYMOND H. ANDERSON
Special to The New York Times

MOSCOW, July 10—A leading Soviet physicist has issued a plea for full intellectual freedom, Soviet-United States cooperation and a worldwide rejection of "demagogic myths" in an urgent program to avert nuclear war and famine.

The 47-year-old scientist, Prof. Andrei D. Sakharov, helped develop the Soviet hydrogen bomb. In a 10,000-word essay, "Thoughts About Progress, Peaceful Co-existence and Intellectual Freedom," expressed fear that the world was "on the brink of disaster." The unpublished work is circulating in Moscow in manuscript.

Professor Sakharov, a member of the Academy of Sciences since 1953, urged a worldwide implementation of the scientific method in politics, economic planning and management, education, the arts and military affairs.

Intellectual freedom is imperative to achieve truth in a complex and changing world, he declared. He denounced Soviet censorship policies as harmful restraint on free inquiry.

The essay called for a thorough investigation into the damaging effects of Stalin's decade of dictatorial rule and demanded that "neo-Stalinists" be ousted from positions of influence.

Discussing foreign affairs, it condemned what was termed the United States' "crimes against humanity" in the Vietnam conflict as a reflection of traditional policies of self-interest. But it also charged that the Soviet Union was responsible for the Israeli-Arab conflict a year ago because of "irresponsible encouragement" of the Arabs.

The essay denounced the Government's action in breaking relations with Israel, protesting that this had damaged efforts for a peaceful settlement of the Middle Eastern conflict and had made more difficult "a necessary diplomatic recognition of Israel by the Arab countries."

Professor Sakharov, with Prof. Igor Y. Tamm, advanced a proposal for a controlled thermonuclear reaction in 1950. Professor Tamm, a leading Soviet scientist, shared a Nobel Prize with two other Russians in 1958 for his work in nuclear physics. Profesor Sakharov received a Stalin Prize.

The Sakharov essay was based on these theses:

¶The estrangement of mankind has put civilization under the perilous shadow of nuclear destruction, famine and ideological myths that leave nations at the mercy of "cruel and treacherous demagogues."

¶The salvation of mankind requires intellectual freedom—freedom to obtain and distribute information, freedom for unprejudiced and unfearing debate, and freedom from intimidation by officialdom.

"Such freedom of thought is the only guarantee against an infection of mankind by mass myths, which, in the hands of treacherous hypocrites and demagogues, can be transformed into bloody dictatorship," Professor Sakharov declared.

"Intellectual freedom is the only guarantee of a scientific-democratic approach to politics, economic development and culture."

Any attempt to preach incompatability between ideologies and nations, the physicist said, is "madness and a crime."

**Need for Debate Stressed**

He called for enactment of a law on the press and information to remove from Glavlit, the Soviet censorship agency, its absolute powers over what appears in print. The law should state explicitly what can be printed and what cannot be printed for state reasons, he suggested, with authority put into the hands of "competent and controlled public figures."

Censorship has killed the "living soul" of Soviet literature, he charged. Equally disturbing, he said, is the impact of censorship on other areas of original thought, causing an absence of "fresh and profound ideas."

"Profound thoughts arise only in debate, with a possibility of counterargument, only when there is a possibility of expressing not only correct but also dubious ideas," he asserted.

"The philosophers of ancient Greece understood this, and it is unlikely that anyone would challenge this today. But, after 50 years of full control over the minds of the entire country, our leadership seems to be afraid of even a hint at such debate."

Referring to the democratic reform under way in Czechoslovakia, Professor Sakharov said that the need for intellectual freedom had been understood there and added: "We must, without doubt, support their bold initiative, which is very important for the fate of Socialism and the whole of mankind."

The essay condemned as shameful the imprisonment of Andrei D. Sinyavsky and Yuli M. Daniel, the writers, and other dissidents sentenced to labor camps. It urged the release of all political prisoners.

In a broader discussion of the perils of nuclear warfare and famine as a result of the world population explosion, the physicist said that mankind could move away from "the brink of disaster" only by a rejection of traditional "empirical-competitive" international politics.

He said that world peace and order in the nuclear age depended upon Soviet-United States agreement on the following basic principles:

¶All peoples in the world have the right to decide their own fate under international guarantees.

¶All military and military-economic forms of exporting revolution or counterrevolution must be forbidden.

¶All countries must strive toward mutual assistance in economic and cultural problems.

¶International policies must reject any exploitation of local conditions for an enlargement of areas of influence or the creation of difficulties for other countries.

Professor Sakharov predicted the emergence of a multi-party political system in the Soviet Union and an ideological evolution toward Socialism in the United States and other capitalist countries.

The essay concluded with the following explanation:

"The author of this essay addresses it to the leadership of our country, to all its citizens and to all people of good-will in the world. The author understands the controversial nature of many points in the essay. His goal is open, frank and public discussion"

July 11, 1968

# 3 Soviet Dissidents Exiled and 2 Jailed

By HENRY KAMM
Special to The New York Times

MOSCOW, Oct. 11 — Three dissidents, including Pavel M Litvinov and Larisa Bogoraz-Daniel, were sentenced today to exile in a remote area of the Soviet Union for having staged a demonstration in Red Square against the invasion of Czechoslovakia.

Two others received jail terms for their part in the brief midday display of posters of protest on Aug. 25 in front of the Kremlin.

Mr. Litvinov, a 30-year-old physicist whose grandfather, Maxim M. Litvinov, was Stalin's Foreign Minister for many years, was sentenced to live for five years in a remote region, as yet undetermined.

Mrs. Daniel, wife of Yuli M. Daniel, who is serving the third year of a five-year term in a prison camp, was banished for four years. Mr. Daniel was sentenced n 1966 for writings critical of the Soviet Union that were published abroad.

Konstantin Babitsky, a 40-year-old scholar at the Russian-language institute of the Soviet Academy of Sciences, was sentenced to exile for three years.

October 12, 1968

# SOVIET SCIENTISTS CRITICIZED AGAIN

## They Are Accused of Wrong Ideological Outlook

By BERNARD GWERTZMAN
Special to The New York Times

MOSCOW, Feb. 22 — Young scientists, an élite group in Soviet society, are coming under increased attack for showing the wrong ideological outlook toward their work.

The latest criticism was leveled yesterday by an academician, Dr. Ivan I. Artobolevsky, the head of Znaniye (Knowledge), a public organization of two million members, drawn from the intelligentsia.

The academician said that among young scientists there sometimes appeared signs of "skepticism, apolitical attitudes, nonclass interpretations of such concepts as democracy, personal freedom and humanism, and a misunderstanding of the roles of the press and other means of mass information."

Dr. Artobolevsky's article, which appeared in the newspaper Sovetskaya Roosiya, did not go into details on the criticism, but apparently was part of the campaign launched last year to instill more ideological awareness in scientists — many of whom have been among those signing petitions in behalf of dissidents brought to trial.

### Sakharov Essay Recalled

Party leaders undoubtedly were also unhappy with the publication last summer in the West of an essay by Andrei D. Sakharov, a noted nuclear physicist, which was sharply critical of Soviet ideological controls over intellectuals and which called among other things for increased cooperation between East and West.

Scientists, especially in the natural sciences, are among the highest paid people in the Soviet Union and are accorded many privileges often denied other citizens.

Because of the importance of their work, scientists have often been free of the ideological harassment that intellectuals in the humanities have complained about.

A press campaign has been under way for several months to bring the scientists and other specialists in line with the stringent resolutions passed at the Communist party plenum last April, which called for more ideological awareness among the Soviet people. The main source of criticism was an article two months ago in Kommunist, the party's theoretical organ, which said that several scientific institutions were failing to cultivate in young people "the finest attributes of the Soviet intelligentsia: party spirit, ideological conviction, industriousness and consciousness of public duty."

### Youth Groups Blamed

Some leaders were charged with having said: "I need scientists, not propagandists; a scientist who deals only with science."

Dr. Artobolevsky tried in his article to avoid straining relations with scientists. He said that the fault in any ideological shortcomings often lay with the Young Communist League organizations.

He said that a recent poll taken of 900 scientific workers under the age of 30 in the Moscow area showed that only 5 per cent said they had no need for any activity outside of their scientific work. He added that 97 per cent said they had followed attentively the international situation and that 60 per cent said they subscribed to periodicals.

This shows, Dr. Artobolevsky said, that the scientific youth is not passive about political matters, but that it has not yet taken its responsibilities seriously.

He urged the young scientists "not only to discover something new in science and technology, but also to propagandize and to bring their knowledge to the people." He said that they would be fulfilling their public duties by taking part in meetings with youth and in holding discussion sessions.

February 23, 1969

# *Soviet Said to Punish Signers Of Human-Rights Plea to U.N.*

By HENRY KAMM
Special to The New York Times

MOSCOW, June 18—Soviet authorities were reliably reported today to be retaliating against signers of a petition addressed to the United Nations last month calling for an investigation into "the repression of basic civil rights in the Soviet Union."

Of the 54 who signed the appeal, five who live in Kharkov were reported to have been dismissed from their jobs. Another signer, from Leningrad, was said to have been confined to a psychiatric hospital within three days of the publication of the letter in Western newspapers.

In Moscow, a student was informed that the academic defense of his dissertation had been canceled, informed sources reported. This has the effect of denying him an academic degree.

A crane operator in Moscow has been threatened with dismissal but remains at work for the time being. In his interrogation, the man was reproached with particular bitterness for being a worker who had joined the intellectual dissidents.

At the same time, a number of signers have expressed the hope that the United Nations will take the appeal into consideration although it has not been formally received. The signers charged that Soviet authorities have kept their letter, mailed late last month, from reaching the United Nations Commission on Human Rights.

Having learned from Western broadcasts that officials at the United Nations had said that the letter had not arrived, signers attempted last week to present copies of the appeal at two offices of the United Nations here. The offices are staffed by Soviet personnel.

The petitioners were told at both offices that their appeal could not be received because the offices were not empowered to accept documents from individuals.

In view of the special circumstances, the signers expressed the wish that the United Nations would dispense with the requirement of physically receiving a petition and take up the appeal.

In a similar attempt, 10 Soviet citizens sent registered letters to the Presidium of the conference of 75 Communist parties that closed here yesterday, as well as to the British and Italian delegations. The letter charged a "rebirth of Stalinist methods."

Two of the signers, Mrs. Pyotr G. Grigorenko and Leonid Petrovsly, a historian, inquired at the press center—the only conference agency accessible to the public—whether the letter had been received. Although they showed a post office receipt, they were told that it had not arrived.

Soviet postal authorities were not the only obstacle to the receipt of the appeal. Reliable sources reported that a member of the Italian party delegation, to whom the letter was offered by an acquaintance, refused to accept it. The Italian Communists are reputed to be the most liberal.

Mrs. Grigorenko, who signed the appeal in place of her husband, a former major general and a leading figure among Soviet dissidents, who is under arrest, was reported today to have been ousted from the Communist party, of which she has been a member for many years.

General Grigorenko is being held in Tashkent, where he went last month to defend a group of Crimean Tatars facing trial for anti-Soviet activities. The Tatars have been thwarted in their efforts to return to the homeland from which Stalin exiled them.

Meanwhile, five political prisoners at the Potma Prison Camp have ended a hunger strike. They went on strike last month to protest the refusal by internal security authorities to allow one of them, Alexsandr Ginzburg, to marry his common-law wife so she would be allowed to visit him.

Security authorities promised that she would be allowed a visit, informed sources reported.

June 19, 1969

## Solzhenitsyn Terms Soviet 'Sick Society'

By JAMES F. CLARITY
Special to The New York Times

MOSCOW, Nov. 14—Aleksandr I. Solzhenitsyn, the Soviet author of "The Cancer Ward" and "The First Circle," has bitterly described the Soviet Union in a letter as a "sick society."

The letter was sent to the writers union of the Russian Federated Republic, which expelled him four days ago. The 51-year-old author also castigated for their "hate-vigilance" those who expelled him. The letter was written Monday and made available today by acquaintances.

Mr. Solzhenitsyn wrote that his expulsion from the local writers union in Ryazan had been approved by the parent union of the Russian Republic before he had a chance to defend himself. "The blind lead the blind." Mr. Solzhenitsyn said in the letter. "In this time of crisis of our seriously sick society, you are not able to suggest anything constructive, anything good, only your hate-vigilance. Shamelessly flouting your own constitution, you expelled me in feverish haste and in my absence, without even sending me a warning telegram, without even giving me the four hours to travel from Ryazan [to Moscow] to be present."

"Was it more convenient for you to invent new accusations against me in my absence?" the letter continued. "Were you afraid that you would have to give me 10 minutes to reply? Your watches are behind the times. The time is near when every one of you will try to find out how you can scrape your signatures off today's resolution."

The expulsion is not expected to affect Mr. Solzhenitsyn's professional life since his works have been banned in the Soviet Union since 1966.

**Silent Since 1967**

The letter marked the first time Mr. Solzhenitsyn, considered by many literary critics as the greatest living Soviet novelist, has answered his enemies or criticized the Soviet Union in two years. In 1967, he proposed that the writers union ban literary censorship and attacked union officials for blocking the publication of his works in the Soviet Union.

Neither "The Cancer Ward" nor "The First Circle" has been published here. Both books became best sellers in the West. The last Solzhenitsyn work published here was a short story in the magazine Novy Mir in January, 1966.

Mr. Solzhenitsyn was expelled from the local union in Ryazan, 110 miles southeast of Moscow, last week during a meting at which he was present. On Monday, the action was approved by the secretariat of the Russian Republic union, in effect stripping him of official status as a writer. Literaturnaya Gazeta, the union's official newspaper, said the expulsion was the result of the author's failure to stem anti-Soviet criticism centering around his name and works.

Mr. Solzhenitsyn became the hero of many Soviet liberals and intellectuals in 1962 with the publication of his short novel, "A Day in the Life of Ivan Denisovich," which depicted life in a Stalinist prison camp. "The Cancer Ward" and "The First Circle" are caustically critical of Stalin and authoritarian aspects of the Soviet political system.

Since his 1967 attack on censorship and on certain union officials, however, he had remained silent. He continued to write, but without serious hope, according to friends, that his work would be published here.

In his letter to the writers union, Mr. Solzhenitsyn also defended two writers, whose expulsions are reportedly being considered by the union. They are Lev Kopolev, a critic who specializes in foreign literature, and Lydia Chukovskaya, the daughter of Kornei Chukovsky, the translator and writer of children's books who died two weeks ago.

Both have signed protests against official harassment and the imprisonment of Soviet writers. In 1967, Mr. Solzhenitsyn reportedly wrote his anti-censorship appeal in Mr. Chukovsky's home. In the letter to the writers union, Mr. Solzhenitsyn said Mr. Kopolev was apparently threatened with expulsion because he had disclosed the proceedings of a secret meeting.

Mr. Solzhenitsyn asked the union why such meetings were necessary.

"The enemy is listening, that's your answer," Mr. Solzhenitsyn said in the letter. "These eternal enemies are the basis of your duties and of your existence. What would you do without your enemies? You would not be able to live without enemies. Hate, hate no less evil than racism, has become your sterile atmosphere."

November 15, 1969

## MEDVEDEV FREED AFTER PROTESTS

### Provisional Release From Asylum Granted by Soviet

Special to The New York Times

MOSCOW, June 17—Zhores A. Medvedev, the biologist whose forced detention in a mental hospital touched off protests from scientists and writers, was provisionally released today and permitted to go home.

Friends of Mr. Medvedev said they understood that Soviet authorities had not given Mr. Medvedev a full discharge and had reserved the right to have him recommitted to the hospital in Kaluga, not far from his home in Obninsk, 60 miles southwest of Moscow.

Although protests from leading Soviet figures against Mr. Medvedev's detention have been widely publicized abroad, the episode has not been reported in the controlled Soviet news media and probably did not come to the attention of the average Russian.

Zhores A. Medvedev

Mr. Medvedev, who made his scientific reputation for his research in molecular biology, ran afoul of authorities for his writings, unpublished here, complaining of restrictions on Soviet scientists' ability to communicate and travel freely abroad. He was dismissed from his job as head of a laboratory in Obninsk, an atomic research center, last year and was without a job for nine months.

He was seized May 29 and taken without any court order to the Kaluga mental hospital. There he was examined by at least five teams of doctors, his friends have reported.

His forced confinement led not only to protests on the legality of the action but assertions of his sanity from such leading scientists as the physicist Pyotr L. Kapitsa, Andrei D. Sakharov and Mikhail A. Leontovich; Boris L. Astaurov, a geneticist, and Vladimir A. Engelhardt, a biochemist. They are all members of the prestigious Academy of Sciences.

**Finding Is Challenged**

In addition, Aleksandr I. Solzhenitsyn, the novelist, wrote a passionate attack on the detention, comparing it to gas chambers. Other literary figures who knew Mr. Medvedev added to their complaints.

According to reliable sources, the decision on releasing Mr. Medvedev, and on the way it was to be done, was reached as a result of a meeting in Moscow last Thursday under the chairmanship of Dr. Boris V. Petrovsky, Minister of Public Health.

At the meeting were Mstislav V. Keldysh, president of the Academy of Sciences, as well as Mr. Sakharov, Mr. Leontovich, Mr. Astaurov and others of Mr. Medvedev's supporters. Mr. Keldysh was reported not to have spoken.

Dr. Viktor Morozov, a psychiatrist who had examined Mr. Medvedev, was reported to have said that he seemed to be suffering from some mental illness. But Mr. Medvedev's supporters said that he was completely sane. In view of the wide support given the detained man, the authorities apparently chose the compromise of provisional release, his friends said.

It is assumed by his supporters that Mr. Medvedev was seized in the first place as a show of official displeasure with his active criticism of such well-established Soviet institutions as censoring of the mail and tight control over travel abroad.

He has said that Soviet science was being held back by these restraints since it blocks quick assimilation of Western ideas and achievements.

Other political dissidents have been committed to mental institutions. But none of them had the kind of impressive support Mr. Medvedev received from the scientific élite, who are presumably regarded by the Soviet leadership with respect.

June 18, 1970

# Solzhenitsyn Is Awarded Nobel Prize in Literature

Special to The New York Times

STOCKHOLM, Oct. 8 — Aleksandr I. Solzhenitsyn, the internationally acclaimed Soviet author whose works are banned in his homeland, won the 1970 Nobel Prize for Literature today.

The writer of the novels "One Day in the Life of Ivan Denisovich," "The First Circle" and "The Cancer Ward" was cited by the Swedish Academy, which makes the annual literature award, "for the ethical force with which he has pursued the indispensable traditions of Russian literature."

The award, to be presented formally at a ceremony here Dec. 10, carries prize money equivalent to about $78,000.

Mr. Solzhenitsyn, who was expelled by the Soviet Writers' Union earlier this year with the suggestion that he go into exile, was hailed today by Dr. Karl-Ragnar Gierow, permanent secretary of the Swedish Academy, as a "son of the Russian revolution, of Lenin's revolution.

"He has never given up his spiritual heritage," Dr. Gierow added.

Mr. Solzhenitsyn, 51 years old, is the second controversial Russian to receive the award in the last 12 years. In 1958, Boris Pasternak, a poet, won the prize mainly for his novel "Doctor Zhivago," but was compelled by the Soviet Union, then led by Nikita S. Khrushchev, to refuse the award.

In 1965, the academy honored Mikhail A. Sholokhov, the Soviet author of "And Quiet Flows the Don." Mr. Sholokhov, who enjoys official favor, made the trip to Stockholm to receive his award.

The award to Mr. Sholokhov was viewed at the time as an attempt to strike a balance with the prize for Mr. Pasternak, which had been assailed in the Soviet Union as a "hostile political act."

In view of this controversy there had been some doubt whether the academy would now risk affronting Moscow again with the selection of an author who was in official disfavor. The vote today was a close one, with Patrick White, an Australian novelist, losing by a narrow margin.

Mr. White lost out last year as well, when the prize went to Samuel Becket, the French-Irish novelist and playwright.

**Based on Experiences**

The novels for which Mr. Solzhenitsyn is best known stem largely from his own experiences in prison, to which he was sent in 1945 for having written a letter to a friend critical of Stalin. He was released in 1953 and deported for life from the European part of the Soviet Union. But in 1957, as a result of Mr. Khrushchev's program of de-Stalinization, he was fully rehabilitated.

The publication in 1962 of his short novel about life in a Stalin labor camp, "One Day in the Life of Ivan Denisovich," brought him wide attention. That book was first published in the Soviet Union, but the two that firmly established his reputation abroad were not.

However, smuggled copies of "The Cancer Ward," which details life in a prison hospital under Stalin, and "The First Circle," which describes life in a Stalinist research center for detained scientists, have circulated among Soviet intellectuals

These two novels were considered too critical of Soviet society to be allowed to appear.

His drama "The Love-Girl and the Innocent," is scheduled to have its world premiere in Minneapolis Oct. 13. The play, which is also scheduled for the 1971-1972 New York season, is described as a love story of two prisoners in a Stalinist labor camp.

A collection of his short stories is being published by Farrar, Straus and Giroux early next year under the title "For the Good of the Cause."

The announcement of the literature award came unusually early this year, as Nobel Prizes are not generally awarded before the middle of October, with the medical one leading the way. However, there is no fixed schedule.

October 9, 1970

# 'The Only Living Soviet Classic'

By HARRISON E. SALISBURY

Yevgeny Yevtushenko, the great young Soviet poet, calls Aleksandr Solzhenitsyn "the only living classic in Russia."

His judgment is shared by many of his literate countrymen as well as critics abroad and readers who have made Solzhenitsyn a best-seller in a dozen languages. The published bulk of Solzhenitsyn's work is small compared with that of most major writers—and far, far smaller in terms of what has been published in his own country. His reputation is based on two major works—"The First Circle" and "The Cancer Ward"—and on "One Day in the Life of Ivan Denisovich," a novella, plus a handful of vignettes and two or three plays.

**An Appraisal**

Of this writing only "One Day in the Life of Ivan Denisovich" and a few of the vignettes have been published (in tiny editions) in the Soviet Union. That is not to say that Soviet readers do not know his other writings, but they have read them only in typescript and mimeograph copies, circulating in a few hundred examples.

**Essential Human Conflict**

From the moment of publication of "One Day in the Life of Ivan Denisovich" there has never been doubt that a great figure in the field of humane letters, a worthy successor to Tolstoy, Dostoyevsky, Turgenev, Chekhov, Bunin and Pasternak had appeared improbably in a Soviet milieu still marked by the harsh repressions of the political censors and the even harsher harassment of the political police.

What are the qualities that have marked Solzhenitsyn's work?

First and immeasurably most important has been his precise and dramatic concern for the essential human conflict of the era, the struggle of the small, ordinary Soviet man and woman to survive under conditions that seem beyond the strength of body and spirit to bear.

No one has captured the pathos of the human condition in the Soviet Union as has Solzhenitsyn, in part, perhaps, because he has lived it all. "One Day in the Life of Ivan Denisovich" was one day in the life of Aleksandr Solzhenitsyn, a "zak,' or prisoner, in one of Stalin's Siberian camps.

It is all there, put down word for word, pain for pain, agony for agony—with the precision of a surgeon and the exactitude of a mathematician, and with the deep understanding that all of humanity is the victim of a system in which some men are brutalized by prison wardens and some are brutalized by being prison wardens.

In a review of "The First Circle" written for The New York Times, this writer said: "The concept of the world as a prison comes naturally to a Russian—his world is a prison."

"The First Circle" was a study of the world of a prisoner, once again the prisoner being Solzhenitsyn himself. But this was no ordinary prisoner for, as the review noted, "it is Solzhenitsyn's camera eye, his absolute sense of pitch, his Tolstoyan power of characterization, his deep humaneness, his almost military discipline, and Greek feeling for the unities which make his work a classic."

Almost all the work of Solzhenitsyn that is now known grows out of the Soviet prison system, but there is no monotony, for the prison system was —and is—as rich and varied as life itself, embracing so large a portion of the population.

**A Towering Figure**

In every country critics and public have hailed Solzhenitsyn as a towering figure in 20th-century literature. And this was also true in the Soviet Union from the inception of his public career under Nikita S. Khrushchev.

But in the dour atmosphere of present-day Russia, another kind of criticism has arisen—a political criticism that characterizes Solzhenitsyn, like other great Russian writers of the past, as rubbish. To which Solzhenitsyn, at the time of his expulsion from the Soviet Writers Union, replied: "The blind lead the blind. The time is near when every one of you will try to find out how you can scrape your signatures off today's resolution."

The body of Solzhenitsyn's known work is comparatively small, and it represents only a part of what he has created. He is now on another major work, one that his friends have said breaks new ground. It is said to be a historical subject, one that some have already begun to compare with Tolstoy's "War and Peace."

Solzhenitsyn, quite clearly, is a living example of a thought he expressed in "The First Circle":

"For a country to have a great writer is like having another government. That's why no regime has ever loved great writers, only minor ones."

October 9, 1970

# Letter by Rostropovich Defends Nobel Award for Solzhenitsyn

## Cellist Assails Curbs

By JAMES F. CLARITY

Special to The New York Times

MOSCOW, Nov. 12 — Mstislav Rostropovich, the virtuoso Soviet cellist, is reported to have written an impassioned defense of the author Aleksandr Solzhenitsyn, whose selection for the 1970 Nobel Prize in literature has been officially denounced here.

Reliable sources made available what they said were copies of an open letter written by the 43-year-old musician to the chief editors of four major Soviet newspapers. The letter, dated Oct. 31, bears the cellist's name at its end.

The letter also assailed recent examples of Soviet censorship of the arts and warned the authorities against returning to Stalin's practices of "destroying talented people" whose works did not conform to official views.

Mr. Rostropovich has been one of the most prestigious Soviet cultural ambassadors abroad, with virtually unrestricted freedom to travel, a privilege denied many ordinary citizens.

As a result of his decision to move openly as Mr. Solzhenitsyn's protector against the wishes of the authorities, he now risks being forbidden to perform abroad or even in the Soviet Union.

His letter was addressed to Pravda, the Communist party newspaper; Izvestia, the Government daily; Literaturnaya Gazeta, the writers union weekly, and Sovetskaya Kultura, the newspaper of the Culture Ministry.

None of these papers has thus far printed the letter, which was critical of Soviet denunciations of the Swedish Academy for having given the Nobel Prize to Mr. Solzhenitsyn.

Soviet newspapers have attacked the award as politically motivated. Mr. Solzhenitsyn's works, though best sellers in the West, have been banned in the Soviet Union on the ground that they depict the Soviet system in too dark a light.

The author, who often stays at Mr. Rostropovich's home, has said he wants to go to Stockholm to accept the prize on Dec. 10. There has been no indication whether he will receive permission to make the trip. All foreign travel by Soviet citizens must be officially approved.

Explaining his intervention on Mr. Solzhenitsyn's behalf, Mr. Rostropovich said in the letter that "it is no longer a secret that A. I. Solzhenitsyn lives a great part of the time in my house near Moscow."

The Rostropovich said he liked many of Mr. Solzhenitsyn's writings and saw "no reason to hide my attitude toward him at a time when a campaign is being waged against him."

Charging in effect that there was duplicity in Soviet policy toward the Nobel award for literature, the letter said:

"This is in my memory already the third time that a Soviet writer has received the Nobel Prize. In two cases out of three, we consider the awarding of the prize a dirty political game, but in one (Sholokhov) a just recognition of the world significance of our literature."

Mikhail A. Sholokhov, the politically conservative author of "And Quiet Flows the Don," received the prize in 1965 and was commended for it by the Soviet authorities. The late Boris Pasternak was given the award in 1958 and was vilified for it. His "Doctor Zhivago" is banned in the Soviet Union.

Discussing the 1958 campaign of vilification against Mr. Pasternak, Mr. Rostropovich recalled "with pride" that he had refused to join in it. He said he had declined to appear at a rally "where I was expected to give a speech in which I had been 'commissioned' to criticize 'Doctor Zhivago' without having read it."

### Selective Acceptance

"It now happens that we selectively sometimes accept Nobel prizes with gratitude, and sometimes we curse them," the letter said.

"What if the next time the prize is awarded to Comrade Kochetov? Of course, it will have to be accepted."

Both Vsevelod A. Kochetov, a conservative novelist and editor of the literary magazine Oktyabr, and Mr. Sholokhov are among critics of Mr. Solzhenitsyn. No Soviet writer of any stature has publicly defended Mr. Solzhenitsyn.

The letter criticized the controlled Soviet newspapers for selectively printing anti-Solzhenitsyn articles from American and Swedish Communist newspapers, while "avoiding the incomparably more popular and important Communist papers like L'Humanité, Lettres Françaises and L'Unità, to say nothing of the non-Communist press."

The letter compared present Soviet literacy criticism with the "nonsense" it said the Soviet press printed in 1948 to attack the music of Dmitri Shostakovich, Sergei Prokofiev and Aram Khatchaturian.

These composers were among cultural figures assailed under Stalin for not conforming to official views of the arts.

"Has that time really not taught us to tread cautiously before destroying talented people," the letter said. "In 1948 there were lists of forbidden works. Now oral prohibitions are preferred, based on the contention that 'opinions exist' that a work is not recommended. It is impossible to establish where that opinion exists and whose it is."

"I don't speak about political or economic questions in our country," the letter said. "There are people who know that better than I, but explain to me please why, just in our literature and art, people absolutely incompetent in this field so often have the final word? Why they are given the right to descredit our art in the eyes of our people?

"I know that after my letter there will undoubtedly be an opinion about me, but I am not afraid and I openly say what I think. Talents of which we are proud must not be subjected to the assaults of the past."

Nov. 13, 1970

# 3 IN RUSSIA MOVE TO DEFEND RIGHTS

## Sakharov Among Physicists Who Establish Committee on Personal Freedom

By BERNARD GWERTZMAN

Special to The New York Times

MOSCOW, Nov. 15 — Dr. Andrei D. Sakharov, a prominent nuclear physicist, and two of his colleagues have formed a Committee for Human Rights to seek ways of guaranteeing personal freedom in the Soviet Union.

A statement of principles, signed by Dr. Sakharov, Andrei N. Tverdokhlebov and Valery N. Chalidze, was made available to Western correspondents today.

The principles appeared to have been composed to avoid direct criticism of the Government, possibly because it is a crime under Soviet law to belong to an "anti-Soviet organization." In fact, the sponsors seem to offer a hand of friendship to the authorities.

But the rules of membership outlined by the three men flatly state that only those who "are not members of a political party" may join. This would rule out members of the Communist party, the only legal political party in the Soviet Union. The three physicists were joined by six other scientists, including Mikhail A. Leontovich, a leading theoretical physicist, in making public a letter protesting last month's sentencing of a Leningrad mathematician, Revolt I. Pimenov, to five years of Siberian exile. The letter was addressed to the Supreme Court of the Russian Federation.

Mr. Pimenov and a friend, Boris B. Vail, a worker in a Kiev puppet theater, were found guilty of slandering the Soviet state. The nine scientists said that the two men had committed no crime in exchanging information in their possession.

Dr. Sakharov, 49 years old, has emerged in recent years as a leading advocate of free speech in the Soviet Union. His writings have been printed abroad and he has protested against the detention and sentencing of several people who have been convicted or sent to psychiatric hospitals for views critical of Soviet society.

Because of his political activity, Dr. Sakharov, a creator of the Soviet hydrogen bomb, has been barred from working on security projects, his friends say. He is believed to be still associated with the Lebedev Physics Institute in Moscow—the Soviet Union's most prestigious physics institute—which recently was criticized by the Central Committee of the Communist party for lax ideological discipline.

The Soviet authorities do not permit the formation of groups over which they do not have control. Article 126 of the Soviet Constitution says that Soviet citizens are guaranteed the right to form public organizations, but adds that the Communist party "is the leading core of all organizations of the working people, both public and state."

Article 72 of the Russian Federation's criminal code makes it a serious crime to participate in "an anti-Soviet organization." It does not state what constitutes such a body.

The principles of Dr. Sakharov's committee said: "The

problem of the maintenance of human rights is important for the creation of favorable conditions for people's lives, the consolidation of peace and the development of mutual understanding."

The statement expressed satisfaction with what it termed successes achieved in the Soviet Union since Stalin's death in 1953, and said that the committee wanted "to cooperate on a consultative basis with the further efforts of the state in the creation of the guarantees for the defense of rights, taking into account the specific character of the problem in the conditions of the socialist system and the specific character of Soviet traditions in this field."

The group said that members of the committee could not be those who are members of a political party "or other organizations claiming participation in governmental management." It also ruled out those who belong to organizations "whose principles allow participation in orthodox or opposition political activity."

### Cooperation With the State

It said that the goals of the committee included "cooperation with organs of state power in the field of the creation and carrying out of guarantees of human rights, either at the initiative of the committee or the initiative of interested organs of power."

The group further said that it would assist those concerned with research into human rights and "the specific character of this problem in the socialist society." It promised "constructive criticism of the contemporary conditions of the system of legal rights of personal freedom in Soviet law." This criticism, it said, would be guided not only by the general principles of the United Nations Declaration on Human Rights, but also by "the specific character of Soviet law" and "the complicated traditions and real difficulties of the state in this area."

The three physicists said that they were prepared for contacts with nonofficial foreign organizations so long as "they proceed from the principles of the United Nations and do not pursue the goal of bringing harm to the Soviet Union."

It is not known how the three physicists plan to recruit members, but it is unlikely that the Soviet authorities will take kindly to the idea.

In May, 1969, a group of 15 political dissidents formed an organization called the Initiative Group for the Defense of Civil Rights in the Soviet Union. This group, however, was openly critical of the Soviet system and appealed to the United Nations' Human Rights Commission for help in stopping the arrests of dissidents.

The United Nations took no action and many members of the group have since been arrested.

November 16, 1970

# Solzhenitsyn Explains Change in Plans

By BERNARD GWERTZMAN
Special to The New York Times

MOSCOW, Nov. 30 — Aleksandr I. Solzhenitsyn has told the Swedish Academy that he changed his mind about going to Stockholm to receive the 1970 Nobel Prize because he assumed, from the suppression of his books, that he would not be permitted to return.

In a letter to the Academy, made public by friends with the author's approval, Mr. Solzhenitsyn said he also thought he would have found the Nobel Prize festivities, beginning Dec. 10 "not in keeping with my character and way of life."

The 51-year-old novelist, whose latest works are banned in his own country because of their frank treatment of the Stalin years, gave the letter to Ambassador Gunnar V. Jarring of Sweden on Friday for transmission to the Academy, which selects the Nobel Prize winner for literature.

When the Swedish Academy announced Oct. 8 that he was this year's recipient of the prize, which carries with it about $78,000, Mr. Solzhenitsyn said he would go to Stockholm if he could. In his letter, he explained his change of heart.

He said he had expressed his intention originally to go to Stockholm although "I anticipated the humiliating procedure, usual in my country for every trip abroad, of filling out questionnaires, obtaining character references from party organizations—even for nonmembers — and being given instructions about behavior."

Soviet citizens do not have the right to travel freely abroad and must apply for exit visas. As Mr. Solzhenitsyn indicated, this is a time-consuming process, with the majority of applications turned down. In addition, a new regulation that went into effect recently requires a fee of 500 rubles ($555) for every private trip to a country outside the Soviet bloc.

Mr. Solzhenitsyn also said, "In recent weeks, the hostile attitude toward my prize, as expressed in the press of my country, and the fact that my books are still suppressed — for reading them, people are dismissed from work or expelled from school — compel me to assume that my journey to Stockholm would be used to cut me off from my native land, simply to prevent me from returning home."

At the time of his expulsion from the official writers union last year, the newspaper Literaturnaya Gazeta suggested that there were no barriers to his emigrating from Russia. It was reliably reported that similar thoughts had been expressed in party circles recently.

Mr. Solzhenitsyn, who lives a hermitlike existence most of the year in the country house of Mstislav Rostropovich, the cellist, has told friends that he has no desire to leave Russia.

He said that he discovered in the program sent him from Stockholm "that in the Nobel celebrations, there are many ceremonies and festivities that would be tiring and not in keeping with my character and way of life."

The novelist said he would be happy to receive the prize in Moscow at the Swedish Embassy and to give the traditional Nobel lecture on literature either orally or in writing. He seemed to be indicating that he might apply for a visa later to give the lecture.

Swedish sources said that Mr. Solzhenitsyn, who has never traveled abroad, had been warned by the academy that he would become the center of press attention in Stockholm.

December 1, 1970

# *U.S. Protests Attack On Two in Moscow*

By BERNARD GWERTZMAN
Special to The New York Times

MOSCOW, Jan. 27 — The United States Embassy protested today against the second assault in the last three days on American newsmen in what appeared to be a campaign to discourage meetings between correspondents and Russian dissidents.

Thompson R. Buchanan, the embassy's political counselor, complained to the Foreign Ministry about the roughing up yesterday of James R. Peipert, of The Associated Press, who was pushed, kicked and had his glasses smashed by at least five persons.

Mr. Peipert said he was convinced the five were members of the State Security Police, who had tapped his phone and knew he was going to meet a dissident on Kalinin Prospect.

The dissident, who was not identified, was also assaulted, Mr. Peipert said. Both of them were able to get into Mr. Peipert's car and drive away.

On Saturday, Anthony Astrachan, correspondent of The Washington Post, was set upon by a group as he got out of his car to pick up a Russian friend whom he was going to take home to dinner. Mr. Astrachan said he had been forced back into his car and the Russian had been seized and taken away. As he started his car to leave, one of the men kicked in a taillight, Mr. Astrachan said.

The embassy protested the harassment of Mr. Astrachan on Monday, a spokesman said today.

Western diplomats said the incidents appeared to be part of a vigilance campaign in preparation for the 24th party congress, which begins March 30.

The diplomats said they did not view them as harassment in retaliation for actions carried out by the Jewish Defense League against Russians in the United States. That campaign has stopped, the embassy believes.

Pressure is being applied in a variety of ways to reduce or eliminate contact between Westerners and Soviet citizens who do not have official business with them.

The drive seems aimed at contacts between newsmen and the few dissidents who have been a source of news about arrests, trials, protest letters and other unofficial information.

Soviet authorities traditionally frown on close ties between Russians and foreigners. The situation is more relaxed these days than in Stalin's time, when merely knowing a foreigner was often grounds for arrest. But periodic press campaigns for vigilance continue.

An article in the party magazine agitator this week said

the West was using contacts with Russians as a means of subversion.

The author, Nikolai V. Zhogin, a deputy prosecutor general, said that Western propagandists "use personal contacts with Soviet people for the purpose of spreading bourgeois influence."

"Sometimes they establish ties with criminal, politically unstable elements, using them for their dirty aims," he said.

He mentioned Andrei Amalrik, who was sentenced last year to three years in a labor camp for spreading anti-Soviet slander. Mr. Amalrik, he said, set up "permanent ties with correspondents of bourgeois newspapers and sent them his writings, which contained slanderous anti - Soviet fabrications."

Semyon K. Tsvigun, the first deputy chairman of the State Security Committee, writing in the same magazine last month, said his agency was waging "a decisive fight against ideological subversion." He listed virtually every form of cultural exchange as suspect. He said Jews were a favorite target of subversion by "international Zionism," which sought to induce "politically immature Soviet Jews to emigrate to Israel."

The current campaign began Dec. 17 when Pravda, the party newspaper, published a lengthy article that said "the Soviet people are increasing their political vigilance and their irreconcilability with rotten bourgeois ideology."

January 28, 1971

# Soviet Repression Leaves The Dissidents in Disarray

By HEDRICK SMITH
Special to The New York Times

MOSCOW, Dec. 10—As the Soviet Union has moved toward improved relations with the West this year, its secret police have mounted a determined campaign of repression against the domestic dissident movement that has left some dissenters feeling weaker, more vulnerable and more on the defensive than at any other time since the mid-nineteen-sixties.

Since the year began, dissident sources report, more than 100 persons have been arrested in the Ukrainian Republic as part of a crackdown against nationalist activities there, and at least a dozen have been given sentences of 3 to 15 years on charges of anti-Soviet activity.

### Publication Is a Target

Eight key activists in Moscow and other major cities have been arrested or tried in a year-old campaign to suppress the Chronicle of Current Events, the most important dissident publication. Since April, 1968, the publication has recorded activities of dissenters, the courts, the secret police and Soviet censors as they affect the rights campaign here.

Some other key activists, arrested previously, have been given long sentences or their terms in mental hospitals have been extended.

The 23-year-old stepdaughter of the physicist Andrei D. Sakharov, now the figurehead leader of the civil rights movement here, has been suspended from Moscow State University, and two of the physicist's colleagues in the rights movement have been forced out of jobs and compelled to find other work.

Although no direct action has been taken against Aleksandr I. Solzhenitsyn, the Nobel Prize-winning author, authorities have reimposed a ban against foreign travel by Mstislav L. Rostropovich, the reknowned cellist at whose home Mr. Solzhenitsyn lives.

But the most severe blow to dissidents recently has been that Pyotr A. Yakir, a 49-year-old historian who until his arrest June 21 was a leading figure in the small, loose dissident coalition known as the Democratic Movement, has reportedly given his police interrogators information about fellow dissenters.

### Some Confront Informant

According to dissident sources, at least 25 persons have been summoned for questioning by the secret police on the basis of information either supplied or confirmed by Mr. Yakir. Some have reportedly been forced by the police to confront Mr. Yakir when they have denied what he had purportedly said.

Among those reportedly called in by the secret police are several scholars at the Institute of History in Moscow, where Mr. Yakir once worked, scientists at the complex of institutes in Obninsk, a city about 75 miles southwest of Moscow, and other intellectuals.

Moreover, close friends said that Mr. Yakir had told his daughter, Irina, during a meeting last month at Lefortovo Prison where he is held, that although he had not abandoned the basic principles of the rights struggle, he had now seen material from previous political trials showing that Soviet dissidents were being used, willingly or unwillingly, by anti-Soviet forces abroad, notably by the Russian émigré organization, the People's Labor Union, known as N.T.S. for its initials in Russia.

To many dissidents, the case of the burly, bearded historian is especially poignant because as the son of Gen. Iona Yakir, a Soviet army officer shot in 1937 at the peak of the Stalinist purges, he spent 16 of his first 30 years in a prison camp. He was rehabilitated by Nikita S. Khrushchev in 1954 and became an active anti-Stalinist and rights campaigner. He was long one of the most regular sources of information on dissident activities for foreign newsmen.

A few months before his arrest and after repeated police warnings that he was engaging in anti-Soviet activities, Mr. Yakir told one foreign reporter: "If they beat me, I will say anything. I know that from my former experience in the camps. But you know it will not be the real me speaking."

From brief contacts, those who have seen Mr. Yakir in the last few weeks report no obvious evidence of physical mistreatment. But he was known widely as a heavy drinker and has reportedly been denied alcohol in prison. Some dissidents said they understood that he had given information to interrogators only after having been hospitalized twice for deprivation of alcohol.

### 'What Movement?'

So demoralized was one Soviet dissident by the latest developments that when he was asked about their impact on the dissident movement, he replied: "What movement?"

Mr. Sakharov, the physicist, has remarked privately that the situation has become worse for dissenters as Soviet relations have improved with Western nations, especially since the visit to Moscow last May of President Nixon. He contends that Soviet authorities now believe that Western public opinion is more concerned with improving relations and trade and will thus ignore police actions against Soviet civil-rights activists. Other dissidents share that view.

The one major exception to the general contraction of the dissident movement is Jewish emigration activity, which has had its periodic ups and downs at critical junctures of Soviet-American diplomacy but still maintains a sense of dynamism.

Dissenters also note that a number of other dissident activities continue. They cite the hunger strike staged by about 35 imprisoned dissidents from Dec. 5 to 10 for the anniversary of the signing of the Universal Declaration of Human Rights at the United Nations, and the silent, one-minute vigil in Pushkin Square here by 25 dissenters, including Mr. Sakharov, on Dec. 5 for the same occasion.

They also note that the Chronicle of Current Events has managed to come out four times this year despite a reported order by the Communist Party's Central Committee last Dec. 30 that it be suppressed by the secret police.

Nonetheless, a number of dissidents acknowledge that the cause of human rights now stirs much less interest among the Soviet scientific and cultural intelligentsia than in the period from 1966 to 1968. At that time, after the trials and conviction of the writers Andrei D. Sinyavsky and Yuli M. Daniel for publishing critical works abroad, hundreds of Soviet citizens signed petitions demanding their release from prison and criticizing the trials.

### More Jews Leaving

Even at its peak, however, the rights movement involved only a tiny group of activists who were generally unknown to the public or else vehemently criticized by the ordinary Soviet citizen.

Dissidents themselves cite a variety of reasons for the present defensive position of their movement.

Among the most prominently mentioned factors is the rise of the Jewish emigration movement. Dissidents say that it not only competes for the energies of activists and gives them one primary interest, but it also deprives the rights movement of the support of those who manage to get exit visas to Israel.

Moreover, the secret police have quietly allowed and even encouraged both Jewish and non-Jewish rights activists to emigrate, with threats of repression if they do not. Among the prominent activists who have left this year are Alexandr Yesenin-Volpin and Roman Rutman, both mathematicians; Yuri Titov, an artist, and his wife, Lena Stroiyeva, and Yuri Glazov, a specialist on Oriental culture.

Another important factor is the sense of despair and impotence among dissident intellectuals after their profusion of petitions and courtroom vigils failed to save Mr. Sinyavsky, Mr. Daniel and others tried in 1966, 1967 and 1968 from long prison sentences or exile to Siberia.

"People started saying, 'What's the point of risking our jobs or even arrest when it does no good?'" commented one active dissident. "They felt they had done all they could and still it had no impact."

Another suggested that in the middle and late sixties, a segment of the intelligensia was still fired by the hope raised in the Khrushchev era that liberalization lay ahead and that they had to help promote it. "They don't believe that any more," this man said. "Things have gotten steadily tougher, and no one believes in liberalization now."

Yet another factor is the relative inactivity of some earlier dissidents when they return from prison, long exiles or mental hospitals. People such as Mrs. Larisa Bogoraz-Daniel, Anatoly T. Marchenko, Aleksandr Ginzburg, Natalya Gorbanevskaya, Mr. Sinyavsky and Mr. Daniel are said to have returned chastened and determined to live private lives rather than resume dissident activities.

**K.G.B. Is Relentless**

But dissidents say that the major factor is relentless pressure shrewdly applied by the secret police, known as the K.G.B. for the initials in Russian. The sweeping methods of Stalinist repression are evidently being avoided in order not to arouse major protests abroad or reawaken domestic fears of a Stalinist purge and thus stimulate opposition, dissidents say.

The figures best known abroad remain active—Mr. Solzhenitsyn, Mr. Sakharov and the two brothers, Roy A. Medvedev, the historian, and Zhores A. Medvedev, the biologist.

Dissenters and Western diplomats believe that these men are protected by their prominence and by the Soviet authorities' fear that arrest of these men would prompt an outcry among Western politicians and intellectuals, including Communists, that could disturb the steady improvement in relations with the West.

The K.G.B. has reportedly been ordered to proceed selectively and in stages against less well-known dissidents.

The two primary targets have been the Ukrainian nationalist movement and the Action Group for Human Rights, which was led by Mr. Yakir and was evidently believed by the police to be largely responsible for the Chronicle of Current Events.

**4-Year or 5-Year Terms**

In the wave of arrests that began in the Ukraine last January, such prominent dissidents as Vyacheslav Chornovil, 34, a journalist; Ivan Svitlichny, 42, a literary critic, and Yevshen Svertsyuk, 43, a literary critic, have been held. At least a dozen persons, including Nina Strokatova, a microbiologist, and Oleksa Riznykiv, a writer, have been tried and sentenced to four or five years in labor camps for alleged "anti-Soviet agitation and propaganda."

In the K.G.B. effort to squelch the Chronicle, at least eight persons have been arrested and held this year and scores of others have been questioned, dissidents say.

In addition to Mr. Yakir, those arrested included Kronid Lyubarsky, 38, an astronomer; Yuri Shikhanovich, a mathematician, Viktor Krasin, an economist, all from Moscow; Yuri Melnik, a 26-year-old astrophysicist from Leningrad; Vatslav Sevruk, a philosopher from Vilnius; Leonid Pilyushch, a cybernetics specialist from Kiev, and Alexander Rybakov, a scientist from Novosibirsk.

Mr. Lyubarsky and Mr. Melnik have already been tried and sentenced to five years and three years respectively for anti-Soviet agitation. Mr. Sevruk has reportedly been ruled insane and detained in a mental hospital.

December 11, 1972

# *Soviet Said to Hold Million in Prison, Including 10,000 on Political Charges*

**By BERNARD GWERTZMAN**
Special to The New York Times

WASHINGTON, Jan. 10 — While Soviet authorities have drastically reduced the size of their prison population in the 20 years since Stalin's death, Western experts believe that more than a million Soviet citizens, including about 10,000 political prisoners, remain in captivity in a network of about 900 prisons and labor camps throughout the country.

Interest in the Soviet penal system has been raised by the publication of Aleksander I. Solzhenitsyn's latest book, "The Gulag Archipelego: 1918-1956," which discussed the system before the prison population was cut to about one million, a figure most Western experts believe has remained constant since the mid-fifties.

Mr. Solzhenitsyn estimated that the total population of Soviet prison camps did not at any time exceed 12 million, of whom half were probably so-called political prisoners. This peak is believed to have been reached just before Stalin's death in 1953. Mr Solzhenitsyn did not offer any over-all total of prison camp inmates for the period of roughly 40 years covered by his statistics.

The Central Intelligence Agency, through the use of satellite photographs, puts the current prison population at 2.4 million to 2.5 million, but State Department and outside experts such as Peter Reddaway, the British specialist on Soviet prisons, believe the number is closer to one million. Of these, according to the estimate of Mr. Reddaway, a senior lecturer at the London School of Economics, about 10,000 can be classed as political prisoners.

On a per-capita basis, this would mean that two and a half times as many Soviet citizens are in captivity as Americans. The United States has the largest prison population in the Western world, about 425,000.

Since the late nineteen-twenties, the Soviet Union has not released information about its crime rate or its prison system and little is known about the mass of ordinary prisoners. But much has been learned about the system in recent years through interviews with former inmates allowed to emigrate to Israel, the United States and other countries.

In addition, Mr. Reddaway and others have done extensive research on the system by carefully analyzing the many written accounts of the camps circulated in underground, typed form known as "samizdat," meaning "self-published."

The political-prisoner group includes intellectuals who have been arrested for circulating dissident documents regarded as anti-Soviet by authorities, those who seek to practice their religion outside the officially approved system of worship, and those who have engaged in activities in support of Soviet minorities.

**Most Go to Labor Camps**

Life in any penal system is grim, of course, but the Soviet system is unique in that almost all prisoners are assigned to labor camps. Only a small percentage spend their terms in prisons, such as the prison in Vladimir, a town northeast of Moscow that is known to tourists for its ancient churches.

Comments about the camps have varied, but in general most recent prisoners tend to agree that the quality of life depends primarily on the type of camp to which a person is assigned.

There are by Soviet law four basic types of camps.

The vast majority of prisoners are assigned to what are called "ordinary regime" camps.

The next grade of severity is known as "hardened regime," and the two most severe grades are called "strict regime," and "special regime." The last two are usually reserved for dangerous criminals or political prisoners.

**Data on All Types**

Many political prisoners, however, particularly first offenders, or those convicted of lesser violations, have served in the "ordinary" camps and as a result, political prisoners have been able to provide information about all types of camps.

These points seem to emerge:

¶Life is difficult in almost every type of camp, but most people survive and are released when their terms expire, something that rarely happened in the Stalin days.

¶As in Soviet society, if a prisoner does not engage in political activity critical of the regime, he is unlikely to suffer any additional penalty. But if he is outspoken in defense of his rights, or engages in the kind of free-thinking that led to his arrest—if he is a political prisoner—he is apt to endure harsh punishment, ranging from isolation in a narrow, dark dungeon, to physical abuse, and he loses such "privileges" as mail and visits.

¶Camps are not totally bleak places. Some former prisoners called the experience "meaningful" because of the opportunity it gave them for introspection. And in some respects, they said, life in prison was interesting because discussions could be held with a cross-section of society not readily available on the outside.

¶Many prisoners are not easily cowed in Soviet camps.

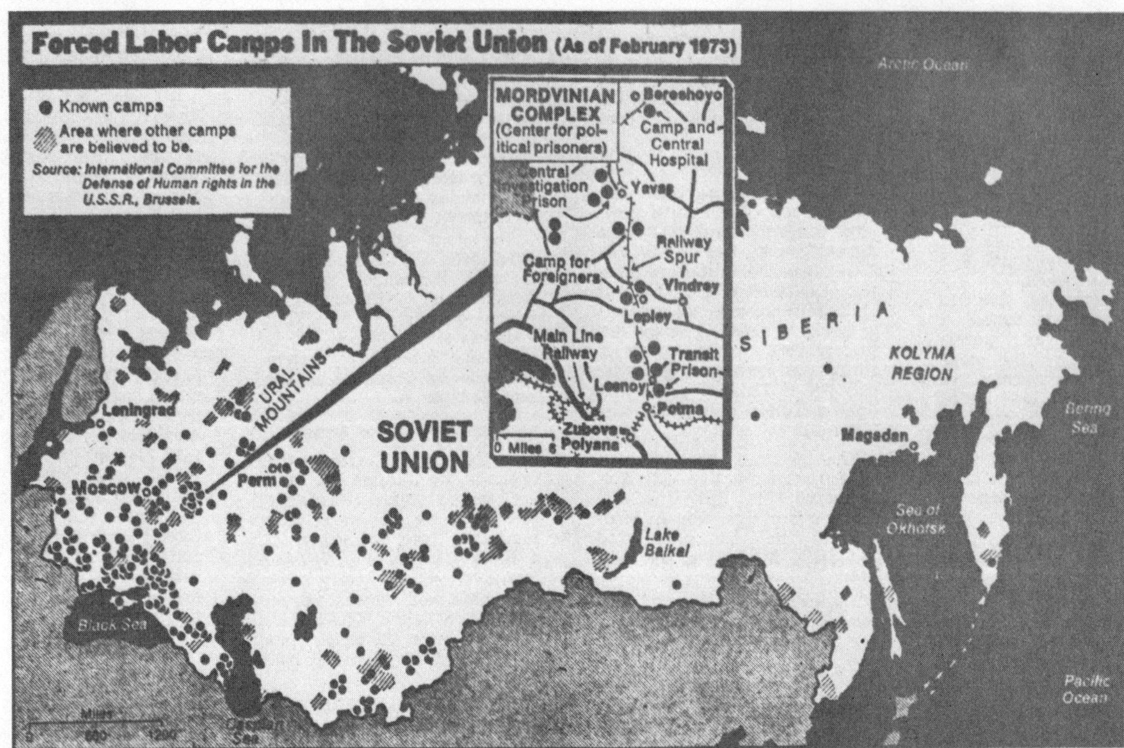


The New York Times/Jan. 13, 1974

Despite threats of punishment, many of them know their rights and when authorities deny them, these captives have engaged in hunger strikes that often have resulted in decisions in their favor. In fact, in the last two years, Moscow has instructed camps to tighten discipline, and in the "strict" regime camps, the bread ration, the mainstay of the diet, has been reduced to less than a pound a day.

**Secret Channels Used**

Prisoners have also been able to send out regular reports and protests through secret channels about camp conditions.

In 1969, for instance, seven political prisoners issued a clandestine statement that said, in part:

"Russia is still crisscrossed by a network of camps where—despite all the international conventions signed by the Soviet Government—forced labor and cruel exploitation are the norm, where people are systematically kept hungry and constantly humiliated, where their human dignity is debased.

"Through these camps passes an uninterrupted human flow, millions strong, which gives back to society physically and morally crippled people. This is the result of a deliberate penal policy, worked out by experts and presented by them in special handbooks with a cynicism worthy of the concentration-camp experts of the Third Reich."

A report by Mr. Reddaway for the International Committee for the Defense of Human Rights in the U.S.S.R. in Brussels last year, said that "the worst single aspect of the conditions in Soviet camps, especially those of strict and special regime, is the constant hunger, which torments and even tortures the prisoners, often for years on end."

**Appeal Smuggled Abroad**

He quoted from the appeal of Yuri Galanskov, a young man arrested in 1967 for having edited an underground journal called Phoenix. He died in 1972 on an operating table in a camp hospital. In that year, Mr. Galanskov had sent the following smuggled appeal to the International Committee of the Red Cross and the United Nations Commission on Human Rights:

"I am ill with a stomach ulcer. Of the food I receive I can eat only a small part, and so every day I undereat. At the same time, in the conditions of a strict-regime camp I am effectively deprived of any real possibility of obtaining from my friends and relatives the food products I need. At night I have terrible pains, and so every day I get too little sleep. I have been undereating and getting too little sleep for five years now. And yet I work eight hours a day. Every day is a torment for me, a daily struggle against pain and illness."

Mr. Galanskov's death at the age of 33 was, however, an exception, Mr. Reddaway believes.

Mr. Reddaway, in an interview in New York where he is spending the academic year at Columbia University, said that although several other political prisoners had died in camps, he believed that Soviet authorities did not as a policy seek the death of prisoners. Rather, "keeping people feeling hungry is part of the punishment," he said.

Anatoly Marchenko, who wrote a book smuggled to the West called "My Testimony" about his experience in camps in the nineteen-sixties, said, "The usual rations are such as to make a person feel perpetual want of food, perpetual malnutrition."

**Woman Describes Diet**

"The daily camp ration — under the strict regime — contains 2,400 calories (enough for a 7- to 11-year-old child) and has to suffice for an adult doing physical labor, day after day for many years, sometimes as many as 15 to 25," he wrote. "The convicts never even set eyes on fresh vegetables, butter and many other indispensible products."

Raiza Palatnik, a Jewish activist in Odessa, was sentenced in 1971 to two years' confinement in an "ordinary regime" camp for allegedly spreading slander about the Soviet state and social system. She emigrated to Israel last year and gave the following description, in answer to a questionnaire, of the daily camp diet in her less severe regime:

"They fed us three times a day. In the morning, a thin soup of gruel, rotten fish and tea with three-quarters of an ounce of sugar. In the evening, the same, only without sugar. The main meal at lunchtime was cabbage soup made from water and bones. The second course at lunch was oatmeal or sometimes a small potato with vegetables. A little more than a pound of bread was distributed daily."

Miss Palatnik said she lived with 23 other women in a room with a floor space of 200 square feet.

In the camp barracks, she said, prisoners slept in two-decker bunks. For mattresses they were given "a dirty ripped sack" that they filled with stuffing. She said an "old" blanket, two sheets and two pillow cases were also handed out, and were expected to be used for as long as a person was in the camp.

"You washed them yourself," she said. "There was no laundry. They give you household soap, about eight ounces a month. It was necessary to buy a toothbrush and comb in the camp store."

"In every barracks, there was a stove, for which they provided 22 pounds of coal and 2 pounds of wood a day," she said. "In general, there were no sanitary conditions to speak of. Often there was no water to wash with after work. In the morning, no one had time to wash. There was one washstand for 120 people where six to seven people could stand at once. They gave you a bath once every 10 days for a half hour. They gave you hot water for laundry once in 10 days."

"Lice were prevalent. The whole time I was in the camp,

there was rampant dysentery," she added.

She said that prisoners could "receive an unlimited number of letters, but a great number of mine were confiscated."

"It was possible to receive a package once every three months, up to a weight of 11 pounds," she said. "A four-hour meeting with friends or relatives was allowed every fourth month. A meeting with a close relative, such as a wife or husband, was permitted once every six months and could last up to three days."

Mr. Reddaway says that the Soviet authorities allow prisoners to have conjugal relations during those meetings, but often use the deprivation of that privilege as a form of punishment.

**Hour a Day Outdoors**

In the camp, Miss Palatnik says, she worked eight hours in a prison clothing factory, and then had the rest of the time free to sleep, walk around, read and write. She said inmates were confined for 23 hours a day and were allowed only one hour outdoors.

For amusement, Miss Palatnik said, prisoners could play chess or checkers. There was a camp library with Soviet books and newspapers. Prisoners were not allowed radios or television sets, but each barracks had a loudspeaker that broadcast the main Moscow radio program. She added that there were concerts by local prisoners and a movie every Sunday.

Once a week, there was a political lecture of about two hours, but she paid no attention to it.

Another former prisoner, Anatoly V. Radygin, said in a questionnaire that political discussions went on constantly "between prisoners of different ideological persuasion, and between prisoners and the camp administration."

"Political study lectures took place weekly, and officially were regarded as voluntary," he said. "The great majority of the prisoners, tired of permanant repression, preferred to sit passively through the lectures, passively listening to the endless portion of demagogy and lies."

**Psychological Maneuvering**

"A minority, much more profound, preferred to avoid the political lectures in general, and as a result were brutally punished," he said. "Others were interested in attacking the lecturers," he said, including himself in this group. They sought a "political dispute, trying by logic and facts to push the lecturer into a corner," he said.

For her work, Miss Palatnik received an average of 60 to 65 rubles (about $75) a month. Half of that went to cover the upkeep of the camp. She had to pay about 15 rubles for her food.

If a prisoner made a legal appeal, he had to pay costs. Any money left over could be spent at the camp store, up to 7 rubles a month, to buy food to supplement the diet.

When released, she was given 108 rubles that she had not yet spent.

Miss Palatnik's experiences at her camp, No. 308/34 in the city of Dneprodzerzhinsk in the Ukraine, were considerably milder than the experiences of some prisoners, particularly those in the complexes situated in the Mordvinian region, in the Volga Hills area of the Russian Republic, where the majority of political prisoners are now sent. An increasing number of political prisoners, however, are now being assigned to the Perm area in the Ural Mountains.

For some released prisoners, the days in camp apparently became a sort of mystical experience because they used the time to examine their views on life and to exchange profound ideas with fellow inmates.

Yuri L. Gendler, who recently emigrated to the United States, remarked in an interview over Radio Liberty, "I must say directly that the camp period of my life was exceptionally interesting, difficult and important."

"It was, perhaps, the most significant experience acquired in my life," he said. "Of course, I am far from idealizing the camp and in no way advertising the "sunny resorts" of Mordvinia. My term—three years—by Soviet standards was short. Beside the spiritual suffering connected with confinement, many experienced physical suffering, because of illness, particularly stomach ailments."

But Mr. Gendler said that despite the drawbacks to camp life, he never before had had "such a possibility" to reexamine himself.

**Philosophical Discussions**

He said that in addition to real criminals, his camp housed "intelligent people, who held completely different views and in meetings with them I was able better to understand and state my own position."

He said that in such meetings, which usually took place in small groups on Sundays, "some specialist from a rather specific field would give a report, for instance on the philosophy of Berdyayev, about the philosophy of Leontyev, about artistry of Dostoyevsky, about the creativity of Gogol."

"I often talked about the novels of Solzhenitsyn, which I had read on my own and understood well," he said.

"The majority of those in the camp did not know the new works of Solzhenitsyn," he said. He had read them prior to his arrest.

"We discussed such themes as the reasons for the drop in morals and morality among the youth of East and West," he said.

"Many of us undertook a very serious self-education," he continued. "For instance, I learned the English language in the camp, after studying the language quite hard. In the camp, there were those who knew English well and had lived for some time in the United States. They helped me very much in mastering the language."

**Prisoners Gave Talks**

Mr. Gendler said that in late 1969, "each of us prepared a talk on the theme, the most important three events which in your opinion took place in the past decade."

"Each of us spoke on three themes and argued why those events were so important," he said. "And of course, after all the speeches, endless arguments began, which lasted into the early morning, sometimes spilling over into the next day."

The camps are run by the Ministry of Internal Affairs, with the subdivision for prisons known as the "Main Directorate for Places of Confinement." It is known by the Russian initials as "GUMZ." In Stalin's time, the title was "Main Directorate for Camps," known by the initials, "GULAG," as in the title of Mr. Solzhenitsyn's book.

**300 Addresses Compiled**

Mr. Reddaway said that he believed there were about 900 camps and that he had compiled about 300 addresses so far. The exact sites have been publicized by those who were released or by the relatives of prisoners.

A major source of information about camps has been provided by the schismatic wing of the Baptist organization in the Soviet Union, which has not agreed to Soviet authority. At any time, several hundred Baptists are in confinement. They usually are not harassed by other prisoners, Mr. Raddaway said, because their dedication to work is respected.

Jewish organizations in the United States report that many of the Jews who have been imprisoned have complained about anti-Semitism in camps, on the part of other prisoners and some camp administrators as well. Baptists have also been subject to punishment from camp officials.

January 13, 1974

# Solzhenitsyn Exiled to West Germany And Stripped of His Soviet Citizenship

By HEDRICK SMITH
Special to The New York Times

MOSCOW, Feb. 13 — The Soviet Union deported Aleksandr I. Solzhenitsyn to West Germany today and issued a decree stripping him of his citizenship for "performing systematically actions that are incompatible with being a citizen."

The action against the Nobel Prize author was the first forced expulsion of a major political dissident since 1929, when Stalin ordered Leon Trotsky exiled to Turkey.

After Mr. Solzhenitsyn telephoned his wife from West Germany to report his safe arrival, Mrs. Solzhenitsyn told newsmen that she and their three sons would join him in exile. "We intend to follow him, certainly, but where, when —we just don't know."

**Family May Join Him**

Tass, the Soviet press agency, said, "Solzhenitsyn's family can join him when they deem it necessary."

Semi-official Soviet sources reported that Mr. Solzhenitsyn, who had always vowed that he would never leave the Soviet Union of his own free will, had agreed to accept exile after meeting with state prosecutors following his arrest last night.

But the 55-year-old author himself, when telephoned by the Moscow bureau of The New York Times, said in Germany that the deportation decree had been shown him only this morning and had been "completely unexpected." He said eight Government aides had accompanied him on the flight to Germany.

"Yesterday they presented me with a grave accusation and today, very unexpectedly, they show me the decree that I was being exiled to Germany," he said. He declined to go into details.

**He Seems in Good Spirits**

Speaking from the country home of the German author Heinrich Böll, he sounded in good spirits and seemed relieved that his fate had been exile rather than criminal prosecution on a major charge and another long imprisonment. He served 11 years in Stalinist camps and in banishment in remote areas of the Soviet Union for having made critical remarks about Stalin during World War II.

His swift and dramatic banishment today, in near total secrecy, dealt a crushing blow to Soviet dissidents and stunned his family.

Diplomats speculated that it would result in a setback to the Soviet policy of improved relations with the West, though not as bad a one as if the Kremlin had decided to put him on trial for publishing his huge new work on the Soviet prison system, "The Gulag Archipelago, 1918-1956."

Only a sketchy picture emerged of the writer's 24 hours in detention after seven police officials burst into his family's apartment and arrested him forcibly. They took him to the Lefortovo secret police prison, and then eight other officials placed him aboard a regularly scheduled Aeroflot TU-154 airliner bound for Frankfurt today. The plane was four hours late taking off, presumably because of complications involved in the Solzhenitsyn deportation, most airport workers and foreign-airline representatives at Moscow's SheremetyevoAir port were unaware that anything unusual was happening.

Even before take-off, a West German Government spokesman announced that the Germans had been informed by the Soviet Government that Mr. Solzhenitsyn was headed for their country. The spokesman disclosed that West Germany was prepared to receive him.

When the Soviet airliner landed after its two-and-one-half-hour flight from Moscow, West German authorities were awaiting Mr. Solzhenitsyn. They sealed off the airport to newsmen and he was whisked off to the country home of his friend, Heinrich Böll, at Langenbroich, not far from Cologne.

In his telephone conversation with The New York Times, Mr. Solzhenitsyn said:

"I've just arrived at Böll's house in the last couple of minutes." It was then shortly after 9 P.M., Moscow time (2 P.M., New York time). "I'm very tired. I want to call my wife. Have you seen my family today? How many hours ago? How are they?"

When told that his wife and sons were safe and in good health, he was relieved. But he was surprised to hear that his wife had seemed disappointed at the news of his exile. "Disappointed?" he asked. But he declined to discuss his own emotions.

After his arrival, Tass distributed a 66-word news item—later read over Soviet radio and television — reporting that the Presidium of the Supreme Soviet had revoked Mr. Solzhenitsyn's citizenship and ordered him exiled.

West German Embassy officials, who reported that they had known nothing of the deportation move in advance, said that it would be no problem for the author's wife and sons to obtain West German entry visas.

February 14, 1974

# Sakharov Named Winner Of '75 Nobel Peace Prize

## Physicist Incurred Wrath of Soviet by Fighting for Civil Liberties

By Reuters

OSLO, Norway, Oct. 9— Andrei D. Sakharov, the father of the Soviet hydrogen bomb, who incurred governmental wrath by becoming the Soviet Union's most outspoken proponent of civil liberties, won the Nobel Peace Prize today.

The decision by the Nobel committee of the Norwegian Parliament was seen as a test of the Soviet Union's sincerity in fulfilling the spirit of the Helsinki agreement on European cooperation and security, which acknowledged the importance of the respect by all nations for human rights and fundamental freedoms.

"Andrei Dimitriyevich Sakharov has addressed his message of peace and justice to all peoples of the world," the committee said in an unusually detailed citation explaining its reasons for choosing him for the 1975 award.

"For him it is a fundamental principle that world peace can have no lasting value unless it is founded on respect for the individual human being in society."

The grey-haired, 54-year-old Dr. Sakharov is the first Soviet citizen to win a Nobel Peace Prize.

Observers here said that Dr. Sakharov would probably not come to Oslo to receive his Peace Prize on Dec. 10, the anniversary of the death of Alfred Nobel, the Swedish inventor of dynamite.

Two Soviet winners of the Nobel Prize for literature, Boris L. Pasternak and Aleksandr I. Solzhenitsyn, decided against going to receive their awards for fear that they would not be allowed back into their country from Sweden. The literature prize is presented in Stockholm.

Pasternak, who wrote "Dr. Zhivago," died in the Soviet Union two years after winning the award in 1958. Solzhenitsyn, winner in 1970, was eventually forced to leave the Soviet Union and now lives in Switzerland.

The five member committee chose Dr. Sakharov for the $140,000 award from about 50 candidates, including President Urho Kekkonen of Finland, whose candidacy was reported to have been championed by the Soviet Union.

Others said to have been considered were Mother Theresa, leader of the Mission of Charity in Calcutta, India, and the Rev. Luis Maria Xirinachs, a Spanish priest who was released this week from a Madrid prison after having served a two-year term for distributing illegal propaganda in his nonviolent campaign for the restoration of civil rights.

Also reported mentioned were the International Press Institute and the International Boy Scout and Girl Scout organizations.

In its citation the committee said: "Uncompromisingly and forcefully, Sakharov has fought not only against the abuse of power and violations of human dignity in all its forms, but he has with equal vigor fought for the ideal of a state founded on the principle of justice for all.

"In a convincing fashion Sakharov has emphasized that the inviolable rights of man can serve as the only sure foundation for a genuine and long-lasting system of international cooperation.

"In this manner he has succeeded very effectively, and under trying conditions, in reinforcing respect for such values as all true friends of peace are anxious to support."

**Position of Defiance**

The soft-spoken Dr. Sakharov, a bespectacled man with thinning hair and a stoop, turned his back on a scientific career showered with honors to speak out against what he believed to be wrong with Soviet society. His world reputation seemingly protected his position of defiance.

Dr. Sakharov has urged the abolition of the Soviet practice of confining political dissidents to psychiatric hospitals; creation of an ombudsman to guard against prison excesses; amnesties for political prisoners; greater freedom of information, and the right of Soviet citizens to travel abroad.

In 1968 he captured the imagination of the West with a 10,000-word essay titled "Progress, Coexistence and Intellectual Freedom." In it he urged Soviet-American cooperation to solve the world's problems and spoke out against nuclear war, hunger, overpopulation and pollution.

"Andrei Sakharov is a firm believer in the brotherhood of man, in genuine coexistence, as the only way to save mankind," the Nobel committee declared.

"Sakharov has warned against the dangers connected with a bogus détente, based on wishful thinking and illusions. As a nuclear physicist he has, with his special insight and sense of responsibility, been able to speak out against the dangers inherent in the armaments race between states," it added.

The citation said Dr. Sakharov's fundamental belief in universal respect for the human being had found expression in several international declarations such as agreements signed this year by 35 states at the security conference in Helsinki. It added:

"The parties acknowledged that the respect for human rights and fundamental freedoms is an important factor in the cause of peace, justice and well-being which is essential to insure the development of friendly relations and cooperation not only among themelves but among all the countries of the world.

"In more forceful terms than others Andrei Sakharov has warned us against not taking this seriously, and he has placed himself in the vanguard of efforts to make the ideals expressed in this paragraph of the Helsinki agreement a living reality.

"Saharov's love of truth and strong belief in the inviolability of the human being, his fight against violence and brutality, his courageous defense of the freedom of the spirit, his unselfishness and strong humanitarian convictions have turned him into the spokesman for the conscience of mankind, which the world so sorely needs today."

Last year the Peace Prize was shared by Sean McBride, the former Foreign Minister of Ireland, and Eisaku Sato, the former Japanese Premier, who died this June.

October 10, 1975

# Soviet Pays in Defections for Conformity

By DAVID K. SHIPLER

MOSCOW—Bobby Fischer never would have made it as a chess player in the Soviet Union. He is just the kind of person that Soviet officialdom cannot tolerate: temperamental, idiosyncratic, arrogant, impudent. Hardly the type to blend smoothly into the collective. Were he Russian instead of American, his bad manners would probably have kept him out of tournaments long before his talents could have been discovered.

This may seem odd for a country with a compulsion to excel at everything from space shots to water polo. But it is an anomaly of Soviet society that, while devoting great resources to cultivating and pampering star athletes, dancers and musicians, the Government is also willing to cast aside fine talent for the sake of political, artistic and behavioral control.

The result has been a flow of Soviet artists and intellectuals to the West through defection, emigration or forced exile. The latest in the series was the chess star, Viktor Korchnoi, who asked for asylum in Amsterdam during a tournament there last week.

Mr. Korchnoi is no Bobby Fischer, but he has been too impulsive and outspoken for Moscow's taste. He has not spelled out clearly his reasons for defecting, but he was reported to be fearful that because of his friction with officials, he would not be allowed to travel abroad again.

Foreign travel is one of the main rewards the Soviet Government bestows on compliant citizens, and withholding the right constitutes a severe punishment for people who thrive on international contacts. This is true not only for chess masters whose medium is international play, but also for painters, sculptors and dancers who often feel starved by the conservative cultural controls in their own country and who need at times to dip into the main currents of artistic innovation in the West.

Such was the case of the sculptor, Ernst Neizvestny, whose work was denounced with an expletive by Nikita Khrushchev in 1962, but who then gained Mr. Khrushchev's admiration by arguing back. Mr. Neizvestny counted 50 occasions on which Soviet authorities rejected his applications to visit abroad in response to professional invitations. His most interesting work never received sanction here; officials tried unsuccessfully to throw him out of his workshop last fall. In April, he emigrated to Israel.

Famous dancers such as Rudolf Nureyev, Natalya Makarova, Mikhail Baryshnikov and Keleriya Fedicheva have described their defections and emigrations to the West as motivated by a desire to escape the artistically stifling atmosphere surrounding dance in Russia. In an interview after arriving in New York last year, Miss Fedicheva indicated that she wanted to dance in modern, Western-style ballets. "We are suffocating from constant management of our minds," she said of the Kirov Ballet Company in Leningrad, where she had danced. "There are gray people who are in charge."

Similarly, Mstislav Rostropovich, the cellist, left the Soviet Union in 1974 and has vowed not to return until artistic freedom is fully restored.

That seems unlikely. As acutely embarrassing as the Kremlin must find the defections, its obsession with control remains paramount. Through history, some of the main upheavals of Soviet society have occurred in periods of disorder, and there is no indication that this Government is at all tempted to relax its centralized authority over all aspects of life just to woo a few talented people.

If anything, the opposite is the case. Prominent, highly-skilled Jewish scientists, sometimes the heads of prestigious scientific research institutes, have suddenly found themselves demoted or jobless after applying for emigration. Many have been sitting for years without work, their skills of no use to the state, apparently as examples to others who might consider following them.

The Soviet people are usually not told by their official press about prominent figures who emigrate or defect, although ordinary Russians who hear the news by foreign radio or word of mouth often react less with envy than with contempt. When Jewish emigration became a major issue here a couple of years ago, the papers carried letters calling for free emigration only with the supreme punishment: that those who leave should never be allowed to return. In this intensely nationalistic country, those who choose to leave the motherland are frequently dismissed as slightly demented, doomed to spiritual drought abroad.

They are also sometimes regarded as greedy and out for personal gain, traits anathema to Soviet ethics, which dictate that in a sense, personal skills are the property of the entire community represented by the state, and personal ambitions must first serve the community's interests, not the individual's.

It is a principle that is not upheld consistently, but the official press is always quick to attack athletes, writers, dancers and others who show signs of becoming infatuated with their stardom. This was the thrust of the Tass attack on Mr. Korchnoi after he defected, although the attack was distributed only abroad, not inside the Soviet Union.

The distaste for personal ambition is so profoundly imbedded in Soviet values that there is even a proverb that describes it, referring to a field of wheat: "Only an empty ear sticks up."

*David K. Shipler is a correspondent for The New York Times, based in Moscow.*

August 1, 1976

# Soviet Defends Drive on Dissidents And Alleges West Is Abetting Them

## Pravda Editorial Concedes Some Pre-Communist Moral Values Still Survive Among Citizens

By DAVID K. SHIPLER
Special to The New York Times

MOSCOW, Feb. 12—The Soviet Union today published a defense of its campaign against dissidents, denouncing them as pawns in a coordinated Western assault on détente and Communism.

The arguments, contained in an editorial in the Communist newspaper Pravda, formed a comprehensive response to the Carter Administration's expressions of concern about observance of human rights in the Soviet Union. Without mentioning the President by name and with only a fleeting gibe at the State Department, the editorial seemed to convey a sense of growing annoyance at the continued debate over the issue.

"These unconcealed enemies of socialism," Pravda said of the dissidents, "are just a handful of individuals who do not represent anyone or anything and are far removed from the Soviet people. What is more, they exist only because they are supported, paid and praised by the West."

In the last 10 days the Soviet authorities have arrested three prominent dissidents: Yuri F. Orlov, a physicist who heads a Moscow group monitoring Soviet compliance with the 1975 Helsinki accords; Mikola Rudenko, a poet who heads a similar group in Kiev, in the Ukraine, and Aleksandr I. Ginzburg, who has been assisting families of political prisoners with money provided by Aleksandr I. Solzhenitsyn, the exiled writer.

The treatment of rights activists has brought expressions of concern from the State Department and from President Carter, who pledged during his campaign that he would make the protection of human rights around the world a theme of his foreign policy.

Pravda provided a partial sketch of the reasons for the crackdown.

"It goes without saying that the little heap of renegades presents no danger to the Soviet system," the editorial said. "But the very fact of its existence shows that remnants of the morals and prejudices of the old society have not been completely eradicated from our life and that individual Soviet citizens still take the bait of bourgeois propaganda, allowing themselves to be dazzled by the tinsel of the bourgeois way of life and to be deceived by fairy tales about the rights and freedoms of people in the capitalist world.

"Therefore it is necessary, as never before, to display a high degree of political vigilance, to give a timely and effective rebuff to bourgeois propaganda, to fight tirelessly against the political indifference and the lack of ideals that still exist in our midst, and to indoctrinate the Soviet people in the spirit of love for the motherland and of loyalty to the cause of the party and lofty Communist ideals."

### Ideological Apathy a Problem

Despite the offhand dismissal of the dissidents as a "heap of renegades," the editorial seemed to suggest some concern that the growing momentum of the small movement might feed on a more widespread absence of ideological commitment and find sympathetic response among broader segments of the population.

The Soviet press has always reacted sensitively to images of American freedom and abundance, and this has been so particularly during the antidissident drive. Pravda recently published an article describing the United States as a land of police surveillance and political arrests. Another article, by the Soviet press agency Tass, said:

"Permanent spying and wiretapping have become everyday practices. Before making a telephone call, an American must now consider that his conversation will be recorded by special secret services."

Today's Pravda editorial offered a Soviet definition of human rights.

"Historical experience has shown that such rights can be insured only by the socialist system," it said. "The right to work, the right to education, to social security, the right to elect and to be elected to government and administrative bodies at all levels, the right to criticize and control the performance of such bodies, the right to participate in discussions and in decision-making, including decisions on matters of national importance—this is our socialist democracy in action."

The editorial contended that Western supporters of dissent were engaged in "a carefully planned and coordinated act of sabotage" against the Soviet Union and the East European countries. They are enemites of détente, Pravda said, attempting to increase tension and weaken the positions of the Communist countries, distract attention from the crises of capitalism and undermine "progressive" forces in the West.

February 13, 1977

# Soviet Dissident Movement Is at Low Ebb

By DAVID K. SHIPLER
Special to The New York Times

MOSCOW, Dec. 27—The small Soviet human-rights movement, which has attracted so much attention around the world though it is probably unrepresentative of any broadly held opinion, is at its lowest point in years after a campaign of arrests, threats and forced exile directed against most of its prominent leaders. Its momentum has been curbed, its political dexterity undermined and its communications network in the Soviet Union badly disrupted.

Yet new people have joined almost as fast as the old have disappeared. Inexperienced for the most part and less dynamic organizers than the previous generation, they have positions of less stature in this supremely status-conscious society, so they may be somewhat less able to generate respect than their predecessors.

### 'Fewer of Us Remain'

But the unending appearance of new names on open letters and of new faces at press conferences supports the dissidents' contention that the movement cannot be pronounced dead. At worst, they predict, it will experience a pause, a lull, a period of somewhat less coordinated activity as a new community of dissent takes shape.

"One part of the movement has gone to the West, another to the east, and fewer of us remain," said Naum Neiman, a mathematics professor, referring to the emigration and the imprisonment that have sapped the front ranks of the activists. "The movement will continue, though, at a higher or lower level. It cannot stop."

Some think Soviet dissent has become "inevitable, a kind of natural phenomenon," in the words of the Yugoslav dissident Milovan Djilas. In part it is a continuing reaction to the latent neo-Stalinism that lurks in this society and to the Stalinist oppression that was suddenly exposed in 1956 by Nikita S. Khrushchev in a secret speech to a Communist Party congress that swept away a patina of falsehood and illusion and allowed the truth to be told.

It is driven also by personal imperatives. "This act is forced on you because you are just trying to keep yourself decent," said Valentin F. Turchin, former head of the Moscow branch of Amnesty International, before he was harassed into emigrating last fall. "I consider myself a scientist mostly and not a political activist. I don't enjoy press conferences—they're not for me. But in this country if you try to behave decently you become a dissident."

### A Question of Importance

How important the dissidents are in political life is subject to debate. Small and unrepresentative though they may be, they act as a pressure point for foreign views of Soviet behavior—views of both

Western governments and some European Communists—and as such they subject the Kremlin's domestic policies to close international scrutiny.

Furthermore, they often elicit expressions of sympathy and regard from other Russians, suggesting that their crusade may have some resonance at home. After Andrei D. Sakharov, the physicist and human-rights advocate, won the Nobel Peace Prize in 1975, an elderly cleaning woman told her Russian employer, "You know, they wanted to raise the price of vodka but Sakharov would not let them." Others have heard the same thing from cab drivers.

After Veniamin G. Levich, a high-ranking physical chemist, was denounced in the press last summer for laziness and anti-Soviet slander because he wanted to emigrate to Israel, a saleswoman in a food store appeared at his apartment with some vobla, a hard-to-get dried and salted fish that she knew he liked. "We read the article," he quoted her as saying. "We were indignant. We know it's all a lie, so please eat some vobla and don't be sad."

### Novelty in Russian History

The phenomenon of open dissent outside the circles of power is relatively new in Russian history, at least in its present form, and a contrast with the clandestine, conspiratorial activity that existed at times under the czars. Even the modicum of debate that was tolerated in the Communist Party during the first years after the Bolshevik Revolution was snuffed out by Stalin's terror and has been kept from re-emerging in the quarter of a century since the dictator's death.

Not until the mid-1960's, near the end of a brief, tentative trend toward liberalization, did the human-rights movement as it is now known spring up. At first it was little more than an assortment of Moscow intellectuals demonstrating and petitioning on behalf of the writers Andrei Sinyavsky and Yuli Daniel, who were tried in February 1966 and convicted of slander against the state.

The writers' supporters made contact with the Western press at the trial, when reporters and sympathizers stood outside the courtroom waiting for news. At first, according to one account, the Russians and the Westerners kept to themselves; then one or two Russians approached American and British correspondents. The information the dissidents provided, sent to the West by news agencies, came pouring back in Russian on broadcasts by the Voice of America and the British Broadcasting Corporation. The newborn dissidents' heady sensation of having their words suddenly amplified so their countrymen could hear began a chain of communication and reinforcement that has persisted despite the repeated efforts of authorities to break it.

### The Pattern for a Decade

Those early months set the pattern for a decade. As intellectuals pleaded for public trial and for compliance with the rights set forth in the Soviet Constitution and as they conveyed reports of injustices in the courts, some were arrested in turn, with those arrests provoking new protests and still more arrests. This produced a rights movement with a constantly changing cast, one almost wholly concerned with ad hoc statements on specific cases rather than proposals for fundamental change or visions of a new political order.

When there has been philosophical discussion it has tended to divide the dissidents by accentuating their differences, for the movement is really a set of parallel, disparate streams that flow together occasionally, then move apart again. At least six such currents can be identified.

The most Western-oriented is that represented by Dr. Sakharov. He and those around him are known here as democrats, for although he has written that he is a socialist, he has advocated the evolution of a multiparty, democratic state tolerant of criticism and diverse opinion. He has also spoken for the right of all to live where they wish, thereby supporting the second large group of dissidents and the one receiving the most vocal defense in the United States: Jews striving to emigrate. (Although some conflict has existed between those who want to leave and those who want to stay and change the system, it has diminished recently in recognition of the impact that free emigration would probably have on making the authorities more responsive to citizens' concerns.)

The third strain of dissent is a form of Russian nationalism, or nostalgia for the roots of Russianness to be found in the Russian Orthodox Church, in the village, in czarism. Its most prominent representative was Aleksandr I. Solzhenitsyn, another Nobel laureate, whose first volume on the Stalinist labor camps, "The Gulag Archipelago," resulted in his expulsion in 1974. Among those left behind are some who see Marxism as an alien, un-Russian ideology and some whose views contain overtones of racism, Russian supremacy in the Soviet Union and anti-Semitism.

### Keeping the Party Pre-eminent

The historian Roy A. Medvedev articulates the fourth line of dissent, the one that might conceivably appeal to some party members, though how many is impossible to say. As described in his book, "On Socialist Democracy," his formula is democratization within the bounds of Communist Party pre-eminence. He believes that free debate is essential rather than anathema to an efficient economy and a robust Communist ideology.

Religious observers make up a fifth tendency. Baptists, Seventh-day Adventists, Pentecostalists, Lithuanian Roman Catholics, Russian Orthodox and others have protested the denial of religious freedom, published undergound journals and the like, usually separately.

Finally, the country is laced with ethnic minorities, such nationalities as Georgians, Lithuanians, Ukrainians and Tatars that struggle for the preservation of their cultures, languages and traditions in the face of Russian dominance.

What began to happen a year and a half ago, and what apparently provoked one of the most carefully executed crackdowns on dissidents in the last decade, was an unprecedented coalition, including democrats, Jews seeking emigration, ethnic nationalists and, to a lesser extent, religious believers.

### The Catalyst in Helsinki

The catalyst was the European security document signed at Helsinki in August 1975 by the United States, the Soviet Union and 33 European states. Its so-called Basket Three provisions called for more humanitarian behavior by governments: reunification of families across frontiers, increased contact among peoples, the improved flow of information internationally. The pact having created common ground for the dissidents, nine activists formed a group in May 1976 to monitor Soviet compliance. Similar "Helsinki watch committees" appeared in Kiev, Tbilisi, Yerevan and Vilnius, and all began issuing periodic reports on violations.

The pace of dissident activity quickened. A broad array of Protestant, Catholic and Orthodox clergy and laymen joined in an open letter to the Soviet leaders pleading for religious freedom. Jews, all wearing bright yellow stars of David, assembled at the reception room of the Supreme Soviet—the legislature—in Moscow to push their demand for emigration, then walked along Karl Marx Prospekt to the offices of the Central Committee of the Communist Party. Other Jews planned a seminar on Judaic culture. Painters formed a group to protest artistic oppression. Activists organized to publicize the use of psychiatric institutions as detention centers.

Yuri F. Orlov, a toughly built physicist who headed the Moscow watch committee, undertook to establish links between the strands of dissent. He introduced Georgian nationalists to Jewish activists in Tbilisi and democrats to religionists in Moscow. Zealous and tireless, he brought the movement a political canniness that Dr. Sakharov, a more academic moralist, did not possess.

At the same time new dissent was emerging in Eastern Europe, long a point of acute sensitivity among Soviet officials on the problems of orthodoxy and control. In Poland workers rioted to protest announced price rises, which the Government was forced to rescind. In Czechoslovakia and Hungary intellectuals signed statements against oppression and in East Germany the number of applications for emigration to the West soared.

The ferment in Eastern Europe must have been worrisome to Moscow, especially as its leadership of the world Communist movement was coming under fresh challenge by West European Communists, particularly the Italian, Spanish and French parties. A centerpiece of this independently minded movement, which came to be known as Eurocommunism, was rejection of the Soviet-style closed political system.

The foundation for a crackdown was laid, then, by the accelerated dissident activity, the growing unification of previously fragmented elements of disaffection, the persistent problems of the Soviet economy and the danger of a coalition between spokesmen for workers' grievances and human-rights activists—plus the centrifugal tendencies in European Communism.

Furthermore, the Russians were apparently distressed at the specter of dissident groups putting out regular statements during the Belgrade follow-up meeting on the Helsinki pacts and they presumably did not want disharmony at the celebrations of the 60th anniversary of the Bolshevik Revolution.

The campaign by the K.G.B., the secret and security police, began in the fall of 1976 when a dozen Jews were seized in the Supreme Soviet's reception area, bused to the outskirts and beaten by plainclothesmen. Jews planning a cultural seminar were subjected to house searches, confiscation of materials and detention. Activists were called in repeatedly for interrogation, told that the K.G.B. had been given more latitude to move against them and warned that criminal cases were being prepared. In January 1977, before Jimmy Carter came into office with his outspokenness on human rights, Mr. Orlov, the head of the Moscow watch committee, was picked up and told that he and others would be prosecuted.

The K.G.B. used a blend of toughness and softness to get rid of key dissidents.

Some who had tried for years to emigrate, such as Vitaly Rubin, a Sinologist and a founding member of the Moscow committee, and Veniamin Fain, chief organizer of the abortive cultural seminar, suddenly found themselves with exit visas.

Some who did not want to leave were threatened and forced to emigrate. The Amnesty International head, Mr. Turchin, a friend of Dr. Sakharov, was informed by the K.G.B. official that he would never work again as a mathematician in the Soviet Union and he was led to believe that he would be arrested if he stayed. Similarly, Tatyana Khodorovich was told to leave or face prosecution, and Dina Kaminskaya, a lawyer who defended many activists, was forced out by threats of imprisonment for her husband.

Sixteen members of Helsinki watch groups have been arrested this year, including Mr. Orlov; Aleksandr Ginzburg, who administered a fund for political prisoners with money sent by Mr. Solzhenitsyn; Anatoly Shcharansky, a Jew who seeks to emigrate and who worked as a consummate public-relations man for the dissidents; Mikola Rudenko, a poet and a head of the Kiev group, and Zviad Gamsakhurdia, a Georgian separatist and head of the Tbilisi committee. Most of the nine founding members of the Moscow group are in jail, in Siberian exile or in the West. Only one remains active—Yelna Bonner, Dr. Sakharov's wife, who has had to go abroad for medical treatment.

Though the watch group has been replenished, the losses have dulled its political acumen. It failed to take advantage of the attention focused on the follow-up conference in Belgrade in October; at one news conference its members were not prepared for questions on their views of the West's handling of human-rights issues at the meeting and declined substantive comment.

The dissidents issued no detailed analysis of the Soviet Constitution adopted in October, nor any appraisal of the political and judicial rights contained and limited in the document.

Lacking friends and colleagues who understand something about Western opinion, Dr. Sakharov has struck some dissidents and Western correspondents as increasingly isolated and even bitter. He has lashed out several times at the American press, accusing it of giving dissent too little attention; reporters have found it difficult to get him to talk about anything else.

**K.G.B. Stunningly Accurate**

He rejected a chance recently to bring some ordinary workers—they had sought his help after haviing been discharged for complaining of corruption and safety violations on the job—into the human-rights movement, partly, a friend said, because he was afraid that simple, relatively unknown people would be hurt and perhaps even slain if they had contact with him. "Unfortunately, unlike Poland, we have no workers in the movement," said Professor Meiman, a watch group member who has been refused permission to go to Israel. "Our people don't really trust the intelligentsia."

Paranoia, always present where the K.G.B. operates, is especially strong now in the wake of disclosures that a trusted "dissident," Dr. Sanya Lipavsky, a Jew, was a police agent. He wrote a letter, published in the Government newspaper Izvestia accusing Mr. Shcharansky and others of working for the Central Intelligence Agency. Mr. Shcharansky is awaiting trial, and his case has cast a chill over dissidents, making people suspect their friends.

The K.G.B. has focused on potentially influential activists with stunning accuracy. The most charismatic and eloquent of the new generation, Aleksandr Podrabinek, has been the target of threats and pressure in the form of a falsified case against his older brother designed to force the family to leave the country—something he has refused to do—or face persecution. A 24-year-old medical assistant, uncannily calm and steady in the face of adversity, he has collected data on the abuse of psychiatry. As others have disappeared from the movement he has stepped in to fill the gap as a clearing house for reports of political arrests.

"I do not want to sit in prison," he said. "I value even the image of freedom, which I have now. I know that in the West I could live freely and receive, finally, a genuine education. I know that there I would not be followed by four or five agents threatening to beat me or push me under a train. I know that there I would not be placed in a concentration camp or a psychiatric hospital for trying to defend the rightless and the oppressed. I know that there I could breathe freely, whereas here—heavily. They stop up your mouth and smother you if you speak too loudly. I know that our country is unhappily doomed to suffering. And therefore I will stay."

"I do not want to sit behind bars, but I am not afraid of prison camp," he continued. "I value my freedom, as I do the freedom of my brother, but I will not sell it. I will not yield to any blackmail. For me a clean conscience is more valuable than everyday well-being. I was born in Russia. It is my country and I must remain in it even if it is difficult here and easy in the West. As much as I can I will try henceforth to defend those whose rights are so crudely trampled in our country. That is my answer. I will stay."

December 30, 1977

# *Dissident Unionists In Moscow Pledge Continuing Struggle*

By CRAIG R. WHITNEY
Special to The New York Times

MOSCOW, Feb. 27—Supporters of an unofficial labor union that was organized here last month said today that five members, including its leader, had disappeared after being arrested and that the authorities had committed two others to psychiatric hospitals.

"But we don't intend to stop now," said Valentin T. Poplavsky, one of the organizers. He said Vladimir Klebanov, a former coal miner who is the union leader, had not been heard from since he was seized by the security police in Moscow on Feb. 7.

Mr. Poplavsky, a former construction engineer from the Donets coal district in the Ukraine, told foreign reporters in a Moscow apartment that he could not confirm a report from another dissident group that Mr. Klebanov was being held in a psychiatric hospital in Donetsk, his home town.

**Union Charter Is Drafted**

A union charter, which Mr. Poplavsky said was drawn up by 43 members on Feb. 1, was made available to the reporters. He said members had been receiving letters of support from Soviet citizens, and he put the membership of the group at 200.

Although some of the charter's aims are similar to those of other rights groups, the labor union seems to have arisen at least in part as a result of class divisions and personality clashes between disaffected workers and dissident intellectuals. Despite tentative approaches over the past year, Mr. Poplavsky said, there is no coordination between his group and other dissidents.

Speaking at a recent meeting of a human rights group, Yelena Bonner, wife of Andrei D. Sakharov, the physicist, expressed support for the principle of a free union. But Mr. Poplavsky and another member, Varvara I. Kucherenko, were disdainful of that support today.

"Those people are swindlers," Mrs. Kucherenko said. "We're a union of free workers." She said she was arrested Feb. 6 and kept in a psychiatric hospital for observation until Feb. 10.

The text of the union charter says membership is open to anyone "whose rights and interests have been unlawfully violated by administrative, governmental party or judicial agencies." It declares that the group, calling itself "Free Trade Union of the Soviet Union," is a legal entity and it expresses confidence that it will be supported by the International Labor Organization, a United Nations agency, and by foreign labor unions.

Although some of the union members are workers who lost their jobs after having complained about injustices or safety violations, the group is not concerned mainly with working conditions and higher wages, Mr. Poplavsky said. "We don't have such a narrow goal," he declared. "We want to help people whose rights have been violated."

February 28, 1978

# Exiles Still Face, and Adjust To Siberia's Inhumanity to Man

By DAVID K. SHIPLER

MOSCOW — For three centuries or more the vast, brooding wilderness of Siberia has held a terrifying fascination for Russians, both as a challenging frontier of great mineral wealth and as a dreaded place of exile. In a push to harness the resources, cities have been built on the permafrost. Pipelines, roads and railroad spurs intersect across the emptiness, and the riches are being released from the frozen land. But still the endless wastes of swamps and forests are dotted with tiny villages so remote and so backward that they are considered fitting only for those sentenced to exile.

Exile in Siberia. It seems like a phrase out of a history of czarist Russia yet it exists today for an untold number of common criminals and political dissidents, just as it did 100 years ago. Their prison is the village, their punishment the hardship of an ordinary villager's everyday life. For the most part they live and work as the local residents do, and although some find it difficult to admit, it can be an interesting experience.

In recent weeks several dissidents have returned from exile, and their stories, combined with others of some years ago, provide a mosaic of images and impressions — of official cruelty and compassion, of peasant stoicism and wariness, of fear and cold, of pain and the tranquility of solitude.

For Iosif Begun, an electrical engineer, the worst of it was the 5,000-mile trip last summer from Moscow into the depths of Siberia, a grueling 68-day journey in which prisoners were jammed like cattle into the cubicles of special railroad cars, then herded off into local prisons along the way. Mr. Begun was placed for a few days at a time in nine different prisons across the country. "It was a frightening thing," he said, "completely inhuman."

A Jewish activist who sought emigration to Israel, he was seized when he tried to enter the United States Embassy in Moscow to deliver a statement of protest. He was convicted of "parasitism," a convenient catch-all aimed at vagrants but now applied with increasing frequency to Jews who lose their jobs after requesting exit visas. After his trial, according to his account, Mr. Begun was put into a small train compartment meant for four passengers but specially outfitted with two extra bunks to hold six. In fact, 25 prisoners were crammed into the space so that it was impossible to lie down. The single window was barred and shuttered, and the door was locked.

During three-to-four-day legs of the journey, nobody was permitted to leave the cubicles except once each morning, when inmates were taken to a toilet at the end of the car. Food rations consisted of half a loaf of black bread a day, plus a cup of water and one or two small pieces of spoiled salted herring that the prisoners were afraid to eat, knowing that it would give them a fierce thirst and that no additional water would be provided.

"People lost their strength and became weak and completely helpless," Mr. Begun said. The hardened criminals preyed on the weaker and the younger, stealing what few possessions they had, especially clothing. At the prisons, 100 inmates were jammed into cells built for 20, and in the constant dampness, lice and other insects thrived.

## In Czarist Times, They Went on Foot

Historically, the trip into exile has been a most difficult phase of a prisoner's experience, often worse than prison or exile itself. In the 17th century, when the czars exiled relatives of merchants who had left the country illegally, later, when landlords could have serfs exiled by turning them over to the authorities, and through most of the 1800's, when waves of persons were exiled for common or political crimes, large parts of the journey were often made on foot, sometimes in chains. After the Trans-Siberian Railroad was built around the turn of the century, exiles were sent by train. Lenin was one of them. Sentenced in 1897 to three years, he managed through connections to gain permission to choose his place of exile. He selected a village in a relatively mild southern region where he befriended the local policeman, who let him maintain communications and continue his political work uninterrupted.

Today the practice is a mixture of soft and hard. Some exiles are allowed to go by themselves, others are taken separately under guard, making the trip easier than in the prison cars. But those sent directly from prison with masses of other detainees usually face special hardships in the first short time after arriving at their destinations. They have nothing but their prison clothes, rarely warm enough for the 60-to-70 below cold of Siberian winters. They have little money for a meal or an overcoat. They are stripped of all papers, so they must carry friends' and family's addresses in their heads. They usually do not even know until the journey has begun for which village they are bound. Nor are their relatives told, so there is no way to wire money or mail clothing until the prisoner himself reaches his destination and gets through by phone or telegram.

Some exiles have told of literally begging for bread and of camping in hotel entranceways until local authorities provided housing. Mr. Begun was lucky. When he arrived in Burkandia, a settlement of 3,000 people who work in a gold mine, he was immediately assigned to a men's dormitory, a considerably more comfortable place than many exiles find. It was a two-story brick building with central heating and cold running water. He managed to call his wife, Alla, who wired him money in a few hours.

He was given work repairing electrical mining equipment, for which he earned $230 a month, the lowest wage possible in that job. When he offered to set up an after-school technical and hobby program for youngsters, he was turned down by Communist Party officials who wanted to keep him out of the school. Even when he agreed to repair the school's only tape recorder, broken for two years, he was not allowed to do so in the building; it was brought to him.

Mr. Begun and others found most local residents curious and wary, afraid to be seen with exiles, but sometimes strangely hospitable. Mr. Begun made friends only with a few people who were latent dissidents themselves, people who were anxious for him to convey appeals on various matters to the authorities when he returned to Moscow.

## Some Natives Think They Are Spies

Andrei Tverdokhlebov, the former secretary of the Moscow chapter of Amnesty International, said recently that many in his village of Nyurbachan, a state farm producing meat and dairy products, were a bit puzzled and hurt that their home town should be used as a prison of sorts. "They said, 'why is our life, which we live all the time, considered a punishment?' " he remarked. He spent nearly two years there, shoveling coal into a heating plant's furnace, but living in a wooden dormitory heated only by a wooden stove. It was so cold inside that anything left on the floor would freeze, and frost formed on the inside of the walls. There was no indoor plumbing, and the wells froze, so water had to be trucked from 12 miles away in wintertime.

Malva Landa, a member of the Moscow dissident group monitoring Soviet observance of the Helsinki accords, said that most people in Vershino-Shakhtama, the village where she was exiled from July 1977 until last month, seemed to think she was a spy. When she tried to explain her struggle for the right to read and write books freely, they thought she had been speculating in books on the black market, a lucrative business in much of the Soviet Union. There was little communication.

Pavel Litvinov, the grandson of Maxim Litvinov, Stalin's

Foreign Minister, had a slightly different experience when he was exiled to Siberia after he and several others demonstrated in Red Square to protest the 1968 Soviet-led invasion of Czechoslovakia. When he arrived with his family, he said, some villagers looked upon him as a guest, a Moscow intellectual with a famous name to whom hospitality must be extended. He remembers a storekeeper putting aside flour, which was in short supply, to sell to him and his wife while other customers went without. Even Communist Party members used to come to his house — usually after dark and on somebody else's motorcycle — for vodka and conversation. Residents became more circumspect later after warnings from the secret police. Mr. Litvinov, a physics teacher who now lives in Tarrytown, N.Y., is one of those who found exile interesting, for he had not had much chance before to know ordinary working people.

Another who gained similar insights into his own country was Andrei Amalrik, the dissident writer who spent two terms in Siberia and wrote a penetrating, witty account of his first exile in his book "Involuntary Journey to Siberia." Before Mr. Amalrik was forced by the authorities to emigrate to the United States two years ago, a visit to his shabby room in a Moscow communal apartment usually entailed a look at a photo album filled with snapshots of him and his smiling wife, Gyuzel, in their Siberian exile. His winter footwear was a snappy pair of reindeer-hide boots purchased during his second term. He now lives in Washington, D.C.

## A Few Do Not Want to Leave

Adam Oelschlager, a young German who visited Muscovy and Tartary from 1633 to 1636, wrote in "The Travels of Olearius" that each exile then was provided "with a tolerable livelihood, in keeping with his personal condition and worth. Magnates are given money, scribes positions in the chancelleries of Siberian cities; soldiers are given places as soldiers, which yield an annual salary and a decent living. There have been instances in which such disgrace worked a great advantage, namely when the exiles' professions or trades were more fruitfully pursued [in Siberia] than in Moscow; some prospered so well that, if they had their wives and children with them, they did not wish to return to Moscow even when released."

According to Miss Landa, some exiles today decide to stay on, although those who are educated are seldom given work consonant with their skills. Mr. Tverdokhlebov, a physicist, was offered a middle-management position after his term at an institute near his place of exile in Yakutia, but did not want to stay.

Miss Landa, a retired geologist who spent time in remote places during much of her career, found life in Vershino-Shakhtama tolerable. She bought a two-room wooden house for $360, kept a small vegetable garden and had neighbors who helped chop wood for her stove. Although most of the villagers had television sets, she had none, and spent most of her time reading and writing. She was indignant because the authorities cut off her mail and telegrams involving dissident affairs, but otherwise, she said, "I was happy, I didn't complain. It was possible to live, and if I had wanted to live quietly, I would have stayed there. If I had thought only of my own personal life, I would have stayed." But she said she wanted to continue the struggle for human rights.

"It was not a typical exile," she added. "It was not a real exile. Real exile can be a nightmare. Some prisoners want to go back to prison." Anatoly Marchenko, for example, a dissident writer now exiled in Chuna, leads an extremely hard life, according to his wife, Larissa, who visits Moscow occasionally. He was given outdoor work hauling heavy logs to a sawmill, and in the deep cold of winter he becomes weak and ill. Outdoor work is often threatened by authorities in an effort to prevent exiles from communicating with dissidents in Moscow.

But it has become clear that at least for political prisoners, who may make up only a fraction of those sent to Siberia, exile from Moscow never ends, even after the formal sentence expires. Mr. Begun, Miss Landa and Mr. Tverdokhlebov returned to the capital to learn that the authorities had refused them permission to live here, apparently to keep them away from the main groups of human rights campaigners and from access to foreign correspondents. Mr. Tverdokhlebov was briefly detained last week on suspicion of staying illegally in Moscow and released with a warning to register outside the Moscow region. "It's double punishment," said Mrs. Begun.

*David K. Shipler is Moscow bureau chief of The New York Times.*

April 30, 1978

# Dissident in Moscow Gets a 7-Year Term

By DAVID K. SHIPLER
Special to The New York Times

MOSCOW, May 18—Yuri F. Orlov, a physicist who organized a dissident group to expose Soviet violations of human rights, was sentenced today to seven years in prison followed by five years of exile, or enforced residence, for the crime of "anti-Soviet agitation."

The severity of the punishment came in defiance of appeals in the West, especially in the United States, for more humane treatment of dissidents. It was evidently meant as a warning to other dissidents that publicity and Western support offered no protection.

A key element of the charge was Mr. Orlov's conveyance of reports on rights violations to foreign correspondents and to Western governments that signed the Helsinki accord on East-West cooperation in 1975. At least 22 members of various self-styled watchdog committees have been arrested thus far in the Soviet Union.

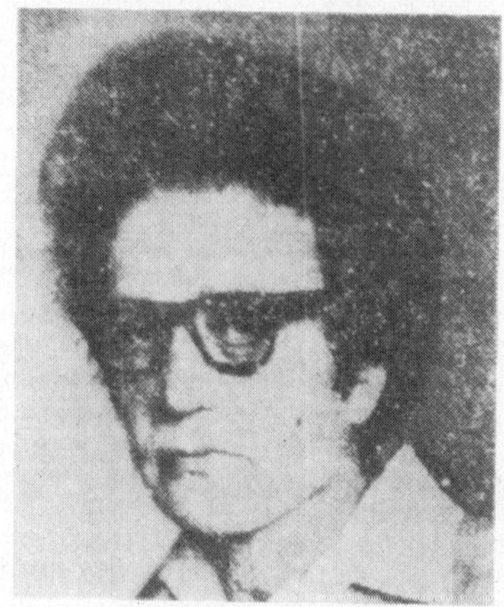
Associated Press
Yuri F. Orlov

The four-day trial of Mr. Orlov, which was closed to the public, was held in the courthouse of Moscow's southeastern Lyublino Borough, a small, out-of-the-way building near a railroad yard. Only his wife, Irina, and his two sons, Dmitri and Aleksandr, were admitted, along with 50 hand-picked spectators who, Mrs. Orlov said, applauded when the sentence was read, shouting, "He should have been given more."

Mr. Orlov, who is 53 years old, was not allowed to call defense witnesses and was denied full opportunity to cross-examine 15 prosecution witnesses who had been brought in to portray the Soviet Union as a land of democracy, decency and freedom, contrary to the picture painted in the statements of his watchdog group.

Despite the handicaps, which included interruptions by the judge and prosecutor, his family felt he had won the case by any objective criteria. When he was brought into court today, Dmitri shouted, "Father, you are the real winner in the trial."

### Refuses to Stand

Throughout the proceedings, Mrs. Orlov said she had refused to stand when the judge, Valentina Lubentsova, entered the courtroom, and today both she and Dmitri refused to stand before the sentence was read. The other son, Aleksandr, was absent, preparing for a defense of his academic dissertation tomorrow.

Three times the judge asked Mrs. Orlov to stand, she said, and she replied, "I do not respect your Soviet court." Two men then seized Dmitri, 25, and forced him to his feet and out of the room. Mrs. Orlov said she had also been held up forcibly before the sentencing.

There was also tension outside the courthouse. Seven dissidents were arrested, five in a scuffle with the police in which Andrei D. Sakharov, the physicist and rights advocate, attempted to argue his way into the building. He and his wife were among those taken into custody after having struck policemen. They were later freed.

Two others were given 1 days in jail, dissidents reported, and Yelena Armand, who was identified as the granddaughter of Inessa Armand, Lenin's mistress, was fined. An eighth dissident, Iosif Begun, who recently returned from exile in Siberia, was arrested last night and charged with violating residence regulations by being in Moscow without permission, his wife said. Residence in Moscow is restricted.

As correspondents drove Mrs. Orlov back to the city center for a news conference, several cars with agents of the K.G.B., the security police, some of them with videotape and still cameras, followed close behind and, at one point, tried to force a reporter's car off the road.

Mrs. Orlov, who is 33, seemed drained and exhausted. With foreign reporters, friends and an American diplomat barred from the courtroom, she had become the main source of information on the proceedings, and the police had subjected her to harassment and humiliation.

She was ordered not to take notes during the trial, and paper was taken away from her. Tape recorders smuggled into the courtroom by Mr. Orlov's two sons were seized. And yesterday she said she had been stripped by policewomen in front of three men until she was wearing only her brassiere, and was searched as she left the courthouse. Today, as she walked away from the building, someone put some tulips and daffodils in her arms.

There are likely to be internal ramifications of the trial of Mr. Orlov, who was known as a zealous organizer who brought together disparate strands of dissent into a movement of growing cohesiveness. Even since his arrest 15 months ago, Soviet dissent has reverted to a shadow of what Mr. Orlov had begun to assemble.

May 19, 1978

## NATIONALIST TENSIONS

# STALINISM SOLVING MINORITIES PROBLEM

**Many Languages and Customs in Soviet Union Are Welded by Communist Party.**

**RACIAL FAVORITISM BARRED**

**Heterogeneous Group in the High Posts of Russia Offers Hope to All Sections.**

**PROGRAMS COVER NATION**

**Aim Is to Foster Pan-Sovietism While Permitting Liberal Measure of Cultural Freedom.**

By WALTER DURANTY.

Special Cable to THE NEW YORK TIMES.

PARIS, June 25.—One of the most evident ways in which Soviet Russia is modifying Marxism is in the matter of nationalities and Soviet federation, for which Joseph Stalin is directly responsible as Commissar of Nationalities during the period prior to 1923, when the Constitution of the Union of Socialist Soviet Republics was adopted and the commissariat in question abolished.

Karl Marx conceived of the establishment of a proletarian dictatorship in a highly industrialized state, where the actual majority of the population would be urban workers speaking the same language and having the same needs, habits and aims. For this homegeneous majority the elimination or absorption of other classes and sections of the population would be a relatively simple matter, once it gained political power and held the economic reins.

**Many Languages and Customs.**

In Russia, however, things were quite different. The urban workers not only formed less than 15 per cent of the population and the peasants more than 80 per cent, but there was a vast divergence of race, language, custom and culture, to say nothing of religion, among the 160,000,000 inhabitants of the Soviet Union. And what, from the Bolshevik point of view, was no less important was the vast difference in "social consciousness" also.

In organizing the U. S. S. R. Stalin was forced to take cognizance of this anomaly from a Marxist doctrinal standpoint. He met it by a compromise, of which even British genius for making two ends meet need not have been ashamed.

Every nationality in the union was allowed full linguistic autonomy and what might have seemed a dangerously lavish degree of cultural and political autonomy. Thus the Jews, who had remained alien expatriates under Czardom, received a small autonomous area with the promise of an independent republic if and when the number of the population concentrated at any one point should justify the augmented status.

At first sight such an arrangement might seem to foster a spirit of petty nationalist and racial antagonism and universal disintegration—that is the exact opposite of what the Bolsheviki are trying to achieve. In a heterogeneous capitalist State—the British Empire, for instance—liberty given minor nationalities must have had a centrifugal effect, but in the U. S. S. R. the Communist party acts as a cement to bind the whole mass together and permit the facile exercise of central control.

For in practice two rules are followed in regard to the Soviet national system. First, the power is progressively restricted to "proletarian elements" of the population—the workers and poor peasants, whether industrialized or not. Secondly, 95 per cent of the political leaders are Communists, and, what is more, it is an almost invariable rule that the national Communist party secretaries and their most important district subordinates are either Russians or members of a different nationality from the people around them.

The strictness of the party discipline does the rest, and, although there have been cases of regional friction and sporadic difficulty, the system on the whole seems to work more smoothly than any organization of a heterogeneous State yet devised by man.

Perhaps one of the secrets of its success is the annual convocation to the centre of the regional party executives for a conference or congress and their relatively frequent switching from one national post to another. It must be admitted also that the Bolsheviki adhere with remarkable steadiness to their creed of Communist equality irrespective of race or color, which assures the members of former "subject" peoples opportunities to rise to the highest central positions and removes any feeling of racial inferiority.

Stalin is a Georgian, Trotsky a Jew, Rudzutak a Lett, Dzerzhinsky was a Pole. These men offer salient examples for Communists of every nationality in the U. S. S. R. It is thus clear that the Soviet federal system, while reinforcing nationalism, did not sacrifice cohesion and centralized direction.

The subsequent evolution of Stalinism tended still further to fuse or coalesce these apparently opposite forces—first, by an intensive and union-wide propaganda for the "defense of the Socialist fatherland against capitalistic intervention." The purpose of the propaganda—and the achievement of it—was to divert and merge the fresh, strong currents of minor nationalism into a mighty river of Pan-Sovietism.

**Construction in All Parts.**

Secondly, the new industrial construction—new dams, railroads, mines and factories, often in remote parts of the union—was concrete proof that each for all and all for each was true. Thirdly, there is the new system of State and collective farms, not the least purpose of which is to bring the advantages of mechanized and organized effort to the humblest Tadzsik peasant or Kasak nomad.

Finally, there is the ever-driving energy of the Communist party, from graybeards to children, which the Kremlin radiates to the remotest edge of the U. S. S. R. like a current that makes all molecules cohere.

To say that this process is fully accomplished is premature, but there is small doubt that Stalinism has already achieved a marked degree of transmutation of petty nationalism into a great Pan-Sovietism—not aggressive, not, the writer firmly believes, "Red imperialism" aroused for world conquest, but strong and potentially dangerous should attack from without provoke it to reprisal.

June 26, 1931

# THREE COUNTRIES VOTE TO BE SOVIETS

## Lithuania, Latvia, Estonia Won by Russia—Ex-Officials Reported Seized

By OTTO D. TOLISCHUS
Wireless to THE NEW YORK TIMES.

STOCKHOLM, Sweden, July 21—Three more independent European countries were wiped off the map today when the three Baltic States, Lithuania, Latvia and Estonia, by formal resolutions of their newly elected, Communist-dominated Parliaments, proclaimed themselves Soviet republics and decided to ask for incorporation into the Union of Soviet Socialist Republics.

The resolutions, adopted unanimously amid the thunderous applause of delegates, acting under the eyes of Russian commissars who have controlled political events in these countries since the Russian military occupation, provide:

1. Creation of Soviet Constitutions and Soviet regimes in the three countries.
2. A petition to the Supreme Council of People's Commissars of the Soviet Union asking for union with Russia.

The petitions of Lithuania and Latvia have already been dispatched to Moscow. The petition of Estonia has been decided upon in principle, but has been referred to a committee for final formulation, and is expected to be passed at a session of Parliament starting at 10 A. M. tomorrow.

There is no doubt what Moscow's answer will be, though the Kremlin obviously desires to accomplish this annexation behind a legalistic front. And the Kremlin will also give the three States their respective numbers in the Soviet constellation.

July 22, 1940

# *Soviet Republics Get Right To Own Armies and Envoys*

By W. H. LAWRENCE
By Wireless to THE NEW YORK TIMES.

MOSCOW, Feb. 1—The Supreme Soviet late tonight unanimously approved a proposal by Foreign Commissar Vyacheslaff M. Molotoff for major changes in the Soviet constitutional system under which each of the sixteen constituent republics will form its own army formations and have separate diplomatic representation abroad.

In less than four hours of debate, including the forty-three-minute opening address by Mr. Molotoff, both chambers approved the constitutional changes by a show of hands without having the full text read to them. They had copies of the proposal in their desks but they waived the reading of it.

On the motion of President Mikhail I. Kalinin, the Supreme Soviet also elected Nikolai Shevrnik as first Vice President of the Presidium of the U.S.S.R. and then adjourned sine die.

While Premier Joseph Stalin looked on from a back-row seat on the platform, Mr. Molotoff gave a general outline of the Government's new plan which, he said, resulted from the political and cultural growth of the constituent Soviet Republics and which, he said, was put forward as a means of strengthening the Soviet Union as a whole.

He gave no details of the specific working out of the plan, saying that it would take some time to work out.

He was interrupted a score of times by applause, the loudest outburst of which greeted his declaration that the war had brought about the creation of a "powerful anti-Hitler coalition headed by the Soviet Union, Britain and the United States, the military and political significance of which for all democratic nations could hardly be overestimated.

Mr. Molotoff said each constituent republic would have its own commissariats for defense and foreign affairs. Until now these two commissariats have been exclusively All-Union. He said the proposal was a new victory for the Lenin-Stalin national policy and a logical development of the growth and progress of the constituent republics.

The diplomatic galleries were packed as Mr. Molotoff delivered his speech. W. Averell Harriman, United States Ambassador, sat in a front row-box with the Canadian Ambassador, L. Dana Wilgress.

Immediately Mr. Molotoff concluded, Yustis Patetskis, who is President of the Lithuanian Soviet Republic, arose to express his approval of the proposed constitutional change and to record the support of his people for the Soviet Union.

Wilhelm Lazis, delegate from Latvia, complained that certain countries, including the United States, continued to recognize the diplomatic representatives of an "old fascist regime," and permitted these representatives to carry on fascist propaganda.

February 2, 1944

# AUTONOMY IS LOST BY 5 SOVIET AREAS

## German Volga Republic Among Those Disestablished—Axis Collaboration a Reason

The Soviet Union has disestablished five of its autonomous national divisions within the past four years and has formally incorporated recently acquired areas into the administrative framework of the country, it is confirmed with the publication in Pravda of a list of all election districts in the U.S.S.R.

This list, appearing in the issue of Oct. 17, which has just reached this country, was published in connection with the elections to the Supreme Soviet scheduled for Feb. 10, 1946. The list provides the most authoritative and complete picture of the administrative-territorial scheme of the Soviet Union that has been available in this country since 1941. It bears out data that had already appeared on recent Soviet maps, but it also reveals many other new changes.

The areas whose autonomy rights were withdrawn are: the German Volga Autonomous Soviet Socialist Republic, the Kalmyk A.S.S.R., the Karachayev Autonomous Region, the Chechen-Ingush A.S.S.R. and the Crimean A.S.S.R.

The reasons for their dissolution, which were never officially announced, are obvious in the case of the German Volga A.S.S.R. As to the dissolution of the other areas, some observers believe that probable collaborationist tendencies in these districts at the time of their occupation by the German Army may have led to the removal of their autonomous status. Except for the German Volga A.S.S.R., all areas in question were either reached or overrun by the Nazis. In any case, strong motives must have been present in a country where the widely publicized policy has been to increase the number of self-administered areas and to encourage cultural and limited political independence for the fifty major nationalities that constitute nearly all its population.

The election district list shows how the disestablished areas were split up among the neighboring administrative units, and how efforts were made to eradicate the languages of the indigenous nationalities by renaming their capitals, towns and villages.

The German Volga A.S.S.R., first to disappear off the map of the U.S.S.R., was abolished soon after the start of the German onslaught on the Soviet Union, and the majority of its population of 570,000 was reported to have been resettled in Siberia. Formerly the German Workers' Commune, founded in October, 1918, it had been the first autonomous national group to be created after the Bolshevik Revolution in 1917. After nearly twenty-three years of self-administration, it was incorporated in 1941 into the adjoining Saratov and Stalingrad Regions (provinces).

In 1943, after the German debacle at Stalingrad, it was the turn of the Kalmyk A.S.S.R., situated in the steppe country on the northwestern shore of the Caspian Sea. Its territory was given to the Stalingrad, Rostov, Stavropol Regions and to the newly formed Astrakhan Region. The name of the capital, Elista, was changed to Russian Stepnoi. The history of this area also dates back to 1920, when it was first established as an Autonomous Region

Near the highest Caucasian peak, Mount Elbrus, lay the small Karachayev Autonomous Region, about the size of the State of Delaware. A small part was assigned to the Stavropol Region, while the Georgian S.S.R. received the bulk of its territory, including the former capital, Mikoyan-Shakhar, which became Georgian Klukhori. The Karachayev A.R. had been formed in 1922.

To the east, in the rich Grozny oil area, the Chechen-Ingush A.S.S.R., created in 1922 as an Autonomous Region, was transformed into a new Grozny Region, a unit of purely administrative character.

Finally, only a few months ago, the Crimea lost its autonomous status, which it had held since 1921, and became the Crimean Region, an administrative unit in the Russian Soviet Federated Socialist Republic (R. S. F. S. R.). This change had been heralded already in December, 1944, when all important towns with Tatar appellations received Russian names.

The Pravda list, furthermore, indicates the position that recently acquired areas occupy in the Soviet administrative set-up. The Petsamo territory, gained as a result of the Finnish armistice of

## INTERNAL CHANGES IN THE SOVIET UNION

Nov. 30, 1945

Five areas that were autonomous prior to the German invasion of Russia and that have lost their autonomy since are indicated on the upper map. The lower map shows the present status.

September, 1944, was made into Pechenga Rayon (county) within the Murmansk Region. The administrative center was moved from Pechenga (Petsamo) to Nikel, in the nickel mining district.

The northern half of East Prussia, acquired at the Berlin Conference in August, 1945, was incorporated into the R. S. F. S. R. as a special Koenigsberg District, separated, however, from the R. S. F. S. R. proper by the Lithuanian and White Russian S. S. Republics.

The Carpatho-Ukraine, ceded by Czechosloxakia in July, 1945, has become the Transcarpathian Region of the Ukrainian S. S. R., and is scheduled to elect three delegates to the Supreme Soviet.

The southern part of Sakhalin Island (Karafuto) and the Kurile Islands, occupied by the Russians as a result of their campaign against Japan, have apparently not yet received their administrative classification, but form, together with northern Sakhalin, one election district.

Tannu-Tuva, which has been incorporated into the Soviet Union as the Tuvinian Autonomous Region, as was already reported, will send six delegates to the Supreme Soviet instead of two as was stated in earlier reports.

A recent change of territory, which as yet does not appear on any map, is the transfer of an area including Viborg (Viipuri) and Kexholm (Kakisalmi) from the Karelo-Finnish S. S. R. to the R. S. F. S. R., giving the latter republic control over the entire Karelian Isthmus.

The list published in Pravda schedules 656 election districts, each electing one delegate to the Soviet of the Union, and 631 districts, each electing one delegate to the Soviet of Nationalities, the two bodies that constitute the Supreme Soviet. While the former includes delegates elected on the basis of population (one for each 300,000 inhabitants), the latter receives twenty-five delegates from each Union Republic, eleven from each A. S. S. R., five from each Autonomous Region, and one from each National District, the lowest type of autonomous unit.

November 30, 1945

# FRONTIER CLEARING SPEEDED BY RUSSIA

### Moscow Transplants Peoples Considered Untrustworthy From Border Areas

By DREW MIDDLETON
Special to THE NEW YORK TIMES.

BERLIN, July 25—During recent months the Russian policy of transplanting border populations considered potentially subversive into the interior of the Soviet Union has been accelerated, Western sources said here today.

These transfers, the sources stated, are difficult to reconcile with the widely advertised Russian policy of autonomy for all national groups within the Soviet Union.

[A dispatch from Prague said that, according to reliable reports, the Soviet Union had deported eastward elements of the population of Lithuania, Latvia and Estonia considered by Moscow to be unreliable. The action was attributed to security reasons in connection with the defense of Leningrad. Full Sovietization of the former Finnish area of Karelia also was reported.]

The latest large-scale move was in June. More than 10,000 Greek Russians were moved to Soviet Central Asia from the Black Sea coast of the Georgian Soviet Socialist Republic, just north of the Turkish frontier. Apparently these Greeks, some of whom are descendants of settlers who came to the area in the Middle Ages, were considered as potentially hostile by the Russian authorities.

Living so close to the Turkish frontier they also probably were considered a bad security risk.

They received two hours' notice to move at 4 o'clock in the morning, were not allowed to take any personal belongings and were shipped to Central Asia in freight cars.

During the last six months, the source said, most of the transferred peoples have been sent to Central Asia rather than to the Urals or Siberia.

The largest transfers have been from the Baltic states, where an estimated 50,000 persons were recently evacuated from Southern Latvia in a few weeks and sent to the same destination by the same means.

Other transfers have been reported from Soviet Bessarabia on the western border of the Russian Ukraine.

Sources here raise the question whether these transfers, all of which have been carried out within the Soviet Union, may not now be extended to the satellite states, where resistance to Communist rule is stronger than in the Soviet Union.

Since the war the Russians have carried out a policy of planting small colonies of Russians of proven loyalty at strategic points in some satellite states and along the frontiers of the Soviet Union.

One such colony was organized astride the Danube, just east of the border between Hungary and Austria. Koenigsberg, in what was formerly East Prussia, has been transformed into a Russian city, populated by Russians and named Kaliningrad.

According to reports reaching here, numbers of Russians have been settled in cities of the Baltic states as well as in the countryside. In some cases they have been lured by promises of monetary bonuses and better living conditions. In others they have been moved by the same arbitrary means employed to evacuate people into the interior of Russia.

July 26, 1949

## RUSSIA SHIFTS POPULATIONS ON DEFENSE LINE

The New York Times July 26, 1949

As a security measure, the Soviet recently moved Russians of Greek origin from the Black Sea coast of the Georgian Republic (1) to the Asian interior. Similar transfers from Soviet Bessarabia and the Ukraine (2) and Byelorussia (3) have been reported. On the outer defenses of Leningrad (4) large numbers of Estonians, Latvians and Lithuanians have been deported eastward, and the Russians have fully consolidated their control of former Finnish territory. Russian colonists have been settled in western Hungary, in a region astride the Danube (5).

# SOVIET CONTINUES MINORITIES' PURGE

### U. S. Observers Consider It a Clue to Kremlin's Concern Over Persistent Nationalism

By HARRY SCHWARTZ

The Soviet Government's hunt for minority group nationalists, begun last summer, is still going strong, with more high-placed individuals falling victims to the accompanying purge, a review of recent Soviet newspapers indicates.

The latest group of important purge victims has been reported from the Kazakh Republic, in Asiatic Russia, where two secretaries of the Young Communist League Central Committee, the editor of the Young Communist newspaper and the chairman of the Kazakhstan branch of the Union of Soviet Writers have been removed from their posts.

As was the case with Communist party officials purged earlier in this area, the newest group of victims were charged either with propagating "bourgeois nationalist" ideas of Kazakh separation or not fighting the expression of such ideas with sufficient vigor. In particular, they were accused of not propagating the "progressive significance of the voluntary union" of Kazakhstan with Czarist Russia.

**Series of Meetings Held**

Throughout the Ukraine in recent weeks a series of meetings have been held at which leading intellectuals, including writers, editors and poets, have confessed in public that they had held "dangerous bourgeois nationalist" ideas that they were now going to give up for the approved ideology.

Little specific information has been published on individuals purged or demoted in this area, but the intensity of Soviet comment and the great amount of space given to the nationalist "heresy" in this area indicate a general shake-up of political and intellectual life to stamp out actual or suspected dissidence.

In Turkmenistan the Communist party Central Committee has launched a sweeping offensive against intellectuals, publishers and Government education officials on similar grounds. The head of the Union of Soviet Writers in Turkmenistan has been accused of having written "obviously bourgeois nationalist poems."

**Folk Epic Outlawed**

The immediate pretext for the hunt in Turkmenistan is a folk epic, "Korkut Ada," which now has been officially outlawed by Communist chiefs as nationalist and representative of the feudal world outlook of the eleventh century. The poem is being denounced because it calls for Allah to bless Turkmen khans, while it "kindles hatred toward non-Moslem peoples and preaches fanatical religious intolerance."

Earlier, a related Moselm folk epic, "Dede Korkut," had been outlawed in Azerbaidzhan on similar grounds. The latest indictment of Turkmen intellectuals accuses them of having tried to pretend that the Turkmen version of this epic was essentially different from and unrelated to the Azerbaidzhan version so that the condemnation there did not apply. This contention has been rejected.

In Uzbekistan, bourgeois nationalism in poetry has come under attack, along with poems written by the head of the Uzbek branch of the Union of Soviet Writers. Some Uzbek poets are being accused of trying to "taint the Uzbek language with Arabic and Turkish terms."

United States Government observers watching the campaign against bourgeois nationalism are inclined to the belief that both the intensity and the duration of the effort are valuable clues to the persistence of nationalist feeling among Soviet minorities and the extent of Kremlin concern over it.

January 6, 1952

# SOVIET MOSLEMS FACE SUBMERSION

## Their Nationalism Suppressed and Past Independence Cut From History Books

By HARRY SCHWARTZ

Recent news of purges in the Soviet republics of Kazakhstan and Turkmenistan gives additional evidence that the 15,000,000 Moslems under Kremlin rule share the same growing nationalistic spirit that is causing current difficulties in the Middle East.

Two secretaries of the Kazakh Communist Party, S. I. Kruglov and I. O. Omarov, have been dismissed for their roles as "protectors of bourgeous nationalist" perversions. Also dismissed were leaders of the Young Communist League and the heads of the Kazakh Academy of Sciences and the Kazakh Union of Soviet Writers.

A plenary session of the Central Committee of the Turkmen Communist party revealed a drive against "bourgeous nationalism" that had penetrated even into the committee's own propaganda and agitation department. Shortly afterward the head of the Turkmen State University and the head of the Turkmen Union of Soviet Writers were dismissed.

Evidence of disaffection among Soviet Moslems was available during World War II when thousands in the Soviet army went over to Germany and fought for the Wehrmacht. Soviet Moslems live mainly in the Caucasus and Central Asia, and include Azerbaijanis, Uzbeks, Kirgis, Kazakhs, Turkmens and others who are religious, cultural and sometimes even blood brothers of Moslem peoples in the Middle East.

From 1945 to the present Soviet leaders have sought to combat this discontent by frequent purges.

For foreign consumption Soviet propaganda gushes over with expressions of friendship for Iran, Egypt and the whole Moslem world. Inside its own borders, the Kremlin has labeled Pan-Iranianism, Pan-Turkism, and Pan-Moslemism as the most serious of "ideological perversions."

Almost all mosques have been closed, except for a few propaganda show places, and all Moslem religious holidays, dietary laws, and the like receive the same condemnation as Christian or Jewish religious customs.

All of the Moslem nations now under Soviet domination have had their histories systematically rewritten in recent years to dim memories of their past independence and to eliminate all evidence of their past friendly ties with Moslem peoples now outside the Soviet orbit. This rewriting of history is now so extensive that almost every Soviet history dealing with these peoples is now condemned in the Soviet Union.

### Area Rich in Resources

A major factor in Moscow's concern over domestic Moslem nationalism is the fact that areas inhabited by the Moslems are among the richest sources of raw materials in the country. Baku, in Soviet Azerbaijan, is still the largest source of Soviet oil while in Moslem-populated Soviet Central Asia are the most important domestic deposits of nonferrous metals, including uranium, as well as the fields that produce the great bulk of Soviet cotton.

Many students of this aspect of Soviet nationalities policy point out that growing Moslem friendship for the Soviet Union in the Middle East would be less likely to continue if there were adequate dissemination there of the facts about these peoples' co-religionists in the Soviet Union.

The Voice of America has tried to disseminate this information in its Middle Eastern broadcasts, but this and related efforts have apparently failed as yet to reach sufficiently large segments of this area's population to make an impact commensurate with the importance of the problem for the Moslem world as a whole.

January 30, 1952

# Soviet Transfers Crimea To the Ukrainian Republic

## Area Lost Autonomy in '45 After Moscow Charged Collaboration in War

By HARRISON E. SALISBURY

Special to THE NEW YORK TIMES.

MOSCOW, Saturday, Feb. 27—The Crimea, which before the war constituted one of the autonomous republics of the Soviet Union, has now become part of the Ukraine under a Government edict made public today.

The Crimea has been one of the oblasts (provinces) of the Russian Soviet Federated Socialist Republic since it lost its republic status at the end of the World War II. The Russian republic is the most important of the sixteen constituent republics that make up the Soviet Union.

The Crimea was deprived of its status as autonomous republic and considerable numbers of its Tartar inhabitants were resettled in the eastern regions of the Soviet Union. The Tartar population had been charged with collaboration with the Germans during the occupation of the region during World War II.

The decision to detach the Crimea from the Russian Republic was announced as designed to assist the "further strengthening of brotherly ties between the Ukrainian and Russian peoples."

The Crimea, which was the locale of the famous Stalin-Roosevelt-Churchill conference held at the seacoast resort city of Yalta, was one of the last Tartar strongholds in the territory now occupied by the Soviet Union.

The New York Times Feb. 27, 1954

The Ukraine (shaded area) now includes the peninsula of the Crimea (cross).

It was not until late in the eighteenth century that the last Tatar khan lost his nominal powers over the region. These khans were successors to those to whom Moscovy princes had long paid tribute.

The population of the Crimea was partly Tatar until World War II and this fact had been recognized by the establishment in 1921 of a special autonomous republic in the Crimean area that existed until 1945 when the republic was dissolved and turned into an ordinary administrative oblast of the Russian Republic. In recent years large numbers of Ukrainians have settled in the Crimea.

In Kremlin ceremonies marking the transfer of the Crimea, Kliment E. Voroshilov, chairman of the Presidium of the Supreme Soviet, declared that Russia's enemies often in the past had sought to wean the Crimea away from Russia in order to utilize the area as a base for attacks against Russia and the Ukraine.

Such attempts, said Mr. Voroshilov, have occurred in the "distant and not so distant past"—an apparent allusion to efforts made by the Germans to alienate the Tatar population of the Crimea during World War II.

Mr. Voroshilov said it had been decided to transfer the Crimea to the Ukraine because of close economic connections and territorial proximity. He also noted that this "friendly act" occurred at a time when Russia and the Ukraine were celebrating the 300th anniversary of their unity.

Today's action once more emphasized the rapidly growing importance of the Ukraine in Soviet affairs.

February 27, 1954

# SOVIET MINORITIES VARY IN FORTUNES

By HARRY SCHWARTZ

Conflicting forces appear to be shaping the fate of the non-Russian minorities who make up roughly half the Soviet population.

Intermarriage and compulsory study of Russian tend to create a culturally and ethnically unified people in many areas. But this process still has a long way to go. Meanwhile, Soviet encouragement for the development of national cultures and national languages among minorities tends to make these groups more conscious of their historic individuality.

For the moment, the crudest techniques of Russification appear to have been suspended. Instead, attacks are being levied at Great Russian chauvinists, attacks that were unthinkable in the last years of Stalin, a Georgian.

The Ukrainians, largest of all Soviet minorities, are being assiduously wooed by the present regime, directed by Russians, Nikita S. Khrushchev, First Secretary of the Communist party, and Premier Nikolai A. Bulganin. A Ukrainian, Alexei I. Kirichenko, was elected to the Presidium of the Communist party Central Committee last July, the first Ukrainian member of that body since the purges of the late Ninteen Thirties.

Vast amounts obviously are being poured into making Kiev, the capital of the Ukraine, one of the most beautiful cities—if not the most beautiful one in the Soviet Union. The special attention being given Kiev is particularly apparent when the city is compared with Minsk, capital of Byelorussia, where building progress is far less advanced.

### Charges Apparently Dropped

Charges of attempted Russification levied in June, 1953, at Leonid G. Melnikov apparently have been rescinded. Mr. Melnikov at that time was removed as head of the Ukrainian Communist party, but the charges were said to be the work of the late secret police chief, Lavrenti P. Beria. Mr. Melnikov now holds a ministerial post in Premier Bulganin's Cabinet.

The Ukrainians and Byelorussians are Slavic peoples like the Great Russians and their languages are related to Russian. Visits to Minsk, Kiev, Kharkov, and Odessa, left the impression that Russification had proceeded far in these cities. Many Russians live in the cities, and most normal businesses are conducted in Russian rather than in Ukrainian or Byelorussian.

No one spoken with in these two minority republics seemed to take very seriously the membership of the Ukraine and Byelorussia in the United Nations.

A visit to the Foreign Ministry of Byelorussia found it occupying part of one floor of a small building. Efforts to elicit a definition of this Foreign Ministry's functions, other than membership in the United Nations, brought from Deputy Foreign Minister G. P. Apostenko only the statement that the Ministry handled all matters "which fall within its competence."

**Poorest of the Cities**

Open dissidence based on nationalism as well as economic factors was found only in Erivan, capital of Armenia. This dissidence exists despite the fact that the Soviet Government has encouraged Armenian cultural institutions and has created Armenia's first modern industry—including one of the world's largest synthetic rubber plants—in Erivan.

Economic discontent was understandable, since Erivan was the poorest Soviet city visited in a five-week tour. Its housing was obviously the worst and its stores had less to sell than those of the other cities.

Armenians openly expressed satisfaction that few Russians lived in Erivan, many Armenians apparently know Russian poorly or not at all. Armenians remember the short-lived independent Armenia after World War I, but longings for independence come up against the hazards of geographical position. One Armenian in Erivan put it this way:

"What are we Armenians to do? Of course morally and religiously we are on the side of the free world, but look at our geographical position. For us it is a choice between Russians and the Turks. Every child among us knows what the Turks have cost us in blood and lives. The Russians at least don't massacre us."

A special problem was created in Armenia by the 100,000 foreign Armenians, including several hundred Americans, who came and settled there after World War II. The news brought by these settlers as to life in the outside world has placed Armenians among the best informed of Soviet minorities about the outside world.

Several of these settlers said many had found life in the Soviet Union the blackest nightmare. Many suicides, cases of hysterical paralysis and the like were said to have resulted.

**American Weeps**

Not until these settlers had given up their foreign citizenship and accepted Soviet citizenship did they learn the low level of material life and the degree of political conformity they would have to accept as Soviet Armenians. At least some apparently have been imprisoned for speaking their opinions too openly.

Many of the settlers manage to live only by selling off their remaining foreign clothes and other goods and by receiving parcels from relatives abroad.

About thirty American Armenians were permitted to visit Erivan this fall in connection with the recent election of the new Catholicos of the Armenian Gregorian Church. At least some of them received a shattering picture of conditions there. One of them said:

"Night after night I retired to my room in Erivan and simply wept uncontrollably at the plight of my people. I had never imagined things could be so bad. Don't worry, there won't be any more emigration of Armenians from the United States to the Soviet Union after we get home."

Other American Armenians visiting Erivan apparently were more impressed, however, by the cultural progress that had been made there.

A number of former Americans who had gone to Soviet Armenia during the last decade begged for help in regaining their American citizenship so they could go back to "paradise and away from hell."

In Tiflis, Georgia, there was reluctance to talk about Beria, who had been a Georgian national hero until he was purged in July, 1953. But in comments on other subjects, Georgians indicated pride in their historic heritage and a determination not to disappear as a people.

In Baku, Azerbaijan, almost all Azerbaijani national and Moslem religious traits appear to have disappeared after almost four decades of Soviet rule. Women go about unveiled, Russian seems the language spoken normally on streets and in stores, and dress seems indistinguishable from that of Soviet citizens everywhere.

But all old customs and local peculiarities evidently have not entirely disappeared. On a bulletin board on the main street of Baku was posted this notice:

"I will exchange one 40-year-old wife with two children for two wives aged 18-20.

"Reception of visitors and examination from 2 to 5 P. M. daily at 71 Stalin Prospect."

November 10, 1955

# *Soviet to Return 750,000 Exiles To Tribal Homes in Caucasus*

## *5 Groups Lost Autonomy Rights in World War II After Alleged Collaboration With Germans—Areas to Be Restored*

By WILLIAM J. JORDEN

Special to The New York Times.

MOSCOW, Feb. 11—The Soviet Union disclosed today that it was going to rehabilitate five minority nationalities uprooted from their Caucasus homes in World War II for disloyalty and shipped off to Central Asia and Kazakhstan.

The nationalities, which will be restored to full membership in the Soviet family of nations, are the Balkars, Chechens, Ingush, Kalmyks and Karachais. Their home territories, which were divided among other political units, are to be revived.

Thus the Soviet Union will seek to erase one of the blackest pages in the history of its treatment of minority groups. However, there was no mention of the Volga Germans or the Tatars of the Crimea, who also were uprooted.

**Groups' Return Scheduled**

The planned restoration of the five groups to their former status and the movement to their home districts was disclosed in a decree dated Jan. 9, that was approved today by the Supreme Soviet, the country's Parliament.

The decree said the movement of the Balkars, Kalmyks and Karachais should be completed next year. The Chechens and the Ingush "because of the larger numbers" would not be resettled fully until 1960.

The total population of the groups, according to the 1939 census, was about 750,000, as follows: Balkars, 42,666; Chechens, 407,690; Ingush, 92,074; Kalmyks, 134,327; Karachais, 75,737.

In addition to returning the five minorities to their former homes, the Soviet Union decided to revive the autonomous political units eliminated when the peoples were moved out.

Thus the Kabardino-Balkar Autonomous Republic will be revived, replacing the Kabardinian Republic, which arose during the war after the Balkars were ousted. The territory of the Balkars, which was absorbed by the Georgian Republic, was restored to the Kabardinian Republic in 1955.

The New York Times Feb. 12, 1957

The Soviet Union intends to restore minority groups to four former republics and an autonomous area (diagonal shading). But no mention was made of two other regions (cross-hatching) that were dissolved under Stalin.

The Chechen-Ingush Autonomous Republic also will be revived. It was dissolved and most of its territory was renamed Grozny Oblast (province).

The Kalmyk Autonomous Republic will be restored as an autonomous oblast. The Karachai will be merged with the neighboring Cherkess minority to form the Karachai-Cherkess Autonomous Oblast.

Soviet embarrassment at past treatment of these five groups was evident in the presentation of the decree today by A. Gorkin, secretary of the Supreme Soviet's Presidium. He described the exile of the minorities as a "violation of the main principles of Leninist nationality policy."

The Communists insist that whole peoples cannot be considered "good" or "bad." Yet because some individuals or groups among them cooperated with the German invaders in World War II, these entire nations were condemned.

The rehabilitation of political units will result in the loss of territory for Soviet Georgia. It was decreed that the Dusheti and Kazbeg districts would be transferred to the Chechen-Ingush Republic.

Elimination of the national units and the forcible movement of their peoples occurred in late 1943 and early 1944 after the Red Army had expelled the Germans from the Caucasus. The Russians charged that these groups had either actively helped the Germans or been too passive in their attitude.

**Two Groups Not Affected**

The ethnic Germans, one of two minority groups not affected by the rehabilitation decree, lived in the former Volga German republic near Saratov.

About 500,000 German residents of this area and ethnic Germans settled elsewhere in the Soviet Union were uprooted at the start of World War II.

The Germans were sent to the east, some to Central Asia and some to Siberia. The Volga German republic was dissolved. Within the last year a number of Volga Germans are known to have been permitted to return to their former homes. But many still reside in exile, especially in Tadzhikistan.

The Germans were remnants of colonies brought into Russia, for the most part, in the late eighteenth century by Catherine II.

The other ethnic group that remains dispersed is the Crimean Tatar population. The Crimean autonomous republic was dissolved in 1945 and about 200,000 Tatars were resettled in the east, mostly in Siberia.

In his secret address to the Twentieth Congress of the Communist party last February, Nikita S. Khrushchev, Soviet party secretary, described Stalin's actions against the national minority groups as monstrous.

The rehabilitation was heralded in 1955 and 1956 when the Soviet press disclosed that the exiled national groups would be permitted to publish books in their native languages.

February 12, 1957

# SECTIONALIST BIAS FOUGHT IN SOVIET

**By WILLIAM J. JORDEN**
Special to The New York Times

**MOSCOW, Feb. 13—Soviet leaders are disturbed by the tendency of some regional economic officials to stress local interests rather than the national welfare.**

**Regional self-interest has emerged as one of the most serious headaches in the vast experiment undertaken last year of transferring control of industrial management to regional economic councils. Freed from the control of centralized ministries in Moscow, regional authorities are said to have begun to shirk their responsibilities for cooperating with other industries and regions.**

**As a result, officials and the press are giving increasing attention to the problem and are rebuking some of the officials most guilty of ignoring their obligations to work closely with other areas.**

**Sectionalism Assailed**

The latest issue of the party journal Kommunist, which reached subscribers today, devoted considerable space to this matter. One article, which dealt with the whole problem of "contradictions" in Socialist society, said that "the appearance of sectionalism" was the "greatest shortcoming" in the program of decentralized management of industry.

Another article said this trend pointed up the necessity for improving the work of the central planning organization.

Under the former system of direction from Moscow, enterprises often had to ship their products to a factory belonging to the same ministry for further processing. Loyalties ran along ministerial lines and the huge Moscow organizations tended to become small empires.

The reorganization was designed to eliminate the inefficiency of such a system. It was also said that decentralization would encourage local initiative.

It now appears that in some cases local initiative has run wild. Some of the regional administrators have begun to think first of the economic welfare of their region and to push aside their obligations to other regions of the Soviet Union.

In some cases products that should have been shipped elsewhere were used within the producing region. In Astrakhan, for example, the regional council turned over to local industries 117,000 cubic meters of lumber that should have been sent to other areas in the Russian Republic and to the Transcaucasus.

February 14, 1958

# *Soviet Absolves Volga Germans, Exiled in 1941, of Charge They Aided Nazis*

By THEODORE SHABAD
Special to The New York Times

MOSCOW, Jan. 5—The Soviet Government announced today the legal rehabilitation of the Volga German minority accused by Stalin of collaboration with the Nazi invaders during World War II.

No provision was made for the restoration of the minority's autonomous republic from which the Germans were exiled in August, 1941, in Siberia and Central Asia.

The Volga Germans are descendants of about 27,000 colonists invited to Russia in 1760 by Catherine the Great to develop uncultivated lands. Special privileges granted them were annulled a century later.

A decree published in the latest issue of the Bulletin of the Supreme Soviet (Parliament) said "life has shown that sweeping accusations [of collaboration] were unfounded and were a manifestation of arbitrary rule under the conditions of Stalin's cult of personality."

"In fact," the decree added, "the overwhelming majority of the ethnic Germans, along with all the Soviet people, through their labor promoted the Soviet Union's victory over Fascist Germany in World War II and have been taking an active part in Communist construction since the war."

The Supreme Soviet decree, dated Aug. 29, put a legal stamp of approval on a de facto restoration of the ethnic Germans' civil and cultural rights that began in 1956. Several other non-Russian minorities banished for alleged treasonable wartime activities were formally vindicated at that time.

The New York Times Jan. 6, 1965

**Cross-hatching marks the former Volga Republic.**

**No explanation was given for the more than seven-year delay of legal action in rehabilitating the German or for the four-month delay in the publication of the decree. Decrees of the Supreme Soviet usually appear in the bulletin within one or two weeks.**

**Unlike the other banished peoples, who were invited by the Soviet Government to return to home regions, the Germans were told to stay where they were.**

**The decree sought to justify the different treatment by saying that the "German population has taken root in new places of residence and their former settlement area [on the Volga River near Saratov] has been occupied [by others]."**

The **administrations in the** Germans' new places of residence were instructed "to continue to assist the German population in economic and cultural development with due regard for their ethnic characteristics and interests."

**Reviewing the de facto revival of ethnic German culture in the last seven years, the decree noted that elementary and secondary schools using German as the language of instruction had been established in areas with German population or that, at least, German language instruction was being offered to children of school age.**

"Radio programs are being **broadcast and newspapers are being published in German, and** other cultural facilities are being provided for the German population, the decree said.

Critics of the Soviet Union's policy toward Jews have cited the German ethnic revival as an example of what can be done for a minority that is scattered throughout the country. The Soviet authorities have sought to justify a shortage of cultural facilities for Jews on the ground that they are not concentrated in a cohesive territory.

The total German population in the Soviet Union in 1941 was 1,600,000. About half lived in the Russian Republic, which includes Siberia.

January 6, 1965

# *Tatars Struggle On Against Moscow*

By HENRY KAMM

Special to The New York Times

MOSCOW, May 2—In September, 1967, the Soviet Government, taking action to right another major wrong done by Stalin, formally absolved the Crimean Tatars of the dictator's accusation of mass collaboration with the Nazis during World War II.

The step was taken quietly; the decree was not published in the national press. The regime, by its actions since, has made it clear that it intends to go no further in restoring the Crimean Tartars' rights, particularly their former autonomous republic.

With all the means at its disposal, the Soviet leadership has been combating the Tatars, who are among the most active and organized pressure groups in the country and who push their demands by concerted action.

As a result, more than 200 have been sentenced to terms of up to seven years in prison camps on charges of anti-Soviet activities or of the circulation of slanders against the state or the social system. Many hundreds more have been summarily tried and jailed for up to 15 days for "petty hooliganism." This charge has been used to quell demonstrations of Tatar nationalism.

### Deported at Gunpoint

The Government wants the Tatars to stay in the regions, mainly in Central Asia, to which they were deported, at gunpoint and in cattle cars, 25 years ago. When Stalin, with a stroke of the pen, ordered the banishment of the nation, about a fourth of the population of the Crimea, it was mainly women, children and the aged who were dragged into exile immediately. The men were still at the fighting front and were not carted off until peace had been restored.

About 250,000 Tatars — a Turkic people commonly known in English as Tartars—lived on the peninsula in the Black Sea when war broke out. About 100,000 died during the exodus in the harsh early days of exile.

The Government has not formally rejected the Tartars' right to return, but very few have been allowed to do so since it insists that they find jobs and homes first. According to Tatar leaders, local officials and managers refuse to register them for residence or hire them.

The assumption is that the policy was instituted because of a fear of creating a new nationality problem in the Ukraine, into which the Crimea has been incorporated, where nationalism, particularly among intellectuals, maintains constant pressure.

Furthermore, it is consistent with de-Stalinization as it was practiced even at its height not to turn the wheel of justice back fully. While Stalin remains controversial, the cloud is never quite lifted from his victims.

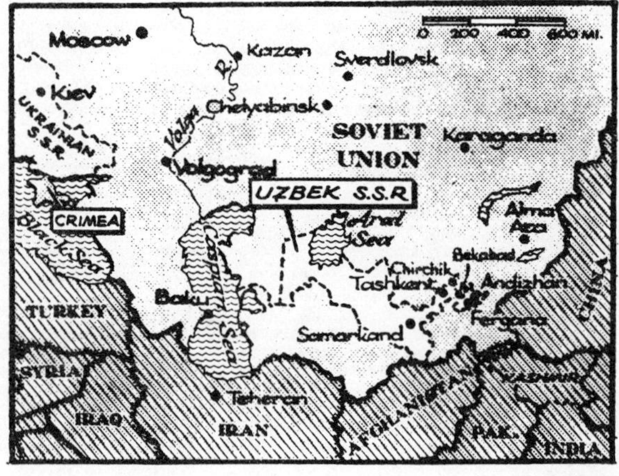


The New York Times May 3, 1969

**Tatars were shifted from Crimea to the Uzbek Republic**

### Volga Germans Too

The only other sizable nationalities without a national territory in this multi-national state are the Jews, who press no territorial claims, and the Volga Germans, who were among the ethnic groups penalized by Stalin during the war and who also were not restored to their homeland.

The Crimean Tatars live close together in the cities, mainly in the republic of Uzbekistan, where they have been settled. They organize protest meetings and keep up a steady flow of petitions to local, regional and national as well as Communist party authorities. They circulate a typewritten newsletter about their activities.

For five years they have maintained a permanent, though unofficial, lobby in Moscow.

On April 17 a group of Tatars presented at the Communist party headquarters four volumes of signatures, totaling 32,808 names, on a new petition demanding full restoration of their rights and protesting the actions against them.

### Paying a High Price

In the Soviet Union, the pressing of demands by concerted action is considered dissidence, and the Tatars have paid the high price of such activity. They have taken pains not to overstep the boundaries of the law, but law is a matter of interpretation.

When Tatars gather outside courthouses where their comrades [illegible]e on trial, the "petty h[illegible]ism" charge is invoked [illegible] up the crow[illegible]

Eleve. Tatars, mainly young intellectuals, are awaiting trail in Tashkent, the Uzbek capital and the scene of most of the trials. The goal of the authorities, according to the Tatars, is to decapitate the movement by concentrating the attack on present and potential leaders.

Tatars who are active in the movement share the fate of all Soviet diddisdents. They have difficulty in finding and keeping jobs. They are expelled from universities and other educa-Soviet dissidents. They have been ousted from the Communist party or its youth movement, a serious blow to a career and social life. They are harassed by the secret police, their homes are searched, their mail opened, their telephones tapped.

Major roundups of Tatar representatives in Moscow took place between May and August of last year. On May 16 and 17, a section of the city near the Exhibition of Economic Achievement was sea ed off and honeycombed. More than 300 Tatars were seized, loaded on a train and sent under escort to Tashkent.

Tatar leaders estimate that 12,000 have been expelled from the Crimea or turned back before reaching it since the 1967 decree. Testimony of cruel treatment, harassment and chicanery have been recorded by many victims as well as witnesses, many not Tatars.

A few days after the decree was published in the Uzbek press, Idris Kaitaz and Kara Izzet gathered up their families and left their collective farm to set out for their Crimean village.

When the two families—each with five children, as well as Mr. Kaitaz's 78-year-old mother — arrived in their village, Uskut, they found that it was now called Privetnoye. The Ukrainians had effaced every trace of the Tatars, who had lived in the Crimea since the Mongol invasion of the 13th century.

The men applied for work at the local state farm and were refused. They asked for lodging at the farm's hostel, but not even the children were given shelter. They slept in the open until the children began to cry from the cold; then they sought refuge in a deserted ruin.

In the morning the district prosecutor arrived with eight policemen and ordered them to leave. The police threw their belongings out a window and pushed the children out after them. Mr. Izzet's 8-year-old daughter landed on her head and lay unconscious.

The other children were pushed about by the policemen. Mrs. Izzet, who was pregnant, was knocked down twice.

For 10 days the two families camped on the outskirts of the village in a tent while the men looked for jobs. On the 11th day policemen struck down the tent, forced the group onto a truck and sent them northward out of the Crimea.

They persuaded the driver to let them off at the city of Simferopol, where they rented an apartment and the men resumed their search for work. One must have a job in the locality to be legally registered as a resident.

After a few days of fruitless search, the men were admitted to see the deputy chairman of the regional council, A. P. Derkach, who shouted: "The decree of Sept. 5 does not give you the right to return to the Crimea! There will never be room for you in the Crimea!"

May 3, 1969

# *Islamic Past of Azerbaijan Republic Frustrates Moscow's Marxist Plans*

**By HEDRICK SMITH**
Special to The New York Times

BAKU, U.S.S.R.—Half a century of Soviet power has done much to modernize the Azerbaijan Republic, but the Azerbaijani style of life, reflecting centuries of Moslem influence, refuses to conform to the Communist model.

As an institution the Islamic faith is weak here. The veil has virtually disappeared. Women as well as men have been educated and moved into jobs in numbers unheard of before the Bolshevik take-over in this region of the Caucasus on April 20, 1920.

The industry of Baku has been modernized and diversified and new plants have been installed in district towns. Phalanxes of square - faced apartment houses surround Baku and have sprouted in new industrial towns like Sumgait. Some Western economists have reckoned that, for many, health care, education and standards of living are higher in Soviet Azerbaijan than in neighboring Iran, where several million ethnic Azerbaijanis live.

But vestiges of the past remain to bedevil and frustrate determined Marxists.

**'For Mercenary Reasons'**

No less a figure than Geidar A. Aliyev, the Communist party chief, has been complaining about nepotism, forced child marriages, corruption on a grand scale, the urge for private ownership and the penchant for private trading—"plundering of socialist property for mercenary reasons," he called it—and the practice of bribing examiners at universities for entrance or graduation.

In two unusually tart speeches in March and October, Mr. Aliyev castigated ideological backsliders of all kinds. He was upset by commercialism in local theaters, painters who copy "the worst models of modern art of the West," the undue pessimism of some novelists, non-Marxist probing of local history, worrisome curiosity about religion among the young and even financial donations to mosques by leading intellectuals.

The New York Times/Dec. 13, 1971

"One reason for bribery is the striving for private property, the basis for which is individualism and selfishness, and worrying only about one's own benefit, and the wish to get as much as possible for oneself and less for society," the party chief declared. "One should not undervalue the influence of bourgeois ideology."

The clannishness of the Azerbaijanis, their skill at arranging deals under the table and their generally undisciplined ways have long been a problem for Communist leaders—apparently at a greater scale than in many other regions. Some local Communists blame centuries of Moslem domination over this southern territory during the conquests by Persians, Arabs and Turks.

"Islam is more aggressive and more reactionary than other religions," asserted Gasham Aslanov, editor of the Communist party youth newspaper Yunost, which circulates 350,000 copies three times a week. "This religion teaches people to think about themselves and their families."

The former party instructor, articulate, fleshy-faced, curly-haired and younger looking than his 37 years, cited what he said were Moslem proverbs to demonstrate the selfishness fostered by Islam.

"We have these proverbs," he said. "'He who sacrifices all of his efforts for the benefits of the people suffers more.' 'First it is necessary to build up the inside of the mosque and then the outside.' 'Each man tries to gather coal under his own stove.'"

"We lived about 1,300 years by this religion, by this ideology," he explained during a chat in a hotel cafe. "We have lived under Soviet power only 50 years. During 50 years it is very difficult to change human nature."

**City With a Hybrid Past**

Actually Baku is an international city with a hybrid past. Its Victorian - style balconied apartments and its tree-lined promenades facing the Caspian Sea give it a Mediterranean flavor.

Russian influence dates from 1806, when the czarist empire won this region from Persia. Attracted by oil, Russians made up a fourth of Baku's population by 1904 are a slightly larger percentage today. Azerbaijanis constitute just half of the city's 1.3 million people.

The language of commerce, politics and advancement is Russian, spoken by most people regardless of ethnic origin. Major public speeches are delivered in Russian. A young journalist recalled his older brother's insistence that he learn Russian at school not only for the sake of his career but so he could date Russian girls.

Nonetheless, it is Islamic tradition and the Azerbaijani character that give the region its distinctive personality. Beside the vast homes of one-time oil magnates, put up on a scale to rival Fifth Avenue mansions, are buildings with the graceful arches of the Islamic world. And the faces of the Azerbaijanis, dark, lively, honey-colored, speak of the nearness of the Middle East.

Formal Islam has withered under the pressure of militant atheism. Local specialists say there are only 16 mosques, two in Baku, for Azerbaijan's 5.1 million people. The Koran, it is reported, was last printed in Russian three years ago and is not available in local bookshops.

Generally the mosques attract only the old, though the leader of the Communist Youth League complained recently that young people, including some of his members, were attending religious rites.

It is less the formal religious structure that disturbs Communist leaders than it is the social influence of Islamic customs—girls dropping out of school for marriages arranged by their families, women left at home by husbands going out to socialize and not advanced properly even in the Communist party, and the undisciplined economic style.

Privately, some people talk like unreconstructed capitalists, eager to display Western watches or fountain pens, boastful about their financial canniness, unashamed that bribes or contacts are the key to success.

"You've got to have money to get what you want," said a well-tanned director of a state farm. "It's the same everywhere—in America, in the Soviet Union, everywhere."

It is that style of life that Mr. Aliyev, formerly chief of the republic's secret police, has pledged to wipe out since being put in charge here in 1969.

He has removed up to 50 senior government and party officials for abuse of office or dereliction. A number of officials have been put on trial for bribery, among them a judge who allegedly took bribes from three men accused of fraud but was caught before he could fix the case. Nonetheless, some Azerbaijanis remain skeptical.

"Let them bring another and another and another," said a workman who described how payoffs helped speed surgical operations. "It will stay the same."

December 13, 1971

# Moscow Deftly Allows Armenia Its Nationalism

By HEDRICK SMITH
Special to The New York Times

ERIVAN, U.S.S.R.—"There is more sausage in Moscow than in Erivan," said a dark-haired Armenian intellectual, acknowledging that living conditions here are not on a par with the distant Soviet capital. "But one doesn't live by sausage alone. I would rather live and work here among my own people, even for 50 rubles less a month."

Such comments are typical of the resurgent national feeling in Soviet Armenia, a nationalism that has been carefully cultivated and deftly controlled by the Communist leadership for its own purposes.

Alone among Soviet minority republics, Armenia has attracted large-scale repatriation from among its 1.5 million nationals abroad. By Soviet count 220,000 Armenians from the Middle East, Europe, Asia and the Americas have returned since the Bolsheviks seized power here in 1920.

Occasionally Armenian patriotism has taken on overtones that have worried Moscow, but because of the deep animosity and fear Armenians harbor for their traditional enemies, the Turks, no serious secessionist movement has developed.

With a dedication that would inspire the envy of an American chamber of commerce, loyal Communists emphasize how Erivan has blossomed from a provincial town of 30,000 in 1920 to a substantial industrial city of nearly 800,000 today.

"This is an entirely reconstructed city," a tourist guide said enthusiastically, pointing out block upon block of recently built Soviet-style stone apartment buildings and ignoring the crumbling homes and shanties that still pockmark parts of this capital of Armenia.

Once only an agricultural region, Armenia now boasts such internationally known scientific centers as the Byurakan Observatory and modern factories that turn out

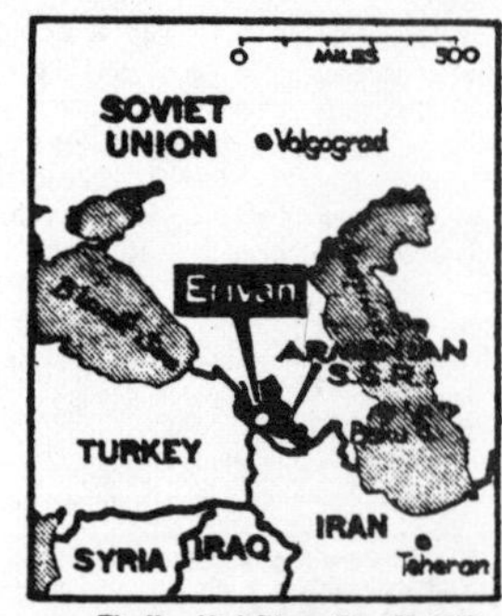

The New York Times/Dec. 20, 1971

computers, chemicals, precision instruments, electrical products and minibuses.

The Armenian Apostolic Church, a focus of national feeling and the principal institution for appealing to the loyalties of overseas Armenians, is enjoying a revival among believers and nonbelievers alike. At Erivan University students are given a compulsory course in Armenian history as well as in Marxism-Leninism.

Language and family ties are especially strong. Armenians have never intermarried with their conquerors—Assyrians, Macedonians, Persians, Arabs, Turks and Mongols—and even now rarely intermarry with Russians, who are less than 3 per cent of Armenia's 2.5 million people. "We have kept our culture pure," a young nationalist said.

Visitors sometimes encounter anti-Russian feelings on a personal level. Not long ago a Western European, seeking batteries for a transistor radio, asked a clerk for them in Russian and was told none were in stock. When the visitor explained that he was a foreigner, the clerk's tone changed. "Oh," he said, "how many do you want?"

From Moscow's point of view the most unnerving outburst of Armenian patriotism in recent years was the unauthorized demonstration of about 100,000 Armenians in Erivan on April 24, 1965, the 50th anniversary of the Turkish massacre of about 1.5 million Armenians during World War I.

Although directed against Turkey rather than Moscow, its strength and spontaneity apparently made the Kremlin uneasy, for a Moscow official denounced it as "anti-Soviet" and "secessionist." A well-known Armenian poet, Silvia Kaputyan, denied any secessionist motive and criticized Moscow for seeking friendly relations with Turkey rather than joining Armenians in mourning the massacre.

More recently Armenian visitors from abroad have found scholars showing interest in the non-Communist government that ruled Armenia briefly in 1920.

Privately, Armenians blame Stalin's secret police for the assassinations of an Armenian Patriarch, Khoren I, in 1938, and a nationalist-minded Communist party leader, Aghassi Khandjan, who was purged in 1936 after he was allegedly in contact with Armenian émigré politicians but has now been officially rehabilitated.

Nonetheless, the prevailing sentiment seems to be that Soviet protection has given Armenia a chance to blossom. Some Armenians even entertain hopes that Moscow can somehow help them recover historic lands held by Turkey.

"Of course, every Armenian wants to get his land back," a writer observed. "What you see here is only a tenth of our land and half of our people. How can the others come back and live among these stones? There's not enough good land."

Between 1920 and 1950, officials say, nearly 200,000 Armenians returned from overseas. Then the repatriation program was suspended because of inadequate facilities. Since 1963, when the program was resumed, about 25,000 more are said to have returned, most of them from Iran.

A small minority have tried to go back overseas, among them some of the few hundred Americans who came here in the immediate post-war period. Some have encountered obstacles and as recently as last spring talked with American newsmen about their difficulties, but this fall, possibly after official warnings, they declined to meet with reporters.

Other Americans have been content here, among them Martic T. Martentz, who returned in 1967 after years of editing the pro-Soviet Armenian newspaper, Raper, in New York. He now surveys the oversees Armenian-language press for the national library.

"There's no deadline, no pressure—it's an easy life," he explained over drinks at the Armenia Hotel. With his wife's salary as a teacher and his daughter's $33-a-a-month stipend at medical school, the family lives on about $385 monthly, helped by the clothes and furnishings brought with them.

Mr. Martentz, who has kept not only his United States passport but some American funds, still dresses nattily in the fashions of the mid-sixties — a trim jacket with narrow lapels, button-down shirt and conservative narrow tie.

He acknowledged some annoying shortages of consumer items here and deficiencies in services "It's easier to build a restaurant than to get a good waiter," he remarked.

There is corruption too, he went on, and it is not uncommon to have to pay an extra ruble or two for some hard-to-get item—from tablespoons to radios.

"But compared with American big cities," he added, "the corruption here is peanuts."

Among Armenians, especially the young, there is great admiration for the United States. "Armenians romanticize American efficiency," Mr. Marentz explained. "They think everyone there is rich. They don't realize how hard people have to work in America."

December 20, 1971

# PROTEST ON SOVIET LAID TO LATVIANS

By BERNARD GWERTZMAN
Special to The New York Times

WASHINGTON, Feb. 26—A letter attributed to 17 Latvian Communists, complaining about what they say are efforts by Moscow to "Russify" their Baltic republic, has been sent to several foreign Communist parties.

A copy of the letter, which has been published in Western Europe, was made available recently to The New York Times by Latvian émigrés here. United States Government analysts who have studied it say they believe it is authentic and consistent with what was already known of the nationalistic tendencies still prevalent in Latvia, which was forcibly annexed to the Soviet Union in 1940.

The Voice of America has already broadcast the full text to the Soviet Union.

The letter is not signed, but in the body of the document the 17 say: "We are Communists and most of us have been such for 25-35 years and more. We wish only well to socialism, Marxism - Leninism and mankind."

They declare, "We cannot sign this letter," but do not say why.

**Russian Chauvinism Charged**

The chief complaint in the 5,000-word document is that the Soviet leaders are practicing "Great Russian chauvinism" and are seeking to force the smaller Soviet ethnic groups, such as the Latvians, to assimilate with the Russians.

Although an effort was made to redress ethnic problems after Stalin's death, the letter says, current policy is to transfer as many Russians, Byelorussians and Ukrainians — all Slavs—to Latvia and the other

Baltic republics of Estonia and Lithuania.

The letter criticizes the creation of new industrial sites in Latvia and the influx of non-Latvian workers. It asserts that the republic now has "a number of large enterprises where there are almost no Latvians among the workers, engineering - technical personnel, and directors."

"There are also those where most of the workers are Latvians but none of the executives understands Latvian," it asserts. "There are entire institutions where there are very few Latvians. The apparatus of the Ministry of Interior in Riga, for example, has 1,500 employes, but only 300 of them are Latvians."

The Interior Ministry supervises the police force.

The letter says that about 65 per cent of the doctors do not speak Latvian "and because of this often make crude mistakes in diagnosing illnesses and prescribing treatment."

**'Just Indignation' Cited**

"All this calls forth just indignation in the local population," it declares.

The letter maintains that priority is given to "the progressive Russification" of all life in Latvia, and the assimilation of the Latvians."

There are now about 2.4 million people in Latvia, of whom only about 57 per cent are ethnically Latvian, a drop of 5 per cent in the last decade. Russians make up 30 per cent of the population, a 3 per cent increase. Poles, Lithuanians, Byelorussians, Jews and Ukrainians make up the remaining 13 per cent.

The decrease in the percentage of Latvians living in Latvia has been due not only to the influx of non-Latvians, but also to the exceptionally low birth rate in the republic, combined with an aging Latvian population.

For instance, in 1969, Latvia recorded a birth rate of only 14 per thousand, which is the smallest of any republic in the Soviet Union. Its death rate was 11.1 per thousand, the second highest after Estonia. This means that its natural increase (birth rate minus death rate) was only 2.9 per thousand, also the smallest in the Soviet Union. The natural increase for the Soviet Union as a whole in 1969 was 8.9 per thousand.

**Russian Broadcasts Noted**

The letter states that although Latvians still are in the majority, two-thirds of the radio and television broadcasts are in Russian. Latvian writers have more difficulty getting their works published than Russians, it says, and "in all republic, city, and district organizations, in most local organizations and in all enterprises, business is conducted in Russian."

"If there is a single Russian in an organization, he will demand that the meeting be conducted in Russian, and his demand will be satisfied," the letter goes on. "If this is not done, then the collective is accused of nationalism."

The letter specifically decries the "loud preaching" of mixed marriages in the republic and says that Latvian language theater groups must produce Russian plays but that Russian language groups rarely have Latvian ones.

The letter was received by the Communist parties of Rumania, Yugoslvaia, France, Austria and Spain among others. It calls on them to use their influence with Soviet leaders to improve the state of the Latvian and other ethnic groups.

February 27, 1972

# SOVIET DISCLOSES UKRAINE UNREST

## Concedes Nationalists Have Ties to Emigre Groups

By THEODORE SHABAD
Special to The New York Times

MOSCOW, June 6—The Soviet Union has conceded the existence of a nationalist movement in the Ukraine having close ties with anti-Communist émigré organizations abroad.

Some Ukrainian intellectuals have long been known to oppose what they view as excessive Russification and an absence of cultural freedom, and have campaigned for more active use of the Ukrainian language in their republic.

Details of the dissident network became available here today in the account of a news conference given in Kiev by Jaroslav Dobosch, a Belgian student of Ukrainian descent, who said he had been sent to the Soviet Union to make contact with the nationalists.

The Belgian's arrest early in January gave rise to a wave of arrests and house searches in which about 20 Ukrainians were seized on charges of defaming the Soviet State. They included Vyacheslav Chornovil, whose accoumt of the nationalist movement, "The Chornovil Papers," has circulated widely abroad.

**Underground Newsletter**

A Ukrainian underground newsletter, Ukrainsky Visnyk, apparently ceased publication at the time of the arrests. Five issues had appeared, starting in early 1970.

Mr. Dobosch, who is 24 years old, was released last Friday after having been detained for five months by the Soviet authorities. He was put on a plane for Brussels a few hours after his public recantation at the Kiev news conference in which he implicated five of the Ukrainian nationalists.

An account of the conference was published Saturday in the Kiev newspaper Pravda Ukrainy, which reached subscribers here today. It provided the most detailed official version yet made public on the Dobosch case and its ramifications.

Mr. Dobosch, in a statement published by the Ukrainian daily, said he had been sent to the Soviet Union by an émigré group known as the Organization of Ukrainian Nationalists to seek out five nationalists in the Ukraine.

**5 Nationalists Identified**

The aim of the journey, according to the Belgian, was to brief the Ukrainians on the émigré activities, make payments to the nationalists and smuggle out anti-Soviet literature.

The student identified the five as Ivan Svitlychny, a literary critic; Zinoviya Franko, granddaughter of Ivan Franko, a Ukrainian revolutionary writer; Leonid Seleznenko, Anna Kotsurova and Stefaniya Gulyk.

"I was supposed to inform them how anti-Soviet nationalist organizations in the West were struggling against the Soviet state with a view to intensifying their activities here in the Ukraine," the Kiev newspaper quoted Mr. Dobosch as having said.

It was one of the most direct acknowledgments yet to appear in the controlled Soviet press that nationalist groups were active in the Ukraine.

In answer to a question at the Kiev news conference, Mr. Dobosch identified a manuscript he sought to smuggle out of the Soviet Union as having been written by S. I. Karavansky, an almost legendary member of the Ukrainian opposition. Mr. Karavansky has spent nearly the entire postwar period in prison camps on charges of espionage and anti-Soviet nationalist activity.

June 7, 1972

# 200 LITHUANIANS REPORTED JAILED

## Second Youth Said to Burn Himself to Death in Protest

By The Associated Press

MOSCOW, June 13—A second youth in two months has burned himself to death and about 200 young people are in jail awaiting trials in the aftermath of two days of rioting in Soviet Lithuania last month, Lithuanian sources reported today.

Street fighting in the city of Kaunas on May 18 and 19 reportedly involved several thousand youths who shouted "Freedom for Lithuania!" and hurled sticks and stones at policemen and paratroopers. Two policemen reportedly died as a result of the rioting.

The rioters, mostly 16 to 24 years old, took to the streets during the funeral of Roman Kalanta, 20, a student who poured nearly a gallon of gasoline over himself in a Kaunas park May 14 and set himself afire. He died 12 hours later.

The sources reported that another youth, apparently inspired by Mr. Kalanta, burned himself to death about 10 days ago in the small city of Varena, about 50 miles south of the Lithuanian capital, Vilna. The informants could not provide the youth's name or age. They said he had climbed to the roof of a four-story building in Varena, poured gasoline over his body, set himself afire and then jumped to the ground. They reported that he died four days later.

The sources said the suicide

The New York Times/June 14, 1972

**Youth burned himself to death in Varena after a similar death in Kaunas.**

had apparently not led to riots like those in Kaunas and that the controlled press had not mentioned it.

**300 Were Released**

They estimated that about 200 youths arrested during the Kaunas rioting in May were in the Lithuanian republic's Investigative Prison at Vilna.

They added that about 300 other people who were taken into custody during the street fighting were later released.

About 20 of the 200 still under detention are students at the Technical and Medical Institutes at Kaunas, the sources said, and the rest are young workers or high school students. The sources said that they did not expect all 200 of the youths to stand trial.

Lithuania, a Baltic republic with a predominantly Roman Catholic population, was annexed by the Soviet Union in 1940. Nationalist sentiment reportedly has been rising in the last six months, with the Catholic community demanding freedom of worship.

One of the sources said that he was a witness to the street fighting in Kaunas in May. The sources recounted that the youths had assembled before Mr. Kalanta's funeral at the home of his parents and then had marched through the streets to the city's Soviet building and then to the secret police headquarters.

The sources said that the demonstrations were strongly nationalistic and that the youths shouted "Freedom! Freedom! Freedom!" "Freedom for Lithuania!" and "Freedom for young people!"

Policemen in front of the secret police headquarters drove the young people away with truncheons, the sources said, and the youths reassembled in the park where Mr. Kalanta had burned himself to death. They said the youths had laid flowers on the spot where the immolation took place but that the police had closed off the area and removed the flowers.

The sources said the streets of Kaunas were still heavily patrolled by the police and by a division of paratroops garrisoned there.

**Firebombings Attempted**

The sources said that the young people had made several attempts to set fires in the city. One firebomb was reportedly thrown at the second story of the Communist party headquarters.

They added that the Kaunas Communist party newspaper, which had tried to discredit Mr. Kalanta by describing him as a mentally deranged drug addict, had published a letter from the youth's mother. The letter expressed sorrow that people had been hurt or killed because of the disturbances, according to the sources.

June 14, 1972

# Soviet Is Pressing the Blending of Its 100 Nationalities

By THEODORE SHABAD
Special to The New York Times

MOSCOW, July 30—After 50 years of trying to knit its more than 100 ethnic groups into a single society, the Soviet Union appears to have made great gains in the educational and cultural development of its nationalities. But it remains well short of the ultimate goal of total harmony.

The continuing existence of ethnic problems has been pointed up in this 50th anniversary year of the establishment of the Union of Soviet Socialist Republics by reports of nationalist unrest in Lithuania, charges of Russification in the Ukraine and attempts to glorify a non-Communist Georgian state that existed briefly more than 50 years ago.

But the most telling evidence of all seems to be the Communist ideologists' own avowed need at this late date to press a campaign for what is known here as "international indoctrination" of citizens, meaning the preaching of a higher degree of ethnic tolerance.

The problems faced by the Soviet Union are perhaps best illustrated by comparison with the United States, also composed of a wide range of ethnic elements.

While the trend in the United States has proceeded from the old melting-pot philosophy to a new affirmation of ethnic identity, a reverse long-term tendency seems evident in the Soviet Union, aimed ultimately at a vaguely defined integration of ethnic groups into a single Soviet nation.

It is the conflict between nationalist aspirations and the integration aim that appears to keep the ethnic issue alive.

Examples of ethnic friction are rarely made public in the controlled press and it is therefore difficult to judge their extent. But chance remarks by Soviet citizens and occasional references in plays and motion pictures suggest vestiges of prejudice and assertions of national feelings.

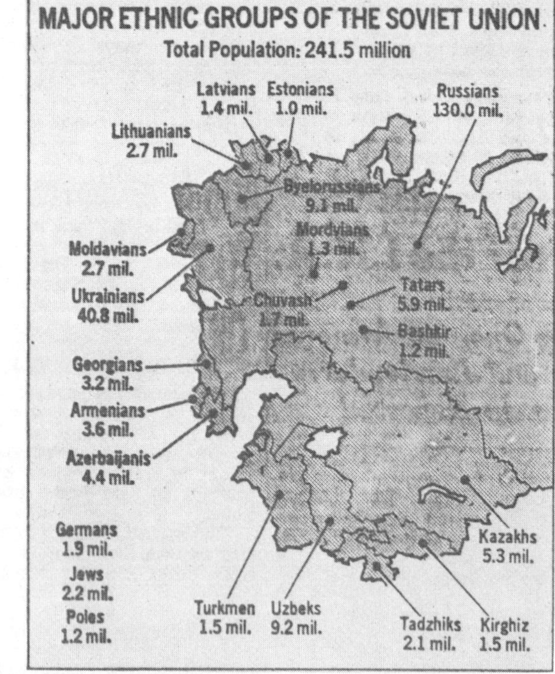


The New York Times/July 31, 1972

One Russian recently remarked at the time of President Nixon's visit to Moscow that he found greater affinity with Americans than with some of the Asian ethnic groups in the Soviet Union.

"I would not want my daughter to marry a Yakut," he asserted. The 300,000 Yakuts, a Turkic - speaking people of northeast Siberia with significant cultural gains under the Soviet regime, are of Mongol stock.

In the 1966 film, "Lebedev Against Lebedev," a bigot introduced to a Georgian physicist comments, "I know those physicists from the Central Market." He was alluding to the Georgian's flair for private enterprise in selling produce at the farmer markets operating outside the Government's retailing system.

In an effort to win the loyalty of the various ethnic groups inhabiting the old Russian empire, the Bolsheviks founded the Soviet state after the 1917 revolution on the principle of a complex network of autonomous ethnic territories coinciding roughly with the historical areas of settlement of the national groups.

Within the limits of its republic, region or other autonomous area, each ethnic group was given the right to foster an education and culture in its own language, but under the over-all umbrella of a Communist ideology. In terms of a widespread slogan, ethnic cultural development became "national in form and socialist in content."

Against this background of ethnic separateness, both the common ideological constraints and the predominant influence of the ethnic Russians—every second Soviet citizen is a Russian—have been major forces working for ultimate integration.

**Next Stage Is Foreseen**

According to Communist doctrine, the blossoming of ethnic cultures is to bring about a further stage of development when national groups will disappear as distinct cultural and linguistic entities and be fused into "a single common socialist culture with a single common language."

In view of the predominant position of Russian, which not only is spoken by the 130 million ethnic Russians but is also the second language of 20 million non-Russians, there appears to be little doubt what the common language would ultimately be.

Nikita S. Khrushchev, the late Soviet leader, sought to accelerate the ethnic integration process by fostering regional economic agencies and other administrative forms of amalgamation in the Baltic republics, in Central Asia and in Transcaucasia. But his measures were abrogated after his fall from power in October,

1964, evidently because of opposition among the integrated republics.

Since then, integration has been encouraged at a more leisurely pace by exchanges of cultural delegations among republics, with Estonian writers and singers traveling, say, to Tadzhikistan in Central Asia, and Uzbek poets and artists touring the Moldavian Republic, adjoining Rumania.

Russians and their fellow Slavs, the Ukrainians and Byelorussians, are probably the most highly mobile and industrially skilled among the Soviet Union's ethnic groups and have been migrating to other republics to help staff construction projects and new industries.

In some areas, as in the Baltic republics of Estonia and Latvia, the Russian influx appears related to the inability of the indigenous population, with a low rate of natural increase, to provide manpower for expanding industry. However, nationalistically minded Latvians and Estonians also fear a deliberate policy aimed at submerging the local cultures through Russian influx.

In Tallinn, the Estonian capital, for example, a new Russian evening newspaper, Vecherny Tallinn (Evening Tallinn), is beginning publication Aug. 1, presumably to meet the needs of the city's growing population. Russians accounted for 30 per cent of the city's population in 1959, and may now represent 40 per cent.

The movement of Russians into Central Asia and Kazakhstan has been associated with intensive industrial development in these regions, combined with apparent reluctance or inability of the indigenous rural population to move to the cities.

Sociological surveys have found that the poor knowledge of Russian among the rural Central Asians has been a major factor inhibiting their migration to cities, where Russian has become the key language in industry.

In the period between the last two population censuses, 1959 to 1970, the ethnic Russian element has been increasing in all non-Russian republics, except one. The exception is the Georgian Republic of Transcaucasia, where a strong feeling of ethnic identity combined with a high level of education and industrial skills has in fact resulted in a net outflow of ethnic Russians over the last decade.

Differences in ethnic attitudes are perhaps best illustrated by two contrasting areas such as culturally strong and homogenous Georgia, on the one hand, and the Republic of Kazakhstan, where the indigenous Kazakh population has been virtually submerged by immigrants and now represents one-third of the total.

In Kazakhstan, where a new resource-oriented industrial economy has been superimposed on the indigenous stock-herding society, the officially controlled press likes to emphasize the "multinational character" of the labor force on construction projects, as representatives of "fraternal republics" join in Kazakhstan's economic development.

In Georgia, where industry and construction projects are staffed to a large extent with locally trained skilled labor, there are few references to outside aid in development projects, although the general ideological point of a rapprochement between the Soviet Union's ethnic groups is also frequently made in the press.

The process of integration probably advances most rapidly among some ethnic communities that, for historical or other reasons, are not concentrated in a particular area of settlement and lack some of the cultural facilities available within autonomous territories.

Largest among these groups is the Jewish community of more than two million, of whom perhaps one per cent live in the Siberian autonomous region of Birobidzhan allocated to the Soviet Union's Jews in the nineteen-thirties.

The absence of instruction in Yiddish and a scarcity of Jewish cultural institutions have fostered the process of assimilation that may portend the ultimate merger of all ethnic groups in the Soviet Union. An undetermined minority of Soviet Jews have sought to assert their ethnic identity by seeking emigration to Israel.

Other ethnic groups without a home area within the Soviet Union are the 1.9 million ethnic Germans and the 1.2 million ethnic Poles. They have been more fortunate than the Jews in asserting themselves as distinct communities, both because of a wider range of cultural facilities granted by the authorities and the fact that both East Germany and Poland are members of the Soviet bloc of nations.

July 31, 1972

# ETHNIC GERMANS SEEK SOVIET EXIT

## They Step Up Pressure for Right to Emigrate Despite Official Reprisals

By CHRISTOPHER S. WREN
Special to The New York Times

MOSCOW, Sept. 11—They come from a minority group that Moscow considers Soviet citizens, but they insist that their true homeland lies beyond the Soviet borders. And to get there, they have increasingly turned to public appeals, hunger strikes and demonstrations despite official reprisals.

Now the warming climate in East-West relations has prompted Soviet authorities to let more of them emigrate, though the activists among them contend that the numbers are not nearly enough.

Those who have received exit visas can be seen evenings in the Belorussian Station, clutching their clumsy bundles of possessions as they nervously wait to board the trains that will carry them westward.

They are not Jews, who have attracted world attention, but rather Soviet citizens of German descent who now are trying to be reunited with relatives in West Germany. For while the issue of Jewish emigration has engaged far greater sympathy abroad, the ethnic Germans have begun waging an almost identical, if considerably less successful, battle for their own right to emigrate.

**Appeal Circulated**

Their situation was dramatized in a letter passed to Western newsmen here this week, in which some 3,500 heads of families, representing about 15,000 ethnic Germans in Central Asia, appealed to Chancellor Helmut Schmidt to help them go to West Germany.

Others have taken bolder action. On Monday, a 51-year-old ethnic German from Estonia sought asylum in the West German Embassy and, according to diplomats, has since refused to leave. He said his daughter was detained by the police on anti-Soviet charges after she had protested the military conscription of her brother, an engineer who had applied to emigrate.

The ethnic Germans, some of whose ancestors settled in the Volga Valley two centuries ago, number about 1.8 million people in the total population of 251 million.

Of these, unofficial German sources here estimate, a half million would like to go to West Germany. The number of those who have actually begun the emigration process has been put at 40,000.

**500 a Month Leaving**

Largely as a result of Bonn's course of accommodation with Moscow, about 500 ethnic Germans a month are now allowed to emigrate. The plight of others who have applied is likely to be discussed during Chancellor Schmidt's visit here at the end of this year.

The emigration figures for ethnic Germans reflect, as in the case of the Jews, the political pragmatism of the Soviet authorities. While only 800 were permitted to leave in 1956, 4,681 left in 1958 and 5,960 the following year, after both countries had signed a consular treaty in 1958.

By 1964, the figure dropped to 262 emigrants. Last year, 4,441 were permitted to emigrate.

Applications by ethnic Germans to go to East Germany are reported to be negligible. The East German Embassy, in response to inquiries, contended that it did not keep such information.

**Many Live in Siberia**

Over half of the Soviet Union's ethnic Germans live in Siberia or the Central Asian republics, principally Kazakhstan, where they were deported by Stalin during World War II. The Germans had their rights fully restored in 1964 but have not been permitted to reclaim their former autonomous republic on the Volga River.

Other ethnic Germans live in the Baltic states, Moldavia and former East Prussia.

Unlike the Jewish emigrants, who reflect a relatively high proportion of educated professionals, the ethnic Germans are usually collective farmers or factory workers. They have not been subjected to loss of employment as have the educated Jews.

Protests by ethnic Germans over the right to emigrate have become more apparent. Last month, four Germans in Estonia were sentenced to prison terms for demonstrations in Moscow last winter. In January, two others occupied the West German Embassy for 11 hours before being persuaded to leave. There have also been reports of hunger strikes among ethnic Germans in the Baltic.

September 12, 1974

# Fires of Independence Smolder in Soviet Georgia

By DAVID K. SHIPLER
Special to The New York Times

TBILISI, U.S.S.R.—Brooding eyes, dark with smoldering anger, look out from behind the raised glass of white wine. To the United States of America, the toast begins, the final bulwark of democracy and freedom. Let the American people not forget the Georgian people, who seek their own democracy and freedom.

**The Talk of Tbilisi**

The toast and the eyes belong to Zviad Gamsakhurdia, an intense Georgian nationalist and separatist who lives a precarious life in advocacy of the independence of Georgia from the Soviet Union. He knows 20 or 30 other Georgians who feel the same way.

If placed on an American political spectrum, these Georgian dissidents would be farther to the right than almost any American conservative, for they would welcome United States military force to help "liberate" Georgia.

"If the Voice of America were to say two words about Georgia," one of them declared hopefully, "the next day—because of the Georgian way of exaggerating—they would be saying that it had talked for two hours."

### An Ancient People

Whatever silent chords of sympathy such separatist sentiments generate within the Georgian population, they lie well beneath the surface of accommodation between Georgian culture and Soviet political rule.

The Georgians are an ancient people, really an array of neighboring tribes and cultures scattered from the Black Sea coast through the foothills and into the mountains of the Caucasus. Their rich heritage of literature, dance, language and religion has remained intact through centuries of conquest and domination by Mongols, Turks and Persians, and now also in a period of Russian pre-eminence, which began in the early 19th century after Orthodox Georgia sought Russia's protection against the Moslems.

In its most overt and apolitical forms, Georgian culture seems as plentiful as the succulent fruit of Georgian vineyards.

### Georgian Culture Common

The Georgian language, with its distinctive alphabet, is used in television broadcasts, films, books and plays. At the Rustaveli Theater recently the program for Brecht's "Caucasian Chalk Circle"—performed in Georgian—was printed only in Georgian, not Russian.

The Georgian-language newspaper, Komunisti, has five times the circulation of its Russian-language counterpart, Zarya Vostoka.

The museums are filled with the frescoes, icons and gold of Georgian artists.

The roots of antiquity are visible everywhere. Filigreed balconies lean out over crooked cobblestone streets. On dry rural hilltops, the ruins of ancient church-fortresses look as if they have grown the rock itself, like the Moorish castles in Spain.

### Two Kinds of Assimilation

In the streets of Tbilisi, the Georgian capital, there is a fluidity and a subtle current of unruliness as different from Moscow as Rome is from London. The busts in the university are mostly of poets and painters, rarely of Lenin.

The wife of a well-known officially approved artist wears a jade cross on a chain around her neck. In the town of Mtskheta, Georgia's capital until the fourth century A.D., a wedding ceremony has just ended in the ornate chapel of the 11th-century Sveti-Tskhoveli Cathedral.

"All Georgians are believers," says the bearded priest. "It is an ancient tradition."

"We've kept our own language through invasions and wars," argues a young woman guide for Intourist, the Soviet travel agency. "My son speaks our own language, and he speaks beautiful Russian, and maybe he'll go to a Russian school. There's no Russification here."

"There are two kinds of assimilation," she continues. "There's natural assimilation, and that's what we do have here. There is forced assimilation, and that is what we do not have."

Still, the relationship between Georgian tradition and Soviet orthodoxy is complex—easy in some fields, strained in others.

Mr. Gamsakhurdia describes a process of Russification: Thirty percent of all Georgian children now attend Russian-language schools by their parents' choice, he maintains. Some take Russian first names; for instance, the Intourist guide, whose Georgian name is Natella, or Nata for short, often calls herself by the Russian name Natasha.

Vocational institutes often assign Georgian graduates to Russian cities for their mandatory three-year tours of duty in their professions, Mr. Gamsakhurdia contends, and he believes that Georgian writers, hampered by censorship, now produce little that is peculiarly Georgian or particularly good.

Last November, the Central Committee of the Georgian Communist Party issued a decree "to intensify the struggle against harmful traditions and customs," a measure aimed at eradicating certain "religious festivities," "name-days for various 'saints,'" animal sacrifices during religious ceremonies, blood feuds and vendettas, arranged marriages, extravagant wedding and funeral feasts, showy marble mausoleums, excessive drinking and other forms of conspicuous consumption for which Georgians are famous throughout the Soviet Union.

The apparent author of this campaign is Eduard A. Shevardnadze, the Georgian party chief, who has aroused so much positive and negative feeling here that rumors circulate of a secret party decree against telling anecdotes about him, or about the party in general.

Just how the campaign is proceeding is unclear. When pressed, several party members conceded that they would be reluctant to admonish anyone they did not know well to avoid traditional customs. One engineer, a party member who could name only seven of the 15 Politburo members, explained over a late-night dinner that there would be "no shouting—just saying, 'you do not need it.'"

Another Communist, a newspaper editor, remarked, "We can't eradicate everything with a magic wand." Then, blushingly citing traditional Georgian hospitality, he opened a bottle of wine. It was 11:30 A.M.

May 15, 1976

# Ethnic Currents Run Deep in the Soviet Republic of Moldavia

By DAVID K. SHIPLER
Special to The New York Times

KISHINEV, U.S.S.R.—In the Soviet Union, where more than a hundred ethnic groups seek, submerge, revere, deny or flaunt their linguistic and cultural traditions in the face of Russian dominance, the question of ethnic assimilation and identity has become exceedingly complex.

In each part of the country, peculiar forces of history, religion and politics shape special patterns of self-definition, governing the degree to which each group sets itself apart from the ethnic Russians, who make up just over half of the country's population.

In Kishinev, the capital of the Soviet Union's Moldavian Republic, there is a particularly complicated confluence of ethnic currents. They run below the surface of a deceptively placid city, one of lush, trimmed parks and tree-lined streets that have the relaxed feeling of a rural town.

In an exhibition hall, a large drawing of two army boots hangs as part of a display of political posters and cartoons. The boots are lying so that their soles can be seen. On one sole is a swastika made of barbed wire; on the other, the barbed wire is twisted into the shape of a Star of David. The caption reads, "Two boots—one pair."

Ostensibly, this is an expression of the Soviet line that Zionism and Israeli policy resemble fascism, an arrgument bolstered last year by the resolution of the United Nations General Assembly equating Zionism with racism. But Kishinev, where prejudice against Jews has ancient roots, the distinction between anti-Zionism and anti-Semitism is virtually invisible. This was one of the principal cities in the Jewish pale, the region where Jews were forced to live in Czarist times. In 1903 it was the scene of a pogrom.

●

Anti-Zionist propaganda is fairly common throughout the Soviet Union, and it has apparently played a role in provoking Jewish emigration. Yuri Shekhtman, a 30-year-old electrician, remembers how his father, after having seen such propaganda on television, turned to him and said, "We must go to Israel to save ourselves, because when Russian men and women see that program they will become more anti-Semitic."

The old man and his wife emigrated to Israel, but the son was denied permission. He is waiting, hoping, with his own wife and his own son, a three-year-old.

The anomaly of Soviet Jews, many of whom gain high professional positions despite anti-Semitism, is explained by Mr. Shekhtman as a function of their willingness to blend into the larger, Russian-oriented society.

"There are Jewish scientists," he said, "and they receive good wages. But they must see nothing, hear nothing, say nothing. And for them it's good. They have been assimilated. I want to live as a Jew. Hebrew language, culture, history. I don't think that Jewish culture can exist here."

By official count, 50,000 Jews live in Kishinev, 14 percent of the population. Once there were about 60 synagogues; now there is one.

●

Linguistically, Kishinev has been Russified. On the streets, in stores, restaurants, offices, the words seem more often Russian than Moldavian. Even

The New York Times/Nov. 8, 1976

**In Kishinev, Moldavia's capital, anti-Semitism has ancient roots.**

some Moldavians speak with one another in Russian, especially in formal, business relationships.

A journalist who edits a Moldavian-language newspaper speaks mostly Russian at home. His wife is Ukrainian, and his daughter attends a school where Russian is the language of instruction. Official documents are in Russian, and Russian is often spoken in his office.

Even at a recent performance of Moldavian folk music and dance in Kishinev, it was in Russian that the master of ceremonies made his announcements and did a comedy routine.

This is partly the result of the large numbers of Russians living in Kishinev. Although the population of the Moldavian Republic was 65 percent Moldavian and 12 percent Russian in the 1970 census, the percentages for Kishinev alone were much different: 37 percent Moldavian and 31 percent Russian. Most of the rest were Ukrainians and Jews, and just over half the city's population named Russian as their first language.

Furthermore, under Russian influence the Moldavian language itself is now written in the Cyrillic alphabet, although it is very close to Rumanian, which is spoken just across the border and is written with Latin letters.

Rumania has long maintained that Moldavians are really Rumanians, both in language and in culture. They share much literature. Barbers, editors and bureaucrats here say they can understand Rumanian without difficulty.

The Rumanian viewpoint has seemed to involve some territorial pretensions, and has fostered friction between Moscow and Bucharest. Bessarabia, as this area was known under the Turks, was annexed by the Czars from the Ottoman Empire in 1812. Rumania seized the area in 1918 and ruled it until the Soviet Union took it back in 1940. The following year it was reoccupied by Rumanian troops, fighting on the side of the Axis forces, and was rewon by the Red Army in 1944.

The Russians have felt it necessary in recent months to have some of their historians write scholarly tracts on the essential differences between Rumanians and Moldavians.

Although this may be one of the world's most esoteric ethnic questions, it was underscored in August when President Nicolae Ceausescu of Rumania stopped in Soviet Moldavia on his way to a meeting with Leonid I. Brezhnev in the Crimea.

It was the first visit to the area by a Rumanian leader since the Soviet annexation. According to a report from Washington, the Rumanians said the visit was designed to establish contacts with the Soviet Moldavians.

November 8, 1976

## 3D SOVIET REGION AFFIRMS OFFICIAL STATE LANGUAGE

MOSCOW, APRIL 24 (Reuters)—A third Soviet republic, Azerbaijan, has affirmed its indigenous language as the republic's official state language, following a precedent set in the adjoining Georgian and Armenian republics.

In Baku, the Azerbaijani capital, a spokesman for the local Communist Party newspaper, Bakinsky Rabochi, said the approved text of the republic's new constitution retained a clause stating that the state language was Azerbaijani, a Turkic tongue.

The constitutions of the three republics, which are situated south of the Caucasus, adjoining Iran and Turkey, have contained such a clause since the early years of the Soviet regime.

During the recent drafting of new constitutions, the Soviet authorities sought to eliminate the special provision to bring the text in line with those of other Soviet republics. However, the use of the indigenous language has long been a sensitive issue in Transcaucasia, especially in Georgia and Armenia, and following reported public protests, the special constitutional provisions were retained.

April 25, 1978

# SOVIET JEWS

**Bolsheviki Forbid Pogroms.**

LONDON, July 31.—The Soviet Government at Moscow has issued a decree against anti-Semitism, a Russian wireless message today announces. There is no place in the Russian scheme for the oppression of nationalities, the decree declares. The Jewish bourgeoisie "is our enemy not as Jews but as bourgeoisie," it continues. The decree invites the working classes to fight against pogroms. All instigators of pogroms and all anti-Semitic agitators will be regarded as outlaws, it is declared.

August 1, 1918

## RUSSIAN COMMUNISTS WAR ON ANTI-SEMITISM

### Central Committee Names Special

### Body to Check Rise of Racial Prejudice in Nation.

In order to check the rise of anti-Semitism in Russia a special meeting of the Central Committee of the Communist Party was held in Moscow on May 8, according to a dispatch to The Jewish Telegraphic Agency. The committee decided to appoint a special co mittee charged with combatting anti-Semitism. The special committee was asked to prepare within a fortnight a plan for its work.

Reports submitted to the special session show that anti-Semitism in Soviet Russia is assuming an intensive character and is affecting even members of the Communist Party and of the Communist youth organization.

Maxim Gorky in a letter to the Ozet, a society for settling Jews on the land, has condemned the rise of anti-Semitic propaganda. Gorky was recently elected an honorary member of the society. In accepting the election he wrote: "I hope the Jewish settlement on the land will somewhat sober up the petty bourgeois anti-Semites, whose brains are again being planted with unsound ideas."

Golovanof, head of the Moscow State Theatre, has been dismissed from his post after an investigating committee found him guilty of anti-Semitic practices. Golovanof attempted to deny he was an anti-Semite, declaring that the Jews were the most musical people on earth. He said, however, that he believed that directors who belong to the national minorities should not be permitted to conduct Russian operas. The investigating committee ordered the dismissal of seven other officials of the State Theatre for their anti-Semitic practices.

Eighteen months imprisonment was the sentence inflicted by a Soviet court upon three employes of the Southwestern Railways at Kief for composing and posting up an anti-Semite verse in the railway administration building, says a Moscow dispatch of May 7 to The Jewish Telegraphic Agency.

May 13, 1928

## Anti-Zionism in Soviet Union Turning Into Anti-Semitism

### Developing Tendency Is Held to Be a Phase of New Campaign Against 'Cosmopolitanism'

By C. L. SULZBERGER
Special to The New York Times.

LAUSANNE, Switzerland, May 1—The Soviet Union's drive against Zionism, which has also extended into the countries under Moscow's control, now appears to be developing into what is at least a minor anti-Semitic—as distinct from an anti-Zionist—trend.

As the Soviet Union is officially against both religion and racism, it is probably logical to presume that this tendency is being developed as one phase of the new campaign against "cosmopolitanism" or any connection with the "outside," "bourgeois" world.

If this deduction is correct, it would appear to be a historically logical development from the original anti-Semitic movement in the Soviet Union that followed the first great purges in the Nineteen Thirties. At that time virtually all Jews of importance in the Foreign Ministry and other major Governmental bureaus were removed from their positions.

In fact, nowadays the only Jew who holds a major position in the Soviet Union is Premier Stalin's old friend Lazar M. Kaganovitch, member of the Political Bureau, whose sister, according to some rumors, was one of Mr. Stalin's wives. The last Jew in the Foreign Office who held a prominent position was former Foreign Minister Maxim V. Litvinov, who has virtually disappeared from the scene. Hardly any Jews are left in the Soviet diplomatic service, which once contained many of them.

#### Impetus for This Tendency

The original impetus for this tendency, it is believed, was based on the theory that Jews were "internationalist" in the sense that they had more cultural connections with the Western world than most other Soviet groups, spoke more foreign languages and actually tended to have more family relationships abroad.

Under the guise of combating Trotskyism and as part of an evident isolationist development, the position of the Jews in the Soviet Governmental hierarchy has been steadily reduced.

Since Moscow began to sponsor an anti-Zionist attitude following the conclusion of the Palestine war, a new anti-Semitic bias has been detectable in the Soviet Union although, presumably because of strict censorship this is not generally known abroad.

While many intellectuals have recently been excoriated for "internationalism" or "cosmopolitanism" and cited as displaying remnants of "bourgeois ideology," the most bitter venom seems to have been reserved for Jews.

Especially sharp digs have been made against people who are "homeless and without kith or kin," which appears to be a phrase employed to describe Jews. That impression is confirmed by the fact that it is frequently coupled with the names of Jewish writers when published in the Soviet press.

These writers, many of whom have "Russianized" their names, are further identified by having their original and clearly quoted Jewish names printed in parentheses after the Slavic version. Such a parenthetical inclusion of the name at birth is, for example, never employed for Mr. Stalin (Djugashvili) or former Foreign Minister Molotov (Scriabin).

#### Literary Gazette Quotes

Yet the Literary Gazette refers to a "malignant putrid story by Melnikov (Melman)" and to "cynical impudent activities of B. Yakovlev (Holzman)."

Theatre critics—of which an especially large proportion of those castigated appear to have been Jewish—have been attacked recently as "double dealers with traitors' souls," "servants of the imperialist West" and "Trotzkyite bandits" in the Moscow press.

N. I. Gusarov, secretary of the Central Committee of the Byelorussian Communist party, told a recent party congress at Minsk that "only one theatre in the republic—the Jewish one—has until recently put on anti-patriotic plays in which the patriarchal life of the Jewish petty bourgeoisie was idealized and life in bourgeois America praised."

The Jewish theatre in Minsk was closed for a time after that, but has since been reopened. There have been recent rumors in Moscow that the Jewish theatre there would be closed, but to date nothing has happened. However, a Jewish paper has been banned and the Jewish anti-Fascist Committee in the Soviet capital dissolved.

Presumably taking their cue from this official propaganda, many lesser Governmental officials have conducted purges in their own departments, removing Jewish subordinates. Additional official and unofficial barriers to the employment of Jews, especially in schools and universities, have appeared.

May 2, 1949

## REDS NAME JEWS PURGED BY SOVIET

### Warsaw Yiddish Newspaper Confirms Execution Under Stalin—Blames Beria

By HARRISON E. SALISBURY

Polish Communist sources have confirmed that Soviet authorities liquidated a large number of Jews prominent in literary, cultural and political fields in the years before Stalin's death in 1953.

A similar purge was carried out during the Nineteen Thirties.

The description of the anti-Semitic excesses was given by the Warsaw Yiddish-language newspaper, Folksshtime, in its edition of April 4, which has just reached New York. Folksshtime is a Communist organ.

The Warsaw newspaper provided the first Communist confirmation of accounts previously published by The New York Times and The Jewish Daily Forward of New York.

The picture painted by the Warsaw report was one of excesses even more extensive than previously rumored. The list of Jewish victims published in Warsaw was longer than any that had been published by anti-Communist groups.

Publication of the Polish newspaper's account increased speculation that Moscow might be preparing to announce that the execution of the Polish Jewish labor leaders, Victor Alter and Henryk Erlich, carried out in December, 1942, was a result of charges that were without foundation in fact.

Mr. Alter and Mr. Erlich were arrested by the Russians when Poland was partitioned by the Soviet Union and Germany in 1939. According to the Soviet version the men were convicted of treason and executed.

The Polish account attributed all the anti-Semitic outrages to Lavrenti P. Beria, former Soviet secret police chief, executed in December, 1953. In fact the Jewish liquidations of the Nineteen Thirties occurred before Stalin brought Beria from Georgia to head the police apparatus in 1938.

Among those listed by Folksshtime as victims of the later Jewish purge of 1948-52 were the writers Itsik Feffer, David Bergelson, Perets Markish, Leib Kvitko, David Hofshtein, Isaac Nusinov, Elijah Spivak, Froyim Kahanovitch, S. Persov and Benjamin Suskin.

Only the first five of these writers had previously positively been known to have been executed in the purge.

The newspaper said that the Jewish Anti-Fascist Committee in Moscow had "suddenly without why or wherefore been liquidated and its leaders sentenced to destruction."

The committee was headed by the prominent Yiddish actor Solomon Mikhoels, whose death previously had been officially attributed to an "automobile accident." The newspaper account suggested that Mr. Mikhoels also was one of the victims of the anti-Semitic campaign.

Mr. Feffer, a poet loyal to the Stalin regime and a Red Army colonel during World War II, was one of the Anti-Fascist Committee leaders. He and Mr. Mikhoels toured the United States in behalf of the Soviet war effort during World War II.

**Victims of Thirties**

Among the Jewish victims of the Nineteen Thirties purges were listed S. Dimanshtein, Ester Frumkin, Rachmael Weinshtein, Moishe Litvakov, Izi Kharik, Moishe Kulbak, H. Duniets, Mikhail Levitan, Yankel Levin, Hershel Brill, Max Erik and Yasha Bronshtein.

Mr. Weinshtein and Mr. Levin were leaders of the Bund, a Jewish Social Democratic organization. Mr. Litvakov was a critic and editor of the Moscow Yiddish newspaper Emes (Truth). Mr. Erik was a leading Yiddish scholar in Kiev.

The Warsaw newspaper also listed a number of other "masters of Yiddish literature" who had been victims of anti-Semitic drives. One of the authors on this list, Samuel Halkin, has been reported recently to be alive in a Leningrad sanatorium.

Among the names on this list were those of Aaron Kushnirov, Lipe Reznik, Ezra Finenberg, Hersh Orland, Noah Lurie, Itsik Kipnis, and Note Lurie.

The text of the Folksshtime report was published by the New York Yiddish-language newspaper Freiheit, a Communist party organ. An extensive account was also published by the Jewish Daily Forward, strongly anti-Communist newspaper, which has long waged a campaign exposing the anti-Semitic excesses in the Soviet Union. The Forward published the confirmation of its charges with the comment "Communists in Warsaw and New York finally tell about Soviet pogrom on Yiddish writers."

April 12, 1956

# JEWS HURT MOST BY BIAS IN SOVIET

## Data Gathered Here Show Other Faiths Suffer Less From Discrimination

**By HARRISON E. SALISBURY**

Soviet restrictive measures are applied more broadly to the Jewish faith than to other religious faiths in the Soviet Union, according to data gathered by Jewish sources here.

The information is based on the observations of travelers in the Soviet Union as well as official material from Soviet more poorly provided for than Russian Orthodox believers.

The study says that members of the Baptist and Evangelical denominations suffer the least discrimination. Members of the Russian Orthodox faith, the largest denomination in the Soviet Union, occupy a middle position. The Jews are at the bottom.

The Jews are twenty-one times worse off in regard to facilities for worship than the Baptists and thirteen times more poorly provided than Russian Orthodox believers.

**Comparative Status**

The following table shows the comparative status of the three faiths:

| | Russian Orthodox. | Baptists. | Jews. |
|---|---|---|---|
| Active in church | 40,000,000 | 340,000 | *1,500,000 |
| Churches or synagogues .... | 22,000 | 500+ | 60-70 |
| Average ......... | 1,800 | 1,100 | 23,000+ |
| Priests or rabbis. | 35,000 | 500+ | 60-70 |
| Average of parishoners per priest or rabbi. | 1,100 | 1,100 | 23,000+ |

*Estimated.

The tendency to discrimination appears in printing and publishing facilities. The Russian Orthodox Church and the Baptists have been permitted to print Bibles in the last year. Moslems have brought out a new edition of the Koran. No Hebrew Bible has been permitted since 1917.

The Russian Orthodox, Baptists and Moslems have all been permitted to print and freely distribute religious calendars. The Jews have been permitted only to issue a photocopy edition of a handwritten calendar.

The Orthodox, Baptists and Moslems each are permitted a nation-wide organization to represent the religious and lay communities. Similar organization for the Jews is forbidden.

Russian and Arabic, essential to the Orthodox and Moslem churches, is taught in state schools. Hebrew is not.

**Differences in Training**

In the field of religious training, discrimination is marked. The Russian Orthodox Church has ten seminaries and academies, which last year had a total of 915 pupils. Several Moslem seminaries and one Baptist seminary exist. The Jews have one seminary, opened less than two years ago. It has only nineteen pupils.

The average age of the sixty to seventy rabbis serving the Jewish community is well over 70 years. At the present rate of training the seminary will not be able to provide replacements as rapidly as the older rabbis die, thus depriving many synagogues of trained religious leaders.

This year the first Jewish prayerbook for general circulation was permitted to be published in many years. The edition numbered 3,000 copies, an average of one per 500 believers, disregarding the fact that considerable numbers of prayer-books were shipped abroad for propaganda purposes. This compares with a Baptist edition of 25,000 hymnals, about one per twenty-one believers.

Whereas large numbers of Russian Orthodox churches that were confiscated by the state in early revolutionary days have been returned to the church in recent years, no confiscated synagogues have been restored. In Kishinev, where forty synagogues existed in 1940, only one is now open.

November 23, 1958

# *Fear Grows Among Soviet Jews At Resurgence of Anti-Semitism*

**By HARRISON E. SALISBURY**

The Jews of Russia, historically the victims of persecution and prejudice, are encountering another time of trouble.

It is milder than past oppressions. There are no pogroms. The old czarist slogan "Beat the Jews and save Russia" may be muttered by some hooligans but it gets no official encouragement. Nor are Jews being executed or shipped off to Siberia as in Stalin's days.

Nonetheless, anti-Semitism—endemic in Russia—again has shown its ugly face, especially in rural areas of the Ukraine and in some parts of Byelorussia and the Moldavian Republic.

Its revival has been stimulated by aggressive official propaganda against the Jewish religion, often couched in terms that blur the boundary between anti-religion and anti-Semitism.

Fear and suspicion, never long absent from the Jewish communities in the Soviet Union, again are on the increase. Jews in many places are reluctant to have contacts with foreigners or co-religionists because of the reprisals that may be visited upon them by the Government.

The same Young Communist League gangs that have been thrown into action by Soviet neo-Stalinists against the Russian Orthodox Church, against restive youth groups and against any manifestation of liberalism in Soviet life have been mobilized to intimidate and browbeat Jewish communities.

The same anti-foreign ruffianism displayed by the neo-Stalinists in other contexts is invoked against Jews.

Among diplomats it is believed that the chief motivation in the drive against Jewish communities and Jewish religious centers is xenophobic rather than anti-religious.

The Jews, the diplomats feel, are feared by the regime. The fear stems from two sources. The first is the phobia that the Communist party persistently displays toward any kind of non-Communist social group, regardless of its basis. The second is the fact that Jews have connections with their co-religionists abroad and have repeatedly demonstrated their sympathy for and interest in Israel.

The Soviet secret police equate an interest in Israel with "security risk" and Israeli representatives, particularly diplomats, are considered to be spies and agents of the United States Central Intelligence Agency.

The revival of active measures against organized Jewish circles in the Soviet Union and the persistence of anti-Semitism have not, however, gone unchallenged in the present liberalized atmosphere of the country.

The Jews now have powerful and articulate allies within the Soviet intellectual community who are actively seeking to arouse Russians to a feeling of shame and anger at the anti-Semitic stain on the national conscience.

**Intellectuals Challenging Anti-Semitic Campaign**

The most spectacular of these voices is that of the flamboyant young poet Yevgeny Yevtushenko, idol of Soviet youth and probably the most popular single figure in Soviet art and letters today.

Mr. Yevtushenko, a non-Jew, has a public platform for his views. His poetic denunciations of the persistence and quasi-official encouragement of anti-Semitism are published by the periodical press. He recites his poems to stormy audiences of students in clubs and assemblies all over Moscow.

When he declaimed his attacks on anti-Semitism last autumn on Poet's Day in Moscow's Mayakovsky Square the crowd of young people was so great that the police finally intervened.

When the youngsters refused to disperse at midnight, police vans were summoned. Dozens of youngsters were loaded into the vehicles and driven twenty miles outside town, dumped out and forced to find their way back to the city as best they might.

The youngsters demonstrated their contempt for the police by reassembling the next night. Again they refused to disperse and again they were carried out of town and dumped on the roadside.

Mr. Yevtushenko's participation in the fight of Russian liberals against anti-Semitism has been spectacular. But he is by no means alone. Another young writer, Vladimir Nekrasov, took a similar stand considerably earlier.

Among the older generations, Ilya Ehrenburg, himself of Jewish origin, has eloquently announced his determination to proclaim as long as anti-Semitism persists, "I am a Jew!" Incidentally, Mr. Ehrenburg has long been a bitter opponent of Zionism and organized Jewish activity.

When the neo-Stalinist poet Aleksei Markov published a slanderous couplet characterizing Mr. Yevtushenko as a "pigmy cosmopolitan," a handwritten poetic "answer to Markov promptly began to circulate among the Moscow intelligentsia.

This compared the Soviet poet to a notorious anti-Semite of the czarist period known as "Markov the Second." The Soviet critic was promptly christened "Markov the Third."

The battle lines in the anti-Semitic controversy are almost identical with those on other issues dividing the two main tendencies in Soviet life today —the neo-Stalinists and the liberals.

However, despite criticism by liberals, the Government-sponsored anti-Jewish program continues.

### One Synagogue Survives In Jewish Area of Kiev

Its effect on the Jewish community can be clearly observed in such a center as Kiev, for example. Kiev, the capital of the Ukraine, was once a great center of Jewish life and culture and had many synagogues.

Today a single synagogue survives in the heart of the old Podol, the poor Jewish quarter of the city. It is a small building, run-down and worn, on a neglected side street.

"Is this the only synagogue in Kiev?" a recent visitor asked in surprise.

"Oh, no, there are others," said the tough-visaged "administrator" of the congregation, probably a nominee of the state security apparatus.

A bearded ancient with a black skull cap shook his head sadly and muttered: "That is not true."

The "other synagogues," it finally developed, were two meeting rooms—one on the second floor and the other to the rear in a kind of storage building. Unfortunately, the keys could not be found so that these "beautiful rooms," as the administrator described them, could not be shown.

"Have any synagogues been closed recently?" the administrator was asked.

He shrugged his shoulders and said he had not heard of any. It might be true. Perhaps there were not enough people to support a synagogue.

"We have complete freedom to worship or not to worship," he said belligerently. "Just as you have in America."

"How many members are there in the congregation?" he was asked.

"We keep no statistics," was the reply.

"How many Jews are there in Kiev?"

"Ask the City Council. That is not our business."

The old man with the beard and the skull cap shook his head in resignation.

Kiev was the scene of one of the worst Nazi massacres of Jews in the Soviet Union. The site of this was a gully called Babi Yar on the outskirts of the city. About 75,000 Jews were taken there and shot. Each group of Jews had to spread a light cover of earth over the earlier victims before being shot.

Kiev is not indifferent to the lives sacrificed during the war. High on the cliffs overlooking the Dnieper there is a monument to all those who died in wartime Kiev, and an eternal flame burns there in memory of the victims. Each day there are pilgrimages and guided tours to the spot.

### Guides Decline to Show Babi Yar to Tourists

But there is no mention at the monument that any Jewish lives were lost in Kiev. And the tourist asks in vain to be taken to see Babi Yar. "It is beyond the city limits," the guides say. "You have to have special permission. There is nothing to see there. It is too difficult."

Actually, there is "nothing to see." The place is a deserted gully. Part of it is used as a city dump. The municipal council has plans for filling in the gully and building a sports center on the spot.

Babi Yar is not a term that Soviet officials like to hear. When the Jewish massacre is mentioned they are quick to say that the Jews were not the only people killed by the Nazis. There were Ukrainian and Russian victims, too.

"Babi Yar," a poem dedicated by Mr. Yevtushenko to the Jewish victims, has been translated into Yiddish. Aaron Vergelis, editor of the new Yiddish language literary journal Sovietish Heimland, has said that the poem will appear in his publication. After four months, however, it still has not appeared.

The symptoms of fear and suspicion observable in the Kiev synagogue are typical of Jewish communities in the Soviet Union today.

A recent visitor to the Moscow synagogue asked about G. R. Pechorsky, head of the Jewish community who was tried in semi-secrecy in October on charges of contact with a foreign power, Israel. "We do not know anything about Pechorsky and we do not want to know anything about Pechorsky," was the response.

There have been administrative moves against the leaders of most of the more important Jewish communities in the Soviet Union in recent months. There have been arrests and trials in Moscow and Leningrad.

In other cities such as Riga, Kiev, Vilna and Tashkent the known and respected Jewish leaders have been compelled to resign and more pliable men have been put in their place.

In a number of cities there has been a calculated effort to create a public image of Jewish graft, corruption and drunkenness. Propaganda stories have been published "exposing" scandals in synagogues and among Jewish communities.

There have been trials of speculators and absconders in which persons with Jewish names are prominently associated. In one such trial in Tiflis, some of the most respected families in the Jewish community were involved. One of the ringleaders was said to be a 94-year-old leader in the local synagogue. He received a death sentence.

The effort to blur the lines and smear the Jews by confusing them with criminal and anti-social elements in the population is identical with the tactics employed by the same coalition of police and Young Communist agents in attacking nonconformist youths and liberal writers. It is obvious that it has the same source and is inspired by the same persons.

### Anti-Jewish Propaganda Circulated in Provinces

Examination of anti-Jewish propaganda materials circulated in the provinces shows the same pattern. For example, an anti-Jewish pamphlet published for local use in Kishinev is filled with "revelations" about drunkenness and speculation by synagogue officials.

This work seeks to link the Jews to the Rumanian forces that occupied Moldavia in World War II. It even hints that the Jews were supporters of the czarist regime.

In Kishinev and other areas pressure has been brought upon members of the Jewish community to "petition" the authorities for permission to close the synagogues on the ground that they no longer are interested in maintaining them.

How many synagogues have been forced to close by such intimidation is not known, but the number is not insubstantial in the rural areas of the Ukraine and Moldavia. The same technique has been used against Russian Orthodox and Roman Catholic congregations.

Most diplomats believe a prime factor in the creation of an atmosphere of permissive anti-Semitism is insensitivity on the Jewish question by Premier Khrushchev. The Soviet leader has frequently discussed Jewish questions and almost invariably has displayed traces, at least, of the anti-Semitic prejudices common to the borderland of the Ukraine where he grew up.

Another factor, in the opinion of many Moscow diplomats, is the hypersensitivity of the Soviet regime to the Zionist question. Soviet relations with Israel are poor at best. With a population of 3,000,000 Jews the Soviet regime suffers from security qualms because of the sympathy of many Soviet Jews for Jews abroad.

In this situation the Soviet authorities are highly suspicious of any links or contacts between Israeli diplomats and Jewish communities in the Soviet Union. In the last two or three years, with the general liberalization of the Soviet regime, such contacts have rapidly broadened and deepened.

### Israeli Diplomats Given Warm Jewish Welcome

In many cities Soviet Jews have demonstratively welcomed Israeli diplomats. In Leningrad, for example, during the celebration of Simhath Torah three years ago about 4,000 Jews turned out and serenaded an Israeli diplomat. The next year 7,000 Jews appeared and last October between 8,000 and 12,000.

This kind of display alarms Soviet security officials. Many diplomats believe it is no coincidence that the secret trials of Jewish community leaders in Leningrad and Moscow quickly followed the Simhath Torah celebration of last fall.

The vigor and intensity of Israeli diplomatic activity in the Soviet Union and its contacts with the Jewish communities are believed by Western diplomats to have stimulated the Soviet Union in its recent widespread reprisals against Jews. The most prominent Jewish victims have been persons who had social and cultural contacts with Israeli diplomats.

There is no sign that any of the Israeli activities were anything but perfectly legal. None of them would have caused the slightest reaction in any country but the Soviet Union.

However, these personal and cultural contacts have aroused the Soviet security apparatus and its propaganda affiliates to a fury of activity.

The Israeli Embassy has been publicly charged with espionage and secret activity of a subversive nature. One Israeli diplomat has been expelled and others threatened with expulsion. And, inevitably, they have been branded "agents of the C.I.A."

Despite all this, so-called "administrative" anti-Semitism —that is, dismissal of Jews from posts or exile and execution—is not occurring as it did in Stalin's day.

At least in Moscow and Leningrad, Jewish students appear to have less difficulty than previously in winning admission to higher educational institutions. Jewish scientists have played a leading role in space and rocket research and this fact has won grudging recognition in high Government circles.

For all that, anti-Semitism is still a blot on the Soviet scene.

# Soviet Spurs Fight On Anti-Semitism

By THEODORE SHABAD
Special to The New York Times

MOSCOW, Sept. 10—A Pravda editorial in which anti-Semitism is condemned is being given unusually wide circulation in the Soviet Union.

The editorial in the Communist party newspaper quotes Lenin as having called for a "tireless struggle" against anti-Jewish bias and warns that "nationalistic survivals and frictions" provide material for anti-Soviet propaganda.

Longtime residents of Moscow cannot recall previous criticism of anti-Semitism in an editorial of the Soviet Union's leading party newspaper, which serves as a vehicle for the views of the inner circles of the Kremlin leadership.

The traditional attitude of Soviet ideologists has been that no "Jewish question" exists in the Soviet Union and that anti-Semitism is not a problem.

In the opinion of foreign observers the publication of the editorial at this time may reflect an increasing sensitivity of the Soviet regime to a flood of Western statements charging religious and cultural suppression of Soviet Jews.

Pravda's reference to anti-Semitism, buried in a lengthy, seemingly routine, editorial on the Leninist friendship of the peoples, a favorite theme of propagandists in this vast nation of more than 100 ethnic and linguistic groups, did not arouse unusual interest here when it first published last Sunday.

**Editorial Being Reprinted**

However, as the week passed, it became evident that the editorial was being reprinted in provincial newspapers throughout the country. Such a wide distribution, presumably prompted by central directive, is ordinarily reserved for major pronouncements on ideological topics judged of particular importance by the Soviet leaders.

This special handling of the editorial led observers to re-study its content and weigh its broader implications.

The editorial's principal theme is that the Bolshevik Revolution "liquidated for all time national inequality" and that the present building of a Communist society is promoting an economic, political, cultural and ideological rapprochement among the peoples of the Soviet Union.

But relations among the country's ethnic groups also have international implications, the editorial notes. Developing countries, it goes on, are looking to relations among the Soviet peoples as a "model" of the way in which groups with different customs, traditions and beliefs can live together.

As for Western opponents of the Soviet Union, the editorial continues, "they do not cease attempts to revive dissension among our peoples."

"Although these attempts are futile," Pravda said, "we must keep them in mind in our ideological work and remember who may benefit from any manifestations whatsoever of nationalistic survivals and frictions."

It was at this point that the editorial recalled that Lenin had "angrily assailed any manifestations of nationalism whatsoever and demanded in particular a tireless 'struggle against anti-Semitism, that malicious exaggeration of racial separateness and national enmity' fostered by the exploiting classes."

The context suggested that this passage was intended both as a warning against persistent evidences of anti-Semitism in the Soviet Union and as a reply to Western charges that such anti-Semitism was officially inspired.

The editorial, it is thought here, is likely to encourage Western critics in a belief that protests about the situation of the Jews in the Soviet Union have played a part in inducing the Soviet leaders to provide religious and cultural facilities that the Soviet Jews lacked in the past.

A delegation of American Orthodox rabbis was assured here last July that three specific grievances of the Jewish religious community were being redressed. The delegation, headed by Rabbi Israel Miller, president of the Rabbinical Council of America was told that the Soviet Jews would be permitted baked matzoh for Passover without special permission, that at least 10,000 prayer books would be published and that the training of future rabbis would not be hampered.

In the cultural field, a Yiddish - language magazine, Sovetish Heimland (Soviet Homeland) has been converted since last January from a bimonthly to a monthly publication, thus doubling the material made available to readers.

A modest Yiddish book publication program has been started.

Yiddish variety shows and folksingers continue to tour the cities with large Jewish audiences, but a permanent Jewish theater that existed in Moscow before being closed by Stalin in 1948 has not been restored.

At a news conference in New York yesterday, Rabbi Miller described these concessions as "cracks of light" but said the over-all situation of Jews in the Soviet Union remained grave and must be a concern of the Western world. He expressed confidence that further protests would elicit additional positive responses from the Soviet leaders.

September 11, 1965

# Soviet Spares Two Jews; Three Get Eased Terms

## Supreme Court Notes That Leningrad Hijacking Plot Was Not Carried Out —Foreign Protests Seen as Factor

By BERNARD GWERTZMAN
Special to The New York Times

MOSCOW, Dec. 31 — The Russian Republic's Supreme Court, noting that a planned hijacking last June was never carried out, today commuted the death sentences given two Jewish defendants in the Leningrad case.

Prison-camp terms for three of the nine other defendants were reduced by the court.

The sentences meted out by a Leningrad city court to the 11 accused—nine of whom are Jews—had aroused widespread concern abroad. Government leaders and Western Communist parties had appealed to the Kremlin to commute the death penalties and ease the prison-camp terms, which ranged from 4 to 15 years. This foreign pressure, as well as Soviet Government concern over a growing fear among Soviet Jews, was thought to have played a major role in the Supreme Court's action today.

Moreover, Spain's commuting of the death sentences of the six Basque nationalists was regarded as an additional inducement to the Kremlin not to execute the two Jews.

Mark Y. Dymshits and Eduard S. Kuznetsov, who had been accused of leading the group—which planned to escape to Sweden or Finland, and from there to Israel—won a reduction of their death sentences to 15 years in prison camp, the maximum period of confinement under Soviet law.

News of the Supreme Court's decision was relayed to a group of Moscow Jews standing in a light snow outside the court's downtown building about noon today. A man who had attended the hearing came out and informed the people. The mood seemed subdued, and several brightened at hearing the news.

A few hours later, Tass, the Soviet press agency, confirmed the news. It said the Supreme Court "proceeded from the fact that the hijacking attempt was averted in time and that under Soviet law, the death penalty is an exceptional measure of punishment."

Tass repeated the contention that the trial was not directed against Jews as such, but against hijacking. It said the Leningrad trial was "in full accord" with United Nations resolutions aimed at combating hijackings.

The press agency said nothing about the reduced prison-camp sentences for three defenadnts. An observer at the trial hearing said the court had reduced the terms of Anatoly Altman from 12 years to 10, of Leib G. Khnokh from 13 to 10, and of Iosif M Mendelevich from 15 to 12.

Meri M. Khnokh, the sister of Mendelevich, was present at today's two-hour hearing, and later told newsmen that she was "very happy" that the terms of her husband and her brother had been reduced.

Ending a silence about the case in the national press, Izvestia, the Government newspaper, tonight printed a long account of the affairs, stressing that 11 had been convicted solely for their crime. It stressed that they might have killed the crew of the Aeroflot plane they had planned to hijack. The prosecution had asked for commuting of the sentences, further underscoring the view that the authorities had made the decisions.

It said the hearing had been held before Lev. N. Smirnov, chief justice, and M.A. Gavrilin and V.M. Timofeyev, associate justices.

Izvestia said the court had decided "that the verdicts of the court of the first instance were complete and justified," but that it was possible to commute the death penalty. Izvestia also listed the prison terms, and this matched the earlier information that three had been lightened.

The 11, most of whm are from Riga, were arrested June 15 at Smolny Airport in Leningrad as they were walking on the tarmac to board a 12-seater

AN-2 plane scheduled to fly to nearby Karelia near the Finnish border. A 12th person arrested at the airport, Vulf I. Zalmanson, will be tried by a court-martial, since he is a lieutenant on active army duty.

On the same day, eight other Jews were arrested at their places of work or at home. And in following days, twelve more were seized. Like the nine connected with the hijacking plot, the 20 others have tried without success to get to Israel. Nine of them are expected to go on trial Jan. 6 in Leningrad.

The Leningrad 11 were charged with treason under Article 64-A, which makes it a capital crime to flee abroad. Article 15 makes an attempted or planned crime as serious as a committed one.

Following are the prison terms and brief backgrounds of the 11 defendants:

Eduard S. Kuznetsov, 31 years old, employed in a Riga mental hospital, previously served seven years for anti-Soviet activity; 15 years in a special camp.

Mark Y. Dymshits, 43, a former air force pilot; 15 years in a strict camp.

Yuri Fyodorov, a Russian from Moscow, who spent time in a prison camp where he met Kuznetsov and Murzhenko; 15 years in special camp.

Aleksei Murzhenko, a Ukrainian; 14 years in special camp.

Iosif M. Mendelevich, 23, former Riga student; 12 years in strict camp.

Silva I. Zalmanson, 26, former wife of Kuznetsov, and industrial designer in Riga; 10 years in strict camp.

Leib Khnokh, 26, electrician from Riga; 10 years in strict camp.

Anatoly Altman, 28, an engraver from Odessa who moved to Riga; 10 years in strict camp.

Boris Penson, 25, an artist from Riga; 10 years in strict camp.

Izrail I. Zalmanson, 21, Riga student, brother of Silva; eight years in strict camp.

Mendel Bodnya, 30, an invalid whose parents are in Israel; four years in an enforced camp.

January 1, 1971

# *The Status of Jews in the Soviet*

By BERNARD GWERTZMAN
Special to The New York Times

MOSCOW, Jan. 4—The recent trial of 11 would-be hijackers, nine of them Jews who sought to flee to Israel, and the impending trial of about 20 other Jews in Leningrad and other cities have again aroused concern abroad and focused attention on the Soviet Union's treatment of its three million Jews. It is an extremely volatile subject. It has led Jewish leaders in the West to talk as if the Jewish population here is faced with annihilation and it has produced anger in the Kremlin and denials that any Jews are persecuted or that any anti-Semitism can exist.

News Analysis

Soviet officials read from background papers to reveal that Soviet Jews live very well by Soviet standards; that Jews hold important and prestigious jobs in society. In a speech four years ago, Premier Aleksei N. Kosygin attacked anti-Semitism publicly, and many Jews say they have no complaints.

**Bitterness Among Youth**

Yet within Soviet society, in recent years, a growing number of Jews, many of them in their twenties, have expressed frustration and bitterness about the restrictions placed in their path; have spoken publicly about cases of anti-Semitism and cultural repression, and have said that their only hope lies in emigrating to Israel.

As the Leningrad hijacking case indicated, at least some of these Jews were ready to take extreme measures to leave the Soviet Union once they were barred by the authorities from receiving exit visas. The group sought to hijack an Aeroflot plane to Sweden, a plan whose seriousness can be seen in the acknowledged harshness of the penalties; nine persons sent to prison camps for terms ranging from 4 to 15 years and two persons condemned to death, although these sentences were commuted last week to 15-years terms in prison camps.

What has developed in the Soviet Union is a complex phenomenon with two distinct types of Jews: The assimilated Jew, such as Maya Plisetskaya, the Bolshoi's prima ballerina, who does very well in Soviet society, and the Jewish nationalist, such as Silva Zalmanson, who received 10 years in a labor camp in the abortive hijacking. Both types see Soviet society from different angles.

The Soviet authorities can readily counter accusations that anti-Semitism is officially sanctioned in the Soviet Union. A Soviet Jew, unlike his forefathers under the czars, is not subject to special legislation or official discrimination because his domestic identity card says he is a Jew and not a Russian, a Ukrainian or a member of some other nationality. Nothing remotely similar to Hitler's racist policies is being carried out in the Soviet Union today.

Assimilated Jews—those who have lost or abandoned their Jewish sense of identity—probably make up a majority of Soviet Jews. They are generally left alone by the authorities and have the same problems adjusting to society as American Jews had about 40 years ago. They encounter anti-Semites in life and undoubtedly are deprived of jobs and opportunities because of their Jewish origin even though they may not be practicing Jews. But in many cases, particularly in such cities as Moscow, they live well and hold good jobs.

But if anti-Semitism as a policy is not followed, Soviet Jews are faced with a policy that is inimical to those who want to identify with their Jewish heritage, who want to live as Jews, to study Jewish history and traditions, to obey the laws of the Torah and to provide Jewish education for their children.

These Jews are culturally starved. They have not one school in the Soviet Union in which they or their children can learn Yiddish or Hebrew. In the Russian language—which most of them speak and read—no books are published about Jewish matters except those harshly critical of the Jewish faith and traditions.

**Petitions to U.N.**

From these Jews have come the angry ones who have sent petitions to the United Nations Commission on Human Rights, who have banded together to study Hebrew secretly, who listen to the Israeli radio and who frequent the synagogue in Moscow not because they are religious but because it is the only "Jewish" place in this city of about half a million Jews.

Soviet leaders have reacted ambiguously to the refusal of these Jews to be assimilated.

Although Lenin and Stalin both predicted that the Jewish nationality would disappear through assimilation as the czarist restrictions were lifted, nothing was done to hasten the assimilation until 1948 when Stalin began a crackdown on all Jewish institutions. Publications and theaters were closed, the Jewish anti-Fascist organization—a sort of central Jewish group—was abolished and leading Jews were executed or imprisoned.

Stalin died before large-scale persecution of the Jews could begin, and after his death, the wave of terror against Jews was stopped. But the damage done to Jewish life has never been significantly repaired.

The authorities seemed to approve the "withering away" of Jewishness as an active way of life, but largely because of foreign pressure, certain Jewish features were restored. A Yiddish journal, a touring Yiddish theater, a few prayer books, a dozen or so books on Jewish subjects in Yiddish all appeared in the last decade.

During this time the tensions in the Middle East have been another pressure on Soviet Jews. The Kremlin has so stoutly supported the Arab cause that every Jew here knows he is suspect if he expresses sympathy with the Israeli side.

The safe course that most Jews have followed has been to avoid discussing the war. Others have chosen to press for permission to emigrate to Israel.

In seeking to leave the Soviet Union, the Jews have run into two imposing barriers. One is the traditional reluctance of the authorities here to let anyone travel abroad freely. An exit visa here is not a right but a privilege. The second is the specific wariness of the authorities toward emigration to Israel.

Moscow is concerned what the propaganda effect would be if thousands of Jews rushed to leave, and is not interested in alarming the Arab states.

Nonetheless, several hundred a year seem to be receiving permission to leave.

No one knows how many Jews would seek permission if the doors were opened. Militant Jews say as many as a million; others, who are happy here, say about 200,000. It is not known how many have actually applied for permission.

January 5, 1971

# Soviet 1970 Census Shows Unexpected 5% Decline in Those Listing Themselves as Jews

By THEODORE SHABAD
Special to The New York Times

MOSCOW, April 16—The Soviet Union made public today its 1970 census results for ethnic groups, showing an unexpected decline in the number of people declaring themselves to be Jewish.

The 5 per cent drop since the last census, in 1959, ran counter to Soviet estimates that had put the number of Jews at three million. There were 2.15 million Jews reported in the 1970 count.

The unusual discrepancy is believed to reflect a strong trend toward assimilation, particularly in the Russian and Ukrainian Republics, where the reduction in the reported Jewish population was particularly pronounced.

The census report, published in tonight's issue of Izvestia, the Government newspaper, also confirmed the effects of a difference in birth rates that has been reducing the size of the ethnic Russian population while the population of Central Asian Moslems has been growing rapidly.

### Influx in Baltic Area

Elsewhere in the Soviet Union, a heavy ethnic Russian influx into the Baltic republics was shown to have reduced the Baltic people's percentage of the populations, particularly in Estonia and Latvia. The Lithuanians, a Roman Catholic people with a higher birth rate, maintained their population level.

Ethnic-distribution figures in the report also reflected the previously reported flight of some minority groups from China in the middle 1960's, particularly the Vigurs of Sinkiang Province.

The census found a generally older Soviet population, the result of an over-all decline in the birth rate and longer life expectancy. It found a reduction in the number of employable people, which helped to explain the current campaign for increases in labor productivity.

The report, covering one-and-one-half pages of the six-page newspaper with data on ethnic groups, age and sex distribution, and educational level, was the second to be made public since the census was held on Jan. 15, 1970. The first report, published a year ago, included total populations of areas and cities and a breakdown of urban and rural figures.

The information about the Jewish component was probably the most startling in the report. Jews are classified as an ethnic group in the Soviet Union, on the same basis as Ukrainians, Georgians, Latvians and other minorities of this ethnically diversified country.

An upsurge of applications by Jews for emigration in recent years has been interpreted by some as reflecting a renewed sense of ethnic identity. Many applicants have charged in public statements that restrictions on Jewish ethnic activities prevent them from leading a "Jewish life" in the Soviet Union.

Foreign students of the Soviet Jewish scene therefore expected the 1970 census to show a substantial increase from the Jewish population of 2,268,000 reported in 1959, because of natural increase and because more Soviet citizens were thought to have declared their Jewish origins.

### Novosti Figures Different

Even the Novosti press agency said in a recently published pamphlet titled "Soviet Jews: Fact and Fiction" that "by now there are about three million" Jews in the Soviet Union.

An analysis of today's figures suggests that many Jews, particularly in the Russian Republic and in the Ukraine, identified themselves as ethnic Russians rather than Jews. Census rules provided that ethnic affiliation was to be accepted on the basis of an oral declaration without documentary proof. The ethnic classification of every Soviet citizen is entered on his official identity card.

Pressures for assimilation appear to be particularly strong in Russia and the Ukraine, where about three-fourths of the Soviet Union's Jews live. Other republics, where Jews have historically retained greater ethnic identity—Byelorussia and Moldavia, for example—showed relative stability or increases.

### Relatively Few Emigrated

Emigration of Jews, estimated at 15,000 in the last 20 years, could account for only a small part of the reported decline. If indeed the actual Jewish population is about three million, it would mean that several hundred thousand, for reasons of their own, had chosen to identify themselves as Russians.

Jews have sometimes been compared with the country's ethnic Germans, also widely scattered and with no concentrated settlement area of their own. The census reported a 14 per cent rise in the German population, from 1.6 million to 1.8 million. While only 17.7 per cent of the Jews declared Yiddish to be their native language, 66.8 per cent of the Germans listed German.

The Moslem minorities of Central Asia recorded an increase up to 52 per cent since the 1959 census, compared with a natural increase of 13 per cent for ethnic Russians. This indicated that despite a large influx of Russians into the Moslem republics, the indigenous peoples accounted for an increasingly large percentage of the population.

Although ethnic Russians, who now number 129 million out of a total Soviet population of 242 million, dropped by 2 percentage points to 53 per cent, they still represent by far the largest ethnic group, with the 41 million Ukrainians second.

April 17, 1971

# New Surge of Emigration By Soviet Jews Reported

Special to The New York Times

MOSCOW, Nov. 5—Jewish sources report that a new surge of emigration to Israel has been permitted in the last two weeks, raising to some 7,500 the number of Jews who have been allowed to leave the Soviet Union this year.

Moscow's Jewish community is alive with the news that several hundred, including some activists in the emigration protest movement and a larger proportion of urban professional people than has previously been permitted to leave, have received exit visas.

On Tuesday, Moscow's airport was the scene of an emotional departure for 40 persons flying to Vienna on their way to Israel. Other Jews in Moscow have been selling furniture and rearranging apartments as they prepare to emigrate.

### 10 Leave Leningrad

In Leningrad, Jewish sources said 10 Jews left by rail for Vienna last night. Fifteen are said to be planning to leave Kiev in a few days, including 11 young people arrested in August for participation in a demonstration at Babi Yar ravine, site of Nazi executions of Soviet Jews during World War II. Others have reportedly been allowed to emigrate from Odessa, Kharkov, and Vilnius.

Among those given permission to leave Moscow was Mikhail N. Kalik, who was once honored for his work as a film director but was expelled from the Union of Cinematographers last December after applying to go to Israel. Since then he has been a vocal exponent of emigration and had returned his state medal of honor in protest over restrictions on emigration.

Another activist granted an exit visa, Jewish sources said, was Dr. I. Nuderman, a surgeon who was among the leaders of a protest demonstration on Oct. 20 in front of the Communist party Central Committe building in downtown Moscow. About 90 demonstrators, including Dr. Nuderman, were reportedly detained temporarily by Soviet police.

### Some Are Refused Visas

Several Jews who took part in that demonstration said that, unlike Dr. Nuderman, they had been told they would not be granted exit visas. In one case, Soviet authorities were said to have promised a visa and then later reversed themselves.

Western diplomats suggested that the upsurge in emigration, reaching more than 350 a week in the period approaching the Nov. 7 celebrations of the revolution, was due largely to pressures of world public opinion. Soviet leaders were reported to have been questioned about their Jewish policy in the foreign capitals that they recently visited.

In the last year, Soviet policy has fluctuated widely on the Jewish issue. At the end of 1970, a year in which only about 1,000 Jews were permitted to emigrate, Soviet authorities convicted 11 Jews of having planned to hijack a Soviet airliner from Leningrad. Following a world protest against the convictions, the Kremlin eased exit restrictions in the spring, allowing more than 2,000 Jews to leave in March and April.

In the summer restrictions were again tightened while other trials of Jews were held in Leningrad and in Kishinev, capital of the Moldavian Republic.

**5,000 Left by August**

Some 5,000 Soviet Jews were reported to have arrived in Israel in the first eight months of 1971. The rate of emigration increased in September and October to about 1,000 a month, or double the flow in July and August, when most of the emigrants were said to be working-class Jews from Georgia, according to specialists.

These specialists say that the year's total may reach 10,000 as some well-placed Soviet sources had predicted privately.

Western diplomats interpret the latest easing of restrictions as an indication that advocates of the hard-line policy lost out when this approach failed to stop the demands of Soviet Jews or to reduce both internal and external pressures for emigration, at a time when Moscow was trying to project an image of moderation to the West.

Nonetheless, some foreign diplomats believe Moscow still faces a problem because the current policy of expanded though controlled emigration has encouraged Soviet Jews and given strength to the emigration movement rather than depriving it of momentum and leadership.

One foreign visitor to a downtown Moscow synagogue recently noticed many young faces in the congregation and found synagogue officials more willing to discuss Jewish activities than they were previously, despite the presence of secret police agents.

Privately, Soviet officials have reportedly said that 50,000 formal applications for visas have been received from Soviet Jews. The total Jewish population was given as 2.15 million in the 1970 census. Jewish sources report that, as emigration increases and the fear of official reprisals diminishes, more and more Jews are applying for visas.

Some Jews, however, still acknowledge a fear of applying to emigrate because they expect reprisals during the usually prolonged period before a visa is granted. They report that in Kishinev, for example, Vladimir J. Gittelman, 51-year-old deputy chief editor of the Moldavian Republic's radio network, was dismissed six months ago after having applied for an exit visa. He was ousted from the Moldavian writers union in late October, making it virtually impossible to get work. Similar cases in Kishinev and elsewhere were cited.

In Moscow, according to Jewish sources, the pregnant wife of an aeronautical engineer was told that while she could emigrate, an exit visa would be denied her husband because of his sensitive work.

Generally, because of a desire to avoid irritating Arab countries as well as to retain skilled workers, the Kremlin has followed the policy outlined last month by Premier Aleksei N. Kosygin in Canada when he said that highly skilled people whose abilities were vital to the Soviet Union would not be permitted to emigrate.

November 6, 1971

# SOVIET JEWS SAY EXIT FEE IS RISING FOR THE EDUCATED

## Range of $5,000-$25,000 Reported to Be Planned in Payment for Schooling

By HEDRICK SMITH
Special to The New York Times

MOSCOW, Aug. 15—Jewish sources reported tonight that Soviet authorities are instituting a new system of heavy exit fees ranging from $5,000 to $25,000 for educated Jews who want to emigrate to Israel.

The sources said they learned of the new measure, replacing the old general fee of about $1,000, while some Jews were applying for exit visas with a branch of the Interior Ministry today. No official confirmation was possible.

The Government explanation, the sources said, was that the fees were necessary repayment to the Government for the costs of state-financed education. A similar reason had long been given for the earlier fee.

**Discrimination Charged**

Earlier today, 10 Jewish intellectuals charged that the Government was discriminating against educated Jews in handling emigration requests and that harassment and delays had increased in the last two months.

Under present Government policies, the 10 said in a joint statement, highly qualified scientists and educated Jews were in danger of becoming "a new category of human beings—the slaves of the 20th century."

The statement was read at a rare news conference by Benjamin G. Levich, a 55-year-old chemist and scholar, the highest-ranking Soviet academician to apply for an exit visa to Israel. He is a corresponding member of the prestigious Academy of Science and so far the only person associated with the academy to apply for permission to emigrate.

**Tensions Said to Rise**

Educated Jews have long encountered more difficulties in emigrating than blue-collar or office workers and tradesmen, and Western diplomats said tensions between Jews and Soviet authorities were evidently rising because more intellectuals had been applying for exit visas lately.

Western diplomats reported that through the first six months of this year about 15,000 Jews had been allowed to emigrate, roughly the same number as in all of 1971.

Some Jews are contending, however, that the flow since midyear has slowed down, reflecting a change in Soviet attitude. So far there has been no official confirmation, nor any confirmation from diplomats who follow such affairs closely.

A new schedule of fees for educated applicants, if put fully into practice, would be aimed not only at blocking those who have already applied but at deterring others from applying, Jewish sources said.

They reported having been told today that Jews who had graduated from a teachers institute faced fees of 4,500 rubles — $5,400. University graduates were to pay 11,000 rubles —$13,200—and holders of the candidate degree, equivalent to a Ph.D. in America, were to be charged 22,000 rubles —$26,400. Other Jewish sources reported slightly different figures but in the same range.

Even without a graduated fee scale, Dr. Levich and his colleagues contended that educated Jews were being discriminated against. "Jews wishing to leave are being divided according to their educational and intellectual level," they said in their statement. "The higher the level, the more difficult it is to get permission to get a visa."

They asserted that obstacles to intellectuals had been increased lately — discharge from work after applying for visas, the threat of prosecution for lack of employment, sudden military call-ups and the danger of trials for those who refused to serve, disconnection of telephones and interference with mail.

These measures, the statement asserted, coincided with new pressures against non-Jewish civil rights activists here and trials of liberals in Czechoslovakia.

Professor Levich, who was demoted since his unsuccessful application for an exit visa last March, said that his son, Yevgeny, a 24-year-old astrophysicist, has been ordered to report for two years' military service despite chronic physical disabilities and despite the normal exemption granted to scientists with Ph.D.'s.

Besides the Leviches, those who endorsed the statement were Dr. David S. Azbel, 61, a retired chemistry professor who spent 16 years in Stalinist prison camps; Prof. Aleksandr V. Voronel, 41, a physicist; Prof. Boris G. Moisheson, 34, mathematician; Dr. Vladimir G. Zaylavsky, 43, molecular biologist; Viktor S. Yakhot, 28, solid-state physicist; Dmitri K. Simis, 24, sociologist formerly with the Institute of World Economics and International Relations; Gregory L. Svechinsky, 32, an engineer and teacher, and Viktor B. Nord, 27, a film director whose recent movie, "The Debut," won critical acclaim.

All said they had begun the complicated procedure for emigration to Israel. Six said they had been rejected. Two said they had had no answer for some months. Two said they had encountered objections from relatives whose consent for emigration was necessary under Soviet regulations.

August 16, 1972

# Soviet Implies It Has Ended Exit Fees

By HEDRICK SMITH
Special to The New York Times

MOSCOW, March 21—Soviet authorities, in a clear bid for American Congressional approval of trade concessions from the United States, sought to convey the impression tonight that the education tax on Jewish emigrants had been lifted permanently.

In the last three days, the heavy fees have been waived for about 60 Jewish families and well-placed Soviet sources have said that the application of the tax law was being "suspended indefinitely" though the law remained on the books.

The American Embassy said, however, that it had no official confirmation for that report. Nor would Soviet sources assert that the taxes would not be reimposed at a later date.

Jewish activists contend that this was Moscow's intention once American trade concessions were granted. They recalled that last November, just before the American Presidential elections, hundreds of educated Jews were exempted from paying the heavy educational fees, but the taxes were reimposed after the elections.

Jewish sources said, moreover, that Soviet authorities were still applying a policy of selective permission and that a number of prominent scientists and activists were still being refused exit visas to Israel.

The latest series of exemptions from the education taxes began Monday. Since then, Soviet authorities have waived fees previously set for the 60 or so Jewish families in Moscow, Leningrad, Riga, Vilna, Smolensk, among other cities. These Jews had previously got permission to emigrate but had been unable to depart because of inability to pay thousands of rubles in education fees.

March 22, 1973

# *Soviet to Tax Funds From Abroad 30%*

By MALCOLM W. BROWNE
Special to The New York Times

MOSCOW, July 1—A new law was made public today under which the Soviet Government will extract a tax of 30 per cent from all money sent from abroad to Soviet citizens.

The law is apparently aimed at depriving dissident groups and individuals in this country of foreign financial assistance. It is expected especially to hurt Jews and others deprived of their jobs because of having applied for emigration visas, and who are largely dependent on help from overseas.

The new levy, to be applied beginning next Jan. 1, is described as a "duty on money transactions to Soviet citizens from abroad." The existence of the new law was reported unofficially last month, but became public only today.

Even before the decree, which was adopted May 23, Soviet citizens had been paying a 30 per cent bank handling charge on funds from abroad, and it remains to be seen whether this charge will continue in addition to the formal government tax.

Individuals may continue to receive certain kinds of funds from abroad without the new tax, the law says.

Among these categories are alimony payments, inheritances, royalties compensation for damages, funds from sale of property abroad, and money belonging to "re-emigrants and repatriates" — Soviet citizens who moved abroad and decided to return.

Apart from actually arresting and imprisoning dissidents, the Soviet state applies various pressures, of which the financial is the most important.

Dissidents are often deprived of jobs and have difficulty surviving without outside help. Another approach is the use of military conscription.

Draft-age Jews seeking to emigrate are generally inducted after applying for passports. Their active service is for three years in addition to a longer period in the military reserves, during which they may not leave.

In a previous move designed to discourage emigration, the Soviet Government a few years ago imposed an education tax on would-be emigrants in an attempt to recover government outlays for higher education which is free in the Soviet Union. The decree was subsequently allowed to lapse in response to protests abroad.

July 2, 1975

# Soviet Revising Bureaucratic Procedure for Would-Be Emigrants

By CHRISTOPHER S. WREN
Special to The New York Times

MOSCOW, Jan. 20—The Soviet Union has quietly begun overhauling some of its complex emigration procedures in an apparent show of formal compliance with the Helsinki declaration's provisions on increased human contacts.

The move, which disclosed by semiofficial Soviet sources and confirmed in part by Western diplomats and Jewish activists, involves a reduction in exit fees and simplification of the bureaucratic process.

Jewish activists have expressed skepticism that the changes, which are mostly still unannounced, would actually permit freer emigration. They said the changes were gestures intended for the West. A Soviet source said he did not expect the modifications to produce any substantial rise in emigration.

The reduction of the emigration visa fee from 400 to 300 rubles means a cutback equivalent to $133. Some recent emigrants told Western consular officials that they had paid the reduced fee.

**Renunciation Costs $665**

However, emigrants to Israel must continue to pay 500 additional rubles ($665) to renounce their Soviet citizenship, which Moscow requires because it has no diplomatic relations with Israel.

Under an amendment enacted Dec. 23 and now published, an applicant refused permission to go abroad will not have to pay passport fees on subsequent applications that are turned down. This seemingly refers to the 40 ruble fee now required with each application.

Both concessions appear to have been aimed at meeting portions of the Helsinki document in which the nations that signed pledged to "lower, where necessary, the fees charged in connection with these applications to insure that they are at a moderate level," and to see that fees for renewed applications "will be charged only when applications are granted."

In another development related to the Helsinki accord, the press agency Tass quoted a Soviet press distribution official today as having said that 18 newspapers from "capitalist countries" including The New York Times, would be on sale in the Soviet Union this year.

**No Details on Papers**

The official, Yevgeny Prokofyev, called this "new testimony" that the Soviet Union was implementing the Helsinki agreement. Normally, only Communist papers from the West have been available to Soviet citizens, and it was not clear how the Western newspapers would be sold.

The emigration legislation reportedly enacted to simplify paperwork has not been published, but Soviet sources described it as follows:

Applications for emigration will be examined by local officials of the Office of Visas and Registrations rather than forwarded for decisions by higher authority. Those refused permission will be entitled to a review of their cases every six months rather than once a year as previously.

The complicated paperwork for visa applications will reportedly be somewhat simplified. One Jewish applicant said a visa official had told him that the character reference needed from a would-be emigrant's employer, would be eliminated, apparently in favor of a simpler affidavit.

A Soviet legal source said he expected some of the procedural changes on emigration to deal with the knowledge-of-secrets issue that has blocked the emigration of some Jewish scientists as well as questions about the emigration of "criminals" and those who would leave behind an obligation such as children or parents.

While most of the reported changes have yet to be confirmed, several Western diplomats thought them probable and believed they were being designed to show that Moscow was doing its part to comply with all provisions of the Helsinki document, signed nearly six months ago at the 35-nation European Conference on Security and Cooperation.

The Soviet Union has been stung by Western charges that it was dragging its feet on the human rights aspects of the agreement. In turn, it accused the Western countries, including the United States, of being the actual violators.

The report of procedural changes comes at a time when there has been little visible movement on the emigration issue. Nearly 12,000 Jews left the Soviet Union last year, according to one knowledgeable Western diplomat. This is about one-third the 1973 total.

Since the Helsinki agreement was signed, no prominent Jewish applicants are known to have been allowed to leave. There has also been little movement on the list of family reunifications submitted by the American embassy to the Soviet Government on Aug. 18. Slightly more than a dozen of the 235 cases presented by the Americans are understood to have been resolved.

January 21, 1976

# Jews in the Ukraine Charge That the Age-Old Anti-Semitism Persists

By CRAIG R. WHITNEY
Special to The New York Times

KIEV, U.S.S.R.—A monument finally stands over Babi Yar, where for 34 years the Soviet Government did little to honor the memory of the 100,000 people, most of them Jews, whom the Nazis rounded up and massacred outside this Ukrainian city in 1941.

Unmarked, the gullies in a wood at the edge of town were mute testimony to the anti-Semitism that was a powerful force in the Ukraine for centuries before the Nazis came. Though the memorial, completed in 1976 after years of dispute and delay, is a powerful statement, there is not a word on it to suggest that Jews were among the victims.

Prejudice was not driven out of here with the Nazis, according to Ukrainian Jews who have tried to stay here as well as to others who have given up and left. One who falls in between is Vladimir Kislik, a 42-year-old scientist who lost his job and his family when he applied to emigrate to Israel in 1973. He has tried to say a prayer at Babi Yar every Sept. 29, the anniversary of the massacre; this year, as in the past, the police arrested him when he tried to go.

"Life for Jews in the Ukraine is still worse today than in any other part of the Soviet Union," he said in a neighbor's tiny apartment, where he hoped to escape constant police surveillance. "There were always too many of us here."

Under the czars the Ukraine was part of the Pale of Settlement, an area established in the late 18th century by Empress Catherine II in which Jews were confined. Today, according to official figures, 152,000 live in Kiev, more than 9 percent of the population. "There is only one very small synagogue for all those people," said Mr. Kislik, who believes the real figure is closer to 300,000. There are nine churches for the city's nearly 2 million Christians.

It has been five years since Mr. Kislik did his last major scientific work, on the effect of radiation on the structure of metals. It has been more than 10 years since he worked for the Government at a secret installation in the Urals. Yet his knowledge of secrets is the reason given by the authorities for refusing to let him go to Israel. His wife and son, now 12, left without him in 1973. He lives with his ailing 75-year-old father, sharing a $100-a-month pension because he cannot get work.

"After I applied to leave I lost my research job at the Institute of Atomic Research in Kiev," Mr. Kislik said. "Until last May I had a job painting

The New York Times

Women of Kiev viewing the war memorial at Babi Yar.

souvenirs in a factory, but they fired me. Everywhere I apply now they tell me my specialty is not needed, yet I am not even allowed to work as a janitor because I am a specialist. The police were asking me the other day why I was not working."

If Mr. Kislik, a tiny man, sounds defiant, it is because he is desperate. He is also terrified of arrest on charges of treason, a capital crime, for trying to send abroad an article he wrote for publication in a scientific journal here in 1972; it was not allowed to appear after he applied to emigrate.

On Sept. 27 a Ukrainian-language newspaper published a long denunciation of him and other Jewish "refuseniks" in Kiev, charging that he had conspired to send abroad a doctoral dissertation in physics and had slandered the Soviet Union. Since September Mr. Kislik has been arrested, kept from traveling to Moscow and interrogated by the K.G.B., the Soviet security and intelligence service.

"They have searched my apartment and taken all my works and all my scientific archives," he related. "They say my case is ready for trial. Where it will end for me I do not know.They think they will break me, I suppose."

A quarter of the Jews who try to emigrate come from the Ukraine. Though the authorities say the experience of what it is to be a Jew in Soviet society is distorted by their disloyalty, official attitudes do seem to have changed, at least on the surface. An Intourist guide even recalls Yevgeny Yevtushenko's anguished 1961 poem, interpreted then as a cry against official anti-Semitism: "No monument stands over Babi Yar. -A drop sheer as a crude gravestone.-I am afraid."

"The first verse of Yevtushenko's poem should be changed," the guide said. "Now there is a monument." Designed by the late Ukrainian sculptor Mikhail G. Lysenko, the massive bronze represents men, women and children being shot with their hands bound and falling backward off a concrete slab into the ravines, now landscaped. The commemorative plaque says in Ukrainian: "Here from 1941 to 1943, the German Fascist invaders shot and killed more than 100,000 citizens of Kiev and military prisoners."

Beneath the surface of Ukrainian attitudes there is at once embarrassment and a sort of disingenuousness about the intolerance that remained after the Nazis were expelled. A student, asked about it, narrows her eyes and says: "This city is 80 percent Jewish, if you want to know the truth. They've got all the best jobs, too." The ballet master of the Ukrainian Dance Ensemble, a man with a Hebrew given name, avoids mentioning his religion and says, when asked about it, that no member of the troupe is Jewish, though other dancers said several Jewish artists performed and worked with it.

Not long ago Izrail Kleiner, a recent Jewish emigrant from the Ukraine, wrote that Ukrainian-Jewish relations were still strained. "Such expressions as 'We can still arrange another Babi Yar for you' every Jew in the Ukraine has heard a dozen times," he remarked.

December 1, 1977

THE SOVIET EXPERIMENT REVIEWED

# RUSSIA IN THE SHADOW

## *By H. G. WELLS*

## First Article: The Collapse in St. Petersburg

*Mr. Wells is regarded by many critics as the foremost English writer; certainly he is among the two or three most distinguished authors of his country. He has won fame as a novelist and essayist. Born 54 years ago, he was educated at private schools and the Royal College of Science, where he won first class honors in zoology. Since "The War of the Worlds," 1898, he has written twoscore books, including the great wartime novel, "Mr. Britling Sees It Through," and a history of the world, "The Outline of History," just published.*

*The articles in the present series on Russia will be published on succeeding Sundays. They are received by cable from London each week as the author completes them.*



IN January, 1914, I visited St. Petersburg and Moscow for a couple of weeks. In September, 1920, I was asked to repeat this visit by Mr. Kameneff of the Russian trade delegation in London. I snatched at this suggestion and went to Russia at the end of September with my son, who speaks a little Russian.

We spent a fortnight and a day in Russia, passing most of our time in St. Petersburg, where we went about freely by ourselves and were shown nearly everything we asked to see. We visited Moscow, and I had a long conversation with Mr. Lenin, which I shall relate.

In St. Petersburg I did not stay at the Hotel International, to which foreign visitors are usually sent, but with my old friend Maxim Gorky. The guide and interpreter assigned to assist us was a lady I had met in Russia in 1914, the niece of a former Russian Ambassador to London. She was educated at Newnham. She had been imprisoned five times by the Bolshevist Government. She is not allowed to leave St. Petersburg because of an attempt to cross the frontier to her children in Esthonia, and she was therefore the last person likely to lend herself to any attempt to hoodwink me. I mention this because on every hand at home and in Russia I had been told that the most elaborate camouflage of realities would go on and I should be kept in blinkers throughout my visit.

#### Facts Cannot Be Hidden.

As a matter of fact, the harsh and terrible realities of the situation in Russia cannot be camouflaged. In the case of special delegations, perhaps a certain distracting tumult of receptions, bands and speeches may be possible and may be attempted, but it is hardly possible to dress up two large cities for the benefit of two stray visitors wandering observantly, often in different directions.

Naturally, when one demands to see a school or a prison one is not shown the worst. Any country would in the circumstances show the best it had and Soviet Russia is no exception. One can allow for that.

Our dominant impression of things Russian is an impression of a vast irreparable breakdown. The great monarchy that was here in 1914, and the administrative, social, financial and commercial systems congregated with it, have under the strains of six years of incessant war fallen down and smashed utterly. Never in all history has there been so great a débâcle before. The fact of the revolution is to our minds altogether dwarfed by the fact of this downfall. By its own inherent rottenness and by the thrusts and strains of aggressive imperialism the Russian part of the old civilized world that existed before 1914 fell and is now gone. The peasant, who was the base of the old pyramid, remains upon the land, living very much as he has always lived. Everything else is broken down or is breaking down.

Amid this vast disorganization, an emergency Government, supported by a disciplined party of perhaps 150,000 adherents, the Communist Party, has taken control. It has at the price of much shooting suppressed brigandage, established a sort of order and security in exhausted towns and set up a crude rationing system. It is, I would say at once, the only possible Government in Russia at the present time. It is the only idea. It supplies the only solidarity left in Russia. But it is a secondary fact. The dominant fact for the Western reader, a threatening and disconcerted fact, is that a social and economic system very like our own and intimately connected with ours has crashed.

#### Empty Palaces, Ragged Streets.

Nowhere in all Russia is the fact of that crash so completely evident as it is in St. Petersburg. St. Petersburg was an artificial creation of Peter the Great. His bronze statue, in a little garden near the Admiralty, still prances amid the ebbing life of the city. Its palaces are still and empty, or strangely furnished with typewriters and tables and plank partitions of a new administration, which is engaged chiefly in a strenuous struggle against famine and the foreign invader.

Its streets were streets of busy shops in 1914. I loafed agreeably in St. Petersburg streets, buying little articles and watching the abundant traffic. All these shops have ceased. There are perhaps half a dozen shops still open in St. Petersburg. There is a Government crockery shop, where I bought a plate or so as souvenirs for seven or eight hundred rubles each, and there are a few flower shops. It is a wonderful fact, I think, that in this city, in which most of the shrinking population is already starving and hardly any one possesses a second suit of clothes or more than a single change of worn and patched linen, flowers can be and are still bought and sold. For 5,000 rubles, which is about 6s. 8d. ($1.50) at the current rate of exchange, one can get a very pleasing bunch of chrysanthemums.

I do not know if the words "all shops have ceased" convey any pictures to the Western reader of what a street looks like in Russia. It is not like Bond Street or Piccadilly on a Sunday with the blinds drawn down in decorous sleep and ready to wake up and begin again on Monday. The shops have an utterly wretched and abandoned look. The paint is peeling off, windows are cracked, some are broken and boarded up. Some still display a few fly-blown relics of stock in the windows. Some have their windows covered with notices. Windows are growing dim, fixtures have gathered two years' dust. They are dead shops. They will never open again.

All the great bazaar-like markets are closed, too, in St. Petersburg now, in a desperate struggle to keep public control of necessities and prevent the profiteer driving up the last vestiges of food to incredible prices. And this cessation of shops makes walking about the streets seem a silly sort of thing to do. Nobody walks about any more. One realizes that a modern city is really nothing but long alleys of shops and restaurants and the like. Shut them up and the meaning of a street has disappeared.

People hurry past in the thin traffic compared with my memories of 1914. Electric street cars are still running, and buses until 6 o'clock. They are the only means of locomotion for ordinary people remaining in town, the last legacy of capitalist enterprise. They became free while we were in St. Petersburg. Previously there had been a charge of 2 or 3 rubles, the hundredth part of the price of an egg. Freeing them made little difference. In their extreme congestion during homegoing hours every one scrambles on a tramcar. If there is no room inside you cluster outside. In the busy hours festoons of people hang outside by any hand-hold possible. They are frequently pushed off and accidents are numerous. We saw a crowd collected around a child cut in half by a tramcar and two people in the little circle in which we moved in St. Petersburg had broken their legs in tramcar accidents.

The roads along which these tramcars run are in frightful condition. They have not been repaired for three or four years. They are full of holes, like shellholes, often two or three feet deep. Frost has eaten out great cavities. Drains have collapsed and the people have torn up the wood pavement for fires. Only once did we see any attempt to repair streets in St. Petersburg. In a side street some mysterious agency had collected a load of wood bricks and two barrels of tar.

#### Motors Run on Kerosene.

Most of our longer journeys about the town were done in official motor cars left over from former times. A drive is an affair of tremendous swerves and concussions. These surviving motor cars are running now on kerosene. They disengage clouds of pale blue smoke and start up with a noise like a machine-gun battle.

Every wooden house was demolished for firing last Winter, and such masonry as there was in those houses remains in ruinous gaps between the houses of stone. Every one is shabby and every one seems to be carrying bundles in both St. Petersburg and Moscow. To walk into some side streets in the twilight and see nothing but ill-clad figures, all hurrying and all carrying loads, gives one an impression as though the entire population was setting out in flight.

That impression is not altogether misleading. Bolshevist statistics I have seen are perfectly frank and honest in the matter.

The population of St. Petersburg has fallen from 1,200,000 to a little over 700,000, and it is still falling. Many of the people have returned to peasant life in the country and many have gone abroad, but hardship has taken an enormous toll of this city. The death rate in St. Petersburg is over 81 per 1,000. Formerly it was high among European cities at 22. The birth rate of the underfed and profoundly depressed population is about 15. It was formerly about 30.

These bundles that every one carries are partly rations of food that are doled out by the Soviet organization. Partly they are materials and the results of illicit trade. The Russian population has always been a trading and bargaining population. Even in 1914 there were but few shops in St. Petersburg whose prices were really fixed prices. Tariffs were abominated in Moscow. Taking a droshky meant always a haggle, ten kopecks at a time.

**Rationing and Food Control.**

Confronted with a shortage of nearly every commodity, a shortage caused partly by the war strain—for Russia has been at war continually now for six years—partly by the general collapse of social organization and partly by the blockade, and with currency in complete disorder, the only possible way to save towns from the chaos of cornering, profiteering, starvation, and at last a mere savage fight for the remnants of food and common necessities, was some sort of collective control and rationing.

The Soviet Government rations on principle, but any Government in Russia now would have to ration. If the war in the West had lasted up to the present time London would be rationing, too, food, clothing and housing.

But in Russia this has to be done on the basis of uncontrollable peasant production, with a population temperamentally undisciplined and self-indulgent. The struggle is necessarily a bitter one. The detected profiteer, the genuine profiteer who profiteers on any considerable scale, gets a short shrift—he is shot.

Quite ordinary trading may be punished severely. All trading is called speculation and is now illegal, but queer street-corner trading in food, &c., is winked at in St. Petersburg and quite openly practiced in Moscow, because only by permitting this can the peasants be induced to bring in food.

There is also much underground trade between buyers and sellers who know each other. Every one who can supplements his public rations in this way, and every railway station at which one stops is an open market. We would find a crowd of peasants at every stopping place waiting to sell milk, eggs, apples, bread, &c. Passengers clamber down and accumulate bundles. An egg or an apple costs 300 rubles.

The peasants look well-fed and I doubt if they are very much worse off than they were in 1914. Probably they are better off. They have more land than they had and they have got rid of their landlords. They will not help in any attempt to overthrow the Soviet Government because they are convinced that while it endure this state of things will continue.

This does not prevent their resisting whenever they can attempts of Red Guards to collect food at regulation prices. Insufficient forces of Red Guards may be attacked and massacred. Such incidents are magnified in the London press as peasant insurrections against the Bolsheviki. They are nothing of the sort. It is just the peasants making themselves comfortable under the existing regime.

**Industrial Breakdown.**

But every class above the peasants, including the official class, is now in a state of extreme privation. The credit and industrial system that produced commodities has broken down, and so far attempts to replace it by some other form of production have been ineffective, so that nowhere are there any new things. About the only things that seem to be fairly well supplied are tea, cigarettes and matches. These are more abundant in Russia than they were in England in 1917, and the Soviet State match is quite a good match. But such things as collars, ties, shoe laces, sheets and blankets, spoons and forks, all haberdashery and crockery and the like are unobtainable. There is no replacing a broken cup or glass except by sedulous search and illegal trading. From St. Petersburg to Moscow we were accommodated with a sleeping car de luxe, but there were no water bottles, glasses, or indeed any loose fittings. They have all gone.

H. G. WELLS

Most of the men one meets strike one at first as being carelessly shaven, and at first we were inclined to regard that as a sign of general apathy, but we understood better how things were when one friend mentioned to my son quite casually that he had been using one safety razor blade for nearly a year.

Drugs and any medicines are equally unobtainable. There is nothing to take for a cold or headache, no packing off to bed with a hot-water bottle. Small ailments develop very easily. Nearly everybody we met struck us as being uncomfortable and a little out of health. A buoyant, healthy person is very rare in this atmosphere of discomforts and petty deficiencies. If any one falls into real illness the outlook is grim indeed.

My son paid a visit to the big Obuchovskaya Hospital, and he tells me things were very miserable there indeed. There was an appalling lack of all sorts of material, and half the beds were not in use through sheer impossibility of dealing with more patients if they came in. Strengthening and stimulating food is out of the question unless the patient's family can by some miracle procure it outside and send it in. Operations are performed only on one day in the week, Dr. Federoff told me, when necessary preparation can be made. On other days they are impossible and the patient must wait.

**Scarcity of Food.**

Hardly any one in St. Petersburg has much more than a change of raiment, and in the great city in which there remains no means of communication but a few overcrowded tramcars, old, leaky and ill-fitting boots are the only footwear.

At times one sees astonishing makeshifts in the way of costumes. The master of a school to which we paid a surprise visit struck me as unusually dapper. He was wearing a dinner suit with a blue serge waistcoat. Several of the distinguished scientific and literary men I met had no collars and wore neck wraps. Gorky possesses only one suit of clothes he wears at gatherings of literary people in St. Petersburg.

Mr. Amphiteatroff, the well-known writer, addressed a long and bitter speech to me. He suffered from the usual delusion that I was blind and stupid and being hoodwinked; he was for taking off the respectable looking coats of all the company present in order that I might see for myself the rags and tatters and pitiful expedients beneath. It was a painful, an unnecessary, speech, but I quote it here to emphasize the effect of the general destitution in this underclad town.

The population in this dismantled and ruinous city is, in spite of all the furtive trading that goes on, appallingly underfed. With the best will in the world the Soviet Government is unable to procure sufficient rations to sustain healthy life.

I went to a district kitchen and saw the normal food distribution going on. The place seemed to us fairly clean and fairly well run, but that does not compensate for lack of material. The lowest grade ration consisted of a basinful of thin skilly and about the same quantity of stewed apple compote.

The people have bread cards and wait in queues for bread, but for three days the St. Petersburg bakeries stopped for lack of flour. The bread varies greatly in quality. Some was good, coarse brown bread and some I found damp, claylike and uneatable.

I do not know how far these disconnected details will suffice to give the Western reader an idea of what ordinary life in St. Petersburg is at the present time. Moscow, they say, is more overcrowded and shorter of fuel than St. Petersburg, but superficially it looked far less grim than St. Petersburg.

We saw these things in October, in a particularly fine and warm October. We saw them in sunshine, in a setting of ruddy and golden foliage. But one day there came a chill, and the yellow leaves went whirling before a drive of snowflakes. It was the first breath of the coming Winter. Every one shivered and looked out of the double windows, already sealed up, and talked to us of the previous year. Then the glow of October returned. It was still glorious sunshine when we left Russia, but when I think of coming Winter my heart sinks.

**Preparing for Winter.**

The Soviet Government, in the Commune of the North, has made extraordinary efforts to prepare for the time of need. There are piles of wood along the quays, along the middle of the main streets, in courtyards, and everywhere where wood can be piled. Last year many people had to live in rooms below the freezing point. Water pipes froze up. Sanitary machinery ceased to work. The reader must imagine what that meant to people who huddled together in ill-lit rooms and kept themselves alive with tea and talk. Presently some Russian novelist will tell us all that this has meant to heart and mind in Russia. This year it may not be quite so bad, as the food situation also, they say, is better, but this I very much doubt.

The railways are now in an extreme state of deterioration. The wood stocked engines are wearing out. Bolts start and rails shift as the trains rumble along at a maximum of twenty-five miles per hour. Even were the railways more efficient, Wrangel has now hold of the Southern food supplies. Soon cold rain will be falling upon these 700,000 souls still left in St. Petersburg and then snow. The

*I saw one passenger steamboat on the Neva crowded with passengers. Usually the river was quite deserted except for a rare Government tug or solitary boatman picking up drift timber.

long nights extend and daylight dwindles.

And this spectacle of misery and ebbing energy is, you will say, the result of Bolshevist rule. I do not believe it is. I will deal with the Bolshevist Government when I have painted the general scenery of our problem. But let me say here that this desolate Russia is not a system that has been attacked and destroyed by something vigorous and malignant. It is an unsound system that has worked itself out and fallen down.

It was not the Communism which built up these great impossible cities, but capitalism. It was not Communism that plunged this huge creaking bankrupt empire into six years of exhausting war, it was European imperialism. Nor is it Communism that has pestered this suffering and perhaps dying Russia with a series of subsidized raids, invasions and insurrections, and inflicted upon it the atrocious blockade. The vindictive French creditor and the journalistic British oaf are far more responsible for these deathbed miseries than any Communist.

But to these questions I will return after I have given a little more description of Russia as we saw it during our visit. It is only when one has some conception of the physical and mental realities of the Russian collapse that we can see and estimate the Bolshevist Government in its proportions.

November 7, 1920

# WINSTON CHURCHILL VS. WELLS

## Further Echoes of the Controversy Over Russian Conditions Under Bolshevist Rule

*Below are extracts from articles by the Right Hon. Winston Churchill, M. P., and H. G. Wells, published in The Sunday Express of London after the appearance of Mr. Wells's series, "Russia in the Shadow." That series was printed in The New York Times on five recent Sundays.*

### CHURCHILL ANSWERS WELLS.

WHEN one has written a history of the world from nebula to the Third International and of the human race from protoplasm to Lord Birkenhead in about a twelvemonth, there ought to be no difficulty in becoming an expert on the internal conditions of Russia after a visit of fourteen days. When a writer of such singular power and imagination as H. G. Wells turns aside from those charming philosophical romances with which he has so often delighted us to give us definite and final guidance on the greatest political question in the world, we ought to examine his conclusions with attention.

These conclusions are set out with great solemnity in the final paragraphs of the articles which Mr. Wells has written upon his visit to Russia.

First—"Russian civilization is in extremis. * * * Nothing like this Russian downfall has ever happened before. If it goes on for a year or so more the process of collapse will be complete. Nothing will be left of Russia but a country of peasants; the towns will be practically deserted and in ruins, the railways will be rusting in disuse. With the railways will go the last vestiges of any general government."

Second—"But this is not the fault of the Bolsheviki or of their communistic system; oh, dear, no. On the contrary, the Bolsheviki 'are the only possible Government that can stave off such a final collapse of Russia * * * if they can be assisted by America and the Western powers.'

Third—"The Bolshevist Government is inexperienced and incapable to an extreme degree" and it must be assisted "generously" to "establish a new social order" in Russia in accordance with the principles of communism, or possibly "a mitigated communism."

Fourth—In order to secure this generous help for the Bolsheviki there must be trade between them and the Western powers and the United States. But as the Bolsheviki regard private traders as "pirates" and all private property as plunder, "there is only one being in Russia with whom the Western world can deal, and that is the Bolshevist Government itself, and there is no way of dealing with that one being safely and effectually, except through some national or, better, some international trust." * * *

[*Mr. Churchill gives a glimpse of advancing civilization and the growth of a class, especially in the large centres of Europe, which laughed at patriotism and developed a cult preaching "better a world of equally hungry slaves than a world of unequally prosperous freemen."*]

These beings, animated by the most ferocious hatreds that the human breast has ever contained, were unable, except in periods of catastrophe, when they immediately rose to the surface, seriously to impede the steady onward march of civilization. From time to time they threw bombs or murdered prominent people as a proof of the faith that was in them. But they bided their time, and at last, when the loosely knit structure of the Russian Empire was shaken by the stress of the great war, their chance came. They represented the principle of death as the consequence of an all-pervading spirit of hate.

With a clang they closed the gates both to the paths which make life tolerable here below and to those which we hope lead on to serener forms of existence, and instead they attempted to thrust upon mankind universal slavery disguised as universal equality under the permanent dictatorship of their own sect.

The doctors tell us that the principle of cancer sleeps in the bodies of great numbers of healthy persons. They tell us that cancer is the revolt of a single cell which proclaims a malignant principle of life and gathers others to its standard and forces an intense effort from the surrounding tissues to wall in and limit the area of rebellion. While the central principle of a man's being is firmly seated on its throne, all the provinces of his body are held in proper subjection, but when that principle is weakened for any reason, then it is that these deadly growths start into activity and enter upon their violent, virulent and inevitably fatal career.

This is what has happened to Russia and is still happening to Russia. We see the Bolshevist cancer eating into the flesh of the wretched being; we see the monstrous growth swelling and thriving upon the emaciated body of its victim. And now Mr. Wells, that philosophical romancer, comes forward with the proposition that the cancer is the only thing that can pull the body around; that we must feed that and cultivate that. After all, it is another form of life. It is "a new social order." Why be so narrow-minded as to draw the line between health and disease, still less between right and wrong? Adopt an impartial attitude. Put your money on the disease if you think it is going to win.

Is this similitude exaggerated? Let us see. The vast majority of thinking men have always proclaimed that the principle of malignant communism, that is to say communism applied by ruthless force to any society, will result in the destruction and death of that society. The Bolsheviki have applied this system by ruthless force to such parts of Russia as they have been able to get a grip of; and those parts of Russia, and only those parts of Russia, are, according to Mr. Wells and to other authorities, some of whom have been there longer than a fortnight, dying, and dying fast. "Nothing will be left of Russia," he says, "but a country of peasants. The towns will be practically deserted and in ruins. The railways will be rusting in disuse." But it is these towns of Russia in which alone it has been found possible to put this system into operation. 'All attempts to enthrall the villages have failed, and none can now succeed in time.

There has never been any work more diabolical in the whole history of the world than that which the Bolsheviki have wrought in Russia. Consciously, deliberately, confidently, ruthlessly—honestly, if you will, in the sense that their wickedness has been the true expression of their nature—they have enforced their theory upon the Russian towns and cities; and these are going to die.

"Ah," says Mr. Wells, "it was not communism that did this, but the blockade." Russia starved by blockade! How is this? Russia is one of the great granaries of the world. Before the war she poured her wheat out to Europe by every channel. During the first three years of the war she required no food from outside. * * *

To find the cause of the famine in Russia we have only to summarize the indisputable facts of the Bolshevist policy toward the peasants in the villages. * * *

They ceased to produce any more grain than that which they could use themselves or be sure of hiding. Hence the famine. It is not the Russian soil which has been ruined; that broad and fertile expanse still lies ready to produce, year by year, in the procession of the seasons, enough for all and to spare. But the motive power, the human effort, the careful direction have been destroyed, and so the cities are starving. Then we come to the final step to which the Bolsheviki are led by the inexorable command of fate—namely, to take over enormous tracts of country and work them by armies of slaves who once were soldiers, in order to wring for a few more months or years, by their efforts under the compulsion of an iron discipline the means of continuing the Bolshevist tyranny in power.

There is nothing in this which is surprising or which is new or which could not have been foreseen or which had not over and over again been predicted in such circumstances. Repeat these steps in any land and you will arrive at the same result. Once the disease is started, if it cannot be excised by a surgical operation, it is fatal.

Thank God, however, Russia is vast and her villages are counted by the tens of thousands. Great masses of the urban population have taken refuge in them or are scattered far and wide in foreign lands. Let them be patient till this tyranny be past. It must pass in time. It can only kill those parts of Russia subjected to its system, and when that system perishes or is abandoned life will flow back by a thousand rills, and then indeed will be the chance for all the world to help.

Mr. Wells may, turning this way and that in his evident intellectual pain, say to me, What is the immediate remedy? It is extremely simple. Let the Bolsheviki drop communism. Let them leave off enforcing this unnatural system which paralyzes human effort and dries up the springs of enterprise and wealth. Instantly the recovery will begin. But then they would cease to be Bolsheviki. They would cease to be communists. They would become only commonplace criminals who had pillaged an empire and installed themselves amid the ruins of its towns. * * *

We must, at any rate, take care that the people of Great Britain, of France, and of the United States are not left in doubt or ignorance as to the causes ard the character of this frightful catastrophe.

---

**WELLS HITS BACK AGAIN.**

*The following excerpts from Mr. Wells's rejoinder to Mr. Churchill appeared in The Sunday Express under the heading "The Anti-Bolshevist Mind."*

Mr. Churchill has not even noted that I do not ascribe the present condition of Russia to the blockade. Instead of a reply there were vehement assertions about Russia and about the world generally, exactly the assertions that Mr. Churchill, inattentive to any reality, unteachable by any experience, has been making for the last two years. * * *

He believes quite naïvely that he belongs to a peculiarly gifted and privileged class of beings to whom the lives and affairs of common men are given over—the raw material for brilliant careers. It seems to him an act of insolence that a common man like myself should form judgments upon matters of statescraft, should venture to dispute the horrible waste of human life and hope—our lives and hopes and the future of our children—that his frantic anti-Russian policy sustains. * * *

Although these Bolsheviki were men of obscure origin they at once set about killing people with a freedom that had hitherto been reserved for their betters. How many they killed is still very much in dispute. Mr. Churchill would fasten upon them the responsibility of a death-roll but little inferior to that of Gallipoli. They ruined Russia, which Mr. Churchill would have us believe was a smiling land of order and plenty in 1917, and they began a sinister but insidious world propaganda which will inevitably destroy all the happy freedoms of the present time unless we devote our whole energies to their overthrow. * * *

While Mr. Churchill seems to be praising this great civilization in which we live, he is really denying that it is a civilization at all. For were it so it would surely have inherent in it a wider and finer future. It would involve developing forces of education and organization, and a power of resistance against error and passion. It would be capable of sane adjustments against war and a proper economy of its resources and energy. It would have no more fear of a little body of impecunious foreign fanatics in insecure control of a bankrupt country than a young lion would have of a mouse. It is just because Mr. Churchill does not really believe in the civilizing forces of the world, and because I do, that he is for stampeding us all into this anti-Bolshevist crusade, and I am for dealing with this very limited and human gang in control of Russia just as we deal with Mr. Churchill's gang and every other form of mischievous or incompetent public activity—patiently, with a steady pressure toward saner things.

I have tried to show the Bolsheviki as I saw them, creatures like ourselves, each one both good and bad, muddled, in a tangle of amazing difficulties. I have sought to draw them to scale. Mrs. Sheridan's frank and amusing diary confirms that story of entirely human beings up to the hilt. But Mr. Churchill will not have that truth. He exalts the Bolsheviki. He makes much of them. He magnifies them to terrific proportions. What vain men there are among them will like Mr. Churchill's account of them much more than they will like mine. Mr. Churchill makes them the leading fact in the whole world, the negative rulers of us all, the "World Cancer." All our lives are to be dictated by what the Bolsheviki say and do. Everything else is to be subordinated to that one supreme antagonism. Bolshevism is to be treated as the male force in human affairs, and our civilization, with no creative plans or powers of its own, is to behave like a nagging, irreconcilable wife. Not for us the manly, "We will." For us the squealing Churchilian "They shan't."

Why is Mr. Churchill making this tremendous fuss about Bolshevism?

It would be interesting to hear some competent psychoanalyst on Mr. Churchill and to trace the forces that have made him, as he undoubtedly is, the anti-Bolshevist leader in Europe. But even an amateur may make a few observations upon his mentality. * * *

Mr. Churchill is incapable of facing the facts of Bolshevism in cold blood; his heat is clear evidence to the discerning of his subconscious struggle; directly he approaches the topic he begins to orate and gesticulate and "work himself up." At any cost, the truth must be shouted aside. Bolshevism, the "World Cancer," is a necessary thing to him. In a fantastic "struggle" against it lies his one hope of escape from the hard constructive work, the discipline and self-abnegation that lies before us all. If he can only keep a fight going with this imaginary Bolshevism, then there will be neither money nor energy for increased education, for improved public health, for any organization of social order beyond the scrambling competition of the present time. The world will be kept unsafe for adventurers. And it does not enter into the Churchill philosophy to care in the least that it will be a sinking and disintegrating world.

**But what a pitiful and dreary project this is—to be an Anti! To have no faith of your own, no plan of your own, to build nothing, to cultivate nothing, but to devote your life to ranting denunciation and to thwarting and overthrowing** the efforts of other men! As a program! As a career! What a spectacle of utter bankruptcy, moral and intellectual, does not Mr. Churchill display! What a prospect he opens before us, of the more and more ragged levies of bankrupt Europe wasting themselves in the desolations of the East! War and war and more war, until the schools are ruined and empty, the factories idle, the towns half desert. But we shall still be saving one precious thing—Freedom, Mr. Churchill's freedom, that is to say—to try one more gamble.

It has been my lot to hear and read much anti-Bolshevism during the last few weeks, because the mere attempt to give even so unflattering a portrait of the Bolshevik as I have done, without the customary expressions of abuse, is enough to raise the typical followers of Mr. Churchill to a frenzy. * * *

One turns the heap over. You find in a little while, after a page or so or a column or so, that the black and horrible Bolshevik is dropping out of the discourse. And other things begin to appear. Denunciations of the education of common people, denunciations of public housing, denunciations of any public care for health. There is such a thing as a real hatred of human welfare. These people betray it. The idea of every one being decently cared for seems in many cases to wound a secret satisfaction. And their indignation sweeps around, almost unaware, upon those who would restrain the currency speculator, who would check gambling with common necessities, who would question a man's misuse of his wealth. "Freedom" they cry, but their "Freedom" has a raucous voice, and it clutches much that does not belong to Freedom at all in its hands. You need but to listen attentively, and you will hear the voice of the money rigger, the forestaller, the knowing watcher of the tape, the sweater and filcher, the smug owner of unearned advantages, the self-indulgent prosperous, breaking through the deep anti-Bolshevisit roar. * * *

Not in a day, not without blood and toil and passion, is a new order brought into the world. But the growth of human sanity and understanding has been a strong and steadfast growth. The history of the past century and a half has been a history of broken and discarded egotists; one adventurer is swept to St. Helena, another to Camden, another to Amerongen. We are getting the spirit of adventure under control.

The dogmas of the Bolshevik and the screams of the anti-Bolshevik are alike incidental inconveniences. The class war is, after all as "anti" a thing as any. Bolshevik and anti-Bolshevik are but left and right of the same thing, two divergent expressions of impatient, undisciplined, and unenlightened minds. There is no despair of this present world for those who take long views, but the impatient and egotistical mind makes its own hell. And, unhappily, opens it to others. Sane men can face the truth about present-day things gravely and with a good heart, and go about their work without haste and without delay. Much is being [illegible], much that is hopeful is being [illegible] over [illegible]. The light increases.

January 9, 1921

---

# DREISER HOME, SEES SOVIET AIMS GAINING

## Author Thinks Principles of Government Will Spread Even to This Country.

## BUT IN A DIFFERENT FORM

### He Declares There Is No Bread-Line or Unemployment in Russia—

Theodore Dreiser, author of "An American Tragedy," returned yesterday with Mrs. Dreiser after spending eleven weeks in Russia studying the Soviet régime. He said he was convinced that its fundamental principles are destined to exert a vast change in the social and economic status of the world.

The author said he believes that while America will drift to these principles, they probably will be manifest in another form, since no nation completely takes over the governing methods of another.

It was explained that Mr. Dreiser had been received in Russia as an emissary of American letters and Joseph Stalin placed at his disposal two secretaries, who were with him and Mrs. Dreiser for their entire stay, traveling with them wherever they went. The Dreisers returned on the Hamburg-American liner Hamburg.

**Varies on Labor Program.**

The writer regarded as splendid the Soviet program as it is applied to the masses, since every one is guaranteed food, shelter and clothing, but he was at variance with their overemphasis of the importance of labor.

He was asked if he had met Trotsky and replied that he was in Moscow at the time of the Russian leader's fall and saw him made a target for a fusillade of overripe tomatoes.

"The Soviet Central Committee, the ruling power in Russia," Mr. Dreiser said, "will not stand for opposition of any character within its ranks. Trotsky and some of his associates in the minority group were in a temper of revolt. Stalin and his group were in the majority. There was nothing left but that Trotsky and his associates be ejected, and though he is a man of tremendous following, he was ejected and exiled. Every Soviet realizes that their strength alone lies in unity, and if there are divisions the scheme must fail."

The writer said that what interested him greatly in Russia is that there is no private property. He said that Stalin lives in a three-room apartment which costs $125 a month and which, like all other apartments, is paid for by the Government.

He was asked if there is not a tendency to adopt capitalistic methods. He said that while Russia already had returned to gold and silver as an exchange, the country seemed apparently determined to centre everything in the nature of property in the Government itself, instead of in individuals and groups of individuals.

When asked what happened to the collector and the connoisseur in Russia, Dreiser said:

"There are none, nor should there be. We people in America have a mania for collecting endless objects. Art and books properly belong where every one can have them, and that is what has happened in Russia with all private collections of art and of libraries.

February 22, 1928

# RED RUSSIA OF TODAY RULED BY STALINISM, NOT BY COMMUNISM

## Kremlin Chief Has Reverted to Autocracy of Early Czars, Dominating Nation.

## 5-YEAR PLAN IS FLEXIBLE

## Soviet Leaders Aim Through It to Direct Masses—Its Relative Success Not Crucial.

## THEORETICAL DAYS PASSING

### Lenin Modified Marxism and Stalin Now Turns Practical Trends of People to His Own Policy.

By WALTER DURANTY.
Special Cable to THE NEW YORK TIMES.

PARIS, June 13.—Russia today cannot be judged by Western standards or interpreted in Western terms. Western Marxists and Socialists go nearly as far wrong about it as the "burgeois" critics because they fail to understand that the dominant principle of the Soviet Union, though called Marxism or Communism, is now a very different thing from the theoretical conception advanced by Karl Marx.

In thirteen years Russia has transformed Marxism—which was only a theory anyway—to suit its racial needs and characteristics, which are strange and peculiar, and fundamentally more Asiatic than European.

The dominant principle in Russia today is not Marxism or even Leninism, although the latter is its official title, but Stalinism—to use a word which Joseph Stalin deprecates and rejects. I mean that, just as Leninism meant Marxian theory plus practical application, plus Russia, so Stalinism denotes a further development from Leninism and bears witness to the prodigious influence of the Russian character and folkways upon what seemed the rigid theory of Marx.

### Operating Principle Is Russian.

Stalinism is a tree that has grown from the alien seed of Marxism planted in Russian soil, and whether Western Socialists like it or not it is a Russian tree.

Old Russia was an amorphous mass, held together by a mystic, half Asian idea of an imperial régime wherein the emperor was exalted to the position of God's vice regent, with limitless power over the bodies, souls, property and even thoughts of his subjects. That, at least, was the theory, and it was only when the Czars themselves began to question it and "act human" that a spirit of doubt and eventual rebellion became manifest.

The Czarist régime was poisoned by the European veneer that was spread over Russia—a veneer that was foreign and at bottom unwelcome to the mass of the Russian people—and one of the things the Bolshevist revolution did was to sweep away this alien crust and give the essential Russianinity underneath an opportunity to breathe and grow. Which explains why the Bolsheviki, who at first were a mere handful among Russia's millions, were able successfully to impose their dominant principle—namely, Marxism—which in superficial appearance was far more alien than the Germanized or Westernized system it overthrew.

The truth is that the ideas outlined in the Communist Manifesto of Marx (which incidentally expounds his whole philosophy far more simply, lucidly and concretely than the ponderous "Das Kapital" and should be learned by heart by any one who wishes to understand the Soviet Union) suited the Russian masses much better than the Western theory of individualism and private enterprise imported by Peter the Great and his successors, who finally perished in the conflict it involved with the native character of Russia.

### Stalin Abolished NEP.

Lenin took and shaped Marxism to fit the Russian foot, and although circumstances compelled him to abandon it temporarily for the New Economic Policy, he always maintained that this political manoeuvre was not a basic change of policy. Sure enough, Stalin, his successor and devout disciple, first emasculated the NEP and then set about abolishing it. Today the NEP is a sorry slave in the outer courts of the Soviet palace.

That is what Stalin did and is doing to our boasted Western individualism and spirit of personal initiative—which was what the NEP meant—not because Stalin is so powerful or cruel and full of hate for the capitalist system as such, but because he has a flair for political management unrivaled since Charles Murphy died.

Stalin is giving the Russian people—the Russian masses, not Westernized landlords, industrialists, bankers and intellectuals, but Russia's 150,000,000 peasants and workers—what they really want, namely, joint effort, communal effort. And communal life is as acceptable to them as it is repugnant to a Westerner. This is one of the reasons why Russian Bolshevism will never succeed in the United States, Great Britain, France or other parts west of the Rhine.

Stalinism, too, has done what Lenin only attempted. It has re-established the semi-divine, supreme autocracy of the imperial idea and has placed itself on the Kremlin throne as a ruler whose lightest word is all in all and whose frown spells death. Try that on free-born Americans, or the British with their tough loyalty to old things, or on France's consciousness of self. But it suits the Russians and is as familiar, natural and right to the Russian mind as it is abominable and wrong to Western nations.

### Key to Stalin's Power.

This Stalin knows and that knowledge is his key to power. Stalin does not think of himself as a dictator or an autocrat, but as the guardian of the sacred flame, or "party line," as the Bolsheviki term it, which for want of a better name must be labeled Stalinism.

Its authority is as absolute as any emperor's—it is an inflexible rule of thought, ethics, conduct and purpose that none may transgress. And its practical expression finds form in what is known as the five-year plan. The Soviet five-year plan is a practical expression of the dominant principle—which for convenience the writer will call Stalinism, although Stalin still terms it Leninism—which rules Russia today with absolute authority.

In a sense it is far more than a plan—and in another sense it is not a plan at all. It is a slogan for a national policy and purpose rather than the glorified budgetary program which it appears at first sight to be. Most persons outside Russia seem to think that if the five-year plan "fails" it will be the end of Bolshevism and that if it "succeeds" it will mean the end of capitalism elsewhere. Nothing could be more absurd or more wrong.

The five-year plan is nothing more or less than applied Stalinism, and its mass of bewildering figures is only the thermometer to measure the degree of heat engendered by the application of the plan, but is not otherwise intrinsically important. The figures have been changed so often and so considerably as to cease to have real value save as an indication of the "tempo," or rate, at which Stalinism is gaining ground.

### Five-Year Plan Provides Goal.

To the rest of the world it is only a menace, in the sense that Bolshevism itself is a menace—which may or may not be true. To Russia it is only a hope or promise in terms of what Bolshevism itself offers. But to the Russian people the five-year plan is infinitely more besides—it is a goal to aim at, and its inception cannot be regarded as a stroke of genius by any one familiar with the Russian nature.

Russians, ignorant or wise, have a positive passion for plans. They almost worship a plan, and the first thing any one, two or more Russians ever do about anything is make a plan for it. That, after making his plan, the Russian feels satisfied and seems to lose sight of the fact that a plan must next be carried out is of the great obstacles Stalin and his associates are now facing.

So, to conceive a whole national policy and everything in the national life as one gigantic plan was the political tour de force that put Stalin in the highest rank. Every one who has employed Russians or worked with Russians or knows Russians finds that if he wants them to jump on a chair, he must tell them to jump on a table, and aiming at the table they will reach the chair. The important thing is that they have something to jump at and make an effort—whether they actually get there all at once or not does not really matter in a country of such vast natural resources and with such a tough and enduring population.

What matters is that they keep on trying, and that is what Stalinism and its five-year plan is set to make them do. In others words, the five-year plan is something for the Russians to measure at, not for the rest of the world to measure Russians by. This sounds confusing, but it is true, and if you cannot understand it you cannot understand Russia.

### Chief Purpose Is Direction.

The whole purpose of the plan is to get the Russians going—that is, to make a nation of eager, conscious workers out of a nation that was a lump of sodden, driven slaves. Outsiders "viewing with alarm" or hooting with disdain as they take and play with Soviet statistics might as well be twiddling their own thumbs for all it really counts.

What does count is that Russia is being speeded up and fermented—and disciplined—into jumping and into making an effort and making it all together in tune to the Kremlin's music. That is why the Soviet press utters shouts of joy about the five-year plan for oil production being accomplished in two and a half years and does not care a rap when some meticulous foreigners comment about the fact that nothing like the five-year amount of oil has actually been produced.

What the Soviet press really means is that in two and a half years the daily production rate—or tempo—has reached the point set for the end of the fifth year of the plan—in short, that Oil has jumped on the table way ahead of time. That the said rate may only be maintained with the utmost difficulty has small importance to Russian logic, and rightly so, because a successful effort has been made and what a man has done once that man can do again.

Russia and Russians and Russian logic are different, but the fact that they are different does not necessarily mean they are wrong.

In succeeding dispatches the writer will try to show what this difference is and how it works. More immediately, how the five-year plan works in practice in this, which the Russians call, the "third and decisive year." And, incidentally, by "decisive" they do not mean critical or deciding of success or failure, but victorious—deciding success only.

June 14, 1931

# SHAW DISCOVERS THE ALMOST PERFECT STATE

*Mr. Shaw's recent visit to Russia attracted world-wide attention, among capitalists as well as Communists. In the article that follows he weighs capitalism against communism, finds the former deplorably deficient and draws what is, if nothing more, at least a striking contrast between the two.*

By GEORGE BERNARD SHAW.



LONDON.

A FRENCH sentimentalist has said that to understand everything is to forgive everything. He was quite wrong. The result of a thorough understanding between reciprocally dangerous parties is that they do their best to kill one another.

They may agree with the Frenchman to the extent of wasting neither time nor virtuous indignation in lecturing one another on their respective morals; but that only makes their warfare more businesslike and implacable.

I am not at all sure that in clearing up the ridiculous misunderstandings between Communist Russia and the capitalist civilization elsewhere I am abating the hostility which they foment. The more light I throw on Russian communism the louder may our capitalist newspapers and imperialist politicians clamor for its destruction.

But if they must clamor, they may as well clamor intelligently as nonsensically. An intelligent agitation is education.

The current American anti-Russian bosh and boloney expresses only the vulgar phobia which leads capitalism to underrate its enemy and overrate itself very dangerously; all the more so as the misunderstanding is not reciprocal. The Communist leaders understand both communism and capitalism. The spokesmen of capitalism understand neither capitalism nor communism.

Stalin may well say, with Archbishop Whately and Palmerston: "The silly people don't understand their own silly business."

### In Russia and at Home.

He might add that even the people who are not silly are so ignorant of the conditions in their own country that they are horrified when they read of conditions in Russia like those which exist within ten minutes' walk of their own doors.

Well-to-do people are brought up in a fool's paradise. They remind us of the crusaders against Negro slavery a century ago, who did not know that in the factories whose smoke darkened their windows, little white children were being more cruelly overworked and beaten than adult Negroes about whose sufferings they told such heartrending tales.

In Russia at present criminals are more leniently and sensibly dealt with than in any other country known to me. In England recently a man convicted of robbery with violence committed suicide in prison after receiving a vindictive sentence of ten years' penal servitude and a flogging.

In France the horrors of Cayenne and Devil's Island, and in America the frightfully long periods of solitary confinement and Delaware's flogging suggest the civilization of fiends rather than of human beings.

### American Racketeering.

The newspapers of the Western World are full of the horrors of American racketeering and portraits of that country's brigand heroes Rascals without sense enough to keep on terms with the Federal Government by paying their income tax have found it so easy to intimidate juries and corrupt the police, even the bench, that it has become a waste of money to smuggle alcohol. It is easier and quite as safe to walk into a shop and inform the shopkeeper that unless he hands over $1,000 he will be shot up presently.

In Soviet Russia the gangster would have as much chance of survival as a rat in a yard full of terriers.

In America families by the million are starving or selling their last sticks of furniture for food without even the dole that in England stands between the unemployed workers and Wall Street. In both countries the governing class is doing nothing to save the situation by social and industrial organization. It is buying off a desperate insurrection against starvation by the charity, voluntary in America, partly compulsory in England, which burns the candle at both ends instead of at the top only.

In Russia there is no unemployment, the people are healthy and carefree and full of hope, going a bit short and working a bit hard, but confident that all the benefit of their work will go to themselves and not be squandered by idlers in luxury hotels from Palm Beach to the Adriatic.

In Russia, though capital punishment is abolished, such idlers are not endowed with millions before they are born; they are either set to work or painlessly shot as not being worth their keep, and they are not replaced.

I might multiply these contrasts; but I have cited enough to make even the most absurd American (and Americans are the most absurd people at present on earth) remember when he feels tempted to lecture Russia on the wickedness of her social and political morals, or the condition of her people, that those who live in glass houses should not throw stones.

The first question a traveler asks for his safety and guidance when he sojourns in a strange State is: "What do these people kill you for?" The next question is: "What do they praise you for?"

In America the answer is simple. They kill you for committing murder and praise you for making money.

In Russia they have abolished capital punishment for murder and substituted four or five years' imprisonment. But if you make money they shoot you ruthlessly.

### Penalty for Too Much Money.

If you walk into a State bank (banking in Russia is a public function, as it should be in every sensible country) and proffer a sum of money on deposit they will pay you 8 per cent interest on it. But if you do this on a scale which suggests you are obtaining more than your fair share, their income tax commissioners will look into the matter; and if they find that you have been speculating or exploiting the labor of others, your relatives will presently miss you and you will not turn up again.

And there will be no visible jury to intimidate, no visible patrolman to corrupt, no visible magistrate or judge with an interest in your booty. Your sole guarantee that this invisible power will not be maliciously used against you is that it is to the interest of the secret tribunal to keep you alive and at work and at large as long as you are of any use to your fellow creatures, and that only when you become or try to become a thief or beggar is it worth any one's while to take the trouble of liquidating you —or shall I say bumping you off?

It was that eminent and highly respectable English Tory property owner, John Ruskin, who pointed out that there are only three possible sorts of persons in human society: workers, beggars and thieves. A Russian would perhaps put it more shortly by admitting only two sorts producers and parasites.

Now the theory of capitalism is that without the incentive of becoming parasites men will not produce and that parasitism is therefore one of the inevitable costs of production. A factory, it declares, is impossible unless there is a landlord to let the land on which it stands for the highest competitive rent he can obtain for it, the capitalist extorting the highest interest his spare cash can command from it, the employer determined to make its profits cover both rent and interest and as much as he can make for himself by keeping down to the utmost the cost of labor which is sold to him at heavily cut prices by workers who must either work or starve.

Russia confutes that theory by showing you factories with full modern equipment, modern American machinery and several Americans on the technical staff who deliberately prefer life in Russia to life in America, working at full pressure without a single parasite. Rent goes into the public exchequer as advised by a deceased American named Henry George, who happened strangely enough to possess some common sense; interest on capital follows it by an obvious deduction from his principles; profit goes the same way and the public fund thereby created is used to build and equip new factories and establish collective farms for the production of food on an unprecedented scale to maintain a formidable army to liquidate Mr. Winston Churchill and Mr. Babbitt if they proceed from anti-revolutionary ink-slinging and platform balderdash to anti-Russian military business and to distribute what is left in more abundant well-being for the workers.

There is no need and no room in the whole process, from beginning to end, for any idler, parasite or exploiter, save only the inevitable Russian baby who preys voraciously on its mother and will not even move across the room unless it is carried. And even the baby has to pay back when it is old enough to work.

There is no longer any use in protesting that all this cannot be done because human nature is greedy and selfish. It is being done. It works. It pays. And even the greedy and selfish do not want to exchange it for life in America.

Also it works without party politics, votes-for-everybody elections and all the rest of the shams and follies which profess to achieve the aims of democracy and, as a matter of fact, make their defeat an automatic certainty.

When the Russians give a man a national job to do they do not set another man to prevent him doing it and amuse themselves by watching the sport and betting on it. They do not allow Fundamentalist farmers to control scientific education, nor ask the opinion of the village wagoner on finance and foreign policy. Yet the neglect of these pseudo-democratic precautions has not restored the tyranny of czars, princes of the church and nobles, nor thrust back the people into serfdom and chattel slavery.

"Strange," says Mr. Babbitt. "How do they do it?"

**Thinking by the Exiles.**

Simply enough. The makers of the Communist Constitution of Soviet Russia in the days of their persecution and exile had plenty of time to think, mostly in Siberia. (In Detroit, Pittsburgh, New York and such places there is no time to think.)

These exiled Russians pondered on the natural history of mankind. They saw that their own cases proved that the curious factor in nature which we call providence always takes care that every human community shall produce the proportion of socially conscientious and intellectually interested persons necessary for governing it, provided every one gets an adequate cultural chance.

These exceptional individuals are easily recognized by their continual clamor for the betterment of the world, their criticisms of society, their greed for books and their consequent knowledge of history and economics, their contempt for vulgar ambitions and cupidities, their lack of reverence for wealth and artificial rank and, when they are poor, by their frequent sentences to imprisonment and even martyrdom.

Such persons as these made the Russian revolution and built up the Soviet State. They were not elected by adult suffrage and would not have stood the smallest chance of being appreciated or understood by Tom, Dick and Harry sufficiently to be chosen as parish beadles. Most of them were thoroughly disliked and feared by their respectable neighbors. Instead of being elected, they occurred. Nature selected them. They still occur. Nature keeps on selecting them.

When they occur in the United States they are vilified, ridiculed, jailed and even electrically chaired.

**When they occur in Russia they are added to the Communist party; and the Communist party and nobody else rules Russia by electing and appointing to the administrative bodies and departments the committees and chairmen and secretaries who carry out the policy of the Supreme Economic Council.**

**This is Russia's original contribution to science and social organization.** Unpopular Americans, from Henry George to Judge Ben Lindsey and Judge Henry Neil, have urged most of the suggestions on which Russians are experimenting; but this solution of the problem of democracy, with its foundation in natural history, mankind and mysterious ways of providence, leaves America a century behind Russia.

Its highest possibilities will not be realized until the field of selection is widened to the uttermost by raising the general level of culture to a point at which no capable person shall be disqualified by ignorance, poverty or lack of opportunity.

**"The Ablest Government."**

**But even at present, when fully qualified persons are so scarce that marginal members of the Communist party are weeded out at the rate of 13 per cent per annum, the Russian Government is the ablest and the most enlightened in the civilized world.** True, it easily might be that without any very extraordinary eminence, but the worse mess we make of public business in the West, the more reason has the East to be thankful for small mercies.

This is desperately puzzling to the simple-minded Westerner who believes that the Mosiac rule of a life for a life and the biblical prophecy that "to him that hath shall be given and he that hath not from him shall be taken even that which he hath," are laws of God. He feels as if he is among mad men who insist that black is white and that two and two make five.

But the madness works in Russia. There are no millionaires nor ladies and gentlemen there. Priests are so scarce that unless you go into a church where they are actually officiating you will not notice their existence. There are no streets of luxury shops and no mendacious commercial advertisements; but nobody seems a penny the worse.

There is no idolatry: the soldier and his officer hobnob on terms of perfect equality off duty; yet discipline is strict in the Russian Army. Children are citizens with civic rights. A beaten child may summons its parent for assault; and marriage, though compulsory on couples who live together, is dissoluble on strict conditions as to provision for children at the will of either party; but family life goes on much as it does among reasonable and kindly people elsewhere.

**The Safety of Possessions.**

Private property is high treason; yet personal possessions are far more secure than they are in London or Chicago. If you are a capitalist, a private trader or successful farmer, you never know the moment at which you may be turned penniless into the street to make a living like any proletarian, or even hailed before a secret tribunal for examination which may end in death taking you unawares; yet private trade and individual farming go on to the full extent needed to cover the ground which the flowing tide of communism has not yet reached.

Eminent statesmen have no private property and receive salaries at which a country bank manager would turn up his nose; but their condition might well be envied by the Presidents, Chancellors and Premiers of the West.

If you doubt it, offer Stalin Mr. Hoover's job and emoluments and see what he will say to you.

Liberty is laughed at as a bourgeois superstition. But in Moscow you can wear what you like, while in New York, to which liberty welcomes all mankind with her waving torch, no man can even choose the sort of hat he is to wear.

In short, nothing in Russia produces the results that respectable Americans have been taught to expect. Foolish, respectable Americans try to save the credit of their teaching by denying the facts and maintaining that the truth must be in accordance with their Babbittiolic logic.

But sensible, respectable Americans will conclude that there must be something wrong with their teaching, even at the cost of facing the stupendous possibility that the United States may have something edifying to learn from Moscow.

August 30, 1931

# As Leon Trotsky Dramatizes the Russian Revolution

## *In Two Volumes He Completes His Version of the Triumph of the Bolsheviks*

***THE HISTORY OF THE RUSSIAN REVOLUTION. Volume Two: The Attempted Counter-Revolution. Volume Three: The Triumph of the Soviets. By Leon Trotsky. 371 and 474 pp. New York: Simon & Schuster. $3.50 per volume.***

***By JOSEPH SHAPLEN***

**THE reader approaching Trotsky's bulky volumes faces a task more complicated than in the usual historical work. What we have before us is a personal account of events in which Trotsky played a leading and decisive part. This circumstance alone opens the road to a partisan interpretation. To a certain extent this is natural and excusable. In the present instance, however, the interpretation calls for particular vigilance, and not only because of the extremely controversial nature of the subject.**

**Trotsky's career and writings do not reveal him as excessively endowed with historical objectivity or generosity toward those who do not happen to see eye to eye with him. He is not a man who brooks criticism. In a preface to the second volume of his history he seeks to anticipate contradiction by branding it in advance as "pedantry," a rather mild word in his vocabulary. What we are confronted with, therefore, is the necessity of disentangling Trotsky's history from Trotsky. This becomes an imperative prerequisite to a proper appreciation of the work. His own contribution to this task by referring to himself throughout in the third person is, to say the least, naive.**

**In these two volumes Trotsky concludes his own story of the events of February-March, 1917. With the first volume, published last year, they cover the period between the overthrow of Czarism and the rise of the Bolsheviks to power. Picking up the narrative where he left it—the eve of the abortive July uprising of the Bolsheviks in March, 1917—Trotsky in the present volumes carries it through the "July days," the Moscow State Conference and Kornilov revolt to the Pre-Parliament, the Bolshevist insurrection and the formation of the Soviet Government.**

**The reader will at once be struck by this limited scope of a work which sets out to be a history of the Russian revolution, but excludes the tremendous events of the fifteen years since October. The revolution is still in progress. To be understood it cannot be divided into compartments to suit the historian, but must be presented as one organic whole. The events from October, 1917, are not only chronologically related to the situation in 1933 but constitute its impetus and its source.**

**As if sensing this deficiency, Trotsky appends to the third voume**

a lengthy argument against Stalin and all those whom he considers responsible for his own downfall. The work becomes thus an argument against the "Compromisers" of February and the "Epigoni" of October, a polemical discourse and personal apologia. This character of the work makes it questionable as belonging properly to the category of scientific historical writing. It is neither Aulard nor Jaurès nor Mathiez. It is Trotsky still addressing a meeting of the Petrograd Soviet. Quite satisfied with the impression, he leaps over a period of fifteen years to settle scores with Stalin and, incidentally, to disclaim responsibility for what he characterizes generally as the bureaucratic degeneration of the Soviet régime since his own elimination as an active factor.

He grants no organic connection between the October revolution as such and this degeneration. The sum total of his dialectic against Stalin, stripped of its verbiage, is that everything would have gone well if only Trotsky had been permitted to guide the destinies of the revolution after Lenin's exit. Not a single important personality of the February régime or of the Stalin government escapes Trotsky's biting ridicule, rapier thrust and rending jeer. Nor does he spare many of the old Bolshevist guard who helped make the October revolution and who, like himself, have since been unceremoniously eliminated from power and influence under the Stalin bureaucracy.

Of all the actors of the revolution only Lenin and Trotsky seem to have understood the meaning and character of events. They alone knew when and how to act. Hardly anything they did that had important repercussions is subject to criticism. If things have now gone wrong it is because Lenin is dead and Trotsky is once more an émigré together with the men of the February revolution. This persistent emphasis of his own and Lenin's omniscience — Lenin never claimed it—finally becomes so monotonous that it defeats itself, as does Trotsky's uninterrupted reviling of his opponents, the other leitmotif of his burning eloquence.

All this does not necessarily vitiate entirely the historical value of the work here under consideration. It remains to be considered as raw material for history, and as such, no doubt, it will be approached by the future historian. Unmoved by Trotsky's threat of being branded as a pedant, the future historian of the revolution will know how to make his way through this maze of dialectics with the aid of the saving instrument of scientific skepticism and an impartial consideration of all the facts.

That no such impartial presentation of the facts can be found in Trotsky is evident from his method without even considering the huge text, a physical impossibility in a brief review.

In the preface, designed to anticipate criticism, Trotsky asserts that "the accuracy of our references and quotations in the first volume no one has yet so far called into question."

> Our opponents [he continues] confine themselves for the most part to reflections upon the topic of how personal prejudice *may* reveal itself in an artificial and one-sided selection of the facts and texts. These observations, although irrefutable in themselves, say nothing about the given work, and still less about its scientific methods. Moreover, we take the liberty to insist firmly that the coefficient of subjectivism is defined, limited and tested not so much by the temperament of the historian, *as by the nature of his method*.

The italics are ours.

It is precisely by his own definition that Trotsky's work falls far short of the requirements. Without dwelling any further on "the temperament of the historian," we find in his work not only an "artificial and one-sided selection of facts and texts" but a method faulty to the extreme. Nor are these faults mitigated by the brilliant pyrotechnic display of argument, the fervid eloquence, the deadly irony, the grand style. On the contrary, these qualities serve only to accentuate the deficiencies in the eyes of the serious student as lending strength to the distortions of fact which the innocent, sympathetic reader may be unable to detect. Because of these elements a European critic of Trotsky's history has observed, not inaptly, that "of all the Bolshevist distortions of the history of the revolution Trotsky's is the ablest."

Trotsky's method is both simple and ingenious. Having determined upon his thesis, the familiar Bolshevist thesis that the "Compromisers," i. e., the men of the provisional government and the non-Bolshevist revolutionary parties, were weaklings, dullards, blunderers, traitors, allies of the "counter-revolution" and "Kornilovists," Trotsky sets out to prove it from their own mouths. He proves it to his own satisfaction. This he does by letting them speak only in so far as their words serve what he terms "the inner logic of the narrative itself." Tseretelli, Chernov, Dan, Martov, Cheidze, Plechanov, Kropotkin, Kerensky and many others get the floor only to the extent to which it suits Trotsky's purpose, i. e., in short snatches arbitrarily torn from contexts and interwoven with Trotsky's ideological pattern to the accompaniment of his ever-present irony. At no time are they permitted to develop their point of view on the revolution, the war, the land problem, and the host of other extremely complex problems that confronted the provisional government and the early Soviets. At no time are they permitted to state without interference from Trotsky their own reasons for their failure.

The inevitable consequence is a one-sided and wholly distorted portrayal of the actual developments and of the moving forces behind them, including the rôle of the Bolsheviks themselves. To make a point against his enemies in the Stalin camp, Trotsky does not conceal that up to the very moment preceding the seizure of the power by the Bolsheviks Lenin was opposed by leading members of the party's central committee, that the Bolsheviks themselves, like the anti-Bolshevist parties, were not a unit, that some of the most important among them doubted the wisdom and advisability of Lenin's policy. Trotsky pours his vitriol on these Bolsheviks, particularly those among them who later turned upon him in the factional struggle with Stalin. They never get a chance in Trotsky's history to speak for themselves.

For the distinterested, serious student of the revolution it is most important to have knowledge from direct sources of the viewpoints of the anti-Bolshevist parties and of those Bolsheviks who did not wish to follow the road of insurrection and overthrow of the provisional government, but were inclined rather to a coalition government of all Socialist parties, including the Bolsheviks. This has an important bearing on what is the most important point in Trotsky's work, namely, whether or not the October revolution was a revolution of the masses, or merely a military conspiracy engineered by a determined group of professional revolutionists.

A proper understanding of this point is essential to an estimate of the true nature of the Soviet régime and of the present situation. Only by an objective interpretation of the events of October, 1917, can we obtain an insight into the question as to whether the Bolshevik dictatorship is, and was from the very beginning, a dictatorship of the proletariat or a dictatorship over the proletariat. With this point clear we can determine for ourselves whether the degeneration of the Soviet régime of which Trotsky now complains is an inevitable consequence of what happened in October, to which Trotsky contributed so much, or merely the consequence of the fact that Trotsky quarreled with somebody.

Trotsky makes it extremely difficult for the reader to obtain an objective view on this all-important question. He deliberately distorts the rôle of the workers and soldiers in the October coup d'état by minimizing the part played by the nondescript soldier mass, under the direction of the Bolshevist Military Revolutionary Committee, which sought to present and did present the Congress of Soviets then in session with a fait accompli.

Several important names crop up in the two volumes in connection with Trotsky's distortion of this fundamental point, notably those of Martov and President Masaryk of Czechoslovakia, who was in Russia at the time of the October coup d'état. Of all the men of the February revolution, Martov, the leader of the Menshevik-Internationalists, is the only one treated with respect by Trotsky, although he by no means escapes misrepresentation. According to Trotsky, Martov was a man of much foresight and understanding. Would it not, therefore, have been a great service to the reader if our historian would have presented clearly and adequately Martov's view of the February and October revolutions? Trotsky carefully avoids doing that. It might seriously dislocate "the inner logic" of his history. Hence Martov is permitted to speak only in a half dozen disjointed snatches scattered through the history.

The same may be said of the treatment accorded by Trotsky to President Masaryk. If Trotsky mentions him at all, it is because

Masaryk is one of the greatest authorities on Russia in Europe. He is the author of a great history of Russian culture, a keen student of Russian political history and of the Russian revolutionary movement. Trotsky mentions him as one of those who consider the Soviet régime as one imposed upon the Russian people from above rather than the creation of a popular revolution. Having mentioned the bare fact, Trotsky proceeds to ignore Masaryk's views and to develop his own. A detailed explanation from Masaryk at this point would be an invaluable contribution to a history of the Russian revolution. Our historian carefully avoids it.

But Trotsky does not confine himself to Russia alone. In his vilification of the men of the February revolution he finds it necessary to go to Spain, Austria and Germany to attack the "Februarists" in these countries. The Spanish revolution does not suit him at all. The Spanish Socialists are counter-revolutionists. The Spanish revolution will not develop along proper lines until it is turned into a civil war against the Socialists and the entire Spanish revolutionary democracy — until Spain has its October revolution.

Similarly, Otto Bauer and Rudolph Hilferding are assailed as copies of the February leaders. Of the entire Socialist and labor movement of Western Europe, Trotsky speaks only with profound derision and contempt. He takes keen pleasure in settling scores with all who refuse to accept his leadership, which includes, of course, the millions of organized workers in Western Europe.

By his method of historical analysis and his formulation of issues Trotsky ceases to be the stern Marxist and becomes a conventional middle-class individualist.

Trotsky's method would not be permissible even in an honest work of frankly polemical character, although some excuse might be found for it, provided the author did not deliberately distort his opponents' views even though he might not present them adequately. In a work pretending to be history it is quite inexcusable. History is not supposed to be the personal interpretation of the author's conception of what happened on the basis of a preconceived theory. It presupposes a just, fair and adequate presentation of all sides with such interpretation as lends itself to critical analysis on the basis of truly objective data. Trotsky's method excludes all possibility of objectivity, although it serves well his own "inner logic."

This alone bars his huge work from the domain of legitimate historical writing. A political pamphlet has never yet risen to the dignity of history by sheer bulk.

# Russia Is 'Still Remote From Communism'

**Stalin's 1927 judgment holds true today. There are classes, coercion, inequalities and want.**

By ISAAC DEUTSCHER

LONDON.

HOW much communism is there in the economic structure of the Soviet Union? Is Soviet society now really passing from socialism to communism, as it is claimed in Moscow?

To answer these questions it is necessary to relate broadly the present condition of Soviet society to the Marxist conception of communism. Every student of European labor movements knows that there have been as many visions of classless, Communist society as there have been schools and trends: Social Democratic, Communist, Anarcho-Syndicalist, Anarchist and so on. It would be irrelevant to view contemporary Russia through the prism of any conception not accepted by that particular school of thought to which Russia's present rulers belong or profess to belong. The question discussed here is, therefore: how much communism is there in Russia according to Bolshevik, or, better still, to Stalin's own standards of communism?

Twenty-two years ago, in an interview with an American labor delegation, Stalin himself gave a fairly concise, if not very precise, formulation of the subject. The question put to him was: "Can you outline briefly the characteristics of the society of the future which communism is trying to create?"

THIS was at the height of the New Economic Policy, when some private capital was still allowed to operate in Russia, when farming was still organized on individualistic lines, and when Stalin himself viewed communism as a remote objective.

"The anatomy of Communist society," he said, "may be described as follows: it is a society in which (a) there will be no private but only social, collective ownership of the means of production; (b) there will be no classes or state, but workers in industry and agriculture, managing their economic affairs as a free association of toilers; (c) national economy, organized according to plan, will be based on the highest technique in both industry and agriculture; (d) there will be no contradiction between town and country, between industry and agriculture; (e) the produce [of labor] will be distributed according to the principle of the old French Communists: 'from each according to his abilities, to each according to his needs'; (f) science and art will enjoy conditions conducive to their highest development; (g) the individual, free from worries about daily bread and from the necessity of cringing to the 'powerful of the earth,' will become really free, etc., etc. Clearly, we are still remote from such a society."

This definition of communism is still frequently quoted by Soviet theoreticians and writers as axiomatic. (Incidentally, it represents no original contribution of Stalin's, for the same ideas, more subtly expounded, could be found in the oldest Marxist textbooks.) Only in one point has Stalin himself revised the formula: in 1939 he told the eighteenth congress of his party that even in a classless Communist society the state would not wither away as long as that society was encircled by hostile capitalist countries.

Let us now see which of these features of communism given by Stalin can be found in Russia today.

UNQUESTIONABLY, the first and basic condition of communism has been largely fulfilled. "Social, collective ownership of the means of production" predominates in the Soviet economy. It is the only form of ownership that exists in industry and transport. Since 1927 Russia has done away with private capital and has built up a vast industry. No matter how much Stalin may be criticized on other counts, it must be admitted that in this very important respect he has brought Russia nearer to the ideal he has been professing.

The picture becomes confused once we turn from industry to agriculture. The old private farm has been superseded by the *kolkhoz* (collective farm); and, according to Soviet theory,

> the latter belongs entirely to the "Socialist sector" of the economy. Yet a *kolkhoz* is not "socially, collectively owned" in the same way in which any Soviet factory or mine is. It is much nearer to the type of a cooperative business, owned by its members, than to a nationalized factory. The members of the *kolkhoz* also possess small plots of land and farmsteads entirely of their own. A very large proportion of the cattle belongs privately to collective farmers and not to the collective farms as bodies. On the other hand, all tractors and most of the agricultural machinery are state-owned and operated by the machine tractor stations which serve the collective farms; and it is on machinery much more than on animal traction that Russian farming now depends.

ON balance, in farming the forms of ownership are mixed. Even after forced collectivization, the Soviet Government has had to make allowance for the individualistic inclinations of the peasantry. The agricultural policy of the Soviets has indeed never ceased to wrestle with the dilemma of how to harness farming to the Socialist economy and how at the same time to give minimum satisfaction to the private interests of the farmers.

The second characteristic of Communist society, given by Stalin—"there will be no classes," only a "free association of toilers"—is in part economic and sociological, in part political; and it has involved Soviet theoreticians and writers in absurd contradictions. They claim, on the one hand, that the peoples of the Soviet Union already form a classless society; and, on the other, they still describe workers and peasants as two distinct and separate social classes. This contradiction in logic has had pathetic consequences: no Russian writer dares to question the axiom that Russia already represents a classless society; but writers who have drawn from this the unrealistic, yet logically consistent, conclusion that the differences between the industrial proletariat and the peasantry have disappeared have brought upon themselves thunders of severe condemnation.

IN this "classless society," still divided into classes, are the workers at least "a free association of toilers"? This would presuppose the liberalization of the state, a progressive, visible, striking abatement of compulsion by the state, if not the "withering away" of the state, previously expected by the Bolsheviks. Instead, we have witnessed a progressive, visible and all too striking growth of the police state. On Stalin's own showing, his second characteristic of a Communist society is still largely absent from Russia.

The same is true of his third point: "national economy, organized according to plan, will be based on the highest technique in both industry and agriculture." The first par[t of] this condition, requiring th[at] the national economy should be organized according to plan, has been fulfilled. Soviet propaganda, no doubt, exaggerates this achievement; but

ISAAC DEUTSCHER is a British journalist who has traveled and lived in Eastern Europe. He is the author of "Stalin: A Political Biography."

**it is true that over the last twenty years the Soviet Government and its planners have developed highly complex, elastic and, on the whole, effective techniques of running their economy according to plan, and that they have thereby kept their country, in peace as well as war, immune from the ups and downs of the trade cycle.**

**THE second part of this condition of communism—that the economy should be organized "on the highest technical basis"—is very far from fulfillment. This point is essential. Yet communism, as Marxists conceive it, is possible only in an economy of plenty.**

**For example, late in the Twenties, when the Soviet Union started its first Five-Year Plan, the entire Soviet footwear industry, working at full capacity, produced no more than about 30,000,000 pairs of shoes per year for a population of more than 150 million people. The 30,000,000 people to whom the 30,000,000 pairs of shoes available were to be allocated would have formed a privileged minority in any case. In actual fact, not thirty, but fifteen or twenty million people, getting more than one pair of shoes, formed that privileged group.**

**At the next stage, enforced inequality itself bred more inequality. The 30,000,000 pairs of shoes (the same might be said about clothing, decent dwellings, educational facilities, etc.) were allocated to key-men in industry, government, education and so on.**

**These people soon had a vested interest in maintaining and increasing their, by American standards, very modest privileges; and the privileges were *up to a point* essential for the industrial and cultural development of the country, for they induced civil servants, technicians, administrators, skilled workers and so on to put their skill and experience at the nation's disposal.**

**TO follow up our illustration, the Russian footwear industry at present produces enough to provide every Soviet citizen with one pair of shoes** (of rather inferior quality) per year. (The production target for 1950 is 240,000,000 pairs of shoes.) This may be regarded as a rough index of the present relation between the needs of society and its capacity to satisfy those needs. For the first time in its history, Russian industry at large has approached a level at which it should be able to supply the barest essentials to the entire population, even while a large part of Russia's national income continues to be spent on capital investment and defense.

IN theory, this creates the basis for an austere sort of equality at the low level of minimum needs. In fact, however, such equality would impede the further economic development of the Soviet Union. It would take away the incentives to work from the intelligentsia and the skilled workers. The Russian economy is thus still an economy of great scarcity with its normal concomitant—great inequality.

What are the prospects?

In February, 1946, Stalin outlined the main production targets for the "next three or four Five-Year Plans." In the light of these targets, Russia will, at best, be approaching within fifteen or twenty years a level which the United States has already surpassed either now or quite a few years ago. But in fifteen or twenty years the population of the Soviet Union should be nearly double the United States' population today. Thus, even after the three or four Five-Year Plans, the Russian economy will not yet be "based on the highest technique," although, if all goes well, it should be able to raise the Russian standard of living to heights undreamt of by the previous Russian generation.

Stalin's next characteristics of Communist society are also absent from Russia, because they are all bound up with an economy of plenty. "There will be no contradiction between town and country." In other words, under communism the differences between rural and urban standards of living, education and leisure are expected to disappear. To fulfill this condition, the vast spaces of the Soviet Union would have to be thoroughly electrified, covered with dense networks of roads, saturated with modern urban civilization. In all these respects the Russians have made some progress, but they still have a very, very long way to go before they bridge the material and cultural gulf between town and countryside. (I think that not more than about one-fifth of the Soviet countryside has been electrified so far.)

"THE produce [of labor] will be distributed according to the principle * * * 'from each according to his abilities, to each according to his needs.'" This again is theoretically possible only in a society whose capacity for producing the necessities and the amenities of life is virtually unlimited.

The principle of Russian wage policy so far has been that each person should be paid for work not according to his or her needs, but in proportion to the quantity and quality of the work performed. Differential wages and salaries, payment by results, incentive bonuses and premiums can be justified on Marxist grounds as features not of Communist society, but of a society that is still in the first phase of its Socialist development. Yet, as Trotsky pointed out, one would have expected that even in that initial phase of socialism the trend would be toward less and not more inequality.

IS inequality tending to grow or to diminish? I would hesitate to say that inequality has been growing, without adding strong qualifications to this answer. Here, too, the Soviet Government wrestles with an awkward dilemma. To spur on productivity and efficiency of labor, it has over the years worked out an elaborate system of incentives. On the other hand, it has periodically shown signs of a grave anxiety lest the differences in incomes should lead to the crystallization of new social classes.

I would venture the following generalization: Russian society does not know such differences *between classes* as exist, for instance, between stockholders or company directors and ordinary workers. But the differences between various sections of the same social class, especially differences *within* the working class itself, are much bigger and wider than those known in any other country.

Here are a few figures to illustrate this assertion: in the Russian coal industry, for instance, the basic pay of a coal-getter at the present time is up to 2,000 rubles per month. The basic pay of an auxiliary over-ground worker is 250 rubles, one-eighth of the coal-getter's wage. The pay of a completely unskilled laborer (a daily woman cleaner) is 150 to 200 rubles per month.

Such discrepancies are characteristic for most Russian industries, especially for those to which the Government attaches great importance. There are twelve categories of wages in the iron and steel industry, eight in machine building, but only six in industries producing consumers' goods. There are nine basic brackets of income in agriculture, but the actual gradations are more numerous. Gradations in the salaries of office employes are more or less comparable to those known in other countries. Thus a manager of a business employing 1,000 workers gets a basic salary of 3,000 rubles per month. A chartered accountant draws 2,500 rubles, an ordinary bookkeeper 500 to 800; a secretary 650; a typist 400 to 600.

**THE actual discrepancies are considerably larger than these figures indicate, because premiums and bonuses for efficiency make big additions to basic rates of payment; and the premiums, nearly always fixed in percentages of the basic pay, fall mainly to people with higher incomes. It must be emphasized that the changes in the structure of industrial wages and agricultural pay that have been carried out since the war have strongly widened the gap between the lower and the higher incomes.**

**While the Government has deliberately and consistently fostered this social differentiation, it has also taken great care that people with high incomes should not be able to transform savings into profit-bearing capital. Where such transformation might occur (for instance, in the countryside) drastic preventive action is taken.**

**A few years ago, it will be remembered, the world was puzzled by stories about "Soviet millionaires" which appeared in the Russian press. In recent years nothing more has been heard about them. Now, those "millionaires" existed in reality—they did not spring from the head of the Kremlin Jupiter. Although they counted their millions in strongly depreciated money, a million rubles still represented the equivalent of the average income of at least fifty Russian peasant families in the early Forties.**

**HOW did people come to accumulate so much money?**

**Some of the "millionaires" were highly paid scientists and artists, Stalin Prize-winners. But most were collective farmers, who got their money not from normal work on the collective farms, but from private trade in foodstuffs carried on at bazaars. This private trade was and still is allowed and encouraged within limits by the Government. It has been officially stated that before the last war 10 per cent of the total turnover in consumers' goods went through the channels of that private or quasi-private trade.**

**This figure almost certainly understated the actual importance of private buying and selling. Bazaar trade may, in fact, have accounted for one-fifth or one-fourth, and during the war for a much higher proportion of the total turnover in consumers' goods.**

**It was in this Russian equivalent of the European gray and black markets that most of the Soviet "millionaires" made their fortunes. During the war the Government encouraged them. It was anxious that private trade should sup-**

ply the agricultural produce which the partly disrupted governmental machinery of distribution was unable to bring to the consumer. Even then, part of the profits of the Soviet "millionaires" was taxed away in "donations" for the Red Army. But the "millionaires" were finally decreed out of existence when, under the currency reform of December, 1947, they were compelled to exchange ten old rubles in cash for one new ruble. One of the main purposes of the reform was indeed to do away with the Soviet "millionaires," so much extolled during the war and now decried as speculators and profiteers.

THE former "millionaire," if he is now left with 100,000 rubles, is still a very wealthy man by Russian standards. (Pravda of June 21, 1949, stated that at present the average money income of a peasant family is 6,000 to 7,000 rubles a year, not counting its income in kind.)

The story of the Soviet "millionaires" provides part of the answer to our question: it shows how circumstances and governmental policy cause new inequalities to grow up, and also, how the Government tries to reduce such inequalities where these threaten to pass beyond its control. The outlook of Russian society, it can be seen from this, is extremely complex; but certainly it is far from that "society of the future" which, as Marxism anticipates, should pay every person "according to his or her needs."

The last two pre-conditions of communism, enumerated by Stalin, sound like an unwitting mockery at the claim that the Soviet Union is passing from socialism to the higher stage of communism. "Science and art will enjoy conditions conducive to their highest development." Even Stalin himself could hardly have thought, when he spoke these words in 1927, that to those conditions belonged the whip constantly cracked over Soviet biologists, economists, writers, artists and musicians, the whip which until recently was wielded by Zhdanov and has now passed into other hands.

"THE individual free from worries about daily bread and from the necessity of cringing to the 'powerful of the earth' will become really free"—said Stalin. It is enough to open any Soviet newspaper with servile "Letters to Our Beloved Leader and Father" filling half its columns, day in, day out, to realize that by this criterion alone Stalin's regime fails to pass the test of communism.

Many things have changed in Russia since 1927, some for the better and some for the worse. But the words in which Stalin then summed up his argument: "Clearly, we are still remote from such a [Communist] society" still stand. *Ipse dixit.*

August 21, 1949

# Enigma of the Russian Character

**It is only to be explained by Russian history, geography and environment. The new Soviet leaders, says an observer, are governed less by ideology than national necessity.**

By HARRISON E. SALISBURY

WHEN the Western Foreign Ministers sit down at Geneva this week they hope that they may be able for the first time to establish whether Russia's "New Look" is something more than a false face designed to lull the unwary West into a fatal mood of bonhomie.

Does real goodwill lie behind the stiff but discernible smiles of Mr. Molotov, the plow-boy-in-the-parlor heartiness of Mr. Khrushchev and the Chesterfieldian gallantry of Mr. Bulganin? Or is it devious Bolshevik cunning?

Something has changed since Stalin's stone face vanished from the iconostasis. But just what?

Many people have leaped to the conclusion that with the coming to power of new men in the Kremlin "the real Russia," long submerged under Stalin's iron diktat, is rising to the surface. It has been suggested that the source of the world's troubles over Russia can be traced to Stalin and his treacherous Byzantine character. Now that "the real Russians"—open-faced, hospitable, free-talking and free-drinking — have taken over, things will be different. So the speculation goes.

If the root of this conduct and the supposed changes in Soviet policy are indeed to be sought in the "real" Russian character, then an examination of this long-standing enigma is very much in order.

HARRISON E. SALISBURY of The New York Times staff served for more than five years as this paper's correspondent in Moscow.

Nothing would be more fatuous than to attempt in so brief an article to try to delineate the enormous complexities of Russian character; the weight of the rich and often tragic Russian history; the maze of cross-pollinations which lie behind the individual and group personalities now ruling the Soviet Union.

Yet it is vital to any understanding of men like Khrushchev, Bulganin, Molotov, Malenkov and Zhukov—or Stalin, for that matter—that we do not view them as isolated phenomena suddenly emerging on the world stage. Nor should we regard them as mere cardboard products stamped out by a didactic and dialectic pseudo-philosophy called communism. Of course something can be learned about these men by studying the ideological tenets of communism. But, more and more, we are coming to realize that Marx is pretty much what Lenin, Stalin or Khrushchev says he is.

THE Soviet leaders are individuals. They are the products of most varied social, cultural, climatic, economic and historic forces. To understand the role and interplay of personality and policy we must know something of their roots and the soil in which they grew.

The Russian character has been studied by men of genius like Tolstoy, Chekhov, Dostoyevsky, Gorky and Klyuchevsky. Times have changed but little of what they wrote has become obsolete. Their works provide a more pertinent guide to Russian character today than do Dickens and Thackeray to the England of 1955.

It has often been remarked, for example, that the clearest explanation of the Moscow purge trials is to be found in Dostoyevsky's "The Brothers Karamazov," written two generations before.

And Firs, the old butler in "The Cherry Orchard," summed up a whole generation, yet unborn, of shoddy, slothful Soviet production workers with the vivid epithet, "nedotyepa," most nearly translated as "stumble bums."

The greatest twentieth century poet of Russia, Alexander Blok, wrote: "* * * We are the Scythians. * * * Yes, Asians, a slant-eyed greedy tribe."

Such readings, of course, can lead to dangerous generalizations. Yet they provide clues to truths that are pertinent to today's problems.

OTHER clues can be found in the Russian language itself, for example the word "nemtsi." Its root means, literally, those without tongues. Mutes. Over the centuries it has become the popular word for "foreigner" and, specifically, for "German." Thus, implicitly, the foreigner is one who cannot be understood. He hasn't even a tongue. There is a wealth of Freudian meaning to be mined here. The "nemtsi" psychology may well play a role in the Russian suspicions. Russian deceit, Russian secrecy and Russian chicanery of which foreigners have complained for hundreds of years.

The French Marquis de Custine went to Russia 115 years ago as a most sympathetic observer (and emerged, as so often happens, a sharp critic) and wrote: "The Russians * * * refuse you nothing, but they accompany you everywhere; courtesy becomes a means of surveillance here * * * The Russians are still convinced of the efficaciousness of the lie. * * * In Russia secrecy presides over everything." It sounds like an Ambassador's report during the Stalin regime.

SHIFT the date back even further, to the time of Catherine the Great, a "liberal." Writing in 1769 a British observer said:

"I do not find it an easy matter to obtain information. * * * No intelligence of a political nature, but as the court chooses to communicate; no views of men and manners and no anecdotes or incidents in domestic life can be collected in the newspapers. The half of Russia may be destroyed and the other half knows nothing about the matter. * * *

"Rumors of conspiracies are secretly propagated; several persons, I have heard, either guilty or suspected of treason, have disappeared; but these things are not noised abroad, they are only mentioned in confidential whispers. The people are prohibited from speaking or writing about politics. * * * The spies are busy; the suspected great men are closely watched."

The 1769 report sounds like extracts from the private correspondence of this correspondent, written from Moscow in the winter of 1953, shortly before Stalin's death.

Clues to the Russian character are present throughout the historic stream of Russian thought and mores. Now that the smoke of Bolshevik revolution has long since cleared away we can see more clearly that a man does not cease being a Russian when he adopts a so-called Communist philosophy.

THIS continuity has led to attempts to evolve some universal doctrine to explain why the Russians behave like Russians. Possibly the most remarkable of these was that of the English anthropologist, Geoffrey Gorer. Mr. Gorer discovered that the Russians swaddle their children in infancy. He deduced that this process built up hidden resentments and repressed conflicts on such a national scale that when the Russians reached adulthood they released their aggressions against other peoples.

It would be quite difficult, of course, to prove that the Russians are more aggressive than a good many other nations. England, for instance. It has often been remarked that it is always the other fellow who is aggressive. Moreover, the American Indians, many Italians and all Eskimos also swaddle their infants without producing the results suggested by Mr. Gorer.

A SOMEWHAT more logical and attractive doctrine was improvised by a second English observer, Edward Crankshaw. Mr. Crankshaw attempted to explain Russian character in terms of the steppes. He saw in these limitless Russian plains a source both of fears and ambitions. The fears arose from the lack of a natural barrier to invasion and the knowledge of many past incursions. Conversely, the steppe offered no barrier to expansion. It seemed to provide Russia with open land space without end.

The vastness of Russia . . . the infiniteness of the steppe. Truly, this does seem to have marked the character of the Russians. Mr. Crankshaw was not the first to note this phenomenon. Gogol more than a hundred years ago captured its essence with high drama:

"Russia! I behold thee * * * poor, neglected and comfortless * * * no many-windowed lofty palaces * * * no ivy-clad houses * * * all is open, desolate, flat; thy lowly towns lie scattered like dots, like specks unseen among the plains; there is nothing to allure or captivate the eye. What is that throb about my heart?

"Russia, what wouldst thou of me * * * thy mighty expanse enfolds me * * * ah, marvelous radiant horizons of which the earth knows nothing!

"Russia!"

THE Russians themselves have objected that their character has been grossly slandered by the West.

They contend, with truth, for instance, that what the world has come to accept as a classic example of official deception, the so-called "Potemkin villages," is a libel invented by an obscure German diplomat. The villages Count Potemkin erected in the Ukraine, they say, were genuine, not sham.

Russians, in their own view, suffer severely in their relations with the West because they lack what has been called the "oil of hypocrisy." Their frankness, they claim, mixes badly with the surface politeness of the West. They merely say out loud the things which Westerners think in private. Russians assert that when Stalin asks: "How many divisions has the Pope?" or Khrushchev raises the question of French bordellos with a Paris delegation this is merely the blunt straightforwardness of simple, honest men.

Russians, say the Russians, are less sophisticated than Western Europeans or Americans. They are less complicated, simpler people, closer to nature.

BUT anyone surveying the depth and complexity of Russian culture; the infinite scrutiny of ethical, spiritual and moral issues which is the benchmark of Russian intellectual life (both before and since Lenin); the intensity with which the most narrow and obscure questions of conduct or philosophy are pursued through mazes of logic and endless ratiocination probably will dispute this Russian self-evaluation.

Nor does the supposed connection between closeness to nature and simple honesty seem valid.

If you have watched the empty blue-eyed innocence of a peasant woman as, under a militia man's very eyes, she blandly tucks beneath her skirt the three chemises which a moment earlier she was illegally offering for sale you may doubt this proposition. Your doubts will increase if you attempt to barter with one of these simple peasant souls over a job of work.

Much of the disillusion and frustration which marked Russian intellectual life in the late years of the nineteenth century sprang from the difficult, sometimes fatal, results of an attempt by the earnest young people known as the "narodniki" to bring culture and enlightenment to the Russian peasants under the mistaken assumption that they were dealing with a variant of Rousseau's "Noble Savages."

The Russian peasant, like peasants the world around, is

canny, suspicious, devious, tough-minded. He readily draws about himself a protective mantle of presumed ignorance. "We are dark people, ignorant people," peasants say. But if ignorance exists it is the ignorance of the book, not the ignorance of life.

The present rulers of Russia are not starry-eyed young intellectuals of the nineteenth century. Nor are they peasants. But they are Russians. And if their character shapes current Soviet policy, it is essential to remember that Russian character is founded upon broad factors of history, geography and environment.

WHAT we so easily forget is that when the Communists changed their country's name to "The Union of Soviet Socialist Republics," they didn't change its geography. And, as Russian Marxists themselves are fond of saying, "you cannot escape history."

Rulers change. Geography and national resources do not. If Russia displays a certain desire for conciliation, the first place to look for the cause is in the balance of international forces. If Russia today is following a "soft" policy in international affairs, we must try to find an explanation in Russia's necessities, her economic position, her technological resources, her own estimate of her defense capabilities. If all the NATO powers in Europe were ranged on the Soviet side; if Russia had long-range bombing bases all around the United States frontiers and a huge lead in nuclear weapons it is just possible that the "New Look" would be a bit more stern.

October 23, 1955

## 1917—The Russian Revolution—1967

# A Balance Sheet of 50 Years of Soviet Rule

*Following is the first of a series of articles by reporters of The New York Times on a half-century of Soviet rule in Russia, to be observed on Nov. 7.*

By HARRISON E. SALISBURY

"WE were one of the most backward of nations and now we are one of the most advanced."

Sitting in his Kremlin office with the summer sun glancing through the window, Anastas I. Mikoyan, member of the Central Committee of the Communist party for 44 years, thus summed up Bolshevik rule in Russia.

Probably no one in Moscow was in a better position to assess the 50 Bolshevik years that will be celebrated Nov. 7 than Mr. Mikoyan, dapper and sparkling-eyed despite his 71 years. No one has stood so close so long to the fulcrum of Soviet power as Mr. Mikoyan—first as one of the young men from the Caucasus, brought up to Moscow in 1926 by Stalin, and later, after Stalin's death, as the right-hand man of Nikita S. Khrushchev.

### Nation Moves Into First Rank

Born the son of a poor Armenian village carpenter, educated in the Armenian seminary in Tiflis, Mr. Mikoyan has seen Russia move from bottom rank among European powers to second in the world to the United States—militarily, industrially, economically. And in space and some areas of technology and science she may be the first.

Mr. Mikoyan is retired now, but his big Kremlin office is the same one he occupied as a member of the party's ruling Politburo and as a First Deputy Premier. Now the sign on the door simply reads: Member, Presidium of the Supreme Soviet. It is the only one on the long red-carpeted corridor so inscribed.

Proudly Mr. Mikoyan ticks off Soviet material gains—elimination of illiteracy, improvement of life, gains in housing, culture, education, standard of living, creature comforts. He concedes that not everything has gone according to plan, that there have been shortfalls from the goals envisaged by Vladimir Ilyich Lenin when he launched his successful coup d'état on Nov. 7, 1917.

By the strength of Mr. Mikoyan's reaffirmation of the doctrine of de-Stalinization he shows concern for the fact that after 15 years the dark stain of Stalin's terror has not been entirely eradicated.

Probably no one has been more aware over the years than Mr. Mikoyan of the gap between Soviet promise and Soviet performance—a gap visible almost from the moment when, 24 hours after having toppled Alexander Kerensky's Provisional Government, Lenin stepped before a cheering crowd at the Smolny Institute in Leningrad and said: "We will now proceed to construct the socialist order."

### Spontaneous Uprising

Lenin on that night was celebrating the success of the Bolshevik seizure of power. The actual revolution, the overthrow of Czar Nicholas II and of the 300-year reign of the House of Romanov occurred the previous March, unaided by Bolsheviks or any other organized group. It was the product of a spontaneous uprising in the streets of Petrograd, largely led by angry women, tired of endless waits in the bread lines.

Now 50 years have passed since the dramatic days of 1917. For 50 years Russia has been ruled as a Soviet state on the principles of what Lenin called the "dictatorship of the proletariat"—actually, dictatorship by the ruling elite of the Communist party.

The Soviet state has held not only the "commanding heights" of industry, but all the means of production. It manages every kind of economic enterprise from street venders of ice cream cones to missile factories. Yet, the "socialist order" of which Lenin spoke remains largely a mirage.

The state has not, as Lenin forecast, withered away. His vision of a new "Soviet man," idealistic and humanitarian, and the utopia he foresaw of a world brotherhood of man are unfulfilled. Young writers like Andrei Voznesensky and Yevgeny Yevtushenko berate the party for banality. Some young Russians simply sneer at it. Within the Politburo quarrels go on behind the scenes over what went wrong and what lines should be followed back to the dream of 1917.

### Influence Is Everywhere

Each day Pravda, the party paper, still publishes next to its name the slogan: "Workers of the world, unite." Nearly one third of the world is under Communist rule of one kind or another. Communist parties, overt or clandestine, exist in all countries. The doctrine of Communism and the politics of the Communist world have influenced world politics and internal regimes almost everywhere. Yet, in the 50th year of the Revolution and the centenary of the appearance of the first volume of Marx's "Kapital," never has conflict so bitter, so intractable, divided Communist revolutionaries from Moscow to Peking, from Havana to Hanoi, from India to the United States.

A brilliant young Soviet economist shook his head and sighed:

"You know, perhaps Marx was right after all:"

He did not mean that after 50 years the Soviet Union was a monument to Marxism. Quite the contrary. He meant that quite possibly Marx was right in believing that the Communist revolution must come first in the West, in industrialized Germany, or England, rather than in dark, vast, peasant Russia. He meant that it might have been better had Russia not attempted to leap from semi-feudalism into a totally organized state system. He meant that perhaps Lenin was wrong when he so boldly insisted on seizing total power, on moving straight into proletarian dictatorship.

Not many Russians articulated their doubts so precisely. Certainly Mr. Mikoyan and the Soviet leadership did not accept this assessment.

Yet, even Mr. Mikoyan conceded that events had not turned out precisely as expected. Lenin and his associates, with the possible exception of Stalin, saw their revolution as merely the first in a wave that would sweep Europe.

"All we Bolsheviks thought until 1924 [when Lenin died] that the world revolution would be victorious in Europe very soon, if not today, then tomorrow," Mr. Mikoyan recalled. "I even put down in my diary: 'Soon the world revolution will be victorious.' I had in view, most of all, Germany. I believed in that."

The world revolution did not come in 1924. By 1967, it seemed so distant that the very phrase hardly passed Russian lips.

Fifty years after the Nov. 7 coup in which, as Mr. Mikoyan recalled, fewer people lost their lives than die in traffic accidents on an ordinary New York weekend, the achievements of Soviet rule were visible throughout Russia. Moscow's world status had risen mightily. But her revolutionary spirit was dim.

### Transformation Misfired

Not only had world revolution failed to occur; the transformation of man that the revolutionaries had expected had misfired. The Soviet state had become the sole owner and employer of labor. But exploitation of man by man, as in Lenin's dream, had not ended. Instead, there had arisen exploitation of man by the world's greatest employer, the Soviet state, with party, courts, secret police, army, press, unions and propaganda to enforce its dictate.

For nearly 30 of Soviet Russia's 50 years, from shortly after Lenin's death in January, 1924, until Stalin's death on March 5, 1953, the figure of Stalin towered over the Soviet state. The memory of his terror, the persistence of his harsh methods, the survival of his police apparatus and, most pervasive, the habits and style that he infused into the monstrous Soviet bureaucracy, threw a shadow over the 50th anniversary celebrations.

There was in Moscow, as the holiday approached, a mood in which questioning and doubt mingled with pride in Soviet achievement. Even in the realm of space, where the Soviet Union had demonstrated brilliant genius, not all the reactions of Muscovites were positive. An angry young writer harshly exclaimed:

"Space—who needs it? The fact is we don't belong there—neither we nor you Americans. There's enough on this earth to occupy ourselves."

### No Place for Skepticism

Such skepticism understandably had no place in the philosophy of Mr. Mikoyan. He had dedicated his life to the material progress of his country. He was proud of its achievements and ticked them off, one by one. He went back to Lenin and his early plans—the Leninist concept that Communism could be defined as "electrification plus Soviet rule," a sort of national Tennessee Valley Authority run by the Bolsheviks.

Lenin launched a plan for national electrification in December, 1920. In 10 to 15 years Soviet power capacity was to be raised to 1,750,000 kilowatts and electric output to 8.5 billion kilowatt-hours. At the time Lenin spoke, Russia's war-ravaged and disorganized electric power industry generated 500 million kilowatt-hours, not enough, Mr. Mikoyan noted, for one small power grid today. Total production under the czars had been 2 billion kilowatt-hours.

"This year we will have an output of 598 billion kilowatt-hours of electricity," Mr. Mikoyan said. "That is more than 6 times what we produced in 1950 when output was 90 billion kilowatt-hours."

Mr. Mikoyan cast back to 1929, the start of Stalin's first five-year plan, the crash program for industrializing Russia.

"I was Commissar of Foreign and Domestic Trade at that time," he recalled. "Steel production had been 4,000,000 tons in Russia before the Revolution. In Lenin's time it had dropped as low as 200,000 tons."

Mr. Mikoyan had a slim folder in front of him. He opened it and took out a sheet on which the latest Soviet production figures had been typed out.

"If anyone had told me, when the first 5-year-plan was presented, that we would produce in my lifetime—in 1967 to be specific—102 million tons of steel," he said, "I would not have believed it."

The Soviet figure was within 20 per cent of United States production for 1967. The prospect seemed excellent that within five years the Soviet Union's production would move ahead of that of its great rival.

Mr. Mikoyan ticked off the figures for 1967 production: textiles—3.3 million square meters in 1950, 8.1 million in 1967; television sets—11,900 in 1950, 4.9 million in 1967; washing machines—300 in 1950, 4,200,000 in 1967; refrigerators—1,200 in 1950, 2,800,000 in 1967 ("Soon it will be 5 million," he interjected). Probably because so much of his career had been devoted to consumer goods production, Mr. Mikoyan chose to measure Soviet economic achievement largely in terms of television sets, refrigerators and other "big ticket" items.

Mr. Mikoyan recalled how he went to the United States in 1936 and saw electric refrigerators being turned out by the hundred thousand by General Electric.

### Refrigerators for Russia

He told the Politburo that the Soviet Union must produce refrigerators.

"I think my colleagues thought I was drunk," Mr. Mikoyan recalled. "'Refrigerators,' they said, 'first you have to have something to put in them. Besides, who needs refrigerators in a cold climate like Russia's?'"

The onset of war made the argument academic. But in 1949 Mr. Mikoyan got Stalin's agreement to turn out 150,000 refrigerators "although everybody thought 50,000 would be too many." He managed to get the refrigerators made by placing orders with defense plants and automobile factories—"our most advanced industries." But he could not sell them. Now, of course, all this has changed. Production of refrigerators cannot keep up with demand generated by the Soviet housing program. There are queues at stores selling refrigerators, waits for delivery and two new factories are going up, each with a projected output of 500,000 a year.

"Yes," mused Mr. Mikoyan. "I think we have made great progress. Formerly, we were a backward nation. Perhaps, the shoes we turn out are still not up to quality. But we have scientists and intelligentsia even in Central Asia where the literacy rate was only 7 per thousand at the time of the Revolution."

Mr. Mikoyan paused and looked out the window of his Kremlin office. The bright sunlight washed the yellow painted walls of the inner courtyard. It was a warm day and the windows were open. A faint murmur could be heard from thousands of tourists and sightseers now roaming through the great Kremlin squares that Stalin had tightly guarded against public entry.

"I think," Mr. Mikoyan resumed, "that the policy of our state deserves respect. All those who intimately assess it cannot but find that we have achieved a high level of culture, science and literacy. We must take pride in our attainments."

The visible symbols of those achievements were everywhere to be seen in the Moscow of 1967—in the new freeway that circles the city, in traffic tunnels and overpasses, in glass-box skyscrapers marching through old, picturesque quarters of the city, in the tangle of automobile traffic that jams the ring boulevards and the narrow streets around the Kremlin.

In the 50th year of Bolshevik power the Soviet Union stands on the edge of the automobile age that the United States entered in the nineteen-twenties. With new production facilities being constructed by Fiat, Renault and others, the Soviet Union will be turning out 1,500,000 passenger cars a year in the early nineteen-seventies, more than five times the present output. But this will not be soon enough to cut off the wave of popular grumbling.

### Soviet Is Unprepared

"When I see that any ordinary worker in Italy or France has a car," said a writer just back from one of his frequent trips to Western Europe, "I wonder what we have been doing in the last 50 years. Of course, there has been progress. But it's not fast enough."

The Soviet Union's entry into the automobile age is not going to be easy. The Russian writer owns a car, a 10-year-old Pobeda. He has to keep it on the street all winter in temperatures of 30 below zero. No garages are available. None are provided in the new apartments or office buildings. Most Moscow car owners drain their radiators every night in winter and fill them in the morning with boiling water to get started. There are three gasoline stations in Moscow selling high-test gasoline. Today there are perhaps 100,000 private cars in Moscow. What will happen when there are a million?

But Moscow life is changing. Galina Serebryakova, Soviet author, wife of the first Soviet Ambassador to London, sat in the dining room of the National Hotel and looked out at the cars streaming through Manezhnaya Square. She remembered the first time she had entered that dining room. Then it served as a commissary for leading Bolshevik revolutionaries in the famine years of 1921-22. There was no gleaming silver, no snowy linen, no fine china on the tables, no buxom waitresses, no jazz band blaring out the latest American numbers. There was no heat, no electricity, nothing but tin plates, tin spoons and a ration of thin gruel or stew. Outside on the street were droshkies with their emaciated horses and their drivers bundled up in sheepskins. Streetcars clanked through Red Square.

Today Moscow has a fine subway system in which neat, new functional stations contrast with the older chandelier-hung and marble-faced underground palaces of Stalin's day.

### Chain of Quality Stores

Moscow has its own fashion industry, its chain of "Svetlana" stores that sell quality goods and Paris imports at high prices. It has foreign currency shops where scarce goods and foreign food, liquor and cigarettes can be purchased at reasonable prices, but only with Western currencies. It has swarms of black-market ruble traders, mostly teen-agers, probably working for the police or with police permission. It has some rather garish prostitutes. It has more food, more consumer goods, more prosperity than in any year since 1917.

But as the 1967 anniversary approached, Moscow's mood was still querulous. Some pined for the end of the anniversary festivities. "It's so dull," one Russian said. "We have read so much about it that we are bored before it ever happens."

Many young people simply paid no heed. "Really," one youthful editor exclaimed, "our young people aren't much interested in this kind of thing. The only subject that arouses them is jazz."

In the summer of 1967, thousands of young Russians put packs on their backs, a roll of blankets over their shoulder, cradled a guitar or an accordion in their arms and wandered off toward the north, a little like the roving tramps of Czarist times. They lived off the countryside, did small chores or begged for their food. They were not hippies, but they were detached from the energetic, purposeful, directed life of the Soviet Union. What they sought was not too clear, but they knew what they did not like — party preaching, xenophobia, Pravda editorials.

"Our young people have definite causes for their rebellion," an American told the poet Andrei Voznesensky. "They are opposing the war in Vietnam or battling for race equality. You have no war in Vietnam and no race problem—what do your young people revolt against?"

Mr. Voznesensky smiled sadly. "Don't worry," he said. "We still have plenty for them to rebel against. It's no problem."

The alienation found expression in a dozen ways. In smaller towns and rural areas short-wave radio hobbyists were broadcasting iconoclastic programs. Some were arrested for their pains. In universities the "underground" student magazine or newspaper became a common phenomenon. Often the young editors would wind up in jail. The sentiments found in this underground press were as subversive of Soviet political and social norms as their equivalents in Berkeley, Calif., or New York's Columbia campus are subversive of the American establishment.

A prized item in the thriving "grey" market, fueled by the contributions of thousands of Soviet tourists returning from abroad, were humorous, rude or obscene buttons from the rich stocks to be found in American campus stores or in Greenwich Village.

Marx called religion the "opiate of the people." Lenin struggled to destroy religion's power in Russia. Stalin compromised to win church support in World War II. Under Nikita S. Khrushchev new campaigns were waged against God. But on the desks of two writers, one an elderly conservative, one a violently alienated youngster, a visitor saw bibles casually displayed. Another writer kept a crucifix on his table.

There is hardly an apartment occupied by the new Soviet middle class that does not have an ikon on the wall. Ostensibly these are art objects. Religious music is being recorded in state studios. The old Russian passion for church bells has been revived after 50 years of desuetude.

The transformation of rural life in Russia in 50 years, or even since World War II, has not been so marked as that of urban life. Relations between Communists and the countryside never proved comfortable. In 1967 the question of whether the Soviet had created a viable, efficient system of food production capable of supporting the new urban technological elite was still an open one.

Some Soviet spokesmen believed that at long last the agricultural problem had been solved. They conceded that Stalin's violent campaign to collectivize agriculture in the years 1928-30, the use of terror, expropriation, exile and execution, was a principal contributor to the problem.

### Collective Farms Formed

Stalin drove the surviving peasants into collective farms. But in the process he sent probably 10 million into exile in Siberia and Central Asia. How many died, starved or perished of deprivation no one has ever been able to estimate. The slaughter of livestock turned the countryside into wasteland. Famine swept the Ukraine and lower Volga. When the fever abated in 1934 the pool of Soviet animals had shrunk. There were 15.4 million horses, instead of 32.1; 33.5 million cattle compared with 60.1; 11.5 million hogs instead of 22; 32.9 million sheep compared with 97.3. In 1953 Mr. Khrushchev revealed the grim truth: in Stalin's last years the grain harvest averaged 10 per cent less than in Czarist Russia.

Today, with investment radically increased, Soviet leaders cautiously hope the corner has been turned.

For the first time since before the Revolution, Soviet Russia in 1967 had a surplus of butter, so large that serious questions of storage arose. Meat and dairy products were available in the cities in ample quantities.

But many kept their fingers crossed. The Soviet Union was importing secondary foods, fruits, vegetables, canned meats and frozen fish from Eastern Europe and the West. As recently as three years ago it had been compelled to enter the international grain market to buy hundreds of thousands of tons of grain to make up a deficit. The Soviet Union was still far from the position of Czarist Russia, one of the world's major food-exporting countries. Hundreds of thousands of rural residents thronged into Moscow each day to shop—often for such commonplace commodities as white bread. No Russian housewife yet could purchase flour at the grocery store whenever she wished or in unlimited quantity. Even before the great holidays like Nov. 7, Easter and May Day purchases were restricted.

The sharp distinction between city and countryside still marked Soviet life. The moment the Moscow city line was passed one entered the world of old Russia, the village with its communal wells, the women beating out their washing on stones beside the pond, the log houses with gaily painted wooden curlicues, the sunflowers beside the picket fences, and here and there a cart with a great wooden yoke over the horse's neck.

But one thing had changed in the summer of 1967, at least in the vicinity of Moscow. No longer was a goat tethered on a scrawny patch of grass before each wooden izba. The goats, so common for three decades that they were called "Moscow cows," had virtually vanished. Today the villagers did not have to rely on goats. Now, they were permitted to own cows.

### More Money in Farms

Yuri Zhukov, Pravda commentator, was one who contended that the farm problem had been solved. Essentially, he said, this was achieved by money. The peasants, for the first time, were being paid liberally to increase production. In his opinion, the basic tasks in industry and agriculture had been solved. The next problem was to improve the lot of the industrial worker—the proletariat. This was the class in whose name, of course, the Revolution had been accomplished.

The workingman was receiving a five-day week as the gift of the 50th year of the revolution. The character of Soviet life was already changing. No longer did Moscow retail stores stay open on Sunday, (except for essential food and services). This had reversed the pattern in the capital city. Instead of 2 or 3 million people pouring into the city on Sunday to shop in the great G.U.M. department store on Red Square and the city's other retail outlets, now hundreds of thousands of Muscovites poured out of the city on Saturday to take advantage of the weekend.

With a decline in working time, the issue of labor productivity was becoming crucial. Mr. Zhukov was critical of the low productivity of Soviet workers. He said it was substantially lower than in the United States, partly because of low wages. He cited the Soviet construction industry as an example. Skills were low. Many workers came directly to the job from rural life. They did not know the meaning of high standards. In the United States, in contrast, the building crafts were among the highest paid and most skilled. The next great task of the Soviet Union, in Mr. Zhukov's opinion, was to lift the skill and productivity of the industrial workers and, along with it, their wages and living standards.

### The 'Tom Sawyer' Tradition

This would not be easy, said a Soviet economist familiar with the United States.

"Really," he said, "there is no comparison between the working energy and efficiency of American workmen and Soviet workmen. The Americans are the best workingmen in the world. They possess the best traditions. After all, it was the energetic, able, skilled people who emigrated to America. They took with them the desire and ability to work hard and well. We have an enormous residue of 19th-century tradition. Only when this is overcome will we begin to get our economy going as well as yours."

He cited the persistence in Russia of what he called the "Tom Sawyer" tradition.

"You remember," he said, "when Tom was painting the fence? All the other boys came along and watched. He was clever enough to get them to do the work for him. Here, however, we are still in the first stage. One man paints, the rest watch."

Even the most self-critical Russians conceded that the persistence of the Tom Sawyer tradition in the age of cosmonauts was an anomaly that hardly could survive much longer.

Fifty years after the Revolution a young Russian writer said: "Somehow, I don't really know how we have survived the last 50 years. We have even begun to make some progress. Fifty years hence, on our 100th anniversary, perhaps we'll really have achieved something worth our dancing in the streets. I hope so and I really think we may."

October 2, 1967

# *Pravda Assails Times Series on Soviet*

Special to The New York Times

MOSCOW, Oct. 18—The New York Times was accused here today of "malicious concotions, lies and slander" in its series of articles analyzing Soviet society on the eve of the 50th anniversary of the Bolshevik Revolution.

The accusation was made by Pravda, newspaper of the Soviet Communist party. The article, printed under the headline "Fumes From Across the Ocean," was signed Vasily Vasin, thought to be a pseudonym.

Pravda directed most of its wrath at Harrison E. Salisbury, an assistant managing editor of The Times. Mr. Salisbury coordinated the preparation of the articles on the Soviet Union, publication of which began Oct. 2 with an analysis of the achievements and failures of the Communist party's 50 years in power.

### Called 'First Violinist'

The party paper called Mr. Salisbury "the first violinist and the conductor of an orchestra of Sovietologists" and described the series of articles as "most strange."

Mr. Salisbury visited Moscow last February for discussions with officials of the Novosti press agency to obtain their cooperation in arranging visits and interviews for Times reporters in economics, science, culture and other fields.

He returned to Moscow in June to gather material for his own articles, and the other Times correspondents came during the spring and early summer to carry out their projects.

Although most of the meetings with Soviet citizens were organized by Novosti, the Pravda writer alleged that Mr. Salisbury had based his articles and interpretations on "imaginary interviews." The paper declared:

"The bosses of the New York Times purportedly want to give American readers 'balanced information' about the various aspects of life in the U.S.S.R. on the 50th anniversary of 'Soviet rule in Russia.'

### 'Donkey Ears of Slanderers'

"It is sufficient, however, to take a quick look at the articles to be convinced that the donkey ears of slanderers and malicious persons project from every page."

Pravda reacted with particular indignation to observations by Mr. Salisbury about the failure of the Soviet regime to transform its dreams of a new society into reality over the last half-century.

Mr. Salisbury wrote:

"Not only had world revolution failed to occur; the transformation of man that the revolutionaries had expected misfired. The Soviet state had become the sole owner and employer of labor. But exploitation of man by man, as in Lenin's dream, had not ended. Instead, there had arisen exploitation of man by the world's greatest employer, the Soviet state, with party, courts, secret police, army, press, unions and propaganda to enforce its dictates."

Pravda retorted:

"With what evidence does he back up these and similar assertions? With none, of course, because it is impossible to back them up."

Pravda also challenged observations by Mr. Salisbury about a revival of interest in religion by Soviet intellectuals despite 50 years of atheist propaganda.

The Communist paper similarly objected to an interpretation by Mr. Salisbury that Soviet young people had become alienated from the programs and propaganda of the party.

Pravda concluded with an allegation that the "dirty campaign" against the Soviet Union had been joined by other United States publications, including the magazines Look, U.S. News & World Report and others.

### Comment by the Times

Turner Catledge, executive editor of The New York Times, said the articles had been produced as a result of fruitful and cooperative arrangements between Soviet authorities and The Times.

"The Times articles are, of course, based on real interviews with real individuals," Mr. Catledge said. "The team of Times reporters worked diligently over a period of several months in the Soviet Union, visiting almost every part of the country and talking with Soviet citizens from the highest to the lowest levels."

October 19, 1967

# Suggested Reading


Billington, James H., *The Icon and the Axe: An Interpretive History of Russian Culture.* New York: Random House, 1970.

Chamberlain, William Henry, *The Russian Revolution.* New York: Grosset & Dunlap, 1965.

Conquest, Robert, *The Great Terror: Stalin's Purge of the Thirties.* New York: Macmillan, 1973

Deutscher, Issaac, *Stalin: A Political Biography.* New York: Oxford University Press.

Johnson, Priscilla, *Khrushchev and the Arts: The Politics of Soviet Culture,* 1962-1964, Boston: MIT PRESS, 1965.

Kopelev, Lev, *To Be Preserved Forever.* New York: Lippincott, 1977.

Lyons, Eugene, *Assignment to Utopia.* New York: Greenwood Press, 1971 [1937].

Medvedev, Roy, *Let History Judge: The Origins and Consequences of Stalinism.* New York: Alfred Knopf, /971.

Mehnert, Klaus, *Soviet Man and His Work.* New York: Greenwood Press, 1976.

Reed, John, *Ten Days That Shook the World.* New York: Random House, 1960.

Salisbury, Harrison E., *Black Night, White Snow: Russia's Revolutions 1905-1917.* New York: Doubleday, 1978.

Salisbury, Harrison E., editor, *The Soviet Union—The Fifty Years. New York: Harcourt, Brace, 1967.*

*Smith, Sedrick, The Russians.* New York: Times Books, 1976.

Solzhenitsyn, Alexander, *One Day in the Life of Ivan Denisovich.* New York: Dutton, 1971 [1963].

Solzhenitsyn, Alexander, *The First Circle.* New York: Bantam Books, 1976.

Solzhenitsyn, Alexander, *The Gulag Archipelago. New York: Harper* & Row, 1974.

Trotsky, Leon, *The History of the Russian Revolution.* Ann Arbor: University of Michigan Press, 1957.

# Index